LEGAL ETHICS: RULES, STATUTES, AND COMPARISONS

2016 Edition

LEGAL ETHICS: RULES, STATUTES, AND COMPARISONS

2016 Edition

Includes ABA and California changes through 2013, a Rule-by-Rule Comparison of the California and Both Old and New ABA Model Rules, and the ABA and California Judicial Codes

Richard Zitrin
Lecturer in Law
University of California, Hastings College of the Law

Kevin E. Mohr
Professor of Law
Western State College of Law

ISBN: 978-1-6328-0952-0 (print)
ISBN: 978-1-6328-0953-7 (ebook)

NOTE TO USERS

To ensure that you are using the latest materials available in this area, please be sure to periodically check the LexisNexis® Law School web site for downloadable updates and supplements at www.lexisnexis.com/lawschool.

Editorial Offices
121 Chanlon Rd, New Providence, NJ 07974 (908) 464-6800
www.lexisnexis.com

MATTHEW◆BENDER   (2015–Pub.3083)

LEGAL ETHICS: RULES, STATUTES AND COMPARISONS 2016 EDITION

Including separate sets of 2002–03 (as amended) and 1983 (as amended) ABA Rules, a "red-lined" edition of the 2002–03 and 1983 rules together, a Rule-by-Rule Comparison of the California Rules and both the 2002–03 and 1983 ABA Rules, and the ABA and California Judicial Codes

Table of Contents

Page

Part I. ABA Model Rules 1

2002 ABA Model Rules of Professional Conduct 1
    2002 ABA Model Rules Table of Contents 1
    2002 ABA Model Rules 1
1983 ABA Model Rules of Professional Conduct, as amended 133
    1983 Model Rules Table of Contents.. 133
    1983 ABA Model Rules, as amended.. 133
    Subject Guide to the 1983 Model Rules.. 239
    Table "A" (Related Sections in the ABA Model Code)..................... 255
2002 ABA Model Rules, legislative ("redlined") style........................ 265
2004 ABA Model Court Rule on Insurance Disclosure 412
2012 ABA Model Rule for Admission by Motion 413
2012 ABA Model Rule on Practice Pending Admission...................... 415

Part II. ABA Model Code 419

ABA Model Code of Professional Responsibility 419
    Model Code Table of Contents 419
    ABA Model Code 422
    Index to the Model Code 515
    Table "B" (Related Sections in the ABA Model Rules) 531

Part III. California — Model Rules Comparisons 539

Comparison Between the 1983 and 2002 ABA Model Rules of
    Professional Conduct and the California Rules of Professional
    Conduct and the California State Bar Act
    (Business & Professions Code).. 539
Table "C" (California Standards Related to Sections of the 1983
    ABA Model Rules of Professional Conduct, as amended............... 587

Part IV. California Rules and Statutes 591

California Rules Table of Contents 591
California Rules of Professional Conduct 591

Selected State Bar of California Resolutions of the Board
  of Trustees... 639
Selected Statutes Table of Contents..................................... 643
Selected Statutes of the California State Bar Act
  (Business & Professions Code).. 643
Selected California Evidence Code Provisions 643
Selected California Rules of Court Regarding
  Multijurisdictional Practice... 705

Part V.   Judicial Codes...727

ABA Model Code of Judicial Conduct 727
California Code of Judicial Ethics....................................... 771

Part VI.   SEC Final Standards of Professional Conduct..... 817

INTRODUCTION and USE NOTE

In 2002, with the assistance of retired California State Bar Court judge Ellen R. Peck, we updated this Rules Book to account for the work of the ABA "Ethics 2000" Commission, which was charged with reviewing the American Bar Association's Model Rules of Professional Conduct and making any necessary revisions. This volume incorporates not only all the changes to the Model Rules adopted by the ABA House of Delegates in August 2001 and February 2002 after its receipt of the "Ethics 2000" Commission's report, but also all substantive changes made to the Model Rules since that time. Most recently, these changes include those proposed by the ABA's "Ethics 20/20" Commission and approved by the House of Delegates in August 2012 and February 2013. We further describe that commission below. We have also included the changes made during that period to the California Rules of Professional Conduct and the selected sections of the California Business & Professions and Evidence Codes included in this book. Further, we have added sections that feature the ABA Model Court Rule on Insurance Disclosure, the ABA Model Rule for Admission by Motion, the ABA Model Rule on Practice Pending Admission, the California Rules of Court adopted to address multijurisdictional concerns, State Bar of California Resolutions concerning the delivery of pro bono and limited scope legal services, and the SEC Attorney Regulations promulgated pursuant to the Sarbanes-Oxley Act.

Beginning with the 2014 Edition, we included the **ABA Model Code of Judicial Conduct (2010)** and the **California Code of Judicial Ethics (2013)**. We continue to include those resources to further assist you in preparing your students for their careers as lawyers.

To summarize, this volume contains the following:

- The Model Rules adopted by the ABA House of Delegates in 2001-2002, as amended in February 2002, August 2003, February 2008, February 2009, August 2009, August 2012, and February 2013. We have designated these Rules the **2002 ABA Model Rules**. They are in Part I.

- The text of the original, now-superseded Model Rules that were adopted in 1983. We have termed these rules the **1983 ABA Model Rules**. These rules, still the basis of the governing disciplinary rules in a diminishing number of jurisdictions, are in the form last amended prior to the Ethics 2000 changes. They follow the 2002 rules in Part I.

- A **"red-lined"** or legislative style copy of the **2002 Rules** (as amended) showing the changes from the 1983 rules, so that the differences between the two sets of rules may be easily reviewed. This "red-line" version has been updated periodically as the Model Rules have been amended, the latest revisions reflecting the aforementioned 2013 amendments. They are also in Part I, and follow "clean" copies of the 2002 and 1983 rules.

- **The 2004 ABA Model Court Rule on Insurance Disclosure,** which can be found in Part I.

- **The 2012 ABA Model Rule for Admission by Motion,** which can be found in Part I.

- **The 2012 ABA Model Rule on Practice Pending Admission,** which can also be found in Part I.

- **The ABA Model Code of Professional Responsibility (1969),** although no state remains a "Code state" (New York was the last such state, but effective April 1, 2009, became a "Model Rule" state.) Nevertheless, we have included the Model Code in Part II and contemplate doing so for the foreseeable future because of its usefulness in tracing the genesis of many of the Model Rules and also because important case law from former Code states refer to the Code sections.

- A **California - Model Rules Comparison** that compares the ABA Model Rules to the California Rules and includes a substantive comparison between the 1983 Model Rules and the 2002 Model Rules. In this way, the 1983 Rules, the 2002 Rules (where substantive changes were made) and the more recent changes to those rules (in 2003, 2008, 2009, 2012, and 2013) are compared to the California Rules and relevant California statutes. This can be found in Part III, together with a table cross-referencing the California standards to the Model Rules.

- **The California Rules of Professional Conduct,** originally adopted in 1989 and 1992 and periodically amended, together with selected provisions of the California State Bar Act from the **California Business & Professions Code.**[1] Both the rules and statutes are in Part IV, together with selected statutes from the California Evidence Code, and State Bar Resolutions on Pro Bono and Limited Scope Legal Services and Selected California Rules of Court Regarding Multijurisdictional Practice.

- **ABA Model Code of Judicial Conduct** and **California Code of Judicial Ethics**. We include the Judicial Codes of the ABA and California. Both Codes are in Part V.

- **SEC Final Standards of Professional Conduct** in Part VI.

---

[1] California, unique among states, has lawyer conduct standards that emanate from both the state legislative process and the state Supreme Court. The Rules of Professional Conduct are proposed and adopted by the State Bar of California and then approved by the California Supreme Court. The legislature, however, also has plenary power to regulate lawyers' conduct, memorialized in the State Bar Act, codified at California Business & Professions Code §§ 6000 et seq. There is, however, no codified plan for the court and legislature to work in concert. As a result, as to those issues that are dealt with directly by legislation, including most significantly confidentiality, the court has historically been reluctant to intrude or impose itself on the legislative process, and has tended to leave modifications up to the legislature.

In particular, we hope the **Rules Comparison** will be of value both in comparing California standards to the ABA standards *and also* the 1983 ABA Rules to the 2002 ABA Rules. As we have with the "red-line" version of the 2002 Rules, we have updated the Rules Comparison periodically as there have been amendments to the Model Rules or the California Rules. However, it is important to note that our intent is not to provide an exhaustive comparison between the 1983 and 2002 versions. For a brief excellent comparison of the two sets of rules that not only discusses the substantive differences, but the reasons for the commission's actions, see Margaret Colgate Love, *The Revised ABA Model Rules of Professional Conduct: Summary of the Work of "Ethics 2000,"* 15 Geo. J. Legal Ethics 441 (2002). In addition, the Ethics 2000 Reporter's Explanation of Changes for each Model Rule is available at: http://www.americanbar.org/ groups/professional responsibility/policy/ethics 2000 commission/e2k report home.html. A compilation of all of the Reporter's Explanations of Changes can be found at: http://www.americanbar.org/content/dam/aba/ migrated/cpr/e2k/10 85rem.pdf.

Since the ABA's adoption of the 2002 Rules, there have been a number of changes not only to the Model Rules, but also to other rules and regulations governing lawyer conduct. We highlight significant changes below.

Changes to the Model Rules Since 2002.

2012-2013 Changes to the Model Rules proposed by the Ethics 20/20 Commission. The ABA Ethics 20/20 Commission was created in 2009 by then-ABA President Carolyn B. Lamm to engage in a thorough review of the Model Rules and the U.S. system of lawyer governance and regulation in light of technological advances and developments in the global practice of law. The Commission's web site can be found at: http://www.americanbar.org/groups/professional responsibility/aba commission on ethics 20 20.html. The Commission completed its work in February 2013.

In August 2012 and again in February 2013, the Commission presented proposals to the ABA House of Delegates that were adopted with only minor revisions. All of the revisions have been included in this volume, not only in the 2002 Model Rules, but also in the redline version comparing the 2002 Model Rules to the 1983 Model Rules and in Part III, which contains the comparison of the Model Rules to the California Rules. Although detailed descriptions of the changes are included in that section, it is appropriate to highlight some of the changes here:

- *Rule 1.1 (Competence).* Two new comments, Comments [6] and [7], have been added to provide guidance concerning a lawyer's responsibilities with respect to outsourcing work to lawyers outside of the firm in which the lawyer works. Perhaps the most publicized Ethics 20/20 revision to the Rules is a clause added to Comment [8] (formerly numbered [6]), which states that to maintain the requisite knowledge and skill, a lawyer should stay current with changes in the law and its practice, "including the benefits and risks associated with relevant technology." Time will tell whether this provision will be viewed as imposing a duty on lawyers to stay current with technology changes or will be seen primarily as a recommended best practice.

- *Rule 1.4 (Communication).* In acknowledgement that clients and lawyers use a variety of technologies to communicate, a comment urging lawyers to return telephone calls now more broadly urges them to "promptly respond to or acknowledge client communications." Such communications include emails and would also appear to include texting and other similar communications.

- *Rule 1.6 (Confidentiality).* Two new sections have been added to the black letter of the rule. New paragraph (b)(7) creates an exception to permit disclosure of confidential information for the limited purpose of clearing law firm conflicts of interest. New paragraph (c) to "make reasonable efforts" to avoid inadvertent or unauthorized disclosure of, or inappropriate access to, confidential client information. New comments have been added to elaborate on the duties imposed by these new sections.

- *Rule 1.18 (Duties to Prospective Clients)*. The definition of "prospective client" has been clarified and an important sentence has been added to Comment [2] to make clear that a person who communicates with a lawyer in order to disqualify the lawyer is not a "prospective client."

- *Rule 4.4 (Respect for Rights of Third Persons)*. Rule 4.4(b) has been revised to expand its application not only to physical "documents" but also to "electronically stored information." The comments to the Rule have similarly been expanded to provide more guidance to lawyers on handling electronic information.

- *Rule 5.3 (Responsibilities Regarding Nonlawyer Assistance)*. The Comment to Rule 5.3 has been substantially revised and supplemented to address a lawyer's responsibilities regarding work that is outsourced to nonlawyers.

- *Rule 5.5 (Unauthorized Practice of Law Multijurisdictional Practice of Law)*. Several revisions have been made to the Rule to conform it to the new Model Rule for Admission by Motion and the new Model Rule on Practice Pending Admission, which are also the work product of the Ethics 20/20 Commission. In addition, several more revisions were made to the rule that, if adopted by a state, would grant foreign lawyers the same kinds of privileges accorded domestic lawyers who work as in-house counsel and who are licensed in United States jurisdictions other than the jurisdiction in which they work.

- *Rules 7.1 (Communications Concerning a Lawyer's Services), 7.2 (Advertising) and 7.3 (Solicitation of Clients)*. Each of these rules has undergone a number of revisions to address issues raised by the various technologies lawyers use to market their legal services. Of particular note is the inclusion of a definition for "solicitation" in new Comment [1] to Rule 7.3.

- *Rule 8.5 (Disciplinary Authority; Choice of Law)*. A comment revision provides that, in determining a lawyer's reasonable belief as to controlling law under paragraph (b)(2), a choice of law agreement, i.e., a written agreement between client and lawyer that specifies a particular jurisdiction, may be considered if the agreement was obtained with the client's informed consent, confirmed in the agreement.

There were also relatively minor revisions to the definition of "writing" in *Rule 1.0 (Terminology)* and to *Model Rule 1.17* (Sale of Law Practice). See Part III for details.

2009 Revisions to the Model Rules: Model Rule 1.10 (imputation and screening). The big news in 2009 was the ABA's adoption, in February and August of 2009, of amendments to Model Rule 1.10 that broadly permit non-consensual screening of lawyers who move from one *private* firm to another *private* firm. In effect, the Model Rule provision places private lawyers more or less on an equal footing with government lawyers, who are governed under MR 1.11, in their ability to be screened. The rule allows such screening even if the screened lawyer had a substantial and direct involvement in the former client's case, and even if the former and current clients' cases were "substantially related." The rule, in effect, changes the presumption that a laterally-moving lawyer would share confidential information with his or her new firm. As of this writing, only two jurisdiction have adopted the Model Rule 1.10(a)(2) screening provisions verbatim: Connecticut and Idaho. Nevertheless, there are 13 other jurisdictions that have adopted screening provisions that broadly permit screening of private lawyers similar to the Model Rule: Delaware, D.C., Illinois, Kentucky, Maryland, Michigan, Montana, North Carolina, Oregon, Pennsylvania, Rhode Island, Utah and Washington. In addition, another 14 jurisdictions permit screening in limited situations, i.e., the jurisdiction's provision permits screening only if a lawyer did not "substantially participate," or was not "substantially involved," did not have a "substantial role," did not have "primary responsibility," etc., in the former client's matter, or when any confidential information that the lawyer might have obtained is deemed not material to the current representation (e.g., Mass.) or "is not likely to be significant" (e.g., Minn.) Jurisdictions that permit screening in such limited situations are: Arizona, Colorado, Indiana, Massachusetts, Minnesota, Nevada, New Hampshire, New Jersey, New Mexico, North Dakota, Ohio, Tennessee, Vermont, and Wisconsin.

2008 Revisions to Model Rule 3.8. After 2003 no further amendments were made to the Model Rules until February 2008, when the House of Delegates adopted Model Rule 3.8, paragraphs (g) and (h). Based on provisions adopted by the New York State Bar Association in November 2007, MR 3.8(g) and (h) codify the duties of prosecutors when they learn of possible false convictions. Paragraph (g) sets forth a prosecutor's minimal duties when the prosecutor "knows of new, credible and material evidence" indicating a defendant was wrongfully convicted. Where the conviction took place in a prosecutor's jurisdiction, paragraph (h) requires the prosecutor "to remedy the conviction."

2003 Revisions to Model Rules 1.6 and 1.13. In August 2003, ABA Model Rules 1.6 (Confidentiality) and 1.13 (Organization as Client), among the most important, underwent material revision following the corporate responsibility debacles in the early part of this decade. Both rules were modified to increase the permissible scope of attorney whistleblowing.

2002 Revisions to Model Rules 5.5 and 8.5 (Multijurisdictional Practice). In August 2002, the ABA House of Delegates adopted substantial revisions to Model Rules 5.5 and 8.5 that the ABA's MJP Commission had recommended in order to address the issues presented by multijurisdictional practice.

The ABA Model Court Rule on Insurance Disclosure

In August 2004, the ABA House of Delegates adopted an important model court rule on malpractice insurance disclosure. This rule requires a lawyer licensed in the jurisdiction to certify on his or her annual registration form whether the lawyer has and intends to maintain professional liability insurance. This model rule can be found at the end of Part I. A total of 24 jurisdictions now have some form of regulation for insurance disclosures. As we note in our introduction to that rule, a number of jurisdictions require lawyers to disclose the fact they do not have malpractice insurance directly to their clients, while still others require attorney disclosure as part of the lawyers' annual dues registration. In 2009, the California Supreme Court adopted a rule of professional conduct, effective January 1, 2010, that requires lawyers to disclose to their clients the fact they do *not* have liability insurance. See Cal. R. Prof. C. 3-410 in Part IV below.

2005 and 2006 ABA Resolutions Concerning the Attorney-Client Privilege

In 2005, the ABA House of Delegates unanimously approved a resolution on the attorney-client privilege that "opposes policies, practices and procedures of governmental agencies that have the effect of eroding the attorney-client privilege and work-product doctrine," and "the routine practice by government officials of seeking to obtain a waiver of the attorney-client privilege or work product doctrine through the granting or denial of any benefit or advantage." The resolution grew out of the work of the ABA's Task Force on Attorney-Client Privilege. This task force was formed in response to concerns that some government agencies have been routinely demanding that those subject to their regulatory oversight, particularly corporations, waive the privilege and work product protections in order to receive favorable treatment during criminal investigations and negotiations.

In 2006, the ABA House of Delegates again unanimously approved a resolution on the attorney-client privilege that opposes "policies, practices and procedures of governmental bodies that have the effect of eroding the attorney-client privilege and work product doctrine" and "the routine practice by government officials of seeking to obtain a waiver of the attorney-client privilege or work product doctrine through the granting or denial of any benefit or advantage."

2002 Sarbanes-Oxley Act & SEC Regulations

The 2002 Sarbanes-Oxley legislation required the SEC to create regulations addressing the duties of attorneys who are confronted by wrongdoing on the part of their "issuer client." While the "Final Standards of Professional Conduct" eventually adopted by the SEC are limited to reporting duties in matters overseen by the SEC, the impact of these regulations has been far broader, and warrants their inclusion in this volume. We direct particular attention to section 205.3, directly addressing reporting, and section 205.2, which contains the definitions used in the SEC standards. See Part VI.

Also of note is a provision in the SEC's proposed draft that the SEC did not include in the Final Standards — the so-called "noisy withdrawal" requirement. That proposal would have required a lawyer to (1) withdraw from the representation if the "issuer client" did not take appropriate action to correct violations of the securities laws; (2) notify the SEC in writing that the lawyer's withdrawal was based on "professional considerations"; and (3) affirmatively disavow any opinions, documents, etc. that the lawyer might have submitted and that the lawyer had discovered were materially misleading. This broad and rather controversial "noisy withdrawal" language still has not, as of this writing, been added to the SEC "Final Standards."

Changes to the California Rules of Professional Conduct, California Rules of Court, and Business & Professions Code Since 2002

In 2004, Section 6068(e) of the California Business & Professions Code, California's statutory duty of confidentiality, was amended to allow for the first time a California lawyer to disclose confidential information to prevent a criminal act reasonably likely to result in death or substantial bodily harm. Soon thereafter, California Rule of Professional Conduct 3-100, which tracks and elaborates upon the statutory exception, was approved by the California Supreme Court. (See footnote 1 above for a discussion of the dual role of legislature and court in drafting California ethics rules.) Both section 6068(e) and rule 3-100 became effective on July 1, 2004. We have described how rule 3-100 differs from Model Rule 1.6 in our California — Model Rules Comparison.

In 2004, the California Supreme Court also approved California Rules of Court 964-967 [subsequently renumbered Rules 9.45 to 9.48], addressing Multijurisdictional Practice ("MJP"). California's approach to regulating MJP thus differs markedly from the ABA, which has addressed MJP in the Model Rules. These rules, together with several other rules of court that address MJP situations, as well as the rule regulating the conduct of certified law students, may be found in the section titled "Selected California Rules of Court Regarding Multijurisdictional Practice" in Part IV. Our California — Model Rules Comparison includes a comparison of the rules of court to ABA Model Rule 5.5.

In 2005, the California legislature reorganized and revised the California statute governing attorney work product, now found at Code Civ. Proc. § 2018.01 to 2018.08 (formerly Code Civ. Proc. § 2018). The revisions became effective on July 1, 2005.

In 2007, the California Supreme Court engaged in a major overhaul of the state's Rules of Court. Effective January 1, 2007, the California Supreme Court implemented a major restructuring, reordering, and renumbering of over 1000 Rules of Court to make them clearer, better organized and easier to read. All of California's rules concerning multijurisdictional practice ("MJP") were given new numbers. We made those changes to those rules but kept the old numbers in brackets for ease of reference. The Court Rules can be found at the end of Part IV.

In 2008, substantive amendments were made to Bus. & Prof. Code §§ 6211-6213, which govern IOLTA deposit accounts. In addition, a new subdivision (c) was added to Bus. & Prof. Code § 6155, which governs Internet attorney matching services.

In July 2009, the California Supreme Court approved two new rules of professional conduct, one rule that became effective immediately and a second rule that become operative on January 1, 2010. The first rule is California Rule 1-650, which is based on Model Rule 6.5, and is intended to facilitate private firm lawyers' participation in limited legal services programs. The second rule, which became operative on January 1, 2010, is the aforementioned rule 3-410, and requires lawyers to disclose to their clients the fact they do not have liability insurance. Both rules can be found in the California Rules of Professional Conduct, in Part IV.

In 2014, several new provisions of the California State Bar Act were enacted, most notably those included in Article 16, Bus. & Prof. Code §§ 6240 – 6242, which is intended to regulate lawyers who provide services under the proposed federal Immigration Reform Act. Although the Act has not yet been passed or signed into law, Article 16 sets forth provisions that will govern lawyer conduct in California once federal legislation becomes operative. By its terms, Article 16 will apply to both members of the California Bar and any other lawyer providing legal services under the Act in California. (Bus. & Prof. Code § 6241.) We have included Article 16 in this volume.

California is one of the few jurisdictions in which evidentiary privileges are governed by statute rather than common law. California courts can neither create new privileges nor add to or abrogate existing privileges. Since our last edition in 2014, important revisions to the California Evidence Code were enacted, including recognition of two new privileges: a human trafficking caseworker-victim privilege (Evid. Code §§ 1038 et seq.) and a lawyer referral service-client privilege (Evid. Code § 965 et seq.) We include the latter, together with the Evidence Code sections relevant to the lawyer-client privilege, in this volume.

FURTHER NOTES ON THE MATERIALS IN THIS BOOK:

Every state empaneled a committee or task force to review the Ethics 2000 Commission's recommended changes to the Model Rules. Forty-eight jurisdictions have now adopted new rules that incorporate post-Ethics 2000 revisions (Alabama, Alaska, Arizona, Arkansas, Colorado, Connecticut, Delaware, District of Columbia, Florida, Hawaii, Idaho, Illinois, Indiana, Iowa, Kansas, Kentucky, Louisiana, Maine, Maryland, Massachusetts, Michigan, Minnesota, Mississippi, Missouri, Montana, Nebraska, Nevada, New Hampshire, New Jersey, New Mexico, New York, North Carolina, North Dakota, Ohio, Oklahoma, Oregon, Pennsylvania, Rhode Island, South Carolina, South Dakota, Tennessee, Utah, Vermont, Virginia, Washington, West Virginia,

Wisconsin and Wyoming). Of particular note, five of those states represent the last of the Code states: Iowa, New York, Nebraska, Ohio and Oregon. Thus, there is no state that still uses the Model Code as its source of lawyer regulation. One state (Georgia) has a committee that is studying the Ethics 2000 changes. The Supreme Court of Texas submitted proposed Rules of Professional Conduct that incorporated Ethics 2000 revisions for a referendum by members of the Texas State Bar, who rejected the proposal. It is not clear when or if new rules might be submitted again for a vote, or if the Supreme Court might act to implement post-Ethics 2000 revisions despite the rejection by referendum. West Virginia's Office of Disciplinary Counsel has submitted proposed rules to the state's Supreme Court. No further information is available at this time.

Finally, in California, the only state whose rules are neither ABA Code- nor ABA Rules-based, in 2010 the State Bar adopted a set of rules that for the first time incorporated the style, format and numbering system of the Model Rules, and that in many respects follow the Model Rules' content. In 2013, the State Bar, in consultation with the California Supreme Court, began submitting proposed rules in a piecemeal fashion to the Court.

However, in September 2014, the Court ended that initial rules revision project and directed the State Bar to empanel a new Rules Commission to re-study and recommend revised California Rules of Professional Conduct. The Supreme Court stated that the second Commission was to "begin with the current [California Rules] and focus on revisions that are necessary to address developments in the law, and that eliminate, where possible, any unnecessary differences between California's rules and those used by a preponderance of the states."[2]

Perhaps most important, the Supreme Court stated the overarching principle that should guide the second Commission's efforts:

> "The second Commission should also be guided in its task by the principle that the [rules'] historical purpose is to regulate the professional conduct of members of the bar, and that as such, the proposed rules should remain a set of minimum disciplinary standards. While the second Commission may be guided by and refer to the American Bar Association's Model Rules of Professional Conduct when appropriate, it should avoid incorporating the purely aspirational or ethical considerations that are present in the Model Rules and Comments."[3]

The second Commission convened for the first time in early spring 2015. The deadline for submission of the revised rules to the Supreme Court is March 31, 2017. As we have done in the past with the first Commission, we will follow and report on the work of this second Commission.

---

[2] September 19, 2015 Letter from Frank McGuire, Court Administrator and Clerk to the Supreme Court, to Senator Joseph Dunn (Ret.), then-Executive Director of the State Bar of California.

[3] *Id.*

Multijurisdictional practice ("MJP") is here to stay. As set out in more detail in the introduction to California's MJP rules, at the time of writing, 46 jurisdictions had adopted a rule either identical to, or similar to Model Rule 5.5, while the review committee in one jurisdiction has recommended the adoption of a form of the rule. The rule is under study in one other jurisdiction. The same is true for Rule 8.5, the other MJP-adopted Model Rule of Professional Conduct, with 46 jurisdictions having adopted some form of the rule, one recommending its adoption, and two having it under study.

While we expect further Model Rule adoptions to occur, two points should be noted. ***First,*** two states continue to operate with rules based on the pre-Ethics 2000 Model Rules (Georgia and Texas). The ABA's Center for Professional Responsibility Policy Implementation Committee provides updates on rules adoptions in the states at http://www.americanbar.org/groups/professional_responsibility/policy.html [last visited 9/6/2015].

Second, and perhaps more important, even those states that have adopted post-Ethics 2000 versions of the Model Rules have not adopted the Model Rules verbatim. We mention this so that users of this book will not use it in their practices without also consulting their own jurisdiction's rules. Even Delaware, the only state we are aware of that has adopted the Model Rules nearly verbatim, has adopted at least two provisions that vary from the Model Rules. One is a rule that permits a lawyer to divide a fee with another lawyer even if the lawyer provides no legal services or does not assume responsibility for the matter (Del. Rule of Prof. Conduct 1.5(e)). Moreover, although Delaware's rule on screening of private lawyers, Delaware Rule 1.10(c), broadly permits screening, it differs in significant respects from Model Rule 1.10(a)(2).

As might be expected, some of the former Code states have diverged significantly from the Model Rules, retaining provisions from their former codes. For example, Oregon rejected the 2003 changes to Model Rule 1.6, used its existing standards on lawyer mediators instead of adopting Model Rule 2.4, and kept a number of its other existing rules, including those addressing screening, sales of law practices, and covert activity. New York has also retained a great number of its former Code provisions in its new rules, and has not officially adopted the Model Rule comments. Divergence from the substance of the Model Rules, however, is not limited to former Code states. For example, both New Jersey and Pennsylvania, Model Rules states of long standing, continue to have rules that depart markedly from the Model Rules in many respects.

California's Second Rules Revision Commission has embarked on its new project to study and recommend revisions to the current California Rules, as described above. Professor Kevin E. Mohr of Western State College of Law, who continues as co-author of this rules volume, remains in his capacity as the Consultant, or "reporter," to the second California Rule Revision Commission, as he was to the first. As such, he is well-placed to update the California materials in this volume.

In future editions of this rules book, we will continue to provide updates and "keep score" as states adopt revisions to their rules, and we will attempt to identify any trends in lawyer regulation as they develop throughout our 50 states and the District of Columbia.

Richard Zitrin
Kevin E. Mohr
September 2015

PART I

AMERICAN BAR ASSOCIATION MODEL RULES OF PROFESSIONAL CONDUCT (2002)

AS AMENDED BY THE HOUSE OF DELEGATES – THROUGH FEBRUARY 2013

Table of Contents

		Page
Preamble: A Lawyer's Responsibilities, and Scope		3

Rule

1.0	Terminology	7
1.1	Competence	10
1.2	Scope of Representation and Allocation of Authority Between Client and Lawyer	12
1.3	Diligence	15
1.4	Communication	16
1.5	Fees	18
1.6	Confidentiality of Information	22
1.7	Conflict of Interest: Current Clients	28
1.8	Conflict of Interest: Current Clients: Specific Rules	37
1.9	Duties to Former Clients	44
1.10	Imputation of Conflicts of Interest: General Rule	47
1.11	Special Conflicts of Interest for Former and Current Government Officers and Employees	50
1.12	Former Judge, Arbitrator, Mediator or Other Third-Party Neutral	54
1.13	Organization as Client	55
1.14	Client with Diminished Capacity	60
1.15	Safekeeping Property	63
1.16	Declining or Terminating Representation	64
1.17	Sale of Law Practice	67
1.18	Duties to Prospective Client	70
2.1	Advisor	72
2.2	Deleted	73

Rule		Page
2.3	Evaluation for Use by Third Persons	73
2.4	Lawyer Serving as Third-Party Neutral	75
3.1	Meritorious Claims and Contentions	77
3.2	Expediting Litigation	77
3.3	Candor toward the Tribunal	78
3.4	Fairness to Opposing Party and Counsel	82
3.5	Impartiality and Decorum of the Tribunal	83
3.6	Trial Publicity	84
3.7	Lawyer as Witness	87
3.8	Special Responsibilities of a Prosecutor	88
3.9	Advocate in Nonadjudicative Proceedings	91
4.1	Truthfulness in Statements to Others	92
4.2	Communication with Person Represented by Counsel	93
4.3	Dealing with Unrepresented Person	95
4.4	Respect for Rights of Third Persons	96
5.1	Responsibilities of Partners, Managers, and Supervisory Lawyers	97
5.2	Responsibilities of a Subordinate Lawyer	99
5.3	Responsibilities Regarding Nonlawyer Assistance	99
5.4	Professional Independence of a Lawyer	101
5.5	Unauthorized Practice of Law Multijurisdictional Practice of Law	102
5.6	Restrictions on Right to Practice	107
5.7	Responsibilities Regarding Law-related Services	108
6.1	Voluntary Pro Bono Publico Service	110
6.2	Accepting Appointments	113
6.3	Membership in Legal Services Organization	114
6.4	Law Reform Activities Affecting Client Interests	114
6.5	Non Profit and Court-Annexed Limited Legal Services Programs	115
7.1	Communications Concerning a Lawyer's Services	116
7.2	Advertising	117
7.3	Solicitation of Clients	120
7.4	Communication of Fields of Practice and Specialization	123
7.5	Firm Names and Letterheads	124
7.6	Political Contributions to Obtain Government Legal Engagements or appointments by Judges	125
8.1	Bar Admission and Disciplinary Matters	126
8.2	Judicial and Legal Officials	127
8.3	Reporting Professional Misconduct	127
8.4	Misconduct	128
8.5	Disciplinary Authority; Choice of Law	130

PREAMBLE: A LAWYER'S RESPONSIBILITIES

[1]   A lawyer, as a member of the legal profession, is a representative of clients, an officer of the legal system and a public citizen having special responsibility for the quality of justice.

[2]   As a representative of clients, a lawyer performs various functions. As advisor, a lawyer provides a client with an informed understanding of the client's legal rights and obligations and explains their practical implications. As advocate, a lawyer zealously asserts the client's position under the rules of the adversary system. As negotiator, a lawyer seeks a result advantageous to the client but consistent with requirements of honest dealings with others. As an evaluator, a lawyer acts by examining a client's legal affairs and reporting about them to the client or to others.

[3]   In addition to these representational functions, a lawyer may serve as a third-party neutral, a nonrepresentational role helping the parties to resolve a dispute or other matter. Some of these Rules apply directly to lawyers who are or have served as third-party neutrals. See, e.g., Rules 1.12 and 2.4. In addition, there are Rules that apply to lawyers who are not active in the practice of law or to practicing lawyers even when they are acting in a nonprofessional capacity. For example, a lawyer who commits fraud in the conduct of a business is subject to discipline for engaging in conduct involving dishonesty, fraud, deceit or misrepresentation. See Rule 8.4.

[4]   In all professional functions a lawyer should be competent, prompt and diligent. A lawyer should maintain communication with a client concerning the representation. A lawyer should keep in confidence information relating to representation of a client except so far as disclosure is required or permitted by the Rules of Professional Conduct or other law.

[5]   A lawyer's conduct should conform to the requirements of the law, both in professional service to clients and in the lawyer's business and personal affairs. A lawyer should use the law's procedures only for legitimate purposes and not to harass or intimidate others. A lawyer should demonstrate respect for the legal system and for those who serve it, including judges, other lawyers and public officials. While it is a lawyer's duty, when necessary, to challenge the rectitude of official action, it is also a lawyer's duty to uphold legal process.

[6]   As a public citizen, a lawyer should seek improvement of the law, access to the legal system, the administration of justice and the quality of service rendered by the legal profession. As a member of a learned profession, a lawyer should cultivate knowledge of the law beyond its use for clients, employ that knowledge in reform of the law and work to strengthen legal education. In addition, a lawyer should further the public's understanding of and confidence in the rule of law and the justice system because legal institutions in a constitutional democracy depend on popular participation and support to maintain their authority. A lawyer should be mindful of deficiencies in the administration of justice and of the fact that the poor, and sometimes persons

who are not poor, cannot afford adequate legal assistance. Therefore, all lawyers should devote professional time and resources and use civic influence to ensure equal access to our system of justice for all those who because of economic or social barriers cannot afford or secure adequate legal counsel. A lawyer should aid the legal profession in pursuing these objectives and should help the bar regulate itself in the public interest.

[7]   Many of a lawyer's professional responsibilities are prescribed in the Rules of Professional Conduct, as well as substantive and procedural law. However, a lawyer is also guided by personal conscience and the approbation of professional peers. A lawyer should strive to attain the highest level of skill, to improve the law and the legal profession and to exemplify the legal profession's ideals of public service.

[8]   A lawyer's responsibilities as a representative of clients, an officer of the legal system and a public citizen are usually harmonious. Thus, when an opposing party is well represented, a lawyer can be a zealous advocate on behalf of a client and at the same time assume that justice is being done. So also, a lawyer can be sure that preserving client confidences ordinarily serves the public interest because people are more likely to seek legal advice, and thereby heed their legal obligations, when they know their communications will be private.

[9]   In the nature of law practice, however, conflicting responsibilities are encountered. Virtually all difficult ethical problems arise from conflict between a lawyer's responsibilities to clients, to the legal system and to the lawyer's own interest in remaining an ethical person while earning a satisfactory living. The Rules of Professional Conduct often prescribe terms for resolving such conflicts. Within the framework of these Rules, however, many difficult issues of professional discretion can arise. Such issues must be resolved through the exercise of sensitive professional and moral judgment guided by the basic principles underlying the Rules. These principles include the lawyer's obligation zealously to protect and pursue a client's legitimate interests, within the bounds of the law, while maintaining a professional, courteous and civil attitude toward all persons involved in the legal system.

[10]   The legal profession is largely self-governing. Although other professions also have been granted powers of self-government, the legal profession is unique in this respect because of the close relationship between the profession and the processes of government and law enforcement. This connection is manifested in the fact that ultimate authority over the legal profession is vested largely in the courts.

[11]   To the extent that lawyers meet the obligations of their professional calling, the occasion for government regulation is obviated. Self-regulation also helps maintain the legal profession's independence from government domination. An independent legal profession is an important force in preserving government under law, for abuse of legal authority is more readily challenged by a profession whose members are not dependent on government for the right to practice.

[12]   The legal profession's relative autonomy carries with it special responsibilities of self-government. The profession has a responsibility to assure that its regulations are conceived in the public interest and not in furtherance of parochial or self-interested concerns of the bar. Every lawyer is responsible for observance of the Rules of Professional Conduct. A lawyer should also aid in securing their observance by other lawyers. Neglect of these responsibilities compromises the independence of the profession and the public interest which it serves.

[13]   Lawyers play a vital role in the preservation of society. The fulfillment of this role requires an understanding by lawyers of their relationship to our legal system. The Rules of Professional Conduct, when properly applied, serve to define that relationship.

SCOPE

[14]   The Rules of Professional Conduct are rules of reason. They should be interpreted with reference to the purposes of legal representation and of the law itself. Some of the Rules are imperatives, cast in the terms "shall" or "shall not." These define proper conduct for purposes of professional discipline. Others, generally cast in the term "may," are permissive and define areas under the Rules in which the lawyer has discretion to exercise professional judgment. No disciplinary action should be taken when the lawyer chooses not to act or acts within the bounds of such discretion. Other Rules define the nature of relationships between the lawyer and others. The Rules are thus partly obligatory and disciplinary and partly constitutive and descriptive in that they define a lawyer's professional role. Many of the Comments use the term "should." Comments do not add obligations to the Rules but provide guidance for practicing in compliance with the Rules.

[15]   The Rules presuppose a larger legal context shaping the lawyer's role. That context includes court rules and statutes relating to matters of licensure, laws defining specific obligations of lawyers and substantive and procedural law in general. The Comments are sometimes used to alert lawyers to their responsibilities under such other law.

[16]   Compliance with the Rules, as with all law in an open society, depends primarily upon understanding and voluntary compliance, secondarily upon reinforcement by peer and public opinion and finally, when necessary, upon enforcement through disciplinary proceedings. The Rules do not, however, exhaust the moral and ethical considerations that should inform a lawyer, for no worthwhile human activity can be completely defined by legal rules. The Rules simply provide a framework for the ethical practice of law.

[17]   Furthermore, for purposes of determining the lawyer's authority and responsibility, principles of substantive law external to these Rules determine whether a client-lawyer relationship exists. Most of the duties flowing from the client-lawyer relationship attach only after the client has requested the lawyer to render legal services and the lawyer has agreed to do so. But there

are some duties, such as that of confidentiality under Rule 1.6, that attach when the lawyer agrees to consider whether a client-lawyer relationship shall be established. See Rule 1.18. Whether a client-lawyer relationship exists for any specific purpose can depend on the circumstances and may be a question of fact.

[18]   Under various legal provisions, including constitutional, statutory and common law, the responsibilities of government lawyers may include authority concerning legal matters that ordinarily reposes in the client in private client-lawyer relationships. For example, a lawyer for a government agency may have authority on behalf of the government to decide upon settlement or whether to appeal from an adverse judgment. Such authority in various respects is generally vested in the attorney general and the state's attorney in state government, and their federal counterparts, and the same may be true of other government law officers. Also, lawyers under the supervision of these officers may be authorized to represent several government agencies in intragovernmental legal controversies in circumstances where a private lawyer could not represent multiple private clients. These Rules do not abrogate any such authority.

[19]   Failure to comply with an obligation or prohibition imposed by a Rule is a basis for invoking the disciplinary process. The Rules presuppose that disciplinary assessment of a lawyer's conduct will be made on the basis of the facts and circumstances as they existed at the time of the conduct in question and in recognition of the fact that a lawyer often has to act upon uncertain or incomplete evidence of the situation. Moreover, the Rules presuppose that whether or not discipline should be imposed for a violation, and the severity of a sanction, depend on all the circumstances, such as the willfulness and seriousness of the violation, extenuating factors and whether there have been previous violations.

[20]   Violation of a Rule should not itself give rise to a cause of action against a lawyer nor should it create any presumption in such a case that a legal duty has been breached. In addition, violation of a Rule does not necessarily warrant any other nondisciplinary remedy, such as disqualification of a lawyer in pending litigation. The Rules are designed to provide guidance to lawyers and to provide a structure for regulating conduct through disciplinary agencies. They are not designed to be a basis for civil liability. Furthermore, the purpose of the Rules can be subverted when they are invoked by opposing parties as procedural weapons. The fact that a Rule is a just basis for a lawyer's self-assessment, or for sanctioning a lawyer under the administration of a disciplinary authority, does not imply that an antagonist in a collateral proceeding or transaction has standing to seek enforcement of the Rule. Nevertheless, since the Rules do establish standards of conduct by lawyers, a lawyer's violation of a Rule may be evidence of breach of the applicable standard of conduct.

[21]   The Comment accompanying each Rule explains and illustrates the meaning and purpose of the Rule. The Preamble and this note on Scope provide general orientation. The Comments are intended as guides to interpretation, but the text of each Rule is authoritative.

RULE 1.0: TERMINOLOGY

(a)　　"Belief" or "believes" denotes that the person involved actually supposed the fact in question to be true. A person's belief may be inferred from circumstances.

(b)　　"Confirmed in writing," when used in reference to the informed consent of a person, denotes informed consent that is given in writing by the person or a writing that a lawyer promptly transmits to the person confirming an oral informed consent. See paragraph (e) for the definition of "informed consent." If it is not feasible to obtain or transmit the writing at the time the person gives informed consent, then the lawyer must obtain or transmit it within a reasonable time thereafter.

(c)　　"Firm" or "law firm" denotes a lawyer or lawyers in a law partnership, professional corporation, sole proprietorship or other association authorized to practice law; or lawyers employed in a legal services organization or the legal department of a corporation or other organization.

(d)　　"Fraud" or "fraudulent" denotes conduct that is fraudulent under the substantive or procedural law of the applicable jurisdiction and has a purpose to deceive.

(e)　　"Informed consent" denotes the agreement by a person to a proposed course of conduct after the lawyer has communicated adequate information and explanation about the material risks of and reasonably available alternatives to the proposed course of conduct.

(f)　　"Knowingly," "known," or "knows" denotes actual knowledge of the fact in question. A person's knowledge may be inferred from circumstances.

(g)　　"Partner" denotes a member of a partnership, a shareholder in a law firm organized as a professional corporation, or a member of an association authorized to practice law.

(h)　　"Reasonable" or "reasonably" when used in relation to conduct by a lawyer denotes the conduct of a reasonably prudent and competent lawyer.

(i)　　"Reasonable belief" or "reasonably believes" when used in reference to a lawyer denotes that the lawyer believes the matter in question and that the circumstances are such that the belief is reasonable.　　*Subjective*

(j)　　"Reasonably should know" when used in reference to a lawyer denotes that a lawyer of reasonable prudence and competence would ascertain the matter in question.　　*Objective*

(k)　　"Screened" denotes the isolation of a lawyer from any participation in a matter through the timely imposition of procedures within a firm that are reasonably adequate under the circumstances to protect information that the isolated lawyer is obligated to protect under these Rules or other law.

(l)   "Substantial" when used in reference to degree or extent denotes a material matter of clear and weighty importance.

(m)   "Tribunal" denotes a court, an arbitrator in a binding arbitration proceeding or a legislative body, administrative agency or other body acting in an adjudicative capacity. A legislative body, administrative agency or other body acts in an adjudicative capacity when a neutral official, after the presentation of evidence or legal argument by a party or parties, will render a binding legal judgment directly affecting a party's interests in a particular matter.

(n)   "Writing" or "written" denotes a tangible or electronic record of a communication or representation, including handwriting, typewriting, printing, photostating, photography, audio or video-recording, and electronic communications. A "signed" writing includes an electronic sound, symbol or process attached to or logically associated with a writing and executed or adopted by a person with the intent to sign the writing.

Comment

Confirmed in Writing

[1]   If it is not feasible to obtain or transmit a written confirmation at the time the client gives informed consent, then the lawyer must obtain or transmit it within a reasonable time thereafter. If a lawyer has obtained a client's informed consent, the lawyer may act in reliance on that consent so long as it is confirmed in writing within a reasonable time there-after.

Firm

[2]   Whether two or more lawyers constitute a firm within paragraph (c) can depend on the specific facts. For example, two practitioners who share office space and occasionally consult or assist each other ordinarily would not be regarded as constituting a firm. However, if they present themselves to the public in a way that suggests that they are a firm or conduct themselves as a firm, they should be regarded as a firm for purposes of the Rules. The terms of any formal agreement between associated lawyers are relevant in determining whether they are a firm, as is the fact that they have mutual access to information concerning the clients they serve. Furthermore, it is relevant in doubtful cases to consider the underlying purpose of the Rule that is involved. A group of lawyers could be regarded as a firm for purposes of the Rule that the same lawyer should not represent opposing parties in litigation, while it might not be so regarded for purposes of the Rule that information acquired by one lawyer is attributed to another.

[3]   With respect to the law department of an organization, including the government, there is ordinarily no question that the members of the department constitute a firm within the meaning of the Rules of Professional Conduct. There can be uncertainty, however, as to the identity of

the client. For example, it may not be clear whether the law department of a corporation represents a subsidiary or an affiliated corporation, as well as the corporation by which the members of the department are directly employed. A similar question can arise concerning an unincorporated association and its local affiliates.

[4]   Similar questions can also arise with respect to lawyers in legal aid and legal services organizations. Depending upon the structure of the organization, the entire organization or different components of it may constitute a firm or firms for purposes of these Rules.

Fraud

[5]   When used in these Rules, the terms "fraud" or "fraudulent" refer to conduct that is characterized as such under the substantive or procedural law of the applicable jurisdiction and has a purpose to deceive. This does not include merely negligent misrepresentation or negligent failure to apprise another of relevant information. For purposes of these Rules, it is not necessary that anyone has suffered damages or relied on the misrepresentation or failure to inform.

Informed Consent

[6]   Many of the Rules of Professional Conduct require the lawyer to obtain the informed consent of a client or other person (e.g., a former client or, under certain circumstances, a prospective client) before accepting or continuing representation or pursuing a course of conduct. See, e.g., Rules 1.2(c), 1.6(a) and 1.7(b). The communication necessary to obtain such consent will vary according to the Rule involved and the circumstances giving rise to the need to obtain informed consent. The lawyer must make reasonable efforts to ensure that the client or other person possesses information reasonably adequate to make an informed decision. Ordinarily, this will require communication that includes a disclosure of the facts and circumstances giving rise to the situation, any explanation reasonably necessary to inform the client or other person of the material advantages and disadvantages of the proposed course of conduct and a discussion of the client's or other person's options and alternatives. In some circumstances it may be appropriate for a lawyer to advise a client or other person to seek the advice of other counsel. A lawyer need not inform a client or other person of facts or implications already known to the client or other person; nevertheless, a lawyer who does not personally inform the client or other person assumes the risk that the client or other person is inadequately informed and the consent is invalid. In determining whether the information and explanation provided are reasonably adequate, relevant factors include whether the client or other person is experienced in legal matters generally and in making decisions of the type involved, and whether the client or other person is independently represented by other counsel in giving the consent. Normally, such persons need less information and explanation than others, and generally a client or other person who is independently represented by other counsel in giving the consent should be assumed to have given informed consent.

[7]   Obtaining informed consent will usually require an affirmative response by the client or other person. In general, a lawyer may not assume consent from a client's or other person's silence. Consent may be inferred, however, from the conduct of a client or other person who has reasonably adequate information about the matter. A number of Rules require that a person's consent be confirmed in writing. See Rules 1.7(b) and 1.9(a). For a definition of "writing" and "confirmed in writing," see paragraphs (n) and (b). Other Rules require that a client's consent be obtained in a writing signed by the client. See, e.g., Rules 1.8(a) and (g). For a definition of "signed," see paragraph (n).

Screened

[8]   This definition applies to situations where screening of a personally disqualified lawyer is permitted to remove imputation of a conflict of interest under Rules 1.10, 1.11, 1.12 or 1.18.

[9]   The purpose of screening is to assure the affected parties that confidential information known by the personally disqualified lawyer remains protected. The personally disqualified lawyer should acknowledge the obligation not to communicate with any of the other lawyers in the firm with respect to the matter. Similarly, other lawyers in the firm who are working on the matter should be informed that the screening is in place and that they may not communicate with the personally disqualified lawyer with respect to the matter. Additional screening measures that are appropriate for the particular matter will depend on the circumstances. To implement, reinforce and remind all affected lawyers of the presence of the screening, it may be appropriate for the firm to undertake such procedures as a written undertaking by the screened lawyer to avoid any communication with other firm personnel and any contact with any firm files or other information, including information in electronic form, relating to the matter, written notice and instructions to all other firm personnel forbidding any communication with the screened lawyer relating to the matter, denial of access by the screened lawyer to firm files or other information, including information in electronic form, relating to the matter and periodic reminders of the screen to the screened lawyer and all other firm personnel.

[10]   In order to be effective, screening measures must be implemented as soon as practical after a lawyer or law firm knows or reasonably should know that there is a need for screening.

RULE 1.1: COMPETENCE

A lawyer shall provide competent representation to a client. Competent representation requires the legal knowledge, skill, thoroughness and preparation reasonably necessary for the representation.

Comment

Legal Knowledge and Skill

[1]   In determining whether a lawyer employs the requisite knowledge and skill in a particular matter, relevant factors include the relative

complexity and specialized nature of the matter, the lawyer's general experience, the lawyer's training and experience in the field in question, the preparation and study the lawyer is able to give the matter and whether it is feasible to refer the matter to, or associate or consult with, a lawyer of established competence in the field in question. In many instances, the required proficiency is that of a general practitioner. Expertise in a particular field of law may be required in some circumstances.

[2]   A lawyer need not necessarily have special training or prior experience to handle legal problems of a type with which the lawyer is unfamiliar. A newly admitted lawyer can be as competent as a practitioner with long experience. Some important legal skills, such as the analysis of precedent, the evaluation of evidence and legal drafting, are required in all legal problems. Perhaps the most fundamental legal skill consists of determining what kind of legal problems a situation may involve, a skill that necessarily transcends any particular specialized knowledge. A lawyer can provide adequate representation in a wholly novel field through necessary study. Competent representation can also be provided through the association of a lawyer of established competence in the field in question.

[3]   In an emergency a lawyer may give advice or assistance in a matter in which the lawyer does not have the skill ordinarily required where referral to or consultation or association with another lawyer would be impractical. Even in an emergency, however, assistance should be limited to that reasonably necessary in the circumstances, for ill-considered action under emergency conditions can jeopardize the client's interest.

[4]   A lawyer may accept representation where the requisite level of competence can be achieved by reasonable preparation. This applies as well to a lawyer who is appointed as counsel for an unrepresented person. See also Rule 6.2.

Thoroughness and Preparation

[5]   Competent handling of a particular matter includes inquiry into and analysis of the factual and legal elements of the problem, and use of methods and procedures meeting the standards of competent practitioners. It also includes adequate preparation. The required attention and preparation are determined in part by what is at stake; major litigation and complex transactions ordinarily require more extensive treatment than matters of lesser complexity and consequence. An agreement between the lawyer and the client regarding the scope of the representation may limit the matters for which the lawyer is responsible. See Rule 1.2(c).

Retaining or contracting with other lawyers

[6]   Before a lawyer retains or contracts with other lawyers outside the lawyer's own firm to provide or assist in the provision of legal services to a client, the lawyer should ordinarily obtain informed consent from the client and must reasonably believe that the other lawyers' services will contribute to the competent and ethical representation of the client. See also Rules 1.2 (allocation

of authority), 1.4 (communication with client), 1.5(e) (fee sharing), 1.6 (confidentiality), and 5.5(a) (unauthorized practice of law). The reasonableness of the decision to retain or contract with other lawyers outside the lawyer's own firm will depend upon the circumstances, including the education, experience and reputation of the nonfirm lawyers; the nature of the services assigned to the nonfirm lawyers; and the legal protections, professional conduct rules, and ethical environments of the jurisdictions in which the services will be performed, particularly relating to confidential information.

[7]   When lawyers from more than one law firm are providing legal services to the client on a particular matter, the lawyers ordinarily should consult with each other and the client about the scope of their respective representations and the allocation of responsibility among them. See Rule 1.2. When making allocations of responsibility in a matter pending before a tribunal, lawyers and parties may have additional obligations that are a matter of law beyond the scope of these Rules.

Maintaining Competence

[8]   To maintain the requisite knowledge and skill, a lawyer should keep abreast of changes in the law and its practice, including the benefits and risks associated with relevant technology, engage in continuing study and education and comply with all continuing legal education requirements to which the lawyer is subject.

RULE 1.2: SCOPE OF REPRESENTATION AND ALLOCATION OF AUTHORITY BETWEEN CLIENT AND LAWYER

(a)   **Subject to paragraphs (c) and (d), a lawyer shall abide by a client's decisions concerning the objectives of representation and, as required by Rule 1.4, shall consult with the client as to the means by which they are to be pursued. A lawyer may take such action on behalf of the client as is impliedly authorized to carry out the representation. A lawyer shall abide by a client's decision whether to settle a matter. In a criminal case, the lawyer shall abide by the client's decision, after consultation with the lawyer, as to a plea to be entered, whether to waive jury trial and whether the client will testify.**

(b)   **A lawyer's representation of a client, including representation by appointment, does not constitute an endorsement of the client's political, economic, social or moral views or activities.**

(c)   **A lawyer may limit the scope of the representation if the limitation is reasonable under the circumstances and the client gives informed consent.**

(d)   **A lawyer shall not counsel a client to engage, or assist a client, in conduct that the lawyer knows is criminal or fraudulent, but a lawyer may discuss the legal consequences of any proposed course of conduct with a client and may counsel or assist a client to make a good faith effort to determine the validity, scope, meaning or application of the law.**

Comment

Allocation of Authority between Client and Lawyer

[1] Paragraph (a) confers upon the client the ultimate authority to determine the purposes to be served by legal representation, within the limits imposed by law and the lawyer's professional obligations. The decisions specified in paragraph (a), such as whether to settle a civil matter, must also be made by the client. See Rule 1.4(a)(1) for the lawyer's duty to communicate with the client about such decisions. With respect to the means by which the client's objectives are to be pursued, the lawyer shall consult with the client as required by Rule 1.4(a)(2) and may take such action as is impliedly authorized to carry out the representation.

[2] On occasion, however, a lawyer and a client may disagree about the means to be used to accomplish the client's objectives. Clients normally defer to the special knowledge and skill of their lawyer with respect to the means to be used to accomplish their objectives, particularly with respect to technical, legal and tactical matters. Conversely, lawyers usually defer to the client regarding such questions as the expense to be incurred and concern for third persons who might be adversely affected. Because of the varied nature of the matters about which a lawyer and client might disagree and because the actions in question may implicate the interests of a tribunal or other persons, this Rule does not prescribe how such disagreements are to be resolved. Other law, however, may be applicable and should be consulted by the lawyer. The lawyer should also consult with the client and seek a mutually acceptable resolution of the disagreement. If such efforts are unavailing and the lawyer has a fundamental disagreement with the client, the lawyer may withdraw from the representation. See Rule 1.16(b)(4). Conversely, the client may resolve the disagreement by discharging the lawyer. See Rule 1.16(a)(3).

[3] At the outset of a representation, the client may authorize the lawyer to take specific action on the client's behalf without further consultation. Absent a material change in circumstances and subject to Rule 1.4, a lawyer may rely on such an advance authorization. The client may, however, revoke such authority at any time.

[4] In a case in which the client appears to be suffering diminished capacity, the lawyer's duty to abide by the client's decisions is to be guided by reference to Rule 1.14.

Independence from Client's Views or Activities

[5] Legal representation should not be denied to people who are unable to afford legal services, or whose cause is controversial or the subject of popular disapproval. By the same token, representing a client does not constitute approval of the client's views or activities.

Agreements Limiting Scope of Representation

[6] The scope of services to be provided by a lawyer may be limited by agreement with the client or by the terms under which the lawyer's services are made available to the client. When a lawyer has been retained by an insurer

to represent an insured, for example, the representation may be limited to matters related to the insurance coverage. A limited representation may be appropriate because the client has limited objectives for the representation. In addition, the terms upon which representation is undertaken may exclude specific means that might otherwise be used to accomplish the client's objectives. Such limitations may exclude actions that the client thinks are too costly or that the lawyer regards as repugnant or imprudent.

[7]   Although this Rule affords the lawyer and client substantial latitude to limit the representation, the limitation must be reasonable under the circumstances. If, for example, a client's objective is limited to securing general information about the law the client needs in order to handle a common and typically uncomplicated legal problem, the lawyer and client may agree that the lawyer's services will be limited to a brief telephone consultation. Such a limitation, however, would not be reasonable if the time allotted was not sufficient to yield advice upon which the client could rely. Although an agreement for a limited representation does not exempt a lawyer from the duty to provide competent representation, the limitation is a factor to be considered when determining the legal knowledge, skill, thoroughness and preparation reasonably necessary for the representation. See Rule 1.1.

[8]   All agreements concerning a lawyer's representation of a client must accord with the Rules of Professional Conduct and other law. See, e.g., Rules 1.1, 1.8 and 5.6.

Criminal, Fraudulent and Prohibited Transactions

[9]   Paragraph (d) prohibits a lawyer from knowingly counseling or assisting a client to commit a crime or fraud. This prohibition, however, does not preclude the lawyer from giving an honest opinion about the actual consequences that appear likely to result from a client's conduct. Nor does the fact that a client uses advice in a course of action that is criminal or fraudulent of itself make a lawyer a party to the course of action. There is a critical distinction between presenting an analysis of legal aspects of questionable conduct and recommending the means by which a crime or fraud might be committed with impunity.

[10]   When the client's course of action has already begun and is continuing, the lawyer's responsibility is especially delicate. The lawyer is required to avoid assisting the client, for example, by drafting or delivering documents that the lawyer knows are fraudulent or by suggesting how the wrongdoing might be concealed. A lawyer may not continue assisting a client in conduct that the lawyer originally supposed was legally proper but then discovers is criminal or fraudulent. The lawyer must, therefore, withdraw from the representation of the client in the matter. See Rule 1.16(a). In some cases, withdrawal alone might be insufficient. It may be necessary for the lawyer to give notice of the fact of withdrawal and to disaffirm any opinion, document, affirmation or the like. See Rule 4.1.

[11]   Where the client is a fiduciary, the lawyer may be charged with special obligations in dealings with a beneficiary.

[12]   Paragraph (d) applies whether or not the defrauded party is a party to the transaction. Hence, a lawyer must not participate in a transaction to effectuate criminal or fraudulent avoidance of tax liability. Paragraph (d) does not preclude undertaking a criminal defense incident to a general retainer for legal services to a lawful enterprise. The last clause of paragraph (d) recognizes that determining the validity or interpretation of a statute or regulation may require a course of action involving disobedience of the statute or regulation or of the interpretation placed upon it by governmental authorities.

[13]   If a lawyer comes to know or reasonably should know that a client expects assistance not permitted by the Rules of Professional Conduct or other law or if the lawyer intends to act contrary to the client's instructions, the lawyer must consult with the client regarding the limitations on the lawyer's conduct. See Rule 1.4(a)(5).

RULE 1.3: DILIGENCE

A lawyer shall act with reasonable diligence and promptness in representing a client.

Comment

[1]   A lawyer should pursue a matter on behalf of a client despite opposition, obstruction or personal inconvenience to the lawyer, and take whatever lawful and ethical measures are required to vindicate a client's cause or endeavor. A lawyer must also act with commitment and dedication to the interests of the client and with zeal in advocacy upon the client's behalf. A lawyer is not bound, however, to press for every advantage that might be realized for a client. For example, a lawyer may have authority to exercise professional discretion in determining the means by which a matter should be pursued. See Rule 1.2. The lawyer's duty to act with reasonable diligence does not require the use of offensive tactics or preclude the treating of all persons involved in the legal process with courtesy and respect.

[2]   A lawyer's work load must be controlled so that each matter can be handled competently.

[3]   Perhaps no professional shortcoming is more widely resented than procrastination. A client's interests often can be adversely affected by the passage of time or the change of conditions; in extreme instances, as when a lawyer overlooks a statute of limitations, the client's legal position may be destroyed. Even when the client's interests are not affected in substance, however, unreasonable delay can cause a client needless anxiety and undermine confidence in the lawyer's trustworthiness. A lawyer's duty to act with reasonable promptness, however, does not preclude the lawyer from agreeing to a reasonable request for a postponement that will not prejudice the lawyer's client.

[4]   Unless the relationship is terminated as provided in Rule 1.16, a lawyer should carry through to conclusion all matters undertaken for a client.

If a lawyer's employment is limited to a specific matter, the relationship terminates when the matter has been resolved. If a lawyer has served a client over a substantial period in a variety of matters, the client sometimes may assume that the lawyer will continue to serve on a continuing basis unless the lawyer gives notice of withdrawal. Doubt about whether a client-lawyer relationship still exists should be clarified by the lawyer, preferably in writing, so that the client will not mistakenly suppose the lawyer is looking after the client's affairs when the lawyer has ceased to do so. For example, if a lawyer has handled a judicial or administrative proceeding that produced a result adverse to the client and the lawyer and the client have not agreed that the lawyer will handle the matter on appeal, the lawyer must consult with the client about the possibility of appeal before relinquishing responsibility for the matter. See Rule 1.4(a)(2). Whether the lawyer is obligated to prosecute the appeal for the client depends on the scope of the representation the lawyer has agreed to provide to the client. See Rule 1.2.

[5] To prevent neglect of client matters in the event of a sole practitioner's death or disability, the duty of diligence may require that each sole practitioner prepare a plan, in conformity with applicable rules, that designates another competent lawyer to review client files, notify each client of the lawyer's death or disability, and determine whether there is a need for immediate protective action. Cf. Rule 28 of the American Bar Association Model Rules for Lawyer Disciplinary Enforcement (providing for court appointment of a lawyer to inventory files and take other protective action in absence of a plan providing for another lawyer to protect the interests of the clients of a deceased or disabled lawyer).

RULE 1.4: COMMUNICATION

(a) A lawyer shall:

(1) promptly inform the client of any decision or circumstance with respect to which the client's informed consent, as defined in Rule 1.0(e), is required by these Rules;

(2) reasonably consult with the client about the means by which the client's objectives are to be accomplished;

(3) keep the client reasonably informed about the status of the matter;

(4) promptly comply with reasonable requests for information; and

(5) consult with the client about any relevant limitation on the lawyer's conduct when the lawyer knows that the client expects assistance not permitted by the Rules of Professional Conduct or other law.

(b) A lawyer shall explain a matter to the extent reasonably necessary to permit the client to make informed decisions regarding the representation.

Comment

[1]   Reasonable communication between the lawyer and the client is necessary for the client effectively to participate in the representation.

Communicating with Client

[2]   If these Rules require that a particular decision about the representation be made by the client, paragraph (a)(1) requires that the lawyer promptly consult with and secure the client's consent prior to taking action unless prior discussions with the client have resolved what action the client wants the lawyer to take. For example, a lawyer who receives from opposing counsel an offer of settlement in a civil controversy or a proffered plea bargain in a criminal case must promptly inform the client of its substance unless the client has previously indicated that the proposal will be acceptable or unacceptable or has authorized the lawyer to accept or to reject the offer. See Rule 1.2(a).

[3]   Paragraph (a)(2) requires the lawyer to reasonably consult with the client about the means to be used to accomplish the client's objectives. In some situations — depending on both the importance of the action under consideration and the feasibility of consulting with the client — this duty will require consultation prior to taking action. In other circumstances, such as during a trial when an immediate decision must be made, the exigency of the situation may require the lawyer to act without prior consultation. In such cases the lawyer must nonetheless act reasonably to inform the client of actions the lawyer has taken on the client's behalf. Additionally, paragraph (a)(3) requires that the lawyer keep the client reasonably informed about the status of the matter, such as significant developments affecting the timing or the substance of the representation.

[4]   A lawyer's regular communication with clients will minimize the occasions on which a client will need to request information concerning the representation. When a client makes a reasonable request for information, however, paragraph (a)(4) requires prompt compliance with the request, or if a prompt response is not feasible, that the lawyer, or a member of the lawyer's staff, acknowledge receipt of the request and advise the client when a response may be expected. A lawyer should promptly respond to or acknowledge client communications.

Explaining Matters

[5]   The client should have sufficient information to participate intelligently in decisions concerning the objectives of the representation and the means by which they are to be pursued, to the extent the client is willing and able to do so. Adequacy of communication depends in part on the kind of advice or assistance that is involved. For example, when there is time to explain a proposal made in a negotiation, the lawyer should review all important provisions with the client before proceeding to an agreement. In litigation a lawyer should explain the general strategy and prospects of success and ordinarily should consult the client on tactics that are likely to result in significant

expense or to injure or coerce others. On the other hand, a lawyer ordinarily will not be expected to describe trial or negotiation strategy in detail. The guiding principle is that the lawyer should fulfill reasonable client expectations for information consistent with the duty to act in the client's best interests, and the client's overall requirements as to the character of representation. In certain circumstances, such as when a lawyer asks a client to consent to a representation affected by a conflict of interest, the client must give informed consent, as defined in Rule 1.0(e).

[6]   Ordinarily, the information to be provided is that appropriate for a client who is a comprehending and responsible adult. However, fully informing the client according to this standard may be impracticable, for example, where the client is a child or suffers from diminished capacity. See Rule 1.14. When the client is an organization or group, it is often impossible or inappropriate to inform every one of its members about its legal affairs; ordinarily, the lawyer should address communications to the appropriate officials of the organization. See Rule 1.13. Where many routine matters are involved, a system of limited or occasional reporting may be arranged with the client.

Withholding Information

[7]   In some circumstances, a lawyer may be justified in delaying transmission of information when the client would be likely to react imprudently to an immediate communication. Thus, a lawyer might withhold a psychiatric diagnosis of a client when the examining psychiatrist indicates that disclosure would harm the client. A lawyer may not withhold information to serve the lawyer's own interest or convenience or the interests or convenience of another person. Rules or court orders governing litigation may provide that information supplied to a lawyer may not be disclosed to the client. Rule 3.4(c) directs compliance with such rules or orders.

RULE 1.5: FEES

(a)   **A lawyer shall not make an agreement for, charge, or collect an unreasonable fee or an unreasonable amount for expenses. The factors to be considered in determining the reasonableness of a fee include the following:**

(1)   **the time and labor required, the novelty and difficulty of the questions involved, and the skill requisite to perform the legal service properly;**

(2)   **the likelihood, if apparent to the client, that the acceptance of the particular employment will preclude other employment by the lawyer;**

(3)   **the fee customarily charged in the locality for similar legal services;**

(4)   **the amount involved and the results obtained;**

(5)   **the time limitations imposed by the client or by the circumstances;**

     (6) the nature and length of the professional relationship with the client;

     (7) the experience, reputation, and ability of the lawyer or lawyers performing the services; and

     (8) whether the fee is fixed or contingent.

     (b) The scope of the representation and the basis or rate of the fee and expenses for which the client will be responsible shall be communicated to the client, preferably in writing, before or within a reasonable time after commencing the representation, except when the lawyer will charge a regularly represented client on the same basis or rate. Any changes in the basis or rate of the fee or expenses shall also be communicated to the client.

[margin handwritten: not mandatory]

     (c) A fee may be contingent on the outcome of the matter for which the service is rendered, except in a matter in which a contingent fee is prohibited by paragraph (d) or other law. A contingent fee agreement shall be in a writing signed by the client and shall state the method by which the fee is to be determined, including the percentage or percentages that shall accrue to the lawyer in the event of settlement, trial or appeal; litigation and other expenses to be deducted from the recovery; and whether such expenses are to be deducted before or after the contingent fee is calculated. The agreement must clearly notify the client of any expenses for which the client will be liable whether or not the client is the prevailing party. Upon conclusion of a contingent fee matter, the lawyer shall provide the client with a written statement stating the outcome of the matter and, if there is a recovery, showing the remittance to the client and the method of its determination.

[margin handwritten: contingency fee allowed]

     (d) A lawyer shall not enter into an arrangement for, charge, or collect:

     (1) any fee in a domestic relations matter, the payment or amount of which is contingent upon the securing of a divorce or upon the amount of alimony or support, or property settlement in lieu thereof; or

     (2) a contingent fee for representing a defendant in a criminal case.

[margin handwritten: No contingency]

     (e) A division of a fee between lawyers who are not in the same firm may be made only if:

[margin handwritten: Have to need both]

     (1) the division is in proportion to the services performed by each lawyer or each lawyer assumes joint responsibility for the representation;

     (2) the client agrees to the arrangement, including the share each lawyer will receive, and the agreement is confirmed in writing; and

     (3) the total fee is reasonable.

Comment

Reasonableness of Fee and Expenses

[1]   Paragraph (a) requires that lawyers charge fees that are reasonable under the circumstances. The factors specified in (1) through (8) are not exclusive. Nor will each factor be relevant in each instance. Paragraph (a) also requires that expenses for which the client will be charged must be reasonable. A lawyer may seek reimbursement for the cost of services performed in-house, such as copying, or for other expenses incurred in-house, such as telephone charges, either by charging a reasonable amount to which the client has agreed in advance or by charging an amount that reasonably reflects the cost incurred by the lawyer.

Basis or Rate of Fee

[2]   When the lawyer has regularly represented a client, they ordinarily will have evolved an understanding concerning the basis or rate of the fee and the expenses for which the client will be responsible. In a new client-lawyer relationship, however, an understanding as to fees and expenses must be promptly established. Generally, it is desirable to furnish the client with at least a simple memorandum or copy of the lawyer's customary fee arrangements that states the general nature of the legal services to be provided, the basis, rate or total amount of the fee and whether and to what extent the client will be responsible for any costs, expenses or disbursements in the course of the representation. A written statement concerning the terms of the engagement reduces the possibility of misunderstanding.

[3]   Contingent fees, like any other fees, are subject to the reasonableness standard of paragraph (a) of this Rule. In determining whether a particular contingent fee is reasonable, or whether it is reasonable to charge any form of contingent fee, a lawyer must consider the factors that are relevant under the circumstances. Applicable law may impose limitations on contingent fees, such as a ceiling on the percentage allowable, or may require a lawyer to offer clients an alternative basis for the fee. Applicable law also may apply to situations other than a contingent fee, for example, government regulations regarding fees in certain tax matters.

Terms of Payment

[4]   A lawyer may require advance payment of a fee, but is obliged to return any unearned portion. See Rule 1.16(d). A lawyer may accept property in payment for services, such as an ownership interest in an enterprise, providing this does not involve acquisition of a proprietary interest in the cause of action or subject matter of the litigation contrary to Rule 1.8 (i). However, a fee paid in property instead of money may be subject to the requirements of Rule 1.8(a) because such fees often have the essential qualities of a business transaction with the client.

[5]   An agreement may not be made whose terms might induce the lawyer improperly to curtail services for the client or perform them in a way contrary to the client's interest. For example, a lawyer should not enter into an

agreement whereby services are to be provided only up to a stated amount when it is foreseeable that more extensive services probably will be required, unless the situation is adequately explained to the client. Otherwise, the client might have to bargain for further assistance in the midst of a proceeding or transaction. However, it is proper to define the extent of services in light of the client's ability to pay. A lawyer should not exploit a fee arrangement based primarily on hourly charges by using wasteful procedures.

Prohibited Contingent Fees

[6]   Paragraph (d) prohibits a lawyer from charging a contingent fee in a domestic relations matter when payment is contingent upon the securing of a divorce or upon the amount of alimony or support or property settlement to be obtained. This provision does not preclude a contract for a contingent fee for legal representation in connection with the recovery of post-judgment balances due under support, alimony or other financial orders because such contracts do not implicate the same policy concerns.

Division of Fee

[7]   A division of fee is a single billing to a client covering the fee of two or more lawyers who are not in the same firm. A division of fee facilitates association of more than one lawyer in a matter in which neither alone could serve the client as well, and most often is used when the fee is contingent and the division is between a referring lawyer and a trial specialist. Paragraph (e) permits the lawyers to divide a fee either on the basis of the proportion of services they render or if each lawyer assumes responsibility for the representation as a whole. In addition, the client must agree to the arrangement, including the share that each lawyer is to receive, and the agreement must be confirmed in writing. Contingent fee agreements must be in a writing signed by the client and must otherwise comply with paragraph (c) of this Rule. Joint responsibility for the representation entails financial and ethical responsibility for the representation as if the lawyers were associated in a partnership. A lawyer should only refer a matter to a lawyer whom the referring lawyer reasonably believes is competent to handle the matter. See Rule 1.1.

[8]   Paragraph (e) does not prohibit or regulate division of fees to be received in the future for work done when lawyers were previously associated in a law firm.

Disputes over Fees

[9]   If a procedure has been established for resolution of fee disputes, such as an arbitration or mediation procedure established by the bar, the lawyer must comply with the procedure when it is mandatory, and, even when it is voluntary, the lawyer should conscientiously consider submitting to it. Law may prescribe a procedure for determining a lawyer's fee, for example, in representation of an executor or administrator, a class or a person entitled to a reasonable fee as part of the measure of damages. The lawyer entitled to such a fee and a lawyer representing another party concerned with the fee should comply with the prescribed procedure.

RULE 1.6: CONFIDENTIALITY OF INFORMATION

(a)   A lawyer shall not reveal information relating to the representation of a client unless the client gives informed consent, the disclosure is impliedly authorized in order to carry out the representation or the disclosure is permitted by paragraph (b).

(b)   A lawyer may reveal information relating to the representation of a client to the extent the lawyer reasonably believes necessary:

(1)   to prevent reasonably certain death or substantial bodily harm;

(2)   to prevent the client from committing a crime or fraud that is reasonably certain to result in substantial injury to the financial interests or property of another and in furtherance of which the client has used or is using the lawyer's services;

(3)   to prevent, mitigate or rectify substantial injury to the financial interests or property of another that is reasonably certain to result or has resulted from the client's commission of a crime or fraud in furtherance of which the client has used the lawyer's services;

(4)   to secure legal advice about the lawyer's compliance with these Rules;

(5)   to establish a claim or defense on behalf of the lawyer in a controversy between the lawyer and the client, to establish a defense to a criminal charge or civil claim against the lawyer based upon conduct in which the client was involved, or to respond to allegations in any proceeding concerning the lawyer's representation of the client;

(6)   to comply with other law or a court order; or

(7)   to detect and resolve conflicts of interest arising from the lawyer's change of employment or from changes in the composition or ownership of a firm, but only if the revealed information would not compromise the attorney-client privilege or otherwise prejudice the client.

(c)   A lawyer shall make reasonable efforts to prevent the inadvertent or unauthorized disclosure of, or unauthorized access to, information relating to the representation of a client.

Comment

[1]   This Rule governs the disclosure by a lawyer of information relating to the representation of a client during the lawyer's representation of the client. See Rule 1.18 for the lawyer's duties with respect to information provided to the lawyer by a prospective client, Rule 1.9(c)(2) for the lawyer's duty not to reveal information relating to the lawyer's prior representation of

a former client and Rules 1.8(b) and 1.9(c)(1) for the lawyer's duties with respect to the use of such information to the disadvantage of clients and former clients.

[2]   A fundamental principle in the client-lawyer relationship is that, in the absence of the client's informed consent, the lawyer must not reveal information relating to the representation. See Rule 1.0(e) for the definition of informed consent. This contributes to the trust that is the hallmark of the client-lawyer relationship. The client is thereby encouraged to seek legal assistance and to communicate fully and frankly with the lawyer even as to embarrassing or legally damaging subject matter. The lawyer needs this information to represent the client effectively and, if necessary, to advise the client to refrain from wrongful conduct. Almost without exception, clients come to lawyers in order to determine their rights and what is, in the complex of laws and regulations, deemed to be legal and correct. Based upon experience, lawyers know that almost all clients follow the advice given, and the law is upheld.

[3]   The principle of client-lawyer confidentiality is given effect by related bodies of law: the attorney-client privilege, the work product doctrine and the rule of confidentiality established in professional ethics. The attorney-client privilege and work-product doctrine apply in judicial and other proceedings in which a lawyer may be called as a witness or otherwise required to produce evidence concerning a client. The rule of client-lawyer confidentiality applies in situations other than those where evidence is sought from the lawyer through compulsion of law. The confidentiality rule, for example, applies not only to matters communicated in confidence by the client but also to all information relating to the representation, whatever its source. A lawyer may not disclose such information except as authorized or required by the Rules of Professional Conduct or other law. See also Scope.

[4]   Paragraph (a) prohibits a lawyer from revealing information relating to the representation of a client. This prohibition also applies to disclosures by a lawyer that do not in themselves reveal protected information but could reasonably lead to the discovery of such information by a third person. A lawyer's use of a hypothetical to discuss issues relating to the representation is permissible so long as there is no reasonable likelihood that the listener will be able to ascertain the identity of the client or the situation involved.

Authorized Disclosure

[5]   Except to the extent that the client's instructions or special circumstances limit that authority, a lawyer is impliedly authorized to make disclosures about a client when appropriate in carrying out the representation. In some situations, for example, a lawyer may be impliedly authorized to admit a fact that cannot properly be disputed or to make a disclosure that facilitates a satisfactory conclusion to a matter. Lawyers in a firm may, in the course of the firm's practice, disclose to each other information relating to a client of the firm, unless the client has instructed that particular information be confined to specified lawyers.

Disclosure Adverse to Client

[6]   Although the public interest is usually best served by a strict rule requiring lawyers to preserve the confidentiality of information relating to the representation of their clients, the confidentiality rule is subject to limited exceptions. Paragraph (b)(1) recognizes the overriding value of life and physical integrity and permits disclosure reasonably necessary to prevent reasonably certain death or substantial bodily harm. Such harm is reasonably certain to occur if it will be suffered imminently or if there is a present and substantial threat that a person will suffer such harm at a later date if the lawyer fails to take action necessary to eliminate the threat. Thus, a lawyer who knows that a client has accidentally discharged toxic waste into a town's water supply may reveal this information to the authorities if there is a present and substantial risk that a person who drinks the water will contract a life-threatening or debilitating disease and the lawyer's disclosure is necessary to eliminate the threat or reduce the number of victims.

[7]   Paragraph (b)(2) is a limited exception to the rule of confidentiality that permits the lawyer to reveal information to the extent necessary to enable affected persons or appropriate authorities to prevent the client from committing a crime or fraud, as defined in Rule 1.0(d), that is reasonably certain to result in substantial injury to the financial or property interests of another and in furtherance of which the client has used or is using the lawyer's services. Such a serious abuse of the client-lawyer relationship by the client forfeits the protection of this Rule. The client can, of course, prevent such disclosure by refraining from the wrongful conduct. Although paragraph (b)(2) does not require the lawyer to reveal the client's misconduct, the lawyer may not counsel or assist the client in conduct the lawyer knows is criminal or fraudulent. See Rule 1.2(d). See also Rule 1.16 with respect to the lawyer's obligation or right to withdraw from the representation of the client in such circumstances, and Rule 1.13(c), which permits the lawyer, where the client is an organization, to reveal information relating to the representation in limited circumstances.

[8]   Paragraph (b)(3) addresses the situation in which the lawyer does not learn of the client's crime or fraud until after it has been consummated. Although the client no longer has the option of preventing disclosure by refraining from the wrongful conduct, there will be situations in which the loss suffered by the affected person can be prevented, rectified or mitigated. In such situations, the lawyer may disclose information relating to the representation to the extent necessary to enable the affected persons to prevent or mitigate reasonably certain losses or to attempt to recoup their losses. Paragraph (b)(3) does not apply when a person who has committed a crime or fraud thereafter employs a lawyer for representation concerning that offense.

[9]   A lawyer's confidentiality obligations do not preclude a lawyer from securing confidential legal advice about the lawyer's personal responsibility to comply with these Rules. In most situations, disclosing information to secure such advice will be impliedly authorized for the lawyer to carry out the

representation. Even when the disclosure is not impliedly authorized, paragraph (b) (2) permits such disclosure because of the importance of a lawyer's compliance with the Rules of Professional Conduct.

[10]   Where a legal claim or disciplinary charge alleges complicity of the lawyer in a client's conduct or other misconduct of the lawyer involving representation of the client, the lawyer may respond to the extent the lawyer reasonably believes necessary to establish a defense. The same is true with respect to a claim involving the conduct or representation of a former client. Such a charge can arise in a civil, criminal, disciplinary or other proceeding and can be based on a wrong allegedly committed by the lawyer against the client or on a wrong alleged by a third person, for example, a person claiming to have been defrauded by the lawyer and client acting together. The lawyer's right to respond arises when an assertion of such complicity has been made. Paragraph (b)(3) does not require the lawyer to await the commencement of an action or proceeding that charges such complicity, so that the defense may be established by responding directly to a third party who has made such an assertion. The right to defend also applies, of course, where a proceeding has been commenced.

[11]   A lawyer entitled to a fee is permitted by paragraph (b)(3) to prove the services rendered in an action to collect it. This aspect of the rule expresses the principle that the beneficiary of a fiduciary relationship may not exploit it to the detriment of the fiduciary.

[12]   Other law may require that a lawyer disclose information about a client. Whether such a law supersedes Rule 1.6 is a question of law beyond the scope of these Rules. When disclosure of information relating to the representation appears to be required by other law, the lawyer must discuss the matter with the client to the extent required by Rule 1.4. If, however, the other law supersedes this Rule and requires disclosure, paragraph (b)(4) permits the lawyer to make such disclosures as are necessary to comply with the law.

Detection of Conflicts of Interest

[13]   Paragraph (b)(7) recognizes that lawyers in different firms may need to disclose limited information to each other to detect and resolve conflicts of interest, such as when a lawyer is considering an association with another firm, two or more firms are considering a merger, or a lawyer is considering the purchase of a law practice. See Rule 1.17, Comment [7]. Under these circumstances, lawyers and law firms are permitted to disclose limited information, but only once substantive discussions regarding the new relationship have occurred. Any such disclosure should ordinarily include no more than the identity of the persons and entities involved in a matter, a brief summary of the general issues involved, and information about whether the matter has terminated. Even this limited information, however, should be disclosed only to the extent reasonably necessary to detect and resolve conflicts of interest that might arise from the possible new relationship. Moreover, the disclosure of any information is prohibited if it would compromise the attorney-client privilege or otherwise prejudice the client (e.g., the fact that a corporate client is seeking

advice on a corporate takeover that has not been publicly announced; that a person has consulted a lawyer about the possibility of divorce before the person's intentions are known to the person's spouse; or that a person has consulted a lawyer about a criminal investigation that has not led to a public charge). Under those circumstances, paragraph (a) prohibits disclosure unless the client or former client gives informed consent. A lawyer's fiduciary duty to the lawyer's firm may also govern a lawyer's conduct when exploring an association with another firm and is beyond the scope of these Rules.

[14] Any information disclosed pursuant to paragraph (b)(7) may be used or further disclosed only to the extent necessary to detect and resolve conflicts of interest. Paragraph (b)(7) does not restrict the use of information acquired by means independent of any disclosure pursuant to paragraph (b)(7). Paragraph (b)(7) also does not affect the disclosure of information within a law firm when the disclosure is otherwise authorized, see Comment [5], such as when a lawyer in a firm discloses information to another lawyer in the same firm to detect and resolve conflicts of interest that could arise in connection with undertaking a new representation.

[15] A lawyer may be ordered to reveal information relating to the representation of a client by a court or by another tribunal or governmental entity claiming authority pursuant to other law to compel the disclosure. Absent informed consent of the client to do otherwise, the lawyer should assert on behalf of the client all nonfrivolous claims that the order is not authorized by other law or that the information sought is protected against disclosure by the attorney-client privilege or other applicable law. In the event of an adverse ruling, the lawyer must consult with the client about the possibility of appeal to the extent required by Rule 1.4. Unless review is sought, however, paragraph (b)(4) permits the lawyer to comply with the court's order.

[16] Paragraph (b) permits disclosure only to the extent the lawyer reasonably believes the disclosure is necessary to accomplish one of the purposes specified. Where practicable, the lawyer should first seek to persuade the client to take suitable action to obviate the need for disclosure. In any case, a disclosure adverse to the client's interest should be no greater than the lawyer reasonably believes necessary to accomplish the purpose. If the disclosure will be made in connection with a judicial proceeding, the disclosure should be made in a manner that limits access to the information to the tribunal or other persons having a need to know it and appropriate protective orders or other arrangements should be sought by the lawyer to the fullest extent practicable.

[17] Paragraph (b) permits but does not require the disclosure of information relating to a client's representation to accomplish the purposes specified in paragraphs (b)(1) through (b)(4). In exercising the discretion conferred by this Rule, the lawyer may consider such factors as the nature of the lawyer's relationship with the client and with those who might be injured by the client, the lawyer's own involvement in the transaction and factors that may extenuate the conduct in question. A lawyer's decision not to disclose as

permitted by paragraph (b) does not violate this Rule. Disclosure may be required, however, by other Rules. Some Rules require disclosure only if such disclosure would be permitted by paragraph (b). See Rules 1.2(d), 4.1(b), 8.1 and 8.3. Rule 3.3, on the other hand, requires disclosure in some circumstances regardless of whether such disclosure is permitted by this Rule. See Rule 3.3(c).

Acting Competently to Preserve Confidentiality

[18]   Paragraph (c) requires a lawyer to act competently to safeguard information relating to the representation of a client against unauthorized access by third parties and against inadvertent or unauthorized disclosure by the lawyer or other persons who are participating in the representation of the client or who are subject to the lawyer's supervision. See Rules 1.1, 5.1 and 5.3. The unauthorized access to, or the inadvertent or unauthorized disclosure of, information relating to the representation of a client does not constitute a violation of paragraph (c) if the lawyer has made reasonable efforts to prevent the access or disclosure. Factors to be considered in determining the reasonableness of the lawyer's efforts include, but are not limited to, the sensitivity of the information, the likelihood of disclosure if additional safeguards are not employed, the cost of employing additional safeguards, the difficulty of implementing the safeguards, and the extent to which the safeguards adversely affect the lawyer's ability to represent clients (e.g., by making a device or important piece of software excessively difficult to use). A client may require the lawyer to implement special security measures not required by this Rule or may give informed consent to forgo security measures that would otherwise be required by this Rule. Whether a lawyer may be required to take additional steps to safeguard a client's information in order to comply with other law, such as state and federal laws that govern data privacy or that impose notification requirements upon the loss of, or unauthorized access to, electronic information, is beyond the scope of these Rules. For a lawyer's duties when sharing information with nonlawyers outside the lawyer's own firm, see Rule 5.3, Comments [3]-[4].

[19]   When transmitting a communication that includes information relating to the representation of a client, the lawyer must take reasonable precautions to prevent the information from coming into the hands of unintended recipients. This duty, however, does not require that the lawyer use special security measures if the method of communication affords a reasonable expectation of privacy. Special circumstances, however, may warrant special precautions. Factors to be considered in determining the reasonableness of the lawyer's expectation of confidentiality include the sensitivity of the information and the extent to which the privacy of the communication is protected by law or by a confidentiality agreement. A client may require the lawyer to implement special security measures not required by this Rule or may give informed consent to the use of a means of communication that would otherwise be prohibited by this Rule. Whether a lawyer may be required to take additional steps in order to comply with other law, such as state and federal laws that govern data privacy, is beyond the scope of these Rules.

Former Client

[20]   The duty of confidentiality continues after the client-lawyer relationship has terminated. See Rule 1.9(c)(2). See Rule 1.9(c)(1) for the prohibition against using such information to the disadvantage of the former client.

RULE 1.7: CONFLICT OF INTEREST: CURRENT CLIENTS

(a)   Except as provided in paragraph (b), a lawyer shall not represent a client if the representation involves a concurrent conflict of interest. A concurrent conflict of interest exists if:

(1)   the representation of one client will be directly adverse to another client; or

(2)   there is a significant risk that the representation of one or more clients will be materially limited by the lawyer's responsibilities to another client, a former client or a third person or by a personal interest of the lawyer.

(b)   Notwithstanding the existence of a concurrent conflict of interest under paragraph (a), a lawyer may represent a client if:

(1)   the lawyer reasonably believes that the lawyer will be able to provide competent and diligent representation to each affected client;

(2)   the representation is not prohibited by law;

(3)   the representation does not involve the assertion of a claim by one client against another client represented by the lawyer in the same litigation or other proceeding before a tribunal; and

(4)   each affected client gives informed consent, confirmed in writing.

Comment

General Principles

[1]   Loyalty and independent judgment are essential elements in the lawyer's relationship to a client. Concurrent conflicts of interest can arise from the lawyer's responsibilities to another client, a former client or a third person or from the lawyer's own interests. For specific Rules regarding certain concurrent conflicts of interest, see Rule 1.8. For former client conflicts of interest, see Rule 1.9. For conflicts of interest involving prospective clients, see Rule 1.18. For definitions of "informed consent" and "confirmed in writing," see Rule 1.0(e) and (b).

[2]   Resolution of a conflict of interest problem under this Rule requires the lawyer to: 1) clearly identify the client or clients; 2) determine whether a conflict of interest exists; 3) decide whether the representation may be undertaken despite the existence of a conflict, i.e., whether the conflict is consentable; and 4) if so, consult with the clients affected under paragraph (a)

and obtain their informed consent, confirmed in writing. The clients affected under paragraph (a) include both of the clients referred to in paragraph (a)(1) and the one or more clients whose representation might be materially limited under paragraph (a)(2).

[3] A conflict of interest may exist before representation is undertaken, in which event the representation must be declined, unless the lawyer obtains the informed consent of each client under the conditions of paragraph (b). To determine whether a conflict of interest exists, a lawyer should adopt reasonable procedures, appropriate for the size and type of firm and practice, to determine in both litigation and non-litigation matters the persons and issues involved. See also Comment to Rule 5.1. Ignorance caused by a failure to institute such procedures will not excuse a lawyer's violation of this Rule. As to whether a client-lawyer relationship exists or, having once been established, is continuing, see Comment to Rule 1.3 and Scope.

[4] If a conflict arises after representation has been undertaken, the lawyer ordinarily must withdraw from the representation, unless the lawyer has obtained the informed consent of the client under the conditions of paragraph (b). See Rule 1.16. Where more than one client is involved, whether the lawyer may continue to represent any of the clients is determined both by the lawyer's ability to comply with duties owed to the former client and by the lawyer's ability to represent adequately the remaining client or clients, given the lawyer's duties to the former client. See Rule 1.9. See also Comments [5] and [29].

[5] Unforeseeable developments, such as changes in corporate and other organizational affiliations or the addition or realignment of parties in litigation, might create conflicts in the midst of a representation, as when a company sued by the lawyer on behalf of one client is bought by another client represented by the lawyer in an unrelated matter. Depending on the circumstances, the lawyer may have the option to withdraw from one of the representations in order to avoid the conflict. The lawyer must seek court approval where necessary and take steps to minimize harm to the clients. See Rule 1.16. The lawyer must continue to protect the confidences of the client from whose representation the lawyer has withdrawn. See Rule 1.9(c).

Identifying Conflicts of Interest: Directly Adverse

[6] Loyalty to a current client prohibits undertaking representation directly adverse to that client without that client's informed consent. Thus, absent consent, a lawyer may not act as an advocate in one matter against a person the lawyer represents in some other matter, even when the matters are wholly unrelated. The client as to whom the representation is directly adverse is likely to feel betrayed, and the resulting damage to the client-lawyer relationship is likely to impair the lawyer's ability to represent the client effectively. In addition, the client on whose behalf the adverse representation is undertaken reasonably may fear that the lawyer will pursue that client's case less effectively out of deference to the other client, i.e., that the representation may be materially limited by the lawyer's interest in retaining the current client. Similarly, a directly adverse

conflict may arise when a lawyer is required to cross-examine a client who appears as a witness in a lawsuit involving another client, as when the testimony will be damaging to the client who is represented in the lawsuit. On the other hand, simultaneous representation in unrelated matters of clients whose interests are only economically adverse, such as representation of competing economic enterprises in unrelated litigation, does not ordinarily constitute a conflict of interest and thus may not require consent of the respective clients.

[7]   Directly adverse conflicts can also arise in transactional matters. For example, if a lawyer is asked to represent the seller of a business in negotiations with a buyer represented by the lawyer, not in the same transaction but in another, unrelated matter, the lawyer could not undertake the representation without the informed consent of each client.

Identifying Conflicts of Interest: Material Limitation

[8]   Even where there is no direct adverseness, a conflict of interest exists if there is a significant risk that a lawyer's ability to consider, recommend or carry out an appropriate course of action for the client will be materially limited as a result of the lawyer's other responsibilities or interests. For example, a lawyer asked to represent several individuals seeking to form a joint venture is likely to be materially limited in the lawyer's ability to recommend or advocate all possible positions that each might take because of the lawyer's duty of loyalty to the others. The conflict in effect forecloses alternatives that would otherwise be available to the client. The mere possibility of subsequent harm does not itself require disclosure and consent. The critical questions are the likelihood that a difference in interests will eventuate and, if it does, whether it will materially interfere with the lawyer's independent professional judgment in considering alternatives or foreclose courses of action that reasonably should be pursued on behalf of the client.

Lawyer's Responsibilities to Former Clients and Other Third Persons

[9]   In addition to conflicts with other current clients, a lawyer's duties of loyalty and independence may be materially limited by responsibilities to former clients under Rule 1.9 or by the lawyer's responsibilities to other persons, such as fiduciary duties arising from a lawyer's service as a trustee, executor or corporate director.

Personal Interest Conflicts

[10]   The lawyer's own interests should not be permitted to have an adverse effect on representation of a client. For example, if the probity of a lawyer's own conduct in a transaction is in serious question, it may be difficult or impossible for the lawyer to give a client detached advice. Similarly, when a lawyer has discussions concerning possible employment with an opponent of the lawyer's client, or with a law firm representing the opponent, such discussions could materially limit the lawyer's representation of the client. In addition, a lawyer may not allow related business interests to affect representation, for example, by referring clients to an enterprise in which the lawyer has an undisclosed financial interest. See Rule 1.8 for specific Rules pertaining

to a number of personal interest conflicts, including business transactions with clients. See also Rule 1.10 (personal interest conflicts under Rule 1.7 ordinarily are not imputed to other lawyers in a law firm).

[11]   When lawyers representing different clients in the same matter or in substantially related matters are closely related by blood or marriage, there may be a significant risk that client confidences will be revealed and that the lawyer's family relationship will interfere with both loyalty and independent professional judgment. As a result, each client is entitled to know of the existence and implications of the relationship between the lawyers before the lawyer agrees to undertake the representation. Thus, a lawyer related to another lawyer, e.g., as parent, child, sibling or spouse, ordinarily may not represent a client in a matter where that lawyer is representing another party, unless each client gives informed consent. The disqualification arising from a close family relationship is personal and ordinarily is not imputed to members of firms with whom the lawyers are associated. See Rule 1.10.

[12]   A lawyer is prohibited from engaging in sexual relationships with a client unless the sexual relationship predates the formation of the client-lawyer relationship. See Rule 1.8(j).

Interest of Person Paying for a Lawyer's Service

[13]   A lawyer may be paid from a source other than the client, including a co-client, if the client is informed of that fact and consents and the arrangement does not compromise the lawyer's duty of loyalty or independent judgment to the client. See Rule 1.8(f). If acceptance of the payment from any other source presents a significant risk that the lawyer's representation of the client will be materially limited by the lawyer's own interest in accommodating the person paying the lawyer's fee or by the lawyer's responsibilities to a payer who is also a co-client, then the lawyer must comply with the requirements of paragraph (b) before accepting the representation, including determining whether the conflict is consentable and, if so, that the client has adequate information about the material risks of the representation.

Prohibited Representations

[14]   Ordinarily, clients may consent to representation notwithstanding a conflict. However, as indicated in paragraph (b), some conflicts are nonconsentable, meaning that the lawyer involved cannot properly ask for such agreement or provide representation on the basis of the client's consent. When the lawyer is representing more than one client, the question of consentability must be resolved as to each client.

[15]   Consentability is typically determined by considering whether the interests of the clients will be adequately protected if the clients are permitted to give their informed consent to representation burdened by a conflict of interest. Thus, under paragraph (b)(1), representation is prohibited if in the circumstances the lawyer cannot reasonably conclude that the lawyer will be able to provide competent and diligent representation. See Rule 1.1 (competence) and Rule 1.3 (diligence).

[16] Paragraph (b)(2) describes conflicts that are nonconsentable because the representation is prohibited by applicable law. For example, in some states substantive law provides that the same lawyer may not represent more than one defendant in a capital case, even with the consent of the clients, and under federal criminal statutes certain representations by a former government lawyer are prohibited, despite the informed consent of the former client. In addition, decisional law in some states limits the ability of a governmental client, such as a municipality, to consent to a conflict of interest.

[17] Paragraph (b)(3) describes conflicts that are nonconsentable because of the institutional interest in vigorous development of each client's position when the clients are aligned directly against each other in the same litigation or other proceeding before a tribunal. Whether clients are aligned directly against each other within the meaning of this paragraph requires examination of the context of the proceeding. Although this paragraph does not preclude a lawyer's multiple representation of adverse parties to a mediation (because mediation is not a proceeding before a "tribunal" under Rule 1.0(m)), such representation may be precluded by paragraph (b)(1).

Informed Consent

[18] Informed consent requires that each affected client be aware of the relevant circumstances and of the material and reasonably foreseeable ways that the conflict could have adverse effects on the interests of that client. See Rule 1.0(e) (informed consent). The information required depends on the nature of the conflict and the nature of the risks involved. When representation of multiple clients in a single matter is undertaken, the information must include the implications of the common representation, including possible effects on loyalty, confidentiality and the attorney-client privilege and the advantages and risks involved. See Comments [30] and [31] (effect of common representation on confidentiality).

[19] Under some circumstances it may be impossible to make the disclosure necessary to obtain consent. For example, when the lawyer represents different clients in related matters and one of the clients refuses to consent to the disclosure necessary to permit the other client to make an informed decision, the lawyer cannot properly ask the latter to consent. In some cases the alternative to common representation can be that each party may have to obtain separate representation with the possibility of incurring additional costs. These costs, along with the benefits of securing separate representation, are factors that may be considered by the affected client in determining whether common representation is in the client's interests.

Consent Confirmed in Writing

[20] Paragraph (b) requires the lawyer to obtain the informed consent of the client, confirmed in writing. Such a writing may consist of a document executed by the client or one that the lawyer promptly records and transmits to the client following an oral consent. See Rule 1.0(b). See also Rule 1.0(n) (writing includes electronic transmission). If it is not feasible to

obtain or transmit the writing at the time the client gives informed consent, then the lawyer must obtain or transmit it within a reasonable time thereafter. See Rule 1.0(b). The requirement of a writing does not supplant the need in most cases for the lawyer to talk with the client, to explain the risks and advantages, if any, of representation burdened with a conflict of interest, as well as reasonably available alternatives, and to afford the client a reasonable opportunity to consider the risks and alternatives and to raise questions and concerns. Rather, the writing is required in order to impress upon clients the seriousness of the decision the client is being asked to make and to avoid disputes or ambiguities that might later occur in the absence of a writing.

Revoking Consent

[21]   A client who has given consent to a conflict may revoke the consent and, like any other client, may terminate the lawyer's representation at any time. Whether revoking consent to the client's own representation precludes the lawyer from continuing to represent other clients depends on the circumstances, including the nature of the conflict, whether the client revoked consent because of a material change in circumstances, the reasonable expectations of the other client and whether material detriment to the other clients or the lawyer would result.

Consent to Future Conflict

[22]   Whether a lawyer may properly request a client to waive conflicts that might arise in the future is subject to the test of paragraph (b). The effectiveness of such waivers is generally determined by the extent to which the client reasonably understands the material risks that the waiver entails. The more comprehensive the explanation of the types of future representations that might arise and the actual and reasonably foreseeable adverse consequences of those representations, the greater the likelihood that the client will have the requisite understanding. Thus, if the client agrees to consent to a particular type of conflict with which the client is already familiar, then the consent ordinarily will be effective with regard to that type of conflict. If the consent is general and open-ended, then the consent ordinarily will be ineffective, because it is not reasonably likely that the client will have understood the material risks involved. On the other hand, if the client is an experienced user of the legal services involved and is reasonably informed regarding the risk that a conflict may arise, such consent is more likely to be effective, particularly if, e.g., the client is independently represented by other counsel in giving consent and the consent is limited to future conflicts unrelated to the subject of the representation. In any case, advance consent cannot be effective if the circumstances that materialize in the future are such as would make the conflict nonconsentable under paragraph (b).

Conflicts in Litigation

[23]   Paragraph (b)(3) prohibits representation of opposing parties in the same litigation, regardless of the clients' consent. On the other hand, simultaneous representation of parties whose interests in litigation may conflict,

such as coplaintiffs or codefendants, is governed by paragraph (a)(2). A conflict may exist by reason of substantial discrepancy in the parties' testimony, incompatibility in positions in relation to an opposing party or the fact that there are substantially different possibilities of settlement of the claims or liabilities in question. Such conflicts can arise in criminal cases as well as civil. The potential for conflict of interest in representing multiple defendants in a criminal case is so grave that ordinarily a lawyer should decline to represent more than one codefendant. On the other hand, common representation of persons having similar interests in civil litigation is proper if the requirements of paragraph (b) are met.

[24]   Ordinarily a lawyer may take inconsistent legal positions in different tribunals at different times on behalf of different clients. The mere fact that advocating a legal position on behalf of one client might create precedent adverse to the interests of a client represented by the lawyer in an unrelated matter does not create a conflict of interest. A conflict of interest exists, however, if there is a significant risk that a lawyer's action on behalf of one client will materially limit the lawyer's effectiveness in representing another client in a different case; for example, when a decision favoring one client will create a precedent likely to seriously weaken the position taken on behalf of the other client. Factors relevant in determining whether the clients need to be advised of the risk include: where the cases are pending, whether the issue is substantive or procedural, the temporal relationship between the matters, the significance of the issue to the immediate and long-term interests of the clients involved and the clients' reasonable expectations in retaining the lawyer. If there is significant risk of material limitation, then absent informed consent of the affected clients, the lawyer must refuse one of the representations or withdraw from one or both matters.

[25]   When a lawyer represents or seeks to represent a class of plaintiffs or defendants in a class-action lawsuit, unnamed members of the class are ordinarily not considered to be clients of the lawyer for purposes of applying paragraph (a)(1) of this Rule. Thus, the lawyer does not typically need to get the consent of such a person before representing a client suing the person in an unrelated matter. Similarly, a lawyer seeking to represent an opponent in a class action does not typically need the consent of an unnamed member of the class whom the lawyer represents in an unrelated matter.

Nonlitigation Conflicts

[26]   Conflicts of interest under paragraphs (a)(1) and (a)(2) arise in contexts other than litigation. For a discussion of directly adverse conflicts in transactional matters, see Comment [7]. Relevant factors in determining whether there is significant potential for material limitation include the duration and intimacy of the lawyer's relationship with the client or clients involved, the functions being performed by the lawyer, the likelihood that disagreements will arise and the likely prejudice to the client from the conflict. The question is often one of proximity and degree. See Comment [8].

[27] For example, conflict questions may arise in estate planning and estate administration. A lawyer may be called upon to prepare wills for several family members, such as husband and wife, and, depending upon the circumstances, a conflict of interest may be present. In estate administration the identity of the client may be unclear under the law of a particular jurisdiction. Under one view, the client is the fiduciary; under another view the client is the estate or trust, including its beneficiaries. In order to comply with conflict of interest rules, the lawyer should make clear the lawyer's relationship to the parties involved.

[28] Whether a conflict is consentable depends on the circumstances. For example, a lawyer may not represent multiple parties to a negotiation whose interests are fundamentally antagonistic to each other, but common representation is permissible where the clients are generally aligned in interest even though there is some difference in interest among them. Thus, a lawyer may seek to establish or adjust a relationship between clients on an amicable and mutually advantageous basis; for example, in helping to organize a business in which two or more clients are entrepreneurs, working out the financial reorganization of an enterprise in which two or more clients have an interest or arranging a property distribution in settlement of an estate. The lawyer seeks to resolve potentially adverse interests by developing the parties' mutual interests. Otherwise, each party might have to obtain separate representation, with the possibility of incurring additional cost, complication or even litigation. Given these and other relevant factors, the clients may prefer that the lawyer act for all of them.

Special Considerations in Common Representation

[29] In considering whether to represent multiple clients in the same matter, a lawyer should be mindful that if the common representation fails because the potentially adverse interests cannot be reconciled, the result can be additional cost, embarrassment and recrimination. Ordinarily, the lawyer will be forced to withdraw from representing all of the clients if the common representation fails. In some situations, the risk of failure is so great that multiple representation is plainly impossible. For example, a lawyer cannot undertake common representation of clients where contentious litigation or negotiations between them are imminent or contemplated. Moreover, because the lawyer is required to be impartial between commonly represented clients, representation of multiple clients is improper when it is unlikely that impartiality can be maintained. Generally, if the relationship between the parties has already assumed antagonism, the possibility that the clients' interests can be adequately served by common representation is not very good. Other relevant factors are whether the lawyer subsequently will represent both parties on a continuing basis and whether the situation involves creating or terminating a relationship between the parties.

[30] A particularly important factor in determining the appropriateness of common representation is the effect on client-lawyer confidentiality and the attorney-client privilege. With regard to the attorney-client privilege,

the prevailing rule is that, as between commonly represented clients, the privilege does not attach. Hence, it must be assumed that if litigation eventuates between the clients, the privilege will not protect any such communications, and the clients should be so advised.

[31]   As to the duty of confidentiality, continued common representation will almost certainly be inadequate if one client asks the lawyer not to disclose to the other client information relevant to the common representation. This is so because the lawyer has an equal duty of loyalty to each client, and each client has the right to be informed of anything bearing on the representation that might affect that client's interests and the right to expect that the lawyer will use that information to that client's benefit. See Rule 1.4. The lawyer should, at the outset of the common representation and as part of the process of obtaining each client's informed consent, advise each client that information will be shared and that the lawyer will have to withdraw if one client decides that some matter material to the representation should be kept from the other. In limited circumstances, it may be appropriate for the lawyer to proceed with the representation when the clients have agreed, after being properly informed, that the lawyer will keep certain information confidential. For example, the lawyer may reasonably conclude that failure to disclose one client's trade secrets to another client will not adversely affect representation involving a joint venture between the clients and agree to keep that information confidential with the informed consent of both clients.

[32]   When seeking to establish or adjust a relationship between clients, the lawyer should make clear that the lawyer's role is not that of partisanship normally expected in other circumstances and, thus, that the clients may be required to assume greater responsibility for decisions than when each client is separately represented. Any limitations on the scope of the representation made necessary as a result of the common representation should be fully explained to the clients at the outset of the representation. See Rule 1.2(c).

[33]   Subject to the above limitations, each client in the common representation has the right to loyal and diligent representation and the protection of Rule 1.9 concerning the obligations to a former client. The client also has the right to discharge the lawyer as stated in Rule 1.16.

Organizational Clients

[34]   A lawyer who represents a corporation or other organization does not, by virtue of that representation, necessarily represent any constituent or affiliated organization, such as a parent or subsidiary. See Rule 1.13(a). Thus, the lawyer for an organization is not barred from accepting representation adverse to an affiliate in an unrelated matter, unless the circumstances are such that the affiliate should also be considered a client of the lawyer, there is an understanding between the lawyer and the organizational client that the lawyer will avoid representation adverse to the client's affiliates, or the lawyer's obligations to either the organizational client or the new client are likely to limit materially the lawyer's representation of the other client.

[35]   A lawyer for a corporation or other organization who is also a member of its board of directors should determine whether the responsibilities of the two roles may conflict. The lawyer may be called on to advise the corporation in matters involving actions of the directors. Consideration should be given to the frequency with which such situations may arise, the potential intensity of the conflict, the effect of the lawyer's resignation from the board and the possibility of the corporation's obtaining legal advice from another lawyer in such situations. If there is material risk that the dual role will compromise the lawyer's independence of professional judgment, the lawyer should not serve as a director or should cease to act as the corporation's lawyer when conflicts of interest arise. The lawyer should advise the other members of the board that in some circumstances matters discussed at board meetings while the lawyer is present in the capacity of director might not be protected by the attorney-client privilege and that conflict of interest considerations might require the lawyer's recusal as a director or might require the lawyer and the lawyer's firm to decline representation of the corporation in a matter.

RULE 1.8: CONFLICT OF INTEREST: CURRENT CLIENTS: SPECIFIC RULES

(a)   A lawyer shall not enter into a business transaction with a client or knowingly acquire an ownership, possessory, security or other pecuniary interest adverse to a client unless:

(1)   the transaction and terms on which the lawyer acquires the interest are fair and reasonable to the client and are fully disclosed and transmitted in writing in a manner that can be reasonably understood by the client;

(2)   the client is advised in writing of the desirability of seeking and is given a reasonable opportunity to seek the advice of independent legal counsel on the transaction; and

(3)   the client gives informed consent, in a writing signed by the client, to the essential terms of the transaction and the lawyer's role in the transaction, including whether the lawyer is representing the client in the transaction.

(b)   A lawyer shall not use information relating to representation of a client to the disadvantage of the client unless the client gives informed consent, except as permitted or required by these Rules.

(c)   A lawyer shall not solicit any substantial gift from a client, including a testamentary gift, or prepare on behalf of a client an instrument giving the lawyer or a person related to the lawyer any substantial gift unless the lawyer or other recipient of the gift is related to the client. For purposes of this paragraph, related persons include a spouse, child, grandchild, parent, grandparent or other relative or individual with whom the lawyer or the client maintains a close, familial relationship.

(d)   Prior to the conclusion of representation of a client, a lawyer shall not make or negotiate an agreement giving the lawyer literary or media rights to a portrayal or account based in substantial part on information relating to the representation.

(e)   A lawyer shall not provide financial assistance to a client in connection with pending or contemplated litigation, except that:

(1)   a lawyer may advance court costs and expenses of litigation, the repayment of which may be contingent on the outcome of the matter; and

(2)   a lawyer representing an indigent client may pay court costs and expenses of litigation on behalf of the client.

(f)   A lawyer shall not accept compensation for representing a client from one other than the client unless:

(1)   the client gives informed consent;

(2)   there is no interference with the lawyer's independence of professional judgment or with the client-lawyer relationship; and

(3)   information relating to representation of a client is protected as required by Rule 1.6.

(g)   A lawyer who represents two or more clients shall not participate in making an aggregate settlement of the claims of or against the clients, or in a criminal case an aggregated agreement as to guilty or nolo contendere pleas, unless each client gives informed consent, in a writing signed by the client. The lawyer's disclosure shall include the existence and nature of all the claims or pleas involved and of the participation of each person in the settlement.

(h)   A lawyer shall not:

(1)   make an agreement prospectively limiting the lawyer's liability to a client for malpractice unless the client is independently represented in making the agreement; or

(2)   settle a claim or potential claim for such liability with an unrepresented client or former client unless that person is advised in writing of the desirability of seeking and is given a reasonable opportunity to seek the advice of independent legal counsel in connection therewith.

(i)   A lawyer shall not acquire a proprietary interest in the cause of action or subject matter of litigation the lawyer is conducting for a client, except that the lawyer may:

(1)   acquire a lien authorized by law to secure the lawyer's fee or expenses; and

(2)   contract with a client for a reasonable contingent fee in a civil case.

(j)   A lawyer shall not have sexual relations with a client unless a consensual sexual relationship existed between them when the client-lawyer relationship commenced.

(k)   While lawyers are associated in a firm, a prohibition in the foregoing paragraphs (a) through (i) that applies to any one of them shall apply to all of them.

Comment

Business Transactions Between Client and Lawyer

[1]   A lawyer's legal skill and training, together with the relationship of trust and confidence between lawyer and client, create the possibility of over-reaching when the lawyer participates in a business, property or financial trans-action with a client, for example, a loan or sales transaction or a lawyer investment on behalf of a client. The requirements of paragraph (a) must be met even when the transaction is not closely related to the subject matter of the representation, as when a lawyer drafting a will for a client learns that the client needs money for unrelated expenses and offers to make a loan to the client. The Rule applies to lawyers engaged in the sale of goods or services related to the practice of law, for example, the sale of title insurance or investment services to existing clients of the lawyer's legal practice. See Rule 5.7. It also applies to lawyers purchasing property from estates they represent. It does not apply to ordinary fee arrange-ments between client and lawyer, which are governed by Rule 1.5, although its requirements must be met when the lawyer accepts an interest in the client's business or other nonmone- tary property as payment of all or part of a fee. In addition, the Rule does not apply to standard commercial transactions between the lawyer and the client for products or services that the client generally mar-kets to others, for example, banking or brokerage services, medical services, products manufactured or distributed by the client, and utilities' services. In such transactions, the lawyer has no advantage in dealing with the client, and the restrictions in paragraph (a) are unnecessary and impracticable.

[2]   Paragraph (a)(1) requires that the transaction itself be fair to the client and that its essential terms be communicated to the client, in writing, in a manner that can be reasonably understood. Paragraph (a)(2) requires that the client also be advised, in writing, of the desirability of seeking the advice of independent legal counsel. It also requires that the client be given a reasonable opportunity to obtain such advice. Paragraph (a)(3) requires that the lawyer obtain the client's informed consent, in a writing signed by the client, both to the essential terms of the transaction and to the lawyer's role. When necessary, the lawyer should discuss both the material risks of the proposed transaction, including any risk presented by the lawyer's involvement, and the existence of reasonably available alternatives and should explain why the advice of independent legal counsel is desirable. See Rule 1.0(e) (definition of informed consent).

[3]   The risk to a client is greatest when the client expects the lawyer to represent the client in the transaction itself or when the lawyer's

financial interest otherwise poses a significant risk that the lawyer's representation of the client will be materially limited by the lawyer's financial interest
in the transaction. Here the lawyer's role requires that the lawyer must comply,
not only with the requirements of paragraph (a), but also with the requirements of Rule 1.7. Under that Rule, the lawyer must disclose the risks associated with the lawyer's dual role as both legal adviser and participant in the
transaction, such as the risk that the lawyer will structure the transaction or
give legal advice in a way that favors the lawyer's interests at the expense of
the client. Moreover, the lawyer must obtain the client's informed consent. In
some cases, the lawyer's interest may be such that Rule 1.7 will preclude the
lawyer from seeking the client's consent to the transaction.

[4]   If the client is independently represented in the transaction,
paragraph (a)(2) of this Rule is inapplicable, and the paragraph (a)(1) requirement for full disclosure is satisfied either by a written disclosure by the lawyer
involved in the transaction or by the client's independent counsel. The fact that
the client was independently represented in the transaction is relevant in
determining whether the agreement was fair and reasonable to the client as
paragraph (a)(1) further requires.

Use of Information Related to Representation

[5]   Use of information relating to the representation to the disadvantage of the client violates the lawyer's duty of loyalty. Paragraph (b) applies
when the information is used to benefit either the lawyer or a third person,
such as another client or business associate of the lawyer. For example, if a
lawyer learns that a client intends to purchase and develop several parcels of
land, the lawyer may not use that information to purchase one of the parcels in
competition with the client or to recommend that another client make such a
purchase. The Rule does not prohibit uses that do not disadvantage the client.

For example, a lawyer who learns a government agency's interpretation
of trade legislation during the representation of one client may properly use
that information to benefit other clients. Paragraph (b) prohibits disadvantageous use of client information unless the client gives informed consent, except
as permitted or required by these Rules. See Rules 1.2(d), 1.6, 1.9(c), 3.3, 4.1(b),
8.1 and 8.3.

Gifts to Lawyers

[6]   A lawyer may accept a gift from a client, if the transaction
meets general standards of fairness. For example, a simple gift such as a present given at a holiday or as a token of appreciation is permitted. If a client
offers the lawyer a more substantial gift, paragraph (c) does not prohibit the
lawyer from accepting it, although such a gift may be voidable by the client
under the doctrine of undue influence, which treats client gifts as presumptively fraudulent. In any event, due to concerns about overreaching and imposition on clients, a lawyer may not suggest that a substantial gift be made to
the lawyer or for the lawyer's benefit, except where the lawyer is related to the
client as set forth in paragraph (c).

[7]   If effectuation of a substantial gift requires preparing a legal instrument such as a will or conveyance the client should have the detached advice that another lawyer can provide. The sole exception to this Rule is where the client is a relative of the donee.

[8]   This Rule does not prohibit a lawyer from seeking to have the lawyer or a partner or associate of the lawyer named as executor of the client's estate or to another potentially lucrative fiduciary position. Nevertheless, such appointments will be subject to the general conflict of interest provision in Rule 1.7 when there is a significant risk that the lawyer's interest in obtaining the appointment will materially limit the lawyer's independent professional judgment in advising the client concerning the choice of an executor or other fiduciary. In obtaining the client's informed consent to the conflict, the lawyer should advise the client concerning the nature and extent of the lawyer's financial interest in the appointment, as well as the availability of alternative candidates for the position.

Literary Rights

[9]   An agreement by which a lawyer acquires literary or media rights concerning the conduct of the representation creates a conflict between the interests of the client and the personal interests of the lawyer. Measures suitable in the representation of the client may detract from the publication value of an account of the representation. Paragraph (d) does not prohibit a lawyer representing a client in a transaction concerning literary property from agreeing that the lawyer's fee shall consist of a share in ownership in the property, if the arrangement conforms to Rule 1.5 and paragraphs (a) and (i).

Financial Assistance

[10]   Lawyers may not subsidize lawsuits or administrative proceedings brought on behalf of their clients, including making or guaranteeing loans to their clients for living expenses, because to do so would encourage clients to pursue lawsuits that might not otherwise be brought and because such assistance gives lawyers too great a financial stake in the litigation. These dangers do not warrant a prohibition on a lawyer lending a client court costs and litigation expenses, including the expenses of medical examination and the costs of obtaining and presenting evidence, because these advances are virtually indistinguishable from contingent fees and help ensure access to the courts. Similarly, an exception allowing lawyers representing indigent clients to pay court costs and litigation expenses regardless of whether these funds will be repaid is warranted.

Person Paying for a Lawyer's Services

[11]   Lawyers are frequently asked to represent a client under circumstances in which a third person will compensate the lawyer, in whole or in part. The third person might be a relative or friend, an indemnitor (such as a liability insurance company) or a co-client (such as a corporation sued along with one or more of its employees). Because third-party payers frequently have interests that differ from those of the client, including interests in minimizing

the amount spent on the representation and in learning how the representation is progressing, lawyers are prohibited from accepting or continuing such representations unless the lawyer determines that there will be no interference with the lawyer's independent professional judgment and there is informed consent from the client. See also Rule 5.4(c) (prohibiting interference with a lawyer's professional judgment by one who recommends, employs or pays the lawyer to render legal services for another).

[12]   Sometimes, it will be sufficient for the lawyer to obtain the client's informed consent regarding the fact of the payment and the identity of the third-party payer. If, however, the fee arrangement creates a conflict of interest for the lawyer, then the lawyer must comply with Rule. 1.7. The lawyer must also conform to the requirements of Rule 1.6 concerning confidentiality. Under Rule 1.7(a), a conflict of interest exists if there is significant risk that the lawyer's representation of the client will be materially limited by the lawyer's own interest in the fee arrangement or by the lawyer's responsibilities to the third-party payer (for example, when the third-party payer is a co-client). Under Rule 1.7(b), the lawyer may accept or continue the representation with the informed consent of each affected client, unless the conflict is nonconsentable under that paragraph. Under Rule 1.7(b), the informed consent must be confirmed in writing.

Aggregate Settlements

[13]   Differences in willingness to make or accept an offer of settlement are among the risks of common representation of multiple clients by a single lawyer. Under Rule 1.7, this is one of the risks that should be discussed before undertaking the representation, as part of the process of obtaining the clients' informed consent. In addition, Rule 1.2(a) protects each client's right to have the final say in deciding whether to accept or reject an offer of settlement and in deciding whether to enter a guilty or nolo contendere plea in a criminal case. The rule stated in this paragraph is a corollary of both these Rules and provides that, before any settlement offer or plea bargain is made or accepted on behalf of multiple clients, the lawyer must inform each of them about all the material terms of the settlement, including what the other clients will receive or pay if the settlement or plea offer is accepted. See also Rule 1.0(e) (definition of informed consent). Lawyers representing a class of plaintiffs or defendants, or those proceeding derivatively, may not have a full client-lawyer relationship with each member of the class; nevertheless, such lawyers must comply with applicable rules regulating notification of class members and other procedural requirements designed to ensure adequate protection of the entire class.

Limiting Liability and Settling Malpractice Claims

[14]   Agreements prospectively limiting a lawyer's liability for malpractice are prohibited unless the client is independently represented in making the agreement because they are likely to undermine competent and diligent representation. Also, many clients are unable to evaluate the desirability of making such an agreement before a dispute has arisen, particularly if they are

then represented by the lawyer seeking the agreement. This paragraph does not, however, prohibit a lawyer from entering into an agreement with the client to arbitrate legal malpractice claims, provided such agreements are enforceable and the client is fully informed of the scope and effect of the agreement. Nor does this paragraph limit the ability of lawyers to practice in the form of a limited-liability entity, where permitted by law, provided that each lawyer remains personally liable to the client for his or her own conduct and the firm complies with any conditions required by law, such as provisions requiring client notification or maintenance of adequate liability insurance. Nor does it prohibit an agreement in accordance with Rule 1.2 that defines the scope of the representation, although a definition of scope that makes the obligations of representation illusory will amount to an attempt to limit liability.

[15]   Agreements settling a claim or a potential claim for malpractice are not prohibited by this Rule. Nevertheless, in view of the danger that a lawyer will take unfair advantage of an unrepresented client or former client, the lawyer must first advise such a person in writing of the appropriateness of independent representation in connection with such a settlement. In addition, the lawyer must give the client or former client a reasonable opportunity to find and consult independent counsel.

Acquiring Proprietary Interest in Litigation

[16]   Paragraph (i) states the traditional general rule that lawyers are prohibited from acquiring a proprietary interest in litigation. Like paragraph (e), the general rule has its basis in common law champerty and maintenance and is designed to avoid giving the lawyer too great an interest in the representation. In addition, when the lawyer acquires an ownership interest in the subject of the representation, it will be more difficult for a client to discharge the lawyer if the client so desires. The Rule is subject to specific exceptions developed in decisional law and continued in these Rules. The exception for certain advances of the costs of litigation is set forth in paragraph (e). In addition, paragraph (i) sets forth exceptions for liens authorized by law to secure the lawyer's fees or expenses and contracts for reasonable contingent fees. The law of each jurisdiction determines which liens are authorized by law. These may include liens granted by statute, liens originating in common law and liens acquired by contract with the client. When a lawyer acquires by contract a security interest in property other than that recovered through the lawyer's efforts in the litigation, such an acquisition is a business or financial transaction with a client and is governed by the requirements of paragraph (a). Contracts for contingent fees in civil cases are governed by Rule 1.5.

Client-Lawyer Sexual Relationships

[17]   The relationship between lawyer and client is a fiduciary one in which the lawyer occupies the highest position of trust and confidence. The relationship is almost always unequal; thus, a sexual relationship between lawyer and client can involve unfair exploitation of the lawyer's fiduciary role, in violation of the lawyer's basic ethical obligation not to use the trust of the client to the client's disadvantage. In addition, such a relationship presents a

significant danger that, because of the lawyer's emotional involvement, the lawyer will be unable to represent the client without impairment of the exercise of independent professional judgment. Moreover, a blurred line between the professional and personal relationships may make it difficult to predict to what extent client confidences will be protected by the attorney-client evidentiary privilege, since client confidences are protected by privilege only when they are imparted in the context of the client-lawyer relationship. Because of the significant danger of harm to client interests and because the client's own emotional involvement renders it unlikely that the client could give adequate informed consent, this Rule prohibits the lawyer from having sexual relations with a client regardless of whether the relationship is consensual and regardless of the absence of prejudice to the client.

[18]   Sexual relationships that predate the client-lawyer relationship are not prohibited. Issues relating to the exploitation of the fiduciary relationship and client dependency are diminished when the sexual relationship existed prior to the commencement of the client-lawyer relationship. However, before proceeding with the representation in these circumstances, the lawyer should consider whether the lawyer's ability to represent the client will be materially limited by the relationship. See Rule 1.7(a)(2).

[19]   When the client is an organization, paragraph (j) of this Rule prohibits a lawyer for the organization (whether inside counsel or outside counsel) from having a sexual relationship with a constituent of the organization who supervises, directs or regularly consults with that lawyer concerning the organization's legal matters.

Imputation of Prohibitions

[20]   Under paragraph (k), a prohibition on conduct by an individual lawyer in paragraphs (a) through (i) also applies to all lawyers associated in a firm with the personally prohibited lawyer. For example, one lawyer in a firm may not enter into a business transaction with a client of another member of the firm without complying with paragraph (a), even if the first lawyer is not personally involved in the representation of the client. The prohibition set forth in paragraph (j) is personal and is not applied to associated lawyers.

RULE 1.9: DUTIES TO FORMER CLIENTS

(a)   **A lawyer who has formerly represented a client in a matter shall not thereafter represent another person in the same or a substantially related matter in which that person's interests are materially adverse to the interests of the former client unless the former client gives informed consent, confirmed in writing.**

(b)   **A lawyer shall not knowingly represent a person in the same or a substantially related matter in which a firm with which the lawyer formerly was associated had previously represented a client**

(1)   **whose interests are materially adverse to that person; and**

(2)   about whom the lawyer had acquired information protected by Rules 1.6 and 1.9(c) that is material to the matter; unless the former client gives informed consent, confirmed in writing.

(c)   A lawyer who has formerly represented a client in a matter or whose present or former firm has formerly represented a client in a matter shall not thereafter:

(1)   use information relating to the representation to the disadvantage of the former client except as these Rules would permit or require with respect to a client, or when the information has become generally known; or

(2)   reveal information relating to the representation except as these Rules would permit or require with respect to a client.

Comment

[1]   After termination of a client-lawyer relationship, a lawyer has certain continuing duties with respect to confidentiality and conflicts of interest and thus may not represent another client except in conformity with this Rule. Under this Rule, for example, a lawyer could not properly seek to rescind on behalf of a new client a contract drafted on behalf of the former client. So also a lawyer who has prosecuted an accused person could not properly represent the accused in a subsequent civil action against the government concerning the same transaction. Nor could a lawyer who has represented multiple clients in a matter represent one of the clients against the others in the same or a substantially related matter after a dispute arose among the clients in that matter, unless all affected clients give informed consent. See Comment [9]. Current and former government lawyers must comply with this Rule to the extent required by Rule 1.11.

[2]   The scope of a "matter" for purposes of this Rule depends on the facts of a particular situation or transaction. The lawyer's involvement in a matter can also be a question of degree. When a lawyer has been directly involved in a specific transaction, subsequent representation of other clients with materially adverse interests in that transaction clearly is prohibited. On the other hand, a lawyer who recurrently handled a type of problem for a former client is not precluded from later representing another client in a factually distinct problem of that type even though the subsequent representation involves a position adverse to the prior client. Similar considerations can apply to the reassignment of military lawyers between defense and prosecution functions within the same military jurisdictions. The underlying question is whether the lawyer was so involved in the matter that the subsequent representation can be justly regarded as a changing of sides in the matter in question.

[3]   Matters are "substantially related" for purposes of this Rule if they involve the same transaction or legal dispute or if there otherwise is a substantial risk that confidential factual information as would normally have

been obtained in the prior representation would materially advance the client's position in the subsequent matter. For example, a lawyer who has represented a businessperson and learned extensive private financial information about that person may not then represent that person's spouse in seeking a divorce. Similarly, a lawyer who has previously represented a client in securing environmental permits to build a shopping center would be precluded from representing neighbors seeking to oppose rezoning of the property on the basis of environmental considerations; however, the lawyer would not be precluded, on the grounds of substantial relationship, from defending a tenant of the completed shopping center in resisting eviction for nonpayment of rent. Information that has been disclosed to the public or to other parties adverse to the former client ordinarily will not be disqualifying. Information acquired in a prior representation may have been rendered obsolete by the passage of time, a circumstance that may be relevant in determining whether two representations are substantially related. In the case of an organizational client, general knowledge of the client's policies and practices ordinarily will not preclude a subsequent representation; on the other hand, knowledge of specific facts gained in a prior representation that are relevant to the matter in question ordinarily will preclude such a representation. A former client is not required to reveal the confidential information learned by the lawyer in order to establish a substantial risk that the lawyer has confidential information to use in the subsequent matter. A conclusion about the possession of such information may be based on the nature of the services the lawyer provided the former client and information that would in ordinary practice be learned by a lawyer providing such services.

Lawyers Moving Between Firms

[4]   When lawyers have been associated within a firm but then end their association, the question of whether a lawyer should undertake representation is more complicated. There are several competing considerations. First, the client previously represented by the former firm must be reasonably assured that the principle of loyalty to the client is not compromised. Second, the rule should not be so broadly cast as to preclude other persons from having reasonable choice of legal counsel. Third, the rule should not unreasonably hamper lawyers from forming new associations and taking on new clients after having left a previous association. In this connection, it should be recognized that today many lawyers practice in firms, that many lawyers to some degree limit their practice to one field or another, and that many move from one association to another several times in their careers. If the concept of imputation were applied with unqualified rigor, the result would be radical curtailment of the opportunity of lawyers to move from one practice setting to another and of the opportunity of clients to change counsel.

[5]   Paragraph (b) operates to disqualify the lawyer only when the lawyer involved has actual knowledge of information protected by Rules 1.6 and 1.9(c). Thus, if a lawyer while with one firm acquired no knowledge or information relating to a particular client of the firm, and that lawyer later

joined another firm, neither the lawyer individually nor the second firm is disqualified from representing another client in the same or a related matter even though the interests of the two clients conflict. See Rule 1.10(b) for the restrictions on a firm once a lawyer has terminated association with the firm.

[6] Application of paragraph (b) depends on a situation's particular facts, aided by inferences, deductions or working presumptions that reasonably may be made about the way in which lawyers work together. A lawyer may have general access to files of all clients of a law firm and may regularly participate in discussions of their affairs; it should be inferred that such a lawyer in fact is privy to all information about all the firm's clients. In contrast, another lawyer may have access to the files of only a limited number of clients and participate in discussions of the affairs of no other clients; in the absence of information to the contrary, it should be inferred that such a lawyer in fact is privy to information about the clients actually served but not those of other clients. In such an inquiry, the burden of proof should rest upon the firm whose disqualification is sought.

[7] Independent of the question of disqualification of a firm, a lawyer changing professional association has a continuing duty to preserve confidentiality of information about a client formerly represented. See Rules 1.6 and 1.9(c).

[8] Paragraph (c) provides that information acquired by the lawyer in the course of representing a client may not subsequently be used or revealed by the lawyer to the disadvantage of the client. However, the fact that a lawyer has once served a client does not preclude the lawyer from using generally known information about that client when later representing another client.

[9] The provisions of this Rule are for the protection of former clients and can be waived if the client gives informed consent, which consent must be confirmed in writing under paragraphs (a) and (b). See Rule 1.0(e). With regard to the effectiveness of an advance waiver, see Comment [22] to Rule 1.7. With regard to disqualification of a firm with which a lawyer is or was formerly associated, see Rule 1.10.

RULE 1.10: IMPUTATION OF CONFLICTS OF INTEREST: GENERAL RULE

(a) While lawyers are associated in a firm, none of them shall knowingly represent a client when any one of them practicing alone would be prohibited from doing so by Rules 1.7 or 1.9, unless

(1) the prohibition is based on a personal interest of the disqualified lawyer and does not present a significant risk of materially limiting the representation of the client by the remaining lawyers in the firm; or

(2) the prohibition is based upon Rule 1.9(a), or (b), and arises out of the disqualified lawyer's association with a prior firm, and

(i)   the disqualified lawyer is timely screened from any participation in the matter and is apportioned no part of the fee therefrom;

(ii)   written notice is promptly given to any affected former client to enable the former client to ascertain compliance with the provisions of this Rule, which shall include a description of the screening procedures employed; a statement of the firm's and of the screened lawyer's compliance with these Rules; a statement that review may be available before a tribunal; and an agreement by the firm to respond promptly to any written inquiries or objections by the former client about the screening procedures; and

(iii)   certifications of compliance with these Rules and with the screening procedures are provided to the former client by the screened lawyer and by a partner of the firm, at reasonable intervals upon the former client's written request and upon termination of the screening procedures.

(b)   When a lawyer has terminated an association with a firm, the firm is not prohibited from thereafter representing a person with interests materially adverse to those of a client represented by the formerly associated lawyer and not currently represented by the firm, unless

(1)   the matter is the same or substantially related to that in which the formerly associated lawyer represented the client; and

(2)   any lawyer remaining in the firm has information protected by Rules 1.6 and 1.9(c) that is material to the matter.

(c)   A disqualification prescribed by this rule may be waived by the affected client under the conditions stated in Rule 1.7.

(d)   The disqualification of lawyers associated in a firm with former or current government lawyers is governed by Rule 1.11.

Comment

Definition of "Firm"

[1]   For purposes of the Rules of Professional Conduct, the term "firm" denotes lawyers in a law partnership, professional corporation, sole proprietorship or other association authorized to practice law; or lawyers employed in a legal services organization or the legal department of a corporation or other organization. See Rule 1.0(c). Whether two or more lawyers constitute a firm within this definition can depend on the specific facts. See Rule 1.0, Comments [2] – [4].

Principles of Imputed Disqualification

[2]   The rule of imputed disqualification stated in paragraph (a) gives effect to the principle of loyalty to the client as it applies to lawyers who practice in a law firm. Such situations can be considered from the premise that a firm of lawyers is essentially one lawyer for purposes of the rules governing loyalty to the client, or from the premise that each lawyer is vicariously bound by the obligation of loyalty owed by each lawyer with whom the lawyer is associated. Paragraph (a)(1) operates only among the lawyers currently associated in a firm. When a lawyer moves from one firm to another, the situation is governed by Rules 1.9(b) and 1.10(a)(2) and 1.10 (b).

[3]   The rule in paragraph (a) does not prohibit representation where neither questions of client loyalty nor protection of confidential information are presented. Where one lawyer in a firm could not effectively represent a given client because of strong political beliefs, for example, but that lawyer will do no work on the case and the personal beliefs of the lawyer will not materially limit the representation by others in the firm, the firm should not be disqualified. On the other hand, if an opposing party in a case were owned by a lawyer in the law firm, and others in the firm would be materially limited in pursuing the matter because of loyalty to that lawyer, the personal disqualification of the lawyer would be imputed to all others in the firm.

[4]   The rule in paragraph (a) also does not prohibit representation by others in the law firm where the person prohibited from involvement in a matter is a nonlawyer, such as a paralegal or legal secretary. Nor does paragraph (a) prohibit representation if the lawyer is prohibited from acting because of events before the person became a lawyer, for example, work that the person did while a law student. Such persons, however, ordinarily must be screened from any personal participation in the matter to avoid communication to others in the firm of confidential information that both the nonlawyers and the firm have a legal duty to protect. See Rules 1.0(k) and 5.3.

[5]   Rule 1.10(b) operates to permit a law firm, under certain circumstances, to represent a person with interests directly adverse to those of a client represented by a lawyer who formerly was associated with the firm. The Rule applies regardless of when the formerly associated lawyer represented the client. However, the law firm may not represent a person with interests adverse to those of a present client of the firm, which would violate Rule 1.7. Moreover, the firm may not represent the person where the matter is the same or substantially related to that in which the formerly associated lawyer represented the client and any other lawyer currently in the firm has material information protected by Rules 1.6 and 1.9(c).

[6]   Rule 1.10(c) removes imputation with the informed consent of the affected client or former client under the conditions stated in Rule 1.7. The conditions stated in Rule 1.7 require the lawyer to determine that the representation is not prohibited by Rule 1.7(b) and that each affected client or former client has given informed consent to the representation, confirmed in writing.

In some cases, the risk may be so severe that the conflict may not be cured by client consent. For a discussion of the effectiveness of client waivers of conflicts that might arise in the future, see Rule 1.7, Comment [22]. For a definition of informed consent, see Rule 1.0(e).

[7]   Rule 1.10(a)(2) similarly removes the imputation otherwise required by Rule 1.10(a), but unlike section (c), it does so without requiring that there be informed consent by the former client. Instead, it requires that the procedures laid out in sections (a)(2)(i)-(iii) be followed. A description of effective screening mechanisms appears in Rule 1.0(k). Lawyers should be aware, however, that, even where screening mechanisms have been adopted, tribunals may consider additional factors in ruling upon motions to disqualify a lawyer from pending litigation.

[8]   Paragraph (a)(2)(i) does not prohibit the screened lawyer from receiving a salary or partnership share established by prior independent agreement, but that lawyer may not receive compensation directly related to the matter in which the lawyer is disqualified.

[9]   The notice required by paragraph (a)(2)(ii) generally should include a description of the screened lawyer's prior representation and be given as soon as practicable after the need for screening becomes apparent. It also should include a statement by the screened lawyer and the firm that the client's material confidential information has not been disclosed or used in violation of the Rules. The notice is intended to enable the former client to evaluate and comment upon the effectiveness of the screening procedures.

[10]   The certifications required by paragraph (a)(2)(iii) give the former client assurance that the client's material confidential information has not been disclosed or used inappropriately, either prior to timely implementation of a screen or thereafter. If compliance cannot be certified, the certificate must describe the failure to comply.

[11]   Where a lawyer has joined a private firm after having represented the government, imputation is governed by Rule 1.11(b) and (c), not this Rule. Under Rule 1.11(d), where a lawyer represents the government after having served clients in private practice, nongovernmental employment or in another government agency, former client conflicts are not imputed to government lawyers associated with the individually disqualified lawyer.

[12]   Where a lawyer is prohibited from engaging in certain transactions under Rule 1.8, paragraph (k) of that Rule, and not this Rule, determines whether that prohibition also applies to other lawyers associated in a firm with the personally prohibited lawyer.

RULE 1.11: SPECIAL CONFLICTS OF INTEREST FOR FORMER AND CURRENT GOVERNMENT OFFICERS AND EMPLOYEES

(a)   Except as law may otherwise expressly permit, a lawyer who has formerly served as a public officer or employee of the government:

(1)   is subject to Rule 1.9(c); and

(2)   shall not otherwise represent a client in connection with a matter in which the lawyer participated personally and substantially as a public officer or employee, unless the appropriate government agency gives its informed consent, confirmed in writing, to the representation.

(b)   When a lawyer is disqualified from representation under paragraph (a), no lawyer in a firm with which that lawyer is associated may knowingly undertake or continue representation in such a matter unless:

(1)   the disqualified lawyer is timely screened from any participation in the matter and is apportioned no part of the fee therefrom; and

(2)   written notice is promptly given to the appropriate government agency to enable it to ascertain compliance with the provisions of this rule.

(c)   Except as law may otherwise expressly permit, a lawyer having information that the lawyer knows is confidential government information about a person acquired when the lawyer was a public officer or employee, may not represent a private client whose interests are adverse to that person in a matter in which the information could be used to the material disadvantage of that person. As used in this Rule, the term "confidential government information" means information that has been obtained under governmental authority and which, at the time this Rule is applied, the government is prohibited by law from disclosing to the public or has a legal privilege not to disclose and which is not otherwise available to the public. A firm with which that lawyer is associated may undertake or continue representation in the matter only if the disqualified lawyer is timely screened from any participation in the matter and is apportioned no part of the fee therefrom.

(d)   Except as law may otherwise expressly permit, a lawyer currently serving as a public officer or employee:

(1)   is subject to Rules 1.7 and 1.9; and

(2)   shall not:

(i)   participate in a matter in which the lawyer participated personally and substantially while in private practice or nongovernmental employment, unless the appropriate government agency gives its informed consent, confirmed in writing; or

(ii)   negotiate for private employment with any person who is involved as a party or as lawyer for a party in a matter in which the lawyer is participating personally and substantially, except that a lawyer serving as a law clerk to a judge, other adjudicative officer or arbitrator may negotiate for private employment as permitted by Rule 1.12(b) and subject to the conditions stated in Rule 1.12(b).

(e)   As used in this Rule, the term "matter" includes:

(1)   any judicial or other proceeding, application, request for a ruling or other determination, contract, claim, controversy, investigation, charge, accusation, arrest or other particular matter involving a specific party or parties, and

(2)   any other matter covered by the conflict of interest rules of the appropriate government agency.

Comment

[1]   A lawyer who has served or is currently serving as a public officer or employee is personally subject to the Rules of Professional Conduct, including the prohibition against concurrent conflicts of interest stated in Rule 1.7. In addition, such a lawyer may be subject to statutes and government regulations regarding conflict of interest. Such statutes and regulations may circumscribe the extent to which the government agency may give consent under this Rule. See Rule 1.0(e) for the definition of informed consent.

[2]   Paragraphs (a)(1), (a)(2) and (d)(1) restate the obligations of an individual lawyer who has served or is currently serving as an officer or employee of the government toward a former government or private client. Rule 1.10 is not applicable to the conflicts of interest addressed by this Rule. Rather, paragraph (b) sets forth a special imputation rule for former government lawyers that provides for screening and notice. Because of the special problems raised by imputation within a government agency, paragraph (d) does not impute the conflicts of a lawyer currently serving as an officer or employee of the government to other associated government officers or employees, although ordinarily it will be prudent to screen such lawyers.

[3]   Paragraphs (a)(2) and (d)(2) apply regardless of whether a lawyer is adverse to a former client and are thus designed not only to protect the former client, but also to prevent a lawyer from exploiting public office for the advantage of another client. For example, a lawyer who has pursued a claim on behalf of the government may not pursue the same claim on behalf of a later private client after the lawyer has left government service, except when authorized to do so by the government agency under paragraph (a). Similarly, a lawyer who has pursued a claim on behalf of a private client may not pursue the claim on behalf of the government, except when authorized to do so by paragraph (d). As with paragraphs (a)(1) and (d)(1), Rule 1.10 is not applicable to the conflicts of interest addressed by these paragraphs.

[4]   This Rule represents a balancing of interests. On the one hand, where the successive clients are a government agency and another client, public or private, the risk exists that power or discretion vested in that agency might be used for the special benefit of the other client. A lawyer should not be

in a position where benefit to the other client might affect performance of the lawyer's professional functions on behalf of the government. Also, unfair advantage could accrue to the other client by reason of access to confidential government information about the client's adversary obtainable only through the lawyer's government service. On the other hand, the rules governing lawyers presently or formerly employed by a government agency should not be so restrictive as to inhibit transfer of employment to and from the government. The government has a legitimate need to attract qualified lawyers as well as to maintain high ethical standards. Thus a former government lawyer is disqualified only from particular matters in which the lawyer participated personally and substantially. The provisions for screening and waiver in paragraph (b) are necessary to prevent the disqualification rule from imposing too severe a deterrent against entering public service. The limitation of disqualification in paragraphs (a)(2) and (d)(2) to matters involving a specific party or parties, rather than extending disqualification to all substantive issues on which the lawyer worked, serves a similar function.

[5]   When a lawyer has been employed by one government agency and then moves to a second government agency, it may be appropriate to treat that second agency as another client for purposes of this Rule, as when a lawyer is employed by a city and subsequently is employed by a federal agency. However, because the conflict of interest is governed by paragraph (d), the latter agency is not required to screen the lawyer as paragraph (b) requires a law firm to do. The question of whether two government agencies should be regarded as the same or different clients for conflict of interest purposes is beyond the scope of these Rules. See Rule 1.13 Comment [6].

[6]   Paragraphs (b) and (c) contemplate a screening arrangement. See Rule 1.0(k) (requirements for screening procedures). These paragraphs do not prohibit a lawyer from receiving a salary or partnership share established by prior independent agreement, but that lawyer may not receive compensation directly relating the lawyer's compensation to the fee in the matter in which the lawyer is disqualified.

[7]   Notice, including a description of the screened lawyer's prior representation and of the screening procedures employed, generally should be given as soon as practicable after the need for screening becomes apparent.

[8]   Paragraph (c) operates only when the lawyer in question has knowledge of the information, which means actual knowledge; it does not operate with respect to information that merely could be imputed to the lawyer.

[9]   Paragraphs (a) and (d) do not prohibit a lawyer from jointly representing a private party and a government agency when doing so is permitted by Rule 1.7 and is not otherwise prohibited by law.

[10]   For purposes of paragraph (e) of this Rule, a "matter" may continue in another form. In determining whether two particular matters are the same, the lawyer should consider the extent to which the matters involve the same basic facts, the same or related parties, and the time elapsed.

RULE 1.12: FORMER JUDGE, ARBITRATOR, MEDIATOR OR OTHER THIRD-PARTY NEUTRAL

(a)   Except as stated in paragraph (d), a lawyer shall not represent anyone in connection with a matter in which the lawyer participated personally and substantially as a judge or other adjudicative officer or law clerk to such a person or as an arbitrator, mediator or other third-party neutral, unless all parties to the proceeding give informed consent, confirmed in writing.

(b)   A lawyer shall not negotiate for employment with any person who is involved as a party or as lawyer for a party in a matter in which the lawyer is participating personally and substantially as a judge or other adjudicative officer or as an arbitrator, mediator or other third-party neutral. A lawyer serving as a law clerk to a judge or other adjudicative officer may negotiate for employment with a party or lawyer involved in a matter in which the clerk is participating personally and substantially, but only after the lawyer has notified the judge, or other adjudicative officer.

(c)   If a lawyer is disqualified by paragraph (a), no lawyer in a firm with which that lawyer is associated may knowingly undertake or continue representation in the matter unless:

   (1)   the disqualified lawyer is timely screened from any participation in the matter and is apportioned no part of the fee therefrom; and

   (2)   written notice is promptly given to the parties and any appropriate tribunal to enable them to ascertain compliance with the provisions of this rule.

(d)   An arbitrator selected as a partisan of a party in a multimember arbitration panel is not prohibited from subsequently representing that party.

Comment

[1]   This Rule generally parallels Rule 1.11. The term "personally and substantially" signifies that a judge who was a member of a multimember court, and thereafter left judicial office to practice law, is not prohibited from representing a client in a matter pending in the court, but in which the former judge did not participate. So also the fact that a former judge exercised administrative responsibility in a court does not prevent the former judge from acting as a lawyer in a matter where the judge had previously exercised remote or incidental administrative responsibility that did not affect the merits. Compare the Comment to Rule 1.11. The term "adjudicative officer" includes such officials as judges pro tempore, referees, special masters, hearing officers and other parajudicial officers, and also lawyers who serve as part-time judges. Compliance Canons A(2), B(2) and C of the Model Code of Judicial Conduct provide that a part-time judge, judge pro tempore or retired judge recalled to active service, may not "act as a lawyer in any proceeding in which he served

as a judge or in any other proceeding related thereto." Although phrased differently from this Rule, those Rules correspond in meaning.

[2]   Like former judges, lawyers who have served as arbitrators, mediators or other third-party neutrals may be asked to represent a client in a matter in which the lawyer participated personally and substantially. This Rule forbids such representation unless all of the parties to the proceedings give their informed consent, confirmed in writing. See Rule 1.0(e) and (b). Other law or codes of ethics governing third-party neutrals may impose more stringent standards of personal or imputed disqualification. See Rule 2.4.

[3]   Although lawyers who serve as third-party neutrals do not have information concerning the parties that is protected under Rule 1.6, they typically owe the parties an obligation of confidentiality under law or codes of ethics governing third-party neutrals. Thus, paragraph (c) provides that conflicts of the personally disqualified lawyer will be imputed to other lawyers in a law firm unless the conditions of this paragraph are met.

[4]   Requirements for screening procedures are stated in Rule 1.0(k). Paragraph (c)(1) does not prohibit the screened lawyer from receiving a salary or partnership share established by prior independent agreement, but that lawyer may not receive compensation directly related to the matter in which the lawyer is disqualified.

[5]   Notice, including a description of the screened lawyer's prior representation and of the screening procedures employed, generally should be given as soon as practicable after the need for screening becomes apparent.

RULE 1.13: ORGANIZATION AS CLIENT

(a)   A lawyer employed or retained by an organization represents the organization acting through its duly authorized constituents.

(b)   If a lawyer for an organization knows that an officer, employee or other person associated with the organization is engaged in action, intends to act or refuses to act in a matter related to the representation that is a violation of a legal obligation to the organization, or a violation of law that reasonably might be imputed to the organization, and that is likely to result in substantial injury to the organization, then the lawyer shall proceed as is reasonably necessary in the best interest of the organization. Unless the lawyer reasonably believes that it is not necessary in the best interest of the organization to do so the lawyer shall refer the matter to higher authority in the organization, including, if warranted by the circumstances, to the highest authority that can act on behalf of the organization as determined by applicable law.

(c)   Except as provided in paragraph (d), if

(1)   despite the lawyer's efforts in accordance with paragraph (b) the highest authority that can act on behalf of

the organization insists upon or fails to address in a timely and appropriate manner an action or a refusal to act, that is clearly a violation of law, and

(2)   the lawyer reasonably believes that the violation is reasonably certain to result in substantial injury to the organization, then the lawyer may reveal information relating to the representation whether or not Rule 1.6 permits such disclosure, but only if and to the extent the lawyer reasonably believes necessary to prevent substantial injury to the organization

(d)   Paragraph (c) shall not apply with respect to information relating to a lawyer's representation of an organization to investigate an alleged violation of law, or to defend the organization or an officer, employee or other constituent associated with the organization against a claim arising out of an alleged violation of law.

(e)   A lawyer who reasonably believes that he or she has been discharged because of the lawyer's actions taken pursuant to paragraphs (b) or (c), or who withdraws under circumstances that require or permit the lawyer to take action under either of those paragraphs, shall proceed as the lawyer reasonably believes necessary to assure that the organization's highest authority is informed of the lawyer's discharge or withdrawal.

(f)   In dealing with an organization's directors, officers, employees, members, shareholders or other constituents, a lawyer shall explain the identity of the client when the lawyer knows or reasonably should know that the organization's interests are adverse to those of the constituents with whom the lawyer is dealing.

(g)   A lawyer representing an organization may also represent any of its directors, officers, employees, members, shareholders or other constituents, subject to the provisions of Rule 1.7. If the organization's consent to the dual representation is required by Rule 1.7, the consent shall be given by an appropriate official of the organization other than the individual who is to be represented, or by the shareholders.

Comment

The Entity as the Client

[1]   An organizational client is a legal entity, but it cannot act except through its officers, directors, employees, shareholders and other constituents. Officers, directors, employees and shareholders are the constituents of the corporate organizational client. The duties defined in this Comment apply equally to unincorporated associations. "Other constituents" as used in this Comment means the positions equivalent to officers, directors, employees and shareholders held by persons acting for organizational clients that are not corporations.

[2]   When one of the constituents of an organizational client communicates with the organization's lawyer in that person's organizational
capacity, the communication is protected by Rule 1.6. Thus, by way of example,
if an organizational client requests its lawyer to investigate allegations of
wrongdoing, interviews made in the course of that investigation between the
lawyer and the client's employees or other constituents are covered by
Rule 1.6. This does not mean, however, that constituents of an organizational
client are the clients of the lawyer. The lawyer may not disclose to such constituents information relating to the representation except for disclosures
explicitly or impliedly authorized by the organizational client in order to
carry out the representation or as otherwise permitted by Rule 1.6.

[3]   When constituents of the organization make decisions for it, the
decisions ordinarily must be accepted by the lawyer even if their utility or prudence is doubtful. Decisions concerning policy and operations, including ones
entailing serious risk, are not as such in the lawyer's province. Paragraph (b)
makes clear, however, that when the lawyer knows that the organization is
likely to be substantially injured by action of an officer or other constituent
that violates a legal obligation to the organization or is in violation of law that
might be imputed to the organization, the lawyer must proceed as is reasonably necessary in the best interest of the organization. As defined in Rule 1.0,
knowledge can be inferred from circumstances, and a lawyer cannot ignore the
obvious.

[4]   In determining how to proceed under paragraph (b), the lawyer
should give due consideration to the seriousness of the violation and its consequences, the responsibility in the organization and the apparent motivation of
the person involved, the policies of the organization concerning such matters,
and any other relevant considerations. Ordinarily, referral to a higher authority
would be necessary. In some circumstances, however, it may be appropriate for
the lawyer to ask the constituent to reconsider the matter; for example, if the
circumstances involve a constituent's innocent misunderstanding of law and
subsequent acceptance of the lawyer's advice, the lawyer may reasonably conclude that the best interest of the organization does not require that the matter
be referred to higher authority. If a constituent persists in conduct contrary to
the lawyer's advice, it will be necessary for the lawyer to take steps to have the
matter reviewed by a higher authority in the organization. If the matter is of
sufficient seriousness and importance or urgency to the organization, referral
to higher authority in the organization may be necessary even if the lawyer has
not communicated with the constituent. Any measures taken should, to the
extent practicable, minimize the risk of revealing information relating to the
representation to persons outside the organization. Even in circumstances
where a lawyer is not obligated by Rule 1.13 to proceed, a lawyer may bring to
the attention of an organizational client, including its highest authority, matters that the lawyer reasonably believes to be of sufficient importance to
warrant doing so in the best interest of the organization.

[5]   Paragraph (b) also makes clear that when it is reasonably
necessary to enable the organization to address the matter in a timely and

appropriate manner, the lawyer must refer the matter to higher authority. Including, if warranted by the circumstances, the highest authority that can act on behalf of the organization under applicable law. The organization's highest authority to whom a matter may be referred ordinarily will be the board of directors or similar governing body. However, applicable law may prescribe that under certain conditions the highest authority reposes elsewhere, for example, in the independent directors of a corporation.

Relation to Other Rules

[6]   The authority and responsibility provided in this Rule are concurrent with the authority and responsibility provided in other Rules. In particular, this Rule does not limit or expand the lawyer's responsibility under Rules 1.8, 1.16, 3.3 or 4.1. Paragraph (c) of this Rule supplements Rule I .6(b) by providing an additional basis upon which the lawyer may reveal information relating to the representation, but does not modify. restrict, or limit the provisions of Rule 1 .6(b)(1) - (6). Under paragraph (c) the lawyer may reveal such information only when the organization's highest authority insists upon or fails to address threatened or ongoing action that is clearly a violation of law, and then only to the extent the lawyer reasonably believes necessary to prevent reasonably certain substantial injury to the organization. It is not necessary that the lawyer's services be used in furtherance of the violation, but it is required that the matter be related to the lawyer's representation of the organization. If the lawyer's services are being used by an organization to further a crime or fraud by the organization, Rules I .6(b)(2) and I .6(b)(3) may permit the lawyer to disclose confidential information. In such circumstances Rule 1.2(d) may also be applicable, in which event, withdrawal from the representation under Rule 1.16(a)(1) may be required.

[7]   Paragraph (d) makes clear that the authority of a lawyer to disclose information relating to a representation in circumstances described in paragraph (c) does not apply with respect to information relating to a lawyer's engagement by an organization to investigate an alleged violation of law or to defend the organization or an officer. employee or other person associated with the organization against a claim arising out of an alleged violation of law. This is necessary in order to enable organizational clients to enjoy the full benefits of legal counsel in conducting an investigation or defending against a claim.

[8]   A lawyer who reasonably believes that he or she has been discharged because of the lawyer's actions taken Pursuant to paragraph (b) or (c). or who withdraws in circumstances that require or permit the lawyer to take action under either of these paragraphs, must Proceed as the lawyer reasonably believes necessary to assure that the organization's highest authority is informed of the lawyer's discharge or withdrawal.

Government Agency

[9]   The duty defined in this Rule applies to governmental organizations. Defining precisely the identity of the client and prescribing the resulting obligations of such lawyers may be more difficult in the government context and is a matter beyond the scope of these Rules. See Scope [18]. Although in some circumstances the client may be a specific agency, it may also be a branch

of government, such as the executive branch, or the government as a whole. For example, if the action or failure to act involves the head of a bureau, either the department of which the bureau is a part or the relevant branch of government may be the client for purposes of this Rule. Moreover, in a matter involving the conduct of government officials, a government lawyer may have authority under applicable law to question such conduct more extensively than that of a lawyer for a private organization in similar circumstances. Thus, when the client is a governmental organization, a different balance may be appropriate between maintaining confidentiality and assuring that the wrongful act is prevented or rectified, for public business is involved. In addition, duties of lawyers employed by the government or lawyers in military service may be defined by statutes and regulation. This Rule does not limit that authority. See Scope.

Clarifying the Lawyer's Role

[10]   There are times when the organization's interest may be or become adverse to those of one or more of its constituents. In such circumstances the lawyer should advise any constituent, whose interest the lawyer finds adverse to that of the organization of the conflict or potential conflict of interest, that the lawyer cannot represent such constituent, and that such person may wish to obtain independent representation. Care must be taken to assure that the individual understands that, when there is such adversity of interest, the lawyer for the organization cannot provide legal representation for that constituent individual, and that discussions between the lawyer for the organization and the individual may not be privileged.

[11]   Whether such a warning should be given by the lawyer for the organization to any constituent individual may turn on the facts of each case.

Dual Representation

[12]   Paragraph (g) recognizes that a lawyer for an organization may also represent a principal officer or major shareholder.

Derivative Actions

[13]   Under generally prevailing law, the shareholders or members of a corporation may bring suit to compel the directors to perform their legal obligations in the supervision of the organization. Members of unincorporated associations have essentially the same right. Such an action may be brought nominally by the organization, but usually is, in fact, a legal controversy over management of the organization.

[14]   The question can arise whether counsel for the organization may defend such an action. The proposition that the organization is the lawyer's client does not alone resolve the issue. Most derivative actions are a normal incident of an organization's affairs, to be defended by the organization's lawyer like any other suit. However, if the claim involves serious charges of wrongdoing by those in control of the organization, a conflict may arise between the lawyer's duty to the organization and the lawyer's relationship with the board. In those circumstances, Rule 1.7 governs who should represent the directors and the organization.

RULE 1.14: CLIENT WITH DIMINISHED CAPACITY

(a)   When a client's capacity to make adequately considered decisions in connection with a representation is diminished, whether because of minority, mental impairment or for some other reason, the lawyer shall, as far as reasonably possible, maintain a normal client-lawyer relationship with the client.

(b)   When the lawyer reasonably believes that the client has diminished capacity, is at risk of substantial physical, financial or other harm unless action is taken and cannot adequately act in the client's own interest, the lawyer may take reasonably necessary protective action, including consulting with individuals or entities that have the ability to take action to protect the client and, in appropriate cases, seeking the appointment of a guardian ad litem, conservator or guardian.

(c)   Information relating to the representation of a client with diminished capacity is protected by Rule 1.6. When taking protective action pursuant to paragraph (b), the lawyer is impliedly authorized under Rule 1.6(a) to reveal information about the client, but only to the extent reasonably necessary to protect the client's interests.

Comment

[1]   The normal client-lawyer relationship is based on the assumption that the client, when properly advised and assisted, is capable of making decisions about important matters. When the client is a minor or suffers from a diminished mental capacity, however, maintaining the ordinary client-lawyer relationship may not be possible in all respects. In particular, a severely incapacitated person may have no power to make legally binding decisions. Nevertheless, a client with diminished capacity often has the ability to understand, deliberate upon, and reach conclusions about matters affecting the client's own well-being. For example, children as young as five or six years of age, and certainly those of ten or twelve, are regarded as having opinions that are entitled to weight in legal proceedings concerning their custody. So also, it is recognized that some persons of advanced age can be quite capable of handling routine financial matters while needing special legal protection concerning major transactions.

[2]   The fact that a client suffers a disability does not diminish the lawyer's obligation to treat the client with attention and respect. Even if the person has a legal representative, the lawyer should as far as possible accord the represented person the status of client, particularly in maintaining communication.

[3]   The client may wish to have family members or other persons participate in discussions with the lawyer. When necessary to assist in the representation, the presence of such persons generally does not affect the

applicability of the attorney-client evidentiary privilege. Nevertheless, the lawyer must keep the client's interests foremost and, except for protective action authorized under paragraph (b), must to look to the client, and not family members, to make decisions on the client's behalf.

[4]   If a legal representative has already been appointed for the client, the lawyer should ordinarily look to the representative for decisions on behalf of the client. In matters involving a minor, whether the lawyer should look to the parents as natural guardians may depend on the type of proceeding or matter in which the lawyer is representing the minor. If the lawyer represents the guardian as distinct from the ward, and is aware that the guardian is acting adversely to the ward's interest, the lawyer may have an obligation to prevent or rectify the guardian's misconduct. See Rule 1.2(d).

Taking Protective Action

[5]   If a lawyer reasonably believes that a client is at risk of substantial physical, financial or other harm unless action is taken, and that a normal client-lawyer relationship cannot be maintained as provided in paragraph (a) because the client lacks sufficient capacity to communicate or to make adequately considered decisions in connection with the representation, then paragraph (b) permits the lawyer to take protective measures deemed necessary. Such measures could include: consulting with family members, using a reconsideration period to permit clarification or improvement of circumstances, using voluntary surrogate decisionmaking tools such as durable powers of attorney or consulting with support groups, professional services, adult-protective agencies or other individuals or entities that have the ability to protect the client. In taking any protective action, the lawyer should be guided by such factors as the wishes and values of the client to the extent known, the client's best interests and the goals of intruding into the client's decisionmaking autonomy to the least extent feasible, maximizing client capacities and respecting the client's family and social connections.

[6]   In determining the extent of the client's diminished capacity, the lawyer should consider and balance such factors as: the client's ability to articulate reasoning leading to a decision, variability of state of mind and ability to appreciate consequences of a decision; the substantive fairness of a decision; and the consistency of a decision with the known long-term commitments and values of the client. In appropriate circumstances, the lawyer may seek guidance from an appropriate diagnostician.

[7]   If a legal representative has not been appointed, the lawyer should consider whether appointment of a guardian ad litem, conservator or guardian is necessary to protect the client's interests. Thus, if a client with diminished capacity has substantial property that should be sold for the client's benefit, effective completion of the transaction may require appointment of a legal representative. In addition, rules of procedure in litigation sometimes provide that minors or persons with diminished capacity must be represented by a guardian or next friend if they do not have a general guardian. In many

circumstances, however, appointment of a legal representative may be more expensive or traumatic for the client than circumstances in fact require. Evaluation of such circumstances is a matter entrusted to the professional judgment of the lawyer. In considering alternatives, however, the lawyer should be aware of any law that requires the lawyer to advocate the least restrictive action on behalf of the client.

Disclosure of the Client's Condition

[8]   Disclosure of the client's diminished capacity could adversely affect the client's interests. For example, raising the question of diminished capacity could, in some circumstances, lead to proceedings for involuntary commitment. Information relating to the representation is protected by Rule 1.6. Therefore, unless authorized to do so, the lawyer may not disclose such information. When taking protective action pursuant to paragraph (b), the lawyer is impliedly authorized to make the necessary disclosures, even when the client directs the lawyer to the contrary. Nevertheless, given the risks of disclosure, paragraph (c) limits what the lawyer may disclose in consulting with other individuals or entities or seeking the appointment of a legal representative. At the very least, the lawyer should determine whether it is likely that the person or entity consulted with will act adversely to the client's interests before discussing matters related to the client. The lawyer's position in such cases is an unavoidably difficult one.

Emergency Legal Assistance

[9]   In an emergency where the health, safety or a financial interest of a person with seriously diminished capacity is threatened with imminent and irreparable harm, a lawyer may take legal action on behalf of such a person even though the person is unable to establish a client-lawyer relationship or to make or express considered judgments about the matter, when the person or another acting in good faith on that person's behalf has consulted with the lawyer. Even in such an emergency, however, the lawyer should not act unless the lawyer reasonably believes that the person has no other lawyer, agent or other representative available. The lawyer should take legal action on behalf of the person only to the extent reasonably necessary to maintain the status quo or otherwise avoid imminent and irreparable harm. A lawyer who undertakes to represent a person in such an exigent situation has the same duties under these Rules as the lawyer would with respect to a client.

[10]   A lawyer who acts on behalf of a person with seriously diminished capacity in an emergency should keep the confidences of the person as if dealing with a client, disclosing them only to the extent necessary to accomplish the intended protective action. The lawyer should disclose to any tribunal involved and to any other counsel involved the nature of his or her relationship with the person. The lawyer should take steps to regularize the relationship or implement other protective solutions as soon as possible. Normally, a lawyer would not seek compensation for such emergency actions taken.

RULE 1.15: SAFEKEEPING PROPERTY

(a)   **A lawyer shall hold property of clients or third persons that is in a lawyer's possession in connection with a representation separate from the lawyer's own property. Funds shall be kept in a separate account maintained in the state where the lawyer's office is situated, or elsewhere with the consent of the client or third person. Other property shall be identified as such and appropriately safeguarded. Complete records of such account funds and other property shall be kept by the lawyer and shall be preserved for a period of [five years] after termination of the representation.**

(b)   **A lawyer may deposit the lawyer's own funds in a client trust account for the sole purpose of paying bank service charges on that account, but only in an amount necessary for that purpose.**

(c)   **A lawyer shall deposit into a client trust account legal fees and expenses that have been paid in advance, to be withdrawn by the lawyer only as fees are earned or expenses incurred.**

(d)   **Upon receiving funds or other property in which a client or third person has an interest, a lawyer shall promptly notify the client or third person. Except as stated in this rule or otherwise permitted by law or by agreement with the client, a lawyer shall promptly deliver to the client or third person any funds or other property that the client or third person is entitled to receive and, upon request by the client or third person, shall promptly render a full accounting regarding such property.**

(e)   **When in the course of representation a lawyer is in possession of property in which two or more persons (one of whom may be the lawyer) claim interests, the property shall be kept separate by the lawyer the dispute is resolved. The lawyer shall promptly distribute all portions of the property as to which the interests are not in dispute.**

Comment

[1]   A lawyer should hold property of others with the care required of a professional fiduciary. Securities should be kept in a safe deposit box, except when some other form of safekeeping is warranted by special circumstances. All property that is the property of clients or third persons, including prospective clients, must be kept separate from the lawyer's business and personal property and, if monies, in one or more trust accounts. Separate trust accounts may be warranted when administering estate monies or acting in similar fiduciary capacities. A lawyer should maintain on a current basis books and records in accordance with generally accepted accounting practice and comply with any recordkeeping rules established by law or court order. See, e.g., ABA Model Financial Recordkeeping Rule.

[2]   While normally it is impermissible to commingle the lawyer's own funds with client funds, paragraph (b) provides that it is permissible when

necessary to pay bank service charges on that account. Accurate records must be kept regarding which part of the funds are the lawyer's.

[3]   Lawyers often receive funds from which the lawyer's fee will be paid. The lawyer is not required to remit to the client funds that the lawyer reasonably believes represent fees owed. However, a lawyer may not hold funds to coerce a client into accepting the lawyer's contention. The disputed portion of the funds must be kept in a trust account and the lawyer should suggest means for prompt resolution of the dispute, such as arbitration. The undisputed portion of the funds shall be promptly distributed.

[4]   Paragraph (e) also recognizes that third parties may have lawful claims against specific funds or other property in a lawyer's custody, such as a client's creditor who has a lien on funds recovered in a personal injury action. A lawyer may have a duty under applicable law to protect such third-party claims against wrongful interference by the client. In such cases, when the third-party claim is not frivolous under applicable law, the lawyer must refuse to surrender the property to the client until the claims are resolved. A lawyer should not unilaterally assume to arbitrate a dispute between the client and the third party, but, when there are substantial grounds for dispute as to the person entitled to the funds, the lawyer may file an action to have a court resolve the dispute.

[5]   The obligations of a lawyer under this Rule are independent of those arising from activity other than rendering legal services. For example, a lawyer who serves only as an escrow agent is governed by the applicable law relating to fiduciaries even though the lawyer does not render legal services in the transaction and is not governed by this Rule.

[6]   A lawyers' fund for client protection provides a means through the collective efforts of the bar to reimburse persons who have lost money or property as a result of dishonest conduct of a lawyer. Where such a fund has been established, a lawyer must participate where it is mandatory, and, even when it is voluntary, the lawyer should participate.

RULE 1.16: DECLINING OR TERMINATING REPRESENTATION

(a)   Except as stated in paragraph (c), a lawyer shall not represent a client or, where representation has commenced, shall withdraw from the representation of a client if:

(1)   the representation will result in violation of the rules of professional conduct or other law;

(2)   the lawyer's physical or mental condition materially impairs the lawyer's ability to represent the client; or

(3)   the lawyer is discharged.

(b)   Except as stated in paragraph (c), a lawyer may withdraw from representing a client if:

(1)   withdrawal can be accomplished without material adverse effect on the interests of the client;

(2)   the client persists in a course of action involving the lawyer's services that the lawyer reasonably believes is criminal or fraudulent;

(3)   the client has used the lawyer's services to perpetrate a crime or fraud;

(4)   the client insists upon taking action that the lawyer considers repugnant or with which the lawyer has a fundamental disagreement;

(5)   the client fails substantially to fulfill an obligation to the lawyer regarding the lawyer's services and has been given reasonable warning that the lawyer will withdraw unless the obligation is fulfilled;

(6)   the representation will result in an unreasonable financial burden on the lawyer or has been rendered unreasonably difficult by the client; or

(7)   other good cause for withdrawal exists.

(c)   A lawyer must comply with applicable law requiring notice to or permission of a tribunal when terminating a representation. When ordered to do so by a tribunal, a lawyer shall continue representation notwithstanding good cause for terminating the representation.

(d)   Upon termination of representation, a lawyer shall take steps to the extent reasonably practicable to protect a client's interests, such as giving reasonable notice to the client, allowing time for employment of other counsel, surrendering papers and property to which the client is entitled and refunding any advance payment of fee or expense that has not been earned or incurred. The lawyer may retain papers relating to the client to the extent permitted by other law.

Comment

[1]   A lawyer should not accept representation in a matter unless it can be performed competently, promptly, without improper conflict of interest and to completion. Ordinarily, a representation in a matter is completed when the agreed-upon assistance has been concluded. See Rules 1.2(c) and 6.5. See also Rule 1.3, Comment [4].

Mandatory Withdrawal

[2]   A lawyer ordinarily must decline or withdraw from representation if the client demands that the lawyer engage in conduct that is illegal or violates the Rules of Professional Conduct or other law. The lawyer is not obliged to decline or withdraw simply because the client suggests such a course of conduct; a client may make such a suggestion in the hope that a lawyer will not be constrained by a professional obligation.

[3]   When a lawyer has been appointed to represent a client, withdrawal ordinarily requires approval of the appointing authority. See also

Rule 6.2. Similarly, court approval or notice to the court is often required by applicable law before a lawyer withdraws from pending litigation. Difficulty may be encountered if withdrawal is based on the client's demand that the lawyer engage in unprofessional conduct. The court may request an explanation for the withdrawal, while the lawyer may be bound to keep confidential the facts that would constitute such an explanation. The lawyer's statement that professional considerations require termination of the representation ordinarily should be accepted as sufficient. Lawyers should be mindful of their obligations to both clients and the court under Rules 1.6 and 3.3.

Discharge

[4]   A client has a right to discharge a lawyer at any time, with or without cause, subject to liability for payment for the lawyer's services. Where future dispute about the withdrawal may be anticipated, it may be advisable to prepare a written statement reciting the circumstances.

[5]   Whether a client can discharge appointed counsel may depend on applicable law. A client seeking to do so should be given a full explanation of the consequences. These consequences may include a decision by the appointing authority that appointment of successor counsel is unjustified, thus requiring self-representation by the client.

[6]   If the client has severely diminished capacity, the client may lack the legal capacity to discharge the lawyer, and in any event the discharge may be seriously adverse to the client's interests. The lawyer should make special effort to help the client consider the consequences and may take reasonably necessary protective action as provided in Rule 1.14.

Optional Withdrawal

[7]   A lawyer may withdraw from representation in some circumstances. The lawyer has the option to withdraw if it can be accomplished without material adverse effect on the client's interests. Withdrawal is also justified if the client persists in a course of action that the lawyer reasonably believes is criminal or fraudulent, for a lawyer is not required to be associated with such conduct even if the lawyer does not further it. Withdrawal is also permitted if the lawyer's services were misused in the past even if that would materially prejudice the client. The lawyer may also withdraw where the client insists on taking action that the lawyer considers repugnant or with which the lawyer has a fundamental disagreement.

[8]   A lawyer may withdraw if the client refuses to abide by the terms of an agreement relating to the representation, such as an agreement concerning fees or court costs or an agreement limiting the objectives of the representation.

Assisting the Client upon Withdrawal

[9]   Even if the lawyer has been unfairly discharged by the client, a lawyer must take all reasonable steps to mitigate the consequences to the client. The lawyer may retain papers as security for a fee only to the extent permitted by law. See Rule 1.15.

RULE 1.17: SALE OF LAW PRACTICE

A lawyer or a law firm may sell or purchase a law practice, or an area of law practice, including good will, if the following conditions are satisfied:

(a)   The seller ceases to engage in the private practice of law, or in the area of practice that has been sold, [in the geographic area] [in the jurisdiction] (a jurisdiction nay elect either version) in which the practice has been conducted;

(b)   The entire practice, or the entire area of practice, is sold to one or more lawyers or law firms;

(c)   The seller gives written notice to each of the seller's clients regarding:

(1)   the proposed sale;

(2)   the client's right to retain other counsel or to take possession of the file; and

(3)   the fact that the client's consent to the transfer of the client's files will be presumed if the client does not take any action or does not otherwise object within ninety (90) days of receipt of the notice.

If a client cannot be given notice, the representation of that client may be transferred to the purchaser only upon entry of an order so authorizing by a court having jurisdiction. The seller may disclose to the court in camera information relating to the representation only to the extent necessary to obtain an order authorizing the transfer of a file.

(d)   The fees charged clients shall not be increased by reason of the sale.

Comment

[1]   The practice of law is a profession, not merely a business. Clients are not commodities that can be purchased and sold at will. Pursuant to this Rule, when a lawyer or an entire firm ceases to practice, or ceases to practice in an area of law, and other lawyers or firms take over the representation, the selling lawyer or firm may obtain compensation for the reasonable value of the practice as may withdrawing partners of law firms. See Rules 5.4 and 5.6.

Termination of Practice by the Seller

[2]   The requirement that all of the private practice, or all of an area of practice, be sold is satisfied if the seller in good faith makes the entire practice, or the area of practice, available for sale to the purchasers. The fact that a number of the seller's clients decide not to be represented by the purchasers but take their matters elsewhere, therefore, does not result in a violation. Return to private practice as a result of an unanticipated change in circumstances does not necessarily result in a violation. For example, a lawyer

who has sold the practice to accept an appointment to judicial office does not violate the requirement that the sale be attendant to cessation of practice if the lawyer later resumes private practice upon being defeated in a contested or a retention election for the office or resigns from a judiciary position.

[3] The requirement that the seller cease to engage in the private practice of law does not prohibit employment as a lawyer on the staff of a public agency or a legal services entity that provides legal services to the poor, or as in-house counsel to a business.

[4] The Rule permits a sale of an entire practice attendant upon retirement from the private practice of law within the jurisdiction. Its provisions, therefore, accommodate the lawyer who sells the practice on the occasion of moving to another state. Some states are so large that a move from one locale therein to another is tantamount to leaving the jurisdiction in which the lawyer has engaged in the practice of law. To also accommodate lawyers so situated, states may permit the sale of the practice when the lawyer leaves the geographical area rather than the jurisdiction. The alternative desired should be indicated by selecting one of the two provided for in Rule 1.17(a).

[5] This Rule also permits a lawyer or law firm to sell an area of practice. If an area of practice is sold and the lawyer remains in the active practice of law, the lawyer must cease accepting any matters in the area of practice that has been sold, either as counsel or co-counsel or by assuming joint responsibility for a matter in connection with the division of a fee with another lawyer as would otherwise be permitted by Rule 1.5(e). For example, a lawyer with a substantial number of estate planning matters and a substantial number of probate administration cases may sell the estate planning portion of the practice but remain in the practice of law by concentrating on probate administration; however, that practitioner may not thereafter accept any estate planning matters. Although a lawyer who leaves a jurisdiction or geographical area typically would sell the entire practice, this Rule permits the lawyer to limit the sale to one or more areas of the practice, thereby preserving the lawyer's right to continue practice in the areas of the practice that were not sold.

Sale of Entire Practice or Entire Area of Practice

[6] The Rule requires that the seller's entire practice, or an entire area of practice, be sold. The prohibition against sale of less than an entire practice area protects those clients whose matters are less lucrative and who might find it difficult to secure other counsel if a sale could be limited to substantial fee-generating matters. The purchasers are required to undertake all client matters in the practice or practice area, subject to client consent. This requirement is satisfied, however, even if a purchaser is unable to undertake a particular client matter because of a conflict of interest.

Client Confidences, Consent and Notice

[7] Negotiations between seller and prospective purchaser prior to disclosure of information relating to a specific representation of an identifiable client no more violate the confidentiality provisions of Model Rule 1.6 than do

preliminary discussions concerning the possible association of another lawyer or mergers between firms, with respect to which client consent is not required. See Rule 1.6(b)(7). Providing the purchaser access to detailed information relating to the representation, such as the client's file, however, requires client consent. The Rule provides that before such information can be disclosed by the seller to the purchaser the client must be given actual written notice of the contemplated sale, including the identity of the purchaser, and must be told that the decision to consent or make other arrangements must be made within 90 days. If nothing is heard from the client within that time, consent to the sale is presumed.

[8]   A lawyer or law firm ceasing to practice cannot be required to remain in practice because some clients cannot be given actual notice of the proposed purchase. Since these clients cannot themselves consent to the purchase or direct any other disposition of their files, the Rule requires an order from a court having jurisdiction authorizing their transfer or other disposition. The Court can be expected to determine whether reasonable efforts to locate the client have been exhausted, and whether the absent client's legitimate interests will be served by authorizing the transfer of the file so that the purchaser may continue the representation. Preservation of client confidences requires that the petition for a court order be considered in camera. (A procedure by which such an order can be obtained needs to be established in jurisdictions in which it presently does not exist).

[9]   All elements of client autonomy, including the client's absolute right to discharge a lawyer and transfer the representation to another, survive the sale of the practice or area of practice.

Fee Arrangements Between Client and Purchaser

[10]   The sale may not be financed by increases in fees charged the clients of the practice. Existing arrangements between the seller and the client as to fees and the scope of the work must be honored by the purchaser.

Other Applicable Ethical Standards

[11]   Lawyers participating in the sale of a law practice or a practice area are subject to the ethical standards applicable to involving another lawyer in the representation of a client. These include, for example, the seller's obligation to exercise competence in identifying a purchaser qualified to assume the practice and the purchaser's obligation to undertake the representation competently (see Rule 1.1); the obligation to avoid disqualifying conflicts, and to secure the client's informed consent for those conflicts that can be agreed to (see Rule 1.7 regarding conflicts and Rule 1.0(e) for the definition of informed consent); and the obligation to protect information relating to the representation (see Rules 1.6 and 1.9).

[12]   If approval of the substitution of the purchasing lawyer for the selling lawyer is required by the rules of any tribunal in which a matter is pending, such approval must be obtained before the matter can be included in the sale (see Rule 1.16).

Applicability of the Rule

[13]   This Rule applies to the sale of a law practice of a deceased, disabled or disappeared lawyer. Thus, the seller may be represented by a non- lawyer representative not subject to these Rules. Since, however, no lawyer may participate in a sale of a law practice which does not conform to the requirements of this Rule, the representatives of the seller as well as the purchasing lawyer can be expected to see to it that they are met.

[14]   Admission to or retirement from a law partnership or professional association, retirement plans and similar arrangements, and a sale of tangible assets of a law practice, do not constitute a sale or purchase governed by this Rule.

[15]   This Rule does not apply to the transfers of legal representation between lawyers when such transfers are unrelated to the sale of a practice or an area of practice.

RULE 1.18: DUTIES TO PROSPECTIVE CLIENT

(a)   A person who consults with a lawyer about the possibility of forming a client-lawyer relationship with respect to a matter is a prospective client.

(b)   Even when no client-lawyer relationship ensues, a lawyer who has learned information from a prospective client shall not use or reveal that information, except as Rule 1.9 would permit with respect to information of a former client.

(c)   A lawyer subject to paragraph (b) shall not represent a client with interests materially adverse to those of a prospective client in the same or a substantially related matter if the lawyer received information from the prospective client that could be significantly harmful to that person in the matter, except as provided in paragraph (d). If a lawyer is disqualified from representation under this paragraph, no lawyer in a firm with which that lawyer is associated may knowingly undertake or continue representation in such a matter, except as provided in paragraph (d).

(d)   When the lawyer has received disqualifying information as defined in paragraph (c), representation is permissible if:

(1)   both the affected client and the prospective client have given informed consent, confirmed in writing, or:

(2)   the lawyer who received the information took reasonable measures to avoid exposure to more disqualifying information than was reasonably necessary to determine whether to represent the prospective client; and

(i)   the disqualified lawyer is timely screened from any participation in the matter and is apportioned no part of the fee therefrom; and

> **(ii)   written notice is promptly given to the prospective client.**

Comment

[1]   Prospective clients, like clients, may disclose information to a lawyer, place documents or other property in the lawyer's custody, or rely on the lawyer's advice. A lawyer's consultations with a prospective client usually are limited in time and depth and leave both the prospective client and the lawyer free (and sometimes required) to proceed no further. Hence, prospective clients should receive some but not all of the protection afforded clients.

[2]   A person becomes a prospective client by consulting with a lawyer about the possibility of forming a client-lawyer relationship with respect to a matter. Whether communications, including written, oral, or electronic communications, constitute a consultation depends on the circumstances. For example, a consultation is likely to have occurred if a lawyer, either in person or through the lawyer's advertising in any medium, specifically requests or invites the submission of information about a potential representation without clear and reasonably understandable warnings and cautionary statements that limit the lawyer's obligations, and a person provides information in response. See also Comment [4]. In contrast, a consultation does not occur if a person provides information to a lawyer in response to advertising that merely describes the lawyer's education, experience, areas of practice, and contact information, or provides legal information of general interest. Such a person communicates information unilaterally to a lawyer, without any reasonable expectation that the lawyer is willing to discuss the possibility of forming a client-lawyer relationship, and is thus not a "prospective client." Moreover, a person who communicates with a lawyer for the purpose of disqualifying the lawyer is not a "prospective client."

[3]   It is often necessary for a prospective client to reveal information to the lawyer during an initial consultation prior to the decision about formation of a client-lawyer relationship. The lawyer often must learn such information to determine whether there is a conflict of interest with an existing client and whether the matter is one that the lawyer is willing to undertake. Paragraph (b) prohibits the lawyer from using or revealing that information, except as permitted by Rule 1.9, even if the client or lawyer decides not to proceed with the representation. The duty exists regardless of how brief the initial conference may be.

[4]   In order to avoid acquiring disqualifying information from a prospective client, a lawyer considering whether or not to undertake a new matter should limit the initial consultation to only such information as reasonably appears necessary for that purpose. Where the information indicates that a conflict of interest or other reason for non-representation exists, the lawyer should so inform the prospective client or decline the representation. If the prospective client wishes to retain the lawyer, and if consent is possible under Rule 1.7, then consent from all affected present or former clients must be obtained before accepting the representation.

[5]   A lawyer may condition a consultation with a prospective client on the person's informed consent that no information disclosed during the consultation will prohibit the lawyer from representing a different client in the matter. See Rule 1.0(e) for the definition of informed consent. If the agreement expressly so provides, the prospective client may also consent to the lawyer's subsequent use of information received from the prospective client.

[6]   Even in the absence of an agreement, under paragraph (c), the lawyer is not prohibited from representing a client with interests adverse to those of the prospective client in the same or a substantially related matter unless the lawyer has received from the prospective client information that could be significantly harmful if used in the matter.

[7]   Under paragraph (c), the prohibition in this Rule is imputed to other lawyers as provided in Rule 1.10, but, under paragraph (d)(1), imputation may be avoided if the lawyer obtains the informed consent, confirmed in writing, of both the prospective and affected clients. In the alternative, imputation may be avoided if the conditions of paragraph (d)(2) are met and all disqualified lawyers are timely screened and written notice is promptly given to the prospective client. See Rule 1.0(k) (requirements for screening procedures). Paragraph (d)(2)(i) does not prohibit the screened lawyer from receiving a salary or partnership share established by prior independent agreement, but that lawyer may not receive compensation directly related to the matter in which the lawyer is disqualified.

[8]   Notice, including a general description of the subject matter about which the lawyer was consulted, and of the screening procedures employed, generally should be given as soon as practicable after the need for screening becomes apparent.

[9]   For the duty of competence of a lawyer who gives assistance on the merits of a matter to a prospective client, see Rule 1.1. For a lawyer's duties when a prospective client entrusts valuables or papers to the lawyer's care, see Rule 1.15.

RULE 2.1: ADVISOR

In representing a client, a lawyer shall exercise independent professional judgment and render candid advice. In rendering advice, a lawyer may refer not only to law but to other considerations such as moral, economic, social and political factors, that may be relevant to the client's situation.

Comment

Scope of Advice

[1]   A client is entitled to straightforward advice expressing the lawyer's honest assessment. Legal advice often involves unpleasant facts and alternatives that a client may be disinclined to confront. In presenting advice, a lawyer endeavors to sustain the client's morale and may put advice in as acceptable a form as honesty permits. However, a lawyer should not be deterred

from giving candid advice by the prospect that the advice will be unpalatable to the client.

[2]   Advice couched in narrow legal terms may be of little value to a client, especially where practical considerations, such as cost or effects on other people, are predominant. Purely technical legal advice, therefore, can sometimes be inadequate. It is proper for a lawyer to refer to relevant moral and ethical considerations in giving advice. Although a lawyer is not a moral advisor as such, moral and ethical considerations impinge upon most legal questions and may decisively influence how the law will be applied.

[3]   A client may expressly or impliedly ask the lawyer for purely technical advice. When such a request is made by a client experienced in legal matters, the lawyer may accept it at face value. When such a request is made by a client inexperienced in legal matters, however, the lawyer's responsibility as advisor may include indicating that more may be involved than strictly legal considerations.

[4]   Matters that go beyond strictly legal questions may also be in the domain of another profession. Family matters can involve problems within the professional competence of psychiatry, clinical psychology or social work; business matters can involve problems within the competence of the accounting profession or of financial specialists. Where consultation with a professional in another field is itself something a competent lawyer would recommend, the lawyer should make such a recommendation. At the same time, a lawyer's advice at its best often consists of recommending a course of action in the face of conflicting recommendations of experts.

Offering Advice

[5]   In general, a lawyer is not expected to give advice until asked by the client. However, when a lawyer knows that a client proposes a course of action that is likely to result in substantial adverse legal consequences to the client, the lawyer's duty to the client under Rule 1.4 may require that the lawyer offer advice if the client's course of action is related to the representation. Similarly, when a matter is likely to involve litigation, it may be necessary under Rule 1.4 to inform the client of forms of dispute resolution that might constitute reasonable alternatives to litigation. A lawyer ordinarily has no duty to initiate investigation of a client's affairs or to give advice that the client has indicated is unwanted, but a lawyer may initiate advice to a client when doing so appears to be in the client's interest.

RULE 2.2 (DELETED)

RULE 2.3: EVALUATION FOR USE BY THIRD PERSONS

(a)   A lawyer may provide an evaluation of a matter affecting a client for the use of someone other than the client if the lawyer reasonably believes that making the evaluation is compatible with other aspects of the lawyer's relationship with the client.

(b)   When the lawyer knows or reasonably should know that the evaluation is likely to affect the client's interests materially and adversely, the lawyer shall not provide the evaluation unless the client gives informed consent.

(c)   Except as disclosure is authorized in connection with a report of an evaluation, information relating to the evaluation is otherwise protected by Rule 1.6.

Comment

Definition

[1]   An evaluation may be performed at the client's direction or when impliedly authorized in order to carry out the representation. See Rule 1.2. Such an evaluation may be for the primary purpose of establishing information for the benefit of third parties; for example, an opinion concerning the title of property rendered at the behest of a vendor for the information of a prospective purchaser, or at the behest of a borrower for the information of a prospective lender. In some situations, the evaluation may be required by a government agency; for example, an opinion concerning the legality of the securities registered for sale under the securities laws. In other instances, the evaluation may be required by a third person, such as a purchaser of a business.

[2]   A legal evaluation should be distinguished from an investigation of a person with whom the lawyer does not have a client-lawyer relationship. For example, a lawyer retained by a purchaser to analyze a vendor's title to property does not have a client-lawyer relationship with the vendor. So also, an investigation into a person's affairs by a government lawyer, or by special counsel by a government lawyer, or by special counsel employed by the government, is not an evaluation as that term is used in this Rule. The question is whether the lawyer is retained by the person whose affairs are being examined. When the lawyer is retained by that person, the general rules concerning loyalty to client and preservation of confidences apply, which is not the case if the lawyer is retained by someone else. For this reason, it is essential to identify the person by whom the lawyer is retained. This should be made clear not only to the person under examination, but also to others to whom the results are to be made available.

Duties Owed to Third Person and Client

[3]   When the evaluation is intended for the information or use of a third person, a legal duty to that person may or may not arise. That legal question is beyond the scope of this Rule. However, since such an evaluation involves a departure from the normal client-lawyer relationship, careful analysis of the situation is required. The lawyer must be satisfied as a matter of professional judgment that making the evaluation is compatible with other functions undertaken in behalf of the client. For example, if the lawyer is acting as advocate in defending the client against charges of fraud, it would normally be incompatible with that responsibility for the lawyer to perform an

evaluation for others concerning the same or a related transaction. Assuming no such impediment is apparent, however, the lawyer should advise the client of the implications of the evaluation, particularly the lawyer's responsibilities to third persons and the duty to disseminate the findings.

Access to and Disclosure of Information

[4]   The quality of an evaluation depends on the freedom and extent of the investigation upon which it is based. Ordinarily a lawyer should have whatever latitude of investigation seems necessary as a matter of professional judgment. Under some circumstances, however, the terms of the evaluation may be limited. For example, certain issues or sources may be categorically excluded, or the scope of search may be limited by time constraints or the noncooperation of persons having relevant information. Any such limitations that are material to the evaluation should be described in the report. If after a lawyer has commenced an evaluation, the client refuses to comply with the terms upon which it was understood the evaluation was to have been made, the lawyer's obligations are determined by law, having reference to the terms of the client's agreement and the surrounding circumstances. In no circumstances is the lawyer permitted to knowingly make a false statement of material fact or law in providing an evaluation under this Rule. See Rule 4.1.

Obtaining Client's Informed Consent

[5]   Information relating to an evaluation is protected by Rule 1.6. In many situations, providing an evaluation to a third party poses no significant risk to the client; thus, the lawyer may be impliedly authorized to disclose information to carry out the representation. See Rule 1.6(a). Where, however, it is reasonably likely that providing the evaluation will affect the client's interests materially and adversely, the lawyer must first obtain the client's consent after the client has been adequately informed concerning the important possible effects on the client's interests. See Rules 1.6(a) and 1.0(e).

Financial Auditors' Requests for Information

[6]   When a question concerning the legal situation of a client arises at the instance of the client's financial auditor and the question is referred to the lawyer, the lawyer's response may be made in accordance with procedures recognized in the legal profession. Such a procedure is set forth in the American Bar Association Statement of Policy Regarding Lawyers' Responses to Auditors' Requests for Information, adopted in 1975.

RULE 2.4: LAWYER SERVING AS THIRD-PARTY NEUTRAL

(a)   **A lawyer serves as a third-party neutral when the lawyer assists two or more persons who are not clients of the lawyer to reach a resolution of a dispute or other matter that has arisen between them. Service as a third-party neutral may include service as an arbitrator, a mediator or in such other capacity as will enable the lawyer to assist the parties to resolve the matter.**

(b)   A lawyer serving as a third-party neutral shall inform unrepresented parties that the lawyer is not representing them. When the lawyer knows or reasonably should know that a party does not understand the lawyer's role in the matter, the lawyer shall explain the difference between the lawyer's role as a third-party neutral and a lawyer's role as one who represents a client.

Comment

[1]   Alternative dispute resolution has become a substantial part of the civil justice system. Aside from representing clients in dispute-resolution processes, lawyers often serve as third-party neutrals. A third-party neutral is a person, such as a mediator, arbitrator, conciliator or evaluator, who assists the parties, represented or unrepresented, in the resolution of a dispute or in the arrangement of a transaction. Whether a third-party neutral serves primarily as a facilitator, evaluator or decisionmaker depends on the particular process that is either selected by the parties or mandated by a court.

[2]   The role of a third-party neutral is not unique to lawyers, although, in some court-connected contexts, only lawyers are allowed to serve in this role or to handle certain types of cases. In performing this role, the lawyer may be subject to court rules or other law that apply either to third- party neutrals generally or to lawyers serving as third-party neutrals. Lawyer- neutrals may also be subject to various codes of ethics, such as the Code of Ethics for Arbitration in Commercial Disputes prepared by a joint committee of the American Bar Association and the American Arbitration Association or the Model Standards of Conduct for Mediators jointly prepared by the American Bar Association, the American Arbitration Association and the Society of Professionals in Dispute Resolution.

[3]   Unlike nonlawyers who serve as third-party neutrals, lawyers serving in this role may experience unique problems as a result of differences between the role of a third-party neutral and a lawyer's service as a client representative. The potential for confusion is significant when the parties are unrepresented in the process. Thus, paragraph (b) requires a lawyer-neutral to inform unrepresented parties that the lawyer is not representing them. For some parties, particularly parties who frequently use dispute-resolution processes, this information will be sufficient. For others, particularly those who are using the process for the first time, more information will be required. Where appropriate, the lawyer should inform unrepresented parties of the important differences between the lawyer's role as third-party neutral and a lawyer's role as a client representative, including the inapplicability of the attorney-client evidentiary privilege. The extent of disclosure required under this paragraph will depend on the particular parties involved and the subject matter of the proceeding, as well as the particular features of the dispute-resolution process selected.

[4]   A lawyer who serves as a third-party neutral subsequently may be asked to serve as a lawyer representing a client in the same matter. The conflicts of interest that arise for both the individual lawyer and the lawyer's law firm are addressed in Rule 1.12.

[5]   Lawyers who represent clients in alternative dispute-resolution processes are governed by the Rules of Professional Conduct. When the dispute-resolution process takes place before a tribunal, as in binding arbitration (see Rule 1.0(m)), the lawyer's duty of candor is governed by Rule 3.3. Otherwise, the lawyer's duty of candor toward both the third-party neutral and other parties is governed by Rule 4.1.

RULE 3.1: MERITORIOUS CLAIMS AND CONTENTIONS

A lawyer shall not bring or defend a proceeding, or assert or controvert an issue therein, unless there is a basis in law and fact for doing so that is not frivolous, which includes a good faith argument for an extension, modification or reversal of existing law. A lawyer for the defendant in a criminal proceeding, or the respondent in a proceeding that could result in incarceration, may nevertheless so defend the proceeding as to require that every element of the case be established.

Comment

[1]   The advocate has a duty to use legal procedure for the fullest benefit of the client's cause, but also a duty not to abuse legal procedure. The law, both procedural and substantive, establishes the limits within which an advocate may proceed. However, the law is not always clear and never is static. Accordingly, in determining the proper scope of advocacy, account must be taken of the law's ambiguities and potential for change.

[2]   The filing of an action or defense or similar action taken for a client is not frivolous merely because the facts have not first been fully substantiated or because the lawyer expects to develop vital evidence only by discovery. What is required of lawyers, however, is that they inform themselves about the facts of their clients' cases and the applicable law and determine that they can make good faith arguments in support of their clients' positions. Such action is not frivolous even though the lawyer believes that the client's position ultimately will not prevail. The action is frivolous, however, if the lawyer is unable either to make a good faith argument on the merits of the action taken or to support the action taken by a good faith argument for an extension, modification or reversal of existing law.

[3]   The lawyer's obligations under this Rule are subordinate to federal or state constitutional law that entitles a defendant in a criminal matter to the assistance of counsel in presenting a claim or contention that otherwise would be prohibited by this Rule. *Δ has a right to fight*

RULE 3.2: EXPEDITING LITIGATION

A lawyer shall make reasonable efforts to expedite litigation consistent with the interests of the client.

Comment

[1]   Dilatory practices bring the administration of justice into disrepute. Although there will be occasions when a lawyer may properly seek a postponement

for personal reasons, it is not proper for a lawyer to routinely fail to expedite litigation solely for the convenience of the advocates. Nor will a failure to expedite be reasonable if done for the purpose of frustrating an opposing party's attempt to obtain rightful redress or repose. It is not a justification that similar conduct is often tolerated by the bench and bar. The question is whether a competent lawyer acting in good faith would regard the course of action as having some substantial purpose other than delay. Realizing financial or other benefit from otherwise improper delay in litigation is not a legitimate interest of the client.

RULE 3.3: CANDOR TOWARD THE TRIBUNAL

(a)   A lawyer shall not knowingly:

(1)   make a false statement of fact or law to a tribunal or fail to correct a false statement of material fact or law previously made to the tribunal by the lawyer;

(2)   fail to disclose to the tribunal legal authority in the controlling jurisdiction known to the lawyer to be directly adverse to the position of the client and not disclosed by opposing counsel; or

Have to tell law

(3)   offer evidence that the lawyer knows to be false. If a lawyer, the lawyer's client, or a witness called by the lawyer, has offered material evidence and the lawyer comes to know of its falsity, the lawyer shall take reasonable remedial measures, including, if necessary, disclosure to the tribunal. A lawyer may refuse to offer evidence, other than the testimony of a defendant in a criminal matter, that the lawyer reasonably believes is false.

"noisy" withdrawal possibly
No testimony except criminal Δ

(b)   A lawyer who represents a client in an adjudicative proceeding and who knows that a person intends to engage, is engaging or has engaged in criminal or fraudulent conduct related to the proceeding shall take reasonable remedial measures, including, if necessary, disclosure to the tribunal.

(c)   The duties stated in paragraphs (a) and (b) continue to the conclusion of the proceeding, and apply even if compliance requires disclosure of information otherwise protected by Rule 1.6.

(d)   In an ex parte proceeding, a lawyer shall inform the tribunal of all material facts known to the lawyer that will enable the tribunal to make an informed decision, whether or not the facts are adverse.

Comment

[1]   This Rule governs the conduct of a lawyer who is representing a client in the proceedings of a tribunal. See Rule 1.0(m) for the definition of "tribunal." It also applies when the lawyer is representing a client in an ancillary proceeding conducted pursuant to the tribunal's adjudicative authority, such as a deposition. Thus, for example, paragraph (a)(3) requires a lawyer to

take reasonable remedial measures if the lawyer comes to know that a client who is testifying in a deposition has offered evidence that is false.

[2]   This Rule sets forth the special duties of lawyers as officers of the court to avoid conduct that undermines the integrity of the adjudicative process. A lawyer acting as an advocate in an adjudicative proceeding has an obligation to present the client's case with persuasive force. Performance of that duty while maintaining confidences of the client, however, is qualified by the advocate's duty of candor to the tribunal. Consequently, although a lawyer in an adversary proceeding is not required to present an impartial exposition of the law or to vouch for the evidence submitted in a cause, the lawyer must not allow the tribunal to be misled by false statements of law or fact or evidence that the lawyer knows to be false.

Representations by a Lawyer

[3]   An advocate is responsible for pleadings and other documents prepared for litigation, but is usually not required to have personal knowledge of matters asserted therein, for litigation documents ordinarily present assertions by the client, or by someone on the client's behalf, and not assertions by the lawyer. Compare Rule 3.1. However, an assertion purporting to be on the lawyer's own knowledge, as in an affidavit by the lawyer or in a statement in open court, may properly be made only when the lawyer knows the assertion is true or believes it to be true on the basis of a reasonably diligent inquiry. There are circumstances where failure to make a disclosure is the equivalent of an affirmative misrepresentation. The obligation prescribed in Rule 1.2(d) not to counsel a client to commit or assist the client in committing a fraud applies in litigation. Regarding compliance with Rule 1.2(d), see the Comment to that Rule. See also the Comment to Rule 8.4(b).

Legal Argument

[4]   Legal argument based on a knowingly false representation of law constitutes dishonesty toward the tribunal. A lawyer is not required to make a disinterested exposition of the law, but must recognize the existence of pertinent legal authorities. Furthermore, as stated in paragraph (a)(2), an advocate has a duty to disclose directly adverse authority in the controlling jurisdiction that has not been disclosed by the opposing party. The underlying concept is that legal argument is a discussion seeking to determine the legal premises properly applicable to the case.

Offering Evidence

[5]   Paragraph (a)(3) requires that the lawyer refuse to offer evidence that the lawyer knows to be false, regardless of the client's wishes. This duty is premised on the lawyer's obligation as an officer of the court to prevent the trier of fact from being misled by false evidence. A lawyer does not violate this Rule if the lawyer offers the evidence for the purpose of establishing its falsity.

[6]   If a lawyer knows that the client intends to testify falsely or wants the lawyer to introduce false evidence, the lawyer should seek to persuade

the client that the evidence should not be offered. If the persuasion is ineffective and the lawyer continues to represent the client, the lawyer must refuse to offer the false evidence. If only a portion of a witness's testimony will be false, the lawyer may call the witness to testify but may not elicit or otherwise permit the witness to present the testimony that the lawyer knows is false.

[7]   The duties stated in paragraphs (a) and (b) apply to all lawyers, including defense counsel in criminal cases. In some jurisdictions, however, courts have required counsel to present the accused as a witness or to give a narrative statement if the accused so desires, even if counsel knows that the testimony or statement will be false. The obligation of the advocate under the Rules of Professional Conduct is subordinate to such requirements. See also Comment [9].

[8]   The prohibition against offering false evidence only applies if the lawyer knows that the evidence is false. A lawyer's reasonable belief that evidence is false does not preclude its presentation to the trier of fact. A lawyer's knowledge that evidence is false, however, can be inferred from the circumstances. See Rule 1.0(f). Thus, although a lawyer should resolve doubts about the veracity of testimony or other evidence in favor of the client, the lawyer cannot ignore an obvious falsehood.

[9]   Although paragraph (a)(3) only prohibits a lawyer from offering evidence the lawyer knows to be false, it permits the lawyer to refuse to offer testimony or other proof that the lawyer reasonably believes is false. Offering such proof may reflect adversely on the lawyer's ability to discriminate in the quality of evidence and thus impair the lawyer's effectiveness as an advocate. Because of the special protections historically provided criminal defendants, however, this Rule does not permit a lawyer to refuse to offer the testimony of such a client where the lawyer reasonably believes but does not know that the testimony will be false. Unless the lawyer knows the testimony will be false, the lawyer must honor the client's decision to testify. See also Comment [7].

Remedial Measures

[10]   Having offered material evidence in the belief that it was true, a lawyer may subsequently come to know that the evidence is false. Or, a lawyer may be surprised when the lawyer's client, or another witness called by the lawyer, offers testimony the lawyer knows to be false, either during the lawyer's direct examination or in response to cross-examination by the opposing lawyer. In such situations or if the lawyer knows of the falsity of testimony elicited from the client during a deposition, the lawyer must take reasonable remedial measures. In such situations, the advocate's proper course is to remonstrate with the client confidentially, advise the client of the lawyer's duty of candor to the tribunal and seek the client's cooperation with respect to the withdrawal or correction of the false statements or evidence. If that fails, the advocate must take further remedial action. If withdrawal from the representation is not permitted or will not undo the effect of the false evidence, the advocate must make such disclosure to the tribunal as is reasonably necessary

to remedy the situation, even if doing so requires the lawyer to reveal information that otherwise would be protected by Rule 1.6. It is for the tribunal then to determine what should be done — making a statement about the matter to the trier of fact, ordering a mistrial or perhaps nothing.

[11]   The disclosure of a client's false testimony can result in grave consequences to the client, including not only a sense of betrayal but also loss of the case and perhaps a prosecution for perjury. But the alternative is that the lawyer cooperate in deceiving the court, thereby subverting the truth-finding process which the adversary system is designed to implement. See Rule 1.2(d). Furthermore, unless it is clearly understood that the lawyer will act upon the duty to disclose the existence of false evidence, the client can simply reject the lawyer's advice to reveal the false evidence and insist that the lawyer keep silent. Thus the client could in effect coerce the lawyer into being a party to fraud on the court.

Preserving Integrity of Adjudicative Process

[12]   Lawyers have a special obligation to protect a tribunal against criminal or fraudulent conduct that undermines the integrity of the adjudicative process, such as bribing, intimidating or otherwise unlawfully communicating with a witness, juror, court official or other participant in the proceeding, unlawfully destroying or concealing documents or other evidence or failing to disclose information to the tribunal when required by law to do so. Thus, paragraph (b) requires a lawyer to take reasonable remedial measures, including disclosure if necessary, whenever the lawyer knows that a person, including the lawyer's client, intends to engage, is engaging or has engaged in criminal or fraudulent conduct related to the proceeding.

Duration of Obligation

[13]   A practical time limit on the obligation to rectify false evidence or false statements of law and fact has to be established. The conclusion of the proceeding is a reasonably definite point for the termination of the obligation. A proceeding has concluded within the meaning of this Rule when a final judgment in the proceeding has been affirmed on appeal or the time for review has passed.

Ex Parte Proceedings

[14]   Ordinarily, an advocate has the limited responsibility of presenting one side of the matters that a tribunal should consider in reaching a decision; the conflicting position is expected to be presented by the opposing party. However, in any ex parte proceeding, such as an application for a temporary restraining order, there is no balance of presentation by opposing advocates. The object of an ex parte proceeding is nevertheless to yield a substantially just result. The judge has an affirmative responsibility to accord the absent party just consideration. The lawyer for the represented party has the correlative duty to make disclosures of material facts known to the lawyer and that the lawyer reasonably believes are necessary to an informed decision.

Withdrawal

[15]   Normally, a lawyer's compliance with the duty of candor imposed by this Rule does not require that the lawyer withdraw from the representation of a client whose interests will be or have been adversely affected by the lawyer's disclosure. The lawyer may, however, be required by Rule 1.16(a) to seek permission of the tribunal to withdraw if the lawyer's compliance with this Rule's duty of candor results in such an extreme deterioration of the client- lawyer relationship that the lawyer can no longer competently represent the client. Also see Rule 1.16(b) for the circumstances in which a lawyer will be permitted to seek a tribunal's permission to withdraw. In connection with a request for permission to withdraw that is premised on a client's misconduct, a lawyer may reveal information relating to the representation only to the extent reasonably necessary to comply with this Rule or as otherwise permitted by Rule 1.6.

RULE 3.4: FAIRNESS TO OPPOSING PARTY AND COUNSEL

A lawyer shall not:

(a)   unlawfully obstruct another party's access to evidence or unlawfully alter, destroy or conceal a document or other material having potential evidentiary value. A lawyer shall not counsel or assist another person to do any such act;

(b)   falsify evidence, counsel or assist a witness to testify falsely, or offer an inducement to a witness that is prohibited by law;

(c)   knowingly disobey an obligation under the rules of a tribunal, except for an open refusal based on an assertion that no valid obligation exists;

(d)   in pretrial procedure, make a frivolous discovery request or fail to make reasonably diligent effort to comply with a legally proper discovery request by an opposing party;

(e)   in trial, allude to any matter that the lawyer does not reasonably believe is relevant or that will not be supported by admissible evidence, assert personal knowledge of facts in issue except when testifying as a witness, or state a personal opinion as to the justness of a cause, the credibility of a witness, the culpability of a civil litigant or the guilt or innocence of an accused; or

(f)   request a person other than a client to refrain from voluntarily giving relevant information to another party unless:

(1)   the person is a relative or an employee or other agent of a client; and

(2)   the lawyer reasonably believes that the person's interests will not be adversely affected by refraining from giving such information.

Comment

[1]   The procedure of the adversary system contemplates that the evidence in a case is to be marshalled competitively by the contending parties. Fair competition in the adversary system is secured by prohibitions against destruction or concealment of evidence, improperly influencing witnesses, obstructive tactics in discovery procedure, and the like.

[2]   Documents and other items of evidence are often essential to establish a claim or defense. Subject to evidentiary privileges, the right of an opposing party, including the government, to obtain evidence through discovery or subpoena is an important procedural right. The exercise of that right can be frustrated if relevant material is altered, concealed or destroyed. Applicable law in many jurisdictions makes it an offense to destroy material for purpose of impairing its availability in a pending proceeding or one whose commencement can be foreseen. Falsifying evidence is also generally a criminal offense. Paragraph (a) applies to evidentiary material generally, including computerized information. Applicable law may permit a lawyer to take temporary possession of physical evidence of client crimes for the purpose of conducting a limited examination that will not alter or destroy material characteristics of the evidence. In such a case, applicable law may require the lawyer to turn the evidence over to the police or other prosecuting authority, depending on the circumstances.

[3]   With regard to paragraph (b), it is not improper to pay a witness's expenses or to compensate an expert witness on terms permitted by law. The common law rule in most jurisdictions is that it is improper to pay an occurrence witness any fee for testifying and that it is improper to pay an expert witness a contingent fee.

[4]   Paragraph (f) permits a lawyer to advise employees of a client to refrain from giving information to another party, for the employees may identify their interests with those of the client. See also Rule 4.2.

RULE 3.5: IMPARTIALITY AND DECORUM OF THE TRIBUNAL

A lawyer shall not:

(a)   seek to influence a judge, juror, prospective juror or other official by means prohibited by law;

(b)   communicate ex parte with such a person during the proceeding unless authorized to do so by law or court order;

(c)   communicate with a juror or prospective juror after discharge of the jury if:

(1)   the communication is prohibited by law or court order;

(2)   the juror has made known to the lawyer a desire not to communicate; or

(3)   the communication involves misrepresentation, coercion, duress or harassment; or

(d)   engage in conduct intended to disrupt a tribunal.

Comment

[1]   Many forms of improper influence upon a tribunal are proscribed by criminal law. Others are specified in the ABA Model Code of Judicial Conduct, with which an advocate should be familiar. A lawyer is required to avoid contributing to a violation of such provisions.

[2]   During a proceeding a lawyer may not communicate ex parte with persons serving in an official capacity in the proceeding, such as judges, masters or jurors, unless authorized to do so by law or court order.

[3]   A lawyer may on occasion want to communicate with a juror or prospective juror after the jury has been discharged. The lawyer may do so unless the communication is prohibited by law or a court order but must respect the desire of the juror not to talk with the lawyer. The lawyer may not engage in improper conduct during the communication.

[4]   The advocate's function is to present evidence and argument so that the cause may be decided according to law. Refraining from abusive or obstreperous conduct is a corollary of the advocate's right to speak on behalf of litigants. A lawyer may stand firm against abuse by a judge but should avoid reciprocation; the judge's default is no justification for similar dereliction by an advocate. An advocate can present the cause, protect the record for subsequent review and preserve professional integrity by patient firmness no less effectively than by belligerence or theatrics.

[5]   The duty to refrain from disruptive conduct applies to any proceeding of a tribunal, including a deposition. See Rule 1.0(m).

RULE 3.6: TRIAL PUBLICITY

(a)   **A lawyer who is participating or has participated in the investigation or litigation of a matter shall not make an extrajudicial statement that the lawyer knows or reasonably should know will be disseminated by means of public communication and will have a substantial likelihood of materially prejudicing an adjudicative proceeding in the matter.**

(b)   **Notwithstanding paragraph (a), a lawyer may state:**

(1)   **the claim, offense or defense involved and, except when prohibited by law, the identity of the persons involved;**

(2)   **information contained in a public record;**

(3)   **that an investigation of a matter is in progress;**

(4)   **the scheduling or result of any step in litigation;**

(5)   **a request for assistance in obtaining evidence and information necessary thereto;**

(6)   **a warning of danger concerning the behavior of a person involved, when there is reason to believe that there exists the likelihood of substantial harm to an individual or to the public interest; and**

(7) **in a criminal case, in addition to subparagraphs (1) through (6):**

(i) **the identity, residence, occupation and family status of the accused;**

(ii) **if the accused has not been apprehended, information necessary to aid in apprehension of that person;**

(iii) **the fact, time and place of arrest; and**

(iv) **the identity of investigating and arresting officers or agencies and the length of the investigation.**

(c) **Notwithstanding paragraph (a), a lawyer may make a statement that a reasonable lawyer would believe is required to protect a client from the substantial undue prejudicial effect of recent publicity not initiated by the lawyer or the lawyer's client. A statement made pursuant to this paragraph shall be limited to such information as is necessary to mitigate the recent adverse publicity.**

(d) **No lawyer associated in a firm or government agency with a lawyer subject to paragraph (a) shall make a statement prohibited by paragraph (a).**

Comment

[1] It is difficult to strike a balance between protecting the right to a fair trial and safeguarding the right of free expression. Preserving the right to a fair trial necessarily entails some curtailment of the information that may be disseminated about a party prior to trial, particularly where trial by jury is involved. If there were no such limits, the result would be the practical nullification of the protective effect of the rules of forensic decorum and the exclusionary rules of evidence. On the other hand, there are vital social interests served by the free dissemination of information about events having legal consequences and about legal proceedings themselves. The public has a right to know about threats to its safety and measures aimed at assuring its security. It also has a legitimate interest in the conduct of judicial proceedings, particularly in matters of general public concern. Furthermore, the subject matter of legal proceedings is often of direct significance in debate and deliberation over questions of public policy.

[2] Special rules of confidentiality may validly govern proceedings in juvenile, domestic relations and mental disability proceedings, and perhaps other types of litigation. Rule 3.4(c) requires compliance with such rules.

[3] The Rule sets forth a basic general prohibition against a lawyer's making statements that the lawyer knows or should know will have a substantial likelihood of materially prejudicing an adjudicative proceeding. Recognizing that the public value of informed commentary is great and the likelihood of prejudice to a proceeding by the commentary of a lawyer who is not involved in the proceeding is small, the rule applies only to lawyers who are, or who have been involved in the investigation or litigation of a case, and their associates.

[4]   Paragraph (b) identifies specific matters about which a lawyer's statements would not ordinarily be considered to present a substantial likelihood of material prejudice, and should not in any event be considered prohibited by the general prohibition of paragraph (a). Paragraph (b) is not intended to be an exhaustive listing of the subjects upon which a lawyer may make a statement, but statements on other matters may be subject to paragraph (a).

[5]   There are, on the other hand, certain subjects that are more likely than not to have a material prejudicial effect on a proceeding, particularly when they refer to a civil matter triable to a jury, a criminal matter, or any other proceeding that could result in incarceration. These subjects relate to:

(1)   the character, credibility, reputation or criminal record of a party, suspect in a criminal investigation or witness, or the identity of a witness, or the expected testimony of a party or witness;

(2)   in a criminal case or proceeding that could result in incarceration, the possibility of a plea of guilty to the offense or the existence or contents of any confession, admission, or statement given by a defendant or suspect or that person's refusal or failure to make a statement;

(3)   the performance or results of any examination or test or the refusal or failure of a person to submit to an examination or test, or the identity or nature of physical evidence expected to be presented;

(4)   any opinion as to the guilt or innocence of a defendant or suspect in a criminal case or proceeding that could result in incarceration;

(5)   information that the lawyer knows or reasonably should know is likely to be inadmissible as evidence in a trial and that would, if disclosed, create a substantial risk of prejudicing an impartial trial; or

(6)   the fact that a defendant has been charged with a crime, unless there is included therein a statement explaining that the charge is merely an accusation and that the defendant is presumed innocent until and unless proven guilty.

[6]   Another relevant factor in determining prejudice is the nature of the proceeding involved. Criminal jury trials will be most sensitive to extrajudicial speech. Civil trials may be less sensitive. Non-jury hearings and arbitration proceedings may be even less affected. The Rule will still place limitations on prejudicial comments in these cases, but the likelihood of prejudice may be different depending on the type of proceeding.

[7]   Finally, extrajudicial statements that might otherwise raise a question under this Rule may be permissible when they are made in response to statements made publicly by another party, another party's lawyer, or third persons, where a reasonable lawyer would believe a public response is required in order to avoid prejudice to the lawyer's client. When prejudicial statements have been publicly made by others, responsive statements may have the

salutary effect of lessening any resulting adverse impact on the adjudicative proceeding. Such responsive statements should be limited to contain only such information as is necessary to mitigate undue prejudice created by the statements made by others.

[8]   See Rule 3.8(f) for additional duties of prosecutors in connection with extrajudicial statements about criminal proceedings.

RULE 3.7: LAWYER AS WITNESS

(a)   A lawyer shall not act as advocate at a trial in which the lawyer is likely to be a necessary witness unless:

> **(1)   the testimony relates to an uncontested issue;**

> **(2)   the testimony relates to the nature and value of legal services rendered in the case; or**

> **(3)   disqualification of the lawyer would work substantial hardship on the client.**

(b)   A lawyer may act as advocate in a trial in which another lawyer in the lawyer's firm is likely to be called as a witness unless precluded from doing so by Rule 1.7 or Rule 1.9.

Comment

[1]   Combining the roles of advocate and witness can prejudice the tribunal and the opposing party and can also involve a conflict of interest between the lawyer and client.

Advocate-Witness Rule

[2]   The tribunal has proper objection when the trier of fact may be confused or misled by a lawyer serving as both advocate and witness. The opposing party has proper objection where the combination of roles may prejudice that party's rights in the litigation. A witness is required to testify on the basis of personal knowledge, while an advocate is expected to explain and comment on evidence given by others. It may not be clear whether a statement by an advocate-witness should be taken as proof or as an analysis of the proof.

[3]   To protect the tribunal, paragraph (a) prohibits a lawyer from simultaneously serving as advocate and necessary witness except in those circumstances specified in paragraphs (a)(1) through (a)(3). Paragraph (a)(1) recognizes that if the testimony will be uncontested, the ambiguities in the dual role are purely theoretical. Paragraph (a)(2) recognizes that where the testimony concerns the extent and value of legal services rendered in the action in which the testimony is offered, permitting the lawyers to testify avoids the need for a second trial with new counsel to resolve that issue. Moreover, in such a situation the judge has firsthand knowledge of the matter in issue; hence, there is less dependence on the adversary process to test the credibility of the testimony.

[4]   Apart from these two exceptions, paragraph (a)(3) recognizes that a balancing is required between the interests of the client and those of the tribunal and the opposing party. Whether the tribunal is likely to be misled or

the opposing party is likely to suffer prejudice depends on the nature of the case, the importance and probable tenor of the lawyer's testimony, and the probability that the lawyer's testimony will conflict with that of other witnesses. Even if there is risk of such prejudice, in determining whether the lawyer should be disqualified, due regard must be given to the effect of disqualification on the lawyer's client. It is relevant that one or both parties could reasonably foresee that the lawyer would probably be a witness. The conflict of interest principles stated in Rules 1.7, 1.9 and 1.10 have no application to this aspect of the problem.

[5] Because the tribunal is not likely to be misled when a lawyer acts as advocate in a trial in which another lawyer in the lawyer's firm will testify as a necessary witness, paragraph (b) permits the lawyer to do so except in situations involving a conflict of interest.

Conflict of Interest

[6] In determining if it is permissible to act as advocate in a trial in which the lawyer will be a necessary witness, the lawyer must also consider that the dual role may give rise to a conflict of interest that will require compliance with Rules 1.7 or 1.9. For example, if there is likely to be substantial conflict between the testimony of the client and that of the lawyer the representation involves a conflict of interest that requires compliance with Rule 1.7. This would be true even though the lawyer might not be prohibited by paragraph (a) from simultaneously serving as advocate and witness because the lawyer's disqualification would work a substantial hardship on the client. Similarly, a lawyer who might be permitted to simultaneously serve as an advocate and a witness by paragraph (a)(3) might be precluded from doing so by Rule 1.9. The problem can arise whether the lawyer is called as a witness on behalf of the client or is called by the opposing party. Determining whether or not such a conflict exists is primarily the responsibility of the lawyer involved. If there is a conflict of interest, the lawyer must secure the client's informed consent, confirmed in writing. In some cases, the lawyer will be precluded from seeking the client's consent. See Rule 1.7. See Rule 1.0(b) for the definition of "confirmed in writing" and Rule 1.0(e) for the definition of "informed consent."

[7] Paragraph (b) provides that a lawyer is not disqualified from serving as an advocate because a lawyer with whom the lawyer is associated in a firm is precluded from doing so by paragraph (a). If, however, the testifying lawyer would also be disqualified by Rule 1.7 or Rule 1.9 from representing the client in the matter, other lawyers in the firm will be precluded from representing the client by Rule 1.10 unless the client gives informed consent under the conditions stated in Rule 1.7.

RULE 3.8: SPECIAL RESPONSIBILITIES OF A PROSECUTOR

The prosecutor in a criminal case shall:

(a)   refrain from prosecuting a charge that the prosecutor knows is not supported by probable cause;

(b)   make reasonable efforts to assure that the accused has been advised of the right to, and the procedure for obtaining, counsel and has been given reasonable opportunity to obtain counsel;

(c)   not seek to obtain from an unrepresented accused a waiver of important pretrial rights, such as the right to a preliminary hearing;

(d)   make timely disclosure to the defense of all evidence or information known to the prosecutor that tends to negate the guilt of the accused or mitigates the offense, and, in connection with sentencing, disclose to the defense and to the tribunal all unprivileged mitigating information known to the prosecutor, except when the prosecutor is relieved of this responsibility by a protective order of the tribunal;

(e)   not subpoena a lawyer in a grand jury or other criminal proceeding to present evidence about a past or present client unless the prosecutor reasonably believes:

(1)   the information sought is not protected from disclosure by any applicable privilege;

(2)   the evidence sought is essential to the successful completion of an ongoing investigation or prosecution; and

(3)   there is no other feasible alternative to obtain the information;

(f)   except for statements that are necessary to inform the public of the nature and extent of the prosecutor's action and that serve a legitimate law enforcement purpose, refrain from making extrajudicial comments that have a substantial likelihood of heightening public condemnation of the accused and exercise reasonable care to prevent investigators, law enforcement personnel, employees or other persons assisting or associated with the prosecutor in a criminal case from making an extrajudicial statement that the prosecutor would be prohibited from making under Rule 3.6 or this Rule.

(g)   When a prosecutor knows of new, credible and material evidence creating a reasonable likelihood that a convicted defendant did not commit an offense of which the defendant was convicted, the prosecutor shall:

(1)   promptly disclose that evidence to an appropriate court or authority, and

(2)   if the conviction was obtained in the prosecutor's jurisdiction,

(A)   promptly disclose that evidence to the defendant unless a court authorizes delay, and

(B)   undertake further investigation, or make reasonable efforts to cause an investigation, to determine

whether the defendant was convicted of an offense that the defendant did not commit.

(h)   When a prosecutor knows of clear and convincing evidence establishing that a defendant in the prosecutor's jurisdiction was convicted of an offense that the defendant did not commit, the prosecutor shall seek to remedy the conviction.

Comment

[1]   A prosecutor has the responsibility of a minister of justice and not simply that of an advocate. This responsibility carries with it specific obligations to see that the defendant is accorded procedural justice and that guilt is decided upon the basis of sufficient evidence, and that special precautions are taken to prevent and to rectify conviction of innocent persons. The extent of mandated remedial action that special precautions are taken to prevent and to rectify is a matter of debate and varies in different jurisdictions. Many jurisdictions have adopted the ABA Standards of Criminal Justice Relating to the Prosecution Function, which in turn are the product of prolonged and careful deliberation by lawyers experienced in both criminal prosecution and defense. Competent representation of the sovereignty may require a prosecutor to undertake some procedural and remedial measures as a matter of obligation. Applicable law may require other measures by the prosecutor and knowing disregard of those obligations or a systematic abuse of prosecutorial discretion could constitute a violation of Rule 8.4.

[2]   In some jurisdictions, a defendant may waive a preliminary hearing and thereby lose a valuable opportunity to challenge probable cause. Accordingly, prosecutors should not seek to obtain waivers of preliminary hearings or other important pretrial rights from unrepresented accused persons. Paragraph (c) does not apply, however, to an accused appearing *pro se* with the approval of the tribunal. Nor does it forbid the lawful questioning of an uncharged suspect who has knowingly waived the rights to counsel and silence.

[3]   The exception in paragraph (d) recognizes that a prosecutor may seek an appropriate protective order from the tribunal if disclosure of information to the defense could result in substantial harm to an individual or to the public interest.

[4]   Paragraph (e) is intended to limit the issuance of lawyer subpoenas in grand jury and other criminal proceedings to those situations in which there is a genuine need to intrude into the client-lawyer relationship.

[5]   Paragraph (f) supplements Rule 3.6, which prohibits extrajudicial statements that have a substantial likelihood of prejudicing an adjudicatory proceeding. In the context of a criminal prosecution, a prosecutor's extrajudicial statement can create the additional problem of increasing public condemnation of the accused. Although the announcement of an indictment, for example, will necessarily have severe consequences for the accused, a prosecutor can, and should, avoid comments which have no legitimate law enforcement purpose and have a substantial likelihood of increasing public opprobrium

of the accused. Nothing in this Comment is intended to restrict the statements which a prosecutor may make which comply with Rule 3.6(b) or 3.6(c).

[6]   Like other lawyers, prosecutors are subject to Rules 5.1 and 5.3, which relate to responsibilities regarding lawyers and nonlawyers who work for or are associated with the lawyer's office. Paragraph (f) reminds the prosecutor of the importance of these obligations in connection with the unique dangers of improper extrajudicial statements in a criminal case. In addition, paragraph (f) requires a prosecutor to exercise reasonable care to prevent persons assisting or associated with the prosecutor from making improper extrajudicial statements, even when such persons are not under the direct supervision of the prosecutor. Ordinarily, the reasonable care standard will be satisfied if the prosecutor issues the appropriate cautions to law- enforcement personnel and other relevant individuals.

[7]   When a prosecutor knows of new, credible and material evidence creating a reasonable likelihood that a person outside the prosecutor's jurisdiction was convicted of a crime that the person did not commit, paragraph (g) requires prompt disclosure to the court or other appropriate authority, such as the chief prosecutor of the jurisdiction where the conviction occurred. If the conviction was obtained in the prosecutor's jurisdiction, paragraph (g) requires the prosecutor to examine the evidence and undertake further investigation to determine whether the defendant is in fact innocent or make reasonable efforts to cause another appropriate authority to undertake the necessary investigation, and to promptly disclose the evidence to the court and, absent court-authorized delay, to the defendant. Consistent with the objectives of Rules 4.2 and 4.3, disclosure to a represented defendant must be made through the defendant's counsel, and, in the case of an unrepresented defendant, would ordinarily be accompanied by a request to a court for the appointment of counsel to assist the defendant in taking such legal measures as may be appropriate.

[8]   Under paragraph (h), once the prosecutor knows of clear and convincing evidence that the defendant was convicted of an offense that the defendant did not commit, the prosecutor must seek to remedy the conviction. Necessary steps may include disclosure of the evidence to the defendant, requesting that the court appoint counsel for an unrepresented indigent defendant and, where appropriate, notifying the court that the prosecutor has knowledge that the defendant did not commit the offense of which the defendant was convicted.

[9]   A prosecutor's independent judgment, made in good faith, that the new evidence is not of such nature as to trigger the obligations of sections (g) and (h), though subsequently determined to have been erroneous, does not constitute a violation of this Rule.

RULE 3.9: ADVOCATE IN NONADJUDICATIVE PROCEEDINGS

A lawyer representing a client before a legislative body or administrative agency in a nonadjudicative proceeding shall disclose

that the appearance is in a representative capacity and shall conform to the provisions of Rules 3.3(a) through (c), 3.4(a) through (c), and 3.5.

Comment

[1]   In representation before bodies such as legislatures, municipal councils, and executive and administrative agencies acting in a rule-making or policy-making capacity, lawyers present facts, formulate issues and advance argument in the matters under consideration. The decision-making body, like a court, should be able to rely on the integrity of the submissions made to it. A lawyer appearing before such a body must deal with it honestly and in conformity with applicable rules of procedure. See Rules 3.3(a) through (c), 3.4(a) through (c) and 3.5.

[2]   Lawyers have no exclusive right to appear before nonadjudicative bodies, as they do before a court. The requirements of this Rule therefore may subject lawyers to regulations inapplicable to advocates who are not lawyers. However, legislatures and administrative agencies have a right to expect lawyers to deal with them as they deal with courts.

[3]   This Rule only applies when a lawyer represents a client in connection with an official hearing or meeting of a governmental agency or a legislative body to which the lawyer or the lawyer's client is presenting evidence or argument. It does not apply to representation of a client in a negotiation or other bilateral transaction with a governmental agency or in connection with an application for a license or other privilege or the client's compliance with generally applicable reporting requirements, such as the filing of income-tax returns. Nor does it apply to the representation of a client in connection with an investigation or examination of the client's affairs conducted by government investigators or examiners. Representation in such matters is governed by Rules 4.1 through 4.4.

RULE 4.1: TRUTHFULNESS IN STATEMENTS TO OTHERS

In the course of representing a client a lawyer shall not knowingly:

(a)   make a false statement of material fact or law to a third person; or

(b)   fail to disclose a material fact when disclosure is necessary to avoid assisting a criminal or fraudulent act by a client, unless disclosure is prohibited by Rule 1.6.

Comment

Misrepresentation

[1]   A lawyer is required to be truthful when dealing with others on a client's behalf, but generally has no affirmative duty to inform an opposing party of relevant facts. A misrepresentation can occur if the lawyer incorporates or affirms a statement of another person that the lawyer knows is false. Misrepresentations can also occur by partially true but misleading statements

or omissions that are the equivalent of affirmative false statements. For dishonest conduct that does not amount to a false statement or for misrepresentations by a lawyer other than in the course of representing a client, see Rule 8.4.

Statements of Fact

[2]   This Rule refers to statements of fact. Whether a particular statement should be regarded as one of fact can depend on the circumstances. Under generally accepted conventions in negotiation, certain types of statements ordinarily are not taken as statements of material fact. Estimates of price or value placed on the subject of a transaction and a party's intentions as to an acceptable settlement of a claim are ordinarily in this category, and so is the existence of an undisclosed principal except where nondisclosure of the principal would constitute fraud. Lawyers should be mindful of their obligations under applicable law to avoid criminal and tortious misrepresentation.

Crime or Fraud by Client

[3]   Under Rule 1.2(d), a lawyer is prohibited from counseling or assisting a client in conduct that the lawyer knows is criminal or fraudulent. Paragraph (b) states a specific application of the principle set forth in Rule 1.2(d) and addresses the situation where a client's crime or fraud takes the form of a lie or misrepresentation. Ordinarily, a lawyer can avoid assisting a client's crime or fraud by withdrawing from the representation. Sometimes it may be necessary for the lawyer to give notice of the fact of withdrawal and to disaffirm an opinion, document, affirmation or the like. In extreme cases, substantive law may require a lawyer to disclose information relating to the representation to avoid being deemed to have assisted the client's crime or fraud. If the lawyer can avoid assisting a client's crime or fraud only by disclosing this information, then under paragraph (b) the lawyer is required to do so, unless the disclosure is prohibited by Rule 1.6.

RULE 4.2: COMMUNICATION WITH PERSON REPRESENTED BY COUNSEL

In representing a client, a lawyer shall not communicate about the subject of the representation with a person the lawyer knows to be represented by another lawyer in the matter, unless the lawyer has the consent of the other lawyer or is authorized to do so by law or a court order.

Comment

[1]   This Rule contributes to the proper functioning of the legal system by protecting a person who has chosen to be represented by a lawyer in a matter against possible overreaching by other lawyers who are participating in the matter, interference by those lawyers with the client-lawyer relationship and the uncounselled disclosure of information relating to the representation.

[2]   This Rule applies to communications with any person who is represented by counsel concerning the matter to which the communication relates.

[3]   The Rule applies even though the represented person initiates or consents to the communication. A lawyer must immediately terminate communication with a person if, after commencing communication, the lawyer learns that the person is one with whom communication is not permitted by this Rule.

[4]   This Rule does not prohibit communication with a represented person, or an employee or agent of such a person, concerning matters outside the representation. For example, the existence of a controversy between a government agency and a private party, or between two organizations, does not prohibit a lawyer for either from communicating with nonlawyer representatives of the other regarding a separate matter. Nor does this Rule preclude communication with a represented person who is seeking advice from a lawyer who is not otherwise representing a client in the matter. A lawyer may not make a communication prohibited by this Rule through the acts of another. See Rule 8.4(a). Parties to a matter may communicate directly with each other, and a lawyer is not prohibited from advising a client concerning a communication that the client is legally entitled to make. Also, a lawyer having independent justification or legal authorization for communicating with a represented person is permitted to do so.

[5]   Communications authorized by law may include communications by a lawyer on behalf of a client who is exercising a constitutional or other legal right to communicate with the government. Communications authorized by law may also include investigative activities of lawyers representing governmental entities, directly or through investigative agents, prior to the commencement of criminal or civil enforcement proceedings. When communicating with the accused in a criminal matter, a government lawyer must comply with this Rule in addition to honoring the constitutional rights of the accused. The fact that a communication does not violate a state or federal constitutional right is insufficient to establish that the communication is permissible under this Rule.

[6]   A lawyer who is uncertain whether a communication with a represented person is permissible may seek a court order. A lawyer may also seek a court order in exceptional circumstances to authorize a communication that would otherwise be prohibited by this Rule, for example, where communication with a person represented by counsel is necessary to avoid reasonably certain injury.

[7]   In the case of a represented organization, this Rule prohibits communications with a constituent of the organization who supervises, directs or regularly consults with the organization's lawyer concerning the matter or has authority to obligate the organization with respect to the matter or whose act or omission in connection with the matter may be imputed to the organization for purposes of civil or criminal liability. Consent of the organization's lawyer is not required for communication with a former constituent. If a constituent of the organization is represented in the matter by his or her own counsel, the consent by that counsel to a communication will be sufficient for

purposes of this Rule. Compare Rule 3.4(f). In communicating with a current or former constituent of an organization, a lawyer must not use methods of obtaining evidence that violate the legal rights of the organization. See Rule 4.4.

[8]   The prohibition on communications with a represented person only applies in circumstances where the lawyer knows that the person is in fact represented in the matter to be discussed. This means that the lawyer has actual knowledge of the fact of the representation; but such actual knowledge may be inferred from the circumstances. See Rule 1.0(f). Thus, the lawyer cannot evade the requirement of obtaining the consent of counsel by closing eyes to the obvious.

[9]   In the event the person with whom the lawyer communicates is not known to be represented by counsel in the matter, the lawyer's communications are subject to Rule 4.3.

RULE 4.3: DEALING WITH UNREPRESENTED PERSON

In dealing on behalf of a client with a person who is not represented by counsel, a lawyer shall not state or imply that the lawyer is disinterested. When the lawyer knows or reasonably should know that the unrepresented person misunderstands the lawyer's role in the matter, the lawyer shall make reasonable efforts to correct the misunderstanding. The lawyer shall not give legal advice to an unrepresented person, other than the advice to secure counsel, if the lawyer knows or reasonably should know that the interests of such a person are or have a reasonable possibility of being in conflict with the interests of the client.

Comment

[1]   An unrepresented person, particularly one not experienced in dealing with legal matters, might assume that a lawyer is disinterested in loyalties or is a disinterested authority on the law even when the lawyer represents a client. In order to avoid a misunderstanding, a lawyer will typically need to identify the lawyer's client and, where necessary, explain that the client has interests opposed to those of the unrepresented person. For misunderstandings that sometimes arise when a lawyer for an organization deals with an unrepresented constituent, see Rule 1.13(d).

[2]   The Rule distinguishes between situations involving unrepresented persons whose interests may be adverse to those of the lawyer's client and those in which the person's interests are not in conflict with the client's. In the former situation, the possibility that the lawyer will compromise the unrepresented person's interests is so great that the Rule prohibits the giving of any advice, apart from the advice to obtain counsel. Whether a lawyer is giving impermissible advice may depend on the experience and sophistication of the unrepresented person, as well as the setting in which the behavior and comments occur. This Rule does not prohibit a lawyer from negotiating the terms of a transaction or settling a dispute with an unrepresented person. So long as

the lawyer has explained that the lawyer represents an adverse party and is not representing the person, the lawyer may inform the person of the terms on which the lawyer's client will enter into an agreement or settle a matter, prepare documents that require the person's signature and explain the lawyer's own view of the meaning of the document or the lawyer's view of the underlying legal obligations.

RULE 4.4: RESPECT FOR RIGHTS OF THIRD PERSONS

(a)   In representing a client, a lawyer shall not use means that have no substantial purpose other than to embarrass, delay, or burden a third person, or use methods of obtaining evidence that violate the legal rights of such a person.

(b)   A lawyer who receives a document or electronically stored information relating to the representation of the lawyer's client and knows or reasonably should know that the document or electronically stored information was inadvertently sent shall promptly notify the sender.

Comment

[1]   Responsibility to a client requires a lawyer to subordinate the interests of others to those of the client, but that responsibility does not imply that a lawyer may disregard the rights of third persons. It is impractical to catalogue all such rights, but they include legal restrictions on methods of obtaining evidence from third persons and unwarranted intrusions into privileged relationships, such as the client-lawyer relationship.

[2]   Paragraph (b) recognizes that lawyers sometimes receive a document or electronically stored information that was mistakenly sent or produced by opposing parties or their lawyers. A document or electronically stored information is inadvertently sent when it is accidentally transmitted, such as when an email or letter is misaddressed or a document or electronically stored information is accidentally included with information that was intentionally transmitted. If a lawyer knows or reasonably should know that such a document or electronically stored information was sent inadvertently, then this Rule requires the lawyer to promptly notify the sender in order to permit that person to take protective measures. Whether the lawyer is required to take additional steps, such as returning the document or [deleting][1] electronically stored information, is a matter of law beyond the scope of these Rules, as is the question of whether the privileged status of a document or electronically stored information has been waived. Similarly, this Rule does

---

[1] **Editors' Note:** We have added the word "deleting" in brackets to conform this sentence with Comment [3], which was revised on the floor of the House of Delegates in August 2012 when it was recognized that "electronically stored information" typically will be deleted rather than returned to the sending party. At the time of publication, it was not known whether this conforming change can be made administratively or whether the rule must be submitted to the House of Delegates.

not address the legal duties of a lawyer who receives a document or electronically stored information that the lawyer knows or reasonably should know may have been inappropriately obtained by the sending person. For purposes of this Rule, "document or electronically stored information" includes, in addition to paper documents, email and other forms of electronically stored information, including embedded data (commonly referred to as "metadata"), that is subject to being read or put into readable form. Metadata in electronic documents creates an obligation under this Rule only if the receiving lawyer knows or reasonably should know that the metadata was inadvertently sent to the receiving lawyer.

[3]   Some lawyers may choose to return a document or delete electronically stored information unread, for example, when the lawyer learns before receiving it that it was inadvertently sent. Where a lawyer is not required by applicable law to do so, the decision to voluntarily return such a document or delete electronically stored information is a matter of professional judgment ordinarily reserved to the lawyer. See Rules 1.2 and 1.4.

RULE 5.1: RESPONSIBILITIES OF PARTNERS, MANAGERS, AND SUPERVISORY LAWYERS

(a)   A partner in a law firm, and a lawyer who individually or together with other lawyers possesses comparable managerial authority in a law firm, shall make reasonable efforts to ensure that the firm has in effect measures giving reasonable assurance that all lawyers in the firm conform to the Rules of Professional Conduct.

(b)   A lawyer having direct supervisory authority over another lawyer shall make reasonable efforts to ensure that the other lawyer conforms to the Rules of Professional Conduct.

(c)   A lawyer shall be responsible for another lawyer's violation of the Rules of Professional Conduct if:

(1)   the lawyer orders or, with knowledge of the specific conduct, ratifies the conduct involved; or

(2)   the lawyer is a partner or has comparable managerial authority in the law firm in which the other lawyer practices, or has direct supervisory authority over the other lawyer, and knows of the conduct at a time when its consequences can be avoided or mitigated but fails to take reasonable remedial action.

Comment

[1]   Paragraph (a) applies to lawyers who have managerial authority over the professional work of a firm. See Rule 1.0(c). This includes members of a partnership, the shareholders in a law firm organized as a professional corporation, and members of other associations authorized to practice law; lawyers having comparable managerial authority in a legal services organization or a law department of an enterprise or government agency; and lawyers who have

intermediate managerial responsibilities in a firm. Paragraph (b) applies to lawyers who have supervisory authority over the work of other lawyers in a firm.

[2]   Paragraph (a) requires lawyers with managerial authority within a firm to make reasonable efforts to establish internal policies and procedures designed to provide reasonable assurance that all lawyers in the firm will conform to the Rules of Professional Conduct. Such policies and procedures include those designed to detect and resolve conflicts of interest, identify dates by which actions must be taken in pending matters, account for client funds and property and ensure that inexperienced lawyers are properly supervised.

[3]   Other measures that may be required to fulfill the responsibility prescribed in paragraph (a) can depend on the firm's structure and the nature of its practice. In a small firm of experienced lawyers, informal supervision and periodic review of compliance with the required systems ordinarily will suffice. In a large firm, or in practice situations in which difficult ethical problems frequently arise, more elaborate measures may be necessary. Some firms, for example, have a procedure whereby junior lawyers can make confidential referral of ethical problems directly to a designated senior partner or special committee. See Rule 5.2. Firms, whether large or small, may also rely on continuing legal education in professional ethics. In any event, the ethical atmosphere of a firm can influence the conduct of all its members the partners may not assume that all lawyers associated with the firm will inevitably conform to the Rules.

[4]   Paragraph (c) expresses a general principle of personal responsibility for acts of another. See also Rule 8.4(a).

[5]   Paragraph (c)(2) defines the duty of a partner or other lawyer having comparable managerial authority in a law firm, as well as a lawyer who has direct supervisory authority over performance of specific legal work by another lawyer. Whether a lawyer has supervisory authority in particular circumstances is a question of fact. Partners and lawyers with comparable authority have at least indirect responsibility for all work being done by the firm, while a partner or manager in charge of a particular matter ordinarily also has supervisory responsibility for the work of other firm lawyers engaged in the matter. Appropriate remedial action by a partner or managing lawyer would depend on the immediacy of that lawyer's involvement and the seriousness of the misconduct. A supervisor is required to intervene to prevent avoidable consequences of misconduct if the supervisor knows that the misconduct occurred. Thus, if a supervising lawyer knows that a subordinate misrepresented a matter to an opposing party in negotiation, the supervisor as well as the subordinate has a duty to correct the resulting misapprehension.

[6]   Professional misconduct by a lawyer under supervision could reveal a violation of paragraph (b) on the part of the supervisory lawyer even though it does not entail a violation of paragraph (c) because there was no direction, ratification or knowledge of the violation.

[7]   Apart from this Rule and Rule 8.4(a), a lawyer does not have disciplinary liability for the conduct of a partner, associate or subordinate. Whether a lawyer may be liable civilly or criminally for another lawyer's conduct is a question of law beyond the scope of these Rules.

[8]   The duties imposed by this Rule on managing and supervising lawyers do not alter the personal duty of each lawyer in a firm to abide by the Rules of Professional Conduct. See Rule 5.2(a).

RULE 5.2: RESPONSIBILITIES OF A SUBORDINATE LAWYER

(a)   A lawyer is bound by the Rules of Professional Conduct notwithstanding that the lawyer acted at the direction of another person.

(b)   A subordinate lawyer does not violate the Rules of Professional Conduct if that lawyer acts in accordance with a supervisory lawyer's reasonable resolution of an arguable question of professional duty.

Comment

[1]   Although a lawyer is not relieved of responsibility for a violation by the fact that the lawyer acted at the direction of a supervisor, that fact may be relevant in determining whether a lawyer had the knowledge required to render conduct a violation of the Rules. For example, if a subordinate filed a frivolous pleading at the direction of a supervisor, the subordinate would not be guilty of a professional violation unless the subordinate knew of the document's frivolous character.

[2]   When lawyers in a supervisor-subordinate relationship encounter a matter involving professional judgment as to ethical duty, the supervisor may assume responsibility for making the judgment. Otherwise a consistent course of action or position could not be taken. If the question can reasonably be answered only one way, the duty of both lawyers is clear and they are equally responsible for fulfilling it. However, if the question is reasonably arguable, someone has to decide upon the course of action. That authority ordinarily reposes in the supervisor, and a subordinate may be guided accordingly. For example, if a question arises whether the interests of two clients conflict under Rule 1.7, the supervisor's reasonable resolution of the question should protect the subordinate professionally if the resolution is subsequently challenged.

RULE 5.3: RESPONSIBILITIES REGARDING NONLAWYER ASSISTANCE

With respect to a nonlawyer employed or retained by or associated with a lawyer:

(a)   a partner, and a lawyer who individually or together with other lawyers possesses comparable managerial authority in a law firm shall make reasonable efforts to ensure that the firm has in

effect measures giving reasonable assurance that the person's conduct is compatible with the professional obligations of the lawyer;

(b)   a lawyer having direct supervisory authority over the nonlawyer shall make reasonable efforts to ensure that the person's conduct is compatible with the professional obligations of the lawyer; and

(c)   a lawyer shall be responsible for conduct of such a person that would be a violation of the Rules of Professional Conduct if engaged in by a lawyer if:

(1)   the lawyer orders or, with the knowledge of the specific conduct, ratifies the conduct involved; or

(2)   the lawyer is a partner or has comparable managerial authority in the law firm in which the person is employed, or has direct supervisory authority over the person, and knows of the conduct at a time when its consequences can be avoided or mitigated but fails to take reasonable remedial action.

Comment

[1]   Paragraph (a) requires lawyers with managerial authority within a law firm to make reasonable efforts to ensure that the firm has in effect measures giving reasonable assurance that nonlawyers in the firm and nonlawyers outside the firm who work on firm matters act in a way compatible with the professional obligations of the lawyer. See Comment [6] to Rule 1.1 (retaining lawyers outside the firm) and Comment [1] to Rule 5.1 (responsibilities with respect to lawyers within a firm). Paragraph (b) applies to lawyers who have supervisory authority over such nonlawyers within or outside the firm. Paragraph (c) specifies the circumstances in which a lawyer is responsible for the conduct of such nonlawyers within or outside the firm that would be a violation of the Rules of Professional Conduct if engaged in by a lawyer.

Nonlawyers within the firm

[2]   Lawyers generally employ assistants in their practice, including secretaries, investigators, law student interns, and paraprofessionals. Such assistants, whether employees or independent contractors, act for the lawyer in rendition of the lawyer's professional services. A lawyer must give such assistants appropriate instruction and supervision concerning the ethical aspects of their employment, particularly regarding the obligation not to disclose information relating to representation of the client, and should be responsible for their work product. The measures employed in supervising non-lawyers should take account of the fact that they do not have legal training and are not subject to professional discipline.

Nonlawyers outside the firm

[3]   A lawyer may use nonlawyers outside the firm to assist the lawyer in rendering legal services to the client. Examples include the retention of an investigative or paraprofessional service, hiring a document management

company to create and maintain a database for complex litigation, sending client documents to a third party for printing or scanning, and using an Internet-based service to store client information. When using such services outside the firm, a lawyer must make reasonable efforts to ensure that the services are provided in a manner that is compatible with the lawyer's professional obligations. The extent of this obligation will depend upon the circumstances, including the education, experience and reputation of the nonlawyer; the nature of the services involved; the terms of any arrangements concerning the protection of client information; and the legal and ethical environments of the jurisdictions in which the services will be performed, particularly with regard to confidentiality. See also Rules 1.1 (competence), 1.2 (allocation of authority), 1.4 (communication with client), 1.6 (confidentiality), 5.4(a) (professional independence of the lawyer), and 5.5(a) (unauthorized practice of law). When retaining or directing a nonlawyer outside the firm, a lawyer should communicate directions appropriate under the circumstances to give reasonable assurance that the nonlawyer's conduct is compatible with the professional obligations of the lawyer.

[4]   Where the client directs the selection of a particular nonlawyer service provider outside the firm, the lawyer ordinarily should agree with the client concerning the allocation of responsibility for monitoring as between the client and the lawyer. See Rule 1.2. When making such an allocation in a matter pending before a tribunal, lawyers and parties may have additional obligations that are a matter of law beyond the scope of these Rules.

RULE 5.4: PROFESSIONAL INDEPENDENCE OF A LAWYER

(a)   **A lawyer or law firm shall not share legal fees with a nonlawyer, except that:**

(1)   **an agreement by a lawyer with the lawyer's firm, partner, or associate may provide for the payment of money, over a reasonable period of time after the lawyer's death, to the lawyer's estate or to one or more specified persons;**

(2)   **a lawyer who purchases the practice of a deceased, disabled, or disappeared lawyer may, pursuant to the provisions of Rule 1.17, pay to the estate or other representative of that lawyer the agreed-upon purchase price;**

(3)   **a lawyer or law firm may include nonlawyer employees in a compensation or retirement plan, even though the plan is based in whole or in part on a profit-sharing arrangement; and**

(4)   **a lawyer may share court-awarded legal fees with a nonprofit organization that employed, retained or recommended employment of the lawyer in the matter.**

(b)   **A lawyer shall not form a partnership with a nonlawyer if any of the activities of the partnership consist of the practice of law.**

(c)   A lawyer shall not permit a person who recommends, employs, or pays the lawyer to render legal services for another to direct or regulate the lawyer's professional judgment in rendering such legal services.

(d)   A lawyer shall not practice with or in the form of a professional corporation or association authorized to practice law for a profit, if:

> (1)   a nonlawyer owns any interest therein, except that a fiduciary representative of the estate of a lawyer may hold the stock or interest of the lawyer for a reasonable time during administration;

> (2)   a nonlawyer is a corporate director or officer thereof or occupies the position of similar responsibility in any form of association other than a corporation; or

> (3)   a nonlawyer has the right to direct or control the professional judgment of a lawyer.

Comment

[1]   The provisions of this Rule express traditional limitations on sharing fees. These limitations are to protect the lawyer's professional independence of judgment. Where someone other than the client pays the lawyer's fee or salary, or recommends employment of the lawyer, that arrangement does not modify the lawyer's obligation to the client. As stated in paragraph (c), such arrangements should not interfere with the lawyer's professional judgment.

[2]   This Rule also expresses traditional limitations on permitting a third party to direct or regulate the lawyer's professional judgment in rendering legal services to another. See also Rule 1.8(f) (lawyer may accept compensation from a third party as long as there is no interference with the lawyer's independent professional judgment and the client gives informed consent).

RULE 5.5: UNAUTHORIZED PRACTICE OF LAW MULTIJURISDICTIONAL PRACTICE OF LAW

(a)   A lawyer shall not practice law in a jurisdiction in violation of the regulation of the legal profession in that jurisdiction, or assist another in doing so.

(b)   A lawyer who is not admitted to practice in this jurisdiction shall not:

> (1)   except as authorized by these Rules or other law, establish an office or other systematic and continuous presence in this jurisdiction for the practice of law; or

> (2)   hold out to the public or otherwise represent that the lawyer is admitted to practice law in this jurisdiction.

(c) A lawyer admitted in another United States jurisdiction, and not disbarred or suspended from practice in any jurisdiction, may provide legal services on a temporary basis in this jurisdiction that:

(1) are undertaken in association with a lawyer who is admitted to practice in this jurisdiction and who actively participates in the matter;

(2) are in or reasonably related to a pending or potential proceeding before a tribunal in this or another jurisdiction, if the lawyer, or a person the lawyer is assisting, is authorized by law or order to appear in such proceeding or reasonably expects to be so authorized;

(3) are in or reasonably related to a pending or potential arbitration, mediation, or other alternative dispute resolution proceeding in this or another jurisdiction, if the services arise out of or are reasonably related to the lawyer's practice in a jurisdiction in which the lawyer is admitted to practice and are not services for which the forum requires pro hac vice admission; or

(4) are not within paragraphs (c)(2) or (c)(3) and arise out of or are reasonably related to the lawyer's practice in a jurisdiction in which the lawyer is admitted to practice.

(d) A lawyer admitted in another United States jurisdiction, or in a foreign jurisdiction, and not disbarred or suspended from practice in any jurisdiction, or the equivalent thereof, may provide legal services through an office or other systematic and continuous presence in this jurisdiction that:

(1) are provided to the lawyer's employer or its organizational affiliates; are not services for which the forum requires pro hac vice admission; and, when performed by a foreign lawyer and requires advice on the law of this or another jurisdiction or of the United States, such advice shall be based upon the advice of a lawyer who is duly licensed and authorized by the jurisdiction to provide such advice; or

(2) are services that the lawyer is authorized to provide by federal law or other law or rule of this jurisdiction.

(e) For purposes of paragraph (d), the foreign lawyer must be a member in good standing of a recognized legal profession in a foreign jurisdiction, the members of which are admitted to practice as lawyers or counselors at law or the equivalent, and are subject to effective regulation and discipline by a duly constituted professional body or a public authority.

Comment

[1] A lawyer may practice law only in a jurisdiction in which the lawyer is authorized to practice. A lawyer may be admitted to practice law in a

jurisdiction on a regular basis or may be authorized by court rule or order or by law to practice for a limited purpose or on a restricted basis. Paragraph (a) applies to unauthorized practice of law by a lawyer, whether through the lawyer's direct action or by the lawyer assisting another person. For example, a lawyer may not assist a person in practicing law in violation of the rules governing professional conduct in that person's jurisdiction.

[2]   The definition of the practice of law is established by law and varies from one jurisdiction to another. Whatever the definition, limiting the practice of law to members of the bar protects the public against rendition of legal services by unqualified persons. This Rule does not prohibit a lawyer from employing the services of paraprofessionals and delegating functions to them, so long as the lawyer supervises the delegated work and retains responsibility for their work. See Rule 5.3.

[3]   A lawyer may provide professional advice and instruction to nonlawyers whose employment requires knowledge of the law; for example, claims adjusters, employees of financial or commercial institutions, social workers, accountants and persons employed in government agencies. Lawyers also may assist independent nonlawyers, such as paraprofessionals, who are authorized by the law of a jurisdiction to provide particular law- related services. In addition, a lawyer may counsel nonlawyers who wish to proceed pro se.

[4]   Other than as authorized by law or this Rule, a lawyer who is not admitted to practice generally in this jurisdiction violates paragraph (b)(1) if the lawyer establishes an office or other systematic and continuous presence in this jurisdiction for the practice of law. Presence may be systematic and continuous even if the lawyer is not physically present here. Such a lawyer must not hold out to the public or otherwise represent that the lawyer is admitted to practice law in this jurisdiction. See also Rules 7.1(a) and 7.5(b).

[5]   There are occasions in which a lawyer admitted to practice in another United States jurisdiction, and not disbarred or suspended from practice in any jurisdiction, may provide legal services on a temporary basis in this jurisdiction under circumstances that do not create an unreasonable risk to the interests of their clients, the public or the courts. Paragraph (c) identifies four such circumstances. The fact that conduct is not so identified does not imply that the conduct is or is not authorized. With the exception of paragraphs (d)(1) and (d)(2), this Rule does not authorize a U.S. or foreign lawyer to establish an office or other systematic and continuous presence in this jurisdiction without being admitted to practice generally here.

[6]   There is no single test to determine whether a lawyer's services are provided on a "temporary basis" in this jurisdiction, and may therefore be permissible under paragraph (c). Services may be "temporary" even though the lawyer provides services in this jurisdiction on a recurring basis, or for an extended period of time, as when the lawyer is representing a client in a single lengthy negotiation or litigation.

[7]   Paragraphs (c) and (d) apply to lawyers who are admitted to practice law in any United States jurisdiction, which includes the District of

Columbia and any state, territory or commonwealth of the United States. Paragraph (d) also applies to lawyers admitted in a foreign jurisdiction. The word "admitted" in paragraphs (c), (d) and (e) contemplates that the lawyer is authorized to practice in the jurisdiction in which the lawyer is admitted and excludes a lawyer who while technically admitted is not authorized to practice, because, for example, the lawyer is on inactive status.

[8] Paragraph (c)(1) recognizes that the interests of clients and the public are protected if a lawyer admitted only in another jurisdiction associates with a lawyer licensed to practice in this jurisdiction. For this paragraph to apply, however, the lawyer admitted to practice in this jurisdiction must actively participate in and share responsibility for the representation of the client.

[9] Lawyers not admitted to practice generally in a jurisdiction may be authorized by law or order of a tribunal or an administrative agency to appear before the tribunal or agency. This authority may be granted pursuant to formal rules governing admission pro hac vice or pursuant to informal practice of the tribunal or agency. Under paragraph (c)(2), a lawyer does not violate this Rule when the lawyer appears before a tribunal or agency pursuant to such authority. To the extent that a court rule or other law of this jurisdiction requires a lawyer who is not admitted to practice in this jurisdiction to obtain admission pro hac vice before appearing before a tribunal or administrative agency, this Rule requires the lawyer to obtain that authority.

[10] Paragraph (c)(2) also provides that a lawyer rendering services in this jurisdiction on a temporary basis does not violate this Rule when the lawyer engages in conduct in anticipation of a proceeding or hearing in a jurisdiction in which the lawyer is authorized to practice law or in which the lawyer reasonably expects to be admitted pro hac vice. Examples of such conduct include meetings with the client, interviews of potential witnesses, and the review of documents. Similarly, a lawyer admitted only in another jurisdiction may engage in conduct temporarily in this jurisdiction in connection with pending litigation in another jurisdiction in which the lawyer is or reasonably expects to be authorized to appear, including taking depositions in this jurisdiction.

[11] When a lawyer has been or reasonably expects to be admitted to appear before a court or administrative agency, paragraph (c)(2) also permits conduct by lawyers who are associated with that lawyer in the matter, but who do not expect to appear before the court or administrative agency. For example, subordinate lawyers may conduct research, review documents, and attend meetings with witnesses in support of the lawyer responsible for the litigation.

[12] Paragraph (c)(3) permits a lawyer admitted to practice law in another jurisdiction to perform services on a temporary basis in this jurisdiction if those services are in or reasonably related to a pending or potential arbitration, mediation, or other alternative dispute resolution proceeding in this or another jurisdiction, if the services arise out of or are reasonably related to the

lawyer's practice in a jurisdiction in which the lawyer is admitted to practice. The lawyer, however, must obtain admission pro hac vice in the case of a court-annexed arbitration or mediation or otherwise if court rules or law so require.

[13]   Paragraph (c)(4) permits a lawyer admitted in another jurisdiction to provide certain legal services on a temporary basis in this jurisdiction that arise out of or are reasonably related to the lawyer's practice in a jurisdiction in which the lawyer is admitted but are not within paragraphs (c)(2) or (c)(3). These services include both legal services and services that nonlawyers may perform but that are considered the practice of law when performed by lawyers.

[14]   Paragraphs (c)(3) and (c)(4) require that the services arise out of or be reasonably related to the lawyer's practice in a jurisdiction in which the lawyer is admitted. A variety of factors evidence such a relationship. The lawyer's client may have been previously represented by the lawyer, or may be resident in or have substantial contacts with the jurisdiction in which the lawyer is admitted. The matter, although involving other jurisdictions, may have a significant connection with that jurisdiction. In other cases, significant aspects of the lawyer's work might be conducted in that jurisdiction or a significant aspect of the matter may involve the law of that jurisdiction. The necessary relationship might arise when the client's activities or the legal issues involve multiple jurisdictions, such as when the officers of a multinational corporation survey potential business sites and seek the services of their lawyer in assessing the relative merits of each. In addition, the services may draw on the lawyer's recognized expertise developed through the regular practice of law on behalf of clients in matters involving a particular body of federal, nationally-uniform, foreign, or international law.

[15]   Paragraph (d) identifies two circumstances in which a lawyer who is admitted to practice in another United States or a foreign jurisdiction, and is not disbarred or suspended from practice in any jurisdiction or the equivalent thereof, may establish an office or other systematic and continuous presence in this jurisdiction for the practice of law. Pursuant to paragraph (c) of this Rule, a lawyer admitted in any U.S. jurisdiction may also provide legal services in this jurisdiction on a temporary basis. See also *Model Rule on Temporary Practice by Foreign Lawyers*. Except as provided in paragraphs (d)(1) and (d)(2), a lawyer who is admitted to practice law in another United States or foreign jurisdiction and who establishes an office or other systematic or continuous presence in this jurisdiction must become admitted to practice law generally in this jurisdiction.

[16]   Paragraph (d)(1) applies to a U.S. or foreign lawyer who is employed by a client to provide legal services to the client or its organizational affiliates, i.e., entities that control, are controlled by, or are under common control with the employer. This paragraph does not authorize the provision of personal legal services to the employer's officers or employees. The paragraph applies to in-house corporate lawyers, government lawyers and others who are employed to render legal services to the employer. The lawyer's ability to represent the employer outside the jurisdiction in which the lawyer is licensed

generally serves the interests of the employer and does not create an unreasonable risk to the client and others because the employer is well situated to assess the lawyer's qualifications and the quality of the lawyer's work. To further decrease any risk to the client, when advising on the domestic law of a United States jurisdiction or on the law of the United States, the foreign lawyer authorized to practice under paragraph (d)(1) of this Rule needs to base that advice on the advice of a lawyer licensed and authorized by the jurisdiction to provide it.

[17]   If an employed lawyer establishes an office or other systematic presence in this jurisdiction for the purpose of rendering legal services to the employer, the lawyer may be subject to registration or other requirements, including assessments for client protection funds and mandatory continuing legal education. See *Model Rule for Registration of In-House Counsel.*

[18]   Paragraph (d)(2) recognizes that a U.S. or foreign lawyer may provide legal services in a jurisdiction in which the lawyer is not licensed when authorized to do so by federal or other law, which includes statute, court rule, executive regulation or judicial precedent. See, e.g., *The ABA Model Rule on Practice Pending Admission.*

[19]   A lawyer who practices law in this jurisdiction pursuant to paragraphs (c) or (d) or otherwise is subject to the disciplinary authority of this jurisdiction. See Rule 8.5(a).

[20]   In some circumstances, a lawyer who practices law in this jurisdiction pursuant to paragraphs (c) or (d) may have to inform the client that the lawyer is not licensed to practice law in this jurisdiction. For example, that may be required when the representation occurs primarily in this jurisdiction and requires knowledge of the law of this jurisdiction. See Rule 1.4(b).

[21]   Paragraphs (c) and (d) do not authorize communications advertising legal services in this jurisdiction by lawyers who are admitted to practice in other jurisdictions. Whether and how lawyers may communicate the availability of their services in this jurisdiction is governed by Rules 7.1 to 7.5.

RULE 5.6: RESTRICTIONS ON RIGHT TO PRACTICE

A lawyer shall not participate in offering or making:

(a)   a partnership, shareholders, operating, employment, or other similar type of agreement that restricts the right of a lawyer to practice after termination of the relationship, except an agreement *Non - compete clause* **concerning benefits upon retirement; or**

(b)   an agreement in which a restriction on the lawyer's right to practice is part of the settlement of a client controversy.

Comment

[1]   An agreement restricting the right of lawyers to practice after leaving a firm not only limits their professional autonomy but also limits the freedom of clients to choose a lawyer. Paragraph (a) prohibits such agreements

except for restrictions incident to provisions concerning retirement benefits for service with the firm.

[2]   Paragraph (b) prohibits a lawyer from agreeing not to represent other persons in connection with settling a claim on behalf of a client.

[3]   This Rule does not apply to prohibit restrictions that may be included in the terms of the sale of a law practice pursuant to Rule 1.17.

RULE 5.7: RESPONSIBILITIES REGARDING LAW-RELATED SERVICES

(a)   **A lawyer shall be subject to the Rules of Professional Conduct with respect to the provision of law-related services, as defined in paragraph (b), if the law-related services are provided:**

>   **(1)   by the lawyer in circumstances that are not distinct from the lawyer's provision of legal services to clients; or**

>   **(2)   in other circumstances by an entity controlled by the lawyer individually or with others if the lawyer fails to take reasonable measures to assure that a person obtaining the law-related services knows that the services are not legal services and that the protections of the client-lawyer relationship do not exist.**

(b)   **The term "law-related services" denotes services that might reasonably be performed in conjunction with and in substance are related to the provision of legal services, and that are not prohibited as unauthorized practice of law when provided by a nonlawyer.**

Comment

[1]   When a lawyer performs law-related services or controls an organization that does so, there exists the potential for ethical problems. Principal among these is the possibility that the person for whom the law- related services are performed fails to understand that the services may not carry with them the protections normally afforded as part of the client-lawyer relationship. The recipient of the law-related services may expect, for example, that the protection of client confidences, prohibitions against representation of persons with conflicting interests, and obligations of a lawyer to maintain professional independence apply to the provision of law-related services when that may not be the case.

[2]   Rule 5.7 applies to the provision of law-related services by a lawyer even when the lawyer does not provide any legal services to the person for whom the law-related services are performed and whether the law-related services are performed through a law firm or a separate entity. The Rule identifies the circumstances in which all of the Rules of Professional Conduct apply to the provision of law-related services. Even when those circumstances do not exist, however, the conduct of a lawyer involved in the provision of law-related services is subject to those Rules that apply generally to lawyer conduct, regardless of whether the conduct involves the provision of legal services. See, e.g., Rule 8.4.

[3]   When law-related services are provided by a lawyer under circumstances that are not distinct from the lawyer's provision of legal services to
clients, the lawyer in providing the law-related services must adhere to the
requirements of the Rules of Professional Conduct as provided in paragraph (a)(1).
Even when the law-related and legal services are provided in circumstances
that are distinct from each other, for example through separate entities or different support staff within the law firm, the Rules of Professional Conduct
apply to the lawyer as provided in paragraph (a)(2) unless the lawyer takes
reasonable measures to assure that the recipient of the law-related services
knows that the services are not legal services and that the protections of the
client-lawyer relationship do not apply.

[4]   Law-related services also may be provided through an entity
that is distinct from that through which the lawyer provides legal services.
If the lawyer individually or with others has control of such an entity's operations, the Rule requires the lawyer to take reasonable measures to assure that
each person using the services of the entity knows that the services provided
by the entity are not legal services and that the Rules of Professional Con-duct
that relate to the client-lawyer relationship do not apply. A lawyer's control of
an entity extends to the ability to direct its operation. Whether a lawyer has
such control will depend upon the circumstances of the particular case.

[5]   When a client-lawyer relationship exists with a person who is
referred by a lawyer to a separate law-related service entity controlled by the
lawyer, individually or with others, the lawyer must comply with Rule 1.8(a).

[6]   In taking the reasonable measures referred to in paragraph (a)(2)
to assure that a person using law-related services understands the practical
effect or significance of the inapplicability of the Rules of Professional Conduct,
the lawyer should communicate to the person receiving the law-related services, in a manner sufficient to assure that the person understands the significance of the fact, that the relationship of the person to the business entity will
not be a client-lawyer relationship. The communication should be made before
entering into an agreement for provision of or providing law- related services,
and preferably should be in writing.

[7]   The burden is upon the lawyer to show that the lawyer has
taken reasonable measures under the circumstances to communicate the
desired understanding. For instance, a sophisticated user of law-related services, such as a publicly held corporation, may require a lesser explanation
than someone unaccustomed to making distinctions between legal services and
law-related services, such as an individual seeking tax advice from a lawyer-
accountant or investigative services in connection with a lawsuit.

[8]   Regardless of the sophistication of potential recipients of law-
related services, a lawyer should take special care to keep separate the provision of law-related and legal services in order to minimize the risk that the
recipient will assume that the law-related services are legal services. The risk
of such confusion is especially acute when the lawyer renders both types of
services with respect to the same matter. Under some circumstances the legal

and law-related services may be so closely entwined that they cannot be distinguished from each other, and the requirement of disclosure and consultation imposed by paragraph (a)(2) of the Rule cannot be met. In such a case a lawyer will be responsible for assuring that both the lawyer's conduct and, to the extent required by Rule 5.3, that of nonlawyer employees in the distinct entity that the lawyer controls complies in all respects with the Rules of Professional Conduct.

[9]   A broad range of economic and other interests of clients may be served by lawyers' engaging in the delivery of law-related services. Examples of law-related services include providing title insurance, financial planning, accounting, trust services, real estate counseling, legislative lobbying, economic analysis, social work, psychological counseling, tax preparation, and patent, medical or environmental consulting.

[10]   When a lawyer is obliged to accord the recipients of such services the protections of those Rules that apply to the client-lawyer relationship, the lawyer must take special care to heed the proscriptions of the Rules addressing conflict of interest (Rules 1.7 through 1.11, especially Rules 1.7(a)(2) and 1.8(a), (b) and (f)), and to scrupulously adhere to the requirements of Rule 1.6 relating to disclosure of confidential information. The promotion of the law- related services must also in all respects comply with Rules 7.1 through 7.3, dealing with advertising and solicitation. In that regard, lawyers should take special care to identify the obligations that may be imposed as a result of a jurisdiction's decisional law.

[11]   When the full protections of all of the Rules of Professional Conduct do not apply to the provision of law-related services, principles of law external to the Rules, for example, the law of principal and agent, govern the legal duties owed to those receiving the services. Those other legal principles may establish a different degree of protection for the recipient with respect to confidentiality of information, conflicts of interest and permissible business relationships with clients. See also Rule 8.4 (Misconduct).

RULE 6.1: VOLUNTARY PRO BONO PUBLICO SERVICE

Every lawyer has a professional responsibility to provide legal services to those unable to pay. A lawyer should aspire to render at least (50) hours of pro bono publico legal services per year. In fulfilling this responsibility, the lawyer should:

(a)   provide a substantial majority of the (50) hours of legal services without fee or expectation of fee to:

(1)   persons of limited means or

(2)   charitable, religious, civic, community, governmental and educational organizations in matters that are designed primarily to address the needs of persons of limited means; and

(b) **provide any additional services through:**

(1) **delivery of legal services at no fee or substantially reduced fee to individuals, groups or organizations seeking to secure or protect civil rights, civil liberties or public rights, or charitable, religious, civic, community, governmental and educational organizations in matters in furtherance of their organizational purposes, where the payment of standard legal fees would significantly deplete the organization's economic resources or would be otherwise inappropriate;**

(2) **delivery of legal services at a substantially reduced fee to persons of limited means; or**

(3) **participation in activities for improving the law, the legal system or the legal profession.**

In addition, a lawyer should voluntarily contribute financial support to organizations that provide legal services to persons of limited means.

Comment

[1] Every lawyer, regardless of professional prominence or professional work load, has a responsibility to provide legal services to those unable to pay, and personal involvement in the problems of the disadvantaged can be one of the most rewarding experiences in the life of a lawyer. The American Bar Association urges all lawyers to provide a minimum of 50 hours of pro bono services annually. States, however, may decide to choose a higher or lower number of hours of annual service (which may be expressed as a percentage of a lawyer's professional time) depending upon local needs and local conditions. It is recognized that in some years a lawyer may render greater or fewer hours than the annual standard specified, but during the course of his or her legal career, each lawyer should render on average per year, the number of hours set forth in this Rule. Services can be performed in civil matters or in criminal or quasi-criminal matters for which there is no government obligation to provide funds for legal representation, such as post-conviction death penalty appeal cases.

[2] Paragraphs (a)(1) and (2) recognize the critical need for legal services that exists among persons of limited means by providing that a substantial majority of the legal services rendered annually to the disadvantaged be furnished without fee or expectation of fee. Legal services under these paragraphs consist of a full range of activities, including individual and class representation, the provision of legal advice, legislative lobbying, administrative rule making and the provision of free training or mentoring to those who represent persons of limited means. The variety of these activities should facilitate participation by government lawyers, even when restrictions exist on their engaging in the outside practice of law.

[3] Persons eligible for legal services under paragraphs (a)(1) and (2) are those who qualify for participation in programs funded by the Legal Services Corporation and those whose incomes and financial resources are

slightly above the guidelines utilized by such programs but nevertheless, cannot afford counsel. Legal services can be rendered to individuals or to organizations such as homeless shelters, battered women's centers and food pantries that serve those of limited means. The term "governmental organizations" includes, but is not limited to, public protection programs and sections of governmental or public sector agencies.

[4]   Because service must be provided without fee or expectation of fee, the intent of the lawyer to render free legal services is essential for the work performed to fall within the meaning of paragraphs (a)(1) and (2). Accordingly, services rendered cannot be considered pro bono if an anticipated fee is uncollected, but the award of statutory attorneys' fees in a case originally accepted as pro bono would not disqualify such services from inclusion under this section. Lawyers who do receive fees in such cases are encouraged to contribute an appropriate portion of such fees to organizations or projects that benefit persons of limited means.

[5]   While it is possible for a lawyer to fulfill the annual responsibility to perform pro bono services exclusively through activities described in paragraphs (a)(1) and (2), to the extent that any hours of service remained unfulfilled, the remaining commitment can be met in a variety of ways as set forth in paragraph (b). Constitutional, statutory or regulatory restrictions may prohibit or impede government and public sector lawyers and judges from performing the pro bono services outlined in paragraphs (a)(1) and (2). Accordingly, where those restrictions apply, government and public sector lawyers and judges may fulfill their pro bono responsibility by performing services outlined in paragraph (b).

[6]   Paragraph (b)(1) includes the provision of certain types of legal services to those whose incomes and financial resources place them above limited means. It also permits the pro bono lawyer to accept a substantially reduced fee for services. Examples of the types of issues that may be addressed under this paragraph include First Amendment claims, Title VII claims and environmental protection claims. Additionally, a wide range of organizations may be represented, including social service, medical research, cultural and religious groups.

[7]   Paragraph (b)(2) covers instances in which lawyers agree to and receive a modest fee for furnishing legal services to persons of limited means. Participation in judicare programs and acceptance of court appointments in which the fee is substantially below a lawyer's usual rate are encouraged under this section.

[8]   Paragraph (b)(3) recognizes the value of lawyers engaging in activities that improve the law, the legal system or the legal profession. Serving on bar association committees, serving on boards of pro bono or legal services programs, taking part in Law Day activities, acting as a continuing legal education instructor, a mediator or an arbitrator and engaging in legislative lobbying to improve the law, the legal system or the profession are a few examples of the many activities that fall within this paragraph.

[9]   Because the provision of pro bono services is a professional responsibility, it is the individual ethical commitment of each lawyer. Nevertheless, there may be times when it is not feasible for a lawyer to engage in pro bono services. At such times a lawyer may discharge the pro bono responsibility by providing financial support to organizations providing free legal services to persons of limited means. Such financial support should be reasonably equivalent to the value of the hours of service that would have otherwise been provided. In addition, at times it may be more feasible to satisfy the pro bono responsibility collectively, as by a firm's aggregate pro bono activities.

[10]   Because the efforts of individual lawyers are not enough to meet the need for free legal services that exists among persons of limited means, the government and the profession have instituted additional programs to provide those services. Every lawyer should financially support such programs, in addition to either providing direct pro bono services or making financial contributions when pro bono service is not feasible.

[11]   Law firms should act reasonably to enable and encourage all lawyers in the firm to provide the pro bono legal services called for by this Rule.

[12]   The responsibility set forth in this Rule is not intended to be enforced through disciplinary process.

RULE 6.2: ACCEPTING APPOINTMENTS

A lawyer shall not seek to avoid appointment by a tribunal to represent a person except for good cause, such as:

(a)   representing the client is likely to result in violation of the Rules of Professional Conduct or other law;

(b)   representing the client is likely to result in an unreasonable financial burden on the lawyer; or

(c)   the client or the cause is so repugnant to the lawyer as to be likely to impair the client-lawyer relationship or the lawyer's ability to represent the client.

Comment

[1]   A lawyer ordinarily is not obliged to accept a client whose character or cause the lawyer regards as repugnant. The lawyer's freedom to select clients is, however, qualified. All lawyers have a responsibility to assist in providing pro bono publico service. See Rule 6.1. An individual lawyer fulfills this responsibility by accepting a fair share of unpopular matters or indigent or unpopular clients. A lawyer may also be subject to appointment by a court to serve unpopular clients or persons unable to afford legal services.

Appointed Counsel

[2]   For good cause a lawyer may seek to decline an appointment to represent a person who cannot afford to retain counsel or whose cause is unpopular. Good cause exists if the lawyer could not handle the matter competently, see Rule 1.1, or if undertaking the representation would result in an improper

conflict of interest, for example, when the client or the cause is so repugnant to the lawyer as to be likely to impair the client-lawyer relationship or the lawyer's ability to represent the client. A lawyer may also seek to decline an appointment if acceptance would be unreasonably burdensome, for example, when it would impose a financial sacrifice so great as to be unjust.

[3]   An appointed lawyer has the same obligations to the client as retained counsel, including the obligations of loyalty and confidentiality, and is subject to the same limitations on the client-lawyer relationship, such as the obligation to refrain from assisting the client in violation of the Rules.

RULE 6.3: MEMBERSHIP IN LEGAL SERVICES ORGANIZATION

A lawyer may serve as a director, officer or member of a legal services organization, apart from the law firm in which the lawyer practices, notwithstanding that the organization serves persons having interests adverse to a client of the lawyer. The lawyer shall not knowingly participate in a decision or action of the organization:

(a)   if participating in the decision or action would be incompatible with the lawyer's obligations to a client under Rule 1.7; or

(b)   where the decision or action could have a material adverse effect on the representation of a client of the organization whose interests are adverse to a client of the lawyer.

Comment

[1]   Lawyers should be encouraged to support and participate in legal service organizations. A lawyer who is an officer or a member of such an organization does not thereby have a client-lawyer relationship with persons served by the organization. However, there is potential conflict between the interests of such persons and the interests of the lawyer's clients. If the possibility of such conflict disqualified a lawyer from serving on the board of a legal services organization, the profession's involvement in such organizations would be severely curtailed.

[2]   It may be necessary in appropriate cases to reassure a client of the organization that the representation will not be affected by conflicting loyalties of a member of the board. Established, written policies in this respect can enhance the credibility of such assurances.

RULE 6.4: LAW REFORM ACTIVITIES AFFECTING CLIENT INTERESTS

A lawyer may serve as a director, officer or member of an organization involved in reform of the law or its administration notwithstanding that the reform may affect the interests of a client of the lawyer. When the lawyer knows that the interests of a client may be materially benefitted by a decision in which the lawyer participates, the lawyer shall disclose that fact but need not identify the client.

Comment

[1]   Lawyers involved in organizations seeking law reform generally do not have a client-lawyer relationship with the organization. Otherwise, it might follow that a lawyer could not be involved in a bar association law reform program that might indirectly affect a client. See also Rule 1.2(b). For example, a lawyer specializing in antitrust litigation might be regarded as disqualified from participating in drafting revisions of rules governing that subject. In determining the nature and scope of participation in such activities, a lawyer should be mindful of obligations to clients under other Rules, particularly Rule 1.7. A lawyer is professionally obligated to protect the integrity of the program by making an appropriate disclosure within the organization when the lawyer knows a private client might be materially benefitted.

RULE 6.5: NONPROFIT AND COURT-ANNEXED LIMITED LEGAL SERVICES PROGRAMS

(a)   **A lawyer who, under the auspices of a program sponsored by a nonprofit organization or court, provides short-term limited legal services to a client without expectation by either the lawyer or the client that the lawyer will provide continuing representation in the matter:**

(1)   **is subject to Rules 1.7 and 1.9(a) only if the lawyer knows that the representation of the client involves a conflict of interest; and**

(2)   **is subject to Rule 1.10 only if the lawyer knows that (a)another lawyer associated with the lawyer in a law firm is disqualified by Rule 1.7 or 1.9(a) with respect to the matter.**

(b)   **Except as provided in paragraph (a)(2), Rule 1.10 is inapplicable to a representation governed by this Rule.**

Comment

[1]   Legal services organizations, courts and various nonprofit organizations have established programs through which lawyers provide short-term limited legal services — such as advice or the completion of legal forms - that will assist persons to address their legal problems without further representation by a lawyer. In these programs, such as legal-advice hotlines, advice-only clinics or pro se counseling programs, a client-lawyer relationship is established, but there is no expectation that the lawyer's representation of the client will continue beyond the limited consultation. Such programs are normally operated under circumstances in which it is not feasible for a lawyer to systematically screen for conflicts of interest as is generally required before undertaking a representation. See, e.g., Rules 1.7, 1.9 and 1.10.

[2]   A lawyer who provides short-term limited legal services pursuant to this Rule must secure the client's informed consent to the limited scope of the representation. See Rule 1.2(c). If a short-term limited representation would not be reasonable under the circumstances, the lawyer may offer

advice to the client but must also advise the client of the need for further assistance of counsel. Except as provided in this Rule, the Rules of Professional Conduct, including Rules 1.6 and 1.9(c), are applicable to the limited representation.

[3]   Because a lawyer who is representing a client in the circumstances addressed by this Rule ordinarily is not able to check systematically for conflicts of interest, paragraph (a) requires compliance with Rules 1.7 or 1.9(a) only if the lawyer knows that the representation presents a conflict of interest for the lawyer, and with Rule 1.10 only if the lawyer knows that another lawyer in the lawyer's firm is disqualified by Rules 1.7 or 1.9(a) in the matter.

[4]   Because the limited nature of the services significantly reduces the risk of conflicts of interest with other matters being handled by the lawyer's firm, paragraph (b) provides that Rule 1.10 is inapplicable to a representation governed by this Rule except as provided by paragraph (a)(2). Paragraph (a)(2) requires the participating lawyer to comply with Rule 1.10 when the lawyer knows that the lawyer's firm is disqualified by Rules 1.7 or 1.9(a). By virtue of paragraph (b), however, a lawyer's participation in a short-term limited legal services program will not preclude the lawyer's firm from undertaking or continuing the representation of a client with interests adverse to a client being represented under the program's auspices. Nor will the personal disqualification of a lawyer participating in the program be imputed to other lawyers participating in the program.

[5]   If, after commencing a short-term limited representation in accordance with this Rule, a lawyer undertakes to represent the client in the matter on an ongoing basis, Rules 1.7, 1.9(a) and 1.10 become applicable.

RULE 7.1: COMMUNICATIONS CONCERNING A LAWYER'S SERVICES

A lawyer shall not make a false or misleading communication about the lawyer or the lawyer's services. A communication is false or misleading if it contains a material misrepresentation of fact or law, or omits a fact necessary to make the statement considered as a whole not materially misleading.

Comment

[1]   This Rule governs all communications about a lawyer's services, including advertising permitted by Rule 7.2. Whatever means are used to make known a lawyer's services, statements about them must be truthful.

[2]   Truthful statements that are misleading are also prohibited by this Rule. A truthful statement is misleading if it omits a fact necessary to make the lawyer's communication considered as a whole not materially misleading. A truthful statement is also misleading if there is a substantial likelihood that it will lead a reasonable person to formulate a specific conclusion about the lawyer or the lawyer's services for which there is no reasonable factual foundation.

[3]   An advertisement that truthfully reports a lawyer's achievements on behalf of clients or former clients may be misleading if presented so as to lead a reasonable person to form an unjustified expectation that the same results could be obtained for other clients in similar matters without reference to the specific factual and legal circumstances of each client's case. Similarly, an unsubstantiated comparison of the lawyer's services or fees with the services or fees of other lawyers may be misleading if presented with such specificity as would lead a reasonable person to conclude that the comparison can be substantiated. The inclusion of an appropriate disclaimer or qualifying language may preclude a finding that a statement is likely to create unjustified expectations or otherwise mislead the public.

[4]   See also Rule 8.4(e) for the prohibition against stating or implying an ability to influence improperly a government agency or official or to achieve results by means that violate the Rules of Professional Conduct or other law.

RULE 7.2: ADVERTISING

(a)   **Subject to the requirements of Rules 7.1 and 7.3, a lawyer may advertise services through written, recorded or electronic communication, including public media.**

(b)   **A lawyer shall not give anything of value to a person for recommending the lawyer's services except that a lawyer may**

     (1)   **pay the reasonable costs of advertisements or communications permitted by this Rule;**

     (2)   **pay the usual charges of a legal service plan or a not-for-profit or qualified lawyer referral service. A qualified lawyer referral service is a lawyer referral service that has been approved by an appropriate regulatory authority;**

     (3)   **pay for a law practice in accordance with Rule 1.17; and**

     (4)   **refer clients to another lawyer or a nonlawyer professional pursuant to an agreement not otherwise prohibited under these Rules that provides for the other person to refer clients or customers to the lawyer, if**

         (i)   **the reciprocal referral agreement is not exclusive, and**

         (ii)   **the client is informed of the existence and nature of the agreement.**

(c)   **Any communication made pursuant to this rule shall include the name and office address of at least one lawyer or law firm responsible for its content.**

Comment

[1]   To assist the public in learning about and obtaining legal services, lawyers should be allowed to make known their services not only through

reputation but also through organized information campaigns in the form of advertising. Advertising involves an active quest for clients, contrary to the tradition that a lawyer should not seek clientele. However, the public's need to know about legal services can be fulfilled in part through advertising. This need is particularly acute in the case of persons of moderate means who have not made extensive use of legal services. The interest in expanding public information about legal services ought to prevail over considerations of tradition. Nevertheless, advertising by lawyers entails the risk of practices that are misleading or overreaching.

[2]   This Rule permits public dissemination of information concerning a lawyer's name or firm name, address, email address, website, and telephone number; the kinds of services the lawyer will undertake; the basis on which the lawyer's fees are determined, including prices for specific services and payment and credit arrangements; a lawyer's foreign language ability; names of references and, with their consent, names of clients regularly represented; and other information that might invite the attention of those seeking legal assistance.

[3]   Questions of effectiveness and taste in advertising are matters of speculation and subjective judgment. Some jurisdictions have had extensive prohibitions against television and other forms of advertising, against advertising going beyond specified facts about a lawyer, or against "undignified" advertising. Television, the Internet, and other forms of electronic communication are now among the most powerful media for getting information to the public, particularly persons of low and moderate income; prohibiting television, Internet, and other forms of electronic advertising, therefore, would impede the flow of information about legal services to many sectors of the public. Limiting the information that may be advertised has a similar effect and assumes that the bar can accurately forecast the kind of information that the public would regard as relevant. But see Rule 7.3(a) for the prohibition against a solicitation through a real-time electronic exchange initiated by the lawyer.

[4]   Neither this Rule nor Rule 7.3 prohibits communications authorized by law, such as notice to members of a class in class action litigation.

Paying Others to Recommend a Lawyer

[5]   Except as permitted under paragraphs (b)(1)-(b)(4), lawyers are not permitted to pay others for recommending the lawyer's services or for channeling professional work in a manner that violates Rule 7.3. A communication contains a recommendation if it endorses or vouches for a lawyer's credentials, abilities, competence, character, or other professional qualities. Paragraph (b)(1), however, allows a lawyer to pay for advertising and communications permitted by this Rule, including the costs of print directory listings, on-line directory listings, newspaper ads, television and radio airtime, domain-name registrations, sponsorship fees, Internet-based advertisements, and group advertising. A lawyer may compensate employees, agents and vendors who are engaged to provide marketing or client-development services, such as publicists, public-relations personnel, business-development staff and website designers. Moreover, a lawyer

may pay others for generating client leads, such as Internet-based client leads, as long as the lead generator does not recommend the lawyer, any payment to the lead generator is consistent with Rules 1.5(e) (division of fees) and 5.4 (professional independence of the lawyer), and the lead generator's communications are consistent with Rule 7.1 (communications concerning a lawyer's services). To comply with Rule 7.1, a lawyer must not pay a lead generator that states, implies, or creates a reasonable impression that it is recommending the lawyer, is making the referral without payment from the lawyer, or has analyzed a person's legal problems when determining which lawyer should receive the referral. See also Rule 5.3 (duties of lawyers and law firms with respect to the conduct of nonlawyers); Rule 8.4(a) (duty to avoid violating the Rules through the acts of another).

[6]   A lawyer may pay the usual charges of a legal service plan or a not-for-profit or qualified lawyer referral service. A legal service plan is a prepaid or group legal service plan or a similar delivery system that assists people who seek to secure legal representation. A lawyer referral service, on the other hand, is any organization that holds itself out to the public as a lawyer referral service. Such referral services are understood by the public to be consumer-oriented organizations that provide unbiased referrals to lawyers with appropriate experience in the subject matter of the representation and afford other client protections, such as complaint procedures or malpractice insurance requirements. Consequently, this Rule only permits a lawyer to pay the usual charges of a not-for-profit or qualified lawyer referral service. A qualified lawyer referral service is one that is approved by an appropriate regulatory authority as affording adequate protections for the public. See, e.g., the American Bar Association's Model Supreme Court Rules Governing Lawyer Referral Services and Model Lawyer Referral and Information Service Quality Assurance Act (requiring that organizations that are identified as lawyer referral services (i) permit the participation of all lawyers who are licensed and eligible to practice in the jurisdiction and who meet reasonable objective eligibility requirements as may be established by the referral service for the protection of the public; (ii) require each participating lawyer to carry reasonably adequate malpractice insurance; (iii) act reasonably to assess client satisfaction and address client complaints; and (iv) do not make referrals to lawyers who own, operate or are employed by the referral service.)

[7]   A lawyer who accepts assignments or referrals from a legal service plan or referrals from a lawyer referral service must act reasonably to assure that the activities of the plan or service are compatible with the lawyer's professional obligations. See Rule 5.3. Legal service plans and lawyer referral services may communicate with the public, but such communication must be in conformity with these Rules. Thus, advertising must not be false or misleading, as would be the case if the communications of a group advertising program or a group legal services plan would mislead the public to think that it was a lawyer referral service sponsored by a state agency or bar association. Nor could the lawyer allow in-person, telephonic, or real-time contacts that would violate Rule 7.3.

[8]   A lawyer also may agree to refer clients to another lawyer or a nonlawyer professional, in return for the undertaking of that person to refer clients or customers to the lawyer. Such reciprocal referral arrangements must not interfere with the lawyer's professional judgment as to making referrals or as to providing substantive legal services. See Rules 2.1 and 5.4(c). Except as provided in Rule 1.5(e), a lawyer who receives referrals from a lawyer or non-lawyer professional must not pay anything solely for the referral, but the lawyer does not violate paragraph (b) of this Rule by agreeing to refer clients to the other lawyer or nonlawyer professional, so long as the reciprocal referral agreement is not exclusive and the client is informed of the referral agreement. Conflicts of interest created by such arrangements are governed by Rule 1.7. Reciprocal referral agreements should not be of indefinite duration and should be reviewed periodically to determine whether they comply with these Rules. This Rule does not restrict referrals or divisions of revenues or net income among lawyers within firms comprised of multiple entities.

RULE 7.3: SOLICITATION OF CLIENTS

(a)   A lawyer shall not by in-person, live telephone or real-time electronic contact, solicit professional employment when a significant motive for the lawyer's doing so is the lawyer's pecuniary gain, unless the person contacted:

(1)   is a lawyer; or

(2)   has a family, close personal, or prior professional relationship with the lawyer.

(b)   A lawyer shall not solicit professional employment from a prospective client by written, recorded or electronic communica-tion or by in-person, telephone or real-time electronic contact even when not otherwise prohibited by paragraph (a), if:

(1)   the target of the solicitation has made known to the lawyer a desire not to be solicited by the lawyer; or

(2)   the solicitation involves coercion, duress or harassment.

(c)   Every written, recorded or electronic communication from a lawyer soliciting professional employment from anyone known to be in need of legal services in a particular matter shall include the words "Advertising Material" on the outside envelope, if any, and at the beginning and ending of any recorded or electronic communica-tion, unless the recipient of the communication is a person specified in paragraphs (a)(1) or (a)(2).

(d)   Notwithstanding the prohibitions in paragraph (a), a lawyer may participate with a prepaid or group legal service plan operated by an organization not owned or directed by the lawyer that uses in-person or telephone contact to solicit memberships or sub-scriptions for the plan from persons who are not known to need legal services in a particular matter covered by the plan.

Comment

[1]   A solicitation is a targeted communication initiated by the lawyer that is directed to a specific person and that offers to provide, or can reasonably be understood as offering to provide, legal services. In contrast, a lawyer's communication typically does not constitute a solicitation if it is directed to the general public, such as through a billboard, an Internet banner advertisement, a website or a television commercial, or if it is in response to a request for information or is automatically generated in response to Internet searches.

[2]   There is a potential for abuse when a solicitation involves direct in-person, live telephone or real-time electronic contact by a lawyer with someone known to need legal services. These forms of contact subject a person to the private importuning of the trained advocate in a direct interpersonal encounter. The person, who may already feel overwhelmed by the circumstances giving rise to the need for legal services, may find it difficult fully to evaluate all available alternatives with reasoned judgment and appropriate self-interest in the face of the lawyer's presence and insistence upon being retained immediately. The situation is fraught with the possibility of undue influence, intimidation, and over-reaching.

[3]   This potential for abuse inherent in direct in-person, live telephone or real-time electronic solicitation justifies its prohibition, particularly since lawyers have alternative means of conveying necessary information to those who may be in need of legal services. In particular, communications can be mailed or transmitted by email or other electronic means that do not involve real-time contact and do not violate other laws governing solicitations. These forms of communications and solicitations make it possible for the public to be informed about the need for legal services, and about the qualifications of available lawyers and law firms, without subjecting the public to direct in-person, telephone or real-time electronic persuasion that may overwhelm a person's judgment.

[4]   The use of general advertising and written, recorded or electronic communications to transmit information from lawyer to the public, rather than direct in-person, live telephone or real-time electronic contact, will help to assure that the information flows cleanly as well as freely. The contents of advertisements and communications permitted under Rule 7.2 can be permanently recorded so that they cannot be disputed and may be shared with others who know the lawyer. This potential for informal review is itself likely to help guard against statements and claims that might constitute false and misleading communications, in violation of Rule 7.1. The contents of direct inperson, live telephone or real-time electronic contact can be disputed and may not be subject to third-party scrutiny. Consequently, they are much more likely to approach (and occasionally cross) the dividing line between accurate representations and those that are false and misleading.

[5]   There is far less likelihood that a lawyer would engage in abusive practices against a former client, or a person with whom the lawyer has close personal or family relationship, or in situations in which the lawyer is motivated by considerations other than the lawyer's pecuniary gain. Nor is

there a serious potential for abuse when the person contacted is a lawyer. Consequently, the general prohibition in Rule 7.3(a) and the requirements of Rule 7.3(c) are not applicable in those situations. Also, paragraph (a) is not intended to prohibit a lawyer from participating in constitutionally protected activities of public or charitable legal-service organizations or bona fide political, social, civic, fraternal, employee or trade organizations whose purposes include providing or recommending legal services to their members or beneficiaries.

[6]   But even permitted forms of solicitation can be abused. Thus, any solicitation which contains information which is false or misleading within the meaning of Rule 7.1, which involves coercion, duress or harassment within the meaning of Rule 7.3(b)(2), or which involves contact with someone who has made known to the lawyer a desire not to be solicited by the lawyer within the meaning of Rule 7.3(b)(1) is prohibited. Moreover, if after sending a letter or other communication as permitted by Rule 7.2 the lawyer receives no response, any further effort to communicate with the recipient of the communication may violate the provisions of Rule 7.3(b).

[7]   This Rule is not intended to prohibit a lawyer from contacting representatives of organizations or groups that may be interested in establishing a group or prepaid legal plan for their members, insureds, beneficiaries or other third parties for the purpose of informing such entities of the availability of and details concerning the plan or arrangement which the lawyer or lawyer's firm is willing to offer. This form of communication is not directed to people who are seeking legal services for themselves. Rather, it is usually addressed to an individual acting in a fiduciary capacity seeking a supplier of legal services for others who may, if they choose, become prospective clients of the lawyer. Under these circumstances, the activity which the lawyer undertakes in communicating with such representatives and the type of information transmitted to the individual are functionally similar to and serve the same purpose as advertising permitted under Rule 7.2.

[8]   The requirement in Rule 7.3(c) that certain communications be marked "Advertising Material" does not apply to communications sent in response to requests of potential clients or their spokespersons or sponsors. General announcements by lawyers, including changes in personnel or office location, do not constitute communications soliciting professional employment from a client known to be in need of legal services within the meaning of this Rule.

[9]   Paragraph (d) of this Rule permits a lawyer to participate with an organization which uses personal contact to solicit members for its group or prepaid legal service plan, provided that the personal contact is not undertaken by any lawyer who would be a provider of legal services through the plan. The organization must not be owned by or directed (whether as manager or otherwise) by any lawyer or law firm that participates in the plan. For example, paragraph (d) would not permit a lawyer to create an organization controlled directly or indirectly by the lawyer and use the organization for the in-person or telephone solicitation of legal employment of the lawyer through memberships in the plan or otherwise. The communication permitted by these

organizations also must not be directed to a person known to need legal services in a particular matter, but is to be designed to inform potential plan members generally of another means of affordable legal services. Lawyers who participate in a legal service plan must reasonably assure that the plan sponsors are in compliance with Rules 7.1, 7.2 and 7.3(b). See 8.4(a).

RULE 7.4: COMMUNICATION OF FIELDS OF PRACTICE AND SPECIALIZATION

(a) **A lawyer may communicate the fact that the lawyer does or does not practice in particular fields of law.**

(b) **A lawyer admitted to engage in patent practice before the United States Patent and Trademark Office may use the designation "Patent Attorney" or a substantially similar designation.**

(c) **A lawyer engaged in Admiralty practice may use the designation "Admiralty," "Proctor in Admiralty" or a substantially similar designation.**

(d) **A lawyer shall not state or imply that a lawyer is certified as a specialist in a particular field of law, unless:**

(1) **the lawyer has been certified as a specialist by an organization that has been approved by an appropriate state authority or that has been accredited by the American Bar Association; and**

(2) **the name of the certifying organization is clearly identified in the communication.**

Comment

[1] Paragraph (a) of this Rule permits a lawyer to indicate areas of practice in communications about the lawyer's services. If a lawyer practices only in certain fields, or will not accept matters except in a specified field or fields, the lawyer is permitted to so indicate. A lawyer is generally permitted to state that the lawyer is a "specialist," practices a "specialty," or "specializes in" particular fields, but such communications are subject to the "false and misleading" standard applied in Rule 7.1 to communications concerning a lawyer's services.

[2] Paragraph (b) recognizes the long-established policy of the Patent and Trademark Office for the designation of lawyers practicing before the Office. Paragraph (c) recognizes that designation of Admiralty practice has a long historical tradition associated with maritime commerce and the federal courts.

[3] Paragraph (d) permits a lawyer to state that the lawyer is certified as a specialist in a field of law if such certification is granted by an organization approved by an appropriate state authority or accredited by the American Bar Association or another organization, such as a state bar association, that has been approved by the state authority to accredit organizations that certify lawyers as specialists. Certification signifies that an objective entity has recognized an

advanced degree of knowledge and experience in the specialty area greater than is suggested by general licensure to practice law. Certifying organizations may be expected to apply standards of experience, knowledge and proficiency to insure that a lawyer's recognition as a specialist is meaningful and reliable. In order to insure that consumers can obtain access to useful information about an organization granting certification, the name of the certifying organization must be included in any communication regarding the certification.

RULE 7.5: FIRM NAMES AND LETTERHEADS

(a)   A lawyer shall not use a firm name, letterhead or other professional designation that violates Rule 7.1. A trade name may be used by a lawyer in private practice if it does not imply a connection with a government agency or with a public or charitable legal services organization and is not otherwise in violation of Rule 7.1.

(b)   A law firm with offices in more than one jurisdiction may use the same name or other professional designation in each jurisdiction, but identification of the lawyers in an office of the firm shall indicate the jurisdictional limitations on those not licensed to practice in the jurisdiction where the office is located.

(c)   The name of a lawyer holding a public office shall not be used in the name of a law firm, or in communications on its behalf, during any substantial period in which the lawyer is not actively and regularly practicing with the firm.

(d)   Lawyers may state or imply that they practice in a partnership or other organization only when that is the fact.

Comment

[1]   A firm may be designated by the names of all or some of its members, by the names of deceased members where there has been a continuing succession in the firm's identity or by a trade name such as the "ABC Legal Clinic." A lawyer or law firm may also be designated by a distinctive website address or comparable professional designation. Although the United States Supreme Court has held that legislation may prohibit the use of trade names in professional practice, use of such names in law practice is acceptable so long as it is not misleading. If a private firm uses a trade name that includes a geographical name such as "Springfield Legal Clinic," an express disclaimer that it is a public legal aid agency may be required to avoid a misleading implication. It may be observed that any firm name including the name of a deceased partner is, strictly speaking, a trade name. The use of such names to designate law firms has proven a useful means of identification. However, it is misleading to use the name of a lawyer not associated with the firm or a predecessor of the firm, or the name of a nonlawyer.

[2]   With regard to paragraph (d), lawyers sharing office facilities, but who are not in fact associated with each other in a law firm, may not denominate themselves as, for example, "Smith and Jones," for that title suggests that they are practicing law together in a firm.

RULE 7.6: POLITICAL CONTRIBUTIONS TO OBTAIN GOVERNMENT LEGAL ENGAGEMENTS OR APPOINTMENTS BY JUDGES

A lawyer or law firm shall not accept a government legal engagement or an appointment by a judge if the lawyer or law firm makes a political contribution or solicits political contributions for the purpose of obtaining or being considered for that type of legal engagement or appointment.

the purpose is important

Comment

[1]   Lawyers have a right to participate fully in the political process, which includes making and soliciting political contributions to candidates for judicial and other public office. Nevertheless, when lawyers make or solicit political contributions in order to obtain an engagement for legal work awarded by a government agency, or to obtain appointment by a judge, the public may legitimately question whether the lawyers engaged to perform the work are selected on the basis of competence and merit. In such a circumstance, the integrity of the profession is undermined.

[2]   The term "political contribution" denotes any gift, subscription, loan, advance or deposit of anything of value made directly or indirectly to a candidate, incumbent, political party or campaign committee to influence or provide financial support for election to or retention in judicial or other government office. Political contributions in initiative and referendum elections are not included. For purposes of this Rule, the term "political contribution" does not include uncompensated services.

[3]   Subject to the exceptions below, (i) the term "government legal engagement" denotes any engagement to provide legal services that a public official has the direct or indirect power to award; and (ii) the term "appointment by a judge" denotes an appointment to a position such as referee, commissioner, special master, receiver, guardian or other similar position that is made by a judge. Those terms do not, however, include (a) substantially uncompensated services; (b) engagements or appointments made on the basis of experience, expertise, professional qualifications and cost following a request for proposal or other process that is free from influence based upon political contributions; and (c) engagements or appointments made on a rotational basis from a list compiled without regard to political contributions.

[4]   The term "lawyer or law firm" includes a political action committee or other entity owned or controlled by a lawyer or law firm.

[5]   Political contributions are for the purpose of obtaining or being considered for a government legal engagement or appointment by a judge if, but for the desire to be considered for the legal engagement or appointment, the lawyer or law firm would not have made or solicited the contributions. The purpose may be determined by an examination of the circumstances in which the contributions occur. For example, one or more contributions that in the aggregate are substantial in relation to other contributions by lawyers or law firms, made for the benefit of an official in a

position to influence award of a government legal engagement, and followed by an award of the legal engagement to the contributing or soliciting lawyer or the lawyer's firm would support an inference that the purpose of the contributions was to obtain the engagement, absent other factors that weigh against existence of the proscribed purpose. Those factors may include among others that the contribution or solicitation was made to further a political, social, or economic interest or because of an existing personal, family, or professional relationship with a candidate.

[6]   If a lawyer makes or solicits a political contribution under circumstances that constitute bribery or another crime, Rule 8.4(b) is implicated.

RULE 8.1: BAR ADMISSION AND DISCIPLINARY MATTERS

An applicant for admission to the bar, or a lawyer in connection with a bar admission application or in connection with a disciplinary matter, shall not:

(a)   knowingly make a false statement of material fact; or

(b)   fail to disclose a fact necessary to correct a misapprehension known by the person to have arisen in the matter, or knowingly fail to respond to a lawful demand for information from an admissions or disciplinary authority, except that this rule does not require disclosure of information otherwise protected by Rule 1.6.

Comment

[1]   The duty imposed by this Rule extends to persons seeking admission to the bar as well as to lawyers. Hence, if a person makes a material false statement in connection with an application for admission, it may be the basis for subsequent disciplinary action if the person is admitted, and in any event may be relevant in a subsequent admission application. The duty imposed by this Rule applies to a lawyer's own admission or discipline as well as that of others. Thus, it is a separate professional offense for a lawyer to knowingly make a misrepresentation or omission in connection with a disciplinary investigation of the lawyer's own conduct. Paragraph (b) of this Rule also requires correction of any prior misstatement in the matter that the applicant or lawyer may have made and affirmative clarification of any misunderstanding on the part of the admissions or disciplinary authority of which the person involved becomes aware.

[2]   This Rule is subject to the provisions of the fifth amendment of the United States Constitution and corresponding provisions of state constitutions. A person relying on such a provision in response to a question, however, should do so openly and not use the right of nondisclosure as a justification for failure to comply with this Rule.

[3]   A lawyer representing an applicant for admission to the bar, or representing a lawyer who is the subject of a disciplinary inquiry or proceeding, is governed by the rules applicable to the client-lawyer relationship, including Rule 1.6 and, in some cases, Rule 3.3.

RULE 8.2: JUDICIAL AND LEGAL OFFICIALS

(a) **A lawyer shall not make a statement that the lawyer knows to be false or with reckless disregard as to its truth or falsity concerning the qualifications or integrity of a judge, adjudicatory officer or public legal officer, or of a candidate for election or appointment to judicial or legal office.**

(b) **A lawyer who is a candidate for judicial office shall comply with the applicable provisions of the Code of Judicial Conduct.**

Comment

[1] Assessments by lawyers are relied on in evaluating the professional or personal fitness of persons being considered for election or appointment to judicial office and to public legal offices, such as attorney general, prosecuting attorney and public defender. Expressing honest and candid opinions on such matters contributes to improving the administration of justice. Conversely, false statements by a lawyer can unfairly undermine public confidence in the administration of justice.

[2] When a lawyer seeks judicial office, the lawyer should be bound by applicable limitations on political activity.

[3] To maintain the fair and independent administration of justice, lawyers are encouraged to continue traditional efforts to defend judges and courts unjustly criticized.

RULE 8.3: REPORTING PROFESSIONAL MISCONDUCT

(a) **A lawyer who knows that another lawyer has committed a violation of the Rules of Professional Conduct that raises a substantial question as to that lawyer's honesty, trustworthiness or fitness as a lawyer in other respects, shall inform the appropriate professional authority.**

(b) **A lawyer who knows that a judge has committed a violation of applicable rules of judicial conduct that raises a substantial question as to the judge's fitness for office shall inform the appropriate authority.**

(c) **This Rule does not require disclosure of information otherwise protected by Rule 1.6 or information gained by a lawyer or judge while participating in an approved lawyers assistance program.**

Comment

[1] Self-regulation of the legal profession requires that members of the profession initiate disciplinary investigation when they know of a violation of the Rules of Professional Conduct. Lawyers have a similar obligation with respect to judicial misconduct. An apparently isolated violation may indicate a pattern of misconduct that only a disciplinary investigation can uncover. Reporting a violation is especially important where the victim is unlikely to discover the offense.

[2]   A report about misconduct is not required where it would involve violation of Rule 1.6. However, a lawyer should encourage a client to consent to disclosure where prosecution would not substantially prejudice the client's interests.

[3]   If a lawyer were obliged to report every violation of the Rules, the failure to report any violation would itself be a professional offense. Such a requirement existed in many jurisdictions but proved to be unenforceable. This Rule limits the reporting obligation to those offenses that a self-regulating profession must vigorously endeavor to prevent. A measure of judgment is, therefore, required in complying with the provisions of this Rule. The term "substantial" refers to the seriousness of the possible offense and not the quantum of evidence of which the lawyer is aware. A report should be made to the bar disciplinary agency unless some other agency, such as a peer review agency, is more appropriate in the circumstances. Similar considerations apply to the reporting of judicial misconduct.

[4]   The duty to report professional misconduct does not apply to a lawyer retained to represent a lawyer whose professional conduct is in question. Such a situation is governed by the Rules applicable to the client-lawyer relationship.

[5]   Information about a lawyer's or judge's misconduct or fitness may be received by a lawyer in the course of that lawyer's participation in an approved lawyers or judges assistance program. In that circumstance, providing for an exception to the reporting requirements of paragraphs (a) and (b) of this Rule encourages lawyers and judges to seek treatment through such a program. Conversely, without such an exception, lawyers and judges may hesitate to seek assistance from these programs, which may then result in additional harm to their professional careers and additional injury to the welfare of clients and the public. These Rules do not otherwise address the confidentiality of information received by a lawyer or judge participating in an approved lawyers assistance program; such an obligation, however, may be imposed by the rules of the program or other law.

RULE 8.4: MISCONDUCT

It is professional misconduct for a lawyer to:

(a)   violate or attempt to violate the Rules of Professional Conduct, knowingly assist or induce another to do so, or do so through the acts of another;

(b)   commit a criminal act that reflects adversely on the lawyer's honesty, trustworthiness or fitness as a lawyer in other respects;

(c)   engage in conduct involving dishonesty, fraud, deceit or misrepresentation;

(d)   engage in conduct that is prejudicial to the administration of justice;

(e)   state or imply an ability to influence improperly a government agency or official or to achieve results by means that violate the Rules of Professional Conduct or other law; or

(f)   knowingly assist a judge or judicial officer in conduct that is a violation of applicable rules of judicial conduct or other law.

Comment

[1]   Lawyers are subject to discipline when they violate or attempt to violate the Rules of Professional Conduct, knowingly assist or induce another to do so or do so through the acts of another, as when they request or instruct an agent to do so on the lawyer's behalf. Paragraph (a), however, does not prohibit a lawyer from advising a client concerning action the client is legally entitled to take.

[2]   Many kinds of illegal conduct reflect adversely on fitness to practice law, such as offenses involving fraud and the offense of willful failure to file an income tax return. However, some kinds of offenses carry no such implication. Traditionally, the distinction was drawn in terms of offenses involving "moral turpitude." That concept can be construed to include offenses concerning some matters of personal morality, such as adultery and comparable offenses, that have no specific connection to fitness for the practice of law. Although a lawyer is personally answerable to the entire criminal law, a lawyer should be professionally answerable only for offenses that indicate lack of those characteristics relevant to law practice. Offenses involving violence, dishonesty, breach of trust, or serious interference with the administration of justice are in that category. A pattern of repeated offenses, even ones of minor significance when considered separately, can indicate indifference to legal obligation.

[3]   A lawyer who, in the course of representing a client, knowingly manifests by words or conduct, bias or prejudice based upon race, sex, religion, national origin, disability, age, sexual orientation or socioeconomic status, violates paragraph (d) when such actions are prejudicial to the administration of justice. Legitimate advocacy respecting the foregoing factors does not violate paragraph (d). A trial judge's finding that peremptory challenges were exercised on a discriminatory basis does not alone establish a violation of this rule.

[4]   A lawyer may refuse to comply with an obligation imposed by law upon a good faith belief that no valid obligation exists. The provisions of Rule 1.2(d) concerning a good faith challenge to the validity, scope, meaning or application of the law apply to challenges of legal regulation of the practice of law.

[5]   Lawyers holding public office assume legal responsibilities going beyond those of other citizens. A lawyer's abuse of public office can suggest an inability to fulfill the professional role of lawyers. The same is true of abuse of positions of private trust such as trustee, executor, administrator, guardian, agent and officer, director or manager of a corporation or other organization.

RULE 8.5: DISCIPLINARY AUTHORITY; CHOICE OF LAW

(a)   **Disciplinary Authority. A lawyer admitted to practice in this jurisdiction is subject to the disciplinary authority of this jurisdiction, regardless of where the lawyer's conduct occurs. A lawyer not admitted in this jurisdiction is also subject to the disciplinary authority of this jurisdiction if the lawyer provides or offers to provide any legal services in this jurisdiction. A lawyer may be subject to the disciplinary authority of both this jurisdiction and another jurisdiction for the same conduct.**

(b)   **Choice of Law. In any exercise of the disciplinary authority of this jurisdiction, the rules of professional conduct to be applied shall be as follows:**

(1)   **for conduct in connection with a matter pending before a tribunal, the rules of the jurisdiction in which the tribunal sits, unless the rules of the tribunal provide otherwise; and**

(2)   **for any other conduct, the rules of the jurisdiction in which the lawyer's conduct occurred, or, if the predominant effect of the conduct is in a different jurisdiction, the rules of that jurisdiction shall be applied to the conduct. A lawyer shall not be subject to discipline if the lawyer's conduct conforms to the rules of a jurisdiction in which the lawyer reasonably believes the predominant effect of the lawyer's conduct will occur.**

Comment

Disciplinary Authority

[1]   It is longstanding law that the conduct of a lawyer admitted to practice in this jurisdiction is subject to the disciplinary authority of this jurisdiction. Extension of the disciplinary authority of this jurisdiction to other lawyers who provide or offer to provide legal services in this jurisdiction is for the protection of the citizens of this jurisdiction. Reciprocal enforcement of a jurisdiction's disciplinary findings and sanctions will further advance the purposes of this Rule. See, Rules 6 and 22, ABA *Model Rules for Lawyer Disciplinary Enforcement*. A lawyer who is subject to the disciplinary authority of this jurisdiction under Rule 8.5(a) appoints an official to be designated by this Court to receive service of process in this jurisdiction. The fact that the lawyer is subject to the disciplinary authority of this jurisdiction may be a factor in determining whether personal jurisdiction may be asserted over the lawyer for civil matters.

Choice of Law

[2]   A lawyer may be potentially subject to more than one set of rules of professional conduct which impose different obligations. The lawyer may be licensed to practice in more than one jurisdiction with differing rules, or may be admitted to practice before a particular court with rules that differ

from those of the jurisdiction or jurisdictions in which the lawyer is licensed to practice. Additionally, the lawyer's conduct may involve significant contacts with more than one jurisdiction.

[3] Paragraph (b) seeks to resolve such potential conflicts. Its premise is that minimizing conflicts between rules, as well as uncertainty about which rules are applicable, is in the best interest of both clients and the profession (as well as the bodies having authority to regulate the profession). Accordingly, it takes the approach of (i) providing that any particular conduct of a lawyer shall be subject to only one set of rules of professional conduct, (ii) making the determination of which set of rules applies to particular conduct as straightforward as possible, consistent with recognition of appropriate regulatory interests of relevant jurisdictions, and (iii) providing protection from discipline for lawyers who act reasonably in the face of uncertainty.

[4] Paragraph (b)(1) provides that as to a lawyer's conduct relating to a proceeding pending before a tribunal, the lawyer shall be subject only to the rules of the jurisdiction in which the tribunal sits unless the rules of the tribunal, including its choice of law rule, provide otherwise. As to all other conduct, including conduct in anticipation of a proceeding not yet pending before a tribunal, paragraph (b)(2) provides that a lawyer shall be subject to the rules of the jurisdiction in which the lawyer's conduct occurred, or, if the predominant effect of the conduct is in another jurisdiction, the rules of that jurisdiction shall be applied to the conduct. In the case of conduct in anticipation of a proceeding that is likely to be before a tribunal, the predominant effect of such conduct could be where the conduct occurred, where the tribunal sits or in another jurisdiction.

[5] When a lawyer's conduct involves significant contacts with more than one jurisdiction, it may not be clear whether the predominant effect of the lawyer's conduct will occur in a jurisdiction other than the one in which the conduct occurred. So long as the lawyer's conduct conforms to the rules of a jurisdiction in which the lawyer reasonably believes the predominant effect will occur, the lawyer shall not be subject to discipline under this Rule. With respect to conflicts of interest, in determining a lawyer's reasonable belief under paragraph (b)(2), a written agreement between the lawyer and client that reasonably specifies a particular jurisdiction as within the scope of that paragraph may be considered if the agreement was obtained with the client's informed consent confirmed in the agreement.

[6] If two admitting jurisdictions were to proceed against a lawyer for the same conduct, they should, applying this rule, identify the same governing ethics rules. They should take all appropriate steps to see that they do apply the same rule to the same conduct, and in all events should avoid proceeding against a lawyer on the basis of two inconsistent rules.

[7] The choice of law provision applies to lawyers engaged in transnational practice, unless international law, treaties or other agreements between competent regulatory authorities in the affected jurisdictions provide otherwise.

AMERICAN BAR ASSOCIATION
MODEL RULES OF PROFESSIONAL CONDUCT
(1983 Version)

THE MODEL RULES OF PROFESSIONAL CONDUCT
WERE ADOPTED BY THE HOUSE OF DELEGATES OF THE
AMERICAN BAR ASSOCIATION ON AUGUST 2, 1983
Reprinted as amended through February 2001

Contents

	Page
Preamble, Scope and Terminology	136

Client-Lawyer Relationship

Rule

1.1	Competence	140
1.2	Scope of Representation	142
1.3	Diligence	144
1.4	Communication	145
1.5	Fees	147
1.6	Confidentiality of Information	150
1.7	Conflict of Interest: General Rule	154
1.8	Conflict of Interest: Prohibited Transactions	158
1.9	Conflict of Interest: Former Client	162
1.10	Imputed Disqualification: General Rule	165
1.11	Successive Government and Private Employment	167
1.12	Former Judge or Arbitrator	170
1.13	Organization as Client	171
1.14	Client under a Disability	175
1.15	Safekeeping Property	176
1.16	Declining or Terminating Representation	178
1.17	Sale of Law Practice	181

Counselor

2.1	Advisor	185
2.2	Intermediary	186
2.3	Evaluation for Use by Third Persons	189

Advocate

Rule		Page
3.1	Meritorius Claims and Contentions	191
3.2	Expediting Litigation	192
3.3	Candor toward the Tribunal	192
3.4	Fairness to Opposing Party and Counsel	196
3.5	Impartiality and Decorum of the Tribunal	198
3.6	Trial Publicity	199
3.7	Lawyer as Witness	202
3.8	Special Responsibilities of a Prosecutor	203
3.9	Advocate in Nonadjudicative Proceedings	205

Transactions with Persons Other Than Clients

4.1	Truthfulness in Statements to Others	206
4.2	Communication with Person Represented by Counsel	207
4.3	Dealing with Unrepresented Person	208
4.4	Respect for Rights of Third Persons	208

Law Firms and Associations

5.1	Responsibilities of a Partner or Supervisory Lawyer	209
5.2	Responsibilities of a Subordinate Lawyer	210
5.3	Responsibilities Regarding Nonlawyer Assistants	211
5.4	Professional Independence of a Lawyer	212
5.5	Unauthorized Practice of Law	213
5.6	Restrictions on Right to Practice	213
5.7	Responsibilities Regarding Law-related Services	214

Public Service

6.1	Voluntary Pro Bono Publico Service	216
6.2	Accepting Appointments	219
6.3	Membership in Legal Services Organization	220
6.4	Law Reform Activities Affecting Client Interests	221

Information About Legal Services

7.1	Communications Concerning a Lawyer's Services	221
7.2	Advertising	222
7.3	Direct Contact with Prospective Clients	224
7.4	Communication of Fields of Practice	227
7.5	Firm Names and Letterheads	229
7.6	Political Contributions to Obtain Government Legal Engagements or Appointments by Judges	230

Maintaining the Integrity of the Profession

Rule   **Page**

8.1   Bar Admission and Disciplinary Matters 232

8.2   Judicial and Legal Officials 233

8.3   Reporting Professional Misconduct 233

8.4   Misconduct 235

8.5   Disciplinary Authority; Choice of Law 236

PREAMBLE:
A LAWYER'S RESPONSIBILITIES

[1] A lawyer is a representative of clients, an officer of the legal system and a public citizen having special responsibility for the quality of justice.

[2] As a representative of clients, a lawyer performs various functions. As advisor, a lawyer provides a client with an informed understanding of the client's legal rights and obligations and explains their practical implications. As advocate, a lawyer zealously asserts the client's position under the rules of the adversary system. As negotiator, a lawyer seeks a result advantageous to the client but consistent with requirements of honest dealing with others. As intermediary between clients, a lawyer seeks to reconcile their divergent interests as an advisor and, to a limited extent, as a spokesperson for each client. A lawyer acts as evaluator by examining a client's legal affairs and reporting about them to the client or to others.

[3] In all professional functions a lawyer should be competent, prompt and diligent. A lawyer should maintain communication with a client concerning the representation. A lawyer should keep in confidence information relating to representation of a client except so far as disclosure is required or permitted by the Rules of Professional Conduct or other law.

[4] A lawyer's conduct should conform to the requirements of the law, both in professional service to clients and in the lawyer's business and personal affairs. A lawyer should use the law's procedures only for legitimate purposes and not to harass or intimidate others. A lawyer should demonstrate respect for the legal system and for those who serve it, including judges, other lawyers and public officials. While it is a lawyer's duty, when necessary, to challenge the rectitude of official action, it is also a lawyer's duty to uphold legal process.

[5] As a public citizen, a lawyer should seek improvement of the law, the administration of justice and the quality of service rendered by the legal profession. As a member of a learned profession, a lawyer should cultivate knowledge of the law beyond its use for clients, employ that knowledge in reform of the law and work to strengthen legal education. A lawyer should be mindful of deficiencies in the administration of justice and of the fact that the poor, and sometimes persons who are not poor, cannot afford adequate legal assistance, and should therefore devote professional time and civic influence in their behalf. A lawyer should aid the legal profession in pursuing these objectives and should help the bar regulate itself in the public interest.

[6] Many of a lawyer's professional responsibilities are prescribed in the Rules of Professional Conduct, as well as substantive and procedural law. However, a lawyer is also guided by personal conscience and the approbation of professional peers. A lawyer should strive to attain the highest level of skill, to improve the law and the legal profession and to exemplify the legal profession's ideals of public service.

[7] A lawyer's responsibilities as a representative of clients, an officer of the legal system and a public citizen are usually harmonious. Thus, when an

opposing party is well represented, a lawyer can be a zealous advocate on behalf of a client and at the same time assume that justice is being done. So also, a lawyer can be sure that preserving client confidences ordinarily serves the public interest because people are more likely to seek legal advice, and thereby heed their legal obligations, when they know their communications will be private.

[8] In the nature of law practice, however, conflicting responsibilities are encountered. Virtually all difficult ethical problems arise from conflict between a lawyer's responsibilities to clients, to the legal system and to the lawyer's own interest in remaining an upright person while earning a satisfactory living. The Rules of Professional Conduct prescribe terms for resolving such conflicts. Within the framework of these Rules, many difficult issues of professional discretion can arise. Such issues must be resolved through the exercise of sensitive professional and moral judgment guided by the basic principles underlying the Rules.

[9] The legal profession is largely self-governing. Although other professions also have been granted powers of self-government, the legal profession is unique in this respect because of the close relationship between the profession and the processes of government and law enforcement. This connection is manifested in the fact that ultimate authority over the legal profession is vested largely in the courts.

[10] To the extent that lawyers meet the obligations of their professional calling, the occasion for government regulation is obviated. Self-regulation also helps maintain the legal profession's independence from government domination. An independent legal profession is an important force in preserving government under law, for abuse of legal authority is more readily challenged by a profession whose members are not dependent on government for the right to practice.

[11] The legal profession's relative autonomy carries with it special responsibilities of self-government. The profession has a responsibility to assure that its regulations are conceived in the public interest and not in furtherance of parochial or self-interested concerns of the bar. Every lawyer is responsible for observance of the Rules of Professional Conduct. A lawyer should also aid in securing their observance by other lawyers. Neglect of these responsibilities compromises the independence of the profession and the public interest which it serves.

[12] Lawyers play a vital role in the preservation of society. The fulfillment of this role requires an understanding by lawyers of their relationship to our legal system. The Rules of Professional Conduct, when properly applied, serve to define that relationship.

SCOPE

[13] The Rules of Professional Conduct are rules of reason. They should be interpreted with reference to the purposes of legal representation and of the law

itself. Some of the Rules are imperatives, cast in the terms "shall" or "shall not." These define proper conduct for purposes of professional discipline. Others, generally cast in the term "may," are permissive and define areas under the Rules in which the lawyer has professional discretion. No disciplinary action should be taken when the lawyer chooses not to act or acts within the bounds of such discretion. Other Rules define the nature of relationships between the lawyer and others. The Rules are thus partly obligatory and disciplinary and partly constitutive and descriptive in that they define a lawyer's professional role. Many of the Comments use the term "should." Comments do not add obligations to the Rules but provide guidance for practicing in compliance with the Rules.

[14] The Rules presuppose a larger legal context shaping the lawyer's role. That context includes court rules and statutes relating to matters of licensure, laws defining specific obligations of lawyers and substantive and procedural law in general. Compliance with the Rules, as with all law in an open society, depends primarily upon understanding and voluntary compliance, secondarily upon reinforcement by peer and public opinion and finally, when necessary, upon enforcement through disciplinary proceedings. The Rules do not, however, exhaust the moral and ethical considerations that should inform a lawyer, for no worthwhile human activity can be completely defined by legal rules. The Rules simply provide a framework for the ethical practice of law.

[15] Furthermore, for purposes of determining the lawyer's authority and responsibility, principles of substantive law external to these Rules determine whether a client-lawyer relationship exists. Most of the duties flowing from the client-lawyer relationship attach only after the client has requested the lawyer to render legal services and the lawyer has agreed to do so. But there are some duties, such as that of confidentiality under Rule 1.6, that may attach when the lawyer agrees to consider whether a client-lawyer relationship shall be established. Whether a client-lawyer relationship exists for any specific purpose can depend on the circumstances and may be a question of fact.

[16] Under various legal provisions, including constitutional, statutory and common law, the responsibilities of government lawyers may include authority concerning legal matters that ordinarily reposes in the client in private client-lawyer relationships. For example, a lawyer for a government agency may have authority on behalf of the government to decide upon settlement or whether to appeal from an adverse judgment. Such authority in various respects is generally vested in the attorney general and the state's attorney in state government, and their federal counterparts, and the same may be true of other government law officers. Also, lawyers under the supervision of these officers may be authorized to represent several government agencies in intragovernmental legal controversies in circumstances where a private lawyer could not represent multiple private clients. They also may have authority to represent the "public interest" in circumstances where a private lawyer would not be authorized to do so. These Rules do not abrogate any such authority.

[17] Failure to comply with an obligation or prohibition imposed by a Rule is a basis for invoking the disciplinary process. The Rules presuppose that disciplinary

assessment of a lawyer's conduct will be made on the basis of the facts and circumstances as they existed at the time of the conduct in question and in recognition of the fact that a lawyer often has to act upon uncertain or incomplete evidence of the situation. Moreover, the Rules presuppose that whether or not discipline should be imposed for a violation, and the severity of a sanction, depend on all the circumstances, such as the willfulness and seriousness of the violation, extenuating factors and whether there have been previous violations.

[18] Violation of a Rule should not give rise to a cause of action nor should it create any presumption that a legal duty has been breached. The Rules are designed to provide guidance to lawyers and to provide a structure for regulating conduct through disciplinary agencies. They are not designed to be a basis for civil liability. Furthermore, the purpose of the Rules can be subverted when they are invoked by opposing parties as procedural weapons. The fact that a Rule is a just basis for a lawyer's self-assessment, or for sanctioning a lawyer under the administration of a disciplinary authority, does not imply that an antagonist in a collateral proceeding or transaction has standing to seek enforcement of the Rule. Accordingly, nothing in the Rules should be deemed to augment any substantive legal duty of lawyers or the extra-disciplinary consequences of violating such a duty.

[19] Moreover, these Rules are not intended to govern or affect judicial application of either the attorney-client or work product privilege. Those privileges were developed to promote compliance with law and fairness in litigation. In reliance on the attorney-client privilege, clients are entitled to expect that communications within the scope of the privilege will be protected against compelled disclosure. The attorney-client privilege is that of the client and not of the lawyer. The fact that in exceptional situations the lawyer under the rules has a limited discretion to disclose a client confidence does not vitiate the proposition that, as a general matter, the client has a reasonable expectation that information relating to the client will not be voluntarily disclosed and that disclosure of such information may be judicially compelled only in accordance with recognized exceptions to the attorney-client and work product privileges.

[20] The lawyer's exercise of discretion not to disclose information under Rule 1.6 should not be subject to reexamination. Permitting such reexamination would be incompatible with the general policy of promoting compliance with law through assurances that communications will be protected against disclosure.

[21] The Comment accompanying each Rule explains and illustrates the meaning and purpose of the Rule. The Preamble and this note on Scope provide general orientation. The Comments are intended as guides to interpretation, but the text of each Rule is authoritative. Research notes were prepared to compare counterparts in the ABA Model Code of Professional Responsibility (adopted 1969, as amended) and to provide selected references to other authorities. The notes have not been adopted, do not constitute part of the Model Rules, and are not intended to affect the application or interpretation of the Rules and Comments.

TERMINOLOGY

"Belief" or "believes" denotes that the person involved actually supposed the fact in question to be true. A person's belief may be inferred from circumstances.

"Consult" or "consultation" denotes communication of information reasonably sufficient to permit the client to appreciate the significance of the matter in question.

"Firm" or "law firm" denotes a lawyer or lawyers in a private firm, lawyers employed in the legal department of a corporation or other organization and lawyers employed in a legal services organization. See Comment, Rule 1.10.

"Fraud" or "fraudulent" denotes conduct having a purpose to deceive and not merely negligent misrepresentation or failure to apprise another of relevant information.

"Knowingly," "known," or "knows" denotes actual knowledge of the fact in question. A person's knowledge may be inferred from circumstances.

"Partner" denotes a member of a partnership and a shareholder in a law firm organized as a professional corporation.

"Reasonable" or "reasonably" when used in relation to conduct by a lawyer denotes the conduct of a reasonably prudent and competent lawyer.

"Reasonable belief" or "reasonably believes" when used in reference to a lawyer denotes that the lawyer believes the matter in question and that the circumstances are such that the belief is reasonable.

"Reasonably should know" when used in reference to a lawyer denotes that a lawyer of reasonable prudence and competence would ascertain the matter in question.

"Substantial" when used in reference to degree or extent denotes a material matter of clear and weighty importance.

CLIENT-LAWYER RELATIONSHIP
RULE 1.1 COMPETENCE

A lawyer shall provide competent representation to a client. Competent representation requires the legal knowledge, skill, thoroughness and preparation reasonably necessary for the representation.

Comment

Legal Knowledge and Skill

[1] In determining whether a lawyer employs the requisite knowledge and skill in a particular matter, relevant factors include the relative complexity and specialized nature of the matter, the lawyer's general experience, the lawyer's training and experience in the field in question, the preparation and study the lawyer is able to give the matter and whether it is feasible to refer the matter to, or associate or consult with, a lawyer of established competence in

the field in question. In many instances, the required proficiency is that of a general practitioner. Expertise in a particular field of law may be required in some circumstances.

[2]   A lawyer need not necessarily have special training or prior experience to handle legal problems of a type with which the lawyer is unfamiliar. A newly admitted lawyer can be as competent as a practitioner with long experience. Some important legal skills, such as the analysis of precedent, the evaluation of evidence and legal drafting, are required in all legal problems. Perhaps the most fundamental legal skill consists of determining what kind of legal problems a situation may involve, a skill that necessarily transcends any particular specialized knowledge. A lawyer can provide adequate representation in a wholly novel field through necessary study. Competent representation can also be provided through the association of a lawyer of established competence in the field in question.

[3]   In an emergency a lawyer may give advice or assistance in a matter in which the lawyer does not have the skill ordinarily required where referral to or consultation or association with another lawyer would be impractical. Even in an emergency, however, assistance should be limited to that reasonably necessary in the circumstances, for ill-considered action under emergency conditions can jeopardize the client's interest.

[4]   A lawyer may accept representation where the requisite level of competence can be achieved by reasonable preparation. This applies as well to a lawyer who is appointed as counsel for an unrepresented person. See also Rule 6.2.

Thoroughness and Preparation

[5]   Competent handling of a particular matter includes inquiry into and analysis of the factual and legal elements of the problem, and use of methods and procedures meeting the standards of competent practitioners. It also includes adequate preparation. The required attention and preparation are determined in part by what is at stake; major litigation and complex transactions ordinarily require more elaborate treatment than matters of lesser consequence.

Maintaining Competence

[6]   To maintain the requisite knowledge and skill, a lawyer should engage in continuing study and education. If a system of peer review has been established, the lawyer should consider making use of it in appropriate circumstances.

Model Code Comparison

DR 6-101(A)(1) provided that a lawyer shall not handle a matter "which he knows or should know that he is not competent to handle, without associating himself with a lawyer who is competent to handle it. "DR 6-101(A)(2) required "preparation adequate in the circumstances." Rule 1.1 more fully particularizes the elements of competence. Whereas DR 6-101(A)(3) prohibited the "[N]eglect of a legal matter," Rule 1.1 does not contain such a prohibition. Instead, Rule 1.1 affirmatively requires the lawyer to be competent.

RULE 1.2 SCOPE OF REPRESENTATION

(a) A lawyer shall abide by a client's decisions concerning the objectives of representation, subject to paragraphs (c), (d) and (e), and shall consult with the client as to the means by which they are to be pursued. A lawyer shall abide by a client's decision whether to accept an offer of settlement of a matter. In a criminal case, the lawyer shall abide by the client's decision, after consultation with the lawyer, as to a plea to be entered, whether to waive jury trial and whether the client will testify.

(b) A lawyer's representation of a client, including representation by appointment, does not constitute an endorsement of the client's political, economic, social or moral views or activities.

(c) A lawyer may limit the objectives of the representation if the client consents after consultation.

(d) A lawyer shall not counsel a client to engage, or assist a client, in conduct that the lawyer knows is criminal or fraudulent, but a lawyer may discuss the legal consequences of any proposed course of conduct with a client and may counsel or assist a client to make a good faith effort to determine the validity, scope, meaning or application of the law.

(e) When a lawyer knows that a client expects assistance not permitted by the rules of professional conduct or other law, the lawyer shall consult with the client regarding the relevant limitations on the lawyer's conduct.

Comment

Scope of Representation

[1]   Both lawyer and client have authority and responsibility in the objectives and means of representation. The client has ultimate authority to determine the purposes to be served by legal representation, within the limits imposed by law and the lawyer's professional obligations. Within those limits, a client also has a right to consult with the lawyer about the means to be used in pursuing those objectives. At the same time, a lawyer is not required to pursue objectives or employ means simply because a client may wish that the lawyer do so. A clear distinction between objectives and means sometimes cannot be drawn, and in many cases the client-lawyer relationship partakes of a joint undertaking. In questions of means, the lawyer should assume responsibility for technical and legal tactical issues, but should defer to the client regarding such questions as the expense to be incurred and concern for third persons who might be adversely affected. Law defining the lawyer's scope of authority in litigation varies among jurisdictions.

[2]   In a case in which the client appears to be suffering mental disability, the lawyer's duty to abide by the client's decisions is to be guided by reference to Rule 1.14.

Independence from Client's Views or Activities

[3] Legal representation should not be denied to people who are unable to afford legal services, or whose cause is controversial or the subject of popular disapproval. By the same token, representing a client does not constitute approval of the client's views or activities.

Services Limited in Objectives or Means

[4] The objectives or scope of services provided by a lawyer may be limited by agreement with the client or by the terms under which the lawyer's services are made available to the client. For example, a retainer may be for a specifically defined purpose. Representation provided through a legal aid agency may be subject to limitations on the types of cases the agency handles. When a lawyer has been retained by an insurer to represent an insured, the representation may be limited to matters related to the insurance coverage. The terms upon which representation is undertaken may exclude specific objectives or means. Such limitations may exclude objectives or means that the lawyer regards as repugnant or imprudent.

[5] An agreement concerning the scope of representation must accord with the Rules of Professional Conduct and other law. Thus, the client may not be asked to agree to representation so limited in scope as to violate Rule 1.1, or to surrender the right to terminate the lawyer's services or the right to settle litigation that the lawyer might wish to continue.

Criminal, Fraudulent and Prohibited Transactions

[6] A lawyer is required to give an honest opinion about the actual consequences that appear likely to result from a client's conduct. The fact that a client uses advice in a course of action that is criminal or fraudulent does not, of itself, make a lawyer a party to the course of action. However, a lawyer may not knowingly assist a client in criminal or fraudulent conduct. There is a critical distinction between presenting an analysis of legal aspects of questionable conduct and recommending the means by which a crime or fraud might be committed with impunity.

[7] When the client's course of action has already begun and is continuing, the lawyer's responsibility is especially delicate. The lawyer is not permitted to reveal the client's wrongdoing, except where permitted by Rule 1.6. However, the lawyer is required to avoid furthering the purpose, for example, by suggesting how it might be concealed. A lawyer may not continue assisting a client in conduct that the lawyer originally supposes is legally proper but then discovers is criminal or fraudulent. Withdrawal from the representation, therefore, may be required.

[8] Where the client is a fiduciary, the lawyer may be charged with special obligations in dealings with a beneficiary.

[9] Paragraph (d) applies whether or not the defrauded party is a party to the transaction. Hence, a lawyer should not participate in a sham transaction; for example, a transaction to effectuate criminal or fraudulent escape of tax liability. Paragraph (d) does not preclude undertaking a criminal defense

incident to a general retainer for legal services to a lawful enterprise. The last clause of paragraph (d) recognizes that determining the validity or interpretation of a statute or regulation may require a course of action involving disobedience of the statute or regulation or of the interpretation placed upon it by governmental authorities.

Model Code Comparison

Paragraph (a) has no counterpart in the Disciplinary Rules of the Model Code. EC 7-7 stated: "In certain areas of legal representation not affecting the merits of the cause or substantially prejudicing the rights of a client, a lawyer is entitled to make decisions on his own. But otherwise the authority to make decisions is exclusively that of the client. . . ." EC 7-8 stated that "[I]n the final analysis, however, the . . . decision whether to forego legally available objectives or methods because of nonlegal factors is ultimately for the client. . . . In the event that the client in a nonadjudicatory matter insists upon a course of conduct that is contrary to the judgment and advice of the lawyer but not prohibited by Disciplinary Rules, the lawyer may withdraw from the employment." DR 7-101(A)(1) provided that a lawyer "shall not intentionally . . . fail to seek the lawful objectives of his client through reasonably available means permitted by law. . . . A lawyer does not violate this Disciplinary Rule, however, by . . . avoiding offensive tactics. . . ."

Paragraph (b) has no counterpart in the Model Code.

With regard to Paragraph (c), DR 7-101(B)(1) provided that a lawyer may, "where permissible, exercise his professional judgment to waive or fail to assert a right or position of his client."

With regard to Paragraph (d), DR 7-102(A)(7) provided that a lawyer shall not "counsel or assist his client in conduct that the lawyer knows to be illegal or fraudulent." DR 7-102(A)(6) provided that a lawyer shall not "participate in the creation or preservation of evidence when he knows or it is obvious that the evidence is false." DR 7-106 provided that a lawyer shall not "advise his client to disregard a standing rule of a tribunal or a ruling of a tribunal . . . but he may take appropriate steps in good faith to test the validity of such rule or ruling." EC 7-5 stated that a lawyer "should never encourage or aid his client to commit criminal acts or counsel his client on how to violate the law and avoid punishment therefore."

With regard to Paragraph (e), DR 2-110(C)(1)(c) provided that a lawyer may withdraw from representation if a client "insists" that the lawyer engage in "conduct that is illegal or that is prohibited under the Disciplinary Rules." DR 9-101(C) provided that "a lawyer shall not state or imply that he is able to influence improperly . . . any tribunal, legislative body or public official."

RULE 1.3 DILIGENCE

A lawyer shall act with reasonable diligence and promptness in representing a client.

Comment

[1] A lawyer should pursue a matter on behalf of a client despite opposition, obstruction or personal inconvenience to the lawyer, and may take whatever lawful and ethical measures are required to vindicate a client's cause or endeavor. A lawyer should act with commitment and dedication to the interests of the client and with zeal in advocacy upon the client's behalf. However, a lawyer is not bound to press for every advantage that might be realized for a client. A lawyer has professional discretion in determining the means by which a matter should be pursued. See Rule 1.2. A lawyer's work load should be controlled so that each matter can be handled adequately.

[2] Perhaps no professional shortcoming is more widely resented than procrastination. A client's interests often can be adversely affected by the passage of time or the change of conditions; in extreme instances, as when a lawyer overlooks a statute of limitations, the client's legal position may be destroyed. Even when the client's interests are not affected in substance, however, unreasonable delay can cause a client needless anxiety and undermine confidence in the lawyer's trustworthiness.

[3] Unless the relationship is terminated as provided in Rule 1.16, a lawyer should carry through to conclusion all matters undertaken for a client. If a lawyer's employment is limited to a specific matter, the relationship terminates when the matter has been resolved. If a lawyer has served a client over a substantial period in a variety of matters, the client sometimes may assume that the lawyer will continue to serve on a continuing basis unless the lawyer gives notice of withdrawal. Doubt about whether a client-lawyer relationship still exists should be clarified by the lawyer, preferably in writing, so that the client will not mistakenly suppose the lawyer is looking after the client's affairs when the lawyer has ceased to do so. For example, if a lawyer has handled a judicial or administrative proceeding that produced a result adverse to the client but has not been specifically instructed concerning pursuit of an appeal, the lawyer should advise the client of the possibility of appeal before relinquishing responsibility for the matter.

Model Code Comparison

DR 6-101(A)(3) required that a lawyer not "[n]eglect a legal matter entrusted to him." EC 6-4 stated that a lawyer should "give appropriate attention to his legal work." Canon 7 stated that "a lawyer should represent a client zealously within the bounds of the law." DR 7-101(A)(1) provided that a lawyer "shall not intentionally . . . fail to seek the lawful objectives of his client through reasonably available means permitted by law and the Disciplinary Rules. . . ." DR 7-101(A)(3) provided that a lawyer "shall not intentionally . . . [p]rejudice or damage his client during the course of the relationship. . . ."

RULE 1.4 COMMUNICATION

(a) A lawyer shall keep a client reasonably informed about the status of a matter and promptly comply with reasonable requests for information.

(b) A lawyer shall explain a matter to the extent reasonably necessary to permit the client to make informed decisions regarding the representation.

Comment

[1]   The client should have sufficient information to participate intelligently in decisions concerning the objectives of the representation and the means by which they are to be pursued, to the extent the client is willing and able to do so. For example, a lawyer negotiating on behalf of a client should provide the client with facts relevant to the matter, inform the client of communications from another party and take other reasonable steps that permit the client to make a decision regarding a serious offer from another party. A lawyer who receives from opposing counsel an offer of settlement in a civil controversy or a proffered plea bargain in a criminal case should promptly inform the client of its substance unless prior discussions with the client have left it clear that the proposal will be unacceptable. See Rule 1.2(a). Even when a client delegates authority to the lawyer, the client should be kept advised of the status of the matter.

[2]   Adequacy of communication depends in part on the kind of advice or assistance involved. For example, in negotiations where there is time to explain a proposal, the lawyer should review all important provisions with the client before proceeding to an agreement. In litigation a lawyer should explain the general strategy and prospects of success and ordinarily should consult the client on tactics that might injure or coerce others. On the other hand, a lawyer ordinarily cannot be expected to describe trial or negotiation strategy in detail. The guiding principle is that the lawyer should fulfill reasonable client expectations for information consistent with the duty to act in the client's best interests, and the client's overall requirements as to the character of representation.

[3]   Ordinarily, the information to be provided is that appropriate for a client who is a comprehending and responsible adult. However, fully informing the client according to this standard may be impracticable, for example, where the client is a child or suffers from mental disability. See Rule 1.14. When the client is an organization or group, it is often impossible or inappropriate to inform every one of its members about its legal affairs; ordinarily, the lawyer should address communications to the appropriate officials of the organization. See Rule 1.13. Where many routine matters are involved, a system of limited or occasional reporting may be arranged with the client. Practical exigency may also require a lawyer to act for a client without prior consultation.

Withholding Information

[4]   In some circumstances, a lawyer may be justified in delaying transmission of information when the client would be likely to react imprudently to an immediate communication. Thus, a lawyer might withhold a psychiatric diagnosis of a client when the examining psychiatrist indicates that disclosure would harm the client. A lawyer may not withhold information to serve the lawyer's own interest or convenience. Rules or court orders governing litigation

may provide that information supplied to a lawyer may not be disclosed to the client. Rule 3.4(c) directs compliance with such rules or orders.

Model Code Comparison

Rule 1.4 has no direct counterpart in the Disciplinary Rules of the Model Code. DR 6-101(A)(3) provided that a lawyer shall not "[n]eglect a legal matter entrusted to him." DR 9-102(B)(1) provided that a lawyer shall "[p]romptly notify a client of the receipt of his funds, securities, or other properties." EC 7-8 stated that a lawyer "should exert his best efforts to insure that decisions of his client are made only after the client has been informed of relevant considerations." EC 9-2 stated that "a lawyer should fully and promptly inform his client of material developments in the matters being handled for the client."

RULE 1.5 FEES

(a)   **A lawyer's fee shall be reasonable. The factors to be considered in determining the reasonableness of a fee include the following:**

(1)   **the time and labor required, the novelty and difficulty of the questions involved, and the skill requisite to perform the legal service properly;**

(2)   **the likelihood, if apparent to the client, that the acceptance of the particular employment will preclude other employment by the lawyer;**

(3)   **the fee customarily charged in the locality for similar legal services;**

(4)   **the amount involved and the results obtained;**

(5)   **the time limitations imposed by the client or by the circumstances;**

(6)   **the nature and length of the professional relationship with the client;**

(7)   **the experience, reputation, and ability of the lawyer or lawyers performing the services; and**

(8)   **whether the fee is fixed or contingent.**

(b)   **When the lawyer has not regularly represented the client, the basis or rate of the fee shall be communicated to the client, preferably in writing, before or within a reasonable time after commencing the representation.**

(c)   **A fee may be contingent on the outcome of the matter for which the service is rendered, except in a matter in which a contingent fee is prohibited by paragraph (d) or other law. A contingent fee agreement shall be in writing and shall state the method by which the fee is to be determined, including the percentage or percentages that shall accrue to the lawyer in the event of settlement, trial or appeal, litigation and other expenses to be deducted from the recovery, and whether such expenses are to be deducted before or after the contingent fee is**

calculated. Upon conclusion of a contingent fee matter, the lawyer shall provide the client with a written statement stating the outcome of the matter and, if there is a recovery, showing the remittance to the client and the method of its determination.

(d)   A lawyer shall not enter into an arrangement for, charge, or collect:

> **(1)   any fee in a domestic relations matter, the payment or amount of which is contingent upon the securing of a divorce or upon the amount of alimony or support, or property settlement in lieu thereof; or**

> **(2)   a contingent fee for representing a defendant in a criminal case.**

(e)   A division of a fee between lawyers who are not in the same firm may be made only if:

> **(1)   the division is in proportion to the services performed by each lawyer or, by written agreement with the client, each lawyer assumes joint responsibility for the representation;**

> **(2)   the client is advised of and does not object to the participation of all the lawyers involved; and**

> **(3)   the total fee is reasonable.**

Comment

Basis or Rate of Fee

[1]   When the lawyer has regularly represented a client, they ordinarily will have evolved an understanding concerning the basis or rate of the fee. In a new client-lawyer relationship, however, an understanding as to the fee should be promptly established. It is not necessary to recite all the factors that underlie the basis of the fee, but only those that are directly involved in its computation. It is sufficient, for example, to state that the basic rate is an hourly charge or a fixed amount or an estimated amount, or to identify the factors that may be taken into account in finally fixing the fee. When developments occur during the representation that render an earlier estimate substantially inaccurate, a revised estimate should be provided to the client. A written statement concerning the fee reduces the possibility of misunderstanding. Furnishing the client with a simple memorandum or a copy of the lawyer's customary fee schedule is sufficient if the basis or rate of the fee is set forth.

Terms of Payment

[2]   A lawyer may require advance payment of a fee, but is obliged to return any unearned portion. See Rule 1.16(d). A lawyer may accept property in payment for services, such as an ownership interest in an enterprise, providing this does not involve acquisition of a proprietary interest in the cause of action or subject matter of the litigation contrary to Rule 1.8(j). However, a fee paid in property instead of money may be subject to special scrutiny because it involves

questions concerning both the value of the services and the lawyer's special knowledge of the value of the property.

[3]   An agreement may not be made whose terms might induce the lawyer improperly to curtail services for the client or perform them in a way contrary to the client's interest. For example, a lawyer should not enter into an agreement whereby services are to be provided only up to a stated amount when it is fore-seeable that more extensive services probably will be required, unless the situation is adequately explained to the client. Otherwise, the client might have to bargain for further assistance in the midst of a proceeding or transac-tion. However, it is proper to define the extent of services in light of the client's ability to pay. A lawyer should not exploit a fee arrangement based primarily on hourly charges by using wasteful procedures. When there is doubt whether a contingent fee is consistent with the client's best interest, the lawyer should offer the client alternative bases for the fee and explain their implications. Applicable law may impose limitations on contingent fees, such as a ceiling on the percentage.

Division of Fee

[4]   A division of fee is a single billing to a client covering the fee of two or more lawyers who are not in the same firm. A division of fee facilitates association of more than one lawyer in a matter in which neither alone could serve the client as well, and most often is used when the fee is contingent and the division is between a referring lawyer and a trial specialist. Paragraph (e) permits the lawyers to divide a fee on either the basis of the proportion of ser-vices they render or by agreement between the participating lawyers if all assume responsibility for the representation as a whole and the client is advised and does not object. It does not require disclosure to the client of the share that each lawyer is to receive. Joint responsibility for the representation entails the obligations stated in Rule 5.1 for purposes of the matter involved.

Disputes over Fees

[5]   If a procedure has been established for resolution of fee disputes, such as an arbitration or mediation procedure established by the bar, the lawyer should conscientiously consider submitting to it. Law may prescribe a procedure for determining a lawyer's fee, for example, in representation of an executor or administrator, a class or a person entitled to a reasonable fee as part of the measure of damages. The lawyer entitled to such a fee and a lawyer represent-ing another party concerned with the fee should comply with the prescribed procedure.

Model Code Comparison

DR 2-106(A) provided that a lawyer "shall not enter into an agreement for, charge, or collect an illegal or clearly excessive fee." DR 2-106(B) provided that a fee is "clearly excessive when, after a review of the facts, a lawyer of ordinary prudence would be left with a definite and firm conviction that the fee is in excess of a reasonable fee." The factors of a reasonable fee in Rule 1.5(a) are substantially identical to those listed in DR 2-106(B). EC 2-17 states that a lawyer "should not charge more than a reasonable fee. . . ."

There was no counterpart to paragraph (b) in the Disciplinary Rules of the Model Code. EC 2-19 stated that it is "usually beneficial to reduce to writing the understanding of the parties regarding the fee, particularly when it is contingent."

There was also no counterpart to paragraph (c) in the Disciplinary Rules of the Model Code. EC 2-20 provided that "[c]ontingent fee arrangements in civil cases have long been commonly accepted in the United States," but that "a lawyer generally should decline to accept employment on a contingent fee basis by one who is able to pay a reasonable fixed fee. . . ."

With regard to paragraph (d), DR 2-106(C) prohibited "a contingent fee in a criminal case." EC 2-20 provided that "contingent fee arrangements in domestic relation cases are rarely justified."

With regard to paragraph (e), DR 2-107(A) permitted division of fees only if: "(1) The client consents to employment of the other lawyer after a full disclosure that a division of fees will be made. (2) The division is in proportion to the services performed and responsibility assumed by each. (3) The total fee does not exceed clearly reasonable compensation. . . ." Paragraph (e) permits division without regard to the services rendered by each lawyer if they assume joint responsibility for the representation.

RULE 1.6 CONFIDENTIALITY OF INFORMATION

(a)   A lawyer shall not reveal information relating to representation of a client unless the client consents after consultation, except for disclosures that are impliedly authorized in order to carry out the representation, and except as stated in paragraph (b).

(b)   A lawyer may reveal such information to the extent the lawyer reasonably believes necessary:

> **(1)   to prevent the client from committing a criminal act that the lawyer believes is likely to result in imminent death or substantial bodily harm; or**

> **(2)   to establish a claim or defense on behalf of the lawyer in a controversy between the lawyer and the client, to establish a defense to a criminal charge or civil claim against the lawyer based upon conduct in which the client was involved, or to respond to allegations in any proceeding concerning the lawyer's representation of the client.**

Comment

[1]   The lawyer is part of a judicial system charged with upholding the law. One of the lawyer's functions is to advise clients so that they avoid any violation of the law in the proper exercise of their rights.

[2]   The observance of the ethical obligation of a lawyer to hold inviolate confidential information of the client not only facilitates the full development of

facts essential to proper representation of the client but also encourages people to seek early legal assistance.

[3] Almost without exception, clients come to lawyers in order to determine what their rights are and what is, in the maze of laws and regulations, deemed to be legal and correct. The common law recognizes that the client's confidences must be protected from disclosure. Based upon experience, lawyers know that almost all clients follow the advice given, and the law is upheld.

[4] A fundamental principle in the client-lawyer relationship is that the lawyer maintain confidentiality of information relating to the representation. The client is thereby encouraged to communicate fully and frankly with the lawyer even as to embarrassing or legally damaging subject matter.

[5] The principle of confidentiality is given effect in two related bodies of law, the attorney-client privilege (which includes the work product doctrine) in the law of evidence and the rule of confidentiality established in professional ethics. The attorney-client privilege applies in judicial and other proceedings in which a lawyer may be called as a witness or otherwise required to produce evidence concerning a client. The rule of client-lawyer confidentiality applies in situations other than those where evidence is sought from the lawyer through compulsion of law. The confidentiality rule applies not merely to matters communicated in confidence by the client but also to all information relating to the representation, whatever its source. A lawyer may not disclose such information except as authorized or required by the Rules of Professional Conduct or other law. See also Scope. The requirement of maintaining confidentiality of information relating to representation applies to government lawyers who may disagree with the policy goals that their representation is designed to advance.

Authorized Disclosure

[6] A lawyer is impliedly authorized to make disclosures about a client when appropriate in carrying out the representation, except to the extent that the client's instructions or special circumstances limit that authority. In litigation, for example, a lawyer may disclose information by admitting a fact that cannot properly be disputed, or in negotiation by making a disclosure that facilitates a satisfactory conclusion.

[7] Lawyers in a firm may, in the course of the firm's practice, disclose to each other information relating to a client of the firm, unless the client has instructed that particular information be confined to specified lawyers.

Disclosure Adverse to Client

[8] The confidentiality rule is subject to limited exceptions. In becoming privy to information about a client, a lawyer may foresee that the client intends serious harm to another person. However, to the extent a lawyer is required or permitted to disclose a client's purposes, the client will be inhibited from revealing facts which would enable the lawyer to counsel against a wrongful course of action. The public is better protected if full and open communication by the client is encouraged than if it is inhibited.

[9] Several situations must be distinguished.

[10] First, the lawyer may not counsel or assist a client in conduct that is criminal or fraudulent. See Rule 1.2(d). Similarly, a lawyer has a duty under

Rule 3.3(a)(4) not to use false evidence. This duty is essentially a special instance of the duty prescribed in Rule 1.2(d) to avoid assisting a client in criminal or fraudulent conduct.

[11] Second, the lawyer may have been innocently involved in past conduct by the client that was criminal or fraudulent. In such a situation the lawyer has not violated Rule 1.2(d), because to "counsel or assist" criminal or fraudulent conduct requires knowing that the conduct is of that character.

[12] Third, the lawyer may learn that a client intends prospective conduct that is criminal and likely to result in imminent death or substantial bodily harm. As stated in paragraph (b)(1), the lawyer has professional discretion to reveal information in order to prevent such consequences. The lawyer may make a disclosure in order to prevent homicide or serious bodily injury which the lawyer reasonably believes is intended by a client. It is very difficult for a lawyer to "know" when such a heinous purpose will actually be carried out, for the client may have a change of mind.

[13] The lawyer's exercise of discretion requires consideration of such factors as the nature of the lawyer's relationship with the client and with those who might be injured by the client, the lawyer's own involvement in the transaction and factors that may extenuate the conduct in question. Where practical, the lawyer should seek to persuade the client to take suitable action. In any case, a disclosure adverse to the client's interest should be no greater than the lawyer reasonably believes necessary to the purpose. A lawyer's decision not to take preventive action permitted by paragraph (b)(1) does not violate this Rule.

Withdrawal

[14] If the lawyer's services will be used by the client in materially furthering a course of criminal or fraudulent conduct, the lawyer must withdraw, as stated in Rule 1.16(a)(1).

[15] After withdrawal the lawyer is required to refrain from making disclosure of the client's confidences, except as otherwise provided in Rule 1.6. Neither this rule nor Rule 1.8(b) nor Rule 1.16(d) prevents the lawyer from giving notice of the fact of withdrawal, and the lawyer may also withdraw or disaffirm any opinion, document, affirmation, or the like.

[16] Where the client is an organization, the lawyer may be in doubt whether contemplated conduct will actually be carried out by the organization. Where necessary to guide conduct in connection with this Rule, the lawyer may make inquiry within the organization as indicated in Rule 1.13(b).

Dispute Concerning a Lawyer's Conduct

[17] Where a legal claim or disciplinary charge alleges complicity of the lawyer in a client's conduct or other misconduct of the lawyer involving representation of the client, the lawyer may respond to the extent the lawyer reasonably

believes necessary to establish a defense. The same is true with respect to a claim involving the conduct or representation of a former client. The lawyer's right to respond arises when an assertion of such complicity has been made.

Paragraph (b)(2) does not require the lawyer to await the commencement of an action or proceeding that charges such complicity, so that the defense may be established by responding directly to a third party who has made such an assertion. The right to defend, of course, applies where a proceeding has been commenced. Where practicable and not prejudicial to the lawyer's ability to establish the defense, the lawyer should advise the client of the third party's assertion and request that the client respond appropriately. In any event, disclosure should be no greater than the lawyer reasonably believes is necessary to vindicate innocence, the disclosure should be made in a manner which limits access to the information to the tribunal or other persons having a need to know it, and appropriate protective orders or other arrangements should be sought by the lawyer to the fullest extent practicable.

[18] If the lawyer is charged with wrongdoing in which the client's conduct is implicated, the rule of confidentiality should not prevent the lawyer from defending against the charge. Such a charge can arise in a civil, criminal or professional disciplinary proceeding, and can be based on a wrong allegedly committed by the lawyer against the client, or on a wrong alleged by a third person; for example, a person claiming to have been defrauded by the lawyer and client acting together. A lawyer entitled to a fee is permitted by paragraph (b)(2) to prove the services rendered in an action to collect it. This aspect of the rule expresses the principle that the beneficiary of a fiduciary relationship may not exploit it to the detriment of the fiduciary. As stated above, the lawyer must make every effort practicable to avoid unnecessary disclosure of information relating to a representation, to limit disclosure to those having the need to know it, and to obtain protective orders or make other arrangements minimizing the risk of disclosure.

Disclosures Otherwise Required or Authorized

[19] The attorney-client privilege is differently defined in various jurisdictions. If a lawyer is called as a witness to give testimony concerning a client, absent waiver by the client, paragraph (a) requires the lawyer to invoke the privilege when it is applicable. The lawyer must comply with the final orders of a court or other tribunal of competent jurisdiction requiring the lawyer to give information about the client.

[20] The Rules of Professional Conduct in various circumstances permit or require a lawyer to disclose information relating to the representation. See Rules 2.2, 2.3, 3.3 and 4.1. In addition to these provisions, a lawyer may be obligated or permitted by other provisions of law to give information about a client. Whether another provision of law supersedes Rule 1.6 is a matter of interpretation beyond the scope of these Rules, but a presumption should exist against such a supersession.

Former Client

[21] The duty of confidentiality continues after the client-lawyer relationship has terminated.

Model Code Comparison

Rule 1.6 eliminates the two-pronged duty under the Model Code in favor of a single standard protecting all information about a client "relating to representation." Under DR 4-101, the requirement applied to information protected by the attorney-client privilege and to information "gained in" the professional relationship that "the client has requested be held inviolate or the disclosure of which would be embarrassing or would be likely to be detrimental to the client." EC 4-4 added that the duty differed from the evidentiary privilege in that it existed "without regard to the nature or source of information or the fact that others share the knowledge." Rule 1.6 imposes confidentiality on information relating to the representation even if it is acquired before or after the relationship existed. It does not require the client to indicate information that is to be confidential, or permit the lawyer to speculate whether particular information might be embarrassing or detrimental.

Paragraph (a) permits a lawyer to disclose information where impliedly authorized to do so in order to carry out the representation. Under DR 4-101(B) and (C), a lawyer was not permitted to reveal "confidences" unless the client first consented after disclosure.

RULE 1.7 CONFLICT OF INTEREST: GENERAL RULE

(a)   A lawyer shall not represent a client if the representation of that client will be directly adverse to another client, unless:

(1)   the lawyer reasonably believes the representation will not adversely affect the relationship with the other client; and

(2)   each client consents after consultation.

(b)   A lawyer shall not represent a client if the representation of that client may be materially limited by the lawyer's responsibilities to another client or to a third person, or by the lawyer's own interests, unless:

(1)   the lawyer reasonably believes the representation will not be adversely affected; and

(2)   the client consents after consultation. When representation of multiple clients in a single matter is undertaken, the consultation shall include explanation of the implications of the common representation and the advantages and risks involved.

Comment

Loyalty to a Client

[1]   Loyalty is an essential element in the lawyer's relationship to a client. An impermissible conflict of interest may exist before representation is undertaken, in which event the representation should be declined. The lawyer should adopt reasonable procedures, appropriate for the size and type of firm and practice, to determine in both litigation and non-litigation matters the parties

and issues involved and to determine whether there are actual or potential conflicts of interest.

[2] If such a conflict arises after representation has been undertaken, the lawyer should withdraw from the representation. See Rule 1.16. Where more than one client is involved and the lawyer withdraws because a conflict arises after representation, whether the lawyer may continue to represent any of the clients is determined by Rule 1.9. See also Rule 2.2(c). As to whether a client-lawyer relationship exists or, having once been established, is continuing, see Comment to Rule 1.3 and Scope.

[3] As a general proposition, loyalty to a client prohibits undertaking representation directly adverse to that client without that client's consent. Paragraph (a) expresses that general rule. Thus, a lawyer ordinarily may not act as advocate against a person the lawyer represents in some other matter, even if it is wholly unrelated. On the other hand, simultaneous representation in unrelated matters of clients whose interests are only generally adverse, such as competing economic enterprises, does not require consent of the respective clients. Paragraph (a) applies only when the representation of one client would be directly adverse to the other.

[4] Loyalty to a client is also impaired when a lawyer cannot consider, recommend or carry out an appropriate course of action for the client because of the lawyer's other responsibilities or interests. The conflict in effect forecloses alternatives that would otherwise be available to the client. Paragraph (b) addresses such situations. A possible conflict does not itself preclude the representation. The critical questions are the likelihood that a conflict will eventuate and, if it does, whether it will materially interfere with the lawyer's independent professional judgment in considering alternatives or foreclose courses of action that reasonably should be pursued on behalf of the client. Consideration should be given to whether the client wishes to accommodate the other interest involved.

Consultation and Consent

[5] A client may consent to representation notwithstanding a conflict. However, as indicated in paragraph (a)(1) with respect to representation directly adverse to a client, and paragraph (b)(1) with respect to material limitations on representation of a client, when a disinterested lawyer would conclude that the client should not agree to the representation under the circumstances, the lawyer involved cannot properly ask for such agreement or provide representation on the basis of the client's consent. When more than one client is involved, the question of conflict must be resolved as to each client. Moreover, there may be circumstances where it is impossible to make the disclosure necessary to obtain consent. For example, when the lawyer represents different clients in related matters and one of the clients refuses to consent to the disclosure necessary to permit the other client to make an informed decision, the lawyer cannot properly ask the latter to consent.

Lawyer's Interests

[6]   The lawyer's own interests should not be permitted to have an adverse effect on representation of a client. For example, a lawyer's need for income should not lead the lawyer to undertake matters that cannot be handled competently and at a reasonable fee. See Rules 1.1 and 1.5. If the probity of a lawyer's own conduct in a transaction is in serious question, it may be difficult or impossible for the lawyer to give a client detached advice. A lawyer may not allow related business interests to affect representation, for example, by referring clients to an enterprise in which the lawyer has an undisclosed interest.

Conflicts in Litigation

[7]   Paragraph (a) prohibits representation of opposing parties in litigation. Simultaneous representation of parties whose interests in litigation may conflict, such as coplaintiffs or codefendants, is governed by paragraph (b). An impermissible conflict may exist by reason of substantial discrepancy in the parties' testimony, incompatibility in positions in relation to an opposing party or the fact that there are substantially different possibilities of settlement of the claims or liabilities in question. Such conflicts can arise in criminal cases as well as civil. The potential for conflict of interest in representing multiple defendants in a criminal case is so grave that ordinarily a lawyer should decline to represent more than one codefendant. On the other hand, common representation of persons having similar interests is proper if the risk of adverse effect is minimal and the requirements of paragraph (b) are met. Compare Rule 2.2 involving intermediation between clients.

[8]   Ordinarily, a lawyer may not act as advocate against a client the lawyer represents in some other matter, even if the other matter is wholly unrelated. However, there are circumstances in which a lawyer may act as advocate against a client. For example, a lawyer representing an enterprise with diverse operations may accept employment as an advocate against the enterprise in an unrelated matter if doing so will not adversely affect the lawyer's relationship with the enterprise or conduct of the suit and if both clients consent upon consultation. By the same token, government lawyers in some circumstances may represent government employees in proceedings in which a government agency is the opposing party. The propriety of concurrent representation can depend on the nature of the litigation. For example, a suit charging fraud entails conflict to a degree not involved in a suit for a declaratory judgment concerning statutory interpretation.

[9]   A lawyer may represent parties having antagonistic positions on a legal question that has arisen in different cases, unless representation of either client would be adversely affected. Thus, it is ordinarily not improper to assert such positions in cases pending in different trial courts, but it may be improper to do so in cases pending at the same time in an appellate court.

Interest of Person Paying for a Lawyer's Service

[10] A lawyer may be paid from a source other than the client, if the client is informed of that fact and consents and the arrangement does not compromise

the lawyer's duty of loyalty to the client. See Rule 1.8(f). For example, when an insurer and its insured have conflicting interests in a matter arising from a liability insurance agreement, and the insurer is required to provide special counsel for the insured, the arrangement should assure the special counsel's professional independence. So also, when a corporation and its directors or employees are involved in a controversy in which they have conflicting interests, the corporation may provide funds for separate legal representation of the directors or employees, if the clients consent after consultation and the arrangement ensures the lawyer's professional independence.

Other Conflict Situations

[11] Conflicts of interest in contexts other than litigation sometimes may be difficult to assess. Relevant factors in determining whether there is potential for adverse effect include the duration and intimacy of the lawyer's relationship with the client or clients involved, the functions being performed by the lawyer, the likelihood that actual conflict will arise and the likely prejudice to the client from the conflict if it does arise. The question is often one of proximity and degree.

[12] For example, a lawyer may not represent multiple parties to a negotiation whose interests are fundamentally antagonistic to each other, but common representation is permissible where the clients are generally aligned in interest even though there is some difference of interest among them.

[13] Conflict questions may also arise in estate planning and estate administration. A lawyer may be called upon to prepare wills for several family members, such as husband and wife, and, depending upon the circumstances, a conflict of interest may arise. In estate administration the identity of the client may be unclear under the law of a particular jurisdiction. Under one view, the client is the fiduciary; under another view the client is the estate or trust, including its beneficiaries. The lawyer should make clear the relationship to the parties involved.

[14] A lawyer for a corporation or other organization who is also a member of its board of directors should determine whether the responsibilities of the two roles may conflict. The lawyer may be called on to advise the corporation in matters involving actions of the directors. Consideration should be given to the frequency with which such situations may arise, the potential intensity of the conflict, the effect of the lawyer's resignation from the board and the possibility of the corporation's obtaining legal advice from another lawyer in such situations. If there is material risk that the dual role will compromise the lawyer's independence of professional judgment, the lawyer should not serve as a director.

Conflict Charged by an Opposing Party

[15] Resolving questions of conflict of interest is primarily the responsibility of the lawyer undertaking the representation. In litigation, a court may raise the question when there is reason to infer that the lawyer has neglected the respon-

sibility. In a criminal case, inquiry by the court is generally required when a lawyer represents multiple defendants. Where the conflict is such as clearly to call in question the fair or efficient administration of justice, opposing counsel may properly raise the question. Such an objection should be viewed with caution, however, for it can be misused as a technique of harassment. See Scope.

Model Code Comparison

DR 5-101(A) provided that "[e]xcept with the consent of his client after full disclosure, a lawyer shall not accept employment if the exercise of his professional judgment on behalf of the client will be or reasonably may be affected by his own financial, business, property, or personal interests." DR 5-105(A) provided that a lawyer "shall decline proffered employment if the exercise of his independent professional judgment in behalf of a client will be or is likely to be adversely affected by the acceptance of the proffered employment, or if it would be likely to involve him in representing differing interests, except to the extent permitted under DR 5-105(C)." DR 5-105(C) provided that "a lawyer may represent multiple clients if it is obvious that he can adequately represent the interest of each and if each consents to the representation after full disclosure of the possible effect of such representation on the exercise of his independent professional judgment on behalf of each." DR 5-107(B) provided that a lawyer "shall not permit a person who recommends, employs, or pays him to render legal services for another to direct or regulate his professional judgment in rendering such services."

Rule 1.7 clarifies DR 5-105(A) by requiring that, when the lawyer's other interests are involved, not only must the client consent after consultation but also that, independent of such consent, the representation reasonably appears not to be adversely affected by the lawyer's other interests. This requirement appears to be the intended meaning of the provision in DR 5-105(C) that "it is obvious that he can adequately represent" the client, and was implicit in EC 5-2, which stated that a lawyer "should not accept proffered employment if his personal interests or desires will, or there is a reasonable probability that they will, affect adversely the advice to be given or services to be rendered the prospective client."

RULE 1.8 CONFLICT OF INTEREST: PROHIBITED TRANSACTIONS

(a)   A lawyer shall not enter into a business transaction with a client or knowingly acquire an ownership, possessory, security or other pecuniary interest adverse to a client unless:

> (1)   the transaction and terms on which the lawyer acquires the interest are fair and reasonable to the client and are fully disclosed and transmitted in writing to the client in a manner which can be reasonably understood by the client;

> (2)   the client is given a reasonable opportunity to seek the advice of independent counsel in the transaction; and

(3)   the client consents in writing thereto.

(b)   A lawyer shall not use information relating to representation of a client to the disadvantage of the client unless the client consents after consultation, except as permitted or required by Rule 1.6 or Rule 3.3.

(c)   A lawyer shall not prepare an instrument giving the lawyer or a person related to the lawyer as parent, child, sibling, or spouse any substantial gift from a client, including a testamentary gift, except where the client is related to the donee.

(d)   Prior to the conclusion of representation of a client, a lawyer shall not make or negotiate an agreement giving the lawyer literary or media rights to a portrayal or account based in substantial part on information relating to the representation.

(e)   A lawyer shall not provide financial assistance to a client in connection with pending or contemplated litigation, except that:

(1)   a lawyer may advance court costs and expenses of litigation, the repayment of which may be contingent on the outcome of the matter; and

(2)   a lawyer representing an indigent client may pay court costs and expenses of litigation on behalf of the client.

(f)   A lawyer shall not accept compensation for representing a client from one other than the client unless:

(1)   the client consents after consultation;

(2)   there is no interference with the lawyer's independence of professional judgment or with the client-lawyer relationship; and

(3)   information relating to representation of a client is protected as required by Rule 1.6.

(g)   A lawyer who represents two or more clients shall not participate in making an aggregate settlement of the claims of or against the clients, or in a criminal case an aggregated agreement as to guilty or nolo contendere pleas, unless each client consents after consultation, including disclosure of the existence and nature of all the claims or pleas involved and of the participation of each person in the settlement.

(h)   A lawyer shall not make an agreement prospectively limiting the lawyer's liability to a client for malpractice unless permitted by law and the client is independently represented in making the agreement, or settle a claim for such liability with an unrepresented client or former client without first advising that person in writing that independent representation is appropriate in connection therewith.

(i)   A lawyer related to another lawyer as parent, child, sibling or spouse shall not represent a client in a representation directly adverse to a person whom the lawyer knows is represented by the other lawyer except upon consent by the client after consultation regarding the relationship.

(j)   A lawyer shall not acquire a proprietary interest in the cause of action or subject matter of litigation the lawyer is conducting for a client, except that the lawyer may:

(1)   acquire a lien granted by law to secure the lawyer's fee or expenses; and

(2)   contract with a client for a reasonable contingent fee in a civil case.

Comment

Transactions Between Client and Lawyer

[1]   As a general principle, all transactions between client and lawyer should be fair and reasonable to the client. In such transactions a review by independent counsel on behalf of the client is often advisable. Furthermore, a lawyer may not exploit information relating to the representation to the client's disadvantage. For example, a lawyer who has learned that the client is investing in specific real estate may not, without the client's consent, seek to acquire nearby property where doing so would adversely affect the client's plan for investment. Paragraph (a) does not, however, apply to standard commercial transactions between the lawyer and the client for products or services that the client generally markets to others, for example, banking or brokerage services, medical services, products manufactured or distributed by the client, and utilities' services. In such transactions, the lawyer has no advantage in dealing with the client, and the restrictions in paragraph (a) are unnecessary and impracticable.

[2]   A lawyer may accept a gift from a client, if the transaction meets general standards of fairness. For example, a simple gift such as a present given at a holiday or as a token of appreciation is permitted. If effectuation of a substantial gift requires preparing a legal instrument such as a will or conveyance, however, the client should have the detached advice that another lawyer can provide. Paragraph (c) recognizes an exception where the client is a relative of the donee or the gift is not substantial.

Literary Rights

[3]   An agreement by which a lawyer acquires literary or media rights concerning the conduct of the representation creates a conflict between the interests of the client and the personal interests of the lawyer. Measures suitable in the representation of the client may detract from the publication value of an account of the representation. Paragraph (d) does not prohibit a lawyer representing a client in a transaction concerning literary property from agreeing that the lawyer's fee shall consist of a share in ownership in the property, if the arrangement conforms to Rule 1.5 and paragraph (j).

Person Paying for a Lawyer's Services

[4]   Paragraph (f) requires disclosure of the fact that the lawyer's services are being paid for by a third party. Such an arrangement must also conform to the

requirements of Rule 1.6 concerning confidentiality and Rule 1.7 concerning conflict of interest. Where the client is a class, consent may be obtained on behalf of the class by court-supervised procedure.

Limiting Liability

[5]   Paragraph (h) is not intended to apply to customary qualifications and limitations in legal opinions and memoranda.

Family Relationships Between Lawyers

[6]   Paragraph (i) applies to related lawyers who are in different firms. Related lawyers in the same firm are governed by Rules 1.7, 1.9, and 1.10. The disqualification stated in paragraph (i) is personal and is not imputed to members of firms with whom the lawyers are associated.

Acquisition of Interest in Litigation

[7]   Paragraph (j) states the traditional general rule that lawyers are prohibited from acquiring a proprietary interest in litigation. This general rule, which has its basis in common law champerty and maintenance, is subject to specific exceptions developed in decisional law and continued in these Rules, such as the exception for reasonable contingent fees set forth in Rule 1.5 and the exception for certain advances of the costs of litigation set forth in paragraph (e).

Model Code Comparison

With regard to paragraph (a), DR 5-104(A) provided that a lawyer "shall not enter into a business transaction with a client if they have differing interests therein and if the client expects the lawyer to exercise his professional judgment therein for the protection of the client, unless the client has consented after full disclosure." EC 5-3 stated that a lawyer "should not seek to persuade his client to permit him to invest in an undertaking of his client nor make improper use of his professional relationship to influence his client to invest in an enterprise in which the lawyer is interested."

With regard to paragraph (b), DR 4-101(B)(3) provided that a lawyer should not use "a confidence or secret of his client for the advantage of himself, or of a third person, unless the client consents after full disclosure."

There was no counterpart to paragraph (c) in the Disciplinary Rules of the Model Code. EC 5-5 stated that a lawyer "should not suggest to his client that a gift be made to himself or for his benefit. If a lawyer accepts a gift from his client, he is peculiarly susceptible to the charge that he unduly influenced or overreached the client. If a client voluntarily offers to make a gift to his lawyer, the lawyer may accept the gift, but before doing so, he should urge that the client secure disinterested advice from an independent, competent person who is cognizant of all the circumstances. Other than in exceptional circumstances, a lawyer should insist that an instrument in which his client desires to name him beneficially be prepared by another lawyer selected by the client."

Paragraph (d) is substantially similar to DR 5-104(B), but refers to "literary or media" rights, a more generally inclusive term than "publication" rights.

Paragraph (e)(1) is similar to DR 5-103(B), but eliminates the requirement that "the client remains ultimately liable for such expenses."

Paragraph (e)(2) has no counterpart in the Model Code.

Paragraph (f) is substantially identical to DR 5-107(A)(1).

Paragraph (g) is substantially identical to DR 5-106.

The first clause of paragraph (h) is similar to DR 6-102(A). There was no counterpart in the Model Code to the second clause of paragraph (h).

Paragraph (i) has no counterpart in the Model Code.

Paragraph (j) is substantially identical to DR 5-103(A).

RULE 1.9 CONFLICT OF INTEREST: FORMER CLIENT

(a)   A lawyer who has formerly represented a client in a matter shall not thereafter represent another person in the same or a substantially related matter in which that person's interests are materially adverse to the interests of the former client unless the former client consents after consultation.

(b)   A lawyer shall not knowingly represent a person in the same or a substantially related matter in which a firm with which the lawyer formerly was associated had previously represented a client

> **(1)   whose interests are materially adverse to that person; and**
>
> **(2)   about whom the lawyer had acquired information protected by Rules 1.6 and 1.9(c) that is material to the matter; unless the former client consents after consultation.**

(c)   A lawyer who has formerly represented a client in a matter or whose present or former firm has formerly represented a client in a matter shall not thereafter:

> **(1)   use information relating to the representation to the disadvantage of the former client except as Rule 1.6 or Rule 3.3 would permit or require with respect to a client, or when the information has become generally known; or**
>
> **(2)   reveal information relating to the representation except as Rule 1.6 or Rule 3.3 would permit or require with respect to a client.**

Comment

[1]   After termination of a client-lawyer relationship, a lawyer may not represent another client except in conformity with this Rule. The principles in Rule 1.7 determine whether the interests of the present and former client are adverse. Thus, a lawyer could not properly seek to rescind on behalf of a new client a contract drafted on behalf of the former client. So also a lawyer who has prosecuted an accused person could not properly represent the accused in a subsequent civil action against the government concerning the same transaction.

[2]   The scope of a "matter" for purposes of this Rule may depend on the facts of a particular situation or transaction. The lawyer's involvement in a matter can also be a question of degree. When a lawyer has been directly involved in a specific transaction, subsequent representation of other clients with materially adverse interests clearly is prohibited. On the other hand, a lawyer who recurrently handled a type of problem for a former client is not precluded from later representing another client in a wholly distinct problem of that type even though the subsequent representation involves a position adverse to the prior client. Similar considerations can apply to the reassignment of military lawyers between defense and prosecution functions within the same military jurisdiction. The underlying question is whether the lawyer was so involved in the matter that the subsequent representation can be justly regarded as a changing of sides in the matter in question.

Lawyers Moving Between Firms

[3]   When lawyers have been associated within a firm but then end their association, the question of whether a lawyer should undertake representation is more complicated. There are several competing considerations. First, the client previously represented by the former firm must be reasonably assured that the principle of loyalty to the client is not compromised. Second, the rule should not be so broadly cast as to preclude other persons from having reasonable choice of legal counsel. Third, the rule should not unreasonably hamper lawyers from forming new associations and taking on new clients after having left a previous association. In this connection, it should be recognized that today many lawyers practice in firms, that many lawyers to some degree limit their practice to one field or another, and that many move from one association to another several times in their careers. If the concept of imputation were applied with unqualified rigor, the result would be radical curtailment of the opportunity of lawyers to move from one practice setting to another and of the opportunity of clients to change counsel.

[4]   Reconciliation of these competing principles in the past has been attempted under two rubrics. One approach has been to seek per se rules of disqualification. For example, it has been held that a partner in a law firm is conclusively presumed to have access to all confidences concerning all clients of the firm. Under this analysis, if a lawyer has been a partner in one law firm and then becomes a partner in another law firm, there may be a presumption that all confidences known by the partner in the first firm are known to all partners in the second firm. This presumption might properly be applied in some circumstances, especially where the client has been extensively represented, but may be unrealistic where the client was represented only for limited purposes. Furthermore, such a rigid rule exaggerates the difference between a partner and an associate in modern law firms.

[5]   The other rubric formerly used for dealing with disqualification is the appearance of impropriety proscribed in Canon 9 of the ABA Model Code of Professional Responsibility. This rubric has a two-fold problem. First, the appearance of impropriety can be taken to include any new client-lawyer

relationship that might make a former client feel anxious. If that meaning were adopted, disqualification would become little more than a question of subjective judgment by the former client. Second, since "impropriety" is undefined, the term "appearance of impropriety" is question-begging. It therefore has to be recognized that the problem of disqualification cannot be properly resolved either by simple analogy to a lawyer practicing alone or by the very general concept of appearance of impropriety.

Confidentiality

[6]   Preserving confidentiality is a question of access to information. Access to information, in turn, is essentially a question of fact in particular circumstances, aided by inferences, deductions or working presumptions that reasonably may be made about the way in which lawyers work together. A lawyer may have general access to files of all clients of a law firm and may regularly participate in discussions of their affairs; it should be inferred that such a lawyer in fact is privy to all information about all the firm's clients. In contrast, another lawyer may have access to the files of only a limited number of clients and participate in discussions of the affairs of no other clients; in the absence of information to the contrary, it should be inferred that such a lawyer in fact is privy to information about the clients actually served but not those of other clients.

[7]   Application of paragraph (b) depends on a situation's particular facts. In such an inquiry, the burden of proof should rest upon the firm whose disqualification is sought.

[8]   Paragraph (b) operates to disqualify the lawyer only when the lawyer involved has actual knowledge of information protected by Rules 1.6 and 1.9(b). Thus, if a lawyer while with one firm acquired no knowledge or information relating to a particular client of the firm, and that lawyer later joined another firm, neither the lawyer individually nor the second firm is disqualified from representing another client in the same or a related matter even though the interests of the two clients conflict. See Rule 1.10(b) for the restrictions on a firm once a lawyer has terminated association with the firm.

[9]   Independent of the question of disqualification of a firm, a lawyer changing professional association has a continuing duty to preserve confidentiality of information about a client formerly represented. See Rules 1.6 and 1.9.

Adverse Positions

[10] The second aspect of loyalty to a client is the lawyer's obligation to decline subsequent representations involving positions adverse to a former client arising in substantially related matters. This obligation requires abstention from adverse representation by the individual lawyer involved, but does not properly entail abstention of other lawyers through imputed disqualification. Hence, this aspect of the problem is governed by Rule 1.9(a). Thus, if a lawyer left one firm for another, the new affiliation would not preclude the firms involved from continuing to represent clients with adverse interests in the same or related matters, so long as the conditions of paragraphs (b) and (c) concerning confidentiality have been met.

[11] Information acquired by the lawyer in the course of representing a client may not subsequently be used or revealed by the lawyer to the disadvantage of the client. However, the fact that a lawyer has once served a client does not preclude the lawyer from using generally known information about that client when later representing another client.

[12] Disqualification from subsequent representation is for the protection of former clients and can be waived by them. A waiver is effective only if there is disclosure of the circumstances, including the lawyer's intended role in behalf of the new client.

[13] With regard to an opposing party's raising a question of conflict of interest, see Comment to Rule 1.7. With regard to disqualification of a firm with which a lawyer is or was formerly associated, see Rule 1.10.

Model Code Comparison

There was no counterpart to this Rule in the Disciplinary Rules of the Model Code. Representation adverse to a former client was sometimes dealt with under the rubric of Canon 9 of the Model Code, which provided: "A lawyer should avoid even the appearance of impropriety." Also applicable were EC 4-6 which stated that the "obligation of a lawyer to preserve the confidences and secrets of his client continues after the termination of his employment" and Canon 5 which stated that "[a] lawyer should exercise independent professional judgment on behalf of a client."

The provision for waiver by the former client in paragraphs (a) and (b) is similar to DR 5-105(C).

The exception in the last clause of paragraph (c)(1) permits a lawyer to use information relating to a former client that is in the "public domain," a use that was also not prohibited by the Model Code, which protected only "confidences and secrets." Since the scope of paragraphs (a) and (b) is much broader than "confidences and secrets," it is necessary to define when a lawyer may make use of information about a client after the client-lawyer relationship has terminated.

RULE 1.10 IMPUTED DISQUALIFICATION: GENERAL RULE

(a)   While lawyers are associated in a firm, none of them shall knowingly represent a client when any one of them practicing alone would be prohibited from doing so by Rules 1.7, 1.8(c), 1.9 or 2.2.

(b)   When a lawyer has terminated an association with a firm, the firm is not prohibited from thereafter representing a person with interests materially adverse to those of a client represented by the formerly associated lawyer and not currently represented by the firm, unless:

(1)   the matter is the same or substantially related to that in which the formerly associated lawyer represented the client; and

(2)   any lawyer remaining in the firm has information pro-tected by Rules 1.6 and 1.9(c) that is material to the matter.

(c)   A disqualification prescribed by this rule may be waived by the affected client under the conditions stated in Rule 1.7.

Comment

Definition of "Firm,"

[1]   For purposes of the Rules of Professional Conduct, the term "firm" includes lawyers in a private firm, and lawyers in the legal department of a corporation or other organization, or in a legal services organization. Whether two or more lawyers constitute a firm within this definition can depend on the specific facts. For example, two practitioners who share office space and occasionally consult or assist each other ordinarily would not be regarded as constituting a firm. However, if they present themselves to the public in a way suggesting that they are a firm or conduct themselves as a firm, they should be regarded as a firm for the purposes of the Rules. The terms of any formal agreement between associated lawyers are relevant in determining whether they are a firm, as is the fact that they have mutual access to information concerning the clients they serve. Furthermore, it is relevant in doubtful cases to consider the under-lying purpose of the Rule that is involved. A group of lawyers could be regarded as a firm for purposes of the rule that the same lawyer should not represent opposing parties in litigation, while it might not be so regarded for purposes of the rule that information acquired by one lawyer is attributed to the other.

[2]   With respect to the law department of an organization, there is ordinarily no question that the members of the department constitute a firm within the meaning of the Rules of Professional Conduct. However, there can be uncertainty as to the identity of the client. For example, it may not be clear whether the law department of a corporation represents a subsidiary or an affiliated corporation, as well as the corporation by which the members of the department are directly employed. A similar question can arise concerning an unincorporated association and its local affiliates.

[3]   Similar questions can also arise with respect to lawyers in legal aid. Lawyers employed in the same unit of a legal service organization constitute a firm, but not necessarily those employed in separate units. As in the case of independent practitioners, whether the lawyers should be treated as associated with each other can depend on the particular rule that is involved, and on the specific facts of the situation.

[4]   Where a lawyer has joined a private firm after having represented the government, the situation is governed by Rule 1.11 (a) and (b); where a lawyer represents the government after having served private clients, the situation is governed by Rule 1.11(c)(1). The individual lawyer involved is bound by the Rules generally, including Rules 1.6, 1.7 and 1.9.

[5]   Different provisions are thus made for movement of a lawyer from one private firm to another and for movement of a lawyer between a private firm and the government. The government is entitled to protection of its client

confidences and, therefore, to the protections provided in Rules 1.6, 1.9 and 1.11. However, if the more extensive disqualification in Rule 1.10 were applied to former government lawyers, the potential effect on the government would be unduly burdensome. The government deals with all private citizens and organizations and, thus, has a much wider circle of adverse legal interests than does any private law firm. In these circumstances, the government's recruitment of lawyers would be seriously impaired if Rule 1.10 were applied to the government. On balance, therefore, the government is better served in the long run by the protections stated in Rule 1.11.

Principles of Imputed Disqualification

[6]   The rule of imputed disqualification stated in paragraph (a) gives effect to the principle of loyalty to the client as it applies to lawyers who practice in a law firm. Such situations can be considered from the premise that a firm of lawyers is essentially one lawyer for purposes of the rules governing loyalty to the client, or from the premise that each lawyer is vicariously bound by the obligation of loyalty owed by each lawyer with whom the lawyer is associated. Paragraph (a) operates only among the lawyers currently associated in a firm. When a lawyer moves from one firm to another, the situation is governed by Rules 1.9(b) and 1.10(b).

[7]   Rule 1.10(b) operates to permit a law firm, under certain circumstances, to represent a person with interests directly adverse to those of a client represented by a lawyer who formerly was associated with the firm. The Rule applies regardless of when the formerly associated lawyer represented the client. However, the law firm may not represent a person with interests adverse to those of a present client of the firm, which would violate Rule 1.7. Moreover, the firm may not represent the person where the matter is the same or substantially related to that in which the formerly associated lawyer represented the client and any other lawyer currently in the firm has material information protected by Rules 1.6 and 1.9(c).

Model Code Comparison

DR 5-105(D) provided that "[i]f a lawyer is required to decline or to withdraw from employment under a Disciplinary Rule, no partner, or associate, or any other lawyer affiliated with him or his firm, may accept or continue such employment."

RULE 1.11 SUCCESSIVE GOVERNMENT AND PRIVATE EMPLOYMENT

(a)   Except as law may otherwise expressly permit, a lawyer shall not represent a private client in connection with a matter in which the lawyer participated personally and substantially as a public officer or employee, unless the appropriate government agency consents after consultation. No lawyer in a firm with which that lawyer is associated may knowingly undertake or continue representation in such a matter unless:

(1)   the disqualified lawyer is screened from any participation in the matter and is apportioned no part of the fee therefrom; and

(2)   written notice is promptly given to the appropriate government agency to enable it to ascertain compliance with the provisions of this rule.

(b)   Except as law may otherwise expressly permit, a lawyer having information that the lawyer knows is confidential government information about a person acquired when the lawyer was a public officer or employee, may not represent a private client whose interests are adverse to that person in a matter in which the information could be used to the material disadvantage of that person. A firm with which that lawyer is associated may undertake or continue representation in the matter only if the disqualified lawyer is screened from any participation in the matter and is apportioned no part of the fee therefrom.

(c)   Except as law may otherwise expressly permit, a lawyer serving as a public officer or employee shall not:

(1)   participate in a matter in which the lawyer participated personally and substantially while in private practice or nongovernmental employment, unless under applicable law no one is, or by lawful delegation may be, authorized to act in the lawyer's stead in the matter; or

(2)   negotiate for private employment with any person who is involved as a party or as lawyer for a party in a matter in which the lawyer is participating personally and substantially, except that a lawyer serving as a law clerk to a judge, other adjudicative officer or arbitrator may negotiate for private employment as permitted by Rule 1.12(b) and subject to the conditions stated in Rule 1.12(b).

(d)   As used in this Rule, the term "matter" includes:

(1)   any judicial or other proceeding, application, request for a ruling or other determination, contract, claim, controversy, investigation, charge, accusation, arrest or other particular matter involving a specific party or parties, and

(2)   any other matter covered by the conflict of interest rules of the appropriate government agency.

(e)   As used in this Rule, the term "confidential government information" means information which has been obtained under governmental authority and which, at the time this rule is applied, the government is prohibited by law from disclosing to the public or has a legal privilege not to disclose, and which is not otherwise available to the public.

Comment

[1]   This Rule prevents a lawyer from exploiting public office for the advantage of a private client. It is a counterpart of Rule 1.10(b), which applies to lawyers moving from one firm to another.

[2] A lawyer representing a government agency, whether employed or specially retained by the government, is subject to the Rules of Professional Conduct, including the prohibition against representing adverse interests stated in Rule 1.7 and the protections afforded former clients in Rule 1.9. In addition, such a lawyer is subject to Rule 1.11 and to statutes and government regulations regarding conflict of interest. Such statutes and regulations may circumscribe the extent to which the government agency may give consent under this Rule.

[3] Where the successive clients are a public agency and a private client, the risk exists that power or discretion vested in public authority might be used for the special benefit of a private client. A lawyer should not be in a position where benefit to a private client might affect performance of the lawyer's professional functions on behalf of public authority. Also, unfair advantage could accrue to the private client by reason of access to confidential government information about the client's adversary obtainable only through the lawyer's government service. However, the rules governing lawyers presently or formerly employed by a government agency should not be so restrictive as to inhibit transfer of employment to and from the government. The government has a legitimate need to attract qualified lawyers as well as to maintain high ethical standards. The provisions for screening and waiver are necessary to prevent the disqualification rule from imposing too severe a deterrent against entering public service.

[4] When the client is an agency of one government, that agency should be treated as a private client for purposes of this Rule if the lawyer thereafter represents an agency of another government, as when a lawyer represents a city and subsequently is employed by a federal agency.

[5] Paragraphs (a)(1) and (b) do not prohibit a lawyer from receiving a salary or partnership share established by prior independent agreement. They prohibit directly relating the lawyer's compensation to the fee in the matter in which the lawyer is disqualified.

[6] Paragraph (a)(2) does not require that a lawyer give notice to the government agency at a time when premature disclosure would injure the client; a requirement for premature disclosure might preclude engagement of the lawyer. Such notice is, however, required to be given as soon as practicable in order that the government agency will have a reasonable opportunity to ascertain that the lawyer is complying with Rule 1.11 and to take appropriate action if it believes the lawyer is not complying.

[7] Paragraph (b) operates only when the lawyer in question has knowledge of the information, which means actual knowledge; it does not operate with respect to information that merely could be imputed to the lawyer.

[8] Paragraphs (a) and (c) do not prohibit a lawyer from jointly representing a private party and a government agency when doing so is permitted by Rule 1.7 and is not otherwise prohibited by law.

[9] Paragraph (c) does not disqualify other lawyers in the agency with which the lawyer in question has become associated.

Model Code Comparison

Paragraph (a) is similar to DR 9-101(B), except that the latter used the terms "in which he had substantial responsibility while he was a public employee." Paragraphs (b), (c), (d) and (e) have no counterparts in the Model Code.

RULE 1.12 FORMER JUDGE OR ARBITRATOR

(a) Except as stated in paragraph (d), a lawyer shall not represent anyone in connection with a matter in which the lawyer participated personally and substantially as a judge or other adjudicative officer, arbitrator or law clerk to such a person, unless all parties to the proceeding consent after consultation.

(b) A lawyer shall not negotiate for employment with any person who is involved as a party or as lawyer for a party in a matter in which the lawyer is participating personally and substantially as a judge or other adjudicative officer or arbitrator. A lawyer serving as a law clerk to a judge, other adjudicative officer or arbitrator may negotiate for employment with a party or lawyer involved in a matter in which the clerk is participating personally and substantially, but only after the lawyer has notified the judge, other adjudicative officer or arbitrator.

(c) If a lawyer is disqualified by paragraph (a), no lawyer in a firm with which that lawyer is associated may knowingly undertake or continue representation in the matter unless:

> **(1) the disqualified lawyer is screened from any participation in the matter and is apportioned no part of the fee therefrom; and**

> **(2) written notice is promptly given to the appropriate tribunal to enable it to ascertain compliance with the provisions of this rule.**

(d) An arbitrator selected as a partisan of a party in a multimember arbitration panel is not prohibited from subsequently representing that party.

Comment

[1] This Rule generally parallels Rule 1.11. The term "personally and substantially" signifies that a judge who was a member of a multimember court, and thereafter left judicial office to practice law, is not prohibited from representing a client in a matter pending in the court, but in which the former judge did not participate. So also the fact that a former judge exercised administrative responsibility in a court does not prevent the former judge from acting as a lawyer in a matter where the judge had previously exercised remote or incidental administrative responsibility that did not affect the merits. Compare the Comment to Rule 1.11. The term "adjudicative officer" includes such officials as judges pro tempore, referees, special masters, hearing officers and other parajudicial officers, and also lawyers who serve as part-time judges. Compliance Canons A(2), B(2) and C of the Model Code of Judicial Conduct

provide that a part-time judge, judge <u>pro tempore</u> or retired judge recalled to active service, may not "act as a lawyer in any proceeding in which he served as a judge or in any other proceeding related thereto." Although phrased differently from this Rule, those rules correspond in meaning.

Model Code Comparison

Paragraph (a) is substantially similar to DR 9-101(A), which provided that a lawyer "shall not accept private employment in a matter upon the merits of which he has acted in a judicial capacity." Paragraph (a) differs, however, in that it is broader in scope and states more specifically the persons to whom it applies. There was no counterpart in the Model Code to paragraphs (b), (c) or (d).

With regard to arbitrators, EC 5-20 stated that "a lawyer [who] has undertaken to act as an impartial arbitrator or mediator, . . . should not thereafter represent in the dispute any of the parties involved." DR 9-101(A) did not permit a waiver of the disqualification applied to former judges by consent of the parties. However, DR 5-105(C) was similar in effect and could be construed to permit waiver.

RULE 1.13 ORGANIZATION AS CLIENT

(a)   A lawyer employed or retained by an organization represents the organization acting through its duly authorized constituents.

(b)   If a lawyer for an organization knows that an officer, employee or other person associated with the organization is engaged in action, intends to act or refuses to act in a matter related to the representation that is a violation of a legal obligation to the organization, or a violation of law which reasonably might be imputed to the organization, and is likely to result in substantial injury to the organization, the lawyer shall proceed as is reasonably necessary in the best interest of the organization. In determining how to proceed, the lawyer shall give due consideration to the seriousness of the violation and its consequences, the scope and nature of the lawyer's representation, the responsibility in the organization and the apparent motivation of the person involved, the policies of the organization concerning such matters and any other relevant considerations. Any measures taken shall be designed to minimize disruption of the organization and the risk of revealing information relating to the representation to persons outside the organization. Such measures may include among others:

(1)   asking reconsideration of the matter;

(2)   advising that a separate legal opinion on the matter be sought for presentation to appropriate authority in the organization; and

(3)   referring the matter to higher authority in the organization, including, if warranted by the seriousness of the matter, referral to the highest authority that can act in behalf of the organization as determined by applicable law.

(c)   If, despite the lawyer's efforts in accordance with paragraph (b), the highest authority that can act on behalf of the organization insists upon action, or a refusal to act, that is clearly a violation of law and is likely to result in substantial injury to the organization, the lawyer may resign in accordance with Rule 1.16.

(d)   In dealing with an organization's directors, officers, employees, members, shareholders or other constituents, a lawyer shall explain the identity of the client when it is apparent that the organization's interests are adverse to those of the constituents with whom the lawyer is dealing.

(e)   A lawyer representing an organization may also represent any of its directors, officers, employees, members, shareholders or other constituents, subject to the provisions of Rule 1.7. If the organization's consent to the dual representation is required by Rule 1.7, the consent shall be given by an appropriate official of the organization other than the individual who is to be represented, or by the shareholders.

Comment

The Entity as the Client

[1]   An organizational client is a legal entity, but it cannot act except through its officers, directors, employees, shareholders and other constituents. Officers, directors, employees and shareholders are the constituents of the corporate organizational client. The duties defined in this Comment apply equally to unincorporated associations. "Other constituents" as used in this Comment means the positions equivalent to officers, directors, employees and shareholders held by persons acting for organizational clients that are not corporations.

[2]   When one of the constituents of an organizational client communicates with the organization's lawyer in that person's organizational capacity, the communication is protected by Rule 1.6. Thus, by way of example, if an organizational client requests its lawyer to investigate allegations of wrongdoing, interviews made in the course of that investigation between the lawyer and the client's employees or other constituents are covered by Rule 1.6. This does not mean, however, that constituents of an organizational client are the clients of the lawyer. The lawyer may not disclose to such constituents information relating to the representation except for disclosures explicitly or impliedly authorized by the organizational client in order to carry out the representation or as otherwise permitted by Rule 1.6.

[3]   When constituents of the organization make decisions for it, the decisions ordinarily must be accepted by the lawyer even if their utility or prudence is doubtful. Decisions concerning policy and operations, including ones entailing serious risk, are not as such in the lawyer's province. However, different considerations arise when the lawyer knows that the organization may be substantially injured by action of a constituent that is in violation of law. In such a circumstance, it may be reasonably necessary for the lawyer to ask the constituent to reconsider the matter. If that fails, or if the matter is of sufficient

seriousness and importance to the organization, it may be reasonably necessary for the lawyer to take steps to have the matter reviewed by a higher authority in the organization. Clear justification should exist for seeking review over the head of the constituent normally responsible for it. The stated policy of the organization may define circumstances and prescribe channels for such review, and a lawyer should encourage the formulation of such a policy. Even in the absence of organization policy, however, the lawyer may have an obligation to refer a matter to higher authority, depending on the seriousness of the matter and whether the constituent in question has apparent motives to act at variance with the organization's interest. Review by the chief executive officer or by the board of directors may be required when the matter is of importance commensurate with their authority. At some point it may be useful or essential to obtain an independent legal opinion.

[4]   In an extreme case, it may be reasonably necessary for the lawyer to refer the matter to the organization's highest authority. Ordinarily, that is the board of directors or similar governing body. However, applicable law may prescribe that under certain conditions highest authority reposes elsewhere, for example, in the independent directors of a corporation.

Relation to Other Rules

[5]   The authority and responsibility provided in paragraph (b) are concurrent with the authority and responsibility provided in other Rules. In particular, this Rule does not limit or expand the lawyer's responsibility under Rule 1.6, 1.8, 1.16, 3.3 or 4.1. If the lawyer's services are being used by an organization to further a crime or fraud by the organization, Rule 1.2(d) can be applicable.

Government Agency

[6]   The duty defined in this Rule applies to governmental organizations. However, when the client is a governmental organization, a different balance may be appropriate between maintaining confidentiality and assuring that the wrongful official act is prevented or rectified, for public business is involved. In addition, duties of lawyers employed by the government or lawyers in military service may be defined by statutes and regulation. Therefore, defining precisely the identity of the client and prescribing the resulting obligations of such lawyers may be more difficult in the government context. Although in some circumstances the client may be a specific agency, it is generally the government as a whole. For example, if the action or failure to act involves the head of a bureau, either the department of which the bureau is a part or the government as a whole may be the client for purpose of this Rule. Moreover, in a matter involving the conduct of government officials, a government lawyer may have authority to question such conduct more extensively than that of a lawyer for a private organization in similar circumstances. This Rule does not limit that authority. See note on Scope.

Clarifying the Lawyer's Role

[7]   There are times when the organization's interest may be or become adverse to those of one or more of its constituents. In such circumstances the

lawyer should advise any constituent, whose interest the lawyer finds adverse to that of the organization of the conflict or potential conflict of interest, that the lawyer cannot represent such constituent, and that such person may wish to obtain independent representation. Care must be taken to assure that the individual understands that, when there is such adversity of interest, the lawyer for the organization cannot provide legal representation for that constituent individual, and that discussions between the lawyer for the organization and the individual may not be privileged.

[8]   Whether such a warning should be given by the lawyer for the organization to any constituent individual may turn on the facts of each case.

Dual Representation

[9]   Paragraph (e) recognizes that a lawyer for an organization may also represent a principal officer or major shareholder.

Derivative Actions

[10] Under generally prevailing law, the shareholders or members of a corporation may bring suit to compel the directors to perform their legal obligations in the supervision of the organization. Members of unincorporated associations have essentially the same right. Such an action may be brought nominally by the organization, but usually is, in fact, a legal controversy over management of the organization.

[11] The question can arise whether counsel for the organization may defend such an action. The proposition that the organization is the lawyer's client does not alone resolve the issue. Most derivative actions are a normal incident of an organization's affairs, to be defended by the organization's lawyer like any other suit. However, if the claim involves serious charges of wrongdoing by those in control of the organization, a conflict may arise between the lawyer's duty to the organization and the lawyer's relationship with the board. In those circumstances, Rule 1.7 governs who should represent the directors and the organization.

Model Code Comparison

There was no counterpart to this Rule in the Disciplinary Rules of the Model Code. EC 5-18 stated that a "lawyer employed or retained by a corporation or similar entity owes his allegiance to the entity and not to a stockholder, director, officer, employee, representative, or other person connected with the entity. In advising the entity, a lawyer should keep paramount its interests and his professional judgment should not be influenced by the personal desires of any person or organization. Occasionally, a lawyer for an entity is requested by a stockholder, director, officer, employee, representative, or other person connected with the entity to represent him in an individual capacity; in such case the lawyer may serve the individual only if the lawyer is convinced that differing interests are not present." EC 5-24 stated that although a lawyer "may be employed by a business corporation with non-lawyers serving as directors or officers, and they necessarily have the right to make decisions of business policy, a lawyer must decline to accept direction of his professional judgment from any layman." DR 5-107(B) provided that a lawyer "shall notpermit a person who ... employs ... him to render legal services for another to direct or regulate his professional judgment in rendering such legal services."

RULE 1.14 CLIENT UNDER A DISABILITY

(a)   When a client's ability to make adequately considered decisions in connection with the representation is impaired, whether because of minority, mental disability or for some other reason, the lawyer shall, as far as reasonably possible, maintain a normal client-lawyer relationship with the client.

(b)   A lawyer may seek the appointment of a guardian or take other protective action with respect to a client only when the lawyer reasonably believes that the client cannot adequately act in the client's own interest.

Comment

[1]   The normal client-lawyer relationship is based on the assumption that the client, when properly advised and assisted, is capable of making decisions about important matters. When the client is a minor or suffers from a mental disorder or disability, however, maintaining the ordinary client-lawyer relationship may not be possible in all respects. In particular, an incapacitated person may have no power to make legally binding decisions. Nevertheless, a client lacking legal competence often has the ability to understand, deliberate upon, and reach conclusions about matters affecting the client's own well-being. Furthermore, to an increasing extent the law recognizes intermediate degrees of competence. For example, children as young as five or six years of age, and certainly those of ten or twelve, are regarded as having opinions that are entitled to weight in legal proceedings concerning their custody. So also, it is recognized that some persons of advanced age can be quite capable of handling routine financial matters while needing special legal protection concerning major transactions.

[2]   The fact that a client suffers a disability does not diminish the lawyer's obligation to treat the client with attention and respect. If the person has no guardian or legal representative, the lawyer often must act as de facto guardian. Even if the person does have a legal representative, the lawyer should as far as possible accord the represented person the status of client, particularly in maintaining communication.

[3]   If a legal representative has already been appointed for the client, the lawyer should ordinarily look to the representative for decisions on behalf of the client. If a legal representative has not been appointed, the lawyer should see to such an appointment where it would serve the client's best interests. Thus, if a disabled client has substantial property that should be sold for the client's benefit, effective completion of the transaction ordinarily requires appointment of a legal representative. In many circumstances, however, appointment of a legal representative may be expensive or traumatic for the client. Evaluation of these considerations is a matter of professional judgment on the lawyer's part.

[4] If the lawyer represents the guardian as distinct from the ward, and is aware that the guardian is acting adversely to the ward's interest, the lawyer may have an obligation to prevent or rectify the guardian's misconduct. See Rule 1.2(d).

Disclosure of the Client's Condition

[5] Rules of procedure in litigation generally provide that minors or persons suffering mental disability shall be represented by a guardian or next friend if they do not have a general guardian. However, disclosure of the client's disability can adversely affect the client's interests. For example, raising the question of disability could, in some circumstances, lead to proceedings for involuntary commitment. The lawyer's position in such cases is an unavoidably difficult one. The lawyer may seek guidance from an appropriate diagnostician.

Model Code Comparison

There was no counterpart to this Rule in the Disciplinary Rules of the Model Code. EC 7-11 stated that the "responsibilities of a lawyer may vary according to the intelligence, experience, mental condition or age of a client. . . . Examples include the representation of an illiterate or an incompetent." EC 7-12 stated that "[a]ny mental or physical condition of a client that renders him incapable of making a considered judgment on his own behalf casts additional responsibilities upon his lawyer. Where an incompetent is acting through a guardian or other legal representative, a lawyer must look to such representative for those decisions which are normally the prerogative of the client to make. If a client under disability has no legal representative, his lawyer may be compelled in court proceedings to make decisions on behalf of the client. If the client is capable of understanding the matter in question or of contributing to the advancement of his interests, regardless of whether he is legally disqualified from performing certain acts, the lawyer should obtain from him all possible aid. If the disability of a client and the lack of a legal representative compel the lawyer to make decisions for his client, the lawyer should consider all circumstances then prevailing and act with care to safeguard and advance the interests of his client. But obviously a lawyer cannot perform any act or make any decision which the law requires his client to perform or make, either acting for himself if competent, or by a duly constituted representative if legally incompetent."

RULE 1.15 SAFEKEEPING PROPERTY

(a) A lawyer shall hold property of clients or third persons that is in a lawyer's possession in connection with a representation separate from the lawyer's own property. Funds shall be kept in a separate account maintained in the state where the lawyer's office is situated, or elsewhere with the consent of the client or third person. Other property shall be identified as such and appropriately safeguarded. Complete records of such account funds and other property shall be

kept by the lawyer and shall be preserved for a period of [five years] after termination of the representation.

(b)   Upon receiving funds or other property in which a client or third person has an interest, a lawyer shall promptly notify the client or third person. Except as stated in this rule or otherwise permitted by law or by agreement with the client, a lawyer shall promptly deliver to the client or third person any funds or other property that the client or third person is entitled to receive and, upon request by the client or third person, shall promptly render a full accounting regarding such property.

(c)   When in the course of representation a lawyer is in possession of property in which both the lawyer and another person claim interests, the property shall be kept separate by the lawyer until there is an accounting and severance of their interests. If a dispute arises concerning their respective interests, the portion in dispute shall be kept separate by the lawyer until the dispute is resolved.

Comment

[1]   A lawyer should hold property of others with the care required of a professional fiduciary. Securities should be kept in a safe deposit box, except when some other form of safekeeping is warranted by special circumstances. All property which is the property of clients or third persons should be kept separate from the lawyer's business and personal property and, if monies, in one or more trust accounts. Separate trust accounts may be warranted when administering estate monies or acting in similar fiduciary capacities.

[2]   Lawyers often receive funds from third parties from which the lawyer's fee will be paid. If there is risk that the client may divert the funds without paying the fee, the lawyer is not required to remit the portion from which the fee is to be paid. However, a lawyer may not hold funds to coerce a client into accepting the lawyer's contention. The disputed portion of the funds should be kept in trust and the lawyer should suggest means for prompt resolution of the dispute, such as arbitration. The undisputed portion of the funds shall be promptly distributed.

[3]   Third parties, such as a client's creditors, may have just claims against funds or other property in a lawyer's custody. A lawyer may have a duty under applicable law to protect such third-party claims against wrongful interference by the client, and accordingly may refuse to surrender the property to the client. However, a lawyer should not unilaterally assume to arbitrate a dispute between the client and the third party. The obligations of a lawyer under this Rule are independent of those arising from activity other than rendering legal services. For example, a lawyer who serves as an escrow agent is governed by the applicable law relating to fiduciaries even though the lawyer does not render legal services in the transaction.

[4]   A "clients' security fund" provides a means through the collective efforts of the bar to reimburse persons who have lost money or property as a result of

dishonest conduct of a lawyer. Where such a fund has been established, a lawyer should participate.

Model Code Comparison

With regard to paragraph (a), DR 9-102(A) provided that "funds of clients" are to be kept in an identifiable bank account in the state in which the lawyer's office is situated. DR 9-102(B)(2) provided that a lawyer shall "identify and label securities and properties of a client . . . and place them in . . . safekeeping. . . ." DR 9-102(B)(3) required that a lawyer "[m]aintain complete records of all funds, securities, and other properties of a client. . . ." Paragraph (a) extends these requirements to property of a third person that is in the lawyer's possession in connection with the representation.

Paragraph (b) is substantially similar to DR 9-102(B)(1), (3) and (4).

Paragraph (c) is similar to DR 9-102(A)(2), except that the requirement regarding disputes applies to property concerning which an interest is claimed by a third person as well as by a client.

RULE 1.16 DECLINING OR TERMINATING REPRESENTATION

(a)   Except as stated in paragraph (c), a lawyer shall not represent a client or, where representation has commenced, shall withdraw from the representation of a client if:

(1)   the representation will result in violation of the rules of professional conduct or other law;

(2)   the lawyer's physical or mental condition materially impairs the lawyer's ability to represent the client; or

(3)   the lawyer is discharged.

(b)   except as stated in paragraph (c), a lawyer may withdraw from representing a client if withdrawal can be accomplished without material adverse effect on the interests of the client, or if:

(1)   the client persists in a course of action involving the lawyer's services that the lawyer reasonably believes is criminal or fraudulent;

(2)   the client has used the lawyer's services to perpetrate a crime or fraud;

(3)   a client insists upon pursuing an objective that the lawyer considers repugnant or imprudent;

(4)   the client fails substantially to fulfill an obligation to the lawyer regarding the lawyer's services and has been given reasonable warning that the lawyer will withdraw unless the obligation is fulfilled;

(5)   the representation will result in an unreasonable financial burden on the lawyer or has been rendered unreasonably difficult by the client; or

(6) other good cause for withdrawal exists.

(c) When ordered to do so by a tribunal, a lawyer shall continue representation notwithstanding good cause for terminating the representation.

(d) Upon termination of representation, a lawyer shall take steps to the extent reasonably practicable to protect a client's interests, such as giving reasonable notice to the client, allowing time for employment of other counsel, surrendering papers and property to which the client is entitled and refunding any advance payment of fee that has not been earned. The lawyer may retain papers relating to the client to the extent permitted by other law.

Comment

[1] A lawyer should not accept representation in a matter unless it can be performed competently, promptly, without improper conflict of interest and to completion.

Mandatory Withdrawal

[2] A lawyer ordinarily must decline or withdraw from representation if the client demands that the lawyer engage in conduct that is illegal or violates the Rules of Professional Conduct or other law. The lawyer is not obliged to decline or withdraw simply because the client suggests such a course of conduct; a client may make such a suggestion in the hope that a lawyer will not be constrained by a professional obligation. When a lawyer has been appointed to represent a client, withdrawal ordinarily requires approval of the appointing authority. See also Rule 6.2. Difficulty may be encountered if withdrawal is based on the client's demand that the lawyer engage in unprofessional conduct. The court may wish an explanation for the withdrawal, while the lawyer may be bound to keep confidential the facts that would constitute such an explanation. The lawyer's statement that professional considerations require termination of the representation ordinarily should be accepted as sufficient.

Discharge

[3] A client has a right to discharge a lawyer at any time, with or without cause, subject to liability for payment for the lawyer's services. Where future dispute about the withdrawal may be anticipated, it may be advisable to prepare a written statement reciting the circumstances.

[4] Whether a client can discharge appointed counsel may depend on applicable law. A client seeking to do so should be given a full explanation of the consequences. These consequences may include a decision by the appointing authority that appointment of successor counsel is unjustified, thus requiring the client to represent himself.

[5] If the client is mentally incompetent, the client may lack the legal capacity to discharge the lawyer, and in any event the discharge may be seriously adverse to the client's interests. The lawyer should make special effort to help

the client consider the consequences and, in an extreme case, may initiate proceedings for a conservatorship or similar protection of the client. See Rule 1.14.

Optional Withdrawal

[6]   A lawyer may withdraw from representation in some circumstances. The lawyer has the option to withdraw if it can be accomplished without material adverse effect on the client's interests. Withdrawal is also justified if the client persists in a course of action that the lawyer reasonably believes is criminal or fraudulent, for a lawyer is not required to be associated with such conduct even if the lawyer does not further it. Withdrawal is also permitted if the lawyer's services were misused in the past even if that would materially prejudice the client. The lawyer also may withdraw where the client insists on a repugnant or imprudent objective.

[7]   A lawyer may withdraw if the client refuses to abide by the terms of an agreement relating to the representation, such as an agreement concerning fees or court costs or an agreement limiting the objectives of the representation.

Assisting the Client upon Withdrawal

[8]   Even if the lawyer has been unfairly discharged by the client, a lawyer must take all reasonable steps to mitigate the consequences to the client. The lawyer may retain papers as security for a fee only to the extent permitted by law.

Whether or not a lawyer for an organization may under certain unusual circumstances have a legal obligation to the organization after withdrawing or being discharged by the organization's highest authority is beyond the scope of these Rules.

Model Code Comparison

With regard to paragraph (a), DR 2-109(A) provided that a lawyer "shall not accept employment . . . if he knows or it is obvious that [the prospective client] wishes to . . . [b]ring a legal action . . . or otherwise have steps taken for him, merely for the purpose of harassing or maliciously injuring any person. . . ." Nor may a lawyer accept employment if the lawyer is aware that the prospective client wishes to "[p]resent a claim or defense . . . that is not warranted under existing law, unless it can be supported by good faith argument for an extension, modification, or reversal of existing law." DR 2-110(B) provided that a lawyer "shall withdraw from employment . . . if:

"(1) He knows or it is obvious that his client is bringing the legal action . . . or is otherwise having steps taken for him, merely for the purpose of harassing or maliciously injuring any person.

"(2) He knows or it is obvious that his continued employment will result in violation of a Disciplinary Rule.

"(3) His mental or physical condition renders it unreasonably difficult for him to carry out the employment effectively.

"(4) He is discharged by his client."

With regard to paragraph (b), DR 2-110(C) permitted withdrawal regardless of the effect on the client if:

"(1)   His client: (a) Insists upon presenting a claim or defense that is not warranted under existing law and cannot be supported by good faith argument for an extension, modification, or reversal of existing law; (b) Personally seeks to pursue an illegal course of conduct; (c) Insists that the lawyer pursue a course of conduct that is illegal or that is prohibited under the Disciplinary Rules; (d) By other conduct renders it unreasonably difficult for the lawyer to carry out his employment effectively; (e) Insists, in a matter not pending before a tribunal, that the lawyer engage in conduct that is contrary to the judgment and advice of the lawyer but not prohibited under the Disciplinary Rules; (f) Deliberately disregards an agreement or obligation to the lawyer as to expenses and fees.

"(2)   His continued employment is likely to result in a violation of a Disciplinary Rule.

"(3)   His inability to work with co-counsel indicates that the best interest of the client likely will be served by withdrawal.

"(4)   His mental or physical condition renders it difficult for him to carry out the employment effectively.

"(5)   His client knowingly and freely assents to termination of his employment.

"(6)   He believes in good faith, in a proceeding pending before a tribunal, that the tribunal will find the existence of other good cause for withdrawal."

With regard to paragraph (c), DR 2-110(A)(1) provided: "If permission for withdrawal from employment is required by the rules of a tribunal, the lawyer shall not withdraw . . . without its permission."

The provisions of paragraph (d) are substantially identical to DR 2-110(A)(2) and (3).

RULE 1.17 SALE OF LAW PRACTICE

A lawyer or a law firm may sell or purchase a law practice, including good will, if the following conditions are satisfied:

(a)   The seller ceases to engage in the private practice of law [in the geographic area] [in the jurisdiction] (a jurisdiction may elect either version) in which the practice has been conducted;

(b)   The practice is sold as an entirety to another lawyer or law firm;

(c)   Actual written notice is given to each of the seller's clients regarding:

(1)   the proposed sale;

(2)   the terms of any proposed change in the fee arrangement authorized by paragraph (d);

(3)   the client's right to retain other counsel or to take possession of the file; and

(4) the fact that the client's consent to the sale will be presumed if the client does not take any action or does not otherwise object within ninety (90) days of receipt of the notice.

If a client cannot be given notice, the representation of that client may be transferred to the purchaser only upon entry of an order so authorizing by a court having jurisdiction. The seller may disclose to the court *in camera* information relating to the representation only to the extent necessary to obtain an order authorizing the transfer of a file.

(d) The fees charged clients shall not be increased by reason of the sale. The purchaser may, however, refuse to undertake the representation unless the client consents to pay the purchaser fees at a rate not exceeding the fees charged by the purchaser for rendering substantially similar services prior to the initiation of the purchase negotiations.

Comment

[1] The practice of law is a profession, not merely a business. Clients are not commodities that can be purchased and sold at will. Pursuant to this Rule, when a lawyer or an entire firm ceases to practice and another lawyer or firm takes over the representation, the selling lawyer or firm may obtain compensation for the reasonable value of the practice as may withdrawing partners of law firms. See Rules 5.4 and 5.6.

Termination of Practice by the Seller

[2] The requirement that all of the private practice be sold is satisfied if the seller in good faith makes the entire practice available for sale to the purchaser. The fact that a number of the seller's clients decide not to be represented by the purchaser but take their matters elsewhere, therefore, does not result in a violation. Neither does a return to private practice as a result of an unanticipated change in circumstances result in a violation. For example, a lawyer who has sold the practice to accept an appointment to judicial office does not violate the requirement that the sale be attendant to cessation of practice if the lawyer later resumes private practice upon being defeated in a contested or a retention election for the office.

[3] The requirement that the seller cease to engage in the private practice of law does not prohibit employment as a lawyer on the staff of a public agency or a legal services entity which provides legal services to the poor, or as in-house counsel to a business.

[4] The Rule permits a sale attendant upon retirement from the private practice of law within the jurisdiction. Its provisions, therefore, accommodate the lawyer who sells the practice upon the occasion of moving to another state. Some states are so large that a move from one locale therein to another is tantamount to leaving the jurisdiction in which the lawyer has engaged in the practice of law. To also accommodate lawyers so situated, states may permit the sale of the practice when the lawyer leaves the geographic area rather than

the jurisdiction. The alternative desired should be indicated by selecting one of the two provided for in Rule 1.17(a).

Single Purchaser

[5] The Rule requires a single purchaser. The prohibition against piecemeal sale of a practice protects those clients whose matters are less lucrative and who might find it difficult to secure other counsel if a sale could be limited to substantial fee-generating matters. The purchaser is required to undertake all client matters in the practice, subject to client consent. If, however, the purchaser is unable to undertake all client matters because of a conflict of interest in a specific matter respecting which the purchaser is not permitted by Rule 1.7 or another rule to represent the client, the requirement that there be a single purchaser is nevertheless satisfied.

Client Confidences, Consent and Notice

[6] Negotiations between seller and prospective purchaser prior to disclosure of information relating to a specific representation of an identifiable client no more violate the confidentiality provisions of Model Rule 1.6 than do preliminary discussions concerning the possible association of another lawyer or mergers between firms, with respect to which client consent is not required. Providing the purchaser access to client-specific information relating to the representation and to the file, however, requires client consent. The Rule provides that before such information can be disclosed by the seller to the purchaser the client must be given actual written notice of the contemplated sale, including the identity of the purchaser and any proposed change in the terms of future representation, and must be told that the decision to consent or make other arrangements must be made within 90 days. If nothing is heard from the client within that time, consent to the sale is presumed.

[7] A lawyer or law firm ceasing to practice cannot be required to remain in practice because some clients cannot be given actual notice of the proposed purchase. Since these clients cannot themselves consent to the purchase or direct any other disposition of their files, the Rule requires an order from a court having jurisdiction authorizing their transfer or other disposition. The Court can be expected to determine whether reasonable efforts to locate the client have been exhausted, and whether the absent client's legitimate interests will be served by authorizing the transfer of the file so that the purchaser may continue the representation. Preservation of client confidences requires that the petition for a court order be considered *in camera*. (A procedure by which such an order can be obtained needs to be established in jurisdictions in which it presently does not exist.)

[8] All the elements of client autonomy, including the client's absolute right to discharge a lawyer and transfer the representation to another, survive the sale of the practice.

Fee Arrangements Between Client and Purchaser

[9] The sale may not be financed by increases in fees charged the clients of the practice. Existing agreements between the seller and the client as to fees and

the scope of the work must be honored by the purchaser, unless the client consents after consultation. The purchaser may, however, advise the client that the purchaser will not undertake the representation unless the client consents to pay the higher fees the purchaser usually charges. To prevent client financing of the sale, the higher fee the purchaser may charge must not exceed the fees charged by the purchaser for substantially similar service rendered prior to the initiation of the purchase negotiations.

[10] The purchaser may not intentionally fragment the practice which is the subject of the sale by charging significantly different fees in substantially similar matters. Doing so would make it possible for the purchaser to avoid the obligation to take over the entire practice by charging arbitrarily higher fees for less lucrative matters, thereby increasing the likelihood that those clients would not consent to the new representation.

Other Applicable Ethical Standards

[11] Lawyers participating in the sale of a law practice are subject to the ethical standards applicable to involving another lawyer in the representation of a client. These include, for example, the seller's obligation to exercise competence in identifying a purchaser qualified to assume the practice and the purchaser's obligation to undertake the representation competently (see Rule 1.1); the obligation to avoid disqualifying conflicts, and to secure client consent after consultation for those conflicts which can be agreed to (see Rule 1.7); and the obligation to protect information relating to the representation (see Rules 1.6 and 1.9).

[12] If approval of the substitution of the purchasing lawyer for the selling lawyer is required by the rules of any tribunal in which a matter is pending, such approval must be obtained before the matter can be included in the sale (see Rule 1.16).

Applicability of the Rule

[13] This Rule applies to the sale of a law practice by representatives of a deceased, disabled or disappeared lawyer. Thus, the seller may be represented by a non-lawyer representative not subject to these Rules. Since, however, no lawyer may participate in a sale of a law practice which does not conform to the requirements of this Rule, the representatives of the seller as well as the purchasing lawyer can be expected to see to it that they are met.

[14] Admission to or retirement from a law partnership or professional association, retirement plans and similar arrangements, and a sale of tangible assets of a law practice, do not constitute a sale or purchase governed by this Rule.

[15] This Rule does not apply to the transfers of legal representation between lawyers when such transfers are unrelated to the sale of a practice.

Model Code Comparison

There was no counterpart to this Rule in the Model Code.

COUNSELOR

RULE 2.1 ADVISOR

In representing a client, a lawyer shall exercise independent professional judgment and render candid advice. In rendering advice, a lawyer may refer not only to law but to other considerations such as moral, economic, social and political factors, that may be relevant to the client's situation.

Comment

Scope of Advice

[1]   A client is entitled to straightforward advice expressing the lawyer's honest assessment. Legal advice often involves unpleasant facts and alternatives that a client may be disinclined to confront. In presenting advice, a lawyer endeavors to sustain the client's morale and may put advice in as acceptable a form as honesty permits. However, a lawyer should not be deterred from giving candid advice by the prospect that the advice will be unpalatable to the client.

[2]   Advice couched in narrowly legal terms may be of little value to a client, especially where practical considerations, such as cost or effects on other people, are predominant. Purely technical legal advice, therefore, can sometimes be inadequate. It is proper for a lawyer to refer to relevant moral and ethical considerations in giving advice. Although a lawyer is not a moral advisor as such, moral and ethical considerations impinge upon most legal questions and may decisively influence how the law will be applied.

[3]   A client may expressly or impliedly ask the lawyer for purely technical advice. When such a request is made by a client experienced in legal matters, the lawyer may accept it at face value. When such a request is made by a client inexperienced in legal matters, however, the lawyer's responsibility as advisor may include indicating that more may be involved than strictly legal considerations.

[4]   Matters that go beyond strictly legal questions may also be in the domain of another profession. Family matters can involve problems within the professional competence of psychiatry, clinical psychology or social work; business matters can involve problems within the competence of the accounting profession or of financial specialists. Where consultation with a professional in another field is itself something a competent lawyer would recommend, the lawyer should make such a recommendation. At the same time, a lawyer's advice at its best often consists of recommending a course of action in the face of conflicting recommendations of experts.

Offering Advice

[5]   In general, a lawyer is not expected to give advice until asked by the client. However, when a lawyer knows that a client proposes a course of action that

is likely to result in substantial adverse legal consequences to the client, duty to the client under Rule 1.4 may require that the lawyer act if the client's course of action is related to the representation. A lawyer ordinarily has no duty to initiate investigation of a client's affairs or to give advice that the client has indicated is unwanted, but a lawyer may initiate advice to a client when doing so appears to be in the client's interest.

Model Code Comparison

There was no direct counterpart to this Rule in the Disciplinary Rules of the Model Code. DR 5-107(B) provided that a lawyer "shall not permit a person who recommends, employs, or pays him to render legal services for another to direct or regulate his professional judgment in rendering such legal services." EC 7-8 stated that "[a]dvice of a lawyer to his client need not be confined to purely legal considerations. . . . In assisting his client to reach a proper decision, it is often desirable for a lawyer to point out those factors which may lead to a decision that is morally just as well as legally permissible. . . . In the final analysis, however, . . . the decision whether to forego legally available objectives or methods because of nonlegal factors is ultimately for the client. . . ."

RULE 2.2 INTERMEDIARY

(a)   A lawyer may act as intermediary between clients if:

(1)   the lawyer consults with each client concerning the implications of the common representation, including the advantages and risks involved, and the effect on the attorney-client privileges, and obtains each client's consent to the common representation;

(2)   the lawyer reasonably believes that the matter can be resolved on terms compatible with the clients' best interests, that each client will be able to make adequately informed decisions in the matter and that there is little risk of material prejudice to the interests of any of the clients if the contemplated resolution is unsuccessful; and

(3)   the lawyer reasonably believes that the common representation can be undertaken impartially and without improper effect on other responsibilities the lawyer has to any of the clients.

(b)   While acting as intermediary, the lawyer shall consult with each client concerning the decisions to be made and the considerations relevant in making them, so that each client can make adequately informed decisions.

(c)   A lawyer shall withdraw as intermediary if any of the clients so requests, or if any of the conditions stated in paragraph (a) is no longer satisfied. Upon withdrawal, the lawyer shall not continue to represent any of the clients in the matter that was the subject of the intermediation.

Comment

[1]   A lawyer acts as intermediary under this Rule when the lawyer represents two or more parties with potentially conflicting interests. A key factor in defining the relationship is whether the parties share responsibility for the lawyer's fee, but the common representation may be inferred from other circumstances. Because confusion can arise as to the lawyer's role where each party is not separately represented, it is important that the lawyer make clear the relationship.

[2]   The Rule does not apply to a lawyer acting as arbitrator or mediator between or among parties who are not clients of the lawyer, even where the lawyer has been appointed with the concurrence of the parties. In performing such a role the lawyer may be subject to applicable codes of ethics, such as the Code of Ethics for Arbitration in Commercial Disputes prepared by a joint Committee of the American Bar Association and the American Arbitration Association.

[3]   A lawyer acts as intermediary in seeking to establish or adjust a relationship between clients on an amicable and mutually advantageous basis; for example, in helping to organize a business in which two or more clients are entrepreneurs, working out the financial reorganization of an enterprise in which two or more clients have an interest, arranging a property distribution in settlement of an estate or mediating a dispute between clients. The lawyer seeks to resolve potentially conflicting interests by developing the parties' mutual interests. The alternative can be that each party may have to obtain separate representation, with the possibility in some situations of incurring additional cost, complication or even litigation. Given these and other relevant factors, all the clients may prefer that the lawyer act as intermediary.

[4]   In considering whether to act as intermediary between clients, a lawyer should be mindful that if the intermediation fails the result can be additional cost, embarrassment and recrimination. In some situations the risk of failure is so great that intermediation is plainly impossible. For example, a lawyer cannot undertake common representation of clients between whom contentious litigation is imminent or who contemplate contentious negotiations. More generally, if the relationship between the parties has already assumed definite antagonism, the possibility that the clients' interests can be adjusted by intermediation ordinarily is not very good.

[5]   The appropriateness of intermediation can depend on its form. Forms of intermediation range from informal arbitration, where each client's case is presented by the respective client and the lawyer decides the outcome, to mediation, to common representation where the clients' interests are substantially though not entirely compatible. One form may be appropriate in circumstances where another would not. Other relevant factors are whether the lawyer subsequently will represent both parties on a continuing basis and whether the situation involves creating a relationship between the parties or terminating one.

Confidentiality and Privilege

[6]   A particularly important factor in determining the appropriateness of intermediation is the effect on client-lawyer confidentiality and the attorney-client privilege. In a common representation, the lawyer is still required both to keep each client adequately informed and to maintain confidentiality of information relating to the representation. See Rules 1.4 and 1.6. Complying with both requirements while acting as intermediary requires a delicate balance. If the balance cannot be maintained, the common representation is improper. With regard to the attorney-client privilege, the prevailing rule is that as between commonly represented clients the privilege does not attach. Hence, it must be assumed that if litigation eventuates between the clients, the privilege will not protect any such communications, and the clients should be so advised.

[7]   Since the lawyer is required to be impartial between commonly represented clients, intermediation is improper when that impartiality cannot be maintained. For example, a lawyer who has represented one of the clients for a long period and in a variety of matters might have difficulty being impartial between that client and one to whom the lawyer has only recently been introduced.

Consultation

[8]   In acting as intermediary between clients, the lawyer is required to consult with the clients on the implications of doing so, and proceed only upon consent based on such a consultation. The consultation should make clear that the lawyer's role is not that of partisanship normally expected in other circumstances.

[9]   Paragraph (b) is an application of the principle expressed in Rule 1.4. Where the lawyer is intermediary, the clients ordinarily must assume greater responsibility for decisions than when each client is independently represented.

Withdrawal

[10] Common representation does not diminish the rights of each client in the client-lawyer relationship. Each has the right to loyal and diligent representation, the right to discharge the lawyer as stated in Rule 1.16, and the protection of Rule 1.9 concerning obligations to a former client.

Model Code Comparison

There was no direct counterpart to this Rule in the Disciplinary Rules of the Model Code. EC 5-20 stated that a "lawyer is often asked to serve as an impartial arbitrator or mediator in matters which involve present or former clients. He may serve in either capacity if he first discloses such present or former relationships." DR 5-105(B) provided that a lawyer "shall not continue multiple employment if the exercise of his independent judgment in behalf of a client will be or is likely to be adversely affected by his representation of another client, or if it would be likely to involve him in representation of differing interests, except to the extent permitted under DR 5-105(C)." DR 5-105(C) provided that "a lawyer may represent multiple clients if it is obvious that he can adequately represent the interests of each and if each consents to the representation after full disclosure of the possible effect of such representation on the exercise of his independent professional judgment on behalf of each."

RULE 2.3 EVALUATION FOR USE BY THIRD PERSONS

(a)   A lawyer may undertake an evaluation of a matter affecting a client for the use of someone other than the client if:

> **(1)   the lawyer reasonably believes that making the evaluation is compatible with other aspects of the lawyer's relationship with the client; and**

> **(2)   the client consents after consultation.**

(b)   Except as disclosure is required in connection with a report of an evaluation, information relating to the evaluation is otherwise protected by Rule 1.6.

Comment

Definition

[1]   An evaluation may be performed at the client's direction but for the primary purpose of establishing information for the benefit of third parties; for example, an opinion concerning the title of property rendered at the behest of a vendor for the information of a prospective purchaser, or at the behest of a borrower for the information of a prospective lender. In some situations, the evaluation may be required by a government agency; for example, an opinion concerning the legality of the securities registered for sale under the securities laws. In other instances, the evaluation may be required by a third person, such as a purchaser of a business.

[2]   Lawyers for the government may be called upon to give a formal opinion on the legality of contemplated government agency action. In making such an evaluation, the government lawyer acts at the behest of the government as the client but for the purpose of establishing the limits of the agency's authorized activity. Such an opinion is to be distinguished from confidential legal advice given agency officials. The critical question is whether the opinion is to be made public.

[3]   A legal evaluation should be distinguished from an investigation of a person with whom the lawyer does not have a client-lawyer relationship. For example, a lawyer retained by a purchaser to analyze a vendor's title to property does not have a client-lawyer relationship with the vendor. So also, an investigation into a person's affairs by a government lawyer, or by special counsel employed by the government, is not an evaluation as that term is used in this Rule. The question is whether the lawyer is retained by the person whose affairs are being examined. When the lawyer is retained by that person, the

general rules concerning loyalty to client and preservation of confidences apply, which is not the case if the lawyer is retained by someone else. For this reason, it is essential to identify the person by whom the lawyer is retained. This should be made clear not only to the person under examination, but also to others to whom the results are to be made available.

Duty to Third Person

[4]   When the evaluation is intended for the information or use of a third person, a legal duty to that person may or may not arise. That legal question is beyond the scope of this Rule. However, since such an evaluation involves a departure from the normal client-lawyer relationship, careful analysis of the situation is required. The lawyer must be satisfied as a matter of professional judgment that making the evaluation is compatible with other functions undertaken in behalf of the client. For example, if the lawyer is acting as advocate in defending the client against charges of fraud, it would normally be incompatible with that responsibility for the lawyer to perform an evaluation for others concerning the same or a related transaction. Assuming no such impediment is apparent, however, the lawyer should advise the client of the implications of the evaluation, particularly the lawyer's responsibilities to third persons and the duty to disseminate the findings.

Access to and Disclosure of Information

[5]   The quality of an evaluation depends on the freedom and extent of the investigation upon which it is based. Ordinarily a lawyer should have whatever latitude of investigation seems necessary as a matter of professional judgment. Under some circumstances, however, the terms of the evaluation may be limited. For example, certain issues or sources may be categorically excluded, or the scope of search may be limited by time constraints or the noncooperation of persons having relevant information. Any such limitations which are material to the evaluation should be described in the report. If after a lawyer has commenced an evaluation, the client refuses to comply with the terms upon which it was understood the evaluation was to have been made, the lawyer's obligations are determined by law, having reference to the terms of the client's agreement and the surrounding circumstances.

Financial Auditors' Requests for Information

[6]   When a question concerning the legal situation of a client arises at the instance of the client's financial auditor and the question is referred to the lawyer, the lawyer's response may be made in accordance with procedures recognized in the legal profession. Such a procedure is set forth in the American Bar Association Statement of Policy Regarding Lawyers' Responses to Auditors' Requests for Information, adopted in 1975.

Model Code Comparison

There was no counterpart to this Rule in the Model Code.

ADVOCATE

RULE 3.1 MERITORIUS CLAIMS AND CONTENTIONS

A lawyer shall not bring or defend a proceeding, or assert or controvert an issue therein, unless there is a basis for doing so that is not frivolous, which includes a good faith argument for an extension, modification or reversal of existing law. A lawyer for the defendant in a criminal proceeding, or the respondent in a proceeding that could result in incarceration, may nevertheless so defend the proceeding as to require that every element of the case be established.

Comment

[1] The advocate has a duty to use legal procedure for the fullest benefit of the client's cause, but also a duty not to abuse legal procedure. The law, both procedural and substantive, establishes the limits within which an advocate may proceed. However, the law is not always clear and never is static. Accordingly, in determining the proper scope of advocacy, account must be taken of the law's ambiguities and potential for change.

[2] The filing of an action or defense or similar action taken for a client is not frivolous merely because the facts have not first been fully substantiated or because the lawyer expects to develop vital evidence only by discovery. Such action is not frivolous even though the lawyer believes that the client's position ultimately will not prevail. The action is frivolous, however, if the client desires to have the action taken primarily for the purpose of harassing or maliciously injuring a person, or, if the lawyer is unable either to make a good faith argument on the merits of the action taken or to support the action taken by a good faith argument for an extension, modification or reversal of existing law.

Model Code Comparison

DR 7-102(A)(1) provided that a lawyer may not "[f]ile a suit, assert a position, conduct a defense, delay a trial, or take other action on behalf of his client when he knows or when it is obvious that such action would serve merely to harass or maliciously injure another." Rule 3.1 is to the same general effect as DR 7-102(A)(1), with three qualifications. First, the test of improper conduct is changed from "merely to harass or maliciously injure another" to the requirement that there be a basis for the litigation measure involved that is "not frivolous." This includes the concept stated in DR 7-102(A)(2) that a lawyer may advance a claim or defense unwarranted by existing law if "it can be supported by good faith argument for an extension, modification, or reversal of existing law." Second, the test in Rule 3.1 is an objective test, whereas DR 7-102(A)(1) applied only if the lawyer "knows or when it is obvious" that the litigation is frivolous. Third, Rule 3.1 has an exception that in a criminal case, or a case in which incarceration of the client may result (for example, certain juvenile proceedings), the lawyer may put the prosecution to its proof even if there is no nonfrivolous basis for defense.

RULE 3.2 EXPEDITING LITIGATION

A lawyer shall make reasonable efforts to expedite litigation consistent with the interests of the client.

Comment

[1]   Dilatory practices bring the administration of justice into disrepute. Delay should not be indulged merely for the convenience of the advocates, or for the purpose of frustrating an opposing party's attempt to obtain rightful redress or repose. It is not a justification that similar conduct is often tolerated by the bench and bar. The question is whether a competent lawyer acting in good faith would regard the course of action as having some substantial purpose other than delay. Realizing financial or other benefit from otherwise improper delay in litigation is not a legitimate interest of the client.

Model Code Comparison

DR 7-101(A)(1) stated that a lawyer does not violate the duty to represent a client zealously "by being punctual in fulfilling all professional commitments." DR 7-102(A)(1) provided that a lawyer "shall not . . . file a suit, assert a position, conduct a defense [or] delay a trial . . . when he knows or when it is obvious that such action would serve merely to harass or maliciously injure another."

RULE 3.3 CANDOR TOWARD THE TRIBUNAL

(a)   **A lawyer shall not knowingly:**

(1)   **make a false statement of material fact or law to a tribunal;**

(2)   **fail to disclose a material fact to a tribunal when disclosure is necessary to avoid assisting a criminal or fraudulent act by the client;**

(3)   **fail to disclose to the tribunal legal authority in the controlling jurisdiction known to the lawyer to be directly adverse to the position of the client and not disclosed by opposing counsel; or**

(4)   **offer evidence that the lawyer knows to be false. If a lawyer has offered material evidence and comes to know of its falsity, the lawyer shall take reasonable remedial measures.**

(b)   **The duties stated in paragraph (a) continue to the conclusion of the proceeding, and apply even if compliance requires disclosure of information otherwise protected by Rule 1.6.**

(c)   **A lawyer may refuse to offer evidence that the lawyer reasonably believes is false.**

(d)   **In an *ex parte* proceeding, a lawyer shall inform the tribunal of all material facts known to the lawyer which will enable the tribunal to make an informed decision, whether or not the facts are adverse.**

Comment

[1]   The advocate's task is to present the client's case with persuasive force. Performance of that duty while maintaining confidences of the client is qualified

by the advocate's duty of candor to the tribunal. However, an advocate does not vouch for the evidence submitted in a cause; the tribunal is responsible for assessing its probative value.

Representations by a Lawyer

[2] An advocate is responsible for pleadings and other documents prepared for litigation, but is usually not required to have personal knowledge of matters asserted therein, for litigation documents ordinarily present assertions by the client, or by someone on the client's behalf, and not assertions by the lawyer. Compare Rule 3.1. However, an assertion purporting to be on the lawyer's own knowledge, as in an affidavit by the lawyer or in a statement in open court, may properly be made only when the lawyer knows the assertion is true or believes it to be true on the basis of a reasonably diligent inquiry. There are circumstances where failure to make a disclosure is the equivalent of an affirmative misrepresentation. The obligation prescribed in Rule 1.2(d) not to counsel a client to commit or assist the client in committing a fraud applies in litigation. Regarding compliance with Rule 1.2(d), see the Comment to that Rule. See also the Comment to Rule 8.4(b).

Misleading Legal Argument

[3] Legal argument based on a knowingly false representation of law constitutes dishonesty toward the tribunal. A lawyer is not required to make a disinterested exposition of the law, but must recognize the existence of pertinent legal authorities. Furthermore, as stated in paragraph (a)(3), an advocate has a duty to disclose directly adverse authority in the controlling jurisdiction which has not been disclosed by the opposing party. The underlying concept is that legal argument is a discussion seeking to determine the legal premises properly applicable to the case.

False Evidence

[4] When evidence that a lawyer knows to be false is provided by a person who is not the client, the lawyer must refuse to offer it regardless of the client's wishes.

[5] When false evidence is offered by the client, however, a conflict may arise between the lawyer's duty to keep the client's revelations confidential and the duty of candor to the court. Upon ascertaining that material evidence is false, the lawyer should seek to persuade the client that the evidence should not be offered or, if it has been offered, that its false character should immediately be disclosed. If the persuasion is ineffective, the lawyer must take reasonable remedial measures.

[6] Except in the defense of a criminal accused, the rule generally recognized is that, if necessary to rectify the situation, an advocate must disclose the existence of the client's deception to the court or to the other party. Such a disclosure can result in grave consequences to the client, including not only a sense of betrayal but also loss of the case and perhaps a prosecution for perjury. But the alternative is that the lawyer cooperate in deceiving the court, thereby subverting the truth-finding process which the adversary system is designed to

implement. See Rule 1.2(d). Furthermore, unless it is clearly understood that the lawyer will act upon the duty to disclose the existence of false evidence, the client can simply reject the lawyer's advice to reveal the false evidence and insist that the lawyer keep silent. Thus the client could in effect coerce the lawyer into being a party to fraud on the court.

Perjury by a Criminal Defendant

[7] Whether an advocate for a criminally accused has the same duty of disclosure has been intensely debated. While it is agreed that the lawyer should seek to persuade the client to refrain from perjurious testimony, there has been dispute concerning the lawyer's duty when that persuasion fails. If the confrontation with the client occurs before trial, the lawyer ordinarily can withdraw. Withdrawal before trial may not be possible, however, either because trial is imminent, or because the confrontation with the client does not take place until the trial itself, or because no other counsel is available.

[8] The most difficult situation, therefore, arises in a criminal case where the accused insists on testifying when the lawyer knows that the testimony is perjurious. The lawyer's effort to rectify the situation can increase the likelihood of the client's being convicted as well as opening the possibility of a prosecution for perjury. On the other hand, if the lawyer does not exercise control over the proof, the lawyer participates, although in a merely passive way, in deception of the court.

[9] Three resolutions of this dilemma have been proposed. One is to permit the accused to testify by a narrative without guidance through the lawyer's questioning. This compromises both contending principles; it exempts the lawyer from the duty to disclose false evidence but subjects the client to an implicit disclosure of information imparted to counsel. Another suggested resolution, of relatively recent origin, is that the advocate be entirely excused from the duty to reveal perjury if the perjury is that of the client. This is a coherent solution but makes the advocate a knowing instrument of perjury. The other resolution of the dilemma is that the lawyer must reveal the client's perjury if necessary to rectify the situation. A criminal accused has a right to the assistance of an advocate, a right to testify and a right of confidential communication with counsel. However, an accused should not have a right to assistance of counsel in committing perjury. Furthermore, an advocate has an obligation, not only in professional ethics but under the law as well, to avoid implication in the commission of perjury or other falsification of evidence. See Rule 1.2(d).

Remedial Measures

[10] If perjured testimony or false evidence has been offered, the advocate's proper course ordinarily is to remonstrate with the client confidentially. If that fails, the advocate should seek to withdraw if that will remedy the situation. If withdrawal will not remedy the situation or is impossible, the advocate should make disclosure to the court. It is for the court then to determine what should be done — making a statement about the matter to the trier of fact, ordering a mistrial or perhaps nothing. If the false testimony was that of the client, the

client may controvert the lawyer's version of their communication when the lawyer discloses the situation to the court. If there is an issue whether the client has committed perjury, the lawyer cannot represent the client in resolution of the issue, and a mistrial may be unavoidable. An unscrupulous client might in this way attempt to produce a series of mistrials and thus escape prosecution. However, a second such encounter could be construed as a deliberate abuse of the right to counsel and as such a waiver of the right to further representation.

Constitutional Requirements

[11] The general rule — that an advocate must disclose the existence of perjury with respect to a material fact, even that of a client — applies to defense counsel in criminal cases, as well as in other instances. However, the definition of the lawyer's ethical duty in such a situation may be qualified by constitutional provisions for due process and the right to counsel in criminal cases. In some jurisdictions these provisions have been construed to require that counsel present an accused as a witness if the accused wishes to testify, even if counsel knows the testimony will be false. The obligation of the advocate under these Rules is subordinate to such a constitutional requirement.

Duration of Obligation

[12] A practical time limit on the obligation to rectify the presentation of false evidence has to be established. The conclusion of the proceeding is a reasonably definite point for the termination of the obligation.

Refusing to Offer Proof Believed to Be False

[13] Generally speaking, a lawyer has authority to refuse to offer testimony or other proof that the lawyer believes is untrustworthy. Offering such proof may reflect adversely on the lawyer's ability to discriminate in the quality of evidence and thus impair the lawyer's effectiveness as an advocate. In criminal cases, however, a lawyer may, in some jurisdictions, be denied this authority by constitutional requirements governing the right to counsel.

Ex Parte Proceedings

[14] Ordinarily, an advocate has the limited responsibility of presenting one side of the matters that a tribunal should consider in reaching a decision; the conflicting position is expected to be presented by the opposing party. However, in any *ex parte* proceeding, such as an application for a temporary restraining order, there is no balance of presentation by opposing advocates. The object of an *ex parte* proceeding is nevertheless to yield a substantially just result. The judge has an affirmative responsibility to accord the absent party just consideration. The lawyer for the represented party has the correlative duty to make disclosures of material facts known to the lawyer and that the lawyer reasonably believes are necessary to an informed decision.

Model Code Comparison

Paragraph (a)(1) is substantially identical to DR 7-102(A)(5), which provided that a lawyer shall not "knowingly make a false statement of law or fact."

Paragraph (a)(2) is implicit in DR 7-102(A)(3), which provided that "a lawyer shall not . . . knowingly fail to disclose that which he is required by law to reveal."

Paragraph (a)(3) is substantially identical to DR 7-106(B)(1).

With regard to paragraph (a)(4), the first sentence of this subparagraph is similar to DR 7-102(A)(4), which provided that a lawyer shall not "knowingly use" perjured testimony or false evidence. The second sentence of paragraph (a)(4) resolves an ambiguity in the Model Code concerning the action required of a lawyer who discovers that the lawyer has offered perjured testimony or false evidence. DR 7-102(A)(4), quoted above, did not expressly deal with this situation, but the prohibition against "use" of false evidence can be construed to preclude carrying through with a case based on such evidence when that fact has become known during the trial. DR 7-102(B)(1), also noted in connection with Rule 1.6, provided that a lawyer "who receives information clearly establishing that . . . [h]is client has . . . perpetrated a fraud upon . . . a tribunal shall [if the client does not rectify the situation] . . . reveal the fraud to the . . . tribunal. . . ." Since use of perjured testimony or false evidence is usually regarded as "fraud" upon the court, DR 7-102(B)(1) apparently required disclosure by the lawyer in such circumstances. However, some states have amended DR 7-102(B)(1) in conformity with an ABA-recommended amendment to provide that the duty of disclosure does not apply when the "information is protected as a privileged communication." This qualification may be empty, for the rule of attorney-client privilege has been construed to exclude communications that further a crime, including the crime of perjury. On this interpretation of DR 7-102(B)(1), the lawyer had a duty to disclose the perjury.

Paragraph (c) confers discretion on the lawyer to refuse to offer evidence that the lawyer "reasonably believes" is false. This gives the lawyer more latitude than DR 7-102(A)(4), which prohibited the lawyer from offering evidence the lawyer "knows" is false.

There was no counterpart in the Model Code to paragraph (d).

RULE 3.4 FAIRNESS TO OPPOSING PARTY AND COUNSEL

A lawyer shall not:

(a)   unlawfully obstruct another party's access to evidence or unlawfully alter, destroy or conceal a document or other material having potential evidentiary value. A lawyer shall not counsel or assist another person to do any such act;

(b)   falsify evidence, counsel or assist a witness to testify falsely, or offer an inducement to a witness that is prohibited by law;

(c)   knowingly disobey an obligation under the rules of a tribunal except for an open refusal based on an assertion that no valid obligation exists;

(d)   in pretrial procedure, make a frivolous discovery request or fail to make reasonably diligent effort to comply with a legally proper discovery request by an opposing party;

(e)   in trial, allude to any matter that the lawyer does not reasonably believe is relevant or that will not be supported by admissible
evidence, assert personal knowledge of facts in issue except when testifying as a witness, or state a personal opinion as to the justness of a
cause, the credibility of a witness, the culpability of a civil litigant or
the guilt or innocence of an accused; or

(f)   request a person other than a client to refrain from voluntarily
giving relevant information to another party unless:

(1)   the person is a relative or an employee or other agent of a
client; and

(2)   the lawyer reasonably believes that the person's interests
will not be adversely affected by refraining from giving such
information.

Comment

[1]   The procedure of the adversary system contemplates that the evidence in
a case is to be marshalled competitively by the contending parties. Fair competition in the adversary system is secured by prohibitions against destruction or
concealment of evidence, improperly influencing witnesses, obstructive tactics
in discovery procedure, and the like.

[2]   Documents and other items of evidence are often essential to establish a
claim or defense. Subject to evidentiary privileges, the right of an opposing
party, including the government, to obtain evidence through discovery or
subpoena is an important procedural right. The exercise of that right can be
frustrated if relevant material is altered, concealed or destroyed. Applicable
law in many jurisdictions makes it an offense to destroy material for purpose
of impairing its availability in a pending proceeding or one whose commencement can be foreseen. Falsifying evidence is also generally a criminal offense.
Paragraph (a) applies to evidentiary material generally, including computerized information.

[3]   With regard to paragraph (b), it is not improper to pay a witness's expenses
or to compensate an expert witness on terms permitted by law. The common
law rule in most jurisdictions is that it is improper to pay an occurrence witness any fee for testifying and that it is improper to pay an expert witness a
contingent fee.

[4]   Paragraph (f) permits a lawyer to advise employees of a client to refrain
from giving information to another party, for the employees may identify their
interests with those of the client. See also Rule 4.2.

Model Code Comparison

With regard to paragraph (a), DR 7-109(A) provided that a lawyer "shall not
suppress any evidence that he or his client has a legal obligation to reveal."
DR 7-109(B) provided that a lawyer "shall not advise or cause a person to
secrete himself . . . for the purpose of making him unavailable as a witness. . . ."
DR 7-106(C)(7) provided that a lawyer shall not "[i]ntentionally or habitually
violate any established rule of procedure or of evidence."

With regard to paragraph (b), DR 7-102(A)(6) provided that a lawyer shall not participate "in the creation or preservation of evidence when he knows or it is obvious that the evidence is false." DR 7-109(C) provided that a lawyer "shall not pay, offer to pay, or acquiesce in the payment of compensation to a witness contingent upon the content of his testimony or the outcome of the case. But a lawyer may advance, guarantee or acquiesce in the payment of:

(1) Expenses reasonably incurred by a witness in attending or testifying;

(2) Reasonable compensation to a witness for his loss of time in attending or testifying; (or) (3) A reasonable fee for the professional services of an expert witness." EC 7-28 stated that witnesses "should always testify truthfully and should be free from any financial inducements that might tempt them to do otherwise."

Paragraph (c) is substantially similar to DR 7-106(A), which provided that "A lawyer shall not disregard . . . a standing rule of a tribunal or a ruling of a tribunal made in the course of a proceeding, but he may take appropriate steps in good faith to test the validity of such rule or ruling."

Paragraph (d) has no counterpart in the Model Code.

Paragraph (e) substantially incorporates DR 7-106(C)(1), (2), (3) and (4). DR 7-106(C)(2) proscribed asking a question "intended to degrade a witness or other person," a matter dealt with in Rule 4.4. DR 7-106(C)(5), providing that a lawyer shall not "fail to comply with known local customs of courtesy or practice," was too vague to be a rule of conduct enforceable as law.

With regard to paragraph (f), DR 7-104(A)(2) provided that a lawyer shall not "give advice to a person who is not represented . . . other than the advice to secure counsel, if the interests of such person are or have a reasonable possibility of being in conflict with the interests of his client."

RULE 3.5 IMPARTIALITY AND DECORUM OF THE TRIBUNAL

A lawyer shall not:

(a) seek to influence a judge, juror, prospective juror or other official by means prohibited by law;

(b) communicate *ex parte* with such a person except as permitted by law; or

(c) engage in conduct intended to disrupt a tribunal.

Comment

[1] Many forms of improper influence upon a tribunal are proscribed by criminal law. Others are specified in the ABA Model Code of Judicial Conduct, with which an advocate should be familiar. A lawyer is required to avoid contributing to a violation of such provisions.

[2] The advocate's function is to present evidence and argument so that the cause may be decided according to law. Refraining from abusive or obstreperous conduct is a corollary of the advocate's right to speak on behalf of litigants. A lawyer may stand firm against abuse by a judge but should avoid

reciprocation; the judge's default is no justification for similar dereliction by an advocate. An advocate can present the cause, protect the record for subsequent review and preserve professional integrity by patient firmness no less effectively than by belligerence or theatrics.

Model Code Comparison

With regard to paragraphs (a) and (b), DR 7-108(A) provided that "[b]efore the trial of a case a lawyer . . . shall not communicate with . . . anyone he knows to be a member of the venire. . . ." DR 7-108(B) provided that during the trial of a case a lawyer "shall not communicate with . . . any member of the jury." DR 7-110(B) provided that a lawyer shall not "communicate . . . as to the merits of the cause with a judge or an official before whom the proceeding is pending, except . . . upon adequate notice to opposing counsel," or as "otherwise authorized by law."

With regard to paragraph (c), DR 7-106(C)(6) provided that a lawyer shall not engage in "undignified or discourteous conduct which is degrading to a tribunal."

RULE 3.6 TRIAL PUBLICITY

(a)   A lawyer who is participating or has participated in the investigation or litigation of a matter shall not make an extrajudicial statement that a reasonable person would expect to be disseminated by means of public communication if the lawyer knows or reasonably should know that it will have a substantial likelihood of materially prejudicing an adjudicative proceeding in the matter.

(b)   Notwithstanding paragraph (a), a lawyer may state:

(1)   the claim, offense or defense involved and, except when prohibited by law, the identity of the persons involved;

(2)   information contained in a public record;

(3)   that an investigation of a matter is in progress;

(4)   the scheduling or result of any step in litigation;

(5)   a request for assistance in obtaining evidence and information necessary thereto;

(6)   a warning of danger concerning the behavior of a person involved, when there is reason to believe that there exists the likelihood of substantial harm to an individual or to the public interest; and

(7)   in a criminal case, in addition to subparagraphs (1) through (6):

(i)   the identity, residence, occupation and family status of the accused;

(ii)   if the accused has not been apprehended, information necessary to aid in apprehension of that person;

(iii)   the fact, time and place of arrest; and

(iv) the identity of investigating and arresting officers or agencies and the length of the investigation.

(c) Notwithstanding paragraph (a), a lawyer may make a statement that a reasonable lawyer would believe is required to protect a client from the substantial undue prejudicial effect of recent publicity not initiated by the lawyer or the lawyer's client. A statement made pursuant to this paragraph shall be limited to such information as is necessary to mitigate the recent adverse publicity.

(d) No lawyer associated in a firm or government agency with a lawyer subject to paragraph (a) shall make a statement prohibited by paragraph (a).

Comment

[1]   It is difficult to strike a balance between protecting the right to a fair trial and safeguarding the right of free expression. Preserving the right to a fair trial necessarily entails some curtailment of the information that may be disseminated about a party prior to trial, particularly where trial by jury is involved. If there were no such limits, the result would be the practical nullification of the protective effect of the rules of forensic decorum and the exclusionary rules of evidence. On the other hand, there are vital social interests served by the free dissemination of information about events having legal consequences and about legal proceedings themselves. The public has a right to know about threats to its safety and measures aimed at assuring its security. It also has a legitimate interest in the conduct of judicial proceedings, particularly in matters of general public concern. Furthermore, the subject matter of legal proceedings is often of direct significance in debate and deliberation over questions of public policy.

[2]   Special rules of confidentiality may validly govern proceedings in juvenile, domestic relations and mental disability proceedings, and perhaps other types of litigation. Rule 3.4(c) requires compliance with such rules.

[3]   The Rule sets forth a basic general prohibition against a lawyer's making statements that the lawyer knows or should know will have a substantial likelihood of materially prejudicing an adjudicative proceeding. Recognizing that the public value of informed commentary is great and the likelihood of prejudice to a proceeding by the commentary of a lawyer who is not involved in the proceeding is small, the rule applies only to lawyers who are, or who have been involved in the investigation or litigation of a case, and their associates.

[4]   Paragraph (b) identifies specific matters about which a lawyer's statements would not ordinarily be considered to present a substantial likelihood of material prejudice, and should not in any event be considered prohibited by the general prohibition of paragraph (a). Paragraph (b) is not intended to be an exhaustive listing of the subjects upon which a lawyer may make a statement, but statements on other matters may be subject to paragraph (a).

[5]   There are, on the other hand, certain subjects which are more likely than not to have a material prejudicial effect on a proceeding, particularly when

they refer to a civil matter triable to a jury, a criminal matter, or any other proceeding that could result in incarceration. These subjects relate to:

(1)   the character, credibility, reputation or criminal record of a party, suspect in a criminal investigation or witness, or the identity of a witness, or the expected testimony of a party or witness;

(2)   in a criminal case or proceeding that could result in incarceration, the possibility of a plea of guilty to the offense or the existence or contents of any confession, admission, or statement given by a defendant or suspect or that person's refusal or failure to make a statement;

(3)   the performance or results of any examination or test or the refusal or failure of a person to submit to an examination or test, or the identity or nature of physical evidence expected to be presented;

(4)   any opinion as to the guilt or innocence of a defendant or suspect in a criminal case or proceeding that could result in incarceration;

(5)   information that the lawyer knows or reasonably should know is likely to be inadmissible as evidence in a trial and that would, if disclosed, create a substantial risk of prejudicing an impartial trial; or

(6)   the fact that a defendant has been charged with a crime, unless there is included therein a statement explaining that the charge is merely an accusation and that the defendant is presumed innocent until and unless proven guilty.

[6]   Another relevant factor in determining prejudice is the nature of the proceeding involved. Criminal jury trials will be most sensitive to extrajudicial speech. Civil trials may be less sensitive. Non-jury hearings and arbitration proceedings may be even less affected. The Rule will still place limitations on prejudicial comments in these cases, but the likelihood of prejudice may be different depending on the type of proceeding.

[7]   Finally, extrajudicial statements that might otherwise raise a question under this Rule may be permissible when they are made in response to statements made publicly by another party, another party's lawyer, or third persons, where a reasonable lawyer would believe a public response is required in order to avoid prejudice to the lawyer's client. When prejudicial statements have been publicly made by others, responsive statements may have the salutary effect of lessening any resulting adverse impact on the adjudicative proceeding. Such responsive statements should be limited to contain only such information as is necessary to mitigate undue prejudice created by the statements made by others.

Model Code Comparison

Rule 3.6 is similar to DR 7-107, except as follows: First, Rule 3.6 adopts the general criterion of "substantial likelihood of materially prejudicing an adjudicative proceeding" to describe impermissible conduct. Second, Rule 3.6 makes clear that only lawyers who are, or have been involved in a proceeding, or their associates, are subject to the Rule. Third, Rule 3.6 omits the particulars in DR 7-107(b), transforming them instead into an illustrative compilation as part of the Rule's commentary that is intended to give fair notice of the kinds of statements that are generally thought to be more likely than other kinds of statements to pose unacceptable dangers to the fair administration of justice. Whether any statement will have a substantial likelihood of materially prejudicially an adjudicatory proceeding will depend upon the facts of each case. The particulars of DR 7-107(c) are retained in Rule 3.6(b), except DR 7-107(C)(7), which provided that a lawyer may reveal "[a]t the time of seizure, a description of the physical evidence seized, other than a confession, admission or statement." Such revelations may be substantially prejudicial and are frequently the subject of pretrial suppression motions whose success would be undermined by disclosure of the suppressed evidence to the press. Finally, Rule 3.6 authorizes a lawyer to protect a client by making a limited reply to adverse publicity substantially prejudicial to the client.

RULE 3.7 LAWYER AS WITNESS

(a)   A lawyer shall not act as advocate at a trial in which the lawyer is likely to be a necessary witness except where:

(1)   the testimony relates to an uncontested issue;

(2)   the testimony relates to the nature and value of legal services rendered in the case; or

(3)   disqualification of the lawyer would work substantial hardship on the client.

(b)   A lawyer may act as advocate in a trial in which another lawyer in the lawyer's firm is likely to be called as a witness unless precluded from doing so by Rule 1.7 or Rule 1.9.

Comment

[1]   Combining the roles of advocate and witness can prejudice the opposing party and can involve a conflict of interest between the lawyer and client.

[2]   The opposing party has proper objection where the combination of roles may prejudice that party's rights in the litigation. A witness is required to testify on the basis of personal knowledge, while an advocate is expected to explain and comment on evidence given by others. It may not be clear whether a statement by an advocate-witness should be taken as proof or as an analysis of the proof.

[3]   Paragraph (a)(1) recognizes that if the testimony will be uncontested, the ambiguities in the dual role are purely theoretical. Paragraph (a)(2) recognizes that where the testimony concerns the extent and value of legal services rendered in the action in which the testimony is offered, permitting the lawyers to testify avoids the need for a second trial with new counsel to resolve that issue. Moreover, in such a situation the judge has firsthand knowledge of the matter in issue; hence, there is less dependence on the adversary process to test the credibility of the testimony.

[4]   Apart from these two exceptions, paragraph (a)(3) recognizes that a balancing is required between the interests of the client and those of the opposing party. Whether the opposing party is likely to suffer prejudice depends

on the nature of the case, the importance and probable tenor of the lawyer's testimony, and the probability that the lawyer's testimony will conflict with that of other witnesses. Even if there is risk of such prejudice, in determining whether the lawyer should be disqualified, due regard must be given to the effect of disqualification on the lawyer's client. It is relevant that one or both parties could reasonably foresee that the lawyer would probably be a witness. The principle of imputed disqualification stated in Rule 1.10 has no application to this aspect of the problem.

[5]   Whether the combination of roles involves an improper conflict of interest with respect to the client is determined by Rule 1.7 or 1.9. For example, if there is likely to be substantial conflict between the testimony of the client and that of the lawyer or a member of the lawyer's firm, the representation is improper.

The problem can arise whether the lawyer is called as a witness on behalf of the client or is called by the opposing party. Determining whether or not such a conflict exists is primarily the responsibility of the lawyer involved. See Comment to Rule 1.7. If a lawyer who is a member of a firm may not act as both advocate and witness by reason of conflict of interest, Rule 1.10 disqualifies the firm also.

Model Code Comparison

DR 5-102(A) prohibited a lawyer, or the lawyer's firm, from serving as advocate if the lawyer "learns or it is obvious that he or a lawyer in his firm ought to be called as a witness on behalf of his client." DR 5-102(B) provided that a lawyer, and the lawyer's firm, may continue representation if the "lawyer learns or it is obvious that he or a lawyer in his firm may be called as a witness other than on behalf of his client . . . until it is apparent that his testimony is or may be prejudicial to his client." DR 5-101(B) permitted a lawyer to testify while representing a client: "(1) If the testimony will relate solely to an uncontested matter; (2) If the testimony will relate solely to a matter of formality and there is no reason to believe that substantial evidence will be offered in opposition to the testimony; (3) If the testimony will relate solely to the nature and value of legal services rendered in the case by the lawyer or his firm to the client; (4) As to any matter if refusal would work a substantial hardship on the client because of the distinctive value of the lawyer or his firm as counsel in the particular case."

The exception stated in paragraph (a)(1) consolidates provisions of DR 5-101(B)(1) and (2). Testimony relating to a formality, referred to in DR 5-101(B)(2), in effect defines the phrase "uncontested issue," and is redundant.

RULE 3.8 SPECIAL RESPONSIBILITIES OF A PROSECUTOR

The prosecutor in a criminal case shall:

(a)   refrain from prosecuting a charge that the prosecutor knows is not supported by probable cause;

(b)   make reasonable efforts to assure that the accused has been advised of the right to, and the procedure for obtaining, counsel and has been given reasonable opportunity to obtain counsel;

(c)   not seek to obtain from an unrepresented accused a waiver of important pretrial rights, such as the right to a preliminary hearing;

(d)   make timely disclosure to the defense of all evidence or information known to the prosecutor that tends to negate the guilt of the accused or mitigates the offense, and, in connection with sentencing, disclose to the defense and to the tribunal all unprivileged mitigating information known to the prosecutor, except when the prosecutor is relieved of this responsibility by a protective order of the tribunal; and

(e)   exercise reasonable care to prevent investigators, law enforcement personnel, employees or other persons assisting or associated with the prosecutor in a criminal case from making an extrajudicial statement that the prosecutor would be prohibited from making under Rule 3.6.

(f)   not subpoena a lawyer in a grand jury or other criminal proceeding to present evidence about a past or present client unless:

(1)   the prosecutor reasonably believes:

(i)   the information sought is not protected from disclosure by any applicable privilege;

(ii)   the evidence sought is essential to the successful completion of an ongoing investigation or prosecution;

(iii)   there is no other feasible alternative to obtain the information; and

(2)   the prosecutor obtains prior judicial approval after an opportunity for an adversarial proceeding.

(g)   except for statements that are necessary to inform the public of the nature and extent of the prosecutor's action and that serve a legitimate law enforcement purpose, refrain from making extrajudicial comments that have a substantial likelihood of heightening public condemnation of the accused.

Comment

[1]   A prosecutor has the responsibility of a minister of justice and not simply that of an advocate. This responsibility carries with it specific obligations to see that the defendant is accorded procedural justice and that guilt is decided upon the basis of sufficient evidence. Precisely how far the prosecutor is required to go in this direction is a matter of debate and varies in different jurisdictions. Many jurisdictions have adopted the ABA Standards of Criminal Justice Relating to the Prosecution Function, which in turn are the product of prolonged and careful deliberation by lawyers experienced in both criminal prosecution and defense. See also Rule 3.3(d), governing *ex parte* proceedings, among which grand jury proceedings are included. Applicable law may require other measures by the prosecutor and knowing disregard of those obligations or a systematic abuse of prosecutorial discretion could constitute a violation of Rule 8.4.

[2]   Paragraph (c) does not apply to an accused appearing *pro se* with the approval of the tribunal. Nor does it forbid the lawful questioning of a suspect who has knowingly waived the rights to counsel and silence.

[3]   The exception in paragraph (d) recognizes that a prosecutor may seek an appropriate protective order from the tribunal if disclosure of information to the defense could result in substantial harm to an individual or to the public interest.

[4]   Paragraph (f) is intended to limit the issuance of lawyer subpoenas in grand jury and other criminal proceedings to those situations in which there is a genuine need to intrude into the client-lawyer relationship. The prosecutor is required to obtain court approval for the issuance of the subpoena after an opportunity for an adversarial hearing is afforded in order to assure an independent determination that the applicable standards are met.

[5]   Paragraph (g) supplements Rule 3.6, which prohibits extrajudicial statements that have a substantial likelihood of prejudicing an adjudicatory proceeding. In the context of a criminal prosecution, a prosecutor's extrajudicial statement can create the additional problem of increasing public condemnation of the accused. Although the announcement of an indictment, for example, will necessarily have severe consequences for the accused, a prosecutor can, and should, avoid comments which have no legitimate law enforcement purpose and have a substantial likelihood of increasing public opprobrium of the accused. Nothing in this Comment is intended to restrict the statements which a prosecutor may make which comply with Rule 3.6(b) or 3.6(c).

Model Code Comparison

DR 7-103(A) provided that a "public prosecutor . . . shall not institute . . . criminal charges when he knows or it is obvious that the charges are not supported by probable cause." DR 7-103(B) provided that "[a] public prosecutor . . . shall make timely disclosure . . . of the existence of evidence, known to the prosecutor . . . that tends to negate the guilt of the accused, mitigate the degree of the offense, or reduce the punishment."

RULE 3.9 ADVOCATE IN NONADJUDICATIVE PROCEEDINGS

A lawyer representing a client before a legislative or administrative tribunal in a nonadjudicative proceeding shall disclose that the appearance is in a representative capacity and shall conform to the provisions of Rules 3.3(a) through (c), 3.4(a) through (c), and 3.5.

Comment

[1]   In representation before bodies such as legislatures, municipal councils, and executive and administrative agencies acting in a rule-making or policy-making capacity, lawyers present facts, formulate issues and advance argument in the matters under consideration. The decision-making body, like a court, should be able to rely on the integrity of the submissions made to it. A lawyer appearing before such a body should deal with the tribunal honestly and in conformity with applicable rules of procedure.

[2]   Lawyers have no exclusive right to appear before nonadjudicative bodies, as they do before a court. The requirements of this Rule therefore may subject lawyers to regulations inapplicable to advocates who are not lawyers. However, legislatures and administrative agencies have a right to expect lawyers to deal with them as they deal with courts.

[3]   This Rule does not apply to representation of a client in a negotiation or other bilateral transaction with a governmental agency; representation in such a transaction is governed by Rules 4.1 through 4.4.

Model Code Comparison

EC 7-15 stated that a lawyer "appearing before an administrative agency, regardless of the nature of the proceeding it is conducting, has the continuing duty to advance the cause of his client within the bounds of the law." EC 7-16 stated that "[w]hen a lawyer appears in connection with proposed legislation, he . . . should comply with applicable laws and legislative rules." EC 8-5 stated that [fraudulent, deceptive, or otherwise illegal conduct by a participant in a proceeding before a . . . legislative body . . . should never be participated in . . . by lawyers."

DR 7-106(B)(1) provided that "[i]n presenting a matter to a tribunal, a lawyer shall disclose . . . [u]nless privileged or irrelevant, the identity of the clients he represents and of the persons who employed him."

TRANSACTIONS WITH PERSONS OTHER THAN CLIENTS

RULE 4.1 TRUTHFULNESS IN STATEMENTS TO OTHERS

In the course of representing a client a lawyer shall not knowingly:

> **(a)   make a false statement of material fact or law to a third person; or**

> **(b)   fail to disclose a material fact to a third person when disclosure is necessary to avoid assisting a criminal or fraudulent act by a client, unless disclosure is prohibited by Rule 1.6.**

Comment

Misrepresentation

[1]   A lawyer is required to be truthful when dealing with others on a client's behalf, but generally has no affirmative duty to inform an opposing party of relevant facts. A misrepresentation can occur if the lawyer incorporates or affirms a statement of another person that the lawyer knows is false. Misrepresentations can also occur by failure to act.

Statements of Fact

[2]   This Rule refers to statements of fact. Whether a particular statement should be regarded as one of fact can depend on the circumstances. Under generally accepted conventions in negotiation, certain types of statements ordinarily are not taken as statements of material fact. Estimates of price or value placed on

the subject of a transaction and a party's intentions as to an acceptable settlement of a claim are in this category, and so is the existence of an undisclosed principal except where nondisclosure of the principal would constitute fraud.

Fraud by Client

[3] Paragraph (b) recognizes that substantive law may require a lawyer to disclose certain information to avoid being deemed to have assisted the client's crime or fraud. The requirement of disclosure created by this paragraph is, however, subject to the obligations created by Rule 1.6.

Model Code Comparison

Paragraph (a) is substantially similar to DR 7-102(A)(5), which stated that "[i]n his representation of a client, a lawyer shall not . . . [k]nowingly make a false statement of law or fact."

With regard to paragraph (b), DR 7-102(A)(3) provided that a lawyer shall not "[c]onceal or knowingly fail to disclose that which he is required by law to reveal."

RULE 4.2 COMMUNICATION WITH PERSON REPRESENTED BY COUNSEL

In representing a client, a lawyer shall not communicate about the subject of the representation with a party the lawyer knows to be represented by another lawyer in the matter, unless the lawyer has the consent of the other lawyer or is authorized by law to do so.

Comment

[1] This Rule does not prohibit communication with a party, or an employee or agent of a party, concerning matters outside the representation. For example, the existence of a controversy between a government agency and a private party, or between two organizations, does not prohibit a lawyer for either from communicating with nonlawyer representatives of the other regarding a separate matter. Also, parties to a matter may communicate directly with each other and a lawyer having independent justification for communicating with the other party is permitted to do so. Communications authorized by law include, for example, the right of a party to a controversy with a government agency to speak with government officials about the matter.

[2] In the case of an organization, this Rule prohibits communications by a lawyer for one party concerning the matter in representation with persons having a managerial responsibility on behalf of the organization, and with any other person whose act or omission in connection with that matter may be imputed to the organization for purposes of civil or criminal liability or whose statement may constitute an admission on the part of the organization. If an agent or employee of the organization is represented in the matter by his or her own counsel, the consent by that counsel to a communication will be sufficient for purposes of this Rule. Compare Rule 3.4(f).

[3] This rule also covers any person, whether or not a party to a formal proceeding, who is represented by counsel concerning the matter in question.

Model Code Comparison

This Rule is substantially identical to DR 7-104(A)(1).

RULE 4.3 DEALING WITH UNREPRESENTED PERSON

In dealing on behalf of a client with a person who is not repre-sented by counsel, a lawyer shall not state or imply that the lawyer is disinterested. When the lawyer knows or reasonably should know that the unrepresented person misunderstands the lawyer's role in the matter, the lawyer shall make reasonable efforts to correct the misunderstanding.

Comment

[1] An unrepresented person, particularly one not experienced in dealing with legal matters, might assume that a lawyer is disinterested in loyalties or is a disinterested authority on the law even when the lawyer represents a client. During the course of a lawyer's representation of a client, the lawyer should not give advice to an unrepresented person other than the advice to obtain counsel.

Model Code Comparison

There was no direct counterpart to this Rule in the Model Code. DR 7-104(A)(2) provided that a lawyer shall not "[g]ive advice to a person who is not repre-sented by a lawyer, other than the advice to secure counsel. . . ."

RULE 4.4 RESPECT FOR RIGHTS OF THIRD PERSONS

In representing a client, a lawyer shall not use means that have no substantial purpose other than to embarrass, delay, or burden a third person, or use methods of obtaining evidence that violate the legal rights of such a person.

Comment

[1] Responsibility to a client requires a lawyer to subordinate the interests of others to those of the client, but that responsibility does not imply that a lawyer may disregard the rights of third persons. It is impractical to catalogue all such rights, but they include legal restrictions on methods of obtaining evidence from third persons.

Model Code Comparison

DR 7-106(C)(2) provided that a lawyer shall not "[a]sk any question that he has no reasonable basis to believe is relevant to the case and that is intended to degrade a witness or other person." DR 7-102(A)(1) provided that a lawyer shall not "take . . . action on behalf of his client when he knows or when it is obvious that such action would serve merely to harass or maliciously injure another." DR 7-108(D) provided that "[a]fter discharge of the jury . . . the lawyer shall not ask questions or make comments to a member of that jury that are calculated merely to harass or embarrass the juror. . . ." DR 7-108(E) provided that a lawyer "shall not conduct . . . a vexatious or harassing investigation of either a venireman or a juror."

LAW FIRMS AND ASSOCIATIONS

RULE 5.1 RESPONSIBILITIES OF A PARTNER OR SUPERVISORY LAWYER

(a)   A partner in a law firm shall make reasonable efforts to ensure that the firm has in effect measures giving reasonable assurance that all lawyers in the firm conform to the Rules of Professional Conduct.

(b)   A lawyer having direct supervisory authority over another lawyer shall make reasonable efforts to ensure that the other lawyer conforms to the Rules of Professional Conduct.

(c)   A lawyer shall be responsible for another lawyer's violation of the Rules of Professional Conduct if:

(1)   the lawyer orders or, with knowledge of the specific conduct, ratifies the conduct involved; or

(2)   the lawyer is a partner in the law firm in which the other lawyer practices, or has direct supervisory authority over the other lawyer, and knows of the conduct at a time when its consequences can be avoided or mitigated but fails to take reasonable remedial action.

Comment

[1]   Paragraphs (a) and (b) refer to lawyers who have supervisory authority over the professional work of a firm or legal department of a government agency. This includes members of a partnership and the shareholders in a law firm organized as a professional corporation; lawyers having supervisory authority in the law department of an enterprise or government agency; and lawyers who have intermediate managerial responsibilities in a firm.

[2]   The measures required to fulfill the responsibility prescribed in paragraphs (a) and (b) can depend on the firm's structure and the nature of its practice. In a small firm, informal supervision and occasional admonition ordinarily might be sufficient. In a large firm, or in practice situations in which intensely difficult ethical problems frequently arise, more elaborate procedures may be necessary. Some firms, for example, have a procedure whereby junior lawyers can make confidential referral of ethical problems directly to a designated senior partner or special committee. See Rule 5.2. Firms, whether large or small, may also rely on continuing legal education in professional ethics. In any event, the ethical atmosphere of a firm can influence the conduct of all its members and a lawyer having authority over the work of another may not assume that the subordinate lawyer will inevitably conform to the Rules.

[3]   Paragraph (c)(1) expresses a general principle of responsibility for acts of another. See also Rule 8.4(a).

[4]   Paragraph (c)(2) defines the duty of a lawyer having direct supervisory authority over performance of specific legal work by another lawyer. Whether a lawyer has such supervisory authority in particular circumstances is a question of fact. Partners of a private firm have at least indirect responsibility

for all work being done by the firm, while a partner in charge of a particular matter ordinarily has direct authority over other firm lawyers engaged in the matter. Appropriate remedial action by a partner would depend on the immediacy of the partner's involvement and the seriousness of the misconduct. The supervisor is required to intervene to prevent avoidable consequences of misconduct if the supervisor knows that the misconduct occurred. Thus, if a supervising lawyer knows that a subordinate misrepresented a matter to an opposing party in negotiation, the supervisor as well as the subordinate has a duty to correct the resulting misapprehension.

Professional misconduct by a lawyer under supervision could reveal a violation of paragraph (b) on the part of the supervisory lawyer even though it does not entail a violation of paragraph (c) because there was no direction, ratification or knowledge of the violation.

[5]   Apart from this Rule and Rule 8.4(a), a lawyer does not have disciplinary liability for the conduct of a partner, associate or subordinate. Whether a lawyer may be liable civilly or criminally for another lawyer's conduct is a question of law beyond the scope of these Rules.

Model Code Comparison

There was no direct counterpart to this Rule in the Model Code. DR 1-103(A) provided that a lawyer "possessing unprivileged knowledge of a violation of DR 1-102 shall report such knowledge to . . . authority empowered to investigate or act upon such violation."

RULE 5.2 RESPONSIBILITIES OF A SUBORDINATE LAWYER

(a)   **A lawyer is bound by the Rules of Professional Conduct notwithstanding that the lawyer acted at the direction of another person.**

(b)   **A subordinate lawyer does not violate the Rules of Professional Conduct if that lawyer acts in accordance with a supervisory lawyer's reasonable resolution of an arguable question of professional duty.**

Comment

[1]   Although a lawyer is not relieved of responsibility for a violation by the fact that the lawyer acted at the direction of a supervisor, that fact may be relevant in determining whether a lawyer had the knowledge required to render conduct a violation of the Rules. For example, if a subordinate filed a frivolous pleading at the direction of a supervisor, the subordinate would not be guilty of a professional violation unless the subordinate knew of the document's frivolous character.

[2]   When lawyers in a supervisor-subordinate relationship encounter a matter involving professional judgment as to ethical duty, the supervisor may assume responsibility for making the judgment. Otherwise a consistent course of action or position could not be taken. If the question can reasonably be answered only one way, the duty of both lawyers is clear and they are equally responsible for fulfilling it. However, if the question is reasonably arguable, someone has to decide upon the course of action. That authority ordinarily

reposes in the supervisor, and a subordinate may be guided accordingly. For example, if a question arises whether the interests of two clients conflict under Rule 1.7, the supervisor's reasonable resolution of the question should protect the subordinate professionally if the resolution is subsequently challenged.

Model Code Comparison

There was no counterpart to this Rule in the Model Code.

RULE 5.3 RESPONSIBILITIES REGARDING NONLAWYER ASSISTANTS

With respect to a nonlawyer employed or retained by or associated with a lawyer:

(a) a partner in a law firm shall make reasonable efforts to ensure that the firm has in effect measures giving reasonable assurance that the person's conduct is compatible with the professional obligations of the lawyer;

(b) a lawyer having direct supervisory authority over the non-lawyer shall make reasonable efforts to ensure that the person's conduct is compatible with the professional obligations of the lawyer; and

(c) a lawyer shall be responsible for conduct of such a person that would be a violation of the Rules of Professional Conduct if engaged in by a lawyer if:

(1) the lawyer orders or, with the knowledge of the specific conduct, ratifies the conduct involved; or

(2) the lawyer is a partner in the law firm in which the person is employed, or has direct supervisory authority over the person, and knows of the conduct at a time when its consequences can be avoided or mitigated but fails to take reasonable remedial action.

Comment

[1] Lawyers generally employ assistants in their practice, including secretaries, investigators, law student interns, and paraprofessionals. Such assistants, whether employees or independent contractors, act for the lawyer in rendition of the lawyer's professional services. A lawyer should give such assistants appropriate instruction and supervision concerning the ethical aspects of their employment, particularly regarding the obligation not to disclose information relating to representation of the client, and should be responsible for their work product. The measures employed in supervising nonlawyers should take account of the fact that they do not have legal training and are not subject to professional discipline.

Model Code Comparison

There was no direct counterpart to this Rule in the Model Code. DR 4-101(D) provided that a lawyer "shall exercise reasonable care to prevent his employees, associates, and others whose services are utilized by him from disclosing or using confidences or secrets of a client. . . ." DR 7-107(J) provided that "[a] lawyer shall exercise reasonable care to prevent his employees and associates from making an extrajudicial statement that he would be prohibited from making under DR 7-107."

RULE 5.4 PROFESSIONAL INDEPENDENCE OF A LAWYER

(a)   A lawyer or law firm shall not share legal fees with a nonlawyer, except that:

(1)   an agreement by a lawyer with the lawyer's firm, partner, or associate may provide for the payment of money, over a reasonable period of time after the lawyer's death, to the lawyer's estate or to one or more specified persons;

(2)   a lawyer who purchases the practice of a deceased, disabled, or disappeared lawyer may, pursuant to the provisions of Rule 1.17, pay to the estate or other representative of that lawyer the agreed-upon purchase price; and

(3)   a lawyer or law firm may include nonlawyer employees in a compensation or retirement plan, even though the plan is based in whole or in part on a profit-sharing arrangement.

(b)   A lawyer shall not form a partnership with a nonlawyer if any of the activities of the partnership consist of the practice of law.

(c)   A lawyer shall not permit a person who recommends, employs, or pays the lawyer to render legal services for another to direct or regulate the lawyer's professional judgment in rendering such legal services.

(d)   A lawyer shall not practice with or in the form of a professional corporation or association authorized to practice law for a profit, if:

(1)   a nonlawyer owns any interest therein, except that a fiduciary representative of the estate of a lawyer may hold the stock or interest of the lawyer for a reasonable time during administration;

(2)   a nonlawyer is a corporate director or officer thereof; or

(3)   a nonlawyer has the right to direct or control the professional judgment of a lawyer.

Comment

[1]   The provisions of this Rule express traditional limitations on sharing fees. These limitations are to protect the lawyer's professional independence of judgment. Where someone other than the client pays the lawyer's fee or salary, or recommends employment of the lawyer, that arrangement does not modify the lawyer's obligation to the client. As stated in paragraph (c), such arrangements should not interfere with the lawyer's professional judgment.

Model Code Comparison

Paragraph (a) is substantially identical to DR 3-102(A).

Paragraph (b) is substantially identical to DR 3-103(A).

Paragraph (c) is substantially identical to DR 5-107(B).

Paragraph (d) is substantially identical to DR 5-107(C).

RULE 5.5 UNAUTHORIZED PRACTICE OF LAW

A lawyer shall not:

(a)   practice law in a jurisdiction where doing so violates the regulation of the legal profession in that jurisdiction; or

(b)   assist a person who is not a member of the bar in the performance of activity that constitutes the unauthorized practice of law.

Comment

[1]   The definition of the practice of law is established by law and varies from one jurisdiction to another. Whatever the definition, limiting the practice of law to members of the bar protects the public against rendition of legal services by unqualified persons. Paragraph (b) does not prohibit a lawyer from employing the services of paraprofessionals and delegating functions to them, so long as the lawyer supervises the delegated work and retains responsibility for their work. See Rule 5.3. Likewise, it does not prohibit lawyers from providing professional advice and instruction to nonlawyers whose employment requires knowledge of law; for example, claims adjusters, employees of financial or commercial institutions, social workers, accountants and persons employed in government agencies. In addition, a lawyer may counsel nonlawyers who wish to proceed *pro se.*

Model Code Comparison

With regard to paragraph (a), DR 3-101(B) of the Model Code provided that "[a] lawyer shall not practice law in a jurisdiction where to do so would be in violation of regulations of the profession in that jurisdiction."

With regard to paragraph (b), DR 3-101(A) of the Model Code provided that "[a] lawyer shall not aid a non-lawyer in the unauthorized practice of law."

RULE 5.6 RESTRICTIONS ON RIGHT TO PRACTICE

A lawyer shall not participate in offering or making:

(a)   a partnership or employment agreement that restricts the right of a lawyer to practice after termination of the relationship, except an agreement concerning benefits upon retirement; or

(b)   an agreement in which a restriction on the lawyer's right to practice is part of the settlement of a controversy between private parties.

Comment

[1]   An agreement restricting the right of partners or associates to practice after leaving a firm not only limits their professional autonomy but also limits the freedom of clients to choose a lawyer. Paragraph (a) prohibits such agreements except for restrictions incident to provisions concerning retirement benefits for service with the firm.

[2] Paragraph (b) prohibits a lawyer from agreeing not to represent other persons in connection with settling a claim on behalf of a client.

[3] This Rule does not apply to prohibit restrictions that may be included in the terms of the sale of a law practice pursuant to Rule 1.17.

Model Code Comparison

This Rule is substantially similar to DR 2-108.

RULE 5.7 RESPONSIBILITIES REGARDING LAW-RELATED SERVICES

(a) A lawyer shall be subject to the Rules of Professional Conduct with respect to the provision of law-related services, as defined in paragraph (b), if the law-related services are provided:

(1) by the lawyer in circumstances that are not distinct from the lawyer's provision of legal services to clients; or

(2) by a separate entity controlled by the lawyer individually or with others if the lawyer fails to take reasonable measures to assure that a person obtaining the law-related services knows that the services of the separate entity are not legal services and that the protections of the client-lawyer relationship do not exist.

(b) The term "law-related services" denotes services that might reasonably be performed in conjunction with and in substance are related to the provision of legal services, and that are not prohibited as unauthorized practice of law when provided by a nonlawyer.

Comment

[1] When a lawyer performs law-related services or controls an organization that does so, there exists the potential for ethical problems. Principal among these is the possibility that the person for whom the law-related services are performed fails to understand that the services may not carry with them the protections normally afforded as part of the client-lawyer relationship. The recipient of the law-related services may expect, for example, that the protection of client confidences, prohibitions against representation of persons with conflicting interests, and obligations of a lawyer to maintain professional independence apply to the provision of law-related services when that may not be the case.

[2] Rule 5.7 applies to the provision of law-related services by a lawyer even when the lawyer does not provide any legal services to the person for whom the law-related services are performed. The Rule identifies the circumstances in which all of the Rules of Professional Conduct apply to the provision of law-related services. Even when those circumstances do not exist, however, the conduct of a lawyer involved in the provision of law-related services is subject to those Rules that apply generally to lawyer conduct, regardless of whether the conduct involves the provision of legal services. See, e.g., Rule 8.4.

[3] When law-related services are provided by a lawyer under circumstances that are not distinct from the lawyer's provision of legal services to clients, the

lawyer in providing the law-related services must adhere to the requirements of the Rules of Professional Conduct as provided in Rule 5.7(a)(1).

[4]   Law-related services also may be provided through an entity that is distinct from that through which the lawyer provides legal services. If the lawyer individually or with others has control of such an entity's operations, the Rule requires the lawyer to take reasonable measures to assure that each person using the services of the entity knows that the services provided by the entity are not legal services and that the Rules of Professional Conduct that relate to the client-lawyer relationship do not apply. A lawyer's control of an entity extends to the ability to direct its operation. Whether a lawyer has such control will depend upon the circumstances of the particular case.

[5]   When a client-lawyer relationship exists with a person who is referred by a lawyer to a separate law-related service entity controlled by the lawyer, individually or with others, the lawyer must comply with Rule 1.8(a).

[6]   In taking the reasonable measures referred to in paragraph (a)(2) to assure that a person using law-related services understands the practical effect or significance of the inapplicability of the Rules of Professional Conduct, the lawyer should communicate to the person receiving the law-related services, in a manner sufficient to assure that the person understands the significance of the fact, that the relationship of the person to the business entity will not be a client-lawyer relationship. The communication should be made before entering into an agreement for provision of or providing law-related services, and preferably should be in writing.

[7]   The burden is upon the lawyer to show that the lawyer has taken reasonable measures under the circumstances to communicate the desired understanding. For instance, a sophisticated user of law-related services, such as a publicly held corporation, may require a lesser explanation than someone unaccustomed to making distinctions between legal services and law-related services, such as an individual seeking tax advice from a lawyer-accountant or investigative services in connection with a lawsuit.

[8]   Regardless of the sophistication of potential recipients of law-related services, a lawyer should take special care to keep separate the provision of law-related and legal services in order to minimize the risk that the recipient will assume that the law-related services are legal services. The risk of such confusion is especially acute when the lawyer renders both types of services with respect to the same matter. Under some circumstances the legal and law-related services may be so closely entwined that they cannot be distinguished from each other, and the requirement of disclosure and consultation imposed by paragraph (a)(2) of the Rule cannot be met. In such a case a lawyer will be responsible for assuring that both the lawyer's conduct and, to the extent required by Rule 5.3, that of nonlawyer employees in the distinct entity which the lawyer controls complies in all respects with the Rules of Professional Conduct.

[9]   A broad range of economic and other interests of clients may be served by lawyers' engaging in the delivery of law-related services. Examples of law- related

services include providing title insurance, financial planning, accounting, trust services, real estate counseling, legislative lobbying, economic analysis social work, psychological counseling, tax preparation, and patent, medical or environmental consulting.

[10] When a lawyer is obliged to accord the recipients of such services the protections of those Rules that apply to the client-lawyer relationship, the lawyer must take special care to heed the proscriptions of the Rules addressing conflict of interest (Rules 1.7 through 1.11, especially Rules 1.7(b) and 1.8(a),(b) and (f)), and to scrupulously adhere to the requirements of Rule 1.6 relating to disclosure of confidential information. The promotion of the law-related services must also in all respects comply with Rules 7.1 through 7.3, dealing with advertising and solicitation. In that regard, lawyers should take special care to identify the obligations that may be imposed as a result of a jurisdiction's decisional law.

[11] When the full protections of all of the Rules of Professional Conduct do not apply to the provision of law-related services, principles of law external to the Rules, for example, the law of principal and agent, govern the legal duties owed to those receiving the services. Those other legal principles may establish a different degree of protection for the recipient with respect to confidentiality of information, conflicts of interest and permissible business relationships with clients. See also Rule 8.4 (Misconduct).

Model Code Comparison

There was no counterpart to this Rule in the Model Code.

PUBLIC SERVICE

RULE 6.1 VOLUNTARY *PRO BONO PUBLICO* SERVICE

A lawyer should aspire to render at least (50) hours of pro bono publico legal services per year. In fulfilling this responsibility, the lawyer should:

(a) provide a substantial majority of the (50) hours of legal services without fee or expectation of fee to:

(1) persons of limited means or

(2) charitable, religious, civic, community, governmental and educational organizations in matters which are designed primarily to address the needs of persons of limited means; and

(b) provide any additional services through:

(1) delivery of legal services at no fee or substantially reduced fee to individuals, groups or organizations seeking to secure or protect civil rights, civil liberties or public rights, or charitable, religious, civic, community, governmental and educational organizations in matters in furtherance of their organizational purposes, where the payment of standard legal fees would significantly

deplete the organization's economic resources or would be otherwise inappropriate;

(2) delivery of legal services at a substantially reduced fee to persons of limited means; or

(3) participation in activities for improving the law, the legal system or the legal profession.

In addition, a lawyer should voluntarily contribute financial support to organizations that provide legal services to persons of limited means.

Comment

[1] Every lawyer, regardless of professional prominence or professional work load, has a responsibility to provide legal services to those unable to pay, and personal involvement in the problems of the disadvantaged can be one of the most rewarding experiences in the life of a lawyer. The American Bar Association urges all lawyers to provide a minimum of 50 hours of pro bono services annually. States, however, may decide to choose a higher or lower number of hours of annual service (which may be expressed as a percentage of a lawyer's professional time) depending upon local needs and local conditions. It is recognized that in some years a lawyer may render greater or fewer hours than the annual standard specified, but during the course of his or her legal career, each lawyer should render on average per year, the number of hours set forth in this Rule. Services can be performed in civil matters or in criminal or quasi-criminal matters for which there is no government obligation to provide funds for legal representation, such as post-conviction death penalty appeal cases.

[2] Paragraphs (a)(1) and (2) recognize the critical need for legal services that exists among persons of limited means by providing that a substantial majority of the legal services rendered annually to the disadvantaged be furnished without fee or expectation of fee. Legal services under these paragraphs consist of a full range of activities, including individual and class representation, the provision of legal advice, legislative lobbying, administrative rule making and the provision of free training or mentoring to those who represent persons of limited means. The variety of these activities should facilitate participation by government lawyers, even when restrictions exist on their engaging in the outside practice of law.

[3] Persons eligible for legal services under paragraphs (a)(1) and (2) are those who qualify for participation in programs funded by the Legal Services Corporation and those whose incomes and financial resources are slightly above the guidelines utilized by such programs but nevertheless, cannot afford counsel. Legal services can be rendered to individuals or to organizations such as homeless shelters, battered women's centers and food pantries that serve those of limited means. The term "governmental organizations" includes, but is not limited to, public protection programs and sections of governmental or public sector agencies.

[4]   Because service must be provided without fee or expectation of fee, the intent of the lawyer to render free legal services is essential for the work performed to fall within the meaning of paragraphs (a)(1) and (2). Accordingly, services rendered cannot be considered pro bono if an anticipated fee is uncollected, but the award of statutory lawyers' fees in a case originally accepted as pro bono would not disqualify such services from inclusion under this section. Lawyers who do receive fees in such cases are encouraged to contribute an appropriate portion of such fees to organizations or projects that benefit persons of limited means.

[5]   While it is possible for a lawyer to fulfill the annual responsibility to perform pro bono services exclusively through activities described in paragraphs (a)(1) and (2), to the extent that any hours of service remained unfulfilled, the remaining commitment can be met in a variety of ways as set forth in paragraph (b). Constitutional, statutory or regulatory restrictions may prohibit or impede government and public sector lawyers and judges from performing the pro bono services outlined in paragraphs (a)(1) and (2). Accordingly, where those restrictions apply, government and public sector lawyers and judges may fulfill their pro bono responsibility by performing services outlined in paragraph (b).

[6]   Paragraph (b)(1) includes the provision of certain types of legal services to those whose incomes and financial resources place them above limited means. It also permits the pro bono lawyer to accept a substantially reduced fee for services. Examples of the types of issues that may be addressed under this paragraph include First Amendment claims, Title VII claims and environmental protection claims. Additionally, a wide range of organizations may be represented, including social service, medical research, cultural and religious groups.

[7]   Paragraph (b)(2) covers instances in which lawyers agree to and receive a modest fee for furnishing legal services to persons of limited means. Participation in judicare programs and acceptance of court appointments in which the fee is substantially below a lawyer's usual rate are encouraged under this section.

[8]   Paragraph (b)(3) recognizes the value of lawyers engaging in activities that improve the law, the legal system or the legal profession. Serving on bar association committees, serving on boards of pro bono or legal services programs, taking part in Law Day activities, acting as a continuing legal education instructor, a mediator or an arbitrator and engaging in legislative lobbying to improve the law, the legal system or the profession are a few examples of the many activities that fall within this paragraph.

[9]   Because the provision of pro bono services is a professional responsibility, it is the individual ethical commitment of each lawyer. Nevertheless, there may be times when it is not feasible for a lawyer to engage in pro bono services. At such times a lawyer may discharge the pro bono responsibility by providing financial support to organizations providing free legal services to persons of limited means. Such financial support should be reasonably equivalent to the value of the hours of service that would have otherwise been provided. In addition, at times it may be more feasible to satisfy the pro bono responsibility collectively, as by a firm's aggregate pro bono activities.

(d)   Any communication made pursuant to this rule shall include the name of at least one lawyer responsible for its content.

Comment

[1]   To assist the public in obtaining legal services, lawyers should be allowed to make known their services not only through reputation but also through organized information campaigns in the form of advertising. Advertising involves an active quest for clients, contrary to the tradition that a lawyer should not seek clientele. However, the public's need to know about legal services can be fulfilled in part through advertising. This need is particularly acute in the case of persons of moderate means who have not made extensive use of legal services. The interest in expanding public information about legal services ought to prevail over considerations of tradition. Nevertheless, advertising by lawyers entails the risk of practices that are misleading or overreaching.

[2]   This Rule permits public dissemination of information concerning a lawyer's name or firm name, address and telephone number; the kinds of services the lawyer will undertake; the basis on which the lawyer's fees are determined, including prices for specific services and payment and credit arrangements; a lawyer's foreign language ability; names of references and, with their consent, names of clients regularly represented; and other information that might invite the attention of those seeking legal assistance.

[3]   Questions of effectiveness and taste in advertising are matters of speculation and subjective judgment. Some jurisdictions have had extensive prohibitions against television advertising, against advertising going beyond specified facts about a lawyer, or against "undignified" advertising. Television is now one of the most powerful media for getting information to the public, particularly persons of low and moderate income; prohibiting television advertising, therefore, would impede the flow of information about legal services to many sectors of the public. Limiting the information that may be advertised has a similar effect and assumes that the bar can accurately forecast the kind of information that the public would regard as relevant.

[4]   Neither this Rule nor Rule 7.3 prohibits communications authorized by law, such as notice to members of a class in class action litigation.

Record of Advertising

[5]   Paragraph (b) requires that a record of the content and use of advertising be kept in order to facilitate enforcement of this Rule. It does not require that advertising be subject to review prior to dissemination. Such a requirement would be burdensome and expensive relative to its possible benefits, and may be of doubtful constitutionality.

Paying Others to Recommend a Lawyer

[6]   A lawyer is allowed to pay for advertising permitted by this Rule and for the purchase of a law practice in accordance with the provisions of Rule 1.17, but otherwise is not permitted to pay another person for channeling professional

work. This restriction does not prevent an organization or person other than the lawyer from advertising or recommending the lawyer's services. Thus, a legal aid agency or prepaid legal services plan may pay to advertise legal services provided under its auspices. Likewise, a lawyer may participate in not-for-profit lawyer referral programs and pay the usual fees charged by such programs. Paragraph (c) does not prohibit paying regular compensation to an assistant, such as a secretary, to prepare communications permitted by this Rule.

Model Code Comparison

With regard to paragraph (a), DR 2-101(B) provided that a lawyer "may publish or broadcast, subject to DR 2-103, . . . in print media . . . or television or radio. . . ."

With regard to paragraph (b), DR 2-101(D) provided that if the advertisement is "communicated to the public over television or radio, . . . a recording of the actual transmission shall be retained by the lawyer."

With regard to paragraph (c), DR 2-103(B) provided that a lawyer "shall not compensate or give anything of value to a person or organization to recommend or secure his employment . . . except that he may pay the usual and reasonable fees or dues charged by any of the organizations listed in DR 2-103(D)." (DR 2-103(D) referred to legal aid and other legal services organizations.) DR 2-101(I) provided that a lawyer "shall not compensate or give anything of value to representatives of the press, radio, television, or other communication medium in anticipation of or in return for professional publicity in a news item."

There was no counterpart to paragraph (d) in the Model Code.

RULE 7.3 DIRECT CONTACT WITH PROSPECTIVE CLIENTS

(a) A lawyer shall not by in-person or live telephone contact solicit professional employment from a prospective client with whom the lawyer has no family or prior professional relationship when a significant motive for the lawyer's doing so is the lawyer's pecuniary gain.

(b) A lawyer shall not solicit professional employment from a prospective client by written or recorded communication or by in-person or telephone contact even when not otherwise prohibited by paragraph (a), if:

(1) the prospective client has made known to the lawyer a desire not to be solicited by the lawyer; or

(2) the solicitation involves coercion, duress or harassment.

(c) Every written or recorded communication from a lawyer soliciting professional employment from a prospective client known to be in need of legal services in a particular matter, and with whom the lawyer has no family or prior professional relationship, shall include the words "Advertising Material" on the outside envelope and at the beginning and ending of any recorded communication.

(d)   Notwithstanding the prohibitions in paragraph (a), a lawyer may participate with a prepaid or group legal service plan operated by an organization not owned or directed by the lawyer which uses in-person or telephone contact to solicit memberships or subscriptions for the plan from persons who are not known to need legal services in a particular matter covered by the plan.

Comment

[1]   There is a potential for abuse inherent in direct in-person or live telephone contact by a lawyer with a prospective client known to need legal services. These forms of contact between a lawyer and a prospective client subject the layperson to the private importuning of the trained advocate in a direct interpersonal encounter. The prospective client, who may already feel overwhelmed by the circumstances giving rise to the need for legal services, may find it difficult fully to evaluate all available alternatives with reasoned judgment and appropriate self-interest in the face of the lawyer's presence and insistence upon being retained immediately. The situation is fraught with the possibility of undue influence, intimidation, and over-reaching.

[2]   This potential for abuse inherent in direct in-person or live telephone solicitation of prospective clients justifies its prohibition, particularly since lawyer advertising and written and recorded communication permitted under Rule 7.2 offer alternative means of conveying necessary information to those who may be in need of legal services. Advertising and written and recorded communications which may be mailed or autodialed make it possible for a prospective client to be informed about the need for legal services, and about the qualifications of available lawyers and law firms, without subjecting the prospective client to direct in-person or telephone persuasion that may overwhelm the client's judgment.

[3]   The use of general advertising and written and recorded communications to transmit information from lawyer to prospective client, rather than direct in-person or live telephone contact, will help to assure that the information flows cleanly as well as freely. The contents of advertisements and communications permitted under Rule 7.2 are permanently recorded so that they cannot be disputed and may be shared with others who know the lawyer. This potential for informal review is itself likely to help guard against statements and claims that might constitute false and misleading communications, in violation of Rule 7.1. The contents of direct in-person or live telephone conversations between a lawyer to a prospective client can be disputed and are not subject to third-party scrutiny. Consequently, they are much more likely to approach (and occasionally cross) the dividing line between accurate representations and those that are false and misleading.

[4]   There is far less likelihood that a lawyer would engage in abusive practices against an individual with whom the lawyer has a prior personal or professional relationship or where the lawyer is motivated by considerations other than the lawyer's pecuniary gain. Consequently, the general prohibition in Rule 7.3(a) and the requirements of Rule 7.3(c) are not applicable in those situations.

[5]   But even permitted forms of solicitation can be abused. Thus, any solicitation which contains information which is false or misleading within the meaning of Rule 7.1, which involves coercion, duress or harassment within the meaning of Rule 7.3(b)(2), or which involves contact with a prospective client who has made known to the lawyer a desire not to be solicited by the lawyer within the meaning of Rule 7.3(b)(1) is prohibited. Moreover, if after sending a letter or other communication to a client as permitted by Rule 7.2 the lawyer receives no response, any further effort to communicate with the prospective client may violate the provisions of Rule 7.3(b).

[6]   This Rule is not intended to prohibit a lawyer from contacting representatives of organizations or groups that may be interested in establishing a group or prepaid legal plan for their members, insureds, beneficiaries or other third parties for the purpose of informing such entities of the availability of and details concerning the plan or arrangement which the lawyer or lawyer's firm is willing to offer. This form of communication is not directed to a prospective client. Rather, it is usually addressed to an individual acting in a fiduciary capacity seeking a supplier of legal services for others who may, if they choose, become prospective clients of the lawyer. Under these circumstances, the activity which the lawyer undertakes in communicating with such representatives and the type of information transmitted to the individual are functionally similar to and serve the same purpose as advertising permitted under Rule 7.2.

[7]   The requirement in Rule 7.3(c) that certain communications be marked "Advertising Material" does not apply to communications sent in response to requests of potential clients or their spokespersons or sponsors. General announcements by lawyers, including changes in personnel or office location, do not constitute communications soliciting professional employment from a client known to be in need of legal services within the meaning of this Rule.

[8]   Paragraph (d) of this Rule would permit a lawyer to participate with an organization which uses personal contact to solicit members for its group or prepaid legal service plan, provided that the personal contact is not undertaken by any lawyer who would be a provider of legal services through the plan. The organization referred to in paragraph (d) must not be owned by or directed (whether as manager or otherwise) by any lawyer or law firm that participates in the plan. For example, paragraph (d) would not permit a lawyer to create an organization controlled directly or indirectly by the lawyer and use the organization for the in-person or telephone solicitation of legal employment of the lawyer through memberships in the plan or otherwise. The communication permitted by these organizations also must not be directed to a person known to need legal services in a particular matter, but is to be designed to inform potential plan members generally of another means of affordable legal services. Lawyers who participate in a legal service plan must reasonably assure that the plan sponsors are in compliance with Rules 7.1, 7.2 and 7.3(b). See 8.4(a).

Model Code Comparison

DR 2-104(A) provided with certain exceptions that "[a] lawyer who has given in-person unsolicited advice to a layperson that he should obtain counsel or take legal action shall not accept employment resulting from that advice. . . ." The exceptions include DR 2-104(A)(1), which provided that a lawyer "may accept employment by a close friend, relative, former client (if the advice is germane to the former employment), or one whom the lawyer reasonably believes to be a client." DR 2-104(A)(2) through DR 2-104(A)(5) provided other exceptions relating, respectively, to employment resulting from public educational programs, recommendation by a legal assistance organization, public speaking or writing and representing members of a class in class action litigation.

RULE 7.4 COMMUNICATION OF FIELDS OF PRACTICE

A lawyer may communicate the fact that the lawyer does or does not practice in particular fields of law. A lawyer shall not state or imply that the lawyer has been recognized or certified as a specialist in a particular field of law except as follows:

(a)   a lawyer admitted to engage in patent practice before the United States Patent and Trademark Office may use the designation "Patent Attorney" or a substantially similar designation;

(b)   a lawyer engaged in Admiralty practice may use the designation "Admiralty," "Proctor in Admiralty" or a substantially similar designation; and

(c)   [for jurisdictions where there is a regulatory authority granting certification or approving organizations that grant certification] a lawyer may communicate the fact that the lawyer has been certified as a specialist in a field of law by a named organization or authority but only if:

(1)   such certification is granted by the appropriate regulatory authority or by an organization which has been approved by the appropriate regulatory authority to grant such certification; or

(2)   such certification is granted by an organization that has not yet been approved by, or has been denied the approval available from, the appropriate regulatory authority, and the absence or denial of approval is clearly stated in the communication, and in any advertising subject to Rule 7.2, such statement appears in the same sentence that communicates the certification.

(c)   [for jurisdictions where there is no procedure either for certification of specialties or for approval of organizations granting certification] a lawyer may communicate the fact that the lawyer has been certified as a specialist in a field of law by a named organization, provided that the communication clearly states that there is no procedure in this jurisdiction for approving certifying organizations. If, however, the named organization has been accredited by the American Bar Association to certify lawyers as specialists in a particular field of law, the communication need not contain such a statement.

Comment

[1] This Rule permits a lawyer to indicate areas of practice in communications about the lawyer's services. If a lawyer practices only in certain fields, or will not accept matters except in a specified field or fields, the lawyer is permitted to so indicate. A lawyer is generally permitted to state that the lawyer is a "specialist," practices a "specialty," or "specializes in" particular fields, but such communications are subject to the "false and misleading" standard applied in Rule 7.1 to communications concerning a lawyer's services.

[2] However, a lawyer may not communicate that the lawyer has been recognized or certified as a specialist in a particular field of law, except as provided by this Rule. Recognition of specialization in patent matters is a matter of long-established policy of the Patent and Trademark Office, as reflected in paragraph (a). Paragraph (b) recognizes that designation of admiralty practice has a long historical tradition associated with maritime commerce and the federal courts.

[3] Paragraph (c) provides for certification as a specialist in a field of law when a state authorizes an appropriate regulatory authority to grant such certification or when the state grants other organizations the right to grant certification. Certification procedures imply that an objective entity has recognized a lawyer's higher degree of specialized ability than is suggested by general licensure to practice law. Those objective entities may be expected to apply standards of competence, experience and knowledge to insure that a lawyer's recognition as a specialist is meaningful and reliable. In order to insure that consumers can obtain access to useful information about an organization granting certification, the name of the certifying organization or agency must be included in any communication regarding the certification.

[4] Lawyers may also be certified as specialists by organizations that either have not yet been approved to grant such certification or have been disapproved. In such instances, the consumer may be misled as to the significance of the lawyer's status as a certified specialist. The Rule therefore requires that a lawyer who chooses to communicate recognition by such an organization also clearly state the absence or denial of the organization's authority to grant such certification. Since lawyer advertising through public media and written or recorded communications invites the greatest danger of misleading consumers, the absence or denial of the organization's authority to grant certification must be clearly stated in such advertising in the same sentence that communicates the certification.

[5] In jurisdictions where no appropriate regulatory authority has a procedure for approving organizations granting certification, the Rule requires that lawyer clearly state such lack of procedure. If, however, the named organization has been accredited by the American Bar Association to certify lawyers as specialists in a particular field of law, the communication need not contain such a statement.

Model Code Comparison

DR 2-105(A) provided that a lawyer "shall not hold himself out publicly as a specialist, as practicing in certain areas of law or as limiting his practice . . . except as follows:

"(1) A lawyer admitted to practice before the United States Patent and Trademark Office may use the designation 'Patents,' 'Patent Attorney,' 'Patent Lawyer,' or 'Registered Patent Attorney' or any combination of those terms, on his letterhead and office sign.

"(2) A lawyer who publicly discloses fields of law in which the lawyer . . . practices or states that his practice is limited to one or more fields of law shall do so by using designations and definitions authorized and approved by [the agency having jurisdiction of the subject under state law].

"(3) A lawyer who is certified as a specialist in a particular field of law or law practice by [the authority having jurisdiction under state law over the subject of specialization by lawyers] may hold himself out as such, but only in accordance with the rules prescribed by that authority."

EC 2-14 stated that "In the absence of state controls to insure the existence of special competence, a lawyer should not be permitted to hold himself out as a specialist, . . . other than in the fields of admiralty, trademark, and patent law where a holding out as a specialist historically has been permitted."

RULE 7.5 FIRM NAMES AND LETTERHEADS

(a) A lawyer shall not use a firm name, letterhead or other professional designation that violates Rule 7.1. A trade name may be used by a lawyer in private practice if it does not imply a connection with a government agency or with a public or charitable legal services organization and is not otherwise in violation of Rule 7.1.

(b) A law firm with offices in more than one jurisdiction may use the same name in each jurisdiction, but identification of the lawyers in an office of the firm shall indicate the jurisdictional limitations on those not licensed to practice in the jurisdiction where the office is located.

(c) The name of a lawyer holding a public office shall not be used in the name of a law firm, or in communications on its behalf, during any substantial period in which the lawyer is not actively and regularly practicing with the firm.

(d) Lawyers may state or imply that they practice in a partnership or other organization only when that is the fact.

Comment

[1] A firm may be designated by the names of all or some of its members, by the names of deceased members where there has been a continuing succession in the firm's identity or by a trade name such as the "ABC Legal Clinic." Although the United States Supreme Court has held that legislation may prohibit the use of trade names in professional practice, use of such names in law practice is acceptable so long as it is not misleading. If a private firm uses a trade name that includes a geographical name such as "Springfield Legal Clinic," an express disclaimer that it is a public legal aid agency may be

required to avoid a misleading implication. It may be observed that any firm name including the name of a deceased partner is, strictly speaking, a trade name. The use of such names to designate law firms has proven a useful means of identification. However, it is misleading to use the name of a lawyer not associated with the firm or a predecessor of the firm.

[2]   With regard to paragraph (d), lawyers sharing office facilities, but who are not in fact partners, may not denominate themselves as, for example, "Smith and Jones," for that title suggests partnership in the practice of law.

Model Code Comparison

With regard to paragraph (a), DR 2-102(A) provided that "[a] lawyer . . . shall not use . . . professional announcement cards . . . letterheads, or similar professional notices or devices, except . . . if they are in dignified form. . . ." DR 2-102(B) provided that "[a] lawyer in private practice shall not practice under a trade name, a name that is misleading as to the identity of the lawyer or lawyers practicing under such name, or a firm name containing names other than those of one or more of the lawyers in the firm, except that . . . a firm may use as . . . its name the name or names of one or more deceased or retired members of the firm or of a predecessor firm in a continuing line of succession."

With regard to paragraph (b), DR 2-102(D) provided that a partnership "shall not be formed or continued between or among lawyers licensed in different jurisdictions unless all enumerations of the members and associates of the firm on its letterhead and in other permissible listings make clear the jurisdictional limitations on those members and associates of the firm not licensed to practice in all listed jurisdictions; however, the same firm name may be used in each jurisdiction." With regard to paragraph (c), DR 2-102(B) provided that "[a] lawyer who assumes a judicial, legislative, or public executive or administrative post or office shall not permit his name to remain in the name of a law firm . . . during any significant period in which he is not actively and regularly practicing law as a member of the firm. . . ."

Paragraph (d) is substantially identical to DR 2-102(C).

RULE 7.6 POLITICAL CONTRIBUTIONS TO OBTAIN GOVERNMENT LEGAL ENGAGEMENTS OR APPOINTMENTS BY JUDGES

A lawyer or law firm shall not accept a government legal engagement or an appointment by a judge if the lawyer or law firm makes a political contribution or solicits political contributions for the purpose of obtaining or being considered for that type of legal engagement or appointment.

Comment

[1]   Lawyers have a right to participate fully in the political process, which includes making and soliciting political contributions to candidates for judicial

and other public office. Nevertheless, when lawyers make or solicit political contributions in order to obtain an engagement for legal work awarded by a government agency, or to obtain appointment by a judge, the public may legitimately question whether the lawyers engaged to perform the work are selected on the basis of competence and merit. In such a circumstance, the integrity of the profession is undermined.

[2] The term "political contribution" denotes any gift, subscription, loan, advance or deposit of anything of value made directly or indirectly to a candidate, incumbent, political party or campaign committee to influence or provide financial support for election to or retention in judicial or other government office. Political contributions in initiative and referendum elections are not included. For purposes of this Rule, the term "political contribution" does not include uncompensated services.

[3] Subject to the exceptions below, (i) the term "government legal engagement" denotes any engagement to provide legal services that a public official has the direct or indirect power to award; and (ii) the term "appointment by a judge" denotes an appointment to a position such as referee, commissioner, special master, receiver, guardian or other similar position that is made by a judge. Those terms do not, however, include (a) substantially uncompensated services; (b) engagements or appointments made on the basis of experience, expertise, professional qualifications and cost following a request for proposal or other process that is free from influence based upon political contributions; and (c) engagements or appointments made on a rotational basis from a list compiled without regard to political contributions.

[4] The term "lawyer or law firm" includes a political action committee or other entity owned or controlled by a lawyer or law firm.

[5] Political contributions are for the purpose of obtaining or being considered for a government legal engagement or appointment by a judge if, but for the desire to be considered for the legal engagement or appointment, the lawyer or law firm would not have made or solicited the contributions. The purpose may be determined by an examination of the circumstances in which the contributions occur. For example, one or more contributions that in the aggregate are substantial in relation to other contributions by lawyers or law firms, made for the benefit of an official in a position to influence award of a government legal engagement, and followed by an award of the legal engagement to the contributing or soliciting lawyer or the lawyer's firm would support an inference that the purpose of the contributions was to obtain the engagement, absent other factors that weigh against existence of the proscribed purpose. Those factors may include among others that the contribution or solicitation was made to further a political, social, or economic interest or because of an existing personal, family, or professional relationship with a candidate.

[6] If a lawyer makes or solicits a political contribution under circumstances that constitute bribery or another crime, Rule 8.4(b) is implicated.

MAINTAINING THE INTEGRITY OF THE PROFESSION

RULE 8.1 BAR ADMISSION AND DISCIPLINARY MATTERS

An applicant for admission to the bar, or a lawyer in connection with a bar admission application or in connection with a disciplinary matter, shall not:

(a)   knowingly make a false statement of material fact; or

(b)   fail to disclose a fact necessary to correct a misapprehension known by the person to have arisen in the matter, or knowingly fail to respond to a lawful demand for information from an admissions or disciplinary authority, except that this rule does not require disclosure of information otherwise protected by Rule 1.6.

Comment

[1]   The duty imposed by this Rule extends to persons seeking admission to the bar as well as to lawyers. Hence, if a person makes a material false statement in connection with an application for admission, it may be the basis for subsequent disciplinary action if the person is admitted, and in any event may be relevant in a subsequent admission application. The duty imposed by this Rule applies to a lawyer's own admission or discipline as well as that of others. Thus, it is a separate professional offense for a lawyer to knowingly make a misrepresentation or omission in connection with a disciplinary investigation of the lawyer's own conduct. This Rule also requires affirmative clarification of any misunderstanding on the part of the admissions or disciplinary authority of which the person involved becomes aware.

[2]   This Rule is subject to the provisions of the fifth amendment of the United States Constitution and corresponding provisions of state constitutions. A person relying on such a provision in response to a question, however, should do so openly and not use the right of nondisclosure as a justification for failure to comply with this Rule.

[3]   A lawyer representing an applicant for admission to the bar, or representing a lawyer who is the subject of a disciplinary inquiry or proceeding, is governed by the rules applicable to the client-lawyer relationship.

Model Code Comparison

DR 1-101(A) provided that a lawyer is "subject to discipline if he has made a materially false statement in, or if he has deliberately failed to disclose a material fact requested in connection with, his application for admission to the bar." DR 1-101(B) provided that a lawyer "shall not further the application for admission to the bar of another person known by him to be unqualified in respect to character, education, or other relevant attribute." With respect to paragraph (b), DR 1-102(A)(5) provided that a lawyer shall not engage in "conduct that is prejudicial to the administration of justice."

RULE 8.2 JUDICIAL AND LEGAL OFFICIALS

(a) A lawyer shall not make a statement that the lawyer knows to be false or with reckless disregard as to its truth or falsity concerning the qualifications or integrity of a judge, adjudicatory officer or public legal officer, or of a candidate for election or appointment to judicial or legal office.

(b) A lawyer who is a candidate for judicial office shall comply with the applicable provisions of the Code of Judicial Conduct.

Comment

[1] Assessments by lawyers are relied on in evaluating the professional or personal fitness of persons being considered for election or appointment to judicial office and to public legal offices, such as attorney general, prosecuting attorney and public defender. Expressing honest and candid opinions on such matters contributes to improving the administration of justice. Conversely, false statements by a lawyer can unfairly undermine public confidence in the administration of justice.

[2] When a lawyer seeks judicial office, the lawyer should be bound by applicable limitations on political activity.

[3] To maintain the fair and independent administration of justice, lawyers are encouraged to continue traditional efforts to defend judges and courts unjustly criticized.

Model Code Comparison

With regard to paragraph (a), DR 8-102(A) provided that a lawyer "shall not knowingly make false statements of fact concerning the qualifications of a candidate for election or appointment to a judicial office." DR 8-102(B) provided that a lawyer "shall not knowingly make false accusations against a judge or other adjudicatory officer."

Paragraph (b) is substantially identical to DR 8-103.

RULE 8.3 REPORTING PROFESSIONAL MISCONDUCT

(a) A lawyer having knowledge that another lawyer has committed a violation of the Rules of Professional Conduct that raises a substantial question as to that lawyer's honesty, trustworthiness or fitness as a lawyer in other respects, shall inform the appropriate professional authority.

(b) A lawyer having knowledge that a judge has committed a violation of applicable rules of judicial conduct that raises a substantial question as to the judge's fitness for office shall inform the appropriate authority.

(c) This Rule does not require disclosure of information otherwise protected by Rule 1.6 or information gained by a lawyer or judge while serving as a member of an approved lawyers assistance program to

the extent that such information would be confidential if it were communicated subject to the attorney-client privilege.

[1]   Self-regulation of the legal profession requires that members of the profession initiate disciplinary investigation when they know of a violation of the Rules of Professional Conduct. Lawyers have a similar obligation with respect to judicial misconduct. An apparently isolated violation may indicate a pattern of misconduct that only a disciplinary investigation can uncover. Reporting a violation is especially important where the victim is unlikely to discover the offense.

[2]   A report about misconduct is not required where it would involve violation of Rule 1.6. However, a lawyer should encourage a client to consent to disclosure where prosecution would not substantially prejudice the client's interests.

[3]   If a lawyer were obliged to report every violation of the Rules, the failure to report any violation would itself be a professional offense. Such a requirement existed in many jurisdictions but proved to be unenforceable. This Rule limits the reporting obligation to those offenses that a self-regulating profession must vigorously endeavor to prevent. A measure of judgment is, therefore, required in complying with the provisions of this Rule. The term "substantial" refers to the seriousness of the possible offense and not the quantum of evidence of which the lawyer is aware. A report should be made to the bar disciplinary agency unless some other agency, such as a peer review agency, is more appropriate in the circumstances. Similar considerations apply to the reporting of judicial misconduct.

[4]   The duty to report professional misconduct does not apply to a lawyer retained to represent a lawyer whose professional conduct is in question. Such a situation is governed by the Rules applicable to the client-lawyer relationship.

[5]   Information about a lawyer's or judge's misconduct or fitness may be received by a lawyer in the course of that lawyer's participation in an approved lawyers' or judges' assistance program. In that circumstance, providing for the confidentiality of such information encourages lawyers and judges to seek treatment through such programs. Conversely, without such confidentiality, lawyers and judges may hesitate to seek assistance from these programs, which may then result in additional harm to their professional careers and additional injury to the welfare of clients and the public. The Rule therefore exempts the lawyer from the reporting requirements of paragraphs (a) and (b) with respect to information that would be privileged if the relationship between the impaired lawyer or judge and the recipient of the information were that of a client and a lawyer. On the other hand, a lawyer who receives such information would nevertheless be required to comply with the Rule 8.3 reporting provisions to report misconduct if the impaired lawyer or judge indicates an intent to engage in illegal activity, for example, the conversion of client funds to his or her use.

Model Code Comparison

DR 1-103(A) provided that "[a] lawyer possessing unprivileged knowledge of a violation of [a Disciplinary Rule] shall report such knowledge to . . . authority empowered to investigate or act upon such violation."

RULE 8.4 MISCONDUCT

It is professional misconduct for a lawyer to:

(a)   violate or attempt to violate the Rules of Professional Conduct, knowingly assist or induce another to do so, or do so through the acts of another;

(b)   commit a criminal act that reflects adversely on the lawyer's honesty, trustworthiness or fitness as a lawyer in other respects;

(c)   engage in conduct involving dishonesty, fraud, deceit or misrepresentation;

(d)   engage in conduct that is prejudicial to the administration of justice;

(e)   state or imply an ability to influence improperly a government agency or official; or

(f)   knowingly assist a judge or judicial officer in conduct that is a violation of applicable rules of judicial conduct or other law.

Comment

[1]   Many kinds of illegal conduct reflect adversely on fitness to practice law, such as offenses involving fraud and the offense of willful failure to file an income tax return. However, some kinds of offense carry no such implication. Traditionally, the distinction was drawn in terms of offenses involving "moral turpitude." That concept can be construed to include offenses concerning some matters of personal morality, such as adultery and comparable offenses, that have no specific connection to fitness for the practice of law. Although a lawyer is personally answerable to the entire criminal law, a lawyer should be professionally answerable only for offenses that indicate lack of those characteristics relevant to law practice. Offenses involving violence, dishonesty, breach of trust, or serious interference with the administration of justice are in that category. A pattern of repeated offenses, even ones of minor significance when considered separately, can indicate indifference to legal obligation.

[2]   A lawyer may refuse to comply with an obligation imposed by law upon a good faith belief that no valid obligation exists. The provisions of Rule 1.2(d) concerning a good faith challenge to the validity, scope, meaning or application of the law apply to challenges of legal regulation of the practice of law.

[3]   Lawyers holding public office assume legal responsibilities going beyond those of other citizens. A lawyer's abuse of public office can suggest an inability

to fulfill the professional role of lawyer. The same is true of abuse of positions of private trust such as trustee, executor, administrator, guardian, agent and officer, director or manager of a corporation or other organization.

Model Code Comparison

With regard to paragraphs (a) through (d), DR 1-102(A) provided that a lawyer shall not:

"(1)　Violate a Disciplinary Rule.

"(2)　Circumvent a Disciplinary Rule through actions of another.

"(3)　Engage in illegal conduct involving moral turpitude.

"(4)　Engage in conduct involving dishonesty, fraud, deceit, or misrepresentation.

"(5)　Engage in conduct that is prejudicial to the administration of justice.

"(6)　Engage in any other conduct that adversely reflects on his fitness to practice law."

Paragraph (e) is substantially similar to DR 9-101(C).

There was no direct counterpart to paragraph (f) in the Disciplinary Rules of the Model Code. EC 7-34 stated in part that "[a] lawyer . . . is never justified in making a gift or a loan to a [judicial officer] except as permitted by . . . the Code of Judicial Conduct." EC 9-1 stated that a lawyer "should promote public confidence in our [legal] system and in the legal profession."

RULE 8.5 DISCIPLINARY AUTHORITY; CHOICE OF LAW

(a)　Disciplinary Authority. A lawyer admitted to practice in this jurisdiction is subject to the disciplinary authority of this jurisdiction, regardless of where the lawyer's conduct occurs. A lawyer may be subject to the disciplinary authority of both this jurisdiction and another jurisdiction where the lawyer is admitted for the same conduct.

(b)　Choice of Law. In any exercise of the disciplinary authority of this jurisdiction, the rules of professional conduct to be applied shall be as follows:

(1)　for conduct in connection with a proceeding in a court before which a lawyer has been admitted to practice (either generally or for purposes of that proceeding), the rules to be applied shall be the rules of the jurisdiction in which the court sits, unless the rules of the court provide otherwise; and

(2)　for any other conduct,

(i)　if the lawyer is licensed to practice only in this jurisdiction, the rules to be applied shall be the rules of this jurisdiction, and

(ii)　if the lawyer is licensed to practice in this and another jurisdiction, the rules to be applied shall be the rules of the

admitting jurisdiction in which the lawyer principally practices; provided, however, that if particular conduct clearly has its predominant effect in another jurisdiction in which the lawyer is licensed to practice, the rules of that jurisdiction shall be applied to that conduct.

Comment

Disciplinary Authority

[1]   Paragraph (a) restates longstanding law.

Choice of Law

[2]   A lawyer may be potentially subject to more than one set of rules of professional conduct which impose different obligations. The lawyer may be licensed to practice in more than one jurisdiction with differing rules, or may be admitted to practice before a particular court with rules that differ from those of the jurisdiction or jurisdictions in which the lawyer is licensed to practice. In the past, decisions have not developed clear or consistent guidance as to which rules apply in such circumstances.

[3]   Paragraph (b) seeks to resolve such potential conflicts. Its premise is that minimizing conflicts between rules, as well as uncertainty about which rules are applicable, is in the best interest of both clients and the profession (as well as the bodies having authority to regulate the profession). Accordingly, it takes the approach of (i) providing that any particular conduct of a lawyer shall be subject to only one set of rules of professional conduct, and (ii) making the determination of which set of rules applies to particular conduct as straight forward as possible, consistent with recognition of appropriate regulatory interests of relevant jurisdictions.

[4]   Paragraph (b) provides that as to a lawyer's conduct relating to a proceeding in a court before which the lawyer is admitted to practice (either generally or pro hac vice), the lawyer shall be subject only to the rules of professional conduct of that court. As to all other conduct, paragraph (b) provides that a lawyer licensed to practice only in this jurisdiction shall be subject to the rules of professional conduct of this jurisdiction, and that a lawyer licensed in multiple jurisdictions shall be subject only to the rules of the jurisdiction where he or she (as an individual, not his or her firm) principally practices, but with one exception: if particular conduct clearly has its predominant effect in another admitting jurisdiction, then only the rules of that jurisdiction shall apply. The intention is for the latter exception to be a narrow one. It would be appropriately applied, for example, to a situation in which a lawyer admitted in, and principally practicing in, State A, but also admitted in State B, handled an acquisition by a company whose headquarters and operations were in State B of another, similar such company. The exception would not appropriately be applied, on the other hand, if the lawyer handled an acquisition by a company whose headquarters and operations were in State A of a company whose headquarters and main operations were in State A, but which also had some operations in State B.

[5]   If two admitting jurisdictions were to proceed against a lawyer for the same conduct, they should, applying this rule, identify the same governing ethics rules. They should take all appropriate steps to see that they do apply the same rule to the same conduct, and in all events should avoid proceeding against a lawyer on the basis of two inconsistent rules.

[6]   The choice of law provision is not intended to apply to transnational practice. Choice of law in this context should be the subject of agreements between jurisdictions or of appropriate international law.

Model Code Comparison

There was no counterpart to this Rule in the Model Code.

SUBJECT GUIDE TO THE ABA MODEL RULES
OF PROFESSIONAL CONDUCT

A

Abuse of process,
  Rule 3.1 (Comment)

Accepting appointments,
  Rule 6.2

Accounting for funds,
  Rule 1.15

Acquiring interest in litigation,
  Rule1.8(f)
contingentfee,
  Rule 1.8(f)(2)

Adjudicative officers,
negotiating for private employment
  Rule 1.12(b)
disqualification of former,
  Rule 1.12(a)

Administration of justice,
conduct prejudicial to,
  Rule 8.4(d)
interference with,
  Rule 8.4 (Comment)
lawyer's duty to seek
improvement in,
  Preamble

Administration of law,
participation in,
  Rule 6.4

Administrative agencies and tribunals,
appearance before,
  Rule 3.9 (Comment)

Administrator,
fee for representation of,
  Rule 1.5 (Comment)

Admiralty practice,
communication of,
  Rule 7.4(b)

Admission to practice,
  Rule 8.1

Advance fee payments,
propriety of,
  Rule 1.5 (Comment)

Adversary system,
duty of lawyer to,
  Preamble

Adverse legal authority,
lawyer's duty to disclose,
  Rule 3.3(a)(3)

Advertising, *See also* Solicitation,
Letterheads, Firm name.
class action members, to notify,
  Rule 7.2 (Comment)
communications concerning a
lawyer's services, generally,
  Rule 7.1
comparisons with services of
other lawyers,
  Rule 7.1(c)
endorsements by clients,
  Rule 7.1 (Comment)
fields of practice,
  Rule 7.4
mail,
  Rule 7.3 permitted forms,
  Rule 7.2
prior results,
  Rule 7.1 (Comment)
specialization,
  Rule 7.4

Advice to client,
candor, duty of,
  Rule 2.1
used to engage in criminal or
fraudulent conduct,
  Rule 1.2 (Comment)
when lawyer not competent in area,
  Rule 1.1

Advisor,
lawyer as,
  Preamble, Rule 2.1

Advocate,
in nonadjudicative proceedings,
  Rule 3.9
lawyer as,
  Preamble

Alteration of documents,
  Rule 3.4(a)

Ancillary businesses (or services)
    Rule 5.7

Appeal,
advising client of possibility,
    Rule 1.3 (Comment), Rule 1.4
        (Comment)
contingent fee,
    Rule 1.5 (Comment)
government lawyer's authority,
    Scope

Appearance of impropriety,
    Rule 1.10 (Comment)

Appointed counsel,
accepting appointments,
    Rule 6.2
discharge by client,
    Rule 1.16 (Comment)
endorsement of client's views,
    Rule 1.2(b)
requirement of competence,
    Rule 1.1
withdrawal by,
    Rule 1.16 (Comment)

Arbitration,
fee disputes,
    Rule 1.5 (Comment)

Arbitrator,
codes of ethics
    Rule 2.2(Comment)
former, negotiating for private
employment,
    Rule 1.12(b)
partisan in multimember panel,
    Rule 1.12(d)

Association with competent
    lawyer,
    Rule 1.1 (Comment)

Associations, unincorporated,
    Rule 1.13 (Comment)

Attorney-client privilege,
    Scope
distinguished from confidentiality rule,
    Rule 1.6 (Comment)
intermediation, effect on,
    Rule 2.2(a)(1)

Attorney general,
authority of,
    Scope

Auditors' requests for information,
    Rule 2.3 (Comment)

Authority of lawyer,
decisionmaking authority,
    Rule 1.2(a)
government lawyer,
    Scope

Autonomy of legal profession,
    Preamble

B

Belief,
defined,
    Terminology

Beneficiary,
fiduciary client, lawyer's obligation
toward,
    Rule 1.2 (Comment)

Board of directors,
lawyer member,
    Rule 1.7 (Comment)
organization as client,
    Rule 1.13

Bodily harm,
client's intent to commit serious,
    Rule 1.6 (Comment)

Breach of trust, offense involving,
    Rule 8.4 (Comment)

Bribery,
of officials,
    Rule 3.5(a)
of witness,
    Rule 3.4(b)

Business affairs of lawyer,
adverse to client,
    Rule 1.8(a)
conflict of interest,
    Rule 1.7 (Comment)
duty to conduct in compliance with law,
    Preamble
law-related services,
    Rule 5.7

C

Candid advice,
    Rule 2.1

Candidate for judicial office,
    Rule 8.2(b)

Candor toward tribunal,
    Rule 3.3

Cause of action,
violation of Rules as basis for,
    Scope

Certification,
as specialist,
    Rule 7.4(a)

Champerty, law of
    Rule 1.8 (Comment)

Child client,
communication with,
    Rule 1.4 (Comment)

Child of lawyer,
gift to,
    Rule 1.8(c)

client of,
    Rule 1.8(i)

Choice of law,
    Rule 8.5

Citizen, lawyer as,
    Preamble

Civil disobedience, Rule 1.2 (Comment)
Civil liability,
violation of Rules as basis for,
    Scope

Class actions,
consent to lawyer's compensation,
    Rule 1.8 (Comment)
fee determination,
    Rule 1.5 (Comment)
notice to members,
    Rule 7.2 (Comment)

Client-lawyer relationship,
existence of defined by substantive law,
    Scope
informed understanding, lawyer's role,
    Preamble
law-related services,
    Rule 5.7

Client's identity,
conflicts of interest,
    Rule 1.10 (Comment)

government agency,
    Rule 1.11 (Comment)
organization,
    Rule 1.13

Client's security fund,
    Rule 1.15 (Comment)

Code of Judicial Conduct,
    Rule 3.5 (Comment), Rule 8.2(b)

Comments,
do not expand lawyer's responsibilities,
    Scope

Communication,
concerning lawyer's services,
    Rule 7.1
duty to maintain with client,
    Preamble, Rule 1.4 (Comment)
with represented party,
    Rule 4.2
with third persons,
    Rule 4.1
with unrepresented persons,
    Rule 4.3
withholding information from client,
    Rule 1.4 (Comment)

Competence,
    Preamble, Rule 1.16 (Comment)

Competent representation,
requirements of,
    Rule 1.1

Compliance with Rules,
    Preamble, Scope

Concealment,
duty to avoid,
    Rule 1.2 (Comment)
of documents,
    Rule 3.4(a)

Confidences of client,
attachment of duty,
    Scope
attorney-client privilege,
    Scope
corporate client,
    Rule 1.13 (Comment)
disclosure of,
    Preamble, Rule 1.6(b)
disclosure to disciplinary authorities,
    Rule 8.1

duty to preserve,
    Preamble, Rule 1.6(a)
evaluation, information used in
        preparing,
    Rule 2.3(b)
former client,
    Rule 1.9 (Comment)
imputed to members of firm,
    Rule 1.10 (Comment)
intermediation, effect of,
    Rule 2.2 (Comment)
perjury by client,
    Rule 3.3(b)
public interest in preserving,
    Preamble, Rule 1.6 (Comment)
withdrawal, facts constituting
explanation for,
    Rule 1.16 (Comment)

Conflict of laws,
    Rule 8.5 (Comment)

Conflict of interest,
acquiring interest in litigation,
    Rule 1.8(j)(2)
advocate, when acting as,
    Rule 1.7 (Comment)
business interests of lawyer,
    Rule 1.7 (Comment)
business transaction with client,
    Rule 1.8(a)
consent of client to,
    Rule 1.7(a)(2), Rule 1.7(b)(2), Rule 1.7
        (Comment),
    Rule 1.8(a)(3), Rule 1.8(b)
co-parties, representation of,
    Rule 1.7 (Comment)
declining employment because of,
    Rule 1.7 (Comment)

estate planning or administration,
    Rule 1.7 (Comment)
existing client, interest adverse to client,
    Rule 1.7(a)
fee paid by one other than client,
    Rule 1.7 (Comment)
former client,
    Rule 1.9
general rule,
    Rule 1.7
interest of lawyer adverse to client,
    Rule 1.7(b)
lawyer as intermediary,
    Rule 2.2 (Comment)

legal services corporation, director of,
    Rule 6.3
"matter" defined,
    Rule 1.9 (Comment)
multiple representation,
    Rule 1.7(b)(2)
negotiation,
    Rule 1.7 (Comment)
opposing party raises,
    Rule 1.7 (Comment)
third person, interest adverse to client,
    Rule 1.7(b)
unrelated matters,
    Rule 1.7 (Comment)
withdrawal because of,
    Rule 1.7 (Comment)

Conflicting responsibilities,
    Preamble

Conscience,
    Preamble

Consent by client,
to conflict of interest,
    Rule 1.7(a)(2), Rule 1.7(b)(2),
    Rule 1.8(a)(3), Rule 1.8(b)
to common representation,
    Rule 2.2(a)(1)
to disclosure of professional misconduct,
    Rule 8.3 (Comment)

to evaluation for use by third persons,
    Rule 2.3(a)(2)

Constitutional law,
governing authority of government
        lawyer,
    Scope

Consultation,
defined,
    Terminology
duty,
    Rule 1.1 (Comment) lawyer as
        intermediary,
    Rule 2.2(a)
with client,
    Rule 1.2
Contingent fee,
civil cases,
    Rule 1.8(j)(2)
costs and expenses advanced by lawyer,
    Rule 1.8(e)(1)
criminal cases,
    Rule 1.5(d)(2)

domestic relations cases,
  Rule 1.5(d)(1)
expert witness,
  Rule 3.4 (Comment)
prohibited representations,
  Rule 1.5(d)
requirements of,
  Rule 1.5(c)

Continuing legal education,
  Rule 1.1 (Comment)

Corporate legal department,
  Terminology, Rule 1.10 (Comment)

Corporate representation,
  See Organization, representation of

Costs advanced to client,
  Rule 1.8(e)(1)

Court, *See also* Tribunal.
authority over legal profession,
  Preamble

candor, duty of,
  Rule 3.3
offering false evidence to,
  Rule 3.3(a)(4)

Court rules, relation to Rules,
  Scope

Creditors of client, claim
funds of client,
  Rule 1.15 (Comment)

Criminal conduct,
by lawyer,
  Rule 8.4(b)
counselling or assisting client to
      engage in,
  Rule 1.2(d), Rule 3.3(a)(2)
disclosure of client's,
  Rule 1.2 (Comment)
withdrawal when client persists in,
  Rule 1.2 (Comment),
  Rule 1.6

(Comment), Rule 1.16(b)(1), Rule 1.13(c)
Criminal representation,
aggregate plea bargain on behalf of
      multiple defendants,
  Rule 1.8(g)
codefendants, representation of,
  Rule 1.7 (Comment)
contingent fee for,
  Rule 1.5(d)(2)

decisionmaking authority,
  Rule 1.2(a)
frivolous defense,
  Rule 3.1
perjury by client,
  Rule 3.3 (Comment)
trial publicity,
  Rule 3.6

D

Deceased lawyer,
payments to estate of,
  Rule 5.4(a)(2)

Deceit by lawyer,
  Rule 8.4(c)

Declining representation, causes,
  Rule 1.16
conflict of interest,
  Rule 1.7 (Comment)
refusing to accept appointment,
  Rule 6.2

Decorum of tribunal,
  Rule 3.5

Delay,
  Rule 3.2 (Comment), Rule 4.4

Delivery of funds or property,
  Rule 1.15(b)

Derivative actions,
  Rule 1.13 (Comment)

Destruction of potential evidence,
  Rule 3.4(a)

Dilatory practices,
  Rule 3.2 (Comment)

Diligence,
  Preamble, Rule 1.3

Direct contact with prospective clients,
  Rule 7.3

Directors of organization
  Rule 1.13

Disability of client,
  Rule 1.2 (Comment),
  Rule 1.14(a),
  Rule 1.4 (Comment)

Disability of lawyer,
  Rule 1.16(a)(2)

Discharge of lawyer,
Rule 1.16(a)

Disciplinary authority,
Rule 8.5

Disciplinary proceedings,
disclosure of client confidences in
connection with,
Rule 1.6 (Comment)
failure to comply with requests
for information,
Rule 8.1(b)
jurisdiction,
Rule 8.5
reporting professional misconduct,
Rule 8.3

Discipline,
violation of Rules as basis for,
Scope

Disclosure of,
client's disability,
Rule 1.14 (Comment)
client's interests when lawyer
participates in law reform activities,
Rule 6.4
fee division,
Rule 1.5 (Comment)

Discovery,
obstructive tactics,
Rule 3.4(d)

Discretion of lawyer,
Scope

Dishonesty, conduct involving,
Rule 8.4(c)

Disruptive conduct,
Rule 3.5(c)

Disputes with client,
confidentiality exception,
Rule 1.6 (Comment) fees,
Rule 1.5 (Comment)

Disqualification, *See also* Imputed
disqualification.
former judge,
Rule 1.12(a)
waiver by client,
Rule 1.9 (Comment), Rule 1.10(d)

Division of fees,
requirements of,
Rule 1.5(e)

with nonlawyer,
Rule 5.4(a)

Documents, alteration of,
Rule 3.4(a)

Domestic relations,
contingent fee in,
Rule 1.5(d)(1)

Dual representation of organization and
constituent,
Rule 1.13(e)

E

Economic factors relevant to client's
situation,
Rule 2.1

Education, legal,
Preamble

Embarrassing third persons,
Rule 4.4

Emergency,
advice in matter,
Rule 1.1 (Comment), Rule 1.2

Employees of client,
Rule 1.13, Rule 3.4.(f)

Employees of lawyer,
responsibility for,
Rule 5.3

Employment agreement restricting right
to practice,
Rule 5.6(a)

Endorsements,
Rule 7.1

Escrow agent,
Rule 1.15 (Comment)

Estate planning,
conflicts of interest in,
Rule 1.7 (Comment)

Evaluation for use by third person,
Rule 2.3

Evaluator,
lawyer as,
Preamble

Evidence,
destruction of,
Rule 3.3(a)

methods of obtaining,
    Rule 4.4
obstructing access to,
    Rule 3.4(a)
offering false,
    Rule 3.3(a)(4)

Ex parte communications with member of
        tribunal,
    Rule 3.5(b)

Ex parte proceedings,
    Rule 3.3(d)

Executor,
lawyer's fee for representation of,
    Rule 1.5 (Comment)

Expediting litigation,
    Rule 3.2

Expenses of litigation,
client's right to determine,
    Rule 1.2 (Comment)
contingent fee,
    Rule 1.5 (Comment)
lawyer advancing to client,
    Rule 1.8(e)(1)
indigent client, paying on behalf of,
    Rule 1.8(e)(2)

Expert witness, *See* Witness.
Expertise,
competent representation,
    Rule 1.1

F

Failure to disclose to tribunal,
adverse legal authority,
    Rule 3.3(a)(3)
material fact,
    Rule 3.3(a)(2)

Fairness to opposing party and counsel,
    Rule 3.4

False communications concerning
        lawyer's services,
    Rule 7.1

False statement to tribunal,
    Rule 3.3(a)(1)

Falsification of evidence,
    Rule 3.4(b)

Family of lawyer,
gift to,
    Rule 1.8(c)
client of lawyer-relative,
    Rule 1.8(i)

Fees,
acquiring ownership interest in
        enterprise as,
    Rule 1.5 (Comment)
advance fee payments,
    Rule 1.5 (Comment)
advertising of,
    Rule 7.2 (Comment)
arbitration of,
    Rule 1.5 (Comment)
communication of to client,
    Rule 1.5(b)
contingent, prohibited
        representations,
    Rule 1.5(d)
contingent, requirements of,
    Rule 1.5(c)
determination of,
    Rule 1.5(a)
disclosure of confidential
information to collect,
    Rule 1.6(b)(2)
division with lawyer,
    Rule 1.5(e)
division with nonlawyer,
    Rule 5.4(a)

former government lawyer representing
        private client,
    Rule 1.11
paid by one other than client,
    Rule 1.7 (Comment), Rule 1.8(f),
    Rule 5.4(c)
risk that client may not pay,
    Rule 1.15 Comment
termination of representation,
    Rule 1.16(d)

Fiduciary
Lawyer's obligation toward
beneficiary,
    Rule 1.2 (Comment)
standard for holding property of others,
    Rule 1.15 (Comment)

Field of practice,
communication of,
    Rule 7.4

Fifth Amendment in bar admission and
    disciplinary matters,
    Rule 8.1 (Comment)

Firm, *See* Law firm.
Former client, *See* Conflict of interest.
Former government lawyer,
"confidential government
information" defined,
    Rule 1.11(e)
"matter" defined,
    Rule 1.11(d)
successive government and private
    employment,
    Rule 1.11

Former judge, *See* Judges.
Fraud,
    Terminology, Rule 8.4(c)

Fraudulent conduct,
counselling or assisting client to
    engage in,
    Rule 1.2(d)
disclosure of client's,
    Rule 1.2 (Comment)

withdrawal when client persists in,
    Rule 1.2 (Comment), Rule 1.6
        (Comment), Rule 1.13(c),
        Rule 1.16(b)(1)

Frivolous claims and defenses,
    Rule 3.1

Frivolous discovery request,
    Rule 3.4(d)

Funds of client,
handling of,
    Rule 1.15(b)
lawyer claims interest in,
    Rule 1.15(c)

G

Gift to lawyer by client,
    Rule 1.8(c)

Government agency,
appearance before,
    Rule 3.9
improper influence on,
    Rule 8.4(e)
representation of,
    Rule 1.13 (Comment)

Government lawyer,
authority of
    Scope
conflict of interest,
    Rule 1.7 (Comment)
duties of,
    Rule 1.13 (Comment)
duty of confidentiality,
    Rule 1.6 (Comment)
opinions on legality of
contemplated agency action,
    Rule 2.3 (Comment)
representing multiple clients,
    Scope
subject to Rules,
    Rule 1.11 (Comment)
supervisory responsibilities,
    Rule 5.1 (Comment)

Guardian of disabled client,
acting adversely toward,
    Rule 1.14 (Comment)
appointment of,
    Rule 1.14(b)

H

Harassment,
    Preamble

Hearing officers, *See* Adjudicative
    officers.
Holiday gifts,
    Rule 1.8 (Comment)

Homicide,
client's intent to commit,
    Rule 1.6 (Comment)

I

Identity of client,
conflicts of interest,
    Rule 1.10 (Comment)
government agency,
    Rule 1.11 (Comment)
organization,
    Rule 1.13

Impartiality and decorum of tribunal,
    Rule 3.5

Imperatives in rules,
    Scope

Imputed disqualification,
firm of former judge or arbitrator,
    Rule 1.12(c)
general rule,
    Rule 1.10
government lawyers,
    Rule 1.11 (Comment)
witness, when member of firm serves as,
    Rule 3.7(b)

Incompetent client,
appointment of guardian for,
    Rule 1.14(b)
discharge of lawyer by,
    Rule 1.16 (Comment)
representation of,
    Rule 1.14(a)

Independence of legal profession,
    Preamble

Independent professional judgment,
    Rule 2.1, Rule 5.4

Indigent,
court costs and expenses of,
    Rule 1.8(e)(2)

legal representation,
    Preamble, Rule 1.2 (Comment),
    Rule 6.1

Information,
used to disadvantage of client,
    Rule 1.8(b)
withholding from client,
    Rule 1.4 (Comment)

Injury,
client's intent to commit serious
bodily,
    Rule 1.6 (Comment)

Insurance representation,
conflict of interest,
    Rule 1.7 (Comment)

Interest, acquisition by lawyer,
adverse to client,
    Rule 1.8(a)
in litigation,
    Rule 1.8(j)

Intermediary,
lawyer as,
    Preamble, Rule 2.2

Intimidation,
    Preamble

Investigation of client's affairs,
    Rule 2.1 (Comment)

J

Judgment, exercise of,
    Preamble

Judges,
duty to show respect for,
    Preamble
ex parte communication with,
    Rule 3.5(b)
former judge, disqualification,
    Rule 1.12
improper influence on,
    Rule 3.5(a)
misconduct by,
    Rule 8.3(b), Rule 8.4(f)
statements about,
    Rule 8.2

Juror,
improper influence on,
    Rule 3.5(a)

Jury trial,
client's right to waive,
    Rule 1.2(a)

K

Knowledge,
defined,
    Terminology
factors,
    Rule 1.1 (Comment)
lawyer's role,
    Preamble
of client's intent to commit
homicide or serious bodily injury,
    Rule 1.6 (Comment)

L

Law clerk,
negotiating for private employment,
    Rule 1.12(b)

Law firm,
defined,
    Terminology, Rule 1.10 (Comment)

disclosure of client information in,
    Rule 1.6 (Comment)

disqualification,
    Rule 1.10 (Comment)
former judge or arbitrator,
        disqualification
    Rule 1.12(c)
name,
    Rule 7.5(a)
nonlawyer assistants,
    Rule 5.3
partner or supervisory lawyer,
    Rule 5.1
subordinate lawyer,
    Rule 5.2

Law reform activities,
affecting clients' interests,
    Rule 6.4

Law-related services,
    Rule 5.7

Lawyer as witness,
    Rule 3.7

Lawyer referral services,
    Rule 6.1 (Comment)
costs of,
    Rule 7.2(c)

Learned profession,
lawyer as member of,
    Preamble

Legal aid,
definition of "firm"
    Rule 1.10 (Comment)
limitations,
    Rule 1.2 (Comment)

Legal assistants,
responsibilities of lawyer,
    Rule 5.3

Legal education,
    Preamble

Legal representative of client under
        disability,
    Rule 1.14 (Comment)

Legal services organization,
costs of,
    Rule 7.2(c)
defined,
    Terminology
membership in,
    Rule 6.3

Legislature,
appearance before,
    Rule 3.9

Letterheads,
false or misleading,
    Rule 7.5(a)
jurisdictional limitations of firm's
members,
    Rule 7.5(b)
public officials,
    Rule 7.5(c)

Liability to client,
agreements limiting,
    Rule 1.8(h)

Licensure statutes,
relation to Rules,
    Scope

Lien to secure fees and expenses,
    Rule 1.8(j)(1)

Literary rights concerning
        representation,
    Rule 1.8(d)

Litigation,
acquiring interest in,
    Rule 1.8(j)
conflict of interest,
    Rule 1.7 (Comment)
expedite, duty to,
    Rule 3.2 information,
    Rule 1.4 (Comment),
    Rule 1.5 (Comment),
    Rule 1.6 (Comment)

Loyalty to client,
    Rule 1.7 (Comment)

M

Mail contact with prospective
        clients,
    Rule 7.3

Maintenance, law of,
    Rule 1.8 (Comment)

Malpractice,
limiting liability to client for,
    Rule 1.8(h)

Mandatory withdrawal,
    Rule 1.16(a)

Media rights concerning representation,
  Rule 1.8(d)

Mediation of fee disputes,
  Rule 1.5 (Comment)

Mediators' codes of ethics,
  Rule 2.2(Comment)

Mental disability of client,
  Rule 1.14(a)
client decisions,
  Rule 1.2 (Comment) communication
    with client,
  Rule 1.4 (Comment)

Mental disability of lawyer,
  Rule 1.16(a)(2)

Memoranda, legal,
limit on malpractice liability,
  Rule 1.8 (Comment)

Meritorious claims and contentions,
  Rule 3.1

Military lawyers,
duties of,
  Rule 1.13 (Comment)
representation of adverse
    interests,
  Rule 1.9 (Comment)

Minor client,
  Rule 1.14(a)

Misconduct,
forms of,
  Rule 8.4
reporting,
  Rule 8.3

Misleading legal argument,
  Rule 3.3 (Comment)

Misrepresentation,
advertisements,
  Rule 7.1
bar admission and disciplinary matters,
  Rule 8.1
firm names and letterhead,
  Rule 7.5 (Comment)
misconduct,
  Rule 8.4(c)
negligent,
  Terminology
to court,
  Rule 3.3 (Comment)

to third person
  Rule 4.1 (Comment)

Moral factors relevant to client's
    situation,
  Rule 2.1

Moral turpitude offenses,
  Rule 8.4 (Comment)

Multiple representation, *See* Conflict of
    interest, Intermediary.

N

Negotiation,
conflicting interest, representation of,
  Rule 1.7 (Comment)
disclosure of information in,
  Rule 1.6 (Comment)
statements made during,
  Rule 4.1 (Comment)

Negotiator,
lawyer as,
  Preamble

Nonadjudicative proceedings,
  Rule 3.9

Nonlawyer assistants,
responsibilities of lawyer,
  Rule 5.3

Nonlawyers,
division of fees with,
  Rule 5.4(a)
partnership,
  Rule 5.4(b)
professional corporation,
  Rule 5.4(d)

Notice of receipt of funds or other
    property,
  Rule 1.15(b)

O

Objectives of the representation,
client's right to determine,
  Rule 1.2(a)
lawyer's right to limit,
  Rule 1.2(c)

Obstruction of party's access to evidence,
  Rule 3.4(a)

Officer of legal system,
    Preamble

Opinions,
evaluation for use by third persons,
    Rule 2.3
limit on malpractice liability,
    Rule 1.8 (Comment)

Opposing party,
communications with represented party,
    Rule 4.2
duty of fairness to,
    Rule 3.4

Optional withdrawal,
    Rule 1.16(b)

Organization, representation of,
board of directors, lawyer on,
    Rule 1.7 (Comment)
communication with,
    Rule 1.4 (Comment)
communication with employees and
        officers of,
    Rule 4.2 (Comment)
conflict of interest,
    Rule 1.7 (Comment)
intended conduct,
    Rule 1.6 (Comment)
constituents, representing,
    Rule 1.13(e)
identity of client,
    Rule 1.13(a), Rule 1.13(d)
law department of,
    Rule 1.10 (Comment)
misconduct, client engaged in,
    Rule 1.13(b)
officers of,
    Rule 1.13

P

Papers, retention of,
    Rule 1.16 (Comment)

Parent of lawyer,
gift to,
    Rule 1.8(c)
client of,
    Rule 1.8(i)

Partner,
defined,
    Terminology

nonlawyer,
    Rule 5.4(b)
supervision of lawyers,
    Rule 5.1
supervision of nonlawyers,
    Rule 5.3

Partnership,
agreement restricting right to practice,
    Rule 5.6(a)

name,
    Rule 7.5(d)

Patent practice,
advertising,
    Rule 7.4(a)

Peer approval,
    Preamble

Peer review agency, reporting misconduct
        to,
    Rule 8.3 (Comment)

Perjury,
criminal defendant,
    Rule 3.3 (Comment)
disclosure of,
    Rule 3.3(b)

Permissive Rules,
    Scope

Personal affairs of lawyer,
duty to conduct in compliance with law,
    Preamble

Physical condition of lawyer,
    Rule 1.16(a)(2)

Plea bargain,
client's right to accept or reject,
    Rule 1.2(a)

Pleadings,
verification of,
    Rule 3.3 (Comment)

Political factors relevant to client's
        situation,
    Rule 2.1

Preamble, role of,
    Scope

Precedent,
failure to disclose to court,
    Rule 3.3(a)(3)

Prepaid legal services,
advertising for,
Rule 7.2 (Comment), Rule 7.3(d)

Privileges,
Scope

Pro bono publico service,
Rule 6.1

Procedural law,
Preamble, Scope

Procedural use of Rules,
Scope

Procrastination,
Rule 1.3 (Comment)

Professional corporation,
defined,
Terminology

formation of,
Rule 5.4(d)
shareholders' responsibilities,
Rule 5.1 (Comment)

Professional role
Scope

Promptness,
Preamble

Property of client,
payment for services,
Rule 1.5 (Comment)
return upon termination of
representation,
Rule 1.16(d)
safekeeping,
Rule 1.15

Prosecutor,
representing former defendant,
Rule 1.9 (Comment)
special responsibilities of,
Rule 3.8
trial publicity,
Rule 3.6, Rule 3.8(g)

Protective order, dispute concerning
lawyer's conduct,
Rule 1.6 (Comment)

Psychiatrist,
withholding diagnosis,
Rule 1.4 (Comment)

Public interest in preserving client
confidences,
Preamble, Rule 1.6 (Comment)

Public citizen,
lawyer's duty as,
Preamble

Public interest,
government lawyer's authority to
represent
Scope

Public interest legal services,
See Pro bono publico service.
Public office,
abuse of,
Rule 8.4 (Comment)
negotiating private employment
while holding,
Rule 1.11(c)(2)

Public officials,
firm's use of name,
Rule 7.5(d)
improper influence,
Rule 8.4(e)
respect for,
Preamble

Public service,
Preamble

Publicity, trial,
Rule 3.6
special responsibilities of prosecutor,
Rule 3.8(e)(g)

Q

Quality of service, improvement,
Preamble

R

Real estate,
lawyer's investment in,
Rule 1.8 (Comment)

Reasonable, defined,
Terminology

Recordkeeping,
property of client,
Rule 1.15(a)

Referral,
to other professionals,
    Rule 2.1 (Comment)
when lawyer not competent to handle
    matter,
    Rule 1.1

Referral services,
    Rule 6.1 (Comment)
costs of,
    Rule 7.2(c)

Referees, See Adjudicative
officers.
Reform of the law,
    Preamble, Rule 6.4

Regulation,
validity or interpretation,
    Rule 1.2 (Comment)

Regulation of legal profession,
self-governance,
    Preamble

Relatives of lawyer, representing inter-
    ests adverse to,
    Rule 1.8(h)

Remedial measures when false evidence
    offered,
    Rule 3.3(a)(4)

Reporting misconduct,
    Rule 8.3

Representation of client,
decisionmaking authority of lawyer and
    client,
    Rule 1.2(a)
declining or terminating,
    Rule 1.16
objectives, lawyer's right to limit,
    Rule 1.2(c)
termination of,
    Rule 1.2 (Comment), Rule 1.16

Representative of clients,
lawyer as,
    Preamble

Representative, legal, of client under
    disability,
    Rule 1.14 (Comment)

Represented party, communication with,
    Rule 4.2

Research notes not part of Rules,
    Scope

Responsibility for observing Rules,
    Preamble

Restrictions on right to practice,
partnership or employment agreement,
    Rule 5.6(a)
settlement agreement,
    Rule 5.6(b)

Retainer for limited purpose,
    Rule 1.2 (Comment)

Rule of reason,
    Scope

S

Safekeeping property,
    Rule 1.15

Sale of law practice,
    Rule 1.17

Sanction,
severity of,
    Scope

Scope of representation,
    Rule 1.2

Screening,
disqualified former government lawyer,
    Rule 1.11

Securities,
safekeeping,
    Rule 1.1.5 (Comment)

Self-regulation,
    Preamble

Settlement, aggregate,
    Rule 1.8(g)
client's right to refuse,
    Rule 1.2(a)
contingent fee,
    Rule 1.5 (Comment)
government lawyer's authority,
    Scope
informing client of settlement offers,
    Rule 1.4 (Comment)
restricting right to practice,
    Rule 5.6(b)

Shareholders of organization,
Rule 1.13

Sibling of lawyer,
gift to,
Rule 1.8(c)
client of,
Rule 1.8(i)

Solicitation,
prohibition on,
Rule 7.3

Special masters, See Adjudicative officers.
Specialization, communication of,
Rule 7.4(c)

Spouse of lawyer,
gift to,
Rule 1.8(c)
client of,
Rule 1.8(i)

State's Attorney,
authority of,
Scope

Statute of limitations,
Rule 1.3 (Comment)

Statutes,
conflict of interest, agency consent to,
Rule 1.11 (Comment)
shape lawyer's role,
Scope
validity or interpretation,
Rule 1.2 (Comment)

Subordinate lawyer,
responsibilities of,
Rule 5.2

Substantive law,
defines existence of
client-lawyer relationship,
Scope
lawyer's professional responsibilities
proscribed by,
Preamble
relation to Rules,
Scope

Supervision of lawyer,
Rule 5.1
nonlawyer,
Rule 5.3

T

Taxation, escaping liability,
Rule 1.2 (Comment)

Termination of representation,
Rule 1.2 (Comment), Rule 1.16

records of funds and other property,
Rule 1.15(a)

Testamentary gifts,
Rule 1.8(c)

Testimony of client in criminal trial,
Rule 1.2(a)

Testimony of lawyer, See Lawyer as
Witness.
Third persons,
evaluation for use by,
Rule 2.3
respect for rights of,
Rule 4.4
statements to,
Rule 4.1

Trade names,
Rule 7.5(a)

Transactions with persons other than
client, See Third persons.
Trial conduct, allusion to irrelevant or
inadmissible evidence,
Rule 3.4(e)
disruptive conduct,
Rule 3.5(c)

Trial publicity,
Rule 3.6
special responsibilities of prosecutor,
Rule 3.8(e)(g)

Tribunal,
continued representation ordered by,
Rule 1.16(c)
disobeying obligation of,
Rule 3.4(c)
impartiality and decorum of,
Rule 3.5

Trust accounts,
Rule 1.15 (Comment)

Truthfulness in statements to third
persons, Rule 4.1

U

Unauthorized practice of law,
assisting in,
    Rule 5.5(b)
engaging in,
    Rule 5.5(a)

Unrepresented person,
dealing with,
    Rule 4.3

Unincorporated associations,
    Rule 1.13 (Comment)

V

Violation of rules of professional conduct,
    See also Misconduct. declining or
    terminating representation,
    Rule 1.16(a)(1)

Violence,
    Rule 8.4 (Comment)

W

Waiver,
prosecutor obtaining from
criminal defendant,
    Rule 3.8(c)

Withdrawal,
    Rule 1.16 (Comment)
conflict of interest,
    Rule 1.7 (Comment)
discharge,
    Rule 1.16(a)(3)
incapacity,
    Rule 1.16(a)(2)
intermediary's,
    Rule 2.2(c)
mandatory,
    Rule 1.16(a)
method of,

Rule 1.3 (Comment)
notice of,
    Rule 1.6 (Comment)
optional,
    Rule 1.16(b)
property of client,
    Rule 1.16(d)

when client persists in criminal or
fraudulent conduct,
    Rule 1.2 (Comment), Rule 1.6
    (Comment), Rule 1.16(b)(1),
    Rule 1.13(c)

Withholding information from client,
        Rule 1.4 (Comment)
Witness,
bribing,
    Rule 3.4(b)
client's right to decide whether to testify,
    Rule 1.2(a)
expenses, payment of,
    Rule 3.4 (Comment)
expert, payment of,
    Rule 3.4 (Comment)
lawyer as,
    Rule 1.6 (Comment), Rule 3.7

Work load management,
    Rule 1.3 (Comment)

Work product privilege,
confidentiality rule,
    Rule 1.6 (Comment)
    Rules do not affect,
    Scope

Z

Zealous representation,
opposing party well-represented,
    Preamble
requirement of,
    Rule 1.3 (Comment)

TABLE A: RELATED SECTIONS
IN THE ABA MODEL CODE OF
PROFESSIONAL RESPONSIBILITY

TABLE A*

ABA MODEL RULES	ABA MODEL CODE
Competence	
Rule 1.1	EC 1-1, EC 1-2, EC 6-1, EC 6-2, EC 6-3, EC 6-4, EC 6-5, DR 6-101(A)
Scope of Representation	
Rule 1.2(a)	EC 5-12, EC 7-7, EC 7-8, DR 7-101(A)(1)
Rule 1.2(b)	EC 7-17
Rule 1.2(c)	EC 7-8, EC 7-9, DR 7-101(B)(1)
Rule 1.2(d)	EC 7-1, EC 7-2, EC 7-5, EC 7-22, DR 7-102(A)(6), (7) & (8), DR 7-106
Rule 1.2(e)	DR 2-110(C)(1)(c), DR 9-101(C)
Diligence	
Rule 1.3	EC 2-31, EC 6-4, EC 7-1, EC 7-38, DR 6-101(A)(3), DR 7-101(A)(1) & (3)
Communication	
Rule 1.4(a)	EC 7-8, EC 9-2, DR 6-101(A)(3), DR 9-102(B)(1)
Rule 1.4(b)	EC 7-8
Fees	
Rule 1.5(a)	EC 2-16, EC 2-17, EC 2-18, DR 2-106(A) & (B)
Rule 1.5(b)	EC 2-19
Rule 1.5(c)	EC 2-20, EC 5-7
Rule 1.5(d)	EC 2-20, DR 2-106(C)
Rule 1.5(e)	EC 2-22, DR 2-107(A)
Confidentiality of Information	
Rule 1.6(a)	EC 4-1, EC 4-2, EC 4-3, EC 4-4, DR 4-101(A), (B) &(C)

---

* Table A provides cross-references to related provisions, but only in the sense that the provisions consider substantially similar subject matter or reflect similar concerns. A cross-reference does not indicate that a provision of the ABA Model Code of Professional Responsibility has been incorporated by the provision of a Model Rule. The Canons of the Code are not cross-referenced.

TABLE A
(Continued)

ABA MODEL RULES	ABA MODEL CODE
Rule 1.6(b)(1)	EC 4-2, DR 4-101(C)(3), DR 7-102(B)
Rule 1.6(b)(2)	DR 4-101(C)(4)

Conflict of Interest

Rule 1.7(a)	EC 5-1, EC 5-14, EC 5-15, EC 5-17, EC 5-21, EC 5-22, DR 5-101(A), DR 5-105(A) & (B), DR 5-107(B)
Rule 1.7(b) & (b)(1)	EC 2-21, EC 5-1, EC 5-2, EC 5-3, EC 5-9, EC 5-11, EC 5-13, EC 5-14, EC 5-15, EC 5-16, EC 5-17, EC 5-19, EC 5-21, EC 5-22, EC 5-23, DR 5-101(A) & (B), DR 5-102, DR 5-104(A), DR 5-105(A), (B) & (C), DR 5-107(A)
Rule 1.7(b)(2)	EC 5-16, EC 5-17, DR 7-106(B)(2)

Prohibited Transactions

Rule 1.8(a)	EC 5-3, EC 5-5, DR 5-104(A)
Rule 1.8(b)	EC 4-5, DR 4-101(B)
Rule 1.8(c)	EC 5-1, EC 5-2, EC 5-5, EC 5-6
Rule 1.8(d)	EC 5-1, EC 5-3, EC 5-4, DR 5-104(B)
Rule 1.8(e)	EC 5-1, EC 5-3, EC 5-7, EC 5-8, DR 5-103(B)
Rule 1.8(f)	EC 2-21, EC 5-1, DR 5-107(A) & (B)
Rule 1.8(g)	EC 5-1, DR 5-106(A)
Rule 1.8(h)	EC 6-6, DR 6-102(A)
Rule 1.8(i)	None
Rule 1.8(j)	EC 5-1, EC 5-7, DR 5-101(A), DR 5-103(A)

Former Client

Rule 1.9(a)	DR 5-105(C)
Rule 1.9(b)	EC 4-5, EC 4-6
Rule 1.9(c)	None

Imputed Disqualification

Rule 1.10(a)	EC 4-5, DR 5-105(D)
Rule 1.10(b)	EC 4-5, DR 5-105(D)
Rule 1.10(c)	DR 5-105(A)

Successive Government and Private Employment

Rule 1.11(a)	EC 9-3, DR 9-101(B)
Rule 1.11(b)	None

TABLE A
(Continued)

ABA MODEL RULES	ABA MODEL CODE
Rule 1.11(c)	EC 8-8
Rule 1.11(d)	None
Rule 1.11(e)	None

Former Judge or Arbitrator

Rule 1.12(a) & (b)	EC 5-20, EC 9-3, DR 9-101(A) & (B)
Rule 1.12(c)	DR 5-105(D)
Rule 1.12(d)	None

Organization as Client

Rule 1.13(a)	EC 5-18, EC 5-24
Rule 1.13(b)	EC 5-18, EC 5-24, DR 5-107(B)
Rule 1.13(c)	EC 5-18, EC 5-24, DR 5-105(D), DR 5-107(B)
Rule 1.13(d)	EC 5-16
Rule 1.13(e)	EC 4-4, EC 5-16, DR 5-105(B) & (C)

Disabled Client

Rule 1.14(a)	EC 7-11, EC 7-12
Rule 1.14(b)	EC 7-12

Safekeeping Property

Rule 1.15	EC 5-7, EC 9-5, EC 9-7, DR 5-103(A)(1), DR 9-102

Declining or Terminating Representation

Rule 1.16(a)(1)	EC 2-30, EC 2-31, EC 2-32, DR 2-103(E), DR 2-104(A), DR 2-109(A), DR 2-110(B)(1) & (2)
Rule 1.16(a)(2)	EC 1-6, EC 2-30, EC 2-31, EC 2-32, DR 2-110(B)(3), DR 2-110(C)(4)
Rule 1.16(a)(3)	EC 2-31, EC 2-32, DR 2-110(B)(4)
Rule 1.16(b)(1)	EC 2-31, EC 2-32, DR 2-110(C)(1)(b) & (c), DR 2-110(C)(2)
Rule 1.16(b)(2)	EC 2-31, EC 2-32, DR 2-110(C)(2)
Rule 1.16(b)(3)	EC 2-30, EC 2-31, EC 2-32, DR 2-110 (C)(1)(d)
Rule 1.16(b)(4)	EC 2-31, EC 2-32, DR 2-110(C)(1)(f)(i)(j)
Rule 1.16(b)(5)	EC 2-32, DR 2-110(C)(1)(d) & (e)
Rule 1.16(b)(6)	EC 2-32, DR 2-110(C)(6)
Rule 1.16(c)	EC 2-32, DR 2-110(A)(1)
Rule 1.16(d)	EC 2-32, DR 2-110(A)(2) & (3)

TABLE A
(Continued)

ABA MODEL RULES   ABA MODEL CODE

Sale of Law Practice
    Rule 1.17   None

Advisor
    Rule 2.1   EC 5-11, EC 7-3, EC 7-8, DR 5-107(B)

Intermediary
    Rule 2.2(a)(1)   EC 4-2, EC 5-14, EC 5-15, EC 5-16,
                              EC 5-20, DR 5-105(A) & (C)
    Rule 2.2(a)(2) & (3)   EC 5-14, EC 5-15, DR 5-105(A) & (C)
    Rule 2.2(b)   EC 5-16
    Rule 2.2(c)   EC 5-15, EC 5-19, DR 5-105(B) & (C)

Evaluation for Use by Third Persons
    Rule 2.3   None

Meritorious Claims and Contentions
    Rule 3.1   EC 7-1, EC 7-4, EC 7-5, EC 7-14,
                              EC 7-25, DR 5-102(A)(5), DR 2-109(A)(B)(1),
                              DR 7-102(A)(1) & (2)

Expediting Litigation
    Rule 3.2   EC 7-20, DR 1-102(A)(5), DR 7-101(A)(1)
                              & (2)

Candor Toward the Tribunal
    Rule 3.3(a)(1)   EC 7-4, EC 7-32, EC 8-5, DR 1-102(A)(4)
                              & (5), DR 7-102(A)(4) & (5)
    Rule 3.3(a)(2)   EC 8-5, DR 1-102(A)(4) & (5),
                              DR 7-102(A)(3), DR 7-102(B)(1),
                              DR 7-109(A)
    Rule 3.3(a)(3)   EC 7-23, DR 1-102(A)(5), DR 7-106(B)(1)
    Rule 3.3(a)(4)   EC 7-5, EC 7-26, EC 8-5, DR 1-102(A)(4)
                              & (5), DR 7-102(A)(7), DR 7-102(B)(1)
    Rule 3.3(b)   EC 8-5, DR 7-102(B)
    Rule 3.3(c)   EC 7-24, EC 7-25
    Rule 3.3(d)   EC 7-24, EC 7-27

Fairness to Opposing Party and Counsel
    Rule 3.4(a)   EC 7-6, EC 7-27, DR 1-102(A)(4) & (5),
                              DR 7-106(C)(7), DR 7-109(A) & (B)

TABLE A
(Continued)

ABA MODEL RULES	ABA MODEL CODE
Rule 3.4(b)	EC 7-6, EC 7-28, DR 1-102(A)(4), (5) & (6), DR 7-102(A)(6), DR 7-109(C)
Rule 3.4(c)	EC 7-22, EC 7-25, EC 7-38, DR 1-102(A)(5), DR 7-106(A), DR 7-106(C)(5) & (7)
Rule 3.4(d)	DR 1-102(A)(5), DR 7-106(A), DR 7-106(C)(7)
Rule 3.4(e)	EC 7-24, EC 7-25, DR 1-102(A)(5), DR 7-106(C)(1), (2), (3) & (4)
Rule 3.4(f)	EC 7-27, DR 1-102(A)(5), DR 7-104(A)(2), DR 7-109(B)

Impartiality and Decorum

Rule 3.5(a)	EC 7-20, EC 7-29, EC 7-31, EC 7-32, EC 7-34, DR 7-106, DR 7-108, DR 7-109, DR 7-110, DR 8-101(A)
Rule 3.5(b)	EC 7-35, DR 7-108, DR 7-110(A) & (B)
Rule 3.5(c)	EC 7-20, EC 7-25, EC 7-36, EC 7-37, DR 7-101(A)(1), DR 7-106(C)(6)

Lawyer as Witness

Rule 3.7(a)	EC 5-9, EC 5-10, DR 5-101(B)(1) & (2), DR 5-102
Rule 3.7(b)	EC 5-9, DR 5-101(B), DR 5-102

Special Responsibilities of a Prosecutor

Rule 3.8(a)	EC 7-11, EC 7-13, EC 7-14, DR 7-103(A)
Rule 3.8(b)	EC 7-11, EC 7-13
Rule 3.8(c)	EC 7-11, EC 7-13, EC 7-18
Rule 3.8(d)	EC 7-11, EC 7-13, DR 7-103(B)
Rule 3.8(e)	None
Rule 3.8(f)	None
Rule 3.8(g)	EC 7-14

Advocate in Nonadjudicative Proceedings

Rule 3.9	EC 7-11, EC 7-15, EC 7-16, EC 8-4, EC 8-5, DR 7-106(B)(2), DR 9-101(C)

Truthfulness to Others

Rule 4.1	EC 7-5, DR 7-102(A)(3), (4), (5) & (7), DR 7-102(B)

TABLE A
(Continued)

ABA MODEL RULES	ABA MODEL CODE

Communication with Represented Persons
Rule 4.2   EC 2-30, EC 7-18, DR 7-104(A)(1)

Dealing with Unrepresented Persons
Rule 4.3   EC 2-3, EC 7-18, DR 7-104(A)(2)

Respect for Rights of Third Persons
Rule 4.4   EC 7-10, EC 7-14, EC 7-21, EC 7-25,
                           EC 7-29, EC 7-30, EC 7-37, DR 2-110(B)
                           (1), DR 7-101(A)(1), DR 7-102(A)(1),
                           DR 7-106(C)(2), DR 7-107(D), (E) & (F),
                           DR 7-108(D), (E), & (F)

Responsibilities of a Partner or Supervisory Lawyer
Rule 5.1(a) & (b)   EC 4-5, DR 4-101(D), DR 7-107(J)
Rule 5.1(c)   DR 1-102(A)(2), DR 1-103(A),
                           DR 7-108(E)

Responsibilities of a Subordinate Lawyer
Rule 5.2   None

Responsibilities Regarding Nonlawyer Assistants
Rule 5.3(a)   EC 3-6, EC 4-2, EC 4-5, EC 7-28,
                           DR 4-101(D), DR 7-107(J)
Rule 5.3(b)   DR 1-102(A)(2), DR 7-107(J),
                           DR 7-108(B), DR 7-108(E)
Rule 5.3(c)   None

Professional Independence of Lawyer
Rule 5.4(a)   EC 2-33, EC 3-8, EC 5-24, DR 2-103(D)
                           (4)(d), (e) & (f), DR 3-102(A),
                           DR 5-107(C)(3)
Rule 5.4(b)   EC 2-33, EC 3-8, DR 3-103(A)
Rule 5.4(c)   EC 2-33, EC 5-23, DR 2-103(C),
                           DR 5-107(B)
Rule 5.4(d)   EC 2-33, EC 3-8, DR 5-107(C)

Unauthorized Practice of Law
Rule 5.5   DR 3-101(A) & (B)

TABLE A
(Continued)

ABA MODEL RULES   ABA MODEL CODE

Restrictions on Right to Practice
   Rule 5.6   DR 2-108

Provision of Ancillary Services
   Rule 5.7   None

Pro Bono Publico Service
   Rule 6.1   EC 1-2, EC 1-4, EC 2-1, EC 2-2, EC 2-16,
                                   EC 2-24, EC 2-25, EC 6-2, EC 8-1,
                                   EC 8-2, EC 8-3, EC 8-7, EC 8-9

Accepting Appointments
   Rule 6.2 (a)   EC 2-1, EC 2-25, EC 2-27, EC 2-28,
                                   EC 2-29, EC 8-3
   Rule 6.2(b)   EC 2-16, EC 2-25, EC 2-29, EC 2-30
   Rule 6.2(c)   EC 2-25, EC 2-27, EC 2-29, EC 2-30

Membership in Legal Services Organization
   Rule 6.3   EC 2-33, DR 5-101(A)

Law Reform Activities Affecting Client Interests
   Rule 6.4   EC 2-33, DR 5-101(A), DR 8-101

Communication Concerning Lawyer's Services
   Rule 7.1(a)   EC 2-8, EC 2-9, EC 2-10, DR 2-101(A),
                                   (B), (C), (E), (F) & (G), DR 2-102(E)
   Rule 7.1(b)   EC 2-5, EC 2-8, EC 2-9, EC 9-4,
                                   DR 2-101(A), (B), (C), (E), (F) & (G),
                                   DR 9-101(C)
   Rule 7.1(c)   EC 2-8, EC 2-9, EC 2-10, DR 2-101(A),
                                     (B), (C), (E), (F) & (G)

Advertising
   Rule 7.2(a)   EC 2-1, EC 2-2, EC 2-6, EC 2-7, EC 2-8,
                                   EC 2-15, DR 2-101(B) & (H), DR
                                   2-102(A) & (B), DR 2-103(B),
                                   DR 2-104(A)(4) & (5)
   Rule 7.2(b)   DR 2-101(D)
   Rule 7.2(c)   EC 2-8, EC 2-15, DR 2-101(I),
                                     DR 2-103(B), (C) & (D)
   Rule 7.2(d)   None

TABLE A
(Continued)

ABA MODEL RULES	ABA MODEL CODE

Direct Contact with Prospective Clients

Rule 7.3 — EC 2-3, EC 2-4, EC 5-6, DR 2-103(A), DR 2-103(C)(1), DR 2-103(D)(4)(b) & (c), DR 2-104(A)(1), (2), (3), & (5)

Communication of Fields of Practice

Rule 7.4 — EC 2-1, EC 2-7, EC 2-8, EC 2-14, DR 2-101(B)(2), DR 2-102(A)(3), DR 2-102(E), DR 2-105(A)

Rule 7.4(a) — DR 2-105(A)(1)

Rule 7.4(b) — EC 2-14

Rule 7.4(c) — DR 2-105(A)(2) & (3)

Firm Names and Letterheads

Rule 7.5(a) — EC 2-11, EC 2-13, DR 2-102(A)(4), DR 2-102(B), (D) & (E), DR 2-105

Rule 7.5(b) — EC 2-11, DR 2-102(D)

Rule 7.5(c) — EC 2-11, EC 2-12, DR 2-102(B)

Rule 7.5(d) — EC 2-11, EC 2-13, DR 2-102(C)

Bar Admission and Disciplinary Matters

Rule 8.1(a) — EC 1-1, EC 1-2, EC 1-3, DR 1-101(A) & (B)

Rule 8.1(b) — DR 1-102(A)(5), DR 1-103(B)

Judges and Legal Officials

Rule 8.2(a) — EC 8-6, DR 8-102

Rule 8.2(b) — DR 8-103

Reporting Professional Misconduct

Rule 8.3 — EC 1-3, DR 1-103(A)

Misconduct

Rule 8.4(a) — EC 1-5, EC 1-6, EC 9-6, DR 1-102(A)(1) & (2), DR 2-103(E), DR 7-102(A) & (B)

Rule 8.4(b) — EC 1-5, DR 1-102(A)(3) & (6), DR 7-102(A)(8), DR 8-101(A)(3)

Rule 8.4(c) — EC 1-5, EC 9-4, DR 1-102(A)(4), DR 8-101(A)(3)

Rule 8.4(d) — EC 3-9, EC 8-3, DR 1-102(A)(5), DR 3-101(B)

TABLE A
(Continued)

<u>ABA MODEL RULES</u>   <u>ABA MODEL CODE</u>
   Rule 8.4(e)   EC 1-5, EC 9-2, EC 9-4, EC 9-6,
                              DR 9-101(C)
   Rule 8.4(f)   EC 1-5, EC 7-34, EC 9-1, DR 1-102(A)(3),
                              (4), (5) & (6), DR 7-110(A),
                              DR 8-101(A)(2)

Jurisdiction
   Rule 8.5   None

AMERICAN BAR ASSOCIATION

MODEL RULES OF PROFESSIONAL CONDUCT REDLINED, SHOWING CHANGES TO 1983 MODEL RULES

INCLUDING AMENDMENTS BY THE HOUSE OF DELEGATES – THROUGH FEBRUARY 2013

PREAMBLE: A LAWYER'S RESPONSIBILITIES

[1] A lawyer, as a member of the legal profession, is a representative of clients, an officer of the legal system and a public citizen having special responsibility for the quality of justice.

[2] As a representative of clients, a lawyer performs various functions. As advisor, a lawyer provides a client with an informed understanding of the client's legal rights and obligations and explains their practical implications. As advocate, a lawyer zealously asserts the client's position under the rules of the adversary system. As negotiator, a lawyer seeks a result advantageous to the client but consistent with requirements of honest dealings with others. ~~As intermediary between clients, a lawyer seeks to reconcile their divergent interests as an advisor and, to a limited extent, as a spokesperson for each client. A~~ As an evaluator, a lawyer acts as evaluator by examining a client's legal affairs and reporting about them to the client or to others.

[2] In addition to these representational functions, a lawyer may serve as a third-party neutral, a nonrepresentational role helping the parties to resolve a dispute or other matter. Some of these Rules apply directly to lawyers who are or have served as third-party neutrals. See, e.g., Rules 1.12 and 2.4. In addition, there are Rules that apply to lawyers who are not active in the practice of law or to practicing lawyers even when they are acting in a nonprofessional capacity. For example, a lawyer who commits fraud in the conduct of a business is subject to discipline for engaging in conduct involving dishonesty, fraud, deceit or misrepresentation. See Rule 8.4.

~~[3]~~ [4] In all professional functions a lawyer should be competent, prompt and diligent. A lawyer should maintain communication with a client concerning the representation. A lawyer should keep in confidence information relating to representation of a client except so far as disclosure is required or permitted by the Rules of Professional Conduct or other law.

{4} [5] A lawyer's conduct should conform to the requirements of the law, both in professional service to clients and in the lawyer's business and personal affairs. A lawyer should use the law's procedures only for legitimate purposes and not to harass or intimidate others. A lawyer should demonstrate respect for the legal system and for those who serve it, including judges, other lawyers and public officials. While it is a lawyer's duty, when necessary, to challenge the rectitude of official action, it is also a lawyer's duty to uphold legal process.

{5} [6] As a public citizen, a lawyer should seek improvement of the law, access to the legal system, the administration of justice and the quality of service rendered by the legal profession. As a member of a learned profession, a lawyer should cultivate knowledge of the law beyond its use for clients, employ that knowledge in reform of the law and work to strengthen legal education. In addition, a lawyer should further the public's understanding of and confidence in the rule of law and the justice system because legal institutions in a constitutional democracy depend on popular participation and support to maintain their authority. A lawyer should be mindful of deficiencies in the administration of justice and of the fact that the poor, and sometimes persons who are not poor, cannot afford adequate legal assistance, and. Therefore, all lawyers should therefore devote professional time and resources and use civic influence in their behalf to ensure equal access to our system of justice for all those who because of economic or social barriers cannot afford or secure adequate legal counsel. A lawyer should aid the legal profession in pursuing these objectives and should help the bar regulate itself in the public interest.

{6} [7] Many of a lawyer's professional responsibilities are prescribed in the Rules of Professional Conduct, as well as substantive and procedural law. However, a lawyer is also guided by personal conscience and the approbation of professional peers. A lawyer should strive to attain the highest level of skill, to improve the law and the legal profession and to exemplify the legal profession's ideals of public service.

{7} [8] A lawyer's responsibilities as a representative of clients, an officer of the legal system and a public citizen are usually harmonious. Thus, when an opposing party is well represented, a lawyer can be a zealous advocate on behalf of a client and at the same time assume that justice is being done. So also, a lawyer can be sure that preserving client confidences ordinarily serves the public interest because people are more likely to seek legal advice, and thereby heed their legal obligations, when they know their communications will be private.

{8} [9] In the nature of law practice, however, conflicting responsibilities are encountered. Virtually all difficult ethical problems arise from conflict between a lawyer's responsibilities to clients, to the legal system and to the lawyer's own interest in remaining an upright ethical person while earning a satisfactory living. The Rules of Professional Conduct often prescribe terms for resolving such conflicts. Within the framework of these Rules, however, many difficult issues of professional discretion can arise. Such issues must be resolved through the exercise of sensitive professional and moral judgment guided by the basic principles underlying the Rules. These principles include the lawyer's obligation zealously to protect and pursue a client's legitimate interests, within the bounds of the law, while maintaining a professional, courteous and civil attitude toward all persons involved in the legal system.

{9} [10] The legal profession is largely self-governing. Although other professions also have been granted powers of self-government, the legal profession is unique in this respect because of the close relationship between the profession and the processes of government and law enforcement. This connection is manifested in the fact that ultimate authority over the legal profession is vested largely in the courts.

{10} [11] To the extent that lawyers meet the obligations of their professional calling, the occasion for government regulation is obviated. Self-regulation also helps maintain the legal profession's independence from government domination. An independent legal profession is an important force in preserving government under law, for abuse of legal authority is more readily challenged by a profession whose members are not dependent on government for the right to practice.

{11} [12] The legal profession's relative autonomy carries with it special responsibilities of self-government. The profession has a responsibility to assure that its regulations are conceived in the public interest and not in furtherance of parochial or self-interested concerns of the bar. Every lawyer is responsible for observance of the Rules of Professional Conduct. A lawyer should also aid in securing their observance by other lawyers. Neglect of these responsibilities compromises the independence of the profession and the public interest which it serves.

{12} [13] Lawyers play a vital role in the preservation of society. The fulfillment of this role requires an understanding by lawyers of their relationship to our legal system. The Rules of Professional Conduct, when properly applied, serve to define that relationship.

SCOPE

{13} [14] The Rules of Professional Conduct are rules of reason. They should be interpreted with reference to the purposes of legal representation and of the law itself. Some of the Rules are imperatives, cast in the terms "shall" or "shall not." These define proper conduct for purposes of professional discipline. Others, generally cast in the term "may," are permissive and define areas under the Rules in which the lawyer has ~~professional~~ discretion to exercise professional judgment. No disciplinary action should be taken when the lawyer chooses not to act or acts within the bounds of such discretion. Other Rules define the nature of relationships between the lawyer and others. The Rules are thus partly obligatory and disciplinary and partly constitu-tive and descriptive in that they define a lawyer's professional role. Many of the Comments use the term "should." Comments do not add obligations to the Rules but provide guidance for practicing in compliance with the Rules.

{14} [15] The Rules presuppose a larger legal context shaping the lawyer's role. That context includes court rules and statutes relating to matters of licensure, laws defining specific obligations of lawyers and substantive and procedural law in general. The Comments are sometimes used to alert lawyers to their responsibilities under such other law.

[16] Compliance with the Rules, as with all law in an open society, depends primarily upon understanding and voluntary compliance, secondarily upon reinforcement by peer and public opinion and finally, when necessary, upon enforcement through disciplinary proceedings. The Rules do not, however, exhaust the moral and ethical considerations that should inform a lawyer, for no worthwhile human activity can be completely defined by legal rules. The Rules simply provide a framework for the ethical practice of law.

[15] [17] Furthermore, for purposes of determining the lawyer's authority and responsibility, principles of substantive law external to these Rules determine whether a client-lawyer relationship exists. Most of the duties flowing from the client-lawyer relationship attach only after the client has requested the lawyer to render legal services and the lawyer has agreed to do so. But there are some duties, such as that of confidentiality under Rule 1.6, that may attach when the lawyer agrees to consider whether a client-lawyer relationship shall be established. See Rule 1.18. Whether a client-lawyer relationship exists for any specific purpose can depend on the circumstances and may be a question of fact.

[16] [18] Under various legal provisions, including constitutional, statutory and common law, the responsibilities of government lawyers may include authority concerning legal matters that ordinarily reposes in the client in private client-lawyer relationships. For example, a lawyer for a government agency may have authority on behalf of the government to decide upon settlement or whether to appeal from an adverse judgment. Such authority in various respects is generally vested in the attorney general and the state's attorney in state government, and their federal counterparts, and the same may be true of other government law officers. Also, lawyers under the supervision of these officers may be authorized to represent several government agencies in intragovernmental legal controversies in circumstances where a private lawyer could not represent multiple private clients. They also may have authority to represent the "public interest" in circumstances where a private lawyer would not be authorized to do so. These Rules do not abrogate any such authority.

[17] [19] Failure to comply with an obligation or prohibition imposed by a Rule is a basis for invoking the disciplinary process. The Rules presuppose that disciplinary assessment of a lawyer's conduct will be made on the basis of the facts and circumstances as they existed at the time of the conduct in question and in recognition of the fact that a lawyer often has to act upon uncertain or incomplete evidence of the situation. Moreover, the Rules presuppose that whether or not discipline should be imposed for a violation, and the severity of a sanction, depend on all the circumstances, such as the willfulness and seriousness of the violation, extenuating factors and whether there have been previous violations.

[18] [20] Violation of a Rule should not itself give rise to a cause of action against a lawyer nor should it create any presumption in such a case that

a legal duty has been breached. <u>In addition, violation of a Rule does not necessarily warrant any other nondisciplinary remedy, such as disqualification of a lawyer in pending litigation.</u> The Rules are designed to provide guidance to lawyers and to provide a structure for regulating conduct through disciplinary agencies. They are not designed to be a basis for civil liability. Furthermore, the purpose of the Rules can be subverted when they are invoked by opposing parties as procedural weapons. The fact that a Rule is a just basis for a lawyer's self-assessment, or for sanctioning a lawyer under the administration of a disciplinary authority, does not imply that an antagonist in a collateral proceeding or transaction has standing to seek enforcement of the Rule. ~~Accordingly, nothing in the Rules should be deemed to augment any substantive legal duty of lawyers or the extra-disciplinary consequences of violating such a duty.~~ <u>Nevertheless, since the Rules do establish standards of conduct by lawyers, a lawyer's violation of a Rule may be evidence of breach of the applicable standard of conduct.</u>

~~[19]   Moreover, these Rules are not intended to govern or affect judicial application of either the attorney-client or work product privilege. Those privileges were developed to promote compliance with law and fairness in litigation. In reliance on the attorney-client privilege, clients are entitled to expect that communications within the scope of the privilege will be protected against compelled disclosure. The attorney-client privilege is that of the client and not of the lawyer. The fact that in exceptional situations the lawyer under the rules has a limited discretion to disclose a client confidence does not vitiate the proposition that, as a general matter, the client has a reasonable expectation that information relating to the client will not be voluntarily disclosed and that disclosure of such information may be judicially compelled only in accordance with recognized exceptions to the attorney-client and work product privileges.~~

~~[20]   The lawyer's exercise of discretion not to disclose information under Rule 1.6 should not be subject to reexamination. Permitting such reexamination would be incompatible with the general policy of promoting compliance with law through assurances that communications will be protected against disclosure.~~

[21]   The Comment accompanying each Rule explains and illustrates the meaning and purpose of the Rule. The Preamble and this note on Scope provide general orientation. The Comments are intended as guides to interpretation, but the text of each Rule is authoritative. ~~Research notes were prepared to compare counterparts in the ABA Model Code of Professional Responsibility (adopted 1969, as amended) and to provide selected references to other authorities. The notes have not been adopted, do not constitute part of the Model Rules, and are not intended to affect the application or interpretation of the Rules and Comments.~~

RULE 1.0: TERMINOLOGY

(a)   "Belief" or "believes" denotes that the person involved actually supposed the fact in question to be true. A person's belief may be inferred from circumstances.

~~"Consult" or "consultation" denotes communication of information reasonably sufficient to permit the client to appreciate the significance of the matter in question.~~

(b)   "Confirmed in writing," when used in reference to the informed consent of a person, denotes informed consent that is given in writing by the person or a writing that a lawyer promptly transmits to the person confirming an oral informed consent. See paragraph (e) for the definition of "informed consent." If it is not feasible to obtain or transmit the writing at the time the person gives informed consent, then the lawyer must obtain or transmit it within a reasonable time thereafter.

(c)   "Firm" or "law firm" denotes a lawyer or lawyers in a ~~private firm,~~ law partnership, professional corporation, sole proprietorship or other association authorized to practice law; or lawyers employed in a legal services organization or the legal department of a corporation or other organization ~~and lawyers employed in a legal services organization. See Comment, Rule 1.10.~~

(d)   "Fraud" or "fraudulent" denotes conduct ~~having~~ that is fraudulent under the substantive or procedural law of the applicable jurisdiction and has a purpose to deceive ~~and not merely negligent misrepresentation or failure to apprise another of relevant information.~~

(e)   "Informed consent" denotes the agreement by a person to a proposed course of conduct after the lawyer has communicated adequate information and explanation about the material risks of and reasonably available alternatives to the proposed course of conduct.

(f)   "Knowingly," "known," or "knows" denotes actual knowledge of the fact in question. A person's knowledge may be inferred from circumstances.

(g)   "Partner" denotes a member of a partnership ~~and,~~ a shareholder in a law firm organized as a professional corporation, or a member of an association authorized to practice law.

(h)   "Reasonable" or "reasonably" when used in relation to conduct by a lawyer denotes the conduct of a reasonably prudent and competent lawyer.

(i)   "Reasonable belief" or "reasonably believes" when used in reference to a lawyer denotes that the lawyer believes the matter in question and that the circumstances are such that the belief is reasonable.

(j)   "Reasonably should know" when used in reference to a lawyer denotes that a lawyer of reasonable prudence and competence would ascertain the matter in question.

(k)   "Screened" denotes the isolation of a lawyer from any participation in a matter through the timely imposition of procedures within a firm that are reasonably adequate under the circumstances to protect information that the isolated lawyer is obligated to protect under these Rules or other law.

(l)   "Substantial" when used in reference to degree or extent denotes a material matter of clear and weighty importance.

(m)   "Tribunal" denotes a court, an arbitrator in a binding arbitration proceeding or a legislative body, administrative agency or other body acting in an adjudicative capacity. A legislative body, administrative agency or other body acts in an adjudicative capacity when a neutral official, after the presentation of evidence or legal argument by a party or parties, will render a binding legal judgment directly affecting a party's interests in a particular matter.

(n)   "Writing" or "written" denotes a tangible or electronic record of a communication or representation, including handwriting, typewriting, printing, photostating, photography, audio or videorecording and electronic communications. A "signed" writing includes an electronic sound, symbol or process attached to or logically associated with a writing and executed or adopted by a person with the intent to sign the writing.

Comment

Confirmed in Writing

[1]   If it is not feasible to obtain or transmit a written confirmation at the time the client gives informed consent, then the lawyer must obtain or transmit it within a reasonable time thereafter. If a lawyer has obtained a client's informed consent, the lawyer may act in reliance on that consent so long as it is confirmed in writing within a reasonable time there-after.

Firm

[2]   Whether two or more lawyers constitute a firm within paragraph (c) can depend on the specific facts. For example, two practitioners who share office space and occasionally consult or assist each other ordinarily would not be regarded as constituting a firm. However, if they present themselves to the public in a way that suggests that they are a firm or conduct themselves as a firm, they should be regarded as a firm for purposes of the Rules. The terms of any formal agreement between associated lawyers are relevant in determining whether they are a firm, as is the fact that they have mutual access to information concerning the clients they serve. Furthermore, it is relevant in doubtful cases to consider the underlying purpose of the Rule that is involved. A group of lawyers could be regarded as a firm for purposes of the Rule that the same lawyer should not represent opposing parties in litigation, while it might not be so regarded for purposes of the Rule that information acquired by one lawyer is attributed to another.

[3]   With respect to the law department of an organization, including the government, there is ordinarily no question that the members of the department constitute a firm within the meaning of the Rules of Professional Conduct. There can be uncertainty, however, as to the identity of the client. For example, it may not be clear whether the law department of a corporation represents a subsidiary or an affiliated corporation, as well as the corporation by which the members of the department are directly employed. A similar question can arise concerning an unincorporated association and its local affiliates.

[4]   Similar questions can also arise with respect to lawyers in legal aid and legal services organizations. Depending upon the structure of the organization, the entire organization or different components of it may constitute a firm or firms for purposes of these Rules.

Fraud

[5]   When used in these Rules, the terms "fraud" or "fraudulent" refer to conduct that is characterized as such under the substantive or procedural law of the applicable jurisdiction and has a purpose to deceive. This does not include merely negligent misrepresentation or negligent failure to apprise another of relevant information. For purposes of these Rules, it is not necessary that anyone has suffered damages or relied on the misrepresentation or failure to inform.

Informed Consent

[6]   Many of the Rules of Professional Conduct require the lawyer to obtain the informed consent of a client or other person (e.g., a former client or, under certain circumstances, a prospective client) before accepting or continuing representation or pursuing a course of conduct. See, e.g, Rules 1.2(c), 1.6(a) and 1.7(b).The communication necessary to obtain such consent will vary according to the Rule involved and the circumstances giving rise to the need to obtain informed consent. The lawyer must make reasonable efforts to ensure that the client or other person possesses information reasonably adequate to make an informed decision. Ordinarily, this will require communication that includes a disclosure of the facts and circumstances giving rise to the situation, any explanation reasonably necessary to inform the client or other person of the material advantages and disadvantages of the proposed course of conduct and a discussion of the client's or other person's options and alternatives. In some circumstances it may be appropriate for a lawyer to advise a client or other person to seek the advice of other counsel. A lawyer need not inform a client or other person of facts or implications already known to the client or other person; nevertheless, a lawyer who does not personally inform the client or other person assumes the risk that the client or other person is inadequately informed and the consent is invalid. In determining whether the information and explanation provided are reasonably adequate, relevant factors include whether the client or other person is experienced in legal matters generally and in making decisions of the type involved, and whether the client or other person is independently represented by other counsel in giving the consent. Normally, such persons need less information and explanation than others, and generally a client or other person who is independently represented by other counsel in giving the consent should be assumed to have given informed consent.

[7]   Obtaining informed consent will usually require an affirmative response by the client or other person. In general, a lawyer may not assume consent from a client's or other person's silence. Consent may be inferred, however, from the conduct of a client or other person who has reasonably adequate information about the matter. A number of Rules require that a person's consent

be confirmed in writing. See Rules 1.7(b) and 1.9(a). For a definition of "writing" and "confirmed in writing," see paragraphs (n) and (b). Other Rules require that a client's consent be obtained in a writing signed by the client. See, e.g., Rules 1.8(a) and (g). For a definition of "signed," see paragraph (n).

Screened

[8]   This definition applies to situations where screening of a personally disqualified lawyer is permitted to remove imputation of a conflict of interest under Rules 1.10, 1.11, 1.12 or 1.18.

[9]   The purpose of screening is to assure the affected parties that confidential information known by the personally disqualified lawyer remains protected. The personally disqualified lawyer should acknowledge the obligation not to communicate with any of the other lawyers in the firm with respect to the matter. Similarly, other lawyers in the firm who are working on the matter should be informed that the screening is in place and that they may not communicate with the personally disqualified lawyer with respect to the matter. Additional screening measures that are appropriate for the particular matter will depend on the circumstances. To implement, reinforce and remind all affected lawyers of the presence of the screening, it may be appropriate for the firm to undertake such procedures as a written undertaking by the screened lawyer to avoid any communication with other firm personnel and any contact with any firm files or other information, including information in electronic form, relating to the matter, written notice and instructions to all other firm personnel forbidding any communication with the screened lawyer relating to the matter, denial of access by the screened lawyer to firm files or other information, including information in electronic form, relating to the matter and periodic reminders of the screen to the screened lawyer and all other firm personnel.

[10]   In order to be effective, screening measures must be implemented as soon as practical after a lawyer or law firm knows or reasonably should know that there is a need for screening.

RULE 1.1: COMPETENCE

A lawyer shall provide competent representation to a client. Competent representation requires the legal knowledge, skill, thoroughness and preparation reasonably necessary for the representation.

Comment

Legal Knowledge and Skill

[1]   In determining whether a lawyer employs the requisite knowledge and skill in a particular matter, relevant factors include the relative complexity and specialized nature of the matter, the lawyer's general experience, the lawyer's training and experience in the field in question, the preparation and study the lawyer is able to give the matter and whether it is feasible to refer the matter to, or associate or consult with, a lawyer of established competence in the field in question. In many instances, the required proficiency is

that of a general practitioner. Expertise in a particular field of law may be required in some circumstances.

[2]   A lawyer need not necessarily have special training or prior experience to handle legal problems of a type with which the lawyer is unfamiliar. A newly admitted lawyer can be as competent as a practitioner with long experience. Some important legal skills, such as the analysis of precedent, the evaluation of evidence and legal drafting, are required in all legal problems. Perhaps the most fundamental legal skill consists of determining what kind of legal problems a situation may involve, a skill that necessarily transcends any particular specialized knowledge. A lawyer can provide adequate representation in a wholly novel field through necessary study. Competent representation can also be provided through the association of a lawyer of established competence in the field in question.

[3]   In an emergency a lawyer may give advice or assistance in a matter in which the lawyer does not have the skill ordinarily required where referral to or consultation or association with another lawyer would be impractical. Even in an emergency, however, assistance should be limited to that reasonably necessary in the circumstances, for ill-considered action under emergency conditions can jeopardize the client's interest.

[4]   A lawyer may accept representation where the requisite level of competence can be achieved by reasonable preparation. This applies as well to a lawyer who is appointed as counsel for an unrepresented person. See also Rule 6.2.

Thoroughness and Preparation

[5]   Competent handling of a particular matter includes inquiry into and analysis of the factual and legal elements of the problem, and use of methods and procedures meeting the standards of competent practitioners. It also includes adequate preparation. The required attention and preparation are determined in part by what is at stake; major litigation and complex transactions ordinarily require more elaborate extensive treatment than matters of lesser complexity and consequence. An agreement between the lawyer and the client regarding the scope of the representation may limit the matters for which the lawyer is responsible. See Rule 1.2(c).

Retaining or contracting with other lawyers

[6]   Before a lawyer retains or contracts with other lawyers outside the lawyer's own firm to provide or assist in the provision of legal services to a client, the lawyer should ordinarily obtain informed consent from the client and must reasonably believe that the other lawyers' services will contribute to the competent and ethical representation of the client. See also Rules 1.2 (allocation of authority), 1.4 (communication with client), 1.5(e) (fee sharing), 1.6 (confidentiality), and 5.5(a) (unauthorized practice of law). The reasonableness of the decision to retain or contract with other lawyers outside the lawyer's own firm will depend upon the circumstances, including the education, experience and reputation of the nonfirm lawyers; the nature of the services

assigned to the nonfirm lawyers; and the legal protections, professional con-duct rules, and ethical environments of the jurisdictions in which the services will be performed, particularly relating to confidential information.

[7]　When lawyers from more than one law firm are providing legal services to the client on a particular matter, the lawyers ordinarily should con-sult with each other and the client about the scope of their respective represen-tations and the allocation of responsibility among them. See Rule 1.2. When making allocations of responsibility in a matter pending before a tribunal, lawyers and parties may have additional obligations that are a matter of law beyond the scope of these Rules.

Maintaining Competence

[6~~8~~]　To maintain the requisite knowledge and skill, a lawyer should keep abreast of changes in the law and its practice, including the benefits and risks associated with relevant technology, engage in continuing study and edu-cation and comply with all continuing legal education requirements to which the lawyer is subject. ~~If a system of peer review has been established, the lawyer should consider making use of it in appropriate circumstance.~~

RULE 1.2: SCOPE OF REPRESENTATION AND ALLOCATION OF AUTHORITY BETWEEN CLIENT AND LAWYER

(a)　~~A~~ Subject to paragraphs (c) and (d), a lawyer shall abide by a client's decisions concerning the objectives of representation~~, subject to para-graphs (c), (d) and (e),~~ and, as required by Rule 1.4, shall consult with the client as to the means by which they are to be pursued. A lawyer may take such action on behalf of the client as is impliedly authorized to carry out the repre-sentation. A lawyer shall abide by a client's decision whether to ~~accept an offer of settlement of~~ settle a matter. In a criminal case, the lawyer shall abide by the client's decision, after consultation with the lawyer, as to a plea to be entered, whether to waive jury trial and whether the client will testify.

(b)　A lawyer's representation of a client, including representation by appointment, does not constitute an endorsement of the client's political, economic, social or moral views or activities.

(c)　A lawyer may limit the ~~objectives~~ scope of the representation if the limitation is reasonable under the circumstances and the client ~~consents after consultation~~ gives informed consent.

(d)　A lawyer shall not counsel a client to engage, or assist a client, in conduct that the lawyer knows is criminal or fraudulent, but a lawyer may discuss the legal consequences of any proposed course of conduct with a client and may counsel or assist a client to make a good faith effort to determine the validity, scope, meaning or application of the law.

~~(e)　When a lawyer knows that a client expects assistance not permitted by the rules of professional conduct or other law, the lawyer shall consult with the client regarding the relevant limitations on the lawyer's conduct.~~

Comment

~~Scope of Representation~~ Allocation of Authority between Client and Lawyer

[1] ~~Both lawyer and client have authority and responsibility in the objectives and means of representation. The~~ Paragraph (a) confers upon the client ~~has~~ the ultimate authority to determine the purposes to be served by legal representation, within the limits imposed by law and the lawyer's professional obligations. ~~Within those limits, a client also has a right to consult with the lawyer about the means to be used in pursuing those objectives. At the same time, a lawyer is not required to pursue objectives or employ means simply because a client may wish that the lawyer do so. A clear distinction between objectives and means sometimes cannot be drawn, and in many cases the client-lawyer relationship partakes of a joint undertaking. In questions of means the lawyer should assume responsibility for technical and legal tactical issues, but should defer to the client regarding such questions as the expense to be incurred and concern for third persons who might be adversely affected. Law defining the lawyer's scope of authority in litigation varies among jurisdictions.~~ The decisions specified in paragraph (a), such as whether to settle a civil matter, must also be made by the client. See Rule 1.4(a)(1) for the lawyer's duty to communicate with the client about such decisions. With respect to the means by which the client's objectives are to be pursued, the lawyer shall consult with the client as required by Rule 1.4(a)(2) and may take such action as is impliedly authorized to carry out the representation.

[2] On occasion, however, a lawyer and a client may disagree about the means to be used to accomplish the client's objectives. Clients normally defer to the special knowledge and skill of their lawyer with respect to the means to be used to accomplish their objectives, particularly with respect to technical, legal and tactical matters. Conversely, lawyers usually defer to the client regarding such questions as the expense to be incurred and concern for third persons who might be adversely affected. Because of the varied nature of the matters about which a lawyer and client might disagree and because the actions in question may implicate the interests of a tribunal or other persons, this Rule does not prescribe how such disagreements are to be resolved. Other law, however, may be applicable and should be consulted by the lawyer. The lawyer should also consult with the client and seek a mutually acceptable resolution of the disagreement. If such efforts are unavailing and the lawyer has a fundamental disagreement with the client, the lawyer may withdraw from the representation. See Rule 1.16(b)(4). Conversely, the client may resolve the disagreement by discharging the lawyer. See Rule 1.16(a)(3).

[3] At the outset of a representation, the client may authorize the lawyer to take specific action on the client's behalf without further consultation. Absent a material change in circumstances and subject to Rule 1.4, a lawyer may rely on such an advance authorization. The client may, however, revoke such authority at any time.

[2] [4] In a case in which the client appears to be suffering ~~mental disability~~ diminished capacity, the lawyer's duty to abide by the client's decisions is to be guided by reference to Rule 1.14.

Independence from Client's Views or Activities

[3] [5] Legal representation should not be denied to people who are unable to afford legal services, or whose cause is controversial or the subject of popular disapproval. By the same token, representing a client does not constitute approval of the client's views or activities.

~~Services Limited in Objectives or Means~~ Agreements Limiting Scope of Representation

[4] [6] The ~~objectives or~~ scope of services to be provided by a lawyer may be limited by agreement with the client or by the terms under which the lawyer's services are made available to the client. ~~For example, a retainer may be for a specifically defined purpose. Representation provided through a legal aid agency may be subject to limitations on the types of cases the agency handles.~~ When a lawyer has been retained by an insurer to represent an insured, for example, the representation may be limited to matters related to the insurance coverage. ~~The~~ A limited representation may be appropriate because the client has limited objectives for the representation. In addition, the terms upon which representation is undertaken may exclude specific ~~objectives or~~ means that might otherwise be used to accomplish the client's objectives. Such limitations may exclude ~~objectives or means~~ actions that the client thinks are too costly or that the lawyer regards as repugnant or imprudent.

[7] Although this Rule affords the lawyer and client substantial latitude to limit the representation, the limitation must be reasonable under the circumstances. If, for example, a client's objective is limited to securing general information about the law the client needs in order to handle a common and typically uncomplicated legal problem, the lawyer and client may agree that the lawyer's services will be limited to a brief telephone consultation. Such a limitation, however, would not be reasonable if the time allotted was not sufficient to yield advice upon which the client could rely.Although an agreement for a limited representation does not exempt a lawyer from the duty to provide competent representation, the limitation is a factor to be considered when determining the legal knowledge, skill, thoroughness and preparation reasonably necessary for the representation. See Rule 1.1.

[5] [8] ~~An agreement~~ All agreements concerning ~~the scope of~~ a lawyer's representation of a client must accord with the Rules of Professional Conduct and other law. ~~Thus, the client may not be asked to agree to representation so limited in scope as to violate Rule 1.1, or to surrender the right to terminate the lawyer's services or the right to settle litigation that the lawyer might wish to continue.~~ See, e.g., Rules 1.1, 1.8 and 5.6.

Criminal, Fraudulent and Prohibited Transactions

[6] [9] ~~A~~ Paragraph (d) prohibits a lawyer from knowingly counseling or assisting a client to commit a crime or fraud. This prohibition, however, does

not preclude the lawyer ~~is required to give~~ from giving an honest opinion about the actual consequences that appear likely to result from a client's conduct. ~~The~~ Nor does the fact that a client uses advice in a course of action that is criminal or fraudulent ~~does not,~~ of itself~~,~~ make a lawyer a party to the course of action. ~~However, a lawyer may not knowingly assist a client in criminal or fraudulent conduct.~~ There is a critical distinction between presenting an analysis of legal aspects of questionable conduct and recommending the means by which a crime or fraud might be committed with impunity.

~~[7]~~ [10] When the client's course of action has already begun and is continuing, the lawyer's responsibility is especially delicate. ~~The lawyer is not permitted to reveal the client's wrongdoing, except where permitted by Rule 1.6. However, the~~ The lawyer is required to avoid ~~furthering the purpose~~ assisting the client, for example, by drafting or delivering documents that the lawyer knows are fraudulent or by suggesting how ~~it~~ the wrongdoing might be concealed. A lawyer may not continue assisting a client in conduct that the lawyer originally ~~supposes is~~ supposed was legally proper but then discovers is criminal or fraudulent. ~~Withdrawal~~ The lawyer must, therefore, withdraw from the representation~~, therefore, may be required~~ of the client in the matter. See Rule 1.16(a). In some cases, withdrawal alone might be insufficient. It may be necessary for the lawyer to give notice of the fact of withdrawal and to disaffirm any opinion, document, affirmation or the like. See Rule 4.1.

~~[8]~~ [11] Where the client is a fiduciary, the lawyer may be charged with special obligations in dealings with a beneficiary.

~~[9]~~ [12] Paragraph (d) applies whether or not the defrauded party is a party to the transaction. Hence, a lawyer ~~should~~ must not participate in a ~~sham~~ transaction~~; for example, a transaction~~ to effectuate criminal or fraudulent ~~escape~~ avoidance of tax liability. Paragraph (d) does not preclude undertaking a criminal defense incident to a general retainer for legal services to a lawful enterprise. The last clause of paragraph (d) recognizes that determining the validity or interpretation of a statute or regulation may require a course of action involving disobedience of the statute or regulation or of the interpretation placed upon it by governmental authorities.

[13]   If a lawyer comes to know or reasonably should know that a client expects assistance not permitted by the Rules of Professional Conduct or other law or if the lawyer intends to act contrary to the client's instructions, the lawyer must consult with the client regarding the limitations on the lawyer's conduct. See Rule 1.4(a)(5).

RULE 1.3: DILIGENCE

A lawyer shall act with reasonable diligence and promptness in representing a client.

Comment

[1]   A lawyer should pursue a matter on behalf of a client despite opposition, obstruction or personal inconvenience to the lawyer, and ~~may~~ take whatever lawful and ethical measures are required to vindicate a client's

cause or endeavor. A lawyer ~~should~~ must also act with commitment and dedication to the interests of the client and with zeal in advocacy upon the client's behalf. ~~However, a~~ A lawyer is not bound, however, to press for every advantage that might be realized for a client. ~~A~~ For example, a lawyer ~~has~~ may have authority to exercise professional discretion in determining the means by which a matter should be pursued. See Rule 1.2. ~~A lawyer's work load should be controlled so that each matter can be handled adequately.~~ The lawyer's duty to act with reasonable diligence does not require the use of offensive tactics or preclude the treating of all persons involved in the legal process with courtesy and respect.

　　　　[2]　　A lawyer's work load must be controlled so that each matter can be handled competently.

　　　　~~[2]~~ [3]　Perhaps no professional shortcoming is more widely resented than procrastination. A client's interests often can be adversely affected by the passage of time or the change of conditions; in extreme instances, as when a lawyer overlooks a statute of limitations, the client's legal position may be destroyed. Even when the client's interests are not affected in substance, however, unreasonable delay can cause a client needless anxiety and undermine confidence in the lawyer's trustworthiness. A lawyer's duty to act with reasonable promptness, however, does not preclude the lawyer from agreeing to a reasonable request for a postponement that will not prejudice the lawyer's client.

　　　　~~[3]~~ [4]　Unless the relationship is terminated as provided in Rule 1.16, a lawyer should carry through to conclusion all matters undertaken for a client. If a lawyer's employment is limited to a specific matter, the relationship terminates when the matter has been resolved. If a lawyer has served a client over a substantial period in a variety of matters, the client sometimes may assume that the lawyer will continue to serve on a continuing basis unless the lawyer gives notice of withdrawal. Doubt about whether a client-lawyer relationship still exists should be clarified by the lawyer, preferably in writing, so that the client will not mistakenly suppose the lawyer is looking after the client's affairs when the lawyer has ceased to do so. For example, if a lawyer has handled a judicial or administrative proceeding that produced a result adverse to the client ~~but has not been specifically instructed concerning pursuit of an~~ and the lawyer and the client have not agreed that the lawyer will handle the matter on appeal, the lawyer ~~should advise~~ must consult with the client of about the possibility of appeal before relinquishing responsibility for the matter. See Rule 1.4(a)(2). Whether the lawyer is obligated to prosecute the appeal for the client depends on the scope of the representation the lawyer has agreed to provide to the client. See Rule 1.2.

　　　　[5]　　To prevent neglect of client matters in the event of a sole practitioner's death or disability, the duty of diligence may require that each sole practitioner prepare a plan, in conformity with applicable rules, that designates another competent lawyer to review client files, notify each client of the lawyer's death or disability, and determine whether there is a need for immediate protective action. Cf. Rule 28 of the American Bar Association Model

Rules for Lawyer Disciplinary Enforcement (providing for court appointment of a lawyer to inventory files and take other protective action in absence of a plan providing for another lawyer to protect the interests of the clients of a deceased or disabled lawyer).

RULE 1.4: COMMUNICATION

(a)   A lawyer shall ~~keep a client reasonably informed about the status of a matter and promptly comply with reasonable requests for information.~~:

> (1)   promptly inform the client of any decision or circumstance with respect to which the client's informed consent, as defined in Rule 1.0(e), is required by these Rules;

> (2)   reasonably consult with the client about the means by which the client's objectives are to be accomplished;

> (3)   keep the client reasonably informed about the status of the matter;

> (4)   promptly comply with reasonable requests for information; and

> (5)   consult with the client about any relevant limitation on the lawyer's conduct when the lawyer knows that the client expects assistance not permitted by the Rules of Professional Conduct or other law.

(b)   A lawyer shall explain a matter to the extent reasonably necessary to permit the client to make informed decisions regarding the representation.

Comment

[1]   Reasonable communication between the lawyer and the client is necessary for the client effectively to participate in the representation.

Communicating with Client

[2]   If these Rules require that a particular decision about the representation be made by the client, paragraph (a)(1) requires that the lawyer promptly consult with and secure the client's consent prior to taking action unless prior discussions with the client have resolved what action the client wants the lawyer to take. For example, a lawyer who receives from opposing counsel an offer of settlement in a civil controversy or a proffered plea bargain in a criminal case must promptly inform the client of its substance unless the client has previously indicated that the proposal will be acceptable or unacceptable or has authorized the lawyer to accept or to reject the offer. See Rule 1.2(a).

[3]   Paragraph (a)(2) requires the lawyer to reasonably consult with the client about the means to be used to accomplish the client's objectives. In some situations - depending on both the importance of the action under consideration and the feasibility of consulting with the client - this duty will

require consultation prior to taking action. In other circumstances, such as during a trial when an immediate decision must be made, the exigency of the situation may require the lawyer to act without prior consultation. In such cases the lawyer must nonetheless act reasonably to inform the client of actions the lawyer has taken on the client's behalf. Additionally, paragraph (a)(3) requires that the lawyer keep the client reasonably informed about the status of the matter, such as significant developments affecting the timing or the substance of the representation.

[4]   A lawyer's regular communication with clients will minimize the occasions on which a client will need to request information concerning the representation. When a client makes a reasonable request for information, however, paragraph (a)(4) requires prompt compliance with the request, or if a prompt response is not feasible, that the lawyer, or a member of the lawyer's staff, acknowledge receipt of the request and advise the client when a response may be expected. A lawyer should promptly respond to or acknowledge client communications.

Explaining Matters

{1} [5] The client should have sufficient information to participate intelligently in decisions concerning the objectives of the representation and the means by which they are to be pursued, to the extent the client is willing and able to do so. For example, a lawyer negotiating on behalf of a client should provide the client with facts relevant to the matter, inform the client of communications from another party and take other reasonable steps that permit the client to make a decision regarding a serious offer from another party. A lawyer who receives from opposing counsel an offer of settlement in a civil controversy or a proffered plea bargain in a criminal case should promptly inform the client of its substance unless prior discussions with the client have left it clear that the proposal will be unacceptable. See Rule 1.2(a). Even when a client delegates authority to the lawyer, the client should be kept advised of the status of the matter. {2} Adequacy of communication depends in part on the kind of advice or assistance that is involved. For example, in negotiations where when there is time to explain a proposal made in a negotiation, the lawyer should review all important provisions with the client before proceeding to an agreement. In litigation a lawyer should explain the general strategy and prospects of success and ordinarily should consult the client on tactics that might are likely to result in significant expense or to injure or coerce others. On the other hand, a lawyer ordinarily cannot will not be expected to describe trial or negotiation strategy in detail. The guiding principle is that the lawyer should fulfill reasonable client expectations for information consistent with the duty to act in the client's best interests, and the client's overall requirements as to the character of representation. In certain circumstances, such as when a lawyer asks a client to consent to a representation affected by a conflict of interest, the client must give informed consent, as defined in Rule 1.0(e).

{3} [6] Ordinarily, the information to be provided is that appropriate for a client who is a comprehending and responsible adult. However, fully informing the client according to this standard may be impracticable, for example, where the client is a child or suffers from ~~mental disability~~ diminished capacity. See Rule 1.14. When the client is an organization or group, it is often impossible or inappropriate to inform every one of its members about its legal affairs; ordinarily, the lawyer should address communications to the appropriate officials of the organization. See Rule 1.13. Where many routine matters are involved, a system of limited or occasional reporting may be arranged with the client. ~~Practical exigency may also require a lawyer to act for a client without prior consultation.~~

Withholding Information

~~[4]~~ [7] In some circumstances, a lawyer may be justified in delaying transmission of information when the client would be likely to react imprudently to an immediate communication. Thus, a lawyer might withhold a psychiatric diagnosis of a client when the examining psychiatrist indicates that disclosure would harm the client. A lawyer may not withhold information to serve the lawyer's own interest or convenience or the interests or convenience of another person. Rules or court orders governing litigation may provide that information supplied to a lawyer may not be disclosed to the client. Rule 3.4(c) directs compliance with such rules or orders.

RULE 1.5: FEES

(a)   A ~~lawyer's fee~~ lawyer shall ~~be reasonable~~ not make an agreement for, charge, or collect an unreasonable fee or an unreasonable amount for expenses. The factors to be considered in determining the reasonableness of a fee include the following:

(1)   the time and labor required, the novelty and difficulty of the questions involved, and the skill requisite to perform the legal service properly;

(2)   the likelihood, if apparent to the client, that the acceptance of the particular employment will preclude other employment by the lawyer;

(3)   the fee customarily charged in the locality for similar legal services;

(4)   the amount involved and the results obtained;

(5)   the time limitations imposed by the client or by the circumstances;

(6)   the nature and length of the professional relationship with the client;

(7)   the experience, reputation, and ability of the lawyer or lawyers performing the services; and

(8)   whether the fee is fixed or contingent.

(b)   ~~When the lawyer has not regularly represented the client,~~ The scope of the representation and the basis or rate of the fee and expenses for which the client will be responsible shall be communicated to the client, preferably in writing, before or within a reasonable time after commencing the representation, except when the lawyer will charge a regularly represented client on the same basis or rate. Any changes in the basis or rate of the fee or expenses shall also be communicated to the client.

(c)   A fee may be contingent on the outcome of the matter for which the service is rendered, except in a matter in which a contingent fee is prohibited by paragraph (d) or other law. A contingent fee agreement shall be in a writing signed by the client and shall state the method by which the fee is to be determined, including the percentage or percentages that shall accrue to the lawyer in the event of settlement, trial or appeal; litigation and other expenses to be deducted from the recovery; and whether such expenses are to be deducted before or after the contingent fee is calculated. The agreement must clearly notify the client of any expenses for which the client will be liable whether or not the client is the prevailing party. Upon conclusion of a contingent fee matter, the lawyer shall provide the client with a written statement stating the outcome of the matter and, if there is a recovery, showing the remittance to the client and the method of its determination.

(d)   A lawyer shall not enter into an arrangement for, charge, or collect:

(1)   any fee in a domestic relations matter, the payment or amount of which is contingent upon the securing of a divorce or upon the amount of alimony or support, or property settlement in lieu thereof; or

(2)   a contingent fee for representing a defendant in acriminal case.

(e)   A division of a fee between lawyers who are not in the same firm may be made only if:

(1)   the division is in proportion to the services performed by each lawyer or, by written agreement with the client, each lawyer assumes joint responsibility for the representation;

(2)   the client is advised of and does not object to the participation of all the lawyers involved agrees to the arrangement, including the share each lawyer will receive, and the agreement is confirmed in writing; and

(3)   the total fee is reasonable.

Comment

Reasonableness of Fee and Expenses

[1]   Paragraph (a) requires that lawyers charge fees that are reasonable under the circumstances. The factors specified in (1) through (8) are not exclusive. Nor will each factor be relevant in each instance. Paragraph (a) also requires that expenses for which the client will be charged must be reasonable. A lawyer may seek reimbursement for the cost of services performed

in-house, such as copying, or for other expenses incurred in-house, such as telephone charges, either by charging a reasonable amount to which the client has agreed in advance or by charging an amount that reasonably reflects the cost incurred by the lawyer.

Basis or Rate of Fee

~~[1]~~ [2] When the lawyer has regularly represented a client, they ordinarily will have evolved an understanding concerning the basis or rate of the fee and the expenses for which the client will be responsible. In a new client-lawyer relationship, however, an understanding as to ~~the fee~~ fees and expenses ~~should~~ must be promptly established. ~~It is not necessary to recite all the factors that underlie the basis of the fee, but only those that are directly involved in its computation. It is sufficient, for example, to state that the basic rate is an hourly charge or a fixed amount or an estimated amount, or to identify the factors that may be taken into account in finally fixing the fee. When developments occur during the representation that render an earlier estimate substantially inaccurate, a revised estimate should be provided to the client.~~ Generally, it is desirable to furnish the client with at least a simple memorandum or copy of the lawyer's customary fee arrangements that states the general nature of the legal services to be provided, the basis, rate or total amount of the fee and whether and to what extent the client will be responsible for any costs, expenses or disbursements in the course of the representation. A written statement concerning the ~~fee~~ terms of the engagement reduces the possibility of misunderstanding. ~~Furnishing the client with a simple memorandum or a copy of the lawyer's customary fee schedule is sufficient if the basis or rate of the fee is set forth.~~

[3] Contingent fees, like any other fees, are subject to the reasonableness standard of paragraph (a) of this Rule. In determining whether a particular contingent fee is reasonable, or whether it is reasonable to charge any form of contingent fee, a lawyer must consider the factors that are relevant under the circumstances. Applicable law may impose limitations on contingent fees, such as a ceiling on the percentage allowable, or may require a lawyer to offer clients an alternative basis for the fee. Applicable law also may apply to situations other than a contingent fee, for example, government regulations regarding fees in certain tax matters.

Terms of Payment

~~[2]~~ [4] A lawyer may require advance payment of a fee, but is obliged to return any unearned portion. See Rule 1.16(d). A lawyer may accept property in payment for services, such as an ownership interest in an enterprise, providing this does not involve acquisition of a proprietary interest in the cause of action or subject matter of the litigation contrary to Rule 1.8~~(j)~~(i). However, a fee paid in property instead of money may be subject to ~~special scrutiny because it involves questions concerning both the value of the services and the lawyer's special knowledge of the value of the property~~ the requirements of Rule 1.8(a) because such fees often have the essential qualities of a business transaction with the client.

~~[3]~~ [5] An agreement may not be made whose terms might induce the lawyer improperly to curtail services for the client or perform them in a way contrary to the client's interest. For example, a lawyer should not enter into an agreement whereby services are to be provided only up to a stated amount when it is foreseeable that more extensive services probably will be required, unless the situation is adequately explained to the client. Otherwise, the client might have to bargain for further assistance in the midst of a proceeding or transaction. However, it is proper to define the extent of services in light of the client's ability to pay. A lawyer should not exploit a fee arrangement based primarily on hourly charges by using wasteful procedures. ~~When there is doubt whether a contingent fee is consistent with the client's best interest, the lawyer should offer the client alternative bases for the fee and explain their implications. Applicable law may impose limitations on contingent fees, such as a ceiling on the percentage.~~

Prohibited Contingent Fees

[6] Paragraph (d) prohibits a lawyer from charging a contingent fee in a domestic relations matter when payment is contingent upon the securing of a divorce or upon the amount of alimony or support or property settlement to be obtained. This provision does not preclude a contract for a contingent fee for legal representation in connection with the recovery of post-judgment balances due under support, alimony or other financial orders because such contracts do not implicate the same policy concerns.

Division of Fee

~~[4]~~ [7] A division of fee is a single billing to a client covering the fee of two or more lawyers who are not in the same firm. A division of fee facilitates association of more than one lawyer in a matter in which neither alone could serve the client as well, and most often is used when the fee is contingent and the division is between a referring lawyer and a trial specialist. Paragraph (e) permits the lawyers to divide a fee ~~on~~ either on the basis of the proportion of services they render or ~~by agreement between the participating lawyers~~ if ~~all assume~~ each lawyer assumes responsibility for the representation as a whole. ~~and~~ In addition, the client ~~is advised and does not object. It does not require disclosure to the client of~~ must agree to the arrangement, including the share that each lawyer is to receive, and the agreement must be confirmed in writing. Contingent fee agreements must be in a writing signed by the client and must otherwise comply with paragraph (c) of this Rule. Joint responsibility for the representation entails ~~the obligations stated in Rule 5.1 for purposes of the matter involved~~ financial and ethical responsibility for the representation as if the lawyers were associated in a partnership. A lawyer should only refer a matter to a lawyer whom the referring lawyer reasonably believes is competent to handle the matter. See Rule 1.1.

[8] Paragraph (e) does not prohibit or regulate division of fees to be received in the future for work done when lawyers were previously associated in a law firm.

Disputes over Fees

~~[5]~~ [9]   If a procedure has been established for resolution of fee disputes, such as an arbitration or mediation procedure established by the bar, the lawyer <u>must comply with the procedure when it is mandatory, and, even when it is voluntary, the lawyer</u> should conscientiously consider submitting to it. Law may prescribe a procedure for determining a lawyer's fee, for example, in representation of an executor or administrator, a class or a person entitled to a reasonable fee as part of the measure of damages. The lawyer entitled to such a fee and a lawyer representing another party concerned with the fee should comply with the prescribed procedure.

RULE 1.6: CONFIDENTIALITY OF INFORMATION

(a)   A lawyer shall not reveal information relating to the representation of a client unless the client ~~consents after consultation, except for disclosures that are~~ <u>gives informed consent, the disclosure is</u> impliedly authorized in order to carry out the representation~~, and except as stated in~~ <u>or the disclosure is permitted by</u> paragraph (b).

(b)   A lawyer may reveal ~~such~~ information <u>relating to the representation of a client</u> to the extent the lawyer reasonably believes necessary:

(1)   to prevent ~~the client from committing a criminal act that the lawyer believes is likely to result in imminent~~ <u>reasonably certain</u> death or substantial bodily harm; ~~or~~

<u>(2)   to prevent the client from committing a crime or fraud that is reasonably certain to result in substantial injury to the financial interests or property of another and in furtherance of which the client has used or is using the lawyer's services;</u>[*1]

<u>(3)   to prevent, mitigate or rectify substantial injury to the financial interests or property of another that is reasonably certain to result or has resulted from the client's commission of a crime or fraud in furtherance of which the client has used the lawyer's services;</u>[*]

<u>(4)   to secure legal advice about the lawyer's compliance with these Rules;</u>

~~(2)~~ <u>(5)</u>   to establish a claim or defense on behalf of the lawyer in a controversy between the lawyer and the client, to establish a defense to a criminal charge or civil claim against the lawyer based upon conduct in which the client was involved, or to respond to allegations in any proceeding concerning the lawyer's representation of the client<u>; or</u>

(6)   to comply with other law or a court order.

<u>(7)   to detect and resolve conflicts of interest arising from the lawyer's change of employment or from changes in the composition or ownership of a firm, but only if the revealed information would not compromise the attorney-client privilege or otherwise prejudice the client.</u>

(c)   A lawyer shall make reasonable efforts to prevent the inadvertent or unauthorized disclosure of, or unauthorized access to, information relating to the representation of a client.

Comment

[1] ~~The lawyer is part of a judicial system charged with upholding the law. One of the lawyer's functions is to advise clients so that they avoid any violation of the law in the proper exercise of their rights.~~

[2] ~~The observance of the ethical obligation of a lawyer to hold inviolate confidential information of the client not only facilitates the full development of facts essential to proper representation of the client but also encourages people to seek early legal assistance.~~

[3] ~~Almost without exception, clients come to lawyers in order to determine what their rights are and what is, in the maze of laws and regulations, deemed to be legal and correct. The common law recognizes that the client's confidences must be protected from disclosure. Based upon experience, lawyers know that almost all clients follow the advice given, and the law is upheld.~~

[1]   This Rule governs the disclosure by a lawyer of information relating to the representation of a client during the lawyer's representation of the client. See Rule 1.18 for the lawyer's duties with respect to information provided to the lawyer by a prospective client, Rule 1.9(c)(2) for the lawyer's duty not to reveal information relating to the lawyer's prior representation of a former client and Rules 1.8(b) and 1.9(c)(1) for the lawyer's duties with respect to the use of such information to the disadvantage of clients and former clients.

[4] [2] A fundamental principle in the client-lawyer relationship is that, in the absence of the client's informed consent, the lawyer ~~maintain confidentiality of~~ must not reveal information relating to the representation. See Rule 1.0(e) for the definition of informed consent. This contributes to the trust that is the hallmark of the client-lawyer relationship. The client is thereby encouraged to seek legal assistance and to communicate fully and frankly with the lawyer even as to embarrassing or legally damaging subject matter. The lawyer needs this information to represent the client effectively and, if necessary, to advise the client to refrain from wrongful conduct. Almost without exception, clients come to lawyers in order to determine their rights and what is, in the complex of laws and regulations, deemed to be legal and correct. Based upon experience, lawyers know that almost all clients follow the advice given, and the law is upheld.

[5] [3] The principle of client-lawyer confidentiality is given effect ~~in two~~ by related bodies of law~~,~~: the attorney-client privilege~~,~~ ~~(which includes~~ the work product doctrine~~) in the law of evidence~~ and the rule of confidentiality established in professional ethics. The attorney-client privilege ~~applies~~ and work-product doctrine apply in judicial and other proceedings in which a lawyer may be called as a witness or otherwise required to produce evidence concerning a client. The rule of client-lawyer confidentiality applies in situations other

than those where evidence is sought from the lawyer through compulsion of law. The confidentiality rule, for example, applies not ~~merely~~ only to matters communicated in confidence by the client but also to all information relating to the representation, whatever its source. A lawyer may not disclose such information except as authorized or required by the Rules of Professional Conduct or other law. See also Scope.

~~[6]   The requirement of maintaining confidentiality of information relating to representation applies to government lawyers who may disagree with the policy goals that their representation is designed to advance.~~

[4]   Paragraph (a) prohibits a lawyer from revealing information relating to the representation of a client. This prohibition also applies to disclosures by a lawyer that do not in themselves reveal protected information but could reasonably lead to the discovery of such information by a third person. A lawyer's use of a hypothetical to discuss issues relating to the representation is permissible so long as there is no reasonable likelihood that the listener will be able to ascertain the identity of the client or the situation involved.

Authorized Disclosure

~~[7]~~ [5] ~~A~~ Except to the extent that the client's instructions or special circumstances limit that authority, a lawyer is impliedly authorized to make disclosures about a client when appropriate in carrying out the representation~~;~~ ~~except to the extent that the client's instructions or special circumstances limit that authority~~. In ~~litigation~~ some situations, for example, a lawyer may ~~disclose information by admitting~~ be impliedly authorized to admit a fact that cannot properly be disputed or~~, in negotiation by making~~ to make a disclosure that facilitates a satisfactory conclusion to a matter. ~~[8]~~ Lawyers in a firm may, in the course of the firm's practice, disclose to each other information relating to a client of the firm, unless the client has instructed that particular information be confined to specified lawyers.

Disclosure Adverse to Client

~~[9]~~ [6] ~~The~~ Although the public interest is usually best served by a strict rule requiring lawyers to preserve the confidentiality of information relating to the representation of their clients, the confidentiality rule is subject to limited exceptions. ~~In becoming privy to information about a client, a lawyer may foresee that the client intends serious harm to another person. However, to the extent a lawyer is required or permitted to disclose a client's purposes, the client will be inhibited from revealing facts which would enable the lawyer to counsel against a wrongful course of action. The public is better protected if full and open communication by the client is encouraged than if it is inhibited.~~ Paragraph (b)(1) recognizes the overriding value of life and physical integrity and permits disclosure reasonably necessary to prevent reasonably certain death or substantial bodily harm. Such harm is reasonably certain to occur if it will be suffered imminently or if there is a present and substantial threat that a person will suffer such harm at a later date if the lawyer fails to take action necessary to eliminate the threat. Thus, a lawyer who knows that a client has accidentally discharged toxic waste into a town's water supply may reveal this information to the authorities if there is a present and substantial risk that a person who drinks the water will contract a life-threatening or debilitating disease and the lawyer's disclosure is necessary to eliminate the threat or reduce the number of victims.

[7] Paragraph (b)(2) is a limited exception to the rule of confidentiality that permits the lawyer to reveal information to the extent necessary to enable affected persons or appropriate authorities to prevent the client from committing a crime or fraud, as defined in Rule 1.0(d), that is reasonably certain to result in substantial injury to the financial or property interests of another and in furtherance of which the client has used or is using the lawyer's services. Such a serious abuse of the client-lawyer relationship by the client forfeits the protection of this Rule. The client can, of course, prevent such disclosure by refraining from the wrongful conduct. Although paragraph (b)(2) does not require the lawyer to reveal the client's misconduct, the lawyer may not counsel or assist the client in conduct the lawyer knows is criminal or fraudulent. See Rule 1.2(d). See also Rule 1.16 with respect to the lawyer's obligation or right to withdraw from the representation of the client in such circumstances, and Rule 1.13(c), which permits the lawyer, where the client is an organization, to reveal information relating to the representation in limited circumstances.*

[8] Paragraph (b)(3) addresses the situation in which the lawyer does not learn of the client's crime or fraud until after it has been consummated. Although the client no longer has the option of preventing disclosure by refraining from the wrongful conduct, there will be situations in which the loss suffered by the affected person can be prevented, rectified or mitigated. In such situations, the lawyer may disclose information relating to the representation to the extent necessary to enable the affected persons to prevent or mitigate reasonably certain losses or to attempt to recoup their losses. Paragraph (b)(3) does not apply when a person who has committed a crime or fraud thereafter employs a lawyer for representation concerning that offense.*

~~[10] Several situations must be distinguished.~~

~~[11] First, the lawyer may not counsel or assist a client in conduct that is criminal or fraudulent. See Rule 1.2(d). Similarly, a lawyer has a duty under Rule 3.3(a)(4) not to use false evidence. This duty is essentially a special instance of the duty prescribed in Rule 1.2(d) to avoid assisting a client in criminal or fraudulent conduct.~~

~~[12] Second, the lawyer may have been innocently involved in past conduct by the client that was criminal or fraudulent. In such a situation the lawyer has not violated Rule 1.2(d), because to "counsel or assist" criminal or fraudulent conduct requires knowing that the conduct is of that character.~~

~~[13] Third, the lawyer may learn that a client intends prospective conduct that is criminal and likely to result in imminent death or substantial bodily harm. As stated in paragraph (b)(1), the lawyer has professional discretion to reveal information in order to prevent such consequences. The lawyer may make a disclosure in order to prevent homicide or serious bodily injury~~

~~which the lawyer reasonably believes is intended by a client. It is very difficult for a lawyer to "know" when such a heinous purpose will actually be carried out, for the client may have a change of mind.~~

~~[14]   The lawyer's exercise of discretion requires consideration of such factors as the nature of the lawyer's relationship with the client and with those who might be injured by the client, the lawyer's own involvement in the transaction and factors that may extenuate the conduct in question. Where practical, the lawyer should seek to persuade the client to take suitable action. In any case, a disclosure adverse to the client's interest should be no greater than the lawyer reasonably believes necessary to the purpose. A lawyer's decision not to take preventive action permitted by paragraph (b)(1) does not violate this Rule.~~

[9]   A lawyer's confidentiality obligations do not preclude a lawyer from securing confidential legal advice about the lawyer's personal responsibility to comply with these Rules. In most situations, disclosing information to secure such advice will be impliedly authorized for the lawyer to carry out the representation. Even when the disclosure is not impliedly authorized, paragraph (b)(2) permits such disclosure because of the importance of a lawyer's compliance with the Rules of Professional Conduct.

~~Dispute Concerning a Lawyer's Conduct~~

~~18]~~[10] Where a legal claim or disciplinary charge alleges complicity of the lawyer in a client's conduct or other misconduct of the lawyer involving representation of the client, the lawyer may respond to the extent the lawyer reasonably believes necessary to establish a defense. The same is true with respect to a claim involving the conduct or representation of a former client. Such a charge can arise in a civil, criminal, disciplinary or other proceeding and can be based on a wrong allegedly committed by the lawyer against the client or on a wrong alleged by a third person, for example, a person claiming to have been defrauded by the lawyer and client acting together. The lawyer's right to respond arises when an assertion of such complicity has been made. Paragraph (b)~~(2)~~(3) does not require the lawyer to await the commencement of an action or proceeding that charges such complicity, so that the defense may be established by responding directly to a third party who has made such an assertion.The right to defend also applies, of course, ~~applies~~ where a proceeding has been commenced. ~~Where practicable and not prejudicial to the lawyer's ability to establish the defense, the lawyer should advise the client of the third party's assertion and request that the client respond appropriately. In any event, disclosure should be no greater than the lawyer reasonably believes is necessary to vindicate innocence, the disclosure should be made in a manner which limits access to the information to the tribunal or other persons having a need to know it, and appropriate protective orders or other arrangements should be sought by the lawyer to the fullest extent practicable.~~

~~[19]~~ [11] ~~If the lawyer is charged with wrongdoing in which the client's conduct is implicated, the rule of confidentiality should not prevent the lawyer from defending against the charge. Such a charge can arise in a civil, criminal~~

~~or professional disciplinary proceeding, and can be based on a wrong allegedly committed by the lawyer against the client, or on a wrong alleged by a third person; for example, a person claiming to have been defrauded by the lawyer and client acting together.~~ A lawyer entitled to a fee is permitted by paragraph (b)~~(2)~~(3) to prove the services rendered in an action to collect it. This aspect of the rule expresses the principle that the beneficiary of a fiduciary relationship may not exploit it to the detriment of the fiduciary.~~As stated above, the lawyer must make every effort practicable to avoid unnecessary disclosure of information relating to a representation, to limit disclosure to those having the need to know it, and to obtain protective orders or make other arrangements minimizing the risk of disclosure.~~

[12]   Other law may require that a lawyer disclose information about a client. Whether such a law supersedes Rule 1.6 is a question of law beyond the scope of these Rules. When disclosure of information relating to the representation appears to be required by other law, the lawyer must discuss the matter with the client to the extent required by Rule 1.4. If, however, the other law supersedes this Rule and requires disclosure, paragraph (b)(4) permits the lawyer to make such disclosures as are necessary to comply with the law.

Detection of Conflicts of Interest

[13]   Paragraph (b)(7) recognizes that lawyers in different firms may need to disclose limited information to each other to detect and resolve conflicts of interest, such as when a lawyer is considering an association with another firm, two or more firms are considering a merger, or a lawyer is considering the purchase of a law practice. See Rule 1.17, Comment [7]. Under these circumstances, lawyers and law firms are permitted to disclose limited information, but only once substantive discussions regarding the new relationship have occurred. Any such disclosure should ordinarily include no more than the identity of the persons and entities involved in a matter, a brief summary of the general issues involved, and information about whether the matter has terminated. Even this limited information, however, should be disclosed only to the extent reasonably necessary to detect and resolve conflicts of interest that might arise from the possible new relationship. Moreover, the disclosure of any information is prohibited if it would compromise the attorney-client privilege or otherwise prejudice the client (e.g., the fact that a corporate client is seeking advice on a corporate takeover that has not been publicly announced; that a person has consulted a lawyer about the possibility of divorce before the person's intentions are known to the person's spouse; or that a person has consulted a lawyer about a criminal investigation that has not led to a public charge). Under those circumstances, paragraph (a) prohibits disclosure unless the client or former client gives informed consent. A lawyer's fiduciary duty to the lawyer's firm may also govern a lawyer's conduct when exploring an association with another firm and is beyond the scope of these Rules.

[14]   Any information disclosed pursuant to paragraph (b)(7) may be used or further disclosed only to the extent necessary to detect and resolve conflicts of interest. Paragraph (b)(7) does not restrict the use of information

acquired by means independent of any disclosure pursuant to paragraph (b)(7). Paragraph (b)(7) also does not affect the disclosure of information within a law firm when the disclosure is otherwise authorized, see Comment [5], such as when a lawyer in a firm discloses information to another lawyer in the same firm to detect and resolve conflicts of interest that could arise in connection with undertaking a new representation.

[15]   A lawyer may be ordered to reveal information relating to the representation of a client by a court or by another tribunal or governmental entity claiming authority pursuant to other law to compel the disclosure. Absent informed consent of the client to do otherwise, the lawyer should assert on behalf of the client all nonfrivolous claims that the order is not authorized by other law or that the information sought is protected against disclosure by the attorney-client privilege or other applicable law. In the event of an adverse ruling, the lawyer must consult with the client about the possibility of appeal to the extent required by Rule 1.4. Unless review is sought, however, paragraph (b)(4) permits the lawyer to comply with the court's order.

[16]   Paragraph (b) permits disclosure only to the extent the lawyer reasonably believes the disclosure is necessary to accomplish one of the purposes specified. Where practicable, the lawyer should first seek to persuade the client to take suitable action to obviate the need for disclosure. In any case, a disclosure adverse to the client's interest should be no greater than the lawyer reasonably believes necessary to accomplish the purpose. If the disclosure will be made in connection with a judicial proceeding, the disclosure should be made in a manner that limits access to the information to the tribunal or other persons having a need to know it and appropriate protective orders or other arrangements should be sought by the lawyer to the fullest extent practicable.

[17]   Paragraph (b) permits but does not require the disclosure of information relating to a client's representation to accomplish the purposes specified in paragraphs (b)(1) through (b)(4). In exercising the discretion conferred by this Rule, the lawyer may consider such factors as the nature of the lawyer's relationship with the client and with those who might be injured by the client, the lawyer's own involvement in the transaction and factors that may extenuate the conduct in question. A lawyer's decision not to disclose as permitted by paragraph (b) does not violate this Rule. Disclosure may be required, however, by other Rules. Some Rules require disclosure only if such disclosure would be permitted by paragraph (b). See Rules 1.2(d), 4.1(b), 8.1 and 8.3. Rule 3.3, on the other hand, requires disclosure in some circumstances regardless of whether such disclosure is permitted by this Rule. See Rule 3.3(c).

Withdrawal

[15]   If the lawyer's services will be used by the client in materially furthering a course of criminal or fraudulent conduct, the lawyer must withdraw, as stated in Rule 1.16(a)(1). [16] After withdrawal the lawyer is required to refrain from making disclosure of the client's confidences, except as otherwise permitted in Rule 1.6. Neither this Rule nor Rule 1.8(b) nor Rule 1.16(d)

~~prevents the lawyer from giving notice of the fact of withdrawal, and the lawyer may also withdraw or disaffirm any opinion, document, affirmation, or the like.~~

~~[17] Where the client is an organization, the lawyer may be in doubt whether contemplated conduct will actually be carried out by the organization. Where necessary to guide conduct in connection with this Rule, the lawyer may make inquiry within the organization as indicated in Rule 1.13(b).~~[*]

~~Disclosures Otherwise Required or Authorized~~

~~[20] The attorney-client privilege is differently defined in various jurisdictions. If a lawyer is called as a witness to give testimony concerning a client, absent waiver by the client, paragraph (a) requires the lawyer to invoke the privilege when it is applicable. The lawyer must comply with the final orders of a court or other tribunal of competent jurisdiction requiring the lawyer to give information about the client.~~

~~[21] The Rules of Professional Conduct in various circumstances permit or require a lawyer to disclose information relating to the representation. See Rules 2.2, 2.3, 3.3 and 4.1. In addition to these provisions, a lawyer may be obligated or permitted by other provisions of law to give information about a client.Whether another provision of law supercedes Rule 1.6 is a matter of interpretation beyond the scope of these Rules, but a presumption should exist against such a supersession.~~

Acting Competently to Preserve Confidentiality

[18] Paragraph (c) requires a lawyer to act competently to safeguard information relating to the representation of a client against unauthorized access by third parties and against inadvertent or unauthorized disclosure by the lawyer or other persons who are participating in the representation of the client or who are subject to the lawyer's supervision. See Rules 1.1, 5.1 and 5.3. The unauthorized access to, or the inadvertent or unauthorized disclosure of, information relating to the representation of a client does not constitute a violation of paragraph (c) if the lawyer has made reasonable efforts to prevent the access or disclosure. Factors to be considered in determining the reasonableness of the lawyer's efforts include, but are not limited to, the sensitivity of the information, the likelihood of disclosure if additional safeguards are not employed, the cost of employing additional safeguards, the difficulty of implementing the safeguards, and the extent to which the safeguards adversely affect the lawyer's ability to represent clients (e.g., by making a device or important piece of software excessively difficult to use). A client may require the lawyer to implement special security measures not required by this Rule or may give informed consent to forgo security measures that would otherwise be required by this Rule. Whether a lawyer may be required to take additional steps to safeguard a client's information in order to comply with other law, such as state and federal laws that govern data privacy or that impose notification requirements upon the loss of, or unauthorized access to, electronic information, is beyond the scope of these Rules. For a lawyer's duties when sharing information with nonlawyers outside the lawyer's own firm, see Rule 5.3, Comments [3]-[4].

[19]   When transmitting a communication that includes information relating to the representation of a client, the lawyer must take reasonable precautions to prevent the information from coming into the hands of unintended recipients. This duty, however, does not require that the lawyer use special security measures if the method of communication affords a reasonable expectation of privacy. Special circumstances, however, may warrant special precautions. Factors to be considered in determining the reasonableness of the lawyer's expectation of confidentiality include the sensitivity of the information and the extent to which the privacy of the communication is protected by law or by a confidentiality agreement. A client may require the lawyer to implement special security measures not required by this Rule or may give informed consent to the use of a means of communication that would otherwise be prohibited by this Rule. Whether a lawyer may be required to take additional steps in order to comply with other law, such as state and federal laws that govern data privacy, is beyond the scope of these Rules.

Former Client

[22] [20]   The duty of confidentiality continues after the client-lawyer relationship has terminated. See Rule 1.9(c)(2). See Rule 1.9(c)(1) for the prohibition against using such information to the disadvantage of the former client.

RULE 1.7: CONFLICT OF INTEREST: ~~GENERAL RULE~~ CURRENT CLIENTS

(a)   A lawyer shall not represent a client if the representation of that client will be directly adverse to another client, unless:

(1)   the lawyer reasonably believes the representation will not adversely affect the relationship with the other client; and

(2)   each client consents after consultation.

(b)   A lawyer shall not represent a client if the representation of that client may be materially limited by the lawyer's responsibilities to another client or to a third person, or by the lawyer's own interests, unless:

(1)   the lawyer reasonably believes the representation will not be adversely affected; and

(2)   the client consents after consultation. When representation of multiple clients in a single matter is undertaken, the consultation shall include explanation of the implications of the common representation and the advantages and risks involved.

(a)   Except as provided in paragraph (b), a lawyer shall not represent a client if the representation involves a concurrent conflict of interest. A concurrent conflict of interest exists if:

(1)   the representation of one client will be directly adverse to another client; or

(2) there is a significant risk that the representation of one or more clients will be materially limited by the lawyer's responsibilities to another client, a former client or a third person or by a personal interest of the lawyer.

(b) Notwithstanding the existence of a concurrent conflict of interest under paragraph (a), a lawyer may represent a client if:

(1) the lawyer reasonably believes that the lawyer will be able to provide competent and diligent representation to each affected client;

(2) the representation is not prohibited by law;

(3) the representation does not involve the assertion of a claim by one client against another client represented by the lawyer in the same litigation or other proceeding before a tribunal; and

(4) each affected client gives informed consent, confirmed in writing.

Comment

~~Loyalty to a Client~~ General Principles

[1] Loyalty ~~is an~~ and independent judgment are essential element elements in the lawyer's relationship to a client. Concurrent conflicts of interest can arise from the lawyer's responsibilities to another client, a former client or a third person or from the lawyer's own interests. For specific Rules regarding certain concurrent conflicts of interest, see Rule 1.8. For former client conflicts of interest, see Rule 1.9. For conflicts of interest involving prospective clients, see Rule 1.18. For definitions of "informed consent" and "confirmed in writing," see Rule 1.0(e) and (b).

[2] Resolution of a conflict of interest problem under this Rule requires the lawyer to: 1) clearly identify the client or clients; 2) determine whether a conflict of interest exists; 3) decide whether the representation may be undertaken despite the existence of a conflict, i.e., whether the conflict is consentable; and 4) if so, consult with the clients affected under paragraph (a) and obtain their informed consent, confirmed in writing. The clients affected under paragraph (a) include both of the clients referred to in paragraph (a)(1) and the one or more clients whose representation might be materially limited under paragraph (a)(2).

[3] ~~An impermissible~~ A conflict of interest may exist before representation is undertaken, in which event the representation ~~should~~ must be declined, unless the lawyer obtains the informed consent of each client under the conditions of paragraph (b). ~~The~~ To determine whether a conflict of interest exists, a lawyer should adopt reasonable procedures, appropriate for the size and type of firm and practice, to determine in both litigation and non-litigation matters the ~~parties~~ persons and issues involved ~~and to determine whether there are actual or potential conflicts of interest~~. See also Comment to Rule 5.1.

Ignorance caused by a failure to institute such procedures will not excuse a lawyer's violation of this Rule. As to whether a client-lawyer relationship exists or, having once been established, is continuing, see Comment to Rule 1.3 and Scope.

{2} [4] If ~~such~~ a conflict arises after representation has been undertaken, the lawyer ~~should~~ ordinarily must withdraw from the representation, unless the lawyer has obtained the informed consent of the client under the conditions of paragraph (b). See Rule 1.16. Where more than one client is involved ~~and the lawyer withdraws because a conflict arises after representation~~, whether the lawyer may continue to represent any of the clients is determined both by the lawyer's ability to comply with duties owed to the former client and by the lawyer's ability to represent adequately the remaining client or clients, given the lawyer's duties to the former client. See Rule 1.9. See also ~~Rule 2.2(c)~~ Comments [5] and [29]. ~~As to whether a client-lawyer relationship exists or, having once been established, is continuing, see Comment to Rule 1.3 and Scope.~~

~~{5}   Unforeseeable developments, such as changes in corporate and other organizational affiliations or the addition or realignment of parties in litigation, might create conflicts in the midst of a representation, as when a company sued by the lawyer on behalf of one client is bought by another client represented by the lawyer in an unrelated matter. Depending on the circumstances, the lawyer may have the option to withdraw from one of the representations in order to avoid the conflict. The lawyer must seek court approval where necessary and take steps to minimize harm to the clients. See Rule 1.16. The lawyer must continue to protect the confidences of the client from whose representation the lawyer has withdrawn. See Rule 1.9(c).~~

Identifying Conflicts of Interest: Directly Adverse

{3} [6] ~~As a general proposition, loyalty~~ Loyalty to a current client prohibits undertaking representation directly adverse to that client without that client's informed consent. ~~Paragraph (a) expresses that general rule.~~ Thus, absent consent, a lawyer ~~ordinarily~~ may not act as an advocate in one matter against a person the lawyer represents in some other matter, even ~~if it is~~ when the matters are wholly unrelated. The client as to whom the representation is directly adverse is likely to feel betrayed, and the resulting damage to the client-lawyer relationship is likely to impair the lawyer's ability to represent the client effectively. In addition, the client on whose behalf the adverse representation is undertaken reasonably may fear that the lawyer will pursue that client's case less effectively out of deference to the other client, i.e., that the representation may be materially limited by the lawyer's interest in retaining the current client. Similarly, a directly adverse conflict may arise when a lawyer is required to cross-examine a client who appears as a witness in a lawsuit involving another client, as when the testimony will be damaging to the client who is represented in the lawsuit. On the other hand, simultaneous representation in unrelated matters of clients whose interests are only ~~generally~~ economically adverse, such as representation of competing economic enterprises in unrelated litigation, does not ordinarily constitute a conflict of interest and thus may not require consent of the respective clients. ~~Paragraph (a) applies only when the representation of one client would be directly adverse to the other.~~

[7] Directly adverse conflicts can also arise in transactional matters. For example, if a lawyer is asked to represent the seller of a business in negotiations with a buyer represented by the lawyer, not in the same transaction but in another, unrelated matter, the lawyer could not undertake the representation without the informed consent of each client.

Identifying Conflicts of Interest: Material Limitation

[4] [8] ~~Loyalty to a client is also impaired when~~ Even where there is no direct adverseness, a conflict of interest exists if there is a significant risk that a ~~lawyer cannot~~ lawyer's ability to consider, recommend or carry out an appropriate course of action for the client ~~because~~ will be materially limited as a result of the lawyer's other responsibilities or interests. For example, a lawyer asked to represent several individuals seeking to form a joint venture is likely to be materially limited in the lawyer's ability to recommend or advocate all possible positions that each might take because of the lawyer's duty of loyalty to the others. The conflict in effect forecloses alternatives that would otherwise be available to the client. ~~Paragraph (b) addresses such situations. A possible conflict~~ The mere possibility of subsequent harm does not itself ~~preclude the representation~~ require disclosure and consent. The critical questions are the likelihood that a ~~conflict~~ difference in interests will eventuate and, if it does, whether it will materially interfere with the lawyer's independent professional judgment in considering alternatives or foreclose courses of action that reasonably should be pursued on behalf of the client. ~~Consideration should be given to whether the client wishes to accommodate the other interest involved.~~

Lawyer's ~~Interests~~ Responsibilities to Former Clients and Other Third Persons

[9] In addition to conflicts with other current clients, a lawyer's duties of loyalty and independence may be materially limited by responsibilities to former clients under Rule 1.9 or by the lawyer's responsibilities to other persons, such as fiduciary duties arising from a lawyer's service as a trustee, executor or corporate director.

Personal Interest Conflicts

[6] [10] The lawyer's own interests should not be permitted to have an adverse effect on representation of a client. For example, ~~a lawyer's need for income should not lead the lawyer to undertake matters that cannot be handled competently and at a reasonable fee. See Rules 1.1 and 1.5. If~~ if the probity of a lawyer's own conduct in a transaction is in serious question, it may be difficult or impossible for the lawyer to give a client detached advice. ~~A~~ Similarly, when a lawyer has discussions concerning possible employment with an opponent of the lawyer's client, or with a law firm representing the opponent, such discussions could materially limit the lawyer's representation of the client. In addition, a lawyer may not allow related business interests to affect representation, for

example, by referring clients to an enterprise in which the lawyer has an undis-closed financial interest. See Rule 1.8 for specific Rules pertaining to a number of personal interest conflicts, including business transactions with clients. See also Rule 1.10 (personal interest conflicts under Rule 1.7 ordinarily are not imputed to other lawyers in a law firm).

[11]   When lawyers representing different clients in the same matter or in substantially related matters are closely related by blood or marriage, there may be a significant risk that client confidences will be revealed and that the lawyer's family relationship will interfere with both loyalty and independent professional judgment. As a result, each client is entitled to know of the existence and implications of the relationship between the lawyers before the lawyer agrees to undertake the representation. Thus, a lawyer related to another lawyer, e.g., as parent, child, sibling or spouse, ordinarily may not represent a client in a matter where that lawyer is representing another party, unless each client gives informed consent. The disqualification arising from a close family relationship is personal and ordinarily is not imputed to members of firms with whom the lawyers are associated. See Rule 1.10.

[12]   A lawyer is prohibited from engaging in sexual relationships with a client unless the sexual relationship predates the formation of the client-lawyer relationship. See Rule 1.8(j).

Interest of Person Paying for a Lawyer's Service

~~[10]~~ [13] A lawyer may be paid from a source other than the client, including a co-client, if the client is informed of that fact and consents and the arrangement does not compromise the lawyer's duty of loyalty or independent judgment to the client. See Rule 1.8(f). ~~For example, when an insurer and its insured have conflicting interests in a matter arising from a liability insurance agreement, and the insurer is required to provide special counsel for the insured, the arrangement should assure the special counsel's professional independence. So also, when a corporation and its directors or employees are involved in a controversy in which they have conflicting inter-ests, the corporation may provide funds for separate legal representation of the directors or employees, if the clients consent after consultation and the arrangement ensures the lawyer's professional independence.~~ If acceptance of the payment from any other source presents a significant risk that the lawyer's representation of the client will be materially limited by the lawyer's own interest in accommodating the person paying the lawyer's fee or by the lawyer's responsibilities to a payer who is also a co-client, then the lawyer must comply with the requirements of paragraph (b) before accepting the representation, including determining whether the conflict is consentable and, if so, that the client has adequate information about the material risks of the representation.

~~Consultation and Consent~~ Prohibited Representations

~~[5]~~ [14] ~~A client~~ Ordinarily, clients may consent to representation not-withstanding a conflict. However, as indicated in paragraph ~~(a)(1) with respect~~

~~to representation directly adverse to a client, and paragraph~~ (b)~~(1) with respect to material limitations on representation of a client, when a disinterested lawyer would conclude that the client should not agree to the representation under the circumstances~~, some conflicts are nonconsentable, meaning that the lawyer involved cannot properly ask for such agreement or provide representation on the basis of the client's consent. When the lawyer is representing more than one client ~~is involved~~, the question of ~~conflict~~ consentability must be resolved as to each client. ~~Moreover, there may be circumstances where it is impossible to make the disclosure necessary to obtain consent. For example, when the lawyer represents different clients in related matters and one of the clients refuses to consent to the disclosure necessary to permit the other client to make an informed decision, the lawyer cannot properly ask the latter to consent.~~

[15]   Consentability is typically determined by considering whether the interests of the clients will be adequately protected if the clients are permitted to give their informed consent to representation burdened by a conflict of interest. Thus, under paragraph (b)(1), representation is prohibited if in the circumstances the lawyer cannot reasonably conclude that the lawyer will be able to provide competent and diligent representation. See Rule 1.1 (competence) and Rule 1.3 (diligence).

[16]   Paragraph (b)(2) describes conflicts that are nonconsentable because the representation is prohibited by applicable law. For example, in some states substantive law provides that the same lawyer may not represent more than one defendant in a capital case, even with the consent of the clients, and under federal criminal statutes certain representations by a former government lawyer are prohibited, despite the informed consent of the former client. In addition, decisional law in some states limits the ability of a governmental client, such as a municipality, to consent to a conflict of interest.

[17]   Paragraph (b)(3) describes conflicts that are nonconsentable because of the institutional interest in vigorous development of each client's position when the clients are aligned directly against each other in the same litigation or other proceeding before a tribunal. Whether clients are aligned directly against each other within the meaning of this paragraph requires examination of the context of the proceeding. Although this paragraph does not preclude a lawyer's multiple representation of adverse parties to a mediation (because mediation is not a proceeding before a "tribunal" under Rule 1.0(m)), such representation may be precluded by paragraph (b)(1).

Informed Consent

[18]   Informed consent requires that each affected client be aware of the relevant circumstances and of the material and reasonably foreseeable ways that the conflict could have adverse effects on the interests of that client. See Rule 1.0(e) (informed consent). The information required depends on the nature of the conflict and the nature of the risks involved. When representation of multiple clients in a single matter is undertaken, the information must include the implications of the common representation, including possible effects on loyalty, confidentiality and the attorney-client privilege and the

advantages and risks involved. See Comments [30] and [31] (effect of common representation on confidentiality).

[19]   Under some circumstances it may be impossible to make the disclosure necessary to obtain consent. For example, when the lawyer represents different clients in related matters and one of the clients refuses to consent to the disclosure necessary to permit the other client to make an informed decision, the lawyer cannot properly ask the latter to consent. In some cases the alternative to common representation can be that each party may have to obtain separate representation with the possibility of incurring additional costs. These costs, along with the benefits of securing separate representation, are factors that may be considered by the affected client in determining whether common representation is in the client's interests.

Consent Confirmed in Writing

[20]   Paragraph (b) requires the lawyer to obtain the informed consent of the client, confirmed in writing. Such a writing may consist of a document executed by the client or one that the lawyer promptly records and transmits to the client following an oral consent. See Rule 1.0(b). See also Rule 1.0(n) (writing includes electronic transmission). If it is not feasible to obtain or transmit the writing at the time the client gives informed consent, then the lawyer must obtain or transmit it within a reasonable time thereafter. See Rule 1.0(b). The requirement of a writing does not supplant the need in most cases for the lawyer to talk with the client, to explain the risks and advantages, if any, of representation burdened with a conflict of interest, as well as reasonably available alternatives, and to afford the client a reasonable opportunity to consider the risks and alternatives and to raise questions and concerns. Rather, the writing is required in order to impress upon clients the seriousness of the decision the client is being asked to make and to avoid disputes or ambiguities that might later occur in the absence of a writing.

Revoking Consent

[21]   A client who has given consent to a conflict may revoke the consent and, like any other client, may terminate the lawyer's representation at any time. Whether revoking consent to the client's own representation precludes the lawyer from continuing to represent other clients depends on the circumstances, including the nature of the conflict, whether the client revoked consent because of a material change in circumstances, the reasonable expectations of the other client and whether material detriment to the other clients or the lawyer would result.

Consent to Future Conflict

[22]   Whether a lawyer may properly request a client to waive conflicts that might arise in the future is subject to the test of paragraph (b). The effectiveness of such waivers is generally determined by the extent to which the client reasonably understands the material risks that the waiver entails. The more comprehensive the explanation of the types of future representations that might arise and the actual and reasonably foreseeable adverse consequences of those

representations, the greater the likelihood that the client will have the requisite understanding. Thus, if the client agrees to consent to a particular type of conflict with which the client is already familiar, then the consent ordinarily will be effective with regard to that type of conflict. If the consent is general and open-ended, then the consent ordinarily will be ineffective, because it is not reasonably likely that the client will have understood the material risks involved. On the other hand, if the client is an experienced user of the legal services involved and is reasonably informed regarding the risk that a conflict may arise, such consent is more likely to be effective, particularly if, e.g., the client is independently represented by other counsel in giving consent and the consent is limited to future conflicts unrelated to the subject of the representation. In any case, advance consent cannot be effective if the circumstances that materialize in the future are such as would make the conflict nonconsentable under paragraph (b).

Conflicts in Litigation

~~[7]~~ [23] Paragraph ~~(a)~~ (b)(3) prohibits representation of opposing parties in the same litigation, regardless of the clients' consent. ~~Simultaneous~~ On the other hand, simultaneous representation of parties whose interests in litigation may conflict, such as coplaintiffs or codefendants, is governed by paragraph ~~(b)~~ (a)(2). ~~An impermissible~~ A conflict may exist by reason of substantial discrepancy in the parties' testimony, incompatibility in positions in relation to an opposing party or the fact that there are substantially different possibilities of settlement of the claims or liabilities in question. Such conflicts can arise in criminal cases as well as civil. The potential for conflict of interest in representing multiple defendants in a criminal case is so grave that ordinarily a lawyer should decline to represent more than one codefendant. On the other hand, common representation of persons having similar interests in civil litigation is proper if ~~the risk of adverse effect is minimal and~~ the requirements of paragraph (b) are met. ~~Compare Rule 2.2 involving intermediation between clients.~~

~~[8] Ordinarily, a lawyer may not act as advocate against a client the lawyer represents in some other matter, even if the other matter is wholly unrelated. However, there are circumstances in which a lawyer may act as advocate against a client. For example, a lawyer representing an enterprise with diverse operations may accept employment as an advocate against the enterprise in an unrelated matter if doing so will not adversely affect the lawyer's relationship with the enterprise or conduct of the suit and if both clients consent upon consultation. By the same token, government lawyers in some circumstances may represent government employees in proceedings in which a government agency is the opposing party. The propriety of concurrent representation can depend on the nature of the litigation. For example, a suit charging fraud entails conflict to a degree not involved in a suit for a declaratory judgment concerning statutory interpretation.~~

~~[9] A lawyer may represent parties having antagonistic positions on a legal question that has arisen in different cases, unless representation of either client would be adversely affected. Thus, it is ordinarily not improper to~~

~~assert such positions in cases pending in different trial courts, but it may be improper to do so in cases pending at the same time in an appellate court.~~

[24]   Ordinarily a lawyer may take inconsistent legal positions in different tribunals at different times on behalf of different clients. The mere fact that advocating a legal position on behalf of one client might create precedent adverse to the interests of a client represented by the lawyer in an unrelated matter does not create a conflict of interest. A conflict of interest exists, however, if there is a significant risk that a lawyer's action on behalf of one client will materially limit the lawyer's effectiveness in representing another client in a different case; for example, when a decision favoring one client will create a precedent likely to seriously weaken the position taken on behalf of the other client. Factors relevant in determining whether the clients need to be advised of the risk include: where the cases are pending, whether the issue is substantive or procedural, the temporal relationship between the matters, the significance of the issue to the immediate and long-term interests of the clients involved and the clients' reasonable expectations in retaining the lawyer. If there is significant risk of material limitation, then absent informed consent of the affected clients, the lawyer must refuse one of the representations or withdraw from one or both matters.

[25]   When a lawyer represents or seeks to represent a class of plaintiffs or defendants in a class-action lawsuit, unnamed members of the class are ordinarily not considered to be clients of the lawyer for purposes of applying paragraph (a)(1) of this Rule. Thus, the lawyer does not typically need to get the consent of such a person before representing a client suing the person in an unrelated matter. Similarly, a lawyer seeking to represent an opponent in a class action does not typically need the consent of an unnamed member of the class whom the lawyer represents in an unrelated matter.

Other Conflict Situations Nonlitigation Conflicts

~~[11]~~ [26] Conflicts of interest under paragraphs (a)(1) and (a)(2) arise in contexts other than litigation ~~sometimes may be difficult to assess~~. For a discussion of directly adverse conflicts in transactional matters, see Comment [7]. Relevant factors in determining whether there is significant potential for ~~adverse effect~~ material limitation include the duration and intimacy of the lawyer's relationship with the client or clients involved, the functions being performed by the lawyer, the likelihood that ~~actual conflict~~ disagreements will arise and the likely prejudice to the client from the conflict ~~if it does arise~~. The question is often one of proximity and degree. See Comment [8].

~~[13]~~ [27] ~~Conflict~~ For example, conflict questions may ~~also~~ arise in estate planning and estate administration. A lawyer may be called upon to prepare wills for several family members, such as husband and wife, and, depending upon the circumstances, a conflict of interest may ~~arise~~ be present. In estate administration the identity of the client may be unclear under the law of a particular jurisdiction. Under one view, the client is the fiduciary; under another view the client is the estate or trust, including its beneficiaries.

~~The~~ In order to comply with conflict of interest rules, the lawyer should make clear the lawyer's relationship to the parties involved.

~~[12]~~ [28] Whether a conflict is consentable depends on the circumstances. For example, a lawyer may not represent multiple parties to a negotiation whose interests are fundamentally antagonistic to each other, but common representation is permissible where the clients are generally aligned in interest even though there is some difference in interest among them. Thus, a lawyer may seek to establish or adjust a relationship between clients on an amicable and mutually advantageous basis; for example, in helping to organize a business in which two or more clients are entrepreneurs, working out the financial reorganization of an enterprise in which two or more clients have an interest or arranging a property distribution in settlement of an estate. The lawyer seeks to resolve potentially adverse interests by developing the parties' mutual interests. Otherwise, each party might have to obtain separate representation, with the possibility of incurring additional cost, complication or even litigation. Given these and other relevant factors, the clients may prefer that the lawyer act for all of them.

Special Considerations in Common Representation

[29] In considering whether to represent multiple clients in the same matter, a lawyer should be mindful that if the common representation fails because the potentially adverse interests cannot be reconciled, the result can be additional cost, embarrassment and recrimination. Ordinarily, the lawyer will be forced to withdraw from representing all of the clients if the common representation fails. In some situations, the risk of failure is so great that multiple representation is plainly impossible. For example, a lawyer cannot undertake common representation of clients where contentious litigation or negotiations between them are imminent or contemplated. Moreover, because the lawyer is required to be impartial between commonly represented clients, representation of multiple clients is improper when it is unlikely that impartiality can be maintained. Generally, if the relationship between the parties has already assumed antagonism, the possibility that the clients' interests can be adequately served by common representation is not very good. Other relevant factors are whether the lawyer subsequently will represent both parties on a continuing basis and whether the situation involves creating or terminating a relationship between the parties.

[30] A particularly important factor in determining the appropriateness of common representation is the effect on client-lawyer confidentiality and the attorney-client privilege. With regard to the attorney-client privilege, the prevailing rule is that, as between commonly represented clients, the privilege does not attach. Hence, it must be assumed that if litigation eventuates between the clients, the privilege will not protect any such communications, and the clients should be so advised.

[31] As to the duty of confidentiality, continued common representation will almost certainly be inadequate if one client asks the lawyer not to

disclose to the other client information relevant to the common representation. This is so because the lawyer has an equal duty of loyalty to each client, and each client has the right to be informed of anything bearing on the representation that might affect that client's interests and the right to expect that the lawyer will use that information to that client's benefit. See Rule 1.4. The lawyer should, at the outset of the common representation and as part of the process of obtaining each client's informed consent, advise each client that information will be shared and that the lawyer will have to withdraw if one client decides that some matter material to the representation should be kept from the other. In limited circumstances, it may be appropriate for the lawyer to proceed with the representation when the clients have agreed, after being properly informed, that the lawyer will keep certain information confidential. For example, the lawyer may reasonably conclude that failure to disclose one client's trade secrets to another client will not adversely affect representation involving a joint venture between the clients and agree to keep that information confidential with the informed consent of both clients.

[32]   When seeking to establish or adjust a relationship between clients, the lawyer should make clear that the lawyer's role is not that of partisanship normally expected in other circumstances and, thus, that the clients may be required to assume greater responsibility for decisions than when each client is separately represented. Any limitations on the scope of the representation made necessary as a result of the common representation should be fully explained to the clients at the outset of the representation. See Rule 1.2(c).

[33]   Subject to the above limitations, each client in the common representation has the right to loyal and diligent representation and the protection of Rule 1.9 concerning the obligations to a former client. The client also has the right to discharge the lawyer as stated in Rule 1.16.

Organizational Clients

[34]   A lawyer who represents a corporation or other organization does not, by virtue of that representation, necessarily represent any constituent or affiliated organization, such as a parent or subsidiary. See Rule 1.13(a). Thus, the lawyer for an organization is not barred from accepting representation adverse to an affiliate in an unrelated matter, unless the circumstances are such that the affiliate should also be considered a client of the lawyer, there is an understanding between the lawyer and the organizational client that the lawyer will avoid representation adverse to the client's affiliates, or the lawyer's obligations to either the organizational client or the new client are likely to limit materially the lawyer's representation of the other client.

[14] [35] A lawyer for a corporation or other organization who is also a member of its board of directors should determine whether the responsibilities of the two roles may conflict. The lawyer may be called on to advise the corporation in matters involving actions of the directors. Consideration should be given to the frequency with which such situations may arise, the potential intensity of the conflict, the effect of the lawyer's resignation from the board and the possibility of the corporation's obtaining legal advice from another

lawyer in such situations. If there is material risk that the dual role will compromise the lawyer's independence of professional judgment, the lawyer should not serve as a director <u>or should cease to act as the corporation's lawyer when conflicts of interest arise. The lawyer should advise the other members of the board that in some circumstances matters discussed at board meetings while the lawyer is present in the capacity of director might not be protected by the attorney-client privilege and that conflict of interest considerations might require the lawyer's recusal as a director or might require the lawyer and the lawyer's firm to decline representation of the corporation in a matter.</u>

~~Conflict Charged by an Opposing Party~~

~~[15] Resolving questions of conflict of interest is primarily the responsibility of the lawyer undertaking the representation. In litigation, a court may raise the question when there is reason to infer that the lawyer has neglected the responsibility. In a criminal case, inquiry by the court is generally required when a lawyer represents multiple defendants. Where the conflict is such as clearly to call in question the fair or efficient administration of justice, opposing counsel may properly raise the question. Such an objection should be viewed with caution, however, for it can be misused as a technique of harassment. See Scope.~~

RULE 1.8: CONFLICT OF INTEREST: ~~PROHIBITED TRANSACTIONS~~ <u>CURRENT CLIENTS: SPECIFIC RULES</u>

(a)   A lawyer shall not enter into a business transaction with a client or knowingly acquire an ownership, possessory, security or other pecuniary interest adverse to a client unless:

(1)   the transaction and terms on which the lawyer acquires the interest are fair and reasonable to the client and are fully disclosed and transmitted in writing ~~to the client~~ in a manner ~~which~~ <u>that</u> can be reasonably understood by the client;

(2)   the client is <u>advised in writing of the desirability of seeking and is</u> given a reasonable opportunity to seek the advice of independent <u>legal</u> counsel in <u>on</u> the transaction; and

(3)   the client ~~consents~~ <u>gives informed consent,</u> in <u>a</u> writing ~~thereto~~ <u>signed by the client, to the essential terms of the transaction and the lawyer's role in the transaction, including whether the lawyer is representing the client in the transaction.</u>

(b)   A lawyer shall not use information relating to representation of a client to the disadvantage of the client unless the client ~~consents after consultation~~ <u>gives informed consent</u>, except as permitted or required by ~~Rule 1.6 or Rule 3.3~~ <u>these Rules</u>.

(c)   A lawyer shall not <u>solicit any substantial gift from a client, including a testamentary gift, or</u> prepare <u>on behalf of a client</u> an instrument giving the lawyer or a person related to the lawyer ~~as parent, child, sibling, or spouse~~ any substantial gift ~~from a client, including a testamentary~~ <u>unless the</u>

lawyer or other recipient of the gift, ~~except where the client~~ is related to the ~~donee~~ client. For purposes of this paragraph, related persons include a spouse, child, grandchild, parent, grandparent or other relative or individual with whom the lawyer or the client maintains a close, familial relationship.

(d)   Prior to the conclusion of representation of a client, a lawyer shall not make or negotiate an agreement giving the lawyer literary or media rights to a portrayal or account based in substantial part on information relating to the representation.

(e)   A lawyer shall not provide financial assistance to a client in connection with pending or contemplated litigation, except that:

(1)   a lawyer may advance court costs and expenses of litigation, the repayment of which may be contingent on the outcome of the matter; and

(2)   a lawyer representing an indigent client may pay court costs and expenses of litigation on behalf of the client.

(f)   A lawyer shall not accept compensation for representing a client from one other than the client unless:

(1)   the client ~~consents after consultation~~ gives informed consent;

(2)   there is no interference with the lawyer's independence of professional judgment or with the client-lawyer relationship; and

(3)   information relating to representation of a client is protected as required by Rule 1.6.

(g)   A lawyer who represents two or more clients shall not participate in making an aggregate settlement of the claims of or against the clients, or in a criminal case an aggregated agreement as to guilty or nolo contendere pleas, unless each client ~~consents after consultation, including~~ gives informed consent, in a writing signed by the client. The lawyer's disclosure ~~of~~ shall include the existence and nature of all the claims or pleas involved and of the participation of each person in the settlement.

(h)   A lawyer shall not:

(1)   make an agreement prospectively limiting the lawyer's liability to a client for malpractice unless ~~permitted by law and~~ the client is independently represented in making the agreement~~;~~; or

(2)   settle a claim or potential claim for such liability with an unrepresented client or former client ~~without first advising~~ unless that person is advised in writing that ~~of~~ the desirability of seeking and is given a reasonable opportunity to seek the advice of independent ~~representation is appropriate~~ legal counsel in connection therewith.

~~(i)   A lawyer related to another lawyer as parent, child, sibling or spouse shall not represent a client in a representation directly adverse to a person whom the lawyer knows is represented by the other lawyer except upon consent by the client after consultation regarding the relationship.~~

~~(j)~~ (i) A lawyer shall not acquire a proprietary interest in the cause of action or subject matter of litigation the lawyer is conducting for a client, except that the lawyer may:

(1) acquire a lien ~~granted~~ authorized by law to secure the lawyer's fee or expenses; and

(2) contract with a client for a reasonable contingent fee in a civil case.

(j) A lawyer shall not have sexual relations with a client unless a consensual sexual relationship existed between them when the client-lawyer relationship commenced.

(k) While lawyers are associated in a firm, a prohibition in the foregoing paragraphs (a) through (i) that applies to any one of them shall apply to all of them.

Comment

Business Transactions Between Client and Lawyer

[1] ~~As a general principle, all transactions between client and lawyer should be fair and reasonable to the client. In such transactions a review by independent counsel on behalf of the client is often advisable. Furthermore, a lawyer may not exploit information relating to the representation to the client's disadvantage. For example, a lawyer who has learned that the client is investing in specific real estate may not, without the client's consent, seek to acquire nearby property where doing so would adversely affect the client's plan for investment. Paragraph (a)~~ A lawyer's legal skill and training, together with the relationship of trust and confidence between lawyer and client, create the possibility of overreaching when the lawyer participates in a business, property or financial transaction with a client, for example, a loan or sales transaction or a lawyer investment on behalf of a client. The requirements of paragraph (a) must be met even when the transaction is not closely related to the subject matter of the representation, as when a lawyer drafting a will for a client learns that the client needs money for unrelated expenses and offers to make a loan to the client. The Rule applies to lawyers engaged in the sale of goods or services related to the practice of law, for example, the sale of title insurance or investment services to existing clients of the lawyer's legal practice. See Rule 5.7. It also applies to lawyers purchasing property from estates they represent. It does not apply to ordinary fee arrangements between client and lawyer, which are governed by Rule 1.5, although its requirements must be met when the lawyer accepts an interest in the client's business or other nonmonetary property as payment of all or part of a fee. In addition, the Rule does not ~~however,~~ apply to standard commercial transactions between the lawyer and the client for products or services that the client generally markets to others, for example, banking or brokerage services, medical services, products manufactured or distributed by the client, and utilities' services. In such transactions, the lawyer has no advantage in dealing with the client, and the restrictions in paragraph (a) are unnecessary and impracticable.

[2]   Paragraph (a)(1) requires that the transaction itself be fair to the client and that its essential terms be communicated to the client, in writing, in a manner that can be reasonably understood. Paragraph (a)(2) requires that the client also be advised, in writing, of the desirability of seeking the advice of independent legal counsel. It also requires that the client be given a reasonable opportunity to obtain such advice. Paragraph (a)(3) requires that the lawyer obtain the client's informed consent, in a writing signed by the client, both to the essential terms of the transaction and to the lawyer's role. When necessary, the lawyer should discuss both the material risks of the proposed transaction, including any risk presented by the lawyer's involvement, and the existence of reasonably available alternatives and should explain why the advice of independent legal counsel is desirable. See Rule 1.0(e) (definition of informed consent).

[3]   The risk to a client is greatest when the client expects the lawyer to represent the client in the transaction itself or when the lawyer's financial interest otherwise poses a significant risk that the lawyer's representation of the client will be materially limited by the lawyer's financial interest in the transaction. Here the lawyer's role requires that the lawyer must comply, not only with the requirements of paragraph (a), but also with the requirements of Rule 1.7. Under that Rule, the lawyer must disclose the risks associated with the lawyer's dual role as both legal adviser and participant in the transaction, such as the risk that the lawyer will structure the transaction or give legal advice in a way that favors the lawyer's interests at the expense of the client. Moreover, the lawyer must obtain the client's informed consent. In some cases, the lawyer's interest may be such that Rule 1.7 will preclude the lawyer from seeking the client's consent to the transaction.

[4]   If the client is independently represented in the transaction, paragraph (a)(2) of this Rule is inapplicable, and the paragraph (a)(1) requirement for full disclosure is satisfied either by a written disclosure by the lawyer involved in the transaction or by the client's independent counsel. The fact that the client was independently represented in the transaction is relevant in determining whether the agreement was fair and reasonable to the client as paragraph (a)(1) further requires.

Use of Information Related to Representation

[5]   Use of information relating to the representation to the disadvantage of the client violates the lawyer's duty of loyalty. Paragraph (b) applies when the information is used to benefit either the lawyer or a third person, such as another client or business associate of the lawyer. For example, if a lawyer learns that a client intends to purchase and develop several parcels of land, the lawyer may not use that information to purchase one of the parcels in competition with the client or to recommend that another client make such a purchase. The Rule does not prohibit uses that do not disadvantage the client. For example, a lawyer who learns a government agency's interpretation of trade legislation during the representation of one client may properly use that information to benefit other clients. Paragraph (b)

prohibits disadvantageous use of client information unless the client gives informed consent, except as permitted or required by these Rules. See Rules 1.2(d), 1.6, 1.9(c), 3.3, 4.1(b), 8.1 and 8.3.

Gifts to Lawyers

~~[2]~~ [6] A lawyer may accept a gift from a client, if the transaction meets general standards of fairness. For example, a simple gift such as a present given at a holiday or as a token of appreciation is permitted. If a client offers the lawyer a more substantial gift, paragraph (c) does not prohibit the lawyer from accepting it, although such a gift may be voidable by the client under the doctrine of undue influence, which treats client gifts as presumptively fraudulent. In any event, due to concerns about overreaching and imposition on clients, a lawyer may not suggest that a substantial gift be made to the lawyer or for the lawyer's benefit, except where the lawyer is related to the client as set forth in paragraph (c).

[7]   If effectuation of a substantial gift requires preparing a legal instrument such as a will or conveyance, ~~however,~~ the client should have the detached advice that another lawyer can provide. ~~Paragraph (c) recognizes an~~ The sole exception to this Rule is where the client is a relative of the donee ~~or the gift is not substantial~~.

[8]   This Rule does not prohibit a lawyer from seeking to have the lawyer or a partner or associate of the lawyer named as executor of the client's estate or to another potentially lucrative fiduciary position. Nevertheless, such appointments will be subject to the general conflict of interest provision in Rule 1.7 when there is a significant risk that the lawyer's interest in obtaining the appointment will materially limit the lawyer's independent professional judgment in advising the client concerning the choice of an executor or other fiduciary. In obtaining the client's informed consent to the conflict, the lawyer should advise the client concerning the nature and extent of the lawyer's financial interest in the appointment, as well as the availability of alternative candidates for the position.

Literary Rights

~~[3]~~ [9] An agreement by which a lawyer acquires literary or media rights concerning the conduct of the representation creates a conflict between the interests of the client and the personal interests of the lawyer. Measures suitable in the representation of the client may detract from the publication value of an account of the representation. Paragraph (d) does not prohibit a lawyer representing a client in a transaction concerning literary property from agreeing that the lawyer's fee shall consist of a share in ownership in the property, if the arrangement conforms to Rule 1.5 and ~~paragraph (j)~~ paragraphs (a) and (i).

Financial Assistance

[10]   Lawyers may not subsidize lawsuits or administrative proceedings brought on behalf of their clients, including making or guaranteeing loans to their clients for living expenses, because to do so would encourage clients to pursue lawsuits that might not otherwise be brought and because such

~~assistance gives lawyers too great a financial stake in the litigation. These dan-gers do not warrant a prohibition on a lawyer lending a client court costs and litigation expenses, including the expenses of medical examination and the costs of obtaining and presenting evidence, because these advances are virtu-ally indistinguishable from contingent fees and help ensure access to the courts. Similarly, an exception allowing lawyers representing indigent clients to pay court costs and litigation expenses regardless of whether these funds will be repaid is warranted.~~

Person Paying for a Lawyer's Services

~~[4]   Paragraph (f) requires disclosure of the fact that the lawyer's services are being paid for by a third party. Such an arrangement must also conform to the requirements of Rule 1.6 concerning confidentiality and Rule 1.7 concerning conflict of interest. Where the client is a class, consent may be obtained on behalf of the class by court-supervised procedure.~~

[11]   Lawyers are frequently asked to represent a client under cir-cumstances in which a third person will compensate the lawyer, in whole or in part. The third person might be a relative or friend, an indemnitor (such as a liability insurance company) or a co-client (such as a corporation sued along with one or more of its employees). Because third-party payers frequently have interests that differ from those of the client, including interests in minimizing the amount spent on the representation and in learning how the representa-tion is progressing, lawyers are prohibited from accepting or continuing such representations unless the lawyer determines that there will be no interfer-ence with the lawyer's independent professional judgment and there is informed consent from the client. See also Rule 5.4(c) (prohibiting interference with a lawyer's professional judgment by one who recommends, employs or pays the lawyer to render legal services for another).

[12]   Sometimes, it will be sufficient for the lawyer to obtain the client's informed consent regarding the fact of the payment and the identity of the third-party payer. If, however, the fee arrangement creates a conflict of interest for the lawyer, then the lawyer must comply with Rule. 1.7. The lawyer must also conform to the requirements of Rule 1.6 concerning confidentiality. Under Rule 1.7(a), a conflict of interest exists if there is significant risk that the lawyer's representation of the client will be materially limited by the law-yer's own interest in the fee arrangement or by the lawyer's responsibilities to the third-party payer (for example, when the third-party payer is a co-client). Under Rule 1.7(b), the lawyer may accept or continue the representation with the informed consent of each affected client, unless the conflict is nonconsent-able under that paragraph. Under Rule 1.7(b), the informed consent must be confirmed in writing.

Aggregate Settlements

[13]   Differences in willingness to make or accept an offer of settlement are among the risks of common representation of multiple clients by a single lawyer. Under Rule 1.7, this is one of the risks that should be discussed before undertaking the representation, as part of the process of

obtaining the clients' informed consent. In addition, Rule 1.2(a) protects each client's right to have the final say in deciding whether to accept or reject an offer of settlement and in deciding whether to enter a guilty or nolo contendere plea in a criminal case. The rule stated in this paragraph is a corollary of both these Rules and provides that, before any settlement offer or plea bargain is made or accepted on behalf of multiple clients, the lawyer must inform each of them about all the material terms of the settlement, including what the other clients will receive or pay if the settlement or plea offer is accepted. See also Rule 1.0(e) (definition of informed consent). Lawyers representing a class of plaintiffs or defendants, or those proceeding derivatively, may not have a full client-lawyer relationship with each member of the class; nevertheless, such lawyers must comply with applicable rules regulating notification of class members and other procedural requirements designed to ensure adequate protection of the entire class.

Limiting Liability and Settling Malpractice Claims

[5] ~~Paragraph (h) is not intended to apply to customary qualifications and limitations in legal opinions and memoranda.~~

[14] Agreements prospectively limiting a lawyer's liability for malpractice are prohibited unless the client is independently represented in making the agreement because they are likely to undermine competent and diligent representation. Also, many clients are unable to evaluate the desirability of making such an agreement before a dispute has arisen, particularly if they are then represented by the lawyer seeking the agreement. This paragraph does not, however, prohibit a lawyer from entering into an agreement with the client to arbitrate legal malpractice claims, provided such agreements are enforceable and the client is fully informed of the scope and effect of the agreement. Nor does this paragraph limit the ability of lawyers to practice in the form of a limited-liability entity, where permitted by law, provided that each lawyer remains personally liable to the client for his or her own conduct and the firm complies with any conditions required by law, such as provisions requiring client notification or maintenance of adequate liability insurance. Nor does it prohibit an agreement in accordance with Rule 1.2 that defines the scope of the representation, although a definition of scope that makes the obligations of representation illusory will amount to an attempt to limit liability.

[15] Agreements settling a claim or a potential claim for malpractice are not prohibited by this Rule. Nevertheless, in view of the danger that a lawyer will take unfair advantage of an unrepresented client or former client, the lawyer must first advise such a person in writing of the appropriateness of independent representation in connection with such a settlement. In addition, the lawyer must give the client or former client a reasonable opportunity to find and consult independent counsel.

~~Family Relationships Between Lawyers~~

[6] ~~Paragraph (i) applies to related lawyers who are in different firms. Related lawyers in the same firm are governed by Rules 1.7, 1.9, and~~

~~1.10. The disqualification stated in paragraph (i) is personal and is not imputed to members of firms with whom the lawyers are associated.~~

~~Acquisition of~~ <u>Acquiring Proprietary</u> Interest in Litigation

~~[7]~~ <u>[16]</u> Paragraph ~~(j)~~ <u>(i)</u> states the traditional general rule that lawyers are prohibited from acquiring a proprietary interest in litigation. ~~This~~ <u>Like paragraph (e), the</u> general rule~~, which~~ has its basis in common law champerty and maintenance, <u>and is designed to avoid giving the lawyer too great an interest in the representation. In addition, when the lawyer acquires an ownership interest in the subject of the representation, it will be more difficult for a client to discharge the lawyer if the client so desires. The Rule</u> is subject to specific exceptions developed in decisional law and continued in these Rules~~, such as the exception for reasonable contingent fees set forth in Rule 1.5 and the exception for certain advances of the costs of litigation set forth in paragraph (e)~~. <u>The exception for certain advances of the costs of litigation is set forth in paragraph (e). In addition, paragraph (i) sets forth exceptions for liens authorized by law to secure the lawyer's fees or expenses and contracts for reasonable contingent fees. The law of each jurisdiction determines which liens are authorized by law. These may include liens granted by statute, liens originating in common law and liens acquired by contract with the client. When a lawyer acquires by contract a security interest in property other than that recovered through the lawyer's efforts in the litigation, such an acquisition is a business or financial transaction with a client and is governed by the requirements of paragraph (a). Contracts for contingent fees in civil cases are governed by Rule 1.5.</u>

<u>Client-Lawyer Sexual Relationships</u>

<u>[17]   The relationship between lawyer and client is a fiduciary one in which the lawyer occupies the highest position of trust and confidence. The relationship is almost always unequal; thus, a sexual relationship between lawyer and client can involve unfair exploitation of the lawyer's fiduciary role, in violation of the lawyer's basic ethical obligation not to use the trust of the client to the client's disadvantage. In addition, such a relationship presents a significant danger that, because of the lawyer's emotional involvement, the lawyer will be unable to represent the client without impairment of the exercise of independent professional judgment. Moreover, a blurred line between the professional and personal relationships may make it difficult to predict to what extent client confidences will be protected by the attorney-client evidentiary privilege, since client confidences are protected by privilege only when they are imparted in the context of the client-lawyer relationship. Because of the significant danger of harm to client interests and because the client's own emotional involvement renders it unlikely that the client could give adequate informed consent, this Rule prohibits the lawyer from having sexual relations with a client regardless of whether the relationship is consensual and regardless of the absence of prejudice to the client.</u>

<u>[18]   Sexual relationships that predate the client-lawyer relationship are not prohibited. Issues relating to the exploitation of the fiduciary</u>

relationship and client dependency are diminished when the sexual relationship existed prior to the commencement of the client-lawyer relationship. However, before proceeding with the representation in these circumstances, the lawyer should consider whether the lawyer's ability to represent the client will be materially limited by the relationship. See Rule 1.7(a)(2).

[19]   When the client is an organization, paragraph (j) of this Rule prohibits a lawyer for the organization (whether inside counsel or outside counsel) from having a sexual relationship with a constituent of the organization who supervises, directs or regularly consults with that lawyer concerning the organization's legal matters.

Imputation of Prohibitions

[20]   Under paragraph (k), a prohibition on conduct by an individual lawyer in paragraphs (a) through (i) also applies to all lawyers associated in a firm with the personally prohibited lawyer. For example, one lawyer in a firm may not enter into a business transaction with a client of another member of the firm without complying with paragraph (a), even if the first lawyer is not personally involved in the representation of the client. The prohibition set forth in paragraph (j) is personal and is not applied to associated lawyers.

RULE 1.9: ~~CONFLICT OF INTEREST:~~ DUTIES TO FORMER ~~CLIENT~~ CLIENTS

(a)   A lawyer who has formerly represented a client in a matter shall not thereafter represent another person in the same or a substantially related matter in which that person's interests are materially adverse to the interests of the former client unless the former client ~~consents after consultation~~ gives informed consent, confirmed in writing.

(b)   A lawyer shall not knowingly represent a person in the same or a substantially related matter in which a firm with which the lawyer formerly was associated had previously represented a client

(1)   whose interests are materially adverse to that person; and

(2)   about whom the lawyer had acquired information protected by Rules 1.6 and 1.9(c) that is material to the matter; unless the former client ~~consents after consultation~~ gives informed consent, confirmed in writing.

(c)   A lawyer who has formerly represented a client in a matter or whose present or former firm has formerly represented a client in a matter shall not thereafter:

(1)   use information relating to the representation to the disadvantage of the former client except as ~~Rule 1.6 or Rule 3.3~~ these Rules would permit or require with respect to a client, or when the information has become generally known; or

(2)   reveal information relating to the representation except as ~~Rule 1.6 or Rule 3.3~~ these Rules would permit or require with respect to a client.

Comment

[1]   After termination of a client-lawyer relationship, a lawyer <u>has certain continuing duties with respect to confidentiality and conflicts of interest and thus</u> may not represent another client except in conformity with this Rule. ~~The principles in Rule 1.7 determine whether the interests of the present and former client are adverse. Thus~~ <u>Under this Rule, for example,</u> a lawyer could not properly seek to rescind on behalf of a new client a contract drafted on behalf of the former client. So also a lawyer who has prosecuted an accused person could not properly represent the accused in a subsequent civil action against the government concerning the same transaction. <u>Nor could a lawyer who has represented multiple clients in a matter represent one of the clients against the others in the same or a substantially related matter after a dispute arose among the clients in that matter, unless all affected clients give informed consent. See Comment [9]. Current and former government lawyers must comply with this Rule to the extent required by Rule 1.11.</u>

[2]   The scope of a "matter" for purposes of this Rule ~~may depend~~ <u>depends</u> on the facts of a particular situation or transaction. The lawyer's involvement in a matter can also be a question of degree. When a lawyer has been directly involved in a specific transaction, subsequent representation of other clients with materially adverse interests <u>in that transaction</u> clearly is prohibited. On the other hand, a lawyer who recurrently handled a type of problem for a former client is not precluded from later representing another client in a ~~wholly~~ <u>factually</u> distinct problem of that type even though the subsequent representation involves a position adverse to the prior client. Similar considerations can apply to the reassignment of military lawyers between defense and prosecution functions within the same military jurisdictions. The underlying question is whether the lawyer was so involved in the matter that the subsequent representation can be justly regarded as a changing of sides in the matter in question.

[3]   <u>Matters are "substantially related" for purposes of this Rule if they involve the same transaction or legal dispute or if there otherwise is a substantial risk that confidential factual information as would normally have been obtained in the prior representation would materially advance the client's position in the subsequent matter. For example, a lawyer who has represented a businessperson and learned extensive private financial information about that person may not then represent that person's spouse in seeking a divorce. Similarly, a lawyer who has previously represented a client in securing environmental permits to build a shopping center would be precluded from representing neighbors seeking to oppose rezoning of the property on the basis of environmental considerations; however, the lawyer would not be precluded, on the grounds of substantial relationship, from defending a tenant of the completed shopping center in resisting eviction for nonpayment of rent. Information that has been disclosed to the public or to other parties adverse to the former client ordinarily will not be disqualifying. Information acquired in a prior representation may have been rendered obsolete by the passage of time, a circumstance that may be relevant in determining whether two representations</u>

are substantially related. In the case of an organizational client, general knowledge of the client's policies and practices ordinarily will not preclude a subsequent representation; on the other hand, knowledge of specific facts gained in a prior representation that are relevant to the matter in question ordinarily will preclude such a representation. A former client is not required to reveal the confidential information learned by the lawyer in order to establish a substantial risk that the lawyer has confidential information to use in the subsequent matter. A conclusion about the possession of such information may be based on the nature of the services the lawyer provided the former client and information that would in ordinary practice be learned by a lawyer providing such services.

Lawyers Moving Between Firms

[3] [4]   When lawyers have been associated within a firm but then end their association, the question of whether a lawyer should undertake representation is more complicated. There are several competing considerations. First, the client previously represented by the former firm must be reasonably assured that the principle of loyalty to the client is not compromised. Second, the rule should not be so broadly cast as to preclude other persons from having reasonable choice of legal counsel. Third, the rule should not unreasonably hamper lawyers from forming new associations and taking on new clients after having left a previous association. In this connection, it should be recognized that today many lawyers practice in firms, that many lawyers to some degree limit their practice to one field or another, and that many move from one association to another several times in their careers. If the concept of imputation were applied with unqualified rigor, the result would be radical curtailment of the opportunity of lawyers to move from one practice setting to another and of the opportunity of clients to change counsel.

[4]   Reconciliation of these competing principles in the past has been attempted under two rubrics. One approach has been to seek per se rules of disqualification. For example, it has been held that a partner in a law firm is conclusively presumed to have access to all confidences concerning all clients of the firm. Under this analysis, if a lawyer has been a partner in one law firm and then becomes a partner in another law firm, there may be a presumption that all confidences known by the partner in the first firm are known to all partners in the second firm. This presumption might properly be applied in some circumstances, especially where the client has been extensively represented, but may be unrealistic where the client was represented only for limited purposes. Furthermore, such a rigid rule exaggerates the difference between a partner and an associate in modern law firms.

[5]   The other rubric formerly used for dealing with disqualification is the appearance of impropriety proscribed in Canon 9 of the ABA Model Code of Professional Responsibility. This rubric has a two-fold problem. First, the appearance of impropriety can be taken to include any new client-lawyer relationship that might make a former client feel anxious. If that meaning were adopted, disqualification would become little more than a question of subjective judgment by the former client. Second, since "impropriety" is undefined, the

~~term "appearance of impropriety" is question-begging. It therefore has to be~~
~~recognized that the problem of disqualification cannot be properly resolved~~
~~either by simple analogy to a lawyer practicing alone or by the very general~~
~~concept of appearance of impropriety.~~

~~Confidentiality~~

~~[8]~~ [5]   Paragraph (b) operates to disqualify the lawyer only when the lawyer involved has actual knowledge of information protected by Rules 1.6 and 1.9~~(b)~~(c). Thus, if a lawyer while with one firm acquired no knowledge or information relating to a particular client of the firm, and that lawyer later joined another firm, neither the lawyer individually nor the second firm is disqualified from representing another client in the same or a related matter even though the interests of the two clients conflict. See Rule 1.10(b) for the restrictions on a firm once a lawyer has terminated association with the firm.

[6]   ~~Preserving confidentiality is a question of access to information.~~ ~~Access to information, in turn, is essentially a question of fact in~~ Application of paragraph (b) depends on a situation's particular ~~circumstances~~ facts, aided by inferences, deductions or working presumptions that reasonably may be made about the way in which lawyers work together. A lawyer may have general access to files of all clients of a law firm and may regularly participate in discussions of their affairs; it should be inferred that such a lawyer in fact is privy to all information about all the firm's clients. In contrast, another lawyer may have access to the files of only a limited number of clients and participate in discussions of the affairs of no other clients; in the absence of information to the contrary, it should be inferred that such a lawyer in fact is privy to information about the clients actually served but not those of other clients. In such an inquiry, the burden of proof should rest upon the firm whose disqualification is sought.

~~[7]~~   ~~Application of paragraph (b) depends on a situation's particular~~ ~~facts. In such an inquiry, the burden of proof should rest upon the firm whose~~ ~~disqualification is sought.~~

~~[9]~~ [7] Independent of the question of disqualification of a firm, a lawyer changing professional association has a continuing duty to preserve confidentiality of information about a client formerly represented. See Rules 1.6 and 1.9(c).

~~Adverse Positions~~

~~[10]   The second aspect of loyalty to a client is the lawyer's obligation~~
~~to decline subsequent representations involving positions adverse to a former~~
~~client arising in substantially related matters. This obligation requires absten-~~
~~tion from adverse representation by the individual lawyer involved, but does~~
~~not properly entail abstention of other lawyers through imputed disqualifica-~~
~~tion. Hence, this aspect of the problem is governed by Rule 1.9(a). Thus, if a~~
~~lawyer left one firm for another, the new affiliation would not preclude the~~
~~firms involved from continuing to represent clients with adverse interests in~~
~~the same or related matters, so long as the conditions of paragraphs (b) and (c)~~
~~concerning confidentiality have been met.~~

[11] [8] ~~Information~~ Paragraph (c) provides that information acquired by the lawyer in the course of representing a client may not subsequently be used or revealed by the lawyer to the disadvantage of the client. However, the fact that a lawyer has once served a client does not preclude the lawyer from using generally known information about that client when later representing another client.

[12] [9] ~~Disqualification from subsequent representation is~~ The provisions of this Rule are for the protection of former clients and can be waived ~~by them. A waiver is effective only if there is disclosure of the circumstances, including the lawyer's intended role in behalf of the new client~~ if the client gives informed consent, which consent must be confirmed in writing under paragraphs (a) and (b). See Rule 1.0(e). [13] With regard to ~~an opposing party's raising a question of conflict of interest~~ the effectiveness of an advance waiver, see Comment [22] to Rule 1.7. With regard to disqualification of a firm with which a lawyer is or was formerly associated, see Rule 1.10.

RULE 1.10: ~~IMPUTED DISQUALIFICATION~~ IMPUTATION OF CONFLICTS OF INTEREST: GENERAL RULE

(a)   While lawyers are associated in a firm, none of them shall knowingly represent a client when any one of them practicing alone would be prohibited from doing so by Rules 1.7, ~~1.8(c), 1.9~~ or ~~2.2.~~1.9, unless

(1)   the prohibition is based on a personal interest of the disqualified lawyer and does not present a significant risk of materially limiting the representation of the client by the remaining lawyers in the firm; or

(2)   the prohibition is based upon Rule 1.9(a), or (b), and arises out of the disqualified lawyer's association with a prior firm, and

(i)   the disqualified lawyer is timely screened from any participation in the matter and is apportioned no part of the fee therefrom;

(ii)   written notice is promptly given to any affected former client to enable the former client to ascertain compliance with the provisions of this Rule, which shall include a description of the screening procedures employed; a statement of the firm's and of the screened lawyer's compliance with these Rules; a statement that review may be available before a tribunal; and an agreement by the firm to respond promptly to any written inquiries or objections by the former client about the screening procedures; and

(iii)   certifications of compliance with these Rules and with the screening procedures are provided to the former client by the screened lawyer and by a partner of the firm, at reasonable intervals upon the former client's written request and upon termination of the screening procedures.

(b)   When a lawyer has terminated an association with a firm, the firm is not ~~prohibited from thereafter representing a person with interests materially adverse to those of a client~~ represented by the formerly associated lawyer and not currently represented by the firm, unless:

(1)   the matter is the same or substantially related to that in which the formerly associated lawyer represented the client; and

(2)   any lawyer remaining in the firm has information protected by Rules 1.6 and 1.9(c) that is material to the matter.

(c)   A disqualification prescribed by this rule may be waived by the affected client under the conditions stated in Rule 1.7.

(d)   The disqualification of lawyers associated in a firm with former or current government lawyers is governed by Rule 1.11.

Comment

Definition of "Firm"

[1]   For purposes of the Rules of Professional Conduct, the term "firm" ~~includes~~ denotes lawyers in a ~~private firm~~ law partnership, ~~and~~ professional corporation, sole proprietorship or other association authorized to practice law; or lawyers employed in a legal services organization or the legal department of a corporation or other organization, ~~or in a legal services organization.~~ See Rule 1.0(c). Whether two or more lawyers constitute a firm within this definition can depend on the specific facts. ~~For example, two practitioners who share office space and occasionally consult or assist each other ordinarily would not be regarded as constituting a firm. However, if they present themselves to the public in a way suggesting that they are a firm or conduct themselves as a firm, they should be regarded as a firm for the purposes of the Rules. The terms of any formal agreement between associated lawyers are relevant in determining whether they are a firm, as is the fact that they have mutual access to information concerning the clients they serve. Furthermore, it is relevant in doubtful cases to consider the underlying purpose of the Rule that is involved. A group of lawyers could be regarded as a firm for purposes of the rule that the same lawyer should not represent opposing parties in litigation while it might not be so regarded for purposes of the rule that information acquired by one lawyer is attributed to the other~~ See Rule 1.0, Comments [2] – [4].

~~[2]   With respect to the law department of an organization, there is ordinarily no question that the members of the department constitute a firm within the meaning of the Rules of Professional Conduct. However, there can be uncertainty as to the identity of the client. For example, it may not be clear whether the law department of a corporation represents a subsidiary or an affiliated corporation, as well as the corporation by which the members of the department are directly employed. A similar question can arise concerning an unincorporated association and its local affiliates.~~

~~[3]   Similar questions can also arise with respect to lawyers in legal aid. Lawyers employed in the same unit of a legal service organization constitute a firm, but not necessarily those employed in separate units. As in the case~~

~~of independent practitioners, whether the lawyers should be treated as associated with each other can depend on the particular rule that is involved, and on the specific facts of the situation.~~

~~[5]   Different provisions are thus made for movement of a lawyer from one private firm to another and for movement of a lawyer between a private firm and the government. The government is entitled to protection of its client confidences and, therefore, to the protections provided in Rules 1.6, 1.9 and 1.11. However, if the more extensive disqualification in Rule 1.10 were applied to former government lawyers, the potential effect on the government would be unduly burdensome. The government deals with all private citizens and organizations and, thus, has a much wider circle of adverse legal interests than does any private law firm. In these circumstances, the government's recruitment of lawyers would be seriously impaired if Rule 1.10 were applied to the government. On balance, therefore, the government is better served in the long run by the protections stated in Rule 1.11.~~

Principles of Imputed Disqualification

[6<u>2</u>]   The rule of imputed disqualification stated in paragraph (a) gives effect to the principle of loyalty to the client as it applies to lawyers who practice in a law firm. Such situations can be considered from the premise that a firm of lawyers is essentially one lawyer for purposes of the rules governing loyalty to the client, or from the premise that each lawyer is vicariously bound by the obligation of loyalty owed by each lawyer with whom the lawyer is associated. Paragraph (a)<u>(1)</u> operates only among the lawyers currently associated in a firm. When a lawyer moves from one firm to another, the situation is governed by Rules 1.9(b) and 1.10(<u>a)(2) and 1.10</u> (b).

<u>[3]   The rule in paragraph (a) does not prohibit representation where neither questions of client loyalty nor protection of confidential information are presented. Where one lawyer in a firm could not effectively represent a given client because of strong political beliefs, for example, but that lawyer will do no work on the case and the personal beliefs of the lawyer will not materially limit the representation by others in the firm, the firm should not be disqualified. On the other hand, if an opposing party in a case were owned by a lawyer in the law firm, and others in the firm would be materially limited in pursuing the matter because of loyalty to that lawyer, the personal disqualification of the lawyer would be imputed to all others in the firm.</u>

<u>[4]   The rule in paragraph (a) also does not prohibit representation by others in the law firm where the person prohibited from involvement in a matter is a nonlawyer, such as a paralegal or legal secretary. Nor does paragraph (a) prohibit representation if the lawyer is prohibited from acting because of events before the person became a lawyer, for example, work that the person did while a law student. Such persons, however, ordinarily must be screened from any personal participation in the matter to avoid communication to others in the firm of confidential information that both the nonlawyers and the firm have a legal duty to protect. See Rules 1.0(k) and 5.3.</u>

{7}[5] Rule 1.10(b) operates to permit a law firm, under certain circumstances, to represent a person with interests directly adverse to those of a client represented by a lawyer who formerly was associated with the firm. The Rule applies regardless of when the formerly associated lawyer represented the client. However, the law firm may not represent a person with interests adverse to those of a present client of the firm, which would violate Rule 1.7. Moreover, the firm may not represent the person where the matter is the same or substantially related to that in which the formerly associated lawyer represented the client and any other lawyer currently in the firm has material information protected by Rules 1.6 and 1.9(c).

[6] Rule 1.10(c) removes imputation with the informed consent of the affected client or former client under the conditions stated in Rule 1.7. The conditions stated in Rule 1.7 require the lawyer to determine that the representation is not prohibited by Rule 1.7(b) and that each affected client or former client has given informed consent to the representation, confirmed in writing. In some cases, the risk may be so severe that the conflict may not be cured by client consent. For a discussion of the effectiveness of client waivers of conflicts that might arise in the future, see Rule 1.7, Comment [22]. For a definition of informed consent, see Rule 1.0(e).

[7] Rule 1.10(a)(2) similarly removes the imputation otherwise required by Rule 1.10(a), but unlike section (c), it does so without requiring that there be informed consent by the former client. Instead, it requires that the procedures laid out in sections (a)(2)(i)-(iii) be followed. A description of effective screening mechanisms appears in Rule 1.0(k). Lawyers should be aware, however, that, even where screening mechanisms have been adopted, tribunals may consider additional factors in ruling upon motions to disqualify a lawyer from pending litigation.

[8] Paragraph (a)(2)(i) does not prohibit the screened lawyer from receiving a salary or partnership share established by prior independent agreement, but that lawyer may not receive compensation directly related to the matter in which the lawyer is disqualified.

[9] The notice required by paragraph (a)(2)(ii) generally should include a description of the screened lawyer's prior representation and be given as soon as practicable after the need for screening becomes apparent. It also should include a statement by the screened lawyer and the firm that the client's material confidential information has not been disclosed or used in violation of the Rules. The notice is intended to enable the former client to evaluate and comment upon the effectiveness of the screening procedures.

[10] The certifications required by paragraph (a)(2)(iii) give the former client assurance that the client's material confidential information has not been disclosed or used inappropriately, either prior to timely implementation of a screen or thereafter. If compliance cannot be certified, the certificate must describe the failure to comply.

{4}[11] Where a lawyer has joined a private firm after having represented the government, the situation imputation is governed by Rule 1.11 (a) and (b) and (c), not this Rule.; Under Rule 1.11(d), where a lawyer represents the government after having served private clients, the situation is governed by Rule 1.11(c)(1). The individual lawyer involved is bound by the Rules generally, including Rules 1.6, 1.7 and 1.9 in private practice, nongovernmental employment or in another government agency, former client conflicts are not imputed to government lawyers associated with the individually disqualified lawyer.

[12]   Where a lawyer is prohibited from engaging in certain transactions under Rule 1.8, paragraph (k) of that Rule, and not this Rule, determines whether that prohibition also applies to other lawyers associated in a firm with the personally prohibited lawyer.

RULE 1.11: SUCCESSIVE SPECIAL CONFLICTS OF INTEREST FOR FORMER AND CURRENT GOVERNMENT OFFICERS AND PRIVATE EMPLOYMENT EMPLOYEES

(a)   Except as law may otherwise expressly permit, a lawyer who has formerly served as a public officer or employee of the government:

(1)   is subject to Rule 1.9(c); and

(2)   shall not otherwise represent a private client in connection with a matter in which the lawyer participated personally and substantially as a public officer or employee, unless the appropriate government agency consents after consultation gives its informed consent, confirmed in writing, to the representation.

(b)   No When a lawyer is disqualified from representation under paragraph (a), no lawyer in a firm with which that lawyer is associated may knowingly undertake or continue representation in such a matter unless:

(1)   the disqualified lawyer is timely screened from any participation in the matter and is apportioned no part of the fee therefrom; and

(2)   written notice is promptly given to the appropriate government agency to enable it to ascertain compliance with the provisions of this rule.

(b) (c)   Except as law may otherwise expressly permit, a lawyer having information that the lawyer knows is confidential government information about a person acquired when the lawyer was a public officer or employee, may not represent a private client whose interests are adverse to that person in a matter in which the information could be used to the material disadvantage of that person. As used in this Rule, the term "confidential government information" means information that has been obtained under governmental authority and which, at the time this Rule is applied, the government is prohibited by law from disclosing to the public or has a legal privilege not to disclose and which is not otherwise available to the public. A firm with which that lawyer is associated may undertake or continue representation in the matter only if the disqualified lawyer is timely screened from any participation in the matter and is apportioned no part of the fee therefrom.

(c) (d)   Except as law may otherwise expressly permit, a lawyer currently serving as a public officer or employee:

> (1)   is subject to Rules 1.7 and 1.9; and

> (2)   shall not:

>> (1) (i)   participate in a matter in which the lawyer participated personally and substantially while in private practice or nongovernmental employment, unless under applicable law no one is, or by lawful delegation may be, authorized to act in the lawyer's stead in the matter the appropriate government agency gives its informed consent, confirmed in writing; or

>> (2) (ii)   negotiate for private employment with any person who is involved as a party or as lawyer for a party in a matter in which the lawyer is participating personally and substantially, except that a lawyer serving as a law clerk to a judge, other adjudicative officer or arbitrator may negotiate for private employment as permitted by Rule 1.12(b) and subject to the conditions stated in Rule 1.12(b).

(d) (e)   As used in this Rule, the term "matter" includes:

> (1)   any judicial or other proceeding, application, request for a ruling or other determination, contract, claim, controversy, investigation, charge, accusation, arrest or other particular matter involving a specific party or parties, and

> (2)   any other matter covered by the conflict of interest rules of the appropriate government agency.

(e)   As used in this Rule, the term "confidential government information" means information which has been obtained under governmental authority and which, at the time this rule is applied, the government is prohibited by law from disclosing to the public or has a legal privilege not to disclose, and which is not otherwise available to the public.

Comment

[1]   This Rule prevents a lawyer from exploiting public office for the advantage of a private client. It is a counterpart of Rule 1.10(b), which applies to lawyers moving from one firm to another.

[2] [1]   A lawyer representing a government agency, whether employed or specially retained by the government, who has served or is currently serving as a public officer or employee is personally subject to the Rules of Professional Conduct, including the prohibition against representing adverse interests concurrent conflicts of interest stated in Rule 1.7 and the protections afforded former clients in Rule 1.9. In addition, such a lawyer is may be subject to Rule 1.11 and to statutes and government regulations regarding conflict of interest. Such statutes and regulations may circumscribe the extent to which the government agency may give consent under this Rule. See Rule 1.0(e) for the definition of informed consent.

[2] Paragraphs (a)(1), (a)(2) and (d)(1) restate the obligations of an individual lawyer who has served or is currently serving as an officer or employee of the government toward a former government or private client. Rule 1.10 is not applicable to the conflicts of interest addressed by this Rule. Rather, paragraph (b) sets forth a special imputation rule for former government lawyers that provides for screening and notice. Because of the special problems raised by imputation within a government agency, paragraph (d) does not impute the conflicts of a lawyer currently serving as an officer or employee of the government to other associated government officers or employees, although ordinarily it will be prudent to screen such lawyers.

[3] Paragraphs (a)(2) and (d)(2) apply regardless of whether a lawyer is adverse to a former client and are thus designed not only to protect the former client, but also to prevent a lawyer from exploiting public office for the advantage of another client. For example, a lawyer who has pursued a claim on behalf of the government may not pursue the same claim on behalf of a later private client after the lawyer has left government service, except when authorized to do so by the government agency under paragraph (a). Similarly, a lawyer who has pursued a claim on behalf of a private client may not pursue the claim on behalf of the government, except when authorized to do so by paragraph (d). As with paragraphs (a)(1) and (d)(1), Rule 1.10 is not applicable to the conflicts of interest addressed by these paragraphs.

[3] [4] ~~Where~~ This Rule represents a balancing of interests. On the one hand, where the successive clients are a ~~public~~ government agency and ~~a private~~ another client, public or private, the risk exists that power or discretion vested in that agency ~~public authority~~ might be used for the special benefit of ~~a private~~ the other client. A lawyer should not be in a position where benefit to ~~a private~~ the other client might affect performance of the lawyer's professional functions on behalf of the government ~~public authority~~. Also, unfair advantage could accrue to the ~~private~~ other client by reason of access to confidential government information about the client's adversary obtainable only through the lawyer's government service. ~~However~~ On the other hand, the rules governing lawyers presently or formerly employed by a government agency should not be so restrictive as to inhibit transfer of employment to and from the government. The government has a legitimate need to attract qualified lawyers as well as to maintain high ethical standards. Thus a former government lawyer is disqualified only from particular matters in which the lawyer participated personally and substantially. The provisions for screening and waiver in paragraph (b) are necessary to prevent the disqualification rule from imposing too severe a deterrent against entering public service. The limitation of disqualification in paragraphs (a)(2) and (d)(2) to matters involving a specific party or parties, rather than extending disqualification to all substantive issues on which the lawyer worked, serves a similar function.

[4] [5] When ~~the client is an agency of~~ a lawyer has been employed by one government agency and then moves to a second government agency, it may be appropriate to treat that second agency ~~should be treated~~ as ~~a private~~ another client for purposes of this Rule ~~if the lawyer thereafter represents an~~

agency of another government, as when a lawyer ~~represents~~ is employed by a city and subsequently is employed by a federal agency. However, because the conflict of interest is governed by paragraph (d), the latter agency is not required to screen the lawyer as paragraph (b) requires a law firm to do. The question of whether two government agencies should be regarded as the same or different clients for conflict of interest purposes is beyond the scope of these Rules. See Rule 1.13 Comment [6].

~~[5]~~ [6] Paragraphs ~~(a)(1) and~~ (b) and (c) contemplate a screening arrangement. See Rule 1.0(k) (requirements for screening procedures). These paragraphs do not prohibit a lawyer from receiving a salary or partnership share established by prior independent agreement. ~~They prohibit,~~ but that lawyer may not receive compensation directly relating the lawyer's compensation to the fee in the matter in which the lawyer is disqualified.

[7] Notice, including a description of the screened lawyer's prior representation and of the screening procedures employed, generally should be given as soon as practicable after the need for screening becomes apparent.

~~[6] Paragraph (a)(2) does not require that a lawyer give notice to the government agency at a time when premature disclosure would injure the client; a requirement for premature disclosure might preclude engagement of the lawyer. Such notice is, however, required to be given as soon as practicable in order that the government agency will have a reasonable opportunity to ascertain that the lawyer is complying with Rule 1.11 and to take appropriate action if it believes the lawyer is not complying.~~

~~[7]~~ [8] Paragraph ~~(b)~~ (c) operates only when the lawyer in question has knowledge of the information, which means actual knowledge; it does not operate with respect to information that merely could be imputed to the lawyer.

~~[8]~~ [9] Paragraphs (a) and ~~(c)~~ (d) do not prohibit a lawyer from jointly representing a private party and a government agency when doing so is permitted by Rule 1.7 and is not otherwise prohibited by law.

~~[9] Paragraph (c) does not disqualify other lawyers in the agency with which the lawyer in question has become associated.~~

[10] For purposes of paragraph (e) of this Rule, a "matter" may continue in another form. In determining whether two particular matters are the same, the lawyer should consider the extent to which the matters involve the same basic facts, the same or related parties, and the time elapsed.

RULE 1.12: FORMER JUDGE ~~OR,~~ ARBITRATOR, MEDIATOR OR OTHER THIRD-PARTY NEUTRAL

(a)   Except as stated in paragraph (d), a lawyer shall not represent anyone in connection with a matter in which the lawyer participated personally and substantially as a judge or other adjudicative officer, ~~arbitrator~~ or law clerk to such a person or as an arbitrator, mediator or other third-party neutral, unless all parties to the proceeding give informed consent ~~after consultation,~~ confirmed in writing.

(b)   A lawyer shall not negotiate for employment with any person who is involved as a party or as lawyer for a party in a matter in which the lawyer is participating personally and substantially as a judge or other adjudicative officer or <u>as an</u> arbitrator<u>, mediator or other third-party neutral</u>. A lawyer serving as a law clerk to a judge<s>,</s> <u>or</u> other adjudicative officer <s>or arbitrator</s> may negotiate for employment with a party or lawyer involved in a matter in which the clerk is participating personally and substantially, but only after the lawyer has notified the judge<s>,</s> <u>or</u> other adjudicative officer <s>or arbitrator</s>.

(c)   If a lawyer is disqualified by paragraph (a), no lawyer in a firm with which that lawyer is associated may knowingly undertake or continue representation in the matter unless:

(1)   the disqualified lawyer is <u>timely</u> screened from any participation in the matter and is apportioned no part of the fee therefrom; and

(2)   written notice is promptly given to the <u>parties and any</u> appropriate tribunal to enable it <u>them</u> to ascertain compliance with the provisions of this rule.

(d)   An arbitrator selected as a partisan of a party in a multi-member arbitration panel is not prohibited from subsequently representing that party.

Comment

[1]   This Rule generally parallels Rule 1.11. The term "personally and substantially" signifies that a judge who was a member of a multimember court, and thereafter left judicial office to practice law, is not prohibited from representing a client in a matter pending in the court, but in which the former judge did not participate. So also the fact that a former judge exercised administrative responsibility in a court does not prevent the former judge from acting as a lawyer in a matter where the judge had previously exercised remote or incidental administrative responsibility that did not affect the merits. Compare the Comment to Rule 1.11. The term "adjudicative officer" includes such officials as judges pro tempore, referees, special masters, hearing officers and other parajudicial officers, and also lawyers who serve as part-time judges. Compliance Canons A(2), B(2) and C of the Model Code of Judicial Conduct provide that a part-time judge, judge pro tempore or retired judge recalled to active service, may not "act as a lawyer in any proceeding in which he served as a judge or in any other proceeding related thereto." Although phrased differently from this Rule, those Rules correspond in meaning.

[2]   <u>Like former judges, lawyers who have served as arbitrators, mediators or other third-party neutrals may be asked to represent a client in a matter in which the lawyer participated personally and substantially. This Rule forbids such representation unless all of the parties to the proceedings give their informed consent, confirmed in writing. See Rule 1.0(e) and (b). Other law or codes of ethics governing third-party neutrals may impose more stringent standards of personal or imputed disqualification. See Rule 2.4.</u>

[3]   Although lawyers who serve as third-party neutrals do not have information concerning the parties that is protected under Rule 1.6, they typically owe the parties an obligation of confidentiality under law or codes of ethics governing third-party neutrals. Thus, paragraph (c) provides that conflicts of the personally disqualified lawyer will be imputed to other lawyers in a law firm unless the conditions of this paragraph are met.

[4]   Requirements for screening procedures are stated in Rule 1.0(k). Paragraph (c)(1) does not prohibit the screened lawyer from receiving a salary or partnership share established by prior independent agreement, but that lawyer may not receive compensation directly related to the matter in which the lawyer is disqualified.

[5]   Notice, including a description of the screened lawyer's prior representation and of the screening procedures employed, generally should be given as soon as practicable after the need for screening becomes apparent.

RULE 1.13: ORGANIZATION AS CLIENT

(a)   A lawyer employed or retained by an organization represents the organization acting through its duly authorized constituents.

(b)   If a lawyer for an organization knows that an officer, employee or other person associated with the organization is engaged in action, intends to act or refuses to act in a matter related to the representation that is a violation of a legal obligation to the organization, or a violation of law that ~~which~~ reasonably might be imputed to the organization, and that is likely to result in substantial injury to the organization, then the lawyer shall proceed as is reasonably necessary in the best interest of the organization. ~~In determining how to proceed, the lawyer shall give due consideration to the seriousness of the violation and its consequences, the scope and nature of the lawyer's representation, the responsibility in the organization and the apparent motivation of the person involved, the policies of the organization concerning such matters and any other relevant considerations. Any measures taken shall be designed to minimize disruption of the organization and the risk of revealing information relating to the representation to persons outside the organization. Such measures may include among others:~~

(1)   ~~asking~~ for reconsideration of the matter;

(2)   ~~advising that a separate legal opinion on the matter be sought for presentation to appropriate authority in the organization; and~~

(3)   ~~referring~~

Unless the lawyer reasonably believes that it is not necessary in the best interest of the organization to do so the lawyer shall refer the matter to higher authority in the organization, including, if warranted by the circumstances, ~~seriousness of the matter, referral~~ to the highest authority that can act on behalf of the organization as determined by applicable law.

(c)   Except as provided in paragraph (d), if,

(1)   despite the lawyer's efforts in accordance with paragraph (b); the highest authority that can act on behalf of the organization insists upon <u>or fails to address in a timely and appropriate manner</u> an action, or a refusal to act, that is clearly a violation of law ~~and is likely to result in substantial injury to the organization,~~ and

(2)   <u>the lawyer reasonably believes that the violation is reasonably certain to result in substantial injury to the organization, then</u> the lawyer may ~~resign in accordance with Rule 1.16~~ <u>reveal information relating to the representation whether or not Rule 1.6 permits such disclosure, but only if and to the extent the lawyer reasonably believes necessary to prevent substantial injury to the organization.</u>

<u>(d)   Paragraph (c) shall not apply with respect to information relating to a lawyer's representation of an organization to investigate an alleged violation of law, or to defend the organization or an officer, employee or other constituent associated with the organization against a claim arising out of an alleged violation of law.</u>

<u>(e)   A lawyer who reasonably believes that he or she has been discharged because of the lawyer's actions taken pursuant to paragraphs (b) or (c), or who withdraws under circumstances that require or permit the lawyer to take action under either of those paragraphs, shall proceed as the lawyer reasonably believes necessary to assure that the organization's highest authority is informed of the lawyer's discharge or withdrawal.</u>

~~(d)~~ <u>(f)</u>   In dealing with an organization's directors, officers, employees, members, shareholders or other constituents, a lawyer shall explain the identity of the client when ~~it is apparent~~ <u>the lawyer knows or reasonably should know</u> that the organization's interests are adverse to those of the constituents with whom the lawyer is dealing.

~~(e)~~ <u>(g)</u>   A lawyer representing an organization may also represent any of its directors, officers, employees, members, shareholders or other constituents, subject to the provisions of Rule 1.7. If the organization's consent to the dual representation is required by Rule 1.7, the consent shall be given by an appropriate official of the organization other than the individual who is to be represented, or by the shareholders.

Comment

The Entity as the Client

[1]   An organizational client is a legal entity, but it cannot act except through its officers, directors, employees, shareholders and other constituents. Officers, directors, employees and shareholders are the constituents of the corporate organizational client. The duties defined in this Comment apply equally to unincorporated associations. "Other constituents" as used in this Comment means the positions equivalent to officers, directors, employees and shareholders held by persons acting for organizational clients that are not corporations.

[2]   When one of the constituents of an organizational client communicates with the organization's lawyer in that person's organizational capacity,
the communication is protected by Rule 1.6. Thus, by way of example, if an organizational client requests its lawyer to investigate allegations of wrongdoing,
interviews made in the course of that investigation between the lawyer and the
client's employees or other constituents are covered by Rule 1.6. This does not
mean, however, that constituents of an organizational client are the clients of
the lawyer. The lawyer may not disclose to such constituents information
relating to the representation except for disclosures explicitly or impliedly
authorized by the organizational client in order to carry out the representation
or as otherwise permitted by Rule 1.6.

[3]   When constituents of the organization make decisions for it, the
decisions ordinarily must be accepted by the lawyer even if their utility or prudence is doubtful. Decisions concerning policy and operations, in-cluding ones
entailing serious risk, are not as such in the lawyer's province. However, different considerations arise Paragraph (b) makes clear, however, that when the
lawyer knows that the organization may is likely to be substantially injured by
action of a an officer or other constituent that violates a legal obligation to the
organization or is in violation of law. In such a cir-cumstance, it may be reasonably necessary for the lawyer to ask the constituent to reconsider the matter. If
that fails, or if the matter is of sufficient seriousness and importance to the
organization, it may be reasonably necessary for the lawyer to take steps to
have the matter reviewed by a higher authority in the organization. Clear
justification should exist for seeking review over the head of the constituent
normally responsible for it. The stated policy of the organization may define
circumstances and prescribe channels for such review, and a lawyer should
encourage the formulation of such a policy. Even in the absence of organization
policy, however, the lawyer may have an obligation to refer a matter to higher
authority, depending on the seriousness of the matter and whether the
constituent in question has apparent motives to act at variance with the organization's interest. Review by the chief executive officer or by the board of
directors may be required when the matter is of importance commensurate
with their authority. At some point it may be useful or essential to obtain an
independent legal opinion. that might be imputed to the organization, the
lawyer must proceed as is reasonably necessary in the best interest of the organization. As defined in Rule 1.0, knowledge can be inferred from circumstances,
and a lawyer cannot ignore the obvious.

[4]   In determining how to proceed under paragraph (b), the lawyer
should give due consideration to the seriousness of the violation and its consequences, the responsibility in the organization and the apparent motivation of
the person involved, the policies of the organization concerning such matters, and
any other relevant considerations. Ordinarily, referral to a higher authority would
be necessary. In some circumstances, however, it may be appropriate for the
lawyer to ask the constituent to reconsider the matter; for example, if the circumstances involve a constituent's innocent misunderstanding of law and subsequent
acceptance of the lawyer's advice, the lawyer may reasonably conclude that the

best interest of the organization does not require that the matter be referred to higher authority. If a constituent persists in conduct contrary to the lawyer's advice, it will be necessary for the lawyer to take steps to have the matter reviewed by a higher authority in the organization. If the matter is of sufficient seriousness and importance or urgency to the organization, referral to higher authority in the organization may be necessary even if the lawyer has not communicated with the constituent. Any measures taken should, to the extent practicable, minimize the risk of revealing information relating to the representation to persons outside the organization. Even in circumstances where a lawyer is not obligated by Rule 1.13 to proceed, a lawyer may bring to the attention of an organizational client, including its highest authority, matters that the lawyer reasonably believes to be of sufficient importance to warrant doing so in the best interest of the organization.

[4] [5] Paragraph (b) also makes clear that when it is reasonably necessary to enable the organization to address the matter in a timely and appropriate manner, the lawyer must refer the matter to higher authority. Including, if warranted by the circumstances, the highest authority that can act on behalf of the organization under applicable law. ~~In an extreme case, it may be reasonably necessary for the lawyer to refer the matter to the~~ The organization's highest authority. ~~Ordinarily, that is~~ to whom a matter may be referred ordinarily will be the board of directors or similar governing body. However, applicable law may prescribe that under certain conditions the highest authority reposes elsewhere, for example, in the independent directors of a corporation.

Relation to Other Rules

[5] [6]   The authority and responsibility provided in ~~paragraph (b)~~ this Rule are concurrent with the authority and responsibility provided in other Rules. In particular, this Rule does not limit or expand the lawyer's responsibility under Rules ~~1.6,~~ 1.8, 1.16, 3.3 or 4.1. Paragraph (c) of this Rule supplements Rule I .6(b) by providing an additional basis upon which the lawyer may reveal information relating to the representation, but does not modify. restrict, or limit the provisions of Rule 1 .6(b)(1) – (6). Under paragraph (c) the lawyer may reveal such information only when the organization's highest authority insists upon or fails to address threatened or ongoing action that is clearly a violation of law, and then only to the extent the lawyer reasonably believes necessary to prevent reasonably certain substantial injury to the organization. It is not necessary that the lawyer's services be used in furtherance of the violation, but it is required that the matter be related to the lawyer's representation of the organization. If the lawyer's services are being used by an organization to further a crime or fraud by the organization, Rules I .6(b)(2) and I .6(b)(3) may permit the lawyer to disclose confidential information. In such circumstances Rule 1.2(d) ~~can~~ may also be applicable, in which event, withdrawal from the representation under Rule 1.16(a)(1) may be required.

[7]   Paragraph (d) makes clear that the authority of a lawyer to disclose information relating to a representation in circumstances described in

paragraph (c) does not apply with respect to information relating to a lawyer's engagement by an organization to investigate an alleged violation of law or to defend the organization or an officer, employee or other person associated with the organization against a claim arising out of an alleged violation of law. This is necessary in order to enable organizational clients to enjoy the full benefits of legal counsel in conducting an investigation or defending against a claim.

[8]   A lawyer who reasonably believes that he or she has been discharged because of the lawyer's actions taken Pursuant to paragraph (b) or (c). or who withdraws in circumstances that require or permit the lawyer to take action under either of these paragraphs, must Proceed as the lawyer reasonably believes necessary to assure that the organization's highest authority is informed of the lawyer's discharge or withdrawal.

Government Agency

[6] [9]   The duty defined in this Rule applies to governmental organizations. ~~However, when the client is a governmental organization, a different balance may be appropriate between maintaining confidentiality and assuring that the wrongful official act is prevented or rectified, for public business is involved. In addition, duties of lawyers employed by the government or lawyers in military service may be defined by statutes and regulation. Therefore, defining~~ Defining precisely the identity of the client and prescribing the resulting obligations of such lawyers may be more difficult in the government context and is a matter beyond the scope of these Rules. See Scope [18]. Although in some circumstances the client may be a specific agency, it ~~is generally~~ may also be a branch of government, such as the executive branch, or the government as a whole. For example, if the action or failure to act involves the head of a bureau, either the department of which the bureau is a part or the relevant branch of government ~~as a whole~~ may be the client for ~~purpose~~ purposes of this Rule. Moreover, in a matter involving the conduct of government officials, a government lawyer may have authority under applicable law to question such conduct more extensively than that of a lawyer for a private organization in similar circumstances. Thus, when the client is a governmental organization, a different balance may be appropriate between maintaining confidentiality and assuring that the wrongful act is prevented or rectified, for public business is involved. In addition, duties of lawyers employed by the government or lawyers in military service may be defined by statutes and regulation. This Rule does not limit that authority. See ~~note on~~ Scope.

Clarifying the Lawyer's Role

[7] [10] There are times when the organization's interest may be or become adverse to those of one or more of its constituents. In such circumstances the lawyer should advise any constituent, whose interest the lawyer finds adverse to that of the organization of the conflict or potential conflict of interest, that the lawyer cannot represent such constituent, and that such person may wish to obtain independent representation. Care must be taken to assure that the individual understands that, when there is such adversity of interest, the lawyer for the organization cannot provide legal representation for that

constituent individual, and that discussions between the lawyer for the organization and the individual may not be privileged.

{8} [11] Whether such a warning should be given by the lawyer for the organization to any constituent individual may turn on the facts of each case.

Dual Representation

{9} [12] Paragraph (e) (g) recognizes that a lawyer for an organization may also represent a principal officer or major shareholder.

Derivative Actions

{10} [13] Under generally prevailing law, the shareholders or members of a corporation may bring suit to compel the directors to perform their legal obligations in the supervision of the organization. Members of unincorporated associations have essentially the same right. Such an action may be brought nominally by the organization, but usually is, in fact, a legal controversy over management of the organization.

{11} [14] The question can arise whether counsel for the organization may defend such an action. The proposition that the organization is the lawyer's client does not alone resolve the issue. Most derivative actions are a normal incident of an organization's affairs, to be defended by the organization's lawyer like any other suit. However, if the claim involves serious charges of wrongdoing by those in control of the organization, a conflict may arise between the lawyer's duty to the organization and the lawyer's relationship with the board. In those circumstances, Rule 1.7 governs who should represent the directors and the organization.

RULE 1.14: CLIENT ~~UNDER A DISABILITY~~ WITH DIMINISHED CAPACITY

(a) When a client's ~~ability~~ capacity to make adequately considered decisions in connection with ~~the~~ a representation is ~~impaired~~ diminished, whether because of minority, mental ~~disability~~ impairment or for some other reason, the lawyer shall, as far as reasonably possible, maintain a normal client-lawyer relationship with the client.

(b) ~~A lawyer may seek the appointment of a guardian or take other protective action with respect to a client only when~~ When the lawyer reasonably believes that the client <u>has diminished capacity, is at risk of substantial physical, financial or other harm unless action is taken and</u> cannot adequately act in the client's own interest<u>, the lawyer may take reasonably necessary protective action, including consulting with individuals or entities that have the ability to take action to protect the client and, in appropriate cases, seeking the appointment of a guardian ad litem, conservator or guardian.</u>

(c) <u>Information relating to the representation of a client with diminished capacity is protected by Rule 1.6. When taking protective action pursuant to paragraph (b), the lawyer is impliedly authorized under Rule 1.6(a) to reveal information about the client, but only to the extent reasonably necessary to protect the client's interests.</u>

Comment

[1]   The normal client-lawyer relationship is based on the assumption that the client, when properly advised and assisted, is capable of making decisions about important matters. When the client is a minor or suffers from a <u>diminished</u> mental <u>capacity</u> ~~disorder or disability~~, however, maintaining the ordinary client-lawyer relationship may not be possible in all respects. In particular, ~~an~~ <u>a severely</u> incapacitated person may have no power to make legally binding decisions. Nevertheless, a client ~~lacking legal competence~~ <u>with diminished capacity</u> often has the ability to understand, deliberate upon, and reach conclusions about matters affecting the client's own well-being. ~~Furthermore, to an increasing extent the law recognizes intermediate degrees of competence.~~ For example, children as young as five or six years of age, and certainly those of ten or twelve, are regarded as having opinions that are entitled to weight in legal proceedings concerning their custody. So also, it is recognized that some persons of advanced age can be quite capable of handling routine financial matters while needing special legal protection concerning major transactions.

[2]   The fact that a client suffers a disability does not diminish the lawyer's obligation to treat the client with attention and respect. ~~If the person has no guardian or legal representative, the lawyer often must act as de facto guardian.~~ Even if the person ~~does have~~ <u>has</u> a legal representative, the lawyer should as far as possible accord the represented person the status of client, particularly in maintaining communication.

[3]   <u>The client may wish to have family members or other persons participate in discussions with the lawyer. When necessary to assist in the representation, the presence of such persons generally does not affect the applicability of the attorney-client evidentiary privilege. Nevertheless, the lawyer must keep the client's interests foremost and, except for protective action authorized under paragraph (b), must to look to the client, and not family members, to make decisions on the client's behalf.</u>

~~[3]~~ <u>[4]</u> If a legal representative has already been appointed for the client, the lawyer should ordinarily look to the representative for decisions on behalf of the client. ~~If a legal representative has not been appointed, the lawyer should see to such an appointment where it would serve the client's best interests. Thus, if a disabled client has substantial property that should be sold for the client's benefit, effective completion of the transaction ordinarily requires appointment of a legal representative. In many circumstances, however, appointment of a legal representative may be expensive or traumatic for the client. Evaluation of these considerations is a matter of professional judgment on the lawyer's part.~~ <u>In matters involving a minor, whether the lawyer should look to the parents as natural guardians may depend on the type of proceeding or matter in which the lawyer is representing the minor.</u> ~~[4]~~ If the lawyer represents the guardian as distinct from the ward, and is aware that the guardian is acting adversely to the ward's interest, the lawyer may have an obligation to prevent or rectify the guardian's misconduct. See Rule 1.2(d).

Taking Protective Action

[5]   If a lawyer reasonably believes that a client is at risk of substantial physical, financial or other harm unless action is taken, and that a normal client-lawyer relationship cannot be maintained as provided in paragraph (a) because the client lacks sufficient capacity to communicate or to make adequately considered decisions in connection with the representation, then paragraph (b) permits the lawyer to take protective measures deemed necessary. Such measures could include: consulting with family members, using a reconsideration period to permit clarification or improvement of circumstances, using voluntary surrogate decisionmaking tools such as durable powers of attorney or consulting with support groups, professional services, adult-protective agencies or other individuals or entities that have the ability to protect the client. In taking any protective action, the lawyer should be guided by such factors as the wishes and values of the client to the extent known, the client's best interests and the goals of intruding into the client's decisionmaking autonomy to the least extent feasible, maximizing client capacities and respecting the client's family and social connections.

[6]   In determining the extent of the client's diminished capacity, the lawyer should consider and balance such factors as: the client's ability to articulate reasoning leading to a decision, variability of state of mind and ability to appreciate consequences of a decision; the substantive fairness of a decision; and the consistency of a decision with the known long-term commitments and values of the client. In appropriate circumstances, the lawyer may seek guidance from an appropriate diagnostician.

[7]   If a legal representative has not been appointed, the lawyer should consider whether appointment of a guardian ad litem, conservator or guardian is necessary to protect the client's interests. Thus, if a client with diminished capacity has substantial property that should be sold for the client's benefit, effective completion of the transaction may require appointment of a legal representative. In addition, rules of procedure in litigation sometimes provide that minors or persons with diminished capacity must be represented by a guardian or next friend if they do not have a general guardian. In many circumstances, however, appointment of a legal representative may be more expensive or traumatic for the client than circumstances in fact require. Evaluation of such circumstances is a matter entrusted to the professional judgment of the lawyer. In considering alternatives, however, the lawyer should be aware of any law that requires the lawyer to advocate the least restrictive action on behalf of the client.

Disclosure of the Client's Condition

[5] [8]   Rules of procedure in litigation generally provide that minors or persons suffering mental disability shall be represented by a guardian or next friend if they do not have a general guardian. However, disclosure Disclosure of the client's disability can diminished capacity could adversely affect the client's interests. For example, raising the question of disability diminished capacity could, in some circumstances, lead to proceedings for

involuntary commitment. <u>Information relating to the representation is protected by Rule 1.6. Therefore, unless authorized to do so, the lawyer may not disclose such information. When taking protective action pursuant to paragraph (b), the lawyer is impliedly authorized to make the necessary disclosures, even when the client directs the lawyer to the contrary. Nevertheless, given the risks of disclosure, paragraph (c) limits what the lawyer may disclose in consulting with other individuals or entities or seeking the appointment of a legal representative. At the very least, the lawyer should determine whether it is likely that the person or entity consulted with will act adversely to the client's interests before discussing matters related to the client.</u> The lawyer's position in such cases is an unavoidably difficult one. ~~The lawyer may seek guidance from an appropriate diagnostician.~~

Emergency Legal Assistance

~~[6]~~ <u>[9]</u> In an emergency where the health, safety or a financial interest of a person ~~under a disability~~ <u>with seriously diminished capacity</u> is threatened with imminent and irreparable harm, a lawyer may take legal action on behalf of such a person even though the person is unable to establish a client-lawyer relationship or to make or express considered judgments about the matter, when the ~~disabled~~ person or another acting in good faith on that person's behalf has consulted <u>with</u> the lawyer. Even in such an emergency, however, the lawyer should not act unless the lawyer reasonably believes that the person has no other lawyer, agent or other representative available. The lawyer should take legal action on behalf of the ~~disabled~~ person only to the extent reasonably necessary to maintain the status quo or otherwise avoid imminent and irreparable harm. A lawyer who undertakes to represent a person in such an exigent situation has the same duties under these Rules as the lawyer would with respect to a client.

~~[7]~~ <u>[10]</u> A lawyer who acts on behalf of a ~~disabled~~ person <u>with seriously diminished capacity</u> in an emergency should keep the confidences of the ~~disabled~~ person as if dealing with a client, disclosing them only to the extent necessary to accomplish the intended protective action. The lawyer should disclose to any tribunal involved and to any other counsel involved the nature of his or her relationship with the ~~disabled~~ person. The lawyer should take steps to regularize the relationship or implement other protective solutions as soon as possible. Normally, a lawyer would not seek compensation for such emergency actions taken ~~on behalf of a disabled person.~~

RULE 1.15: SAFEKEEPING PROPERTY

(a)   A lawyer shall hold property of clients or third persons that is in a lawyer's possession in connection with a representation separate from the lawyer's own property. Funds shall be kept in a separate account maintained in the state where the lawyer's office is situated, or elsewhere with the consent of the client or third person. Other property shall be identified as such and appropriately safeguarded. Complete records of such account funds and other property shall be kept by the lawyer and shall be preserved for a period of [five years] after termination of the representation.

(b)   A lawyer may deposit the lawyer's own funds in a client trust account for the sole purpose of paying bank service charges on that account, but only in an amount necessary for that purpose.

(c)   A lawyer shall deposit into a client trust account legal fees and expenses that have been paid in advance, to be withdrawn by the lawyer only as fees are earned or expenses incurred.

~~(b)~~ (d)   Upon receiving funds or other property in which a client or third person has an interest, a lawyer shall promptly notify the client or third person. Except as stated in this rule or otherwise permitted by law or by agreement with the client, a lawyer shall promptly deliver to the client or third person any funds or other property that the client or third person is entitled to receive and, upon request by the client or third person, shall promptly render a full accounting regarding such property.

~~(c)~~ (e)   When in the course of representation a lawyer is in possession of property in which ~~both~~ two or more persons (one of whom may be the lawyer ~~and another person~~) claim interests, the property shall be kept separate by the lawyer until ~~there is an accounting and severance of their interests. If a dispute arises concerning their respective interests, the portion in dispute shall be kept separate by the lawyer until~~ the dispute is resolved. The lawyer shall promptly distribute all portions of the property as to which the interests are not in dispute.

Comment

[1]   A lawyer should hold property of others with the care required of a professional fiduciary. Securities should be kept in a safe deposit box, except when some other form of safekeeping is warranted by special circumstances. All property that is the property of clients or third persons ~~should,~~ including prospective clients, must be kept separate from the lawyer's business and personal property and, if monies, in one or more trust accounts. Separate trust accounts may be warranted when administering estate monies or acting in similar fiduciary capacities. A lawyer should maintain on a current basis books and records in accordance with generally accepted accounting practice and comply with any recordkeeping rules established by law or court order. See, e.g., ABA Model Financial Recordkeeping Rule.

[2]   While normally it is impermissible to commingle the lawyer's own funds with client funds, paragraph (b) provides that it is permissible when necessary to pay bank service charges on that account. Accurate records must be kept regarding which part of the funds are the lawyer's.

~~[2]~~ [3]   Lawyers often receive funds from ~~third parties from~~ which the lawyer's fee will be paid. ~~If there is risk that the client may divert the funds without paying the fee, the~~ The lawyer is not required to remit ~~the portion from which the fee is to be paid~~ to the client funds that the lawyer reasonably believes represent fees owed. However, a lawyer may not hold funds to coerce a client into accepting the lawyer's contention. The disputed portion of the funds ~~should~~ must be kept in a trust account and the lawyer should suggest means for prompt resolution of the dispute, such as arbitration. The undisputed portion of the funds shall be promptly distributed.

[3] [4]   ~~Third~~ Paragraph (e) also recognizes that third parties~~, such as a client's creditors,~~ may have ~~just~~ lawful claims against specific funds or other property in a lawyer's custody, such as a client's creditor who has a lien on funds recovered in a personal injury action. A lawyer may have a duty under applicable law to protect such third-party claims against wrongful interference by the client~~, and accordingly may.~~ In such cases, when the third-party claim is not frivolous under applicable law, the lawyer must refuse to surrender the property to the client until the claims are resolved. ~~However, a~~ A lawyer should not unilaterally assume to arbitrate a dispute between the client and the third party, but, when there are substantial grounds for dispute as to the person entitled to the funds, the lawyer may file an action to have a court resolve the dispute.

[4] [5]   The obligations of a lawyer under this Rule are independent of those arising from activity other than rendering legal services. For example, a lawyer who serves only as an escrow agent is governed by the applicable law relating to fiduciaries even though the lawyer does not render legal services in the transaction and is not governed by this Rule.

[5] [6]   A "~~clients' security~~ lawyers' fund" for client protection provides a means through the collective efforts of the bar to reimburse persons who have lost money or property as a result of dishonest conduct of a lawyer. Where such a fund has been established, a lawyer must participate where it is mandatory, and, even when it is voluntary, the lawyer should participate.

RULE 1.16: DECLINING OR TERMINATING REPRESENTATION

(a)   Except as stated in paragraph (c), a lawyer shall not represent a client or, where representation has commenced, shall withdraw from the representation of a client if:

(1)   the representation will result in violation of the rules of professional conduct or other law;

(2)   the lawyer's physical or mental condition materially impairs the lawyer's ability to represent the client; or

(3)   the lawyer is discharged.

(b)   Except as stated in paragraph (c), a lawyer may withdraw from representing a client if:

(1)   withdrawal can be accomplished without material adverse effect on the interests of the client~~, or if:~~;

(1) (2)   the client persists in a course of action involving the lawyer's services that the lawyer reasonably believes is criminal or fraudulent;

(2) (3)   the client has used the lawyer's services to perpetrate a crime or fraud;

~~(3)~~ (4) ~~a~~ the client insists upon ~~pursuing an objective~~ taking action that the lawyer considers repugnant or ~~imprudent~~ with which the lawyer has a fundamental disagreement;

~~(4)~~ (5) the client fails substantially to fulfill an obligation to the lawyer regarding the lawyer's services and has been given reasonable warning that the lawyer will withdraw unless the obligation is fulfilled;

~~(5)~~ (6) the representation will result in an unreasonable financial burden on the lawyer or has been rendered unreasonably difficult by the client; or

~~(6)~~ (7) other good cause for withdrawal exists.

(c) A lawyer must comply with applicable law requiring notice to or permission of a tribunal when terminating a representation. When ordered to do so by a tribunal, a lawyer shall continue representation notwithstanding good cause for terminating the representation.

(d) Upon termination of representation, a lawyer shall take steps to the extent reasonably practicable to protect a client's interests, such as giving reasonable notice to the client, allowing time for employment of other counsel, surrendering papers and property to which the client is entitled and refunding any advance payment of fee or expense that has not been earned or incurred. The lawyer may retain papers relating to the client to the extent permitted by other law.

Comment

[1] A lawyer should not accept representation in a matter unless it can be performed competently, promptly, without improper conflict of interest and to completion. Ordinarily, a representation in a matter is completed when the agreed-upon assistance has been concluded. See Rules 1.2(c) and 6.5. See also Rule 1.3, Comment [4].

Mandatory Withdrawal

[2] A lawyer ordinarily must decline or withdraw from representation if the client demands that the lawyer engage in conduct that is illegal or violates the Rules of Professional Conduct or other law. The lawyer is not obliged to decline or withdraw simply because the client suggests such a course of conduct; a client may make such a suggestion in the hope that a lawyer will not be constrained by a professional obligation.

[3] When a lawyer has been appointed to represent a client, withdrawal ordinarily requires approval of the appointing authority. See also Rule 6.2. Similarly, court approval or notice to the court is often required by applicable law before a lawyer withdraws from pending litigation. Difficulty may be encountered if withdrawal is based on the client's demand that the lawyer engage in unprofessional conduct. The court may wish request an explanation for the withdrawal, while the lawyer may be bound to keep confidential the facts that would constitute such an explanation. The lawyer's statement that

professional considerations require termination of the representation ordinarily should be accepted as sufficient. Lawyers should be mindful of their
obligations to both clients and the court under Rules 1.6 and 3.3.

Discharge

[4]   A client has a right to discharge a lawyer at any time, with or
without cause, subject to liability for payment for the lawyer's services. Where
future dispute about the withdrawal may be anticipated, it may be advisable to
prepare a written statement reciting the circumstances.

[5]   Whether a client can discharge appointed counsel may depend
on applicable law. A client seeking to do so should be given a full explanation of
the consequences. These consequences may include a decision by the appointing authority that appointment of successor counsel is unjustified, thus
requiring self-representation by the client.

[6]   If the client is mentally incompetent has severely diminished
capacity, the client may lack the legal capacity to discharge the lawyer, and in
any event the discharge may be seriously adverse to the client's interests. The
lawyer should make special effort to help the client consider the consequences
and, in an extreme case, may initiate proceedings for a conservatorship or similar protection of the client. See take reasonably necessary protective action as
provided in Rule 1.14.

Optional Withdrawal

[7]   A lawyer may withdraw from representation in some circumstances. The lawyer has the option to withdraw if it can be accomplished
without material adverse effect on the client's interests. Withdrawal is also
justified if the client persists in a course of action that the lawyer reasonably
believes is criminal or fraudulent, for a lawyer is not required to be associated
with such conduct even if the lawyer does not further it. Withdrawal is also
permitted if the lawyer's services were misused in the past even if that would
materially prejudice the client. The lawyer may also withdraw where the client
insists on a taking action that the lawyer considers repugnant or imprudent
objective with which the lawyer has a fundamental disagreement.

[8]   A lawyer may withdraw if the client refuses to abide by the
terms of an agreement relating to the representation, such as an agreement
concerning fees or court costs or an agreement limiting the objectives of the
representation.

Assisting the Client upon Withdrawal

[9]   Even if the lawyer has been unfairly discharged by the client, a
lawyer must take all reasonable steps to mitigate the consequences to the
client. The lawyer may retain papers as security for a fee only to the extent
permitted by law. Whether or not a lawyer for an organization may under
certain unusual circumstances have a legal obligation to the organization after
withdrawing or being discharged by the organization's highest authority is
beyond the scope of these Rules. See Rule 1.15.

RULE 1.17: SALE OF LAW PRACTICE

A lawyer or a law firm may sell or purchase a law practice, <u>or an area of practice,</u> including good will, if the following conditions are satisfied:

(a)   The seller ceases to engage in the private practice of law<u>, or in the area of practice that has been sold,</u> [in the geographic area] [in the jurisdiction] (a jurisdiction may elect either version) in which the practice has been conducted;

(b)   The <u>entire</u> practice<u>, or the entire area of practice,</u> is sold ~~as an entirety~~ to ~~another lawyer~~ <u>one or more lawyers</u> or law ~~firm~~ <u>firms</u>;

(c)   ~~Actual~~ <u>The seller gives</u> written notice ~~is given~~ to each of the seller's clients regarding:

(1)   the proposed sale;

~~(2)   the terms of any proposed change in the fee arrangement authorized by paragraph (d);~~

~~(3)~~ <u>(2)</u>   the client's right to retain other counsel or to take possession of the file; and

~~(4)~~ <u>(3)</u>   the fact that the client's consent to the sale <u>transfer of the client's files</u> will be presumed if the client does not take any action or does not otherwise object within ninety (90) days of receipt of the notice.

If a client cannot be given notice, the representation of that client may be transferred to the purchaser only upon entry of an order so authorizing by a court having jurisdiction. The seller may disclose to the court in camera information relating to the representation only to the extent necessary to obtain an order authorizing the transfer of a file.

(d)   The fees charged clients shall not be increased by reason of the sale. ~~The purchaser may, however, refuse to undertake the representation unless the client consents to pay the purchaser fees at a rate not exceeding the fees charged by the purchaser for rendering substantially similar services prior to the initiation of the purchase negotiations.~~

Comment

[1]   The practice of law is a profession, not merely a business. Clients are not commodities that can be purchased and sold at will. Pursuant to this Rule, when a lawyer or an entire firm ceases to practice<u>, or ceases to practice in an area of law,</u> and ~~another lawyer~~ <u>other lawyers</u> or ~~firm takes~~ <u>firms take</u> over the representation, the selling lawyer or firm may obtain compensation for the reasonable value of the practice as may withdrawing partners of law firms. See Rules 5.4 and 5.6.

Termination of Practice by the Seller

[2]   The requirement that all of the private practice<u>, or all of an area of practice,</u> be sold is satisfied if the seller in good faith makes the entire practice<u>, or the area of practice,</u> available for sale to the ~~purchaser~~ <u>purchasers</u>.

The fact that a number of the seller's clients decide not to be represented by the ~~purchaser~~ purchasers but take their matters elsewhere, therefore, does not result in a violation. ~~Neither does a return~~ Return to private practice as a result of an unanticipated change in circumstances does not necessarily result in a violation. For example, a lawyer who has sold the practice to accept an appointment to judicial office does not violate the requirement that the sale be attendant to cessation of practice if the lawyer later resumes private practice upon being defeated in a contested or a retention election for the office or resigns from a judiciary position.

[3] The requirement that the seller cease to engage in the private practice of law does not prohibit employment as a lawyer on the staff of a public agency or a legal services entity that provides legal services to the poor, or as in-house counsel to a business.

[4] The Rule permits a sale of an entire practice attendant upon retirement from the private practice of law within the jurisdiction. Its provisions, therefore, accommodate the lawyer who sells the practice upon the occasion of moving to another state. Some states are so large that a move from one locale therein to another is tantamount to leaving the jurisdiction in which the lawyer has engaged in the practice of law. To also accommodate lawyers so situated, states may permit the sale of the practice when the lawyer leaves the geographic area rather than the jurisdiction. The alternative desired should be indicated by selecting one of the two provided for in Rule 1.17(a).

[5] This Rule also permits a lawyer or law firm to sell an area of practice. If an area of practice is sold and the lawyer remains in the active practice of law, the lawyer must cease accepting any matters in the area of practice that has been sold, either as counsel or co-counsel or by assuming joint responsibility for a matter in connection with the division of a fee with another lawyer as would otherwise be permitted by Rule 1.5(e). For example, a lawyer with a substantial number of estate planning matters and a substantial number of probate administration cases may sell the estate planning portion of the practice but remain in the practice of law by concentrating on probate administration; however, that practitioner may not thereafter accept any estate planning matters. Although a lawyer who leaves a jurisdiction or geographical area typically would sell the entire practice, this Rule permits the lawyer to limit the sale to one or more areas of the practice, thereby preserving the lawyer's right to continue practice in the areas of the practice that were not sold.

~~Single Purchaser~~ Sale of Entire Practice or Entire Area of Practice

~~[5]~~ [6] The Rule requires ~~a single purchaser~~ that the seller's entire practice, or an entire area of practice, be sold. The prohibition against ~~piecemeal~~ sale of ~~a~~ less than an entire practice area protects those clients whose matters are less lucrative and who might find it difficult to secure other counsel if a sale could be limited to substantial fee-generating matters. The ~~purchaser is~~ purchasers are required to undertake all client matters in the practice or practice area, subject to client consent. ~~If~~ This requirement is satisfied, however, ~~the~~ even if a purchaser is unable to undertake ~~all~~ a particular client ~~matters~~ matter because of a conflict of interest ~~in a specific matter respecting which the purchaser is not permitted by Rule 1.7 or another rule to represent the client, the requirement that there be a single purchaser is nevertheless satisfied~~.

Client Confidences, Consent and Notice

~~[6]~~ [7] Negotiations between seller and prospective purchaser prior to disclosure of information relating to a specific representation of an identifiable client no more violate the confidentiality provisions of Model Rule 1.6 than do preliminary discussions concerning the possible association of another lawyer or mergers between firms, with respect to which client consent is not required. See Rule 1.6(b)(7). Providing the purchaser access to ~~client-specific~~ detailed information relating to the representation, ~~and to~~ such as the client's file, however, requires client consent. The Rule provides that before such information can be disclosed by the seller to the purchaser the client must be given actual written notice of the contemplated sale, including the identity of the purchaser ~~and any proposed change in the terms of future representation~~, and must be told that the decision to consent or make other arrangements must be made within 90 days. If nothing is heard from the client within that time, consent to the sale is presumed.

~~[7]~~ [8] A lawyer or law firm ceasing to practice cannot be required to remain in practice because some clients cannot be given actual notice of the proposed purchase. Since these clients cannot themselves consent to the purchase or direct any other disposition of their files, the Rule requires an order from a court having jurisdiction authorizing their transfer or other disposition. The Court can be expected to determine whether reasonable efforts to locate the client have been exhausted, and whether the absent client's legitimate interests will be served by authorizing the transfer of the file so that the purchaser may continue the representation. Preservation of client confidences requires that the petition for a court order be considered in camera. (A procedure by which such an order can be obtained needs to be established in jurisdictions in which it presently does not exist.)

~~[8]~~ [9] All the elements of client autonomy, including the client's absolute right to discharge a lawyer and transfer the representation to another, survive the sale of the practice or area of practice.

Fee Arrangements Between Client and Purchaser

~~[9]~~ [10] The sale may not be financed by increases in fees charged the clients of the practice. Existing agreements between the seller and the client as to fees and the scope of the work must be honored by the purchaser~~, unless the client consents after consultation. The purchaser may, however, advise the client that the purchaser will not undertake the representation unless the client consents to pay the higher fees the purchaser usually charges. To prevent client financing of the sale, the higher fee the purchaser may charge must not exceed the fees charged by the purchaser for substantially similar service rendered prior to the initiation of the purchase negotiations~~.

[10]   ~~The purchaser may not intentionally fragment the practice which is the subject of the sale by charging significantly different fees in substantially similar matters. Doing so would make it possible for the purchaser to avoid the obligation to take over the entire practice by charging arbitrarily higher fees for less lucrative matters, thereby increasing the likelihood that those clients would not consent to the new representation.~~

Other Applicable Ethical Standards

[11]   Lawyers participating in the sale of a law practice <u>or a practice area</u> are subject to the ethical standards applicable to involving another lawyer in the representation of a client. These include, for example, the seller's obligation to exercise competence in identifying a purchaser qualified to assume the practice and the purchaser's obligation to undertake the representation competently (see Rule 1.1); the obligation to avoid disqualifying conflicts, and to secure ~~client~~ <u>the client's informed</u> consent ~~after consultation~~ for those conflicts that can be agreed to (see Rule 1.7 <u>regarding conflicts and Rule 1.0(e) for the definition of informed consent</u>); and the obligation to protect information relating to the representation (see Rules 1.6 and 1.9).

[12]   If approval of the substitution of the purchasing lawyer for the selling lawyer is required by the rules of any tribunal in which a matter is pending, such approval must be obtained before the matter can be included in the sale (see Rule 1.16).

Applicability of the Rule

[13]   This Rule applies to the sale of a law practice by representatives of a deceased, disabled or disappeared lawyer. Thus, the seller may be represented by a non-lawyer representative not subject to these Rules. Since, however, no lawyer may participate in a sale of a law practice which does not conform to the requirements of this Rule, the representatives of the seller as well as the purchasing lawyer can be expected to see to it that they are met.

[14]   Admission to or retirement from a law partnership or professional association, retirement plans and similar arrangements, and a sale of tangible assets of a law practice, do not constitute a sale or purchase governed by this Rule.

[15]   This Rule does not apply to the transfers of legal representation between lawyers when such transfers are unrelated to the sale of a practice <u>or an area of practice</u>.

RULE 1.18: <u>DUTIES TO PROSPECTIVE CLIENT</u>

<u>(a)   A person who consults with a lawyer about the possibility of forming a client-lawyer relationship with respect to a matter is a prospective client.</u>

<u>(b)   Even when no client-lawyer relationship ensues, a lawyer who learned information from a prospective client shall not use or reveal that information, except as Rule 1.9 would permit with respect to information of a former client.</u>

(c)   A lawyer subject to paragraph (b) shall not represent a client with interests materially adverse to those of a prospective client in the same or a substantially related matter if the lawyer received information from the prospective client that could be significantly harmful to that person in the matter, except as provided in paragraph (d). If a lawyer is disqualified from representation under this paragraph, no lawyer in a firm with which that lawyer is associated may knowingly undertake or continue representation in such a matter, except as provided in paragraph (d).

(d)   When the lawyer has received disqualifying information as defined in paragraph (c), representation is permissible if:

(1)   both the affected client and the prospective client have given informed consent, confirmed in writing, or:

(2)   the lawyer who received the information took reasonable measures to avoid exposure to more disqualifying information than was reasonably necessary to determine whether to represent the prospective client; and

(i)   the disqualified lawyer is timely screened from any participation in the matter and is apportioned no part of the fee therefrom; and

(ii)   written notice is promptly given to the prospective client.

Comment

[1]   Prospective clients, like clients, may disclose information to a lawyer, place documents or other property in the lawyer's custody, or rely on the lawyer's advice. A lawyer's consultations with a prospective client usually are limited in time and depth and leave both the prospective client and the lawyer free (and sometimes required) to proceed no further. Hence, prospective clients should receive some but not all of the protection afforded clients.

[2]   A person becomes a prospective client by consulting with a lawyer about the possibility of forming a client-lawyer relationship with respect to a matter. Whether communications, including written, oral, or electronic communications, constitute a consultation depends on the circumstances. For example, a consultation is likely to have occurred if a lawyer, either in person or through the lawyer's advertising in any medium, specifically requests or invites the submission of information about a potential representation without clear and reasonably understandable warnings and cautionary statements that limit the lawyer's obligations, and a person provides information in response. See also Comment [4]. In contrast, a consultation does not occur if a person provides information to a lawyer in response to advertising that merely describes the lawyer's education, experience, areas of practice, and contact information, or provides legal information of general interest. Such a person communicates information unilaterally to a lawyer, without any reasonable expectation that the lawyer is willing to discuss the possibility of forming a client-lawyer relationship, and is thus not a "prospective client." Moreover, a

person who communicates with a lawyer for the purpose of disqualifying the lawyer is not a "prospective client."

[3] It is often necessary for a prospective client to reveal information to the lawyer during an initial consultation prior to the decision about formation of a client-lawyer relationship. The lawyer often must learn such information to determine whether there is a conflict of interest with an existing client and whether the matter is one that the lawyer is willing to undertake. Paragraph (b) prohibits the lawyer from using or revealing that information, except as permitted by Rule 1.9, even if the client or lawyer decides not to proceed with the representation. The duty exists regardless of how brief the initial conference may be.

[4] In order to avoid acquiring disqualifying information from a prospective client, a lawyer considering whether or not to undertake a new matter should limit the initial consultation to only such information as reasonably appears necessary for that purpose. Where the information indicates that a conflict of interest or other reason for non-representation exists, the lawyer should so inform the prospective client or decline the representation. If the prospective client wishes to retain the lawyer, and if consent is possible under Rule 1.7, then consent from all affected present or former clients must be obtained before accepting the representation.

[5] A lawyer may condition consultations with a prospective client on the person's informed consent that no information disclosed during the consultation will prohibit the lawyer from representing a different client in the matter. See Rule 1.0(e) for the definition of informed consent. If the agreement expressly so provides, the prospective client may also consent to the lawyer's subsequent use of information received from the prospective client.

[6] Even in the absence of an agreement, under paragraph (c), the lawyer is not prohibited from representing a client with interests adverse to those of the prospective client in the same or a substantially related matter unless the lawyer has received from the prospective client information that could be significantly harmful if used in the matter.

[7] Under paragraph (c), the prohibition in this Rule is imputed to other lawyers as provided in Rule 1.10, but, under paragraph (d)(1), imputation may be avoided if the lawyer obtains the informed consent, confirmed in writing, of both the prospective and affected clients. In the alternative, imputation may be avoided if the conditions of paragraph (d)(2) are met and all disqualified lawyers are timely screened and written notice is promptly given to the prospective client. See Rule 1.0(k) (requirements for screening procedures). Paragraph (d)(2)(i) does not prohibit the screened lawyer from receiving a salary or partnership share established by prior independent agreement, but that lawyer may not receive compensation directly related to the matter in which the lawyer is disqualified.

[8] Notice, including a general description of the subject matter about which the lawyer was consulted, and of the screening procedures

employed, generally should be given as soon as practicable after the need for screening becomes apparent.

[9]   For the duty of competence of a lawyer who gives assistance on the merits of a matter to a prospective client, see Rule 1.1. For a lawyer's duties when a prospective client entrusts valuables or papers to the lawyer's care, see Rule 1.15.

RULE 2.1: ADVISOR

In representing a client, a lawyer shall exercise independent professional judgment and render candid advice. In rendering advice, a lawyer may refer not only to law but to other considerations such as moral, economic, social and political factors, that may be relevant to the client's situation.

Comment

Scope of Advice

[1]   A client is entitled to straightforward advice expressing the lawyer's honest assessment. Legal advice often involves unpleasant facts and alternatives that a client may be disinclined to confront. In presenting advice, a lawyer endeavors to sustain the client's morale and may put advice in as acceptable a form as honesty permits. However, a lawyer should not be deterred from giving candid advice by the prospect that the advice will be unpalatable to the client.

[2]   Advice couched in narrow legal terms may be of little value to a client, especially where practical considerations, such as cost or effects on other people, are predominant. Purely technical legal advice, therefore, can sometimes be inadequate. It is proper for a lawyer to refer to relevant moral and ethical considerations in giving advice.Although a lawyer is not a moral advisor as such, moral and ethical considerations impinge upon most legal questions and may decisively influence how the law will be applied.

[3]   A client may expressly or impliedly ask the lawyer for purely technical advice. When such a request is made by a client experienced in legal matters, the lawyer may accept it at face value. When such a request is made by a client inexperienced in legal matters, however, the lawyer's responsibility as advisor may include indicating that more may be involved than strictly legal considerations.

[4]   Matters that go beyond strictly legal questions may also be in the domain of another profession. Family matters can involve problems within the professional competence of psychiatry, clinical psychology or social work; business matters can involve problems within the competence of the accounting profession or of financial specialists. Where consultation with a professional in another field is itself something a competent lawyer would recommend, the lawyer should make such a recommendation. At the same time, a lawyer's advice at its best often consists of recommending a course of action in the face of conflicting recommendations of experts.

Offering Advice

[5]   In general, a lawyer is not expected to give advice until asked by the client. However, when a lawyer knows that a client proposes a course of action that is likely to result in substantial adverse legal consequences to the client, the lawyer's duty to the client under Rule 1.4 may require that the lawyer act offer advice if the client's course of action is related to the representation. Similarly, when a matter is likely to involve litigation, it may be necessary under Rule 1.4 to inform the client of forms of dispute resolution that might constitute reasonable alternatives to litigation. A lawyer ordinarily has no duty to initiate investigation of a client's affairs or to give advice that the client has indicated is unwanted, but a lawyer may initiate advice to a client when doing so appears to be in the client's interest.

RULE 2.2: INTERMEDIARY

(a)   A lawyer may act as intermediary between clients if:

(1)   the lawyer consults with each client concerning the implications of the common representation, including the advantages and risks involved, and the effect on the attorney-client privileges, and obtains each client's consent to the common representation;

(2)   the lawyer reasonably believes that the matter can be resolved on terms compatible with the clients' best interests, that each client will be able to make adequately informed decisions in the matter and that there is little risk of material prejudice to the interests of any of the clients if the contemplated resolution is unsuccessful; and

(3)   the lawyer reasonably believes that the common representation can be undertaken impartially and without improper effect on other responsibilities the lawyer has to any of the clients.

(b)   While acting as intermediary, the lawyer shall consult with each client concerning the decisions to be made and the considerations relevant in making them, so that each client can make adequately informed decisions.

(c)   A lawyer shall withdraw as intermediary if any of the clients so requests, or if any of the conditions stated in paragraph (a) is no longer satisfied. Upon withdrawal, the lawyer shall not continue to represent any of the clients in the matter that was the subject of the intermediation.

Comment

[1]   A lawyer acts as intermediary under this Rule when the lawyer represents two or more parties with potentially conflicting interests. A key factor in defining the relationship is whether the parties share responsibility for the lawyer's fee, but the common representation may be inferred from other circumstances. Because confusion can arise as to the lawyer's role where each party is not separately represented, it is important that the lawyer make clear the relationship.

~~[2] The Rule does not apply to a lawyer acting as arbitrator or mediator between or among parties who are not clients of the lawyer, even where the lawyer has been appointed with the concurrence of the parties. In performing such a role the lawyer may be subject to applicable codes of ethics, such as the Code of Ethics for Arbitration in Commercial Disputes prepared by a joint Committee of the American Bar Association and the American Arbitration Association.~~

~~[3] A lawyer acts as intermediary in seeking to establish or adjust a relationship between clients on an amicable and mutually advantageous basis; for example, in helping to organize a business in which two or more clients are entrepreneurs, working out the financial reorganization of an enterprise in which two or more clients have an interest, arranging a property distribution in settlement of an estate or mediating a dispute between clients. The lawyer seeks to resolve potentially conflicting interests by developing the parties' mutual interests. The alternative can be that each party may have to obtain separate representation, with the possibility in some situations of incurring additional cost, complication or even litigation. Given these and other relevant factors, all the clients may prefer that the lawyer act as intermediary.~~

~~[4] In considering whether to act as intermediary between clients, a lawyer should be mindful that if the intermediation fails the result can be additional cost, embarrassment and recrimination. In some situations the risk of failure is so great that intermediation is plainly impossible. For example, a lawyer cannot undertake common representation of clients between whom contentious litigation is imminent or who contemplate contentious negotiations. More generally, if the relationship between the parties has already assumed definite antagonism, the possibility that the clients' interests can be adjusted by intermediation ordinarily is not very good.~~

~~[5] The appropriateness of intermediation can depend on its form. Forms of intermediation range from informal arbitration, where each client's case is presented by the respective client and the lawyer decides the outcome, to mediation, to common representation where the clients' interests are substantially though not entirely compatible. One form may be appropriate in circumstances where another would not. Other relevant factors are whether the lawyer subsequently will represent both parties on a continuing basis and whether the situation involves creating a relationship between the parties or terminating one.~~

~~Confidentiality and Privilege~~

~~[6] A particularly important factor in determining the appropriateness of intermediation is the effect on client-lawyer confidentiality and the attorney-client privilege. In a common representation, the lawyer is still required both to keep each client adequately informed and to maintain confidentiality of information relating to the representation. See Rules 1.4 and 1.6. Complying with both requirements while acting as intermediary requires a delicate balance. If the balance cannot be maintained, the common representation is improper. With regard to the attorney-client privilege, the prevailing~~

~~rule is that as between commonly represented clients the privilege does not attach. Hence, it must be assumed that if litigation eventuates between the clients, the privilege will not protect any such communications, and the clients should be so advised.~~

~~[7] Since the lawyer is required to be impartial between commonly represented clients, intermediation is improper when that impartiality cannot be maintained. For example, a lawyer who has represented one of the clients for a long period and in a variety of matters might have difficulty being impartial between that client and one to whom the lawyer has only recently been introduced.~~

~~Consultation~~

~~[8] In acting as intermediary between clients, the lawyer is required to consult with the clients on the implications of doing so, and proceed only upon consent based on such a consultation. The consultation should make clear that the lawyer's role is not that of partisanship normally expected in other circumstances.~~

~~[9] Paragraph (b) is an application of the principle expressed in Rule 1.4. Where the lawyer is intermediary, the clients ordinarily must assume greater responsibility for decisions than when each client is independently represented.~~

~~Withdrawal~~

~~[10] Common representation does not diminish the rights of each client in the client-lawyer relationship. Each has the right to loyal and diligent representation, the right to discharge the lawyer as stated in Rule 1.16, and the protection of Rule 1.9 concerning obligations to a former client.~~

RULE 2.3: EVALUATION FOR USE BY THIRD PERSONS

(a) A lawyer may ~~undertake~~ <u>provide</u> an evaluation of a matter affecting a client for the use of someone other than the client if~~: (1)~~ the lawyer reasonably believes that making the evaluation is compatible with other aspects of the lawyer's relationship with the client~~; and~~<u>.</u>

~~(2)~~ <u>(b)</u> <u>When the lawyer knows or reasonably should know that the evaluation is likely to affect the client's interests materially and adversely, the lawyer shall not provide the evaluation unless</u> the client ~~consents after consultation~~ <u>gives informed consent</u>.

~~(b)~~ <u>(c)</u> Except as disclosure is ~~required~~ <u>authorized</u> in connection with a report of an evaluation, information relating to the evaluation is otherwise protected by Rule 1.6.

Comment

Definition

[1] An evaluation may be performed at the client's direction ~~but~~ <u>or</u> <u>when impliedly authorized in order to carry out the representation. See Rule 1.2.</u>

<u>Such an evaluation may be</u> for the primary purpose of establishing information for the benefit of third parties; for example, an opinion concerning the title of property rendered at the behest of a vendor for the information of a prospective purchaser, or at the behest of a borrower for the information of a prospective lender. In some situations, the evaluation may be required by a government agency; for example, an opinion concerning the legality of the securities registered for sale under the securities laws. In other instances, the evaluation may be required by a third person, such as a purchaser of a business.

~~[2] Lawyers for the government may be called upon to give a formal opinion on the legality of contemplated government agency action. In making such an evaluation, the government lawyer acts at the behest of the government as the client but for the purpose of establishing the limits of the agency's authorized activity. Such an opinion is to be distinguished from confidential legal advice given agency officials. The critical question is whether the opinion is to be made public.~~

~~[3]~~ [2] A legal evaluation should be distinguished from an investigation of a person with whom the lawyer does not have a client-lawyer relationship. For example, a lawyer retained by a purchaser to analyze a vendor's title to property does not have a client-lawyer relationship with the vendor. So also, an investigation into a person's affairs by a government lawyer, or by special counsel by a government lawyer, or by special counsel employed by the government, is not an evaluation as that term is used in this Rule. The question is whether the lawyer is retained by the person whose affairs are being examined. When the lawyer is retained by that person, the general rules concerning loyalty to client and preservation of confidences apply, which is not the case if the lawyer is retained by someone else. For this reason, it is essential to identify the person by whom the lawyer is retained. This should be made clear not only to the person under examination, but also to others to whom the results are to be made available.

~~Duty~~ Duties Owed to Third Person and Client

~~[4]~~ [3] When the evaluation is intended for the information or use of a third person, a legal duty to that person may or may not arise. That legal question is beyond the scope of this Rule. However, since such an evaluation involves a departure from the normal client-lawyer relationship, careful analysis of the situation is required. The lawyer must be satisfied as a matter of professional judgment that making the evaluation is compatible with other functions undertaken in behalf of the client. For example, if the lawyer is acting as advocate in defending the client against charges of fraud, it would normally be incompatible with that responsibility for the lawyer to perform an evaluation for others concerning the same or a related transaction. Assuming no such impediment is apparent, however, the lawyer should advise the client of the implications of the evaluation, particularly the lawyer's responsibilities to third persons and the duty to disseminate the findings.

Access to and Disclosure of Information

{5} [4]   The quality of an evaluation depends on the freedom and extent of the investigation upon which it is based. Ordinarily a lawyer should have whatever latitude of investigation seems necessary as a matter of professional judgment. Under some circumstances, however, the terms of the evaluation may be limited. For example, certain issues or sources may be categorically excluded, or the scope of search may be limited by time constraints or the non-cooperation of persons having relevant information. Any such limitations that are material to the evaluation should be described in the report. If after a lawyer has commenced an evaluation, the client refuses to comply with the terms upon which it was understood the evaluation was to have been made, the lawyer's obligations are determined by law, having reference to the terms of the client's agreement and the surrounding circumstances. In no circumstances is the lawyer permitted to knowingly make a false statement of material fact or law in providing an evaluation under this Rule. See Rule 4.1.

Obtaining Client's Informed Consent

[5]   Information relating to an evaluation is protected by Rule 1.6. In many situations, providing an evaluation to a third party poses no significant risk to the client; thus, the lawyer may be impliedly authorized to disclose information to carry out the representation. See Rule 1.6(a). Where, however, it is reasonably likely that providing the evaluation will affect the client's interests materially and adversely, the lawyer must first obtain the client's consent after the client has been adequately informed concerning the important possible effects on the client's interests. See Rules 1.6(a) and 1.0(e).

Financial Auditors' Requests for Information

[6]   When a question concerning the legal situation of a client arises at the instance of the client's financial auditor and the question is referred to the lawyer, the lawyer's response may be made in accordance with procedures recognized in the legal profession. Such a procedure is set forth in the American Bar Association Statement of Policy Regarding Lawyers' Responses to Auditors' Requests for Information, adopted in 1975.

RULE 2.4: LAWYER SERVING AS THIRD-PARTY NEUTRAL

(a)   A lawyer serves as a third-party neutral when the lawyer assists two or more persons who are not clients of the lawyer to reach a resolution of a dispute or other matter that has arisen between them. Service as a third-party neutral may include service as an arbitrator, a mediator or in such other capacity as will enable the lawyer to assist the parties to resolve the matter.

(b)   A lawyer serving as a third-party neutral shall inform unre-presented parties that the lawyer is not representing them.When the lawyer knows or reasonably should know that a party does not understand the lawyer's role in the matter, the lawyer shall explain the difference between the lawyer's role as a third-party neutral and a lawyer's role as one who represents a client.

Comment

[1]   Alternative dispute resolution has become a substantial part of the civil justice system. Aside from representing clients in dispute-resolution processes, lawyers often serve as third-party neutrals. A third-party neutral is a person, such as a mediator, arbitrator, conciliator or evaluator, who assists the parties, represented or unrepresented, in the resolution of a dispute or in the arrangement of a transaction. Whether a third-party neutral serves primarily as a facilitator, evaluator or decisionmaker depends on the particular process that is either selected by the parties or mandated by a court.

[2]   The role of a third-party neutral is not unique to lawyers, although, in some court-connected contexts, only lawyers are allowed to serve in this role or to handle certain types of cases. In performing this role, the lawyer may be subject to court rules or other law that apply either to third-party neutrals generally or to lawyers serving as third-party neutrals. Lawyer-neutrals may also be subject to various codes of ethics, such as the Code of Ethics for Arbitration in Commercial Disputes prepared by a joint committee of the American Bar Association and the American Arbitration Association or the Model Standards of Conduct for Mediators jointly prepared by the American Bar Association, the American Arbitration Association and the Society of Professionals in Dispute Resolution.

[3]   Unlike nonlawyers who serve as third-party neutrals, lawyers serving in this role may experience unique problems as a result of differences between the role of a third-party neutral and a lawyer's service as a client representative. The potential for confusion is significant when the parties are unrepresented in the process. Thus, paragraph (b) requires a lawyer-neutral to inform unrepresented parties that the lawyer is not representing them. For some parties, particularly parties who frequently use dispute-resolution processes, this information will be sufficient. For others, particularly those who are using the process for the first time, more information will be required. Where appropriate, the lawyer should inform unrepresented parties of the important differences between the lawyer's role as third-party neutral and a lawyer's role as a client representative, including the inapplicability of the attorney-client evidentiary privilege. The extent of disclosure required under this paragraph will depend on the particular parties involved and the subject matter of the proceeding, as well as the particular features of the dispute-resolution process selected.

[4]   A lawyer who serves as a third-party neutral subsequently may be asked to serve as a lawyer representing a client in the same matter. The conflicts of interest that arise for both the individual lawyer and the lawyer's law firm are addressed in Rule 1.12.

[5]   Lawyers who represent clients in alternative dispute-resolution processes are governed by the Rules of Professional Conduct. When the dispute-resolution process takes place before a tribunal, as in binding arbitration (see Rule 1.0(m)), the lawyer's duty of candor is governed by Rule 3.3. Otherwise, the lawyer's duty of candor toward both the third-party neutral and other parties is governed by Rule 4.1.

RULE 3.1: MERITORIOUS CLAIMS AND CONTENTIONS

A lawyer shall not bring or defend a proceeding, or assert or controvert an issue therein, unless there is a basis <u>in law and fact</u> for doing so that is not frivolous, which includes a good faith argument for an extension, modification or reversal of existing law. A lawyer for the defendant in a criminal proceeding, or the respondent in a proceeding that could result in incarceration, may nevertheless so defend the proceeding as to require that every element of the case be established.

Comment

[1]   The advocate has a duty to use legal procedure for the fullest benefit of the client's cause, but also a duty not to abuse legal procedure. The law, both procedural and substantive, establishes the limits within which an advocate may proceed. However, the law is not always clear and never is static. Accordingly, in determining the proper scope of advocacy, account must be taken of the law's ambiguities and potential for change.

[2]   The filing of an action or defense or similar action taken for a client is not frivolous merely because the facts have not first been fully substantiated or because the lawyer expects to develop vital evidence only by discovery. <u>What is required of lawyers, however, is that they inform themselves about the facts of their clients' cases and the applicable law and determine that they can make good faith arguments in support of their clients' positions.</u> Such action is not frivolous even though the lawyer believes that the client's position ultimately will not prevail. The action is frivolous, however, if the ~~client desires to have the action taken primarily for the purpose of harassing or maliciously injuring a person, or, if the~~ lawyer is unable either to make a good faith argument on the merits of the action taken or to support the action taken by a good faith argument for an extension, modification or reversal of existing law.

[3]   <u>The lawyer's obligations under this Rule are subordinate to federal or state constitutional law that entitles a defendant in a criminal matter to the assistance of counsel in presenting a claim or contention that otherwise would be prohibited by this Rule.</u>

RULE 3.2: EXPEDITING LITIGATION

A lawyer shall make reasonable efforts to expedite litigation consistent with the interests of the client.

Comment

[1]   Dilatory practices bring the administration of justice into disrepute. ~~Delay should not be indulged merely for the convenience of the advocates, or~~ <u>Although there will be occasions when a lawyer may properly seek a postponement for personal reasons, it is not proper for a lawyer to routinely fail to expedite litigation solely for the convenience of the advocates. Nor will a failure to expedite be reasonable if done</u> for the purpose of frustrating an opposing party's attempt to obtain rightful redress or repose. It is not a justification that similar conduct is

often tolerated by the bench and bar. The question is whether a competent lawyer acting in good faith would regard the course of action as having some substantial purpose other than delay. Realizing financial or other benefit from otherwise improper delay in litigation is not a legitimate interest of the client.

RULE 3.3: CANDOR TOWARD THE TRIBUNAL

(a)   A lawyer shall not knowingly:

(1)   make a false statement of ~~material~~ fact or law to a tribunal <u>or fail to correct a false statement of material fact or law previously made to the tribunal by the lawyer</u>;

~~(2)   fail to disclose a material fact to a tribunal when disclosure is necessary to avoid assisting a criminal or fraudulent act by the client;~~

~~(3)~~ <u>(2)</u>   fail to disclose to the tribunal legal authority in the controlling jurisdiction known to the lawyer to be directly adverse to the position of the client and not disclosed by opposing counsel; or

~~(4)~~ <u>(3)</u>   offer evidence that the lawyer knows to be false. If a lawyer<u>, the lawyer's client, or a witness called by the lawyer,</u> has offered material evidence and <u>the lawyer</u> comes to know of its falsity, the lawyer shall take reasonable remedial measures<u>, including, if necessary, disclosure to the tribunal. A lawyer may refuse to offer evidence, other than the testimony of a defendant in a criminal matter, that the lawyer reasonably believes is false</u>.

<u>(b)   A lawyer who represents a client in an adjudicative proceeding and who knows that a person intends to engage, is engaging or has engaged in criminal or fraudulent conduct related to the proceeding shall take reasonable remedial measures, including, if necessary, disclosure to the tribunal.</u>

~~(b)~~ <u>(c)</u>   The duties stated in ~~paragraph~~ <u>paragraphs</u> (a) <u>and (b)</u> continue to the conclusion of the proceeding, and apply even if compliance requires disclosure of information otherwise protected by Rule 1.6.

~~(c)   A lawyer may refuse to offer evidence that the lawyer reasonably believes is false.~~

(d)   In an ex parte proceeding, a lawyer shall inform the tribunal of all material facts known to the lawyer that will enable the tribunal to make an informed decision, whether or not the facts are adverse.

Comment

<u>[1]   This Rule governs the conduct of a lawyer who is representing a client in the proceedings of a tribunal. See Rule 1.0(m) for the definition of "tribunal." It also applies when the lawyer is representing a client in an ancillary proceeding conducted pursuant to the tribunal's adjudicative authority, such as a deposition. Thus, for example, paragraph (a)(3) requires a lawyer to take reasonable remedial measures if the lawyer comes to know that a client who is testifying in a deposition has offered evidence that is false.</u>

~~[1]~~ [2] ~~The advocate's task is~~ This Rule sets forth the special duties of lawyers as officers of the court to avoid conduct that undermines the integrity of the adjudicative process. A lawyer acting as an advocate in an adjudicative proceeding has an obligation to present the client's case with persuasive force. Performance of that duty while maintaining confidences of the client, however, is qualified by the advocate's duty of candor to the tribunal. ~~However~~ Consequently, ~~an advocate does~~ although a lawyer in an adversary proceeding is not required to present an impartial exposition of the law or to vouch for the evidence submitted in a cause~~;~~, the lawyer must not allow the tribunal ~~is responsible for assessing its probative value~~ to be misled by false statements of law or fact or evidence that the lawyer knows to be false.

Representations by a Lawyer

~~[2]~~ [3] An advocate is responsible for pleadings and other documents prepared for litigation, but is usually not required to have personal knowledge of matters asserted therein, for litigation documents ordinarily present assertions by the client, or by someone on the client's behalf, and not assertions by the lawyer. Compare Rule 3.1. However, an assertion purporting to be on the lawyer's own knowledge, as in an affidavit by the lawyer or in a statement in open court, may properly be made only when the lawyer knows the assertion is true or believes it to be true on the basis of a reasonably diligent inquiry. There are circumstances where failure to make a disclosure is the equivalent of an affirmative misrepresentation. The obligation prescribed in Rule 1.2(d) not to counsel a client to commit or assist the client in committing a fraud applies in litigation. Regarding compliance with Rule 1.2(d), see the Comment to that Rule. See also the Comment to Rule 8.4(b).

~~Misleading~~ Legal Argument

~~[3]~~ [4] Legal argument based on a knowingly false representation of law constitutes dishonesty toward the tribunal. A lawyer is not required to make a disinterested exposition of the law, but must recognize the existence of pertinent legal authorities. Furthermore, as stated in paragraph (a)~~(3)~~(2), an advocate has a duty to disclose directly adverse authority in the controlling jurisdiction that has not been disclosed by the opposing party. The underlying concept is that legal argument is a discussion seeking to determine the legal premises properly applicable to the case.

~~False~~ Offering Evidence

~~[4]   When evidence that a lawyer knows to be false is provided by a person who is not the client, the lawyer must refuse to offer it regardless of the client's wishes.~~

~~[5]   When false evidence is offered by the client, however, a conflict may arise between the lawyer's duty to keep the client's revelations confidential and the duty of candor to the court. Upon ascertaining that material evidence is false, the lawyer should seek to persuade the client that the evidence should not be offered or, if it has been offered, that its false character should~~

~~immediately be disclosed. If the persuasion is ineffective, the lawyer must take reasonable remedial measures.~~

[5] Paragraph (a)(3) requires that the lawyer refuse to offer evidence that the lawyer knows to be false, regardless of the client's wishes. This duty is premised on the lawyer's obligation as an officer of the court to prevent the trier of fact from being misled by false evidence. A lawyer does not violate this Rule if the lawyer offers the evidence for the purpose of establishing its falsity.

[6] If a lawyer knows that the client intends to testify falsely or wants the lawyer to introduce false evidence, the lawyer should seek to persuade the client that the evidence should not be offered. If the persuasion is ineffective and the lawyer continues to represent the client, the lawyer must refuse to offer the false evidence. If only a portion of a witness's testimony will be false, the lawyer may call the witness to testify but may not elicit or otherwise permit the witness to present the testimony that the lawyer knows is false.

[7] The duties stated in paragraphs (a) and (b) apply to all lawyers, including defense counsel in criminal cases. In some jurisdictions, however, courts have required counsel to present the accused as a witness or to give a narrative statement if the accused so desires, even if counsel knows that the testimony or statement will be false. The obligation of the advocate under the Rules of Professional Conduct is subordinate to such requirements. See also Comment [9].

[8] The prohibition against offering false evidence only applies if the lawyer knows that the evidence is false. A lawyer's reasonable belief that evidence is false does not preclude its presentation to the trier of fact. A lawyer's knowledge that evidence is false, however, can be inferred from the circumstances. See Rule 1.0(f). Thus, although a lawyer should resolve doubts about the veracity of testimony or other evidence in favor of the client, the lawyer cannot ignore an obvious falsehood.

~~Refusing to Offer Proof Believed to Be False~~

~~[14]~~ [9] ~~Generally speaking,~~ Although paragraph (a)(3) only prohibits a lawyer ~~has authority~~ from offering evidence the lawyer knows to be false, it permits the lawyer to refuse to offer testimony or other proof that the lawyer reasonably believes is ~~untrustworthy~~ false. Offering such proof may reflect adversely on the lawyer's ability to discriminate in the quality of evidence and thus impair the lawyer's effectiveness as an advocate. ~~In criminal cases, however, a lawyer may, in some jurisdictions, be denied this authority by constitutional requirements governing the right to counsel.~~ Because of the special protections historically provided criminal defendants, however, this Rule does not permit a lawyer to refuse to offer the testimony of such a client where the lawyer reasonably believes but does not know that the testimony will be false. Unless the lawyer knows the testimony will be false, the lawyer must honor the client's decision to testify. See also Comment [7].

~~Perjury by a Criminal Defendant~~

~~[7]   Whether an advocate for a criminally accused has the same duty of disclosure has been intensely debated. While it is agreed that the lawyer should seek to persuade the client to refrain from perjurious testimony, there has been dispute concerning the lawyer's duty when that persuasion fails. If the confrontation with the client occurs before trial, the lawyer ordinarily can withdraw. Withdrawal before trial may not be possible, however, either because trial is imminent, or because the confrontation with the client does not take place until the trial itself, or because no other counsel is available.~~

~~[8]   The most difficult situation, therefore, arises in a criminal case where the accused insists on testifying when the lawyer knows that the testimony is perjurious. The lawyer's effort to rectify the situation can increase the likelihood of the client's being convicted as well as opening the possibility of a prosecution for perjury. On the other hand, if the lawyer does not exercise control over the proof, the lawyer participates, although in a merely passive way, in deception of the court.~~

~~[9]   Three resolutions of this dilemma have been proposed. One is to permit the accused to testify by a narrative without guidance through the lawyer's questioning. This compromises both contending principles; it exempts the lawyer from the duty to disclose false evidence but subjects the client to an implicit disclosure of information imparted to counsel. Another suggested resolution, of relatively recent origin, is that the advocate be entirely excused from the duty to reveal perjury if the perjury is that of the client. This is a coherent solution but makes the advocate a knowing instrument of perjury.~~

~~[10]   The other resolution of the dilemma is that the lawyer must reveal the client's perjury if necessary to rectify the situation. A criminal accused has a right to the assistance of an advocate, a right to testify and a right of confidential communication with counsel. However, an accused should not have a right to assistance of counsel in committing perjury. Furthermore, an advocate has an obligation, not only in professional ethics but under the law as well, to avoid implication in the commission of perjury or other falsification of evidence. See Rule 1.2(d).~~

Remedial Measures

~~[11]~~ [10]   ~~If perjured testimony or false~~ Having offered material evidence ~~has been offered~~ in the belief that it was true, a lawyer may subsequently come to know that the evidence is false. Or, a lawyer may be surprised when the lawyer's client, or another witness called by the lawyer, offers testimony the lawyer knows to be false, either during the lawyer's direct examination or in response to cross-examination by the opposing lawyer. In such situations or if the lawyer knows of the falsity of testimony elicited from the client during a deposition, the lawyer must take reasonable remedial measures. In such situations, the advocate's proper course ~~ordinarily~~ is to remonstrate with the client confidentially, advise the client of the lawyer's duty of candor to the tribunal and seek the client's cooperation with respect to the withdrawal or correction of the false statements or evidence. If that fails, the advocate ~~should~~

~~seek to withdraw if that will remedy the situation~~ must take further remedial action. If withdrawal from the representation is not permitted or will not ~~remedy the situation or is impossible~~ undo the effect of the false evidence, the advocate ~~should~~ must make such disclosure to the ~~court~~ tribunal as is reasonably necessary to remedy the situation, even if doing so requires the lawyer to reveal information that otherwise would be protected by Rule 1.6. It is for the ~~court~~ tribunal then to determine what should be done — making a statement about the matter to the trier of fact, ordering a mistrial or perhaps nothing. ~~If the false testimony was that of the client, the client may controvert the lawyer's version of their communication when the lawyer discloses the situation to the court. If there is an issue whether the client has committed perjury, the lawyer cannot represent the client in resolution of the issue, and a mistrial may be unavoidable. An unscrupulous client might in this way attempt to produce a series of mistrials and thus escape prosecution. However, a second such encounter could be construed as a deliberate abuse of the right to counsel and as such a waiver of the right to further representation.~~

~~[6]~~ [11] ~~Except in the defense of a criminal accused, the rule generally recognized is that, if necessary to rectify the situation, an advocate must disclose the existence of the client's deception to the court or to the other party.~~ ~~Such a~~ The disclosure of a client's false testimony can result in grave consequences to the client, including not only a sense of betrayal but also loss of the case and perhaps a prosecution for perjury. But the alternative is that the lawyer cooperate in deceiving the court, thereby subverting the truth-finding process which the adversary system is designed to implement. See Rule 1.2(d). Furthermore, unless it is clearly understood that the lawyer will act upon the duty to disclose the existence of false evidence, the client can simply reject the lawyer's advice to reveal the false evidence and insist that the lawyer keep silent. Thus the client could in effect coerce the lawyer into being a party to fraud on the court.

Preserving Integrity of Adjudicative Process

[12]   Lawyers have a special obligation to protect a tribunal against criminal or fraudulent conduct that undermines the integrity of the adjudicative process, such as bribing, intimidating or otherwise unlawfully communicating with a witness, juror, court official or other participant in the proceeding, unlawfully destroying or concealing documents or other evidence or failing to disclose information to the tribunal when required by law to do so. Thus, paragraph (b) requires a lawyer to take reasonable remedial measures, including disclosure if necessary, whenever the lawyer knows that a person, including the lawyer's client, intends to engage, is engaging or has engaged in criminal or fraudulent conduct related to the proceeding.

~~Constitutional Requirements~~

[12]   The general rule that an advocate must reveal the existence of perjury with respect to a material fact, even that of a client –applies to defense counsel in criminal cases, as well as in other instances. However, the definition of the lawyer's ethical duty in such a situation may be qualified by constitutional

provisions for due process and the right to counsel in criminal cases. In some jurisdictions these provisions have been construed to require that counsel present an accused as a witness if the accused wishes to testify, even if counsel knows the testimony will be false. The obligation of the advocate under these Rules is subordinate to such a constitutional requirement.

Duration of Obligation

[13]   A practical time limit on the obligation to rectify the presentation of false evidence or false statements of law and fact has to be established. The conclusion of the proceeding is a reasonably definite point for the termination of the obligation. A proceeding has concluded within the meaning of this Rule when a final judgment in the proceeding has been affirmed on appeal or the time for review has passed.

Ex Parte Proceedings

[15] [14]   Ordinarily, an advocate has the limited responsibility of presenting one side of the matters that a tribunal should consider in reaching a decision; the conflicting position is expected to be presented by the opposing party. However, in any ex parte proceeding, such as an application for a temporary restraining order, there is no balance of presentation by opposing advocates.The object of an ex parte proceeding is nevertheless to yield a substantially just result. The judge has an affirmative responsibility to accord the absent party just consideration. The lawyer for the represented party has the correlative duty to make disclosures of material facts known to the lawyer and that the lawyer reasonably believes are necessary to an informed decision.

Withdrawal

[15]   Normally, a lawyer's compliance with the duty of candor imposed by this Rule does not require that the lawyer withdraw from the representation of a client whose interests will be or have been adversely affected by the lawyer's disclosure. The lawyer may, however, be required by Rule 1.16(a) to seek permission of the tribunal to withdraw if the lawyer's compliance with this Rule's duty of candor results in such an extreme deterioration of the client-lawyer relationship that the lawyer can no longer competently represent the client. Also see Rule 1.16(b) for the circumstances in which a lawyer will be permitted to seek a tribunal's permission to withdraw. In connection with a request for permission to withdraw that is premised on a client's misconduct, a lawyer may reveal information relating to the representation only to the extent reasonably necessary to comply with this Rule or as otherwise permitted by Rule 1.6.

RULE 3.4: FAIRNESS TO OPPOSING PARTY AND COUNSEL

A lawyer shall not:

(a)   unlawfully obstruct another party's access to evidence or unlawfully alter, destroy or conceal a document or other material having potential evidentiary value. A lawyer shall not counsel or assist another person to do any such act;

     (b)   falsify evidence, counsel or assist a witness to testify falsely, or offer an inducement to a witness that is prohibited by law;

     (c)   knowingly disobey an obligation under the rules of a tribunal, except for an open refusal based on an assertion that no valid obligation exists;

     (d)   in pretrial procedure, make a frivolous discovery request or fail to make reasonably diligent effort to comply with a legally proper discovery request by an opposing party;

     (e)   in trial, allude to any matter that the lawyer does not reasonably believe is relevant or that will not be supported by admissible evidence, assert personal knowledge of facts in issue except when testifying as a witness, or state a personal opinion as to the justness of a cause, the credibility of a witness, the culpability of a civil litigant or the guilt or innocence of an accused; or

     (f)   request a person other than a client to refrain from voluntarily giving relevant information to another party unless:

          (1)   the person is a relative or an employee or other agent of a client; and

          (2)   the lawyer reasonably believes that the person's interests will not be adversely affected by refraining from giving such information.

Comment

     [1]   The procedure of the adversary system contemplates that the evidence in a case is to be marshalled competitively by the contending parties. Fair competition in the adversary system is secured by prohibitions against destruction or concealment of evidence, improperly influencing witnesses, obstructive tactics in discovery procedure, and the like.

     [2]   Documents and other items of evidence are often essential to establish a claim or defense. Subject to evidentiary privileges, the right of an opposing party, including the government, to obtain evidence through discovery or subpoena is an important procedural right. The exercise of that right can be frustrated if relevant material is altered, concealed or destroyed. Applicable law in many jurisdictions makes it an offense to destroy material for purpose of impairing its availability in a pending proceeding or one whose commencement can be foreseen. Falsifying evidence is also generally a criminal offense. Paragraph (a) applies to evidentiary material generally, including computerized information. <u>Applicable law may permit a lawyer to take temporary possession of physical evidence of client crimes for the purpose of conducting a limited examination that will not alter or destroy material characteristics of the evidence. In such a case, applicable law may require the lawyer to turn the evidence over to the police or other prosecuting authority, depending on the circumstances.</u>

     [3]   With regard to paragraph (b), it is not improper to pay a witness's expenses or to compensate an expert witness on terms permitted by law.

The common law rule in most jurisdictions is that it is improper to pay an occurrence witness any fee for testifying and that it is improper to pay an expert witness a contingent fee.

[4]   Paragraph (f) permits a lawyer to advise employees of a client to refrain from giving information to another party, for the employees may identify their interests with those of the client. See also Rule 4.2.

RULE 3.5: IMPARTIALITY AND DECORUM OF THE TRIBUNAL

A lawyer shall not:

(a)   seek to influence a judge, juror, prospective juror or other official by means prohibited by law;

(b)   communicate ex parte with such a person except as permitted during the proceeding unless authorized to do so by law or court order;

(c)   communicate with a juror or prospective juror after discharge of the jury if:

(1)   the communication is prohibited by law or court order;

(2)   the juror has made known to the lawyer a desire not to communicate; or

(3)   the communication involves misrepresentation, coercion, duress or harassment; or

(c) (d)   engage in conduct intended to disrupt a tribunal.

Comment

[1]   Many forms of improper influence upon a tribunal are proscribed by criminal law. Others are specified in the ABA Model Code of Judicial Conduct, with which an advocate should be familiar. A lawyer is required to avoid contributing to a violation of such provisions.

[2]   During a proceeding a lawyer may not communicate ex parte with persons serving in an official capacity in the proceeding, such as judges, masters or jurors, unless authorized to do so by law or court order.

[3]   A lawyer may on occasion want to communicate with a juror or prospective juror after the jury has been discharged. The lawyer may do so unless the communication is prohibited by law or a court order but must respect the desire of the juror not to talk with the lawyer. The lawyer may not engage in improper conduct during the communication.

[2] [4]   The advocate's function is to present evidence and argument so that the cause may be decided according to law. Refraining from abusive or obstreperous conduct is a corollary of the advocate's right to speak on behalf of litigants. A lawyer may stand firm against abuse by a judge but should avoid reciprocation; the judge's default is no justification for similar dereliction by an advocate. An advocate can present the cause, protect the record for subsequent review and preserve professional integrity by patient firmness no less effectively than by belligerence or theatrics.

[5] The duty to refrain from disruptive conduct applies to any proceeding of a tribunal, including a deposition. See Rule 1.0(m).

RULE 3.6: TRIAL PUBLICITY

(a) A lawyer who is participating or has participated in the investigation or litigation of a matter shall not make an extrajudicial statement that a reasonable person would expect to the lawyer knows or reasonably should know will be disseminated by means of public communication if the lawyer knows or reasonably should know that it and will have a substantial likelihood of materially prejudicing an adjudicative proceeding in the matter.

(b) Notwithstanding paragraph (a), a lawyer may state:

(1) the claim, offense or defense involved and, except when prohibited by law, the identity of the persons involved;

(2) information contained in a public record;

(3) that an investigation of a matter is in progress;

(4) the scheduling or result of any step in litigation;

(5) a request for assistance in obtaining evidence and information necessary thereto;

(6) a warning of danger concerning the behavior of a person involved, when there is reason to believe that there exists the likelihood of substantial harm to an individual or to the public interest; and

(7) in a criminal case, in addition to subparagraphs (1) through (6):

(i) the identity, residence, occupation and family status of the accused;

(ii) if the accused has not been apprehended, information necessary to aid in apprehension of that person;

(iii) the fact, time and place of arrest; and

(iv) the identity of investigating and arresting officers or agencies and the length of the investigation.

(c) Notwithstanding paragraph (a), a lawyer may make a statement that a reasonable lawyer would believe is required to protect a client from the substantial undue prejudicial effect of recent publicity not initiated by the lawyer or the lawyer's client. A statement made pursuant to this paragraph shall be limited to such information as is necessary to mitigate the recent adverse publicity.

(d) No lawyer associated in a firm or government agency with a lawyer subject to paragraph (a) shall make a statement prohibited by paragraph (a).

Comment

[1] It is difficult to strike a balance between protecting the right to a fair trial and safeguarding the right of free expression. Preserving the right

to a fair trial necessarily entails some curtailment of the information that may be disseminated about a party prior to trial, particularly where trial by jury is involved. If there were no such limits, the result would be the practical nullification of the protective effect of the rules of forensic decorum and the exclusionary rules of evidence. On the other hand, there are vital social interests served by the free dissemination of information about events having legal consequences and about legal proceedings themselves. The public has a right to know about threats to its safety and measures aimed at assuring its security. It also has a legitimate interest in the conduct of judicial proceedings, particularly in matters of general public concern. Furthermore, the subject matter of legal proceedings is often of direct significance in debate and deliberation over questions of public policy.

[2]   Special rules of confidentiality may validly govern proceedings in juvenile, domestic relations and mental disability proceedings, and perhaps other types of litigation. Rule 3.4(c) requires compliance with such rules.

[3]   The Rule sets forth a basic general prohibition against a lawyer's making statements that the lawyer knows or should know will have a substantial likelihood of materially prejudicing an adjudicative proceeding. Recognizing that the public value of informed commentary is great and the likelihood of prejudice to a proceeding by the commentary of a lawyer who is not involved in the proceeding is small, the rule applies only to lawyers who are, or who have been involved in the investigation or litigation of a case, and their associates.

[4]   Paragraph (b) identifies specific matters about which a lawyer's statements would not ordinarily be considered to present a substantial likelihood of material prejudice, and should not in any event be considered prohibited by the general prohibition of paragraph (a). Paragraph (b) is not intended to be an exhaustive listing of the subjects upon which a lawyer may make a statement, but statements on other matters may be subject to paragraph (a).

[5]   There are, on the other hand, certain subjects that are more likely than not to have a material prejudicial effect on a proceeding, particularly when they refer to a civil matter triable to a jury, a criminal matter, or any other proceeding that could result in incarceration. These subjects relate to:

> (1) the character, credibility, reputation or criminal record of a party, suspect in a criminal investigation or witness, or the identity of a witness, or the expected testimony of a party or witness;

> (2) in a criminal case or proceeding that could result in incarceration, the possibility of a plea of guilty to the offense or the existence or contents of any confession, admission, or statement given by a defendant or suspect or that person's refusal or failure to make a statement;

> (3) the performance or results of any examination or test or the refusal or failure of a person to submit to an

examination or test, or the identity or nature of physical evidence expected to be presented;

(4) any opinion as to the guilt or innocence of a defendant or suspect in a criminal case or proceeding that could result in incarceration;

(5) information that the lawyer knows or reasonably should know is likely to be inadmissible as evidence in a trial and that would, if disclosed, create a substantial risk of prejudicing an impartial trial; or

(6) the fact that a defendant has been charged with a crime, unless there is included therein a statement explaining that the charge is merely an accusation and that the defendant is presumed innocent until and unless proven guilty.

[6] Another relevant factor in determining prejudice is the nature of the proceeding involved. Criminal jury trials will be most sensitive to extrajudicial speech. Civil trials may be less sensitive. Non-jury hearings and arbitration proceedings may be even less affected. The Rule will still place limitations on prejudicial comments in these cases, but the likelihood of prejudice may be different depending on the type of proceeding.

[7] Finally, extrajudicial statements that might otherwise raise a question under this Rule may be permissible when they are made in response to statements made publicly by another party, another party's lawyer, or third persons, where a reasonable lawyer would believe a public response is required in order to avoid prejudice to the lawyer's client. When prejudicial statements have been publicly made by others, responsive statements may have the salutary effect of lessening any resulting adverse impact on the adjudicative proceeding. Such responsive statements should be limited to contain only such information as is necessary to mitigate undue prejudice created by the statements made by others.

[8] See Rule 3.8(f) for additional duties of prosecutors in connection with extrajudicial statements about criminal proceedings.

RULE 3.7: LAWYER AS WITNESS

(a) A lawyer shall not act as advocate at a trial in which the lawyer is likely to be a necessary witness except where unless:

(1) the testimony relates to an uncontested issue;

(2) the testimony relates to the nature and value of legal services rendered in the case; or

(3) disqualification of the lawyer would work substantial hardship on the client.

(b) A lawyer may act as advocate in a trial in which another lawyer in the lawyer's firm is likely to be called as a witness unless precluded from doing so by Rule 1.7 or Rule 1.9.

Comment

[1]   Combining the roles of advocate and witness can prejudice the tribunal and the opposing party and can also involve a conflict of interest between the lawyer and client.

Advocate-Witness Rule

[2]   The tribunal has proper objection when the trier of fact may be confused or misled by a lawyer serving as both advocate and witness. The opposing party has proper objection where the combination of roles may prejudice that party's rights in the litigation. A witness is required to testify on the basis of personal knowledge, while an advocate is expected to explain and comment on evidence given by others. It may not be clear whether a statement by an advocate-witness should be taken as proof or as an analysis of the proof.

[3]   To protect the tribunal, paragraph (a) prohibits a lawyer from simultaneously serving as advocate and necessary witness except in those circumstances specified in paragraphs (a)(1) through (a)(3). Paragraph (a)(1) recognizes that if the testimony will be uncontested, the ambiguities in the dual role are purely theoretical. Paragraph (a)(2) recognizes that where the testimony concerns the extent and value of legal services rendered in the action in which the testimony is offered, permitting the lawyers to testify avoids the need for a second trial with new counsel to resolve that issue. Moreover, in such a situation the judge has firsthand knowledge of the matter in issue; hence, there is less dependence on the adversary process to test the credibility of the testimony.

[4]   Apart from these two exceptions, paragraph (a)(3) recog-nizes that a balancing is required between the interests of the client and those of the tribunal and the opposing party. Whether the tribunal is likely to be misled or the opposing party is likely to suffer prejudice depends on the nature of the case, the importance and probable tenor of the lawyer's testimony, and the probability that the lawyer's testimony will conflict with that of other witnesses. Even if there is risk of such prejudice, in determining whether the lawyer should be disqualified, due regard must be given to the effect of disqualification on the lawyer's client. It is relevant that one or both parties could reasonably foresee that the lawyer would probably be a wit-ness. The ~~principle of imputed disqualification~~ conflict of interest principles stated in ~~Rule~~ Rules 1.7, 1.9 and 1.10 ~~has~~ have no application to this aspect of the problem.

[5]   Because the tribunal is not likely to be misled when a lawyer acts as advocate in a trial in which another lawyer in the lawyer's firm will testify as a necessary witness, paragraph (b) permits the lawyer to do so except in situations involving a conflict of interest.

Conflict of Interest

~~[5]~~ [6]   ~~Whether the combination of roles involves an improper~~ In determining if it is permissible to act as advocate in a trial in which the lawyer will be a necessary witness, the lawyer must also consider that the dual role may give rise to a conflict of interest ~~with respect to the client is determined by Rule~~ that will require compliance with Rules 1.7 or 1.9. For example, if there is likely to be substantial conflict between the testimony of the client and that of the lawyer ~~or a member of the lawyer's firm~~, the representation ~~is improper~~ <u>involves a conflict of interest that requires compliance with Rule 1.7. This would be true even though the lawyer might not be prohibited by paragraph (a) from simultaneously serving as advocate and witness because the lawyer's disqualification would work a substantial hardship on the client. Similarly, a lawyer who might be permitted to simultaneously serve as an advocate and a witness by paragraph (a)(3) might be precluded from doing so by Rule 1.9</u>. The problem can arise whether the lawyer is called as a witness on behalf of the client or is called by the opposing party. Determining whether or not such a conflict exists is primarily the responsibility of the lawyer involved. <u>If there is a conflict of interest, the lawyer must secure the client's informed consent, confirmed in writing. In some cases, the lawyer will be precluded from seeking the client's consent.</u> See ~~Comment to~~ Rule 1.7. ~~If a lawyer who is a member of a firm may not act as both advocate and witness by reason of conflict of interest, Rule 1.10 disqualifies the firm also.~~ <u>See Rule 1.0(b) for the definition of "confirmed in writing" and Rule 1.0(e) for the definition of "informed consent."</u>

[7] <u>Paragraph (b) provides that a lawyer is not disqualified from serving as an advocate because a lawyer with whom the lawyer is associated in a firm is precluded from doing so by paragraph (a). If, however, the testifying lawyer would also be disqualified by Rule 1.7 or Rule 1.9 from representing the client in the matter, other lawyers in the firm will be precluded from representing the client by Rule 1.10 unless the client gives informed consent under the conditions stated in Rule 1.7.</u>

RULE 3.8: SPECIAL RESPONSIBILITIES OF A PROSECUTOR

The prosecutor in a criminal case shall:

(a)   refrain from prosecuting a charge that the prosecutor knows is not supported by probable cause;

(b)   make reasonable efforts to assure that the accused has been advised of the right to, and the procedure for obtaining, counsel and has been given reasonable opportunity to obtain counsel;

(c)   not seek to obtain from an unrepresented accused a waiver of important pretrial rights, such as the right to a preliminary hearing;

(d)   make timely disclosure to the defense of all evidence or information known to the prosecutor that tends to negate the guilt of the accused or mitigates the offense, and, in connection with sentencing, disclose to the defense and to the tribunal all unprivileged mitigating information known to the prosecutor, except when the prosecutor is relieved of this responsibility by a protective order of the tribunal;

~~(e)~~   [See paragraph (f).]

~~(f)~~ <u>(e)</u>   not subpoena a lawyer in a grand jury or other criminal proceeding to present evidence about a past or present client unless the prosecutor reasonably believes:

(1)   the information sought is not protected from disclosure by any applicable privilege;

(2)   the evidence sought is essential to the successful completion of an ongoing investigation or prosecution; and

(3)   there is no other feasible alternative to obtain the information~.~;

~(g)~ (f)   except for statements that are necessary to inform the public of the nature and extent of the prosecutor's action and that serve a legitimate law enforcement purpose, refrain from making extrajudicial comments that have a substantial likelihood of heightening public condemnation of the accused and ~(e)~ exercise reasonable care to prevent investigators, law enforcement personnel, employees or other persons assisting or associated with the prosecutor in a criminal case from making an extrajudicial statement that the prosecutor would be prohibited from making under Rule 3.6 or this Rule.

(g)   When a prosecutor knows of new, credible and material evidence creating a reasonable likelihood that a convicted defendant did not commit an offense of which the defendant was convicted, the prosecutor shall:

(1)   promptly disclose that evidence to an appropriate court or authority, and

(2)   if the conviction was obtained in the prosecutor's jurisdiction,

(A)   promptly disclose that evidence to the defendant unless a court authorizes delay, and

(B)   undertake further investigation, or make reasonable efforts to cause an investigation, to determine whether the defendant was convicted of an offense that the defendant did not commit.

(h)   When a prosecutor knows of clear and convincing evidence establishing that a defendant in the prosecutor's jurisdiction was convicted of an offense that the defendant did not commit, the prosecutor shall seek to remedy the conviction.

Comment

[1]   A prosecutor has the responsibility of a minister of justice and not simply that of an advocate. This responsibility carries with it specific obligations to see that the defendant is accorded procedural justice, ~and~ that guilt is decided upon the basis of sufficient evidence, ~Precisely how far~ and that special precautions are taken to prevent and to rectify the ~prosecutor is required to go in this direction~ conviction of innocent persons. The extent of mandated remedial action is a matter of debate and varies in different jurisdictions. Many jurisdictions have adopted the ABA Standards of Criminal Justice Relating to the Prosecution Function, which ~in turn~ are the product of prolonged and careful deliberation by lawyers experienced in both criminal prosecution and defense. Competent representation of the sovereignty may require a prosecutor to undertake some procedural and remedial measures as a matter of obligation.

~~See also Rule 3.3(d), governing *ex parte* proceedings, among which grand jury~~ ~~proceedings are included.~~ Applicable law may require other measures by the prosecutor and knowing disregard of those obligations or a systematic abuse of prosecutorial discretion could constitute a violation of Rule 8.4.

[2] In some jurisdictions, a defendant may waive a preliminary hearing and thereby lose a valuable opportunity to challenge probable cause. Accordingly, prosecutors should not seek to obtain waivers of preliminary hearings or other important pretrial rights from unrepresented accused persons. Paragraph (c) does not apply, however, to an accused appearing *prose* with the approval of the tribunal. Nor does it forbid the lawful questioning of ~~a~~ an uncharged suspect who has knowingly waived the rights to counsel and silence.

[3] The exception in paragraph (d) recognizes that a prosecutor may seek an appropriate protective order from the tribunal if disclosure of information to the defense could result in substantial harm to an individual or to the public interest.

[4] Paragraph ~~(f)~~ (e) is intended to limit the issuance of lawyer subpoenas in grand jury and other criminal proceedings to those situations in which there is a genuine need to intrude into the client-lawyer relationship.

[5] Paragraph ~~(g)~~ (f) supplements Rule 3.6, which prohibits extrajudicial statements that have a substantial likelihood of prejudicing an adjudicatory proceeding. In the context of a criminal prosecution, a prosecutor's extrajudicial statement can create the additional problem of increasing public condemnation of the accused. Although the announcement of an indictment, for example, will necessarily have severe consequences for the accused, a prosecutor can, and should, avoid comments which have no legitimate law enforcement purpose and have a substantial likelihood of increasing public opprobrium of the accused. Nothing in this Comment is intended to restrict the statements which a prosecutor may make which comply with Rule 3.6(b) or 3.6(c).

[6] Like other lawyers, prosecutors are subject to Rules 5.1 and 5.3, which relate to responsibilities regarding lawyers and nonlawyers who work for or are associated with the lawyer's office. Paragraph (f) reminds the prosecutor of the importance of these obligations in connection with the unique dangers of improper extrajudicial statements in a criminal case. In addition, paragraph (f) requires a prosecutor to exercise reasonable care to prevent persons assisting or associated with the prosecutor from making improper extra-judicial statements, even when such persons are not under the direct supervision of the prosecutor. Ordinarily, the reasonable care standard will be satisfied if the prosecutor issues the appropriate cautions to law enforcement personnel and other relevant individuals.

[7] When a prosecutor knows of new, credible and material evidence creating a reasonable likelihood that a person outside the prosecutor's jurisdiction was convicted of a crime that the person did not commit, paragraph (g) requires prompt disclosure to the court or other appropriate authority, such as the chief prosecutor of the jurisdiction where the conviction occurred. If the conviction was obtained in the prosecutor's jurisdiction, paragraph (g)

requires the prosecutor to examine the evidence and undertake further investigation to determine whether the defendant is in fact innocent or make reasonable efforts to cause another appropriate authority to undertake the necessary investigation, and to promptly disclose the evidence to the court and, absent court-authorized delay, to the defendant. Consistent with the objectives of Rules 4.2 and 4.3, disclosure to a represented defendant must be made through the defendant's counsel, and, in the case of an unrepresented defendant, would ordinarily be accompanied by a request to a court for the appointment of counsel to assist the defendant in taking such legal measures as may be appropriate.

[8]   Under paragraph (h), once the prosecutor knows of clear and convincing evidence that the defendant was convicted of an offense that the defendant did not commit, the prosecutor must seek to remedy the conviction. Necessary steps may include disclosure of the evidence to the defendant, requesting that the court appoint counsel for an unrepresented indigent defendant and, where appropriate, notifying the court that the prosecutor has knowledge that the defendant did not commit the offense of which the defendant was convicted.

[9]   A prosecutor's independent judgment, made in good faith, that the new evidence is not of such nature as to trigger the obligations of sections (g) and (h), though subsequently determined to have been erroneous, does not constitute a violation of this Rule.

RULE 3.9: ADVOCATE IN NONADJUDICATIVE PROCEEDINGS

A lawyer representing a client before a legislative body or administrative tribunal agency in a nonadjudicative proceeding shall disclose that the appearance is in a representative capacity and shall conform to the provisions of Rules 3.3(a) through (c), 3.4(a) through (c), and 3.5.

Comment

[1]   In representation before bodies such as legislatures, municipal councils, and executive and administrative agencies acting in a rule-making or policy-making capacity, lawyers present facts, formulate issues and advance argument in the matters under consideration. The decision-making body, like a court, should be able to rely on the integrity of the submissions made to it. A lawyer appearing before such a body should must deal with the tribunal it honestly and in conformity with applicable rules of procedure. See Rules 3.3(a) through (c), 3.4(a) through (c) and 3.5.

[2]   Lawyers have no exclusive right to appear before nonadjudicative bodies, as they do before a court. The requirements of this Rule therefore may subject lawyers to regulations inapplicable to advocates who are not lawyers. However, legislatures and administrative agencies have a right to expect lawyers to deal with them as they deal with courts.

[3]   This Rule only applies when a lawyer represents a client in connection with an official hearing or meeting of a governmental agency or a

legislative body to which the lawyer or the lawyer's client is presenting evi-dence or argument. It does not apply to representation of a client in a negotia-tion or other bilateral transaction with a governmental agency; representation or in connection with an application for a license or other privilege or the cli-ent's compliance with generally applicable reporting requirements, such as the filing of income-tax returns. Nor does it apply to the representation of a client in connection with an investigation or examination of the client's affairs con-ducted by government investigators or examiners. Representation in such a transaction matters is governed by Rules 4.1 through 4.4.

RULE 4.1: TRUTHFULNESS IN STATEMENTS TO OTHERS

In the course of representing a client a lawyer shall not knowingly:

(a)   make a false statement of material fact or law to a third person; or

(b)   fail to disclose a material fact when disclosure is necessary to avoid assisting a criminal or fraudulent act by a client, unless disclosure is prohibited by Rule 1.6.

Comment

Misrepresentation

[1]   A lawyer is required to be truthful when dealing with others on a client's behalf, but generally has no affirmative duty to inform an opposing party of relevant facts. A misrepresentation can occur if the lawyer incorpo-rates or affirms a statement of another person that the lawyer knows is false. Misrepresentations can also occur by failure to act partially true but mis-leading statements or omissions that are the equivalent of affirmative false statements. For dishonest conduct that does not amount to a false statement or for misrepresentations by a lawyer other than in the course of representing a client, see Rule 8.4.

Statements of Fact

[2]   This Rule refers to statements of fact. Whether a particular statement should be regarded as one of fact can depend on the circumstances. Under generally accepted conventions in negotiation, certain types of state-ments ordinarily are not taken as statements of material fact. Estimates of price or value placed on the subject of a transaction and a party's intentions as to an acceptable settlement of a claim are ordinarily in this category, and so is the existence of an undisclosed principal except where nondisclosure of the principal would constitute fraud. Lawyers should be mindful of their obliga-tions under applicable law to avoid criminal and tortious misrepresentation.

Crime or Fraud by Client

[3]   Under Rule 1.2(d), a lawyer is prohibited from counseling or assisting a client in conduct that the lawyer knows is criminal or fraudulent. Paragraph (b) recognizes that states a specific application of the principle set forth in Rule 1.2(d) and addresses the situation where a client's crime or fraud

takes the form of a lie or misrepresentation. Ordinarily, a lawyer can avoid assisting a client's crime or fraud by withdrawing from the representation. Sometimes it may be necessary for the lawyer to give notice of the fact of withdrawal and to disaffirm an opinion, document, affirmation or the like. In extreme cases, substantive law may require a lawyer to disclose ~~certain~~ information relating to the representation to avoid being deemed to have assisted the client's crime or fraud. ~~The requirement of~~ If the lawyer can avoid assisting a client's crime or fraud only by disclosing this information, then under paragraph (b) the lawyer is required to do so, unless the disclosure ~~created by this paragraph is, however, subject to the obligations created~~ is prohibited by Rule 1.6.

RULE 4.2: COMMUNICATION WITH PERSON REPRESENTED BY COUNSEL

In representing a client, a lawyer shall not communicate about the subject of the representation with a person the lawyer knows to be represented by another lawyer in the matter, unless the lawyer has the consent of the other lawyer or is authorized to do so by law ~~to do so~~ or a court order.

Comment

[1] This Rule contributes to the proper functioning of the legal system by protecting a person who has chosen to be represented by a lawyer in a matter against possible overreaching by other lawyers who are participating in the matter, interference by those lawyers with the client-lawyer relationship and the uncounselled disclosure of information relating to the representation.

~~[3]~~ [2] This Rule also applies to communications with any person~~,~~ ~~whether or not a party to a formal adjudicative proceeding, contract or nego-~~ ~~tiation,~~ who is represented by counsel concerning the matter to which the communication relates.

[3] The Rule applies even though the represented person initiates or consents to the communication. A lawyer must immediately terminate communication with a person if, after commencing communication, the lawyer learns that the person is one with whom communication is not permitted by this Rule.

~~[1]~~ [4] This Rule does not prohibit communication with a represented person, or an employee or agent of such a person, concerning matters outside the representation. For example, the existence of a controversy between a government agency and a private party, or between two organizations, does not prohibit a lawyer for either from communicating with nonlawyer representatives of the other regarding a separate matter. ~~Also, parties~~ Nor does this Rule preclude communication with a represented person who is seeking advice from a lawyer who is not otherwise representing a client in the matter. A lawyer may not make a communication prohibited by this Rule through the acts of another. See Rule 8.4(a). Parties to a matter may communicate directly with each other, and a lawyer is not prohibited from advising a client concerning a communication that the client is legally entitled to make.Also, a lawyer having independent jus-tification or legal authorization for communicating with a represented person is permitted to do so. ~~Communications authorized by law include, for example, the right of a party to a controversy with a government agency to speak with government officials about the matter.~~

[5] Communications authorized by law may include communica-tions by a lawyer on behalf of a client who is exercising a constitutional or other legal right to communicate with the government. ~~[2]~~ Communications authorized by law may also include ~~constitutionally permissible~~ investigative activities of lawyers representing governmental entities, directly or through investigative agents, prior to the commencement of criminal or civil enforce-ment proceedings, ~~when there is applicable judicial precedent that either has found the activity permissible under this Rule or has found this Rule inappli-cable. However, the Rule imposes ethical restrictions that go beyond those imposed by constitutional provisions~~. When communicating with the accused in a criminal matter, a government lawyer must comply with this Rule in addition to honoring the constitutional rights of the accused. The fact that a communication does not violate a state or federal constitutional right is insuf-ficient to establish that the communication is permissible under this Rule.

[6] A lawyer who is uncertain whether a communication with a represented person is permissible may seek a court order. A lawyer may also seek a court order in exceptional circumstances to authorize a communication that would otherwise be prohibited by this Rule, for example, where communi-cation with a person represented by counsel is necessary to avoid reason-ably certain injury.

~~[4]~~ [7] In the case of ~~an~~ a represented organization, this Rule prohibits communications ~~by a lawyer for another person or entity concerning the matter in representation~~ with ~~persons having a managerial responsibility on behalf~~ a constituent of the organization, ~~and with any other person~~ who supervises, directs or regularly consults with the organization's lawyer concerning the matter or has authority to obligate the organization with respect to the matter or whose act or omission in connection with ~~that~~ the matter may be imputed to the organization for purposes of civil or criminal liability ~~or whose statement may constitute an admission on the part of the organization~~. Consent of the organization's lawyer is not required for communication with a former constituent. If ~~an agent or employee~~ a constituent of the organization is repre-sented in the matter by his or her own counsel, the consent by that counsel to a communication will be sufficient for purposes of this Rule. Compare Rule 3.4(f). In communicating with a current or former constituent of an orga-nization, a lawyer must not use methods of obtaining evidence that violate the legal rights of the organization. See Rule 4.4.

~~[5]~~ [8] The prohibition on communications with a represented person only applies, ~~however,~~ in circumstances where the lawyer knows that the person is in fact represented in the matter to be discussed. This means that the lawyer has actual knowledge of the fact of the representation; but such actual knowledge may be inferred from the circumstances. See ~~Terminology Rule 1.0(f). Such an inference may arise in circumstances where there is substantial reason to believe that the person with whom communication is sought is represented in the matter to be discussed.~~ Thus, the lawyer cannot evade the requirement of obtaining the consent of counsel by closing eyes to the obvious.

~~[6]~~ [9] In the event the person with whom the lawyer communicates is not known to be represented by counsel in the matter, the lawyer's communications are subject to Rule 4.3.

RULE 4.3: DEALING WITH UNREPRESENTED PERSON

In dealing on behalf of a client with a person who is not represented by counsel, a lawyer shall not state or imply that the lawyer is disinterested. When the lawyer knows or reasonably should know that the unrepresented person misunderstands the lawyer's role in the matter, the lawyer shall make reasonable efforts to correct the misunderstanding. <u>The lawyer shall not give legal advice to an unrepresented person, other than the advice to secure counsel, if the lawyer knows or reasonably should know that the interests of such a person are or have a reasonable possibility of being in conflict with the interests of the client.</u>

Comment

[1]   An unrepresented person, particularly one not experienced in dealing with legal matters, might assume that a lawyer is disinterested in loyalties or is a disinterested authority on the law even when the lawyer represents a client. ~~During the course of a lawyer's representation of a client, the lawyer should not give advice to an unrepresented person other than the advice to obtain counsel.~~ <u>In order to avoid a misunderstanding, a lawyer will typically need to identify the lawyer's client and, where necessary, explain that the client has interests opposed to those of the unrepresented person. For misunderstandings that sometimes arise when a lawyer for an organization deals with an unrepresented constituent, see Rule 1.13(d).</u>

[2]   <u>The Rule distinguishes between situations involving unrepresented persons whose interests may be adverse to those of the lawyer's client and those in which the person's interests are not in conflict with the client's. In the former situation, the possibility that the lawyer will compromise the unrepresented person's interests is so great that the Rule prohibits the giving of any advice, apart from the advice to obtain counsel. Whether a lawyer is giving impermissible advice may depend on the experience and sophistication of the unrepresented person, as well as the setting in which the behavior and comments occur. This Rule does not prohibit a lawyer from negotiating the terms of a transaction or settling a dispute with an unrepresented person. So long as the lawyer has explained that the lawyer represents an adverse party and is not representing the person, the lawyer may inform the person of the terms on which the lawyer's client will enter into an agreement or settle a matter, prepare documents that require the person's signature and explain the lawyer's own view of the meaning of the document or the lawyer's view of the underlying legal obligations.</u>

RULE 4.4: RESPECT FOR RIGHTS OF THIRD PERSONS

(a)　　In representing a client, a lawyer shall not use means that have no substantial purpose other than to embarrass, delay, or burden a third person, or use methods of obtaining evidence that violate the legal rights of such a person.

(b)　　A lawyer who receives a document or electronically stored information relating to the representation of the lawyer's client and knows or reasonably should know that the document or electronically stored information was inadvertently sent shall promptly notify the sender.

Comment

[1]　　Responsibility to a client requires a lawyer to subordinate the interests of others to those of the client, but that responsibility does not imply that a lawyer may disregard the rights of third persons. It is impractical to catalogue all such rights, but they include legal restrictions on methods of obtaining evidence from third persons and unwarranted intrusions into privileged relationships, such as the client-lawyer relationship.

[2]　　Paragraph (b) recognizes that lawyers sometimes receive a document or electronically stored information that was mistakenly sent or produced by opposing parties or their lawyers. A document or electronically stored information is inadvertently sent when it is accidentally transmitted, such as when an email or letter is misaddressed or a document or electronically stored information is accidentally included with information that was intentionally transmitted. If a lawyer knows or reasonably should know that a such a document or electronically stored information was sent inadvertently, then this Rule requires the lawyer to promptly notify the sender in order to permit that person to take protective measures. Whether the lawyer is required to take additional steps, such as returning the document or [deleting][1] electronically stored information, is a matter of law beyond the scope of these Rules, as is the question of whether the privileged status of a document or electronically stored information has been waived. Similarly, this Rule does not address the legal duties of a lawyer who receives a document or electronically stored information that the lawyer knows or reasonably should know may have been inappropriately obtained by the sending person. For purposes of this Rule, "document or electronically stored information" includes, in addition to paper documents, email and other forms of electronically stored information, including embedded data (commonly referred to as "metadata"), that is subject to being read or put into readable form. Metadata in electronic documents creates an obligation under this Rule only if the receiving lawyer knows or reasonably should know that the metadata was inadvertently sent to the receiving lawyer.

---

[1] **Editors' Note:** We have added the word "deleting" in brackets to conform this sentence with Comment [3], which was revised on the floor of the House of Delegates in August 2012 when it was recognized that "electronically stored information" typically will be deleted rather than returned to the sending party. At the time of publication, it was not known whether this conforming change can be made administratively or whether the rule must be submitted to the House of Delegates.

[3]   Some lawyers may choose to return a document or delete elec-tronically stored information unread, for example, when the lawyer learns before receiving it that it was inadvertently sent. Where a lawyer is not required by applicable law to do so, the decision to voluntarily return such a document or delete electronically stored information is a matter of professional judgment ordinarily reserved to the lawyer. See Rules 1.2 and 1.4.

RULE 5.1: RESPONSIBILITIES OF A PARTNER OR PARTNERS, MANAGERS, AND SUPERVISORY LAWYER LAWYERS

(a)   A partner in a law firm, and a lawyer who individually or together with other lawyers possesses comparable managerial authority in a law firm, shall make reasonable efforts to ensure that the firm has in effect measures giving reasonable assurance that all lawyers in the firm conform to the Rules of Professional Conduct.

(b)   A lawyer having direct supervisory authority over another lawyer shall make reasonable efforts to ensure that the other lawyer conforms to the Rules of Professional Conduct.

(c)   A lawyer shall be responsible for another lawyer's violation of the Rules of Professional Conduct if:

(1)   the lawyer orders or, with knowledge of the specific conduct, ratifies the conduct involved; or

(2)   the lawyer is a partner or has comparable managerial authority in the law firm in which the other lawyer practices, or has direct supervisory authority over the other lawyer, and knows of the conduct at a time when its consequences can be avoided or mitigated but fails to take reasonable remedial action.

Comment

[1]   Paragraphs Paragraph (a) and (b) refer applies to lawyers who have supervisory managerial authority over the professional work of a firm or legal department of a government agency. See Rule 1.0(c). This includes members of a partnership and, the shareholders in a law firm organized as a professional corporation, and members of other associations authorized to practice law; lawyers having supervisory comparable managerial authority in the a legal services organization or a law department of an enterprise or government agency; and lawyers who have intermediate managerial responsibilities in a firm. Paragraph (b) applies to lawyers who have supervisory authority over the work of other lawyers in a firm.

[2]   Paragraph (a) requires lawyers with managerial authority within a firm to make reasonable efforts to establish internal policies and procedures designed to provide reasonable assurance that all lawyers in the firm will conform to the Rules of Professional Conduct. Such policies and procedures include those designed to detect and resolve conflicts of interest, identify dates

by which actions must be taken in pending matters, account for client funds and property and ensure that inexperienced lawyers are properly supervised.

[2] [3] The Other measures that may be required to fulfill the responsibility prescribed in paragraphs paragraph (a) and (b) can depend on the firm's structure and the nature of its practice. In a small firm of experienced lawyers, informal supervision and occasional admonition periodic review of compliance with the required systems ordinarily might be sufficient will suffice. In a large firm, or in practice situations in which intensely difficult ethical problems frequently arise, more elaborate procedures measures may be necessary. Some firms, for example, have a procedure whereby junior lawyers can make confidential referral of ethical problems directly to a designated senior partner or special committee. See Rule 5.2. Firms, whether large or small, may also rely on continuing legal education in professional ethics. In any event, the ethical atmosphere of a firm can influence the conduct of all its members and a lawyer having authority over the work of another the partners may not assume that the subordinate lawyer all lawyers associated with the firm will inevitably conform to the Rules.

[3] [4] Paragraph (c)(1) expresses a general principle of personal responsibility for acts of another. See also Rule 8.4(a).

[4] [5] Paragraph (c)(2) defines the duty of a partner or other lawyer having comparable managerial authority in a law firm, as well as a lawyer who has direct supervisory authority over performance of specific legal work by another lawyer. Whether a lawyer has supervisory authority in particular circumstances is a question of fact. Partners of a private firm and lawyers with comparable authority have at least indirect responsibility for all work being done by the firm, while a partner or manager in charge of a particular matter ordinarily also has direct authority over supervisory responsibility for the work of other firm lawyers engaged in the matter. Appropriate remedial action by a partner or managing lawyer would depend on the immediacy of the partner's that lawyer's involvement and the seriousness of the misconduct. The A supervisor is required to intervene to prevent avoidable consequences of misconduct if the supervisor knows that the misconduct occurred. Thus, if a supervising lawyer knows that a subordinate misrepresented a matter to an opposing party in negotiation, the supervisor as well as the subordinate has a duty to correct the resulting misapprehension.

[5] [6] Professional misconduct by a lawyer under supervision could reveal a violation of paragraph (b) on the part of the supervisory lawyer even though it does not entail a violation of paragraph (c) because there was no direction, ratification or knowledge of the violation.

[6] [7] Apart from this Rule and Rule 8.4(a), a lawyer does not have disciplinary liability for the conduct of a partner, associate or subordinate. Whether a lawyer may be liable civilly or criminally for another lawyer's conduct is a question of law beyond the scope of these Rules.

[8] The duties imposed by this Rule on managing and supervising lawyers do not alter the personal duty of each lawyer in a firm to abide by the Rules of Professional Conduct. See Rule 5.2(a).

RULE 5.2: RESPONSIBILITIES OF A SUBORDINATE LAWYER

(a) A lawyer is bound by the Rules of Professional Conduct notwithstanding that the lawyer acted at the direction of another person.

(b) A subordinate lawyer does not violate the Rules of Professional Conduct if that lawyer acts in accordance with a supervisory lawyer's reasonable resolution of an arguable question of professional duty.

Comment

[1] Although a lawyer is not relieved of responsibility for a violation by the fact that the lawyer acted at the direction of a supervisor, that fact may be relevant in determining whether a lawyer had the knowledge required to render conduct a violation of the Rules. For example, if a subordinate filed a frivolous pleading at the direction of a supervisor, the subordinate would not be guilty of a professional violation unless the subordinate knew of the document's frivolous character.

[2] When lawyers in a supervisor-subordinate relationship encounter a matter involving professional judgment as to ethical duty, the supervisor may assume responsibility for making the judgment. Otherwise a consistent course of action or position could not be taken. If the question can reasonably be answered only one way, the duty of both lawyers is clear and they are equally responsible for fulfilling it. However, if the question is reasonably arguable, someone has to decide upon the course of action. That authority ordinarily reposes in the supervisor, and a subordinate may be guided accordingly. For example, if a question arises whether the interests of two clients conflict under Rule 1.7, the supervisor's reasonable resolution of the question should protect the subordinate professionally if the resolution is subsequently challenged.

RULE 5.3: RESPONSIBILITIES REGARDING NONLAWYER ASSISTANTSCE

With respect to a nonlawyer employed or retained by or associated with a lawyer:

(a) a partner, and a lawyer who individually or together with other lawyers possesses comparable managerial authority in a law firm shall make reasonable efforts to ensure that the firm has in effect measures giving reasonable assurance that the person's conduct is compatible with the professional obligations of the lawyer;

(b) a lawyer having direct supervisory authority over the nonlawyer shall make reasonable efforts to ensure that the person's conduct is compatible with the professional obligations of the lawyer; and

(c)   a lawyer shall be responsible for conduct of such a person that would be a violation of the Rules of Professional Conduct if engaged in by a lawyer if:

(1)   the lawyer orders or, with the knowledge of the specific conduct, ratifies the conduct involved; or

(2)   the lawyer is a partner <u>or has comparable managerial authority</u> in the law firm in which the person is employed, or has direct supervisory authority over the person, and knows of the conduct at a time when its consequences can be avoided or mitigated but fails to take reasonable remedial action.

Comment

<u>[1]   Paragraph (a) requires lawyers with managerial authority within a law firm to make reasonable efforts to ensure that the firm has in effect measures giving reasonable assurance that nonlawyers in the firm and nonlawyers outside the firm who work on firm matters act in a way compatible with the professional obligations of the lawyer. See Comment [6] to Rule 1.1 (retaining lawyers outside the firm) and Comment [1] to Rule 5.1 (responsibilities with respect to lawyers within a firm). Paragraph (b) applies to lawyers who have supervisory authority over such nonlawyers within or outside the firm. Paragraph (c) specifies the circumstances in which a lawyer is responsible for the conduct of such nonlawyers within or outside the firm that would be a violation of the Rules of Professional Conduct if engaged in by a lawyer.</u>

Nonlawyers within the firm

[~~1~~2]   Lawyers generally employ assistants in their practice, including secretaries, investigators, law student interns, and paraprofessionals. Such assistants, whether employees or independent contractors, act for the lawyer in rendition of the lawyer's professional services. A lawyer ~~should~~ <u>must</u> give such assistants appropriate instruction and supervision concerning the ethical aspects of their employment, particularly regarding the obligation not to disclose information relating to representation of the client, and should be responsible for their work product. The measures employed in supervising nonlawyers should take account of the fact that they do not have legal training and are not subject to professional discipline.

Nonlawyers outside the firm

<u>[3]   A lawyer may use nonlawyers outside the firm to assist the lawyer in rendering legal services to the client. Examples include the retention of an investigative or paraprofessional service, hiring a document management company to create and maintain a database for complex litigation, sending client documents to a third party for printing or scanning, and using an Internet-based service to store client information. When using such services outside the firm, a lawyer must make reasonable efforts to ensure that the services are provided in a manner that is compatible with the lawyer's professional</u>

obligations. The extent of this obligation will depend upon the circumstances, including the education, experience and reputation of the nonlawyer; the nature of the services involved; the terms of any arrangements concerning the protection of client information; and the legal and ethical environments of the jurisdictions in which the services will be performed, particularly with regard to confidentiality. See also Rules 1.1 (competence), 1.2 (allocation of authority), 1.4 (communication with client), 1.6 (confidentiality), 5.4(a) (professional independence of the lawyer), and 5.5(a) (unauthorized practice of law). When retaining or directing a nonlawyer outside the firm, a lawyer should communicate directions appropriate under the circumstances to give reasonable assurance that the nonlawyer's conduct is compatible with the professional obligations of the lawyer.

[4]   Where the client directs the selection of a particular nonlawyer service provider outside the firm, the lawyer ordinarily should agree with the client concerning the allocation of responsibility for monitoring as between the client and the lawyer. See Rule 1.2. When making such an allocation in a matter pending before a tribunal, lawyers and parties may have additional obligations that are a matter of law beyond the scope of these Rules.

RULE 5.4: PROFESSIONAL INDEPENDENCE OF A LAWYER

(a)   A lawyer or law firm shall not share legal fees with a non-lawyer, except that:

(1)   an agreement by a lawyer with the lawyer's firm, partner, or associate may provide for the payment of money, over a reasonable period of time after the lawyer's death, to the lawyer's estate or to one or more specified persons;

(2)   a lawyer who purchases the practice of a deceased, disabled, or disappeared lawyer may, pursuant to the provisions of Rule 1.17, pay to the estate or other representative of that lawyer the agreed-upon purchase price; and

(3)   a lawyer or law firm may include nonlawyer employees in a compensation or retirement plan, even though the plan is based in whole or in part on a profit-sharing arrangement; and

(4)   a lawyer may share court-awarded legal fees with a nonprofit organization that employed, retained or recommended employment of the lawyer in the matter.

(b)   A lawyer shall not form a partnership with a nonlawyer if any of the activities of the partnership consist of the practice of law.

(c)   A lawyer shall not permit a person who recommends, employs, or pays the lawyer to render legal services for another to direct or regulate the lawyer's professional judgment in rendering such legal services.

(d)   A lawyer shall not practice with or in the form of a professional corporation or association authorized to practice law for a profit, if:

(1)   a nonlawyer owns any interest therein, except that a fiduciary representative of the estate of a lawyer may hold the stock or interest of the lawyer for a reasonable time during administration;

(2)   a nonlawyer is a corporate director or officer thereof <u>or occupies the position of similar responsibility in any form of association other than a corporation</u>; or

(3)   a nonlawyer has the right to direct or control the professional judgment of a lawyer.

Comment

[1]   The provisions of this Rule express traditional limitations on sharing fees. These limitations are to protect the lawyer's professional independence of judgment. Where someone other than the client pays the lawyer's fee or salary, or recommends employment of the lawyer, that arrangement does not modify the lawyer's obligation to the client. As stated in paragraph (c), such arrangements should not interfere with the lawyer's professional judgment.

[2]   <u>This Rule also expresses traditional limitations on permitting a third party to direct or regulate the lawyer's professional judgment in rendering legal services to another. See also Rule 1.8(f) (lawyer may accept compensation from a third party as long as there is no interference with the lawyer's independent professional judgment and the client gives informed consent).</u>

RULE 5.5: ~~UNAUTHORIZED PRACTICE OF LAW~~ <u>MULTIJURISDICTIONAL PRACTICE OF LAW</u>

<u>(a)</u>   A lawyer shall not~~: (a)~~ practice law in a jurisdiction ~~where doing so violates~~ <u>in violation of</u> the regulation of the legal profession in that jurisdiction<u>;</u>, or ~~(b)~~ assist ~~a person who is not a member of the bar~~ <u>another</u> in ~~the performance of activity that constitutes the unauthorized practice of law~~ <u>doing so.</u>

<u>(b)</u>   <u>A lawyer who is not admitted to practice in this jurisdiction shall not:</u>

<u>(1)   except as authorized by these Rules or other law, establish an office or other systematic and continuous presence in this jurisdiction for the practice of law; or</u>

<u>(2)   hold out to the public or otherwise represent that the lawyer is admitted to practice law in this jurisdiction.</u>

<u>(c)   A lawyer admitted in another United States jurisdiction, and not disbarred or suspended from practice in any jurisdiction, may provide legal services on a temporary basis in this jurisdiction that:</u>

<u>(1)   are undertaken in association with a lawyer who is admitted to practice in this jurisdiction and who actively participates in the matter;</u>

(2)   are in or reasonably related to a pending or potential proceeding before a tribunal in this or another jurisdiction, if the lawyer, or a person the lawyer is assisting, is authorized by law or order to appear in such proceeding or reasonably expects to be so authorized;

(3)   are in or reasonably related to a pending or potential arbitration, mediation, or other alternative dispute resolution proceeding in this or another jurisdiction, if the services arise out of or are reasonably related to the lawyer's practice in a jurisdiction in which the lawyer is admitted to practice and are not services for which the forum requires pro hac vice admission; or

(4)   are not within paragraphs (c)(2) or (c)(3) and arise out of or are reasonably related to the lawyer's practice in a jurisdiction in which the lawyer is admitted to practice.

(d)   A lawyer admitted in another United States jurisdiction or in a foreign jurisdiction, and not disbarred or suspended from practice in any jurisdiction or the equivalent thereof, may provide legal services through an office or other systematic and continuous presence in this jurisdiction that:

(1)   are provided to the lawyer's employer or its organizational affiliates; and are not services for which the forum requires pro hac vice admission; and, when performed by a foreign lawyer and requires advice on the law of this or another jurisdiction or of the United States, such advice shall be based upon the advice of a lawyer who is duly licensed and authorized by the jurisdiction to provide such advice; or

(2)   are services that the lawyer is authorized to provide by federal law or other law or rule of this jurisdiction.

(e)   For purposes of paragraph (d), the foreign lawyer must be a member in good standing of a recognized legal profession in a foreign jurisdiction, the members of which are admitted to practice as lawyers or counselors at law or the equivalent, and are subject to effective regulation and discipline by a duly constituted professional body or a public authority.

Comment

[1]   A lawyer may practice law only in a jurisdiction in which the lawyer is authorized to practice. A lawyer may be admitted to practice law in a jurisdiction on a regular basis or may be authorized by court rule or order or by law to practice for a limited purpose or on a restricted basis. Paragraph (a) applies to unauthorized practice of law by a lawyer, whether through the lawyer's direct action or by the lawyer assisting another person. For example, a lawyer may not assist a person in practicing law in violation of the rules governing professional conduct in that person's jurisdiction.

[1] [2] The definition of the practice of law is established by law and varies from one jurisdiction to another. Whatever the definition, limiting the practice of law to members of the bar protects the public against rendition of

legal services by unqualified persons. ~~Paragraph (b)~~ This Rule does not prohibit a lawyer from employing the services of paraprofessionals and delegating functions to them, so long as the lawyer supervises the delegated work and retains responsibility for their work. See Rule 5.3.

[3]   ~~Likewise, it does not prohibit lawyers from providing~~ A lawyer may provide professional advice and instruction to nonlawyers whose employment requires knowledge of the law; for example, claims adjusters, employees of financial or commercial institutions, social workers, accountants and persons employed in government agencies. Lawyers also may assist independent nonlawyers, such as paraprofessionals, who are authorized by the law of a jurisdiction to provide particular law-related services. In addition, a lawyer may counsel nonlawyers who wish to proceed prose.

[4]   Other than as authorized by law or this Rule, a lawyer who is not admitted to practice generally in this jurisdiction violates paragraph (b) if the lawyer establishes an office or other systematic and continuous presence in this jurisdiction for the practice of law. Presence may be systematic and continuous even if the lawyer is not physically present here. Such a lawyer must not hold out to the public or otherwise represent that the lawyer is admitted to practice law in this jurisdiction. See also Rules 7.1(a) and 7.5(b).

[5]   There are occasions in which a lawyer admitted to practice in another United States jurisdiction, and not disbarred or suspended from practice in any jurisdiction, may provide legal services on a temporary basis in this jurisdiction under circumstances that do not create an unreasonable risk to the interests of their clients, the public or the courts. Paragraph (c) identifies four such circumstances. The fact that conduct is not so identified does not imply that the conduct is or is not authorized. With the exception of paragraphs (d)(1) and (d)(2), this Rule does not authorize a U.S. or foreign lawyer to establish an office or other systematic and continuous presence in this jurisdiction without being admitted to practice generally here.

[6]   There is no single test to determine whether a lawyer's services are provided on a "temporary basis" in this jurisdiction, and may therefore be permissible under paragraph (c). Services may be "temporary" even though the lawyer provides services in this jurisdiction on a recurring basis, or for an extended period of time, as when the lawyer is representing a client in a single lengthy negotiation or litigation.

[7]   Paragraphs (c) and (d) apply to lawyers who are admitted to practice law in any United States jurisdiction, which includes the District of Columbia and any state, territory or commonwealth of the United States. Paragraph (d) also applies to lawyers admitted in a foreign jurisdiction. The word "admitted" in paragraphs (c), (d) and (e) contemplates that the lawyer is authorized to practice in the jurisdiction in which the lawyer is admitted and excludes a lawyer who while technically admitted is not authorized to practice, because, for example, the lawyer is on inactive status.

[8]   Paragraph (c)(1) recognizes that the interests of clients and the public are protected if a lawyer admitted only in another jurisdiction

associates with a lawyer licensed to practice in this jurisdiction. For this paragraph to apply, however, the lawyer admitted to practice in this jurisdiction must actively participate in and share responsibility for the representation of the client.

[9] Lawyers not admitted to practice generally in a jurisdiction may be authorized by law or order of a tribunal or an administrative agency to appear before the tribunal or agency. This authority may be granted pursuant to formal rules governing admission prohac vice or pursuant to informal practice of the tribunal or agency. Under paragraph (c)(2), a lawyer does not violate this Rule when the lawyer appears before a tribunal or agency pursuant to such authority. To the extent that a court rule or other law of this jurisdiction requires a lawyer who is not admitted to practice in this jurisdiction to obtain admission prohac vice before appearing before a tribunal or administrative agency, this Rule requires the lawyer to obtain that authority.

[10] Paragraph (c)(2) also provides that a lawyer rendering services in this jurisdiction on a temporary basis does not violate this Rule when the lawyer engages in conduct in anticipation of a proceeding or hearing in a jurisdiction in which the lawyer is authorized to practice law or in which the lawyer reasonably expects to be admitted prohac vice. Examples of such conduct include meetings with the client, interviews of potential witnesses, and the review of documents. Similarly, a lawyer admitted only in another jurisdiction may engage in conduct temporarily in this jurisdiction in connection with pending litigation in another jurisdiction in which the lawyer is or reasonably expects to be authorized to appear, including taking depositions in this jurisdiction.

[11] When a lawyer has been or reasonably expects to be admitted to appear before a court or administrative agency, paragraph (c)(2) also permits conduct by lawyers who are associated with that lawyer in the matter, but who do not expect to appear before the court or administrative agency. For example, subordinate lawyers may conduct research, review documents, and attend meetings with witnesses in support of the lawyer responsible for the litigation.

[12] Paragraph (c)(3) permits a lawyer admitted to practice law in another jurisdiction to perform services on a temporary basis in this jurisdiction if those services are in or reasonably related to a pending or potential arbitration, mediation, or other alternative dispute resolution proceeding in this or another jurisdiction, if the services arise out of or are reasonably related to the lawyer's practice in a jurisdiction in which the lawyer is admitted to practice. The lawyer, however, must obtain admission prohac vice in the case of a court-annexed arbitration or mediation or otherwise if court rules or law so require.

[13] Paragraph (c)(4) permits a lawyer admitted in another jurisdiction to provide certain legal services on a temporary basis in this jurisdiction that arise out of or are reasonably related to the lawyer's practice in a jurisdiction

in which the lawyer is admitted but are not within paragraphs (c)(2) or (c)(3). These services include both legal services and services that nonlawyers may perform but that are considered the practice of law when performed by lawyers.

[14]   Paragraphs (c)(3) and (c)(4) require that the services arise out of or be reasonably related to the lawyer's practice in a jurisdiction in which the lawyer is admitted. A variety of factors evidence such a relationship. The lawyer's client may have been previously represented by the lawyer, or may be resident in or have substantial contacts with the jurisdiction in which the lawyer is admitted. The matter, although involving other jurisdictions, may have a significant connection with that jurisdiction. In other cases, significant aspects of the lawyer's work might be conducted in that jurisdiction or a significant aspect of the matter may involve the law of that jurisdiction. The necessary relationship might arise when the client's activities or the legal issues involve multiple jurisdictions, such as when the officers of a multinational corporation survey potential business sites and seek the services of their lawyer in assessing the relative merits of each. In addition, the services may draw on the lawyer's recognized expertise developed through the regular practice of law on behalf of clients in matters involving a particular body of federal, nationally-uniform, foreign, or international law.

[15]   Paragraph (d) identifies two circumstances in which a lawyer who is admitted to practice in another United States or a foreign jurisdiction, and is not disbarred or suspended from practice in any jurisdiction or the equivalent thereof, may establish an office or other systematic and continuous presence in this jurisdiction for the practice of law. Pursuant to paragraph (c) of this Rule, a lawyer admitted in any U.S. jurisdiction may also provide legal services in this jurisdiction on a temporary basis. See also *Model Rule on Temporary Practice by Foreign Lawyers*. Except as provided in paragraphs (d)(1) and (d)(2), a lawyer who is admitted to practice law in another United States or foreign jurisdiction and who establishes an office or other systematic or continuous presence in this jurisdiction must become admitted to practice law generally in this jurisdiction.

[16]   Paragraph (d)(1) applies to a U.S. or foreign lawyer who is employed by a client to provide legal services to the client or its organizational affiliates, i.e., entities that control, are controlled by, or are under common control with the employer. This paragraph does not authorize the provision of personal legal services to the employer's officers or employees. The paragraph applies to in-house corporate lawyers, government lawyers and others who are employed to render legal services to the employer. The lawyer's ability to represent the employer outside the jurisdiction in which the lawyer is licensed generally serves the interests of the employer and does not create an unreasonable risk to the client and others because the employer is well situated to assess the lawyer's qualifications and the quality of the lawyer's work. To further decrease any risk to the client, when advising on the domestic law of a United States jurisdiction or on the law of the United States, the foreign lawyer authorized to practice under paragraph (d)(1) of this Rule needs to

~~base that advice on the advice of a lawyer~~ licensed and authorized by the jurisdiction to provide it.

[17] If an employed lawyer establishes an office or other systematic presence in this jurisdiction for the purpose of rendering legal services to the employer, the lawyer may be subject to registration or other requirements, including assessments for client protection funds and mandatory continuing legal education. See *Model Rule for Registration of In-House Counsel.*

[18] Paragraph (d)(2) recognizes that a U.S. or foreign lawyer may provide legal services in a jurisdiction in which the lawyer is not licensed when authorized to do so by federal or other law, which includes statute, court rule, executive regulation or judicial precedent. See, e.g., *The ABA Model Rule on Practice Pending Admission.*

[19] A lawyer who practices law in this jurisdiction pursuant to paragraphs (c) or (d) or otherwise is subject to the disciplinary authority of this jurisdiction. See Rule 8.5(a).

[20] In some circumstances, a lawyer who practices law in this jurisdiction pursuant to paragraphs (c) or (d) may have to inform the client that the lawyer is not licensed to practice law in this jurisdiction. For example, that may be required when the representation occurs primarily in this jurisdiction and requires knowledge of the law of this jurisdiction. See Rule 1.4(b).

[21] Paragraphs (c) and (d) do not authorize communications advertising legal services in this jurisdiction by lawyers who are admitted to practice in other jurisdictions. Whether and how lawyers may communicate the availability of their services in this jurisdiction is governed by Rules 7.1 to 7.5.

RULE 5.6: RESTRICTIONS ON RIGHT TO PRACTICE

A lawyer shall not participate in offering or making:

(a) a partnership ~~or,~~ shareholders, operating, employment, or other similar type of agreement that restricts the right of a lawyer to practice after termination of the relationship, except an agreement concerning benefits upon retirement; or

(b) an agreement in which a restriction on the lawyer's right to practice is part of the settlement of a <u>client</u> controversy ~~between private parties~~.

Comment

[1] An agreement restricting the right of ~~partners or associates~~ lawyers to practice after leaving a firm not only limits their professional autonomy but also limits the freedom of clients to choose a lawyer. Paragraph (a) prohibits such agreements except for restrictions incident to provisions concerning retirement benefits for service with the firm.

[2] Paragraph (b) prohibits a lawyer from agreeing not to represent other persons in connection with settling a claim on behalf of a client.

[3] This Rule does not apply to prohibit restrictions that may be included in the terms of the sale of a law practice pursuant to Rule 1.17.

RULE 5.7: RESPONSIBILITIES REGARDING LAW-RELATED SERVICES

(a)   A lawyer shall be subject to the Rules of Professional Conduct with respect to the provision of law-related services, as defined in paragraph (b), if the law-related services are provided:

> (1)   by the lawyer in circumstances that are not distinct from the lawyer's provision of legal services to clients; or

> (2)   in other circumstances by a~~ separate~~ an entity controlled by the lawyer individually or with others if the lawyer fails to take reasonable measures to assure that a person obtaining the law-related services knows that the services ~~of the separate entity~~ are not legal services and that the protections of the client-lawyer relationship do not exist.

(b)   The term "law-related services" denotes services that might reasonably be performed in conjunction with and in substance are related to the provision of legal services, and that are not prohibited as unauthorized practice of law when provided by a nonlawyer.

Comment

[1]   When a lawyer performs law-related services or controls an organization that does so, there exists the potential for ethical problems. Principal among these is the possibility that the person for whom the law-related services are performed fails to understand that the services may not carry with them the protections normally afforded as part of the client-lawyer relationship. The recipient of the law-related services may expect, for example, that the protection of client confidences, prohibitions against representation of persons with conflicting interests, and obligations of a lawyer to maintain professional independence apply to the provision of law-related services when that may not be the case.

[2]   Rule 5.7 applies to the provision of law-related services by a lawyer even when the lawyer does not provide any legal services to the person for whom the law-related services are performed and whether the law-related services are performed through a law firm or a separate entity. The Rule identifies the circumstances in which all of the Rules of Professional Conduct apply to the provision of law-related services. Even when those circumstances do not exist, however, the conduct of a lawyer involved in the provision of law-related services is subject to those Rules that apply generally to lawyer conduct, regardless of whether the conduct involves the provision of legal services. See, e.g., Rule 8.4.

[3]   When law-related services are provided by a lawyer under circumstances that are not distinct from the lawyer's provision of legal services to clients, the lawyer in providing the law-related services must adhere to the requirements of the Rules of Professional Conduct as provided in ~~Rule 5.7~~ paragraph (a)(1). Even when the law-related and legal services are provided in circumstances that are distinct from each other, for example through separate

entities or different support staff within the law firm, the Rules of Professional Conduct apply to the lawyer as provided in paragraph (a)(2) unless the lawyer takes reasonable measures to assure that the recipient of the law-related services knows that the services are not legal services and that the protections of the client-lawyer relationship do not apply.

[4]   Law-related services also may be provided through an entity that is distinct from that through which the lawyer provides legal services. If the lawyer individually or with others has control of such an entity's operations, the Rule requires the lawyer to take reasonable measures to assure that each person using the services of the entity knows that the services provided by the entity are not legal services and that the Rules of Professional Conduct that relate to the client-lawyer relationship do not apply. A lawyer's control of an entity extends to the ability to direct its operation. Whether a lawyer has such control will depend upon the circumstances of the particular case.

[5]   When a client-lawyer relationship exists with a person who is referred by a lawyer to a separate law-related service entity controlled by the lawyer, individually or with others, the lawyer must comply with Rule 1.8(a).

[6]   In taking the reasonable measures referred to in paragraph (a) (2) to assure that a person using law-related services understands the practical effect or significance of the inapplicability of the Rules of Professional Conduct, the lawyer should communicate to the person receiving the law-related services, in a manner sufficient to assure that the person understands the significance of the fact, that the relationship of the person to the business entity will not be a client-lawyer relationship. The communication should be made before entering into an agreement for provision of or providing law-related services, and preferably should be in writing.

[7]   The burden is upon the lawyer to show that the lawyer has taken reasonable measures under the circumstances to communicate the desired understanding. For instance, a sophisticated user of law-related services, such as a publicly held corporation, may require a lesser explanation than someone unaccustomed to making distinctions between legal services and law-related services, such as an individual seeking tax advice from a lawyer-accountant or investigative services in connection with a lawsuit.

[8]   Regardless of the sophistication of potential recipients of law-related services, a lawyer should take special care to keep separate the provision of law-related and legal services in order to minimize the risk that the recipient will assume that the law-related services are legal services. The risk of such confusion is especially acute when the lawyer renders both types of services with respect to the same matter. Under some circumstances the legal and law-related services may be so closely entwined that they cannot be distinguished from each other, and the requirement of disclosure and consultation imposed by paragraph (a)(2) of the Rule cannot be met. In such a case a lawyer will be responsible for assuring that both the lawyer's conduct and, to the extent required by Rule 5.3, that of nonlawyer employees in the distinct entity that the lawyer controls complies in all respects with the Rules of Professional Conduct.

[9]   A broad range of economic and other interests of clients may be served by lawyers' engaging in the delivery of law-related services. Examples of law-related services include providing title insurance, financial planning, accounting, trust services, real estate counseling, legislative lobbying, economic analysis, social work, psychological counseling, tax preparation, and patent, medical or environmental consulting.

[10]   When a lawyer is obliged to accord the recipients of such services the protections of those Rules that apply to the client-lawyer relationship, the lawyer must take special care to heed the proscriptions of the Rules addressing conflict of interest (Rules 1.7 through 1.11, especially Rules 1.7~~(b)~~ (a)(2) and 1.8(a), (b) and (f)), and to scrupulously adhere to the requirements of Rule 1.6 relating to disclosure of confidential information. The promotion of the law-related services must also in all respects comply with Rules 7.1 through 7.3, dealing with advertising and solicitation. In that regard, lawyers should take special care to identify the obligations that may be imposed as a result of a jurisdiction's decisional law.

[11]   When the full protections of all of the Rules of Professional Conduct do not apply to the provision of law-related services, principles of law external to the Rules, for example, the law of principal and agent, govern the legal duties owed to those receiving the services. Those other legal principles may establish a different degree of protection for the recipient with respect to confidentiality of information, conflicts of interest and permissible business relationships with clients. See also Rule 8.4 (Misconduct).

RULE 6.1: VOLUNTARY PRO BONO PUBLICO SERVICE

Every lawyer has a professional responsibility to provide legal services to those unable to pay. A lawyer should aspire to render at least (50) hours of pro bono publico legal services per year. In fulfilling this responsibility, the lawyer should:

(a)   provide a substantial majority of the (50) hours of legal services without fee or expectation of fee to:

(1)   persons of limited means or

(2)   charitable, religious, civic, community, governmental and educational organizations in matters that are designed primarily to address the needs of persons of limited means; and

(b)   provide any additional services through:

(1)   delivery of legal services at no fee or substantially reduced fee to individuals, groups or organizations seeking to secure or protect civil rights, civil liberties or public rights, or charitable, religious, civic, community, governmental and educational organizations in matters in furtherance of their organizational purposes, where the payment of standard legal fees would significantly deplete the organization's economic resources or would be otherwise inappropriate;

(2)   delivery of legal services at a substantially reduced fee to persons of limited means; or

(3) participation in activities for improving the law, the legal system or the legal profession.

In addition, a lawyer should voluntarily contribute financial support to organizations that provide legal services to persons of limited means.

Comment

[1] Every lawyer, regardless of professional prominence or professional work load, has a responsibility to provide legal services to those unable to pay, and personal involvement in the problems of the disadvantaged can be one of the most rewarding experiences in the life of a lawyer. The American Bar Association urges all lawyers to provide a minimum of 50 hours of pro bono services annually. States, however, may decide to choose a higher or lower number of hours of annual service (which may be expressed as a percentage of a lawyer's professional time) depending upon local needs and local conditions. It is recognized that in some years a lawyer may render greater or fewer hours than the annual standard specified, but during the course of his or her legal career, each lawyer should render on average per year, the number of hours set forth in this Rule. Services can be performed in civil matters or in criminal or quasi-criminal matters for which there is no government obligation to provide funds for legal representation, such as post-conviction death penalty appeal cases.

[2] Paragraphs (a)(1) and (2) recognize the critical need for legal services that exists among persons of limited means by providing that a substantial majority of the legal services rendered annually to the disadvantaged be furnished without fee or expectation of fee. Legal services under these paragraphs consist of a full range of activities, including individual and class representation, the provision of legal advice, legislative lobbying, administrative rule making and the provision of free training or mentoring to those who represent persons of limited means. The variety of these activities should facilitate participation by government lawyers, even when restrictions exist on their engaging in the outside practice of law.

[3] Persons eligible for legal services under paragraphs (a)(1) and (2) are those who qualify for participation in programs funded by the Legal Services Corporation and those whose incomes and financial resources are slightly above the guidelines utilized by such programs but nevertheless, cannot afford counsel. Legal services can be rendered to individuals or to organizations such as homeless shelters, battered women's centers and food pantries that serve those of limited means. The term "governmental organizations" includes, but is not limited to, public protection programs and sections of governmental or public sector agencies.

[4] Because service must be provided without fee or expectation of fee, the intent of the lawyer to render free legal services is essential for the work performed to fall within the meaning of paragraphs (a)(1) and (2). Accordingly, services rendered cannot be considered pro bono if an anticipated fee is uncollected, but the award of statutory attorneys' fees in a case originally accepted as pro bono would not disqualify such services from inclusion under

this section. Lawyers who do receive fees in such cases are encouraged to contribute an appropriate portion of such fees to organizations or projects that benefit persons of limited means.

[5]   While it is possible for a lawyer to fulfill the annual responsibility to perform pro bono services exclusively through activities described in paragraphs (a)(1) and (2), to the extent that any hours of service remained unfulfilled, the remaining commitment can be met in a variety of ways as set forth in paragraph (b). Constitutional, statutory or regulatory restrictions may prohibit or impede government and public sector lawyers and judges from performing the pro bono services outlined in paragraphs (a)(1) and (2). Accordingly, where those restrictions apply, government and public sector lawyers and judges may fulfill their pro bono responsibility by performing services outlined in paragraph (b).

[6]   Paragraph (b)(1) includes the provision of certain types of legal services to those whose incomes and financial resources place them above limited means. It also permits the probono lawyer to accept a substantially reduced fee for services. Examples of the types of issues that may be addressed under this paragraph include First Amendment claims, Title VII claims and environmental protection claims. Additionally, a wide range of organizations may be represented, including social service, medical research, cultural and religious groups.

[7]   Paragraph (b)(2) covers instances in which lawyers agree to and receive a modest fee for furnishing legal services to persons of limited means. Participation in judicare programs and acceptance of court appointments in which the fee is substantially below a lawyer's usual rate are encouraged under this section.

[8]   Paragraph (b)(3) recognizes the value of lawyers engaging in activities that improve the law, the legal system or the legal profession. Serving on bar association committees, serving on boards of pro bono or legal services programs, taking part in Law Day activities, acting as a continuing legal education instructor, a mediator or an arbitrator and engaging in legislative lobbying to improve the law, the legal system or the profession are a few examples of the many activities that fall within this paragraph.

[9]   Because the provision of probono services is a professional responsibility, it is the individual ethical commitment of each lawyer. Nevertheless, there may be times when it is not feasible for a lawyer to engage in probono services. At such times a lawyer may discharge the probono responsibility by providing financial support to organizations providing free legal services to persons of limited means. Such financial support should be reasonably equivalent to the value of the hours of service that would have otherwise been provided. In addition, at times it may be more feasible to satisfy the probono responsibility collectively, as by a firm's aggregate probono activities.

[10]   Because the efforts of individual lawyers are not enough to meet the need for free legal services that exists among persons of limited

means, the government and the profession have instituted additional programs to provide those services. Every lawyer should financially support such programs, in addition to either providing direct pro bono services or making financial contributions when pro bono service is not feasible.

[11]   Law firms should act reasonably to enable and encourage all lawyers in the firm to provide the pro bono legal services called for by this Rule.

[11] [12]   The responsibility set forth in this Rule is not intended to be enforced through disciplinary process.

RULE 6.2: ACCEPTING APPOINTMENTS

A lawyer shall not seek to avoid appointment by a tribunal to represent a person except for good cause, such as:

(a)   representing the client is likely to result in violation of the Rules of Professional Conduct or other law;

(b)   representing the client is likely to result in an unreasonable financial burden on the lawyer; or

(c)   the client or the cause is so repugnant to the lawyer as to be likely to impair the client-lawyer relationship or the lawyer's ability to represent the client.

Comment

[1]   A lawyer ordinarily is not obliged to accept a client whose character or cause the lawyer regards as repugnant. The lawyer's freedom to select clients is, however, qualified. All lawyers have a responsibility to assist in providing probono publico service. See Rule 6.1. An individual lawyer fulfills this responsibility by accepting a fair share of unpopular matters or indigent or unpopular clients. A lawyer may also be subject to appointment by a court to serve unpopular clients or persons unable to afford legal services.

Appointed Counsel

[2]   For good cause a lawyer may seek to decline an appointment to represent a person who cannot afford to retain counsel or whose cause is unpopular. Good cause exists if the lawyer could not handle the matter competently, see Rule 1.1, or if undertaking the representation would result in an improper conflict of interest, for example, when the client or the cause is so repugnant to the lawyer as to be likely to impair the client-lawyer relationship or the lawyer's ability to represent the client. A lawyer may also seek to decline an appointment if acceptance would be unreasonably burdensome, for example, when it would impose a financial sacrifice so great as to be unjust.

[3]   An appointed lawyer has the same obligations to the client as retained counsel, including the obligations of loyalty and confidentiality, and is subject to the same limitations on the client-lawyer relationship, such as the obligation to refrain from assisting the client in violation of the Rules.

RULE 6.3: MEMBERSHIP IN LEGAL SERVICES ORGANIZATION

A lawyer may serve as a director, officer or member of a legal services organization, apart from the law firm in which the lawyer practices, notwithstanding that the organization serves persons having interests adverse to a client of the lawyer. The lawyer shall not knowingly participate in a decision or action of the organization:

(a)   if participating in the decision or action would be incompatible with the lawyer's obligations to a client under Rule 1.7; or

(b)   where the decision or action could have a material adverse effect on the representation of a client of the organization whose interests are adverse to a client of the lawyer.

Comment

[1]   Lawyers should be encouraged to support and participate in legal service organizations. A lawyer who is an officer or a member of such an organization does not thereby have a client-lawyer relationship with persons served by the organization. However, there is potential conflict between the interests of such persons and the interests of the lawyer's clients. If the possibility of such conflict disqualified a lawyer from serving on the board of a legal services organization, the profession's involvement in such organizations would be severely curtailed.

[2]   It may be necessary in appropriate cases to reassure a client of the organization that the representation will not be affected by conflicting loyalties of a member of the board. Established, written policies in this respect can enhance the credibility of such assurances.

RULE 6.4: LAW REFORM ACTIVITIES AFFECTING CLIENT INTERESTS

A lawyer may serve as a director, officer or member of an organization involved in reform of the law or its administration notwithstanding that the reform may affect the interests of a client of the lawyer. When the lawyer knows that the interests of a client may be materially benefitted by a decision in which the lawyer participates, the lawyer shall disclose that fact but need not identify the client.

Comment

[1]   Lawyers involved in organizations seeking law reform generally do not have a client-lawyer relationship with the organization. Otherwise, it might follow that a lawyer could not be involved in a bar association law reform program that might indirectly affect a client. See also Rule 1.2(b). For example, a lawyer specializing in antitrust litigation might be regarded as disqualified from participating in drafting revisions of rules governing that subject. In determining the nature and scope of participation in such activities, a lawyer should be mindful of obligations to clients under other Rules, particularly Rule 1.7. A lawyer is professionally obligated to protect the integrity of

the program by making an appropriate disclosure within the organization when the lawyer knows a private client might be materially benefitted.

RULE 6.5: NONPROFIT AND COURT-ANNEXED LIMITED LEGAL SERVICES PROGRAMS

(a)   A lawyer who, under the auspices of a program sponsored by a nonprofit organization or court, provides short-term limited legal services to a client without expectation by either the lawyer or the client that the lawyer will provide continuing representation in the matter:

(1)   is subject to Rules 1.7 and 1.9(a) only if the lawyer knows that the representation of the client involves a conflict of interest; and

(2)   is subject to Rule 1.10 only if the lawyer knows that another lawyer associated with the lawyer in a law firm is disqualified by Rule 1.7 or 1.9(a) with respect to the matter.

(b)   Except as provided in paragraph (a)(2), Rule 1.10 is inapplicable to a representation governed by this Rule.

Comment

[1]   Legal services organizations, courts and various nonprofit organizations have established programs through which lawyers provide short-term limited legal services — such as advice or the completion of legal forms - that will assist persons to address their legal problems without further representation by a lawyer. In these programs, such as legal-advice hotlines, advice-only clinics or prose counseling programs, a client-lawyer relationship is established, but there is no expectation that the lawyer's representation of the client will continue beyond the limited consultation. Such programs are normally operated under circumstances in which it is not feasible for a lawyer to systematically screen for conflicts of interest as is generally required before undertaking a representation. See, e.g., Rules 1.7, 1.9 and 1.10.

[2]   A lawyer who provides short-term limited legal services pursuant to this Rule must secure the client's informed consent to the limited scope of the representation. See Rule 1.2(c). If a short-term limited representation would not be reasonable under the circumstances, the lawyer may offer advice to the client but must also advise the client of the need for further assistance of counsel. Except as provided in this Rule, the Rules of Professional Conduct, including Rules 1.6 and 1.9(c), are applicable to the limited representation.

[3]   Because a lawyer who is representing a client in the circumstances addressed by this Rule ordinarily is not able to check systematically for conflicts of interest, paragraph (a) requires compliance with Rules 1.7 or 1.9(a) only if the lawyer knows that the representation presents a conflict of interest for the lawyer, and with Rule 1.10 only if the lawyer knows that another lawyer in the lawyer's firm is disqualified by Rules 1.7 or 1.9(a) in the matter.

[4] Because the limited nature of the services significantly reduces the risk of conflicts of interest with other matters being handled by the lawyer's firm, paragraph (b) provides that Rule 1.10 is inapplicable to a representation governed by this Rule except as provided by paragraph (a)(2). Paragraph (a)(2) requires the participating lawyer to comply with Rule 1.10 when the lawyer knows that the lawyer's firm is disqualified by Rules 1.7 or 1.9(a). By virtue of paragraph (b), however, a lawyer's participation in a short-term limited legal services program will not preclude the lawyer's firm from undertaking or continuing the representation of a client with interests adverse to a client being represented under the program's auspices. Nor will the personal disqualification of a lawyer participating in the program be imputed to other lawyers participating in the program.

[5] If, after commencing a short-term limited representation in accordance with this Rule, a lawyer undertakes to represent the client in the matter on an ongoing basis, Rules 1.7, 1.9(a) and 1.10 become applicable.

RULE 7.1: COMMUNICATIONS CONCERNING A LAWYER'S SERVICES

A lawyer shall not make a false or misleading communication about the lawyer or the lawyer's services. A communication is false or misleading if it: (a) contains a material misrepresentation of fact or law, or omits a fact necessary to make the statement considered as a whole not materially misleading;

(b) is likely to create an unjustified expectation about results the lawyer can achieve, or states or implies that the lawyer can achieve results by means that violate the Rules of Professional Conduct or other law; or

(c) compares the lawyer's services with other lawyers' services, unless the comparison can be factually substantiated.

Comment

[1] This Rule governs all communications about a lawyer's services, including advertising permitted by Rule 7.2. Whatever means are used to make known a lawyer's services, statements about them should must be truthful. The prohibition in paragraph (b) of statements that may create "unjustified expectations" would ordinarily preclude advertisements about results obtained on behalf of a client, such as the amount of a damage award or the lawyer's record in obtaining favorable verdicts, and advertisements containing client endorsements. Such information may create the unjustified expectation that similar results can be obtained for others without reference to the specific factual and legal circumstances.

[2] Truthful statements that are misleading are also prohibited by this Rule. A truthful statement is misleading if it omits a fact necessary to make the lawyer's communication considered as a whole not materially misleading. A truthful statement is also misleading if there is a substantial

likelihood that it will lead a reasonable person to formulate a specific conclusion about the lawyer or the lawyer's services for which there is no reasonable factual foundation.

[3]   An advertisement that truthfully reports a lawyer's achievements on behalf of clients or former clients may be misleading if presented so as to lead a reasonable person to form an unjustified expectation that the same results could be obtained for other clients in similar matters without reference to the specific factual and legal circumstances of each client's case. Similarly, an unsubstantiated comparison of the lawyer's services or fees with the services or fees of other lawyers may be misleading if presented with such specificity as would lead a reasonable person to conclude that the comparison can be substantiated. The inclusion of an appropriate disclaimer or qualifying language may preclude a finding that a statement is likely to create unjustified expectations or otherwise mislead the public.

[4]   See also Rule 8.4(e) for the prohibition against stating or implying an ability to influence improperly a government agency or official or to achieve results by means that violate the Rules of Professional Conduct or other law.

RULE 7.2: ADVERTISING

(a)   Subject to the requirements of Rules 7.1 and 7.3, a lawyer may advertise services through written, recorded or electronic communication, including public media.

(b)   A lawyer shall not give anything of value to a person for recommending the lawyer's services except that a lawyer may

(1)   pay the reasonable costs of advertisements or communications permitted by this Rule;

(2)   pay the usual charges of a legal service plan or a not-for-profit or qualified lawyer referral service. A qualified lawyer referral service is a lawyer referral service that has been approved by an appropriate regulatory authority;

(3)   pay for a law practice in accordance with Rule 1.17;and

(4)   refer clients to another lawyer or a nonlawyer professional pursuant to an agreement not otherwise prohibited under these Rules that provides for the other person to refer clients or customers to the lawyer, if

(i) the reciprocal referral agreement is not exclusive, and

(ii) the client is informed of the existence and nature of the agreement.

(c)   Any communication made pursuant to this rule shall include the name and office address of at least one lawyer or law firm responsible for its content.

Comment

[1]   To assist the public in <u>learning about and</u> obtaining legal services, lawyers should be allowed to make known their services not only through reputation but also through organized information campaigns in the form of <u>advertising</u>. <u>Advertising</u> involves an active quest for clients, contrary to the tradition that a lawyer should not seek clientele. However, the public's need to know about legal services can be fulfilled in part through advertising. This need is particularly acute in the case of persons of moderate means who have not made extensive use of legal services. The interest in expanding public information about legal services ought to prevail over considerations of tradition. Nevertheless, advertising by lawyers entails the risk of practices that are misleading or overreaching.

[2]   This Rule permits public dissemination of information concerning a lawyer's name or firm name, address<u>, email address, website,</u> and telephone number; the kinds of services the lawyer will undertake; the basis on which the lawyer's fees are determined, including prices for specific services and payment and credit arrangements; a lawyer's foreign language ability; names of references and, with their consent, names of clients regularly represented; and other information that might invite the attention of those seeking legal assistance.

[3]   Questions of effectiveness and taste in advertising are matters of speculation and subjective judgment. Some jurisdictions have had extensive prohibitions against television <u>and other forms of</u> advertising, against advertising going beyond specified facts about a lawyer, or against "undignified" advertising. Television<u>, the Internet, and other forms of electronic communication are</u> ~~is~~ now ~~one of~~ <u>among</u> the most powerful media for getting information to the public, particularly persons of low and moderate income; prohibiting television<u>, Internet, and other forms of electronic</u> advertising, therefore, would impede the flow of information about legal services to many sectors of the public. Limiting the information that may be advertised has a similar effect and assumes that the bar can accurately forecast the kind of information that the public would regard as relevant. ~~Similarly, electronic media, such as the Internet, can be an important source of information about legal services, and lawful communication by electronic mail is permitted by this Rule.~~ But see Rule 7.3(a) for the prohibition against ~~the~~ <u>a</u> solicitation ~~of a prospective client~~ through a real-time electronic exchange ~~that is not initiated by the prospective client~~ <u>initiated by the lawyer</u>.

[4]   Neither this Rule nor Rule 7.3 prohibits communications authorized by law, such as notice to members of a class in class action litigation.

Paying Others to Recommend a Lawyer

[5]   <u>Except as permitted under paragraphs (b)(1)-(b)(4),</u> ~~Lawyers~~ <u>lawyers</u> are not permitted to pay others for ~~channeling professional work~~ <u>recommending the lawyer's services or for channeling professional work in a manner that violates Rule 7.3. A communication contains a recommendation if</u>

~~it endorses or vouches for a lawyer's credentials, abilities, competence, character, or other professional qualities~~. Paragraph (b)(1), however, allows a lawyer to pay for advertising and communications permitted by this Rule, including the costs of print directory listings, on-line directory listings, newspaper ads, television and radio airtime, domain-name registrations, sponsorship fees, ~~banner ads~~ Internet-based advertisements, and group advertising. A lawyer may compensate employees, agents and vendors who are engaged to provide marketing or client-development services, such as publicists, public-relations personnel, business-development staff and website designers. Moreover, a lawyer may pay others for generating client leads, such as Internet-based client leads, as long as the lead generator does not recommend the lawyer, any payment to the lead generator is consistent with Rules 1.5(e) (division of fees) and 5.4 (professional independence of the lawyer), and the lead generator's communications are consistent with Rule 7.1 (communications concerning a lawyer's services). To comply with Rule 7.1, a lawyer must not pay a lead generator that states, implies, or creates a reasonable impression that it is recommending the lawyer, is making the referral without payment from the lawyer, or has analyzed a person's legal problems when determining which lawyer should receive the referral. See also See Rule 5.3 ~~for the~~ (duties of lawyers and law firms with respect to the conduct of nonlawyers); ~~who prepare marketing materials for them~~ Rule 8.4(a) (duty to avoid violating the Rules through the acts of another).

[6] A lawyer may pay the usual charges of a legal service plan or a not-for-profit or qualified lawyer referral service. A legal service plan is a prepaid or group legal service plan or a similar delivery system that assists ~~prospective clients~~ people who seek to secure legal representation. A lawyer referral service, on the other hand, is any organization that holds itself out to the public as a lawyer referral service. Such referral services are understood by ~~laypersons~~ the public to be consumer-oriented organizations that provide unbiased referrals to lawyers with appropriate experience in the subject matter of the representation and afford other client protections, such as complaint procedures or malpractice insurance requirements. Consequently, this Rule only permits a lawyer to pay the usual charges of a not-for-profit or qualified lawyer referral service. A qualified lawyer referral service is one that is approved by an appropriate regulatory authority as affording adequate protections for ~~prospective clients~~the public. See, e.g., the American Bar Association's Model Supreme Court Rules Governing Lawyer Referral Services and Model Lawyer Referral and Information Service Quality Assurance Act (requiring that organizations that are identified as lawyer referral services (i) permit the participation of all lawyers who are licensed and eligible to practice in the jurisdiction and who meet reasonable objective eligibility requirements as may be established by the referral service for the protection of ~~prospective clients~~the public; (ii) require each participating lawyer to carry reasonably adequate malpractice insurance; (iii) act reasonably to assess client satisfaction and address client complaints; and (iv) do not make referrals ~~prospective clients~~ to lawyers who own, operate or are employed by the referral service.)

[7]   A lawyer who accepts assignments or referrals from a legal service plan or referrals from a lawyer referral service must act reasonably to assure that the activities of the plan or service are compatible with the lawyer's professional obligations. See Rule 5.3. Legal service plans and lawyer referral services may communicate with ~~prospective clients~~the public, but such communication must be in conformity with these Rules. Thus, advertising must not be false or misleading, as would be the case if the communications of a group advertising program or a group legal services plan would mislead ~~prospective clients~~ the public to think that it was a lawyer referral service sponsored by a state agency or bar association. Nor could the lawyer allow in-person, telephonic, or real-time contacts that would violate Rule 7.3.

[8]   A lawyer also may agree to refer clients to another lawyer or a nonlawyer professional, in return for the undertaking of that person to refer clients or customers to the lawyer. Such reciprocal referral arrangements must not interfere with the lawyer's professional judgment as to making referrals or as to providing substantive legal services. See Rules 2.1 and 5.4(c). Except as provided in Rule 1.5(e), a lawyer who receives referrals from a lawyer or nonlawyer professional must not pay anything solely for the referral, but the lawyer does not violate paragraph (b) of this Rule by agreeing to refer clients to the other lawyer or nonlawyer professional, so long as the reciprocal referral agreement is not exclusive and the client is informed of the referral agreement. Conflicts of interest created by such arrangements are governed by Rule 1.7. Reciprocal referral agreements should not be of indefinite duration and should be reviewed periodically to determine whether they comply with these Rules. This Rule does not restrict referrals or divisions of revenues or net income among lawyers within firms comprised of multiple entities.

RULE 7.3: ~~DIRECT CONTACT WITH PROSPECTIVE~~ SOLICITATION OF CLIENTS

(a)   A lawyer shall not by in-person ~~or,~~ live telephone or real-time electronic contact solicit professional employment ~~from a prospective client with whom the lawyer has no family or prior professional relationship~~ when a significant motive for the lawyer's doing so is the lawyer's pecuniary gain, unless the person contacted:

          (1)   is a lawyer; or

          (2)   has a family, close personal, or prior professional relationship with the lawyer.

(b)   A lawyer shall not solicit professional employment from a prospective client by written ~~or,~~ recorded or electronic communication or by in-person ~~or,~~ telephone or real-time electronic contact even when not otherwise prohibited by paragraph (a), if:

          (1)   the ~~prospective client~~ target of the solicitation has made known to the lawyer a desire not to be solicited by the lawyer; or

          (2)   the solicitation involves coercion, duress or harassment.

(c)   Every written ~~or,~~ recorded or electronic communication from a lawyer soliciting professional employment from ~~a prospective client~~ anyone known to be in need of legal services in a particular matter~~, and with whom the lawyer has no family or prior professional relationship,~~ shall include the words "Advertising Material" on the outside envelope, if any, and at the beginning and ending of any recorded or electronic communication, unless the recipient of the communication is a person specified in paragraphs (a)(1) or (a)(2).

(d)   Notwithstanding the prohibitions in paragraph (a), a lawyer may participate with a prepaid or group legal service plan operated by an organization not owned or directed by the lawyer that uses in-person or telephone contact to solicit memberships or subscriptions for the plan from persons who are not known to need legal services in a particular matter covered by the plan.

Comment

[1]   A solicitation is a targeted communication initiated by the lawyer that is directed to a specific person and that offers to provide, or can reasonably be understood as offering to provide, legal services. In contrast, a lawyer's communication typically does not constitute a solicitation if it is directed to the general public, such as through a billboard, an Internet banner advertisement, a website or a television commercial, or if it is in response to a request for information or is automatically generated in response to Internet searches.

[~~1~~2]   There is a potential for abuse ~~inherent in~~ when a solicitation involves direct in-person ~~or,~~ live telephone or real-time electronic contact by a lawyer with ~~a prospective client~~ someone known to need legal services. These forms of contact ~~between a lawyer and a prospective client~~ subject ~~the layperson~~ a person to the private importuning of the trained advocate in a direct interpersonal encounter. The ~~prospective client~~person, who may already feel overwhelmed by the circumstances giving rise to the need for legal services, may find it difficult fully to evaluate all available alternatives with reasoned judgment and appropriate self-interest in the face of the lawyer's presence and insistence upon being retained immediately. The situation is fraught with the possibility of undue influence, intimidation, and over-reaching.

[~~2~~3]   This potential for abuse inherent in direct in-person ~~or,~~ live telephone or real-time electronic solicitation ~~of prospective clients~~ justifies its prohibition, particularly since lawyers have ~~advertising and written and recorded communication permitted under Rule 7.2 offer~~ alternative means of conveying necessary information to those who may be in need of legal services. ~~Advertising and written and recorded~~ In particular, communications ~~which may~~ can be mailed ~~or autodialed~~ or transmitted by email or other electronic means that do not involve real-time contact and do not violate other laws governing solicitations. These forms of communications and solicitations make it possible for ~~a prospective client~~the public to be informed about the need for legal services, and about the qualifications of available lawyers and law firms, without subjecting the ~~prospective client~~public to direct in-person ~~or,~~ telephone or real-time electronic persuasion that may overwhelm ~~the client's~~ a person's judgment.

[~~3~~4] The use of general advertising and written ~~and,~~ recorded or electronic communications to transmit information from lawyer to ~~prospective client~~the public, rather than direct in-person ~~or,~~ live telephone or real-time electronic contact, will help to assure that the information flows cleanly as well as freely. The contents of advertisements and communications permitted under Rule 7.2 ~~are~~ can be permanently recorded so that they cannot be disputed and may be shared with others who know the lawyer. This potential for informal review is itself likely to help guard against statements and claims that might constitute false and misleading communications, in violation of Rule 7.1. The contents of direct in-person ~~or,~~ live telephone or real-time electronic ~~conversations between a lawyer to~~ and a ~~prospective client~~ contact can be disputed and ~~are~~ may not ~~be~~ subject to third-party scrutiny. Consequently, they are much more likely to approach (and occasionally cross) the dividing line between accurate representations and those that are false and misleading.

[~~4~~5] There is far less likelihood that a lawyer would engage in abusive practices against ~~an individual~~ a former client, or a person with whom the lawyer has a ~~prior~~ close personal or ~~professional~~ family relationship, or ~~where~~ in situations in which the lawyer is motivated by considerations other than the lawyer's pecuniary gain. Nor is there a serious potential for abuse when the person contacted is a lawyer. Consequently, the general prohibition in Rule 7.3(a) and the requirements of Rule 7.3(c) are not applicable in those situations. Also, paragraph (a) is not intended to prohibit a lawyer from participating in constitutionally protected activities of public or charitable legal-service organizations or bonafide political, social, civic, fraternal, employee or trade organizations whose purposes include providing or recommending legal services to their members or beneficiaries.

[~~5~~6] But even permitted forms of solicitation can be abused. Thus, any solicitation which contains information which is false or misleading within the meaning of Rule 7.1, which involves coercion, duress or harassment within the meaning of Rule 7.3(b)(2), or which involves contact with ~~a prospective client~~someone who has made known to the lawyer a desire not to be solicited by the lawyer within the meaning of Rule 7.3(b)(1) is prohibited. Moreover, if after sending a letter or other communication ~~to a client~~ as permitted by Rule 7.2 the lawyer receives no response, any further effort to communicate with the ~~prospective client~~recipient of the communication may violate the provisions of Rule 7.3(b).

[~~6~~7] This Rule is not intended to prohibit a lawyer from contacting representatives of organizations or groups that may be interested in establishing a group or prepaid legal plan for their members, insureds, beneficiaries or other third parties for the purpose of informing such entities of the availability of and details concerning the plan or arrangement which the lawyer or lawyer's firm is willing to offer. This form of communication is not directed to ~~a prospective client~~people who are seeking legal services for themselves. Rather, it is usually addressed to an individual acting in a fiduciary capacity seeking a sup-plier of legal services for others who may, if they choose, become prospective clients of the lawyer. Under these circumstances, the activity which the lawyer undertakes in communicating with such representatives and the type of information transmitted to the individual are functionally similar to and serve the same purpose as advertising permitted under Rule 7.2.

[~~7~~8]   The requirement in Rule 7.3(c) that certain communications be marked "Advertising Material" does not apply to communications sent in response to requests of potential clients or their spokespersons or sponsors. General announcements by lawyers, including changes in personnel or office location, do not constitute communications soliciting professional employment from a client known to be in need of legal services within the meaning of this Rule.

[~~8~~9]   Paragraph (d) of this Rule ~~would permit~~ permits a lawyer to participate with an organization which uses personal contact to solicit mem-bers for its group or prepaid legal service plan, provided that the personal contact is not undertaken by any lawyer who would be a provider of legal ser-vices through the plan. The organization ~~referred to in paragraph (d)~~ must not be owned by or directed (whether as manager or otherwise) by any lawyer or law firm that participates in the plan. For example, paragraph (d) would not permit a lawyer to create an organization controlled directly or indirectly by the lawyer and use the organization for the in-person or telephone solicitation of legal employment of the lawyer through memberships in the plan or other-wise. The communication permitted by these organizations also must not be directed to a person known to need legal services in a particular matter, but is to be designed to inform potential plan members generally of another means of affordable legal services. Lawyers who participate in a legal service plan must reasonably assure that the plan sponsors are in compliance with Rules 7.1, 7.2 and 7.3(b). See 8.4(a).

RULE 7.4: COMMUNICATION OF FIELDS OF PRACTICE AND SPECIALIZATION

(a)   A lawyer may communicate the fact that the lawyer does or does not practice in particular fields of law. ~~A lawyer shall not state or imply that the lawyer has been recognized or certified as a specialist in a particular field of law except as follows:~~

~~(a)~~ (b)   ~~a~~ A lawyer admitted to engage in patent practice before the United States Patent and Trademark Office may use the designation "Patent Attorney" or a substantially similar designation~~;~~.

~~(b)~~ (c)   ~~a~~ A lawyer engaged in Admiralty practice may use the desig-nation "Admiralty," "Proctor in Admiralty" or a substantially similar designa-tion~~; and~~.

~~(c)   [for jurisdictions where there is a regulatory authority grant-ing certification or approving organizations that grant certification] a lawyer may communicate the fact that the lawyer has been certified as a specialist in a field of law by a named organization or authority but only if:~~

~~(1)   such certification is granted by the appropriate regulatory authority or by an organization which has been approved by the appropriate regulatory authority to grant such certification; or~~

~~(2)   such certification is granted by an organization that has not yet been approved by, or has been denied the approval available from, the appropriate regulatory authority, and the absence or denial of approval is clearly stated in the communication, and in any advertising subject to Rule 7.2, such statement appears in the same sentence that communicates the certification.~~

~~(c)   [for jurisdictions where there is no procedure either for certification of specialties or for approval of organizations granting certification] a lawyer may communicate the fact that the lawyer has been certified as a specialist in a field of law by a named organization, provided that the communication clearly states that there is no procedure in this jurisdiction for approving certifying organizations. If, however, the named organization has been accredited by the American Bar Association to certify lawyers as specialists in a particular field of law, the communication need not contain such a statement.~~

<u>(d)   A lawyer shall not state or imply that a lawyer is certified as a specialist in a particular field of law, unless:</u>

<u>(1)   the lawyer has been certified as a specialist by an organization that has been approved by an appropriate state authority or that has been accredited by the American Bar Association; and</u>

<u>(2)   the name of the certifying organization is clearly identified in the communication.</u>

Comment

[1]   ~~This~~ <u>Paragraph (a) of this</u> Rule permits a lawyer to indicate areas of practice in communications about the lawyer's services. If a lawyer practices only in certain fields, or will not accept matters except in a specified field or fields, the lawyer is permitted to so indicate. A lawyer is generally permitted to state that the lawyer is a "specialist," practices a "specialty," or "specializes in" particular fields, but such communications are subject to the "false and misleading" standard applied in Rule 7.1 to communications concerning a lawyer's services.

[2]   ~~However, a lawyer may not communicate that the lawyer has been recognized or certified as a specialist in a particular field of law, except as provided by this Rule. Recognition of specialization in patent matters is a matter of~~ <u>Paragraph (b) recognizes the</u> long-established policy of the Patent and Trademark Office~~, as reflected in paragraph (a)~~ <u>for the designation of lawyers practicing before the Office</u>. Paragraph ~~(b)~~ <u>(c)</u> recognizes that designation of ~~admiralty~~ <u>Admiralty</u> practice has a long historical tradition associated with maritime commerce and the federal courts.

[3]   Paragraph ~~(c) provides for certification~~ <u>(d) permits a lawyer to state that the lawyer is certified</u> as a specialist in a field of law ~~when a state authorizes an appropriate regulatory authority to grant such certification or~~

~~when the state grants other organizations the right to grant certification~~ if such certification is granted by an organization approved by an appropriate state authority or accredited by the American Bar Association or another organization, such as a state bar association, that has been approved by the state authority to accredit organizations that certify lawyers as specialists. Certification ~~procedures imply~~ signifies that an objective entity has recognized ~~a lawyer's higher~~ an advanced degree of ~~specialized ability~~ knowledge and experience in the specialty area greater than is suggested by general licensure to practice law. ~~Those objective entities~~ Certifying organizations may be expected to apply standards of ~~competence,~~ experience ~~and,~~ knowledge and proficiency to insure that a lawyer's recognition as a specialist is meaningful and reliable. In order to insure that consumers can obtain access to useful information about an organization granting certification, the name of the certifying organization ~~or agency~~ must be included in any communication regarding the certification.

~~[4]   Lawyers may also be certified as specialists by organizations that either have not yet been approved to grant such certification or have been disapproved. In such instances, the consumer may be misled as to the significance of the lawyer's status as a certified specialist. The Rule therefore requires that a lawyer who chooses to communicate recognition by such an organization also clearly state the absence or denial of the organization's authority to grant such certification. Since lawyer advertising through public media and written or recorded communications invites the greatest danger of misleading consumers, the absence or denial of the organization's authority to grant certification must be clearly stated in such advertising in the same sentence that communicates the certification.~~

~~[5]   In jurisdictions where no appropriate regulatory authority has a procedure for approving organizations granting certification, the Rule requires that a lawyer clearly state such lack of procedure. If, however, the named organization has been accredited by the American Bar Association to certify lawyers as specialists in a particular field of law, the communication need not contain such a statement.~~

RULE 7.5: FIRM NAMES AND LETTERHEADS

(a)   A lawyer shall not use a firm name, letterhead or other professional designation that violates Rule 7.1. A trade name may be used by a lawyer in private practice if it does not imply a connection with a government agency or with a public or charitable legal services organization and is not otherwise in violation of Rule 7.1.

(b)   A law firm with offices in more than one jurisdiction may use the same name or other professional designation in each jurisdiction, but identification of the lawyers in an office of the firm shall indicate the jurisdictional limitations on those not licensed to practice in the jurisdiction where the office is located.

(c)   The name of a lawyer holding a public office shall not be used in the name of a law firm, or in communications on its behalf, during any substantial period in which the lawyer is not actively and regularly practicing with the firm.

(d)   Lawyers may state or imply that they practice in a partnership or other organization only when that is the fact.

Comment

[1]   A firm may be designated by the names of all or some of its members, by the names of deceased members where there has been a continuing succession in the firm's identity or by a trade name such as the "ABC Legal Clinic." A lawyer or law firm may also be designated by a distinctive website address or comparable professional designation. Although the United States Supreme Court has held that legislation may prohibit the use of trade names in professional practice, use of such names in law practice is acceptable so long as it is not misleading. If a private firm uses a trade name that includes a geographical name such as "Springfield Legal Clinic," an express disclaimer that it is a public legal aid agency may be required to avoid a misleading implication. It may be observed that any firm name including the name of a deceased partner is, strictly speaking, a trade name. The use of such names to designate law firms has proven a useful means of identification. <u>However, it is misleading to use the name of a lawyer not associated with the firm or a predecessor of the firm, or the name of a nonlawyer.</u>

[2]   With regard to paragraph (d), lawyers sharing office facilities, but who are not in fact associated with each other in a law firm, may not denominate themselves as, for example, "Smith and Jones," for that title suggests that they are practicing law together in a firm.

RULE 7.6: POLITICAL CONTRIBUTIONS TO OBTAIN GOVERNMENT LEGAL ENGAGEMENTS OR APPOINTMENTS BY JUDGES

A lawyer or law firm shall not accept a government legal engagement or an appointment by a judge if the lawyer or law firm makes a political contribution or solicits political contributions for the purpose of obtaining or being considered for that type of legal engagement or appointment.

Comment

[1]   Lawyers have a right to participate fully in the political process, which includes making and soliciting political contributions to candidates for judicial and other public office. Nevertheless, when lawyers make or solicit political contributions in order to obtain an engagement for legal work awarded by a government agency, or to obtain appointment by a judge, the public may legitimately question whether the lawyers engaged to perform the work are selected on the basis of competence and merit. In such a circumstance, the integrity of the profession is undermined.

[2]   The term "political contribution" denotes any gift, subscription, loan, advance or deposit of anything of value made directly or indirectly to a candidate, incumbent, political party or campaign committee to influence or provide financial support for election to or retention in judicial or other government office. Political contributions in initiative and referendum elections are not included. For purposes of this Rule, the term "political contribution" does not include uncompensated services.

[3]   Subject to the exceptions below, (i) the term "government legal engagement" denotes any engagement to provide legal services that a public official has the direct or indirect power to award; and (ii) the term "appointment by a judge" denotes an appointment to a position such as referee, commissioner, special master, receiver, guardian or other similar position that is made by a judge. Those terms do not, however, include (a) substantially uncompensated services; (b) engagements or appointments made on the basis of experience, expertise, professional qualifications and cost following a request for proposal or other process that is free from influence based upon political contributions; and (c) engagements or appointments made on a rotational basis from a list compiled without regard to political contributions.

[4]   The term "lawyer or law firm" includes a political action committee or other entity owned or controlled by a lawyer or law firm.

[5]   Political contributions are for the purpose of obtaining or being considered for a government legal engagement or appointment by a judge if, but for the desire to be considered for the legal engagement or appointment, the lawyer or law firm would not have made or solicited the contributions. The purpose may be determined by an examination of the circumstances in which the contributions occur. For example, one or more contributions that in the aggregate are substantial in relation to other contributions by lawyers or law firms, made for the benefit of an official in a position to influence award of a government legal engagement, and followed by an award of the legal engagement to the contributing or soliciting lawyer or the lawyer's firm would support an inference that the purpose of the contributions was to obtain the engagement, absent other factors that weigh against existence of the proscribed purpose. Those factors may include among others that the contribution or solicitation was made to further a political, social, or economic interest or because of an existing personal, family, or professional relationship with a candidate.

[6]   If a lawyer makes or solicits a political contribution under circumstances that constitute bribery or another crime, Rule 8.4(b) is implicated.

RULE 8.1: BAR ADMISSION AND DISCIPLINARY MATTERS

An applicant for admission to the bar, or a lawyer in connection with a bar admission application or in connection with a disciplinary matter, shall not:

(a)   knowingly make a false statement of material fact; or

(b)   fail to disclose a fact necessary to correct a misapprehension known by the person to have arisen in the matter, or knowingly fail to respond to a lawful demand for information from an admissions or disciplinary authority, except that this rule does not require disclosure of information otherwise protected by Rule 1.6.

Comment

[1]   The duty imposed by this Rule extends to persons seeking admission to the bar as well as to lawyers. Hence, if a person makes a material false statement in connection with an application for admission, it may be the basis for subsequent disciplinary action if the person is admitted, and in any event may be relevant in a subsequent admission application. The duty imposed by this Rule applies to a lawyer's own admission or discipline as well as that of others. Thus, it is a separate professional offense for a lawyer to knowingly make a misrepresentation or omission in connection with a disciplinary investigation of the lawyer's own conduct. ~~This~~ Paragraph (b) of this Rule also requires correction of any prior misstatement in the matter that the applicant or lawyer may have made and affirmative clarification of any misunderstanding on the part of the admissions or disciplinary authority of which the person involved becomes aware.

[2]   This Rule is subject to the provisions of the fifth amendment of the United States Constitution and corresponding provisions of state constitutions. A person relying on such a provision in response to a question, however, should do so openly and not use the right of nondisclosure as a justification for failure to comply with this Rule.

[3]   A lawyer representing an applicant for admission to the bar, or representing a lawyer who is the subject of a disciplinary inquiry or proceeding, is governed by the rules applicable to the client-lawyer relationship, including Rule 1.6 and, in some cases, Rule 3.3.

RULE 8.2: JUDICIAL AND LEGAL OFFICIALS

(a)   A lawyer shall not make a statement that the lawyer knows to be false or with reckless disregard as to its truth or falsity concerning the qualifications or integrity of a judge, adjudicatory officer or public legal officer, or of a candidate for election or appointment to judicial or legal office.

(b)   A lawyer who is a candidate for judicial office shall comply with the applicable provisions of the Code of Judicial Conduct.

Comment

[1]   Assessments by lawyers are relied on in evaluating the professional or personal fitness of persons being considered for election or appointment to judicial office and to public legal offices, such as attorney general, prosecuting attorney and public defender. Expressing honest and candid opinions on such matters contributes to improving the administration of justice. Conversely, false statements by a lawyer can unfairly undermine public confidence in the administration of justice.

~~[2]   When a lawyer seeks judicial office, the lawyer should be bound~~ by applicable limitations on political activity.

[3]   To maintain the fair and independent administration of justice, lawyers are encouraged to continue traditional efforts to defend judges and courts unjustly criticized.

RULE 8.3: REPORTING PROFESSIONAL MISCONDUCT

(a)   A lawyer ~~having knowledge~~ who knows that another lawyer has committed a violation of the Rules of Professional Conduct that raises a substantial question as to that lawyer's honesty, trustworthiness or fitness as a lawyer in other respects, shall inform the appropriate professional authority.

(b)   A lawyer ~~having knowledge~~ who knows that a judge has committed a violation of applicable rules of judicial conduct that raises a substantial question as to the judge's fitness for office shall inform the appropriate authority.

(c)   This Rule does not require disclosure of information otherwise protected by Rule 1.6 or information gained by a lawyer or judge while ~~serving as a member of~~ participating in an approved lawyers assistance program ~~to the extent that such information would be confidential if it were communicated subject to the attorney-client privilege.~~

Comment

[1]   Self-regulation of the legal profession requires that members of the profession initiate disciplinary investigation when they know of a violation of the Rules of Professional Conduct. Lawyers have a similar obligation with respect to judicial misconduct. An apparently isolated violation may indicate a pattern of misconduct that only a disciplinary investigation can uncover. Reporting a violation is especially important where the victim is unlikely to discover the offense.

[2]   A report about misconduct is not required where it would involve violation of Rule 1.6. However, a lawyer should encourage a client to consent to disclosure where prosecution would not substantially prejudice the client's interests.

[3]   If a lawyer were obliged to report every violation of the Rules, the failure to report any violation would itself be a professional offense. Such a requirement existed in many jurisdictions but proved to be unenforceable. This Rule limits the reporting obligation to those offenses that a self-regulating profession must vigorously endeavor to prevent. A measure of judgment is, therefore, required in complying with the provisions of this Rule. The term "substantial" refers to the seriousness of the possible offense and not the quantum of evidence of which the lawyer is aware. A report should be made to the bar disciplinary agency unless some other agency, such as a peer review agency, is more appropriate in the circumstances. Similar considerations apply to the reporting of judicial misconduct.

[4] The duty to report professional misconduct does not apply to a lawyer retained to represent a lawyer whose professional conduct is in question. Such a situation is governed by the Rules applicable to the client-lawyer relationship.

[5] Information about a lawyer's or judge's misconduct or fitness may be received by a lawyer in the course of that lawyer's participation in an approved lawyers or judges assistance program. In that circumstance, providing for ~~the confidentiality of such information~~ an exception to the reporting requirements of paragraphs (a) and (b) of this Rule encourages lawyers and judges to seek treatment through such a program. Conversely, without such ~~confidentiality~~ an exception, lawyers and judges may hesitate to seek assistance from these programs, which may then result in additional harm to their professional careers and additional injury to the welfare of clients and the public. ~~The Rule therefore exempts the lawyer from the reporting requirements of paragraphs (a) and (b) with respect to information that would be privileged if the relationship between the impaired lawyer or judge and the recipient of the information were that of a client and a lawyer. On the other hand, a lawyer who receives such information would nevertheless be required to comply with the Rule 8.3 reporting provisions to report misconduct if the impaired lawyer or judge indicates an intent to engage in illegal activity, for example, the conversion of client funds to his or her use.~~ These Rules do not otherwise address the confidentiality of information received by a lawyer or judge participating in an approved lawyers assistance program; such an obligation, however, may be imposed by the rules of the program or other law.

RULE 8.4: MISCONDUCT

It is professional misconduct for a lawyer to:

(a) violate or attempt to violate the Rules of Professional Conduct, knowingly assist or induce another to do so, or do so through the acts of another;

(b) commit a criminal act that reflects adversely on the lawyer's honesty, trustworthiness or fitness as a lawyer in other respects;

(c) engage in conduct involving dishonesty, fraud, deceit or misrepresentation;

(d) engage in conduct that is prejudicial to the administration of justice;

(e) state or imply an ability to influence improperly a government agency or official or to achieve results by means that violate the Rules of Professional Conduct or other law; or

(f) knowingly assist a judge or judicial officer in conduct that is a violation of applicable rules of judicial conduct or other law.

Comment

[1] Lawyers are subject to discipline when they violate or attempt to violate the Rules of Professional Conduct, knowingly assist or induce another to do so or do so through the acts of another, as when they request or

instruct an agent to do so on the lawyer's behalf. Paragraph (a), however, does not prohibit a lawyer from advising a client concerning action the client is legally entitled to take.

[1] [2] Many kinds of illegal conduct reflect adversely on fitness to practice law, such as offenses involving fraud and the offense of willful failure to file an income tax return. However, some kinds of offenses carry no such implication. Traditionally, the distinction was drawn in terms of offenses involving "moral turpitude." That concept can be construed to include offenses concerning some matters of personal morality, such as adultery and comparable offenses, that have no specific connection to fitness for the practice of law. Although a lawyer is personally answerable to the entire criminal law, a lawyer should be professionally answerable only for offenses that indicate lack of those characteristics relevant to law practice. Offenses involving violence, dishonesty, breach of trust, or serious interference with the administration of justice are in that category. A pattern of repeated offenses, even ones of minor significance when considered separately, can indicate indifference to legal obligation.

[2] [3] A lawyer who, in the course of representing a client, knowingly manifests by words or conduct, bias or prejudice based upon race, sex, religion, national origin, disability, age, sexual orientation or socioeconomic status, violates paragraph (d) when such actions are prejudicial to the administration of justice. Legitimate advocacy respecting the foregoing factors does not violate paragraph (d). A trial judge's finding that peremptory challenges were exercised on a discriminatory basis does not alone establish a violation of this rule.

[3] [4] A lawyer may refuse to comply with an obligation imposed by law upon a good faith belief that no valid obligation exists. The provisions of Rule 1.2(d) concerning a good faith challenge to the validity, scope, meaning or application of the law apply to challenges of legal regulation of the practice of law.

[4] [5] Lawyers holding public office assume legal responsibilities going beyond those of other citizens. A lawyer's abuse of public office can suggest an inability to fulfill the professional role of lawyers. The same is true of abuse of positions of private trust such as trustee, executor, administrator, guardian, agent and officer, director or manager of a corporation or other organization.

RULE 8.5: DISCIPLINARY AUTHORITY; CHOICE OF LAW

(a)   Disciplinary Authority. A lawyer admitted to practice in this jurisdiction is subject to the disciplinary authority of this jurisdiction, regardless of where the lawyer's conduct occurs. A lawyer not admitted in this jurisdiction is also subject to the disciplinary authority of this jurisdiction if the lawyer provides or offers to provide any legal services in this jurisdiction. A lawyer may be subject to the disciplinary authority of both this jurisdiction and another jurisdiction where the lawyer is admitted for the same conduct.

(b)   Choice of Law. In any exercise of the disciplinary authority of this jurisdiction, the rules of professional conduct to be applied shall be as follows:

(1)   for conduct in connection with a ~~proceeding in~~ matter pending before a ~~court before which a lawyer has been admitted to practice (either generally or for purposes of that proceeding)~~ tribunal, the rules ~~to be applied shall be the rules~~ of the jurisdiction in which the ~~court~~ tribunal sits, unless the rules of the ~~court~~ tribunal provide otherwise; and

(2)   for any other conduct, the rules of the jurisdiction in which the lawyer's conduct occurred, or, if the predominant effect of the conduct is in a different jurisdiction, the rules of that jurisdiction shall be applied to the conduct. A lawyer shall not be subject to discipline if the lawyer's conduct conforms to the rules of a jurisdiction in which the lawyer reasonably believes the predominant effect of the lawyer's conduct will occur.

~~(i)   if the lawyer is licensed to practice only in this jurisdiction, the rules to be applied shall be the rules of this jurisdiction, and~~

~~(ii)   if the lawyer is licensed to practice in this and another jurisdiction, the rules to be applied shall be the rules of the admitting jurisdiction in which the lawyer principally practices; provided, however, that if particular conduct clearly has its predominant effect in another jurisdiction in which the lawyer is licensed to practice, the rules of that jurisdiction shall be applied to that conduct.~~

Comment

Disciplinary Authority

[1]   ~~Paragraph (a) restates~~ It is longstanding law that the conduct of a lawyer admitted to practice in this jurisdiction is subject to the disciplinary authority of this jurisdiction. Extension of the disciplinary authority of this jurisdiction to other lawyers who provide or offer to provide legal services in this jurisdiction is for the protection of the citizens of this jurisdiction. Reciprocal enforcement of a jurisdiction's disciplinary findings and sanctions will further advance the purposes of this Rule. *See,* Rules 6 and 22, ABA *Model Rules for Lawyer Disciplinary Enforcement.* A lawyer who is subject to the disciplinary authority of this jurisdiction under Rule 8.5(a) appoints an official to be designated by this Court to receive service of process in this jurisdiction. The fact that the lawyer is subject to the disciplinary authority of this jurisdiction may be a factor in determining whether personal jurisdiction may be asserted over the lawyer for civil matters.

Choice of Law

[2]   A lawyer may be potentially subject to more than one set of rules of professional conduct which impose different obligations. The lawyer

~~may be licensed to practice in more than one jurisdiction with differing rules,~~ or may be admitted to practice before a particular court with rules that differ from those of the jurisdiction or jurisdictions in which the lawyer is licensed to practice. ~~In the past, decisions have not developed clear or consistent guidance as to which rules apply in such circumstances.~~ Additionally, the lawyer's conduct may involve significant contacts with more than one jurisdiction.

[3]   Paragraph (b) seeks to resolve such potential conflicts. Its premise is that minimizing conflicts between rules, as well as uncertainty about which rules are applicable, is in the best interest of both clients and the profession (as well as the bodies having authority to regulate the profession). Accordingly, it takes the approach of (i) providing that any particular conduct of a lawyer shall be subject to only one set of rules of professional conduct, ~~and~~ (ii) making the determination of which set of rules applies to particular conduct as straightforward as possible, consistent with recognition of appropriate regulatory interests of relevant jurisdictions, and (iii) providing protection from discipline for lawyers who act reasonably in the face of uncertainty.

[4]   Paragraph (b)(1) provides that as to a lawyer's conduct relating to a proceeding ~~in~~ pending before a ~~court before which the lawyer is admitted to practice (either generally or pro hac vice)~~ tribunal, the lawyer shall be subject only to the rules of ~~professional conduct of that court~~ the jurisdiction in which the tribunal sits unless the rules of the tribunal, including its choice of law rule, provide otherwise. As to all other conduct, including conduct in anticipation of a proceeding not yet pending before a tribunal, paragraph (b)(2) provides that a lawyer ~~licensed to practice only in this jurisdiction shall be subject to the rules of professional conduct of this jurisdiction, and that a lawyer licensed in multiple jurisdictions shall be subject only to the rules of the jurisdiction where he or she (as an individual, not his or her firm) principally practices, but with one exception: if particular conduct clearly has its predominant effect in another admitting jurisdiction, then only the rules of that jurisdiction shall apply. The intention is for the latter exception to be a narrow one. It would be appropriately applied, for example, to a situation in which a lawyer admitted in, and principally practicing in, State A, but also admitted in State B, handled an acquisition by a company whose headquarters and operations were in State B of another, similar such company. The exception would not appropriately be applied, on the other hand, if the lawyer handled an acquisition by a company whose headquarters and operations were in State A of a company whose headquarters and main operations were in State A, but which also had some operations in State B~~ shall be subject to the rules of the jurisdiction in which the lawyer's conduct occurred, or, if the predominant effect of the conduct is in another jurisdiction, the rules of that jurisdiction shall be applied to the conduct. In the case of conduct in anticipation of a proceeding that is likely to be before a tribunal, the predominant effect of such conduct could be where the conduct occurred, where the tribunal sits or in another jurisdiction.

[5]   When a lawyer's conduct involves significant contacts with more than one jurisdiction, it may not be clear whether the predominant effect of the lawyer's conduct will occur in a jurisdiction other than the one in which the conduct occurred. So long as the lawyer's conduct conforms to the rules of a jurisdiction in which the lawyer reasonably believes the predominant effect will occur, the lawyer shall not be subject to discipline under this Rule. With respect to conflicts of interest, in determining a lawyer's reasonable belief under paragraph (b)(2), a written agreement between the lawyer and client that reasonably specifies a particular jurisdiction as within the scope of that paragraph may be considered if the agreement was obtained with the client's informed consent confirmed in the agreement.

~~[5]~~ [6] If two admitting jurisdictions were to proceed against a lawyer for the same conduct, they should, applying this rule, identify the same governing ethics rules. They should take all appropriate steps to see that they do apply the same rule to the same conduct, and in all events should avoid proceeding against a lawyer on the basis of two inconsistent rules.

~~[6]~~ [7] The choice of law provision ~~is not intended to apply to~~ applies to lawyers engaged in transnational practice, unless international law, treaties or other agreements between competent regulatory authorities in the affected jurisdictions provide otherwise. ~~Choice of law in this context should be the subject of agreements between jurisdictions or of appropriate international law.~~

I. AMERICAN BAR ASSOCIATION MODEL COURT RULE ON INSURANCE DISCLOSURE (2004)

2016 Editors' Introduction. In August 2004, the ABA House of Delegates adopted a Model Court Rule on Insurance Disclosure. At present, 24 states require lawyers licensed in the state to make some form of disclosure about whether they carry malpractice insurance.

Seven states, through a rule of professional conduct, require lawyers who do *not* have insurance coverage or carry inadequate coverage to disclose directly to the client: Alaska, California, New Hampshire, New Mexico, Ohio, Pennsylvania and South Dakota. New Mexico lawyers have to advise clients in writing if they carry less than $100,000 in liability insurance per claim or less than $300,000 in aggregate coverage. South Dakota goes so far as to require lawyers to include the information on their letterhead, in a type size "no smaller than the type used for showing the individual lawyer's names." S.D. Rule of Prof. Conduct 7.5.

As of this writing, 17 states (Arizona, Colorado, Delaware, Hawaii, Idaho, Illinois, Kansas, Massachusetts, Michigan, Minnesota, Nebraska, Nevada, North Dakota, Rhode Island, Virginia, Washington, and West Virginia) require lawyers licensed in those states to disclose on their annual bar registration forms whether they carry the insurance. These states then make the information available to the public, either on their web sites or in answer to inquiries from clients or prospective clients. Since this volume was last published, one state (North Carolina) withdrew its rule requiring disclosure on the annual bar registration.

Six other states are currently considering adoption of an insurance disclosure rule (Maine, New Jersey, New York, South Carolina, Utah and Vermont).

To date, five states, Arkansas, Connecticut, Florida, Kentucky, and Texas have declined to adopt an insurance disclosure rule.

Effective January 1, 2010, California Rule of Professional Conduct 4-210, requires a lawyer who does not carry professional liability insurance to disclose that fact to a client in writing at the time of engagement whenever the actual representation exceeds four hours. A lawyer also has to inform an existing client within 30 days if the lawyer ceases to carry insurance. The Rule does not apply to government lawyers and in-house counsel.

Finally, only one state, Oregon, currently requires lawyers to carry malpractice insurance.

ABA MODEL COURT RULE ON INSURANCE DISCLOSURE
AUGUST 2004

Copyright © 2005 by the American Bar Association.

RULE ___. INSURANCE DISCLOSURE

A.   **Each lawyer admitted to the active practice of law shall certify to the [highest court of the jurisdiction] on or before [December 31 of each year]: 1) whether the lawyer is engaged in the private practice of law; 2) if engaged in the private practice of law, whether the lawyer is currently covered by professional liability insurance; 3) whether the lawyer intends to maintain insurance during the period of time the lawyer is engaged in the private practice of law; and 4) whether the lawyer is exempt from the provisions of this Rule because the lawyer is engaged in the practice of law as a full-time government lawyer or is counsel employed by an organizational client and does not represent clients outside that capacity. Each lawyer admitted to the active practice of law in this jurisdiction who reports being covered by professional liability insurance shall notify [the highest court in the jurisdiction] in writing within 30 days if the insurance policy providing coverage lapses, is no longer in effect or terminates for any reason.**

B.   **The foregoing shall be certified by each lawyer admitted to the active practice of law in this jurisdiction in such form as may be prescribed by the [highest court of the jurisdiction]. The information submitted pursuant to this Rule will** be made available to the public by such means as may be designated by the [highest court of the jurisdiction].

C. Any lawyer admitted to the active practice of law who fails to comply with this Rule in a timely fashion, as defined by the [highest court in the jurisdiction], may be suspended from the practice of law until such time as the lawyer complies. Supplying false information in response to this Rule shall subject the lawyer to appropriate disciplinary action.

II. AMERICAN BAR ASSOCIATION MODEL RULE FOR ADMISSION BY MOTION (2012)

Editors' Introduction. In August 2012, the ABA House of Delegates approved revisions to the Model Rule for Admission By Motion as part of the Ethics 20/20 Commission's proposals related to multijurisdictional practice.

ABA MODEL RULE FOR ADMISSION BY MOTION
AUGUST 2012

Copyright © 2012 by the American Bar Association.

Reprinted with permission. This information or any or portion thereof may not be copied or disseminated in any form or by any means or stored in an electronic database or retrieval system without the express written consent of the American Bar Association.

RULE ___. ADMISSION BY MOTION

1. An applicant who meets the requirements of (a) through (g) of this Rule may, upon motion, be admitted to the practice of law in this jurisdiction. The applicant shall:

(a) have been admitted to practice law in another state, territory, or the District of Columbia;

(b) hold a J.D. or LL.B. degree from a law school approved by the Council of the Section of Legal Education and Admissions to the Bar of the American Bar Association at the time the applicant matriculated or graduated;

(c) have been primarily engaged in the active practice of law in one or more states, territories or the District of Columbia for five three of the seven five years immediately preceding the date upon which the application is filed;

(d) establish that the applicant is currently a member in good standing in all jurisdictions where admitted;

(e) establish that the applicant is not currently subject to lawyer discipline or the subject of a pending disciplinary matter in any jurisdiction;

>   (f)   establish that the applicant possesses the character
>   and fitness to practice law in this jurisdiction; and
>
>   (g)   designate the Clerk of the jurisdiction's highest
>   court for service of process.

2.   For purposes of this Rule, the "active practice of law" shall
     include the following activities, if performed in a jurisdic-
     tion in which the applicant is admitted and authorized to
     practice, or if performed in a jurisdiction that affirmatively
     permits such activity by a lawyer not admitted in that juris-
     diction; however, in no event shall any activities that were
     performed pursuant to the Model Rule on Practice Pending
     Admission or in advance of bar admission in some state,
     territory, or the District of Columbia be accepted toward
     the durational requirement:

     (a)   Representation of one or more clients in the private
           practice of law;

     (b)   Service as a lawyer with a local, state, territorial or
           federal agency, including military service;

     (c)   Teaching law at a law school approved by the
           Council of the Section of Legal Education and
           Admissions to the Bar of the American Bar
           Association;

     (d)   Service as a judge in a federal, state, territorial or
           local court of record;

     (e)   Service as a judicial law clerk; or

     (f)   Service as in-house counsel provided to the law-
           yer's employer or its organizational affiliates.

3.   For purposes of this Rule, the active practice of law shall
     not include work that, as undertaken, constituted the unau-
     thorized practice of law in the jurisdiction in which it was
     performed or in the jurisdiction in which the clients
     receiving the unauthorized services were located.

4.   An applicant who has failed a bar examination adminis-
     tered in this jurisdiction within five years of the date of fil-
     ing an application under this Rule shall not be eligible for
     admission on motion.

III. AMERICAN BAR ASSOCIATION MODEL RULE ON PRACTICE PENDING ADMISSION (2012)

Editors' Introduction. In August 2012, the ABA House of Delegates the
Model Rule on Practice Pending Admission as part of the Ethics 20/20
Commission's proposals related to multijurisdictional practice.

ABA MODEL RULE ON PRACTICE PENDING ADMISSION
AUGUST 2012

Copyright © 2012 by the American Bar Association.

RULE ___. PRACTICE PENDING ADMISSION

1. A lawyer currently holding an active license to practice law in another U.S. jurisdiction and who has been engaged in the active practice of law for three of the last five years, may provide legal services in this jurisdiction through an office or other systematic and continuous presence for no more than [365] days, provided that the lawyer:

    a. is not disbarred or suspended from practice in any jurisdiction and is not currently subject to discipline or a pending disciplinary matter in any jurisdiction;

    b. has not previously been denied admission to practice in this jurisdiction or failed this jurisdiction's bar examination;

    c. notifies Disciplinary Counsel and the Admissions Authority in writing prior to initiating practice in this jurisdiction that the lawyer will be doing so pursuant to the authority in this Rule;

    d. submits within [45] days of first establishing an office or other systematic and continuous presence for the practice of law in this jurisdiction a complete application for admission by motion or by examination;

    e. reasonably expects to fulfill all of this jurisdiction's requirements for that form of admission;

    f. associates with a lawyer who is admitted to practice in this jurisdiction;

    g. complies with Rules 7.1 and 7.5 of the Model Rules of Professional Conduct [or jurisdictional equivalent] in all communications with the public and clients regarding the nature and scope of the lawyer's practice authority in this jurisdiction; and

    h. pays any annual client protection fund assessment.

2. A lawyer currently licensed as a foreign legal consultant in another U.S. jurisdiction may provide legal services in this jurisdiction through an office or other systematic and

continuous presence for no more than [365] days, provided that the lawyer:

    a. provides services that are limited to those that may be provided in this jurisdiction by foreign legal consultants;

    b. is a member in good standing of a recognized legal profession in the foreign jurisdiction, the members of which are admitted to practice as lawyers or counselors at law or the equivalent, and are subject to effective regulation and discipline by a duly constituted professional body or a public authority;

    c. submits within [45] days of first establishing an office or other systematic and continuous presence for the practice of law in this jurisdiction a complete application for admission to practice as a foreign legal consultant;

    d. reasonably expects to fulfill all of this jurisdiction's requirements for admission as a foreign legal consultant; and

    e. meets the requirements of paragraphs 1(a), (b), (c), (f), (g), and (h) of this Rule.

3. Prior to admission by motion, through examination, or as a foreign legal consultant, the lawyer may not appear before a tribunal in this jurisdiction that requires pro hac vice admission unless the lawyer is granted such admission.

4. The lawyer must immediately notify Disciplinary Counsel and the Admissions Authority in this jurisdiction if the lawyer becomes subject to a disciplinary matter or disciplinary sanctions in any other jurisdiction at any time during the [365] days of practice authorized by this Rule. The Admissions Authority shall take into account such information in determining whether to grant the lawyer's application for admission to this jurisdiction.

5. The authority in this Rule shall terminate immediately if:

    a. the lawyer withdraws the application for admission by motion, by examination, or as a foreign legal consultant, or if such application is denied, prior to the expiration of [365] days;

    b. the lawyer fails to file the application for admission within [45] days of first establishing an office or other systematic and continuous presence for the practice of law in this jurisdiction;

    c. the lawyer fails to remain in compliance with Paragraph 1 of this Rule;

     d.   the lawyer is disbarred or suspended in any other jurisdiction in which the lawyer is licensed to practice law; or

     e.   the lawyer has not complied with the notification requirements of Paragraph 4 of this Rule.

6.   Upon the termination of authority pursuant to Paragraph 5, the lawyer, within [30] days, shall:

     a.   cease to occupy an office or other systematic and continuous presence for the practice of law in this jurisdiction unless authorized to do so pursuant to another Rule;

     b.   notify all clients being represented in pending matters, and opposing counsel or co-counsel of the termination of the lawyer's authority to practice pursuant to this Rule;

     c.   not undertake any new representation that would require the lawyer to be admitted to practice law in this jurisdiction; and

     d.   take all other necessary steps to protect the interests of the lawyer's clients.

7.   Upon the denial of the lawyer's application for admission by motion, by examination, or as a foreign legal consultant, the Admissions Authority shall immediately notify Disciplinary Counsel that the authority granted by this Rule has terminated.

8.   The Court, in its discretion, may extend the time limits set forth in this Rule for good cause shown.

Comment

[1]   This Rule recognizes that a lawyer admitted in another jurisdiction may need to relocate to or commence practice in this jurisdiction, sometimes on short notice. The admissions process can take considerable time, thus placing a lawyer at risk of engaging in the unauthorized practice of law and leaving the lawyer's clients without the benefit of their chosen counsel. This Rule closes this gap by authorizing the lawyer to practice in this jurisdiction for a limited period of time, up to 365 days, subject to restrictions, while the lawyer diligently seeks admission. The practice authority provided pursuant to this Rule commences immediately upon the lawyer's establishment of an office or other systematic and continuous presence for the practice of law.

[2]   Paragraph 1(f) requires a lawyer practicing in this jurisdiction pursuant to the authority granted under this Rule to associate with a lawyer who is admitted to practice law in this jurisdiction. The association between the incoming lawyer and the lawyer licensed in this jurisdiction is akin to that between a local lawyer and a lawyer practicing in a jurisdiction on a temporary basis pursuant to Model Rule of Professional Conduct 5.5(c)(1).

[3]   While exercising practice authority pursuant to this Rule, a lawyer cannot hold out to the public or otherwise represent that the lawyer is admitted to practice in this jurisdiction. See Model Rule of Professional Conduct 5.5(b)(2). Because such a lawyer will typically be assumed to be admitted to practice in this jurisdiction, that lawyer must disclose the limited practice authority and jurisdiction of licensure in all communications with potential clients, such as on business cards, websites, and letterhead. Further, the lawyer must disclose the limited practice authority to all potential clients before agreeing to represent them. See Model Rules 7.1 and 7.5(b).

[4]   The provisions of paragraph 5 (a) through (d) of this Rule are necessary to avoid prejudicing the rights of existing clients or other parties. Thirty days should be sufficient for the lawyer to wind up his or her practice in this jurisdiction in an orderly manner.

PART II

ABA MODEL CODE OF PROFESSIONAL RESPONSIBILITY (1969)

Table of Contents

	Page
PREAMBLE AND PRELIMINARY STATEMENT	422

CANON 1.   A LAWYER SHOULD ASSIST IN MAINTAINING THE INTEGRITY AND COMPETENCE OF THE LEGAL PROFESSION 425

	Page
Ethical Considerations	425
Disciplinary Rules	426
DR 1-101 Maintaining Integrity and Competence of the Legal Profession	426
DR 1-102 Misconduct	426
DR 1-103 Disclosure of Information to Authorities	427

CANON 2.   A LAWYER SHOULD ASSIST THE LEGAL PROFESSION IN FULFILLING ITS DUTY TO MAKE LEGAL COUNSEL AVAILABLE 430

	Page
Ethical Considerations	430
Recognition of Legal Problems	430
Selection of a Lawyer	431
Selection of a Lawyer: Lawyer Advertising	432
Financial Ability to Employ Counsel: Generally	434
Financial Ability to Employ Counsel: Persons Able to Pay Reasonable Fees	434
Financial Ability to Employ Counsel: Persons Unable to Pay Reasonable Fees	435
Acceptance and Retention of Employment	436
Disciplinary Rules	437
DR 2-101 Publicity in General	437
DR 2-102 Professional Notices, Letterheads, Offices	440
DR 2-103 Recommendation of Professional Employment	441
DR 2-104 Suggestion of Need of Legal Services	443
DR 2-105 Limitation of Practice	444

DR 2-106   Fees for Legal Services 444
DR 2-107   Division of Fees Among Lawyers 445
DR 2-108   Agreements Restricting the Practice of a Lawyer 445
DR 2-109   Acceptance of Employment 445
DR 2-110   Withdrawal from Employment 445

CANON 3.   A LAWYER SHOULD ASSIST IN PREVENTING THE UNAUTHORIZED PRACTICE OF LAW 456

Ethical Considerations 456
Disciplinary Rules 457
DR 3-101   Aiding Unauthorized Practice of Law 457
DR 3-102   Dividing Legal Fees with a Nonlawyer 458
DR 3-103   Forming a Partnership with a Nonlawyer 458

CANON 4.   A LAWYER SHOULD PRESERVE THE CONFIDENCES AND SECRETS OF A CLIENT 460

Ethical Considerations 460
Disciplinary Rules 461
DR 4-101   Preservation of Confidences and Secrets 461

CANON 5.   A LAWYER SHOULD EXERCISE INDEPENDENT PROFESSIONAL JUDGMENT ON BEHALF OF A CLIENT 465

Ethical Considerations 465
Interests of a Lawyer That May Affect His Judgment 465
Interests of Multiple Clients 468
Desires of Third Persons 469
Disciplinary Rules 470
DR 5-101   Refusing Employment When the Interests of the Lawyer May Impair His Independent Professional Judgment 470
DR 5-102   Withdrawal as Counsel When the Lawyer Becomes a Witness 471
DR 5-103   Avoiding Acquisition of Interest in Litigation 471
DR 5-104   Limiting Acquisition of Interest in Litigation 471
DR 5-105   Refusing to Accept or Continue Employment if the Interests of Another Client May Impair the Independent Professional Judgment of the Lawyer 472
DR 5-106   Settling Similar Claims of Clients 472
DR 5-107   Avoiding Influence by Others Than the Client 472

CANON 6.   A LAWYER SHOULD REPRESENT A CLIENT COMPETENTLY 478

Ethical Considerations 478
Disciplinary Rules 479

DR 6-101   Failing to Act Competently 479

DR 6-102   Limiting Liability to Client 479

**CANON 7. A LAWYER SHOULD REPRESENT A CLIENT
ZEALOUSLY WITHIN THE BOUNDS OF THE LAW** 480

Ethical Considerations 480

Duty of the Lawyer to a Client 481

Duty of the Lawyer to the Adversary System of Justice 484

Disciplinary Rules 488

DR 7-101   Representing a Client Zealously 488

DR 7-102   Representing a Client within the Bounds of the Law 488

DR 7-103   Performing the Duty of Public Prosecutor or Other
Government Lawyer 489

DR 7-104   Communicating with One of Adverse Interest 489

DR 7-105   Threatening Criminal Prosecution 490

DR 7-106   Trial Conduct 490

DR 7-107   Trial Publicity 490

DR 7-108   Communication with or Investigation of Jurors 493

DR 7-109   Contact with Witnesses 494

DR 7-110   Contact with Officials 494

**CANON 8. A LAWYER SHOULD ASSIST IN IMPROVING THE
LEGAL SYSTEM** 505

Ethical Considerations 505

Disciplinary Rules 507

DR 8-101   Action as a Public Official 507

DR 8-102   Statements Concerning Judges and Other
Adjudicatory Officers 507

DR 8-103   Lawyer Candidate for Judicial Office 507

**CANON 9. A LAWYER SHOULD AVOID EVEN THE
APPEARANCE OF PROFESSIONAL IMPROPRIETY** ... 509

Ethical Considerations 509

Disciplinary Rules 510

DR 9-101   Avoiding Even the Appearance of Impropriety 510

DR 9-102   Preserving Identity of Funds and Property of a Client 511

DEFINITIONS 513

ABA MODEL CODE OF PROFESSIONAL RESPONSIBILITY

Preamble And Preliminary Statement

Preamble[1]

The continued existence of a free and democratic society depends upon recognition of the concept that justice is based upon the rule of law grounded in respect for the dignity of the individual and his capacity through reason for enlightened self-government.[2] Law so grounded makes justice possible, for only through such law does the dignity of the individual attain respect and protection. Without it, individual rights become subject to unrestrained power, respect for law is destroyed, and rational self-government is impossible.

Lawyers, as guardians of the law, play a vital role in the preservation of society. The fulfillment of this role requires an understanding by lawyers of their relationship with and function in our legal system.[3] A consequent obligation of lawyers is to maintain the highest standards of ethical conduct.

In fulfilling his professional responsibilities, a lawyer necessarily assumes various roles that require the performance of many difficult tasks. Not every situation which he may encounter can be foreseen,[4] but fundamental ethical principles are always present to guide him. Within the framework of these principles a lawyer must with courage and foresight be able and ready to shape the body of the law to the every-changing relationships of society.[5]

The Model Code of Professional Responsibility points the way to the aspiring and provides standards by which to judge the transgressor. Each lawyer must find within his own conscience the touchstone against which to test the extent to which his actions should rise above minimum standards. But in the last analysis it is the desire for the respect and confidence of the members of his profession and of the society which he serves that should provide to a lawyer the incentive for the highest possible degree of ethical conduct. The possible loss of that respect and confidence is the ultimate sanction. So long as its practitioners are guided by these principles, the law will continue to be a noble profession. This is its greatness and its strength, which permit of no compromise.

Preliminary Statement

In furtherance of the principles stated in the Preamble, the American Bar Association has promulgated this Model Code of Professional Responsibility, consisting of three separate but interrelated parts: Canons, Ethical Considerations, and Disciplinary Rules.[6] The Model Code is designed to be adopted by appropriate agencies both as an inspirational guide to the members of the profession and as a basis for disciplinary action when the conduct of a lawyer falls below the required minimum standards stated in the Disciplinary Rules.

Obviously the Canons, Ethical Considerations, and Disciplinary Rules cannot apply to non-lawyers; however, they do define the type of ethical conduct that the public has a right to expect not only of lawyers but also of their non-professional employees and associates in all matters pertaining to professional employment. A lawyer should ultimately be responsible for the conduct of his employees and associates in the course of the professional representation of the client.

The Canons are statements of axiomatic norms, expressing in general terms the standards of professional conduct expected of lawyers in their relationships with the public, with the legal system, and with the legal profession. They embody the general concepts from which the Ethical Consideration and the Disciplinary Rules are derived.

The Ethical Considerations are aspirational in character and represent the objectives toward which every member of the profession should strive. They constitute a body of principles upon which the lawyer can rely for guidance in many specific situations.[7]

The Disciplinary Rules, unlike the Ethical Considerations, are mandatory in character. The Disciplinary Rules state the minimum level of conduct below which no lawyer can fall without being subject to disciplinary action. Within the framework of fair trial,[8] the Disciplinary Rules should be uniformly applied to all lawyers,[9] regardless of the nature of their professional activities.[10] The Model Code makes no attempt to prescribe either disciplinary procedures or penalties[11] for violation of a Disciplinary Rule,[12] nor does it undertake to define standards for civil liability of lawyers for professional conduct. The severity of judgment against one found guilty of violating a Disciplinary Rule should be determined by the character of the offense and the attendant circumstances.[13] An enforcing agency, in applying the Disciplinary Rules, may find interpretive guidance in the basic principles embodied in the Canons and in the objectives reflected in the Ethical Considerations.

NOTES

1. The footnotes are intended merely to enable the reader to relate the provisions of this Model Code to the ABA Canons of Professional Ethics adopted in 1908, as amended, the Opinions of the ABA Committee on Professional Ethics, and a limited number of other sources; they are not intended to be an annotation of the views taken by the ABA Special Committee on Evaluation of Ethical Standards. Footnotes citing ABA Canons refer to the ABA Canons of Professional Ethics, adopted in 1908, as amended.

2. *Cf.* ABA CANONS OF PROFESSIONAL ETHICS, Preamble (1908).

3. "[T]he lawyer stands today in special need of a clear understanding of his obligations and of the vital connection between these obligations and the role his profession plays in society." *Professional Responsibility: Report of the Joint Conference*, 44 A.B.A.J. 1159, 1160 (1958).

4. "No general statement of the responsibilities of the legal profession can encompass all the situations in which the lawyer may be placed. Each position held by him makes its own peculiar demands. These demands the lawyer must clarify for himself in the light of the particular role in which he serves. *Professional Responsibility: Report of the Joint Conference*, 44 A.B.A.J. 1159, 1218 (1958).

5. "The law and its institutions change as social conditions change. They must change if they are to preserve, much less advance, the political and social values from which they derive their purposes and their life. This is true of the most important of legal institutions, the profession of law. The profession, too, much change when conditions change in order to preserve and advance the social values that are its reasons for being."

Cheatham, *Availability of Legal Services: The Responsibility of the Individual Lawyer and the Organized Bar*, 12 U.C.L.A. L. REV. 438, 440 (1965).

6. The Supreme Court of Wisconsin adopted a Code of Judicial Ethics in 1967. "The code is divided into standards and rules, the standards being statements of what the general desirable level of conduct should be, the rules being particular canons, the violation of which shall subject an individual judge to sanctions." In re Promulgation of a Code of Judicial Ethics, 36 Wis. 2d 252, 255, 153 N.W. 2d 873, 874 (1967).

The portion of the Wisconsin Code of Judicial Ethics entitled "Standards" states that "[t]he following standards set forth significant qualities of the ideal judge...." *Id.*, 36 Wis.2d at 256, 153 N.W. 2d at 875. The portion entitled "Rules" states that "[t]he court promulgates the following rules because the requirements of judicial conduct embodied therein are of sufficient gravity to warrant sanctions if they are not obeyed...." *Id.*, 36 Wis.2d at 259, 153 N.W. 2d at 876.

7. "Under the conditions of modern practice it is peculiarly necessary that the lawyer should understand, not merely the established standards of professional conduct, but the reasons underlying these standards. Today the lawyer plays a changing and increasingly varied role. In many developing fields the precise contribution of the legal profession is as yet undefined." *Professional Responsibility: Report of the Joint Conference*, 44 A.B.A.J. 1159 (1958).

"A true sense of professional responsibility must derive from an understanding of the reasons that lie back of specific restraints, such as those embodied in the Canons. The grounds for the lawyer's peculiar obligations are to be found in the nature of his calling. The lawyer who seeks a clear understanding of his duties will be led to reflect on the special services his profession renders to society and the services it might render if its full capacities were realized. When the lawyer fully understands the nature of his office, he will then discern what restraints are necessary to keep that office wholesome and effective." *Id.*

8. "Disbarment, designed to protect the public, is a punishment or penalty imposed on the lawyer.... He is accordingly entitled to procedural due process, which includes fair notice of the charge." In re Ruffalo, 390 U.S. 544, 550, 20 L. Ed. 2d 117, 122 88 S. Ct. 1222, 1226 (1968), *rehearing denied*, 391 U.S. 961, 20 L. Ed. 2d 874, 88 S. Ct. 1833 (1968).

"A State cannot exclude a person from the practice of law or from any other occupation in a manner or for reasons that contravene the Due Process or Equal Protection Clause of the Fourteenth Amendment.... A State can require high standards of qualification... but any qualification must have a rational connection with the applicant's fitness or capacity to practice law." Schware v. Bd. of Bar Examiners, 353 U.S. 232, 239, 1 L. Ed. 2d 796, 801-02, 77 S. Ct. 752, 756 (1957).

"[A]n accused lawyer may expect that he will not be condemned out of a capricious self-righteousness or denied the essentials of a fair hearing." Kingsland v. Dorsey, 338 U.S. 318, 320, 94 L. Ed. 123, 126, 70 S. Ct. 123, 124-25 (1949).

"The attorney and counsellor being, by the solemn judicial act of the court, clothed with his office, does not hold it as a matter of grace and favor. The right which it confers upon him to appear for suitors, and to argue causes, is something more than a mere indulgence, revocable at the pleasure of the court, or at the command of the legislature. It is a right of which he can only be deprived by the judgment of the court, for moral or professional delinquency." Ex parte Garland, 71 U.S. (4 Wall.) 333, 378-79, 18 L. Ed. 366, 370 (1866).

See generally Comment, *Procedural Due Process and Character Hearings for Bar Applicants*, 15 STAN. L. REV. 500 (1963).

9. "The canons of professional ethics must be enforced by the Courts and must be respected by members of the Bar if we are to maintain public confidence in the integrity and impartiality of the administration of justice." In re Meeker, 76 N.M. 354, 357, 414 P.2d 862, 864 (1966), *appeal dismissed*, 385 U.S. 449 (1967).

10. See ABA CANON OF PROFESSIONAL ETHICS, CANON 45 (1908).

11. "Other than serving as a model or derivative source, the American Bar Association Model Code of Professional Responsibility plays no part in the disciplinary proceeding, except as a guide for consideration in adoption of local applicable rules for the regulation of conduct on the part of legal practitioners." ABA COMM. ON PROFESSIONAL ETHICS, INFORMAL OPINION NO. 1420 (1978) [hereinafter each Formal Opinion is cited as *ABA Opinion*]. For the purposes and intended effect of the American Bar Association Model Code of Professional Responsibility and of the opinions of the Standing Committee on Ethics and Professional Responsibility, see Informal Opinion No. 1420.

"There is generally no prescribed discipline for any particular type of improper conduct. The disciplinary measures taken are discretionary with the courts, which may disbar, suspend, or merely censure the attorney as the nature of the offense and past indicia of character may warrant." Note, 43 CORNELL L.Q. 489, 495 (1958).

12. The Model Code seeks only to specify conduct for which a lawyer should be disciplined by courts and governmental agencies which have adopted it. Recommendations as to the procedures to be used in disciplinary actions are within the jurisdiction of the American Bar Association Standing Committee on Professional Discipline.

13. "The severity of the judgment of this court should be in proportion to the gravity of the offenses, the moral turpitude involved, and the extent that the defendant's acts and conduct affect his professional qualifications to practice law." Louisiana State Bar Ass'n v. Steiner, 204 La. 1073, 1092-93, 16 So. 2d 843, 850 (1944) (Higgins, J., concurring in decree).

"Certainly an erring lawyer who has been disciplined and who having paid the penalty has given satisfactory evidence of repentance and has been rehabilitated and restored to his place at the bar by the court which knows him best ought not to have what amounts to an order of permanent disbarment entered against him by a federal court solely on the basis of an earlier criminal record and without regard to his subsequent rehabilitation and present good character.... We think, therefore, that the district court should reconsider the appellant's application for admission and grant it unless the court finds it to be a fact that the appellant is not presently of good moral or professional character." In re Dreier, 258 F.2d 68, 69-70 (3d Cir. 1958).

CANON 1

A Lawyer Should Assist in Maintaining the Integrity and Competence of the Legal Profession

ETHICAL CONSIDERATIONS

EC 1-1 A basic tenet of the professional responsibility of lawyers is that every person in our society should have ready access to the independent professional services of a lawyer of integrity and competence. Maintaining the integrity and improving the competence of the bar to meet the highest standards is the ethical responsibility of every lawyer.

EC 1-2 The public should be protected from those who are not qualified to be lawyers by reason of a deficiency in education[1] or moral standards[2] or of other relevant factors[3] but who nevertheless seek to practice law. To assure the maintenance of high moral and educational standards of the legal profession, lawyers should affirmatively assist courts and other appropriate bodies in promulgating, enforcing, and improving requirements for admission to the bar.[4] In like manner, the bar has a positive obligation to aid in the continued improvement of all phases of pre-admission and post-admission legal education.

EC 1-3 Before recommending an applicant for admission, a lawyer should satisfy himself that the applicant is of good moral character. Although a lawyer should not become a self-appointed investigator or judge of applicants for admission, he should report to proper officials all unfavorable information he possesses relating to the character or other qualifications of an applicant.[5]

EC 1-4 The integrity of the profession can be maintained only if conduct of lawyers in violation of the Disciplinary Rules is brought to the attention of the proper officials. A lawyer should reveal voluntarily to those officials all unprivileged knowledge of conduct of lawyers which he believes clearly to be in violation of the Disciplinary Rules.[6] A lawyer should, upon request serve on and assist committees and boards having responsibility for the administration of the Disciplinary Rules.[7]

EC 1-5 A lawyer should maintain high standards of professional conduct and should encourage fellow lawyers to do likewise. He should be temperate and dignified, and he should refrain from all illegal and morally reprehensible conduct.[8] Because of his position in society, even minor violations of law by a lawyer may tend to lessen public confidence in the legal profession. Obedience to law exemplifies respect for law. To lawyers especially, respect for the law should be more than a platitude.

EC 1-6 An applicant for admission to the bar or a lawyer may be unqualified, temporarily or permanently, for other than moral and educational reasons, such as mental or emotional instability. Lawyers should be diligent in taking steps to see that during a period of disqualification such person is not granted a license or, if licensed, is not permitted to practice.[9] In like manner, when the disqualification has terminated, members of the bar should assist such person in being licensed, or, if licensed, in being restored to his full right to practice.

DISCIPLINARY RULES

DR 1-101   Maintaining Integrity and Competence of the Legal Profession.

(A)   A lawyer is subject to discipline if he has made a materially false statement in, or if he has deliberately failed to disclose a material fact requested in connection with, his application for admission to the bar.[10]

(B)   A lawyer shall not further the application for admission to the bar of another person known by him to be unqualified in respect to character, education, or other relevant attribute.[11]

DR 1-102   Misconduct.

(A)   A lawyer shall not:

(1)   Violate a Disciplinary Rule.

(2)   Circumvent a Disciplinary Rule through actions of another.[12]

(3)   Engage in illegal conduct involving moral turpitude.[13]

(4)   Engage in conduct involving dishonesty, fraud, deceit, or misrepresentation.

(5) Engage in conduct that is prejudicial to the administration of justice.

(6) Engage in any other conduct that adversely reflects on his fitness to practice law.[14]

DR 1-103   Disclosure of Information to Authorities.

(A) A lawyer possessing unprivileged knowledge of a violation of DR 1-102 shall report such knowledge to a tribunal or other authority empowered to investigate or act upon such violation.[15]

(B) A lawyer possessing unprivileged knowledge or evidence concerning another lawyer or a judge shall reveal fully such knowledge or evidence upon proper request of a tribunal or other authority empowered to investigate or act upon the conduct of lawyers or judges.[16]

NOTES

1. "[W]e cannot conclude that all educational restrictions [on bar admission] are unlawful. We assume that few would deny that a grammar school education requirement, before taking the bar examination, was reasonable. Or that an applicant had to be able to read or write. Once we conclude that *some* restriction is proper, then it becomes a matter of degree — the problem of drawing the line.
    ....
"We conclude the fundamental question here is whether Rule IV, Section 6 of the Rules Pertaining to Admission of Applicants to the State Bar of Arizona is 'arbitrary, capricious and unreasonable.' We conclude an educational requirement of graduation from an accredited law school is not." Hackin v. Lockwood, 361 F.2d 499, 503-4 (9th Cir. 1966), *cert. denied*, 385 U.S. 960, 17 L. Ed.2d 305, 87 S. Ct. 396 (1966).

2. "Every state in the United States, as a prerequisite for admission to the practice of law, requires that applicants possess 'good moral character.' Although the requirement is of judicial origin, it is now embodied in legislation in most states." Comment, *Procedural Due Process and Character Hearings for Bar Applicants*, 15 STAN. L. REV. 500 (1963).

"Good character in the members of the bar is essential to the preservation of the integrity of the courts. The duty and power of the court to guard its portals against intrusion by men and women who are mentally and morally dishonest, unfit because of bad character, evidenced by their course of conduct, to participate in the administrative law, would seem to be unquestioned in the matter of preservation of judicial dignity and integrity." In re Monaghan, 126 Vt. 53, 222 A.2d 665, 670 (1966).

"Fundamentally, the question involved in both situations [i.e. admission and disciplinary proceedings] is the same — is the applicant for admission or the attorney sought to be disciplined a fit and proper person to be permitted to practice law, and that usually turns upon whether he has committed or is likely to continue to commit acts of moral turpitude. At the time of oral argument the attorney for respondent frankly conceded that the test for admission and for discipline is and should be the same. We agree with this concession." Hallinan v. Comm. of Bar Examiners, 65 Cal.2d 447, 453, 421 P.2d 76, 81, 55 Cal.Rptr. 228, 233 (1966).

3. "Proceedings to gain admission to the bar are for the purpose of protecting the public and the courts from the ministrations of persons unfit to practice the profession. Attorneys are officers of the court appointed to assist the court in the administration of justice. Into their hands are committed the property, the liberty and sometimes the lives of their clients. This commitment demands a high degree of intelligence, knowledge of

the law, respect for its function is society, sound and faithful judgment and, above all else, integrity of character in private and professional conduct." In re Monaghan, 126 Vt. 53, 222 A.2d 665, 676 (1966) (Holden, C.J., dissenting).

4. "A bar composed of lawyers of good moral character is a worthy objective but it is unnecessary to sacrifice vital freedoms in order to obtain that goal. It is also important both to society and the bar itself that lawyers be unintimidated — free to think, speak, and act as members of an Independent Bar." Konigsberg v. State Bar, 353 U.S. 252, 273, 1 L. Ed. 2d 810, 825, 77 S. Ct. 722, 733 (1957).

5. See ABA CANONS OF PROFESSIONAL ETHICS, CANON 29 (1908).

6. ABA CANONS OF PROFESSIONAL ETHICS, CANON 28 (1908) designates certain conduct as unprofessional and then states that: "A duty to the public and to the profession devolves upon every member of the Bar having knowledge of such practices upon the part of any practitioner immediately to inform thereof, to the end that the offender may be disbarred." ABA CANON 29 states a broader admonition: "Lawyers should expose without fear or favor before the proper tribunals corrupt or dishonest conduct in the profession."

7. "It is the obligation of the organized Bar and the individual lawyer to give unstinted cooperation and assistance to the highest court of the state in discharging its function and duty with respect to discipline and in purging the profession of the unworthy." *Report of the Special Committee on Disciplinary Procedures*, 80 A.B.A. REP. 463, 470 (1955).

8. *Cf.* ABA CANONS OF PROFESSIONAL ETHICS, CANON 32 (1908).

9. "We decline, on the present record, to disbar Mr. Sherman or to reprimand him — not because we condone his actions, but because, as heretofore indicated, we are concerned with whether he is mentally responsible for what he has done.

"The logic of the situation would seem to dictate the conclusion that, if he was mentally responsible for the conduct we have outlined, he should be disbarred; and, if he was not mentally responsible, he should not be permitted to practice law.

"However, the flaw in the logic is that he may have been mentally irresponsible [at the time of his offensive conduct]..., and, yet, have sufficiently improved in the almost two and one-half years intervening to be able to capably and competently represent his clients....

"We would make clear that we are satisfied that a case has been made against Mr. Sherman, warranting a refusal to permit him to further practice law in this state unless he can establish his mental irresponsibility at the time of the offenses charged. The burden of proof is upon him.

"If he establishes such mental irresponsibility, the burden is then upon him to establish his present capability to practice law." In re Sherman, 58 Wash. 2d 1, 6-7, 354 P.id 888, 890 (1960), *cert. denied*, 371 U.S. 951, 9 L. Ed. 2d 499, 83 S. Ct. 506 (1963).

10. "This Court has the inherent power to revoke a license to practice law in this State, where such license was issued by this Court, and its issuance was procured by the fraudulent concealment, or by the false and fraudulent representation by the applicant of a fact which was manifestly material to the issuance of the license." North Carolina ex rel. Attorney General v. Gorson, 209 N.C. 320, 326, 183 S.E. 392, 395 (1936), *cert. denied*, 298 U.S. 662, 80 L. Ed. 1387, 56 S. Ct. 752 (1936).

See also Application of Patterson, 318 P.2d 907, 913 (Or. 1957), *cert. denied*, 356 U.S. 947, 2 L. Ed. 2d 822, 78 S. Ct. 795 (1958).

11. See ABA CANONS OF PROFESSIONAL ETHICS, CANON 29 (1908).

12. In *ABA Opinion 95* (1933), which held that a municipal attorney could not permit police officers to interview persons with claims against the municipality when the attorney knew the claimants to be represented by counsel, the Committee on Professional Ethics said:

"The law officer is, of course, responsible for the acts of those in his department who are under his supervision and control. *Opinion 85. In re Robinson*, 136 N.Y.S. 548

(affirmed 209 N.Y. 354-1912) held that was a matter of disbarment for an attorney to adopt a general course of approving the unethical conduct of employees of his client, even though he did not actively participate therein.

"'... The attorney should not advise or sanction acts by his client which he himself should not do.' *Opinion 75*."

13. "The most obvious non-professional ground for disbarment is conviction for a felony. Most states make conviction for a felony grounds for automatic disbarment. Some of these states, including New York, make disbarment mandatory upon conviction for any felony, while others require disbarment only for those felonies which involve moral turpitude. There are strong arguments that some felonies, such as involuntary manslaughter, reflect neither on an attorney's fitness, trustworthiness, nor competence and, therefore, should not be grounds for disbarment, but most states tend to disregard these arguments and, following the common law rule, make disbarment mandatory on conviction for any felony." Note, 43 CORNELL L.Q. 489, 490 (1958).

"Some states treat conviction for misdemeanors as grounds for automatic disbarment.... However, the vast majority, accepting the common law rule, require that the misdemeanor involve moral turpitude. While the definition of moral turpitude may prove difficult, it seems only proper that those minor offenses which do not affect the attorney's fitness to continue in the profession should not be grounds for disbarment. A good example is an assault and battery conviction which would not involve moral turpitude unless done with malice and deliberation." *Id*. at 491.

"The term 'moral turpitude' has been used in the law for centuries. It has been the subject of many decisions by the courts but has never been clearly defined because of the nature of the term. Perhaps the best general definition of the term 'moral turpitude' is that it imparts an act of baseness, vileness or depravity in the duties which one person owes to another or to society in general, which is contrary to the usual, accepted and customary rule of right and duty which a person should follow. 58 C.J.S. at page 1201. Although offenses against revenue laws have been held to be crimes of moral turpitude, it has also been held that the attempt to evade the payment of taxes due to the government or any subdivision thereof, while wrong and unlawful, does not involve moral turpitude. 58 C.J.S. at page 1205." Comm. on Legal Ethics v. Scheer, 149 W. Va. 721, 726-27, 143 S.E.2d 141, 145 (1965).

"The right and power to discipline an attorney, as one of its officers, is inherent in the court.... This power is not limited to those instances of misconduct wherein he has been employed, or has acted, in a professional capacity; but, on the contrary, this power may be exercised where his misconduct outside the scope of his professional relations shows him to be an unfit person to practice law." In re Wilson, 391 S.W.2d 914, 917-18 (Mo. 1965).

14. "It is a fair characterization of the lawyer's responsibility in our society that he stands 'as a shield,' to quote Devlin, J., in defense of right and to ward off wrong. From a profession charged with these responsibilities there must be exacted those qualities of truthspeaking, of a high sense of honor, of granite discretion, of the strictest observance of fiduciary responsibility, that have, throughout the centuries, been compendiously described as 'moral character.'" Schware v. Bd. of Bar Examiners, 353 U.S. 232, 247 1 L. Ed. 2d 796, 806, 77 S. Ct. 752, 761 (1957) (Frankfurter, J., *concurring*).

"Particularly applicable here is Rule 4.47 providing that 'A lawyer should always maintain his integrity; and shall not willfully commit any act against the interest of the public; *nor shall he violate his duty to the courts or his clients; nor shall he, by any misconduct, commit any offense against the laws of Missouri or the United States of America, which amounts to a crime involving acts done by him contrary to justice, honesty, modesty or good morals*; nor shall he be guilty of any other misconduct whereby, for the protection of the public and those charged with the administration of justice, he should no longer be entrusted with the duties and responsibilities belonging to the office of an attorney.'" In re Wilson, 391 S.W.2d 914, 917 (Mo. 1965).

15. See ABA CANONS OF PROFESSIONAL ETHICS, CANON 29 (1908); cf. ABA CANONS OF PROFESSIONAL ETHICS, CANON 28 (1908).

16. *Cf.* ABA CANONS OF PROFESSIONAL ETHICS, CANONS 28 and 29 (1908).

CANON 2

A Lawyer Should Assist the Legal Profession in Fulfilling Its Duty to Make Legal Counsel Available

ETHICAL CONSIDERATIONS

EC 2-1 The need of members of the public for legal services[1] is met only if they recognize their legal problems, appreciate the importance of seeking assistance,[2] and are able to obtain the services of acceptable legal counsel.[3] Hence, important functions of the legal profession are to educate laymen to recognize their problems, to facilitate the process of intelligent selection of lawyers, and to assist in making legal services fully available.[4]

Recognition of Legal Problems

EC 2-2 The legal profession should assist laypersons to recognize legal problems because such problems may not be self-revealing and often are not timely noticed. Therefore, lawyers should encourage and participate in educational and public relations programs concerning our legal system with particular reference to legal problems that frequently arise. Preparation of advertisements and professional articles for lay publications[5] and participation in seminars, lectures, and civic programs should be motivated by a desire to educate the public to an awareness of legal needs and to provide information relevant to the selection of the most appropriate counsel rather than to obtain publicity for particular lawyers. The problems of advertising on television require special consideration, due to the style, cost, and transitory nature of such media. If the interests of laypersons in receiving relevant lawyer advertising are not adequately served by print media and radio advertising, and if adequate safeguards to protect the public can reasonably be formulated, television advertising may serve a public interest.

EC 2-3 Whether a lawyer acts properly in volunteering in-person advice to a layperson to seek legal services depends upon the circumstances.[6] The giving of advice that one should take legal action could well be in fulfillment of the duty of the legal profession to assist laypersons in recognizing legal problems.[7] The advice is proper only if motivated by a desire to protect one who does not recognize that he may have legal problems or who is ignorant of his legal rights or obligations. It is improper if motivated by a desire to obtain personal benefit, secure personal publicity, or cause legal action to be taken merely to harass or injure another. A lawyer should not initiate an in-person contact with a non-client, personally or through a representative, for the purpose of being retained to represent him for compensation.

EC 2-4 Since motivation is subjective and often difficult to judge, the motives of a lawyer who volunteers in-person advice likely to produce legal controversy may well be suspect if he receives professional employment or other benefits as a result.[8] A lawyer who volunteers in-person advice that one should obtain the services of a lawyer generally should not himself accept employment, compensation, or other benefit in connection with that matter. However, it is not improper for a lawyer to volunteer such advice and render resulting legal services to close friends, relatives, former clients (in regard to matters germane to former employment), and regular clients.[9]

EC 2-5 A lawyer who writes or speaks for the purpose of educating members of the public to recognize their legal problems should carefully refrain from giving or appearing to give a general solution applicable to all apparently similar individual problems,[10] since slight changes in fact situations may require a material variance in the applicable advice; otherwise, the public may be mislead and misadvised. Talks and writings by lawyers for laypersons should caution them not to attempt to solve individual problems upon the basis of the information contained therein.[11]

Selection of a Lawyer

EC 2-6 Formerly a potential client usually knew the reputations of local lawyers for competency and integrity and therefore could select a practitioner in whom he had confidence. This traditional selection process worked well because it was initiated by the client and the choice was an informed one.

EC 2-7 Changed conditions, however, have seriously restricted the effectiveness of the traditional selection process. Often the reputations of lawyers are not sufficiently known to enable laypersons to make intelligent choices.[12] The law has become increasingly complex and specialized. Few lawyers are willing and competent to deal with every kind of legal matter, and many laypersons have difficulty in determining the competence of lawyers to render different types of legal services. The selection of legal counsel is particularly difficult for transients, persons moving into new areas, persons of limited education or means, and others who have little or no contact with lawyers.[13] Lack of information about the availability of lawyers, the qualifications of particular lawyers, and the expense of legal representation leads laypersons to avoid seeking legal advice.

EC 2-8 Selection of a lawyer by a layperson should be made on an informed basis. Advice and recommendation of third parties — relatives, friends, acquaintances, business associates, or other lawyers — and disclosure of relevant information about the lawyer and his practice may be helpful. A layperson is best served if the recommendation is disinterested and informed. In order that the recommendation be disinterested, a lawyer should not seek to influence another to recommend his employment. A lawyer should not compensate another person for recommending him, for influencing a prospective client to employ him, or to encourage future recommendations.[14] Advertisements and public communications, whether in law lists, telephone directories, newspapers, other forms of print media, television or radio, should be formulated to convey only information that is necessary to make an appropriate selection. Such information includes: (1) office information, such as, name, including name of law firm and names of professional associates; addresses; telephone numbers; credit card acceptability; fluency in foreign languages; and office hours; (2) relevant biographical information; (3) description of the practice, but only by using designations and definitions authorized by [the agency having jurisdiction of the subject under state law], for example, one or more fields of law in which the lawyer or law firm practices; a statement that practice is limited to one or more fields of law; and/or a statement that the lawyer or law firm specializes in a particular field of law practice, but only by using designations, definitions and standards authorized by [the agency having jurisdiction of the subject under state law]; and (4) permitted fee information. Self-laudation should be avoided.[15]

Selection of a Lawyer: Lawyer Advertising

EC 2-9 The lack of sophistication on the part of many members of the public concerning legal services, the importance of the interests affected by the choice of a lawyer and prior experience with unrestricted lawyer advertising, require that special care be taken by lawyers to avoid misleading the public and to assure that the information set forth in any advertising is relevant to the selection of a lawyer. The lawyer must be mindful that the benefits of lawyer advertising depend upon its reliability and accuracy. Examples of information in lawyer advertising that would be deceptive include misstatements of fact, suggestions that the ingenuity or prior record of a lawyer rather than the justice of the claim are the principal factors likely to determine the result, inclusion of information irrelevant to selecting a lawyer, and representations concerning the quality of service, which cannot be measured or verified. Since lawyer advertising is calculated and not spontaneous, reasonable regulation of lawyer advertising designed to foster compliance with appropriate standards serves the public interest without impeding the flow of useful, meaningful, and relevant information to the public.

EC 2-10 A lawyer should ensure that the information contained in any advertising which the lawyer publishes, broadcasts or causes to be published or broadcast is relevant, is disseminated in an objective and understandable fashion, and would facilitate the prospective client's ability to compare the qualifications of the lawyers available to represent him. A lawyer should strive to communicate such information without undue emphasis upon style and advertising stratagems which serve to hinder rather than to facilitate intelligent selection of counsel. Because technological change is a recurrent feature of communications forms, and because perceptions of what is relevant in lawyer selection may change, lawyer advertising regulations should not be cast in rigid, unchangeable terms. Machinery is therefore available to advertisers and consumers for prompt consideration of proposals to change the rules governing lawyer advertising. The determination of any request for such change should depend upon whether the proposal is necessary in light of existing Code provisions, whether the proposal accords with standards of accuracy, reliability and truthfulness, and whether the proposal would facilitate informed selection of lawyers by potential consumers of legal services. Representatives of lawyers and consumers should be heard in addition to the applicant concerning any proposed change. Any change which is approved should be promulgated in the form of an amendment to the Code so that all lawyers practicing in the jurisdiction may avail themselves of its provisions.

EC 2-11 The name under which a lawyer conducts his practice may be a factor in the selection process.[16] The use of a trade name or an assumed name could mislead laypersons concerning the identity, responsibility, and status of those practicing thereunder.[17] Accordingly, a lawyer in private practice should practice only under a designation containing his own name, the name of a lawyer employing him, the name of one or more of the lawyers practicing in a partnership, or, if permitted by law, the name of a professional legal corporation, which should be clearly designated as such. For many years some law firms have used a firm name retaining one or more names of deceased or retired partners and such practice is not improper if the firm is a bona fide successor of a firm in which the deceased or retired person was a member, if the use of the name is authorized by law or by contract, and if the public is not misled thereby.[18] However, the name of a partner who withdraws from a firm but continues to practice law should be omitted from the firm, name in order to avoid misleading the public.

EC 2-12 A lawyer occupying a judicial, legislative, or public executive or administrative position who has the right to practice law concurrently may allow his name to remain in the name of the firm if he actively continues to practice law as a member thereof. Otherwise, his name should be removed from the firm name,[19] and he should not be identified as a past or present member of the firm; and he should not hold himself out as being a practicing lawyer.

EC 2-13 In order to avoid the possibility of misleading persons with whom he deals, a lawyer should be scrupulous in the representation of his professional status.[20] He should not hold himself out as being a partner or associate of a law firm if he is not one in fact,[21] and thus should not hold himself out as a partner or associate if he only shares offices with another lawyer.[22]

EC 2-14 In some instances a lawyer confines his practice to a particular field of law.[23] In the absence of state controls to insure the existence of special competence, a lawyer should not be permitted to hold himself out as a specialist or as having official recognition as a specialist, other than in the fields of admiralty, trademark, and patent law where a holding out as a specialist historically has been permitted. A lawyer may, however, indicate in permitted advertising, if it is factual, a limitation of his practice or one or more particular areas or fields of law in which he practices using designations and definitions authorized for that purpose by [the state agency having jurisdiction]. A lawyer practicing in a jurisdiction which certifies specialists must also be careful not to confuse laypersons as to his status. If a lawyer discloses areas of law in which he practices or to which he limits his practice, but is not certified in [the jurisdiction], he, and the designation authorized in [the jurisdiction], should avoid any implication that he is in fact certified.

EC 2-15 The legal profession has developed lawyer referral systems designed to aid individuals who are able to pay fees but need assistance in locating lawyers competent to handle their particular problems. Use of a lawyer referral system enables a layman to avoid an uninformed selection of a lawyer because such a system makes possible the employment of competent lawyers who have indicated an interest in the subject matter involved. Lawyers should support the principle of lawyer referral systems and should encourage the evolution of other ethical plans which aid in the selection of qualified counsel.

Financial Ability to Employ Counsel: Generally

EC 2-16 The legal profession cannot remain a viable force in fulfilling its role in our society unless its members receive adequate compensation for services rendered, and reasonable fees[24] should be charged in appropriate cases to clients able to pay them. Nevertheless, persons unable to pay all or a portion of a reasonable fee should be able to obtain necessary legal services,[25] and lawyers should support and participate in ethical activities designed to achieve that objective.[26]

Financial Ability to Employ Counsel: Persons Able to Pay Reasonable Fees

EC 2-17 The determination of a proper fee requires consideration of the interests of both client and lawyer.[27] A lawyer should not charge more than a reasonable fee,[28] for excessive cost of legal service would deter laymen from utilizing the legal system in protection of their rights. Furthermore, an excessive charge abuses the professional relationship between lawyer and client. On the other hand, adequate compensation is necessary in order to enable the lawyer to serve his client effectively and to preserve the integrity and independence of the profession.[29]

EC 2-18 The determination of the reasonableness of a fee requires consideration of all relevant circumstances,[30] including those stated in the Disciplinary Rules. The fees of a lawyer will vary according to many factors, including the time required, his experience, ability, and reputation, the nature of the employment, the responsibility involved, and the results obtained. It is a commendable and long-standing tradition of the bar that special consideration is given in the fixing of any fee for services rendered a brother lawyer or a member of his immediate family.

EC 2-19 As soon as feasible after a lawyer has been employed, it is desirable that he reach a clear agreement with his client as to the basis of the fee charges to be made. Such a course will not only prevent later misunderstanding but will also work for good relations between the lawyer and the client. It is usually beneficial to reduce to writing the understanding of the parties regarding the fee, particularly when it is contingent. A lawyer should be mindful that many persons who desire to employ him may have had little or no experience with fee charges of lawyers, and for this reason he should explain fully to such persons the reasons for the particular fee arrangement he proposes.

EC 2-20 Contingent fee arrangements[31] in civil cases have long been commonly accepted in the United States in proceedings to enforce claims. The historical bases of their acceptance are that (1) they often, and in a variety of circumstances, provide the only practical means by which one having a claim against another can economically afford, finance, and obtain the services of a competent lawyer to prosecute his claim, and (2) a successful prosecution of the claim produces a *res* out of which the fee can be paid.[32] Although a lawyer generally should decline to accept employment on a contingent fee basis by one who is able to pay a reasonable fixed fee, it is not necessarily improper for a lawyer, where justified by the particular circumstances of a case, to enter into a contingent fee contract in a civil case with any client who, after being fully informed of all relevant factors, desires that arrangement. Because of the human relationships involved and the unique character of the proceedings, contingent fee arrangements in domestic relation cases are rarely justified. In administrative agency proceedings contingent fee contracts should be governed by the same consideration as in other civil cases. Public policy properly condemns contingent fee arrangements in criminal cases, largely on the ground that legal services in criminal cases do not produce a res with which to pay the fee.

EC 2-21 A lawyer should not accept compensation or any thing of value incident to his employment or services from one other than his client without the knowledge and consent of his client after full disclosure.[33]

EC 2-22 Without the consent of his client, a lawyer should not associate in a particular matter another lawyer outside his firm. A fee may properly be divided between lawyers[34] properly associated if the division is in proportion to the services performed and the responsibility assumed by each lawyer[35] and if the total fee is reasonable.

EC 2-23 A lawyer should be zealous in his efforts to avoid controversies over fees with clients[36] and should attempt to resolve amicably and differences on the subject.[37] He should not sue a client for a fee unless necessary to prevent fraud or gross imposition by the client.[38]

Financial Ability to Employ Counsel: Persons Unable to Pay Reasonable Fees

EC 2-24 A layman whose financial ability is not sufficient to permit payment of any fee cannot obtain legal services, other than in cases where a contingent fee is appropriate, unless the services are provided for him. Even a person of moderate means may be unable to pay a reasonable fee which is large because of the complexity, novelty, or difficulty of the problem or similar factors.[39]

EC 2-25 Historically, the need for legal services of those unable to pay reasonable fees has been met in part by lawyers who donated their services or accepted court appointments on behalf of such individuals. The basic responsibility for providing legal services for those unable to pay ultimately rests upon the individual lawyer, and personal involvement in the problems of the disadvantaged can be one of the most rewarding experiences in the life a lawyer. Every lawyer, regardless of professional prominence or professional workload, should find time to participate in serving the disadvantaged. The rendition of free legal services to those unable to pay reasonable fees continues to be an obligation of each lawyer, but the efforts of individual lawyers are often not enough to meet the need.[40] Thus it has been necessary for the profession to institute additional programs to provide legal services.[41] Accordingly, legal aid offices,[42] lawyer referral services, and other related programs have been developed, and others will be developed, by the profession.[43] Every lawyer should support all proper efforts to meet this need for legal services.[44]

Acceptance and Retention of Employment

EC 2-26 A lawyer is under no obligation to act as adviser or advocate for every person who may wish to become his client; but in furtherance of the objective of the bar to make legal services fully available, a lawyer should not lightly decline proffered employment. The fulfillment of this objective requires acceptance by a lawyer of his share of tendered employment which may be unattractive both to him and the bar generally.[45]

EC 2-27 History is replete with instances of distinguished and sacrificial services by lawyers who have represented unpopular clients and causes. Regardless of his personal feelings, a lawyer should not decline representation because a client or a cause is unpopular or community reaction is adverse.[46]

EC 2-28 The personal preference of a lawyer to avoid adversary alignment against judges, other lawyers,[47] public officials, or influential members of the community does not justify his rejection of tendered employment.

EC 2-29 When a lawyer is appointed by a Court or requested by a bar association to undertake representation of a person unable to obtain counsel, whether for financial or other reasons, he should not seek to be excused from undertaking the representation except for compelling reasons.[48] Compelling reasons do not include such factors as the repugnance of the subject matter of the proceeding, the identity[49] or position of a person involved in the case, the belief of the lawyer that the defendant in a criminal proceeding is guilty,[50] or the belief of the lawyer regarding the merits of the civil case.[51]

EC 2-30 Employment should not be accepted by a lawyer when he is unable to render competent service[52] or when he knows or it is obvious that the person seeking to employ him desires to institute or maintain an action merely for the purpose of harassing or maliciously injuring another.[53] Likewise, a lawyer should decline employment if the intensity of his personal feeling, as distinguished from a community attitude, may impair his effective representation of a prospective client. If a lawyer knows a client has previously obtained counsel, he should not accept employment in the matter unless the other counsel approves[54] or withdraws, or the client terminates the prior employment.[55]

EC 2-31 Full availability of legal counsel requires both that persons be able to obtain counsel and that lawyers who undertake representation complete the work involved. Trial counsel for a convicted defendant should continue to represent his client by advising whether to take an appeal and, if the appeal is prosecuted, by representing him through the appeal unless new counsel is substituted or withdrawal is permitted by the appropriate court.

EC 2-32 A decision by a lawyer to withdrawn should be made only on the basis of compelling circumstances,[56] and in a matter pending before a tribunal he must comply with the rules of the tribunal regarding withdrawal. A lawyer should not withdraw without considering carefully and endeavoring to minimize the possible adverse effect on the rights of his client and the possibility of prejudice to his client[57] as a result of his withdrawal. Even when he justifiably withdraws, a lawyer should protect the welfare of his client by giving due notice of his withdrawal,[58] suggesting employment of other counsel, delivering to the client all papers and property to which the client is entitled, cooperating with counsel subsequently employed, and otherwise endeavoring to minimize the possibility of harm. Further, he should refund to the client any compensation not earned during the employment.[59]

EC 2-33 As a part of the legal profession's commitment to the principle that high quality legal services should be available to all, attorneys are encouraged to cooperate with qualified legal assistance organizations providing prepaid legal services. Such participation should at all times be in accordance with the basic tenets of the profession: independence, integrity, competence and devotion to the interests of individual clients. An attorney so participating should make certain that his relationship with a qualified legal assistance organization in no way interferes with his independent, professional representation of the interests of the individual client. An attorney should avoid situations in which officials of the organization who are not lawyers attempt to direct attorneys concerning the manner in which legal services are performed for individual members, and should also avoid situations in which considerations of economy are given undue weight in determining the attorneys employed by an organization or the legal services to be performed for the member or beneficiary rather than competence and quality of service. An attorney interested in maintaining the historic traditions of the profession and preserving the function of a lawyer as a trusted and independent advisor to individual members of society should carefully assess such factors when accepting employment by, or otherwise participating in, a particular qualified legal assistance organization, and while so participating should adhere to the highest professional standards of effort and competence.[60]

DISCIPLINARY RULES

DR 2-101   Publicity.

(A)   A lawyer shall not, on behalf of himself, his partner, associate or any other lawyer affiliated with him or his firm, use or participate in the use of any form of public communication containing a false, fraudulent, misleading, deceptive, self-laudatory or unfair statement or claim.

(B)   In order to facilitate the process of informed selection of a lawyer by potential consumers of legal services, a lawyer may publish or broadcast, subject to DR 2-103, the following information in print media distributed or over television or radio broadcast in the geographic area or areas in which the lawyer resides or maintains offices or in which a significant part of the lawyer's clientele resides, provided that the information disclosed by the lawyer in such publication or broadcast complies with DR 2-101 (A), and is presented in a dignified manner:[61]

    (1)   Name, including name of law firm and names of professional associates; addresses and telephone numbers;

    (2)   One or more fields of law in which the lawyer or law firm practices, a statement that practice is limited to one or more fields of law, or a statement that the lawyer or law firm specializes in a particular field of law practice, to the extent authorized under DR 2-105;

(3)   Date and place of birth;

(4)   Date and place of admission to the bar of state and federal courts;

(5)   Schools attended, with dates of graduation, degrees and other scholastic distinctions;

(6)   Public or quasi-public offices;

(7)   Military service;

(8)   Legal authorships;

(9)   Legal teaching positions;

(10)   Memberships, offices, and committee assignments, in bar associations;

(11)   Membership and offices in legal fraternities and legal societies;

(12)   Technical and professional licenses;

(13)   Memberships in scientific, technical and professional associations and societies;

(14)   Foreign language ability;

(15)   Names and addresses of bank references;

(16)   With their written consent, names of clients regularly represented;

(17)   Prepaid or group legal services programs in which the lawyer participates;

(18)   Whether credit cards or other credit arrangements are accepted;

(19)   Office and telephone answering service hours;

(20)   Fee for an initial consultation;

(21)   Availability upon request of a written schedule of fees and/or an estimate of the fee to be charged for specific services;

(22)   Contingent fee rates subject to DR 2-106(C), provided that the statement discloses whether percentages are computed before or after deduction of costs;

(23)   Range of fees for services, provided that the statement discloses that the specific fee within the range which will be charged will vary depending upon the particular matter to be handled for each client and the client is entitled without obligation to an estimate of the fee within the range likely to be charged, in print size equivalent to the largest print used in setting forth the fee information;

(24)   Hourly rate, provided that the statement discloses that the total fee charged will depend upon the number of hours which must be devoted to the particular matter to be handled for each client and the client is entitled to without obligation an estimate of the fee likely to be charged, in print size at least equivalent to the largest print used in setting forth the fee information;

(25)   Fixed fees for specific legal services,

* the description of which would not be misunderstood or be deceptive, provided that the statement discloses that the quoted fee will be available only to clients whose matters fall into the services described and that the client is entitled without obligation to a specific estimate of the fee likely to be charged in print size at least equivalent to the largest print used in setting forth the fee information.

(C)   Any person desiring to expand the information authorized for disclosure in DR 2-101(B), or to provide for its dissemination through other forums may apply to [the agency having jurisdiction under state law]. Any such application shall be served upon [the agencies having jurisdiction under state law over the regulation of the legal profession and consumer matters] who shall be heard, together with the applicant, on the issue of whether the proposal is necessary in light of the existing provisions of the Code, accords with standards of accuracy, reliability and truthfulness, and would facilitate the process of informed selection of lawyers by potential consumers of legal services. The relief granted in response to any such application shall be promulgated as an amendment to DR 2-101(B), universally applicable to all lawyers.**

(D)   If the advertisement is communicated to the public over television or radio, it shall be prerecorded, approved for broadcast by the lawyer, and a recording of the actual transmission shall be retained by the lawyer.[62]

(E)   If a lawyer advertises a fee for a service, the lawyer must render that service for no more than the fee advertised.

(F)   Unless otherwise specified in the advertisement if a lawyer publishes any fee information authorized under DR 2-101(B) in a publication that is published more frequently than one time per month, the lawyer shall be bound by any representation made therein for a period of not less than 30 days after such publication. If a lawyer publishes any fee information authorized under DR 2-101(B) in a publication that is published once a month or less frequently, he shall be bound by any representation made therein until the publication of the succeeding issue. If a lawyer publishes any fee information authorized under DR 2-101(B) in a publication which has no fixed date for publication of a succeeding issue, the lawyer shall be bound by any representation made therein for a reasonable period of time after publication but in no event less than one year.

(G)   Unless otherwise specified, if a lawyer broadcasts any fee information authorized under DR 2-101(B), the lawyer shall be bound by any representation made therein for a period of not less than 30 days after such broadcast.

(H)   This rule does not prohibit limited and dignified identification of a lawyer as a lawyer as well as by name:

---

* The agency having jurisdiction under state law may desire to issue appropriate guidelines defi ning "specific legal services."

** The agency having jurisdiction under state law should establish orderly and expeditious procedures for ruling on such applications.

    (1)   In political advertisements when his professional status is germane to the political campaign or to a political issue.

    (2)   In public notices when the name and profession of a lawyer are required or authorized by law or are reasonably pertinent for a purpose other than the attraction of potential clients.

    (3)   In routine reports and announcements of a bona fide business, civic, professional, or political organization in which he serves as a director or officer.

    (4)   In and on legal documents prepared by him.

    (5)   In and on legal textbooks, treatises, and other legal publications, and in dignified advertisements thereof.

(I)   A lawyer shall not compensate or give any thing of value to representatives of the press, radio, television, or other communication medium in anticipation of or in return for professional publicity in a news item.

DR 2-102   Professional Notices, Letterheads and Offices.

(A)   A lawyer or law firm shall not use or participate in the use of[63] professional cards, professional announcement cards, office signs, letterheads, or similar professional notices or devices, except that the following may be used if they are in dignified form:

    (1)   A professional card of a lawyer identifying him by name and as a lawyer, and giving his addresses, telephone numbers, the name of his law firm, and any information permitted under DR 2-105. A professional card of a law firm may also give the names of members and associates. Such cards may be used for identification.

    (2)   A brief professional announcement card stating new or changed associations or addresses, change of firm name, or similar matters pertaining to the professional offices of a lawyer or law firm, which may be mailed to lawyers, clients, former clients, personal friends, and relatives.[64] It shall not state biographical data except to the extent reasonably necessary to identify the lawyer or to explain the change in his association, but it may state the immediate past position of the lawyer.[65] It may give the names and dates of predecessor firms in a continuing line of succession. It shall not state the nature of the practice except as permitted under DR 2-105.[66]

    (3)   A sign on or near the door of the office and in the building directory identifying the law office. The sign shall not state the nature of the practice, except as permitted under DR 2-105.

    (4)   A letterhead of a lawyer identifying him by name and as a lawyer, and giving his addresses, telephone numbers, the name of his law firm, associates and any information permitted under DR 2-105. A letterhead of a law firm may also give the names of members and associates,[67] and names and dates relating to deceased and retired members.[68] A lawyer may be designated "Of Counsel" on a letterhead if he has a continuing relationship with a lawyer or law firm, other than as a partner or associate. A lawyer or law firm may be

designated as "General Counsel" or by similar professional reference on stationery of a client if he or the firm devotes a substantial amount of professional time in the representation of that client.[69] The letterhead of a law firm may give the names and dates of predecessor firms in a continuing line of succession.

(B) A lawyer in private practice shall not practice under a trade name, a name that is misleading as to the identity of the lawyer or lawyers practicing under such name, or a firm name containing names other than those of one or more of the lawyers in the firm, except that the name of a professional corporation or professional association may contain "P.C." or "P.A." or similar symbols indicating the nature of the organization, and if otherwise lawful a firm may use as, or continue to include in, its name the name or names of one or more deceased or retired members of the firm or of a predecessor firm in a continuing line of succession.[70] A lawyer who assumes a judicial, legislative, or public executive or administrative post or office shall not permit his name to remain in the name of a law firm or to be used in professional notices of the firm during any significant period in which he is not actively and regularly practicing law as a member of the firm,[71] and during such period other members of the firm shall not use his name in the firm name or in professional notices of the firm.[72]

(C) A lawyer shall not hold himself out as having a partnership with one or more other lawyers or professional corporations[73] unless they are in fact partners.[74]

(D) A partnership shall not be formed or continued between or among lawyers licensed in different jurisdictions unless all enumerations of the members and associates of the firm on its letterhead and in other permissible listings make clear the jurisdictional limitations on those members and associates of the firm not licensed to practice in all listed jurisdictions;[75] however, the same firm name may be used in each jurisdiction.

(E) Nothing contained herein shall prohibit a lawyer from using or permitting the use of, in connection with his name, an earned degree or title derived therefrom indicating his training in the law.[76]

DR 2-103   Recommendation of Professional Employment.[77]

(A) A lawyer shall not, except as authorized in DR 2-101 (B), recommend employment as a private practitioner,[78] of himself, his partner, or associate to a layperson who has not sought his advice regarding employment of a lawyer.[79]

(B) A lawyer shall not compensate or give anything of value to a person or organization to recommend or secure his employment[80] by a client, or as a reward for having made a recommendation resulting in his employment[81] by a client, except that he may pay the usual and reasonable fees or dues charged by any of the organizations listed in DR 2-103(D).[82]

(C) A lawyer shall not request a person or organization to recommend or promote the use of his services or those of his partner or associate, or

~~any other lawyer affiliated with him or his firm, as a private practi-~~ tioner[83], except as authorized in DR 2-101, and except that

(1)　He may request referrals from a lawyer referral service operated, sponsored, or approved by a bar association and may pay its fees incident thereto.[84]

(2)　He may cooperate with the legal service activities of any of the offices or organizations enumerated in DR 2-103(D)(1) through (4) and may perform legal services for those to whom he was recommended by it to do such work if:

   (a)　The person to whom the recommendation is made is a member or beneficiary of such office or organization; and

   (b)　The lawyer remains free to exercise his independent professional judgment on behalf of his client.[85]

(D)　A lawyer or his partner or associate or any other lawyer affiliated with him or his firm may be recommended, employed or paid by, or may cooperate with, one of the following offices or organizations that promote the use of his services or those of his partner or associate or any other lawyer affiliated with him or his firm if there is no interference with the exercise of independent professional judgment in behalf of his client:

(1)　A legal aid office or public defender office:

   (a)　Operated or sponsored by a duly accredited law school.

   (b)　Operated or sponsored by a bona fide nonprofit community organization.

   (c)　Operated or sponsored by a governmental agency.

   (d)　Operated, sponsored, or approved by a bar association.[86]

(2)　A military legal assistance office.

(3)　A lawyer referral service operated, sponsored, or approved by a bar association.

(4)　Any bona fide organization that recommends, furnishes or pays for legal services to its members or beneficiaries[87] provided the following conditions are satisfied:

   (a)　Such organization, including any affiliate, is so organized and operated that no profit is derived by it from the rendition of legal services by lawyers, and that, if the organization is organized for profit, the legal services are not rendered by lawyers employed, directed, supervised or selected by it except in connection with matters where such organization bears ultimate liability of its member or beneficiary.

   (b)　Neither the lawyer, nor his partner, nor associate, nor any other lawyer affiliated with him or his firm, nor any non-lawyer, shall have initiated or promoted such organization for the primary purpose of providing financial or other benefit to such lawyer, partner, associate or affiliated lawyer.

(c) Such organization is not operated for the purpose of procuring legal work or financial benefit for any lawyer as a private practitioner outside of the legal services program of the organization.

(d) The member or beneficiary to whom the legal services are furnished, and not such organization, is recognized as the client of the lawyer in the matter.

(e) Any member or beneficiary who is entitled to have legal services furnished or paid for by the organization may, if such member or beneficiary so desires, select counsel other than that furnished, selected or approved by the organization for the particular matter involved; and the legal service plan of such organization provides appropriate relief for any member or beneficiary who asserts a claim that representation by counsel furnished, selected or approved would be unethical, improper or inadequate under the circumstances of the matter involved and the plan provides an appropriate procedure for seeking such relief.

(f) The lawyer does not know or have cause to know that such organization is in violation of applicable laws, rules of court and other legal requirements that govern its legal service operations.

(g) Such organization has filed with the appropriate disciplinary authority at least annually a report with respect to its legal service plan, if any, showing its terms, its schedule of benefits, its subscription charges, agreements with counsel, and financial results of its legal service activities or, if it has failed to do so, the lawyer does not know or have cause to know of such failure.[88]

(E) A lawyer shall not accept employment when he knows or it is obvious that the person who seeks his services does so as a result of conduct prohibited under this Disciplinary Rule.

DR 2-104   Suggestion of Need of Legal Services.[89, 90]

(A) A lawyer who has given in-person unsolicited advice to a layperson that he should obtain counsel or take legal action shall not accept employment resulting from the advice,[91] except that:

(1) A lawyer may accept employment by a close friend, relative, former client (if the advice is germane to the former employment), or one whom the lawyer reasonably believes to be a client.[92]

(2) A lawyer may accept employment that results from his participation in activities designed to educate laypersons to recognize legal problems, to make intelligent selection of counsel, or to utilize available legal services if such activities are conducted or sponsored by a qualified legal assistance organization.[93]

(3) A lawyer who is recommended, furnished or paid by a qualified legal assistance organization enumerated in DR 2-103 (D)(1) through (4)[94] may represent a member or beneficiary thereof, to the extent and under the conditions prescribed therein.

(4) Without affecting his right to accept employment, a lawyer may speak publicly or write for publication on legal topics[95] so long as he does not emphasize his own professional experience or reputation and does not undertake to give individual advice.

(5) If success in asserting rights or defenses of his client in litigation in the nature of a class action is dependent upon the joinder of others, a lawyer may accept, but shall not seek, employment from those contacted for the purpose of obtaining their joinder.[96]

DR 2-105   Limitation of Practice.[97]

(A) A lawyer shall not hold himself out publicly as a specialist, as practicing in certain areas of law or as limiting his practice permitted under DR 2-101(B), except as follows:

(1) A lawyer admitted to practice before the United States Patent and Trademark Office may use the designation "Patents," "Patent Attorney," "Patent Lawyer," or "Registered Patent Attorney" or any combination of those terms, on his letterhead and office sign.

(2) A lawyer who publicly discloses fields of law in which the lawyer or the law firm practices or states that his practice is limited to one or more fields of law shall do so by using designations and definitions authorized and approved by [the agency having jurisdiction of the subject under state law].

(3) A lawyer who is certified as a specialist in a particular field of law or law practice by [the authority having jurisdiction under state law over the subject of specialization by lawyers] may hold himself out as such, but only in accordance with the rules prescribed by that authority.[98]

DR 2-106   Fees for Legal Services.[99]

(A) A lawyer shall not enter into an agreement for, charge, or collect an illegal or clearly excessive fee.[100]

(B) A fee is clearly excessive when, after a review of the facts, a lawyer of ordinary prudence would be left with a definite and firm conviction that the fee is in excess of a reasonable fee. Factors to be considered as guides in determining the reasonableness of a fee include the following:

(1) The time and labor required, the novelty and difficulty of the questions involved, and the skill requisite to perform the legal service properly.

(2) The likelihood, if apparent to the client, that the acceptance of the particular employment will preclude other employment by the lawyer.

(3) The fee customarily charged in the locality for similar legal services.

(4) The amount involved and the results obtained.

(5) The time limitations imposed by the client or by the circumstances.

(6) The nature and length of the professional relationship with the client.

(7)   The experience, reputation, and ability of the lawyer or lawyers performing the services.

(8)   Whether the fee is fixed or contingent.[101]

(C)   A lawyer shall not enter into an arrangement for, charge, or collect a contingent fee for representing a defendant in a criminal case.[102]

DR 2-107   Division of Fees Among Lawyers.

(A)   A lawyer shall not divide a fee for legal services with another lawyer who is not a partner in or associate of his law firm or law office, unless:

(1)   The client consents to employment of the other lawyer after a full disclosure that a division of fees will be made.

(2)   The division is made in proportion to the services performed and responsibility assumed by each.[103]

(3)   The total fee of the lawyers does not clearly exceed reasonable compensation for all legal services they rendered the client.[104]

(B)   This Disciplinary Rule does not prohibit payment to a former partner or associate pursuant to a separation or retirement agreement.

DR 2-108   Agreements Restricting the Practice of a Lawyer.

(A)   A lawyer shall not be a party to or participate in a partnership or employment agreement with another lawyer that restricts the right of a lawyer to practice law after the termination of a relationship created by the agreement, except as a condition to payment of retirement benefits.[105]

(B)   In connection with the settlement of a controversy or suit, a lawyer shall not enter into an agreement that restricts his right to practice law.

DR 2-109   Acceptance of Employment.

(A)   A lawyer shall not accept employment on behalf of a person if he knows or it is obvious that such person wishes to:

(1)   Bring a legal action, conduct a defense, or assert a position in litigation, or otherwise have steps taken for him, merely for the purpose of harassing or maliciously injuring any person.[106]

(2)   Present a claim or defense in litigation that is not warranted under existing law, unless it can be supported by good faith argument for an extension, modification, or reversal of existing law.

DR 2-110   Withdrawal from Employment.[107]

(A)   In general.

(1)   If permission for withdrawal from employment is required by the rules of a tribunal, a lawyer shall not withdraw from employment is a proceeding before that tribunal without its permission.

(2)   In any event, a lawyer shall not withdraw from employment until he has taken reasonable steps to avoid foreseeable prejudice to the

rights of his client, including giving due notice to his client, allowing time for employment of other counsel, delivering to the client all papers and property to which the client is entitled, and complying with applicable laws and rules.

(3) A lawyer who withdraws from employment shall refund promptly any part of a fee paid in advance that has not been earned.

(B) Mandatory withdrawal.

A lawyer representing a client before a tribunal, with its permission if required by its rules, shall withdraw from employment, and a lawyer representing a client in other matters shall withdraw from employment, if:

(1) He knows or it is obvious that his client is bringing the legal action, conducting the defense, or asserting a position in the litigation, or is otherwise having steps taken for him merely for the purpose of harassing or maliciously injuring any person.

(2) He knows or it is obvious that his continued employment will result in violation of a Disciplinary Rule.[108]

(3) His mental or physical condition renders it unreasonably difficult for him to carry out the employment effectively.

(4) He is discharged by his client.

(C) Permissive withdrawal.[109]

If DR 2-110 (B) is not applicable, a lawyer may not request permission to withdraw in matters pending before a tribunal, and may not withdraw in other matters, unless such request or such withdrawal is because:

(1) His client:

(a) Insists upon presenting a claim or defense that is not warranted under existing law and cannot be supported by good faith argument for an extension, modification, or reversal of existing law.[110]

(b) Personally seeks to pursue an illegal course of conduct.

(c) Insists that the lawyer pursue a course of conduct that is illegal or that is prohibited under the Disciplinary Rules

(d) By other conduct renders it unreasonably difficult for the lawyer to carry out his employment effectively.

(e) Insists, in a matter not pending before a tribunal, that the lawyer engage in conduct that is contrary to the judgment and advice of the lawyer but not prohibited under the Disciplinary Rules.

(f) Deliberately disregards an agreement or obligation to the lawyer as to expenses or fees.

(2) His continued employment is likely to result in a violation of a Disciplinary Rule.

(3) His inability to work with co-counsel indicates that the best interest of the client likely will be served by withdrawal.

(4) His mental or physical condition renders it difficult for him to carry out the employment effectively.

(5) His client knowingly and freely assents to termination of his employment.

(6) He believes in good faith, in a proceeding pending before a tribunal, that the tribunal will find the existence of other good cause for withdrawal.

NOTES

1. "Men have need for more than a system of law; they have need for a system of law which functions, and that means they have need for lawyers." Cheatham, *The Lawyer's Role and Surroundings*, 25 ROCKY MT. L. REV. 405 (1953).

2. "Law is not self-applying; men must apply and utilize it in concrete cases. But the ordinary man is incapable. He cannot know the principles of law or the rules guiding the machinery of law administration; he does not know how to formulate his desires with precision and to put them into writing; he is ineffective in the presentation of his claims." *Id.*

3. "This need [to provide legal services] was recognized by... Mr. [Lewis F.] Powell [Jr., President, American Bar Association, 1963-64], who said: 'Looking at contemporary America realistically, we must admit that despite all our efforts to date (and these have not been insignificant), far too many persons are not able to obtain equal justice under law. This usually results because their poverty or their ignorance has prevented them from obtaining legal counsel.'" Address by E. Clinton Bamberger, Association of American Law Schools 1965 Annual Meeting, Dec. 28, 1965, in PROCEEDINGS, PART II, 1965, 61, 63-64 (1965).

"A wide gap separates the need for legal services and its satisfaction, as numerous studies reveal. Looked at from the side of the layman, one reason for the gap is poverty and the consequent inability to pay legal fees. Another set of reasons is ignorance of the need for and the value of legal services, and ignorance of where to find a dependable lawyer. There is fear of the mysterious processes and delays of the law, and there is fear of overreaching and overcharging by lawyers, a fear stimulated by the occasional exposure of shysters." Cheatham, *Availability of Legal Services: The Responsibility of the Individual Lawyer and of the Organized Bar*, 12 U.C.L.A. L. REV. 438 (1965).

4. "It is not only the right but the duty of the profession as a whole to utilize such methods as may be developed to bring the services of its members to those who need them, so long as this can be done ethically and with dignity." ABA Opinion 320 (1968).

"[T]here is a responsibility on the bar to make legal services available to those who need them. The maxim, 'privilege brings responsibilities,' can be expanded to read, exclusive privilege to render public service brings responsibility to assure that the service is available to those in need of it." Cheatham, Availability of Legal Services: The Responsibility of the Individual Lawyer and of the Organized Bar, 12 U.C.L.A. L. REV. 438, 443 (1965). "The obligation to provide legal services for those actually caught up in litigation carries with it the obligation to make preventive legal advice accessible to all. It is among those unaccustomed to business affairs and fearful of the ways of the law that such advice is often most needed. If it is not received in time, the most valiant and skillful representation in court may come too late." *Professional Responsibility: Report of the Joint Conference*, 44 A.B.A.J. 1159, 1216 (1958).

5. "A lawyer may with propriety write articles for publications in which he gives information upon the law...." ABA CANONS OF PROFESSIONAL ETHICS, CANON 40 (1908).

6. See ABA CANONS OF PROFESSIONAL ETHICS, CANNON 28 (1908).

7. This question can assume constitutional dimensions: "We meet at the outset the contention that "solicitation' is wholly outside the area of freedoms protected by the First Amendment. To this contention there are two answers. The first is that a State cannot foreclose the exercise of constitutional rights by mere labels. The second is that abstract discussion is not the only species of communication which the Constitution protects; the First Amendment also protects vigorous advocacy, certainly of lawful ends, against governmental intrusion....

"However valid may be Virginia's interest in regulating the traditionally illegal practice of barratry, maintenance and champerty, that interest does not justify the prohibition of the NAACP activities disclosed by this record. Malicious intent was of the essence of the common-law offenses of fomenting or stirring up litigation. And whatever may be or may have been true of suits against governments in other countries, the exercise in our own, as in this case of First Amendment rights to enforce Constitutional rights through litigation, as a matter of law, cannot be deemed malicious." NAACP v. Button, 371 U.S. 415, 429, 439-40, 9 L. Ed. 2d 405, 415-16, 422, 83 S. Ct. 328, 336, 341 (1963).

8. "It is disreputable for an attorney to breed litigation by seeking out those who have claims for personal injuries or other grounds of action in order to secure them as clients, or to employ agents or runners, or to reward those who bring or influence the bringing of business to his office.... Moreover, it tends quite easily to the institution of baseless litigation and the manufacture of perjured testimony. From early times, this danger has been recognized in the law by the condemnation of the crime of common barratry, or the stirring up of suits or quarrels between individuals at law or otherwise." In re Ades, 6 F.Supp. 467, 474-75 (D. Mary. 1934).

9. "Rule 2.

"'a....

"[A] member of the State Bar shall not solicit professional employment by

"(1) Volunteering counsel or advice except where ties of blood relationship or trust make it appropriate." CAL. BUSINESS AND PROFESSIONS CODE § 6076 (West 1962).

10. "Rule 18... A member of the State Bar shall not advise inquirers or render opinions to them through or in connection with a newspaper, radio or other publicity medium of any kind in respect to their specific legal problems, whether or not such attorney shall be compensated for his services." CAL. BUSINESS AND PROFESSIONS CODE § 6076 (West 1962).

11. "In any case where a member might well apply the advice given in the opinion to his individual affairs, the lawyer rendering the opinion [concerning problems common to members of an association and distributed to the members through a periodic bulletin] should specifically state that this opinion should not be relied on by any member as a basis for handling his individual affairs, but that in every case he should consult his counsel. In the publication of the opinion the association should make a similar statement." ABA Opinion 273 (1946).

12. "A group of recent interrelated changes bears directly on the availability of legal services.... [One] change is the constantly accelerating urbanization of the country and the decline of personal and neighborhood knowledge of whom to retain as a professional man." Cheatham, *Availability of Legal Services: The Responsibility of the Individual Lawyer and of the Organized Bar*, 12 U.C.L.A. L. REV. 438, 440 (1965).

13. *Cf.* Cheatham, *A Lawyer When Needed: Legal Services for the Middle Classes*, 63 COLUM. L. REV. 973, 974 (1963).

14. See ABA CANONS OF PROFESSIONAL ETHICS, CANON 28 (1908).

15. Amended, August 1978, House Informational Report No. 130.

16. *Cf.* ABA Opinion 303 (1961).

17. See ABA CANONS OF PROFESSIONAL ETHICS, CANON 33 (1908).

18. *Id.*

"The continued use of a firm name by one or more surviving partners after the death of a member of the firm whose name is in the firm title is expressly permitted by the Canons of Ethics. The reason for this is that all of the partners have by their joint and several efforts over a period of years contributed to the good will attached to the firm name.In the case of a firm having widespread connections, this good will is disturbed by a change in firm name every time a name partner dies, and that reflects a loss in some degree of the good will to the building up of which the surviving partners have contributed their time, skill and labor through a period of years. To avoid this loss the firm name is continued, and to meet the requirements of the Canon the individuals constituting the firm from time to time are listed." ABA Opinion 267 (1945).

"Accepted local custom in New York recognizes that the name of a law firm does not necessarily identify the individual members of the firm, and hence the continued use of a firm name after the death of one or more partners is not a deception and is permissible.... The continued use of a deceased partner's name in the firm title is not affected by the fact that another partner withdraws from the firm and his name is dropped, or the name of the new partner is added to the firm name." Opinion No. 45, Committee on Professional Ethics, New York State Bar Ass'n, 39 N.Y.St.B.J. 455 (1967).

Cf. ABA Opinion 258 (1943).

19. Cf. ABA CANONS OF PROFESSIONAL ETHICS, CANON 33 (1908) and ABA Opinion 315 (1965).

20. Cf. ABA Opinions 283 (1950) and 81 (1932).

21. See ABA Opinion 316 (1967).

22. "The word 'associates' has a variety of meanings. Principally through custom the word when used on the letterheads of law firms has come to be regarded as describing those who are employees of the firm. Because the word has acquired this special significance in connection with the practice of the law the use of the word to describe lawyer relationships other than employer-employee is likely to be misleading." In re Sussman and Tanner, 241 Ore. 246, 248, 405 P.2d 355, 356 (1965).

According to ABA Opinion 310 (1963), use of the term "associates" would be misleading in two situations: (1) where two lawyers are partners and they share both responsibility and liability for the partnership; and (2) where two lawyers practice separately, sharing no responsibility or liability, and only share a suite of offices and some costs.

23. "For a long time, many lawyers have, of necessity, limited their practice to certain branches of law. The increasing complexity of the law and the demand of the public for more expertness on the part of the lawyer has, in the past few years — particularly in the last ten years — brought about specialization on an increasing scale." Report of the Special Committee on Specialization and Specialized Legal Services, 79 A.B.A. REP. 582, 584 (1954).

24. See ABA CANONS OF PROFESSIONAL ETHICS, CANON 12 (1908).

25. Cf. ABA CANONS OF PROFESSIONAL ETHICS, CANON 12 (1908).

26. "If there is any fundamental proposition of government on which all would agree, it is that one of the highest goals of society must be to achieve and maintain equality before the law. Yet this ideal remains an empty form of words unless the legal profession is ready to provide adequate representation for those unable to pay the usual fees." Professional Representation: Report of the Joint Conference, 44 A.B.A.J. 1159, 1216 (1958).

27. See ABA CANONS OF PROFESSIONAL ETHICS, CANON 12 (1958).

28. Cf. ABA CANONS OF PROFESSIONAL ETHICS, CANON 12 (1908).

29. "When members of the Bar are induced to render legal services for inadequate compensation, as a consequence the quality of the service rendered may be lowered, the welfare of the profession injured and the administration of justice made less efficient." ABA Opinion 302 (1961).

Cf. ABA Opinion 307 (1962).

30. See ABA CANONS OF PROFESSIONAL ETHICS, CANON 12 (1908).

31. See ABA CANONS OF PROFESSIONAL ETHICS, CANON 13; see also MACKINNON, CONTINGENT FEES FOR LEGAL SERVICES (1964) (A report of the American Bar Foundation).

"A contract for a reasonable contingent fee where sanctioned by law is permitted by Canon 13, but the client must remain responsible to the lawyer for expenses advanced by the latter. 'There is to be no barter of the privilege of prosecuting a cause for gain in exchange for the promise of the attorney to prosecute at his own expense.' (Cardozo, C.J. in Matter of Gilman, 251 N.Y. 265, 270-271.)" ABA Opinion 246 (1942).

32. See Comment, *Providing Legal Services for the Middle Class in Civil Matters: The Problem, the Duty and a Solution*, 26 U. PITT. L. REV. 811, 829 (1965).

33. See ABA CANONS OF PROFESSIONAL ETHICS, CANON 38 (1908).

"Of course, as... [Informal Opinion 679] points out, there must be full disclosure of the arrangement [that an entity other than the client pays the attorney's fee] by the attorney to the client. ..." ABA Opinion 320 (1968).

34. "Only lawyers may share in... a division of fees, but... it is not necessary that both lawyers be admitted to practice in the same state, so long as the division was based on the division of services or responsibility." ABA Opinion 316 (1967).

35. See ABA CANONS OF PROFESSIONAL ETHICS, CANON 34 (1908).

"We adhere to our previous rulings that where a lawyer merely brings about the employment of another lawyer *but renders no service and assumes no responsibility in the matter*, a division of the latter's fee is improper. Opinions 18 and 153)."

"It is assumed that the bar, generally, understands what acts or conduct of a lawyer may constitute 'services' to a client within the intendment of Canon 12. Such acts or conduct invariably, if not always, involve 'responsibility' on the part of the lawyer, whether the word 'responsibility' be construed to denote the possible resultant legal or moral liability on the part of the lawyer to the client or to others, or the onus of deciding what should or should not be done in behalf of the client. The word 'services' in Canon 12 must be construed in this broad sense and may apply to the selection and retainer of associate counsel as well as to other acts or conduct in the client's behalf." ABA Opinion 204 (1940).

36. See ABA CANONS OF PROFESSIONAL ETHICS, CANON 14 (1908).

37. *Cf.* ABA Opinion 320 (1968).

38. See ABA CANONS OF PROFESSIONAL ETHICS, CANON 14 (1908).

"Ours is a learned profession, not a mere money-getting trade.... Suits to collect fees should be avoided. Only where the circumstances imperatively require, should resort be had to a suit to compel payment. And where a lawyer does resort to a suit to enforce payment of fees which involves a disclosure, he should carefully avoid any disclosure not clearly necessary to obtaining or defending his rights." ABA Opinion 250 (1943).

But cf. ABA Opinion 320 (1968).

39. "As a society increases in size, sophistication and technology, the body of laws which is required to control that society also increases in size, scope and complexity. With this growth, the law directly affects more and more facets of individual behavior, creating an expanding need for legal services on the part of the individual members of the society.... As legal guidance in social and commercial behavior increasingly becomes necessary, there will come a concurrent demand from the layman that such guidance be made available to him. This demand will not come from those who are able to employ the best legal talent, nor from those who can obtain legal assistance at little or no cost. In will come from the large forgotten middle income class,' who can neither afford to pay proportionately large fees nor qualify for ultra-low-cost services. The legal profession must recognize this inevitable demand and consider methods whereby it can be satisfied. If the profession fails to provide such methods, the laity will." Comment, *Providing*

Legal Services for the Middle Class in Civil Matters: "The Problem, the Duty and a Solution, 26 U. PITT. L. REV. 811, 811-12 (1965).

"The issue is not whether we shall do something or do nothing. The demand for ordinary everyday legal justice is so great and the moral nature of the demand is so strong that the issue has become whether we devise, maintain, and support suitable agencies able to satisfy the demand, or by our own default, force the government to take over the job, supplant us, and ultimately dominate us." Smith, *Legal Service Offices for Persons of Moderate Means*, 1949 WIS. L. REV. 416, 418 (1949).

40. "Lawyers have peculiar responsibilities for the just administration of the law, and these responsibilities include providing advice and representation for needy persons. To a degree not always appreciated by the public at large, the bar has performed these obligations with zeal and devotion. The Committee is persuaded, however, that a system of justice that attempts, in midtwentieth century America, to meet the needs of the financially incapacitated accused through primary or exclusive reliance on the uncompensated services of counsel will prove unsuccessful and inadequate.... A system of adequate representation, therefore, should be structured and financed in a manner reflecting its public importance.... We believe that fees for private appointed counsel should be set by the court within maximum limits established by the statute." REPORT OF THE ATT'Y GEN'S COMM. ON POVERTY AND THE ADMINISTRATION OF CRIMINAL JUSTICE 41-43 (1963).

41. "At present this representation [of those unable to pay usual fees] is being supplied in some measure through the spontaneous generosity of individual lawyers, through legal aid societies, and — increasingly — through the organized efforts of the Bar. If those who stand in need of this service know of its availability and their need is in fact adequately met, the precise mechanism by which this service is provided becomes of secondary importance. It is of great importance, however, that both the impulse to render this service, and the plan for making that impulse effective, should arise within the legal profession itself." *Professional Responsibility: Report of the Joint Conference*, 44 A.B.A.J. 1159, 1216 (1958).

42. "Free legal clinics carried on by the organized bar are not ethically objectionable. On the contrary, they serve a very worthwhile purpose and should be encouraged." ABA Opinion 191 (1939).

43. "Whereas the American Bar Association believes that it is a fundamental duty of the bar to see to it that all persons requiring legal advice be able to attain it, irrespective of their economic status. ...

"Resolved, that the Association approves and sponsors the setting up by state and local bar associations of lawyer referral plans and low-cost legal service methods for the purpose of dealing with cases of persons who might not otherwise have the benefit of legal advice. ..." *Proceedings of the House of Delegates of the American Bar Association*, Oct. 30, 1946, 71 A.B.A. REP. 103, 109-10 (1946).

44. "The defense of indigent citizens, without compensation, is carried on throughout the country by lawyers representing legal aid societies, not only with the approval, but with the commendation of those acquainted with the work. Not infrequently services are rendered out of sympathy or for other philanthropic reasons, by individual lawyers who do not represent legal aid societies. There is nothing whatever in the Canons to prevent a lawyer from performing such an act, nor should there be." ABA Opinion 148 (1935).

45. But cf. ABA CANNONS OF PROFESSIONAL ETHICS, CANON 31 (1908).

46. "One of the highest services the lawyer can render to society is to appear in court on behalf of clients whose causes are in disfavor with the general public." *Professional Responsibility: Report of the Joint Conference*, 44 A.B.A.J. 1159, 1216 (1958).

One author proposes the following proposition to be included in "A Proper Oath for Advocates": "I recognize that it is sometimes difficult for clients with unpopular causes to obtain proper legal representation. I will do all that I can to assure that the client with the unpopular cause is properly represented, and that the lawyer representing such a client receives credit from and support of the bar for handling such a matter." Thode, *The Ethical Standard for the Advocate*, 39 TEXAS L. REV. 575, 592 (1961).

"'6068.... It is the duty of an attorney:

"(h) Never to reject, for any consideration personal to himself, the cause of the defenseless or the oppressed." CAL. BUSINESS AND PROFESSIONS CODE § 6068 (West 1962). Virtually the same language is found in the oregon statutes at ORE. REV. STATS. Ch. 9 § 9.460(8).

See Rostow, *The Lawyer and His Client*, 48 A.B.A.J. 25 and 146 (1962).

47. See ABA CANONS OF PROFESSIONAL ETHICS, CANONS 7 and 29 (1908).

"We are of the opinion that it is not professionally improper for a lawyer to accept employment to compel another lawyer to honor the just claim of a layman. Unfortunately, there appears to be a widespread feeling among laymen that it is difficult, if not impossible, to obtain justice when they have claims against members of the Bar because other lawyers will not accept employment to proceed against them. The honor of the profession, whose members proudly style themselves officers of the court, must surely be sullied if its members bind themselves by custom to refrain from enforcing just claims of laymen against lawyers." ABA Opinion 144 (1935).

48. ABA CANONS OF PROFESSIONAL ETHICS, CANON 4 (1908) uses a slightly different test, saying, "A lawyer assigned as counsel for an indigent prisoner ought not to ask to be excused for any trivial reason. ..."

49. *Cf.* ABA CANONS OF PROFESSIONAL ETHICS, CANON 7 (1908).

50. See ABA CANONS OF PROFESSIONAL ETHICS, CANON 5 (1908).

51. Dr. Johnson's reply to Boswell upon being asked what he thought of "supporting a cause which you know to be bad" was: "Sir, you do not know it to be good or bad till the Judge determines it.I have said that you are to state facts fairly; so that your thinking, or what you call knowing, a cause to be bad, must be from reasoning, must be from supposing your arguments to be weak and inconclusive. But, Sir, that is not enough. An argument which does not convince yourself, may convince the Judge to whom you urge it: and if it does convince him, why, then, Sir, you are wrong, and he is right." 2 BOSWELL, THE LIFE OF JOHNSON 47-48 (Hill ed. 1887).

52. "The lawyer deciding whether to undertake a case must be able to judge objectively whether he is capable of handling it and whether he can assume its burdens without prejudice to previous commitments. ..." *Professional Responsibility: Report of the Joint Conference*, 44 A.B.A.J. 1158, 1218 (1958).

53. "The lawyer must decline to conduct a civil cause or to make a defense when convinced that it is intended merely to harass or to injure the opposite party or to work oppression or wrong." ABA CANONS OF PROFESSIONAL ETHICS, CANON 30 (1908).

54. See ABA CANONS OF PROFESSIONAL ETHICS, CANON 7 (1908).

55. *Id.*

"From the facts stated we assume that the client has discharged the first attorney and given notice of the discharge. Such being the case, the second attorney may properly accept employment. Canon 7; Opinions 10, 130, 149." ABA Opinion 209 (1941).

56. See ABA CANONS OF PROFESSIONAL ETHICS, CANON 44 (1908).

"I will carefully consider, before taking a case, whether it appears that I can fully represent the client within the framework of law. If the decision is in the affirmative, then it will take extreme circumstances to cause me to decide later that I cannot so represent him." Thode, *The Ethical Standard for the Advocate*, 39 TEXAS L. REV. 575, 592 (1961) (from "A Proper Oath for Advocates").

57. ABA Opinion 314 (1965) held that a lawyer should not disassociate himself from a cause when "it is obvious that the very act of disassociation would have the effect of violating Canon 37."

58. ABA CANON 44 enumerates instances in which "... the lawyer may be warranted in withdrawing on due notice to the client, allowing him time to employ another lawyer."

59. See ABA CANONS OF PROFESSIONAL ETHICS, CANON 44 (1908).

60. Amended, February 1975, House Informational Report No. 110.

61. Amended, August 1978, House Informational Report No. 130.

62. *Id.*

63. Amended, February 1976, House Informational Report No. 100.

64. See ABA Opinion 301 (1961).

65. "[I]t has become commonplace for many lawyers to participate in government service; to deny them the right, upon their return to private practice, to refer to their prior employment in a brief and dignified manner, would place an undue limitation upon a large element of our profession. It is entirely proper for a member of the profession to explain his absence from private practice, where such is the primary purpose of the announcement, by a brief and dignified reference to the prior employment.

"... [A]ny such announcement should be limited to the immediate past connection of the lawyer with the government, made upon his leaving that position to enter private practice." ABA Opinion 301 (1961).

66. See ABA Opinion 251 (1943).

67. "Those lawyers who are working for an individual lawyer or a law firm may be designated on the letterhead and in other appropriate places as 'associates'." ABA Opinion 310 (1963).

68. See ABA CANONS OF PROFESSIONAL ETHICS, CANON 33 (1908).

69. But see ABA Opinion 285 (1951).

70. See ABA CANONS OF PROFESSIONAL ETHICS, CANON 33 (1908); cf. ABA Opinions 318 (1967), 267 (1945), 219 (1941), 208 (1940), 192 (1939), 97 (1933), and 6 (1925).

71. ABA Opinion 318 (1967) held, "anything to the contrary in Formal Opinion 315 or in the other opinions cited notwithstanding that: "Where a partner whose name appears in the name of a law firm is elected or appointed to high local, state or federal office, which office he intends to occupy only temporarily, at the end of which time he intends to return to his position with the firm, and provided that he is not precluded by holding such office from engaging in the practice of law and does not in fact sever his relationship with the firm but only takes a leave of absence, and provided that there is no local law, statute or custom to the contrary, his name may be retained in the firm name during his term or terms of office, but only if proper precautions are taken not to mislead the public as to his degree of participation in the firm's affairs."

Cf. ABA Opinion 143 (1935), New York County Opinion 67, and New York City Opinions 36 and 798; but cf. ABA Opinion 192 (1939) and Michigan Opinion 164.

72. *Cf.* ABA CANONS OF PROFESSIONAL ETHICS, CANON 33 (1908).

73. Amended, February 1979, House Informational Report No. 123.

74. See ABA Opinion 277 (1948); cf. ABA CANONS OF PROFESSIONAL ETHICS, CANON 33 (1908) and ABA Opinions 318 (1967), 126 (1935), 115 (1934), 106 (1934), and i 1383 (1977).

75. See ABA Opinions 318 (1967) and 316 (1967); cf. ABA CANONS OF PROFESSIONAL ETHICS, CANON 33 (1908).

76. DR 2-102(E) was deleted and DR 2-102(F) was redesignated as DR 2-102(E) in February 1980, House Informational Report No. 107.

77. *Cf.* ABA CANONS OF PROFESSIONAL ETHICS, CANON 28 (1908).

78. "We think it clear that a lawyer's seeking employment in an ordinary law office, or appointment to a civil service position, is not prohibited by... [Canon 27]." ABA Opinion 197 (1939).

79. "[A] lawyer may not seek from persons not his clients the opportunity to perform... a [legal] check-up." ABA Opinion 307 (1962).

80. *Cf.* ABA Opinion 78 (1932).

81. "'No financial connection of any kind between the Brotherhood and any lawyer is permissible. No lawyer can properly pay any amount whatsoever to the Brotherhood or any of its departments, officers or members as compensation, reimbursement of expenses or gratuity in connection with the procurement of a case.'" In re Brotherhood of R.R. Trainmen, 13 Ill. 2d 391, 398, 150 N.E. 2d 163, 167 (1958), *quoted in* In re Ratner, 194 Kan. 362, 372, 399 P.2d 865, 873 (1965).

See ABA Opinion 147 (1935).

82. Amended, February 1975, House Informational Report No. 110.

83. "This Court has condemned the practice of ambulance chasing through the media of runners and touters. In similar fashion we have with equal emphasis condemned the practice of direct solicitation by a lawyer. We have classified both offenses as serious breaches of the Canons of Ethics demanding severe treatment of the offending lawyer." State v. Dawson, 111 So. 2d 427, 431 (Fla. 1959).

84. "Registrants [of a lawyer referral plan] may be required to contribute to the expense of operating it by a reasonable registration charge or by a reasonable percentage of fees collected by them." ABA Opinion 291 (1956).

Cf. ABA Opinion 227 (1941).

85. Amended, February 1975, House Informational Report No. 110.

86. *Cf.* ABA Opinion 148 (1935).

87. United Mine Workers v. Ill. State Bar Ass'n., 389 U.S. 217, 19 L. Ed. 2d 426, 88 S. Ct. 353 (1967); Brotherhood of R.R. Trainmen v. Virginia, 371 U.S. 1, 12 L. Ed. 2d 89, 84 S. Ct. 1113 (1964); NAACP v. Button, 371 U.S. 415, 9 L. Ed. 2d 405, 83 S. Ct. 328 (1963). Also see ABA Opinion 332 (1973) and 333 (1973).

88. Amended, February 1975, House Informational Report No. 110.

89. "If a bar association has embarked on a program of institutional advertising for an annual legal check-up and provides brochures and reprints, it is not improper to have these available in the lawyer's office for persons to read and take." ABA Opinion 307 (1962).

Cf. ABA Opinion 121 (1934).

90. ABA CANONS OF PROFESSIONAL ETHICS, CANON 28 (1908).

91. *Cf.* ABA Opinions 229 (1941) and 173 (1937).

92. "It certainly is not improper for a lawyer to advise his regular clients of new statutes, court decisions, and administrative rulings, which may affect the client's interests, provided the communication is strictly limited to such information. ...

"When such communications go to concerns or individuals other than regular clients of the lawyer, they are thinly disguised advertisements for professional employment, and are obviously improper." ABA Opinion 213 (1941).

"It is our opinion that where the lawyer has no reason to believe that he has been supplanted by another lawyer, it is not only his right, but it might even be his duty to advise his client of any change of fact or law which might defeat the client's testamentary purpose as expressed in the will.

"Periodic notices might be sent to the client for whom a lawyer has drawn a will, suggesting that it might be wise for the client to reexamine his will to determine whether or not there has been any change in his situation requiring a modification of his will." ABA Opinion 210 (1941).

Cf. ABA CANONS OF PROFESSIONAL ETHICS, CANON 28 (1908).

93. Amended, March 1974, House Informational Report No. 127.

94. Amended, February 1975, House Informational Report No. 110.

95. *Cf.* ABA Opinion 168 (1937).

96. But cf. ABA Opinion 111 (1934).

97. See ABA CANONS OF PROFESSIONAL ETHICS, CANON 45 (1908); cf. ABA CANONS OF PROFESSIONAL ETHICS, CANONS 43, and 46 (1908).

98. This provision is included to conform to action taken by the ABA House of Delegates at the Mid-Winter Meeting, January, 1969.

99. See ABA CANONS OF PROFESSIONAL ETHICS, CANON 12 (1908).

100. The charging of a "clearly excessive fee" is a ground for discipline. State ex rel. Nebraska State Bar Ass'n. v. Richards. 165 Neb. 80, 90, 84 N.W.2d 136, 143 (1957).

"An attorney has the right to contract for any fee he chooses so long as it is not excessive (see Opinion 190), and this Committee is not concerned with the amount of such fees unless so excessive as to constitute a misappropriation of the client's funds (see Opinion 27)." Aba o/pinion 320 (1968).

Cf. ABA Opinions 209 (1940), 190 (1939), and 27 (1930) and State ex rel. Lee v. Buchanan, 191 So.2d 33 (Fla. 1966).

101. *Cf.* ABA CANONS OF PROFESSIONAL ETHICS, CANON 13 (1908); see generally MACKINNON, CONTINGENT FEES FOR LEGAL SERVICES (1964) (A Report of the American Bar Foundation).

102. "Contingent fees, whether in civil or criminal cases, are a special concern of the law. ...

"In criminal cases, the rule is stricter because of the danger of corrupting justice. The second part of Section 542 of the Restatement [of Contracts] reads; 'A bargain to conduct a criminal case... in consideration of a promise of a fee contingent on success is illegal. ...'" Peyton v. Margiotti, 398 Pa. 86, 156 A.2d 865, 967 (1959).

"The third area of practice in which the use of the contingent fee is generally considered to be prohibited is the prosecution and defense of criminal cases. However, there are so few cases, and these are predominantly old, that it is doubtful that there can be said to be any current law on the subject.... In the absence of cases on the validity of contingent fees for defense attorneys, it is necessary to rely on the consensus among commentators that such a fee is void as against public policy. The nature of criminal practice itself makes unlikely the use of contingent fee contracts." MACKINNON, CONTINGENT FEES FOR LEGAL SERVICES 52 (1964) (A Report of the American Bar Foundation).

103. See ABA CANONS OF PROFESSIONAL ETHICS, CANON 34 (1908) and ABA Opinions 316 (1967) and 294 (1958); see generally ABA Opinions 265 (1945), 204 (1940), 190 (1939), 171 (1937), 153 (1936), 97 (1933), 63 (1932), 28 (1930), 27 (1930), and 18 (1930).

104. "Canon 12 contemplates that a lawyer's fee should not exceed *the value of the services rendered.* ...

"Canon 12 applies, whether joint or separate fees are charged [by associate attorneys]. ..." ABA Opinion 204 (1940).

105. "[A] general covenant restricting an employed lawyer, after leaving the employment, from practicing in the community for a stated period, appears to this Committee to be an unwarranted restriction on the right of a lawyer to choose here he will practice and inconsistent with our professional status. Accordingly, the Committee is of the opinion it would be improper for the employing lawyer to require the covenant and likewise for the employed lawyer to agree to it." ABA Opinion 300 (1961).

106. See ABA CANONS OF PROFESSIONAL ETHICS, CANON 30 (1908).

"Rule 13.... A member of the State Bar shall not accept employment to prosecute or defend a case solely out of spite, or solely for the purpose of harassing or delaying another. ..." CAL. BUSINESS AND PROFESSIONS CODE § 6067 (West 1962).

107. *Cf.* ABA CANONS OF PROFESSIONAL ETHICS, CANON 44 (1908).

108. See also MODEL CODE OF PROFESSIONAL RESPONSIBILITY, DR 5-102 and DR 5-105.

109. *Cf.* ABA CANONS OF PROFESSIONAL ETHICS, CANON 4 (1908).

110. *Cf.* Anders v. California, 386 U.S. 738, 18 L. Ed. 2d 493, 87 S. Ct. 1396 (1967), *rehearing denied,* 388 U.S. 924, 18 L. Ed. 2d 1377, 87 S. Ct. 2094 (1967).

CANON 3

A Lawyer Should Assist in Preventing the Unauthorized Practice of Law

ETHICAL CONSIDERATIONS

EC 3-1 The prohibition against the practice of law by a layman is grounded in the need of the public for integrity and competence of those who undertake to render legal services. Because of the fiduciary and personal character of the lawyer-client relationship and the inherently complex nature of our legal system, the public can better be assured of the requisite responsibility and competence if the practice of law is confined to those who are subject to the requirements and regulations imposed upon members of the legal profession.

EC 3-2 The sensitive variations in the considers that bear on legal determinations often make it difficult even for a lawyer to exercise appropriate professional judgment, and it is therefore essential that the personal nature of the relationship of client and lawyer be preserved. Competent professional judgment is the product of a trained familiarity with law and legal processes, a disciplined, analytical approach to legal problems, and a firm ethical commitment.

EC 3-3 A non-lawyer who undertakes to handle legal matters is not governed as to integrity or legal competence by the same rules that govern the conduct of a lawyer. A lawyer is not only subject to that regulation but also is committed to high standards of ethical conduct. The public interest is best served in legal matters by a regulated profession committed to such standards.[1] The Disciplinary Rules protect the public in that they prohibit a lawyer from seeking employment by improper overtures, from acting in cases of divided loyalties, and from submitting to the control of others in the exercise of his judgment. Moreover, a person who entrusts legal matters to a lawyer is protected by the attorney-client privilege and by the duty of the lawyer to hold inviolate the confidences and secrets of his client.

EC 3-4 A layman who seeks legal services often is not in a position to judge whether he will receive proper professional attention. The entrustment of a legal matter may well involve the confidences, the reputation, the property, the freedom, or even the life of the client. Proper protection of members of the public demands that no person be permitted to act in the confidential and demanding capacity of a lawyer unless he is subject to the regulations of the legal profession.

EC 3-5 It is neither necessary nor desirable to attempt the formulation of a single, specific definition of what constitutes the practice of law.[2] Functionally, the practice of law relates to the rendition of services for others that call for the professional judgment of a lawyer. The essence of the professional judgment of the lawyer is his educated ability to relate the general body and philosophy of law to a specific legal problem of a client; and thus, the public interest will be better served if only lawyers are permitted to act in matters involving professional judgment. Where this professional judgment is not involved, non-lawyers, such as court clerks, police officers, abstracters, and many governmental employees, may engage in occupations that require a special knowledge of law in certain areas. But the services of a lawyer are essential in the public interest whenever the exercise of professional legal judgment is required.

EC 3-6 A lawyer often delegates tasks to clerks, secretaries, and other lay persons. Such delegation is proper if the lawyer maintains a direct relationship with his client, supervises the delegated work, and has complete professional responsibility for the work product.[3] This delegation enables a lawyer to render legal service more economically and efficiently.

EC 3-7 The prohibition against a non-lawyer practicing law does not prevent a layman from representing himself, for then he is ordinarily exposing only himself to possible injury. The purpose of the legal profession is to make educated legal representation available to the public; but anyone who does not wish to avail himself of such representation is not required to do so. Even so, the legal profession should help members of the public to recognize legal problems and to understand why it may be unwise for them to act for themselves in matters having legal consequences.

EC 3-8 Since a lawyer should not aid or encourage a layman to practice law, he should not practice law in association with a layman or otherwise share legal fees with a layman.[4] This does not mean, however, that the pecuniary value of the interest of a deceased lawyer in his firm or practice may not be paid to his estate or specified persons such as his widow or heirs.[5] In like manner, profit-sharing retirement plans of a lawyer or law firm which include non-lawyer office employees are not improper.[6] These limited exceptions to the rule against sharing legal fees with laymen are permissible since they do not aid or encourage laymen to practice law.

EC 3-9 Regulation of the practice of law is accomplished principally by the respective states.[7] Authority to engage in the practice of law conferred in any jurisdiction is not per se a grant of the right to practice elsewhere, and it is improper for a lawyer to engage in practice where he is not permitted by law or by court order to do so. However, the demands of business and the mobility of our society pose distinct problems in the regulation of the practice of law by the states.[8] In furtherance of the public interest, the legal profession should discourage regulation that unreasonably imposes territorial limitations upon the right of a lawyer to handle the legal affairs of his client or upon the opportunity of a client to obtain the services of a lawyer of his choice in all matters including the presentation of a contested matter in a tribunal before which the lawyer is not permanently admitted to practice.[9]

DISCIPLINARY RULES

DR 3-101   Aiding Unauthorized Practice of Law.[10]

(A) A lawyer shall not aid a non-lawyer in the unauthorized practice of law.[11]

(B) A lawyer shall not practice law in a jurisdiction where to do so would be in violation of regulations of the profession in that jurisdiction.[12]

DR 3-102   Dividing Legal Fees with a Non-Lawyer.

(A) A lawyer or law firm shall not share legal fees with a non-lawyer,[13] except that:

(1) An agreement by a lawyer with his firm, partner, or associate may provide for the payment of money, over a reasonable period of time after his death, to his estate or to one or more specified persons.[14]

(2) A lawyer who undertakes to complete unfinished legal business of a deceased lawyer may pay to the estate of the deceased lawyer that proportion of the total compensation which fairly represents the services rendered by the deceased lawyer.

(3) A lawyer or law firm may include non-lawyer employees in a compensation or retirement plan, even though the plan is based in whole or in part on a profit-sharing arrangement,[15] providing such plan does not circumvent another Disciplinary Rule.[16, 17]

DR 3-103   Forming a Partnership with a Non-Lawyer.

(A) A lawyer shall not form a partnership with a non-lawyer if any of the activities of the partnership consist of the practice of law.[18]

NOTES

1. "The condemnation of the unauthorized practice of law is designed to protect the public from legal services by persons unskilled in the law. The prohibition of lay intermediaries is intended to insure the loyalty of the lawyer to the client unimpaired by intervening and possibly conflicting interests." Cheatham, *Availability of Legal Services: The Responsibility of the Individual Lawyer and of the Organized Bar*, 12 U.C.L.A. L. REV. 438, 439 (1965).

2. What constitutes unauthorized practice of the law in a particular jurisdiction is a matter for determination by the courts of that jurisdiction." ABA Opinion 198 (1939).

"In the light of the historical development of the lawyer's functions, it is impossible to lay down an exhaustive definition of 'the practice of law' by attempting to enumerate every conceivable act performed by lawyers in the normal course of their work." State Bar of Arizona v. Arizona Land Title & Trust Co., 90 Ariz., 76, 87, 366 P.2d 1, 8-9 (1961), modified, 91 Ariz. 293, 371 P.2d 1020 (1962).

3. "A lawyer can employ lay secretaries, lay investigators, lay detectives, lay researchers, accountants, lay scriveners, nonlawyer draftsmen or nonlawyer researchers. In fact, he may employ nonlawyers to do any task for him except counsel clients about law matters, engage directly in the practice of law, appear in court or appear in formal proceedings a part of the judicial process, so long as it is he who takes the work and vouches for it to the client and becomes responsible to the client." ABA Opinion 316 (1967).

ABA Opinion 316 (1967) also stated that if a lawyer practices law as part of a law firm which includes lawyers from several states, he may delegate tasks to firm members in other states so long as he "is the person who, on behalf of the firm, vouched for the work of all of the others and, with the client and in the courts, did the legal acts defined by that state as the practice of law."

"A lawyer cannot delegate his professional responsibility to a law student employed in his office. He may avail himself of the assistance of the student in many of the fields of the lawyer's work, such as examination of case law, finding and interviewing witnesses, making collections of claims, examining court records, delivering papers, conveying important messages, and other similar matters. But the student is not permitted, until he is admitted to the Bar, to perform the professional functions of a lawyer, such as conducting court trials, giving professional advice to clients or drawing legal documents for them. The student in all his work must act as agent for the lawyer employing him, who must supervise his work and be responsible for his good conduct." ABA Opinions 85 (1932).

4. "No division of fees for legal services is proper, except with another lawyer. ..." ABA CANONS OF PROFESSIONAL ETHICS, CANON 34 (1908). Otherwise, according to ABA Opinion 316 (1967), "[t]he Canons of Ethics do not examine into the method by which such persons are remunerated by the lawyer.... They may be paid a salary, a per diem charge, a flat fee, a contract price, etc."

See ABA CANONS OF PROFESSIONAL ETHICS, CANONS 33 and 47 (1908).

5. "Many partnership agreements provide that the active partners, on the death of any on of them, are to make payments to the estate or to the nominee of a deceased partner on a pre-determined formula. It is only where the effect of such an arrangement is to make the estate or nominee a member of the partnership along with the surviving partners that it is prohibited by Canon 34. Where the payments are made in accordance with a pre-existing agreement entered into by the deceased partner during his lifetime and providing for a fixed method for determining their amount based upon the value of services rendered during the partner's lifetime and providing for a fixed period over which the payments are to be made, this is not the case. Under these circumstances, whether the payments are considered to be delayed payment of compensation earned but withheld during the partner's lifetime, or whether they are considered to be an approximation of his interest in matters pending at the time of his death, is immaterial. In either event, as Henry S. Drinker says in his book, LEGAL ETHICS, at page 189: 'It would seem, however, that a reasonable agreement to pay the estate a proportion of the receipts for a reasonable period is a proper practical settlement for the lawyer's services to his retirement or death.'" ABA Opinion 308 (1963).

6. *Id.* ABA Opinion 311 (1964).

7. "That the States have broad power to regulate the practice of law is, of course, beyond question." United Mine Workers v. Ill. State Bar Ass'n, 389 U.S. 217, 222 (1967).

"It is a matter of law, not of ethics, as to where an individual may practice law. Each state has its own rules." ABA Opinion 316 (1967).

8. "Much of clients' business crosses state lines. People are mobile, moving from state to state. Many metropolitan areas cross state lines. It is common today to have a single economic and social community involving more than one state. The business of a single client may involve legal problems in several states." ABA Opinion 316 (1967).

9. "[We] reaffirmed the general principle that legal services to New Jersey residents with respect to New Jersey matters may ordinarily be furnished only by New Jersey counsel; but we pointed out that there may be multistate transactions where strict adherence to this thesis would not be in the public interest and that, under the circumstances, it would have been not only more costly to the client but also 'grossly impractical and inefficient' to have had the settlement negotiations conducted by separate lawyers from different states." In re Estate of Waring, 47 N.J. 367, 376, 221 A.2d 193, 197 (1966).

Id. ABA Opinion 316 (1967).

10. Conduct permitted by the Disciplinary Rules of Canons 2 and 5 does not violate DR 3-101.

11. See ABA CANONS OF PROFESSIONAL ETHICS, CANON 47 (1908).

12. It should be noted, however, that a lawyer may engage in conduct, otherwise prohibited by this Disciplinary Rule, where such conduct is authorized by preemptive federal legislation. See Sperry v. Florida, 373 U.S. 379, 10 L. Ed. 2d 428, 83 S. Ct. 1322 (1963).

13. See ABA CANONS OF PROFESSIONAL ETHICS, CANON 34 (1908) and ABA Opinions 316 (1967), 180 (1938), and 48 (1931).

"The receiving attorney shall not under any guise or form share his fee for legal services with a lay agency, personal or corporate, without prejudice, however, to the right of the lay forwarder to charge and collect from the creditor proper compensation for non-legal services rendered by the law [sic] forwarder which are separate and apart from the services performed by the receiving attorney." ABA Opinion 294 (1958).

14. See ABA Opinion 266 (1945).

15. *Id*. ABA Opinion 311 (1964).

16. See ABA Opinion i1440.

17. Amended, February 1980, House Informational Report No. 107.

18. See ABA CANONS OF PROFESSIONAL ETHICS, CANON 33 (1908); cf. ABA Opinions 239 (1942) and 201 (1940).

ABA Opinion 316 (1967) states that lawyers licensed in different jurisdictions may, under certain conditions, enter "into an arrangement for the practice of law" and that a lawyer licensed in State A is not, for such purpose, a layman in State B.

CANON 4

A Lawyer Should Preserve the Confidences and Secrets of a Client

ETHICAL CONSIDERATIONS

EC 4-1 Both the fiduciary relationship existing between lawyer and client and the proper functioning of the legal system require the preservation by the lawyer of confidences and secrets of one who has employed or sought to employ him.[1] A client must feel free to discuss whatever he wishes with his lawyer and a lawyer must be equally free to obtain information beyond that volunteered by his client.[2] A lawyer should be fully informed of all the facts of the matter he is handling in order for his client to obtain the full advantage of our legal system. It is for the lawyer in the exercise of his independent professional judgment to separate the relevant and important from the irrelevant and unimportant. The observance of the ethical obligation of a lawyer to hold inviolate the confidences and secrets of his client not only facilitates the full development of facts essential to proper representation of the client but also encourages laymen to seek early legal assistance.

EC 4-2 The obligation to protect confidences and secrets obviously does not preclude a lawyer from revealing information when his client consents after full disclosure,[3] when necessary to perform his professional employment, when permitted by a Disciplinary Rule, or when required by law. Unless the client otherwise directs, a lawyer may disclose the affairs of his client to partners or associates of his firm. It is a matter of common knowledge that the normal operation of a law office exposes confidential professional information to non-lawyer employees of the office, particularly secretaries and those having access to the files; and this obligates a lawyer to exercise care in selecting and training his employees so that the sanctity of all confidences and secrets of his clients may be preserved. If the obligation extends to two or more clients as to the same information, a lawyer should obtain the permission of all before revealing the information. A lawyer must always be sensitive to the rights and wishes of his client and act scrupulously in the making of decisions which may involve the disclosure of information obtained in his professional relationship.[4] Thus, in the absence of consent of his client after full disclosure, a lawyer should not associate another lawyer in the handling of a matter; nor should he, in the absence of consent, seek counsel from another lawyer if there is a reasonable possibility that the identity of the client or his confidences or secrets would be revealed to such lawyer. Both social amenities and professional duty should cause a lawyer to shun indiscreet conversations concerning his clients.

EC 4-3   Unless the client otherwise directs, it is not improper for a lawyer to give limited information from his files to an outside agency necessary for statistical, bookkeeping, accounting, data processing, banking, printing, or other legitimate purposes, provided he exercises due care in the selection of the agency and warns the agency that the information must be kept confidential.

EC 4-4   The attorney-client privilege is more limited than the ethical obligation of a lawyer to guard the confidences and secrets of his client. This ethical precept, unlike the evidentiary privilege, exists without regard to the nature or source of information or the fact that others share the knowledge. A lawyer should endeavor to act in a manner which preserves the evidentiary privilege; for example, he should avoid professional discussions in the presence of persons to whom the privilege does not extend. A lawyer owes an obligation to advise the client of the attorney-client privilege and timely to assert the privilege unless it is waived by the client.

EC 4-5   A lawyer should not use information acquired in the course of the representation of a client to the disadvantage of the client and a lawyer should not use, except with the consent of his client after full disclosure, such information for his own purposes.[5] Likewise, a lawyer should be diligent in his efforts to prevent the misuse of such information by his employees and associates.[6] Care should be exercised by a lawyer to prevent the disclosure of the confidences and secrets of one client to another,[7] and no employment should be accepted that might require such disclosure.

EC 4-6   The obligation of a lawyer to preserve the confidences and secrets of his client continues after the termination of his employment.[8] Thus a lawyer should not attempt to sell a law practice as a going business because, among other reasons, to do so would involve the disclosure of confidences and secrets.[9] A lawyer should also provide for the protection of the confidences and secrets of his client following the termination of the practice of the lawyer, whether termination is due to death, disability, or retirement. For example, a lawyer might provide for the personal papers of the client to be returned to him and for the papers of the lawyer to be delivered to another lawyer or to be destroyed. In determining the method of disposition, the instructions and wishes of the client should be a dominant consideration.

DISCIPLINARY RULES

DR 4-101   Preservation of Confidences and Secrets of a Client.[10]

(A)   "Confidence" refers to information protected by the attorney-client privilege under applicable law, and "secret" refers to other information gained in the professional relationship that the client has requested be held inviolate or the disclosure of which would be embarrassing or would be likely to be detrimental to the client.

(B) Except when permitted under DR 4-101 (C), a lawyer shall not knowingly:

    (1) Reveal a confidence or secret of his client.[11]

    (2) Use a confidence or secret of his client to the disadvantage of the client.

    (3) Use a confidence or secret of his client for the advantage of himself[12] or of a third person,[13] unless the client consents after full disclosure.

(C) A lawyer may reveal:

    (1) Confidences or secrets with the consent of the client or clients affected, but only after a full disclosure to them.[14]

    (2) Confidences or secrets when permitted under Disciplinary Rules or required by law or court order.[15]

    (3) The intention of his client to commit a crime[16] and the information necessary to prevent the crime.[17]

    (4) Confidences or secrets necessary to establish or collect his fee[18] or to defend himself or his employees or associates against an accusation of wrongful conduct.[19]

(D) A lawyer shall exercise reasonable care to prevent his employees, associates, and others whose services are utilized by him from disclosing or using confidences or secrets of a client, except that a lawyer may reveal the information allowed by DR 4-101 (C) through an employee.

NOTES

1. See ABA CANONS OF PROFESSIONAL ETHICS, CANONS 6 and 37 (1908) and ABA Opinion 287 (1953).

"The reason underlying the rule with respect to confidential communications between attorney and client is well stated in MECHEM ON AGENCY, 2d Ed., Vol. 2, § 2297, as follows: 'The purposes and necessities of the relation between a client and his attorney require, in many cases, on the part of the client, the fullest and freest disclosures to the attorney of the client's objects, motives and acts. This disclosure is made in the strictest confidence, relying upon the attorney's honor and fidelity. To permit the attorney to reveal to others what is so disclosed, would be not only a gross violation of a sacred trust upon his part, but it would utterly destroy and prevent the usefulness and benefits to be derived from professional assistance. Based upon considerations of public policy, therefore, the law wisely declares that all confidential communications and disclosures, made by a client to his legal adviser for the purpose of obtaining his professional aid or advice, shall be strictly priviledged; — that the attorney shall not be permitted, without the consent of his client, — and much less will he be compelled — to reveal or disclose communications made to him under such circumstances.'" ABA Opinion 250 (1943).

"While it is true that complete revelation of relevant facts should be encouraged for trial purposes, nevertheless an attorney's dealings with his client, if both are sincere, and if the dealings involve more than mere technical matters, should be immune to discovery proceedings. There must be freedom from fear of revealment of matters disclosed to an attorney because of the peculiarly intimate relationshp existing." Ellis-Foster Co. v. Union Carbide & Carbon Corp., 159 F.Supp. 917, 919 (D.N.J. 1958).

Id. ABA Opinions 314 (1965), 274 (1946) and 268 (1945).

2. "While it is the great purpose of law to ascertain the truth, there is the countervailing necessity of insuring the right of every person to freely and fully confer and confide in one having knowledge of the law, and skilled in its practice, in order that the former may have adequate advice and a proper defense. This assistance can be made safely and readily available only when the client is free from the consequences of apprehension of disclosure by reason of the subsequent statements of the skilled lawyer. Baird v. Koerner, 279 F.2d 623, 629-30 (9th Cir. 1960)

Id. ABA Opinion 150 (1936).

3. "Where... [a client] knowingly and after full disclosure participates in a [legal fee] financing plan which requires the furnishing of certain information to the bank, clearly by his conduct he has waived any privilege as to that information." ABA Opinion 320 (1968).

4. "The lawyer must decide when he takes a case whether it is a suitable one for him to undertake and after his client by exposing injurious evidence entrusted to him.... [D]oing something intrinsically regrettable, because the only alternative involves worse consequences, is a necessity in every profession." WILLISTON, LIFE AND LAW 271 (1940).

Id. ABA Opinions 177 (1938) and 83 (1932).

5. See ABA CANONS OF PROFESSIONAL ETHICS, CANON 11 (1908).

6. See ABA CANONS OF PROFESSIONAL ETHICS, CANON 37 (1908).

7. See ABA CANONS OF PROFESSIONAL ETHICS, CANONS 6 and 37 (1908).

"[An] attorney must not accept professional employment against a client or a former client which will, or even may require him to use confidential information obtained by the attorney in the course of his professional relations with such client regarding the subject matter of the employment. ..." ABA Opinion 165 (1936).

8. See ABA CANONS OF PROFESSIONAL ETHICS, CANON 37 (1908).

"Confidential communications between an attorney and his client, made because of the relationship and concerning the subject-matter of the attorney's employment, are generally privileged from disclosure without the consent of the client, and this privilege outlasts the attorney's employment.Canon 37." ABA Opinion 154 (1936).

9. *Id.* ABA Opinion 266 (1945).

10. See ABA CANONS OF PROFESSIONAL ETHICS, CANON 37 (1908); cf. ABA CANONS OF PROFESSIONAL ETHICS, CANON 6 (1908).

11. " § 6068... It is the duty of an attorney:

"(e) To maintain inviolate the confidence, and at every peril to himself to preserve the secrets, of his client." CAL. BUSINESS AND PROFESSIONS CODE § 6068 (West 1962). Virtually the same provision is found in the Oregon statutes. ORE. REV. STATS. ch. 9 § 9.460(5).

"Communications between lawyer and client are privileged (WIGMORE ON EVIDENCE, 3d Ed., Vol. 8, §§ 2290-2329). The modern theory underlying the privilege is subjective and is to give the client freedom of apprehension in consulting his legal adviser (ibid., § 2290, p. 548). The privilege applies to communications made in seeking legal advice for any purpose (ibid.,§ 2294, p. 563). The mere circumstance that the advice is given without charge therefor does not nullify the privilege (ibid., § 2303)." ABA Opinion 216 (1941).

"It is the duty of an attorney to maintain the confidence and preserve inviolate the secrets of his client. ..." ABA Opinion 155 (1936).

12. See ABA CANONS OF PROFESSIONAL ETHICS, CANON 11 (1908).

"The provision respecting employment is in accord with the general rule announced in the adjudicated cases that a lawyer may not make use of knowledge or information acquired by him through his professional relations with his client, or in the conduct of his client's business, to his own advantage or profit (7 C.J.S., § 125, p. 958; Healy v. Gray, 184 Iowa 111, 168 N.W. 222; Baumgardner v. Hudson, D.C. App., 277 F. 552; Goodrum v. Clement, D.C. App., 277 F. 586)." ABA Opinion 250 (1943).

13. See ABA Opinion 177 (1938).

14. "[A lawyer] may not divulge confidential communications, information, and secrets imparted to him by the client or acquired during their professional relations, unless he is authorized to do so by the client (People v. Gerold, 265 Ill. 448, 107 N.E. 165, 178; Murphy v. Riggs, 238 Mich. 151, 213 N.W. 110, 112; Opinion of this Committee, No. 91)." ABA Opinion 202 (1940).

Id. ABA Opinion 91 (1933).

15. "A defendant in a criminal case when admitted to bail is not only regarded as in the custody of his bail, but he is also in the custody of the law, and admission to bail does not deprive the court of its inherent power to deal with the person of the prisoner. Being in lawful custody, the defendant is guilty of an escape when he gains his liberty before he is delivered in due process of law, and is guilty of a separate offense for which he may be punished. In failing to disclose his client's whereabouts as a fugitive under these circumstances the attorney would not only be aiding his client to escape trial on the charge for which he was indicted, but would likewise be aiding him in evading prosecution for the additional offense of escape.

"It is the opinion of the committee that under such circumstances the attorney's knowledge of his client's whereabouts is not privileged, and that he may be disciplined for failing to disclose that information to the proper authorities. ..." ABA Opinion 155 (1936).

"We held in Opinion 155 that a communication by a client to his attorney in respect to the future commission of an unlawful act or to a continuing wrong is not privileged from disclosure. Public policy forbids that the relation of attorney and client should be used to conceal wrongdoing on the part of this client.

"When an attorney representing a defendant in a criminal case applies on his behalf for probation or suspension of sentence, he represents to the court, by implication at least, that his client will abide by the terms and conditions of the court's order. When that attorney is later advised of a violation of that order, it is his duty to advise his client of the consequences of his act, and endeavor to prevent a continuance of the wrongdoing. If his client thereafter persists in violating the terms and conditions of his probation, it is the duty of the attorney as an officer of the court to advise the proper authorities concerning his client's conduct. Such information, even though coming to the attorney from the client in the course of his professional relations with respect to other matters in which he represents the defendant, is not privileged from disclosure. ..."

See ABA Opinion 156 (1936).

16. ABA Opinion 314 (1965) indicates that a lawyer must disclose even the confidences of his clients if "the facts in the attorney's possession indicate beyond reasonable doubt that a crime will be committed."

See ABA Opinion 155 (1936).

17. See ABA CANONS OF PROFESSIONAL ETHICS, CANON 37 (1908) and ABA Opinion 202 (1940).

18. *Id.* ABA Opinion 250 (1943).

19. See ABA CANONS OF PROFESSIONAL ETHICS, CANON 37 (1908) and ABA Opinions 202 (1940) and 19 (1930).

"[The] adjudicated cases recognize an exception to the rule [that a lawyer shall not reveal the confidences of his client], where disclosure is necessary to protect the attorney's interests arising out of the relation of attorney and client in which disclosure was made.

"The exception is stated in MECHEM ON AGENCY, 2d Ed., Vol. 2, § 2313, as follows: 'But the attorney may disclose information received from the client when it becomes necessary for his own protection, as if the client should bring an action against the attorney for negligence or misconduct, and it became necessary for the attorney to show what his instructions were, or what was the nature of the duty which the client expected him to perform. So if it became necessary for the attorney to bring an action against the client, the client's privilege could not prevent the attorney from disclosing what was essential as a means of obtaining or defending his own rights.'

"Mr. Jones, in his COMMENTARIES ON EVIDENCE, 2d Ed., Vol. 5, § 2165, states the exception thus: 'It has frequently been held that the rule as to privileged communications does not apply when litigation arises between attorney and client to the extent that their communications are relevant to the issue. In such cases, if the disclosure of privileged communications becomes necessary to protect the attorney's rights, he is released from those obligations of secrecy which the law places upon him. He should not, however, disclose more than is necessary for his own protection. It would be a manifest injustice to allow the client to take advantage of the rule of exclusion as to professional confidence to the prejudice of his attorney, or that it should be carried to the extent of depriving the attorney of the means of obtaining or defending his own rights. In such cases the attorney is exempted from the obligations of secrecy.'" ABA Opinion 250 (1943).

CANON 5

A Lawyer Should Exercise Independent Professional Judgment on Behalf of a Client

ETHICAL CONSIDERATIONS

EC 5-1 The professional judgment of a lawyer should be exercised, within the bounds of the law, solely for the benefit of his client and free of compromising influences and loyalties.[1] Neither his personal interests, the interests of other clients, nor the desires of third persons should be permitted to dilute his loyalty to his client.

Interests of a Lawyer That May Affect His Judgment

EC 5-2 A lawyer should not accept proffered employment if his personal interests or desires will, or there is a reasonable probability that they will, affect adversely the advice to be given or services to be rendered the prospective client.[2] After accepting employment, a lawyer carefully should refrain from acquiring a property right or assuming a position that would tend to make his judgment less protective of the interests of his client.

EC 5-3 The self-interest of a lawyer resulting from his ownership of property in which his client also has an interest or which may affect property of his client may interfere with the exercise of free judgment on behalf of his client. If such interference would occur with respect to a prospective client, a lawyer should decline employment proffered by him. After accepting employment, a lawyer should not acquire property rights that would adversely affect his professional judgment in the presentation of his client. Even if the property interests of a lawyer do not presently interfere with the exercise of his independent judgment, but the likelihood of interference can reasonably be foreseen by him, a lawyer should explain the situation to his client and should decline employment or withdraw unless the client consents to the continuance of the relationship after full disclosure. A lawyer should not seek to persuade his client to permit him to invest in an undertaking of his client nor make improper use of his professional relationship to influence his client to invest in an enterprise in which the lawyer is interested.

EC 5-4 If, in the course of his representation of a client, a lawyer is permitted to receive from his client a beneficial ownership in publication rights relating to the subject matter of the employment, he may be tempted to subordinate the interests of his client to his own anticipated pecuniary gain. For example, a lawyer in a criminal case who obtains from his client television, radio, motion picture, newspaper, magazine, book, or other publication rights with respect to the case may be influenced, consciously or unconsciously, to a course of conduct that will enhance the value of his publication rights to the prejudice of his client. To prevent these potentially differing interests, such arrangements should be scrupulously avoided prior to the termination of all aspects of the matter giving rise to the employment, even though his employment has previously ended.

EC 5-5 A lawyer should not suggest to his client that a gift be made to himself or for his benefit. If a lawyer accepts a gift from his client, he is peculiarly susceptible to the charge that he unduly influenced or over-reached the client. If a client voluntarily offers to make a gift to his lawyer, the lawyer may accept the gift, but before doing so, he should urge that his client secure disinterested advice from an independent, competent person who is cognizant of all the circumstances.[3] Other than in exceptional circumstances, a lawyer should insist that an instrument in which his client desires to name him beneficially be prepared by another lawyer selected by the client.[4]

EC 5-6 A lawyer should not consciously influence a client to name him as executor, trustee, or lawyer in an instrument. In those cases where a client wishes to name his lawyer as such, care should be taken by the lawyer to avoid even the appearance of impropriety.[5]

EC 5-7 The possibility of an adverse effect upon the exercise of free judgment by a lawyer on behalf of his client during litigation generally makes it undesirable for the lawyer to acquire a proprietary interest in the cause of his client or otherwise to become financially interested in the outcome of the litigation.[6] However, it is not improper for a lawyer to protect his right to collect a fee for his services by the assertion of legally permissible liens, even though by doing so he may acquire an interest in the outcome of litigation. Although a contingent fee arrangement[7] gives a lawyer a financial interest in the outcome of litigation, a reasonable contingent fee is permissible in civil cases because it may be the only means by which a layman can obtain the services of a lawyer of his choice. But a lawyer, because he is in a better position to evaluate a cause of action, should enter into a contingent fee arrangement only in those instances where the arrangement will be beneficial to the client.

EC 5-8 A financial interest in the outcome of litigation also results if monetary advances are made by the lawyer to his client.[8] Although this assistance generally is not encouraged, there are instances when it is not improper to make loans to a client. For example, the advancing or guaranteeing of payment of the costs and expenses of litigation by a lawyer may be the only way a client can enforce his cause of action,[9] but the ultimate liability for such costs and expenses must be that of the client.

EC 5-9 Occasionally a lawyer is called upon to decide in a particular case whether he will be a witness or an advocate. If a lawyer is both counsel and witness, he becomes more easily impeachable for interest and thus may be a less effective witness. Conversely, the opposing counsel may be handicapped in challenging the credibility of the lawyer when the lawyer also appears as an advocate in the case. An advocate who becomes a witness is in the unseemly and ineffective position of arguing his own credibility. The roles of an advocate and of a witness are inconsistent; the function of an advocate is to advance or argue the cause of another, while that of a witness is to state facts objectively.

EC 5-10 Problems incident to the lawyer-witness relationship arise at different stages; they relate either to whether a lawyer should accept employment or should withdraw from employment.[10] Regardless of when the problem arises, his decision is to be governed by the same basic considerations. It is not objectionable for a lawyer who is a potential witness to be an advocate if it is unlikely that he will be called as a witness because his testimony would be merely cumulative or if his testimony will relate only to an uncontested issue.[11] In the exceptional situation where it will be manifestly unfair to the client for the lawyer to refuse employment or to withdraw when he will likely be a witness on a contested issue, he may serve as advocate even though he may be a witness.[12] In making such decision, he should determine the personal or financial sacrifice of the client that may result from his refusal of employment or withdrawal therefrom, the materiality of his testimony, and the effectiveness of his representation in view of his personal involvement. In weighing these factors, it should be clear that refusal or withdrawal will impose an unreasonable hardship upon the client before the lawyer accepts or continues the employment.[13] Where the question arises, doubts should be resolved in favor of the lawyer testifying and against his becoming or continuing as an advocate.[14]

EC 5-11 A lawyer should not permit his personal interests to influence his advice relative to a suggestion by his client that additional counsel be employed.[15] In like manner, his personal interests should not deter him from suggesting that additional counsel be employed; on the contrary, he should be alert to the desirability of recommending additional counsel when, in his judgment, the proper representation of his client requires it. However, a lawyer should advise his client not to employ additional counsel suggested by the client if the lawyer believes that such employment would be a disservice to the client, and he should disclose the reasons for his belief.

EC 5-12 Inability of co-counsel to agree on a matter vital to the representation of their client requires that their disagreement be submitted by them jointly to their client for his resolution, and the decision of the client shall control the action to be taken.[16]

EC 5-13 A lawyer should not maintain membership in or be influenced by any organization of employees that undertakes to prescribe, direct, or suggest when or how he should fulfill his professional obligations to a person or organization that employs him as a lawyer. Although it is not necessarily improper for a lawyer employed by a corporation or similar entity to be a member of an organization of employees, he should be vigilant to safeguard his fidelity as a lawyer to his employer, free from outside influences.

Interests of Multiple Clients

EC 5-14 Maintaining the independence of professional judgment required of a lawyer precludes his acceptance or continuation of employment that will adversely affect his judgment on behalf of or dilute his loyalty to a client.[17] This problem arises whenever a lawyer is asked to represent two or more clients who may have differing interests, whether such interests be conflicting, inconsistent, diverse, or otherwise discordant.[18]

EC 5-15 If a lawyer is requested to undertake or to continue representation of multiple clients having potentially differing interests, he must weigh carefully the possibility that his judgment may be impaired or his loyalty divided if he accepts or continues the employment. He should resolve all doubts against the propriety of the representation. A lawyer should never represent in litigation multiple clients with differing interests;[19] and there are few situations in which he would be justified in representing in litigation multiple clients with potentially differing interests. If a lawyer accepted such employment and the interests did become actually differing, he would have to withdraw from employment with likelihood of resulting hardship on the clients; and for this reason it is preferable that he refuse the employment initially. On the other hand, there are many instances in which a lawyer may properly serve multiple clients having potentially differing interests in matters not involving litigation. If the interests vary only slightly, it is generally likely that the lawyer will not be subjected to an adverse influence and that he can retain his independent judgment on behalf of each client; and if the interests become differing, withdrawal is less likely to have a disruptive effect upon the causes of his clients.

EC 5-16 In those instances in which a lawyer is justified in representing two or more clients having differing interests, it is nevertheless essential that each client be given the opportunity to evaluate his need for representation free of any potential conflict and to obtain other counsel if he so desires.[20] Thus before a lawyer may represent multiple clients, he should explain fully to each client the implications of the common representation and should accept or continue employment only if the clients consent.[21] If there are present other circumstances that might cause any of the multiple clients to question the undivided loyalty of the lawyer, he should also advise all of the clients of those circumstances.[22]

EC 5-17 Typically recurring situations involving potentially differing interests are those in which a lawyer is asked to represent co-defendants in a criminal case, co-plaintiffs in a personal injury case, an insured and his insurer,[23] and beneficiaries of the estate of a decedent. Whether a lawyer can fairly and adequately protect the interests of multiple clients in these and similar situations depends upon an analysis of each case. In certain circumstances, there may exist little chance of the judgment of the lawyer being adversely affected by the slight possibility that the interests will become actually differing; in other circumstances, the chance of adverse effect upon his judgment is not unlikely.

EC 5-18 A lawyer employed or retained by a corporation or similar entity owes his allegiance to the entity and not to a stockholder, director, officer, employee, representative, or other person connected with the entity. In advising the entity, a lawyer should keep paramount its interests and his professional judgment should not be influenced by the personal desires of any person or organization. Occasionally a lawyer for an entity is requested by a stockholder, director, officer, employee, representative, or other person connected with the entity to represent him in an individual capacity; in such case the lawyer may serve the individual only if the lawyer is convinced that differing interests are not present.

EC 5-19 A lawyer may represent several clients whose interests are not actually or potentially differing. Nevertheless, he should explain any circumstances that might cause a client to question his undivided loyalty.[24] Regardless of the belief of a lawyer that he may properly represent multiple clients, he must defer to a client who holds the contrary belief and withdraw from representation of that client.

EC 5-20 A lawyer is often asked to serve as an impartial arbitrator or mediator in matters which involve present or former clients. He may serve in either capacity if he first discloses such present or former relationships. After a lawyer has undertaken to act as an impartial arbitrator or mediator, he should not thereafter represent in the dispute any of the parties involved.

Desires of Third Persons

EC 5-21 The obligation of a lawyer to exercise professional judgment solely on behalf of his client requires that he disregard the desires of others that might impair his free judgment.[25] The desires of a third person will seldom adversely affect a lawyer unless that person is in a position to exert strong economic, political, or social pressures upon the lawyer. These influences are often subtle, and a lawyer must be alert to their existence. A lawyer subjected to outside pressures should make full disclosure of them to his client;[26] and if he or his client believes that the effectiveness of his representation has been or will be impaired thereby, the lawyer should take proper steps to withdraw from representation of his client.

EC 5-22 Economic, political, or social pressures by third persons are less likely to impinge upon the independent judgment of a lawyer in a matter in which he is compensated directly by his client and his professional work is exclusively with his client. On the other hand, if a lawyer is compensated from a source other than his client, he may feel a sense of responsibility to someone other than his client.

EC 5-23 A person or organization that pays or furnishes lawyers to represent others possesses a potential power to exert strong pressures against the independent judgment of those lawyers. Some employers may be interested in furthering their own economic, political, or social goals without regard to the professional responsibility of the lawyer to his individual client. Others may be far more concerned with establishment or extension of legal principles than in the immediate protection of the rights of the lawyer's individual client. On some occasions, decisions on priority of work may be made by the employer rather than the lawyer with the result that prosecution of work already under-taken for clients is postponed to their detriment. Similarly, an employer may seek, consciously or unconsciously, to further its own economic interests through the action of the lawyers employed by it. Since a lawyer must always be free to exercise his professional judgment without regard to the interests or motives of a third person, the lawyer who is employed by one to represent another must constantly guard against erosion of his professional freedom.[27]

EC 5-24 To assist a lawyer in preserving his professional independence, a number of courses are available to him. For example, a lawyer should not prac-tice with or in the form of a professional legal corporation, even though the corporate form is permitted by law,[28] if any director, officer, or stockholder of it is a non-lawyer. Although a lawyer may be employed by a business corporation with non-lawyers serving as directors or officers, and they necessarily have the right to make decisions of business policy, a lawyer must decline to accept direction of his professional judgment from any layman. Various types of legal aid offices are administered by boards of directors composed of lawyers and laymen. A lawyer should not accept employment from such an organization unless the board sets only broad policies and there is no interference in the relationship of the lawyer and the individual client he serves. Where a lawyer is employed by an organization, a written agreement that defines the relation-ship between him and the organization and provides for his independence is desirable since it may serve to prevent misunderstanding as to their respective roles. Although other innovations in the means of supplying legal counsel may develop, the responsibility of the lawyer to maintain his professional independence remains constant, and the legal profession must insure that changing circumstances do not result in loss of the professional independence of the lawyer.

DISCIPLINARY RULES

DR 5-101   Refusing Employment When the Interests of the Lawyer May Impair His Independent Professional Judgment.

(A) Except with the consent of his client after full disclosure, a lawyer shall not accept employment if the exercise of his professional judgment on behalf of his client will be or reasonably may be affected by his own financial, business, property, or personal interests.[29]

(B) A lawyer shall not accept employment in contemplated or pending liti-gation if he knows or it is obvious that he or a lawyer in his firm ought to be called as a witness, except that he may undertake the employment and he or a lawyer in his firm may testify:

(1)   If the testimony will relate solely to an uncontested matter.

(2)   If the testimony will relate solely to a matter of formality and there is no reason to believe that substantial evidence will be offered in opposition to the testimony.

(3)   If the testimony will relate solely to the nature and value of legal services rendered in the case by the lawyer or his firm to the client.

(4)   As to any matter, if refusal would work a substantial hardship on the client because of the distinctive value of the lawyer or his firm as counsel in the particular case.

DR 5-102   Withdrawal as Counsel When the Lawyer Becomes a Witness.[30]

(A)   If, after undertaking employment in contemplated or pending litigation, a lawyer learns or it is obvious that he or a lawyer in his firm ought to be called as a witness on behalf of his client, he shall withdraw from the conduct of the trial and his firm, if any, shall not continue representation in the trial, except that he may continue the representation and he or a lawyer in his firm may testify in the circumstances enumerated in DR 5-101(B) (1) through (4).

(B)   If, after undertaking employment in contemplated or pending litigation, a lawyer learns or it is obvious that he or a lawyer in his firm may be called as a witness other than on behalf of his client, he may continue the representation until it is apparent that his testimony is or may be prejudicial to his client.[31]

DR 5-103   Avoiding Acquisition of Interest in Litigation.

(A)   A lawyer shall not acquire a proprietary interest in the cause of action or subject matter of litigation he is conducting for a client,[32] except that he may:

(1)   Acquire a lien granted by law to secure his fee or expenses.

(2)   Contract with a client for a reasonable contingent fee in a civil case.[33]

(B)   While representing a client in connection with contemplated or pending litigation, a lawyer shall not advance or guarantee financial assistance to his client,[34] except that a lawyer may advance or guarantee the expenses of litigation, including court costs, expenses of investigation, expenses of medical examination, and costs of obtaining and presenting evidence, provided the client remains ultimately liable for such expenses.

DR 5-104   Limiting Acquisition of Interest in Litigation.

(A)   A lawyer shall not enter into a business transaction with a client if they have differing interests therein and if the client expects the lawyer to exercise his professional judgment therein for the protection of the client, unless the client has consented after full disclosure.

(B) Prior to conclusion of all aspects of the matter giving rise to his employment, a lawyer shall not enter into any arrangement or understanding with a client or a prospective client by which he acquires an interest in publication rights with respect to the subject matter of his employment or proposed employment.

DR 5-105   Refusing to Accept or Continue Employment if the Interests of Another Client May Impair the Independent Professional Judgment of the Lawyer.

(A) A lawyer shall decline proffered employment if the exercise of his independent professional judgment in behalf of a client will be or is likely to be adversely affected by the acceptance of the proffered employment,[35] or if it would be likely to involve him in representing differing interests[36], except to the extent permitted under DR 5-105(C).[37]

(B) A lawyer shall not continue multiple employment if the exercise of his independent professional judgment in behalf of a client will be or is likely to be adversely affected by his representation of another client, or if it would be likely to involve him in representing differing interests,[38] except to the extent permitted under DR 5-105(C).[39]

(C) In the situations covered by DR 5-105 (A) and (B), a lawyer may represent multiple clients if it is obvious that he can adequately represent the interest of each and if each consents to the representation after full disclosure of the possible effect of such representation on the exercise of his independent professional judgment on behalf of each.

(D) If a lawyer is required to decline employment or to withdraw from employment under a Disciplinary Rule, no partner, or associate, or any other lawyer affiliated with him[40] or his firm, may accept or continue such employment.

DR 5-106   Settling Similar Claims of Clients.[41]

(A) A lawyer who represents two or more clients shall not make or participate in the making of an aggregate settlement of the claims of or against his clients, unless each client has consented to the settlement after being advised of the existence and nature of all the claims involved in the proposed settlement, of the total amount of the settlement, and of the participation of each person in the settlement.

DR 5-107   Avoiding Influence by Others Than the Client.

(A) Except with the consent of his client after full disclosure, a lawyer shall not:

   (1) Accept compensation for his legal services from one other than his client.

   (2) Accept from one other than his client any thing of value related to his representation of or his employment by his client.[42]

(B) A lawyer shall not permit a person who recommends, employs, or pays him to render legal services for another to direct or regulate his professional judgment in rendering such legal services.[43]

(C)   A lawyer shall not practice with or in the form of a professional corporation or association authorized to practice law for a profit, if:

    (1)   A non-lawyer owns any interest therein,[44] except that a fiduciary representative of the estate of a lawyer may hold the stock or interest of the lawyer for a reasonable time during administration;

    (2)   A non-lawyer is a corporate director or officer thereof;[45] or

    (3)   A non-lawyer has the right to direct or control the professional judgment of a lawyer.[46]

NOTES

1. *Cf.* ABA CANONS OF PROFESSIONAL ETHICS, CANON 35 (1908).

"[A lawyer's] fiduciary duty is of the highest order and he must not represent interests adverse to those of the client. It is true that because of his professional responsibility and the confidence and trust which his client may legitimately repose in him, he must adhere to a high standard of honesty, integrity and good faith in dealing with his client. He is not permitted to take advantage of his position or superior knowledge to impose upon the client; nor to conceal facts or law, nor in any way deceive him without being held responsible therefor." Smoot v. Lund, 13 Utah 2d 168, 172, 369 P.2d 933, 936 (1962).

"When a client engages the services of a lawyer in a given piece of business he is entitled to feel that, until that business is finally disposed of in some manner, he has the undivided loyalty of the one upon whom he looks as his advocate and champion. If, as in this case, he is sued and his home attached by his own attorney, who is representing him in another matter, all feeling of loyalty is necessarily destroyed, and the profession is exposed to the charge that it is interested only in money." Grievance Comm. v. Rattner, 152 Conn. 59, 65, 203 A.2d 82, 84 (1964).

"One of the cardinal principles confronting every attorney in the representation of a client is the requirement of complete loyalty and service in good faith to the best of his ability. In a criminal case the client is entitled to a fair trial, but not a perfect one. These are fundamental requirements of due process under the Fourteenth Amendment.... The same principles are applicable in Sixth Amendment cases (not pertinent herein) and suggest that an attorney should have no conflict of interest and that he must devote his full and faithful efforts toward the defense of his client." Johns v. Smyth, 176 F. Supp. 949, 952 (E.D. Va. 1959), modified, United States ex rel. Wilkins v. Banmiller, 205 F. Supp. 123, 128 n. 5 (E.D. Pa. 1962), aff'd, 325 F.2d 514 (3d Cir. 1963), *cert. denied*, 379 U.S. 847, 13 L.Ed. 2d 51, 85 S.Ct. 87 (1964).

2. "Attorneys must not allow their private interests to conflict with those of their clients.... They owe their entire devotion to the interests of their clients." United States v. Anonymous, 215 F. Supp. 111, 113 (E.D. Tenn. 1963).

"[The] court [below] concluded that a firm may not accept any action against a person whom they are presently representing even though there is no relationship between the two cases. In arriving at this conclusion, the court cites an opinion of the Committee on Professional Ethics of the New York County Lawyers' Association which stated in part: 'While under the circumstances *** there may be no actual conflict of interest *** "maintenance of public confidence in the Bar requires an attorney who has accepted representation of a client to decline, while representing such client, any employment from an adverse party in any matter even though wholly unrelated to the original retainer." See Question and Answer No. 350, N.Y. County L. Ass'n, Questions and Answer No. 450 (June 21, 1956).'" Grievance Comm. v. Rattner, 152 Conn. 59, 65, 203 A.2d 82, 84 (1964).

3. "Courts of equity will scrutinize with jealous vigilance transactions between parties occupying fiduciary relations toward each other.... A deed will not be held

invalid, however, if made by the grantor with full knowledge of its nature and effect, and because of the deliberate, voluntary and intelligent desire of the grantor.... Where a fiduciary relation exists, the burden of proof is on the grantee or beneficiary of an instrument executed during the existence of such relationship to show the fairness of the transaction, that it was equitable and just and that it did not proceed from undue influence.... The same rule has application where an attorney engages in a transaction with a client during the existence of the relation and is benefited thereby.... Conversely, an attorney is not prohibited from dealing with his client or buying his property, and such contracts, if open, fair and honest, when deliberately made, are as valid as contracts between other parties.... [Important] factors in determining whether a transaction is fair include a showing by the fiduciary (1) that he made a full and frank disclosure of all the relevant information that he had; (2) that the consideration was adequate; and (3) that the principal had independent advice before completing the transaction." McFail v. Braden, 19 Ill. 2d 108, 117-18, 166 N.E. 2d 46, 52 (1960).

4. See State ex rel. Nebraska State Bar Ass'n v. Richards, 165 Neb. 80, 94-95, 84 N.W. 2d 136, 146 (1957).

5. See ABA CANONS OF PROFESSIONAL ETHICS, CANON 9 (1908).

6. See ABA CANONS OF PROFESSIONAL ETHICS, CANON 10 (1908).

7. See MODEL CODE OF PROFESSIONAL RESPONSIBILITY, EC 2-20.

8. See ABA CANONS OF PROFESSIONAL ETHICS, CANON 42 (1908).

9. "Rule 3a.... A member of the State Bar shall not directly or indirectly pay or agree to pay, or represent or sanction the representation that he will pay, medical, hospital or nursing bills or other personal expenses incurred by or for a client, prospective or existing; provided this rule shall not prohibit a member:

"(1)   with the consent of the client, from paying or agreeing to pay to third persons such expenses from funds collected or to be collected for the client; or

(2)   after he has been employed, from lending money to his client upon the client's promise in writing to repay such loan; or

(3)   from advancing the costs of prosecuting or defending a claim or action. Such costs within the meaning of this subparagraph (3) include all taxable costs or disbursements, costs or investigation and costs of obtaining and presenting evidence." CAL. BUSINESS AND PROFESSIONS CODE @ 6076 (West Supp. 1967).

10. "When a lawyer knows, prior to trial, that he will be a necessary witness, except as to merely formal matters such as identification or custody of a document or the like, neither he nor his firm or associates should conduct the trial. If, during the trial, he discovers that the ends of justice require his testimony, he should, from that point on, if feasible and not prejudicial to his client's case, leave further conduct of the trial to other counsel. If circumstances do not permit withdrawal from the conduct of the trial, the lawyer should not argue the credibility of his own testimony." *A Code of Trial Conduct: Promulgated by the American College of Trial Lawyers,* 43 A.B.A.J. 223, 224-25 (1957).

11. *cf.* ABA CANONS OF PROFESSIONAL ETHICS, CANON 19 (1908); "When a lawyer is a witness for his client, except as to merely formal matters, such as the attestation or custody of an instrument and the like, he should leave the trial of the case to other counsel."

12. "It is the general rule that a lawyer may not testify in litigation in which he is an advocate unless circumstances arise which could not be anticipated and it is necessary to prevent a miscarriage of justice. In those rare cases where the testimony of an attorney is needed to protect his client's interests, it is not only proper but mandatory that it be forthcoming." Schwartz v. Wenger, 267 Minn. 40, 43-44, 124 N.W. 2d 489, 492 (1963).

13. "The great weight of authority in this country holds that the attorney who acts as counsel and witness, in behalf of his client, in the same cause on a material matter, not of a merely formal character, and not in an emergency, but having knowledge that he

would be required to be a witness in ample time to have secured other counsel and given up his service in the case, violates a highly important provision of the Code of Ethics and a rule of professional conduct, but does not commit a legal error in so testifying, as a result of which a new trial will be granted." Erwin M. Jennings Co. v. DiGenova, 107 Conn. 491, 499, 141A. 866, 869 (1928).

14. "[C]ases may arise, and in practice often do arise, in which there would be a failure of justice should the attorney withhold his testimony. In such a case it would be a vicious professional sentiment which would deprive the client of the benefit of his attorney's testimony." Connolly v. Straw, 53 Wis. 645, 649, 11 N.W. 17, 19 (1881).

But see ABA CANONS OF PROFESSIONAL ETHICS, CANON 19 (1908): "Except when essential to the ends of justice, a lawyer should avoid testifying in court in behalf of his client."

15. cf. ABA CANONS OF PROFESSIONAL ETHICS, CANON 7 (1908).

16. See ABA CANONS OF PROFESSIONAL ETHICS, CANON 7 (1908).

17. See ABA CANONS OF PROFESSIONAL ETHICS, CANON 6 (1908); cf. ABA Opinions 261 (1944), 242 (1942), 142 (1935), and 30 (1931).

18. The ABA Canons speak of "conflicting interests" rather than "differing interests" but make no attempt to define such other than the statement in Canon 6: "Within the meaning of this canon, a lawyer represents conflicting interests when, in behalf of one client, it is his duty to contend for that which duty to another client requires him to oppose."

19. "Canon 6 of the Canons of Professional Ethics, adopted by the American Bar Association on September 30, 1937, and by the Pennsylvania Bar Association on January 7, 1938, provides in part that 'It is unprofessional to represent conflicting interests, except by express consent of all concerned given after a full disclosure of the facts. Within the meaning of this Canon, a lawyer represents conflicting interests when, in behalf of one client, it is his duty to contend for that which duty to another client requires him to oppose.' The full disclosure required by this canon contemplates that the possibly adverse effect of the conflict be fully explained by the attorney to the client to be affected and by him thoroughly understood. ...

"The foregoing canon applies to cases where the circumstances are such that possibly conflicting interests may permissibly be represented by the same attorney. But manifestly, there are instances where the conflicts of interest are so critically adverse as not to admit of one attorney's representing both sides. Such is the situation which this record presents. No one could conscionably contend that the same attorney may represent both the plaintiff and defendant in an adversary action. Yet, that is what is being done in this case." Jedwabny v. Philadelphia Transportation Co., 309 Pa. 231, 235, 135 A.2d 252, 254 (1957), cert. denied, 355 U.S. 966, 2 L. Ed 2d 541, 78 S. Ct. 557 (1958).

20. "Glasser wished the benefit of the undivided assistance of counsel of his own choice. We think that such a desire on the part of an accused should be respected. Irrespective of any conflict of interest, the additional burden of representing another party may conceivably impair counsel's effectiveness.

"To determine the precise degree of prejudice sustained by Glasser as a result of the court's appointment of Stewart as counsel for Kretske is at once difficult and unnecessary. The right to have the assistance of counsel is too fundamental and absolute to allow courts to indulge in nice calculations as to the amount of prejudice arising from its denial." Glasser v. United States, 315 U.S. 60, 75-76, 86 L. Ed. 680, 702 S. Ct. 457, 467 (1942).

21. See ABA CANONS OF PROFESSIONAL ETHICS, CANON 6 (1908).

22. Id.

23. cf. ABA Opinion 282 (1950).

"When counsel, although paid by the casualty company, undertakes to represent the policyholder and files his notice of appearance, he owes to his client, the assured, and undeviating and single allegiance. His fealty embraces the requirement to produce in court all witnesses, fact and expert, who are available and necessary for the proper protection of the rights of his client. ...

"... The Canons of Professional Ethics make it pellucid that there are not two standards, one applying to counsel privately retained by a client, and the other to counsel paid by an insurance carrier." American Employers Ins. Co. v. Goble Aircraft Specialties, 205 Misc. 1066, 1075, 131 N.Y.S.2d 393, 401 (1954), *motion to withdraw appeal granted*, 1 App. Div. 2d 1008, 154 N.Y.S.2d 835 (1956).

"[C]ounsel, selected by State Farm to defend Dorothy Walker's suit for $50,000 damages, was apprised by Walker that his earlier version of the accident was untrue and that actually the accident occurred because he lost control of his car in passing a Cadillac just ahead. At that point, Walker's counsel should have refused to participate further in view of the conflict of interest between Walker and State Farm.... Instead he participated in the ensuing deposition of the Walkers, even took an ex parte sworn statement from Mr. Walker in order to advise State Farm what action it should take, and later used the statement against Walker in the District Court. This action appears to contravene an Indiana attorney's duty 'at every peril to himself, to preserve the secrets of his client'. ..." State Farm Mut. Auto Ins. Co. v. Walker, 382 F.2d 548, 552 (1967), *cert. denied*, 389 U.S. 1045, 19 L. Ed. 2d 837, 88 S. Ct. 789 (1968).

24. See ABA CANONS OF PROFESSIONAL ETHICS, CANON 6 (1908).

25. See ABA CANONS OF PROFESSIONAL ETHICS, CANON 35 (1908).

"Objection to the intervention of a lay intermediary, who may control litigation or otherwise interfere with the rendering of legal services in a confidential relationship,... derives from the element of pecuniary gain. Fearful of dangers thought to arise from that element, the courts of several States have sustained regulations aimed at these activities. We intimate no view one way or the other as to the merits of those decisions with respect to the particular arrangements against which they are directed. It is enough that the superficial resemblance in form between those arrangements and that at bar cannot obscure the vital fact that here the entire arrangement employs constitutionally privileged means of expression to secure constitutionally guaranteed civil rights." NAACP v. Button, 371 U.S. 415, 441-42, 9 L. Ed. 2d 405, 423-24, 83 S. Ct. 328, 342-43 (1963).

26. *cf.* ABA CANONS OF PROFESSIONAL ETHICS, CANON 38 (1908).

27. "Certainly it is true that 'the professional relationship between an attorney and his client is highly personal, involving an intimate appreciation of each individual client's particular problem.' And this Committee does not condone practices which interfere with that relationship. However, the mere fact the lawyer is actually paid by some entity other than the client does not affect that relationship, so long as the lawyer is selected by and is directly responsible to the client. See Informal Opinions 469 and 679. Of course, as the latter decision points out, there must be full disclosure of the arrangement by the attorney to the client. ..." ABA Opinion 320 (1968).

"[A] third party may pay the cost of legal services as long as control remains in the client and the responsibility of the lawyer is solely to the client. Informal Opinions 469 ad [sic] 679. See also Opinion 237." *Id.*

28. ABA Opinion 303 (1961) recognized that "[s]tatutory provisions now exist in several states which are designed to make [the practice of law in a form that will be classified as a corporation for federal income tax purposes] legally possible, either as a result of lawyers incorporating or forming associations with various corporate characteristics."

29. *cf.* ABA CANONS OF PROFESSIONAL ETHICS, CANON 6 (1908) and ABA Opinions 181 (1938), 104 (1934), 103 (1933), 72 (1932), 50 (1931), 49 (1931), and 33 (1931).

"New York County [Opinion] 203.... [A lawyer] should not advise a client to employ an investment company in which he is interested, without informing him of this." DRINKER, LEGAL ETHICS 956 (1953).

"In Opinions 72 and 49 this Committee held: The relations of partners in a law firm are such that neither the firm nor any member or associate thereof, may accept any professional employment which any member of the firm cannot properly accept.

"In Opinion 16 this Committee held that a member of a law firm could not represent a defendant in a criminal case which was being prosecuted by another member of the firm who was public prosecuting attorney. The Opinion stated that it was clearly unethical for one member of the firm to oppose the interest of the state while another member represented those interests.... Since the prosecutor himself could not represent both the public and the defendant, no member of his law firm could either." ABA Opinion 296 (1959).

30. *cf.* ABA CANONS OF PROFESSIONAL ETHICS, CANON 19 (1908) and ABA Opinions 220 (1941), 185 (1938), 50 (1931), and 33 (1931); but *cf.* Erwin M. Jennings Co. v. DiGenova, 107 Conn. 491, 498-99, 141 A. 866, 868 (1928).

31. This Canon [19] of Ethics needs no elaboration to be applied to the facts here. Apparently, the object of this precept is to avoid putting a lawyer in the obviously embarrassing predicament of testifying and then having to argue the credibility and effect of his own testimony. It was not designed to permit a lawyer to call opposing counsel as a witness and thereby disqualify him as counsel." Galarowicz v. Ward, 119 Utah 611, 620, 230 P.2d 576, 580 (1951).

32. ABA CANONS OF PROFESSIONAL ETHICS, CANON 10 (1908) and ABA Opinions 279 (1949), 246 (1942), and 176 (1938).

33. See MODEL CODE OF PROFESSIONAL RESPONSIBILITY, DR 2-106(C).

34. See ABA CANONS OF PROFESSIONAL ETHICS, CANON 42 (1908); *cf.* ABA Opinion 288 (1954).

35. See ABA CANONS OF PROFESSIONAL ETHICS, CANON 6 (1908) *cf.* ABA Opinions 167 (1937), 60 (1931), and 40 (1931).

36. Amended, March 1974, House Informational Report No. 127.

37. ABA Opinion 247 (1942) held that an attorney could not investigate a night club shooting on behalf of one of the owner's liability insurers, obtaining the co-operation of the owner, and later represent the injured patron in an action against the owner and a different insurance company unless the attorney obtain the "express consent of all concerned given after a full disclosure of the facts," since to do so would be to represent conflicting interests.

See ABA Opinions 247 (1942), 224 (1941), 222 (1941), 218 (1941), 112 (1934), 86 (1932), and 83 (1932).

38. Amended, March 1974, House Informational Report No. 127.

39. *cf.* ABA Opinions 231 (1941) and 160 (1936).

40. Amended, March 1974, House Informational Report No. 127.

41. *cf.* ABA Opinion 235 (1941).

42. See ABA CANONS OF PROFESSIONAL ETHICS, CANON 38 (1908).

"A lawyer who receives a commission (whether delayed or not) from a title insurance company or guaranty fund for recommending or selling the insurance to his client, or for work done for the client or the company, without either fully disclosing to the client his financial interest in the transaction, or crediting the client's bill with the amount thus received, is guilty of unethical conduct." ABA Opinion 304 (1962).

43. See ABA CANONS OF PROFESSIONAL ETHICS, CANON 35 (1908); *cf.* ABA Opinion 237 (1941).

"When the lay forwarder, as agent for the creditor, forwards a claim to an attorney, the direct relationship of attorney and client shall then exist between the attorney and the creditor, and the forwarder shall not interpose itself as an intermediary to control the activities of the attorney." ABA Opinion 294 (1958).

44. "Permanent beneficial and voting rights in the organization set up to practice law, whatever its form, must be restricted to lawyers while the organization is engaged in the practice of law." ABA Opinion 303 (1961).

45. "Canon 33… promulgates underlying principles that must be observed no matter in what form of organization lawyers practice law. Its requirement that no person shall be admitted or held out as a practitioner or member who is not a member of the legal profession duly authorized to practice, and amenable to professional discipline, makes it clear that any centralized management must be in lawyers to avoid a violation of this Canon." ABA Opinion 303 (1961).

46. "There is no intervention of any lay agency between lawyer and client when centralized management provided only by lawyers may give guidance or direction to the services being rendered by a lawyer-member of the organization to a client. The language in Canon 35 that a lawyer should avoid all relations which direct the performance of his duties by or in the interest of an intermediary refers to lay intermediaries and not lawyer intermediaries with whom he is associated in the practice of law." ABA Opinion 303 (1961).

CANON 6

A Lawyer Should Represent a Client Competently

ETHICAL CONSIDERATIONS

EC 6-1 Because of his vital role in the legal process, a lawyer should act with competence and proper care in representing clients. He should strive to become and remain proficient in his practice[1] and should accept employment only in matters which he is or intends to become competent to handle.

EC 6-2 A lawyer is aided in attaining and maintaining his competence by keeping abreast of current legal literature and developments, participating in continuing legal education programs,[2] concentrating in particular areas of the law, and by utilizing other available means. He has the additional ethical obligation to assist in improving the legal profession, and he may do so by participating in bar activities intended to advance the quality and standards of members of the profession. Of particular importance is the careful training of his younger associates and the giving of sound guidance to all lawyers who consult him. In short, a lawyer should strive at all levels to aid the legal profession in advancing the highest possible standards of integrity and competence and to meet those standards himself.

EC 6-3 While the licensing of a lawyer is evidence that he has met the standards then prevailing for admission to the bar, a lawyer generally should not accept employment in any area of the law in which he is not qualified.[3] However, he may accept such employment if in good faith he expects to become qualified through study and investigation, as long as such preparation would not result in unreasonable delay or expense to his client. Proper preparation and representation may require the association by the lawyer of professionals in other disciplines. A lawyer offered employment in a matter in which he is not and does not expect to become so qualified should either decline the employment or, with the consent of his client, accept the employment and associate a lawyer who is competent in the matter.

EC 6-4 Having undertaken representation, a lawyer should use proper care to safeguard the interests of his client. If a lawyer has accepted employment in a matter beyond his competence but in which he expected to become competent, he should diligently undertake the work and study necessary to qualify himself. In addition to being qualified to handle a particular matter, his obligation to his client requires him to prepare adequately for and give appropriate attention to his legal work.

EC 6-5 lawyer should have pride in his professional endeavors. His obligation to act competently calls for higher motivation than that arising from fear of civil liability or disciplinary penalty.

EC 6-6 A lawyer should not seek, by contract or other means, to limit his individual liability to his client for his malpractice. A lawyer who handles the affairs of his client properly has no need to attempt to limit his liability for his professional activities and one who does not handle the affairs of his client properly should not be permitted to do so. A lawyer who is a stockholder in or is associated with a professional legal corporation may, however, limit his liability for malpractice of his associates in the corporation, but only to the extent permitted by law.[4]

DISCIPLINARY RULES

DR 6-101   Failing to Act Competently.

(A)   A lawyer shall not:

   (1)   Handle a legal matter which he knows or should know that he is not competent to handle, without associating with him a lawyer who is competent to handle it.

   (2)   Handle a legal matter without preparation adequate in the circumstances.

   (3)   Neglect a legal matter entrusted to him.[5]

DR 6-102   Limiting Liability to Client.

(A)   A lawyer shall not attempt to exonerate himself from or limit his liability to his client for his personal malpractice.

NOTES

1. "[W]hen a citizen is faced with the need for a lawyer, he wants, and is entitled to, the best informed counsel he can obtain. Changing times produce changes in our laws and legal procedures. The natural complexities of law require continuing intensive study by a lawyer if he is to render his clients a maximum of efficient service. And, in so doing, he maintains the high standards of the legal profession; and he also increases respect and confidence by the general public." Rochelle & Payne, *The Struggle for Public Understanding*, 25 TEXAS B.J. 109, 160 (1962).

"We have undergone enormous changes in the last fifty years within the lives of most of the adults living today who may be seeking advice. Most of these changes have been accompanied by changes and developments in the law.... Every practicing lawyer encounters these problems and is often perplexed with his own inability to keep up, not only with changes in the law, but also with changes in the lives of his clients and their legal problems.

"To be sure, no client has a right to expect that his lawyer will have all of the answers at the end of his tongue or even in the back of his head at all times. But the client does have the right to expect that the lawyer will have devoted his time and energies to maintaining and improving his competence to know where to look for the answers, to know how to deal with the problems, and to know how to advise to the best of his legal talents and abilities." Levy & Sprague, *Accounting and Law: Is Dual Practice in the Public Interest?*, 52 A.B.A.J. 1110, 1112 (1966).

2. "The whole purpose of continuing legal education, so enthusiastically supported by the ABA, is to make it possible for lawyers to make themselves better lawyers. But there are no nostrums for proficiency in the law; it must come through the hard work of the lawyer himself. To the extent that that work, whether it be in attending institutes or lecture courses, in studying after hours or in the actual day in and day out practice of his profession, can be concentrated within a limited field, the greater the proficiency and expertness that can be developed." *Report of the Special Committee on Specialization and Specialized Legal Education*, 79 A.B.A. REP. 582, 588 (1954).

3. "If the attorney is not competent to skillfully and properly perform the work, he should not undertake the service." Degen v. Steinbrink, 202 App. Div. 477, 481, 195 N.Y.S. 810, 814 (1922), aff'd mem., 236 N.Y. 669 142 N.E. 328 (1923).

4. See ABA Opinion 303 (1961); *cf.* CODE OF PROFESSIONAL RESPONSIBILITY, EC 2-11.

5. The annual report for 1967-1968 of the Committee on Grievances of the Association of the Bar of the City of New York showed a receipt of 2,232 complaints; of the 828 offenses against clients, 76 involved conversion, 49 involved "overreaching," and 452, or more than half of all such offenses, involved neglect. *Annual Report of the Committee on Grievances of the Association of the Bar of the City of New York*, N.Y.L.J., Sept. 12, 1968, at 4, col. 5.

CANON 7

A Lawyer Should Represent a Client Zealously Within the Bounds of the Law

ETHICAL CONSIDERATIONS

EC 7-1 The duty of a lawyer, both to his client[1] and to the legal system, is to represent his client zealously[2] within the bounds of the law,[3] which includes Disciplinary Rules and enforceable professional regulations.[4] The professional responsibility of a lawyer derives from his membership in a profession which has the duty of assisting members of the public to secure and protect available legal rights and benefits. In our government of laws and not of men, each member of our society is entitled to have his conduct judged and regulated in accordance with the law;[5] to seek any lawful objective[6] through legally permissible means;[7] and to present for adjudication any lawful claim, issue, or defense.

EC 7-2 The bounds of the law in a given case are often difficult to ascertain[8]. The language of legislative enactments and judicial opinions may be uncertain as applied to varying factual situations. The limits and specific meaning of apparently relevant law may be made doubtful by changing or developing constitutional interpretations, inadequately expressed statutes or judicial opinions, and changing public and judicial attitudes. Certainty of law ranges from well-settled rules through areas of conflicting authority to areas without precedent.

EC 7-3 Where the bounds of law are uncertain, the action of a lawyer may depend on whether he is serving as advocate or adviser. A lawyer may serve simultaneously as both advocate and adviser, but the two roles are essentially different.[9] In asserting a position on behalf of his client, an advocate for the most par deals with past conduct and must take the facts as he finds them. By contrast, a lawyer serving as adviser primarily assists his client in determining the course of future conduct and relationships. While serving as advocate, a lawyer should resolve in favor of his client doubts as to the bounds of the law.[10] In serving a client as adviser, a lawyer in appropriate circumstances should give his professional opinion as to what the ultimate decisions of the courts would likely be as to the applicable law.

Duty of the Lawyer to a Client

EC 7-4 The advocate may urge any permissible construction of the law favorable to his client, without regard to his professional opinion as to the likelihood that the construction will ultimately prevail.[11] His conduct is within the bounds of the law, and therefore permissible, if the position taken is supported by the law or is supportable by a good faith argument for an extension, modification, or reversal of the law. However, a lawyer is not justified in asserting a position in litigation that is frivolous.[12]

EC 7-5 A lawyer as adviser furthers the interest of his client by giving his professional opinion as to what he believes would likely be the ultimate decision of the courts on the matter at hand and by informing his client of the practical effect of such decision.[13] He may continue in the representation of his client even though his client has elected to pursue a course of conduct contrary to the advice of the lawyer so long as he does not thereby knowingly assist the client to engage in illegal conduct or to take a frivolous legal position. A lawyer should never encourage or aid his client to commit criminal acts or counsel his client on how to violate the law and avoid punishment therefor.[14]

EC 7-6 Whether the proposed action of a lawyer is within the bounds of the law may be a perplexing question when his client is contemplating a course of conduct having legal consequences that vary according to the client's intent, motive, or desires at the time of the action. Often a lawyer is asked to assist his client in developing evidence relevant to the state of mind of the client at a particular time. He may properly assist his client in the development and preservation of evidence of existing motive, intent, or desire; obviously, he may not do anything furthering the creation or preservation of false evidence. In many cases a lawyer may not be certain as to the state of mind of his client, and in those situations he should resolve reasonable doubts in favor of his client.

EC 7-7 In certain areas of legal representation not affecting the merits of the cause of substantially prejudicing the rights of a client, a lawyer is entitled to make decisions on his own. But otherwise the authority to make decisions is exclusively that of the client and, if made within the framework of the law, such decisions are binding on his lawyer. As typical examples in civil cases, it is for the client to decide whether he will accept a settlement offer or whether he will waive his right to plead an affirmative defense. A defense lawyer in a criminal case has the duty to advise his client fully on whether a particular plea to a charge appears to be desirable and as to the prospects of success on appeal, but it is for the client to decide what plea should be entered and whether an appeal should be taken.[15]

EC 7-8 A lawyer should exert his best efforts to insure that decisions of his client are made only after the client has been informed of relevant considerations. A lawyer ought to initiate this decision-making process if the client does not do so. Advice of a lawyer to his client need not be confined to purely legal considerations.[16] A lawyer should advise his client of the possible effect of each legal alternative.[17] A lawyer should bring to bear upon this decision-making process the fullness of his experience as well as his objective viewpoint.[18] In assisting his client to reach a proper decision, it is often desirable for a lawyer to point out those factors which may lead to a decision that is morally just as well as legally permissible.[19] He may emphasize the possibility of harsh consequences that might result from assertion of legally permissible positions. In the final analysis, however, the lawyer should always remember that the decision whether to forego legally available objectives or methods because of non-legal factors is ultimately for the client and not for himself. In the event that the client in a non-adjudicatory matter insists upon a course of conduct that is contrary to the judgment and advice of the lawyer but not prohibited by Disciplinary Rules, the lawyer may withdraw from the employment.[20]

EC 7-9 In the exercise of his professional judgment on those decisions which are for his determination in the handling of a legal matter,[21] a lawyer should always act in a manner consistent with the best interests of his client.[22] However, when an action in the best interest of his client seems to him to be unjust, he may ask his client for permission to forego such action.

EC 7-10 The Duty of a lawyer to represent his client with zeal does not militate against his concurrent obligation to treat with consideration all persons involved in the legal process and to avoid the infliction of needless harm.

EC 7-11 The responsibilities of a lawyer may vary according to the intelligence, experience, mental condition or age of a client, the obligation of a public officer, or the nature of a particular proceeding. Examples include the representation of an illiterate or an incompetent, service as a public prosecutor or other government lawyer, and appearances before administrative and legislative bodies.

EC 7-12 Any mental or physical condition of a client that renders him incapable of making a considered judgment on his own behalf casts additional responsibilities upon his lawyer. Where an incompetent is acting through a guardian or other legal representative, a lawyer must look to such representative for those decisions which are normally the prerogative of the client to make. If a client under disability has no legal representative, his lawyer may be compelled in court proceedings to make decisions on behalf of the client. If the client is capable of understanding the matter in question or of contributing to the advancement of his interests, regardless of whether he is legally disqualified from performing certain acts, the lawyer should obtain from him all possible aid. If the disability of a client and the lack of a legal representative compel the lawyer to make decisions for his client, the lawyer should consider all circumstances then prevailing and act with care to safeguard and advance the interests of his client. But obviously a lawyer cannot perform any act or make any decision which the law requires his client to perform or make, either acting for himself if competent, or by a duly constituted representative if legally incompetent.

EC 7-13 The responsibility of a public prosecutor differs from that of the usual advocate; his duty is to seek justice, not merely to convict.[23] This special duty exists because: (1) the prosecutor represents the sovereign and therefore should use restraint in the discretionary exercise of governmental powers, such as in the selection of cases to prosecute; (2) during trial the prosecutor is not only an advocate but he also may make decisions normally made by an individual client, and those affecting the public interest should be fair to all; and (3) in our system of criminal justice the accused is to be given the benefit of all reasonable doubts. With respect to evidence and witnesses, the prosecutor has responsibilities different from those of a lawyer in private practice: the prosecutor should make timely disclosure to the defense of available evidence, known to him, that tends to negate the guilt of the accused, mitigate the degree of the offense, or reduce the punishment. Further, a prosecutor should not intentionally avoid pursuit of evidence merely because he believes it will damage the prosecutor's case or aid the accused.

EC 7-14 A government lawyer who has discretionary power relative to litigation should refrain from instituting or continuing litigation that is obviously unfair. A government lawyer not having such discretionary power who believes there is lack of merit in a controversy submitted to him should so advise his superiors and recommend the avoidance of unfair litigation. A government lawyer in a civil action or administrative proceeding has the responsibility to seek justice and to develop a full and fair record, and he should not use his position or the economic power of the government to harass parties or to bring about unjust settlements or results.

EC 7-15 The nature and purpose of proceedings before administrative agencies vary widely. The proceedings may be legislative or quasi-judicial, or a combination of both. They may be ex parte in character, in which event they may originate either at the instance of the agency or upon motion of an interested party. The scope of an inquiry may be purely investigative or it may be truly adversary looking toward the adjudication of specific rights of a party or of classes of parties. The foregoing are but examples of some of the types of proceedings conducted by administrative agencies. A lawyer appearing before an administrative agency,[25] regardless of the nature of the proceeding it is conducting, has the continuing duty to advance the cause of his client within the bounds of the law. Where the applicable rules of the agency impose specific obligations upon a lawyer, it is his duty to comply therewith, unless the lawyer has a legitimate basis for challenging the validity thereof. In all appearances before administrative agencies, a lawyer should identify himself, his client if identity of his client is not privileged,[26] and the representative nature of his appearance. It is not improper, however, for a lawyer to seek from an agency information available to the public without identifying his client.

EC 7-16 The primary business of a legislative body is to enact laws rather than to adjudicate controversies, although on occasion to activities of a legislative body may take on the characteristics of an adversary proceeding, particularly in investigative and impeachment matters. The role of a lawyer supporting or opposing proposed legislation normally is quite different from his role in representing a person under investigation or on trial by a legislative body. When a lawyer appears in connection with proposed legislation, he seeks to affect the lawmaking process, but when he appears on behalf of a client in investigatory or impeachment proceedings, he is concerned with the protection of the rights of his client. In either event, he should identify himself and his client, if identity of his client is not privileged, and should comply with applicable laws and legislative rules.[27]

EC 7-17 The obligation of loyalty to his client applies only to a lawyer in the discharge of his professional duties and implies no obligation to adopt a personal viewpoint favorable to the interests or desires of his client.[28] While a lawyer must act always with circumspection in order that his conduct will not adversely affect the rights of a client in a matter he is then handling, he may take positions on public issues and espouse legal reforms he favors without regard to the individual views of any client.

EC 7-18 The legal system in its broadest sense functions best when persons in need of legal advice or assistance are represented by their own counsel. For this reason a lawyer should not communicate on the subject matter of the representation of his client with a person he knows to be represented in the matter by a lawyer, unless pursuant to law or rule of court or unless he has the consent of the lawyer for that person.[29] If one is not represented by counsel, a lawyer representing another may have to deal directly with the unrepresented person; in such an instance, a lawyer should not undertake to give advice to the person who is attempting to represent himself,[30] except that he may advise him to obtain a lawyer.

Duty of the Lawyer to the Adversary System of Justice

EC 7-19 Our legal system provides for the adjudication of disputes governed by the rules of substantive, evidentiary, and procedural law. An adversary presentation counters the natural human tendency to judge too swiftly in terms of the familiar that which is not yet fully known,[31] the advocate, by his zealous preparation and presentation of facts and law, enables the tribunal to come to the hearing with an open and neutral mind and to render impartial judgments.[32] The duty of a lawyer to his client and his duty to the legal system are the same: to represent his client zealously within the bounds of the law.[33]

EC 7-20 In order to function properly, our adjudicative process requires an informed, impartial tribunal capable of administering justice promptly and efficiently[34] according to procedures that command public confidence and respect.[35] Not only must there be competent, adverse presentation of evidence and issues, but a tribunal must be aided by rules appropriate to an effective and dignified process. The procedures under which tribunals operate in our adversary system have been prescribed largely by legislative enactments, court rules and decisions, and administrative rules. Through the years certain concepts of proper professional conduct have become rules of law applicable to the adversary adjudicative process. Many of these concepts are the bases for standards of professional conduct set forth in the Disciplinary Rules.

EC 7-21 The civil adjudicative process is primarily designed for the settlement of disputes between parties, while the criminal process is designed for the protection of society as a whole. Threatening to use, or using, the criminal process to coerce adjustment of private civil claims or controversies is a subversion of that process,[36] further, the person against whom the criminal process is so misused may be deterred from asserting his legal rights and thus the usefulness of the civil process in settling private disputes is impaired. As in all cases of abuse of judicial process, the improper use of criminal process tends to diminish public confidence in our legal system.

EC 7-22 Respect for judicial rulings is essential to the proper administration of justice; however, a litigant or his lawyer may, in good faith and within the framework of the law, take steps to test the correctness of a ruling of a tribunal.[37]

EC 7-23 The complexity of law often makes it difficult for a tribunal to be fully informed unless the pertinent law is presented by the lawyers in the cause. A tribunal that is fully informed on the applicable law is better able to make a fair and accurate determination of the matter before it. The adversary system contemplates that each lawyer will present and argue the existing law in the light most favorable to his client.[38] Where a lawyer knows of legal authority in the controlling jurisdiction directly adverse to the position of his client, he should inform the tribunal of its existence unless his adversary has done so; but, having made such disclosure, he may challenge its soundness in whole or in part.[39]

EC 7-24 In order to bring about just and informed decisions, evidentiary and procedural rules have been established by tribunals to permit the inclusion of relevant evidence and argument and the exclusion of all other considerations. The expression by a lawyer of his personal opinion as to the justness of a cause, as to the credibility of a witness, as to the culpability of a civil litigant, or as to the guilt or innocence of an accused is not a proper subject for argument to the trier of fact.[40] It is improper as to factual matters because admissible evidence possessed by a lawyer should be presented only as sworn testimony. It is improper as to all other matters because, were the rule otherwise, the silence of a lawyer on a given occasion could be construed unfavorably to his client. However, a lawyer may argue, on his analysis of the evidence, for any position or conclusion with respect to any of the foregoing matters.

EC 7-25 Rules of evidence and procedure are designed to lead to just decisions and are part of the framework of the law. Thus while a lawyer may take steps in good faith and within the framework of the law to test the validity of rules, he is not justified in consciously violating such rules and he should be diligent in his efforts to guard against his unintentional violation of them.[41] As examples, a lawyer should subscribe to or verify only those pleadings that he believes are in compliance with applicable law and rules; a lawyer should not make any prefatory statement before a tribunal in regard to the purported facts of the case on trial unless he believes that his statement will be supported by admissible evidence; a lawyer should not ask a witness a question solely for the purpose of harassing or embarrassing him; and a lawyer should not by subterfuge put before a jury matters which it cannot properly consider.

EC 7-26 The law and Disciplinary Rules prohibit the use of fraudulent, false, or perjured testimony or evidence.[42] A lawyer who knowingly[43] participates in introduction of such testimony or evidence is subject to discipline. A lawyer should, however, present any admissible evidence his client desires to have presented unless he knows, or from facts within his knowledge should know, that such testimony or evidence is false, fraudulent, or perjured.[44]

EC 7-27 Because it interferes with the proper administration of justice, a lawyer should not suppress evidence that he or his client has a legal obligation to reveal or produce. In like manner, a lawyer should not advise or cause a person to secrete himself or to leave the jurisdiction of a tribunal for the purpose of making him unavailable as a witness therein.[45]

EC 7-28 Witnesses should always testify truthfully[46] and should be free from any financial inducements that might tempt them to do otherwise.[47] A lawyer should not pay or agree to pay a non-expert witness an amount in excess of reimbursement for expenses and financial loss incident to his being a witness; however, a lawyer may pay or agree to pay an expert witness a reasonable fee for his services as an expert. But in no event should a lawyer pay or agree to pay a contingent fee to any witness. A lawyer should exercise reasonable diligence to see that his client and lay associates conform to these standards.[48]

EC 7-29 To safeguard the impartiality that is essential to the judicial process, veniremen and jurors should be protected against extraneous influences.[49] When impartiality is present, public confidence in the judicial system is enhanced. There should be no extrajudicial communication with veniremen prior to trial or with jurors during trial by or on behalf of a lawyer connected with the case. Furthermore, a lawyer who is not connected with the case should not communicate with or cause another to communicate with a venireman or a juror about the case. After the trial, communication by a lawyer with jurors is permitted so long as he refrains from asking questions or making comments that tend to harass or embarrass the juror[50] or to influence actions of the juror in future cases. Were a lawyer to be prohibited from communicating after trial with a juror, he could not ascertain if the verdict might be subject to legal challenge, in which event the invalidity of a verdict might go undetected.[51] When an extrajudicial communication by a lawyer with a juror is permitted by law, it should be made considerately and with deference to the personal feelings of the juror.

EC 7-30 Vexatious or harassing investigations of veniremen or jurors seriously impair the effectiveness of our jury system. For this reason, a lawyer or anyone on his behalf who conducts an investigation of veniremen or jurors should act with circumspection and restraint.

EC 7-31 Communications with or investigations of members of families of veniremen or jurors by a lawyer or by anyone on his behalf are subject to the restrictions imposed upon the lawyer with respect to his communications with or investigations of veniremen and jurors.

EC 7-32 Because of his duty to aid in preserving the integrity of the jury system, a lawyer who learns of improper conduct by or towards a venireman, a juror, or a member of the family of either should make a prompt report to the court regarding such conduct.

EC 7-33 A goal of our legal system is that each party shall have his case, criminal or civil, adjudicated by an impartial tribunal. The attainment of this goal may be defeated by dissemination of news or comments which tend to influence judge or jury.[52] Such news or comments may prevent prospective jurors from being impartial at the outset of the trial[53] and may also interfere with the obligation of jurors to base their verdict solely upon the evidence admitted in the trial.[54] The release by a lawyer of out-of-court statements regarding and anticipated or pending trial may improperly affect the impartiality of the tribunal.[55] For these reasons, standards for permissible and prohibited conduct of a lawyer with respect to trial publicity have been established.

EC 7-34 The impartiality of a public servant in our legal system may be impaired by the receipt of gifts or loans. A lawyer,[56] therefore, is never justified in making a gift or a loan to a judge, a hearing officer, or an official or employee of a tribunal except as permitted by Section C(4) of Canon 5 of the Code of Judicial Conduct, but a lawyer may make a contribution to the campaign fund of a candidate for judicial office in conformity with Section B(2) under Canon 7 of the Code of Judicial Conduct.[57, 58]

EC 7-35 All litigants and lawyers should have access to tribunals on an equal basis. Generally, in adversary proceedings a lawyer should not communicate with a judge relative to a matter pending before, or which is to be brought before, a tribunal over which he presides in circumstances which might have the effect or give the appearance of granting undue advantage to one party.[59] For example, a lawyer should not communicate with a tribunal by a writing unless a copy thereof is promptly delivered to opposing counsel or to the adverse party if he is not represented by a lawyer. Ordinarily an oral communication by a lawyer with a judge or hearing officer should be made only upon adequate notice to opposing counsel, or, if there is none, to the opposing party. A lawyer should not condone or lend himself to private importunities by another with a judge or hearing officer on behalf of himself or his client.

EC 7-36 Judicial hearing ought to be conducted through dignified and orderly procedures designed to protect the rights of all parties. Although a lawyer has the duty to represent his client zealously, he should not engage in any conduct that offends the dignity and decorum of proceedings.[60] While maintaining his independence, a lawyer should be respectful, courteous, and above-board in his relations with a judge or hearing officer before whom he appears.[61] He should avoid undue solicitude for the comfort or convenience of judge or jury and should avoid any other conduct calculated to gain special consideration.

EC 7-37 In adversary proceedings, clients are litigants and though ill feeling may exist between clients, such ill feeling should not influence a lawyer in his conduct, attitude, and demeanor towards opposing lawyers.[62] A lawyer should not make unfair or derogatory personal reference to opposing counsel. Haranguing and offensive tactics by lawyers interfere with the orderly administration of justice and have no proper place in our legal system.

EC 7-38 A lawyer should be courteous to opposing counsel and should accede to reasonable requests regarding court proceedings, settings, continuances, waiver of procedural formalities, and similar matters which do not prejudice the rights of his client.[63] He should follow local customs of courtesy or practice, unless he gives timely notice to opposing counsel of his intention not to do so.[64] A lawyer should be punctual in fulfilling all professional commitments.[65]

EC 7-39 In the final analysis, proper functioning of the adversary system depends upon co-operation between lawyers and tribunals in utilizing procedures which will preserve the impartiality of tribunals and make their decisional processes prompt and just, without impinging upon the obligation of lawyers to represent their clients zealously within the framework of the law.

DISCIPLINARY RULES

DR 7-101　Representing a Client Zealously.

(A)　A lawyer shall not intentionally:[66]

(1)　Fail to seek the lawful objectives of his client through reasonably available means[67] permitted by law and the Disciplinary Rules, except as provided by DR 7-101 (B). A lawyer does not violate this Disciplinary Rule, however, by acceding to reasonable requests of opposing counsel which do not prejudice the rights of his client, by being punctual in fulfilling all professional commitments, by avoiding offensive tactics, or by treating with courtesy and consideration all persons involved in the legal process.

(2)　Fail to carry out a contract of employment entered into with a client for professional services, but he may withdraw as permitted under DR 2-110, DR 5-102, and DR 5-105.

(3)　Prejudice or damage his client during the course of the professional relationship,[68] except as required under DR 7-102 (B).

(B)　In his representation of a client, a lawyer may:

(1)　Where permissible, exercise his professional judgment to waive or fail to assert a right or position of his client.

(2)　Refuse to aid or participate in conduct that he believes to be unlawful, even though there is some support for an argument that the conduct is legal.

DR 7-102　Representing a Client Within the Bounds of the Law.

(A)　In his representation of a client, a lawyer shall not:

(1) File a suit, assert a position, conduct a defense, delay a trial, or take other action on behalf of his client when he knows or when it is obvious that such action would serve merely to harass or maliciously injure another.[69]

(2) Knowingly advance a claim or defense that is unwarranted under existing law, except that he may advance such claim or defense if it can be supported by good faith argument for an extension, modification, or reversal of existing law.

(3) Conceal or knowingly fail to disclose that which he is required by law to reveal.

(4) Knowingly use perjured testimony or false evidence.[70]

(5) Knowingly make a false statement of law or fact.

(6) Participate in the creation or preservation of evidence when he knows or it is obvious that the evidence is false.

(7) Counsel or assist his client in conduct that the lawyer knows to be illegal or fraudulent.

(8) Knowingly engage in other illegal conduct or conduct contrary to a Disciplinary Rule.

(B) A lawyer who receives information clearly establishing that:

(1) His client has, in the course of the representation, perpetrated a fraud upon a person or tribunal shall promptly call upon his client to rectify the same, and if his client refuses or is unable to do so, he shall reveal the fraud to the affected person or tribunal, except when the information is protected as a privileged communication.[71, 72]

(2) A person other than his client has perpetrated a fraud upon a tribunal shall promptly reveal the fraud to the tribunal.[73]

DR 7-103   Performing the Duty of Public Prosecutor or Other Government Lawyer.[74]

(A) A public prosecutor or other government lawyer shall not institute or cause to be instituted criminal charges when he knows or it is obvious that the charges are not supported by probable cause.

(B) A public prosecutor or other government lawyer in criminal litigation shall make timely disclosure to counsel for the defendant, or to the defendant if he has no counsel, of the existence of evidence, known to the prosecutor or other government lawyer, that tends to negate the guilt of the accused, mitigate the degree of the offense, or reduce the punishment.

DR 7-104   Communicating With One of Adverse Interest.[75]

(A) During the course of his representation of a client a lawyer shall not:

(1) Communicate or cause another to communicate on the subject of the representation with a party he knows to be represented by a lawyer in that matter unless he has the prior consent of the lawyer representing such other party[76] or is authorized by law to do so.

(2) Give advice to a person who is not represented by a lawyer, other than the advice to secure counsel,[77] if the interests of such person are or have a reasonable possibility of being in conflict with the interests of his client.[78]

DR 7-105   Threatening Criminal Prosecution.

(A) A lawyer shall not present, participate in presenting, or threaten to present criminal charges solely to obtain an advantage in a civil matter.

DR 7-106   Trial Conduct.

(A) A lawyer shall not disregard or advise his client to disregard a standing rule of a tribunal or a ruling of a tribunal made in the course of a proceeding, but he may take appropriate steps in good faith to test the validity of such rule or ruling.

(B) In presenting a matter to a tribunal, a lawyer shall disclose.[79]

 (1) Legal authority in the controlling jurisdiction known to him to be directly adverse to the position of his client and which is not disclosed by opposing counsel.[80]

 (2) Unless privileged or irrelevant, the identities of the clients he represents and of the persons who employed him.[81]

(C) In appearing in his professional capacity before a tribunal, a lawyer shall not:

 (1) State or allude to any matter that he has no reasonable basis to believe is relevant to the case or that will not be supported by admissible evidence.[82]

 (2) Ask any question that he has no reasonable basis to believe is relevant to the case and that is intended to degrade a witness or other person.[83]

 (3) Assert his personal knowledge of the facts in issue, except when testifying as a witness.

 (4) Assert his personal opinion as to the justness of a cause, as to the credibility of a witness, as to the culpability of a civil litigant, or as to the guilt or innocence of an accused;[84] but he may argue, on his analysis of the evidence, for any position or conclusion with respect to the matters stated herein.

 (5) Fail to comply with known local customs of courtesy or practice of the bar or a particular tribunal without giving to opposing counsel timely notice of his intent not to comply.[85]

 (6) Engage in undignified or discourteous conduct which is degrading to a tribunal.

 (7) Intentionally or habitually violate any established rule of procedure or of evidence.

DR 7-107   Trial Publicity.[86]

(A) A lawyer participating in or associated with the investigation of a criminal matter shall not make or participate in making an extrajudicial statement that a reasonable person would expect to be disseminated by means of public communication and that does more than state without elaboration:

(1) Information contained in a public record.

(2) That the investigation is in progress.

(3) The general scope of the investigation including a description of the offense and, if permitted by law, the identity of the victim.

(4) A request for assistance in apprehending a suspect or assistance in other matters and the information necessary thereto.

(5) A warning to the public of any dangers.

(B) A lawyer or law firm associated with the prosecution or defense of a criminal matter shall not, from the time of the filing of a complaint, information, or indictment, the issuance of an arrest warrant, or arrest until the commencement of the trial or disposition without trial, make or participate in making an extrajudicial statement that a reasonable person would expect to be disseminated by means of public communication and that relates to:

(1) The character, reputation, or prior criminal record (including arrests, indictments, or other charges of crime) of the accused.

(2) The possibility of a plea of guilty to the offense charged or to a lesser offense.

(3) The existence or contents of any confession, admission, or statement given by the accused or his refusal or failure to make a statement.

(4) The performance or results of any examinations or tests or the refusal or failure of the accused to submit to examinations or tests.

(5) The identity, testimony, or credibility of a prospective witness.

(6) Any opinion as to the guilt or innocence of the accused, the evidence, or the merits of the case.

(C) DR 7-107 (B) does not preclude a lawyer during such period from announcing:

(1) The name, age, residence, occupation, and family status of the accused.

(2) If the accused has not been apprehended, any information necessary to aid in his apprehension or to warn the public of any dangers he may present.

(3) A request for assistance in obtaining evidence.

(4) The identity of the victim of the crime.

(5) The fact, time, and place of arrest, resistance, pursuit, and use of weapons.

(6) The identity of investigating and arresting officers or agencies and the length of the investigation.

(7) At the time of seizure, a description of the physical evidence seized, other than a confession, admission, or statement.

(8)   The nature, substance, or text of the charge.

(9)   Quotations from or references to public records of the court in the case.

(10) The scheduling or result of any step in the judicial proceedings.

(11) That the accused denies the charges made against him.

(D) During the selection of a jury or the trial of a criminal matter, a lawyer or law firm associated with the prosecution or defense of a criminal matter shall not make or participate in making an extra-judicial statement that a reasonable person would expect to be disseminated by means of public communication and that relates to the trial, parties, or issues in the trial or other matters that are reasonably likely to interfere with a fair trial, except that he may quote from or refer without comment to public records of the court in the case.

(E) After the completion of a trial or disposition without trial of a criminal matter and prior to the imposition of sentence, a lawyer or law firm associated with the prosecution or defense shall not make or participate in making an extrajudicial statement that a reasonable person would expect to be disseminated by public communication and that is reasonably likely to affect the imposition of sentence.

(F) The foregoing provisions of DR 7-107 also apply to professional disciplinary proceedings and juvenile disciplinary proceedings when pertinent and consistent with other law applicable to such proceedings.

(G) A lawyer or law firm associated with a civil action shall not during its investigation or litigation make or participate in making an extrajudicial statement, other than a quotation from or reference to public records, that a reasonable person would expect to be disseminated by means of public communication and that relates to:

(1)   Evidence regarding the occurrence or transaction involved.

(2)   The character, credibility, or criminal record of a party, witness, or prospective witness.

(3)   The performance or results of any examinations or tests or the refusal or failure of a party to submit to such.

(4)   His opinion as to the merits of the claims or defenses of a party, except as required by law or administrative rule.

(5)   Any other matter reasonably likely to interfere with a fair trial of the action.

(H) During the pendency of an administrative proceeding, a lawyer or law firm associated therewith shall not make or participate in making a statement, other than a quotation from or reference to public records, that a reasonable person would expect to be disseminated by means of public communication if it is made outside the official course of the proceeding and relates to:

(1) Evidence regarding the occurrence or transaction involved.

(2) The character, credibility, or criminal record of a party, witness, or prospective witness.

(3) Physical evidence or the performance or results of any examinations or tests or the refusal or failure of a party to submit to such.

(4) His opinion as to the merits of the claims, defenses, or positions of an interested person.

(5) Any other matter reasonably likely to interfere with a fair hearing.

(I) The foregoing provisions of DR 7-107 do not preclude a lawyer from replying to charges of misconduct publicly made against him or from participating in the proceedings of legislative, administrative, or other investigative bodies.

(J) A lawyer shall exercise reasonable care to prevent his employees and associates from making an extrajudicial statement that he would be prohibited from making under DR 7-107.

DR 7-108 Communication with or Investigation of Jurors.

(A) Before the trial of a case a lawyer connected therewith shall not communicate with or cause another to communicate with anyone he knows to be a member of the venire from which the jury will be selected for the trial of the case.

(B) During the trial of a case:

(1) A lawyer connected therewith shall not communicate with or cause another to communicate with any member of the jury.[87]

(2) A lawyer who is not connected therewith shall not communicate with or cause another to communicate with a juror concerning the case.

(C) DR 7-108 (A) and (B) do not prohibit a lawyer from communicating with veniremen or jurors in the course of official proceedings.

(D) After discharge of the jury from further consideration of a case with which the lawyer was connected, the lawyer shall not ask questions of or make comments to a member of that jury that are calculated merely to harass or embarrass the juror or to influence his actions in future jury service.[88]

(E) A lawyer shall not conduct or cause, by financial support or otherwise, another to conduct a vexatious or harassing investigation of either a venireman or a juror.

(F) All restrictions imposed by DR 7-108 upon a lawyer also apply to communications with or investigations of members of a family of a venireman or a juror.

(G) A lawyer shall reveal promptly to the court improper conduct by a venireman or a juror, or by another toward a venireman or a juror or a member of his family, of which the lawyer has knowledge.

DR 7-109   Contact with Witnesses.

(A) A lawyer shall not suppress any evidence that he or his client has a legal obligation to reveal or produce.[89]

(B) A lawyer shall not advise or cause a person to secrete himself or to leave the jurisdiction of a tribunal for the purpose of making him unavailable as a witness therein.[90]

(C) A lawyer shall not pay, offer to pay, or acquiesce in the payment of compensation to a witness contingent upon the content of his testimony or the outcome of the case.[91] But a lawyer may advance, guarantee, or acquiesce in the payment of:

(1) Expenses reasonably incurred by a witness in attending or testifying.

(2) Reasonable compensation to a witness for his loss of time in attending or testifying.

(3) A reasonable fee for the professional services of an expert witness.

DR 7-110   Contact with Officials.[92]

(A) A lawyer shall not give or lend any thing of value to a judge, official, or employee of a tribunal except as permitted by Section C(4) of Canon 5 of the Code of Judicial Conduct, but a lawyer may make a contribution to the campaign fund of a candidate for judicial office in conformity with Section B(2) under Canon 7 of the Code of Judicial Conduct.[93]

(B) In an adversary proceeding, a lawyer shall not communicate, or cause another to communicate, as to the merits of the cause with a judge or an official before whom the proceeding is pending, except:

(1) In the course of official proceedings in the cause.

(2) In writing if he promptly delivers a copy of the writing to opposing counsel or to the adverse party if he is not represented by a lawyer.

(3) Orally upon adequate notice to opposing counsel or to the adverse party if he is not represented by a lawyer.

(4) As otherwise authorized by law, or by Section A(4) under Canon 3 of the Code of Judicial Conduct.[94, 95]

NOTES

1. "The right to be heard would be, in many cases, of little avail if it did not comprehend the right to be heard by counsel. Even the intelligent and educated layman has small and sometimes no skill in the science of law." Powell v. Alabama, 287 U.S. 45, 68-69, 77 L. Ed. 158, 170, 53 S. Ct. 55, 64 (1932).

2. *Cf.* ABA CANONS OF PROFESSIONAL ETHICS, CANON 4 (1908).

"At times... [the tax lawyer] will be wise to discard some arguments and he should exercise discretion to emphasize the arguments which in his judgment are most likely to be persuasive. But this process involves legal judgment rather than moral attitudes. The tax lawyer should put aside private disagreements with Congressional and Treasury polices. His own notions of policy, and his personal view of what the law should be, are irrelevant. The job entrusted to him by his client is to use all his learning and ability to protect his client's rights, not to help in the process of promoting a better tax system.

The tax lawyer need not accept his client's economic and social opinions, but the client is paying for technical attention and undivided concentration upon his affairs. He is equally entitled to performance unfettered by his attorney's economic and social predilections." Paul, *The Lawyer as a Tax Adviser*, 25 ROCKY MT. L. REV. 412, 418 (1953).

3. See ABA CANONS OF PROFESSIONAL ETHICS, CANONS 15 and 32 (1908).

ABA Canon 5, although only speaking of one accused of crime, imposes a similar obligation on the lawyer: "[T]he lawyer is bound, by all fair and honorable means, to present every defense that the law of the land permits, to the end that no person may be deprived of life or liberty, but by due process of law."

"Any persuasion or pressure on the advocate which deters him from planning and carrying out the litigation on the basis of 'what, within the framework of the law, is best for my client's interest?' interferes with the obligation to represent the client fully within the law.

"This obligation, in its fullest sense, is the heart of the adversary process. Each attorney, as an advocate, acts for and seeks that which in his judgment is best for his client, within the bounds authoritatively established. The advocate does not decide what is just in this case — he would be usurping the function of the judge and jury — he acts for and seeks for his client that which he is entitled to under the law. He can do no less and properly represent the client." Thode, *The Ethical Standard for the Advocate*, 39 TEXAS L. REV. 575, 584 (1961).

"The [Texas public opinion] survey indicates that distrust of the lawyer can be traced directly to certain factors. Foremost of these is a basic misunderstanding of the function of the lawyer as an advocate in an adversary system.

"Lawyers are accused of taking advantage of 'loopholes' and 'technicalities' to win. Persons who make this charge are unaware, or do not understand, that the lawyer is hired to win, and if he does not exercise every legitimate effort in his client's behalf, then he is betraying a sacred trust." Rochelle & Payne, *The Struggle for Public Understanding*, 25 TEXAS B.J. 109, 159 (1962).

"The importance of the attorney's undivided allegiance and faithful service to one accused of crime, irrespective of the attorney's personal opinion as to the guilt of his client, lies in Canon 5 of the American Bar Association Canon of Ethics.

"The difficulty lies, of course, in ascertaining whether the attorney has been guilty of an error of judgment, such as an election with respect to trial tactics, or has otherwise been actuated by his conscience or belief that his client should be convicted in any event. All too frequently courts are called upon to review actions of defense counsel which are, at the most, errors of judgment, not properly reviewable on habeas corpus unless the trial is a farce and a mockery of justice which requires the court to intervene.... But when defense counsel, in a truly adverse proceeding, admits that his conscience would not permit him to adopt certain customary trial procedures, this extends beyond the realm of judgment and strongly suggests an invasion of constitutional rights." Johns v. Smyth, 176 F. Supp. 949, 952 (E.D. Va. 1959), modified, United States ex rel. Wilkins v. Banmiller, 205 F. Supp. 123, 128, n. 5 (E.D. Pa. 1962), aff'd, 325 F. 2d 514 (3d Cir. 1963), *cert. denied*, 379 U.S. 847, 13 L. Ed. 2d 51, 85 S. Ct. 87 (1964).

"The adversary system in law administration bears a striking resemblance to the competitive economic system. In each we assume that the individual through partisanship or through self-interest will strive mightily for his side, and that kind of striving we must have. But neither system would be tolerable without restraints and modifications, and at times without outright departures from the system itself. Since the legal profession is entrusted with the system of law administration, a part of its task is to develop in its members appropriate restraints without impairing the values of partisan striving. An accompanying task is to aid in the modification of the adversary system or departure from it in areas to which the system is unsuited." Cheatham, *The Lawyer's Role and Surroundings*, 25 ROCKY MT. L. REV. 405, 410 (1953).

4. "Rule 4.15 prohibits, in the pursuit of a client's cause, 'any manner of fraud or chicane'; Rule 4.22 requires 'candor and fairness' in the conduct of the lawyer, and forbids the making of knowing misquotations; Rule 4.47 provides that a lawyer 'should always maintain his integrity,' and generally forbids all misconduct injurious to the interests of the public, the courts, or his clients, and acts contrary to 'justice, honesty, modesty or good morals.' Our Commissioner has accurately paraphrased these rules as follows: 'An attorney does not have the duty to do all and whatever he can that may enable him to win his client's cause or to further his client's interest. His duty and efforts in these respects, although they should be prompted by his "entire devotion" to the interest of his client, must be within and not without the bounds of the law.'" In re Wines, 370 S.W.2d 328, 333 (Mo. 1963).

See Note, 38 TEXAS L. REV. 107, 110 (1959).

5. "Under our system of government the process of adjudication is surrounded by safeguards evolved from centuries of experience. These safeguards are not designed merely to lend formality and decorum to the trial of causes. They are predicated on the assumption that to secure for any controversy a truly informed and dispassionate decision is a difficult thing, requiring for its achievement a special summoning and organization of human effort and the adoption of measures to exclude the biases and prejudgments that have free play outside the courtroom. All of this goes for naught if the man with an unpopular cause is unable to find a competent lawyer courageous enough to represent him. His chance to have his day in court loses much of its meaning if his case is handicapped from the outset by the very kind of prejudgment our rules of evidence and procedure are intended to prevent." *Professional Responsibility: Report of the Joint Conference*, 44 A.B.A.J. 1159, 1216 (1958).

6. "[I]t is... [the tax lawyer's] positive duty to show the client how to avail himself to the full of what the law permits. He is not the keeper of the Congressional conscience." Paul, *The Lawyer as a Tax Adviser*, 25 ROCKY MT. L. REV. 412, 418 (1953).

7. See ABA CANONS OF PROFESSIONAL ETHICS, CANONS 15 and 30 (1908).

8. "The fact that it desired to evade the law, as it is called, is immaterial, because the very meaning of a line in the law is that you intentionally may go as close to it as you can if you do not pass it.... It is a matter of proximity and degree as to which minds will differ...." Justice Holmes, in Superior Oil Co. v. Mississippi, 280 U.S. 390, 395-96, 74 L. Ed 504, 508, 50 S. Ct. 169, 170 (1930).

9. "Today's lawyers perform two distinct types of functions, and our ethical standards should, but in the main do not, recognize these two functions. Judge Philbrick McCoy recently reported to the American Bar Association the need for a reappraisal of the Canons in light of the new and distinct function of counselor, as distinguished from advocate, which today predominates in the legal profession....

"... In the first place, any revision of the canons must take into account and speak to this new and now predominant function of the lawyer.... It is beyond the scope of this paper to discuss the ethical standards to be applied to the counselor except to state that in my opinion such standards should require a greater recognition and protection for the interest of the public generally than is presently expressed in the canons. Also, the counselor's obligation should extend to requiring him to inform and to impress upon the client a just solution of the problem, considering all interests involved." Thode, *The Ethical Standard for the Advocate*, 39 TEXAS L. REV. 575, 578-79 (1961).

"The man who has been called into court to answer for his own actions is entitled to fair hearing. Partisan advocacy plays its seeential part in such a hearing, and the lawyer pleading his client's case may properly present it in the most favorable light. A similar resolution of doubts in one direction becomes inappropriate when the lawyer acts as counselor. The reasons that justify and even require partisan advocacy in the trial of a cause do not grant any license to the lawyer to participate as legal advisor in a line of conduct that is immoral, unfair, or of doubtful legality. In saving himself from this unworthy involvement, the lawyer cannot be guided solely by an unreflective inner sense of good faith; he must be at pains to preserve a sufficient detachment from his client's interests so that he remains capable of a sound and objective appraisal of the propriety of what his client proposes to do." *Professional Responsibility: Report of the Joint Conference*, 44 A.B.A.J. 1159, 1161 (1958).

10. "[A] lawyer who is asked to advise his client... may freely urge the statement of positions most favorable to the client just as long as there is reasonable basis for those positions." ABA Opinion 314 (1965).

11. "The lawyer... is not an umpire, but an advocate. He is under no duty to refrain from making every proper argument in support of any legal point because he is not convinced of its inherent soundness.... His personal belief in the soundness of his cause or of the authorities supporting it, is irrelevant." ABA Opinion 280 (1949).

"Counsel apparently misconceived his role. It was his duty to honorably present his client's contentions in the light most favorable to his client. Instead he presumed to advise the court as to the validity and sufficiency of prisoner's motion, by letter.We therefore conclude that prisoner had no effective assistance of counsel and remand this case to the District Court with instructions to set aside the Judgment, appoint new counsel to represent the prisoner if he makes no objection thereto, and proceed anew." McCartney v. United States, 343 F.2d 471, 472 (9th Cir. 1965).

12. "Here the court-appointed counsel had the transcript but refused to proceed with the appeal because he found no merit in it.... We cannot say that there was a finding of frivolity by either of the California courts or that counsel acted in any greater capacity than merely as amicus curiae which was condemned in *Ellis, supra*. Hence California's procedure did not furnish petitioner with counsel acting in the role of an advocate nor did it provide that full consideration and resolution of the matter as is obtained when counsel is acting in that capacity....

"The constitutional requirement of substantial equality and fair process can only be attained where counsel acts in the role of an active advocate in behalf of his client, as opposed to that of amicus curiae. The nomerit letter and the procedure it triggers do not reach that dignity. Counsel should, and can with honor and without conflict, be of more assistance to his client and to the court. His role as advocate requires that he support his client's appeal to the best of his ability. Of course, if counsel finds his case to be wholly frivolous, after a conscientious examination of it, he should so advise the court and request permission to withdraw. That request must, however, be accompanied by a brief referring to anything in the record that might arguably support the appeal. A copy of counsel's brief should be furnished the indigent and time allowed him to raise any points that he chooses; the court — not counsel — then proceeds, after a full examination of all the proceedings, to decide whether the case is wholly frivolous. If it so finds it may grant counsel's request to withdraw and dismiss the appeal insofar as federal requirements are concerned, or proceed to a decision on the merits, if state law so requires. On the other hand, if it finds any of the legal points arguable on their merits (and therefore not frivolous) it must, prior to decision, afford the indigent the assistance of counsel to argue the appeal." Anders v. California, 386 U.S. 738, 744, 18 L. Ed. 2d 493, 498, 87 S. Ct. 1396, 1399-1400 (1967), *rehearing denied*, 388 U.S. 924, 18 L. Ed. 2d 1377, 87 S. Ct. 2094 (1967).

See Paul, *The Lawyer as a Tax Adviser*, 25 ROCKY MT. L. REV. 412, 432 (1953).

13. See ABA CANONS OF PROFESSIONAL ETHICS, CANON 32 (1908).

14. "For a lawyer to represent a syndicate notoriously engaged in the violation of the law for the purpose of advising the members how to break the law and at the same time escape it, is manifestly improper. While a lawyer may see to it that anyone accused of crime, no matter how serious and flagrant, has a fair trial, and present all available defenses, he may not co-operate in planning violations of the law. There is a sharp distinction, of course, between advising what can lawfully be done and advising how

unlawful acts can be done in a way to avoid conviction. Where a lawyer accepts a retainer from an organization, known to be unlawful, and agrees in advance to defend its members when from time to time they are accused of crime arising out of its unlawful activities, this is equally improper."

"See also Opinion 155." ABA Opinion 281 (1952).

15. See ABA Special Committee on Minimum Standards for the Administration of Criminal Justice, *Standards Relating to Pleas of Guilty* pp. 69-70 (1968).

16. "First of all, a truly great lawyer is a wise counselor to all manner of men in the varied crises of their lives when they most need disinterested advice. Effective counseling necessarily involves a thoroughgoing knowledge of the principles of the law not merely as they appear in the books but as they actually operate in action." Vanderbilt, *The Five Functions of the Lawyer: Service to Clients and the Public*, 40 A.B.A.J. 31 (1954).

17. "A lawyer should endeavor to obtain full knowledge of his client's cause before advising thereon...." ABA CANONS OF PROFESSIONAL ETHICS, CANON 8 (1908).

18. "[I]n devising charters of collaborative effort the lawyer often acts where all of the affected parties are present as participants. But the lawyer also performs a similar function in situations where this is not so, as, for example, in planning estates and drafting wills. Here the instrument defining the terms of collaboration may affect persons not present and often not born. Yet here, too, the good lawyer does not serve merely as a legal conduit for his client's desires, but as a wise counselor, experienced in the art of devising arrangements that will put in workable order the entangled affairs and interests of human beings." *Professional Responsibility: Report of the Joint Conference*, 44 A.B.A.J. 1159, 1162 (1958).

19. See ABA CANONS OF PROFESSIONAL ETHICS, CANON 8 (1908).

"Vital as is the lawyer's role in adjudication, it should not be though that it is only as an advocate pleading in open court that he contributes to the administration of the law. The most effective realization of the law's aims often takes place in the attorney's office, where litigation is forestalled by anticipating its outcome, where the lawyer's quite counsel takes the place of public force. Contrary to popular belief, the compliance with the law thus brought about is not generally lip-serving and narrow, for by reminding him of its long-run costs the lawyer often deters his client from a course of conduct technically permissible under existing law, though inconsistent with its underlying spirit and purpose." *Professional Responsibility: Report of the Joint Conference*, 44 A.B.A.J. 1159, 1161 (1958).

20. "My summation of Judge Sharswood's view of the advocate's duty to the client is that he owes to the client the duty to use all legal means in support of the client's case. However, at the same time Judge Sharswood recognized that many advocates would find this obligation unbearable if applicable without exception. Therefore, the individual lawyer is given the choice of representing his client fully within the bounds set by the law or of telling his client that he cannot do so, so that the client may obtain another attorney if he wishes." Thode, *The Ethical Standard for the Advocate*, 39 TEXAS L. REV. 575, 582 (1961).

Cf. MODEL CODE OF PROFESSIONAL RESPONSIBILITY, DR 2-110(C).

21. See ABA CANONS OF PROFESSIONAL ETHICS, CANON 24 (1908).

22. Thode, The Ethical Standard for the Advocate, 39 TEXAS L. REV. 575, 592 (1961).

23. See ABA CANONS OF PROFESSIONAL ETHICS, CANON 5 (1908) and Berger v. United States, 295 U.S. 78, 79 L. Ed. 1314, 55 S. Ct. 629 (1935).

"The public prosecutor cannot take as a guide for the conduct of his office the standards of an attorney appearing on behalf of an individual client. The freedom elsewhere wisely granted to a partisan advocate must be severely curtailed if the prosecutor's duties are to be properly discharged. The public prosecutor must recall that he occupies a dual role, being obligated, on the one hand, to furnish that adversary element essential to the informed decision of any controversy, but being possessed, on the other, of important governmental powers that are pledged to the accomplishment of one objective only, that of impartial justice. Where the prosecutor is recreant to the trust implicit in his office, he undermines confidence, not only in his profession, but in government and the very ideal of justice itself." *Professional Responsibility: Report of the Joint Conference*, 44 A.B.A.J. 1159, 1218 (1958).

"The prosecuting attorney is the attorney for the state, and it is his primary duty not to convict but to see that justice is done." ABA Opinion 150 (1936).

24. As to appearances before a department of government, ABA CANONS OF PROFESSIONAL ETHICS, Canon 26 (1908) provides: "A lawyer openly... may render professional services... in advocacy of claims before departments of government, upon the same principles of ethics which justify his appearance before the Courts...."

25. "But as an advocate before a service which itself represents the adversary point of view, where his client's case is fairly arguable, a lawyer is under no duty to disclose its weaknesses, any more than he would be to make such a disclosure to a brother lawyer. The limitations within which he must operate are best expressed in Canon 22...." ABA Opinion 314 (1965).

26. See Baird v. Koerner, 279 F.2d 623 (9th Cir. 1960).

27. See ABA CANONS OF PROFESSIONAL ETHICS, CANON 26 (1908).

28. "Law should be so practiced that the lawyer remains free to make up his own mind how he will vote, what causes he will support, what economic and political philosophy he will espouse. It is one of the glories of the profession that it admits of this freedom. Distinguished examples can be cited of lawyers whose views were at variance from those of their clients, lawyers whose skill and wisdom make them valued advisers to those who had little sympathy with their views as citizens." *Professional Responsibility: Report of the Joint Conference,* 44 A.B.A.J. 1159, 1217 (1958).

"No doubt some tax lawyers feel constrained to abstain from activities on behalf of a better tax system because they think that their clients may object. Clients have no right to object if the tax adviser handles their affairs competently and faithfully and independently of his private views as to tax policy. They buy his expert services, not his private opinions or his silence on issues that gravely affect the public interest." Paul, *The Lawyer as a Tax Adviser*, 25 ROCKY MT. L. REV. 412, 434 (1953).

29. See ABA CANONS OF PROFESSIONAL ETHICS, CANON 9 (1908).

30. *Id.*

31. See *Professional Responsibility: Report of the Joint Conference*, 44 A.B.A.J. 1159, 1160 (1958).

32. "Without the participation of someone who can act responsibly for each of the parties, this essential narrowing of the issues [by exchange of written pleadings or stipulations of counsel] becomes impossible. But here again the true significance of partisan advocacy lies deeper, touching once more the integrity of the adjudicative process itself. It is only through the advocate's participation that the hearing may remain in fact what it purports to be in theory: a public trial of the facts and issues. Each advocate comes to the hearing prepared to present his proofs and arguments, knowing at the same time that his arguments may fail to persuade and that his proof may be rejected as inadequate.... The deciding tribunal, on the other hand, comes to the hearing uncommitted. It has not represented to the public that any fact can be proved, that any argument is sound, or that any particular way of stating a litigant's case is the most effective expression of its merits." *Professional Responsibility: Report of the Joint Conference*, 44 A.B.A.J. 1159, 1160-61 (1958).

33. *Cf.* ABA CANONS OF PROFESSIONAL ETHICS, CANONS 15 and 32 (1908).

34. *Cf.* ABA CANONS OF PROFESSIONAL ETHICS, CANON 21 (1908).

35. See *Professional Responsibility: Report of the Joint Conference*, 44 A.B.A.J. 1159, 1216 (1958).

36. "We are of the opinion that the letter in question was improper, and that in writing and sending it respondent was guilty of unprofessional conduct. This court has heretofore expressed its disapproval of using threats of criminal prosecution as a means of forcing settlement of civil claims....

"Respondent has been guilty of a violation of a principle which condemns any confusion of threats of criminal prosecution with the enforcement of civil claims. For this misconduct he should be severely censured." Matter of Gelman, 230 App. Div. 524, 527, N.Y.S. 416, 419 (1930).

37. "An attorney has the duty to protect the interests of his client. He has a right to press legitimate argument and to protest an erroneous ruling." Gallagher v. Municipal Court, 31 Cal. 2d 784, 796, 192 P.2d 905, 913 (1948).

"There must be protection, however, in the far more frequent case of the attorney who stands on his rights and combats the order in good faith and without disrespect believing with good cause that it is void, for it is here that the independence of the bar becomes valuable." Note, 39 COLUM. L. REV. 433, 438 (1939).

38. "Too many do not understand that accomplishment of the layman's abstract ideas of justice is the function of the judge and jury, and that it is the lawyer's sworn duty to portray his client's case in its most favorable light." Rochelle and Payne, *The Struggle for Public Understanding*, 25 TEXAS B.J. 109, 159 (1962).

39. "We are of the opinion that this Canon requires the lawyer to disclose such decisions [that are adverse to his client's contentions] to the court. He may, of course, after doing so, challenge the soundness of the decisions or present reasons which he believes would warrant the court in not following them in the pending case." ABA Opinion 146 (1935).

Cf. ABA Opinion 280 (1949) and Thode, *The Ethical Standard for the Advocate*, 39 TEXAS L. REV. 575, 585-86 (1961).

40. See ABA CANONS OF PROFESSIONAL ETHICS, CANON 15 (1908).

"The traditional duty of an advocate is that he honorably uphold the contentions of his client. He should not voluntarily undermine them." Harders v. State of California, 373 F.2d 839, 842 (9th Cir. 1967).

41. See ABA CANONS OF PROFESSIONAL ETHICS, CANON 22 (1908).

42. *Id.*; *cf.* ABA CANONS OF PROFESSIONAL ETHICS, CANON 41 (1908).

43. See generally ABA Opinion 287 (1953) as to a lawyer's duty when he unknowingly participates in introducing perjured testimony.

44. "Under any standard of proper ethical conduct an attorney should not sit by silently and permit his client to commit what may have been perjury, and which certainly would mislead to the court and the opposing party on a matter vital to the issue under consideration....

"Respondent next urges that it was his duty to observe the utmost good faith toward his client, and therefore he could not divulge any confidential information. This duty to the client of course does not extend to the point of authorizing collaboration with him in the commission of fraud." In re Carroll, 244 S.W.2d 474, 474-75 (Ky. 1951).

45. See ABA CANONS OF PROFESSIONAL ETHICS, CANON 5 (1908); *cf.* ABA Opinion 131 (1935).

46. *Cf.* ABA CANONS OF PROFESSIONAL ETHICS, CANON 39 (1908).

47. "The prevalence of perjury is a serious menace to the administration of justice, to prevent which no means have as yet been satisfactorily devised. But there certainly can be no greater incentive to perjury than to allow a party to make payments to its opponents witnesses under any guise or on any excuse, and at least attorneys who are officers of the court to aid it in the administration of justice, must keep themselves clear of any connection which in the slightest degree tends to induce witnesses to testify in favor of their clients." In re Robinson, 151 App. Div. 589, 600, 136 N.Y.S. 548, 556-57 (1912), aff'd, 209 N.Y. 354, 103 N.E. 160 (1913).

48. "It will not do for an attorney who seeks to justify himself against charges of this kind to show that he has escaped criminal responsibility under the Penal Law, nor can he blindly shut his eyes to a system which tends to suborn witnesses, to produce perjured testimony, and to suppress the truth. He has an active affirmative duty to protect the administration of justice from perjury and fraud, and that duty is not performed by allowing his subordinates and assistants to attempt to subvert justice and procure results for his clients based upon false testimony and perjured witnesses." *Id.*, 151 App. Div. at 592, 136 N.Y.S. at 551.

49. See ABA CANONS OF PROFESSIONAL ETHICS, CANON 23 (1908).

50. "[I]t is unfair to jurors to permit a disappointed litigant to pick over their private associations in search of something to discredit them and their verdict. And it would be unfair to the public too if jurors should understand that they cannot convict a man of means without risking an inquiry of that kind by paid investigators, with, to boot, the distortions an inquiry of that kind can produce." State v. LaFera, 42 N.J. 97, 107, 199 A.2d 630, 636 (1964).

51. ABA Opinion 319 (1968) points out that "[m]any courts today, and the trend is in this direction, allow the testimony of jurors as to all irregularities in and out of the courtroom except those irregularities whose existence can be determined only by exploring the consciousness of a single particular juror, New Jersey v. Kociolek, 20 N.J. 92, 118 A.2d 812 (1955). Model Code of Evidence Rule 301. Certainly as to states in which the testimony and affidavits of jurors may be received in support of or against a motion for new trial, a lawyer, in his obligation to protect his client, must have the tools for ascertaining whether or not grounds for a new trial exist and it is not unethical for him to talk to and question jurors."

52. Generally see ABA ADVISORY COMMITTEE ON FAIR TRIAL AND FREE PRESS, STANDARDS RELATING TO FAIR TRIAL AND FREE PRESS (1966).

"[T]he trial court might well have proscribed extrajudicial statements by any lawyer, party, witness, or court official which divulged prejudicial matters.... See State v. Van Dwyne, 43 N.J. 369, 389, 204 A.2d 841, 852 (1964), in which the court interpreted Canon 20 of the American Bar Association's Canons of Professional Ethics to prohibit such statements. Being advised of the great public interest in the case, the mass coverage of the press, and the potential prejudicial impact of publicity, the court could also have requested the appropriate city and county officials to promulgate a regulation with respect to dissemination of information about the case by their employees. In addition, reporters who wrote or broadcast prejudicial stories, could have been warned as to the impropriety of publishing material not introduced in the proceedings.... In this manner, Sheppard's right to a trial free from outside interference would have been given added protection without corresponding curtailment of the news media. Had the judge, the other officers of the court, and the police placed the interest of justice first, the news media would have soon learned to be content with the task of reporting the case as it unfolded in the courtroom — not pieced together from extrajudicial statements." Sheppard v. Maxwell, 384 U.S. 333, 361-62, 16 L. Ed. 2d 600, 619-20, 86 S. Ct. 1507, 1521-22 (1966).

"Court proceedings are held for the solemn purpose of endeavoring to ascertain the truth which is the sine qua non of a fair trial. Over the centuries Anglo-American courts have devised careful safeguards by rule and otherwise to protect and facilitate the performance of this high function. As a result, as this time those safeguards do not permit the televising and photographing of a criminal trial, save in two States and there only under restrictions. The federal courts prohibit it by specific rule. This is weighty evidence that our concepts of a fair trial do not tolerate such an indulgence. We have always held that the atmosphere essential to the preservation of a fair trial — the most fundamental of all freedoms — must be maintained at all costs." Estes v. State of Texas, 381 U.S. 532, 540, 14 L. Ed. 2d 543, 549, 85 S. Ct. 1628, 1631-32 (1965), *rehearing denied*, 382 U.S. 875, 15 L. Ed. 2d 118, 86 S. Ct. 18 (1965).

53. "Pretrial can create a major problem for the defendant in a criminal case. Indeed, it may be more harmful than publicity during the trial for it may well set the community opinion as to guilt or innocence.... The trial witnesses present at the hearing, as well as the original jury panel, were undoubtedly made aware of the peculiar public importance of the case by the press and television coverage being provided, and by the fact that they themselves were televised live and their pictures rebroadcast on the evening show." *Id.*, 381 U.S. at 536-37, 14 L. Ed. 2d at 546-47, 85 S.Ct. at 1629-30.

54. "The undeviating rule of this Court was expressed by Mr. Justice Holmes over half a century ago in Patterson v. Colorado, 205 U.S. 454, 462 (1907):

The theory of our system is that the conclusions to be reached in a case will be induced only by evidence and argument in open court, and not by any outside influence, whether of private talk or public print."

Sheppard v. Maxwell, 384 U.S. 333, 351, 16 L. Ed. 2d 600, 614, 86 S. Ct. 1507, 1516 (1966).

"The trial judge has a large discretion in ruling on the issue of prejudice resulting from the reading by jurors of news articles concerning the trial.... Generalizations beyond that statement are not profitable, because each case must turn on its special facts. We have here the exposure of jurors to information of a character which the trial judge ruled was so prejudicial it could not be directly offered as evidence. The prejudice to the defendant is almost certain to be as great when that evidence reaches the jury through news accounts as when it is a part of the prosecution's evidence.... It may indeed be greater for it is then not tempered by protective procedures." Marshall v. United States, 360 U.S. 310, 312-13, 3 L. Ed. 2d 1250, 1252, 79 S. Ct. 1171, 1173 (1959).

"The experienced trial lawyer knows that an adverse public opinion is a tremendous disadvantage to the defense of his client. Although grand jurors conduct their deliberations in secret, they are selected from the body of the public. They are likely to know what the general public knows and to reflect the public attitude. Trials are open to the public, and aroused public opinion respecting the merits of a legal controversy creates a court room atmosphere which, without any vocal expression in the presence of the petit jury, makes itself felt and has its effect upon the action of the petit jury. Our fundamental concepts of justice and our American sense of fair play require that the petit jury shall be composed of persons with fair and impartial minds and without preconceived views as to the merits of the controversy, and that it shall determine the issues presented to it solely upon the evidence adduced at the trial and according to the law given in the instructions of the trial judge.

"While we may doubt that the effect of public opinion would sway or bias the judgment of the trial judge in an equity proceeding, the defendant should not be called upon to run that risk and the trial court should not have his work made more difficult by any dissemination of statements to the public that would be calculated to create a public demand for a particular judgment in a prospective or pending case." ABA Opinion 199 (1940).

Cf. Estes v. State of Texas, 381 U.S. 532, 544-45, 144 L. Ed. 2d 543, 551, 85 S. Ct. 1628, 1634 (1965), *rehearing denied*, 381 U.S. 875, 15 L. Ed. 2d 118, 86 S. Ct. 18 (1965).

56. Canon 3 observes that a lawyer "deserves rebuke and denunciation for any device or attempt to gain from a Judge special personal consideration or favor."

See ABA CANONS OF PROFESSIONAL ETHICS, CANON 32 (1908).

57. "Judicial Canon 32 provides:

A judge should not accept any presents or favors from litigants, or from lawyers practicing before him or from others whose interests are likely to be submitted to him for judgment.

The language of this Canon is perhaps broad enough to prohibit campaign contributions by lawyers, practicing before the court upon which the candidate hopes to sit. However, we do not think it was intended to prohibit such contributions when the candidate is obligated, by force of circumstances over which he has no control, to conduct a campaign, the expense of which exceeds that which he should reasonably be expected to personally bear!" ABA Opinion 226 (1941).

58. Amended, March 1974, House Informational Report No. 127.

59. See ABA CANONS OF PROFESSIONAL ETHICS, CANONS 3 and 32 (1908).

60. *Cf.* ABA CANONS OF PROFESSIONAL ETHICS, CANON 18 (1908).

61. See ABA CANONS OF PROFESSIONAL ETHICS, CANONS 1 and 3 (1908).

62. See ABA CANONS OF PROFESSIONAL ETHICS, CANON 17 (1908).

63. See ABA CANONS OF PROFESSIONAL ETHICS, CANON 24 (1908).

64. See ABA CANONS OF PROFESSIONAL ETHICS, CANON 25 (1908).

65. See ABA CANONS OF PROFESSIONAL ETHICS, CANON 21 (1908).

66. See ABA CANONS OF PROFESSIONAL ETHICS, CANON 15 (1908).

67. See ABA CANONS OF PROFESSIONAL ETHICS, CANONS 5 and 15 (1908); *cf.* ABA CANONS 4 and 32 (1908).

68. *Cf.* ABA CANONS OF PROFESSIONAL ETHICS, CANON 24 (1908).

69. See ABA CANONS OF PROFESSIONAL ETHICS, CANON 30 (1908).

70. *Cf.* ABA CANONS OF PROFESSIONAL ETHICS, CANONS 22 and 29 (1908).

71. See ABA CANONS OF PROFESSIONAL ETHICS, CANON 41 (1908); *cf.* Hinds v. State Bar, 19 Cal.2d 87, 92-93, 119 P.2d 134, 137 (1941); but see ABA Opinion 287 (1953) and TEXAS CANON 38. Also see MODEL CODE OF PROFESSIONAL RESPONSIBILITY, DR 4-101(C)(2).

72. Amended, March 1974, House Informational Report No. 127.

73. See Precision Inst. Mfg. Co. v. Automotive M.M. Co., 324 U.S. 806, 89 L. Ed. 1381, 65 S. C. 993 (1945).

74. *Cf.* ABA CANONS OF PROFESSIONAL ETHICS, CANON 5 (1908).

75. "Rule 12.... A member of the State Bar shall not communicate with a party represented by counsel upon a subject of controversy, in the absence and without the consent of such counsel. This rule shall not apply to communications with a public officer, board, committee or body." CAL. BUSINESS AND PROFESSIONS CODE § 6076 (West 1962).

76. See ABA CANONS OF PROFESSIONAL ETHICS, CANON 9 (1908); *Cf.* ABA Opinions 124 (1934), 108 (1934), 95 (1933), and 75 (1932); also see In re Schwabe, 242 Or. 169, 174-75, 408 P.2d 922, 924 (1965).

"It is clear from the earlier opinions of this committee that Canon 9 is to be construed literally and does not allow a communication with an opposing party, without the consent of his counsel, though the purpose merely be to investigate the facts. Opinions 117, 55, 66," ABA Opinion 187 (1938).

77. *Cf.* ABA Opinion 102 (1933).

78. *Cf.* ABA CANONS OF PROFESSIONAL ETHICS, CANON 9 (1908) and ABA Opinion 58 (1931).

79. *Cf.* Note, 38 TEXAS L. REV. 107, 108-09 (1959).

80. "In the brief summary in the 1947 edition of the Committee's decisions (p. 17), Opinion 146 was thus summarized: Opinion 146 — A lawyer should disclose to the court a decision directly adverse to his client s case that is unknown to his adversary.

"We would not confine the Opinion to 'controlling authorities' — i.e., those decisive of the pending case — but, in accordance with the tests hereafter suggested, would apply it to a decision directly adverse to any proposition of law on which the lawyer expressly relies, which would reasonably be considered important by the judge sitting on the case.

"... The test in every case should be: Is the decision which opposing counsel has overlooked one which the court should clearly consider in deciding the case? Would a reasonable judge properly feel that a lawyer who advanced, as the law, a proposition adverse to the undisclosed decision, was lacking in candor and fairness to him? Might the judge consider himself misled by an implied representation that the lawyer knew of no adverse authority?" ABA Opinion 280 (1949).

81. "The authorities are substantially uniform against any privilege as applied to the fact of retainer or identity of the client. The privilege is limited to confidential communications, and a retainer is not a confidential communication, although it cannot come into existence without some communication between the attorney and the — at that stage prospective — client." United States v. Pape, 144 F.2d 778, 782 (2d Cir. 1944), *cert. denied,* 323 U.S. 752, 89 L. Ed. 2d 602, 65 S. Ct. 86 (1944).

"To be sure, there may be circumstances under which the identification of a client may amount to the prejudicial disclosure of a confidential communication, as where the substance of a disclosure has already been revealed but not its source." Colton v. United States, 306 F.2d 633, 637 (2d Cir. 1962).

82. See ABA CANONS OF PROFESSIONAL ETHICS, CANON 22 (1908); *cf.* ABA CANONS OF PROFESSIONAL ETHICS, CANON 17 (1908).

"The rule allowing counsel when addressing the jury the widest latitude in discussing the evidence and presenting the client's theories falls far short of authorizing the statement by counsel of matter not in evidence, or indulging in argument founded on no proof, or demanding verdicts for purposes other than the just settlement of the matters at issue between the litigants, or appealing to prejudice or passion. The rule confining counsel to legitimate argument is not based on etiquette, but on justice. Its violation is not merely an overstepping of the bounds of propriety, but a violation of a party's rights. The jurors must determine the issues upon the evidence. Counsel's address should help them do this, not tend to lead them astray." Cherry Creek Nat. Bank v. Fidelity & Cas. Co., 207 App. Div. 787, 790-91, 202 N.Y.S. 611, 614 (1924).

83. *Cf.* ABA CANONS OF PROFESSIONAL ETHICS, CANON 18 (1908).

§ 6068.... It is the duty of an attorney:

"(f) To abstain from all offensive personality, and to advance no fact prejudicial to the honor or reputation of a party or witness, unless required by the justice of the cause with which he is charged." CAL. BUSINESS AND PROFESSIONS CODE § 6068 (West 1962).

84. "The record in the case at bar was silent concerning the qualities and character of the deceased. It is especially improper, in addressing the jury in a murder case, for the prosecuting attorney to make reference to his knowledge of the good qualities of the deceased where there is no evidence in the record bearing upon his character.... A prosecutor should never inject into his argument evidence not introduced at the trial." People v. Dukes, 12 Ill. 2d 334, 341, 146 N.E.2d 14, 17-18 (1957).

85. "A lawyer should not ignore known customs or practice of the Bar or of a particular Court, even when the law permits, without giving timely notice to the opposing counsel." ABA CANONS OF PROFESSIONAL ETHICS, CANON 25 (1908).

86. The provisions of Section (A), (B), (C), and (D) of this Disciplinary Rule incorporate the fair trial-free press standards which apply to lawyers as adopted by the ABA House of Delegates, Feb. 19, 1968, upon the recommendation of the Fair Trial and Free Press Advisory Committee of the ABA Special Committee on Minimum Standards for the Administration of Criminal Justice.

Cf. ABA CANONS OF PROFESSIONAL ETHICS, CANON 20 (1908); see generally ABA ADVISORY COMMITTEE ON FAIR TRIAL AND FREE PRESS, STANDARDS RELATING TO FAIR TRIAL AND FREE PRESS (1966).

"From the cases coming here we note that unfair and prejudicial news comment on pending trials has become increasingly prevalent. Due process requires that the accused receive a trial by an impartial jury free from outside influences. Given the pervasiveness of modern communications and the difficulty of effacing prejudicial publicity from the minds of the jurors, the trial courts must take strong measures to ensure that the balance is never weighed against the accused. And appellate tribunals have the duty to make an independent evaluation of the circumstances. Of course, there is nothing that prescribes the press from reporting events that transpire in the courtroom. But where there is a reasonable likelihood that prejudicial news prior to trial will prevent a fair trial, the judge should continue the case until the threat abates, or transfer it to another county not so permeated with publicity.... The courts must take such steps by rule and regulation that will protect their processes from prejudicial outside interferences. Neither prosecutors, counsel for defense, the accused, witnesses, court staff nor enforcement officers coming under the jurisdiction of the court should be permitted to frustrate its function. Collaboration between counsel and the press as to information affecting the fairness of a criminal trial is not only subject to regulation, but is highly censurable and worthy of disciplinary measures." Sheppard v. Maxwell, 384 U.S. 333, 362-63, 16 L. Ed. 2d 600, 620, 86 S. Ct. 1507, 1522 (1966).

87. See ABA CANONS OF PROFESSIONAL ETHICS, CANON 23 (1908).

88. "[I]t would be unethical for a lawyer to harass, entice, induce or exert influence on a juror to obtain his testimony." ABA Opinion 319 (1968).

89. See ABA CANONS OF PROFESSIONAL ETHICS, CANON 5 (1908).

90. *Cf.* ABA CANONS OF PROFESSIONAL ETHICS, CANON 5 (1908).

"Rule 15.... A member of the State Bar shall not advise a person, whose testimony could establish or tend to establish a material fact, to avoid service of process, or secrete himself, or otherwise to make his testimony unavailable." CAL. BUSINESS AND PROFESSIONS CODE § 6076 (West 1962).

91. See In re O'Keefe, 49 Mont. 369, 142 P. 638 (1914).

92. *Cf.* ABA CANONS OF PROFESSIONAL ETHICS, CANON 3 (1908).

93. Amended, March 1974, House Informational Report No. 127.

94. "Rule 16.... A member of the State Bar shall not, in the absence of opposing counsel, communicate with or argue to a judge or judicial officer except in open court upon the merits of a contested matter pending before such judge or judicial officer; nor shall he, without furnishing opposing counsel with a copy thereof, address a written communication to a judge or judicial officer concerning the merits of a contested matter pending before such judge or judicial officer. This rule shall not apply to ex parte matters." CAL. BUSINESS AND PROFESSIONS CODE § 6076 (West 1962).

95. Amended, March 1974, House Informational Report No. 127.

CANON 8

A Lawyer Should Assist in Improving the Legal System

ETHICAL CONSIDERATIONS

EC 8-1 Changes in human affairs and imperfections in human institutions make necessary constant efforts to maintain and improve our legal system.[1] This system should function in a manner that commands public respect and fosters the use of the legal remedies to achieve redress of grievances. By reason of education and experience, lawyers are especially qualified to recognize deficiencies in the legal system and to initiate corrective measures therein. Thus they should participate in proposing and supporting legislation and programs to improve the system,[2] without regard to the general interests or desires of clients or former clients.[3]

EC 8-2 Rules of law are deficient if they are not just, understandable, and responsive to the needs of society. If a lawyer believes that the existence or absence of a rule of law, substantive or procedural, causes or contributes to an unjust result, he should endeavor by lawful means to obtain appropriate changes in the law. He should encourage the simplification of laws and the repeal or amendment of laws that are outmoded.[4] Likewise, legal procedures should be improved whenever experience indicates a change is needed.

EC 8-3 The fair administration of justice requires the availability of competent lawyers. Members of the public should be educated to recognize the existence of legal problems and the resultant need for legal services, and should be provided methods for intelligent selection of counsel. Those persons unable to pay for legal services should be provided needed services. Clients and lawyers should not be penalized by undue geographical restraints upon representation in legal matters, and the bar should address itself to improvements in licensing, reciprocity, and admission procedures consistent with the needs of modern commerce.

EC 8-4 Whenever a lawyer seeks legislative or administrative changes, he should identify the capacity in which he appears, whether on behalf of himself, a client, or the public.[5] A lawyer may advocate such changes on behalf of a client even though he does not agree with them. But when a lawyer purports to act on behalf of the public, he should espouse only those changes which he conscientiously believes to be in the public interest.

EC 8-5 Fraudulent, deceptive, or otherwise illegal conduct by a participant in a proceeding before a tribunal or legislative body is inconsistent with fair administration of justice, and it should never be participated in or condoned by lawyers. Unless constrained by his obligation to preserve the confidences and secrets of his client, a lawyer should reveal to appropriate authorities any knowledge he may have of such improper conduct.

EC 8-6 Judges and administrative officials having adjudicatory powers ought to be persons of integrity, competence, and suitable temperament. Generally, lawyers are qualified, by personal observation or investigation, to evaluate the qualifications of persons seeking or being considered for such public offices, and for this reason they have a special responsibility to aid in the selection of only those who are qualified.[6] It is the duty of lawyers to endeavor to prevent political considerations from outweighing judicial fitness in the selection of judges. Lawyers should protest earnestly against the appointment or election of those who are unsuited for the bench and should strive to have elected[7] or appointed thereto only those who are willing to forego pursuits, whether of a business, political, or other nature, that may interfere with the free and fair consideration of questions presented for adjudication. Adjudicatory officials, not being wholly free to defend themselves, are entitled to receive the support of the bar against unjust criticism.[8] While a lawyer as a citizen has a right to criticize such officials publicly,[9] he should be certain of the merit of his complaint, use appropriate language, and avoid petty criticisms, for unrestrained and intemperate statements tend to lessen public confidence in our legal system.[10] Criticisms motivated by reasons other than a desire to improve the legal system are not justified.

EC 8-7 Since lawyers are a vital part of the legal system, they should be persons of integrity, of professional skill, and of dedication to the improvement of the system. Thus a lawyer should aid in establishing, as well as enforcing, standards of conduct adequate to protect the public by insuring that those who practice law are qualified to do so.

EC 8-8 Lawyers often serve as legislators or as holders of other public offices. This is highly desirable, as lawyers are uniquely qualified to make significant contributions to the improvement of the legal system. A lawyer who is a public officer, whether full or part-time, should not engage in activities in which his personal or professional interests are or foreseeably may be in conflict with his official duties.[11]

EC 8-9 The advancement of our legal system is of vital importance in maintaining the rule of law and in facilitating orderly changes; therefore, lawyers should encourage, and should aid in making, needed changes and improvements.

DISCIPLINARY RULES

DR 8-101   Action as a Public Official.

(A)   A lawyer who holds public office shall not:

(1)   Use his public position to obtain, or attempt to obtain, a special advantage in legislative matters for himself or for a client under circumstances where he knows or it is obvious that such action is not in the public interest.

(2)   Use his public position to influence, or attempt to influence, a tribunal to act in favor of himself or of a client.

(3)   Accept any thing of value from any person when the lawyer knows or it is obvious that the offer is for the purpose of influencing his action as a public official.

DR 8-102   Statements Concerning Judges and Other Adjudicatory Officers.[12]

(A)   A lawyer shall not knowingly make false statements of fact concerning the qualifications of a candidate for election or appointment to a judicial office.

(B)   A lawyer shall not knowingly make false accusations against a judge or other adjudicatory officer.

DR 8-103   Lawyer Candidate for Judicial Office.

(A)   A lawyer who is a candidate for judicial office shall comply with the applicable provisions of Canon 7 of the Code of Judicial Conduct.[13]

NOTES

1. "... [another] task of the great lawyer is to do his part individually and as a member of the organized bar to improve his profession, the courts, and the law. As President Theodore Roosevelt aptly put it, 'Every man owes some of his time to the upbuilding of the profession to which he belongs.' Indeed, this obligation is one of the great things which distinguishes a profession from a business. The soundness and the necessity of

President Roosevelt's admonition insofar as it relates to the legal profession cannot be doubted. The advances in natural science and technology are so startling and the velocity of change in business and in social life is so great that the law along with the other social sciences, and even human life itself, is in grave danger of being extinguished by new gods of its own invention if it does not awake from its lethargy." *Vanderbilt, The Five Functions of the Lawyer: Service of Clients and the Public,* 40 A.B.A.J. 31, 31-32 (1954).

2. See ABA CANONS OF PROFESSIONAL ETHICS, CANON 29 (1908); *Cf.* Cheatham, *The Lawyer's Role and Surroundings,* 25 ROCKY MT. L. REV. 405, 406-07 (1953).

"The lawyer tempted by repose should recall the heavy costs paid by his profession when needed legal reform has to be accomplished through the initiative of public-spirited laymen. Where change must be thrust from without upon an unwilling Bar, the public's least flattering picture of the lawyer seems confirmed. The lawyer concerned for the standing of his profession will, therefore, interest himself actively in the improvement of the law. In doing so he will not only help to maintain confidence in the Bar, but will have the satisfaction of meeting a responsibility inhering in the nature of his calling." *Professional Responsibility: Report of the Joint Conference,* 44 A.B.A.J. 1159, 1217 (1958).

3. See Stayton, Cum Honore Officium, 19 TEX. B.J. 765, 766 (1956); *Professional Responsibility: Report of the Joint Conference,* 44 A.B.A.J. 1159, 1162 (1958); and Paul, *The Lawyer as a Tax Adviser,* 25 ROCKY MT. L. REV. 412, 433-34 (1953).

4. "There are few great figures in the history of the Bar who have not concerned themselves with the reform and improvement of the law. The special obligation of the profession with respect to legal reform rests on considerations too obvious to require enumeration. Certainly it is the lawyer who has both the best chance to know when the law is working badly and the special competence to put it in order." *Professional Responsibility: Report of the Joint Conference,* 44 A.B.A.J. 1159, 1217 (1958).

5. "Rule 14. ... A member of the State Bar shall not communicate with, or appear before, a public officer, board, committee or body, in his professional capacity, without first disclosing that he is an attorney representing interests that may be affected by action of such officer, board, committee or body." CAL. BUSINESS AND PROFESSIONS CODE § 6076 (West 1962).

6. See ABA CANONS OF PROFESSIONAL ETHICS, CANON 2 (1908).

"Lawyers are better able than laymen to appraise accurately the qualifications of candidates for judicial office. It is proper that they should make that appraisal known to the voters in a proper and dignified manner. A lawyer may with propriety endorse a candidate for judicial office and seek like endorsement from other lawyers. But the lawyer who endorses a judicial candidate or seeks that endorsement from other lawyers should be actuated by a sincere belief in the superior qualifications of the candidate for judicial service and not by personal or selfish motives; and a lawyer should not use or attempt to use the power or prestige of the judicial office to secure such endorsement. On the other hand, the lawyer whose endorsement is sought, if he believes the candidate lacks the essential qualifications for the office or believes the opposing candidate is better qualified, should have the courage and moral stamina to refuse the request for endorsement." ABA Opinion 189 (1938).

7. "[W]e are of the opinion that, whenever a candidate for judicial office merits the endorsement and support of lawyers, the lawyers may make financial contributions toward the campaign if its cost, when reasonably conducted, exceeds that which the candidate would be expected to bear personally." ABA Opinion 226 (1941).

8. See ABA CANONS OF PROFESSIONAL ETHICS, CANON 1 (1908).

9. "Citizens have a right under our constitutional system to criticize governmental officials and agencies. Courts are not, and should not be, immune to such criticism." Konigsberg v. State Bar of California, 353 U.S. 252, 269 (1957).

10. "[E]very lawyer, worthy of respect, realizes that public confidence in our courts is the cornerstone of our governmental structure, and will refrain from unjustified attack on the character of the judges, while recognizing the duty to denounce and expose a corrupt or dishonest judge." Kentucky State Bar Ass'n v. Lewis, 282 S.W. 2d 321, 326 (Ky. 1955).

"We should be the last to deny that Mr. Meeker has the right to uphold the honor of the profession and to expose without fear or favor corrupt or dishonest conduct in the profession, whether the conduct be that of a judge or not. ... However, this Canon [29] does not permit one to make charges which are false and untrue and unfounded in fact. When one's fancy leads him to make false charges, attacking the character and integrity of others, he does so at his peril. He should not do so without adequate proof of his charges and he is certainly not authorized to make careless, untruthful and vile charges against his professional brethren." In re Meeker, 76 N.M. 354, 364-65, 414 P.2d 862, 869 (1966), *appeal dismissed*, 385 U.S. 449, 17 L. Ed. 2d 510, 87 S. Ct. 613 (1967).

11. "Opinions 16, 30, 34, 77, 118 and 134 relate to Canon 6, and pass on questions concerning the propriety of the conduct of an attorney who is a public officer, in representing private interests adverse to those of the public body which he represents. The principle applied in those opinions is that an attorney holding public office should avoid all conduct which might lead the layman to conclude that the attorney is utilizing his public position to further his professional success or personal interests." ABA Opinion 192 (1939).

"The next question is whether a lawyer-member of a legislative body may appear as counsel or co-counsel at hearings before a zoning board of appeals, or similar tribunal, created by the legislative group of which he is a member. We are of the opinion that he may practice before fact-finding officers, hearing bodies and commissioners, since under our views he may appear as counsel in the courts where his municipality is a party. Decisions made at such hearings are usually subject to administrative review by the courts upon the record there made. It would be inconsistent to say that a lawyer-member of a legislative body could not participate in a hearing at which the record is made, but could appear thereafter when the cause is heard by the courts on administrative review. This is subject to an important exception. He should not appear as counsel where the matter is subject to review by the legislative body of which he is a member. ... We are of the opinion that where a lawyer does so appear there would be conflict of interests between his duty as an advocate for his client on the one hand and the obligation to his governmental unit on the other." In re Becker, 16 Ill. 2d 488, 494-95, 158 N.E. 2d 753, 756-57 (1959).

Cf. ABA Opinions 186 (1938), 136 (1935), 118 (1934), and 77 (1932).

12. *Cf.* ABA CANONS OF PROFESSIONAL ETHICS, CANONS 1 and 2 (1908).

13. Amended, March 1974, House Informational Report No. 127.

CANON 9

A Lawyer Should Avoid Even the Appearance of Professional Impropriety

ETHICAL CONSIDERATIONS

EC 9-1 Continuation of the American concept that we are to be governed by rules of law requires that the people have faith that justice can be obtained through our legal system.[1] A lawyer should promote public confidence in our system and in the legal profession.[2]

EC 9-2 Public confidence in law and lawyers may be eroded by irresponsible or improper conduct of a lawyer. On occasion, ethical conduct of a lawyer may appear to laymen to be unethical. In order to avoid misunderstandings and hence to maintain confidence, a lawyer should fully and promptly inform his client of material developments in the matters being handled for the client. While a lawyer should guard against otherwise proper conduct that has a tendency to diminish public confidence in the legal system or in the legal profession, his duty to clients or to the public should never be subordinate merely because the full discharge of his obligation may be misunderstood or may tend to subject him or the legal profession to criticism. When explicit ethical guidance does not exist, a lawyer should determine his conduct by acting in a manner that promotes public confidence in the integrity and efficiency of the legal system and the legal profession.[3]

EC 9-3 After a lawyer leaves judicial office or other public employment, he should not accept employment in connection with any matter in which he had substantial responsibility prior to his leaving, since to accept employment would give the appearance of impropriety even if none exists.[4]

EC 9-4 Because the very essence of the legal system is to provide procedures by which matters can be presented in an impartial manner so that they may be decided solely upon the merits, any statement or suggestion by a lawyer that he can or would attempt to circumvent those procedures is detrimental to the legal system and tends to undermine public confidence in it.

EC 9-5 Separation of the funds of a client from those of his lawyer not only serves to protect the client but also avoids even the appearance of impropriety, and therefore commingling of such funds should be avoided.

EC 9-6 Every lawyer owes a solemn duty to uphold the integrity and honor of his profession; to encourage respect for the law and for the courts and the judges thereof; to observe the Code of Professional Responsibility; to act as a member of a learned profession, one dedicated to public service; to cooperate with his brother lawyers in supporting the organized bar through the devoting of his time, efforts, and financial support as his professional standing and ability reasonably permit; to conduct himself so as to reflect credit on the legal profession and to inspire the confidence, respect, and trust of his clients and of the public; and to strive to avoid not only professional impropriety but also the appearance of impropriety.[5]

EC 9-7 A lawyer has an obligation to the public to participate in collective efforts of the bar to reimburse persons who have lost money or property as a result of the misappropriation or defalcation of another lawyer, and contribution to a clients' security fund is an acceptable method of meeting this obligation.[6]

DISCIPLINARY RULES

DR 9-101   Avoiding Even the Appearance of Impropriety.[7]

  (A) A lawyer shall not accept private employment in a matter upon the merits of which he has acted in a judicial capacity.[8]

  (B) A lawyer shall not accept private employment in a matter in which he had substantial responsibility while he was a public employee.[9]

(C)   A lawyer shall not state or imply that he is able to influence improperly or upon irrelevant grounds any tribunal, legislative body,[10] or public official.

DR 9-102   Preserving Identity of Funds and Property of a Client.[11]

(A)   All funds of clients paid to a lawyer or law firm, other than advances for costs and expenses, shall be deposited in one or more identifiable bank accounts maintained in the state in which the law office is situated and no funds belonging to the lawyer or law firm shall be deposited therein except as follows:

   (1)   Funds reasonably sufficient to pay bank charges may be deposited therein.

   (2)   Funds belonging in part to a client and in part presently or potentially to the lawyer or law firm must be deposited therein, but the portion belonging to the lawyer or law firm may be withdrawn when due unless the right of the lawyer or law firm to receive it is disputed by the client, in which event the disputed portion shall not be withdrawn until the dispute is finally resolved.

(B)   A lawyer shall:

   (1)   Promptly notify a client of the receipt of his funds, securities, or other properties.

   (2)   Identify and label securities and properties of a client promptly upon receipt and place them in a safe deposit box or other place of safekeeping as soon as practicable.

   (3)   Maintain complete records of all funds, securities, and other properties of a client coming into the possession of the lawyer and render appropriate accounts to his client regarding them.

   (4)   Promptly pay or deliver to the client as requested by a client the funds, securities, or other properties in the possession of the lawyer which the client is entitled to receive.

NOTES

1. "Integrity is the very breath of justice. Confidence in our law, our courts, and in the administration of justice is our supreme interest. No practice must be permitted to prevail which invites towards the administration of justice a doubt or distrust of its integrity." Erwin M. Jennings Co. v. DiGenova, 107 Conn. 491, 499, 141 A. 866, 868 (1928).

2. "A lawyer should never be reluctant or too proud to answer unjustified criticism of his profession, of himself, or of his brother lawyer. He should guard the reputation of his profession and of his brothers as zealously as he guards his own." Rochelle and Payne, *The Struggle for Public Understanding*, 25 TEXAS B.J. 109, 162 (1962).

3. See ABA CANONS OF PROFESSIONAL ETHICS, CANON 29 (1908).

4. See ABA CANONS OF PROFESSIONAL ETHICS, CANON 36 (1908).

5. "As said in Opinion 49, of the Committee on Professional Ethics and Grievances of the American Bar Association, page 134: 'An attorney should not only avoid impropriety but should avoid the appearance of impropriety.'" State ex rel. Nebraska State Bar Ass'n v. Richards, 165 Neb. 80, 93, 84 N.W.2d 136, 145 (1957).

"It would also be preferable that such contribution [to the campaign of a candidate for judicial office] be made to a campaign committee rather than to the candidate personally. In so doing, possible appearances of impropriety would be reduced to a minimum." ABA Opinion 226 (1941). "The lawyer assumes high duties, and has imposed upon him grave responsibilities. He may be the means of much good or much mischief. Interests of vast magnitude are entrusted to him; confidence is reposed in him; life, liberty, character and property should be protected by him. He should guard, with jealous watchfulness, his own reputation, as well as that of his profession." People ex rel. Cutler v. Ford, 54 Ill. 520, 522 (1870), and also quoted in State Board of Law Examiners v. Sheldon, 43 Wyo. 522, 526, 7 P.2d 226, 227 (1932).

See ABA Opinion 150 (1936).

6. Amended, February 1980, House Informational Report No. 105.

7. Cf. MODEL CODE OF PROFESSIONAL RESPONSIBILITY, EC 5-6.

8. See ABA CANONS OF PROFESSIONAL ETHICS, CANON 36 (1908).

"It is the duty of the judge to rule on questions of law and evidence in misdemeanor cases and examinations in felony cases. That duty calls for impartial and uninfluenced judgment, regardless of the effect on those immediately involved or others who may, directly or indirectly, be affected. Discharge of that duty might be greatly interfered with if the judge, in another capacity, were permitted to hold himself out to employment by those who are to be, or who may be, brought to trial in felony cases, even though he did not conduct the examination. His private interests as a lawyer in building up his clientele, his duty as such zealously to espouse the cause of his private clients and to defend against charges of crime brought by law-enforcement agencies of which he is a part, might prevent, or even destroy, that unbiased judicial judgment which is so essential in the administration of justice.

"In our opinion, acceptance of a judgeship with the duties of conducting misdemeanor trials, and examinations in felony cases to determine whether those accused should be bound over for trial in a higher court, ethically bars the judge from acting as attorney for the defendants upon such trial, whether they were examined by him or by some other judge. Such a practice would not only diminish public confidence in the administration of justice in both courts, but would produce serious conflict between the private interests of the judge as a lawyer, and of his clients, and his duties as a judge in adjudicating important phases of criminal processes in other cases. The public and private duties would be incompatible. The prestige of the judicial office would be diverted to private benefit, and the judicial office would be demeaned thereby." ABA Opinion 242 (1942).

"A lawyer, who has previously occupied a judicial position or acted in a judicial capacity, should refrain from accepting employment in any matter involving the same facts as were involved in any specific question which he acted upon in a judicial capacity and, for the same reasons, should also refrain from accepting any employment which might reasonably appear to involve the same facts." ABA Opinion 49 (1931).

See ABA Opinion 101 (1934).

9. See ABA Opinions 135 (1935) and 134 (1935); cf. ABA CANONS OF PROFESSIONAL ETHICS, CANON 36 (1980) and ABA Opinions 39 (1931) and 26 (1930). But see ABA Option 37 (1931).

10. "[A statement by a governmental department or agency with regard to a lawyer resigning from its staff that includes a laudation of his legal ability] carries implications, probably not founded in fact, that the lawyer's acquaintance and previous relations with the personnel of the administrative agencies of the government place him in an advantageous position in practicing before such agencies. So to imply would not only represent what probably is untrue, but would be highly reprehensible." ABA Opinion 184 (1938).

11. See ABA CANONS OF PROFESSIONAL ETHICS, CANON 11 (1908).

"Rule 9.... A member of the State Bar shall not commingle the money or other property of a client with his own; and he shall promptly report to the client the receipt by him of all money and other property belonging to such client. Unless the client otherwise directs in writing, he shall promptly deposit his client's funds in a bank or trust company ... in a bank account separate from his own account and clearly designated as 'Clients' Funds Account' or 'Trust Funds Account' or words of similar import. Unless the client otherwise directs in writing, securities of a client in bearer form shall be kept by the attorney in a safe deposit box at a bank or trust company. ... which safe deposit box shall be clearly designated as 'Clients' Account' or 'Trust Account' or words of similar import, and be bank or trust company, ... which safe deposit box CAL. BUSINESS AND PROFESSIONS CODE § 6076 (West 1962). "[C]ommingling is committed when a client's money is intermingled with that of his attorney and its separate identity lost so that it may be used for the attorney's personal expenses or subjected to claims of his creditors.... The rule against commingling was adopted to provide against the probability in some cases, the possibility in many cases, and the danger in all cases that such commingling will result in the loss of clients' money." Black v. State Bar, 57 Cal. 2d 219, 225-26, 368 P.2d 118, 122, 18 Cal. Rptr. 518, 522 (1962).

DEFINITIONS*

As used in the Disciplinary Rules of the Model Code of Professional Responsibility:

(1) "Differing interests" include every interest that will adversely affect either the judgment or the loyalty of a lawyer to a client, whether it be a conflicting, inconsistent, diverse, or other interest.

(2) "Law firm" includes a professional legal corporation.

(3) "Person" includes a corporation, an association, a trust, a partnership, and any other organization or legal entity.

(4) "Professional legal corporation" means a corporation, or an association treated as a corporation, authorized by law to practice law for profit.

(5) "State" includes the District of Columbia, Puerto Rico, and other federal territories and possessions.

(6) "Tribunal" includes all courts and all other adjudicatory bodies.

(7) "A bar association" includes a bar association of specialists as referred to in DR 2-105 (A) (1) or (4)·

(8) "Qualified legal assistance organization" means an office or organization of one of the four types listed in DR 2-103(D)(1)-(4), inclusive that meets all the requirements thereof

---

* Confidence" and "secret" are defi ned in DR 4-101(A).

INDEX TO MODEL CODE

A

Acceptance of Employment. *See*
   Employment, acceptance of
Acquiring interest in litigation. *See*
   Adverse effect on professional
   judgment, interests of lawyer
Address change, notification of,
   DR 2-102(A)(2)
Administrative agencies and tribunals'
   former employee, rejection of
   employment by,
   DR 9-101(B)
   improper influences on,
   EC 5-13, EC 5-21, EC 5-24,
   DR 5-107 (A), (B), EC 8-5,
   EC 8-6, DR 8-101 (A)
   representation of client, generally,
   Canon 7, EC 7-15, EC 7-16,
   EC 8-4, EC 8-8, DR 8-101 (A)
Admiralty practitioners,
   EC 2-14
Admission to practice,
   duty of lawyers as to applicants,
   EC 1-2, DR 1-101 (B)
   requirements for,
   EC 1-2, EC 1-3, EC 1-6,
   DR 1-101 (A)
Advancing funds to clients,
   EC 1-2, EC 1-3, EC 1-6,
   DR 1-101 (A)
   court costs,
   EC 5-8, DR 5-103 (B)
   investigation expenses,
   EC 5-8, DR 5-103 (B)
   medical examination,
   EC 5-8, DR 5-103 (B)
   personal expenses,
   EC 5-8, DR 5-103 (B)
Adversary system, duty of lawyer to,
   Canon 7
Adverse legal authority, duty to reveal,
   EC 7-23, DR 7-106 (B) (1)
Adverse effect
   on professional judgment of lawyer,
   Canon 5
      desires of third persons,
      EC 5-21, EC 5-24, DR 5-107
      interests of lawyer,
      EC 5-2 - EC 5-24, DR 5-101,
      DR 5-104
      interests of other clients,
      EC 5-14 - EC 5-20, DR 5-105,
      DR 5-106
Advertising. *See also* Name, use of.
   EC 2-6 - EC 2-15, DR 2-101,
   DR 2-102
   announcement of change of
      association,
      DR 2-102 (A) (2)
   announcement of change of firm name,
      DR 2-102 (A) (2)
   announcement of change of office
      address,
      DR 2-102 (A) (2)
   announcement of establishment of law
      office,
      DR 2-102 (A) (2)
   announcement of office opening,
      DR 2-102 (A) (2)
   books written by lawyer,
      DR 2-101 (H) (5)
   building directory,
      DR 2-102 (A) (3)
   cards, professional announcement,
      DR 2-102 (A) (1), (2)
   commercial publicity,
      EC 2-8 - EC 2-10, DR 2-101
   compensation for,
      EC 2-8, DR 2-101 (B),
      DR 2-101 (1)
   jurisdictional limitations of members of
      firm, required notice of,
      DR 2-102 (D)
   legal documents,
      DR 2-101 (H) (4)
   letterheads,
      of clients,
      DR 2-102 (A) (4)
      of law firm,
      DR 2-102 (A) (4), DR 2-102 (B)
      of lawyer,

DR 2-102 (A) (4) DR 2-102 (B)
limited practice,
    EC 2-14, DR 2-101 (B) (2),
    DR 2-105
magazine,
    DR 2-101 (B), DR 2-101 (I)
name, *See* Name, use of
newspaper,
    DR 2-101 (B), DR 2-101 (I)
office address change,
    DR 2-102 (A) (2)
office building directory,
    DR 2-102 (A) (3)
office establishment,
    DR 2-102 (A) (2)
office, identification of,
    DR 2-101 (B), DR 2-102 (A)
office sign,
    DR 2-102 (A) (3)
political,
    DR 2-101 (H) (1)
public notices,
    DR 2-101 (H) (2)
radio,
    DR 2-101 (B), DR 2-101 (D),
    DR 2-101 (I)
reasons for regulating,
    EC 2-6 - EC 2-10
sign,
    DR 2-102 (A) (3)
specialization,
    EC 2-14, DR 2-101 (B) (2),
    DR 2-105
television,
    EC 2-8, DR 2-101 (B) (D)
textbook,
    DR 2-101 (H) (5)
treatises,
    DR 2-101 (H) (5)
Advice by lawyer to secure legal services,
    EC 2-4 - EC 2-5, DR 2-104
client, former or regular,
    EC 2-4, DR 2-104 (A) (1)
close friend,
    EC 2-4, DR 2-104 (A) (1)
employment resulting from,
    EC 2-4, DR 2-104
motivation, effect of,
    EC 2-4

other laymen parties to class action,
    DR 2-104 (A) (5)
relative,
    EC 2-4, DR 2-104 (A) (1)
volunteered,
    EC 2-4, DR 2-104
within permissible legal service
    programs
    DR 2-104 (A) (3)
Advocacy, professional,
    Canon 7
Aiding unauthorized practice of law,
    Canon 3
Ambulance chasing. *See*
    Recommendation of professional
    employment.
Announcement card. *See* Advertising,
    cards, professional announcement.
Appearance of impropriety, avoiding,
    EC 55-6, Canon 9
Appearance of lawyer. *See*
    Administrative agencies,
    representation of client before; Courts,
    representation
    of client before; Legislature,
    representation of client before; Witness,
    lawyer acting as.
Applicant for bar admission. *See*
    Admission to practice.
Arbitrator, lawyer acting as,
    EC 5-20
Argument,
    before administrative agency,
        EC 7-15
    before jury,
        EC 7-24, EC 7-25, DR 7-106(C)
    before legislature,
        EC 7-16
    before tribunal,
        EC 7-19 - EC 7-25, DR 7-102, DR
        7-106
Associates of lawyer, duty to control,
    EC 1-4, DR 2-103, EC 3-8,
    EC 3-9, EC 4-2, DR 4-101 (D),
    DR 7-107
Association of counsel. *See also*
    Co-counsel; Division of legal fees.
client's suggestion of,
    EC 5-10, EC 5-11

lawyer's suggestion of,
 EC 5-10, EC 5-11, EC 6-3,
 DR 6-101 (1)
Assumed name. *See* Name, use of,
 assumed name
Attempts to exert personal influence on
 tribunal,
 EC 7-24, EC 7-29, EC 7-33,
 EC 7-36, DR 7-106 (C),
 DR 7-108, DR 7-110
Attorney-client privilege. *See also*
 Confidences of client;
 Secrets of client.
 EC 4-4, DR 4-101 (A),
 DR 7-102 (B) (1)
Attorney's lien. *See* Fee for legal services,
 collection of.
Availability of counsel,
 EC 2-1, EC 2-7, EC 2-24
 - EC 2-33

B

Bank accounts for clients' funds,
 EC 9-5, DR 9-102
Bar applicant. *See* Admission to
 practice.
 bar examiners, assisting,
 EC 1-2
Bar associations,
 disciplinary authority, assisting,
 EC 1-4, DR 1-103
 educational activities,
 EC 6-2
 lawyer referral service,
 DR 2-103 (C) (1), DR 2-103
 (D) (3)
 legal aid office,
 DR 2-103 (D) (1) (d)
Barratry. *See* Advice by lawyer to
 secure legal services;
 Recommendation of professional
 employment.
Bequest by client to lawyer,
 EC 5-5
Best efforts. *See* Zeal.
Bounds of law,
 difficulty of ascertaining,
 EC 7-2, 7-3, 7-4, 7-6

duty to observe,
 EC 7-1, DR 7-102
 generally,
 Canon 7
Bribes. *See* Gifts to tribunal officer or
 employee by lawyer.
Building directory. *See* Advertising,
 building directory.
Business card. *See* Advertising, cards,
 professional.

C

Calling card. *See* Advertising, cards,
 professional.
Candidate. *See* Political activity.
Canons, purpose and function of,
 Preamble & Preliminary
 Statement
Cards. *See* Advertising, cards.
Change of office address. *See*
 Advertising, announcement of change
 of office address.
Change of association. *See*
 Advertising, announcement of change
 of association.
Change of firm name. *See* Advertising,
 announcement of change of firm name.
Character requirements,
 EC 1-3
Class Action. *See* Advice by lawyer to
 secure legal services, parties to legal
 action.
Clients. *See also* Employment; Adverse
 effect on professional judgment of
 lawyer; Fee for legal services;
 Indigent parties, representation of;
 Unpopular party, representation of.
 appearance as witness for,
 EC 5-9, EC 5-10, DR 5-101 (B),
 DR 5-102
 attorney-client privilege,
 Canon 4
 commingling of funds of,
 EC 9-5, DR 9-102
 confidence of,
 Canon 4
 counseling,
 EC 7-5, EC 7-7, EC 7-8,

EC 7-9, EC 7-12, DR 7-102 (A)
    (7), (B) (1), DR 7-109 (B)

Clients' security funds,
    EC 9-7
Co-counsel. *See also* Association of
    counsel.
    division of fee with,
        DR 2-107
    inability to work with,
        DR 2-110 (C) (3)
Commercial publicity. *See*
    Advertising, commercial publicity.
Commingling of funds,
    EC 9-5, DR 9-102
Communications with
    one of adverse interests,
        DR 7-104
    judicial officers,
        EC 7-34, EC 7-35, EC 7-36,
        DR 7-104
    jurors,
        EC 7-29, DR 7-108
    opposing party,
        DR 7-104
    veniremen,
        EC 7-29, EC 7-31, DR 7-108
    witnesses,
        EC 7-28, DR 7-109
Compensation for recommendation of
    employment, prohibition against,
        DR 2-103 (B)
Competence, Mental. *See* Instability,
    mental or emotional; Mental
    competence of client, effect on
    representation.
Competence, professional,
    EC 2-30, Canon 6
Confidences of client,
    Canon 4
Conflicting interests. *See* Adverse
    effect on professional judgment of
    lawyer.
Consent of client, requirement of
    acceptance of employment though
    interests conflict,
        EC 5-14, EC 5-15, EC 5-16,
        EC 5-17, EC 5-18, EC 5-19,
        EC 5-20, DR 5-101, DR 5-105

acceptance of value from third
    person,
        EC 2-21, EC 5-22, EC 5-23,
        DR 5-107 (A), (B)
    advice requested from another
        lawyer, EC 4-2
    aggregate settlement of claims,
        DR 5-106 (A)
    association of lawyer,
        EC 2-22, DR 2-107 (A) (1)
    foregoing legal action,
        EC 7-7, EC 7-8
    multiple representation,
        EC 5-16, DR 5-105 (C)
    revelation of client's confidences and
        secrets,
        EC 4-2, EC 4-5, DR 4-101 (B) (3),
        DR 4-101 (C) (1)
    use of client's confidences and
        secrets,
        EC 4-2, EC 4-5, DR 4-101 (B) (3),
        DR 4-101 (C) (1)
    withdrawal from employment,
        EC 2-32, DR 2-110 (A) (2),
        DR 2-110 (C) (5)
Consent of tribunal to lawyer's
    withdrawal, requirement of,
        EC 2-32, DR 2-110 (A) (1),
        DR 2-110 (C)
Consultant. *See* Advertising,
    availability as consultant
Contingent fee, propriety of
    in civil actions,
        EC 2-20, EC 5-7, DR 5-103 (A) (2)
    in criminal actions,
        EC 2-20, DR 2-106 (C)
    in domestic relation cases,
        EC 2-20
Continuing legal education programs,
    EC 6-2
Contract of employment,
    fee provisions, desirability of
        writing,
        EC 2-19
    restrictive covenant in,
        DR 2-108
Controversy over fee, avoiding,
    EC 2-23

Copyright practitioner,
EC 2-14, DR 2-105 (A) (1)
Corporation, lawyer employed by,
EC 5-18

Counsel, designation as,
"General Counsel" designation,
DR 2-102 (A) (4)
"Of Counsel" designation,
DR 2-102 (A) (4)
Corporation, professional
legal. See Professional legal
corporation.
Counseling. See Client, counseling.
Courts. See also Consent of tribunal to
lawyer's withdrawal, requirement of;
Evidence, conduct regarding; Trial
tactics.
appointment of lawyers as counsel,
EC 2-29
courtesy, known customs of,
EC 7-36, EC 7-38, DR 7-106 (C)
(5), (6)
personal influence, prohibitions against
exerting,
EC 7-35, EC 7-36, DR 7-110
representation of client before,
Canon 7
Criminal conduct,
as basis for discipline of lawyer,
EC 1-5, DR 1-102 (A) (3)
duty to reveal information as to,
EC 1-4, DR 1-103
providing counsel for those accused of,
EC 2-27, EC 2-29
Criticism of judges and administrative
officials,
EC 8-6, DR 8-102
Cross-examination of witness. See
Witnesses, communications with.

D

Deceased lawyer,
payment to estate of,
EC 3-8, DR 3-102 (A) (1)
use of name by law firm,
EC 2-11, DR 2-102 (B)
De facto specialization,
EC 2-14, DR 2-105

Defender, public. See Public defender
office, working with.
Defense against accusation by client,
privilege to disclose confidences and
secrets,
DR 4-101 (C) (4)
Defense of those accused of crime,
EC 2-29, EC 2-31
Definitions,
p. 245
Delegation by lawyer of tasks,
EC 3-6
Desires of third parties, duty to avoid
influence of,
EC 5-21, EC 5-22, EC 5-23,
EC 5-24, DR 5-107
Differing interests. See also Adverse
effect on professional judgment of
lawyer.
Canon 5
Directory listing. See Advertising,
directories.
Discipline of lawyer, grounds for
advancement of funds to client
improper,
DR 5-103 (B)
advertising, improper,
DR 1-102, DR 2-102
associates, failure to exercise
reasonable care toward,
DR 4-101 (D)
bribery of legal officials,
DR 7-110 (A)
circumvention of disciplinary rule,
DR 1-102 (A) (3)
clients' funds, mismanagement of,
DR 9-102
communication with adverse party,
improper,
DR 7-104
communications with jurors,
improper,
DR 7-108
confidential information, disclosure of,
DR 4-101 (B)
conflicting interests, representation of,
DR 5-105, DR 5-106, DR 5-107
crime of moral turpitude,
DR 1-102 (A) (3)

criminal conduct,
DR 1-102, DR 7-102 (A) (7), (8),
DR 7-109 (A)
differing interests, improper
representation of,
DR 5-105 (A), (B)
disregard of tribunal ruling,
DR 7-106 (A)
division of fee, improper.
DR 7-107 (A)
employees, failure to exercise
reasonable care toward,
DR 3-102, DR 4-101 (D)
evidence, false or misleading use of,
DR 7-102 (A) (4), (6)
extra judicial statement, improper,
DR 7-107
failure to act competently,
DR 6-101
failure to act zealously,
DR 7-101 (A)
failure to disclose information
concerning another lawyer or
judge,
DR 1-103
failure to disclose information to
tribunal,
DR 7-102 (A) (3), DR 7-106 (B)
false accusations,
DR 8-102
false statement in bar application,
DR 1-101 (A)
fees
charging illegal or clearly
excessive,
DR 2-106 (A)
charging contingent fee in criminal
case,
DR 2-106 (C)
failure to return unearned,
DR 2-110 (A) (3)
further application of unqualified bar
applicant,
DR 2-101 (B)
guaranty of financial assistance,
DR 5-103 (B)
holding out as having limited
practice,
DR 2-105

holding out as a specialist,
DR 2-105
illegal conduct,
DR 1-102 (A) (3), DR 7-102 (A)
(7)
improper argument before
tribunal,
DR 7-106 (C)
institution of criminal charges,
DR 7-103 (A)
investigation of jurors,
DR 7-108
malpractice,
DR 6-102
moral turpitude, crime of,
DR 1-102 (A) (3)
public office, improper use of,
DR 8-101 (A)
publicity, improper,
DR 2-101
recommendation of professional
employment, prohibited,
DR 2-103
restrictive covenant, entering
prohibited,
DR 2-108
secrets, disclosure of,
DR 4-101
solicitation of business,
DR 2-103, DR 2-104
specialization, notice of,
DR 2-105
suggestion of need of legal services,
prohibited,
DR 2-104
unauthorized practice of the law, aiding
laymen in,
DR 2-104
violation of disciplinary rule,
DR 2-102 (A) (1)
withdrawal, improper,
DR 2-110 (A)
Disclosure of improper conduct
of another lawyer,
EC 1-4, DR 1-103
of bar applicant,
EC 1-2, EC 1-3, DR 1-101 (B)
of judge,
DR 1-103 (B)

toward juror or venireman,
EC 7-32, DR 7-108 (G)
Discretion of government lawyer,
exercise of,
EC 7-14
Discussion of pending litigation with
news media. *See* Trial publicity.
Diverse interests. *See* Adverse effect on
professional judgment of lawyer.
Division of legal fees,
consent of client, when required for,
EC 2-22, DR 2-107 (A) (1)
reasonableness of total fee,
requirement of,
EC 2-22, DR 2-107 (A) (3)
with associated lawyer,
EC 2-22, DR 2-107 (A)
with estate of deceased lawyer,
EC 3-8, DR 3-102 (A) (2), (3)
with laymen,
EC 3-8, DR 3-102 (A)

E

Education,
continuing legal education programs,
EC 6-2
of laymen to recognize legal
problems,
EC 2-1 - EC 2-5, EC 8-1
of laymen to select lawyers,
EC 2-6 - EC 2-15, EC 8-1
requirement of bar for applicant,
EC 1-2
Elections. *See* Political activity
Emotional instability. *See* Instability,
mental or emotional.
Employees of lawyer,
delegation of tasks,
EC 3-6
duty of lawyer to control,
EC 4-2, EC 4-3, DR 4-101 (D)
Employment. *See also* Advice by
lawyer to secure legal services;
Recommendation of professional
employment.
acceptance of,
generally,
EC 2-6 - EC 2-33
indigent client on behalf of,

EC 2-25
instances when improper,
EC 2-3, EC 2-4, EC 2-30,
DR 2-103, DR 2-104, Canon 5,
EC 6-1, EC 6-3, DR 6-101 (A)
(1), EC 9-3, DR 9-101 (A), (B)
public retirement from,
EC 9-3, DR 9-1101 (A), (B)
rejection of,
EC 2-26 - EC 2-33, DR 2-103
(E), DR 2-104, DR 2-109,
DR 2-110, EC 4-5, Canon 5,
EC 6-1, EC 6-3, DR 6-101 (A),
EC 9-3, DR 9-101 (A), (B)
unpopular cause, on behalf of,
EC 2-27
unpopular client, on behalf of,
EC 2-27
when able to render competent
service,
EC 2-30, EC 6-1, EC 6-3,
DR 6-101 (A) (1)
contract of,
desirability of,
EC 2-19
restrictive covenant in,
withdrawal from,
generally,
EC 2-32, DR 2-110, Canon 5,
EC 7-8
harm to client, avoidance of,
EC 2-32, DR 2-110 (B), Canon 5
permissive withdrawal,
DR 2-110 (C), Canon 5, EC 7-8
refund of unearned fee paid in
advance, requirement of,
EC 2-32, DR 2-110 (A) (3)
tribunal, consent to,
EC 2-32, DR 2-110
when arbitrator or mediator,
EC 5-20
Estate of deceased lawyer, *See* Division of
legal fees, with estate of deceased
lawyer.
Ethical considerations, purpose and
function of,
Preliminary Statement
Evidence, conduct regarding,
EC 7-24, EC 7-25, DR 7-102 (A),
(3) - (6)

Excessive fee. *See* Fee for legal
    services, amount of, excessive.
Expenses of client, advancing or
    guaranteeing payment of,
        EC 5-8, DR 5-103

F

Fee for legal services,
    adequate fee, need for,
        EC 2-17
    agreement, as to,
        EC 2-19, DR 2-106 (A)
    amount of
        excessive, clearly,
            DR 2-106
        reasonableness, desirability of,
            EC 2-17, EC 2-18
    collection of,
        avoiding litigation with client,
            EC 2-23
        client's secrets, use of in
        collecting or establishing,
            DR 4-101 (C) (4)
        liens, use of,
            EC 5-7, DR 5-103 (A) (1)
    contingent fee,
        EC 2-20, DR 2-106 (B) (8),
        DR 2-106 (C), EC 5-7,
        DR 5-103 (A) (2)
    contract as to, desirability of,
        written,
            EC 2-19
    controversy over, avoiding,
        EC 2-23
    determination of, factors to consider
        ability of lawyer,
            EC 2-19, DR 2-106 (B) (7)
        amount involved,
            DR 2-106 (B) (4)
        customary,
            DR 2-106 (B) (1)
        effort required,
            DR 2-106 (B) (1)
        employment, likelihood of pre-
        clusion of other,
            DR 2-106 (B) (2)
        experience of lawyer,
            EC 2-18, DR 2-106 (B) (7)

fee customarily charged in
    locality,
        DR 2-106 (B) (3)
    interests of client and lawyer,
        EC 2-17
    labor required,
        DR 2-106 (B) (1)
    nature of employment,
        EC 2-18
    question involved, difficulty and
        novelty of,
        DR 2-106 (B) (1)
    relationship with client,
        professional,
        EC 2-17, DR 2-106 (B) (6)
    reputation of lawyer,
        EC 2-18, DR 2-106 (7)
    responsibility assumed by
        lawyer,
        EC 2-18
    results obtained,
        EC 2-19, DR 2-106 (B) (4)
    skill requisite to services,
        EC 2-18
    time required,
        EC 2-18, DR 2-106 (B) (1)
    type of fee, fixed or contingent,
        EC 2-18, DR 2-106 (B) (8)
division of,
    EC 2-22, DR 2-107, DR 3-102
establishment of fee, use of client's
    confidences and secrets,
        DR 4-101 (C) (4)
excessive fee,
    EC 2-17, DR 2-106 (A)
explanation of,
    EC 2-17, EC 2-18
illegal fee, prohibition against,
    DR 2-106 (A)
persons able to pay reasonable fee,
    EC 2-17, EC 2-18
persons only able to pay a partial
    fee,
        EC 2-16
persons without means to pay a fee,
    EC 2-24, EC 2-25
reasonable fee, rationale against
    overcharging,
        EC 2-17

refund of unearned portion to client,
DR 2-110 (A) (3)
Felony. *See* Discipline of lawyer, grounds
for, illegal conduct.
Firm name. *See* Name, use of, firm name.
Framework of law. *See* Bounds of law.
Frivolous position, avoiding,
EC 7-4, DR 7-102 (A) (1)
Funds of client, protection of,
EC 9-5, DR 9-102
Future conduct of client, counseling as to.
See Clients, counseling.

G

"General counsel" designation,
DR 2-102 (A) (4)
Gift to lawyer by client,
EC 5-5
Gifts to tribunal officer or employee by
lawyer,
DR 7-110 (A)
Government legal agencies, working with,
DR 2-103 (C) (2), DR 2-103 (D)
(1) (C)
Grievance committee. *See* Bar
associations, disciplinary authority,
assisting.
Guaranteeing payment of client's cost
and expenses,
EC 5-8, DR 5-103 (B)

H

Harassment, duty to avoid litigation
involving,
EC 2-30, DR 2-109 (A) (1),
DR 7-102 (A) (1)
as limiting practice,
EC 2-8, EC 2-14, DR 2-101 (B)
(2), DR 2-105
as partnership,
EC 2-13, DR 2-102 (C)
as specialist,
EC 2-8, EC 2-14, DR 2-101 (B)
(2), DR 2-105

I

Identity of client, duty to reveal,
EC 7-16, EC 8-5

Illegal conduct, as cause for discipline,
EC 1-5, DR 1-102(A) (3),
DR 7-102 (A) (7)
Impartiality of tribunal, aiding in the,
Canon 7
Instability, mental or emotional
of bar applicant,
EC 1-6
of lawyer,
EC 1-6, DR 2-110 (B) (3),
DR 2-110 (C) (4)
recognition of rehabilitation,
EC 1-6
Improper influences,
gift or loan to judicial officer,
EC 7-34, DR 7-110 (A)
on judgment of lawyer. *See* Adverse
effect on professional judgment of
lawyer.
Improvement of legal system,
EC 8-1, EC 8-2, EC 8-9
Incompetence, mental. *See* Instability,
mental or emotional; Mental
competence of client.
Incompetence, professional. *See*
Competence, professional.
Independent professional judgment,
duty to preserve,
Canon 5
Indigent parties,
provision of legal services to,
EC 2-24, EC 2-25
representation of,
EC 2-25
Integrity of legal profession,
maintaining,
Preamble, EC 1-1, EC 1-4,
DR 1-101, EC 8-7
Intent of client, as factor in giving advice,
EC 7-5, EC 7-6, DR 7-102
Interests of lawyer. *See* Adverse effect on
professional judgment of lawyer,
interests of lawyer.
Interests of other client. *See* Adverse
effect on professional judgment of
lawyer, interests of other clients.
Interests of third person. *See* Adverse
effect on professional judgment of
lawyer, desires of third persons.

Intermediary, prohibition against
  use of,
    EC 5-21, EC 5-23, EC 5-24,
    DR 5-107 (A), (B)
Interview,
  with opposing party,
    DR 7-104
  with news media,
    EC 7-33, DR 7-109
Investigation expenses, advancing
  or guaranteeing payment,
    EC 5-8, DR 5-103 (B)

J

Judges,
  false statements concerning,
    DR 8-102
  improper influences on
    gifts to,
      EC 7-34, DR 7-110 (A)
    private communication with,
      EC 7-39, DR 7-110 (B)
  misconduct toward,
    criticisms of,
      EC 8-6
    disobedience of orders,
      EC 7-36, DR 7-106 (A)
    false statement regarding,
      DR 8-102
  name in partnership, use of,
    EC 2-12, DR 2-102 (B)
  retirement from bench,
    EC 9-3
  selection of,
    EC 8-6
Judgment of lawyer. See Adverse
  effect on professional judgment
  of lawyer.
Jury,
  arguments before,
    EC 7-25, DR 7-102 (A) (4), (5), (6)
  investigation of members,
    EC 7-30, DR 7-108 (E)
  misconduct of, duty to reveal,
    EC 7-32, DR 7-108 (G)
  questioning members after their
    dismissal,
    EC 7-29, DR 7-108 (D)

K

Knowledge of intended crime,
  revealing,
    DR 4-101 (C) (3)

L

Law firm. See Partnership.
Law office. See Partnership.
Law school, working with legal
  aid office or public defender office
  sponsored by,
    DR 2-103 (D) (1) (a)
Lawyer-client privilege. See Attorney-
  client privilege.
Lawyer referral services,
  fee for listing, propriety of paying,
    DR 2-103 (C) (1)
  request for referrals, propriety of,
    DR 2-103 (D)
  working with,
    EC 2-15, DR 2-103 (C), (D)
Laymen. See also Unauthorized
  practice of law.
  need of legal services,
    EC 2-6, EC 2-7, EC 2-8
  recognition of legal problems, need
    to improve,
    EC 2-2, EC 8-3
  selection of lawyer, need to
    facilitate,
    EC 2-9, EC 2-10, EC 8-3
Legal aid offices, working with,
    EC 2-25, DR 2-103 (D) (1)
Legal corporation. See professional legal
  corporation.
Legal directory. See Advertising, legal
  directories.
Legal documents of clients, duty to
  safeguard,
    EC 4-2, EC 4-3
Legal education programs. See
  Continuing legal education
  programs.
Legal problems, recognition
  of by laymen,
    EC 2-2, EC 8-3
Legal system, duty to improve,
    Canon 8

Legislature,
  improper influence upon,
    EC 9-2, EC 9-3, EC 9-4,
    DR 8-101 (A), DR 9-101 (B), DR
    9-101 (C)
  representation of client before,
    EC 7-17, EC 8-4, EC 8-5
  serving as a member of,
    EC 8-8, DR 8-101
Letterhead, *See* Advertising,
  letterheads.
Liability to client,
    Preamble, Canon 7
Licensing of lawyers,
  control of,
    EC 3-1, EC 3-3, EC 3-4,
    EC 3-5, EC 3-6, EC 3-9,
    DR 3-101
  modernization of,
    EC 3-5, EC 3-9, EC 8-3
Liens, attorneys',
    EC 5-7, DR 5-103 (A)
Limited practice, holding out as
  having,
    EC 2-14, DR 2-101 (B) (2),
    DR 2-1-5
Litigation,
  acquiring an interest in,
    EC 5-7, EC 5-8, DR 5-103 (A)
  expenses of advancing or
  guaranteeing payment of,
    EC 5-7, EC 5-8, DR 5-103 (B)
  pending, discussion of in the media,
    EC 7-33, DR 7-107
  responsibility for conduct of,
    EC 7-4, EC 7-5, EC 7-7,
    EC 7-10, EC 7-13, EC 7-14,
    EC 7-20, EC 7-22, EC 7-23,
    EC 7-24, DR 7-102, DR 7-103,
    DR 7-106
  to harass another, duty to avoid,
    EC 2-30, DR 2-110 (B),
    DR 2-109 (A) (1), EC 7-10,
    EC 7-14, DR 7-102 (A) (1),
    DR 7-103 (A)
  to maliciously harm another, duty to
  avoid,
    EC 2-30, DR 2-110 (B),
    DR 2-109 (A) (1), EC 7-10,

    EC 7-14, DR 7-102 (A) (1),
    DR 7-103 (A)
Living expenses of client, advances to
  client,
    EC 5-8, DR 5-103 (B)
Loan to judicial officer,
    EC 7-34, DR 7-110 (A)
Loyalty to client. *See* Zeal.
Lump-sum settlements,
    DR 5-106

M

Mandatory withdrawal. *See*
  Employment, withdrawal from,
  mandatory.
Mediator, lawyer serving as,
    EC 5-20
Medical expenses,
    EC 5-8, DR 5-103 (B)
Mental competence of client, effect on
  representation,
    EC 7-11, EC 7-12
Medical competence of lawyer. *See*
  Instability, mental or emotional.
Military legal service officers, being
  recommended by and collaborating
  with,
    DR 2-103 (D) (2)
Minimum fee schedule. *See* Fee for legal
  services, determination of, factors to
  consider, minimum fee schedule.
Misappropriation,
  confidences and secrets of client,
    EC 4-1, EC 4-5, EC 4-6,
    DR 4-101 (B) (3)
  property of client,
    EC 9-5, EC 9-6, DR 9-102
Misconduct. *See also* Discipline of lawyer.
  of client,
    EC 2-23, EC 2-26, EC 2-30,
    DR 2-110 (A), DR 2-110 (B) (1),
    DR 2-110 (C) (1), DR 4-101 (C),
    EC 7-5, EC 7-8, EC 7-9, EC 7-10
  of juror,
    DR 7-108 (D), DR 7-108 (F),
    DR 7-108 (G)
  of lawyer, duty to reveal to proper
    officials,

DR 1-103

Misleading advertisement or professional notice, prohibition of,
EC 2-9, EC 2-11, EC 2-13,
EC 2-14, DR 2-101, DR 2-102 (B), (C)

Moral character, requirement of,
EC 1-2, EC 1-3, EC 1-5,
DR 1-102

Moral factors considered in counseling,
EC 7-3, EC 7-5, EC 7-9

Moral turpitude, crime of as ground for discipline,
DR 1-102 (A) (3)

Multiple clients, representation of,
EC 5-14, EC 5-20, DR 5-105, DR 5-106

N

Name, use of
assumed name,
EC 2-11, DR 2-102 (B)
deceased partner's,
EC 2-11, DR 2-102 (A) (4),
DR 2-102 (B)
firm name,
EC 2-11, EC 2-12, DR 2-102 (B)
misleading name,
EC 2-11, DR 2-102 (B)
partners who hold public office,
EC 2-12, DR 2-102 (B)
predecessor firms,
EC 2-11, DR 2-102 (A) (4), (B)
retired partner,
EC 2-11, DR 2-102 (A) (4), (B)
trade name,
EC 2-11, DR 2-102 (B)
withdrawn partner's,
EC 2-11, DR 2-104 (B)

Need for legal services, suggestion of. *See* Advice by lawyer to secure legal services.

Negligence of lawyer,
Canon 6

Negotiations with opposite party,
EC 7-18, EC 7-20, DR 7-104,
DR 7-105

Neighborhood law offices, working with,
EC 2-6, EC 2-7, DR 2-103 (D) (1) (b)

Newspapers,
advertising in,
EC 2-8, EC 2-9, EC 2-10, DR 2-101 (A), (B), (C), (E), (F), (I)
news stories in,
EC 2-5, DR 2-104 (4)
news releases in, during or pending trial
EC 7-33, DR 7-107

Non-meritorious position, duty to avoid,
DR 2-109(A) (2), (3), EC 7-4,
EC 7-5, EC 7-14, DR 7-102 (A) (1), (2), DR 7-103 (A)

Non-profit organizations, legal aid services of,
EC 2-24, EC 2-25, DR 2-103 (D) (1), (4), DR 2-104 (A) (2), (3)

Notices. *See* Advertising.

O

Objectives of client, duty to seek,
EC 7-1, EC 7-10, DR 7-102

"Of Counsel" designation,
DR 2-102 (A) (4)

Offensive tactics by lawyer,
EC 7-4, EC 7-5, EC 7-10,
DR 7-102, DR 7-104, DR 7-105

Office building directory. *See* Advertising, building directory.

Office sign,
DR 2-102 (A) (3)

Opposing counsel,
EC 5-9, EC 7-20, EC 7-23,
EC 7-35, EC 7-37, EC 7-38,
DR 7-104, DR 7-106 (C) (5),
DR 7-110 (B) (2), (3)

Opposing party, communications with,
EC 7-18, DR 7-104

P

Partnership,
advertising. *See* Advertising.
conflicts of interest,
DR 5-105
deceased member,
payments to estate of,
EC 3-8

use of name,
  EC 2-11, DR 2-102 (A) (4), (B)
dissolved, use of name of,
  EC 2-11, EC 2-12, EC 2-13,
  DR 2-102 (A) (4), (B), (C)
holding out as, falsely,
  EC 2-13, DR 2-102 (B), (C)
members licensed in different
  jurisdictions,
  DR 2-102 (D)
name,
  EC 2-11, EC 2-12, DR 2-102 (B)
nonexistent, holding out falsely,
  EC 2-13, DR 2-102 (B), (C)
non-lawyer, with,
  EC 3-8, DR 3-103
professional corporation, with,
  DR 2-102 (C)
recommending professional
  employment of,
  EC 2-9
Patent practitioner,
  EC 2-14, DR 2-105 (A) (1)
Payment to obtain recommendation or
  employment, prohibition against,
  EC 2-8, DR 2-103 (B), (D)
Pending litigation, discussion of in media,
  EC 7-33, DR 7-107
Perjury,
  EC 7-5, EC 7-6, EC 7-26,
  EC 7- 28, DR 7-102 (A) (4), (6),
  (7), DR 7-102 (B)
Personal opinion of client's cause,
  EC 2-27, EC 2-28, EC 2-29,
  EC 7- 24, DR 7-106 (C) (4)
Political activity,
  EC 8-8, DR 8-101, DR 8-103
Political considerations in selection of
  judges
  EC 8-6, DR 8-103
Potentially differing interests. See
  Adverse effect on professional
  judgment of lawyer.
Practice of law, unauthorized,
  Canon 3
Prejudice to right of client, duty to avoid,
  EC 2-32, DR 2-110 (A) (2), (C)
  (3), (C) (4), DR 7-101 (A) (3)

Preservation of confidences of client,
  Canon 4
Preservation of secrets of client,
  Canon 4
Pressure on lawyer by third person. See
  Adverse effect on professional
  judgment of lawyer.
Privilege, attorney client. See
  Attorney-client privilege.
Procedures, duty to help improve,
  EC 8-1, EC 8-2, EC 8-9
Professional card of lawyer. See
  Advertising, cards, professional.
Professional impropriety, avoiding
  appearance of,
  EC 5-1, Canon 9
Professional judgment, duty to protect
  independence of,
  Canon 5
Professional legal corporations,
  Definitions (2), (4)
  DR 2-102 (B), EC 5-24,
  DR 5-107 (C)
Professional notices. See Advertising.
Professional status, responsibility not to
  mislead concerning,
  EC 2-11, EC 2-12, EC 2-14,
  DR 2-102 (B), (C), (D)
Profit-sharing with lay employees,
  authorization of,
  EC 3-8, DR 3-102 (A) (3)
Property of client, handling,
  EC 9-5, DR 9-102
Prosecuting attorney, duty of,
  EC 7-13, EC 7-14, DR 7-103
Public defender office, working with,
  DR 2-103 (C) (2), DR 2-103 (D) (1)
Public employment, retirement from,
  EC 9-3, DR 9-101 (B)
Public office, duty of holder,
  EC 8-8, DR 8-101
Public opinion, irrelevant to
  acceptance of employment,
  EC 2-26, EC 2-27, EC 2-29
Public prosecutor. See Prosecuting
  attorney, duty of.
Publication of articles for lay press,
  EC 2-2, EC 2-5

Publicity, commercial. *See* Advertising, commercial publicity.

Publicity, trial. *See* Trial publicity.

Q

Quasi-judicial proceedings,
    EC 7-15, EC 7-16, DR 7-107 (H),
    EC 8-4

R

Radio broadcasting. *See* Advertising, radio.

Reasonable fee. *See* Fee for legal services, amount of.

Rebate, propriety of accepting,
    EC 2-24, EC 2-25

Recognition of legal problems, aiding laymen in,
    EC 2-1, EC 2-5

Recommendation of bar applicant, duty of lawyer to satisfy himself that applicant is qualified,
    EC 1-3, DR 1-101 (B)

Recommendation of professional employment,
    EC 2-8, EC 2-15, DR 2-103

Records of funds, securities, and properties of clients,
    EC 9-5, DR 9-102 (B)

Referral service. *See* Lawyer referral services.

Rehabilitation of bar applicant or lawyer, recognition of,
    EC 1-6

Refund of unearned fee when withdrawing, duty to give to client,
    EC 2-32, DR 2-110

Regulation of legal profession,
    Canons 3 and 8, EC 3-1, EC 3-3,
    EC 3-9, EC 8-7

Representation of multiple clients. *See* Adverse effect on professional judgment of lawyer, interest of other clients.

Reputation of lawyer,
    EC 2-6, EC 2-7

Requests for recommendation for employment,
    EC 2-8, DR 2-103 (C)

Requirements for bar admission,
    EC 1-2, EC 1-6, DR 1-101 (B)

Respect for law,
    EC 1-5

Restrictive covenant,
    DR 2-108

Retention of employment. *See* Employment.

Retirement. *See also* Name, use of retired partner.
    from judicial office,
        EC 9-3, DR 9-101 (A)
    from public employment,
        EC 9-3, DR 9-101 (B)
    plan for laymen employees,
        EC 3-8, DR 3-102 (3)

Revealing of confidences,
    EC 4-1, EC 4-2, EC 4-6,
    DR 4- 101 (B) (1), (C), (D)

Revealing to tribunal jury misconduct,
    EC 7-32, DR 7-108 (G)

Runner, prohibition against use of,
    EC 2-8, DR 2-103 (B)

S

Sanction for violating disciplinary rules,
    Preliminary Statement

Secrets of client,
    Canon 4

Selection of lawyer,
    EC 2-6, EC 2-7, EC 2-8,
    EC 2-9, EC 2-11, EC 2-14,
    EC 2-15, DR 2-101

Selection of judges, duty of lawyers,
    EC 8-6, DR 8-102 (A)

Self-interest of lawyer. *See* Adverse effect on professional judgment of lawyer, interests of lawyer.

Self-representation, privilege of,
    EC 3-7

Settlement agreement,
    DR 5-106

Solicitation of business. *See* Advertising: Recommendation of professional employment.

Specialist, holding out as,
    EC 2-14, DR 2-105

Specialization,
admiralty,
EC 2-14
holding out as having,
EC 2-14, DR 2-105
patents,
EC 2-14, DR 2-105 (A) (1)
trademark,
EC 2-14, DR 2-105 (A) (1)
Speeches to lay groups,
EC 2-2, EC 2-5
State of mind of client, effect of in
advising him,
EC 7-11, EC 7-12
State's attorney. *See* Prosecuting
attorney.
"Stirring up litigation." *See* Advertising:
Advice by lawyer to secure
legal services; Recommendation of
professional employment.
Stockholders of corporation, corporate
counsel's allegiance to,
EC 5-18
Suit to harass another, duty to avoid,
EC 2-30, DR 2-109 (A) (1),
EC 7-10, EC 7-14, DR 7-102
(A) (1)
Suggested fee schedule. *See* Fees for
legal services, determination
of minimum fee schedule.
Suggestion of need for legal
services. *See* Advice by lawyer
to secure legal services.
Suppression of evidence,
EC 7-27, DR 7-102 (A) (2),
DR 7-103 (B), DR 7-106 (C) (7)

T

Technical and professional licenses,
DR 2-101 (B)(12), DR 2-102 (E)
Termination of employment. *See*
Confidences of client; Employment,
withdrawal from.
Third persons, desires of. *See* Adverse
effects on professional judgment of
lawyer, desires of third persons.
Threatening criminal process,
EC 7-21, DR 7-105 (A)

Trademark practitioner,
EC 2-14, DR 2-105 (A) (1)
Trade name. *See* Name, use of trade
name.
Trial publicity,
EC 7-33, DR 7-107
Trial tactics,
Canon 7
Tribunal, representation of client
before,
Canon 7
Trustee, client naming lawyer as,
EC 5-6

U

Unauthorized practice of law. *See also*
Division of legal fees; Partnership,
non-lawyer, with.
aiding a layman in the, prohibited,
EC 3-8, DR 3-101 (A)
distinguished from delegation of
tasks to subprofessionals,
EC 3-5, EC 3-6, DR 3-102 (A) (3)
functional meaning of,
EC 3-5, EC 3-9
self-representation by layman not
included in,
EC 3-7
Undignified conduct, duty to avoid,
EC 7-37, EC 7-38
Unlawful conduct, aiding client in,
DR 7-102 (A) (6), (7), (B) (1)
Unpopular party, representation of,
EC 2-27, EC 2-29, EC 2-30,
EC 2-31
Unreasonable fees. *See* Fee for legal
services, amount of.
Unsolicited advice. *See* Advice by lawyer
to obtain legal services.

V

Varying interests of clients. *See*
Adverse effect on professional
judgment of a lawyer, interests of other
clients.
Veniremen. *See* Jury.
Violation of disciplinary rule as cause for
discipline.
DR 1-102 (A) (1), (2)

Violation of law as cause for
discipline,
   EC 1-5, DR 1-102 (3), (4),
   EC 7-26, DR 7-102 (A) (3) - (8)
Voluntary gifts by clients to lawyer,
   EC 5-5
Volunteered advice to secure legal
services. *See* Advice by lawyer to secure
legal services.

W

Waiver of position of client,
   DR 7-101 (B) (1)
Will of client, gift to lawyer in,
   EC 5-5
Withdrawal. *See* Employment,
withdrawal from.
Witness,
communications with,
   EC 7-27, EC 7-28, DR 7-109
false testimony by,
   EC 7-26, EC 7-28, DR 7-102 (B) (2)
lawyer acting as,
   EC 5-9, EC 5-10, DR 5-101 (B),
DR 5-102
member of lawyer's firm acting as,
   DR 5-101 (B), DR 5-102
payment to,
   EC 7-28, DR 7-109 (C)
Writing for lay publication,
avoiding appearance of giving
general
solution,
   EC 2-5

Z

Zeal,
general duty of,
   EC 7-1, DR 7-101
limitations upon,
   EC 7-1, EC 7-2, EC 7-3,
   EC 7-5, EC 7-6, EC 78-7,
   EC 7-8, EC 7-9, EC 7-10,
   EC 7-15, EC 7-16, EC 7-17,
   EC 7-21, EC 7-22, EC 7-25,
   EC 7-26, EC 7-27, EC 7-36,
   EC 7-37, EC 7-38, EC 7-39,
   DR 7-101, DR 7-102, DR 7-105

TABLE B: RELATED SECTIONS IN
THE ABA MODEL RULES OF
PROFESSIONAL CONDUCT

TABLE B*

ABA MODEL CODE	ABA MODEL RULES
Canon 1: Integrity of Profession	
EC 1-1	Rule 1.1, 8.1(a)
EC 1-2	Rules 1.1, 6.1, 8.1(a)
EC 1-3	Rules 8.1(a), 8.3
EC 1-4	Rule 6.1
EC 1-5	Rule 8.4(a), (b), (c), (e) & (f)
EC 1-6	Rules 1.16(a)(2), 8.4(a)
DR 1-101	Rule 8.1(a)
DR 1-102(A)(1)	Rule 8.4(a)
DR 1-102(A)(2)	Rules 5.1(c), 5.3(b), 8.4(a)
DR 1-102(A)(3)	Rule 8.4(b) & (f)
DR 1-102(A)(4)	Rules 3.3(a)(1), (2) & (4), 3.4(a) & (b), 8.4(c) & (f)
DR 1-102(A)(5)	Rules 3.1, 3.2, 3.3(a)(1), (2) & (4), 3.4, 8.4(d) & (f)
DR 1-102(A)(6)	Rules 3.4(b), 8.4(b) & (f)
DR 1-103(A)	Rules 5.1(c), 8.3
DR 1-103(B)	Rule 8.1(b)
Canon 2: Making Counsel Available	
EC 2-1	Rules 6.1, 6.2(a), 7.2(a), 7.4
EC 2-2	Rules 6.1, 7.2(a)
EC 2-3	Rules 4.3, 7.3
EC 2-4	Rule 7.3
EC 2-5	Rule 7.1(b)
EC 2-6	Rule 7.2(a)
EC 2-7	Rules 7.2(a), 7.4
EC 2-8	Rules 7.1, 7.2(a) & (c), 7.4
EC 2-9	Rule 7.1
EC 2-10	Rule 7.1(a) & (c)
EC 2-11	Rule 7.5
EC 2-12	Rule 7.5(c)
EC 2-13	Rule 7.5(a) & (d)
EC 2-14	Rule 7.4
EC 2-15	Rule 7.2(a) & (c)
EC 2-16	Rules 1.5(a), 6.1, 6.2(b)

---

* Table B provides cross-reference to related provisions, but only in the sense that the provisions consider substantially similar subject matter or reflect similar concerns. A cross-reference does not indicate that a provision of the ABA Model Code of Professional Responsibility has been incorporated by the provision of a Model Rule. The Canons of the Code are not cross-referenced.

TABLE B
(Continued)

ABA MODEL CODE	ABA MODEL RULES
EC 2-17	Rule 1.5(a)
EC 2-18	Rule 1.5(a)
EC 2-19	Rule 1.5(b)
EC 2-20	Rule 1.5(c) & (d)
EC 2-21	Rules 1.7(b), 1.8(f)
EC 2-22	Rule 1.5(e)
EC 2-23	None
EC 2-24	Rule 6.1
EC 2-25	Rules 6.1, 6.2
EC 2-26	None
EC 2-27	Rule 6.2(a) & (c)
EC 2-28	Rule 6.2(a)
EC 2-29	Rule 6.2
EC 2-30	Rules 1.16(a)(1) & (2), 1.16(b)(3), 4.2, 6.2(b) & (c)
EC 2-31	Rules 1.3, 1.16(a) & (b)
EC 2-32	Rule 1.16(a), (b), (c) & (d)
EC 2-33	Rules 5.4, 6.3, 6.4
DR 2-101(A)	Rule 7.1
DR 2-101(B)	Rules 7.1, 7.2(a)
DR 2-101(C)	Rule 7.1
DR 2-101(D)	Rule 7.2(b)
DR 2-101(E)	Rule 7.1
DR 2-101(F)	Rule 7.1
DR 2-101(G)	Rule 7.1
DR 2-101(H)	Rule 7.2
DR 2-101(I)	Rule 7.2(c)
DR 2-102(A)	Rules 7.2(a), 7.4
DR 2-102(B)	Rules 7.2(a), 7.5(a) & (c)
DR 2-102(C)	Rule 7.5(d)
DR 2-102(D)	Rule 7.5(a) & (b)
DR 2-102(E)	Rules 7.1(a), 7.4, 7.5(a)
DR 2-103(A)	Rule 7.3
DR 2-103(B)	Rule 7.2(a) & (c)
DR 2-103(C)	Rules 5.4(a), 7.2(c), 7.3
DR 2-103(D)	Rules 1.16(a)(1), 5.4(a), 7.2(c), 7.3
DR 2-103(E)	Rules 1.16(a), 7.2(a), 7.3
DR 2-104	Rules 1.16(a), 7.3
DR 2-105	Rule 7.4
DR 2-106(A)	Rule 1.5(a)
DR 2-106(B)	Rule 1.5(a)
DR 2-106(C)	Rule 1.5(d)
DR 2-107(A)	Rule 1.5(e)
DR 2-107(B)	Rule 5.4(a)(1)

TABLE B
(Continued)

ABA MODEL CODE	**ABA MODEL RULES**
DR 2-108(A)	Rule 5.6
DR 2-108(B)	Rule 5.6
DR 2-109(A)	Rules 1.16(a)(1), 3.1
DR 2-110(A)	Rule 1.16(c) & (d)
DR 2-110(B)	Rules 1.16(a), 3.1, 4.4
DR 2-110(C)	Rules 1.2(e), 1.16(a) & (b)

Canon 3: Unauthorized Practice

EC 3-1	None
EC 3-2	None
EC 3-3	Rule 8.4(e)
EC 3-4	None
EC 3-5	None
EC 3-6	Rule 5.3(a)
EC 3-7	None
EC 3-8	Rule 5.4(a), (b) & (d)
EC 3-9	Rule 8.4(d)
DR 3-101(A)	Rule 5.5
DR 3-101(B)	Rules 5.5, 8.4(d)
DR 3-102	Rule 5.4(a)
DR 3-103	Rule 5.4(b)

Canon 4: Confidences and Secrets

EC 4-1	Rule 1.6(a)
EC 4-2	Rules 1.6(a) & (b)(1), 2.2(a)(1), 5.3(a)
EC 4-3	Rule 1.6(a)
EC 4-4	Rules 1.6(a), 1.13(e)
EC 4-5	Rules 1.8(b), 1.9(b), 1.10(a) & (b), 5.1(a) & (c), 5.3(a)
EC 4-6	Rule 1.9(b)
DR 4-101(A)	Rule 1.6(a)
DR 4-101(B)	Rules 1.6(a), 1.8(b), 1.9(b)
DR 4-101(C)	Rule 1.6(a) & (b)
DR 4-101(D)	Rules 5.1(a) & (b), 5.3(a) & (b)

Canon 5: Independent Judgment

EC 5-1	Rules 1.7(a) & (b), 1.8(c), (d), (e), (f), (g) & (j)
EC 5-2	Rules 1.7(b), 1.8(c)
EC 5-3	Rules 1.7(b), 1.8(a), (d) & (e)
EC 5-4	Rule 1.8(d)
EC 5-5	Rule 1.8(a) & (c)
EC 5-6	Rules 1.8(c), 7.3
EC 5-7	Rules 1.5(c), 1.8(e) & (j), 1.15
EC 5-8	Rule 1.8(e)
EC 5-9	Rules 1.7(b), 3.7

TABLE B
(Continued)

ABA MODEL CODE	ABA MODEL RULES
EC 5-10	Rule 3.7(a)
EC 5-11	Rules 1.7(b), 2.1
EC 5-12	Rule 1.2(a)
EC 5-13	Rule 1.7(b)
EC 5-14	Rules 1.7(a), 2.2(a)
EC 5-15	Rules 1.7, 2.2(a) & (c)
EC 5-16	Rules 1.7(b), 1.10(d), 1.13(d) & (e), 2.2(a)(1) & (b)
EC 5-17	Rule 1.7
EC 5-18	Rule 1.13(a), (b) & (c)
EC 5-19	Rules 1.7(b), 2.2(c)
EC 5-20	Rules 1.12(a) & (b), 2.2(a)(1)
EC 5-21	Rule 1.7
EC 5-22	Rule 1.7
EC 5-23	Rules 1.7(b), 5.4(c)
EC 5-24	Rules 1.13(a),(b) & (c), 5.4(a)
DR 5-101(A)	Rules 1.7, 1.8(j), 6.3, 6.4
DR 5-101(B)	Rules 1.7(b), 3.7
DR 5-102(A)	Rules 1.7(b), 3.7
DR 5-102(B)	Rules 1.7(b), 3.7
DR 5-103(A)	Rules 1.8(j), 1.15
DR 5-103(B)	Rule 1.8(e)
DR 5-104(A)	Rules 1.7(b), 1.8(a)
DR 5-104(B)	Rule 1.8(d)
DR 5-105(A)	Rules 1.7, 1.10(c), 2.2(a)
DR 5-105(B)	Rules 1.7, 1.13(e), 2.2(c)
DR 5-105(C)	Rules 1.7(b), 1.13(e), 1.9(a), 2.2
DR 5-105(D)	Rules 1.10(a), 1.12(c), 1.13(c)
DR 5-106	Rule 1.8(g)
DR 5-107(A)	Rules 1.7(b), 1.8(f)
DR 5-107(B)	Rules 1.7(a), 1.8(f), 1.13(b) & (c), 2.1, 5.4(c)
DR 5-107(C)	Rule 5.4(a) & (d)
Canon 6: Competence	
EC 6-1	Rule 1.1
EC 6-2	Rules 1.1, 5.1(a) & (b), 6.1
EC 6-3	Rule 1.1
EC 6-4	Rules 1.1, 1.3
EC 6-5	Rule 1.1
EC 6-6	Rule 1.8(h)
DR 6-101	Rules 1.1, 1.3, 1.4(a)
DR 6-102	Rule 1.8(h)

TABLE B
(Continued)

ABA MODEL CODE	ABA MODEL RULES
Canon 7: Zeal Within the Law	
EC 7-1	Rules 1.2(d), 1.3, 3.1
EC 7-2	Rule 1.2(d)
EC 7-3	Rule 2.1
EC 7-4	Rules 3.1, 3.3(a)(1)
EC 7-5	Rules 1.2(d), 3.1, 3.3(a)(4), 4.1
EC 7-6	Rule 3.4(a) & (b)
EC 7-7	Rule 1.2(a)
EC 7-8	Rules 1.2(a) & (c), 1.4, 2.1
EC 7-9	Rule 1.2(c)
EC 7-10	Rule 4.4
EC 7-11	Rules 1.14(a), 3.8(a), (b), (c) & (d), 3.9
EC 7-12	Rule 1.14
EC 7-13	Rule 3.8
EC 7-14	Rules 3.1, 3.8(a)(g), 4.4
EC 7-15	Rule 3.9
EC 7-16	Rule 3.9
EC 7-17	Rule 1.2(b)
EC 7-18	Rules 3.8(c), 4.2, 4.3
EC 7-19	None
EC 7-20	Rules 3.2, 3.5(a) & (c)
EC 7-21	Rule 4.4
EC 7-22	Rules 1.2(d), 3.4(c)
EC 7-23	Rule 3.3(a)(3)
EC 7-24	Rules 3.3(c) & (d), 3.4(e)
EC 7-25	Rules 3.1, 3.3(c), 3.4(c) & (e), 3.5(c), 3.6, 4.4
EC 7-26	Rule 3.3(a)(4)
EC 7-27	Rules 3.3(d), 3.4(a) & (f)
EC 7-28	Rules 3.4(b), 5.3(a)
EC 7-29	Rules 3.5(a), 4.4
EC 7-30	Rule 4.4
EC 7-31	Rules 3.5(a)
EC 7-32	Rules 3.3(a)(1), 3.5(a)
EC 7-33	Rule 3.6
EC 7-34	Rules 3.5(a), 8.4(f)
EC 7-35	Rule 3.5(b)
EC 7-36	Rule 3.5(c)
EC 7-37	Rules 3.5(c), 4.4
EC 7-38	Rules 1.3, 3.4(c)
EC 7-39	None
DR 7-101(A)	Rules 1.2(a), 1.3, 3.2, 3.5(c), 4.4

TABLE B
(Continued)

ABA MODEL CODE	ABA MODEL RULES
DR 7-101(B)	Rules 1.2(b), 1.16(b)
DR 7-102(A)(1)	Rules 3.1, 4.4
DR 7-102(A)(2)	Rule 3.1
DR 7-102(A)(3)	Rules 3.3(a)(2), 4.1
DR 7-102(A)(4)	Rules 3.3(a) & (c), 4.1
DR 7-102(A)(5)	Rules 3.3(a)(1), 4.1
DR 7-102(A)(6)	Rules 1.2(d), 3.4(b)
DR 7-102(A)(7)	Rules 1.2,(d), 3.3(a)(4), 4.1
DR 7-102(A)(8)	Rules 1.2(d), 8.4(a) & (b)
DR 7-102(B)	Rules 1.6(b)(1), 3.3(b), 4.1
DR 7-103(A)	Rule 3.8(a)
DR 7-103(B)	Rule 3.8(d)
DR 7-104	Rules 3.4(f), 4.2, 4.3
DR 7-105	None
DR 7-106(A)	Rules 1.2(d), 3.4(c) & (d), 3.5(a)
DR 7-106(B)	Rules 1.7(b)(2), 3.3(a)(3), 3.9
DR 7-106(C)	Rules 3.4(a), (c), (d) & (e), 3.5(c), 4.4
DR 7-107(A)-(I)	Rule 3.6
DR 7-107(D)-(F)	Rule 4.4
DR 7-107(J)	Rules 5.1(a) & (b), 5.3(a) & (b)
DR 7-108(A)	Rule 3.5(a) & (b)
DR 7-108(B)	Rules 3.5(a), (b), (c), (d) & (f), 5.3(b)
DR 7-108(C)	Rule 3.5(a) & (b)
DR 7-108(D)	Rule 4.4
DR 7-108(E)	Rules 4.4, 5.1(c), 5.3(b)
DR 7-108(F)	Rule 4.4
DR 7-108(G)	None
DR 7-109(A)	Rules 3.3(a)(2), 3.4(a)
DR 7-109(B)	Rule 3.4(a) & (f)
DR 7-109(C)	Rule 3.4(b)
DR 7-110(A)	Rules 3.5(a), 8.4(f)
DR 7-110(B)	Rule 3.5(a) & (b)

Canon 8: Improving Legal System

EC 8-1	Rule 6.1
EC 8-2	Rule 6.1
EC 8-3	Rules 6.1, 6.2(a), 8.4 (d)
EC 8-4	Rule 3.9
EC 8-5	Rules 3.3(a)(1), (2) & (4), 3.3(b), 3.9
EC 8-6	Rule 8.2(a)
EC 8-7	Rule 6.1
EC 8-8	Rule 1.11(c)
EC 8-9	Rule 6.1
DR 8-101	Rules 3.5, 8.4(b), (c) & (f)
DR 8-102	Rule 8.2(a)
DR 8-103	Rule 8.2(b)

TABLE B
(Continued)

ABA MODEL CODE	ABA MODEL RULES

Canon 9: Appearance of Impropriety

EC 9-1	Rule 8.4(f)
EC 9-2	Rules 1.4(a), 8.4(e)
EC 9-3	Rules 1.11(a), 1.12(a) & (b)
EC 9-4	Rules 7.1(b), 8.4(c) & (e)
EC 9-5	Rule 1.15
EC 9-6	Preamble, Rule 8.4(e)
EC 9-7	Rule 1.15
DR 9-101(A)	Rule 1.12(a) & (b)
DR 9-101(B)	Rules 1.11(a), 1.12(a) & (b)
DR 9-101(C)	Rules 1.2(e), 3.9, 7.1(b), 8.4(e)
DR 9-102	Rules 1.4(a), 1.15

COMPARISON BETWEEN THE ABA MODEL RULES OF PROFESSIONAL CONDUCT, 1983 AND 2002 VERSIONS, AS AMENDED, AND BETWEEN THE ABA MODEL RULES, 1983 AND 2002 VERSIONS, AND THE CALIFORNIA RULES OF PROFESSIONAL CONDUCT AND RELEVANT STATUTES

Table of Contents

ABA Model Rule	**Page**
MR 1.0	541
MR 1.1	542
MR 1.2	543
MR 1.3	544
MR 1.4	545
MR 1.5	545
MR 1.6	547
MR 1.7	550
MR 1.8	552
MR 1.9	554
MR 1.10	555
MR 1.11	556
MR 1.12	557
MR 1.13	557
MR 1.14	558
MR 1.15	558
MR 1.16	559
MR 1.17	561
MR 1.18	562
MR 2.1	563
MR 2.2	563
MR 2.3	563
MR 2.4	564
MR 3.1	564
MR 3.2	565
MR 3.3	565
MR 3.4	566
MR 3.5	567
MR 3.6	568
MR 3.7	568
MR 3.8	568
MR 3.9	569

ABA Model Rule	Page
MR 4.1	569
MR 4.2	569
MR 4.3	570
MR 4.4	570
MR 5.1	571
MR 5.2	572
MR 5.3	572
MR 5.4	573
MR 5.5	573
MR 5.6	577
MR 5.7	577
MR 6.1	577
MR 6.2	578
MR 6.3	578
MR 6.4	578
MR 6.5	578
MRs 7.1 - 7.5	579
MR 7.6	583
MR 8.1	583
MR 8.2	584
MR 8.3	584
MR 8.4	584
MR 8.5	585

ABA Model Rule 1.0

1983 Model Rules:

There was no MR 1.0 prior to the 2002 revisions.

2002 Model Rules:

MR 1.0 is entirely new. It adds as black-letter rule the former terminology section that was not part of the rules themselves.

MR 1.0(a) does not substantively change the definition of "belief" or "believes." California does not have this definition in any standard. The definition of "consult" or "consultation" was completely deleted.

MR 1.0(b) adds a new definition of "confirmed in writing." to mean informed consent given in writing *or* a writing that a lawyer promptly transmits to the person confirming an oral informed consent. An exception is made if a delayed transmittal is necessary.

Cal. Rule 3-310(A), the principal conflicts rule, contains a definition of "informed written consent" as being "the client's or former client's written agreement to the representation following written disclosure." In its turn, "disclosure" is defined as informing of "the actual and reasonably foreseeable adverse consequences" and "written" is defined by the Cal. Evidence Code standard. This California standard thus requires significantly more than the concept of "confirmed in writing" used in MR 1.0.

MR 1.0(c) amends the definition of "firm" or "law firm" to include law partnership, professional corporation, sole proprietorship or other association authorized to practice law; or lawyers employed in a legal services organization or the legal department of a corporation or other organization. Cal. Rule 1-100(B)(1) is worded differently but is substantially similar.

MR 1.0(d) changes the definition of "fraud" or "fraudulent" to include conduct that is fraudulent under the substantive or procedural law of the applicable jurisdiction and has a purpose to deceive. The definition deletes the comparison to negligent misrepresentation.

MR 1.0(e) provides a new definition for "informed consent": an agreement by a person to a proposed course of conduct after the lawyer has communicated adequate information and explanation about the material risks of and reasonably available alternatives to the proposed course of conduct.

Cal. Rule 3-310(A) contains a definition of "informed written consent", described above, which is similar, but requires a writing.

MR 1.0(f) made no substantive changes to the definitions of "knowingly," "known," or "knows." These terms are not defined by California's professional standards.

MR 1.0(g) added to the definition of "partner" a member of an association authorized to practice law. California professional standards do not define "partner."

MR 1.0(h) made no substantive changes to "reasonable" or "reasonably." California professional standards do not define these terms.

MR 1.0(i) made no substantive changes to "reasonable belief" or "reasonably believes." California professional standards do not define these terms.

MR 1.0(j) made no substantive changes to "reasonably should know." California professional standards do not define these terms.

MR 1.0(k) adds a definition of "screened" to mean "the isolation of a lawyer from any participation in a matter through the timely imposition of procedures within a firm that are reasonably adequate under the circumstances to protect information that the isolated lawyer is obligated to protect under these Rules or other law." California professional standards do not define these terms and currently are silent about whether screening is prohibited.

MR 1.0(l) made no substantive changes to the term "substantial". California professional standards do not define this term.

MR 1.0(m) added a definition of "tribunal" to mean a court, arbitrator in binding arbitration or a legislative body, administrative agency or other body acting in an adjudicative capacity. California professional standards contain no definition of this term.

MR 1.0(n) added definitions for the terms "writing" or "written" to mean a tangible or electronic record of a communication or representation, including handwriting, typewriting, printing, photo stating, photography, audio or video recording and, in 2012, added "electronic communications." A "signed" writing includes an electronic sound, symbol or process attached to or logically associated with a writing and executed or adopted by a person with the intent to sign the writing. Cal. Rule 3-310(A) incorporates the definition of "written" as defined for evidentiary purposes by Evidence Code §250. California's rules do not define "signed."

ABA Model Rule 1.1

1983 Model Rules:

Cal. Rule 3-110 prohibits a member from "intentionally, recklessly or repeatedly" failing to provide legal services with "competence," while MR 1.1 has a simpler and broader definition: "competent representation." In a separate rule, MR 1.3 re quires a lawyer to act with reasonable diligence and promptness in representing a client. Cal. Rule 3-110 combines the duties found in Model Rules 1.1 and 1.3 into a single rule by including "diligence" in the definition of "competence," though without further defining "diligence" in the Discussion section. See below for the Rule 1.3 comparison.

Cal. Rule 3-110 defines "competence" to mean the 1) diligence, 2) learning and skill, and 3) mental, emotional and physical ability reasonably necessary for the performance of services. MR 1.1 defines "competent representation" to mean the legal knowledge, skill, thoroughness and preparation necessary for representation. The "mental, emotional and physical ability" component found in Cal. Rule 3-110 is not found in MR 1.1.

Cal. Rule 3-110 allows a member who does not have sufficient learning and skill when the legal service is undertaken to take on the client's matter by

1) associating with or, where appropriate, professionally consulting another lawyer reasonably believed to be competent, or 2) acquiring sufficient learning and skill before performance is required. MR 1.1 does not contain this provision in the rule itself, but discusses these approaches with approval in the Comment to the rule.

Unlike MR 1.1, Cal. Rule 3-110, in its Discussion section, includes the duty to supervise the work of subordinate attorney and non-attorney employees or agents. However, both Cal. Rule 3-110 and MR 1.1 create a limited exception to the duty of competence in an emergency situation. Both state, the Cal. Rule in its Discussion, the Model Rule in its Comment, that in an emergency a lawyer may give advice or assistance in a matter in which the lawyer does not have the skill ordinarily required where referral to or consultation with another lawyer would be impractical. However, both note that even in an emergency, assistance should be limited to that reasonably necessary in the circumstances.

2002 Model Rules:

Rule 1.1 and comments [1]-[5] remained unchanged in the 2002 revisions. In 2012, new Comments [6] and [7], on "retaining or contracting with other lawyers," were added to identify factors lawyers should take into consideration when associating with non-firm lawyers in the representation of a client, Comment [6], and to provide guidance on allocating responsibility when lawyers not ordinarily associated with one another joinly represent a client, Comment [7]. In 2002, Comment [8] (previously numbered [6]), on maintaining competence, added that a lawyer should keep abreast of changes in the law and its practice and that a lawyer should comply with all required continuing legal educational requirements. References to peer review were deleted. In 2012, Comment [8] expressly identified an understanding of "the benefits and risks associated with relevant technology" as part of a lawyer's obligation to keep abreast of changes in the law and its practice.

Cal. Rule 3-110 is silent about these subjects. However, California lawyers are subject to mandatory continuing legal education requirements. (Ca.Bus. & Prof. Code §6070.)

ABA Model Rule 1.2

1983 Model Rules:

There is no California Rule of Professional Conduct that parallels MR 1.2 or directly addresses an attorney's duty to abide by the client's decision. Cal. Rule 3-510 requires an attorney to promptly communicate to the client the terms of criminal settlement offers and any written settlement offer in all other matters. Implicit in this and in case law, is the client's right to decide ultimate outcomes.

There is no California Rule of Professional Conduct that parallels MR 1.2(b) or addresses the topic of endorsement of a client's views.

There is no California Rule of Professional Conduct that parallels MR 1.2(c) or addresses this topic directly. However, in 2009, the Board of Governors of the State Bar recognized the importance of providing "short-term" limited-scope representation in a legal-services setting, both by approving Rule 1-650 (later approved by the California Supreme Court), and by adopting a resolution supporting "the expansion of limited scope legal assistance as part of the ongoing effort to increase access to legal services" in California. See Cal. Rule 1-650 and the Limited Scope Legal Assistance (Unbundling) Resolution, both in Part IV.

Additionally, Cal. Rule 3-400 prohibits an attorney from contracting with a client prospectively to limit the attorney's liability to the client for the attorney's professional malpractice. Cal. B&P Code § 6148 requires that the general nature of legal services to be provided the client be set forth in a fee agreement for a fixed or hourly fee. Also, case law discusses examining the fee contract to determine the scope of representation, at least from a malpractice point of view.

Similar to MR 1.2(d), Cal. Rule 3-210 prohibits an attorney from advising the violation of any law, rule, or ruling of a tribunal unless the attorney believes in good faith that such law, rule, or ruling is invalid. Cal. Rule 3-210 permits an attorney to take appropriate steps in good faith to test the validity of any law, rule, or ruling of a tribunal.

MR 1.2(e), which was moved into the Comment in 2002, addresses the topic of a lawyer limiting a representation due to ethical structures. Cal. Rule 3-500 and Cal. B&P Code §6068(m) are the closest counterparts. Both require that an attorney keep clients reasonably informed about significant developments relating to the representation, which would implicitly mandate the disclosure of any limitations on the scope of representation. Cal. Rule 3-700 requires that an attorney withdraw from representation where the attorney knows or should know that continuing to assist the client will result in a violation of the California Rules of Professional Conduct or the State Bar Act.

2002 Model Rules:

MR 1.2(a) adds that a lawyer shall consult with the client about the means by which the client's objectives are to be pursued, consistent with MR 1.4, but also adds that a lawyer may act on behalf of the client if the actions are impliedly authorized to carry out the representation.

MR 1.2(c) was amended to require that limitations upon the scope of representation be reasonable. See comparison of California rules and statutes to the 1983 version of MR 1.2(c).

MR 1.2(e), requiring a lawyer to consult with the client on objectives inconsistent with the rules, was deleted from the black-letter rule and placed in comment [13]. See comparison of California rules and statutes to the 1983 version of MR 1.2(e).

ABA Model Rule 1.3

1983 Model Rules:

Cal. Rule 3-110 combines the duties found in ABA Model Rules 1.1 and 1.3 into a single rule. See our comment under MR 1.1. Paragraph 1 of the Comment to MR 1.3 shapes the definition of "diligence" in its first two sentences, while the second sentence adds that a lawyer should act "with zeal in advocacy upon the client's behalf." The California rule on competence, which serves to cover diligence, does not further define the term. The Model Rule 1.3 comment continues the concept of zealous advocacy found in the ABA Model Code (see DR 7-101), with the caveat that a lawyer "is not bound" to "press for every advantage" on behalf of a client. California rules contain no requirement of zeal or of zealous advocacy.

2002 Model Rules:

No change was made to the black letter rule.

Comment [1] added language that diligence does not require the use of offensive tactics or treating third parties with lack or respect and courtesy. New comment [2] suggests that a lawyer's work load should be controlled so that each matter may be competently handled. Comment [3] adds language suggesting that a lawyer may agree to postponements of events which do not prejudice the client. New comment [5] suggests that diligence may require sole practitioners to provide for handling of client their matters in the event of the lawyer's death or disability. California has no similar comment under its Rule 3-110.

***

ABA Model Rule 1.4

1983 Model Rules:

Cal. Rule 3-500 is substantially similar to MR 1.4(a). It requires an attorney to keep the client reasonably informed about significant developments relating to the engagement and to promptly comply with reasonable requests for information. There is no California rule that parallels MR 1.4(b), describing the extent to which a lawyer must keep the client informed. However, the concept of informed consent of the client is mentioned in several places in the California Rules. See, e.g., Rule 3-310 and Rule 4-200.

2002 Model Rules:

MR 1.4(a) was amended in 2002 to require the lawyer to promptly inform the client of any matter requiring the client's informed consent to reasonably consult about the means of accomplishing the client's objectives, and to consult with the client when the lawyer's conduct is not permitted by the Rules of Professional Conduct or other law. In 2012, Comment [4] was revised to state more generally that "[a] lawyer should promptly respond to or acknowledge client communications," however received. Previously, the comment had been limited to returning client telephone calls.

The California rules do not contain any counterparts to the additions to MR 1.4(a) or Comment [4].

***

ABA Model Rule 1.5

1983 Model Rules:

MR 1.5 (a) requires lawyers to charge a reasonable fee. The standard under Cal. Rule 4-200(A) concerns making an agreement for charging, or collecting an *unconscionable or illegal* fee. This appears to set a higher threshold for discipline, though there is little empirical evidence that these new rules are enforced differently.

As opposed to the Model Rule's eight factors, Cal. Rule 4-200 contains eleven factors to be used in considering the reasonableness of a fee. Factor (1) of MR 1.5 appears in the California rule as two different factors. One factor mentioned in MR 1.5 is *not* present in the California rule — the fee customarily charged in the community for the legal services. This factor, taken directly from Model Code DR 2-106, was also not present in former Cal. Rule 2-107. The history of the 1989 revision indicates that the Rules Commission never considered adding this provision.

The California rule considers the following enumerated factors not in MR 1.5: (1) the amount of the fee in proportion to the value of the services; (2) the relative sophistication of the attorney and client; and (11) the client's informed consent. Factors (1) and (2) were added by the 1989 rules revision. Consent was also considered in former rule 2-107. It is unclear how factor (1) is distinguishable from California factor (3), which tracks the intent of MR 1.5(a)(1).

The California rule's reference to informed consent tracks Ca. B&P Code §§6147 and 6148, which require contingent fees (§6147) and hourly and, with exceptions, fixed fees (§6148) to be in writing. Note that the standard for failing to meet the requirements of these two sections is to allow the lawyer a "reasonable" fee. These sections thus set different standards for voiding fee contracts than those used for discipline.

These sections are at variance from the ABA rule. MR 1.5(c) requires contingent fee agreements to be in writing, but MR 1.5(b), governing other fees, *prefers* but does not require writing, merely requiring that the basis of the fee be communicated to the client.

Until 1989, former Cal. Rule 2-107's enumerated factors ambiguously referred to both "unconscionable" and "unreasonable" fees. In 1989, the Rules Commission adopted the uniform standard of "unconscionable," thereby rejecting the ABA standard of "reasonableness" (see MR 1.5(a)). This is despite the fact that the Ca. B&P Code fee agreement sections themselves adopt the "reasonableness" standard (failure to comply with the sections' requirements results in a contract voidable at the client's election and allows the recovery of a "reasonable" fee).

The Ca. B&P Code also has provisions requiring a lawyer to notify a client of the client's right to mandatory fee dispute arbitration before the lawyer may sue the client for fees (§§ 6299 et seq.). The Model Rules have no such requirement.

MR 1.5(e), concerning splitting fees among lawyers from different firms, varies materially from Cal. Rule 2-200. MR 1.5 takes the more traditional view, requiring that the second lawyer may not receive a fee unless it is either proportional to that attorney's participation in the matter or, with client consent, the second attorney undertakes "joint responsibility" for the case. The California rule allows "bare" referral fees, i.e., without the second lawyer either participating in the representation or assuming joint responsibility, so long as certain specific requirements are satisfied. Under paragraph (a), those requirements are that the fee division is subject to the client's written consent after full disclosure and that the total fee is not increased as a result of the fee division. Paragraph (b) permits lawyers to give an after-the-fact *unexpected* gratuity, not subject to a prior arrangement. The Cal. Rule has been interpreted to allow payments to contract attorneys. This rule is consistent with former Cal. Rule 2-108, which had been liberalized in the early 1980's.

2002 Model Rules:

MR 1.5(a) was amended to add a prohibition against unreasonable amounts for expenses. While unreasonable fees are subject to fee arbitration (Ca. B&P Code §§6200 et seq.) California continues to discipline only for unconscionable or illegal fees.

MR 1.5 (b) was amended to require communication as to the scope of the representation; the basis or rate of expenses for which the client will be responsible; and any changes in the basis or rate of the fee or expenses. Similarly, Ca. B&P Code §6148 requires setting forth in a written fee agreement any other standard rates and charges applicable to the case (subd.(a)(1)) and the general nature of the legal services to be performed (subd.(a)(2)).

Comment [4] notes that a fee paid in property may be regarded as a "business transaction" subject to MR 1.8(a). While California has no corresponding rule or comment, case law covers this issue.

MR 1.5(c) added a provision that a contingency fee agreement must clearly notify the client of any expenses for which the client will be liable whether or not the client is the prevailing party. California contains no similar provisions. Comment [3] clarifies that a contingent fee is subject to the reasonableness standard. Comment [5] deleted a suggestion that a lawyer should offer a client an alternative to a contingent fee in certain circumstances.

MR 1.5(e) requires a client's agreement to all fee splits among lawyers, in addition to maintaining that the division be in proportion to the services performed and to the share each lawyer will receive. The agreement must be confirmed in writing, but need not be signed by the client. This contrasts with Cal. Rule 2-200(A)(1) which requires the client's consent in writing and, as noted above, sets a more liberal standard for fee-splitting.

ABA Model Rule 1.6

1983 Model Rules:

California Rule of Professional Conduct 3-100 is analogous to Model Rule 1.6. Until July 1, 2004, California was the sole jurisdiction in the country in which there were no express exceptions to the absolute statutory duty of confidentiality. This absolute duty had been embodied in California Business and Professions Code section 6068(e): "to maintain inviolate the confidence, and at every peril to himself or herself to preserve the secrets, of his or her client." Anomalously, Ca. Evid. Code § 956.5 had provided that there was no attorney client *privilege* if the lawyer believed that disclosure of privileged information

was necessary to prevent the client's commission of a criminal act that the
lawyer believes is likely to result in death or substantial bodily harm, the same
standard used in MR 1.6.

In 2003, the California legislature passed, and the governor signed, AB 1101,
modifying B&P Code § 6068(e) effective July 1, 2004. The language of subsection (e) was placed into section (e)(1); subsection (e)(2) creates an exception
that closely conforms to the 1983 version of MR 1.6(b)(1). As with the 1983 version of MR 1.6, the new California statute uses the standard of a lawyer's reasonable belief in the necessity of disclosure, and permits (but does not require)
an attorney to disclose confidential information to prevent a criminal act that
would result in death or substantial bodily harm. The California code section,
however, does not require that the harm be "imminent."

In addition to providing the first express exception to confidentiality in
California, the legislation also resolved the inconsistency between Evidence
Code §956.5 and B&P Code § 6068(e).

In addition to § 6068(e)(2), AB 1101 also provided that a Task Force
appointed by the President of the State Bar, in consultation with the Supreme
Court, make recommendations for a rule of professional conduct that would
address certain issues the legislature had identified would arise in the implementation of the code section. For example, two issues identified in AB 1101
for consideration by the Task Force were (1) whether an attorney must inform
the client of the attorney's discretion under § 6068(e)(2) to reveal the client's
confidential information, and (2) whether an attorney must take steps to
attempt to dissuade the client from committing the perceived criminal conduct before revealing the client's confidential information. Paragraph (C)(2) of
rule 3-100 requires an attorney, "if reasonable under the circumstances," to
inform the client of the attorney's ability to confidential information pursuant
to § 6068(e)(2), and paragraph (C)(1) provides that an attorney, "if reasonable
under the circumstances," must "make a good faith effort to persuade the
client" not to commit the perceived criminal conduct before the attorney
reveals the client's confidential information. In addition, rule 3-100(E)
expressly provides that an attorney who chooses not to reveal confidential
information, even when permitted under the rule, does not violate the rule.
Neither the 1983 nor the 2002 version of Model Rule 1.6 have provisions analogous to paragraphs (C)(1), (C)(2) or (E).

MR 1.6(b)(2) has no California equivalent, though case law indicates a
lawyer may disclose confidential information to defend a claim brought against
a lawyer by the client. See, e.g., *Arden v. State Bar*, 52 Cal.2d 310, 320, 341
P.2d 6 (1959); *Carlson Collins v. Banducci* 257 Cal.App.2d 212, 227-28, 64 Cal.
Rptr. 915 (1967).

2002 Model Rules:

MR 1.6 has undergone three extensive revisions since 1983, one in
August 2002, a second in August 2003, and a third in August 2012. As amended
in 2002, MR 1.6(b)(1) permits disclosure of confidential information to prevent
reasonably certain death or substantial bodily harm. This is a substantial

change from the 1983 rule, which required that the harm be a *criminal act* by *the client*, that the harm be *imminent*, and expressly referred to the *lawyer's belief of the likelihood* of harm. Outside of the absence of the word "imminent," the new California code section tracks the 1983 language, and is not consistent with these changes. See discussion of Cal. Rule 3-100 under "1983 Model Rules," above.

MR 1.6(b)(2) and (b)(3) were both amended in 2003. Both subsections concern permitted disclosures of otherwise confidential information where the lawyer's legal services have been used to further a client's commission of a crime or fraud. Subsection (b)(2) permits a lawyer to reveal confidences to *prevent* the client from committing a crime or fraud seriously injurious to the financial interests of another. Subsection (b)(2) permits revelation to "mitigate or rectify" such substantial financial injury resulting from the client's crime or fraud *after* it has occurred. California has no corresponding rule or statute.

New MR 1.6(b)(4), added in 2002, permits disclosure of confidential information to enable the lawyer to secure legal advice about the lawyer's compliance with the Model Rules. There is no corresponding California rule or statute.

MR 1.6(b)(6), added in 2002, permits disclosure of confidential information to comply with other law or a court order. There is no similar California rule or statute.

In 2012, new section (b)(7) was added. It provides that confidential information may be disclosed to the limited extent necessary to clear potential conflicts of interest that might arise from a lawyer's migration from one firm to another or changes in the composition or ownership of a law firm, provided "the revealed information would not compromise the attorney-client privilege or otherwise prejudice the client." Two comments, discussed below, elaborate on new paragraph (b)(7). There is no similar California rule or statute.

Also in 2012, new paragraph (c) was added. It requires that a lawyer "make reasonable efforts to prevent the inadvertent or unauthorized disclosure of, or unauthorized access to" confidential client information. A comment, discussed below, has been extensively revised to elaborate on the duties provided in new paragraph (c). There is no similar California rule or statute.

The comments to MR 1.6 were also changed significantly in 2002. The most important of these changes appear in Comment paragraphs (6), (7), and (8). Comment paragraph 6 explains the removal of the word "imminent" from the rule, noting that "present and substantial" harm at a future date, such as "discharg[ing] toxic waste into a town's water supply," is equally dangerous and equally disclosable. Comment paragraphs (7) and (8) expand on the justifications for the amendments to (b)(2) and (b)(3) respectively. California has no such commentary, as it has no (b)(2) or (b)(3) equivalent. Moreover, the statute contains no commentary.

In addition to the 2002 revisions, Comments [13] and [14] were added in 2012 to elaborate upon and provide guidance concerning new section (b)(7) on clearing conflicts of interest, described above. Comment [13] states that limited disclosure is permitted "only once substantive discussions regarding the new relationship have occurred," and provides examples of when disclosure is strictly prohibited. Comment [14] includes an important exception to restricting the use of such information, i.e., there is no restriction on the use of information acquired by means independent of any disclosures pursuant to (b)(7). There is no similar California rule or statute.

Further, in 2012 Comments [18] (formerly numbered [16]) and [19] (formerly numbered [17]) were amended to elaborate upon and provide guidance concerning new paragraph (c) on duties with respect to inadvertent or unauthorized disclosure of confidential information, as described above. Under Comment [18], for example, a lawyer's reasonable efforts to prevent access to or disclosure of the information would avoid a violation of paragraph (c). Comment [19] added a sentence cautioning lawyers that the Model Rule is not exclusive in this area and that "other law, such as state and federal laws that govern data privacy," may require the lawyer to take additional steps to protect confidential client information. There is no similar California rule or statute, though there is California case law addressing these issues.

ABA Model Rule 1.7

1983 Model Rules:

Cal. Rule 3-310 is the California conflict of interest rule that parallels MR 1.7. MR 1.7 addresses conflicts of interest generally, focusing on an attorney's loyalty to and impartial representation of each client. In contrast, Cal. Rule 3-310 defines specific situations in which an attorney's loyalty to an individual client or former client may be impaired and requires the attorney to take specific steps to address each specific situation.

Where MR 1.7 always requires client consent after consultation, though not explicitly *written* consent, Cal. Rule 3-310 always requires written attorney disclosure to the client, but does not always require client consent following disclosure. Written disclosure under the California rule is broader than in MR 1.7, including a requirement that the lawyer inform the client of "the relevant circumstances and of the actual and reasonably foreseeable adverse consequences" to the client. MR 1.7, unlike Cal. Rule 3-310, contains an absolute bar to representation based upon an attorney's "reasonable belief" regarding the adverse impact of a conflict of interest. Moreover, paragraph (5) of the Comment to MR 1.7 states that when a client should not objectively agree to waive a limitation on the loyalty of the attorney, the lawyer cannot appropriately ask for such waiver even where the client would be willing to consent.

MR 1.7(a) addresses representation of one client that is directly adverse to another client, while MR 1.7(b) addresses representations that may be materially limited by the attorney's relationship with another client or a third person, or by the attorney's own interests. Cal. Rule 3-310(B), by contrast, defines four specific situations where an attorney must disclose to the client in writing "the actual and reasonably foreseeable adverse consequences to the client" of the attorney's relationships or interests. These situations include where the attorney: 1) has a legal, business, financial, professional, or personal relationship with a party or witness in the same matter; 2) knows or reasonably should know that the attorney previously had such a relationship, and that the previous relationship would substantially affect the attorney's representation; 3) has or had such a relationship with another who would be affected substantially by the resolution of the matter; or 4) has or had a legal, business, financial, or professional interest in the subject matter of the representation.

The Discussion section clarifies that 3-310(B) deals with the issues of adequate disclosure to the present clients of the attorney and is not intended to require either the disclosure to a former client. The Discussion also clarifies that 3-310(B) is not intended to apply to the relationship of an attorney to another party's lawyer, a relationship governed by Cal. Rule 3-320.

MR 1.7(b)(2) addresses representation of multiple clients in a single matter. Cal. Rule 3-310(C), its parallel, states that an attorney may not, without the informed written consent of each client, either accept representation of more than one client in a matter in which the interests of the clients *potentially* conflict (3-310(C)(1)), or accept or continue representation of more than one client in a matter in which the interests of the clients *actually* conflict [3-310(C) (2)]. "Informed written consent" is defined in sub-section (A) of the Cal. Rule. While MR 1.7(b)(2), again, refers only to consent after consultation, without the explicit understanding that the consent be written, the rule also requires that the consultation include an explanation of the implications of the joint representation and the discussion of both the risks and advantages.

Cal. Rule 3-310(C)(3) specifically addresses the conflict of interest when a lawyer concurrently represents a client in one matter against the interests of an entity which is a client in a second matter. This specific admonition seems to be within the purview of both MR 1.7(a) and MR 1.7(b), depending on the circumstances in which the situation arises.

2002 Model Rules:

MR 1.7, has been renamed to clarify that it covers only conflicts of interest among *current* clients. It has also been substantially reorganized. However, the substantive standards are essentially unchanged. New MR 1.7(a) articulates direct aversity and the "materially limited" representation contained in MR 1.7(b) in the 1983 version. MR 1.7(a) adds the requirement that there be a "significant risk" of this material limitation. MR 1.7(b)(1)-(3) provide the prerequisites to representation notwithstanding the conflict.

MR 1.7(b)(4) is new. It requires that each affected client gives informed consent confirmed in writing as an additional prerequisites to representation notwithstanding the conflict. This moves the Model Rule conflict provisions substantially closer to the California requirement of the client's written consent after written disclosure.

Comment [5] is new. It sets forth options for how the lawyer may respond to "unforeseen developments" that give rise to a conflict during the course of a representation.

A lawyer's obligation to withdraw where a conflict arises after a representation has begun will be reviewed in several contexts, including common representations. Where more than one client is involved, the question is whether a lawyer must terminate both representations, and whether client consent is sufficient to permit the lawyer to continue any participation in the matter.

Comment [12] provides for client revocation of consent and termination of the lawyer. Comment [22] permits a client's prospective consent to conflicts, but not where they are open-ended or would waive "non-consentable" conflicts.

New comment [24] provides that a lawyer may generally take inconsistent positions on behalf of different clients. Comment [25] addresses class actions. It states that "unnamed members of the class are not ordinarily considered to be clients." New comment [34] suggests that a lawyer may take adverse positions to a corporate affiliate as corporate family conflicts. California's rules and statutes do not expressly cover these subjects. There is a California case law that indicates that passive class members in a class action may be considered clients of the lawyer *after* the class has been certified.

Since MR 2.2 ("Lawyer as Intermediary") has been deleted, this rule and commentary now cover multiple client representation formerly discussed in MR 2.2. Ca. Rule 3-310(C)(1) and (2) cover multiple client representation.

ABA Model Rule 1.8

1983 Model Rules:

The extensive breadth of MR 1.8 covers territory found in several different California rules. We review each sub-section of MR 1.8 in turn.

MR 1.8(a): This rule and Cal. Rule 3-300 are substantially similar, except that the Cal. Rule additionally requires that the client be advised *in writing* about seeking the advice of an independent lawyer. Cal. Rule 3-300, unlike MR 1.8(a), expressly addresses the timing of the client's consent, mandating that such consent is only possible after the disclosure requirements of the rule are met.

MR 1.8(b): There is no California Rule of Professional Conduct which parallels MR 1.8(b) or addresses this topic. However, by implication, the duties of competence (Cal. Rule 3-110) and confidentiality (Cal. B&P Code §6068(e)) would generally prohibit this behavior.

MR 1.8(c): Like MR 1.8(c), Cal. Rule 4-400 prohibits an attorney from inducing a client to make a substantial gift, including a testamentary gift, to the member or to the member's immediate family. But the Cal. Rule does not specifically address the preparation of donative instruments.

MR 1.8(d): There is no California Rule of Professional Conduct that parallels MR 1.8(d) or expressly addresses this topic. However, there is California case law which has permitted such agreements when accompanied by appropriate disclosures and consent. See *Maxwell v. Superior Court*, 30 Cal. 3d 606 (1982).

MR 1.8(e): Cal. Rule 4-210 is similar to but broader than MR 1.8(e). It addresses not only the payment of, but the offer to pay, personal and business expenses of a prospective or existing client. Cal. Rule 4-210 permits an attorney to advance the costs of prosecuting or defending a claim or action or otherwise protecting or promoting the client's interests, the repayment of which may be contingent on the outcome of the matter. Cal. Rule 4-210, unlike MR 1.8(e), permits the attorney: 1) with the consent of the client, to pay and agree to pay expenses to third persons from funds collected or to be collected for the client as a result of the representation; and (2) after employment, to lend money to the client upon the client's promise in writing to repay such loan. Unlike MR 1.8(e), Cal. Rule 4-210 does not address the representation of indigent clients.

MR 1.8(f): Cal. Rule 3-310(F) is similar, except that 3-310(F) requires that the client's consent be in writing and provides limited express exceptions to the duty of attorney disclosure and client consent.

MR 1.8(g): Cal. Rule 3-310(D) is similar, prohibiting an attorney who represents two more clients from entering into an aggregate settlement of the claims regarding those clients without the informed written consent of each client. The California Rule makes no specific reference to criminal matters.

MR 1.8(h): Both MR 1.8(h) and Cal. Rule 3-400(B) allow an attorney to settle an existing claim with the client for the attorney's professional malpractice. Cal. Rule 3-400(B), unlike MR 1.8(h), also expressly allows an attorney to settle a potential claim. Unlike the ABA rule, Cal. Rule 3-400(A) flatly prohibits an attorney from contracting prospectively with a client to limit the attorney's liability.

While both MR 1.8(h) and Cal. Rule 3-400(B) require that, prior to settling a malpractice claim, the client be informed in writing that the client may seek the advice of an independent lawyer, Cal. Rule 3-400(B) applies this requirement to *all* clients, not just unrepresented ones, as in MR 1.8(h). Additionally, Cal. Rule 3-400(B) adds the requirement that such written notice include a reasonable opportunity to seek such advice.

MR 1.8(i): Cal. Rule 3-320 addresses the relationships between attorneys discussed in MR 1.8(i), and provides somewhat broader prohibitions. The California Rule prohibits an attorney from representing a client in a matter in which another party's lawyer is a spouse, parent, child or sibling of the attorney, lives with the attorney, is a client of the attorney, or has an intimate personal relationship with the attorney, unless the attorney informs the client in writing of the relationship. However, Cal. Rule 3-320 does not expressly require client consent following disclosure.

MR 1.8(j): Cal. Rule 3-300 covers this area. The Discussion section of Cal. Rule 3-300 clarifies that this rule is intended to apply where the attorney takes a lien to secure expenses, but is not intended to apply where the attorney enters into a contingent fee contract with the client.

2002 Model Rules:

MR 1.8(a) has been amended to require that the client be advised *in writing* about seeking the advice of an independent lawyer, bringing it much closer to Ca. Rule 3-300.

MR 1.8(i) has been deleted. Old MR 1.8(j) has been renumbered 1.8(i).

New MR 1.8(j) prohibits a lawyer from having sexual relations with a client unless a consensual relationship predated the attorney-client relationship. California's standards do not prohibit client sexual relationships per se unless they are accompanied by threats to the lawyer's competence or are a product of a lawyer's coercion, undue influence, or intimidation. Consensual sexual relationships predating the attorney-client relationship are exempted. However, sexual relationships between spouses are separately exempted. [Cal. Rule 3-120.] Ca. B&P Code §6106.9 also exempts domestic relationships equivalent to spouses. It is unclear whether those exemptions are intended to permit spousal-like relationships if they begin after formation of the attorney-client relationship.

New MR 1.8(k) makes subparts (a)-(i) applicable to all members in the law firm. This is inconsistent with the California rules, which have a personal responsibility model for disciplinary purposes. However, California and the Model Rules are consistent in permitting lawyer/client consensual sexual relationships where the lawyer involved is not actually providing legal services.

ABA Model Rule 1.9

1983 Model Rules:

Cal. Rule 3-310(E) treats representation adverse to a former client in the same way it deals with representation adverse to a current client. (Cal. Rule 3-310(C)(3) contains further prohibitions against representing a current client.) Cal. Rule 3-310(E) prohibits a lawyer from accepting a matter adverse to a client or a former client whenever the attorney has obtained confidential information "material to the employment" during the representation of that client or former client. The client or former client may consent in writing to such representation.

Unlike MR 1.9, the California Rule does not directly embody the "substantial relationship test" of representation adverse to a former client. However, generally, the receipt of "information material to the employment" will turn on whether the former and current representation are substantially related. While not part of the rules of professional conduct per se, the "substantial relationship test" enjoys healthy respect in California case law. (See, for example, *Trone v. Smith*, 621 F.2d 994 (9th Cir. 1980) and *Global Van Lines, Inc. v. Superior Court*, 144 Cal.App. 3d 483, 192 Cal. Rptr. 609 (1983).)

2002 Model Rules:

MR 1.9 has been amended to require the client's informed consent, confirmed in writing. This moves the Model Rules substantially closer to California's requirements that the client consent in writing after written disclosure. (Ca. Rules 3-310(E) and (A).)

ABA Model Rule 1.10

1983 Model Rules:

California does not have an imputed disqualification rule. However, the Discussion to Cal. Rule 3-310 clarifies that Cal. Rule 3-310(B) is intended to apply and require written disclosure to the current client where the attorney knows that a partner or associate in the same firm as the attorney has or had a relationship with another party or witness in the matter or has or had an interest in the subject matter of the representation. Moreover, there exists case law which imputes disqualification to an entire law firm. (See, e.g., *Henriksen v. Great America Savings & Loan*, 11 Cal.App. 4th 109 (1992).) On the issue of "screening," see discussion under 2002 Model Rules, below.

2002 Model Rules:

MR 1.10(a) has been amended to exempt conflicts "based on a personal interest of the prohibited lawyer" that do not "present a significant risk of materially limiting the representation of the client by the remaining lawyers in the firm." This is consistent with a similar change in MR 1.7(a)(2). Of greater significance is that in February 2009, the ABA amended MR 1.10(a) to broadly permit a law firm to create an "ethical screen" around a lawyer who has a personal interest that would interfere with the law firm's representation under MR 1.7, or who had involvement in the case of a former client, regardless of whether that lawyer acquired (or is presumed to have acquired) confidential information of the former client.

Under revised MR 1.10, the involved lawyer may be screened even if the lawyer's involvement was direct and substantial on behalf of the former client, and even if the former client's case is substantially related to the law firm's new case. For example, a screen would be permitted even if the lawyer had been the lead trial lawyer for the former client and the matter is now on appeal. In effect, the new Model Rule provision would place private lawyers more or less on equal footing with government lawyers, whose conflicts are governed by MR 1.11.

Finally, in August 2009, the ABA House of Delegates approved "housekeeping amendments" to MR 1.10(a)(2) that limit the availability of screening to a lawyer who has moved laterally from another firm.

As of this writing, only two jurisdiction have adopted the Model Rule 1.10(a)(2) screening provisions verbatim: Connecticut and Idaho. Nevertheless, there are 13 other jurisdictions that have adopted screening provisions that broadly permit screening of private lawyers similar to the Model Rule: Delaware, D.C., Illinois, Kentucky, Maryland, Michigan, Montana, North Carolina, Oregon, Pennsylvania, Rhode Island, Utah and Washington. In addition, another 14 jurisdictions permit screening in limited situations, i.e., the jurisdiction's provision permits screening only if a lawyer did not "substantially participate," or was not "substantially involved," did not have a "substantial role," did not have "primary responsibility," etc., in the former client's matter, or when any confidential information that the lawyer might have obtained is deemed not material to the current representation (e.g., Mass.) or "is not likely to be significant" (e.g., Minn.) Jurisdictions that permit screening in such limited situations are: Arizona, Colorado, Indiana, Massachusetts, Minnesota, Nevada, New Hampshire, New Jersey, New Mexico, North Dakota, Ohio, Tennessee, Vermont, and Wisconsin.

California rules and standards do not provide disqualification standards, although they have been used to disqualify lawyers pursuant to the cases cited above and in the Rule 1.9 comparison. In 2010, the California Court of Appeal issued its opinion in *Kirk v. First American Title Ins. Co.*, 183 Cal. App.4th 776 (2010), *rev. denied* (6/23/2010), which concluded that a non-consented-to ethical screen might effectively rebut the presumption that a lawyer in possession of confidential information of a former client would share that information with lawyers in the new firm, thus refuting the need to disqualify the new firm. In reaching its decision, the *Kirk* court provided a comprehensive summary California case law on vicarious disqualification and screening, suggesting the broad kind of screening as permitted under MR 1.10(a)(2) would also be available in California. However, because the case involved only a preliminary discussion between the tainted lawyer and a prospective client, and not substantial involvement by the lawyer in the same matter, it is arguably dicta.

ABA Model Rule 1.11

1983 Model Rules:

California does not have a specific conflict of interest rule on successive government and private employment. However, Cal. Rule 3-310(E) would apply generally to all attorneys, including those who leave government to work in the private sector.

While there is no California parallel to paragraph 3 of the Comment to MR 1.11, California case law does exist which supports limited "screening" for the government lawyer once that attorney has entered private practice. (See, e.g., *Klein v. Superior Court*, 198 Cal.App.3d 894, 142 Cal. Rptr. 226 (1988).)

However, Ca. B&P Code §6131 creates criminal penalties and requires disbarment for any attorney that participates in any criminal defense where the lawyer participated as a criminal prosecutor in the same matter or if the lawyer's partner formerly participated in the same prosecution.

2002 Model Rules:

MR 1.11 has been amended to clarify that former government attorneys are subject to MR 1.9(c) [MR 1.11(a)]; that those imputed conflicts of interest also apply to governmental lawyers [MR 1.11(b)]; that the government may consent to MR 1.9 conflicts through informed consent, confirmed in writing; and that current government lawyers are subject to MR 1.7 and 1.9 [MR 1.11(d).] Similarly, California's conflicts rules apply equally to publicly-employed lawyers as well as lawyers in private practice. (See e.g., Ca. Rules 3-310, 1-100(B)(2).)

ABA Model Rule 1.12

1983 Model Rules:

California does not have a specific conflict of interest rule regarding former judges or arbitrators. However, Cal. Rule 3-310 would apply to all attorneys generally, including one who represents a client in connection with a matter in which the lawyer had participated personally as a judge, adjudicative officer or arbitrator.

2002 Model Rules:

No substantive changes to the Model Rule. However, the California Judicial Council has proposed standards of conduct for arbitrators and mediators which include conflict of interest provisions.

ABA Model Rule 1.13

1983 Model Rules:

Cal. Rule 3-600 is substantially similar to MR 1.13. However, the California Rule emphasizes the absolute duty to protect the corporate client's confidences and secrets, as well as the duty not to mislead constituents of the corporation that the attorney represents them individually. Moreover, since MR 1.13 must be read in light of MR 1.6 (see paragraph 6 of the Comment), it is significant to note that Cal. Rule 3-600 must be read in light of the stronger, more absolute language of Cal. B&P Code §6068(e). (See MR 1.6 rule comparison.)

Both the Comment to MR 1.13 (see paragraphs 8 through 12) and the Discussion section of Cal. Rule 3-600 (see the last paragraph) are intended to give guidance to lawyers whose duties and loyalties become confl icting. Paragraph 7 of the Comment specifically addresses the "difficult" problems faced by governmental attorneys. Cal. Rule 3-600 contains no such discussion.

2002 Model Rules:

The significant changes to MR 1.13 occurred in 2003. First, subsection (b) no longer requires an "up the ladder" protocol for lawyers who perceive acts substantially injurious to the organization. A lawyer is now presumptively *mandated* to refer such matters to higher organizational authority, including, "if warranted by the circumstances," the highest authority, unless the lawyer believes that the best interests of the organization are not served by such a referral.

The second major change, or series of changes, falls within subsection (c). Where the organization's highest authority fails in a timely manner to address the issue at hand and that failure clearly violates the law, a lawyer *may* reveal information outside the organization to the extent the lawyer believes necessary to prevent substantial injury to the organization. No longer is a lawyer limited to resigning silently. In order for such outside revelation to be made, there must be a violation of law that the lawyer is "reasonably certain" will result in substantial injury to the organization. However, if these conditions exist, subsection (c) explicitly allows disclosure whether or not MR 1.6 would permit it.

Unlike the new SEC regulations, disclosure under MR 1.13 remains grounded in a determination of the best interests of the organization, rather than the effect on individuals, entities, or regulatory agencies outside the organization. There is no California rule equivalent to these new changes.

ABA Model Rule 1.14

1983 Model Rules:

There is no California Rule of Professional Conduct that parallels MR 1.14 or addresses this topic. Cal. Rule 3-110 makes it the duty of an attorney to represent a client competently.

2002 Model Rules:

MR 1.14 changes the term "disability" to "diminished capacity." MR 1.14(b) refines the definition of "protective action" to what is "reasonably necessary." MR 1.14(b) gives examples of such protective action.

New MR 1.14 (c) provides that revealing a diminished capacity client's confidences pursuant to MR 1.6 is impliedly authorized to the extent reasonably necessary to take protective action in the client's best interests.

California has no provisions corresponding to these requirements.

ABA Model Rule 1.15

1983 Model Rules:

Cal. Rule 4-100 parallels MR 1.15, but is considerably more detailed. Cal. Rule 4-100 provides descriptive titles for the attorney's client trust account and specifically requires that "all funds received or held for the benefit of clients by a member or law firm, including advances for costs and expenses" be placed in such account. Like MR 1.15, Cal. Rule 4-100 allows the client trust account to be maintained in a jurisdiction outside the state, but unlike MR 1.15, requires the client's *written* consent to do so.

MR 1.15 requires generally that client or third party funds be held separately from the attorney's funds. Cal. Rule 4-100(A) is more specific, requiring in the case of funds belonging in part to the client and in part to the attorney, that the portion belonging to the attorney be withdrawn at the earliest reasonable time after the attorney's interest in that portion becomes fixed. However, when the right of the attorney or law firm to receive a portion of trust funds is disputed by the client, Cal. Rule 4-100(A) requires that the disputed portion not be withdrawn until the dispute is finally resolved.

Cal. Rule 4-100(B) closely tracks MR 1.15(b). Unlike MR 1.15, Cal. Rule 4-100(B) expressly requires that the attorney comply with any order for an audit of such records issued by the State Bar of California.

Cal. Rule 4-100(C) authorizes the State Bar to develop detailed record keeping Standards, requiring that the attorney maintain a written ledger for each client on whose behalf funds are held, a written journal for each bank account containing client funds and all bank statements and cancelled checks for each bank account. These Standards, while not part of the Rules of Professional Conduct themselves, are authorized by the California Supreme Court's approval of 4-100(C). No such standards are found in MR 1.15.

The standards also have the following requirements. Attorneys are required to prepare a monthly reconciliation of the client ledger, bank account and cancelled checks. Additionally, attorneys are required to maintain a written journal that specifies: 1) each item of security and property held; 2) the person on whose behalf the security or property is held; 3) the date of receipt of the security or property; 4) the date of distribution of the security or property; and 5) the person to whom the security or property was distributed.

2002 Model Rules:

New MR 1.15 (b) clarifies that a lawyer may deposit the lawyer's own funds in a client trust account for the sole purpose of paying bank service charges on that account, but only in an amount necessary for that purpose. This is similar to Ca. Rule 4-100(A)(1).

New MR 1.15 (c) clarifies that a lawyer shall deposit legal fees and expenses that have been paid in advance into a client trust account, to be withdrawn by the lawyer only as fees are earned or expenses incurred. California's Rule 4-100(A) is similar to the extent it requires deposit of advanced costs and expenses in a clients' trust account, but does not require the deposit of advanced *fees*. (*Baranowski v. State Bar* 24 Cal.3d 153, 163 (1979).)

ABA Model Rule 1.16

1983 Model Rules:

MR 1.16 addresses both acceptance and termination of legal representation. Three California rules apply in these areas. Cal. Rule 3-700 specifically addresses the termination of representation. Cal. Rule 2-400 prohibits discrimination in the acceptance or termination of representation, while Cal. Rule 3-200 addresses prohibited objectives of legal employment.

Both Cal. Rule 3-700 and MR 1.16 address withdrawal from representation of a client before a tribunal. Cal. Rule 3-700(A)(1) forbids an attorney from withdrawing from employment in a proceeding before that tribunal without its permission. MR 1.16(c) requires an attorney to continue representation when ordered to do so by the tribunal. In withdrawing from employment, Cal. Rule 3-700(A)(2) and MR 1.16(d) both require that an attorney take reasonable steps to avoid prejudice to the rights of the client, including giving due notice to the client, allowing time for employment of other counsel, returning unearned advance fees and other papers and property of the client that the client has requested be returned. MR 1.16(d) allows an attorney to retain client papers to the extent permitted by law, while Cal. Rule 3-700(D)(1) recognizes that the duty to return client papers is subject to protective orders or non-disclosure agreements.

In evaluating *mandatory* withdrawal, Cal. Rule 3-700(B)(1), unlike MR 1.16(a), adds the requirement that the attorney withdraw from representation where the attorney knows or should know that the client is acting without probable cause and for the purpose of harassing or injuring another. Cal. Rule 3-700(B), however, does not expressly contain the provision found in MR 1.16(a)(3) that withdrawal is mandatory when the attorney is discharged by the client. However, California case law gives the client the absolute right to discharge the attorney at any time. MR 1.16(a)(1) requires that an attorney withdraw from representation where the representation will violate rules of professional conduct or other law. On the other hand, the California counterpart to MR 1.16(a)(1), Cal. Rule 3-700(B)(2) requires a lawyer to withdraw where the representation will result in a violation of the rules of professional conduct "or of the State Bar Act." The ultimate effect is probably de minimis because by incorporation, provisions in the California Rules and the State Bar Act prohibit more general violations of law. For example, Cal. Rule 3-210 prohibits a lawyer from advising the violation of the law, rule 3-200 identifies prohibited objectives of a representation, and Business & Professions Code § 6106 imposes sanctions on a lawyer for acts of "moral turpitude, dishonesty or corruption," whether or not in the course of a representation. Both rules require that an attorney withdraw from representation where the attorney's mental or physical condition "materially impairs" (MR 1.16) or "renders it unreasonably difficult" (Cal. Rule 3-700) to carry out the representation effectively.

In evaluating *permissive* withdrawal, Cal. Rule 3-700(C) provides eleven permissive reasons for withdrawal, while MR 1.16(b) provides six such reasons. MR 1.16(b)'s reasons are not exclusive. In contrast, Cal. Rule 3-700(C) expressly forbids withdrawal from representation unless one of its eleven enumerated reasons is present. However, when appearing before a tribunal, Cal. Rule 3-700(C) contains a "catch-all" provision allowing for withdrawal whenever the tribunal finds "good cause."

Cal. Rule 3-700(C) permits withdrawal where the client: 1) insists upon presenting a claim or defense that is not warranted under existing law and cannot be supported by good faith argument for an extension, modification, or reversal of existing law; 2) seeks to pursue an illegal course of conduct; 3) renders it "unreasonably difficult" for the attorney to continue; 4) insists that the member pursue an illegal or unethical course of conduct; 5) insists, in a matter not pending before a tribunal, that the attorney engage in conduct that is contrary to the lawyer's judgment and advice; or 6) breaches an agreement to pay expenses or fees. These reasons are similar to the first five reasons found in MR 1.16(b), although their content and wording are not exact. For example, MR 1.16(b)(3) adds a client's "repugnant" objective as a reason for permissive withdrawal. MR 1.16(b)(4) allows for permissive withdrawal where the client fails to substantially fulfill any obligation to the attorney, not just obligations as to expenses or fees. MR 1.16(b)(5) also permits withdrawal where the representation will result in an "unreasonable financial burden" on the attorney.

Unlike MR 1.16(b), Cal. Rule 3-700 adds the following permissive reasons for withdrawal: 1) the continued employment is likely to result in an ethical violation of the rules; 2) the inability to work with co-counsel; 3) the attorney's mental or physical condition renders it difficult for the member to continue effectively; 4) the client consents to withdrawal; or 5) the tribunal finds the existence of "other good cause" for withdrawal. MR 1.16(b)(6) is broader, allowing permissive withdrawal for "other good cause" regardless of whether the matter is pending before a tribunal.

Cal. Rule 3-200 says that a lawyer "shall not seek, accept, or continue employment" where the objective of the representation is either (1) to act in a manner without probable cause and for the purpose of harassing or injuring another; or (2) to present a claim or defense that is not warranted under existing law and cannot be supported by good faith argument for an extension, modification, or reversal of existing law. Anomalously, while Cal. Rule 3-200 seems to *require* that, in these circumstances, a lawyer must withdraw, the second circumstance is enumerated in Cal. Rule 3-700(C) as a grounds for *permissive* withdrawal.

Cal. Rule 2-400 prohibits discrimination in the acceptance or termination of representing any client. However, Cal. Rule 2-400(C) mandates that no disciplinary investigation may be initiated unless a tribunal has first made a fiding that unlawful conduct has occurred.

2002 Model Rules:

Clarifying changes only have been made, with no material substantive changes.

ABA Model Rule 1.17

1983 Model Rules:

Cal. Rule 2-300 parallels MR 1.17, but is considerably more detailed and somewhat more permissive. Both rules permit the sale of a law practice, including goodwill, to another lawyer so long as clients are given written notice, and fees charged to clients are not increased by reason of such sale. The notice requirements of both rules are substantially similar.

Cal. Rule 2-300, unlike MR 1.17, does not contain the requirement that such sale may occur only where the seller ceases to engage in the private practice of law in the geographic area or jurisdiction in which the practice has been conducted. Additionally, Cal. Rule 2-300, unlike MR 1.17: 1) permits the sale of less than the entirety of a law practice; 2) requires a client's written consent regarding any transfer of that client's matter; 3) distinguishes situations where the seller represents a decedent; 4) addresses situations where substitution of counsel is required by the rules of a tribunal; and 5) addresses confidentiality and conflict of interest issues.

2002 Model Rules:

In 2002, MR 1.17 was amended to permit the sale or purchase of an entire area of practice. This amendment is more liberal than Cal. Rule 2-300, which permits the purchase or sale of "substantially" all of the law practice. In 2012, Comment [7] was amended to provide a cross-reference to new subparagraph (b)(7) of MR 1.6 on clearing conflicts of interest.

ABA Model Rule 1.18

1983 Model Rules:

There was no MR 1.18 prior to the 2002 revisions.

2002 Model Rules:

MR 1.18, regarding duties to prospective clients, was entirely new in 2002 and was substantially amended in 2012.

MR 1.18(a) defines a "prospective client" as a person who consults with a lawyer about the possibility of forming a client-lawyer relationship with respect to a matter. In addition, the Ethics 20/20 Commission recommended removing the term "prospective client" in all other instances in which it appears in the Model Rules where it did not have the same meaning as contained in MR 1.18(a), See the comparison discussions of MR 5.5, cmt. [21], MR 7.1, cmt. [3], MR 7.2, cmts. [3], [6] and [7], MR 7.3, Title, MR 7.3(b)(1) and (c), and MR 7.3, cmts. [2], [3], [4], [6] and [7]. In each of those places, the term referred to a member of the public and thus might be viewed in the most general sense as a prospective client. Accordingly, in each of those places the term has either been deleted or replaced by the term "the public."

MR 1.18(b), modified in 2012, prohibits the use or revelation of information learned from a prospective client, except as Rule 1.9 would permit.

MR 1.18(c) prohibits a lawyer who has received confidences from a prospective client from representing anyone with interests materially adverse to the prospective client. The MR 1.9 standard that the matters be "substantially related" is used, except that the information must rise to what "could be significantly harmful" to the prospective client.

MR 1.18(d) limits law firm imputation and permits representation by the firm if the lawyer who received the information took reasonable measures to avoid exposure to more disqualifying information than was reasonably necessary to determine whether to represent the prospective client; and the disqualified lawyer is timely screened, with written notice promptly given the prospective client.

In 2012, Comments [1], [4] and [5] to MR 1.18 were amended for consistency by substituting the word "consultations" or "consultation" for the words "discussions," "interview," and "conversations," respectively. The uniform use of the word "consultation" – rather than "discussion" and/or "interview" – may have the effect of narrowing the scope of who constitutes a prospective client. Comment [2] was substantially revised to provide an example of when a prospective client consultation exists, and an example where a person who makes a "unilateral" communication would not be deemed to be a prospective client. Further, a sentence was added to the end of Comment [2] that provides: "a person who communicates with a lawyer for the purpose of disqualifying the lawyer is not a 'prospective client.'" This sentence is intended to address situations such as "beauty contests" where a person might consult with a number of lawyers primarily for the purpose of preventing his or her opponent from retaining them.

While California has no express equivalent to MR 1.18, the definition of a prospective client in Ca. Evid. Code §951 has been applied to the duties of confidentiality of Ca. B&P Code §6068(e) through ethics opinions, e.g., Cal. State Bar Formal Opns. 2003-161 and 2004-168, and case law has applied the provisions of Cal. Rule 3-310(E) to conflicts arising from consultations with prospective clients. (See e.g. *Marriage of Zimmerman* 16 Cal.App.4th 556, 20 Cal. Rptr.2d 132 (1993).) Similarly, the topic of unilateral communications by a person in the context of an Internet communication is addressed in S.D. County Bar Ass'n Ethics Opn. 2006-1. Finally, California case law holds that where a person communicates with a lawyer who is not holding himself or herself out as a lawyer, the person is not a prospective client. *People v. Gionis*, 9 Cal.4th 1196, 40 Cal.Rptr.2d 456 (1995).

ABA Model Rule 2.1

1983 Model Rules:

There is no Cal. Rule of Professional Conduct that parallels MR 2.1, either regarding the attorney as advisor, or the independent judgment of the lawyer. Cal. Rule 1-600 prohibits an attorney from participating in a nongovernmental legal service program which allows any third person or organization to interfere with the member's independence of professional judgment.

2002 Model Rules: No substantive changes to the Model Rule.

ABA Model Rule 2.2

1983 Model Rules:

There is no California Rule of Professional Conduct that directly parallels MR 2.2 regarding the lawyer acting as an intermediary. However, Cal. Rule 3-310(C) prohibits an attorney, without the informed written consent of each client, from: 1) accepting representation of more than one client in a matter in which the interests of the clients potentially conflict; or 2) accepting or continuing representation of more than one client in a matter in which the interests of the clients actually conflict. In obtaining each client's informed written consent, the attorney must inform each client of the relevant circumstances and of the actual and reasonably foreseeable adverse consequences to each client.

2002 Model Rules: This rule was deleted in its entirety.

ABA Model Rule 2.3

1983 Model Rules:

There is no California Rule of Professional Conduct that parallels MR 2.3 or addresses this topic, regarding evaluations made by the lawyer for a client to third parties, so long as the evaluation is "compatible" with the lawyer's relationship with the client.

2002 Model Rules:

MR 2.3(b) was added to expressly prohibit a lawyer from providing an evaluation to a third party when the lawyer knows or reasonably should know that the evaluation is likely to affect the client's interests materially and adversely.

———

ABA Model Rule 2.4

2002 Model Rules:

MR 2.4, regarding lawyers who serve as third-party neutrals, is completely new. MR2.4 (a) defines a lawyer third-party neutral as a person that assists two or more non-clients to reach a resolution of a dispute or other matter that has arisen between them, including service as an arbitrator or a mediator or in another capacity to assist the parties to resolve the matter.

MR 2.4(b) requires a third-party neutral lawyer to inform unrepresented parties that the lawyer does not represent them and, where warranted, to explain the difference between the lawyer's role as a third-party neutral and a lawyer's role in representing a client.

While there is no California counterpart, the California Judicial Council has proposed standards of conduct for arbitrators and mediators which include disclosure requirements.

———

ABA Model Rule 3.1

1983 Model Rules:

Cal. Rule 3-200 parallels MR 3.1. Like MR 3.1, Cal. Rule 3-200 prohibits an attorney from seeking, accepting or continuing employment if the attorney knows or should know that the objective of such employment is to present a claim or defense in litigation that is not warranted under existing law, unless it can be supported by a good faith argument for an extension, modification or reversal of such existing law.

Unlike MR 3.1, Cal. Rule 3-200 also prohibits an attorney from seeking, accepting or continuing employment if the attorney knows or should know that the objective of such employment is to bring an action, conduct a defense, assert a position in litigation or take an appeal, without probable cause and for the purpose of harassing or maliciously injuring any person. Moreover, Cal. B&P Code § 6068(c) requires that a lawyer maintain actions, proceedings or defenses only as appear to be just.

Cal. Rule 3-200 does not address the representation of criminal defendants, though California case law interpretations of criminal and constitutional law would comport with the last sentence of MR 3.1. Moreover, Cal. B&P Code § 6068(c) specifically exempts the defense of a person charged with a crime from the requirement of maintaining only those defenses "as appear to be just."

2002 Model Rules: No substantive changes to the Model Rule.

ABA Model Rule 3.2

There is no California Rule of Professional Conduct that parallels MR 3.2 on expediting litigation, or addresses this topic.

2002 Model Rules: No substantive changes to the Model Rule.

ABA Model Rule 3.3

1983 Model Rules:

Cal. Rule 5-200 is the California rule that most closely parallels MR 3.3. Like MR 3.3, Cal. Rule 5-200 requires that an attorney appearing before a tribunal employ only means consistent with the truth, and not make a false statement of fact or law. Cal. B&P Code § 6068(d) parallels these requirements.

Cal. Rule 5-200 and Cal. B&P Code § 6068(d) also require that the lawyer never mislead either the judge or jury by any "artifice." Cal. Rule 5-200 also prohibits an attorney from asserting personal knowledge of the facts at issue, except when the attorney is a witness. Cal. B&P Code § 6128(a) makes it a misdemeanor for any attorney who acts with deceit or collusion with intent to deceive the court or any party. These requirements are similar but not identical to those contained in MR 3.3.

MR 3.3(a)(3) requires that a lawyer must disclose legal authority in the controlling jurisdiction directly adverse to the lawyer's client's position. Cal. Rule 5-200(C) and (D) do not directly say this. They do refer to the requirement that a lawyer neither misquote a book, statute or decision, nor knowingly cite invalid or unconstitutional authority.

Unlike MR 3.3, the California rules do not expressly address the known offering of false evidence, material omissions of fact or law, or candor to the tribunal in ex parte proceedings. Moreover, unlike MR 3.3(c), the California rules contain no provision allowing a lawyer to refuse to offer evidence when the lawyer "reasonably believes" that it is false.

The California rules diverge sharply from MR 3.3 regarding the disclosure of client confidences to a tribunal. MR 3.3(b) requires disclosure of client confidences where necessary to fulfill the duties in sub-part (a), including the offering of evidence that the lawyer knows to be false. Moreover, in cases of false evidence, the lawyer is obligated to take "reasonable remedial measures." By contrast, in California, the duty to maintain client confidences and secrets remains absolute pursuant to Business and Professions Code § 6068(e).

In sum, the ABA Model Rule, with its extensive Comment section, offers substantially more specific guidance on the issues raised by that rule than can be found in the California Rules or B&P Code. On the other hand, Cal. B&P Code §6068(e) offers a clear and absolute statement of an attorney's obligations regarding confidences and secrets.

2002 Model Rules:

MR 3.3(a)(1) deletes the word "material" from the phrase "false statement of material fact or law," and adds a duty to correct a false statement of *material* fact or law previously made by the lawyer.

MR 3.3(a)(2), which provided that a lawyer shall disclose material facts when disclosure is necessary to avoid assisting a criminal or fraudulent act by the client, has been deleted and replaced by MR 3.3(b).

MR 3.3(a)(3) was expanded to add to the requirement that a lawyer "take reasonable remedial measures," in those situations in which the lawyer's client or a witness called by the lawyer has offered false evidence. Such measures shall include disclosure if necessary. Also, a lawyer is still permitted to refuse to offer evidence that the lawyer *reasonably believes* (but does not *know*) is false, except in the case of the testimony of a defendant in a criminal matter.

MR 3.3(b) replaces former 3.3(a)(2) and adds language about remedial measures including disclosure that parallel 3.3(a)(3). There is no California counterpart to this rule.

MR 3.3(c) was formerly subsection (b).

ABA Model Rule 3.4

1983 Model Rules:

MR 3.4 addresses several specific topics that are found in separate California rules and statutes.

MR 3.4(a): A similar, albeit narrower, prohibition is contained in Cal. Rule 5-220, which prohibits an attorney from suppressing any evidence when there is a legal obligation to reveal it. More generally, Cal. B&P Code § 6068(d) and Cal. Rule 5-200(A) and (B) require lawyers to use "such means only as are consistent with truth," and Cal. B&P Code § 6128(a) makes it a misdemeanor for a lawyer to use deceit or collusion to deceive the court or any party.

MR 3.4(b): Other than the general provisions noted above, Cal. Rule 5-200 and Cal. B&P Code §§ 6068(d) and 6128(a), there is no further provision against the falsification of evidence. Cal. Rule 5-310(B) prevents an illegal inducement to a witness in the form of payment, by prohibiting direct or indirect payment to a witness in return for that witness's testimony or dependent on the outcome of the case. There is no specific California provision that relates to counseling a witness to testify falsely. However, Cal. Rule 5-310(A) prohibits a lawyer from advising or assisting a witness to avoid the jurisdiction of a court, or making that witness unavailable.

MR 3.4(c): Cal. Rule 3-210 forbids a lawyer from advising the violation of a law, rule or ruling unless the member believes in good faith that it is invalid. It does not directly address the lawyer's own disobedience.

MR 3.4(d): There is no California ethics rule that specifically addresses frivolous discovery. The closest California rule is Cal. Rule 3-200, containing a general prohibition against unwarranted defenses and positions, and Cal. B&P Code § 6068(c), contains similar language.

MR 3.4(e): Despite its wide breadth, MR 3.4(e) has no parallel in the California ethics rules, except for the prohibition against an attorney asserting personal knowledge of facts. That prohibition, with a similar exception when the attorney is testifying as a witness, is contained in Cal. Rule 5-200.

Nor is there a direct prohibition against a lawyer presenting evidence that the attorney does not reasonably believe is relevant or supported by admissible evidence. There is no specific provision which prevents an attorney from stating a personal opinion as to the merits of a cause. However, California case law prohibits both these practices.

MR 3.4(f): There is no California rule that specifically parallels this provision. However, Cal. Rule 5-310(A) does prohibit a lawyer from advising a person to avoid the jurisdiction of a court when that person may be a witness.

2002 Model Rules: No substantive changes to the Model Rule.

ABA Model Rule 3.5

1983 Model Rules:

Cal. Rule 5-300 and 5-320 are the California rules that most closely parallel MR 3.5.

MR 3.5(a): Cal. Rule 5-300 addresses conduct directed toward judges; Cal. Rule 5-320 addresses conduct directed toward jurors. Cal. Rule 5-300(A) defines in considerable detail the limitations on a lawyer giving anything to a judge or employee of a tribunal. Cal. Rule 5-320(E) prohibits an investigation of a juror or venire person in a manner likely to influence the state of mind of such a person.

MR 3.5(b): Cal. Rule 5-300(B) defines in significant detail the limitations on a lawyer's direct or indirect communications with a judicial officer. Cal. Rule 5-320, which contains nine sub-sections, details with specificity the conduct which is prohibited when lawyers are dealing with jurors. The prohibited conduct includes limitations on contact with jurors after they have been discharged or excused, and in sub-section (F), extends to members of a family of a juror or venire person.

MR 3.5(c): The closest requirement to the prohibition of engaging in conduct "intended to disrupt a tribunal" is Cal. B&P Code § 6068(b), which requires a lawyer to maintain the respect due to the courts. Section 6068(f) also includes the admonition that lawyers must "abstain from all offensive personality." However, this subsection has been widely criticized as unconstitutionally vague.

2002 Model Rules:

MR 3.5(b) was amended to limit the prohibition against ex parte communications to the period during the proceeding. Post discharge communication with jurors is now governed by MR 3.5(c).

MR 3.5(c) was added to prohibit communication with a juror or prospective juror after the jury is discharged if: the communication is prohibited by law or court order; the juror has made known a desire not to communicate; or the communication involves misrepresentation, coercion, duress or harassment.

Cal. Rule 5-320(D) is similar to MR 3.5(c) in that it prohibits a lawyer from asking questions or making comments to a member of a discharged jury that are intended to harasss or embarrass the juror or influence the juror's future jury service.

ABA Model Rule 3.6

1983 Model Rules:

There is no Cal. Rule of Professional Conduct comparable to ABA MR 3.6. In 1986, the State Bar of California, following consideration of MR 3.6, declined to adopt a rule comparable to MR 3.6. As of the date of publication of this volume, the State Bar of California, pursuant to a mandate of the state legislature, had transmitted proposed Cal. Rule 5-120 to the state Supreme Court for its review. The rule was transmitted to the court without state bar endorsement.

As drafted, proposed Cal. Rule 5-120 is significantly narrower than MR 3.6. First, it uses a narrower "clear and present danger" standard in assessing the possible prejudice. Second, it limits its application to criminal or civil jury trials as opposed to all adjudicative proceedings, as defined in MR 3.6(a). Third, it does not contain the vicarious prohibition set forth in MR 3.6(d); rather it limits statements made "by or on behalf" of a particular attorney.

2002 Model Rules: No substantive changes to the Model Rule.

ABA Model Rule 3.7

1983 Model Rules:

Cal. Rule 5-210 is the rule which addresses the attorney acting as a witness. Both MR 3.7 and Cal. Rule 5-210 allow an attorney to act as both an advocate and a witness where the attorney's testimony relates to an uncontested matter or where the testimony relates to the nature and value of legal services rendered in the case.

There are two significant differences between MR 3.7 and Cal. Rule 5-210. First, MR 3.7 applies to all trials, regardless of whether they are heard before a judge or jury, while Cal. Rule 5-210 applies only to jury trials. Second, Cal. Rule 5-210, unlike MR 3.7, also allows an attorney to act as an advocate and a witness whenever the attorney has the informed, written consent of the client. MR 3.7 allows an attorney to act in this dual capacity only where disqualification of the attorney would work substantial hardship on the client. Both MR 3.7 and Cal. Rule 5-210 do not apply where another lawyer in the attorney's firm will be a witness, although MR 3.7 notes that the attorney may still be precluded from acting as an advocate by MR 1.7 or MR 1.9.

2002 Model Rules: No substantive changes to the Model Rule.

ABA Model Rule 3.8

1983 Model Rules:

There is no rule in California with the broad scope found in MR 3.8. Cal. Rule 5-110 refers generally to government lawyers, and includes a prohibition against filing criminal charges that are not supported by probable cause. There is, however, no California ethics rule that addresses: 1) obtaining waivers from unrepresented defendants; 2) disclosure of mitigating evidence to the defense in criminal cases; 3) extrajudicial statements by law enforcement personnel or prosecutorial staff; or 4) subpoenas of lawyers in grand jury or other criminal proceedings.

2002 Model Rules: No substantive changes to the 1983 Model Rule.

2008 Amendments to Model Rule 3.8: In February 2008, the ABA House of Delegates adopted paragraphs (g) and (h), and corresponding comments. Based on provisions adopted by the New York State Bar Association in November 2007, MR 3.8(g) and (h) codify the duties of prosecutors when they learn of possible false convictions. Paragraph (g) sets forth a prosecutor's minimal duties when the prosecutor "knows of new, credible and material evidence" indicating a defendant was wrongfully convicted. Where the conviction took place in a prosecutor's jurisdiction, paragraph (h) requires the prosecutor "to remedy the conviction." As of the date of writing (October 2008), no state has yet adopted paragraphs (g) and (h). The New York Rule awaits approval by the courts.

ABA Model Rule 3.9

1983 Model Rules:

There is no California ethics rule that parallels MR 3.9 or addresses this topic.

2002 Model Rules: No substantive changes to the Model Rule.

ABA Model Rule 4.1

1983 Model Rules:

There is no California ethics rule that parallels MR 4.1 or addresses this topic directly. California has only the general prohibitions of Cal. Rule 5-200 and Cal. B&P Code §§ 6068(d) and 6128(a), previously discussed with respect to other ABA rules. Also, B&P Code § 6106 makes the commission of any act "involving moral turpitude, dishonesty or corruption" a cause for discipline.

2002 Model Rules: No substantive changes to the Model Rule.

ABA Model Rule 4.2 1983 Model Rules:

The parallel rule to MR 4.2 is Cal. Rule 2-100. The California rule expressly prohibits direct *and indirect* communications. While both rules contain an exception for communications authorized by law, the California rule adds exceptions not found in MR 4.2 regarding communications with public officers, boards and so on, or those initiated by a party seeking advice or representation from an independent lawyer chosen by that party. The Discussion to Cal. Rule 2-100 makes specific reference to case law governing defining which employees of a corporation are considered a "party" for purposes of such communication.

Both rules define who is included in the term "party," the California rule in the rule itself, and the ABA rule in the Comment. Finally, neither rule expressly requires that an attorney ask a party if the party is represented before engaging in communication.

2002 Model Rules:

MR 4.2 was amended to permit communication with a represented party if permitted by court order. Ca. Rule 2-100(C)(3) permits communications with represented parties that are otherwise authorized by law.

ABA Model Rule 4.3

1983 Model Rules:

There is no California ethics rule that parallels MR 4.3 or addresses this topic directly, though Cal. B&P Code §6128(a) makes it a misdemeanor offense for any attorney who is guilty of any deceit or collusion, or who consents to any deceit or collusion, with intent to deceive any "party."

2002 Model Rules:

MR 4.3 adds a requirement that a lawyer not give legal advice to an unrepresented person other than the advice to secure counsel, if the lawyer knows or reasonably should know that the interests of such a person are or have a reasonable possibility of being in conflict with the interests of the lawyer's client.

California has no similar rule or standards.

ABA Model Rule 4.4

1983 Model Rules:

There is no California ethics rule that directly parallels MR 4.4. Cal. B&P Code §6068(f), though of dubious validity as to the first quoted phrase, requires an attorney to "abstain from all offensive personality, and to advance no fact prejudicial to the honor or the reputation of a party or witness," unless it is necessary under the circumstances. Moreover, Cal. Rule 3-200 prohibits a lawyer from engaging in a matter for the purpose of harassing or injuring another.

2002 Model Rules:

In 2002, MR 4.4 added paragraph (b), which imposed a requirement that a lawyer who receives a document relating to the representation of the lawyer's client who knows or reasonably should know that the document was inadvertently sent shall promptly notify the sender. California has no corresponding rule or statute. However, the civil duty to notify the sender of inadvertently disclosed documents is similar. The current requirements under California law are spelled out by the State Supreme Court in *Rico v. Mitsubishi Motors Corp.*, 42 Cal. 4th 807 (2007). *Rico* in turn relied on the California Court of Appeal's reasoning in *State Compensation Ins. Fund v. WPS, Inc.*, 70 Cal.App.4th 644 (1999), which in turn relied in part on ABA Formal Ethics Opn. 98-368. Interestingly, the ABA Opinion has been superseded by MR 4.4(b) and ABA Formal Ethics Opn. 05-437. The earlier ABA opinion imposed an obligation on the lawyer not only to notify the sender, but also to refrain from reading the document and return or destroy the document as instructed by the other party. The latter ABA opinion, relying on MR 4.4(b), limits the requirement to informing the opposing side. Thus, the current approach in California may require the lawyer to do more than merely notify the other party as required under MR 4.4(b).

In 2012, MR 4.4 underwent several substantial amendments to both the black letter rule and the comments. Paragraph (b) was amended to impose the notification obligation when a lawyer receives inadvertently disclosed "electronically stored information" as well as when the lawyer receives a physical "document." Comment [2] was revised to include a definition of "inadvertently sent": "A document or electronically stored information is inadvertently sent when it is accidentally transmitted, such as when an email or letter is misaddressed or a document or electronically stored information is accidentally included with information that was intentionally transmitted." Further, the comment notes that the obligations under Rule 4.4(b) apply not only to "inadvertently sent" information, but also to information that may have been "inappropriately obtained" by the sending person, for example, when a former employee provides a lawyer with documents from the employee's former employer to which the employee is not entitled.

In California, a Court of Appeal case, *Clark v. Superior Court*, 196 Cal. App.4th 37 (2011), similarly holds that a lawyer's obligations under *Rico v. Mitsubishi* apply to inappropriately obtained documents or information, and not just documents or information that have been sent inadvertently. Finally, in 2012 MR 4.4, cmt. [2], was revised to explain its application to data that is electronically embedded in an electronic document (i.e., "metadata"). For obligations concerning metadata in California, see, e.g., Cal. State Bar Ethics Opns. 2007-174 and 2010-179.

ABA Model Rule 5.1

1983 Model Rules:

There is no California ethics rule that directly parallels MR 5.1. However, the Discussion to Cal. Rule 3-110 clarifies that the duty to act competently includes the duty to supervise the work of subordinate attorney and non-attorney employees or agents. The California State Bar has disciplined lawyers for failing adequately to supervise both subordinate attorney and non-attorney personnel. Cal. Rule 2-400 prohibits an attorney, in the management or operation of a law practice, from unlawfully discriminating against another person.

2002 Model Rules:

MR 5.1(a) was revised to include lawyers with "managerial authority" along with partners of law firms as those lawyers in a law office who are responsible for supervising nonlawyer employees and nonlawyer contract hires. The addition was made in part in recognition that law offices other than private law firms (e.g., government law offices, in-house corporate law offices) have supervisors who are not "partners" in the traditional sense of that term.

MR 1.0(c), the definition of "firm" or "law firm," was added in 2002 and includes "lawyers employed in a legal services organization or the legal department of a corporation or other organization."

ABA Model Rule 5.2

1983 Model Rules:

There is no California ethics rule that parallels MR 5.2(b)'s "safe harbor" or subordinate lawyers. Under California rules, an attorney is subject to discipline or a "willful" breach of any of the California Rules of Professional Conduct, pursuant to Cal. Rule 1-100.

2002 Model Rules: No substantive changes to the Model Rule.

ABA Model Rule 5.3

1983 Model Rules:

There is no California ethics rule that directly parallels MR 5.3. The Discussion to Cal. Rule 3-110 clarifies that the duty to act competently includes the duty to supervise the work of subordinate attorney and non-attorney employees or agents.

2002 Model Rules:

In 2002, MR 5.3(a) was revised to include lawyers with "managerial authority" along with partners of law firms as those lawyers who are responsible for supervising nonlawyer employees and nonlawyer contract hires. The addition was made in part in recognition that law offices other than private law firms (e.g., government law offices, in-house corporate law offices) have supervisors who are not "partners" in the traditional sense of that term. MR 1.0(c), the definition of "firm" or "law firm," was added in 2002 and includes "lawyers employed in a legal services organization or the legal department of a corporation or other organization."

In 2012, the title of the rule was amended to substitute "Assistance" for "Assistants," so that it now states more broadly: "Responsibilities Regarding Nonlawyer Assistance." In addition, the comments to MR 5.3 were substantially revised to address the issue of outsourcing. Former Comment [2] was moved and renumbered as Comment [1] and revised to provide that lawyers with managerial authority have to make "reasonable efforts to ensure that the firm has in effect measures giving reasonable assurance" that not only nonlawyers employed in the firm but also nonlawyers outside the firm who are retained to work on firm matters "act in a way compatible with the professional obligations of a lawyer." Former Comment [1] is now renumbered Comment [2] under a new heading, "Nonlawyers within the firm." New Comments [3] and [4], were also added under a new heading, "Nonlawyers outside the firm," to elaborate on supervisory lawyers' duties with respect to outsourced work of the firm. Comment [3] gives examples of outsourced work and provides factors to consider in determining the level of supervision that might be appropriate. Comment [4] provides that when a outside nonlawyer is utilized at the direction of the client, the lawyer and client should agree on allocating their respective responsibilities for supervising the nonlawyer.

Although California has no similar comprehensive treatment of outsourcing, the clarification in the Discussion to Cal. Rule 3-110 that the duty to act competently includes the duty to supervise the work of subordinate agents suggests that California lawyers have similar duties with respect to outsourced work. Compare Cal. State Bar Ethics Opn. 2004-165 (concerning duties with respect to work outsourced to contract lawyers).

ABA Model Rule 5.4

1983 Model Rules:

The topics addressed in MR 5.4 are found in separate California rules and statutes.

Cal. Rule 1-320 is substantially similar to MR 5.4(a). The California rule adds an additional exception to the general prohibition against sharing legal fees with a non-lawyer to allow an attorney to pay a prescribed fee to a lawyer referral service. Cal. Rule 1-320 also prohibits an attorney from compensating a non-lawyer for recommending or securing a client for the attorney or the attorney's law firm. Cal. Rule 1-320 also prohibits an attorney from giving anything of value to any representative of the media in return for publicity.

Cal. Rule 1-310 is virtually identical to MR 5.4(b).

Cal. Rule 1-600 parallels MR 5.4(c), but contains somewhat more extensive language. It specifically refers to the state bar's minimum standards for lawyer referral services, as defining those referral services to which an attorney may acceptably belong. Cal. Rule 3-310(F) prohibits an attorney from accepting compensation from one other than the client unless there is no interference with the attorney's independence of professional judgment or with the client-lawyer relationship.

Law corporations in California must be created, registered and administered in accordance with Cal. B&P Code § 6160 *et seq.* As with MR 5.4(d), shareholders of law corporations must be attorneys.

2002 Model Rules:

New MR 5.4(a)(4) permits a lawyer to share court-awarded legal fees with a nonprofit organization that employed, retained or recommended employment of the lawyer in the matter. There is no corresponding California provision.

MR 5.4(d)(2) was amended to expand the definition of a non-lawyer's responsibility to include similar responsibility to a corporate director or officer in any form of association.

ABA Model Rule 5.5

1983 Model Rules:

Cal. Rule 1-300 is virtually identical to the 1983 version of MR 5.5. Cal. Rule 1-300 prohibits an attorney from aiding any person or entity in the unauthorized practice of law, or practicing law in a jurisdiction where to do so violates that jurisdiction's rules. However, Cal. Rules of Court 9.45 to 9.48, effective on November 15, 2004, substantially expand the situations under which an out-of-state attorney not licensed in California may practice law in California without first being admitted to practice there. Rules 9.45 to 9.48 are discussed more fully under "2002 Model Rules," below.

2002 Model Rule:

In 2002, MR 5.5 was expanded significantly as a result of the work and recommendations of the ABA's Multijurisdictional Practice Commission. MR 5.5(a) retained the prohibition against a lawyer practicing in a jurisdiction where that lawyer is not admitted and where the regulations of that jurisdiction prohibit such law practice. MR 5.5(a) is still consistent with Cal. Rule 1-300. In 2012, a sentence was added to the end of Comment [1] to clarify the prohibition of MR 5.5(a). California has no similar Discussion section, rule or statute.

MR 5.5(b)(1) expands the prohibition of paragraph (a) by prohibiting establishing offices or other "systematic and continuous" presence in a jurisdiction or holding out oneself as entitled to practice in a jurisdiction where not admitted. See, however, the discussion of MR 5.5(d), which was amended in 2012, below. Similar prohibitions may be found in paragraph (c)(2) of Cal. Rule of Court 9.47, which governs lawyers who practice temporarily in California as part of litigation, and in paragraph (c)(2) of Cal. Rule of Court 9.48, governing non-litigating lawyers who are temporarily in California to provide legal services. MR 5.5(b)(2) prohibits lawyers not admitted to practice in a jurisdiction from holding themselves out to the public or representing that they are admitted to practice law. MR 5.5(b)(1) is consistent with the "virtual practice of law" prohibition established by the California Supreme Court in *Birbrower, Montalbano, Condon & Frank, P.C. v. Superior Ct.,* 17 Cal.4th 119, 128-129, 70 Cal.Rptr.2d 304 (1998) (hereinafter *Birbrower.*) MR 5.5(b)(2) is consistent with Calif. Business & Professions Code § 6126(a), and similar prohibitions in paragraph (c)(1) of Cal. Rule of Court 9.47 and in paragraph (c)(1) of Cal. Rule of Court 9.48.

MR 5.5(c) substantially expands the scope of permitted legal services that a lawyer may provide on a "temporary" basis in a jurisdiction where the lawyer is not admitted, if: (1) the lawyer is acting in association with an admitted lawyer; (2) the services are in connection with a court proceeding and the lawyer obtains authorization to proceed (such as by pro hac vice admission); (3) the services are in connection with an alternative dispute resolution proceeding arising out of the lawyer's own jurisdiction and the other jurisdiction does not require pro hac vice admission for ADR matters); or (4) where the services are reasonably related to the lawyer's practice in the "home" state.

MR 5.5(c)(1) [association with a lawyer admitted to practice in the jurisdiction] is inconsistent with *Birbrower, supra,* 17 Cal.4th at p. 126, fn.3 (noting there is no statutory exception to Bus. & Prof. Code § 6125's proscription on an out-of-state lawyer practicing in California that would permit such practice if the out-of-state lawyer were to associate with a California lawyer). Although there is no provision in rules 9.45 to 9.48 identical to paragraph (c)(1), rule 9.45 permits a lawyer not licensed in California to practice law under the supervision of a California-licensed attorney employed by a "qualifying legal service provider." Cal. Rule of Court 9.45(j)(1)(A). Unlike Model Rule 5.5(c)(1), which applies to any lawyer, only registered legal services lawyers come within the provisions of rule 9.45.

MR 5.5(c)(2) [when authorized by law to appear before a tribunal or reasonably expects to be so authorized] is partly consistent with Cal. Rule of Court 9.40 governing pro hac vice admission. It authorizes performance of legal services before admission pro hac vice, which is also authorized under subparagraphs (b)(2)-(4) of Cal. Rule of Court 9.47, governing lawyers who practice temporarily in California as part of litigation.

MR 5.5(c)(3) [performance of services in an alternative dispute resolution proceeding related to lawyer's practice] appears consistent with new California law passed in the wake of *Birbrower, supra.* Statutes include: Cal. Code of Civ. Proc. § 297.351 on international arbitrations, §1282.4 (g) and (i) on statutory collective bargaining arbitrations, § 1282.4(f) on legal services in connection with an arbitration pending in the jurisdiction in which the lawyer is admitted, and § 1282.4 and Cal. Rule of Ct. 9.43, governing pro hac vice admission to appear in other arbitrations. In addition, California Rule of Court 9.47 would also permit the same kinds of activities permitted under MR 5.5(c)(3). See Cal. Rule of Court 9.47(g)(1), which defines "formal legal proceeding" as "litigation, arbitration, mediation, or a legal action before an administrative decision-maker."

MR 5.5(c)(4) [legal services reasonably related to the lawyer's practice in a jurisdiction in which the lawyer is admitted to practice] has its counterpart in Cal. Rule of Court 9.48, governing non-litigating lawyers who are temporarily in California to provide legal services.

MR 5.5(d)(1) seeks to resolve the issue of in-house corporate counsel by permitting an out-of-jurisdiction lawyer to provide transactional (i.e., not requiring pro hac vice admission) legal services to an employer or its affiliates. Although this appears to be inconsistent with Calif. Bus. & Prof. Code §6125, Cal. Rule of Court 9.46 permits registered in-house counsel to provide the same kinds of legal services (i.e., those that do not require pro hac vice admission) to an employer or its affiliates.

Further, in 2002, MR 5.5(d)(2) was added as a clarifying change to recognize federal supremacy principles and that states themselves have adopted many statutory and regulatory exceptions to unauthorized practice of law. MR 5.5(d)(2) permits a lawyer to provide legal services where authorized by such laws. This is consistent with California case law, statutes and Cal. Rule of Court 9.48(b)(2). That rule expressly provides that an attorney meeting the rule's requirements, may provide "legal assistance or legal advice in California on an issue of federal law or of the law of a jurisdiction other than California *to attorneys licensed to practice law in California.*" (Emphasis added). See also generally Vapnek, et al. *California Practice Guide Professional Responsibility*

(The Rutter Group) at pp. 1-37 – 1-38; 1-50 – 1-59. In 2012, MR 5.5(d)(2) was amended to expand permitted practice not only when authorized by "federal or other law" of the jurisdiction, but also when permitted by a "rule" of the jurisdiction. This change was made specifically to permit a lawyer to take advantage of the ABA Model Rule on Practice Pending Admission, which was also adopted by the House of Delegates as proposed by the Ethics 2020 Commission. There is no corresponding California Rule or statute. A cross-reference to the Model Rule on Practice Pending Admission was also added to Comment [18] to MR 5.5.

In 2012, also as part of the adoption of the Ethics 2020 Commission's recommendations concerning its proposed Model Rule on Practice Pending Admission, the introductory paragraph of MR 5.5(d) was amended to permit lawyers to provide legal services "through an office or other systematic and continuous presence" in a jurisdiction to which the lawyer has moved provided that the lawyer also satisfies MR 5.5(d)(1) or (d)(2). This change in essence clarifies that a recently-moved lawyer may maintain "an office or other systematic and continuous presence" in providing legal services to a client who has moved to a jurisdiction in which the lawyer has not yet been authorized to practice law. California has no similar provision that would permit a lawyer to retain such a presence in California pending admission to California Bar.

In addition, in 2012, references to "prospective client" in Comment [21] were deleted. See discussion of the definition of "prospective client" under the Model Rule 1.18 comparison, above.

In 2013, among the final recommendations of the Ethics 20/20 Commission were revisions to Model Rule 5.5. These revisions all relate to granting foreign lawyers the same kinds of privileges accorded lawyers who work as in-house counsel and who are licensed in United States jurisdictions other than the jurisdiction in which they work.

Among the changes were: (1) revising the introductory clause of paragraph (d) by referring not only to a lawyer admitted in another U.S. jurisdiction, but also "in a foreign jurisdiction"; and (2) revising subparagraph (d)(1) extensively to permit such a foreign lawyer to provide legal services to the employer client but, if such legal services include advice on the law of a U.S. jurisdiction or of the United States, the foreign lawyer may do so only based upon the advice of a lawyer licensed by the jurisdiction to provide such advice. As noted in the resolution submitted to the ABA House of Delegates, these revision "provide a limited authority to practice for the foreign lawyer's employer on matters that do not involve U.S. law, unless the foreign lawyer consults with a U.S. lawyer authorized to provide such advice."

A new paragraph (e) was also added. It defines a "foreign lawyer" in "good standing" as a lawyer in his or her home country, admitted as a lawyer, counselor at law or the equivalent, and subject to "effective regulation and discipline" in the home country.

Conforming changes were made to the rule comment, including Comments [5], [7], [15], [16], [17] and [18].

California has no corresponding provisions in its counterpart rule of court, rule 9.46 ("Registered In-house Counsel"), whose application is limited to an "[a]ctive member in good standing of the bar of a United States state, jurisdiction, possession, territory, or dependency." Rule 9.46, paragraphs (a)(2) and (c)(1). Foreign legal consultants, who may register with the State Bar of California pursuant to California Rule of Court 9.44, are limited to providing advice on the law of the foreign country in which they are admitted. Rule 9.44, paragraphs (c) and (d). Rule 9.44 is provided in the section of this book entitled, "Selected California Rules Of Court Regarding Multijurisdictional Practice."

Finally, the Ethics 20/20 Commission also recommended, and the ABA House of Delegates adopted, conforming changes to the ABA Model Rule for Registration of In-House Counsel.

ABA Model Rule 5.6

1983 Model Rules:

Cal. Rule 1-500 is substantially similar to MR 5.6, but is broader and more detailed. Cal. Rule 1-500 generally prohibits an attorney from being a party to or participating in offering or making an agreement, whether in connection with the settlement of a lawsuit or otherwise, if the agreement restricts the right of a member to practice law. Cal. Rule 1-500 expressly permits such a restrictive agreement where it: 1) is a part of certain employment, shareholders' or partnership agreements; 2) requires payments to a member upon the attorney's retirement; or 3) is authorized by Business and Professions Code sections regarding agreements in lieu of discipline.

Unlike MR 5.6, Cal. Rule 1-500 expressly prohibits an attorney from being a party to or participating in offering or making an agreement that prevents the reporting of a violation of the California Rules of Professional Conduct. The Discussion to Cal. Rule 1-500 expressly clarifies that settling a case on the condition that an attorney refrain from representing other clients in similar litigation is prohibited.

2002 Model Rules: No substantive changes to the Model Rule.

ABA Model Rule 5.7

1983 Model Rules:

There is no California Rule of Professional Conduct that parallels MR 5.7 or addresses the topic of law-related services.

2002 Model Rules: No substantive changes to the Model Rule.

ABA Model Rule 6.1

1983 Model Rules:

There is no California Rule of Professional Conduct comparable to MR 6.1. While MR 6.1 creates an aspirational goal of 50 hours of pro bono public legal services per year, the California Rules of Professional Conduct are silent on this issue. However, the Board of Governors of the State Bar adopted a resolution in 1989 that was revised in 2002, which among other things, urges lawyers "to devote a reasonable amount of time, at least 50 hours per year, to provide or enable the direct delivery of legal services, without expectation of compensation other than reimbursement of expenses, to indigent individuals." See Pro Bono Resolution, in Part IV. Cal. B&P Code §6068(h) also states that it is the "duty" of an attorney "[n]ever to reject, for any consideration personal to himself or herself, the cause of the defenseless or the oppressed."

2002 Model Rules:

MR 6.1 was strengthened by adding a first sentence that states that every lawyer "has a professional responsibility to provide legal services to those unable to pay." This language stops short of a binding requirement, however.

ABA Model Rule 6.2

1983 Model Rules:

There is no California Rule of Professional Conduct that parallels MR 6.2 or addresses this topic. Cal B&P Code §6068(h) makes it the duty of an attorney never to reject, for any consideration personal to the attorney, the cause of the defenseless or the oppressed.

2002 Model Rules: No substantive changes to the Model Rule.

ABA Model Rule 6.3

1983 Model Rules:

Cal. Rule 1-600 is the California rule that parallels MR 6.3. Cal. Rule 1-600 prohibits an attorney from participating in a organization furnishing legal services if there is interference with the attorney's independence of professional judgment, or with the client-lawyer relationship, or if it allows unlicensed persons to practice law or receive part of the attorney's fee.

2002 Model Rules: No substantive changes to the Model Rule.

ABA Model Rule 6.4

1983 Model Rules:

There is no California Rule of Professional Conduct that parallels MR 6.4 or addresses the topic of law reform.

2002 Model Rules: No substantive changes to the Model Rule.

ABA Model Rule 6.5

There was no MR 6.5 prior to the 2002 revisions.

2002 Model Rules:

MR 6.5, regarding discrete task representation, or "unbundled" legal services, was entirely new in 2002. There was no California counterpart until 2009 (see discussion below).

MR 6.5(a) provides that a lawyer that provides limited legal services under the auspices of a program sponsored by a nonprofit organization or court is subject to the conflict of interest rules set forth in MRs 1.7 and 1.9(a) only if the lawyer knows that the representation of the client involves a conflict of interest and is subject to MR 1.10 only if the lawyer knows that another lawyer associated with the lawyer in a law firm is disqualified by MRs 1.7 or 1.9(a).

MR 6.5 (b) provides that MR 1.10 is inapplicable to these limited legal services except as provided above.

Comment [2] clarifies that a lawyer who provides short-term limited legal services pursuant to this Rule must secure the client's informed consent to the limited scope of the representation under MR 1.2(c).

California's new rule 1-650 is similar. The legal service organizations set forth in subsection (a) of the California rule specifically include government agencies, law schools, and bar associations and so may be interpreted more broadly than under MR 6.5. The California rule also states in part (C) that even if the individual lawyer providing the legal services is disqualified, that disqualification would not be imputed to any other lawyers participating in the legal services program.

ABA Model Rules 7.1 – 7.5

1983 Model Rules:

These rules all address the extent to which lawyers may communicate to the public about their legal services. We address them together here because the California Rules have a single rule which addresses the subject, Cal. Rule 1-400. Moreover, under authority authorized by Cal. Rule 1-400(E), the State Bar of California has promulgated sixteen "standards" which were not subject to state supreme court approval. These standards raise a rebuttable presumption of a violation of the rules of conduct. Cal. B&P Code §§ 6150 - 6159 also address advertising and communication issues, including lawyer referral services.

Unlike the Model Rules, Cal. Rule 1-400 expressly defines the words "communication" and "solicitation." Moreover, Cal. B&P Code §6157 expressly defines the word "advertisement." Finally, Cal. Rule 1-400(C), prohibiting certain solicitations, expressly recognizes that some solicitations are protected by the constitutions of both the United States and the State of California. The rules thus pay specific deference to the series of United States Supreme Court opinions on the issues of lawyer advertising and solicitation.

MR 7.1: Like MR 7.1 on misleading communications, Cal. Rule 1-400 and Cal. B&P Code §6157.1 prohibit false or misleading communications. Regarding advertisements by electronic media, including radio, television and computer networks, Business and Professions Code section 6158 requires that the advertisement as a whole must not be false, misleading or deceptive and must be factually substantiated.

Cal. Rule 1-400 specifically prohibits communications that: 1) contain any untrue statement; 2) contain any matter, or present or arrange any matter in a manner or format which is false, deceptive or which tends to confuse, deceive or mislead the public; 3) fail to state facts necessary to make the communications not misleading; 4) fail to state expressly or in context that it is a solicitation; or 5) are coercive or harassing.

Cal. B&P Code §6157.2 specifically prohibits advertisements containing: 1) guarantees regarding the outcome of a matter; 2) statements about attorneys getting quick cash results; 3) impersonations or dramatization of the attorney or of clients without disclosure; 4) a spokesperson used without disclosure; and 5) statements concerning contingency fees unless the statements disclose the client's responsibility for costs. Several of the state bar standards appended to Cal. Rule 1-400 address these concerns as well. Unlike MR 7.1, neither the California rule nor the statutes directly prohibit a comparison of the attorney's services with those of another lawyer.

MR 7.2: Like MR 7.2(b), Cal. Rule 1-400(F) requires that copies of communications be retained for two years, while the Cal. B&P Code §6159.1 requires retention of copies of advertisements for one year. Like MR 7.2(c), Cal. Rule 1-320 prohibits an attorney from compensating any person for recommending or securing clients and also prohibits an attorney from compensating the media in return for publicity.

Standard 12 to Cal. Rule 1-400 creates a presumption that a communication is misleading if it does not contain the name of at least one attorney responsible for it. This parallels MR 7.2(d). Cal. B&P Code §6157.3 requires that where an advertisement made on behalf of an attorney is paid for by someone other than the attorney, the business relationship between the attorney and that person must be disclosed.

MR 7.3: Like MR 7.3 on solicitation, Cal. Rule 1-400 prohibits in-person and telephone solicitation of clients with whom the attorney has no family or prior professional relationship, subject, however, to constitutional limitations. Like MR 7.3(c), Standard 5 to Cal. Rule 1-400 prohibits an unsolicited mailed communication which does not contain the words "Advertisement," "Newsletter" or the like. The standard details the manner of setting forth such words; however, it only creates a presumption that the communication is misleading.

MR 7.4: While Cal. Rule 1-400 does not address communication of fields of practice specifically, Cal. B&P Code §6158.2 presumes that such a communication is acceptable, so long as the communication as a whole is not false, misleading or deceptive. Regarding MR 7.4(c) on certified specialists, Standard 11 of Cal. Rule 1-400 creates a presumption that a communication is misleading unless it states the complete name of the entity which granted the certification as a specialist. However, there is no longer a limitation to State Bar certification programs.

MR 7.5: Several standards of Cal. Rule 1-400 create the presumption that a communication is misleading due to its reference to a firm name, trade name or fictitious name. These restrictions include stating or implying: 1) a relationship between an attorney and a government agency or legal services organization; and 2) that an attorney has a relationship to any other lawyer or law firm unless that relationship in fact exists.

The standards attached to Cal. Rule 1-400 create a number of other presumptions, not found in the Model Rules, that a communication is misleading where the communication: 1) contains guarantees, warranties or predictions regarding the result of the representation; 2) contains testimonials or endorsements with express disclaimers; 3) is delivered to a potential client whom the attorney knows or should reasonably know is in such a physical, emotional, or mental state that he or she would not be expected to exercise reasonable judgment in retaining counsel; 4) is transmitted at the scene of an accident or the like; 5) implies that the attorney is participating in a lawyer referral service unless the service is State Bar certified; 6) contains a dramatization without a disclaimer; 7) states or implies "no fee without recovery" without disclosing whether the client will be liable for costs; 8) states or implies that an attorney is able to provide legal services in a language other than English unless the lawyer can actually provide legal services in that language or the communication also states the employment title of the person who speaks such language; and 9) sets forth specific fees for a particular service where, in fact, the member charges a greater fee than advertised.

Cal. B&P Code §6158.1 also creates rebuttable presumptions, not found in the Model Rules, that an advertisement is misleading where it contains: 1) a message about the ultimate result; 2) displays or portrayals of injuries or accident scenes; and 3) a reference to money received for a client in a particular case or to potential monetary recovery for a prospective client.

2002 Model Rules:

MR 7.1: The revision deleted from the definition of false and misleading communications those statements that are likely to create an unjustified expectation about results the lawyer can achieve; state or imply results achieved by means that violate the ethics rules or other law; or compare the lawyer's services with other lawyers' services. These rules have been made admonitions by adding Comments [2], [3], and [4]. California did not adopt these definitions. In 2012, Comment [3] was amended to substitute "the public" for the phrase "a prospective client." See discussion of the definition of "prospective client" under the Model Rule 1.18 comparison, above.

MR 7.2: MR 7.2(a) deleted specific references to types of public media and added electronic media as a permissive means of lawyer advertising subject to the limitations in other advertising rules.

Former MR 7.2(b), requiring a lawyer to keep records of advertisements for a period of two years after distribution or broadcast, was deleted. Cal. Rule 1-400(F) and Cal. B & P Code §6159 continue to require that copies of advertisements be maintained for two years and one year, respectively.

MR 7.2(b)(1) was amended to expand the permitted payments by a lawyer to include the usual charges of a legal service plan or a not-for-profit or qualified lawyer referral service "approved by an appropriate regulatory authority." This expansion makes the exception similar to Cal. Rule 1-320(A)(4), and B&P Code §§6155 et seq.

MR 7.2(b)(4) has been added to permit strategic alliances among lawyers, law firms and non-lawyers and their entities. This new rule permits non-exclusive reciprocal referring relationships with the client disclosure. This rule appears to be at material variance with current California law. Reciprocal referrals from a non-lawyer businessperson or entity may be prohibited if it involves in-person solicitation [Cal. Rule 1-400(B)(C)]; and may be prohibited as promising something of value (future referrals) in exchange for a referral [Cal. Rule 1-320(B)]. Neither of these foregoing rules turn on disclosure to or consent by the client. However, referral agreements and reciprocal referrals between lawyers and law firms may be permitted in California with disclosure and client consent [Cal. Rule 2-200(B)].

In 2012, a number of amendments were made to the comments to MR 7.2. As noted in the discussion of the definition of "prospective client" under the Model Rule 1.18 comparison, above, references to "prospective client" were deleted or substituted in Comments [3], [6] and [7], and minor additions were made to Comments [1] through [3]. The most significant changes were made to Comment [5], which elaborates on permitted payments to third persons for generating client leads, including Internet-based client leads, as well as the limitations on such payments.

MR 7.3: In 2012, the title of MR 7.3 was changed from "Direct Contact with Prospective Clients" to "Solicitation of Clients." See discussion of the definition of "prospective client" under the Model Rule 1.18 comparison, above.

In 2002, MR 7.3(a) was amended to provide that in-person solicitation is committed when a lawyer solicits professional employment through "real-time electronic contact" (such as on-line real-time interactive chat rooms.) The amended rule also allows contact with other lawyers and close personal friends.

Cal. Rule 4-100(B) defines contact subject to the unlawful solicitation rule as being only personal or telephonic. But compare Cal. State Bar Formal Ethics Opn. 2004-166. Cal. Rule 4-100(C) continues to exempt only prior professional and familial relationships from the definition of a prospective client.

MR 7.3(b) adds electronic communication and real-time electronic contact to the means of contacting prospective clients that may be prohibited under the circumstances of the rule. Cal. Rule 1-400(A) and (D) contain similar prohibitions since all media communications, including electronic, are within the scope of the rule. In 2012, references to "prospective client" in MR 7.3(b)(1) and (c) were replaced by "target of the solicitation" and "anyone," respectively.

Also in 2012, a number of changes were made to the MR 7.3 comments. Most significantly, a new Comment [1], providing a definition of "solicitation," was added and the remaining comments were renumbered. Under that definition, a "solicitation" is a targeted communication "initiated by the lawyer that is directed to a specific person and that offers to provide, or can reasonably be understood as offering to provide, legal services." Cal. Rule 1-400(B), on the other hand, defines "solicitation" more narrowly, i.e., it must be "delivered in person or by telephone" or "directed to a person known to the sender to be represented by counsel in a matter which is the subject of the communication." Further, the term "prospective client" is replaced throughout the comments. See discussion of the definition of "prospective client" under the Model Rule 1.18 comparison, above.

MR 7.4: MR 7.4(c), concerning what statements about certified specialties were permitted, was deleted in its entirety. New subd. (d) was added. It provides that a lawyer shall not state or imply that a lawyer is certified as a specialist in a particular field of law unless the organization that has been approved by appropriate state authority or accredited by the American Bar Association, and the name of the certifying organization is clearly identified. This provision is substantially similar to Cal. Rule 1-400(D)(6).

MR 7.5, Comment 1: A new sentence was added to the end of comment [1] providing that it is misleading to use the name of a lawyer not associated with the firm, a predecessor of the firm or the name of a nonlawyer.

MR 7.5, Comment 1 is consistent with standards (7) and (8) to Cal. Rule 1-400(E), which presume any designation or statement of relationship (including "of counsel") where no relationship exists to be misleading. The prohibition in use of a nonlawyer name in a law practice is implied by Bus. & Prof Code §§6125, 6126 and Cal. Rules 1-300(A) [aiding a person or entity in the unauthorized practice of law] and 1-310 [forming a partnership with a nonlawyer where the activities of the partnership include the practice of law].

ABA Model Rule 7.6

1983 Model Rules:

MR 7.6 prohibits lawyers from accepting government legal engagement or appointments by a judge if the lawyer or law firm makes a political contribution or solicits political contributions for the purpose of being considered for such legal engagement. Other than the general prohibition contained in Cal. B.& P. Code §6106 not to engage in an act of corruption, California has no specific corresponding standard.

2002 Model Rules: No substantive changes to Model Rule.

ABA Model Rule 8.1

1983 Model Rules:

Cal. Rule 1-200 is the California rule that parallels MR 8.1. Like MR 8.1, Cal. Rule 1-200 prohibits an attorney from knowingly make a false statement regarding a material fact or knowingly fail to disclose a material fact in connection with an application for admission to the State Bar. Unlike MR 8.1, Cal. Rule 1-200 also expressly prohibits an attorney from furthering another's application for admission if the attorney knows that person to be unqualified in character, education or other relevant attributes.

2002 Model Rules: No substantive changes to Model Rule.

_____

ABA Model Rule 8.2

1983 Model Rules:

There is no California Rule of Professional Conduct that parallels MR 8.2 or addresses the topics of commenting on judges' qualifications or running for judicial office. However, California Rule 1-710 directs members of the Bar to comply with Canon 6D of the Code of Judicial Ethics whenever they act a temporary judges, referees or court-appointed arbitrators. (Canon 6D sets forth which provisions of the Code of Judicial Ethics apply to temporary judges, referees, etc.) There is no similar provision in the ABA Model Rules.

2002 Model Rules: No substantive changes to Model Rule.

_____

ABA Model Rule 8.3

1983 Model Rules:

There is no California Rule of Professional Conduct comparable to MR 8.3. The California Rules of Professional Conduct are silent on the issue of whether lawyers must report professional misconduct. Thus, a member of the State Bar of California has no duty to report the known professional misconduct of another lawyer to either the State Bar or another "appropriate professional authority."

2002 Model Rules: No substantive changes to Model Rule.

_____

ABA Model Rule 8.4

1983 Model Rules:

Many of the topics addressed in MR 8.4 are found in separate California rules and statutes.

MR 8.4(a): Cal. Rule 1-120 makes it professional misconduct for an attorney to knowingly assist in, solicit or induce any violation of the California Rules of Professional Conduct or the State Bar Act.

MR 8.4(b): Cal. B&P Code § 6101 makes conviction of a felony or misdemeanor involving moral turpitude a cause for disbarment or suspension. Cal. B&P Code §6068(a) makes it the duty of an attorney to support the Constitution and laws of the United States and California.

MR 8.4(c): Cal. B&P Code §6106 is similar. It makes the commission of any act involving moral turpitude, dishonesty or corruption grounds for attorney discipline, whether the act is committed while acting as an attorney or not.

MR 8.4(d): There is no California rule which specifically prohibits conduct prejudicial to the administration of justice. However, several sub-sections of Cal. B&P Code §6068, (b), (c), (d), (f) and (g), prohibit specific conduct which could constitute prejudice to the administration of justice. Moreover, Cal. Rules 3-200 and 3-210 prohibit similar conduct.

MR 8.4(e): There is no California Rule of Professional Conduct or Cal. B&P Code statute that parallels this provision or addresses the topic of claiming influence over a government agency.

MR 8.4(f): There is no California Rule of Professional Conduct or Cal. B&P Code statute that parallels this provision or addresses the topic of assisting a judge's improper conduct.

2002 Model Rules: No substantive changes to Model Rule.

ABA Model Rule 8.5

Cal. Rule 1-100(D) approximates MR 8.5. Cal. Rule 1-100(D) provides that, as to attorneys who are members of the State Bar of California, the California Rules of Professional Conduct govern the activities of such attorneys in and outside California, except where such attorneys practicing outside California are specifically required by a jurisdiction in which they are practicing to follow rules of professional conduct different from the California rules. Regarding attorneys from other jurisdictions who are not members of the State Bar of California, Cal. Rule 1-100(D) provides that the California Rules of Professional Conduct govern the activities of such attorneys while engaged in the performance of lawyer functions in California.

2002 Model Rules:

MR 8.5(a) extends the scope of disciplinary jurisdiction to regulate non-admitted lawyers that provide or offer to provide legal services in the jurisdiction.

MR 8.5(a) is consistent with Cal. Rule 1-100(D)(2) [lawyers performing lawyer functions in this state] and *Birbrower, Montalbano, Condon & Frank, P.C. v. Superior Ct.*, 17 Cal.4th 119, 128-129, 70 Cal.Rptr.2d 304 (1998), which evaluates at length the limits on out-of-state lawyers' practice in California, including the issue of lawyers appearing "virtually" in California.

MR 8.5(b)(1) changes the focus from court to "tribunal," deletes the requirement that the lawyer needs to be admitted before the court, and directs that the disciplinary law should be the law of the jurisdiction where the tribunal sits. Cal. Rule 1-100(D)(2) does not make this distinction, but the distinction is not inconsistent with California case law. (See e.g., *Birbrower, Montalbano, Condon & Frank, P.C. v. Super.* Ct, supra, 17 Cal.4th 119, 128-129, 70 Cal. Rptr.2d 304 [California disciplinary rules apply because the arbitration was in California]; *In re Mortgage & Realty Trust* 195 BR 740 (Bktcy. Ct. C.D. Cal. 1996) [court should apply disciplinary rules of the situs of the court].

MR 8.5(b)(2) adds new choice of law provisions for conduct outside the lawyer's "home" tribunal: The disciplinary rules of the jurisdiction in which the conduct occurred apply, unless the "predominant effect" of the conduct occurs in a different jurisdiction, in which case, the disciplinary rules of the affected jurisdiction apply. The rule also creates a safe harbor: a lawyer is not subject to discipline if the lawyer's conduct conforms to the rules of the jurisdiction which the lawyer reasonably believes is the predominant locale.

In 2013, among the final recommendations of the Ethics 20/20 Commission was a revision to Model Rule 8.5, Comment [5], which provides that in determining a lawyer's reasonable belief as to controlling law under paragraph (b)(2), a choice of law agreement, i.e., a written agreement between client and lawyer that specifies a particular jurisdiction may be considered if the agreement was obtained with the client's informed consent, confirmed in the agreement.

California has no such provision. Moreover, inasmuch as MR 8.5(b)(2) permits California to lose disciplinary jurisdiction covered by Cal Rule 1-100(D), it would be inconsistent with that rule. The "reasonable belief" safe harbor provision is also inconsistent with the California law that has a "willful" breach standard (Cal. Rule 1-100(A), Bus. & Prof. Code §6077.)

———

TABLE C   CALIFORNIA RULES OF PROFESSIONAL CONDUCT   587

TABLE C: CALIFORNIA STANDARDS RELATED TO SECTIONS OF THE ABA MODEL RULES OF PROFESSIONAL CONDUCT

CALIFORNIA RULES & CODE	1983 ABA MODEL RULES as amended
Rules of Professional Conduct	
Rule 1-100	MR 5.2, MR 8.5
Rule 1-110(D)	MR 8.5
Rule 1-110	[No ABA rule]
Rule 1-120	MR 8.4(a)
Rule 1-200	MR 8.1
Rule 1-300	MR 5.5
Rule 1-310	MR 5.4(b)
Rule 1-311	[No ABA rule]
Rule 1-320	MR 5.4(a), MR 7.2(c)
Rule 1-400	MR 7.1 - 7.5
Rule 1-400(F)	MR 7.2(b)
Standards [per 1-400(E)]	MR 7.3(c), MR 7.4, MR 7.5
Rule 1-500	MR 5.6
Rule 1-600	MR 2.1, MR 5.4(c), MR 6.3
Rule 1-700	MR 8.2(b)
Rule 2-100	MR 4.2
Rule 2-200	MR 1.5(e)
Rule 2-300	MR 1.17
Rule 2-400	MR 1.16, MR 5.1
Rule 3-110	MR 1.1, MR 1.3, MR 1.8(b), MR 1.14, MR 5.1, MR 5.3
Rule 3-200	MR 8.4(d), MR 1.16, MR 3.3, MR 3.4(d), MR 4.4
Rule 3-210	MR 1.2(d), MR 3.4(c), MR 8.4(d)
Rule 3-300	MR 1.8(a), MR 1.8(j)
Rule 3-310	MR 1.4(b), MR 1.7, MR 1.1
Rule 3-310(B)	MR 1.10
Rule 3-310(C)	MR 2.2
Rule 3-310(C)(3)	MR 1.9, MR 1.11
Rule 3-310(D)	MR 1.8(g)
Rule 3-310(E)	MR 1.9, MR 1.11

TABLE C
(Continued)

CALIFORNIA RULES & CODE	ABA MODEL RULES
Rule 3-400	MR 1.2, MR 1.2(c)
Rule 3-400(A)	MR 1.8(h)
Rule 3-400(B)	MR 1.8(h)
Rule 3-500	MR 1.2(e), MR 1.4(a)
Rule 3-510	MR 1.2
Rule 3-600	MR 1.13
Rule 3-700	MR 1.2(e), MR 1.16
Rule 4-100	MR 1.15
Rule 4-100(B)	MR 1.15(b)
Rule 4-200	MR 1.4(b), MR 1.5
Rule 4-210	MR 1.8(e)
Rule 4-300	[no ABA rule]
Rule 4-400	MR 1.8(c)
Rule 5-100	[no ABA rule]
Rule 5-110	MR 3.8
Rule 5-120	MR 3.6
Rule 5-200	MR 3.3, MR 3.4(e), MR 3.7, MR 4.1
Rule 5-210	MR 3.7
Rule 5-220	MR 3.4
Rule 5-220(A)	MR 3.4(a), (b)
Rule 5-220(B)	MR 3.4(a), (b)
Rule 5-300	MR 3.5
Rule 5-300(A)	MR 3.5(a)
Rule 5-300(B)	MR 3.5(b)
Rule 5-310	MR 3.4(b), (f)
Rule 5-320	MR 3.5
Rule 5-320(E)	MR 3.5(a)
Rule 5-320(F)	MR 3.5(b)
Business & Professions Code	
§ 6068(a)	MR 8.4(b)
§ 6068(b)	MR 3.5(c), MR 8.4(d)
§ 6068(c)	MR 8.4(d), MR 3.1, MR 3.4(d)
§ 6068(d)	MR 8.4(d), MR 3.3, MR 3.4(a), (b), MR 4.1

TABLE C   CALIFORNIA RULES OF PROFESSIONAL CONDUCT   589

TABLE C
(Continued)

CALIFORNIA RULES & CODE	ABA MODEL RULES
§ 6068(e)	MR 1.6, MR 1.8(b), MR 1.13, MR 3.3
§ 6068(f)	MR 3.5(c), MR 4.4, MR 8.4(d)
§ 6068(g)	MR 8.4(d)
§ 6068(h)	MR 6.1, MR 6.2
§ 6068(m)	MR 1.2(e)
§ 6101	MR 8.4(b)
§ 6106	MR 4.1, MR 8.4(c)
§ 6128(a)	MR 3.3, MR 3.4(a), (b), MR 4.1, MR 4.3
§ 6147	MR 1.5(b), (c)
§ 6148	MR 1.2, MR 1.5(b), (c)
§ 6157.1	MR 7.1
§ 6157.2	MR 7.1
§ 6158	MR 7.1
§ 6158.1	MR 7.5
§ 6158.2	MR 7.4

PART IV

CALIFORNIA RULES AND STATUTES

California Rules Table of Contents 591

California Rules of Professional Conduct 591

Selected Statutes Table of Contents.. 643

Selected Statutes of the California State Bar Act
(Business & Professions Code) 643

Selected Provisions of the California Evidence Code................................... 643

Selected California Rules of Court Regarding
Multijurisdictional Practice.. 705

CALIFORNIA RULES OF PROFESSIONAL CONDUCT

(Approved by the California Supreme Court on November 28, 1988, as amended, operative on January 1, 2010)

TABLES OF RULES

CHAPTER 1. PROFESSIONAL INTEGRITY IN GENERAL

Rule		Page
1-100.	Rules of Professional Conduct, in General......................................	595
1-110.	Disciplinary Authority of the State Bar..	597
1-120.	Assisting, Soliciting, or Inducing Violations..................................	597
1-200.	False Statement Regarding Admission to the State Bar	597
1-300.	Unauthorized Practice of Law..	597
1-310.	Forming a Partnership With a Non-Lawyer.....................................	597
1-311.	Employment of Disbarred, Suspended, Resigned, or Involuntarily Inactive Member..	598
1-320.	Financial Arrangements With Non-Lawyers..................................	600
1-400.	Advertising and Solicitation..	601
1-500.	Agreements Restricting a Member's Practice...............................	605
1-600.	Legal Service Programs	605
1-650.	Limited Legal Services Programs	606
1-700.	Member as Candidate for Judicial Office.......................................	607
1-710.	Member as Temporary Judge, Referee, or Court-Appointed Arbitrator	608

CHAPTER 2. RELATIONSHIP AMONG MEMBERS

Rule   **Page**

2-100. Communication With a Represented Party 608

2-200. Financial Arrangements Among Lawyers 609

2-300. Sale or Purchase of a Law Practice of a Member,
Living or Deceased 610

2-400. Prohibited Discriminatory Conduct in a Law Practice. 612

CHAPTER 3. PROFESSIONAL RELATIONSHIP WITH CLIENTS

3-100. Confidential Information of a Client 613

3-110. Failing to Act Competently 618

3-120. Sexual Relations With Client. 619

3-200. Prohibited Objectives of Employment 620

3-210. Advising the Violation of Law 620

3-300. Avoiding Interests Adverse to a Client 620

3-310. Avoiding the Representation of Adverse Interests 621

3-320. Relationship With Other Party's Lawyer 624

3-400. Limiting Liability to Client 624

3-410. Disclosure of Professional Liability Insurance 625

3-500. Communication 626

3-510. Communication of Settlement Offer 626

3-600. Organization as Client 627

3-700. Termination of Employment 628

CHAPTER 4. FINANCIAL RELATIONSHIP WITH CLIENTS

4-100. Preserving Identity of Funds and Property of a Client 630

4-200. Fees for Legal Services 632

4-210. Payment of Personal or Business Expenses Incurred
by or for a Client 633

4-300. Purchasing Property at a Foreclosure or a Sale Subject
to Judicial Review 633

4-400. Gifts From Client 634

CHAPTER 5. ADVOCACY AND REPRESENTATION

5-100. Threatening Criminal, Administrative,
or Disciplinary Charges 634

5-110. Performing the Duty of Member in Government Service 635

Rule		Page
5-120.	Trial Publicity	635
5-200.	Trial Conduct	636
5-210.	Member as Witness	636
5-220.	Suppression of Evidence	637
5-300.	Contact With Officials	637
5-310.	Prohibited Contact With Witnesses	637
5-320.	Contact With Jurors	638

CHAPTER 1. Professional Integrity in General

Rule 1-100. Rules of Professional Conduct, in General

(A)   Purpose and Function.

The following rules are intended to regulate professional conduct of members of the State Bar through discipline. They have been adopted by the Board of Governors of the State Bar of California and approved by the Supreme Court of California pursuant to Business and Professions Code sections 6076 and 6077 to protect the public and to promote respect and confidence in the legal profession. These rules together with any standards adopted by the Board of Governors pursuant to these rules shall be binding upon all members of the State Bar.

For a willful breach of any of these rules, the Board of Governors has the power to discipline members as provided by law.

The prohibition of certain conduct in these rules is not exclusive. Members are also bound by applicable law including the State Bar Act (Bus. & Prof. Code, §6000 et seq.) and opinions of California courts. Although not binding, opinions of ethics committees in California should be consulted by members for guidance on proper professional conduct. Ethics opinions and rules and standards promulgated by other jurisdictions and bar associations may also be considered.

These rules are not intended to create new civil causes of action. Nothing in these rules shall be deemed to create, augment, diminish, or eliminate any substantive legal duty of lawyers or the non-disciplinary consequences of violating such a duty.

(B)   Definitions.

   (1)   "Law Firm" means:

      (a)   two or more lawyers whose activities constitute the practice of law, and who share its profits, expenses, and liabilities; or

      (b)   a law corporation which employs more than one lawyer; or

      (c)   a division, department, office, or group within a business entity, which includes more than one lawyer who performs legal services for the business entity; or

      (d)   a publicly funded entity which employs more than one lawyer to perform legal services.

   (2)   "Member" means a member of the State Bar of California.

   (3)   "Lawyer" means a member of the State Bar of California or a person who is admitted in good standing of and eligible to practice before the bar of any United States court or the highest court of the District of Columbia or any state, territory, or

insular possession of the United States, or is licensed to practice law in, or is admitted in good standing and eligible to practice before the bar of the highest court of, a foreign country or any political subdivision thereof.

(4)   "Associate" means an employee or fellow employee who is employed as a lawyer.

(5)   "Shareholder" means a shareholder in a professional corporation pursuant to Business and Professions Code section 6160 et seq.

(C)   Purpose of Discussions. Because it is a practical impossibility to convey in black letter form all of the nuances of these disciplinary rules, the comments contained in the Discussions of the rules, while they do not add independent basis for imposing discipline, are intended to provide guidance for interpreting the rules and practicing in compliance with them.

(D)   Geographic Scope of Rules.

(1)   As to members: These rules shall govern the activities of members in and outside this state, except as members lawfully practicing outside this state may be specifically required by a jurisdiction in which they are practicing to follow rules of professional conduct different from these rules.

(2)   As to lawyers from other jurisdictions who are not members: These rules shall also govern the activities of lawyers while engaged in the performance of lawyer functions in this state; but nothing contained in these rules shall be deemed to authorize the performance of such functions by such persons in this state except as otherwise permitted by law.

(E)   These rules may be cited and referred to as "Rules of Professional Conduct of the State Bar of California."

Discussion:

The Rules of Professional Conduct are intended to establish the standards for members for purposes of discipline. (See *Ames v. State Bar* (1973) 8 Cal.3d 910 [106 Cal.Rptr. 489].) The fact that a member has engaged in conduct that may be contrary to these rules does not automatically give rise to a civil cause of action. (See *Noble v. Sears, Roebuck & Co.* (1973) 33 Cal.App.3d 654 [109 Cal. Rptr. 269]; *Wilhelm v. Pray, Price, Williams & Russell* (1986) 186 Cal.App.3d 1324 [231 Cal.Rptr. 355].) These rules are not intended to supersede existing law relating to members in non-disciplinary contexts. (See, e.g., *Klemm v. Superior Court* (1977) 75 Cal.App.3d 893 [142 Cal.Rptr. 509] (motion for disqualification of counsel due to a conflict of interest); *Academy of California Optometrists, Inc. v Superior Court* (1975) 51 Cal.App.3d 999 [124 Cal. Rptr. 668] (duty to return client fi les); *Chronometrics, Inc. v. Sysgen, Inc.* (1980) 110 Cal.App.3d 597 [168 Cal.Rptr. 196] (disqualification of member appropriate remedy for improper communication with adverse party).

Law firm, as defined by subparagraph (B)(1), is not intended to include an association of lawyers who do not share profits, expenses, and liabilities. The subparagraph is not intended to imply that a law firm may include a person who is not a member in violation of the law governing the unauthorized practice of law. (Amended by order of the Supreme Court, operative September 14, 1992.)

Rule 1-110. Disciplinary Authority of the State Bar

A member shall comply with conditions attached to public or private reprovals or other discipline administered by the State Bar pursuant to Business and Professions Code sections 6077 and 6078 and rule 9.19, California Rules of Court. (Amended by order the Supreme Court, operative July 11, 2008.)

Rule 1-120. Assisting, Soliciting, or Inducing Violations

A member shall not knowingly assist in, solicit, or induce any violation of these rules or the State Bar Act.

Rule 1-200. False Statement Regarding Admission to the State Bar

(A)   A member shall not knowingly make a false statement regarding a material fact or knowingly fail to disclose a material fact in connection with an application for admission to the State Bar.

(B)   A member shall not further an application for admission to the State Bar of a person whom the member knows to be unqualified in respect to character, education, or other relevant attributes.

(C)   This rule shall not prevent a member from serving as counsel of record for an applicant for admission to practice in proceedings related to such admission.

Discussion:

For purposes of rule 1-200, "admission" includes readmission.

Rule 1-300. Unauthorized Practice of Law

(A)   A member shall not aid any person or entity in the unauthorized practice of law.

(B)   A member shall not practice law in a jurisdiction where to do so would be in violation of regulations of the profession in that jurisdiction.

Rule 1-310. Forming a Partnership With a Non-Lawyer

A member shall not form a partnership with a person who is not a lawyer if any of the activities of that partnership consist of the practice of law.

Discussion:

Rule 1-310 is not intended to govern members' activities which cannot be considered to constitute the practice of law. It is intended solely to preclude a member from being involved in the practice of law with a person who is not a lawyer. (Amended by order of Supreme Court, operative September 14, 1992.)

Rule 1-311. Employment of Disbarred, Suspended, Resigned, or Involuntarily Inactive Member.

(A)   For purposes of this rule:

    (1)   "Employ" means to engage the services of another, including employees, agents, independent contractors and consultants, regardless of whether any compensation is paid;

    (2)   "Involuntarily inactive member" means a member who is ineligible to practice law as a result of action taken pursuant to Business and Professions Code sections 6007, 6203(d)(1)[1], or California Rule of Court 9.31; and

    (3)   "Resigned member" means a member who has resigned from the State Bar while disciplinary charges are pending.

(B)   A member shall not employ, associate professionally with, or aid a person the member knows or reasonably should know is a disbarred, suspended, resigned, or involuntarily inactive member to perform the following on behalf of the member's client:

    (1)   Render legal consultation or advice to the client;

    (2)   Appear on behalf of a client in any hearing or proceeding or before any judicial officer, arbitrator, mediator, court, public agency, referee, magistrate, commissioner, or hearing officer;

    (3)   Appear as a representative of the client at a deposition or other discovery matter;

    (4)   Negotiate or transact any matter for or on behalf of the client with third parties;

    (5)   Receive, disburse or otherwise handle the client's funds; or

    (6)   Engage in activities which constitute the practice of law.

(C)   A member may employ, associate professionally with, or aid a disbarred, suspended, resigned, or involuntarily inactive member to perform research, drafting or clerical activities, including but not limited to:

    (1)   Legal work of a preparatory nature, such as legal research, the assemblage of data and other necessary information, drafting of pleadings, briefs, and other similar documents;

---

[1] **Editors' Note:** During its consideration of this rule, the California State Bar Rules Revision Commission ("RRC") determined that the reference in paragraph (A)(2) to Business & Professions Code § 6203(c) was incorrect. The reference should be to section 6203(d)(1). Although this "housekeeping" change to rule 1-311 has not yet been officially adopted, the RRC has endorsed it, so we made the anticipated change beginning with the 2006 edition.

(2)   Direct communication with the client or third parties regarding matters such as scheduling, billing, updates, confirmation of receipt or sending of correspondence and messages; or

(3)   Accompanying an active member in attending a deposition or other discovery matter for the limited purpose of providing clerical assistance to the active member who will appear as the representative of the client.

(D)   Prior to or at the time of employing a person the member knows or reasonably should know is a disbarred, suspended, resigned, or involuntarily inactive member, the member shall serve upon the State Bar written notice of the employment, including a full description of such person's current bar status. The written notice shall also list the activities prohibited in paragraph (B) and state that the disbarred, suspended, resigned, or involuntarily inactive member will not perform such activities. The member shall serve similar written notice upon each client on whose specific matter such person will work, prior to or at the time of employing such person to work on the client's specific matter. The member shall obtain proof of service of the client's written notice and shall retain such proof and a true and correct copy of the client's written notice for two years following termination of the member's employment with the client.

(E)   A member may, without client or State Bar notification, employ a disbarred, suspended, resigned, or involuntarily inactive member whose sole function is to perform office physical plant or equipment maintenance, courier or delivery services, catering, reception, typing or transcription, or other similar support activities.

(F)   Upon termination of the disbarred, suspended, resigned, or involuntarily inactive member, the member shall promptly serve upon the State Bar written notice of the termination.

Discussion:

For discussion of the activities that constitute the practice of law, see Farnham v. State Bar (1976) 17 Cal.3d 605 [131Cal.Rptr. 611]; Bluestein v. State Bar (1974) 13 Cal.3d 162 [118 Cal.Rptr. 175]; Baron v. City of Los Angeles (1970) 2 Cal.3d 535 [86 Cal.Rptr. 673]; Crawford v. State Bar (1960) 54 Cal.2d 659 [7 Cal.Rptr. 746]; People v. Merchants Protective Corporation (1922) 189 Cal. 531, 535 [209 P. 363]; People v. Landlords Professional Services (1989) 215 Cal. App.3d 1599 [264 Cal.Rptr. 548]; and People v. Sipper (1943) 61 Cal.App.2d Supp. 844 [142 P.2d 960].)

Paragraph (D) is not intended to prevent or discourage a member from fully discussing with the client the activities that will be performed by the disbarred, suspended, resigned, or involuntarily inactive member on the client's matter.

If a member's client is an organization, then the written notice required by paragraph (D) shall be served upon the highest authorized officer, employee, or constituent overseeing the particular engagement. (See rule 3-600.)

Nothing in rule 1-311 shall be deemed to limit or preclude any activity engaged in pursuant to rules 9.40, 9.41, 9.42, and 9.44 of the California Rules of Court, or any local rule of a federal district court concerning admission pro hac vice. (Added by Order of Supreme Court, operative August 1, 1996. Amended by order of the Supreme Court, operative July 11, 2008.)

Rule 1-320. Financial Arrangements With Non-Lawyers

(A)   Neither a member nor a law firm shall directly or indirectly share legal fees with a person who is not a lawyer, except that:

    (1)   An agreement between a member and a law firm, partner, or associate may provide for the payment of money after the member's death to the member's estate or to one or more specified persons over a reasonable period of time; or

    (2)   A member or law firm undertaking to complete unfinished legal business of a deceased member may pay to the estate of the deceased member or other person legally entitled thereto that proportion of the total compensation which fairly represents the services rendered by the deceased member;

    (3)   A member or law firm may include non-member employees in a compensation, profit-sharing, or retirement plan even though the plan is based in whole or in part on a profit-sharing arrangement, if such plan does not circumvent these rules or Business and Professions Code section 6000 et seq.; or

    (4)   A member may pay a prescribed registration, referral, or participation fee to a lawyer referral service established, sponsored, and operated in accordance with the State Bar of California's Minimum Standards for a Lawyer Referral Service in California.

(B)   A member shall not compensate, give, or promise anything of value to any person or entity for the purpose of recommending or securing employment of the member or the member's law firm by a client, or as a reward for having made a recommendation resulting in employment of the member or the member's law firm by a client. A member's offering of or giving a gift or gratuity to any person or entity having made a recommendation resulting in the employment of the member or the member's law firm shall not of itself violate this rule, provided that the gift or gratuity was not offered or given in consideration of any promise, agreement, or understanding that such a gift or gratuity would be forthcoming or that referrals would be made or encouraged in the future.

(C)   A member shall not compensate, give, or promise anything of value to any representative of the press, radio, television, or other communication medium in anticipation of or in return for publicity of the member, the law firm, or any other member as such in a news item, but the incidental provision of food or beverage shall not of itself violate this rule.

Discussion:

Rule 1-320(C) is not intended to preclude compensation to the communications media in exchange for advertising the member's or law firm's availability for professional employment.

Rule 1-400. Advertising and Solicitation

(A)   For purposes of this rule, "communication" means any message or offer made by or on behalf of a member concerning the availability for professional employment of a member or a law firm directed to any former, present, or prospective client, including but not limited to the following:

   (1)   Any use of firm name, trade name, fictitious name, or other professional designation of such member or law firm; or

   (2)   Any stationery, letterhead, business card, sign, brochure, or other comparable written material describing such member, law firm, or lawyers; or

   (3)   Any advertisement (regardless of medium) of such member or law firm directed to the general public or any substantial portion thereof; or

   (4)   Any unsolicited correspondence from a member or law firm directed to any person or entity.

(B)   For purposes of this rule, a "solicitation" means any communication:

   (1)   Concerning the availability for professional employment of a member or a law firm in which a significant motive is pecuniary gain; and

   (2)   Which is;

      (a)   delivered in person or by telephone, or

      (b)   directed by any means to a person known to the sender to be represented by counsel in a matter which is a subject of the communication.

(C)   A solicitation shall not be made by or on behalf of a member or law firm to a prospective client with whom the member or law firm has no family or prior professional relationship, unless the solicitation is protected from abridgment by the Constitution of the United States or by the Constitution of the State of California. A solicitation to a former or present client in the discharge of a member's or law firm's professional duties is not prohibited.

(D)   A communication or a solicitation (as defined herein) shall not:

   (1)   Contain any untrue statement; or

   (2)   Contain any matter, or present or arrange any matter in a manner or format which is false, deceptive, or which tends to confuse, deceive, or mislead the public; or

    (3)   Omit to state any fact necessary to make the statements made, in the light of circumstances under which they are made, not misleading to the public; or

    (4)   Fail to indicate clearly, expressly, or by context, that it is a communication or solicitation, as the case may be; or

    (5)   Be transmitted in any manner which involves intrusion, coercion, duress, compulsion, intimidation, threats, or vexatious or harassing conduct; or

    (6)   State that a member is a "certified specialist" unless the member holds a current certificate as a specialist issued by the Board of Legal Specialization, or any other entity accredited by the State Bar to designate specialists pursuant to standards adopted by the Board of Governors, and states the complete name of the entity which granted certification.

(E)   The Board of Governors of the State Bar shall formulate and adopt standards as to communications which will be presumed to violate this rule 1-400. The standards shall only be used as presumptions affecting the burden of proof in disciplinary proceedings involving alleged violations of these rules. "Presumption affecting the burden of proof" means that presumption defined in Evidence Code sections 605 and 606. Such standards formulated and adopted by the Board, as from time to time amended, shall be effective and binding on all members.

(F)   A member shall retain for two years a true and correct copy or recording of any communication made by written or electronic media. Upon written request, the member shall make any such copy or recording available to the State Bar, and, if requested, shall provide to the State Bar evidence to support any factual or objective claim contained in the communication.

Standards:

Pursuant to rule 1-400(E) the Board of Governors of the State Bar has adopted the following standards, effective May 27, 1989 as forms of "communication" defined in Rule 1-400(A) which are presumed to be in violation of Rule 1-400:

    (1)   A "communication" which contains guarantees, warranties, or predictions regarding the result of the representation.

    (2)   A "communication" which contains testimonials about or endorsements of a member unless such communication also contains an express disclaimer such as "this testimonial or endorsement does not constitute a guarantee, warranty, or prediction regarding the outcome of your legal matter."

    (3)   A "communication" which is delivered to a potential client whom the member knows or should reasonably know is in such a physical, emotional, or mental state that he or she would not be expected to exercise reasonable judgment as to the retention of counsel.

(4)   A "communication" which is transmitted at the scene of an accident or at or en route to a hospital, emergency care center, or other health care facility.

(5)   A "communication," except professional announcements, seeking professional employment for pecuniary gain, which is transmitted by mail or equivalent means which does not bear the word "Advertisement," "Newsletter" or words of similar import in 12 point print on the first page. If such communication, including firm brochures, newsletters, recent legal development advisories, and similar materials, is transmitted in an envelope, the envelope shall bear the word "Advertisement," "Newsletter" or words of similar import on the outside thereof.

(6)   A "communication" in the form of a firm name, trade name, fictitious name, or other professional designation which states or implies a relationship between any member in private practice and a government agency or instrumentality or a public or non-profit legal services organization.

(7)   A "communication" in the form of a firm name, trade name, fictitious name, or other professional designation which states or implies that a member has a relationship to any other lawyer or a law firm as a partner or associate, or officer or shareholder pursuant to Business and Professions Code sections 6160-6172 unless such relationship in fact exists.

(8)   A "communication" which states or implies that a member or law firm is "of counsel" to another lawyer or a law firm unless the former has a relationship with the latter (other than as a partner or associate, or officer or shareholder pursuant to Business and Professions Code sections 6160-6172) which is close, personal, continuous, and regular.

(9)   A "communication" in the form of a firm name, trade name, fictitious name, or other professional designation used by a member or law firm in private practice which differs materially from any other such designation used by such member or law firm at the same time in the same community.

(10)   A "communication" which implies that the member or law firm is participating in a lawyer referral service which has been certified by the State Bar of California or as having satisfied the Minimum Standards for Lawyer Referral Services in California, when that is not the case.

Standard (11) was repealed effective June 1, 1997.

[(11)   A "communication" which states or implies that a member is a "certified specialist" unless such communication also states the complete name of the entity which granted the certification as a specialist. (**Editors' Note:** *Standard (11) was repealed by order of the California Supreme Court, effective June 1, 1997.*

Rule 1-400(D)(6) contains operative language on this subject similar to this former standard.)]

[The remaining standards 12-16 were <u>not</u> renumbered.]

(12)   A "communication," except professional announcements in the form of an advertisement primarily directed to seeking professional employment primarily for pecuniary gain transmitted to the general public or any substantial portion thereof by mail or equivalent means or by means of television, radio, newspaper, magazine or other form of commercial mass media which does not state the name of the member responsible for the communication. When the communication is made on behalf of a law firm, the communication shall state the name of at least one member responsible for it.

(13)   A "communication" which contains a dramatization unless such communication contains a disclaimer which states "this is a dramatization" or words of similar import.

(14)   A "communication" which states or implies "no fee without recovery" unless such communication also expressly discloses whether or not the client will be liable for costs.

(15)   A "communication" which states or implies that a member is able to provide legal services in a language other than English unless the member can actually provide legal services in such language or the communication also states in the language of the communication (a) the employment title of the person who speaks such language and (b) that the person is not a member of the State Bar of California, if that is the case.

(16)   An unsolicited "communication" transmitted to the general public or any substantial portion thereof primarily directed to seeking professional employment primarily for pecuniary gain which sets forth a specific fee or range of fees for a particular service where, in fact, the member charges a greater fee than advertised in such communication within a period of 90 days following dissemination of such communication, unless such communication expressly specifies a shorter period of time regarding the advertised fee. Where the communication is published in the classified or "yellow pages" section of telephone, business or legal directories or in other media not published more frequently than once a year, the member shall conform to the advertised fee for a period of one year from initial publication, unless such communication expressly specifies a shorter period of time regarding the advertised fee. (Amended by order of Supreme Court, operative September 14, 1992. Standard (5) amended by the Board of Governors, effective May 11, 1994. Standards (12) - (16) added by the Board of Governors, effective May 11, 1994.)

(Amended by order of Supreme Court, operative September 14, 1992. Standard (5) amended by the Board of Governors, effective May 11, 1994. Standards (12) - (16) added by the Board of Governors, effective May 11, 1994. Standard (11) *repealed June 1, 1997*)

Rule 1-500. Agreements Restricting a Member's Practice

(A) A member shall not be a party to or participate in offering or making an agreement, whether in connection with the settlement of a lawsuit or otherwise, if the agreement restricts the right of a member to practice law, except that this rule shall not prohibit such an agreement which:

    (1) Is a part of an employment, shareholders', or partnership agreement among members provided the restrictive agreement does not survive the termination of the employment, shareholder, or partnership relationship; or

    (2) Requires payments to a member upon the member's retirement from the practice of law; or

    (3) Is authorized by Business & Professions Code sections 6092.5, subdivision (i) or 6093.

(B) A member shall not be a party to or participate in offering or making an agreement which precludes the reporting of a violation of these rules.

Discussion:

Paragraph (A) makes it clear that the practice, in connection with settlement agreements, of proposing that a member refrain from representing other clients in similar litigation, is prohibited. Neither counsel may demand or suggest such provisions nor may opposing counsel accede or agree to such provisions.

Paragraph (A) permits a restrictive covenant in a law corporation, partnership, or employment agreement. The law corporation shareholder, partner, or associate may agree not to have a separate practice during the existence of the relationship; however, upon termination of the relationship (whether voluntary or involuntary), the member is free to practice law without any contractual restriction except in the case of retirement from the active practice of law. (Amended by order of Supreme Court, operative September 14, 1992.)

Rule 1-600. Legal Service Programs

(A) A member shall not participate in a nongovernmental program, activity, or organization furnishing, recommending, or paying for legal services, which allows any third person or organization to interfere with the member's independence of professional judgment, or with the client-lawyer relationship, or allows unlicensed persons to practice law, or allows any third person or organization to receive directly or indirectly any part of the consideration paid to the member except as permitted by these rules, or otherwise violates the State Bar Act or these rules.

(B)   The Board of Governors of the State Bar shall formulate and adopt
        Minimum Standards for Lawyer Referral Services, which, as from time
        to time amended, shall be binding on members.

Discussion:

The participation of a member in a lawyer referral service established, sponsored, supervised, and operated in conformity with the Minimum Standards for a Lawyer Referral Service in California is encouraged and is not, of itself, a violation of these rules.

Rule 1-600 is not intended to override any contractual agreement or relationship between insurers and insureds regarding the provision of legal services.

Rule 1-600 is not intended to apply to the activities of a public agency responsible for providing legal services to a government or to the public.

For purposes of paragraph (A), "a nongovernmental program, activity, or organization" includes, but is not limited to group, prepaid, and voluntary legal service programs, activities, or organizations.

Rule 1-650. Limited Legal Services Programs

(A)   A member who, under the auspices of a program sponsored by a court, government agency, bar association, law school, or nonprofit organization, provides short-term limited legal services to a client without expectation by either the member or the client that the member will provide continuing representation in the matter:

    (1)   is subject to rule 3-310 only if the member knows that the representation of the client involves a conflict of interest; and

    (2)   has an imputed conflict of interest only if the member knows that another lawyer associated with the member in a law firm would have a conflict of interest under rule 3-310 with respect to the matter.

(B)   Except as provided in paragraph (A)(2), a conflict of interest that arises from a member's participation in a program under paragraph (A) will not be imputed to the member's law firm.

(C)   The personal disqualification of a lawyer participating in the program will not be imputed to other lawyers participating in the program.

Discussion:

[1] Courts, government agencies, bar associations, law schools and various nonprofit organizations have established programs through which lawyers provide short-term limited legal services – such as advice or the completion of legal forms – that will assist persons in addressing their legal problems without further representation by a lawyer. In these programs, such as legal-advice hotlines, advice-only clinics or prose counseling programs, whenever a lawyer-client relationship is established, there is no expectation that the lawyer's representation of the client will continue beyond that limited consultation. Such programs are normally operated under circumstances in which it is not feasible

for a lawyer to systematically screen for conflicts of interest as is generally required before undertaking a representation.

[2]   A member who provides short-term limited legal services pursuant to rule 1-650 must secure the client's informed consent to the limited scope of the representation. If a short-term limited representation would not be reasonable under the circumstances, the member may offer advice to the client but must also advise the client of the need for further assistance of counsel. See rule 3-110. Except as provided in this rule 1-650, the Rules of Professional Conduct and the State Bar Act, including the member's duty of confidentiality under Business and Professions Code § 6068(e)(1), are applicable to the limited representation.

[3]   A member who is representing a client in the circumstances addressed by rule 1-650 ordinarily is not able to check systematically for conflicts of interest. Therefore, paragraph (A)(1) requires compliance with rule 3-310 only if the member knows that the representation presents a conflict of interest for the member. In addition, paragraph (A)(2) imputes conflicts of interest to the member only if the member knows that another lawyer in the member's law firm would be disqualified under rule 3-310.

[4]   Because the limited nature of the services significantly reduces the risk of conflicts of interest with other matters being handled by the member's law firm, paragraph (B) provides that imputed conflicts of interest are inapplicable to a representation governed by this rule except as provided by paragraph (A)(2). Paragraph (A)(2) imputes conflicts of interest to the participating member when the member knows that any lawyer in the member's firm would be disqualified under rule 3-310. By virtue of paragraph (B), moreover, a member's participation in a short-term limited legal services program will not be imputed to the member's law firm or preclude the member's law firm from undertaking or continuing the representation of a client with interests adverse to a client being represented under the program's auspices. Nor will the personal disqualifi cation of a lawyer participating in the program be imputed to other lawyers participating in the program.

[5]   If, after commencing a short-term limited representation in accordance with rule 1-650, a member undertakes to represent the client in the matter on an ongoing basis, rule 3-310 and all other rules become applicable.

Rule 1-700. Member as Candidate for Judicial Office

(A)   A member who is a candidate for judicial office in California shall comply with Canon 5 of the Code of Judicial Ethics.

(B)   For purposes of this rule, "candidate for judicial office" means a member seeking judicial office by election. The determination of when a member is a candidate for judicial office is defined in the terminology section of the California Code of Judicial Ethics. A member's duty to comply with paragraph (A) shall end when the member announces withdrawal of the member's candidacy or when the results of the election are final, whichever occurs first.

Discussion:

Nothing in rule 1-700 shall be deemed to limit the applicability of any other rule or law. (Approved by order of the Supreme Court, effective November 21, 1997.)

Rule 1-710. Member as Temporary Judge, Referee, or Court-Appointed Arbitrator

A member who is serving as a temporary judge, referee, or court-appointed arbitrator, and is subject under the Code of Judicial Ethics to Canon 6D, shall comply with the terms of that canon.

Discussion

This rule is intended to permit the State Bar to discipline members who violate applicable portions of the Code of Judicial Ethics while acting in a judicial capacity pursuant to an order or appointment by a court. (Added by order of the California Supreme Court, effective March 18, 1999.)

CHAPTER 2. Relationship Among Members

Rule 2-100. Communication With a Represented Party

(A)   While representing a client, a member shall not communicate directly or indirectly about the subject of the representation with a party the member knows to be represented by another lawyer in the matter, unless the member has the consent of the other lawyer.

(B)   For purposes of this rule, a "party" includes:

    (1)   An officer, director, or managing agent of a corporation or association, and a partner or managing agent of a partnership; or

    (2)   An association member or an employee of an association, corporation, or partnership, if the subject of the communication is any act or omission of such person in connection with the matter which may be binding upon or imputed to the organization for purposes of civil or criminal liability or whose statement may constitute an admission on the part of the organization.

(C)   This rule shall not prohibit:

    (1)   Communications with a public officer, board, committee, or body;

    (2)   Communications initiated by a party seeking advice or representation from an independent lawyer of the party's choice; or

    (3)   Communications otherwise authorized by law.

Discussion:

Rule 2-100 is intended to control communications between a member and persons the member knows to be represented by counsel unless a statutory scheme or case law will override the rule. There are a number of express statutory schemes which authorize communications between a member and person who would otherwise be subject to this rule. These statutes protect a variety of other rights such as the right of employees to organize and to engage in collective bargaining, employee health and safety, or equal employment opportunity. Other applicable law also includes the authority of government prosecutors and investigators to conduct criminal investigations, as limited by the relevant decisional law.

Rule 2-100 is not intended to prevent the parties themselves from communicating with respect to the subject matter of the representation, and nothing in the rule prevents a member from advising the client that such communication can be made. Moreover, the rule does not prohibit a member who is also a party to a legal matter from directly or indirectly communicating on his or her own behalf with a represented party. Such a member has independent rights as a party which should not be abrogated because of his or her professional status. To prevent any possible abuse in such situations, the counsel for the opposing party may advise that party (1) about the risks and benefits of communications with a lawyer-party, and (2) not to accept or engage in communications with the lawyer-party.

Rule 2-100 also addresses the situation in which member A is contacted by an opposing party who is represented and, because of dissatisfaction with that party's counsel, seeks A's independent advice. Since A is employed by the opposition, the member cannot give independent advice.

As used in paragraph (A), "the subject of the representation," "matter," and "party" are not limited to a litigation context.

Paragraph (B) is intended to apply only to persons employed at the time of the communication. (See *Triple A Machine Shop, Inc. v. State of California* (1989) 213 Cal.App.3d 131 [261 Cal.Rptr. 493].).

Subparagraph (C)(2) is intended to permit a member to communicate with a party seeking to hire new counsel or to obtain a second opinion. A member contacted by such a party continues to be bound by other Rules of Professional Conduct. (See, e.g., rules 1-400 and 3-310.). (Amended by order of Supreme Court, operative September 14, 1992.)

Rule 2-200. Financial Arrangements Among Lawyers

(A)   A member shall not divide a fee for legal services with a lawyer who is not a partner of, associate of, or shareholder with the member unless:

    (1)   The client has consented in writing thereto after a full disclosure has been made in writing that a division of fees will be made and the terms of such division; and

    (2)   The total fee charged by all lawyers is not increased solely by reason of the provision for division of fees and is not unconscionable as that term is defined in rule 4-200.

(B)   Except as permitted in paragraph (A) of this rule or rule 2-300, a member shall not compensate, give, or promise anything of value to any lawyer for the purpose of recommending or securing employment of the member or the member's law firm by a client, or as a reward for having made a recommendation resulting in employment of the member or the member's law firm by a client. A member's offering of or giving a gift or gratuity to any lawyer who has made a recommendation resulting in the employment of the member or the member's law firm shall not of itself violate this rule, provided that the gift or gratuity was not offered in consideration of any promise, agreement, or understanding that such a gift or gratuity would be forthcoming or that referrals would be made or encouraged in the future.

Rule 2-300. Sale or Purchase of a Law Practice of a Member, Living or Deceased

All or substantially all of the law practice of a member, living or deceased, including goodwill, may be sold to another member or law firm subject to all the following conditions:

(A)   Fees charged to clients shall not be increased solely by reason of such sale.

(B)   If the sale contemplates the transfer of responsibility for work not yet completed or responsibility for client files or information protected by Business and Professions Code section 6068, subdivision (e), then;

      (1)   if the seller is deceased, or has a conservator or other person acting in a representative capacity, and no member has been appointed to act for the seller pursuant to Business and Professions Code section 6180.5, then prior to the transfer;

            (a)   the purchaser shall cause a written notice to be given to the client stating that the interest in the law practice is being transferred to the purchaser; that the client has the right to retain other counsel; that the client may take possession of any client papers and property, as required by rule 3-700(D); and that if no response is received to the notification within 90 days of the sending of such notice, or in the event the client's rights would be prejudiced by a failure to act during that time, the purchaser may act on behalf of the client until otherwise notified by the client. Such notice shall comply with the requirements as set forth in rule 1-400(D) and any provisions relating to attorney-client fee arrangements, and

            (b)   the purchaser shall obtain the written consent of the client provided that such consent shall be presumed until otherwise notified by the client if no response is received to the notification specified in subparagraph within 90 days of the date of the sending of such notification to the client's last address as shown on the records of the seller, or the client's rights would be prejudiced by a failure to act during such 90-day period.

    (2)   in all other circumstances, not less than 90 days prior to the transfer;

        (a)   the seller, or the member appointed to act for the seller pursuant to Business and Professions Code section 6180.5, shall cause a written notice to be given to the client stating that the interest in the law practice is being transferred to the purchaser; that the client has the right to retain other counsel; that the client may take possession of any client papers and property, as required by rule 3-700(D); and that if no response is received to the notification within 90 days of the sending of such notice, the purchaser may act on behalf of the client until otherwise notified by the client. Such notice shall comply with the requirements as set forth in rule 1-400(D) and any provisions relating to attorney-client fee arrangements, and

        (b)   the seller, or the member appointed to act for the seller pursuant to Business and Professions Code section 6180.5, shall obtain the written consent of the client prior to the transfer provided that such consent shall be presumed until otherwise notified by the client if no response is received to the notification specified in subparagraph (a) within 90 days of the date of the sending of such notification to the client's last address as shown on the records of the seller.

(C)   If substitution is required by the rules of a tribunal in which a matter is pending, all steps necessary to substitute a member shall be taken.

(D)   All activity of a purchaser or potential purchaser under this rule shall be subject to compliance with rules 3-300 and 3-310 where applicable.

(E)   Confidential information shall not be disclosed to a nonmember in connection with a sale under this rule.

(F)   Admission to or retirement from a law partnership or law corporation, retirement plans and similar arrangements, or sale of tangible assets of a law practice shall not be deemed a sale or purchase under this rule.

Discussion:

Paragraph (A) is intended to prohibit the purchaser from charging the former clients of the seller a higher fee than the purchaser is charging his or her existing clients.

"All or substantially all of the law practice of a member" means, for purposes of rule 2-300, that, for example, a member may retain one or two clients who have such a longstanding personal and professional relationship with the member that transfer of those clients' files is not feasible. Conversely, rule 2-300 is not intended to authorize the sale of a law practice in a piecemeal fashion except as may be required by subparagraph (B)(1)(a) or paragraph (D).

Transfer of individual client matters, where permitted, is governed by rule 2-200. Payment of a fee to a non-lawyer broker for arranging the sale or purchase of a law practice is governed by rule 1-320. (Amended by order of Supreme Court, operative September 14, 1992.)

Rule 2-400. Prohibited Discriminatory Conduct in a Law Practice.

(A)   For purposes of this rule:

    (1)   "law practice" includes sole practices, law partnerships, law corporations, corporate and governmental legal departments, and other entities which employ members to practice law;

    (2)   "knowingly permit" means a failure to advocate correction action where the member knows of a discriminatory policy or practice which results in the unlawful discrimination prohibited in paragraph (B); and

    (3)   "unlawfully" and "unlawful" shall be determined by reference to applicable state or federal statutes or decisions making unlawful discrimination in employment and in offering goods and services to the public.

(B)   In the management or operation of a law practice, a member shall not unlawfully discriminate or knowingly permit unlawful discrimination on the basis of race, national origin, sex, sexual orientation, religion, age or disability in:

    (1)   hiring, promoting, discharging, or otherwise determining the conditions of employment of any person; or

    (2)   accepting or terminating representation of any client.

(C)   No disciplinary investigation or proceeding may be initiated by the State Bar against a member under this rule unless and until a tribunal of competent jurisdiction, other than a disciplinary tribunal, shall have first adjudicated a complaint of alleged discrimination and found that unlawful conduct occurred. Upon such adjudication, the tribunal finding or verdict shall then be admissible evidence of the occurrence or non-occurrence of the alleged discrimination in any disciplinary proceeding initiated under this rule. In order for discipline to be imposed under this rule, however, the finding of unlawfulness must be upheld and final after appeal, the time for filing an appeal must have expired, or the appeal must have been dismissed.

Discussion

In order for discriminatory conduct to be actionable under this rule, it must first be found to be unlawful by an appropriate civil administrative or judicial tribunal under applicable state or federal law. Until there is a finding of civil unlawfulness, there is no basis for disciplinary action under this rule.

A complaint of misconduct based on this rule may be filed with the State Bar following a finding of unlawfulness in the first instance even though that finding is thereafter appealed.

A disciplinary investigation or proceeding for conduct coming within this rule may be initiated and maintained, however, if such conduct warrants discipline under California Business and Professions Code sections 6106 and 6068, the California Supreme Court's inherent authority to impose discipline, or other disciplinary standard. (Added by order of Supreme Court, effective March 1, 1995.)

CHAPTER 3. Professional Relationship With Clients

Rule 3-100. Confidential Information of a Client[2]

(A)   A member shall not reveal information protected from disclosure by Business and Professions Code section 6068, subdivision (e)(1) without the informed consent of the client, or as provided in paragraph (B) of this rule.

(B)   A member may, but is not required to, reveal confidential information relating to the representation of a client to the extent that the member reasonably believes the disclosure is necessary to prevent a criminal act that the member reasonably believes is likely to result in death of, or substantial bodily harm to, an individual.

(C)   Before revealing confidential information to prevent a criminal act as provided in paragraph (B), a member shall, if reasonable under the circumstances:

  (1)   make a good faith effort to persuade the client: (i) not to commit or to continue the criminal act or (ii) to pursue a course of conduct that will prevent the threatened death or substantial bodily harm; or do both (i) and (ii); and

  (2)   inform the client, at an appropriate time, of the member's ability or decision to reveal information as provided in paragraph (B).

(D)   In revealing confidential information as provided in paragraph (B), the member's disclosure must be no more than is necessary to prevent the criminal act, given the information known to the member at the time of the disclosure.

(E)   A member who does not reveal information permitted by paragraph (B) does not violate this rule.

---

[2] California Rule of Professional Conduct 3-100 was approved by the California Supreme Court on June 23, 2004, and became effective on July 1, 2004. Rule 3-100 was drafted pursuant to Assembly Bill 1101 ("AB 1101"), which amended the California Business & Professions Code by adding § 6068(e)(2), thus creating the first express exception to the duty of confidentiality in California. The rule was intended to address certain issues that the legislature had identified would arise in the implementation of § 6068(e)(2), for example, (1) whether an attorney must inform the client of the attorney's discretion under § 6068(e)(2) to reveal the client's confidential information, and (2) whether an attorney must take steps to attempt to dissuade the client from committing the perceived criminal conduct before revealing the client's confidential information. The rule squarely addresses those issues in paragraphs (C)(2) and (C)(1), respectively, and in the corresponding Discussion sections.

Discussion:

[1] *Duty of confidentiality.* Paragraph (A) relates to a member's obligations under Business and Professions Code section 6068, subdivision (e)(1), which provides it is a duty of a member: "To maintain inviolate the confidence, and at every peril to himself or herself to preserve the secrets, of his or her client." A member's duty to preserve the confidentiality of client information involves public policies of paramount importance. (*In Re Jordan* (1974) 12 Cal.3d 575, 580 [116 Cal.Rptr. 371].) Preserving the confidentiality of client information contributes to the trust that is the hallmark of the client-lawyer relationship. The client is thereby encouraged to seek legal assistance and to communicate fully and frankly with the lawyer even as to embarrassing or legally damaging subject matter. The lawyer needs this information to represent the client effectively and, if necessary, to advise the client to refrain from wrongful conduct. Almost without exception, clients come to lawyers in order to determine their rights and what is, in the complex of laws and regulations, deemed to be legal and correct. Based upon experience, lawyers know that almost all clients follow the advice given, and the law is upheld. Paragraph (A) thus recognizes a fundamental principle in the client-lawyer relationship, that, in the absence of the client's informed consent, a member must not reveal information relating to the representation. (See, e.g., *Commercial Standard Title Co. v. Superior Court* (1979) 92 Cal.App.3d 934, 945 [155 Cal.Rptr.393].)

[2] *Client-lawyer confidentiality encompasses the attorney-client privilege, the work-product doctrine and ethical standards of confidentiality.* The principle of client-lawyer confidentiality applies to information relating to the representation, whatever its source, and encompasses matters communicated in confidence by the client, and therefore protected by the attorney-client privilege, matters protected by the work product doctrine, and matters protected under ethical standards of confidentiality, all as established in law, rule and policy. (See *In the Matter of Johnson* (Rev. Dept. 2000) 4 Cal. State Bar Ct. Rptr. 179; *Goldstein Lees* (1975) 46 Cal.3d 614, 621 [120 Cal. Rptr. 253].) The attorney-client privilege and work-product doctrine apply in judicial and other proceedings in which a member may be called as a witness or be otherwise compelled to produce evidence concerning a client. A member's ethical duty of confidentiality is not so limited in its scope of protection for the client-lawyer relationship of trust and prevents a member from revealing the client's confidential information even when not confronted with such compulsion. Thus, a member may not reveal such information except with the consent of the client or as authorized or required by the State Bar Act, these rules, or other law.

[3] *Narrow exception to duty of confidentiality under this Rule.* Notwithstanding the important public policies promoted by lawyers adhering to the core duty of confidentiality, the overriding value of life permits disclosures otherwise prohibited under Business & Professions Code section 6068(e), subdivision (1). Paragraph (B), which restates Business and Professions Code section 6068, subdivision (e)(2), identifies a narrow confidentiality exception, absent the client's informed consent, when a member reasonably believes that disclosure is necessary to prevent a criminal act

that the member reasonably believes is likely to result in the death of, or substantial bodily harm to an individual. Evidence Code section 956.5, which relates to the evidentiary attorney-client privilege, sets forth a similar express exception. Although a member is not permitted to reveal confidential information concerning a client's past, completed criminal acts, the policy favoring the preservation of human life that underlies this exception to the duty of confidentiality and the evidentiary privilege permits disclosure to prevent a future or ongoing criminal act.

[4] *Member not subject to discipline for revealing confidential information as permitted under this Rule.* Rule 3-100, which restates Business and Professions Code section 6068, subdivision (e)(2), reflects a balancing between the interests of preserving client confidentiality and of preventing a criminal act that a member reasonably believes is likely to result in death or substantial bodily harm to an individual. A member who reveals information as permitted under this rule is not subject to discipline.

[5] *No duty to reveal confidential information.* Neither Business and Professions Code section 6068, subdivision (e)(2) nor this rule imposes an affirmative obligation on a member to reveal information in order to prevent harm. (See rule 1-100(A).) A member may decide not to reveal confidential information. Whether a member chooses to reveal confidential information as permitted under this rule is a matter for the individual member to decide, based on all the facts and circumstances, such as those discussed in paragraph [6] of this discussion.

[6] *Deciding to reveal confidential information as permitted under paragraph (B).* Disclosure permitted under paragraph (B) is ordinarily a last resort, when no other available action is reasonably likely to prevent the criminal act. Prior to revealing information as permitted under paragraph (B), the member must, if reasonable under the circumstances, make a good faith effort to persuade the client to take steps to avoid the criminal act or threatened harm. Among the factors to be considered in determining whether to disclose confidential information are the following:

(1)   the amount of time that the member has to make a decision about disclosure;

(2)   whether the client or a third party has made similar threats before and whether they have ever acted or attempted to act upon them;

(3)   whether the member believes the member's efforts to persuade the client or a third person not to engage in the criminal conduct have or have not been successful;

(4)   the extent of adverse effect to the client's rights under the Fifth, Sixth and Fourteenth Amendments of the United States Constitution and analogous rights and privacy rights under Article 1 of the Constitution of the State of California that may result from disclosure contemplated by the member;

(5)   the extent of other adverse effects to the client that may result from disclosure contemplated by the member; and

(6)   the nature and extent of information that must be disclosed to prevent the criminal act or threatened harm.

A member may also consider whether the prospective harm to the victim or victims is imminent in deciding whether to disclose the confidential information. However, the imminence of the harm is not a prerequisite to disclosure and a member may disclose the information without waiting until immediately before the harm is likely to occur.

[7]   *Counseling client or third person not to commit a criminal act reasonably likely to result in death of substantial bodily harm.* Subparagraph (C)(1) provides that before a member may reveal confidential information, the member must, if reasonable under the circumstances, make a good faith effort to persuade the client not to commit or to continue the criminal act, or to persuade the client to otherwise pursue a course of conduct that will prevent the threatened death or substantial bodily harm, or if necessary, do both. The interests protected by such counseling is the client's interest in limiting disclosure of confidential information and in taking responsible action to deal with situations attributable to the client. If a client, whether in response to the member's counseling or otherwise, takes corrective action – such as by ceasing the criminal act before harm is caused – the option for permissive disclosure by the member would cease as the threat posed by the criminal act would no longer be present. When the actor is a nonclient or when the act is deliberate or malicious, the member who contemplates making adverse disclosure of confidential information may reasonably conclude that the compelling interests of the member or others in their own personal safety preclude personal contact with the actor. Before counseling an actor who is a nonclient, the member should, if reasonable under the circumstances, first advise the client of the member's intended course of action. If a client or another person has already acted but the intended harm has not yet occurred, the member should consider, if reasonable under the circumstances, efforts to persuade the client or third person to warn the victim or consider other appropriate action to prevent the harm. Even when the member has concluded that paragraph (B) does not permit the member to reveal confidential information, the member nevertheless is permitted to counsel the client as to why it may be in the client's best interest to consent to the attorney's disclosure of that information.

[8]   *Disclosure of confidential information must be no more than is reasonably necessary to prevent the criminal act.* Under paragraph (D), disclosure of confidential information, when made, must be no more extensive than the member reasonably believes necessary to prevent the criminal act. Disclosure should allow access to the confidential information to only those persons who the member reasonably believes can act to prevent the harm. Under some circumstances, a member may determine that the best course to pursue is to make an anonymous disclosure to the potential victim or relevant law-enforcement authorities. What particular measures are reasonable depends on the circumstances known to the member. Relevant circumstances include the time available, whether the victim might be unaware of the threat, the member's prior

course of dealings with the client, and the extent of the adverse effect on the client that may result from the disclosure contemplated by the member.

[9] Informing client of member's ability or decision to reveal confidential *information under subparagraph (C)(2)*. A member is required to keep a client reasonably informed about significant developments regarding the employment or representation. Rule 3-500; Business and Professions Code, section 6068, subdivision (m). Paragraph (C)(2), however, recognizes that under certain circumstances, informing a client of the member's ability or decision to reveal confidential information under paragraph (B) would likely increase the risk of death or substantial bodily harm, not only to the originally-intended victims of the criminal act, but also to the client or members of the client's family, or to the member or the member's family or associates. Therefore, paragraph (C)(2) requires a member to inform the client of the member's ability or decision to reveal confidential information as provided in paragraph (B) only if it is reasonable to do so under the circumstances. Paragraph (C)(2) further recognizes that the appropriate time for the member to inform the client may vary depending upon the circumstances. (See paragraph [10] of this discussion.) Among the factors to be considered in determining an appropriate time, if any, to inform a client are:

(1) whether the client is an experienced user of legal services;

(2) the frequency of the member's contact with the client;

(3) the nature and length of the professional relationship with the client;

(4) whether the member and client have discussed the member's duty of confidentiality or any exceptions to that duty;

(5) the likelihood that the client's matter will involve information within paragraph (B);

(6) the member's belief, if applicable, that so informing the client is likely to increase the likelihood that a criminal act likely to result in the death of, or substantial bodily harm to, an individual; and

(7) the member's belief, if applicable, that good faith efforts to persuade a client not to act on a threat have failed.

[10] *Avoiding a chilling effect on the lawyer-client relationship*. The foregoing flexible approach to the member's informing a client of his or her ability or decision to reveal confidential information recognizes the concern that informing a client about limits on confidentiality may have a chilling effect on client communication. (See Discussion paragraph [1].) To avoid that chilling effect, one member may choose to inform the client of the member's ability to reveal information as early as the outset of the representation, while another member may choose to inform a client only at a point when that client has imparted information that may fall under paragraph (B), or even choose not to inform a client until such time as the member attempts to counsel the client as contemplated in Discussion paragraph [7]. In each situation, the member will have discharged properly the requirement under subparagraph (C)(2), and will not be subject to discipline.

[11] *Informing client that disclosure has been made; termination of the lawyer-client relationship.* When a member has revealed confidential information under paragraph (B), in all but extraordinary cases the relationship between member and client will have deteriorated so as to make the member's representation of the client impossible. Therefore, the member is required to seek to withdraw from the representation (see rule 3-700(B)), unless the member is able to obtain the client's informed consent to the member's continued representation. The member must inform the client of the fact of the member's disclosure unless the member has a compelling interest in not informing the client, such as to protect the member, the member's family or a third person from the risk of death or substantial bodily harm.

[12] *Other consequences of the member's disclosure.* Depending upon the circumstances of a member's disclosure of confidential information, there may be other important issues that a member must address. For example, if a member will be called as a witness in the client's matter, then rule 5-210 should be considered. Similarly, the member should consider his or her duties of loyalty and competency (rule 3-110).

[13] *Other exceptions to confidentiality under California law.* Rule 3-100 is not intended to augment, diminish, or preclude reliance upon, any other exceptions to the duty to preserve the confidentiality of client information recognized under California law.

Rule 3-110. Failing to Act Competently.

(A)   A member shall not intentionally, recklessly, or repeatedly fail to perform legal services with competence.

(B)   For purposes of this rule, "competence" in any legal service shall mean to apply the 1) diligence, 2) learning and skill, and 3) mental, emotional, and physical ability reasonably necessary for the performance of such service.

(C)   If a member does not have sufficient learning and skill when the legal service is undertaken, the member may nonetheless perform such services competently by 1) associating with or, where appropriate, professionally consulting another lawyer reasonably believed to be competent, or 2) by acquiring sufficient learning and skill before performance is required.

Discussion:

The duties set forth in rule 3-110 include the duty to supervise the work of subordinate attorney and non-attorney employees or agents. (See, e.g., *Waysman v. State Bar* (1986) 41 Cal.3d 452; *Tousil v. State Bar* (1985) 38 Cal.3d 337, 342 [211 Cal.Rptr. 525]; *Palomo v. State Bar* (1984) 36 Cal.3d 785 [205 Cal.Rptr. 834]; *Crane v. State Bar* (1981) 30 Cal.3d 117, 122; *Black v. State Bar* (1972) 7 Cal.3d 676, 692 [103 Cal.Rptr. 288; 499 P.2d 968]; *Vaughn v. State Bar* (1972) 6 Cal.3d 847, 857-858 [100 Cal.Rptr. 713; 494 P.2d 1257]; *Moore v. State Bar* (1964) 62 Cal.2d 74, 81 [41 Cal.Rptr. 161; 396 P.2d 577].).

In an emergency a lawyer may give advice or assistance in a matter in which the lawyer does not have the skill ordinarily required where referral to or consultation with another lawyer would be impractical. Even in an emergency, however, assistance should be limited to that reasonably necessary in the circumstances.

Rule 3-120. Sexual Relations With Client.

(A)   For purposes of this rule, "sexual relations" means sexual intercourse or the touching of an intimate part of another person for the purpose of sexual arousal, gratification, or abuse.

(B)   A member shall not:

   (1)   Require or demand sexual relations with a client incident to or as a condition of any professional representation; or

   (2)   Employ coercion, intimidation, or undue influence in entering into sexual relations with a client; or

   (3)   Continue representation of a client with whom the member has sexual relations if such sexual relations cause the member to perform legal services incompetently in violation of rule 3-110.

(C)   Paragraph (B) shall not apply to sexual relations between members and their spouses or to ongoing consensual sexual relationships which predate the initiation of the lawyer-client relationship.

(D)   Where a lawyer in a firm has sexual relations with a client but does not participate in the representation of that client, the lawyers in the firm shall not be subject to discipline under this rule solely because of the occurrence of such sexual relations.

Discussion

Rule 3-120 is intended to prohibit sexual exploitation by a lawyer in the course of a professional representation. Often, based upon the nature of the underlying representation, a client exhibits great emotional vulnerability and dependence upon the advice and guidance of counsel. Attorneys owe the utmost duty of good faith and fidelity to clients. (See, e.g., *Greenbaum v. State Bar* (1976) 15 Cal.3d 893, 903 [126 Cal.Rptr. 785]; *Alkow v. State Bar* (1971) 3 Cal.3d 924, 935 [92 Cal.Rptr. 278]; *Cutler v. State Bar* (1969) 71 Cal.2d 241, 251 [78 Cal.Rptr 172]; *Clancy v. State Bar* (1969) 71 Cal.2d 140, 146 [77 Cal.Rptr. 657].) The relationship between an attorney and client is a fiduciary relationship of the very highest character and all dealings between an attorney and client that are beneficial to the attorney will be closely scrutinized with the utmost strictness for unfairness. (See, e.g., *Giovanazzi v. State Bar* (1980) 28 Cal.3d 465, 472 [169 Cal.Rptr.581]; *Benson v. State Bar* (1975) 13 Cal.3d 581, 586 [119 Cal. Rptr. 297]; *Lee v. State Bar* (1970) 2 Cal.3d 927, 939 [88 Cal.Rptr. 361]; *Clancy v. State Bar* (1969) 71 Cal.2d 140, 146 [77 Cal.Rptr.657].) Where attorneys exercise undue influence over clients or take unfair advantage of clients, discipline is appropriate. (See, e.g., *Magee v. State Bar* (1962) 58 Cal.2d 423 [24 Cal. Rptr. 839]; *Lantz v. State Bar* (1931) 212 Cal. 213 [298 P. 497].)

In all client matters, a member is advised to keep clients' interests paramount in the course of the member's representation.

For purposes of this rule, if the client is an organization, any individual overseeing the representation shall be deemed to be the client. (See rule 3-600.).

Although paragraph (C) excludes representation of certain clients from the scope of rule 3-120, such exclusion is not intended to preclude the applicability of other Rules of Professional Conduct, including rule 3-110. (Added by order of Supreme Court, operative September 14, 1992.)

Rule 3-200. Prohibited Objectives of Employment

A member shall not seek, accept, or continue employment if the member knows or should know that the objective of such employment is:

(A)   To bring an action, conduct a defense, assert a position in litigation, or take an appeal, without probable cause and for the purpose of harassing or maliciously injuring any person; or

(B)   To present a claim or defense in litigation that is not warranted under existing law, unless it can be supported by a good faith argument for an extension, modification, or reversal of such existing law.

Rule 3-210. Advising the Violation of Law

A member shall not advise the violation of any law, rule, or ruling of a tribunal unless the member believes in good faith that such law, rule, or ruling is invalid. A member may take appropriate steps in good faith to test the validity of any law, rule, or ruling of a tribunal.

Discussion:

Rule 3-210 is intended to apply not only to the prospective conduct of a client but also to the interaction between the member and client and to the specific legal service sought by the client from the member. An example of the former is the handling of physical evidence of a crime in the possession of the client and offered to the member. (See *People v. Meredith* (1981) 29 Cal.3d 682 [175 Cal.Rptr. 612].) An example of the latter is a request that the member negotiate the return of stolen property in exchange for the owner's agreement not to report the theft to the police or prosecutorial authorities. (See *People v. Pic'l* (1982) 31 Cal.3d 731 [183 Cal.Rptr. 685].)

Rule 3-300. Avoiding Interests Adverse to a Client

A member shall not enter into a business transaction with a client; or knowingly acquire an ownership, possessory, security, or other pecuniary interest adverse to a client, unless each of the following requirements has been satisfied:

(A)   The transaction or acquisition and its terms are fair and reasonable to the client and are fully disclosed and transmitted in writing to the client in a manner which should reasonably have been understood by the client; and

(B)   The client is advised in writing that the client may seek the advice of an independent lawyer of the client's choice and is given a reasonable opportunity to seek that advice; and

(C)   The client thereafter consents in writing to the terms of the transaction or the terms of the acquisition.

Discussion:

Rule 3-300 is not intended to apply to the agreement by which the member is retained by the client, unless the agreement confers on the member an ownership, possessory, security, or other pecuniary interest adverse to the client. Such an agreement is governed, in part, by rule 4-200.

Rule 3-300 is not intended to apply where the member and client each make an investment on terms offered to the general public or a significant portion thereof. For example, rule 3-300 is not intended to apply where A, a member, invests in a limited partnership syndicated by a third party. B, A's client, makes the same investment. Although A and B are each investing in the same business, A did not enter into the transaction "with" B for the purposes of the rule.

Rule 3-300 is intended to apply where the member wishes to obtain an interest in client's property in order to secure the amount of the member's past due or future fees. (Amended by order of Supreme Court, operative September 14, 1992.)

Rule 3-310. Avoiding the Representation of Adverse Interests

(A)   For purposes of this rule:

    (1)   "Disclosure" means informing the client or former client of the relevant circumstances and of the actual and reasonably foreseeable adverse consequences to the client or former client;

    (2)   "Informed written consent" means the client's or former client's written agreement to the representation following written disclosure;

    (3)   "Written" means any writing as defi ned in Evidence Code section 250.

(B)   A member shall not accept or continue representation of a client without providing written disclosure to the client where:

    (1)   The member has a legal, business, financial, professional, or personal relationship with a party or witness in the same matter; or

    (2)   The member knows or reasonably should know that:

        (a)   the member previously had a legal, business, financial, professional, or personal relationship with a party or witness in the same matter; and

        (b)   the previous relationship would substantially affect the member's representation; or

(3)   The member has or had a legal, business, financial, professional, or personal relationship with another person or entity the member knows or reasonably should know would be affected substantially by resolution of the matter; or

(4)   The member has or had a legal, business, financial, or professional interest in the subject matter of the representation.

(C)   A member shall not, without the informed written consent of each client:

(1)   Accept representation of more than one client in a matter in which the interests of the clients potentially conflict; or

(2)   Accept or continue representation of more than one client in a matter in which the interests of the clients actually conflict; or

(3)   Represent a client in a matter and at the same time in a separate matter accept as a client a person or entity whose interest in the first matter is adverse to the client in the first matter.

(D)   A member who represents two or more clients shall not enter into an aggregate settlement of the claims or against the clients without the informed written consent of each client.

(E)   A member shall not, without the informed written consent of the client or former client, accept employment adverse to the client or former client where, by reason of the representation of the client or former client, the member has obtained confidential information material to the employment.

(F)   A member shall not accept compensation for representing a client from one other than the client unless:

(1)   There is no interference with the member's independence of professional judgment or with the client-lawyer relationship; and

(2)   Information relating to representation of the client is protected as required by Business and Professions Code section 6068, subdivision (e); and

(3)   The member obtains the client's informed written consent, provided that no disclosure or consent is required if:

(a)   such nondisclosure is otherwise authorized by law; or

(b)   the member is rendering legal services on behalf of any public agency which provides legal services to other public agencies or the public.

By order of Supreme Court, operative March 3, 2003, the Discussion to rule 3-310 was amended to add a new paragraph after paragraph 8 of the Discussion, as indicated in the underlined text. No change was made to the black letter rule.]

Discussion:

Rule 3-310 is not intended to prohibit a member from representing parties having antagonistic positions on the same legal question that has arisen in different cases, unless representation of either client would be adversely affected.

Other rules and laws may preclude making adequate disclosure under this rule. If such disclosure is precluded, informed written consent is likewise precluded. (See, e.g., Business and Professions Code section 6068, subsection (e).)

Paragraph (B) is not intended to apply to the relationship of a member to another party's lawyer. Such relationships are governed by rule 3-320.

Paragraph (B) is not intended to require either the disclosure of the new engagement to a former client or the consent of the former client to the new engagement. However, such disclosure or consent is required if paragraph (E) applies.

While paragraph (B) deals with the issues of adequate disclosure to the present client or clients of the members present or past relationships to other parties or witnesses or present interest in the subject matter of the representation, paragraph (E) is intended to protect the confidences of another present or former client. These two paragraphs are to apply as complementary provisions.

Paragraph (B) is intended to apply only to a member's own relationships or interests, unless the member knows that a partner or associate in the same firm as the member has or had a relationship with another party or witness or has or had an interest in the subject matter of the representation.

Subparagraphs (C)(1) and (C)(2) are intended to apply to all types of legal employment, including the concurrent representation of multiple parties in litigation or in a single transaction or in some other common enterprise or legal relationship. Examples of the latter include the formation of a partnership for several partners or a corporation for several shareholders, the preparation of an ante-nuptial agreement, or joint or reciprocal wills for a husband and wife, or the resolution of an "uncontested" marital dissolution. In such situations, for the sake of convenience or economy, the parties may well prefer to employ a single counsel, but a member must disclose the potential adverse aspects of such multiple representation (e.g., Evid. Code §962) and must obtain the informed written consent of the clients thereto pursuant to subparagraph (C)(1). Moreover, if the potential adversity should become actual, the member must obtain the further informed written consent of the clients pursuant to subparagraph (C)(2).

Subparagraph (C)(3) is intended to apply to representations of clients in both litigation and transactional matters.

In *State Farm Mutual Automobile Insurance Company v. Federal Insurance Company* (1999) 72 Cal.App. 4th 1422 [86 Cal.Rptr.2d 20], the court held that subparagraph (C)(3) was violated when a member, retained by an insurer to defend one suit, and while that suit was still pending, filed a direct action against the same insurer in an unrelated action without securing the insurer's consent. Notwithstanding State Farm, subparagraph (C)(3) is not intended to apply with respect to the relationship between an insurer and a member when, in each matter, the insurer's interest is only as an indemnity provider and not as a direct party to the action.

There are some matters in which the conflicts are such that written consent may not suffice for non-disciplinary purposes. (See *Woods v. Superior Court* (1983) 149 Cal.App.3d 931 [197 Cal.Rptr. 185]; *Klemm v. Superior Court* (1977) 75 Cal.App.3d 893 [142 Cal.Rptr. 509]; *Ishmael v. Millington* (1966) 241 Cal. App.2d 520 [50 Cal.Rptr. 592].).

Paragraph (D) is not intended to apply to class action settlements subject to court approval.

Paragraph (F) is not intended to abrogate existing relationships between insurers and insureds whereby the insurer has the contractual right to unilaterally select counsel for the insured, where there is no conflict of interest. *(See San Diego Navy Federal Credit Union v. Cumis Insurance Society* (1984) 162 Cal.App.3d 358 [208 Cal.Rptr. 494].) (Amended by order of Supreme Court, operative September 14, 1992.)

Rule 3-320. Relationship With Other Party's Lawyer

A member shall not represent a client in a matter in which another party's lawyer is a spouse, parent, child, or sibling of the member, lives with the member, is a client of the member, or has an intimate personal relationship with the member, unless the member informs the client in writing of the relationship.

Discussion:

Rule 3-320 is not intended to apply to circumstances in which a member fails to advise the client of a relationship with another lawyer who is merely a partner or associate in the same law firm as the adverse party's counsel, and who has no direct involvement in the matter. (Amended by order of Supreme Court, operative September 14, 1992.)

Rule 3-400. Limiting Liability to Client

A member shall not:

(A)   Contract with a client prospectively limiting the member's liability to the client for the member's professional malpractice; or

(B)   Settle a claim or potential claim for the member's liability to the client for the member's professional malpractice, unless the client is informed in writing that the client may seek the advice of an independent lawyer of the client's choice regarding the settlement and is given a reasonable opportunity to seek that advice.

Discussion:

Rule 3-400 is not intended to apply to customary qualifications and limitations in legal opinions and memoranda, nor is it intended to prevent a member from reasonably limiting the scope of the member's employment or representation. (Amended by order of Supreme Court, operative September 14, 1992.)

Rule 3-410. Disclosure of Professional Liability Insurance

(A)   A member who knows or should know that he or she does not have professional liability insurance shall inform a client in writing, at the time of the client's engagement of the member, that the member does not have professional liability insurance whenever it is reasonably foreseeable that the total amount of the member's legal representation of the client in the matter will exceed four hours.

(B)   If a member does not provide the notice required under paragraph (A) at the time of a client's engagement of the member, and the member subsequently knows or should know that he or she no longer has professional liability insurance during the representation of the client, the member shall inform the client in writing within thirty days of the date that the member knows or should know that he or she no longer has professional liability insurance.

(C)   This rule does not apply to a member who is employed as a government lawyer or in-house counsel when that member is representing or providing legal advice to a client in that capacity.

(D)   This rule does not apply to legal services rendered in an emergency to avoid foreseeable prejudice to the rights or interests of the client.

(E)   This rule does not apply where the member has previously advised the client under Paragraph (A) or (B) that the member does not have professional liability insurance.

Discussion:

[1]   The disclosure obligation imposed by Paragraph (A) of this rule applies with respect to new clients and new engagements with returning clients.

[2]   A member may use the following language in making the disclosure required by Rule 3-410(A), and may include that language in a written fee agreement with the client or in a separate writing:

> "Pursuant to California Rule of Professional Conduct 3-410, I am informing you in writing that I do not have professional liability insurance."

[3]   A member may use the following language in making the disclosure required by Rule 3-410(B):

> "Pursuant to California Rule of Professional Conduct 3-410, I am informing you in writing that I no longer have professional liability insurance."

[4]   Rule 3-410(C) provides an exemption for a "government lawyer or in-house counsel when that member is representing or providing legal advice to a client in that capacity." The basis of both exemptions is essentially the same. The purpose of this rule is to provide information directly to a client if

a member is not covered by professional liability insurance. If a member is employed directly by and provides legal services directly for a private entity or a federal, state or local governmental entity, that entity presumably knows whether the member is or is not covered by professional liability insurance. The exemptions under this rule are limited to situations involving direct employment and representation, and do not, for example, apply to outside counsel for a private or governmental entity, or to counsel retained by an insurer to represent an insured. (Added by order of the Supreme Court, operative January 1, 2010.)

Rule 3-500. Communication

A member shall keep a client reasonably informed about significant developments relating to the employment or representation, including promptly complying with reasonable requests for information and copies of significant documents when necessary to keep the client so informed.

Discussion

Rule 3-500 is not intended to change a member's duties to his or her clients. It is intended to make clear that, while a client must be informed of significant developments in the matter, a member will not be disciplined for failing to communicate insignificant or irrelevant information. (See Bus. & Prof. Code, §6068, subd. (m).)

A member may contract with the client in their employment agreement that the client assumes responsibility for the cost of copying significant documents. This rule is not intended to prohibit a claim for the recovery of the member's expense in any subsequent legal proceeding.

Rule 3-500 is not intended to create, augment, diminish, or eliminate any application of the work product rule. The obligation of the member to provide work product to the client shall be governed by relevant statutory and decisional law. Additionally, this rule is not intended to apply to any document or correspondence that is subject to a protective order or non-disclosure agreement, or to override applicable statutory or decisional law requiring that certain information not be provided to criminal defendants who are clients of the member. (Amended by order of the Supreme Court, operative June 5, 1997)

Rule 3-510. Communication of Settlement Offer

(A)   A member shall promptly communicate to the member's client:

       (1)   All terms and conditions of any offer made to the client in a criminal matter; and

       (2)   All amounts, terms, and conditions of any written offer of settlement made to the client in all other matters.

(B)   As used in this rule, "client" includes a person who possesses the authority to accept an offer of settlement or plea, or, in a class action, all the named representatives of the class.

Discussion:

Rule 3-510 is intended to require that counsel in a criminal matter convey all offers, whether written or oral, to the client, as give and take negotiations are less common in criminal matters, and, even were they to occur, such negotiations should require the participation of the accused.

Any oral offers of settlement made to the client in a civil matter should also be communicated if they are "significant" for the purposes of rule 3-500.

Rule 3-600. Organization as Client

(A)   In representing an organization, a member shall conform his or her representation to the concept that the client is the organization itself, acting through its highest authorized officer, employee, body, or constituent overseeing the particular engagement.

(B)   If a member acting on behalf of an organization knows that an actual or apparent agent of the organization acts or intends or refuses to act in a manner that is or may be a violation of law reasonably imputable to the organization, or in a manner which is likely to result in substantial injury to the organization, the member shall not violate his or her duty of protecting all confidential information as provided in Business and Professions Code section 6068, subdivision (e). Subject to Business and Professions Code section 6068, subdivision (e), the member may take such actions as appear to the member to be in the best lawful interest of the organization. Such actions may include among others:

   (1)   Urging reconsideration of the matter while explaining its likely consequences to the organization; or

   (2)   Referring the matter to the next higher authority in the organization, including, if warranted by the seriousness of the matter, referral to the highest internal authority that can act on behalf of the organization.

(C)   If, despite the member's actions in accordance with paragraph (B), the highest authority that can act on behalf of the organization insists upon action or a refusal to act that is a violation of law and is likely to result in substantial injury to the organization, the member's response is limited to the member's right, and, where appropriate, duty to resign in accordance with rule 3-700.

(D)   In dealing with an organization's directors, officers, employees, members, shareholders, or other constituents, a member shall explain the identity of the client for whom the member acts, whenever it is or becomes apparent that the organization's interests are or may become adverse to those of the constituent(s) with whom the member is dealing. The member shall not mislead such a constituent into believing that the constituent may communicate confidential information to the member in a way that will not be used in the organization's interest if that is or becomes adverse to the constituent.

(E)   A member representing an organization may also represent any of its directors, officers, employees, members, shareholders, or other constituents, subject to the provisions of rule 3-310. If the organization's consent to the dual representation is required by rule 3-310, the consent shall be given by an appropriate constituent of the organization other than the individual or constituent who is to be represented, or by the shareholder(s) or organization members.

Discussion:

Rule 3-600 is not intended to enmesh members in the intricacies of the entity and aggregate theories of partnership. Rule 3-600 is not intended to prohibit members from representing both an organization and other parties connected with it, as for instance (as simply one example) in establishing employee benefit packages for closely held corporations or professional partnerships.

Rule 3-600 is not intended to create or to validate artificial distinctions between entities and their officers, employees, or members, nor is it the purpose of the rule to deny the existence or importance of such formal distinctions. In dealing with a close corporation or small association, members commonly perform professional engagements for both the organization and its major constituents. When a change in control occurs or is threatened, members are faced with complex decisions involving personal and institutional relationships and loyalties and have frequently had difficulty in perceiving their correct duty. (See *People ex rel Deukmejian v. Brown* (1981) 29 Cal.3d 150 [172 Cal.Rptr. 478]; *Goldstein v. Lees* (1975) 46 Cal.App.3d 614 [120 Cal.Rptr. 253]; *Woods v. Superior Court* (1983) 149 Cal.App.3d 931 [197 Cal.Rptr.185]; *In re Banks* (1978) 283 Ore. 459 [584 P.2d 284]; 1 A.L.R.4th 1105.) In resolving such multiple relationships, members must rely on case law.

Rule 3-700. Termination of Employment

(A)   In General.

(1)   If permission for termination of employment is required by the rules of a tribunal, a member shall not withdraw from employment in a proceeding before that tribunal without its permission.

(2)   A member shall not withdraw from employment until the member has taken reasonable steps to avoid reasonably foreseeable prejudice to the rights of the client, including giving due notice to the client, allowing time for employment of other counsel, complying with rule 3-700(D), and complying with applicable laws and rules.

(B)   Mandatory Withdrawal.

A member representing a client before a tribunal shall withdraw from employment with the permission of the tribunal, if required by its rules, and a member representing a client in other matters shall withdraw from employment, if:

(1) The member knows or should know that the client is bringing an action, conducting a defense, asserting a position in litigation, or taking an appeal, without probable cause and for the purpose of harassing or maliciously injuring any person; or

(2) The member knows or should know that continued employment will result in violation of these rules or of the State Bar Act; or

(3) The member's mental or physical condition renders it unreasonably difficult to carry out the employment effectively.

(C) Permissive Withdrawal.

If rule 3-700(B) is not applicable, a member may not request permission to withdraw in matters pending before a tribunal, and may not withdraw in other matters, unless such request or such withdrawal is because:

(1) The client

    (a) insists upon presenting a claim or defense that is not warranted under existing law and cannot be supported by good faith argument for an extension, modification, or reversal of existing law, or

    (b) seeks to pursue an illegal course of conduct, or

    (c) insists that the member pursue a course of conduct that is illegal or that is prohibited under these rules or the State Bar Act, or

    (d) by other conduct renders it unreasonably difficult for the member to carry out the employment effectively, or

    (e) insists, in a matter not pending before a tribunal, that the member engage in conduct that is contrary to the judgment and advice of the member but not prohibited under these rules or the State Bar Act, or

    (f) breaches an agreement or obligation to the member as to expenses or fees.

(2) The continued employment is likely to result in a violation of these rules or of the State Bar Act; or

(3) The inability to work with co-counsel indicates that the best interests of the client likely will be served by withdrawal; or

(4) The member's mental or physical condition renders it difficult for the member to carry out the employment effectively; or

(5) The client knowingly and freely assents to termination of the employment; or

(6) The member believes in good faith, in a proceeding pending before a tribunal, that the tribunal will find the existence of other good cause for withdrawal.

(D)   Papers, Property, and Fees.

A member whose employment has terminated shall:

(1)   Subject to any protective order or non-disclosure agreement, promptly release to the client, at the request of the client, all the client papers and property. "Client papers and property" includes correspondence, pleadings, deposition transcripts, exhibits, physical evidence, expert's reports, and other items reasonably necessary to the client's representation, whether the client has paid for them or not; and

(2)   Promptly refund any part of a fee paid in advance that has not been earned. This provision is not applicable to a true retainer fee which is paid solely for the purpose of ensuring the availability of the member for the matter.

Discussion:

Subparagraph (A)(2) provides that "a member shall not withdraw from employment until the member has taken reasonable steps to avoid reasonably foreseeable prejudice to the rights of the clients." What such steps would include, of course, will vary according to the circumstances. Absent special circumstances, "reasonable steps" do not include providing additional services to the client once the successor counsel has been employed and rule 3-700(D) has been satisfied.

Paragraph (D) makes clear the member's duties in the recurring situation in which new counsel seeks to obtain client files from a member discharged by the client. It codifies existing case law. (See *Academy of California Optometrists v. Superior Court* (1975) 51 Cal.App.3d 999 [124 Cal.Rptr. 668]; *Weiss v. Marcus* (1975) 51 Cal.App.3d 590 [124 Cal.Rptr. 297].) Paragraph (D) also requires that the member "promptly" return unearned fees paid in advance. If a client disputes the amount to be returned, the member shall comply with rule 4-100(A)(2).

Paragraph (D) is not intended to prohibit a member from making, at the member's own expense, and retaining copies of papers released to the client, nor to prohibit a claim for the recovery of the member's expense in any subsequent legal proceeding.

CHAPTER 4. Financial Relationship With Clients

Rule 4-100. Preserving Identity of Funds and Property of a Client

(A)   All funds received or held for the benefit of clients by a member or law firm, including advances for costs and expenses, shall be deposited in one or more identifiable bank accounts labelled "Trust Account," "Client's Funds Account" or words of similar import, maintained in the State of California, or, with written consent of the client, in any other jurisdiction where there is a substantial relationship between the client or the client's business and the other jurisdiction. No funds belonging to the member or the law firm shall be deposited therein or otherwise commingled therewith except as follows:

(1)   Funds reasonably sufficient to pay bank charges.

(2)   In the case of funds belonging in part to a client and in part presently or potentially to the member or the law firm, the portion belonging to the member or law firm must be withdrawn at the earliest reasonable time after the member's interest in that portion becomes fixed. However, when the right of the member or law firm to receive a portion of trust funds is disputed by the client, the disputed portion shall not be withdrawn until the dispute is finally resolved.

(B)   A member shall:

(1)   Promptly notify a client of the receipt of the client's funds, securities, or other properties.

(2)   Identify and label securities and properties of a client promptly upon receipt and place them in a safe deposit box or other place of safekeeping as soon as practicable.

(3)   Maintain complete records of all funds, securities, and other properties of a client coming into the possession of the member or law firm and render appropriate accounts to the client regarding them; preserve such records for a period of no less than five years after final appropriate distribution of such funds or properties; and comply with any order for an audit of such records issued pursuant to the Rules of Procedure of the State Bar.

(4)   Promptly pay or deliver, as requested by the client, any funds, securities, or other properties in the possession of the member which the client is entitled to receive.

(C)   The Board of Governors of the State Bar shall have the authority to formulate and adopt standards as to what "records" shall be maintained by members and law firms in accordance with subparagraph (B)(3). The standards formulated and adopted by the Board, as from time to time amended, shall be effective and binding on all members.

Standards:

Pursuant to rule 4-100(C) the Board of Governors of the State Bar adopted the following standards as to what "records" shall be maintained by members and law firms in accordance with subparagraph (B)(3).

(1)   A member shall, from the date of receipt of client funds through the period ending five years from the date of appropriate disbursement of such funds, maintain:

(a)   a written ledger for each client on whose behalf funds are held that sets forth:

(i)   the name of such client,

(ii)   the date, amount and source of all funds received on behalf of such client,

> (iii) the date, amount, payee and purpose of each disbursement made on behalf of such client, and
>
> (iv) the current balance for such client;
>
> (b) a written journal for each bank account that sets forth:
>
> (i) the name of such account,
>
> (ii) the date, amount and client affected by each debit and credit, and
>
> (iii) the current balance in such account;
>
> (c) all bank statements and cancelled checks for each bank account; and
>
> (d) each monthly reconciliation (balancing) of (a), (b), and (c).

(2) A member shall, from the date of receipt of all securities and other properties held for the benefit of client through the period ending five years from the date of appropriate disbursement of such securities and other properties, maintain a written journal that specifies:

> (a) each item of security and property held;
>
> (b) the person on whose behalf the security or property is held;
>
> (c) the date of receipt of the security or property;
>
> (d) the date of distribution of the security or property; and
>
> (e) person to whom the security or property was distributed.

(Trust Account Record Keeping Standards as Adopted by the Board of Governors on July 11, 1992, effective January 1, 1993).

Rule 4-200. Fees for Legal Services

(A) A member shall not enter into an agreement for, charge, or collect an illegal or unconscionable fee.

(B) Unconscionability of a fee shall be determined on the basis of all the facts and circumstances existing at the time the agreement is entered into except where the parties contemplate that the fee will be affected by later events. Among the factors to be considered, where appropriate, in determining the conscionability of a fee are the following:

> (1) The amount of the fee in proportion to the value of the services performed.
>
> (2) The relative sophistication of the member and the client.
>
> (3) The novelty and difficulty of the questions involved and the skill requisite to perform the legal service properly.
>
> (4) The likelihood, if apparent to the client, that the acceptance of the particular employment will preclude other employment by the member.

(5)   The amount involved and the results obtained.

(6)   The time limitations imposed by the client or by the circumstances.

(7)   The nature and length of the professional relationship with the client.

(8)   The experience, reputation, and ability of the member or members performing the services.

(9)   Whether the fee is fixed or contingent.

(10)   The time and labor required.

(11)   The informed consent of the client to the fee.

Rule 4-210. Payment of Personal or Business Expenses Incurred by or for a Client

(A)   A member shall not directly or indirectly pay or agree to pay, guarantee, represent, or sanction a representation that the member or member's law firm will pay the personal or business expenses of a prospective or existing client, except that this rule shall not prohibit a member:

(1)   With the consent of the client, from paying or agreeing to pay such expenses to third persons from funds collected or to be collected for the client as a result of the representation; or

(2)   After employment, from lending money to the client upon the client's promise in writing to repay such loan; or

(3)   From advancing the costs of prosecuting or defending a claim or action or otherwise protecting or promoting the client's interests, the repayment of which may be contingent on the outcome of the matter. Such costs within the meaning of this subparagraph (3) shall be limited to all reasonable expenses of litigation or reasonable expenses in preparation for litigation or in providing any legal services to the client.

(B)   Nothing in rule 4-210 shall be deemed to limit rules 3-300, 3-310, and 4-300.

Rule 4-300. Purchasing Property at a Foreclosure or a Sale Subject to Judicial Review

(A)   A member shall not directly or indirectly purchase property at a probate, foreclosure, receiver's, trustee's, or judicial sale in an action or proceeding in which such member or any lawyer affiliated by reason of personal, business, or professional relationship with that member or with that member's law firm is acting as a lawyer for a party or as executor, receiver, trustee, administrator, guardian, or conservator.

(B)   A member shall not represent the seller at a probate, foreclosure, receiver, trustee, or judicial sale in an action or proceeding in which the purchaser is a spouse or relative of the member or of another lawyer in the member's law firm or is an employee of the member or the member's law firm.

Rule 4-400. Gifts From Client

A member shall not induce a client to make a substantial gift, including a testamentary gift, to the member or to the member's parent, child, sibling, or spouse, except where the client is related to the member.

Discussion:

A member may accept a gift from a member's client, subject to general standards of fairness and absence of undue influence. The member who participates in the preparation of an instrument memorializing a gift which is otherwise permissible ought not to be subject to professional discipline. On the other hand, where impermissible influence occurred, discipline is appropriate. (See *Magee v. State Bar* (1962) 58 Cal.2d 423 [24 Cal.Rptr. 839].)

CHAPTER 5. Advocacy and Representation

Rule 5-100. Threatening Criminal, Administrative, or Disciplinary Charges

(A)   A member shall not threaten to present criminal, administrative, or disciplinary charges to obtain an advantage in a civil dispute.

(B)   As used in paragraph (A) of this rule, the term "administrative charges" means the filing or lodging of a complaint with a federal, state, or local governmental entity which may order or recommend the loss or suspension of a license, or may impose or recommend the imposition of a fine, pecuniary sanction, or other sanction of a quasi-criminal nature but does not include filing charges with an administrative entity required by law as a condition precedent to maintaining a civil action.

(C)   As used in paragraph (A) of this rule, the term "civil dispute" means a controversy or potential controversy over the rights and duties of two or more parties under civil law, whether or not an action has been commenced, and includes an administrative proceeding of a quasi-civil nature pending before a federal, state, or local governmental entity.

Discussion:

Rule 5-100 is not intended to apply to a member's threatening to initiate contempt proceedings against a party for a failure to comply with a court order.

Paragraph (B) is intended to exempt the threat of filing an administrative charge which is a prerequisite to filing a civil complaint on the same transaction or occurrence.

For purposes of paragraph (C), the definition of "civil dispute" makes clear that the rule is applicable prior to the formal filing of a civil action.

Rule 5-110. Performing the Duty of Member in Government Service

A member in government service shall not institute or cause to be instituted criminal charges when the member knows or should know that the charges are not supported by probable cause. If, after the institution criminal charges, the member in government service having responsibility for prosecuting the charges becomes aware that those charges are not supported by probable cause, the member shall promptly so advise the court in which the criminal matter is pending.

Rule 5-120. Trial Publicity

(A) A member who is participating or has participated in the investigation or litigation of a matter shall not make an extrajudicial statement that a reasonable person would expect to be disseminated by means of public communication if the member knows or reasonably should know that it will have a substantial likelihood of materially prejudicing an adjudicative proceeding in the matter.

(B) Notwithstanding paragraph (A), a member may state:

(1) the claim, offense or defense involved and, except when prohibited by law, the identity of the persons involved;

(2) the information contained in a public record;

(3) that an investigation of the matter is in progress;

(4) the scheduling or result of any step in litigation;

(5) a request for assistance in obtaining evidence and information necessary thereto;

(6) a warning of danger concerning the behavior of a person involved, when there is reason to believe that there exists the likelihood of substantial harm to an individual or the public interest; and

(7) in a criminal case, in addition to subparagraphs (1) through (6):

(a) the identity, residence, occupation, and family status of the accused;

(b) if the accused has not been apprehended, the information necessary to aid in apprehension of that person;

(c) the fact, time, and place of arrest; and

(d) the identity of investigating and arresting officers or agencies and the length of the investigation.

(C) Notwithstanding paragraph (A), a member may make a statement that a reasonable member would believe is required to protect a client from the substantial undue prejudicial effect of recent publicity not initiated by the member or the member's client. A statement made pursuant to this paragraph shall be limited to such information as is necessary to mitigate the recent adverse publicity.

Discussion:

Rule 5-120 is intended to apply equally to prosecutors and criminal defense counsel.

Whether an extrajudicial statement violates rule 5-120 depends on many factors, including: (1) whether the extrajudicial statement presents information clearly inadmissible as evidence in the matter for the purpose of proving or disproving a material fact in issue; (2) whether the extrajudicial statement presents information the member knows is false, deceptive, or the use of which would violate Business and Professions Code section 6068(d); (3) whether the extrajudicial statement violates a lawful "gag" order, or protective order, statute, rule of court, or special rule of confidentiality (for example, in juvenile, domestic, mental disability, and certain criminal proceedings); and (4) the timing of the statement.

Paragraph (A) is intended to apply to statements made by or on behalf of the member.

Subparagraph (B)(6) is not intended to create, augment, diminish, or eliminate any application of the lawyer-client privilege or of Business and Professions Code section 6068(e) regarding the member's duty to maintain client confidence and secrets. (Passed by the Supreme Court and effective October 1, 1995)

Rule 5-200. Trial Conduct

In presenting a matter to a tribunal, a member:

(A)   Shall employ, for the purpose of maintaining the causes confided to the member such means only as are consistent with truth;

(B)   Shall not seek to mislead the judge, judicial officer, or jury by an artifice or false statement of fact or law;

(C)   Shall not intentionally misquote to a tribunal the language of a book, statute, or decision;

(D)   Shall not, knowing its invalidity, cite as authority a decision that has been overruled or a statute that has been repealed or declared unconstitutional; and

(E)   Shall not assert personal knowledge of the facts at issue, except when testifying as a witness.

Rule 5-210. Member as Witness

A member shall not act as an advocate before a jury which will hear testimony from the member unless:

(A)   The testimony relates to an uncontested matter; or

(B)   The testimony relates to the nature and value of legal services rendered in the case; or

(C)   The member has the informed, written consent of the client. If the member represents the People or a governmental entity, the consent shall be obtained from the head of the office or a designee of the head of the office by which the member is employed and shall be consistent with principles of recusal.

Discussion:

Rule 5-210 is intended to apply to situations in which the member knows or should know that he or she ought to be called as a witness in litigation in which there is a jury. This rule is not intended to encompass situations in which the member is representing the client in an adversarial proceeding and is testifying before a judge. In non-adversarial proceedings, as where the member testifies on behalf of the client in a hearing before a legislative body, rule 5-210 is not applicable.

Rule 5-210 is not intended to apply to circumstances in which a lawyer in an advocate's firm will be a witness. (Amended by order of Supreme Court, operative September 14, 1992.)

Rule 5-220. Suppression of Evidence

A member shall not suppress any evidence that the member or the member's client has a legal obligation to reveal or to produce.

Rule 5-300. Contact With Officials

(A) A member shall not directly or indirectly give or lend anything of value to a judge, official, or employee of a tribunal unless the personal or family relationship between the member and the judge, official, or employee is such that gifts are customarily given and exchanged. Nothing contained in this rule shall prohibit a member from contributing to the campaign fund of a judge running for election or confirmation pursuant to applicable law pertaining to such contributions.

(B) A member shall not directly or indirectly communicate with or argue to a judge or judicial officer upon the merits of a contested matter pending before such judge or judicial officer, except:

    (1) In open court; or

    (2) With the consent of all other counsel in such matter; or

    (3) In the presence of all other counsel in such matter; or

    (4) In writing with a copy thereof furnished to such other counsel; or

    (5) In ex parte matters.

(C) As used in this rule, "judge" and "judicial officer" shall include law clerks, research attorneys, or other court personnel who participate in the decision-making process. (Amended by order of Supreme Court, operative September 14, 1992.)

Rule 5-310. Prohibited Contact With Witnesses

A member shall not:

(A) Advise or directly or indirectly cause a person to secrete himself or herself or to leave the jurisdiction of a tribunal for the purpose of making that person unavailable as a witness therein.

(B)   Directly or indirectly pay, offer to pay, or acquiesce in the payment of compensation to a witness contingent upon the content of the witness's testimony or the outcome of the case. Except where prohibited by law, a member may advance, guarantee, or acquiesce in the payment of:

  (1)   Expenses reasonably incurred by a witness in attending or testifying.

  (2)   Reasonable compensation to a witness for loss of time in attending or testifying.

  (3)   A reasonable fee for the professional services of an expert witness.

Rule 5-320. Contact With Jurors

(A)   A member connected with a case shall not communicate directly or indirectly with anyone the member knows to be a member of the venire from which the jury will be selected for trial of that case.

(B)   During trial a member connected with the case shall not communicate directly or indirectly with any juror.

(C)   During trial a member who is not connected with the case shall not communicate directly or indirectly concerning the case with anyone the member knows is a juror in the case.

(D)   After discharge of the jury from further consideration of a case a member shall not ask questions of or make comments to a member of that jury that are intended to harass or embarrass the juror or to influence the juror's actions in future jury service.

(E)   A member shall not directly or indirectly conduct an out of court investigation of a person who is either a member of the venire or a juror in a manner likely to influence the state of mind of such person in connection with present or future jury service.

(F)   All restrictions imposed by this rule also apply to communications with or investigations of members of the family of a person who is either a member of the venire or a juror.

(G)   A member shall reveal promptly to the court improper conduct by a person who is either a member of a venire or a juror, or by another toward a person who is either a member of a venire or a juror or a member of his or her family, of which the member has knowledge.

(H)   This rule does not prohibit a member from communicating with persons who are members of a venire or jurors as a part of the official proceedings.

(I)   For purposes of this rule, "juror" means any empaneled, discharged, or excused juror. (Amended by order of Supreme Court, operative September 14, 1992.)

STATE BAR OF CALIFORNIA
RESOLUTIONS OF THE BOARD OF TRUSTEES

Pro Bono Resolution..640

Limited Scope Legal Assistance (Unbundling) Resolution...........................641

STATE BAR OF CALIFORNIA
PRO BONO RESOLUTION

(Adopted by the Board of Governors of the State Bar of California at its December 9, 1989 Meeting and amended at its June 22, 2002 Meeting)

RESOLVED that the Board hereby adopts the following resolution and urges local bar associations to adopt similar resolutions:

WHEREAS, there is an increasingly dire need for pro bono legal services for the needy and disadvantaged; and

WHEREAS, the federal, state and local governments are not providing sufficient funds for the delivery of legal services to the poor and disadvantaged; and

WHEREAS, lawyers should ensure that all members of the public have equal redress to the courts for resolution of their disputes and access to lawyers when legal services are necessary; and

WHEREAS, the Chief Justice of the California Supreme Court, the Judicial Council of California and Judicial Officers throughout California have consistently emphasized the pro bono responsibility of lawyers and its importance to the fair and efficient administration of justice; and

WHEREAS, California Business and Professions Code Section 6068(h) establishes that it is the duty of a lawyer "Never to reject, for any consideration personal to himself or herself, the cause of the defenseless or the oppressed"; now, therefore, it is

RESOLVED that the Board of Governors of the State Bar of California:

(1) Urges all attorneys to devote a reasonable amount of time, at least 50 hours per year, to provide or enable the direct delivery of legal services, without expectation of compensation other than reimbursement of expenses, to indigent individuals, or to not-for-profit organizations with a primary purpose of providing services to the poor or on behalf of the poor or disadvantaged, not-for-profit organizations with a purpose of improving the law and the legal system, or increasing access to justice;

(2) Urges all law firms and governmental and corporate employers to promote and support the involvement of associates and partners in pro bono and other public service activities by counting all or a reasonable portion of their time spent on these activities, at least 50 hours per year, toward their billable hour requirements, or by otherwise giving actual work credit for these activities;

(3) Urges all law schools to promote and encourage the participation of law students in pro bono activities, including requiring any law firm wishing to recruit on campus to provide a written statement of its policy, if any, concerning the involvement of its attorneys in public service and pro bono activities; and

(4) Urges all attorneys and law firms to contribute financial support to not-for-profit organizations that provide free legal services to the poor, especially those attorneys who are precluded from directly rendering pro bono services.

STATE BAR OF CALIFORNIA
LIMITED SCOPE LEGAL ASSISTANCE (UNBUNDLING)
RESOLUTION

(Adopted by the Board of Governors of the State Bar of California at its May 15, 2009 Meeting)

Whereas, limited scope legal assistance is defined as a relationship between an attorney and a person seeking legal services in which it is agreed that the scope of the legal services will be limited to the defined tasks that the person asks the attorney to perform;

Whereas the need for legal services for all Californians continues to increase and limited scope representation can help fill that need by providing legal assistance and specific representation at critical points in the legal process;

Whereas limited scope practice has been recognized by the State Bar Board of Governors as well as by the Judicial Council through the adoption of Rules of Court and Court Forms to facilitate providing legal services;

Whereas the Standing Committee on the Delivery of Legal Services has promoted the use of limited scope legal assistance as a way to address the unmet legal need of low and moderate income Californians; they have sponsored or co-sponsored multiple trainings on Limited Scope Representation at numerous conferences and local bar associations statewide to educate State Bar members on the ethical and competent practice of Limited Scope Legal Assistance;

Whereas various segments of the legal profession can play an important role in promoting and expanding limited scope practice and State Bar members can enhance their practices by providing services on a limited scope basis;

RESOLVED that the State Bar supports the expansion of limited scope legal assistance as part of the ongoing effort to increase access to legal services; that it is important to continue to identify ways in which attorneys can appropriately provide "unbundled" legal services to provide limited and specific services to litigants without undertaking full case representation;

RESOLVED FURTHER that limited scope legal assistance must be performed with a sound understanding of the ethical obligations, and that all education programs must clearly explain that limits on the scope of legal assistance do not limit the ethical obligations of the attorney to the client nor the obligations of counsel to other parties or to the court, the attorney's exposure to liability for the work he or she agreed to perform is not limited, and that the attorney continues to have an obligation to warn a client about issues outside the scope of representation which the client should address, and for which the client should consider seeking counsel, Attorneys and clients must be thoughtful in their approach to establishing the scope of services, and an attorney should not undertake such an engagement without a careful analysis of the client's capabilities, the complexity of the case, as well as the alternatives available.

THEREFORE the following steps should be pursued:

- **State Bar Section members**, particularly the Family Law, Solo and Small Firm Practice, Business Law, Real Property and Trusts & Estates Sections, should be encouraged to develop education for their membership and to expand the use of limited scope representation in their respective practice areas, and should emphasize the benefits to their members if they offer limited scope legal assistance;

- **Law schools** should be encouraged to expand their efforts to raise awareness of limited scope legal assistance, particularly through their legal clinics, so that their students can competently incorporate it into their private practices after graduation. Law schools can also help by developing a quality teaching curriculum including the concept of limited scope representation to supplement their clinical offerings;

- **State Bar Certified Lawyer Referral Services** should be encouraged to create and expand subject matter panels to include limited scope representation in a greater number of practice areas and to provide additional training for increased participation of panel attorneys;

- **Errors and Omissions insurance carriers** should be encouraged to offer training on limited scope representation;

- **The Judicial Council** should continue to be involved with the coordination of strategies for educating the legal profession and the judiciary as to the need for and implementation of increased limited scope representation; and

- **The State Bar** should continue to coordinate with experts in the field and with legal training providers to present training programs on limited scope representation on a statewide and local basis, with programs offered live and online to maximize training opportunities and the expanded limited scope practice.

The State Bar Board of Governors will continue to review the efforts to expand the use of limited scope representation on an annual basis to further support and promote these efforts.

SELECTED STATUTES OF THE CALIFORNIA STATE BAR ACT

(BUSINESS AND PROFESSIONS CODE)

(As amended, 2015)

Division 3 Professions and Vocations Generally

Chapter 4 Attorneys

Article 1 General Provisions

Section		Page
6000.	Citation of Chapter	648
6001.1	State Bar - Protection of the Public as the Highest Priority	648

Article 4 Admission to Practice of Law

6067.	Oath	648
6068.	Duties of Attorney	648

Article 5 Disciplinary Authority of Board of Trustees

6077.	Rules of Professional Conduct Binding; Board's Authority to Discipline Members for Wilful Breach	650
6078.	Board's Authority to Recommend Disbarment or Suspension or to Discipline Members	651
6079.4.	Exercise of Fifth Amendment Privilege or Other Constitutional or Statutory Privileges	651
6082.	Review of Board Action	651
6085.	Rights of Person Complained Against	651
6086.8.	Report of Judgment Against Attorney for Fraud, Misrepresentation, Breach of Fiduciary Duty, or Gross Negligence Committed in a Professional Capacity; Report of Claim or Action for Damages	652
6087.	Disciplinary Authority of Supreme Court	652

Article 5.5 Miscellaneous Disciplinary Provisions

6090.5.	Attorney/Client Agreement Not to File Complaint — Cause for Discipline	652
6091.	Client Trust Fund: Filing of Complaint; Investigation and Audit; Written Request for Complete Statement	653

Article 6 Disciplinary Authority of the Courts

6100.	Disbarment or Suspension	653
6101.	Conviction of Crime; Notice of Pendency of Action; Record of Conviction; Proceedings	653

Section		Page
6102.	Conviction of Crime Suspension and Disbarment Procedure	654
6103.	Disobedience of Court Order; Violation of Oath or Attorney's Duties	655
6103.5.	Written Offers of Settlement; Required Communication to Client; Discovery	656
6103.6.	Violation of Probate Code Section 15687 or Part 3.5 of Division 11 of Probate Code Grounds for Discipline	656
6104.	Unauthorized Appearance	656
6105.	Permitting Misuse of Name	656
6106	Moral Turpitude, Dishonesty or Corruption Irrespective of Criminal Conviction	656
6106.1.	Advocacy of Overthrow of Government	656
6106.2	Violation of Civil Code Section 55.3, 55.31 and 55.32 - Grounds for Discipline	657
6106.2	Violation of Civil Code Sections 55.3 - Ground for Discipline [Operative January 1, 2016]	657
6106.5.	Insurance Claims; Frauds	657
6106.7.	Professional Sport Service Contracts; Violation of Requirements	657
6106.8.	Sexual Involvement Between Lawyers and Clients; Rule of Professional Conduct	658
6106.9.	Sexual Relations Between Attorney and Client; Cause for Discipline; Complaints to State Bar	658
6107.	Proceedings on Grounds Other Than the Conviction of Felony or Misdemeanor Involving Moral Turpitude	659

Article 7 Unlawful Practice of Law

6125.	Restriction of practice of law to active members of the State Bar	659
6126.	Advertising or Holding Oneself Out As Practicing or Entitled to Practice Law Without Being Active Member of State Bar	659
6126.5	Relief	660
6127.	Contempt of Court: Acts or Omissions in Practice of Law; Proceedings	661
6127.5.	Inapplicability of Provisions for Law Corporations	661
6128.	Deceit, Collusion, Delay of Suit and Improper Receipt of Money as Misdemeanor	661
6129.	Buying Claim as Misdemeanor	661
6130.	Disbarred or Suspended Attorney Suing as Assignee	662
6131.	Aiding Defense Where Partner or Self Has Acted as Public Prosecutor; Misdemeanor and Disbarment	662
6132.	Removal of Name of Disbarred Attorney From Law Firm's Business Name	662
6133.	Employment of Resigned, Suspended or Disbarred Attorney	662

Section   **Page**

Article 8.5 Fee Agreements

6146.   Limitations; Periodic Payments 663

6147.   Contingency Fee Contract Requirements; Exclusion
         for Recovery of Workers' Compensation Benefits 664

6147.5. Contingency Fee Contracts; Recovery of Claims Between
         Merchants 664

6148.   Fee Agreements Involving Expenses in Excess of
         One Thousand Dollars; Exclusions 665

6149.   Written Fee Contract as Confidential Communication 666

6149.5. Notification by Insurer of Settlement of Third-Party
         Liability Claim 666

Article 9 Unlawful Solicitation

6151.   Definitions 666

6152.   Prohibition of Solicitation 667

6153.   Penalties for Violating Provisions 667

6154.   Invalidity of Contract for Services 668

6155.   Lawyer Referral Services: Requirements; Operation;
         Exclusions; Minimum Standards 668

6156.   Civil Penalty for Violation of Requirements as the Operation
         of Lawyer Referral Services 671

Article 9.5 Legal Advertising

6157.   Definitions 672

6157.1. Prohibited Statements 672

6157.2. Prohibited Contents 672

6157.3. Disclosure of Business Relationship 673

6157.4. Lawyer Referral Service Advertisements 673

6158.   Advertising by Electronic Media; "Message;" Prohibition
         of False, Misleading, or Deceptive Message 673

6158.1. Rebuttable Presumption as to False, Misleading,
         or Deceptive Messages 673

6158.2. Information Presumed to Be in Compliance with Article 674

6158.3. Required Disclosure in Advertising by Electronic Media 674

6158.7. Violation of Prohibition of False, Misleading, or Deceptive
         Advertisement in Electronic Media as Cause
         for Disciplinary Action 675

6159.   Report of Violation 675

6159.1. Retention of Copy of Advertisement 675

6159.2. Effect of Article 675

6159.5   Legal Aid Organizations – Legislative Findings 675

Section		**Page**
6159.51	Legal Aid Organizations – Defined	676
6159.52	Legal Aid Organizations – Use of Terms; Prohibitions	676
6159.53	Legal Aid Organizations – Remedies for Violation of Section 6159.52	676

Article 13 Arbitration of Attorney's Fees

6200.	Establishment and Administration of Procedure by Board; Exceptions	677
6201.	Action against Client for Recovery of Fees: Written Notice to Client; Request for arbitration; Waiver of Client's Right to Arbitration	678
6202.	Disclosure of Privileged Matters in Connection with Arbitration	679
6203.	Arbitration Award	679
6204.	Trial After Arbitration: Entitlement; Initiation; Prevailing Party	681

Article 14 Funds for the Provision of Legal Services to Indigent Persons

6210.	Legislative Intent Concerning Provision of Legal Services to Indigent Persons	682
6211.	Demand Trust Accounts	682
6212.	Provisions Governing Demand Trust Accounts	683
6213.	Definitions	684
6214.	Qualified Legal Services Projects	687
6214.5.	Eligibility of Law School Program	687
6215.	Qualified Support Centers	687
6216.	Distribution of Funds	688
6217.	Recipient Obligations in Connection with Provision of Legal Assistance	689
6218.	Financial Eligibility Guidelines for Indigent Persons; Use of Funds for Designated Purposes	689
6219.	Use of Funds for Disadvantaged Law Students	690
6220.	Services to Pro Bono Attorneys	690
6221.	Services to Disadvantaged Groups	690
6222.	Submission of Annual Financial Statement by Recipients	690
6223.	Prohibitions Regarding Use of Funds	690
6224.	Authority to Deny Funding; Hearings for Denial	691
6225.	Adoption of Implementing Regulations	691
6226.	Implementation of Article; Resolutions	691
6227.	Credit of State Not Pledged	691
6228.	Severability	692

Article 16 Attorneys Providing Immigration Reform Act Services

6240.   Definitions 692

6241.   Applicability of Article 692

6242.   Immigration Reform Act Services; Refunding of Advance Payment; Statement of Accounting 693

6243.   Written Contract for Legal Services; Reporting of Complaints; Languages for Form of Notice; Failure to Comply 693

Article 1   General Provisions

§ 6000.   Citation of chapter

This chapter of the Business and Professions Code constitutes the chapter on attorneys. It may be cited as the State Bar Act.

§ 6001.1   State Bar - Protection of the Public as the Highest Priority

Protection of the public shall be the highest priority for the State Bar of California and the board of trustees in exercising their licensing, regulatory, and disciplinary functions. Whenever the protection of the public is inconsistent with other interests sought to be promoted, the protection of the public shall be paramount.

Article 4   Admission to Practice of Law

§ 6067.   Oath

Every person on his admission shall take an oath to support the Constitution of the United States and the Constitution of the State of California, and faithfully to discharge the duties of any attorney at law to the best of his knowledge and ability. A certificate of the oath shall be indorsed upon his license.[1]

§ 6068.   Duties of Attorney

It is the duty of an attorney to do all of the following:

(a)   To support the Constitution and laws of the United States and of this state.

(b)   To maintain the respect due to the courts of justice and judicial officers.

(c)   To counsel or maintain those actions, proceedings, or defenses only as appear to him or her legal or just, except the defense of a person charged with a public offense.

(d)   To employ, for the purpose of maintaining the causes confided to him or her those means only as are consistent with truth, and never to seek to mislead the judge or any judicial officer by an artifice or false statement of fact or law.

(e)(1)To maintain inviolate the confidence, and at every peril to himself or herself to preserve the secrets, of his or her client.

(2)   Notwithstanding paragraph (1), an attorney may, but is not required to, reveal confidential information relating to the representation of a client to the extent that the attorney reasonably believes the disclosure is necessary to

---

[1] **Editors' Note**: Effective May 27, 2014, Rule of Court 9.4 was adopted. It provides:

> In addition to the language required by Business and Professions Code section 6067, the oath to be taken by every person on admission to practice law is to conclude with the following: "As an officer of the court, I will strive to conduct myself at all times with dignity, courtesy and integrity."

It is unknown when section 6067 might be amended to conform to Rule 9.4.

prevent a criminal act that the attorney reasonably believes is likely to result in death of, or substantial bodily harm to, an individual.*

(f)   To advance no fact prejudicial to the honor or reputation of a party or witness, unless required by the justice of the cause with which he or she is charged.

(g)   Not to encourage either the commencement or the continuance of an action or proceeding from any corrupt motive of passion or interest.

(h)   Never to reject, for any consideration personal to himself or herself, the cause of the defenseless or the oppressed.

(i)   To cooperate and participate in any disciplinary investigation or other regulatory or disciplinary proceeding pending against himself or herself. However, this subdivision shall not be construed to deprive an attorney of any privilege guaranteed by the Fifth Amendment to the Constitution of the United States or any other constitutional or statutory privileges. This subdivision shall not be construed to require an attorney to cooperate with a request that requires him or her to waive any constitutional or statutory privilege or to comply with a request for information or other matters within an unreasonable period of time in light of the time constraints of the attorney's practice. Any exercise by an attorney of any constitutional or statutory privilege shall not be used against the attorney in a regulatory or disciplinary proceeding against him or her.

(j)   To comply with the requirements of Section 6002.1.

(k)   To comply with all conditions attached to any disciplinary probation, including a probation imposed with the concurrence of the attorney.

(l)   To keep all agreements made in lieu of disciplinary prosecution with the agency charged with attorney discipline.

(m)   To respond promptly to reasonable status inquiries of clients and to keep clients reasonably informed of significant developments in matters with regard to which the attorney has agreed to provide legal services.

(n)   To provide copies to the client of certain documents under time limits and as prescribed in a rule of professional conduct which the board shall adopt

(o)   To report to the agency charged with attorney discipline, in writing, within 30 days of the time the attorney has knowledge of any of the following:

(1)   The filing of three or more lawsuits in a 12-month period against the attorney for malpractice or other wrongful conduct committed in a professional capacity.

---

* added by Calif. AB 1101 (Steinberg), and signed into law October 10, 2003, effective July 1, 2004. This legislation also changed the language of Evidence Code section 956.5 to make it consistent with the Business & Professions Code. Section 3 of the act requested formation of a task force "to study and make recommendations for a rule of professional conduct regarding professional responsibility issues related to the imple- mentation of this act." The rule that resulted from the work of that Task Force is California Rule of Professional Conduct 3-100.

(2)   The entry of judgment against the attorney in a civil action for fraud, misrepresentation, breach of fiduciary duty, or gross negligence committed in a professional capacity.

(3)   The imposition of judicial sanctions against the attorney, except for sanctions for failure to make discovery or monetary sanctions of less than one thousand dollars ($1,000).

(4)   The bringing of an indictment or information charging a felony against the attorney.

(5)   The conviction of the attorney, including any verdict of guilty, or plea of guilty or no contest, of a felony, or a misdemeanor committed in the course of the practice of law, or in any manner in which a client of the attorney was the victim, or a necessary element of which, as determined by the statutory or common law definition of the misdemeanor, involves improper conduct of an attorney, including dishonesty or other moral turpitude, or an attempt or a conspiracy or solicitation of another to commit a felony or a misdemeanor of that type.

(6)   The imposition of discipline against the attorney by a professional or occupational disciplinary agency or licensing board, whether in California or elsewhere.

(7)   Reversal of judgment in a proceeding based in whole or in part upon misconduct, grossly incompetent representation, or willful misrepresentation by an attorney.

(8)   As used in this subdivision, "against the attorney" includes claims and proceedings against any firm of attorneys for the practice of law in which the attorney was a partner at the time of the conduct complained of and any law corporation in which the attorney was a shareholder at the time of the conduct complained of unless the matter has to the attorney's knowledge already been reported by the law firm or corporation.

(9)   The State Bar may develop a prescribed form for the making of reports required by this section, usage of which it may require by rule or regulation.

(10) This subdivision is only intended to provide that the failure to report as required herein may serve as a basis of discipline. (Origin: Code Civ. Proc., § 282. Amended by Stats. 1985, ch. 453; Stats. 1986, ch. 475; Stats. 1988, ch. 1159; Stats. 1990, ch. 1639; Stats. 1999, ch. 221; Stats. 1999, ch. 342; Stats. 2001, ch. 24; Stats.2003, ch. 765)

Article 5   Disciplinary Authority of Board of Trustees

§ 6077.   Rules of Professional Conduct Binding; Board's Authority to Discipline Members for Wilful Breach

The rules of professional conduct adopted by the board, when approved by the Supreme Court, are binding upon all members of the State Bar.

For a wilful breach of any of these rules, the board has power to discipline members of the State Bar by reproval, public or private, or to recommend to the

Supreme Court the suspension from practice for a period not exceeding three years of members of the State Bar.

§ 6078.   Board's Authority to Recommend Disbarment or Suspension or to Discipline Members

After a hearing for any of the causes set forth in the laws of the State of California warranting disbarment, suspension or other discipline, the board has the power to recommend to the Supreme Court the disbarment or suspension from practice of members or to discipline them by reproval, public or private, without such recommendation.

The board may pass upon all petitions for reinstatement.

§ 6079.4.   Exercise of Fifth Amendment Privilege or Other Constitutional or Statutory Privileges

The exercise by an attorney of his or her privilege under the Fifth Amendment to the Constitution of the United Sates, or of any other constitutional or statutory privileges shall not be deemed a failure to cooperate within the meaning of subdivision (i) of Section 6068.

§ 6082.   Review of Board Action

Any person complained against and any person whose reinstatement the board may refuse to recommend may have the action of the board, or of any committee authorized by it to make a determination on its behalf, pursuant to the provisions of this chapter, reviewed by the California Supreme Court or by a California Court of Appeal in accordance with the procedure prescribed by the California Supreme Court.

§ 6085.   Rights of Person Complained Against

Any person complained against shall be given Any person complained against shall be given fair, adequate and reasonable notice and have a fair, adequate and reasonable opportunity and right:

(a) To defend against the charge by the introduction of evidence.

(b) To receive any and all exculpatory evidence from the State Bar after the initiation of a disciplinary proceeding in State Bar Court, and thereafter when this evidence is discovered and available. This subdivision shall not require the disclosure of mitigating evidence.

(c) To be represented by counsel.

(d) To examine and cross-examine witnesses.

(e) To exercise any right guaranteed by the California Constitution or the United States Constitution, including the right against self-incrimination.

He or she shall also have the right to the issuance of subpoenas for attendance of witnesses to appear and testify or produce books and papers, as provided in this chapter.

§ 6086.8.   Report of Judgment against Attorney for Fraud, Misrepresentation, Breach of Fiduciary Duty, or Gross Negligence Committed in a Professional Capacity; Report of Claim or Action for Damages

(a)   Within 20 days after a judgment by a court of this state that a member of the State Bar of California is liable for any damages resulting in a judgment against the attorney in any civil action for fraud, misrepresentation, breach of fiduciary duty, or gross negligence committed in a professional capacity, the court which rendered the judgment shall report that fact in writing to the State Bar of California.

(b)   Every claim or action for damages against a member of the State Bar of California for fraud, misrepresentation, breach of fiduciary duty, or negligence committed in a professional capacity shall be reported to the State Bar of California within 30 days of receipt by the admitted insurer or licensed surplus brokers providing professional liability insurance to that member of the State Bar.

(c)   An attorney who does not possess professional liability insurance shall send a complete written report to the State Bar as to any settlement, judgment, or arbitration award described in subdivision (b), in the manner specified in that subdivision.

§ 6087.   Disciplinary Authority of Supreme Court

Nothing in this chapter shall be construed as limiting or altering the powers of the Supreme Court of this State to disbar or discipline members of the bar as this power existed prior to the enactment of Chapter 34 of the Statutes of 1927, relating to the State Bar of California.

Notwithstanding any other provision of law, the Supreme Court may by rule authorize the State Bar to take any action otherwise reserved to the Supreme Court in any matter arising under this chapter or initiated by the Supreme Court; provided, that any such action by the State Bar shall be reviewable by the Supreme Court pursuant to such rules as the Supreme Court may prescribe.

Article 5.5 Miscellaneous Disciplinary Provisions

§ 6090.5.   Attorney/Client Agreement Not to File Complaint — Cause for Discipline

(a)   It is cause for suspension, disbarment, or other discipline for any member, whether as a party or as an attorney for a party, to agree or seek agreement, that:

    (1)   The professional misconduct or the terms of a settlement of a claim for professional misconduct shall not be reported to the disciplinary agency.

(2)   The plaintiff shall withdraw a disciplinary complaint or shall not cooperate with the investigation or prosecution conducted by the disciplinary agency.

(3)   The record of any civil action for professional misconduct shall be sealed from review by the disciplinary agency.

(b)   This section applies to all settlements, whether made before or after the commencement of a civil action.

§ 6091.   Client Trust Fund: Filing of Complaint; Investigation and Audit; Written Request for Complete Statement

If a client files a complaint with the State Bar alleging that his or her trust fund is being mishandled, the State Bar shall investigate and may require an audit if it determines that circumstances warrant.

At the client's written request, the attorney shall furnish the client with a complete statement of the funds received and disbursed and any charges upon the trust account, within 10 calendar days after receipt of the request. Such requests may not be made more often than once each 30 days unless a client files a complaint with the State Bar and the State Bar determines that more statements are warranted.

Article 6   Disciplinary Authority of the Courts

§ 6100.   Disbarment or Suspension

For any of the causes provided in this article, arising after an attorney's admission to practice, he or she may be disbarred or suspended by the Supreme Court. Nothing in this article limits the inherent power of the Supreme Court to discipline, including to summarily disbar, any attorney.

§ 6101.   Conviction of Crime; Notice of Pendency of Action; Record of Conviction; Proceedings

(a)   Conviction of a felony or misdemeanor, involving moral turpitude, constitutes a cause for disbarment or suspension.

In any proceeding, whether under this article or otherwise, to disbar or suspend an attorney on account of that conviction, the record of conviction shall be conclusive evidence of guilt of the crime of which he or she has been convicted.

(b)   The district attorney, city attorney, or other prosecuting agency shall notify the Office of the State Bar of the State Bar of California of the pendency of an action against an attorney charging a felony or misdemeanor immediately upon obtaining information that the defendant is an attorney. The notice shall identify the attorney and describe the crimes charged and the alleged facts. The prosecuting agency shall also notify the clerk of the court in which the action is pending that the defendant is an attorney, and the clerk shall record prominently in the file that the defendant is an attorney.

(c)   The clerk of the court in which an attorney is convicted of a crime shall, within 48 hours after the conviction, transmit a certified copy of the record of conviction to the Office of the State Bar. Within five days of receipt, the Office of the State Bar shall transmit the record of any conviction which involves or may involve moral turpitude to the Supreme Court with such other records and information as may be appropriate to establish the Supreme Court's jurisdiction. The State Bar of California may procure and transmit the record of conviction to the Supreme Court when the clerk has not done so or when the conviction was had in a court other than a court of this state.

(d)   The proceedings to disbar or suspend an attorney on account of such a conviction shall be undertaken by the Supreme Court pursuant to the procedure provided in this section and Section 6102, upon the receipt of the certified copy of the record of conviction.

(e)   A plea or verdict of guilty or a conviction after a plea of nolo contendere is deemed to be a conviction within the meaning of those sections.

§ 6102.   Conviction of Crime-Suspension and Disbarment Procedure

(a)   Upon the receipt of the certified copy of the record of conviction, if it appears therefrom that the crime of which the attorney was convicted involved, or that there is probable cause to believe that it involved, moral turpitude or is a felony under the laws of California, the United States, or any state or territory thereof, the Supreme Court shall suspend the attorney until the time for appeal has elapsed, if no appeal has been taken, or until the judgment of conviction has been affirmed on appeal, or has otherwise become final, and until the further order of the court. Upon its own motion or upon good cause shown, the court may decline to impose, or may set aside, the suspension when it appears to be in the interest of justice to do so, with due regard being given to maintaining the integrity of, and confidence in, the profession.

(b)   For the purposes of this section, a crime is a felony under the law of California if it is declared to be so specifically or by subdivision (a) of Section 17 of the Penal Code, unless it is charged as a misdemeanor pursuant to paragraph (4) or (5) of subdivision (b) of Section 17 of the Penal Code, irrespective of whether in a particular case the crime may be considered a misdemeanor as a result of postconviction proceedings, including proceedings resulting in punishment or probation set forth in paragraph (1) or (3) of subdivision (b) of Section 17 of the Penal Code.

(c)   After the judgment of conviction of an offense specified in subdivision (a) has become final or, irrespective of any subsequent order under Section 1203.4 of the Penal Code or similar statutory provision, an order granting probation has been made suspending the imposition of sentence, the Supreme Court shall summarily disbar the attorney if the offense is a felony under the laws of California, the United States, or any state or territory thereof, and an element of the offense is the specific intent to deceive, defraud, steal, or make or suborn a false statement, or involved moral turpitude.

(d)   For purposes of this section, a conviction under the laws of another state or territory of the United States shall be deemed a felony if:

(1)   The judgment or conviction was entered as a felony irrespective of any subsequent order suspending sentence or granting probation and irrespective of whether the crime may be considered a misdemeanor as a result of postconviction proceedings.

(2)   The elements of the offense for which the member was convicted would constitute a felony under the laws of the State of California at the time the offense was committed.

(e)   Except as provided in subdivision (c), if after adequate notice and opportunity to be heard (which hearing shall not be had until the judgment of conviction has become final or, irrespective of any subsequent order under Section 1203.4 of the Penal Code, an order granting probation has been made suspending the imposition of sentence), the court finds that the crime of which the attorney was convicted, or the circumstances of its commission, involved moral turpitude, it shall enter an order disbarring the attorney or suspending him or her from practice for a limited time, according to the gravity of the crime and the circumstances of the case; otherwise it shall dismiss the proceedings. In determining the extent of the discipline to be imposed in a proceeding pursuant to this article, any prior discipline imposed upon the attorney may be considered.

(f)   The court may refer the proceedings or any part thereof or issue therein, including the nature or extent of discipline, to the State Bar for hearing, report, and recommendation.

(g)   The record of the proceedings resulting in the conviction, including a transcript of the testimony therein, may be received in evidence.

(h)   The Supreme Court shall prescribe rules for the practice and procedure in proceedings conducted pursuant to this section and Section 6101.

(i)   The other provisions of this article providing a procedure for the disbarment or suspension of an attorney do not apply to proceedings pursuant to this section and Section 6101, unless expressly made applicable.

§ 6103.   Disobedience of Court Order; Violation of Oath or Attorney's Duties

A willful disobedience or violation of an order of the court requiring him to do or forbear an act connected with or in the course of his profession, which he ought in good faith to do or forbear, and any violation of the oath taken by him, or of his duties as such attorney, constitute causes for disbarment or suspension.

§ 6103.5.   Written Offers of Settlement; Required Communication to Client; Discovery

(a) A member of the State Bar shall promptly communicate to the member's client all amounts, terms, and conditions of any written offer of settlement made by or on behalf of an opposing party. As used in this section, "client" includes any person employing the member of the State Bar who possesses the authority to accept an offer of settlement, or in a class action, who is a representative of the class.

(b) Any written offer of settlement or any required communication of a settlement offer, as described in subdivision (a), shall be discoverable by either party in any action in which the existence or communication of the offer of settlement is an issue before the trier of fact.

§6103.6.   Violation of Probate Code Section 15687 or Part 3.5 of Division 11 of Probate Code-Grounds for Discipline

Violation of Section 15687 of the Probate Code, or of Part 3.5 (commencing with Section 21350) of Division 11 of the Probate Code, shall be grounds for discipline, if the attorney knew or should have known of the facts leading to the violation. This section shall only apply to violations that occur on or after January 1, 1994.

§ 6104.   Unauthorized Appearance

Corruptly or wilfully and without authority appearing as attorney for a party to an action or proceeding constitutes a cause for disbarment or suspension.

§ 6105.   Permitting Misuse of Name

Lending his name to be used as attorney by another person who is not an attorney constitutes a cause for disbarment or suspension.

§ 6106.   Moral Turpitude, Dishonesty or Corruption Irrespective of Criminal Conviction

The commission of any act involving moral turpitude, dishonesty or corruption, whether the act is committed in the course of his relations as an attorney or otherwise, and whether the act is a felony or misdemeanor or not, constitutes a cause for disbarment or suspension.

If the act constitutes a felony or misdemeanor, conviction thereof in a criminal proceeding is not a condition precedent to disbarment or suspension from practice therefor.

§ 6106.1.   Advocacy of Overthrow of Government as Cause for Disbarment or Suspension

Advocating the overthrow of the Government of the United States or of this State by force, violence, or other unconstitutional means, constitutes a cause for disbarment or suspension.

§ 6106.2   Violation of Civil Code Sections 55.3, 55.31 and 55.32 - Grounds for Discipline

(a)   It shall constitute cause for the imposition of discipline of an attorney within the meaning of this chapter for an attorney to engage in any conduct in violation of Section 55.3 of the Civil Code. [**Editors' Note:** Civil Code § 55.3 imposes duties on lawyers who file actions against a building or business owner under federal or state statutes proscribing discrimination on the basis of disability, e.g., The Americans with Disabilities Act.]

(b)   Commencing January 1, 2013, it shall constitute cause for the imposition of discipline of an attorney within the meaning of this chapter for an attorney to engage in any conduct in violation of subdivision (b) or (c) of Section 55.31, or paragraph (3) of subdivision (a) or subdivision (b) of Section 55.32 of the Civil Code, or paragraph (2) of subdivision (a) of Section 55.32 of the Civil Code as provided in subdivision (c) of that section. [**Editors' Note:** The referenced paragraphs in sections 55.31 and 55.32 of the Civil Code place limitations on the contents of a demand letter sent by a lawyer that alleges a construction-related accessibility claim and requires a lawyer to provide a copy of any such letter to the State Bar.]

(c)   This section shall remain in effect only until January 1, 2016, and as of that date is repealed, unless a later enacted statute, that is enacted before January 1, 2016, deletes or extends that date. [**Editors' Note:** On January 1, 2016, a revised § 6106.2 will become operative, which will combine paragraphs (a) and (b) into a single paragraph. See SB 1186 [2010-2012 Session], Chaptered 9/19/2012. "See below."]

§ 6106.2   Violation of Civil Code Sections 55.3 - Ground for Discipline [Operative January 1, 2016]

(a)   It shall constitute cause for the imposition of discipline of an attorney within the meaning of this chapter for an attorney to engage in any conduct in violation of Section 55.3, subdivision (b) or (c) of Section 55.31, or paragraph (2) of subdivision (a) or subdivision (b) of Section 55.32 of the Civil Code.

(b)   This section shall become operative on January 1, 2016. (Added by Stats. 2012, ch. 383, operative September 19, 2012.)

§6106.5   Insurance Claims; Fraud

It shall constitute cause for disbarment or suspension for an attorney to engage in any conduct prohibited under Section 1871.4 of the Insurance Code or Section 550 of the Penal Code.

§ 6106.7.   Professional Sport Service Contracts; Violation of Requirements

(a)   It shall constitute cause for the imposition of discipline of an attorney within the meaning of this chapter for an attorney to negotiate a professional sport service contract, as defined by subdivision (d) of Section 1500 of the Labor

Code, and in willful violation of subdivision (b) of Section 1531 of the Labor Code, to collect a fee that in any calendar year exceeds 10 percent of the compensation the athlete is receiving in that calendar year under the contract.

(b)   Willful violation of Section 1530.5, subdivision (b) or (c) of Section 1531, or Section 1535.5, 1535.7, or 1539 of the Labor Code constitutes cause for the imposition of discipline of an attorney within the meaning of this chapter.

§ 6106.8.   Sexual Involvement Between Lawyers and Clients; Rule of Professional Conduct

(a)   The Legislature hereby finds and declares that there is no rule that governs propriety of sexual relationships between lawyers and clients. The Legislature further finds and declares that it is difficult to separate sound judgment from emotion or bias which may result from sexual involvement between a lawyer and his or her client during the period that an attorney-client relationship exists, and that emotional detachment is essential to the lawyer's ability to render competent legal services. Therefore, in order to ensure that a lawyer acts in the best interest of his or her client, a rule of professional conduct governing sexual relations between attorneys and their clients shall be adopted.

(b)   With the approval of the Supreme Court, the State Bar shall adopt a rule of professional conduct governing sexual relations between attorneys and their clients in cases involving, but not limited to, probate matters and domestic relations, including dissolution proceedings, child custody cases, and settlement proceedings.

(c)   The State Bar shall submit the proposed rule to the Supreme Court for approval no later than January 1, 1991.

(d)   Intentional violation of this rule shall constitute a cause for suspension or disbarment.

§ 6106.9.   Sexual Relations Between Attorney and Client; Cause for Discipline; Complaints to State Bar

(a)   It shall constitute cause for the imposition of discipline of an attorney within the meaning of this chapter for an attorney to do any of the following:

(1)   Expressly or impliedly condition the performance of legal services for a current or prospective client upon the client's willingness to engage in sexual relations with the attorney.

(2)   Employ coercion, intimidation, or undue influence in entering into sexual relations with a client.

(3)   Continue representation of a client with whom the attorney has sexual relations if the sexual relations cause the attorney to perform legal services incompetently in violation of Rule 3-110 of the Rules of Professional Conduct of the State Bar of California, or if the sexual relations would, or would be likely to, damage or prejudice the client's case.

(b)   Subdivision (a) shall not apply to sexual relations between attorneys and their spouses or persons in an equivalent domestic relationship or to ongoing consensual sexual relationships that predate the initiation of the attorney-client relationship.

(c)   Where an attorney in a firm has sexual relations with a client but does not participate in the representation of that client, the attorneys in the firm shall not be subject to discipline under this section solely because of the occurrence of those sexual relations.

(d)   For the purposes of this section, "sexual relations" means sexual intercourse or the touching of an intimate part of another person for the purpose of sexual arousal, gratification, or abuse.

(e)   Any complaint made to the State Bar alleging a violation of subdivision (a) shall be verified under oath by the person making the complaint.

§ 6107.   Proceedings on Grounds Other Than the Conviction of Felony or Misdemeanor Involving Moral Turpitude

The proceedings to disbar or suspend an attorney, on grounds other than the conviction of a felony or misdemeanor, involving moral turpitude, may be taken by the court for the matters within its knowledge, or may be taken upon the information of another.

Article 7   Unlawful Practice of Law

§ 6125.   Restriction of Practice of Law to Active Members of the State Bar

No person shall practice law in California unless the person is an active member of the State Bar.

§ 6126.   Advertising or Holding Oneself Out as Practicing or Entitled to Practice Law Without Being Active Member of State Bar

(a)   Any person advertising or holding himself or herself out as practicing or entitled to practice law or otherwise practicing law who is not an active member of the State Bar, is guilty of a misdemeanor.

(b)   Any person who has been involuntarily enrolled as an inactive member of the State Bar, or has been suspended from membership from the State Bar, or has been disbarred, or has resigned from the State Bar with charges pending, and thereafter advertises or holds himself or herself out as practicing or otherwise entitled to practice law, is guilty of a crime punishable by imprisonment pursuant to subdivision (h) of Section 1170 of the Penal Code or in a county jail for a period not to exceed six months. However, any person who has been involuntarily enrolled as an inactive member of the State Bar pursuant to paragraph (1) of subdivision (e) of Section 6007 and who knowingly thereafter advertises or holds himself or herself out as practicing or otherwise entitled to practice law, is guilty of a crime punishable by imprisonment pursuant to subdivision (h) of Section 1170 of the Penal Code or in a county jail for a period not to exceed six months.

(c)   The willful failure of a member of the State Bar, or one who has resigned or been disbarred, to comply with an order of the Supreme Court to comply with Rule 9.20 of the California Rules of Court, constitutes a crime punishable by imprisonment in the state prison or county jail.

(d)   The penalties provided in this section are cumulative to each other and to any other remedies or penalties provided by law.

§ 6126.5.   Relief

(a)   In addition to any remedies and penalties available in any enforcement action brought in the name of the people of the State of California by the Attorney General, a district attorney, or a city attorney, acting as a public prosecutor, the court shall award relief in the enforcement action of any person who obtained services offered or provided in violation of Section 6125 or 6126 or who purchased any goods, services, or real or personal property in connection with services offered or provided in violation of Section 6125 or 6126 against the person who violated Section 6125 or 6126, or who sold goods, services, or property in connection with that violation. The court shall consider the following relief:

(1)   Actual damages.

(2)   Restitution of all amounts paid.

(3)   The amount of penalties and tax liabilities incurred in connection with the sale or transfer of assets to pay for any goods, services, or property.

(4)   Reasonable attorney's fees and costs expended to rectify errors made in the unlawful practice of law.

(5)   Prejudgment interest at the legal rate from the date of loss to the date of judgment.

(6)   Appropriate equitable relief, including the rescission of sales made in connection with a violation of law.

(b)   The relief awarded under paragraphs (1) to (6), inclusive, of subdivision (a) shall be distributed to, or on behalf of, the person for whom it was awarded or, if it is impracticable to do so, shall be distributed as may be directed by the court pursuant to its equitable powers.

(c)   The court shall also award the Attorney General, district attorney, or city attorney reasonable attorney's fees and costs and, in the court's discretion, exemplary damages as provided in Section 3294 of the Civil Code.

(d)   This section shall not be construed to create, abrogate, or otherwise affect claims, rights, or remedies, if any, that may be held by a person or entity other than those law enforcement agencies described in subdivision (a). The remedies provided in this section are cumulative to each other and to the remedies and penalties provided under other laws. (Added by Stats. 2001, ch. 304.)

§ 6127.   Contempt of Court: Acts or Omissions in Practice of Law; Proceedings

The following acts or omissions in respect to the practice of law are contempts of the authority of the courts:

(a)   Assuming to be an officer or attorney of a court and acting as such, without authority.

(b)   Advertising or holding oneself out as practicing or as entitled to practice law or otherwise practicing law in any court, without being an active member of the State Bar.

Proceedings to adjudge a person in contempt of court under this section are to be taken in accordance with the provisions of Title V of Part III of the Code of Civil Procedure.

§ 6127.5.   Inapplicability of Provisions for Law Corporations

Nothing in Sections 6125, 6126 and 6127 shall be deemed to apply to the acts and practices of a law corporation duly certificated pursuant to the Professional Corporation Act, as contained in Part 4 (commencing with Section 13400) of Division 3 of Title 1 of the Corporations Code, and pursuant to Article 10 (commencing with Section 6160) of Chapter 4 of Division 3 of this code, when the law corporation is in compliance with the requirements of (a) the Professional Corporation Act; (b) Article 10 (commencing with Section 6160) of Chapter 4 of Division 3 of this code; and (c) all other statutes and all rules and regulations now or hereafter enacted or adopted pertaining to such corporation and the conduct of its affairs.

§ 6128.   Deceit, Collusion, Delay of Suit and Improper Receipt of Money as Misdemeanor

Every attorney is guilty of a misdemeanor who either:

(a)   Is guilty of any deceit or collusion, or consents to any deceit or collusion, with intent to deceive the court or any party.

(b)   Willfully delays his client's suit with a view to his own gain.

(c)   Willfully receives any money or allowance for or on account of any money which he has not laid out or become answerable for.

Any violation of the provisions of this section is punishable by imprisonment in the county jail not exceeding six months, or by a fine not exceeding two thousand five hundred dollars ($ 2,500), or by both.

§ 6129.   Buying Claim as Misdemeanor

Every attorney who, either directly or indirectly, buys or is interested in buying any evidence of debt or thing in action, with intent to bring suit thereon, is guilty of a misdemeanor.

Any violation of the provisions of this section is punishable by imprisonment in the county jail not exceeding six months, or by a fine not exceeding two thousand five hundred dollars ($ 2,500), or by both.

§ 6130.   Disbarred or Suspended Attorney Suing as Assignee

No person, who has been an attorney, shall while a judgment of disbarment or suspension is in force appear on his own behalf as plaintiff in the prosecution of any action where the subject of the action has been assigned to him subsequent to the entry of the judgment of disbarment or suspension and solely for purpose of collection.

§ 6131.   Aiding Defense Where Partner or Self Has Acted as Public Prosecutor; Misdemeanor and Disbarment

Every attorney is guilty of a misdemeanor and, in addition to the punishment prescribed therefor, shall be disbarred:

(a)   Who directly or indirectly advises in relation to, or aids, or promotes the defense of any action or proceeding in any court the prosecution of which is carried on, aided or promoted by any person as district attorney or other public prosecutor with whom such person is directly or indirectly connected as a partner.

(b)   Who, having himself prosecuted or in any manner aided or promoted any action or proceeding in any court as district attorney or other public prosecutor, afterwards, directly or indirectly, advises in relation to or takes any part in the defense thereof, as attorney or otherwise, or who takes or receives any valuable consideration from or on behalf of any defendant in any such action upon any understanding or agreement whatever having relation to the defense thereof.

This section does not prohibit an attorney from defending himself in person, as attorney or counsel, when prosecuted, either civilly or criminally.

§ 6132.   Removal of Name of Disbarred Attorney from Law Firm's Business Name

Any law firm, partnership, corporation, or association which contains the name of an attorney who is disbarred, or who resigned with charges pending, in its business name shall remove the name of that attorney from its business name, and from all signs, advertisements, letterhead, and other materials containing that name, within 60 days of the disbarment or resignation.

§ 6133.   Employment of Resigned, Suspended or Disbarred Attorney

Any attorney or any law firm, partnership, corporation, or association employing an attorney who has resigned, or who is under actual suspension from the practice of law, or is disbarred, shall not permit that attorney to practice law or so advertise or hold himself or herself out as practicing law and shall supervise him or her in any other assigned duties. A willful violation of this section constitutes a cause for discipline.

Article 8.5 Fee Agreements

§ 6146.   Limitations; Periodic Payments

(a)   An attorney shall not contract for or collect a contingency fee for representing any person seeking damages in connection with an action for injury or damage against a health care provider based upon such person's alleged professional negligence in excess of the following limits:

(1)   Forty percent of the first fifty thousand dollars ($ 50,000) recovered.

(2)   Thirty-three and one-third percent of the next fifty thousand dollars ($ 50,000) recovered.

(3)   Twenty-five percent of the next five hundred thousand dollars ($ 500,000) recovered.

(4)   Fifteen percent of any amount on which the recovery exceeds six hundred thousand dollars ($ 600,000).

The limitations shall apply regardless of whether the recovery is by settlement, arbitration, or judgment, or whether the person for whom the recovery is made is a responsible adult, an infant, or a person of unsound mind.

(b)   If periodic payments are awarded to the plaintiff pursuant to Section 667.7 of the Code of Civil Procedure, the court shall place a total value on these payments based upon the projected life expectancy of the plaintiff and include this amount in computing the total award from which attorney's fees are calculated under this section.

(c)   For purposes of this section:

(1)   "Recovered" means the net sum recovered after deducting any disbursements or costs incurred in connection with prosecution or settlement of the claim. Costs of medical care incurred by the plaintiff and the attorney's office overhead costs or charges are not deductible disbursements or costs for such purpose.

(2)   "Health care provider" means any person licensed or certified pursuant to Division 2 (commencing with Section 500), or licensed pursuant to the Osteopathic Initiative Act, or the Chiropractic Initiative Act, or licensed pursuant to Chapter 2.5 (commencing with Section 1440) of Division 2 of the Health and Safety Code; and any clinic, health dispensary, or health facility, licensed pursuant to Division 2 (commencing with Section 1200) of the Health and Safety Code. "Health care provider" includes the legal representatives of a health care provider.

(3)   "Professional negligence" is a negligent act or omission to act by a health care provider in the rendering of professional services, which act or omission is the proximate cause of a personal injury or wrongful death, provided that the services are within the scope of services for which the provider is

licensed and which are not within any restriction imposed by the licensing agency or licensed hospital.

§ 6147.   Contingency Fee Contract Requirements; Exclusion for Recovery of Workers' Compensation Benefits

(a)   An attorney who contracts to represent a client on a contingency fee basis shall, at the time the contract is entered into, provide a duplicate copy of the contract, signed by both the attorney and the client, or the client's guardian or representative, to the plaintiff, or to the client's guardian or representative. The contract shall be in writing and shall include, but is not limited to, all of the following:

(1)   A statement of the contingency fee rate that the client and attorney have agreed upon.

(2)   A statement as to how disbursements and costs incurred in connection with the prosecution or settlement of the claim will affect the contingency fee and the client's recovery.

(3)   A statement as to what extent, if any, the client could be required to pay any compensation to the attorney for related matters that arise out of their relationship not covered by their contingency fee contract. This may include any amounts collected for the plaintiff by the attorney.

(4)   Unless the claim is subject to the provisions of Section 6146, a statement that the fee is not set by law but is negotiable between attorney and client.

(5)   If the claim is subject to the provisions of Section 6146, a statement that the rates set forth in that section are the maximum limits for the contingency fee agreement, and that the attorney and client may negotiate a lower rate.

(b   Failure to comply with any provision of this section renders the agreement voidable at the option of the plaintiff, and the attorney shall thereupon be entitled to collect a reasonable fee.

(c)   This section shall not apply to contingency fee contracts for the recovery of workers' compensation benefits.

(d)   This section shall become operative on January 1, 1997.

§ 6147.5.   Contingency Fee Contracts; Recovery of Claims Between Merchants

(a)   Sections 6147 and 6148 shall not apply to contingency fee contracts for the recovery of claims between merchants as defined in Section 2104 of the Commercial Code, arising from the sale or lease of goods or services rendered, or money loaned for use, in the conduct of a business or profession if the merchant contracting for legal services employs 10 or more individuals.

(b)   (1) In the instances in which no written contract for legal services exists as permitted by subdivision (a), an attorney shall not contract for or collect a contingency fee in excess of the following limits:

(A)   Twenty percent of the first three hundred dollars ($ 300) collected.

(B)   Eighteen percent of the next one thousand seven hundred dollars ($ 1,700) collected.

(C)   Thirteen percent of sums collected in excess of two thousand dollars ($ 2,000).

(2)   However, the following minimum charges may be charged and collected:

(A)   Twenty-five dollars ($ 25) in collections of seventy-five dollars ($ 75) to one hundred twenty-five dollars ($ 125).

(B)   Thirty-three and one-third percent of collections less than seventy-five dollars ($ 75).

§ 6148.   Fee Agreements Involving Expenses in Excess of One Thousand Dollars; Exclusions

(a)   In any case not coming within Section 6147 in which it is reasonably foreseeable that total expense to a client, including attorney fees, will exceed one thousand dollars ($ 1,000), the contract for services in the case shall be in writing. At the time the contract is entered into, the attorney shall provide a duplicate copy of the contract signed by both the attorney and the client, or the client's guardian or representative, to the client or to the client's guardian or representative. The written contract shall contain all of the following:

(1)   Any basis of compensation including, but not limited to, hourly rates, statutory fees or flat fees, and other standard rates, fees, and charges applicable to the case.

(2)   The general nature of the legal services to be provided to the client.

(3)   The respective responsibilities of the attorney and the client as to the performance of the contract.

(b)   All bills rendered by an attorney to a client shall clearly state the basis thereof. Bills for the fee portion of the bill shall include the amount, rate, basis for calculation, or other method of determination of the attorney's fees and costs. Bills for the cost and expense portion of the bill shall clearly identify the costs and expenses incurred and the amount of the costs and expenses. Upon request by the client, the attorney shall provide a bill to the client no later than 10 days following the request unless the attorney has provided a bill to the client within 31 days prior to the request, in which case the attorney may provide a bill to the client no later than 31 days following the date the most recent bill was provided. The client is entitled to make similar requests at intervals of no less than 30 days following the initial request. In providing responses to client requests for billing information, the attorney may use billing data that is currently effective on the date of the request, or, if any fees or costs to that date cannot be accurately determined, they shall be described and estimated.

(c)   Failure to comply with any provision of this section renders the agreement voidable at the option of the client, and the attorney shall, upon the agreement being voided, be entitled to collect a reasonable fee.

(d)   This section shall not apply to any of the following:

(1)   Services rendered in an emergency to avoid foreseeable prejudice to the rights or interests of the client or where a writing is otherwise impractical.

(2)   An arrangement as to the fee implied by the fact that the attorney's services are of the same general kind as previously rendered to and paid for by the client.

(3)   If the client knowingly states in writing, after full disclosure of this section, that a writing concerning fees is not required.

(4)   If the client is a corporation.

(e)   This section applies prospectively only to fee agreements following its operative date.

(f)   This section shall become operative on January 1, 1997.

§ 6149.   Written Fee Contract as Confidential Communication

A written fee contract shall be deemed to be a confidential communication within the meaning of subdivision (e) of Section 6068 and of Section 952 of the Evidence Code.

§ 6149.5.   Notification by Insurer of Settlement of Third-Party Liability Claim

(a)   Upon the payment of one hundred dollars ($ 100) or more in settlement of any third-party liability claim the insurer shall provide written notice to the claimant if both of the following apply:

(1)   The claimant is a natural person.

(2)   The payment is delivered to the claimant's lawyer or other representative by draft, check, or otherwise.

(b)   For purposes of this section, "written notice" includes providing to the claimant a copy of the cover letter sent to the claimant's attorney or other representative that accompanied the settlement payment.

(c)   This section shall not create any cause of action for any person against the insurer based upon the insurer's failure to provide the notice to a claimant required by this section. This section shall not create a defense for any party to any cause of action based upon the insurer's failure to provide this notice.

Article 9   Unlawful Solicitation

§ 6151.   Definitions

As used in this article:

(a)   A runner or capper is any person, firm, association or corporation acting for consideration in any manner or in any capacity as an agent for an attorney at law or law firm, whether the attorney or any member of the law firm is admitted in California or any other jurisdiction, in the solicitation or procure-ment of business for the attorney at law or law firm as provided in this article.

(b)   An agent is one who represents another in dealings with one or more third persons.

§ 6152.   Prohibition of Solicitation

(a)   It is unlawful for:

(1)   Any person, in an individual capacity or in a capacity as a public or private employee, or for any firm, corporation, partnership or association to act as a runner or capper for any attorneys or to solicit any business for any attorneys in and about the state prisons, county jails, city jails, city prisons, or other places of detention of persons, city receiving hospitals, city and county receiving hospitals, county hospitals, superior courts, or in any public institution or in any public place or upon any public street or highway or in and about private hospitals, sanitariums or in and about any private institution or upon private property of any character whatsoever.

(2)   Any person to solicit another person to commit or join in the commission of a violation of subdivision (a).

(b)   A general release from a liability claim obtained from any person dur-ing the period of the first physical confinement, whether as an inpatient or outpatient, in a clinic or health facility, as defined in Sections 1203 and 1250 of the Health and Safety Code, as a result of the injury alleged to have given rise to the claim and primarily for treatment of the injury, is presumed fraudulent if the release is executed within 15 days after the commencement of confine-ment or prior to release from confinement, whichever occurs first.

(c)   Nothing in this section shall be construed to prevent the recommenda-tion of professional employment where that recommendation is not prohibited by the Rules of Professional Conduct of the State Bar of California.

(d)   Nothing in this section shall be construed to mean that a public defender or assigned counsel may not make known his or her services as a criminal defense attorney to persons unable to afford legal counsel whether those per-sons are in custody or otherwise.

§ 6153.   Penalties for Violating Provisions

Any person, firm, partnership, association, or corporation violating subdivi-sion (a) of Section 6152 is punishable, upon a first conviction by imprisonment in a county jail for not more than one year. Upon a second or subsequent con-viction, a person, firm, partnership, association, or corporation is punishable by imprisonment in a county jail for not more than one year, or by imprisonment pursuant to subdivision (h) of Section 1170 of the Penal Code for two, three or four years, or by a fine not exceeding fifteen thousand dollars ($ 10,000), or by both that imprisonment and fine.

Any person employed either as an officer, director, trustee, clerk, servant or agent of this state or of any county or other municipal corporation or subdivision thereof, who is found guilty of violating any of the provisions of this article, shall forfeit the right to his office and employment in addition to any other penalty provided in this article.

§ 6154.   Invalidity of Contract for Services

(a)   Any contract for professional services secured by any attorney at law or law firm in this state through the services of a runner or capper is void. In any action against any attorney or law firm under the Unfair Practices Act, Chapter 4 (commencing with Section 17000) of Division 7, or Chapter 5 (commencing with Section 17200) of Division 7, any judgment shall include an order divesting the attorney or law firm of any fees and other compensation received pursuant to any such void contract. Those fees and compensation shall be recoverable as additional civil penalties under Chapter 4 (commencing with Section 17000) or Chapter 5 (commencing with Section 17200) of Division 7.

(b)   Notwithstanding Section 17206 or any other provision of law, any fees recovered pursuant to subdivision (a) in an action involving professional services related to the provision of workers' compensation shall be allocated as follows: if the action is brought by the Attorney General, one-half of the penalty collected shall be paid to the State General Fund, and one-half of the penalty collected shall be paid to the Workers' Compensation Fraud Account in the Insurance Fund; if the action is brought by a district attorney, one-half of the penalty collected shall be paid to the treasurer of the county in which the judgment was entered, and one-half of the penalty collected shall be paid to the Workers' Compensation Fraud Account in the Insurance Fund; if the action is brought by a city attorney or city prosecutor, one-half of the penalty collected shall be paid to the treasurer of the city in which the judgment was entered, and one-half of the penalty collected shall be paid to the Workers' Compensation Fraud Account in the Insurance Fund. Moneys deposited into the Workers' Compensation Fraud Account pursuant to this subdivision shall be used in the investigation and prosecution of workers' compensation fraud, as appropriated by the Legislature.

§ 6155.   Lawyer Referral Services: Requirements; Operation; Exclusions; Minimum Standards

(a)   An individual, partnership, corporation, association, or any other entity shall not operate for the direct or indirect purpose, in whole or in part, of referring potential clients to attorneys, and no attorney shall accept a referral of such potential clients, unless all of the following requirements are met:

(1)   The service is registered with the State Bar of California and (a) on July 1, 1988, is operated in conformity with minimum standards for a lawyer referral service established by the State Bar, or (b) upon approval by the Supreme Court of minimum standards for a lawyer referral service, is operated in conformity with those standards.

(2)   The combined charges to the potential client by the referral service and the attorney to whom the potential client is referred do not exceed the total cost that the client would normally pay if no referral service were involved.

(b)   A referral service shall not be owned or operated, in whole or in part, directly or indirectly, by those lawyers to whom, individually or collectively, more than 20 percent of referrals are made. For purposes of this subdivision, a referral service that is owned or operated by a bar association, as defined in the minimum standards, shall be deemed to be owned or operated by its governing committee so long as the governing committee is constituted and functions in the manner prescribed by the minimum standards.

(c)   Except as provided in subdivision (d), a lawyer referral service includes, but is not limited to, a service provided over the Internet that operates for the direct or indirect purpose, in whole or in part, of matching of referring potential clients to California attorneys.

(d)   None of the following is a lawyer referral service:

(1)   A plan of legal insurance as defined in Section 119.6 of the Insurance Code.

(2)   A group or prepaid legal plan, whether operated by a union, trust, mutual benefit or aid association, public or private corporation, or other entity or person, which meets both of the following conditions:

(A)   It recommends, furnishes, or pays for legal services to its members or beneficiaries.

(B)   It provides telephone advice or personal consultation.

(3)   A program having as its purpose the referral of clients to attorneys for representation on a pro bono basis.

(e)   The following are in the public interest and do not constitute an unlawful restraint of trade or commerce:

(1)   An agreement between a referral service and a participating attorney to eliminate or restrict the attorney's fee for an initial office consultation for each potential client or to provide free or reduced fee services.

(2)   Requirements by a referral service that attorneys meet reasonable participation requirements, including experience, education, and training requirements.

(3)   Provisions of the minimum standards as approved by the Supreme Court.

(4)   Requirements that the application and renewal fees for certification as a lawyer referral service be determined, in whole or in part, by a consideration of any combination of the following factors: a referral service's gross annual revenues, number of panels, number of panel members, amount of fees charged to panel members, or for-profit or nonprofit status; provided that the application and renewal fees do not exceed ten thousand dollars ($ 10,000) or 1 percent of the gross annual revenues, whichever is less.

(5)   Requirements that, to increase access to the justice system for all Californians, lawyer referral services establish separate ongoing activities or arrangements that serve persons of limited means.

(f)   A violation or threatened violation of this section may be enjoined by any person.

(g)   With the approval of the Supreme Court, the State Bar shall formulate and enforce rules and regulations for carrying out this section, including rules and regulations that do the following:

(1)   Establish minimum standards for lawyer referral services. The minimum standards shall include provisions ensuring that panel membership shall be open to all attorneys practicing in the geographical area served who are qualified by virtue of suitable experience, and limiting attorney registration and membership fees to reasonable sums that do not discourage widespread attorney membership.

(2)   Require that an entity seeking to qualify as a lawyer referral service register with the State Bar and obtain from the State Bar a certificate of compliance with the minimum standards for lawyer referral services.

(3)   Require that the certificate may be obtained, maintained, suspended, or revoked pursuant to procedures set forth in the rules and regulations.

(4)   Require the lawyer referral service to pay an application and renewal fee for the certificate in such reasonable amounts as may be determined by the State Bar. The State Bar shall adopt rules authorizing the waiver or reduction of the fees upon a demonstration of financial necessity. The State Bar may require that the application and renewal fees for certification as a lawyer referral service be determined, in whole or in part, by a consideration of any combination of the following factors: a referral service's gross annual revenues, number of panels, number of panel members, amount of fees charged to panel members, or for-profit or nonprofit status; provided that the application and renewal fees do not exceed ten thousand dollars ($ 10,000) or 1 percent of the gross annual revenues, whichever is less.

(5)   Require that, to increase access to the justice system for all Californians, lawyer referral services establish separate ongoing activities or arrangements that serve persons of limited means.

(6)   Require each lawyer who is a member of a certified lawyer referral service to comply with all applicable professional standards, rules, and regulations, and to possess a policy of errors and omissions insurance in an amount not less than one hundred thousand dollars ($ 100,000) for each occurrence and three hundred thousand dollars ($ 300,000) aggregate, per year. By rule, the State Bar may provide for alternative proof of financial responsibility to meet this requirement.

(h)   Provide that cause for denial of certification or recertification or revocation of certification of a lawyer referral service shall include, but not be limited to:

(1)   Noncompliance with the statutes or minimum standards governing lawyer referral services as adopted and from time to time amended.

(2)   Sharing common or cross ownership, interests, or operations with any entity that engages in referrals to licensed or unlicensed health care providers.

(3)   Direct or indirect consideration regarding referrals between an owner, operator, or member of a lawyer referral service and any licensed or unlicensed health care provider.

(4)   Advertising on behalf of attorneys in violation of the Rules of Professional Conduct or the Business and Professions Code.

(i)   This section shall not be construed to prohibit attorneys from jointly advertising their services.

(1)   Permissible joint advertising, among other things, identifies by name the advertising attorneys or law firms whom the consumer of legal services may select and initiate contact with.

(2)   Certifiable referral activity involves, among other things, some person or entity other than the consumer and advertising attorney or law firms which, in person, electronically, or otherwise, refers the consumer to an attorney or law firm not identified in the advertising.

(j)   A lawyer referral service certified under this section and operating in full compliance with this section, and in full compliance with the minimum standards and the rules and regulations of the State Bar governing lawyer referral services, shall not be deemed to be in violation of Section 3215 of the Labor Code or Section 750 of the Insurance Code.

(k)   The payment by an attorney or law firm member of a certified referral service of the normal fees of that service shall not be deemed to be in violation of Section 3215 of the Labor Code or Section 750 of the Insurance Code, provided that the attorney or law firm member is in full compliance with the minimum standards and the rules and regulations of the State Bar governing lawyer referral services.

(l)   Certifications of lawyer referral services issued by the State Bar shall not be transferable.

§ 6156.   Civil Penalty for Violation of Requirements as the Operation of Lawyer Referral Services

(a)   Any individual, partnership, association, corporation, or other entity, including, but not limited to, any person or entity having an ownership interest in a lawyer referral service, which engages, has engaged, or proposes to engage in violations of Section 6155, shall be liable for a civil penalty as defined in Sections 17206, 17206.1, and 17536, respectively, which shall be assessed and recovered in a civil action brought:

(1)   In the manner specified in subdivision (a) of Section 17206 or Section 17536.

(2)   By the State Bar of California.

(b)   If the action is brought pursuant to subdivision (a), the court shall determine the reasonable expenses, if any, incurred by the State Bar in its investigation and prosecution of the action. In these cases, before any penalty collected is paid out pursuant to subdivision (b) of Section 17206 or 17536, the amount of the reasonable expenses incurred by the State Bar shall be paid to the State Bar and shall be deposited and used as provided in subdivision (c).

(c)   If the action is brought pursuant to paragraph (2) of subdivision (a), the civil penalty shall be paid to the State Bar and shall be deposited into a special fund to be used first for the investigation and prosecution of other such cases by the State Bar, with any excess to be used for the investigation and prosecution of attorney discipline cases.

Article 9.5 Legal Advertising

§ 6157.   Definitions

As used in this article, the following definitions apply:

(a)   "Member" means a member in good standing of the State Bar and includes any agent of the member and any law firm or law corporation doing business in the State of California.

(b)   "Lawyer" means a member of the State Bar or a person who is admitted in good standing and eligible to practice before the bar of any United States court or the highest court of the District of Columbia or any state, territory, or insular possession of the United States, or is licensed to practice law in, or is admitted in good standing and eligible to practice before the bar of the highest court of, a foreign country or any political subdivision thereof, and includes any agent of the lawyer or law firm or law corporation doing business in this state.

(c)   "Advertise" or "advertisement" means any communication, disseminated by television or radio, by any print medium including, but not limited to, newspapers and billboards, or by means of a mailing directed generally to members of the public and not to a specific person, that solicits employment of legal services provided by a member, and is directed to the general public and is paid for by, or on the behalf of, an attorney.

(d)   "Electronic medium" means television, radio, or computer networks.

§ 6157.1.   Prohibited Statements

No advertisement shall contain any false, misleading, or deceptive statement or omit to state any fact necessary to make the statements made, in light of circumstances under which they are made, not false, misleading, or deceptive.

§ 6157.2.   Prohibited Contents

No advertisement shall contain or refer to any of the following:

(a)   Any guarantee or warranty regarding the outcome of a legal matter as a result of representation by the member.

(b)   Statements or symbols stating that the member featured in the advertisement can generally obtain immediate cash or quick settlements. (c)(1) An impersonation of the name, voice, photograph, or electronic image of any person other than the lawyer, directly or implicitly purporting to be that of a lawyer.

(2)   An impersonation of the name, voice, photograph, or electronic image of any person, directly or implicitly purporting to be a client of the member featured in the advertisement, or a dramatization of events, unless disclosure of the impersonation or dramatization is made in the advertisement.

(3)   A spokesperson, including a celebrity spokesperson, unless there is disclosure of the spokesperson's title.

(d)   A statement that a member offers representation on a contingent basis unless the statement also advises whether a client will be held responsible for any costs advanced by the member when no recovery is obtained on behalf of the client. If the client will not be held responsible for costs, no disclosure is required.

§ 6157.3.   Disclosure of Business Relationship

Any advertisement made on behalf of a member, which is not paid for by the member, shall disclose any business relationship, past or present, between the member and the person paying for the advertisement.

§ 6157.4.   Lawyer Referral Service Advertisements

Any advertisement that is created or disseminated by a lawyer referral service shall disclose whether the attorneys on the organization's referral list, panel, or system, paid any consideration, other than a proportional share of actual cost, to be included on that list, panel, or system.

§ 6158.   Advertising by Electronic Media; "Message"; Prohibition of False, Misleading, or Deceptive Message

In advertising by electronic media, to comply with Sections 61571.1 and 6157.2, the message as a whole may not be false, misleading, or deceptive, and the message as a whole must be factually substantiated. The message means the effect in combination of the spoken word, sound, background, action, symbols, visual image, or any other technique employed to create the message. Factually substantiated means capable of verification by a credible source.

§ 6158.1.   Rebuttable Presumption as to False, Misleading, or Deceptive Messages

There shall be a rebuttable presumption affecting the burden of producing evidence that the following messages are false, misleading, or deceptive within the meaning of Section 6158:

(a)   A message as to the ultimate result of a specific case or cases presented out of context without adequately providing information as to the facts or law giving rise to the result.

(b)   The depiction of an event through methods such as the use of displays of injuries, accident scenes, or portrayals of other injurious events which may or may not be accompanied by sound effects and which may give rise to a claim for compensation.

(c)   A message referring to or implying money received by or for a client in a particular case or cases, or to potential monetary recovery for a prospective client. A reference to money or monetary recovery includes, but is not limited to, a specific dollar amount, characterization of a sum of money, monetary symbols, or the implication of wealth.

§ 6158.2.   Information Presumed to Be in Compliance with Article

The following information shall be presumed to be in compliance with this article for purposes of advertising by electronic media, provided the message as a whole is not false, misleading, or deceptive:

(a)   Name, including name of law firm, names of professional associates, addresses, telephone numbers, and the designation "lawyer," "attorney," "law firm," or the like.

(b)   Fields of practice, limitation of practice, or specialization.

(c)   Fees for routine legal services, subject to the requirements of subdivision (d) of Section 6157.2 and the Rules of Professional Conduct.

(d)   Date and place of birth.

(e)   Date and place of admission to the bar of state and federal courts.

(f)   Schools attended, with dates of graduation, degrees, and other scholastic distinctions.

(g)   Public or quasi-public offices.

(h)   Military service.

(i)   Legal authorship.

(j)   Legal teaching positions.

(k)   Memberships, offices, and committee assignments in bar associations.

(l)   Memberships and offices in legal fraternities and legal societies.

(m)   Technical and professional licenses.

(n)   Memberships in scientific, technical, and professional associations and societies.

(o)   Foreign language ability of the advertising lawyer or a member of lawyer's firm.

§ 6158.3.   Required Disclosure in Advertising by Electronic Media

In addition to any disclosure required by Section 6157.2, Section 6157.3, and the Rules of Professional Conduct, the following disclosure shall appear in advertising by electronic media. Use of the following disclosure alone may not rebut any presumption created in Section 6158.1. If an advertisement in the electronic media conveys a message portraying a result in a particular case or cases, the advertisement must state, in either an oral or printed communication, either of the following disclosures: The advertisement must adequately disclose the factual and legal circumstances that justify the result portrayed in the message, including the basis for liability and the nature of injury or damage sustained, or the advertisement must state that the result portrayed in the advertisement was dependent on the facts of that case, and that the results will differ if based on different facts.

§ 6158.7.   Violation of Prohibition of False, Misleading, or Deceptive Advertisement in Electronic Media as Cause for Disciplinary Action

A violation of Section 6158, 6158.1, or 6158.3 by a member shall be cause for discipline by the State Bar. In addition to the existing grounds for initiating a disciplinary proceeding set forth in a statute or in the Rules of Professional Conduct, the State Bar may commence an investigation based upon a complaint filed by a person pursuant to Section 6158.4. The State Bar's decision pursuant to subdivision (a) of Section 6158.4 shall be admissible, but shall not be determinative, in any disciplinary proceeding brought as a result of that complaint.

§ 6159.   Report of Violation

The court shall report the name, address, and professional license number of any person found in violation of this article to the appropriate professional licensing agency for review and possible disciplinary action.

§ 6159.1.   Retention of Copy of Advertisement

A true and correct copy of any advertisement made by a person or member shall be retained for one year by the person or member who pays for an advertisement soliciting employment of legal services.

§ 6159.2.   Effect of Article

(a)   Nothing in this article shall be deemed to limit or preclude enforcement of any other provision of law, or of any court rule, or of the State Bar Rules of Professional Conduct.

(b)   Nothing in this article shall limit the right of advertising protected under the Constitution of the State of California or of the United States. If any provision of this article is found to violate either Constitution, that provision is severable and the remaining provisions shall be enforceable without the severed provision.

§ 6159.5   Legal Aid Organizations – Legislative Findings

The Legislature hereby finds and declares all of the following:

(a)   Legal aid programs provide a valuable service to the public by providing free legal services to the poor.

(b)   Private, for-profit organizations that have no lawyers have been using the name "legal aid" in order to obtain business from people who believe they are obtaining services from a nonprofit legal aid organization.

(c)   Public opinion research has shown that the term "legal aid" is commonly understood by the public to mean free legal assistance for the poor.

(d)   Members of the public seeking free legal assistance are often referred by telephone and other directory assistance information providers to for-profit organizations that charge a fee for their services, and there are a large number of listings in many telephone directories for "legal aid" that are not nonprofit but are actually for-profit organizations.

(e)   The Los Angeles Superior Court has held that there is a common law trademark on the name "legal aid," which means legal services for the poor provided by a nonprofit organization.

(f)   The public will be benefited if for-profit organizations are prohibited from using the term "legal aid," in order to avoid confusion.

§ 6159.51   Legal Aid Organizations – Defined

For purposes of this article, "legal aid organization" means a nonprofit organization that provides civil legal services for the poor without charge.

§ 6159.52   Legal Aid Organizations – Use of Terms; Prohibitions

It is unlawful for any person or organization to use the term "legal aid," "legal aide," or any confusingly similar name in any firm name, trade name, fictitious business name, or any other designation, or on any advertisement, letterhead, business card, or sign, unless the person or organization is a legal aid organization subject to fair use principles for nominative, descriptive, or noncommercial use.

§ 6159.53   Legal Aid Organizations – Remedies for Violation of Section 6159.52

(a)   Any consumer injured by a violation of Section 6159.52 may file a complaint and seek injunctive relief, restitution, and damages in the superior court of any county in which the defendant maintains an office, advertises, or is listed in a telephone directory.

(b)   A person who violates Section 6159.52 shall be subject to an injunction against further violation of Section 6159.52 by any legal aid organization that maintains an office in any county in which the defendant maintains an office, advertises, or is listed in a telephone directory. In an action under this subdivision, it is not necessary to allege or prove actual damage to the plaintiff, and irreparable harm and interim harm to the plaintiff shall be presumed.

(c)   Reasonable attorney's fees shall be awarded to the prevailing plaintiff in any action under this section.

Article 13 Arbitration of Attorney's Fees

§ 6200.   Establishment and Administration of Procedure by Board; Exceptions

(a)   The board of trustees shall, by rule, establish, maintain, and administer a system and procedure for the arbitration, and may establish, maintain, and administer a system and procedure for mediation of disputes concerning fees, costs, or both, charged for professional services by members of the State Bar or by members of the bar of other jurisdictions. The rules may include provision for a filing fee in such amount as the board may, from time to time, determine.

(b)   This article shall not apply to any of the following:

(1)   Disputes where a member of the State Bar of California is also admitted to practice in another jurisdiction or where an attorney is only admitted to practice in another jurisdiction, and he or she maintains no office in the State of California, and no material portion of the services were rendered in the State of California.

(2)   Claims for affirmative relief against the attorney for damages or otherwise based upon alleged malpractice or professional misconduct, except as provided in subdivision (a) of Section 6203.

(3)   Disputes where the fee or cost to be paid by the client or on his or her behalf has been determined pursuant to statute or court order.

(c)   Arbitration under this article shall be voluntary for a client and shall be mandatory for an attorney if commenced by a client. Mediation under this article shall be voluntary for an attorney and a client.

(d)   The board of trustees shall adopt rules to allow arbitration and mediation of attorney fee and cost disputes under this article to proceed under arbitration and mediation systems sponsored by local bar associations in this state. Rules of procedure promulgated by local bar associations are subject to review by the board to insure that they provide for a fair, impartial, and speedy hearing and award.

(e)   In adopting or reviewing rules of arbitration under this section the board shall provide that the panel shall include one attorney member whose area of practice is either, at the option of the client, civil law, if the attorney's representation involved civil law, or criminal law, if the attorney's representation involved criminal law, as follows:

(1)   If the panel is composed of three members the panel shall include one attorney member whose area of practice is either, at the option of the client, civil or criminal law, and shall include one lay member.

(2)   If the panel is composed of one member, that member shall be an attorney whose area of practice is either, at the option of the client, civil or criminal law.

(f)   In any arbitration or mediation conducted pursuant to this article by the State Bar or by a local bar association, pursuant to rules of procedure approved by the board of trustees, an arbitrator or mediator, as well as the arbitrating association and its directors, officers, and employees, shall have the same immunity which attaches in judicial proceedings.

(g)   In the conduct of arbitrations under this article the arbitrator or arbitrators may do all of the following:

(1)   Take and hear evidence pertaining to the proceeding.

(2)   Administer oaths and affirmations.

(3)   Compel, by subpoena, the attendance of witnesses and the production of books, papers, and documents pertaining to the proceeding.

(h)   Participation in mediation is a voluntary consensual process, based on direct negotiations between the attorney and his or her client, and is an extension of the negotiated settlement process. All discussions and offers of settlement are confidential and may not be disclosed in any subsequent arbitration or other proceedings.

§ 6201.   Action against Client for Recovery of Fees: Written Notice to Client; Request for Arbitration; Waiver of Client's Right to Arbitration

(a)   The rules adopted by the board of trustees shall provide that an attorney shall forward a written notice to the client prior to or at the time of service of summons or claim in an action against the client for recovery of fees, costs, or both, covered by the provisions of this article. The written notice shall be in the form that the board of trustees prescribes, and shall include a statement of the client's right to arbitration under this article. Failure to give this notice shall be a ground for the dismissal of the action.

The rules adopted by the board of trustees shall provide that the client's failure to request arbitration within 30 days after receipt of notice from the attorney shall be deemed a waiver of the client's right to arbitration under the provisions of this article.

(b)   If an attorney, or the attorney's assignee, subject to the provisions of this article, commences an action in any court, and the dispute is not one to which subdivision (b) of Section 6200 applies, the client may stay the action by serving and filing a request for arbitration in accordance with the rules established by the board of trustees pursuant to subdivision (a) of Section 6200. The request for arbitration shall be served and filed prior to the filing of an answer in the action; failure to so request arbitration prior to the filing of an answer shall be deemed a waiver of the client's right to arbitration under the provisions of this article if notice of the client's right to arbitration was given pursuant to subdivision (a).

(c)   Upon filing and service of the request for arbitration, the action shall be stayed, without the necessity of court order, until the award of the arbitrators is issued or the arbitration is otherwise terminated, and the time of she continuance of the stay shall not be part of the time limited for the commencement of the action. The stay may be vacated in whole or in part, after a hearing duly noticed by any party or the court, if the court finds that the matter, or any part of it, is not an appropriate one for arbitration under the provisions of this article. The action may thereafter proceed subject to the provisions of Section 6204.

(d)   A client's right to request or maintain arbitration under the provisions of this article is waived by the client commencing an action or filing any pleading seeking either of the following:

(1)   Judicial resolution of a fee dispute to which this article applies.

(2)   Affirmative relief against the attorney for damages or otherwise based upon alleged malpractice or professional misconduct.

(e)   If the client waives the right to arbitration under this article, the parties may stipulate to set aside the waiver and to proceed with arbitration.

§ 6202.   Disclosure of Privileged Matters in Connection with Arbitration

The provisions of Article 3 (commencing with Section 950) of Chapter 4 of Division 8 of the Evidence Code shall not prohibit the disclosure of any relevant communication, nor shall the provisions of Chapter 4 (commencing with Section 2018.010) of Title 4 of Part 4 of the Code of Civil Procedure be construed to prohibit the disclosure of any relevant work product of the attorney in connection with: (1) an arbitration hearing pursuant to this article; (2) a trial after arbitration; or (3) judicial confirmation, correction, or vacation of an arbitration award. In no event shall such disclosure be deemed a waiver of the confidential character of such matters for any other purpose.

§ 6203.   Arbitration Award

(a)   The award shall be in writing and signed by the arbitrators concurring therein. It shall include a determination of all the questions submitted to the arbitrators, the decision of which is necessary in order to determine the controversy. The award shall not include any award to either party for attorney's fees incurred, notwithstanding any contract between the parties providing for such an award or attorney's fees. However, this section shall not preclude an award of attorney's fees to either party by a court pursuant to subdivision (c) of this section or of subdivision (d) of Section 6204.The State Bar, or the local bar association delegated by the State Bar to conduct the arbitration, shall deliver to each of the parties with the award, an original declaration of service of the award.

Evidence relating to claims of malpractice and professional misconduct, shall be admissible only to the extent that those claims bear upon the fees, costs, or both, to which the attorney is entitled. The arbitrators shall not award affirmative relief, in the form of damages or offset or otherwise, for injuries underlying any such claim. Nothing in this section shall be construed to prevent the arbitrators from awarding the client a refund of unearned fees, costs, or both previously paid to the attorney.

(b) Even if the parties to the arbitration have not agreed in writing to be bound, the arbitration award shall become binding upon the passage of 30 days after mailing of notice of the award, unless a party has, within the 30 days, sought a trial after arbitration pursuant to Section 6204. If an action has previously been filed in any court, any petition to confirm, correct, or vacate the award shall be to the court in which the action is pending, and may be served by mail on any party who has appeared, as provided in Chapter 4 (commencing with Section 1003) of Title 14 of Part 2 of the Code of Civil Procedure; otherwise it shall be in the same manner as provided in Chapter 4 (commencing with Section 1285) of Title 9 of Part 3 of the Code of Civil Procedure. If no action is pending in any court, the award may be confirmed, corrected, or vacated by petition to the court having jurisdiction over the amount of the arbitration award, but otherwise in the same manner as provided in Chapter 4 (commencing with Section 1285) of Title 9 of Part 3 of the Code of Civil Procedure.

(c) A court confirming, correcting, or vacating an award under this section may award to the prevailing party reasonable fees and costs including, if applicable, fees or costs on appeal, incurred in obtaining confirmation, correction, or vacation of the award. The party obtaining judgment confirming, correcting, or vacating the award shall be the prevailing party except that, without regard to consideration of who the prevailing party may be, if a party did not appear at the arbitration hearing in the manner provided by the rules adopted by the board of trustees, that party shall not be entitled to attorney's fees or costs upon confirmation, correction, or vacation of the award.
(d)(1) In any matter in which (A) the award of the arbitrators includes a refund of fees or costs, or both, to the client; (B) the award is binding or has become binding by operation of law or has become a judgment either after confirmation under subdivision (c) or after a trial after arbitration under Section 6204; and (C) the attorney has not complied with that award, the State Bar shall enforce the award by placing the attorney on involuntary inactive status until the award has been paid.

(2) The State Bar shall provide for an administrative procedure to determine whether an award should be enforced pursuant to this subdivision. An award shall be so enforced if either of the following applies:

(A) The State Bar shows that the attorney has failed to comply with a binding fee arbitration award rendered pursuant to this article.

(B) The attorney has not proposed a payment plan acceptable to the client or the State Bar. However, the award shall not be so enforced if the attorney has demonstrated that he or she (i) is not personally responsible for making or ensuring payment of the award, or (ii) is unable to pay the award.

(3) An attorney who has failed to comply with a binding award shall pay administrative penalties or reasonable costs, or both, as directed by the State Bar. Penalties imposed shall not exceed 20 percent of the amount awarded to the client or one thousand dollars ($ 1,000), whichever is greater. Any penalties or costs, or both, that are not paid shall be added to the membership fee of the attorney for the next calendar year.

(4)   The board shall terminate the inactive enrollment upon proof that the attorney has complied with the award and upon payment of any costs or penalties, or both, assessed as a result of the attorney's failure to comply.

(5)   A request for enforcement under this subdivision shall be made within four years from the date the arbitration award was mailed. However, in no event shall a request be made prior to 100 days from the date of the service of a signed copy of the award. In cases where the award is appealed, a request shall not be made prior to 100 days from the date the award has become final as set forth in this section.

§ 6204.   Trial after Arbitration: Entitlement; Initiation; Prevailing Party

(a)   The parties may agree in writing to be bound by the award of the arbitrators. In the absence of such an agreement, either party shall be entitled to a trial after arbitration if sought within 30 days, pursuant to subdivisions (b) and (c), except that if either party willfully fails to appear at the arbitration hearing in the manner provided by the rules adopted by the board of trustees, that party shall not be entitled to a trial after arbitration. The determination of willfulness shall be made by the court. The party who failed to appear at the arbitration shall have the burden of proving that the failure to appear was not willful. In making its determination, the court may consider any fi ndings made by the arbitrators on the subject of a party's failure to appear.

(b)   If there is an action pending, the trial after arbitration shall be initiated by filing a rejection of arbitration award and request for trial after arbitration in that action within 30 days after mailing of notice of the award. If the rejection of arbitration award has been filed by the plaintiff in the pending action, all defendants shall file a responsive pleading within 30 days following service upon the defendant of the rejection of arbitration award and request for trial after arbitration. If the rejection of arbitration award has been filed by the defendant in the pending action, all defendants shall file a responsive pleading within 30 days after the filing of the rejection of arbitration award and request for trial after arbitration. Service may be made by mail on any party who has appeared; otherwise service shall be made in the manner provided in Chapter 4 (commencing with Section 413.10) of Title 5 of Part 2 of the Code of Civil Procedure. Upon service and filing of the rejection of arbitration award, any stay entered pursuant to Section 6201 shall be vacated, without the necessity of a court order.

(c)   If no action is pending, the trial after arbitration shall be initiated by the commencement of an action in the court having jurisdiction over the amount of money in controversy within 30 days after mailing of notice of the award. After the filing of such an action, the action shall proceed in accordance with the provisions of Part 2 (commencing with Section 307) of the Code of Civil Procedure, concerning civil actions generally.

(d)   The party seeking a trial after arbitration shall be the prevailing party if that party obtains a judgment more favorable than that provided by the arbitration award, and in all other cases the other party shall be the prevailing party. The prevailing party may, in the discretion of the court, be entitled to an allowance for reasonable attorneys' fees and costs incurred in the trial after arbitration, which allowance shall be fixed by the court. In fixing the attorneys' fees, the court shall consider the award and determinations of the arbitrators, in addition to any other relevant evidence.

(e)   Except as provided in this section, the award and determinations of the arbitrators shall not be admissible nor operate as collateral estoppel or res judicata in any action or proceeding.

Article 14 Funds for the Provision of Legal Services to Indigent Persons

§ 6210.   Legislative Intent Concerning Provision of Legal Services to Indigent Persons

The Legislature finds that, due to insufficient funding, existing programs providing free legal services in civil matters to indigent persons, especially underserved client groups, such as the elderly, the disabled, juveniles, and non-English-speaking persons, do not adequately meet the needs of these persons. It is the purpose of this article to expand the availability and improve the quality of existing free legal services in civil matters to indigent persons, and to initiate new programs that will provide services to them. The Legislature finds that the use of funds collected by the State Bar pursuant to this article for these purposes is in the public interest, is a proper use of the funds, and is consistent with essential public and governmental purposes in the judicial branch of government. The Legislature further finds that the expansion, improvement, and initiation of legal services to indigent persons will aid in the advancement of the science of jurisprudence and the improvement of the administration of justice.

§ 6211.   Demand Trust Accounts

(a)   An attorney or law firm that, in the course of the practice of law receives or disburses trust funds shall establish and maintain an IOLTA account in which the attorney or law firm shall deposit or invest all client deposits or funds that are nominal in amount or are on deposit or invested for a short period of time. All such client funds may be deposited or invested in a single unsegregated account. The interest and dividends earned on all those accounts shall be paid to the State Bar of California to be used for the purposes set forth in this article.

(b)   Nothing in this article shall be construed to prohibit an attorney or law firm from establishing one or more interest bearing bank trust deposit accounts or dividend-paying trust investment accounts as may be permitted by the Supreme Court, with the interest or dividends earned on the accounts payable to clients for trust funds not deposited or invested in accordance with subdivision (a).

(c)   With the approval of the Supreme Court, the State Bar may formulate and enforce rules of professional conduct pertaining to the use by attorneys or law firms of an IOLTA account for unsegregated client funds pursuant to this article.

(d)   Nothing in this article shall be construed as affecting or impairing the disciplinary powers and authority of the Supreme Court or of the State Bar or as modifying the statutes and rules governing the conduct of members of the State Bar.

§ 6212.   Provisions Governing Demand Trust Accounts

An attorney who, or a law firm that, establishes an IOLTA account pursuant to subdivision (a) of Section 6211 shall comply with all of the following provisions:

(a)   The IOLTA account shall be established and maintained with an eligible institution offering or making available an IOLTA account that meets the requirements of this article. The IOLTA account shall be established and maintained consistent with the attorney's or law firm's duties of professional responsibility. An eligible financial institution shall have no responsibility for selecting the deposit or investment product chosen for the IOLTA account.

(b)   The Except as provided in subdivision (e), the rate of interest or dividends payable on any IOLTA account shall not be less than the interest rate or dividends generally paid by the eligible institution to nonattorney customers on accounts of the same type meeting the same minimum balance and other eligibility requirements as the IOLTA account. In determining the interest rate or dividend payable on any IOLTA account, an eligible institution may consider, in addition to the balance in the IOLTA account, risk or other factors customarily considered by the eligible institution when setting the interest rate or dividends for its non-IOLTA accounts, provided that the factors do not discriminate between IOLTA customers and non-IOLTA customers and that these factors do not include the fact that the account is an IOLTA account. The eligible institution shall calculate interest and dividends in accordance with its standard practice for non-IOLTA customers. Nothing in this article shall preclude an eligible institution from paying a higher interest rate or dividend on an IOLTA account or from electing to waive any fees and service charges on an IOLTA account.

(c)   Reasonable fees may be deducted from the interest or dividends remitted on an IOLTA account only at the rates and in accordance with the customary practices of the eligible institution for non-IOLTA customers. No other fees or service charges may be deducted from the interest or dividends earned on an IOLTA account. Unless and until the State Bar enacts regulations exempting from compliance with subdivision (a) of Section 6211 those accounts for which maintenance fees exceed the interest or dividends paid, an eligible institution may deduct the fees and service charges in excess of the interest or dividends paid on an IOLTA account from the aggregate interest and dividends remitted to the State Bar. Fees and service charges other than reasonable fees shall be the sole responsibility of, and may only be charged to, the attorney or law firm maintaining the IOLTA account. Fees and charges shall not be assessed against or deducted from the principal of any IOLTA account. It is the intent of the Legislature that the State Bar develop policies so that eligible institutions do not incur uncompensated administrative costs in adapting their systems to comply with the provisions of Chapter 422 of the Statutes of 2007 or in making investment products available to IOLTA members.

(d)   The eligible institution shall be directed to do all of the following:

(1)   To remit interest or dividends on the IOLTA account, less reasonable fees, to the State Bar, at least quarterly.

(2)   To transmit to the State Bar with each remittance a statement showing the name of the attorney or law firm for which the remittance is sent, for each account the rate of interest applied or dividend paid, the amount and type of fees deducted, if any, and the average balance for each account for each month of the period for which the report is made.

(3)   To transmit to the attorney or law firm customer at the same time a report showing the amount paid to the State Bar for that period, the rate of interest or dividend applied, the amount of fees and service charges deducted, if any, and the average daily account balance for each month of the period for which the report is made.

(e)   An eligible institution has no affirmative duty to offer or make investment products available to IOLTA customers. However, if an eligible institution offers or makes investment products available to non-IOLTA customers, in order to remain an IOLTA eligible institution, it shall make those products available to IOLTA customers or pay an interest rate on the IOLTA deposit account that is comparable to the rate of return or the dividends generally paid on that investment product for similar customers meeting the same minimum balance and other requirements applicable to the investment product. If the eligible institution elects to pay that higher interest rate, the eligible institution may subject the IOLTA deposit account to equivalent fees and charges assessable against the investment product. (Added by Stats. 1981, ch. 789. Amended by Stats. 2007, ch. 422; Stats. 2008, ch. 179.)

§ 6213.   Definitions

As used in this article:

(a)   "Qualified legal services project" means either of the following:

(1)   A nonprofit project incorporated and operated exclusively in California which provides as its primary purpose and function legal services without charge to indigent persons and which has quality control procedures approved by the State Bar of California.

(2)   A program operated exclusively in California by a nonprofit law school accredited by the State Bar of California which meets the requirements of subparagraphs (A) and (B).

(A)   The program shall have operated for at least two years at a cost of at least twenty thousand dollars ($ 20,000) per year as an identifiable law school unit with a primary purpose and function of providing legal services without charge to indigent persons.

(B) The program shall have quality control procedures approved by the State Bar of California.

(b) "Qualified support center" means an incorporated nonprofit legal services center, which has as its primary purpose and function the provision of legal training, legal technical assistance, or advocacy support without charge and which actually provides through an office in California a significant level of legal training, legal technical assistance, or advocacy support without charge to qualified legal services projects on a statewide basis in California.

(c) "Recipient" means a qualified legal services project or support center receiving financial assistance under this article.

(d) "Indigent person" means a person whose income is

(1) 125 percent or less of the current poverty threshold established by the United States Office of Management and Budget, or

(2) who is eligible for Supplemental Security Income or free services under the Older Americans Act or Developmentally Disabled Assistance Act. With regard to a project that provides free services of attorneys in private practice without compensation, "indigent person" also means a person whose income is 75 percent or less of the maximum levels of income for lower income households as defined in Section 50079.5 of the Health and Safety Code. For the purpose of this subdivision, the income of a person who is disabled shall be determined after deducting the costs of medical and other disability-related special expenses.

(e) "Fee generating case" means a case or matter that, if undertaken on behalf of an indigent person by an attorney in private practice, reasonably may be expected to result in payment of a fee for legal services from an award to a client, from public funds, or from the opposing party. A case shall not be considered fee generating if adequate representation is unavailable and any of the following circumstances exist:

(1) The recipient has determined that free referral is not possible because of any of the following reasons:

(A) The case has been rejected by the local lawyer referral service, or if there is no such service, by two attorneys in private practice who have experience in the subject matter of the case.

(B) Neither the referral service nor any attorney will consider the case without payment of a consultation fee.

(C) The case is of the type that attorneys in private practice in the area ordinarily do not accept, or do not accept without prepayment of a fee.

(D) Emergency circumstances compel immediate action before referral can be made, but the client is advised that, if appropriate and consistent with professional responsibility, referral will be attempted at a later time.

(2)   Recovery of damages is not the principal object of the case and a request for damages is merely ancillary to an action for equitable or other nonpecuniary relief, or inclusion of a counterclaim requesting damages is necessary for effective defense or because of applicable rules governing joinder of counterclaims.

(3)   A court has appointed a recipient or an employee of a recipient pursuant to a statute or a court rule or practice of equal applicability to all attorneys in the jurisdiction.

(4)   The case involves the rights of a claimant under a publicly supported benefit program for which entitlement to benefit is based on need.

(f)   "Legal Services Corporation" means the Legal Services Corporation established under the Legal Services Corporation Act of 1974 (P.L. 93-355; 42 U.S.C. Sec. 2996 et seq.).

(g)   "Older Americans Act" means the Older Americans Act of 1965, as amended (Public Law 89-73; 42 U.S.C. Sec. 3001 et seq.).

(h)   "Developmentally Disabled Assistance Act" means the Developmentally Disabled Assistance and Bill of Rights Act of 1975, as amended (Public Law 94-103; 42 U.S.C. Sec. 6001 et seq.).

(i)   "Supplemental security income recipient" means an individual receiving or eligible to receive payments under Title XVI of the federal Social Security Act, or payments under Chapter 3 (commencing with Section 12000) of Part 3 of Division 9 of the Welfare and Institutions Code.

(j)   "IOLTA account" means an account or investment product established and maintained pursuant to subdivision (a) of Section 6211 that is any of the following:

(1)   An interest-bearing checking account.

(2)   An investment sweep product that is a daily (overnight) financial institution repurchase agreement or an open-end money-market fund.

(3)   An investment product authorized by California Supreme Court rule or order. A daily financial institution repurchase agreement shall be fully collateralized by United States Government Securities or other comparably conservative debt securities, and may be established only with any eligible institution that is "well-capitalized" or "adequately capitalized" as those terms are defined by applicable federal statutes and regulations. An open-end money-market fund shall be invested solely in United States Government Securities or repurchase agreements fully collateralized by United States Government Securities or other comparably conservative debt securities, shall hold itself out as a "money-market fund" as that term is defined by federal statutes and regulations under the Investment Company Act of 1940 (15 U.S.C. Sec. 80a-1 et seq.), and, at the time of the investment, shall have total assets of at least two hundred fifty million dollars ($250,000,000).

(k)   "Eligible institution" means a bank or any other type of financial institution authorized by the Supreme Court. (Added by Stats. 1981, ch. 789. Amended by Stats. 1984, ch. 784; Stats. 2007, ch. 422; Stats. 2008, ch. 179.)

§ 6214.   Qualified Legal Services Projects

(a)   Projects meeting the requirements of subdivision (a) of Section 6213 which are funded either in whole or part by the Legal Services Corporation or with Older American Act funds shall be presumed qualified legal services projects for the purpose of this article.

(b)   Projects meeting the requirements of subdivision (a) of Section 6213 but not qualifying under the presumption specified in subdivision (a) shall qualify for funds under this article if they meet all of the following additional criteria:

(1)   They receive cash funds from other sources in the amount of at least twenty thousand dollars ($ 20,000) per year to support free legal representation to indigent persons.

(2)   They have demonstrated community support for the operation of a viable ongoing program.

(3)   They provide one or both of the following special services:

(A)   The coordination of the recruitment of substantial numbers of attorneys in private practice to provide free legal representation to indigent persons or to qualified legal services projects in California.

(B)   The provision of legal representation, training, or technical assistance on matters concerning special client groups, including the elderly, the disabled, juveniles, and non-English-speaking groups, or on matters of specialized substantive law important to the special client groups.

§ 6214.5.   Eligibility of Law School Program

A law school program that meets the definition of a "qualified legal services project" as defined in paragraph (2) of subdivision (a) of Section 6213, and that applied to the State Bar for funding under this article not later than February 17, 1984, shall be deemed eligible for all distributions of funds made under Section 6216.

§ 6215.   Qualified Support Centers

(a)   Support centers satisfying the qualifications specified in subdivision (b) of Section 6213 which were operating an office and providing services in California on December 31, 1980, shall be presumed to be qualified support centers for the purposes of this article.

(b)   Support centers not qualifying under the presumption specified in subdivision (a) may qualify as a support center by meeting both of the following additional criteria:

(1)   Meeting quality control standards established by the State Bar.

(2)   Being deemed to be of special need by a majority of the qualified legal services projects.

§ 6216.   Distribution of Funds

The State Bar shall distribute all moneys received under the program established by this article for the provision of civil legal services to indigent persons. The funds first shall be distributed 18 months from the effective date of this article, or upon such a date, as shall be determined by the State Bar, that adequate funds are available to initiate the program. Thereafter, the funds shall be distributed on an annual basis. All distributions of funds shall be made in the following order and in the following manner:

(a) To pay the actual administrative costs of the program, including any costs incurred after the adoption of this article and a reasonable reserve therefor.

(b) Eighty-five percent of the funds remaining after payment of administrative costs allocated pursuant to this article shall be distributed to qualified legal services projects. Distribution shall be by a pro rata county-by-county formula based upon the number of persons whose income is 125 percent or less of the current poverty threshold per county. For the purposes of this section, the source of data identifying the number of persons per county shall be the latest available figures from the United States Department of Commerce, Bureau of the Census. Projects from more than one county may pool their funds to operate a joint, multicounty legal services project serving each of their respective counties.

(1) (A) In any county which is served by more than one qualified legal services project, the State Bar shall distribute funds for the county to those projects which apply on a pro rata basis, based upon the amount of their total budget expended in the prior year for legal services in that county as compared to the total expended in the prior year for legal services by all qualified legal services projects applying therefor in the county. In determining the amount of funds to be allocated to a qualified legal services project specified in paragraph (2) of subdivision (a) of Section 6213, the State Bar shall recognize only expenditures attributable to the representation of indigent persons as constituting the budget of the program.

(B) The State Bar shall reserve 10 percent of the funds allocated to the county for distribution to programs meeting the standards of subparagraph (A) of paragraph (3) and paragraphs (1) and (2) of subdivision (b) of Section 6214 and which perform the services described in subparagraph (A) of paragraph (3) of Section 6214 as their principal means of delivering legal services. The State Bar shall distribute the funds for that county to those programs which apply on a pro rata basis, based upon the amount of their total budget expended for free legal services in that county as compared to the total expended for free legal services by all programs meeting the standards of subparagraph (A) of paragraph (3) and paragraphs (1) and (2) of subdivision (b) of Section 6214 in that county. The State Bar shall distribute any funds for which no program has qualified pursuant hereto, in accordance with the provisions of subparagraph of paragraph (1) of this subdivision.

(2) In any county in which there is no qualified legal services projects providing services, the State Bar shall reserve for the remainder of the fiscal year for distribution the pro rata share of funds as provided for by this article. Upon application of a qualified legal services project proposing to provide legal services to the indigent of the county, the State Bar shall distribute the funds to the project. Any funds not so distributed shall be added to the funds to be distributed the following year.

(c) Fifteen percent of the funds remaining after payment of administrative costs allocated for the purposes of this article shall be distributed equally by the State Bar to qualified support centers which apply for the funds. The funds provided to support centers shall be used only for the provision of legal services within California. Qualified support centers that receive funds to provide services to qualified legal services projects from sources other than this article, shall submit and shall have approved by the State Bar a plan assuring that the services funded under this article are in addition to those already funded for qualified legal services projects by other sources.

§ 6217.   Recipient Obligations in Connection with Provision of Legal Assistance

With respect to the provision of legal assistance under this article, each recipient shall ensure all of the following:

(a) The maintenance of quality service and professional standards.

(b) The expenditure of funds received in accordance with the provisions of this article.

(c) The preservation of the attorney-client privilege in any case, and the protection of the integrity of the adversary process from any impairment in furnishing legal assistance to indigent persons.

(d) That no one shall interfere with any attorney funded in whole or in part by this article in carrying out his or her professional responsibility to his or her client as established by the rules of professional responsibility and this chapter.

§ 6218.   Financial Eligibility Guidelines for Indigent Persons; Use of Funds for Designated Purposes

All legal services projects and support centers receiving funds pursuant to this article shall adopt financial eligibility guidelines for indigent persons.

(a) Qualified legal services programs shall ensure that funds appropriated pursuant to this article shall be used solely to defray the costs of providing legal services to indigent persons or for such other purposes as set forth in this article.

(b) Funds received pursuant to this article by support centers shall only be used to provide services to qualified legal services projects as defined in subdivision (a) of Section 6213 which are used pursuant to a plan as required by subdivision (c) of Section 6216, or as permitted by Section 6219.

§ 6219.   Use of Funds for Disadvantaged Law Students

Qualified legal services projects and support centers may use funds provided under this article to provide work opportunities with pay, and where feasible, scholarships for disadvantaged law students to help defray their law school expenses.

§ 6220.   Services to Pro Bono Attorneys

Attorneys in private practice who are providing legal services without charge to indigent persons shall not be disqualified from receiving the services of the qualified support centers.

§ 6221.   Services to Disadvantaged Groups

Qualified legal services projects shall make significant efforts to utilize 20 percent of the funds allocated under this article for increasing the availability of services to the elderly, the disabled, juveniles, or other indigent persons who are members of disadvantaged and underserved groups within their service area.

§ 6222.   Submission of Annual Financial Statement by Recipients

A recipient of funds allocated pursuant to this article annually shall submit a financial statement to the State Bar, including an audit of the funds by a certified public accountant or a fiscal review approved by the State Bar, a report demonstrating the programs on which they were expended, a report on the recipient's compliance with the requirements of Section 6217, and progress in meeting the service expansion requirements of Section 6221.

The Board of Trustees of the State Bar shall include a report of receipts of funds under this article, expenditures for administrative costs, and disbursements of the funds, on a county-by-county basis, in the annual report of State Bar receipts and expenditures required pursuant to Section 6145.

§ 6223.   Prohibitions Regarding Use of Funds

No funds allocated by the State Bar pursuant to this article shall be used for any of the following purposes:

(a)   The provision of legal assistance with respect to any fee generating case, except in accordance with guidelines which shall be promulgated by the State Bar.

(b)   The provision of legal assistance with respect to any criminal proceeding.

(c)   The provision of legal assistance, except to indigent persons or except to provide support services to qualified legal services projects as defined by this article.

§ 6224.   Authority to Deny Funding; Hearings for Denial

The State Bar shall have the power to determine that an applicant for funding is not qualified to receive funding, to deny future funding, or to terminate existing funding because the recipient is not operating in compliance with the requirements or restrictions of this article.

A denial of an application for funding or for future funding or an action by the State Bar to terminate an existing grant of funds under this article shall not become final until the applicant or recipient has been afforded reasonable notice and an opportunity for a timely and fair hearing. Pending final determination of any hearing held with reference to termination of funding, financial assistance shall be continued at its existing level on a month-to-month basis. Hearings for denial shall be conducted by an impartial hearing officer whose decision shall be final. The hearing officer shall render a decision no later than 30 days after the conclusion of the hearing. Specific procedures governing the conduct of the hearings of this section shall be determined by the State Bar pursuant to Section 6225.

§ 6225.   Adoption of Implementing Regulations

The Board of Trustees of the State Bar shall adopt the regulations and procedures necessary to implement this article and to ensure that the funds allocated herein are utilized to provide civil legal services to indigent persons, especially underserved client groups such as but not limited to the elderly, the disabled, juveniles, and non-English-speaking persons.

In adopting the regulations the Board of Trustees shall comply with the following procedures:

(a)   The board shall publish a preliminary draft of the regulations and procedures, which shall be distributed, together with notice of the hearings required by subdivision (b), to commercial banking institutions, to members of the State Bar, and to potential recipients of funds.

(b)   The board shall hold at least two public hearings, one in southern California and one in northern California where affected and interested parties shall be afforded an opportunity to present oral and written testimony regarding the proposed regulations and procedures.

§ 6226.   Implementation of Article; Resolutions

The program authorized by this article shall become operative only upon the adoption of a resolution by the Board of Trustees of the State Bar stating that regulations have been adopted pursuant to Section 6225 which conform the program to all applicable tax and banking statutes, regulations, and rulings.

§ 6227.   Credit of State Not Pledged

Nothing in this article shall create an obligation or pledge of the credit of the State of California or of the State Bar of California. Claims arising by reason of acts done pursuant to this article shall be limited to the moneys generated hereunder.

§ 6228.   Severability

If any provision of this article or the application thereof to any group or circumstances is held invalid, such invalidity shall not affect the other provisions or applications of this article which can be given effect without the invalid provision or application, and to this end the provisions of this article are severable.

ARTICLE 16 ATTORNEYS PROVIDING IMMIGRATION REFORM ACT SERVICES

§ 6240   Definitions

For purposes of this article, the following definitions apply:

(a)   "Immigration reform act" means any pending or future act of Congress that is enacted after the effective date of this section but before January 1, 2017, including, but not limited to, the federal act known as the "Border Security, Economic Opportunity, and Immigration Modernization Act" (S. 744, 2013), that authorizes an undocumented immigrant who either entered the United States without inspection or who did not depart after the expiration of a nonimmigrant visa, to attain a lawful status under federal law. The State Bar shall announce and post on its Internet Web site when an immigration reform act has been enacted.

(b)   "Immigration reform act services" means services offered in connection with an immigration reform act that are necessary in the preparation of an application and other related initial processes in order for an undocumented immigrant, who either entered the United States without inspection or who did not depart after the expiration of a nonimmigrant visa, to attain a lawful status under an immigration reform act. (Added by Stats. 2013, ch. 574.)

§ 6241   Applicability of Article

This article shall apply to the following:

(a)   An attorney who is an active member of the State Bar who provides immigration reform act services.

(b)   An attorney who is not an active member of the State Bar, but who meets both of the following:

   (1)   The attorney is authorized by federal law to practice law and to represent persons before the Board of Immigration Appeals or the United States Citizenship and Immigration Services.

   (2)   The attorney is providing immigration reform act services in an office or business in California. (Added by Stats. 2013, ch. 574.)

§ 6242   Immigration Reform Act Services; Refunding of Advance Payment; Statement of Accounting

(a)   It is unlawful for an attorney to demand or accept the advance payment of any funds from a person for immigration reform act services before the enactment of an immigration reform act.

(b)   Any funds received after the effective date of this section, but before the enactment of an immigration reform act, shall be refunded to the client promptly, but no later than 30 days after the receipt of the funds.

(c)   (1) If an attorney providing immigration reform act services accepted funds for immigration reform act services prior to the effective date of this section, and the services to be performed in connection with payment of those funds were rendered, the attorney shall promptly, but no later than 30 days after the effective date of this section, provide the client with a statement of accounting describing the services rendered.

    (2)   (A)Any funds received before the effective date of this section for which immigration reform act services were not rendered prior to the effective date of this section, shall be either refunded to the client or deposited in a client trust account

    (B)If an attorney deposits funds in a client trust account pursuant to this paragraph, he or she shall provide a written notice, in both English and the client's native language, informing the client of the following:

        (i)   That there are no benefits or relief available, and that no application for such benefits or relief may be processed, until enactment of an immigration reform act and the related necessary federal regulations or forms, and that, commencing with the effective date of this section, it is unlawful for an attorney to demand or accept the advance payment of any funds from a person for immigration reform act services before the enactment of an immigration reform act.

        (ii)   That he or she may report complaints to the Executive Office for Immigration Review of the United States Department of Justice, to the State Bar of California, or to the bar of the court of any state, possession, territory, or commonwealth of the United States or of the District of Columbia where the attorney is admitted to practice law. The notice shall include the toll-free telephone numbers and Internet Web sites of those entities. (Added by Stats. 2013, ch. 574.)

§ 6243   Written Contract for Legal Services; Reporting of Complaints; Languages for Form of Notice; Failure to Comply

(a)   (1) When a contract for legal services is required in writing pursuant to Section 6148, or is subject to Section 1632 of the Civil Code, an attorney providing immigration reform act services shall provide a written notice informing the client that he or she may report complaints to the Executive Office for Immigration Review of the United States Department of Justice, to the State Bar of California, or to the bar of the court of any state, possession, territory, or commonwealth of the United States or of the District of Columbia where the attorney is admitted to practice law. The notice shall include the toll-free telephone numbers and Internet Web sites of those entities.

(2) The notice shall be in English and in one of the languages of the forms translated by the State Bar pursuant to paragraph (1) of subdivision (b), if the contract for immigration reform act services was negotiated in one of those languages.

(3) The notice shall be attached or incorporated into any written contract for immigration reform act services. If the notice is attached to a written contract, it shall be signed by both the attorney and the client.

(b) (1) The State Bar shall provide the form of the notice required in subdivision (a) and shall post the form and translations on its Internet Web site. The State Bar shall translate the form into the following languages: Spanish, Chinese, Tagalog, Vietnamese, Korean, Armenian, Persian, Japanese, Russian, Hindi, Arabic, French, Punjabi, Portuguese, Mon-Khmer, Hmong, Thai, Gujarati. The State Bar, upon request, may translate the forms into other languages.

(2) Notwithstanding paragraph (1), an attorney providing immigration reform act services who meets the criteria of subdivision (b) of Section 6241 shall be responsible for adding and translating the name of, toll-free telephone number of, and information on the Internet Web site for, the bar of the court of any state, possession, territory, or commonwealth of the United States or the District of Columbia in which he or she is admitted to practice law.

(c) Failure to comply with any provision of this section renders the contract voidable at the option of the client, and the attorney shall, upon the contract being voided, be entitled to collect a reasonable fee.

This section shall become operative when the State Bar posts on its Internet Web site the form and translations required by paragraph (1) of subdivision (b). The State Bar shall post the form and translations as soon as practicable, but no later than 45 days after the effective date of this section. (Added by Stats. 2013, ch. 574.)

SELECTED PROVISIONS OF THE CALIFORNIA EVIDENCE CODE

250.   Writing... 695
905.   Presiding Officer 696
911.   No Privilege to Refuse to Be Witness, to Disclose or to Produce 696
912.   Privilege, Waiver 696
913.   Comments on, or Inferences from, Exercise of Privilege 697
914.   Determining Claim of Privilege; Limitations on Punishment and
        Contempt.. 697
915.   Disclosure of Privileged Information to Determine Claim 697
916.   Duties of Presiding Officer 698
917.   Confidential Communications – Presumptions, Burden of Proof...... 698
918.   Claim of Privilege; Error In Overruling... 699
919.   Erroneously Compelled Disclosure 699
920.   No Repeal By Implication.. 699

Article 3 Lawyer-Client Privilege

950.   Lawyer Defined 699
951.   Client Defined 699
952.   Confidential Communication Defined... 700
953.   Holder of Privilege Defined 700
954.   Who May Claim The Privilege 700
955.   When Lawyer May Claim Privilege 701
956.   Crime or Fraud.. 701
956.5. Life-Threatening Criminal Act... 701
957.   Deceased Client... 701
958.   Breach of Duty Arising Out of Lawyer-Client Relationship.............. 701
959.   Intention or Competence of Deceased Client 701
960.   Intention of Deceased Client to Affect Property Interest 701
961.   Validity of Writing Executed by Deceased Client 702
962.   Common Interest Clients 702

Article 3.5 Lawyer Referral Service-Client Privilege

965.   Lawyer Referral Service-Client Privilege–Definitions 702
966.   Lawyer Referral Service-Client Privilege... 703
967.   Lawyer Referral Service-Client Privilege–Claiming of Privilege....... 703
968.   Lawyer Referral Service-Client Privilege–Exceptions to Privilege.... 703

§ 250.   Writing

"Writing" means handwriting, typewriting, printing, photostating, photograph-ing, photocopying, transmitting by electronic mail or facsimile, and every other means of recording upon any tangible thing, any form of communication or representation, including letters, words, pictures, sounds, or symbols, or combinations thereof, and any record thereby created, regardless of the manner in which the record has been stored.

§ 905.   Presiding Officer

"Presiding officer" means the person authorized to rule on a claim of privilege in the proceeding in which the claim is made.

§ 911.   No Privilege to Refuse to Be Witness, to Disclose or to Produce

Except as otherwise provided by statute:

(a)   No person has a privilege to refuse to be a witness.

(b)   No person has a privilege to refuse to disclose any matter or to refuse to produce any writing, object, or other thing.

(c)   No person has a privilege that another shall not be a witness or shall not disclose any matter or shall not produce any writing, object, or other thing.

§ 912.   Privilege, Waiver

(a)   Except as otherwise provided in this section, the right of any person to claim a privilege provided by Section 954 (lawyer-client privilege), 966 (lawyer referral service-client privilege), 980 (privilege for confidential marital communications), 994 (physician-patient privilege), 1014 (psychotherapist-patient privilege), 1033 (privilege of penitent), 1034 (privilege of clergy member), 1035.8 (sexual assault counselor-victim privilege), 1037.5 (domestic violence counselor-victim privilege), or 1038 (human trafficking caseworker-victim privilege) is waived with respect to a communication protected by the privilege if any holder of the privilege, without coercion, has disclosed a significant part of the communication or has consented to disclosure made by anyone. Consent to disclosure is manifested by any statement or other conduct of the holder of the privilege indicating consent to the disclosure, including failure to claim the privilege in any proceeding in which the holder has legal standing and the opportunity to claim the privilege.

(b)   Where two or more persons are joint holders of a privilege provided by Section 954 (lawyer-client privilege), 966 (lawyer referral service-client privilege), 994 (physician-patient privilege), 1014 (psychotherapist-patient privilege), 1035.8 (sexual assault counselor-victim privilege), 1037.5 (domestic violence counselor-victim privilege), or 1038 (human trafficking caseworker-victim privilege), a waiver of the right of a particular joint holder of the privilege to claim the privilege does not affect the right of another joint holder to claim the privilege. In the case of the privilege provided by Section 980 (privilege for confidential marital communications), a waiver of the right of one spouse to claim the privilege does not affect the right of the other spouse to claim the privilege.

(c)   A disclosure that is itself privileged is not a waiver of any privilege.

(d)   A disclosure in confidence of a communication that is protected by a privilege provided by Section 954 (lawyer-client privilege), 966 (lawyer referral service-client privilege), 994 (physician-patient privilege), 1014 (psychotherapist-patient privilege), 1035.8 (sexual assault counselor-victim privilege), 1037.5 (domestic violence counselor-victim privilege), or 1038 (human trafficking caseworker-victim privilege), when disclosure is reasonably necessary for the accomplishment of the purpose for which the lawyer, lawyer referral service, physician, psychotherapist, sexual assault counselor, domestic violence counselor, or human trafficking caseworker was consulted, is not a waiver of the privilege.

§ 913.   Comments on, or Inferences from, Exercise of Privilege

(a)   If in the instant proceeding or on a prior occasion a privilege is or was exercised not to testify with respect to any matter, or to refuse to disclose or to prevent another from disclosing any matter, neither the presiding officer nor counsel may comment thereon, no presumption shall arise because of the exercise of the privilege, and the trier of fact may not draw any inference therefrom as to the credibility of the witness or as to any matter at issue in the proceeding.

(b)   The court, at the request of a party who may be adversely affected because an unfavorable inference may be drawn by the jury because a privilege has been exercised, shall instruct the jury that no presumption arises because of the exercise of the privilege and that the jury may not draw any inference therefrom as to the credibility of the witness or as to any matter at issue in the proceeding.

§ 914.   Determining Claim of Privilege; Limitations on Punishment and Contempt

(a)   The presiding officer shall determine a claim of privilege in any proceeding in the same manner as a court determines such a claim under Article 2 (commencing with Section 400) of Chapter 4 of Division 3.

(b)   No person may be held in contempt for failure to disclose information claimed to be privileged unless he has failed to comply with an order of a court that he disclose such information. This subdivision does not apply to any governmental agency that has constitutional contempt power, nor does it apply to hearings and investigations of the Industrial Accident Commission, nor does it impliedly repeal Chapter 4 (commencing with Section 9400) of Part 1 of Division 2 of Title 2 of the Government Code. If no other statutory procedure is applicable, the procedure prescribed by Section 1991 of the Code of Civil Procedure shall be followed in seeking an order of a court that the person disclose the information claimed to be privileged.

§ 915.   Disclosure of Privileged Information to Determine Claim

(a)   Subject to subdivision (b), the presiding officer may not require disclosure of information claimed to be privileged under this division or attorney work product under subdivision (a) of Section 2018.030 of the Code of Civil Procedure in order to rule on the claim of privilege; provided, however, that in any hearing conducted pursuant to subdivision (c) of Section 1524 of the Penal Code in which a claim of privilege is made and the court determines that there is no other feasible means to rule on the validity of the claim other than to require disclosure, the court shall proceed in accordance with subdivision (b).

(b)   When a court is ruling on a claim of privilege under Article 9 (commencing with Section 1040) of Chapter 4 (official information and identity of informer) or under Section 1060 (trade secret) or under subdivision (b) of Section 2018.030 of the Code of Civil Procedure (attorney work product) and is unable to do so without requiring disclosure of the information claimed to be privileged, the court may require the person from whom disclosure is sought or the person authorized to claim the privilege, or both, to disclose the information in chambers out of the presence and hearing of all persons except the person authorized to claim the privilege and any other persons as the person authorized to claim the privilege is willing to have present. If the judge determines that the information is privileged, neither the judge nor any other person may ever disclose, without the consent of a person authorized to permit disclosure, what was disclosed in the course of the proceedings in chambers.

§ 916.   Duties of Presiding Officer

(a)   The presiding officer, on his own motion or on the motion of any party, shall exclude information that is subject to a claim of privilege under this division if:

> (1)   The person from whom the information is sought is not a person authorized to claim the privilege; and
>
> (2)   There is no party to the proceeding who is a person authorized to claim the privilege.

(b)   The presiding officer may not exclude information under this section if:

> (1)   He is otherwise instructed by a person authorized to permit disclosure; or
>
> (2)   The proponent of the evidence establishes that there is no person authorized to claim the privilege in existence.

§ 917.   Confidential Communications – Presumptions, Burden of Proof

(a)   If a privilege is claimed on the ground that the matter sought to be disclosed is a communication made in confidence in the course of the lawyer-client, lawyer referral service-client, physician-patient, psychotherapist-patient, clergy-penitent, husband-wife, sexual assault counselor-victim, domestic violence counselor-victim, or human trafficking caseworker-victim relationship, the communication is presumed to have been made in confidence and the opponent of the claim of privilege has the burden of proof to establish that the communication was not confidential.

(b)   A communication between persons in a relationship listed in subdivision (a) does not lose its privileged character for the sole reason that it is communicated by electronic means or because persons involved in the delivery, facilitation, or storage of electronic communication may have access to the content of the communication.

(c)   For purposes of this section, "electronic" has the same meaning provided in Section 1633.2 of the Civil Code.

§ 918.   Claim of Privilege; Error In Overruling

A party may predicate error on a ruling disallowing a claim of privilege only if he is the holder of the privilege, except that a party may predicate error on a ruling disallowing a claim of privilege by his spouse under Section 970 or 971.

§ 919.   Erroneously Compelled Disclosure

(a)   Evidence of a statement or other disclosure of privileged information is inadmissible against a holder of the privilege if:

(1)   A person authorized to claim the privilege claimed it but nevertheless disclosure erroneously was required to be made; or

(2)   The presiding officer did not exclude the privileged information as required by Section 916.

(b)   If a person authorized to claim the privilege claimed it, whether in the same or a prior proceeding, but nevertheless disclosure erroneously was required by the presiding officer to be made, neither the failure to refuse to disclose nor the failure to seek review of the order of the presiding officer requiring disclosure indicates consent to the disclosure or constitutes a waiver and, under these circumstances, the disclosure is one made under coercion.

§ 920.   No Repeal By Implication

Nothing in this division shall be construed to repeal by implication any other statute relating to privileges.

Article 3.   Lawyer-Client Privilege

§ 950.   Lawyer Defined

As used in this article, "lawyer" means a person authorized, or reasonably believed by the client to be authorized, to practice law in any state or nation.

§ 951.   Client Defined

As used in this article, "client" means a person who, directly or through an authorized representative, consults a lawyer for the purpose of retaining the lawyer or securing legal service or advice from him in his professional capacity, and includes an incompetent (a) who himself so consults the lawyer or (b) whose guardian or conservator so consults the lawyer in behalf of the incompetent.

§ 952.   Confidential Communication Defined

As used in this article, "confidential communication between client and lawyer" means information transmitted between a client and his or her lawyer in the course of that relationship and in confidence by a means which, so far as the client is aware, discloses the information to no third persons other than those who are present to further the interest of the client in the consultation or those to whom disclosure is reasonably necessary for the transmission of the information or the accomplishment of the purpose for which the lawyer is consulted, and includes a legal opinion formed and the advice given by the lawyer in the course of that relationship.

§ 953.   Holder of Privilege Defined

As used in this article, "holder of the privilege" means:

(a)   The client, if the client has no guardian or conservator.

(b)   A guardian or conservator of the client, if the client has a guardian or conservator.

(c)   The personal representative of the client if the client is dead, including a personal representative appointed pursuant to Section 12252 of the Probate Code.

(d)   A successor, assign, trustee in dissolution, or any similar representative of a firm, association, organization, partnership, business trust, corporation, or public entity that is no longer in existence.

§ 954.   Who May Claim The Privilege

Subject to Section 912 and except as otherwise provided in this article, the client, whether or not a party, has a privilege to refuse to disclose, and to prevent another from disclosing, a confidential communication between client and lawyer if the privilege is claimed by:

(a)   The holder of the privilege;

(b)   A person who is authorized to claim the privilege by the holder of the privilege; or

(c)   The person who was the lawyer at the time of the confidential communication, but such person may not claim the privilege if there is no holder of the privilege in existence or if he is otherwise instructed by a person authorized to permit disclosure. The relationship of attorney and client shall exist between a law corporation as defined in Article 10 (commencing with Section 6160) of Chapter 4 of Division 3 of the Business and Professions Code and the persons to whom it renders professional services, as well as between such persons and members of the State Bar employed by such corporation to render services to such persons. The word "persons" as used in this subdivision includes partnerships, corporations, limited liability companies, associations and other groups and entities.

§ 955.   When Lawyer May Claim Privilege

The lawyer who received or made a communication subject to the privilege under this article shall claim the privilege whenever he is present when the communication is sought to be disclosed and is authorized to claim the privilege under subdivision (c) of Section 954.

§ 956.   Crime or Fraud

There is no privilege under this article if the services of the lawyer were sought or obtained to enable or aid anyone to commit or plan to commit a crime or a fraud.

§ 956.5.   Life-Threatening Criminal Act

There is no privilege under this article if the lawyer reasonably believes that disclosure of any confidential communication relating to representation of a client is necessary to prevent a criminal act that the lawyer reasonably believes is likely to result in the death of, or substantial bodily harm to, an individual.

§ 957.   Deceased Client

There is no privilege under this article as to a communication relevant to an issue between parties all of whom claim through a deceased client, regardless of whether the claims are by testate or intestate succession, nonprobate transfer, or inter vivos transaction.

§ 958.   Breach of Duty Arising Out of Lawyer-Client Relationship

There is no privilege under this article as to a communication relevant to an issue of breach, by the lawyer or by the client, of a duty arising out of the lawyer-client relationship.

§ 959.   Intention or Competence of Deceased Client

There is no privilege under this article as to a communication relevant to an issue concerning the intention or competence of a client executing an attested document of which the lawyer is an attesting witness, or concerning the execution or attestation of such a document.

§ 960.   Intention of Deceased Client to Affect Property Interest

There is no privilege under this article as to a communication relevant to an issue concerning the intention of a client, now deceased, with respect to a deed of conveyance, will, or other writing, executed by the client, purporting to affect an interest in property.

§ 961.   Validity of Writing Executed by Deceased Client

There is no privilege under this article as to a communication relevant to an issue concerning the validity of a deed of conveyance, will, or other writing, executed by a client, now deceased, purporting to affect an interest in property.

§ 962.   Common Interest Clients

Where two or more clients have retained or consulted a lawyer upon a matter of common interest, none of them, nor the successor in interest of any of them, may claim a privilege under this article as to a communication made in the course of that relationship when such communication is offered in a civil proceeding between one of such clients (or his successor in interest) and another of such clients (or his successor in interest).

Article 3.5 Lawyer Referral Service-Client Privilege

§ 965.   Lawyer Referral Service-Client Privilege–Definitions

For purposes of this article, the following terms have the following meanings:

(a)   "Client" means a person who, directly or through an authorized representative, consults a lawyer referral service for the purpose of retaining, or securing legal services or advice from, a lawyer in his or her professional capacity, and includes an incompetent who consults the lawyer referral service himself or herself or whose guardian or conservator consults the lawyer referral service on his or her behalf.

(b)   "Confidential communication between client and lawyer referral service" means information transmitted between a client and a lawyer referral service in the course of that relationship and in confidence by a means that, so far as the client is aware, does not disclose the information to third persons other than those who are present to further the interests of the client in the consultation or those to whom disclosure is reasonably necessary for the transmission of the information or the accomplishment of the purpose for which the lawyer referral service is consulted.

(c)   "Holder of the privilege" means any of the following:

　　(1)   The client, if the client has no guardian or conservator.

　　(2)   A guardian or conservator of the client, if the client has a guardian or conservator.

　　(3)   The personal representative of the client if the client is dead, including a personal representative appointed pursuant to Section 12252 of the Probate Code.

　　(4)   A successor, assign, trustee in dissolution, or any similar representative of a firm, association, organization, partnership, business trust, corporation, or public entity that is no longer in existence.

(d) "Lawyer referral service" means a lawyer referral service certified under, and operating in compliance with, Section 6155 of the Business and Professions Code or an enterprise reasonably believed by the client to be a lawyer referral service certified under, and operating in compliance with, Section 6155 of the Business and Professions Code. (Added by Stats. 2013, ch. 123.)

§ 966.   Lawyer Referral Service-Client Privilege

Subject to Section 912 and except as otherwise provided in this article, the client, whether or not a party, has a privilege to refuse to disclose, and to prevent another from disclosing, a confidential communication between client and lawyer if the privilege is claimed by:

(a) Subject to Section 912 and except as otherwise provided in this article, the client, whether or not a party, has a privilege to refuse to disclose, and to prevent another from disclosing, a confidential communication between client and lawyer referral service if the privilege is claimed by any of the following:

(1) The holder of the privilege.

(2) A person who is authorized to claim the privilege by the holder of the privilege.

(3) The lawyer referral service or a staff person thereof, but the lawyer referral service or a staff person thereof may not claim the privilege if there is no holder of the privilege in existence or if the lawyer referral service or a staff person thereof is otherwise instructed by a person authorized to permit disclosure.

(b) The relationship of lawyer referral service and client shall exist between a lawyer referral service, as defined in Section 965, and the persons to whom it renders services, as well as between such persons and anyone employed by the lawyer referral service to render services to such persons. The word "persons" as used in this subdivision includes partnerships, corporations, limited liability companies, associations, and other groups and entities. (Added by Stats. 2013, ch. 123.)

§ 967.   Lawyer Referral Service-Client Privilege–Claiming of Privilege

A lawyer referral service that has received or made a communication subject to the privilege under this article shall claim the privilege if the communication is sought to be disclosed and the client has not consented to the disclosure. (Added by Stats. 2013, ch. 123.)

§ 968.   Lawyer Referral Service-Client Privilege–Exceptions to Privilege

There is no privilege under this article if either of the following applies:

(a) The services of the lawyer referral service were sought or obtained to enable or aid anyone to commit or plan to commit a crime or a fraud.

(b)   A staff person of the lawyer referral service who receives a confidential communication in processing a request for legal assistance reasonably believes that disclosure of the confidential communication is necessary to prevent a criminal act that the staff person of the lawyer referral service reasonably believes is likely to result in the death of, or substantial bodily harm to, an individual. (Added by Stats. 2013, ch. 123.)

SELECTED CALIFORNIA RULES OF COURT REGARDING MULTIJURISDICTIONAL PRACTICE

2016 Editors' Introduction. On March 10, 2004, the California Supreme Court Multijurisdictional Practice Implementation Committee issued its Final Report, including proposed Rules of Court 964-967, concerning multijurisdictional practice in California. The Supreme Court adopted the Implementation Committee's recommended rules, which became effective on November 15, 2004. In addition to the Rules of Court, the California State Bar has promulgated rules governing the registration of out-of-state lawyers as "registered legal service attorneys" under rule 964 and "registered in-house counsel" under rule 965. Rule 966 governs lawyers who practice temporarily in California as part of litigation, and Rule 967 governs non-litigating lawyers who are temporarily in California to provide legal services. Included as part of each rule is a "Statement of Purpose" that summarizes each rule's intent. These rules are analogous to Model Rule 5.5.

These rules were subsequently renumbered 9.45 to 9.48, respectively, as part of a major reorganization of the California Rules of Court, which became effective on January 1, 2007. We have inserted the rules' new numbers, and placed the old numbers in brackets, below.

As of this writing, 13 jurisdictions have adopted a rule identical to Model Rule 5.5, and 33 (including California) have adopted a rule similar to Model Rule 5.5.One state's reviewing committee has recommended adoption of a rule identical to the model rule (Mississippi), and in a second state, a rule substantially similar to the model rule is before the state's highest court (New York). Another jurisdiction has the rule under review (Texas). Three states (Hawaii, Kansas, and Montana) appear to have rejected the post-Ethics 2000 revisions to Model Rule 5.5.

As to Model Rule 8.5, the other Model Rule of Professional Conduct that was substantially revised in light of MJP concerns, 25 jurisdictions have adopted an identical rule, 21 have adopted a similar rule, and one state's reviewing committee has recommended the adoption of an identical rule (Mississippi). Two other jurisdictions are studying the rule for possible adoption (Alabama and Texas). Two states (Hawaii and Kansas) appear to have rejected the adoption of the post-Ethics 2000 revisions to Model Rule 8.5.

The ABA's Final Multijurisdictional Practice Report, adopted in August 2002, proposed other rules and procedures in addition to Model Rules 5.5 and 8.5, including proposed model rules concerning *pro hac vice* admission and licensing of foreign legal consultants. California has rules of court governing *pro hac vice* admission (rule 9.40) and foreign legal consultant registration (rule 9.44). California also has rules of court governing appearances by military counsel in California courts (rule 9.41) and appearances by out-of state attorney arbitration counsel (rule 9.43). These rules have also been included in the supplement. In addition, we have included rule 9.42, which regulates the conduct of certified law students.

The ABA Commission on Ethics 20/20 completed its work in February 2013. The Commission engaged in a thorough review of the Model Rules and the U.S. system of lawyer governance and regulation in light of technological advances and developments in law practice globally. In light of its charge to study the global practice of law, many of the Commission's proposals concerned multi-jurisdictional practice in the international arena. The Commission's proposals were put before the ABA House of Delegates in August 2012 and February 2013, and adopted with only minor revisions. An overview of these changes is set forth in the Introduction and Use Note and more detailed descriptions of the changes can be found in the Model Rule – California Rules Comparison section, Model Rules 5.5 and 8.5 (Part III).

Rule   **Page**

9.45 [964].   Registered Legal Services Attorneys 706

9.46 [965].   Registered In-House Counsel 710

9.47 [966].   Attorneys Practicing Law Temporarily in California
               as Part of Litigation 713

9.48 [967].   Non Litigating Attorneys Temporarily in California
               to Provide Legal Services 715

9.40 [983].   Counsel *Pro Hac Vice* 717

9.41 [983.1]. Appearances by Military Counsel 718

9.42 [983.2]   Certified Law Students 720

9.43 [983.4]. Out-of-State Attorney Arbitration Counsel 722

9.44 [988].   Registered Foreign Legal Consultant 723

Statement of Purpose [Rule 9.45]. The purpose of this rule is to permit an attorney who relocates to California and who is licensed to practice law in one or more jurisdictions in the United States other than California to practice law in California under a registration system without becoming a member of the State Bar of California. An attorney so registered may practice law in California for no more than three years and during that period must do so under the supervision of an attorney employed by a qualifying legal service provider.

Rule 9.45 [964]. Registered Legal Services Attorneys

(a) **[Scope of practice]** Subject to all applicable rules, regulations, and statutes, an attorney practicing law under this rule is permitted to practice law in California only while working, with or without pay, at a qualifying legal services provider, as defined in this rule, and, at that institution and only on behalf of its clients, may engage, under supervision, in all forms of legal practice that are permissible for a member of the State Bar of California.

(b) **[Requirements]** For an attorney to practice law under this rule, the attorney must:

(1) Be an active member in good standing of the bar of a United States state, jurisdiction, possession, territory, or dependency;

(2) Register with the State Bar of California and file an Application for Determination of Moral Character;

(3) Meet all of the requirements for admission to the State Bar of California, except that the attorney:

(A) Need not take the California bar examination or the Multistate Professional Responsibility Examination; and

(B) May practice law while awaiting the result of his or her *Application for Determination of Moral Character*;

(4) Comply with the rules adopted by the Board of Governors relating to the State Bar Registered Legal Services Attorney Program;

(5) Practice law exclusively for a single qualifying legal services provider, except that if so qualified, an attorney may, while practicing under this rule, simultaneously practice law as registered in-house counsel;

(6) Practice law under the supervision of an attorney who is employed by the qualifying legal services provider and who is a member in good standing of the State Bar of California;

(7) Abide by all of the laws and rules that govern members of the State Bar of California, including the Minimum Continuing Legal Education (MCLE) requirements;

(8) Satisfy in his or her first year of practice under this rule all of the MCLE requirements, including ethics education, that members of the State Bar of California must complete every three years; and

(9) Not have taken and failed the California bar examination within five years immediately preceding application to register under this rule.

(c) **[Application]** To qualify to practice law as a registered legal services attorney, the attorney must:

(1) Register as an attorney applicant and file an *Application for Determination of Moral Character* with the Committee of Bar Examiners;

(2) Submit to the State Bar of California a declaration signed by the attorney agreeing that he or she will be subject to the disciplinary authority of the Supreme Court of California and the State Bar of California and attesting that he or she will not practice law in California other than under supervision at a qualifying legal services provider during the time he or she practices law as a registered legal services attorney in California, except that if so qualified, the attorney may, while practicing under this rule, simultaneously practice law as registered in-house counsel; and

(3)   Submit to the State Bar of California a declaration signed by a qualifying supervisor on behalf of the qualifying legal services provider in California attesting that the applicant will work, with or without pay, as an attorney for the organization; that the applicant will be supervised as specified in this rule; and that the qualifying legal services provider and the supervising attorney assume professional responsibility for any work performed by the applicant under this rule.

(d)   [Duration of practice] An attorney may practice for no more than a total of three years under this rule.

(e)   [Fees] The State Bar of California may set appropriate initial and annual registration fees, as well as application fees, to be paid by registered legal services attorneys.

(f)   [State Bar Registered Legal Services Attorney Program] The State Bar may establish and administer a program for registering California legal services attorneys under rules adopted by the Board of Governors of the State Bar.

(g)   [Supervision] To meet the requirements of this rule, an attorney supervising a registered legal services attorney:

(1)   Must be an active member in good standing of the State Bar of California;

(2)   Must have actively practiced law in California and been a member in good standing of the State Bar of California for at least the two years immediately preceding the time of supervision;

(3)   Must have practiced law as a full-time occupation for at least four years;

(4)   Must not supervise more than two registered legal services attorneys concurrently;

(5)   Must assume professional responsibility for any work that the registered legal services attorney performs under the supervising attorney's supervision;

(6)   Must assist, counsel, and provide direct supervision of the registered legal services attorney in the activities authorized by this rule and review such activities with the supervised attorney, to the extent required for the protection of the client;

(7)   Must read, approve, and personally sign any pleadings, briefs, or other similar documents prepared by the registered legal services attorney before their filing, and must read and approve any documents prepared by the registered legal services attorney for execution by any person who is not a member of the State Bar of California before their submission for execution; and

(8) May, in his or her absence, designate another attorney meeting the requirements of (1) through (7) to provide the supervision required under this rule.

(h) [Inherent power of Supreme Court] Nothing in this rule is to be construed as affecting the power of the Supreme Court of California to exercise its inherent jurisdiction over the practice of law in California.

(i) [Effect of rule on multijurisdictional practice] Nothing in this rule limits the scope of activities permissible under existing law by attorneys who are not members of the State Bar of California.

(j) [Definitions] The following definitions apply to terms used in this rule:

(1) "Qualifying legal services provider" means either of the following, provided that the qualifying legal services provider follows quality-control procedures approved by the State Bar of California:

(A) A nonprofit entity incorporated and operated exclusively in California that as its primary purpose and function provides legal services without charge in civil matters to indigent persons, especially underserved client groups, such as the elderly, persons with disabilities, juveniles, and non-English- speaking persons; or

(B) A program operated exclusively in California by a nonprofit law school approved by the American Bar Association or accredited by the State Bar of California that has operated for at least two years at a cost of at least $20,000 per year as an identifiable law school unit with a primary purpose and function of providing legal services without charge to indigent persons.

(2) "Active member in good standing of the bar of a United States state, jurisdiction, possession, territory, or dependency" means an attorney who meets all of the following criteria:

(A) Is a member in good standing of the entity governing the practice of law in each jurisdiction in which the member is licensed to practice law;

(B) Remains an active member in good standing of the entity governing the practice of law in at least one United States state, jurisdiction, possession, territory, or dependency other than California while practicing law as a registered legal services attorney in California; and

(C) Has not been disbarred, has not resigned with charges pending, or is not suspended from practicing law in any other jurisdiction.

Statement of Purpose [Rule 9.46]. The purpose of this rule is to permit an attorney who resides in California and who is licensed to practice law in one or more jurisdictions in the United States other than California to register to provide legal services as in-house counsel for a single qualifying institution in California without becoming a member of the State Bar of California.

Rule 9.46 [965]. Registered In-House Counsel

(a) **[Scope of practice]** Subject to all applicable rules, regulations, and statutes, an attorney practicing law under this rule:

    (1) Is permitted to provide legal services in California only to the qualifying institution that employs him or her;

    (2) Is not permitted to make court appearances in California state courts or to engage in any other activities for which pro hac vice admission is required if they are performed in California by an attorney who is not a member of the State Bar of California; and

    (3) Is not permitted to provide personal or individual representation to any customers, shareholders, owners, partners, officers, employees, servants, or agents of the qualifying institution.

(b) **[Requirements]** For an attorney to practice law under this rule, the attorney must:

    (1) Be an active member in good standing of the bar of a United States state, jurisdiction, possession, territory, or dependency;

    (2) Register with the State Bar of California and file an *Application for Determination of Moral Character*;

    (3) Meet all of the requirements for admission to the State Bar of California, except that the attorney:

        (A) Need not take the California bar examination or the Multistate Professional Responsibility Examination; and

        (B) May practice law while awaiting the result of his or her *Application for Determination of Moral Character*;

    (4) Comply with the rules adopted by the Board of Governors relating to the State Bar Registered In-House Counsel Program;

    (5) Practice law exclusively for a single qualifying institution, except that, while practicing under this rule, the attorney may, if so qualified, simultaneously practice law as a registered legal services attorney;

    (6) Abide by all of the laws and rules that govern members of the State Bar of California, including the Minimum Continuing Legal Education (MCLE) requirements;

    (7) Satisfy in his or her first year of practice under this rule all of the MCLE requirements, including ethics education, that members of

the State Bar of California must complete every three years and, thereafter, satisfy the MCLE requirements applicable to all members of the State Bar; and

(8)   Reside in California.

(c)   **[Application]** To qualify to practice law as registered in-house counsel, an attorney must:

(1)   Register as an attorney applicant and file an *Application for Determination of Moral Character* with the Committee of Bar Examiners;

(2)   Submit to the State Bar of California a declaration signed by the attorney agreeing that he or she will be subject to the disciplinary authority of the Supreme Court of California and the State Bar of California and attesting that he or she will not practice law in California other than on behalf of the qualifying institution during the time he or she is registered in-house counsel in California, except that if so qualified, the attorney may, while practicing under this rule, simultaneously practice law as a registered legal services attorney; and

(3)   Submit to the State Bar of California a declaration signed by an officer, a director, or a general counsel of the applicant's employer, on behalf of the applicant's employer, attesting that the applicant is employed as an attorney for the employer, that the nature of the employment conforms to the requirements of this rule, that the employer will notify the State Bar of California within 30 days of the cessation of the applicant's employment in California, and that the person signing the declaration believes, to the best of his or her knowledge after reasonable inquiry, that the applicant qualifies for registration under this rule and is an individual of good moral character.

(d)   **[Duration of practice]** Registered in-house counsel must renew his or her registration annually. There is no limitation on the number of years in-house counsel may register under this rule. Registered in-house counsel may practice law under this rule only for as long as he or she remains employed by the same qualifying institution that provided the declaration in support of his or her application. If an attorney practicing law as registered in-house counsel leaves the employment of his or her employer or changes employers, he or she must notify the State Bar of California within 30 days. If an attorney wishes to practice law under this rule for a new employer, he or she must first register as in-house counsel for that employer.

(e)   **[Eligibility]** It will not be grounds for denial of an application to register under this rule if the attorney applicant has practiced law in California as in-house counsel before the effective date of this rule. Further, it will not be grounds for denial of an application to register under this rule if the attorney applicant is practicing law as in-house counsel at or after the effective date of this rule, provided that the attorney applies under this rule within six months of its effective date.

(f) **[Fees]** The State Bar of California may set appropriate initial and annual registration fees, as well as application fees, to be paid by registered in- house counsel.

(g) **[State Bar Registered In-House Counsel Program]** The State Bar may establish and administer a program for registering California in- house counsel under rules adopted by the Board of Governors.

(h) **[Inherent power of Supreme Court]** Nothing in this rule is to be construed as affecting the power of the Supreme Court of California to exercise its inherent jurisdiction over the practice of law in California.

(i) **[Effect of rule on multijurisdictional practice]** Nothing in this rule limits the scope of activities permissible under existing law by attorneys who are not members of the State Bar of California.

(j) **[Definitions]** The following definitions apply to terms used in this rule:

(1) "Qualifying institution" means a corporation, a partnership, an association, or other legal entity, including its subsidiaries and organizational affiliates. Neither a governmental entity nor an entity that provides legal services to others can be a qualifying institution for purposes of this rule. A qualifying institution must:

(A) Employ at least 10 employees full-time in California; or

(B) Employ in California an attorney who is an active member in good standing of the State Bar of California.

(2) "Active member in good standing of the bar of a United States state, jurisdiction, possession, territory, or dependency" means an attorney who meets all of the following criteria:

(A) Is a member in good standing of the entity governing the practice of law in each jurisdiction in which the member is licensed to practice law;

(B) Remains an active member in good standing of the entity governing the practice of law in at least one United States state, jurisdiction, possession, territory, or dependency, other than California, while practicing law as registered in-house counsel in California; and

(C) Has not been disbarred, has not resigned with charges pending, or is not suspended from practicing law in any other jurisdiction.

Statement of Purpose [Rule 9.47]. The purpose of this rule is to permit an attorney who is licensed to practice law in a jurisdiction in the United States other than California, and who is in California temporarily as part of litigation, to perform litigation tasks in California under specified circumstances. An attorney practicing in accordance with this rule is not engaged in the unauthorized practice of law in California.

Rule 9.47 [966].   Attorneys practicing law temporarily in California as part of litigation

(a) **[Requirements]** For an attorney to practice law under this rule, the attorney must:

(1)   Maintain an office in a United States jurisdiction other than California and in which the attorney is licensed to practice law;

(2)   Already be retained by a client in the matter for which the attorney is providing legal services in California, except that the attorney may provide legal advice to a potential client, at the potential client's request, to assist the client in deciding whether to retain the attorney;

(3)   Indicate on any Web site or other advertisement that is accessible in California either that the attorney is not a member of the State Bar of California or that the attorney is admitted to practice law only in the states listed; and

(4)   Be an active member in good standing of the bar of a United States state, jurisdiction, possession, territory, or dependency.

(b) **[Permissible activities]** An attorney meeting the requirements of this rule, who complies with all applicable rules, regulations, and statutes, is not engaging in the unauthorized practice of law in California if the attorney's services are part of:

(1)   A formal legal proceeding that is pending in another jurisdiction and in which the attorney is authorized to appear;

(2)   A formal legal proceeding that is anticipated but is not yet pending in California and in which the attorney reasonably expects to be authorized to appear;

(3)   A formal legal proceeding that is anticipated but is not yet pending in another jurisdiction and in which the attorney reasonably expects to be authorized to appear; or

(4)   A formal legal proceeding that is anticipated or pending and in which the attorney's supervisor is authorized to appear or reasonably expects to be authorized to appear. The attorney whose anticipated authorization to appear in a formal legal proceeding serves as the basis for practice under this rule must seek that authorization promptly after it becomes possible to do so. Failure to seek that authorization promptly, or denial of that authorization, ends eligibility to practice under this rule.

(c) **[Restrictions]** To qualify to practice law in California under this rule, an attorney must not:

    (1)   Hold out to the public or otherwise represent that he or she is admitted to practice law in California;

    (2)   Establish or maintain a resident office or other systematic or continuous presence in California for the practice of law;

    (3)   Be a resident of California;

    (4)   Be regularly employed in California;

    (5)   Regularly engage in substantial business or professional activities in California; or

    (6)   Have been disbarred, have resigned with charges pending, or be suspended from practicing law in any other jurisdiction.

(d) **[Conditions]** By practicing law in California pursuant to this rule, an attorney agrees that he or she is providing legal services in California subject to:

    (1)   The jurisdiction of the State Bar of California;

    (2)   The jurisdiction of the courts of this state to the same extent as is a member of the State Bar of California; and

    (3)   The laws of the State of California relating to the practice of law, the State Bar Rules of Professional Conduct, the rules and regulations of the State Bar of California, and these rules.

(e) **[Inherent power of Supreme Court]** Nothing in this rule is to be construed as affecting the power of the Supreme Court of California to exercise its inherent jurisdiction over the practice of law in California.

(f) **[Effect of rule on multijurisdictional practice]** Nothing in this rule limits the scope of activities permissible under existing law by attorneys who are not members of the State Bar of California.

(g) **[Definitions]** The following definitions apply to the terms used in this rule:

    (1)   "A formal legal proceeding" means litigation, arbitration, mediation, or a legal action before an administrative decisionmaker.

    (2)   "Authorized to appear" means the attorney is permitted to appear in the proceeding by the rules of the jurisdiction in which the formal legal proceeding is taking place or will be taking place.

    (3)   "Active member in good standing of the bar of a United States state, jurisdiction, possession, territory, or dependency" means an attorney who meets all of the following criteria:

        (A)   Is a member in good standing of the entity governing the practice of law in each jurisdiction in which the member is licensed to practice law;

        (B)   Remains an active member in good standing of the entity governing the practice of law in at least one United States state, jurisdiction, possession, territory, or dependency while practicing law under this rule; and

(C) Has not been disbarred, has not resigned with charges pending, or is not suspended from practicing law in any other jurisdiction.

Statement of Purpose [Rule 9.48].   The purpose of this rule is to permit an attorney who is licensed to practice law in a jurisdiction in the United States other than California, and who is in California temporarily other than as part of litigation, to practice law to a limited extent in California. An attorney practicing under this rule is not engaged in the unauthorized practice of law in California.

Rule 9.48 [967].   Non litigating attorneys temporarily in California to provide legal services

(a)   **[Requirements]** For an attorney to practice law under this rule, the attorney must:

(1)   Maintain an office in a United States jurisdiction other than California and in which the attorney is licensed to practice law;

(2)   Already be retained by a client in the matter for which the attorney is providing legal services in California, except that the attorney may provide legal advice to a potential client, at the potential client's request, to assist the client in deciding whether to retain the attorney;

(3)   Indicate on any Web site or other advertisement that is accessible in California either that the attorney is not a member of the State Bar of California or that the attorney is admitted to practice law only in the states listed; and

(4)   Be an active member in good standing of the bar of a United States state, jurisdiction, possession, territory, or dependency.

(b)   **[Permissible activities]** An attorney who meets the requirements of this rule and who complies with all applicable rules, regulations, and statutes is not engaging in the unauthorized practice of law in California if the attorney:

(1)   Provides legal assistance or legal advice in California to a client concerning a transaction or other nonlitigation matter, a material aspect of which is taking place in a jurisdiction other than California and in which the attorney is licensed to provide legal services;

(2)   Provides legal assistance or legal advice in California on an issue of federal law or of the law of a jurisdiction other than California to attorneys licensed to practice law in California; or

(3)   Is an employee of a client and provides legal assistance or legal advice in California to the client or to the client's subsidiaries or organizational affiliates.

(c)   **[Restrictions]** To qualify to practice law in California pursuant to this rule, an attorney must not:

(1)   Hold out to the public or otherwise represent that he or she is admitted to practice law in California;

(2)   Establish or maintain a resident office or other systematic or continuous presence in California for the practice of law;

(3)   Be a resident of California;

(4)   Be regularly employed in California;

(5)   Regularly engage in substantial business or professional activities in California; or

(6)   Have been disbarred, have resigned with charges pending, or be suspended from practicing law in any other jurisdiction.

(d)   [Conditions] By practicing law in California pursuant to this rule, an attorney agrees that he or she is providing legal services in California subject to:

(1)   The jurisdiction of the State Bar of California;

(2)   The jurisdiction of the courts of this state to the same extent as is a member of the State Bar of California; and

(3)   The laws of the State of California relating to the practice of law, the State Bar Rules of Professional Conduct, the rules and regulations of the State Bar of California, and these rules.

(e)   [Scope of practice] An attorney is permitted by this rule to provide legal assistance or legal services concerning only a transaction or other nonlitigation matter.

(f)   [Inherent power of Supreme Court] Nothing in this rule is to be construed as affecting the power of the Supreme Court of California to exercise its inherent jurisdiction over the practice of law in California.

(g)   [Effect of rule on multijurisdictional practice] Nothing in this rule limits the scope of activities permissible under existing law by attorneys who are not members of the State Bar of California.

(h)   [Definitions] The following definitions apply to terms used in this rule:

(1)   "A transaction or other nonlitigation matter" includes any legal matter other than litigation, arbitration, mediation, or a legal action before an administrative decision-maker.

(2)   "Active member in good standing of the bar of a United States state, jurisdiction, possession, territory, or dependency" means an attorney who meets all of the following criteria:

(A)   Is a member in good standing of the entity governing the practice of law in each jurisdiction in which the member is licensed to practice law;

(B)   Remains an active member in good standing of the entity governing the practice of law in at least one United States state, jurisdiction, possession, territory, or dependency other than California while practicing law under this rule; and

(C)   Has not been disbarred, has not resigned with charges pending, or is not suspended from practicing law in any other jurisdiction.

Rule 9.40 [983].   Counsel *pro hac vice*

[Eligibility] A person who is not a member of the State Bar of California but who is a member in good standing of and eligible to practice before the bar of any United States court or the highest court in any state, territory or insular possession of the United States, and who has been retained to appear in a particular cause pending in a court of this state, may in the discretion of such court be permitted upon written application to appear as counsel *pro hac vice*, provided that an active member of the State Bar of California is associated as attorney of record. No person is eligible to appear as counsel *pro hac vice* pursuant to this rule if

(1)   he is a resident of the State of California, or

(2)   he is a resident of the State of California, or

(3)   he is regularly engaged in substantial business, professional, or other activities in the State of California.

Absent special circumstances, repeated appearances by any person pursuant to this rule shall be a cause for denial of an application.

(b)   [Application; notice of hearing] A person desiring to appear as counsel *pro hac vice* in a superior, municipal, or justice court shall file with the court a verified application together with proof of service by mail in accordance with section 1013a of the Code of Civil Procedure of a copy of the application and of the notice of hearing of the application upon all parties who have appeared in the cause and upon the State Bar of California at its San Francisco office. The notice of hearing shall be given at the time prescribed in section 1005 of the Code of Civil Procedure unless the court has prescribed a shorter period.

An application to appear as counsel *pro hac vice* in the Supreme Court or a Court of Appeal shall be made as provided in rule 41, with proof of service upon all parties who have appeared in the cause and upon the State Bar of California at its San Francisco office.

The application shall state:

(1)   the applicant's residence and office address;

(2)   the courts to which the applicant has been admitted to practice and the dates of admission;

(3)   that the applicant is a member in good standing in those courts;

(4)   that the applicant is not currently suspended or disbarred in any court;

(5) the title of court and cause in which the applicant has filed an application to appear as counsel pro hac vice in this state in the preceding two years, the date of each application, and whether or not it was granted; and

(6) the name, address, and telephone number of the active member of the State Bar of California who is attorney of record.

(c) **[Fee]** An applicant for permission to appear as counsel *pro hac vice* pursuant to this rule shall pay a reasonable fee not exceeding $50 to the State Bar of California with the copy of the application and the notice of hearing that is served upon the State Bar. The amount of the fee shall be fixed by the Board of Governors of the State Bar of California

(1) to defray the expenses of administering the provisions of this rule which are applicable to the State Bar and the incidental consequences resulting from such provisions, and

(2) partially to defray the expenses of administering the board's other responsibilities to enforce the provisions of the State Bar Act relating to the competent delivery of legal services and the incidental consequences resulting therefrom.

(d) **[Contempt and other court sanctions; discipline]** A person permitted to appear as counsel *pro hac vice* pursuant to this rule shall be subject to the jurisdiction of the courts of this state with respect to the law of this state governing the conduct of attorneys to the same extent as a member of the State Bar of California. He shall familiarize himself and comply with the standards of professional conduct required of members of the State Bar of California and shall be subject to the disciplinary jurisdiction of the State Bar with respect to any of his acts occurring in the course of such appearance. Article 5, Chapter 4, Division III of the California Business and Professions Code and the Rules of Procedure of the State Bar shall govern in any investigation or proceeding conducted by the State Bar under this rule.

(e) This rule does not preclude the Supreme Court or a Court of Appeal from permitting argument in a particular case from a person who is not a member of the State Bar, but who is licensed to practice in another jurisdiction and who possesses special expertise in the particular field affected by the proceeding.

Rule 9.41 [983.1].   Appearances by military counsel

(a) A judge advocate (as that term is defined at 10 United States Code section 801(13)) who is not a member of the State Bar of California but who is a member in good standing of and eligible to practice before the bar of any United States court or of the highest court in any state, territory, or insular possession of the United States may, in the discretion of a court of this state, be permitted to appear in that court to represent a person in the military service in a particular cause pending before that court, pursuant to the Soldiers' and Sailors' Civil Relief Act of 1940, 50 United States Code Appendix section 501 et seq., if:

(1) the judge advocate has been made available by the cognizant Judge Advocate General (as that term is defined at 10 United States Code section 801(1)), or a duly designated representative; and

(2) the court finds that retaining civilian counsel likely would cause substantial hardship for the person in military service or that person's family; and

(3) the court appoints a judge advocate as attorney to represent the person in military service pursuant to the Soldiers' and Sailors' Civil Relief Act of 1940.

Under no circumstances is the determination of availability of a judge advocate to be made by any court within this state, or reviewed by any court of this state. In determining the likelihood of substantial hardship as a result of the retention of civilian counsel, the court may take judicial notice of the prevailing pay scales for persons in the mili- tary service.

(b) The clerk of the court considering appointment of a judge advocate pursuant to this rule shall provide written notice of that fact to all parties who have appeared in the cause. A copy of the notice, together with proof of service by mail in accordance with section 1013a of the Code of Civil Procedure, shall be filed by the clerk of the court. Any party who has appeared in the matter may file a written objection to the appointment within 10 days of the date on which notice was given unless the court has prescribed a shorter period. If the court determines to hold a hearing in relation to the appointment, notice of the hearing shall be given at least 10 days before the date designated for the hearing unless the court has prescribed a shorter period.

(c) A judge advocate permitted to appear pursuant to this rule 983.1 shall be subject to the jurisdiction of the courts of this state with respect to the law of this state governing the conduct of attorneys to the same extent as a member of the State Bar of California. The judge advocate shall become familiar with and comply with the standards of professional conduct required of members of the State Bar of California and shall be subject to the disciplinary jurisdiction of the State Bar of California. Division 3, chapter 4, article 5 of the California Business and Professions Code and the Rules of Procedure of the State Bar of California shall govern any investigation or proceeding conducted by the State Bar under this rule.

(d) A judge advocate permitted to appear pursuant to this rule shall be subject to rights and obligations with respect to attorney-client privilege, work-product privilege, and other professional privileges to the same extent as a member of the State Bar of California.

Rule 9.42.   Certified law students

(a) Definition

(1)   A "certified law student" is a law student who has a currently effective certificate of registration as a certified law student from the State Bar.

(2)   A "supervising attorney" is a member of the State Bar who agrees to supervise a certified law student under rules established by the State Bar and whose name appears on the application for certification.

(Subd (a) amended effective January 1, 2007.)

(b) State Bar Certified Law Student Program

The State Bar must establish and administer a program for registering law students under rules adopted by the Board of Governors of the State Bar.

(Subd (b) amended effective January 1, 2007.)

(c) Eligibility for certification

To be eligible to become a certified law student, an applicant must:

(1)   Have successfully completed one full year of studies (minimum of 270 hours) at a law school accredited by the American Bar Association or the State Bar of California, or both, or have passed the first year law students' examination;

(2)   Have been accepted into, and be enrolled in, the second, third, or fourth year of law school in good academic standing or have graduated from law school, subject to the time period limitations specified in the rules adopted by the Board of Governors of the State Bar; and

(3)   Have either successfully completed or be currently enrolled in and attending academic courses in evidence and civil procedure.

(d) Permitted activities

Subject to all applicable rules, regulations, and statutes, a certified law student may:

(1)   Negotiate for and on behalf of the client subject to final approval thereof by the supervising attorney or give legal advice to the client, provided that the certified law student:

(A)   Obtains the approval of the supervising attorney to engage in the activities;

(B)   Obtains the approval of the supervising attorney regarding the legal advice to be given or plan of negotiation to be undertaken by the certified law student; and

(C)   Performs the activities under the general supervision of the supervising attorney;

(2)   Appear on behalf of the client in depositions, provided that the certified law student:

   (A)   Obtains the approval of the supervising attorney to engage in the activity;

   (B)   Performs the activity under the direct and immediate supervision and in the personal presence of the supervising attorney (or, exclusively in the case of government agencies, any deputy, assistant, or other staff attorney authorized and designated by the supervising attorney); and

   (C)   Obtains a signed consent form from the client on whose behalf the certified law student acts (or, exclusively in the case of government agencies, from the chief counsel or prosecuting attorney) approving the performance of such acts by such certified law student or generally by any certified law student;

(3)   Appear on behalf of the client in any public trial, hearing, arbitration, or proceeding, or before any arbitrator, court, public agency, referee, magistrate, commissioner, or hearing officer, to the extent approved by such arbitrator, court, public agency, referee, magistrate, commissioner, or hearing officer, provided that the certified law student:

   (A)   Obtains the approval of the supervising attorney to engage in the activity;

   (B)   Performs the activity under the direct and immediate supervision and in the personal presence of the supervising attorney (or, exclusively in the case of government agencies, any deputy, assistant, or other staff attorney authorized and designated by the supervising attorney);

   (C)   Obtains a signed consent form from the client on whose behalf the certified law student acts (or, exclusively in the case of government agencies, from the chief counsel or prosecuting attorney) approving the performance of such acts by such certified law student or generally by any certified law student; and

   (D)   As a condition to such appearance, either presents a copy of the consent form to the arbitrator, court, public agency, referee, magistrate, commissioner, or hearing officer, or files a copy of the consent form in the court case file; and

(4)   Appear on behalf of a government agency in the prosecution of criminal actions classified as infractions or other such minor criminal offenses with a maximum penalty or a fine equal to the maximum fine for infractions in California, including any public trial:

   (A)   Subject to approval by the court, commissioner, referee, hearing officer, or magistrate presiding at such public trial; and

(B) Without the personal appearance of the supervising attorney or any deputy, assistant, or other staff attorney authorized and designated by the supervising attorney, but only if the supervising attorney or the designated attorney has approved in writing the performance of such acts by the certified law student and is immediately available to attend the proceeding.

(Subd (d) amended effective January 1, 2007.)

(e) Failure to comply with program

A certified law student who fails to comply with the requirements of the State Bar Certified Law Student Program must have his or her certification withdrawn under rules adopted by the Board of Governors of the State Bar.

(Subd (e) amended effective January 1, 2007.)

(f) Fee and penalty

The State Bar has the authority to set and collect appropriate fees and penalties for this program.

(Subd (f) amended effective January 1, 2007.)

(g) Inherent power of Supreme Court

Nothing in these rules may be construed as affecting the power of the Supreme Court to exercise its inherent jurisdiction over the practice of law in California.

(Subd (g) amended effective January 1, 2007.)

Rule 9.42 amended and renumbered effective January 1, 2007; adopted as rule 983.2 by the Supreme Court effective December 29, 1993.

Rule 9.43 [983.4].   Out-of-State Attorney Arbitration Counsel

(a) [Definition]

(1) An "Out-of-State Attorney Arbitration Counsel" is an attorney who is not a member of the State Bar of California but who is a member in good standing of and eligible to practice before the bar of any United States court or the highest court in any state, territory or insular possession of the United States, and who has been retained to appear in the course of, or in connection with, an arbitration proceeding in this state; and

(2) has served a certificate in accordance with the requirements of Code of Civil Procedure section 1282.4 upon the arbitrator, the arbitrators, or the arbitral forum, the State Bar of California, and all other parties and counsel in the arbitration whose addresses are known to the attorney; and

(3) whose appearance has been approved by the arbitrator, the arbitrators or the arbitral forum.

(b) **[The State Bar Out-of-State Attorney Arbitration Counsel Program]** The State Bar of California shall establish and administer a program to implement the State Bar of California's responsibilities under Code of Civil Procedure section 1282.4. The State Bar of California's program shall be operative only as long as the applicable provisions of Code of Civil Procedure section 1282.4 remain in effect.

(c) **[Eligibility to appear as an Out-of-State Attorney Arbitration Counsel]** To be eligible to appear as an Out-of-State Attorney Arbitration Counsel, an attorney must comply with all of the applicable provisions of Code of Civil Procedure section 1282.4 and the requirements of this rule and the rules and regulations adopted by the State Bar of California pursuant to this rule.

(d) **[Discipline]** An attorney who files a certificate containing false information or who otherwise fails to comply with the standards of professional conduct required of members of the State Bar or California shall be subject to the disciplinary jurisdiction of the State Bar with respect to any of his or her acts occurring in the course of the arbitration.

(e) **[Disqualification]** Failure to timely file a certificate or, absent special circumstances, appearances in multiple separate arbitration matters shall be grounds for disqualification from serving in the arbitration in which the certificate was filed.

(f) **[Fee]** Out-of-State Attorney Arbitration Counsel shall pay a reasonable fee not exceeding $50 to the State Bar of California with the copy of the certificate that is served upon the State Bar.

(g) **[Inherent power of Supreme Court]** Nothing in these rules shall be constructed as affecting the power of the Supreme Court to exercise its inherent jurisdiction over the practice of law in California.

Rule 9.44 [988].   Registered foreign legal consultant

(a) **[Definition]** A "Registered Foreign Legal Consultant" is a person who

(1) is admitted to practice and is in good standing as an attorney or counselor at law or the equivalent in a foreign country; and

(2) has a currently effective Certificate of Registration as a Registered Foreign Legal Consultant from the State Bar.

(b) **[State Bar Registered Foreign Legal Consultant program]** The State Bar shall establish and administer a program for registering foreign attorneys or counselors at law or the equivalent under rules adopted by the Board of Governors of the State Bar.

(c) **[Eligibility for certification]** To be eligible to become a Registered Foreign Legal Consultant, an applicant must:

(1) Present satisfactory proof that the applicant has been admitted to practice and has been in good standing as an attorney or counselor at law or the equivalent in a foreign country for at least four of the

six years immediately preceding the application, and while so admitted, has actually practiced the law of that country;

(2)   Present satisfactory proof that the applicant possesses the good moral character requisite for a person to be licensed as a member of the State Bar of California;

(3)   Agree to comply with the provisions of the rules adopted by the Board of Governors of the State Bar relating to security for claims against a Foreign Legal Consultant by his or her clients;

(4)   Agree to comply with the provisions of the rules adopted by the Board of Governors of the State Bar relating to maintaining an address of record for State Bar purposes;

(5)   Agree to notify the State Bar of any change in his or her status in any jurisdiction where he or she is admitted to practice or of any discipline with respect to such admission;

(6)   Agree to be subject to the jurisdiction of the courts of this state with respect to the laws of the State of California governing the conduct of attorneys, to the same extent as a member of the State Bar of California;

(7)   Agree to become familiar with and comply with the standards of professional conduct required of members of the State Bar of California;

(8)   Agree to be subject to the disciplinary jurisdiction of the State Bar of California;

(9)   Agree to be subject to the rights and obligations with respect to attorney client privilege, work-product privilege, and other professional privileges, to the same extent as attorneys admitted to practice law in California; and

(10) Agree to comply with the laws of the State of California, the Rules and Regulations of the State Bar of California, and these Rules.

(d)   [Authority to practice law] Subject to all applicable rules, regulations, and statutes, a Registered Foreign Legal Consultant may render legal services in California, except that he or she may not:

(1)   Appear for a person other than himself or herself as attorney in any court, or before any magistrate or other judicial officer, in this state or prepare pleadings or any other papers or issue subpoenas in any action or proceeding brought in any court or before any judicial officer;

(2)   Prepare any deed, mortgage, assignment, discharge, lease, or any other instrument affecting title to real estate located in the United States;

(3)   Prepare any will or trust instrument affecting the disposition on death of any property located in the United States and owned by a

resident or any instrument relating to the administration of a decedent's estate in the United States;

(4) Prepare any instrument in respect of the marital relations, rights or duties of a resident of the United States, or the custody or care of the children of a resident; or

(5) Otherwise render professional legal advice on the law of the State of California, any other state of the United States, the District of Columbia, the United States, or of any jurisdiction other than the jurisdiction(s) named in satisfying the requirements of subdivision (c) of this rule, whether rendered incident to preparation of legal instruments or otherwise.

(e) **[Failure to comply with program]** A Registered Foreign Legal Consultant who fails to comply with the requirements of the Registered Foreign Legal Consultant program of the State Bar shall have her or his certification suspended or revoked under rules adopted by the Board of Governors of the State Bar.

(f) **[Fee and penalty]** The State Bar shall have the authority to set and collect appropriate fees and penalties for this program.

(g) **[Inherent power of Supreme Court]** Nothing in these rules shall be construed as affecting the power of the Supreme Court to exercise its inherent jurisdiction over the practice of law in California.

PART V

AMERICAN BAR ASSOCIATION AND CALIFORNIA JUDICIAL CODES

American Bar Association Model Code of Judicial Conduct 727

California Code of Judicial Ethics 771

AMERICAN BAR ASSOCIATION MODEL CODE OF JUDICIAL CONDUCT

Table of Contents

	Page
PREAMBLE	730
SCOPE	730
TERMINOLOGY	731
APPLICATION	734

CANON 1. A JUDGE SHALL UPHOLD AND PROMOTE THE INDEPENDENCE, INTEGRITY, AND IMPARTIALITY OF THE JUDICIARY, AND SHALL AVOID IMPROPRIETY AND THE APPEARANCE OF IMPROPRIETY

Rule

1.1	Compliance with the Law	737
1.2	Promoting Confidence in the Judiciary	737
1.3	Avoiding Abuse of the Prestige of Judicial Office	738

CANON 2. A JUDGE SHALL PERFORM THE DUTIES OF JUDICIAL OFFICE IMPARTIALLY, COMPETENTLY, AND DILIGENTLY

2.1	Giving Precedence to the Duties of Judicial Office	738
2.2	Impartiality and Fairness	739
2.3	Bias, Prejudice and Harassment	739
2.4	External Influences on Judicial Conduct	740

Rule		Page
2.5	Competence, Diligence, and Cooperation	740
2.6	Ensuring the Right to Be Heard	741
2.7	Responsibility to Decide	742
2.8	Decorum, Demeanor, and Communication with Jurors	742
2.9	Ex Parte Communications	743
2.10	Judicial Statements on Pending and Impending Cases	744
2.11	Disqualification	745
2.12	Supervisory Duties	748
2.13	Administrative Appointments	748
2.14	Disability and Impairment	749
2.15	Responding to Judicial and Lawyer Misconduct	749
2.16	Cooperation with Disciplinary Authorities	750

CANON 3. A JUDGE SHALL CONDUCT THE JUDGE'S PERSONAL AND EXTRAJUDICIAL ACTIVITIES TO MINIMIZE THE RISK OF CONFLICT WITH THE OBLIGATIONS OF JUDICIAL OFFICE.

3.1	Extrajudicial Activities in General	751
3.2	Appearances before Governmental Bodies and Consultation with Government Officials	752
3.3	Testifying as a Character Witness	752
3.4	Appointments to Governmental Positions	753
3.5	Use of Nonpublic Information.	753
3.6	Affiliation with Discriminatory Organizations	753
3.7	Participation in Educational, Religious, Charitable, Fraternal, or Civic Organizations and Activities	754
3.8	Appointments to Fiduciary Positions	756
3.9	Service as Arbitrator or Mediator	757
3.10	Practice of Law	757
3.11	Financial, Business, or Remunerative Activities	757
3.12	Compensation for Extrajudicial Activities	758
3.13	Acceptance and Reporting of Gifts, Loans, Bequests, Benefits, or Other Things of Value	758
3.14	Reimbursement of Expenses and Waivers of Fees or Charges	761
3.15	Reporting Requirements	762

CANON 4. JUDGE OR CANDIDATE FOR JUDICIAL OFFICE SHALL NOT ENGAGE IN POLITICAL OR CAMPAIGN ACTIVITY THAT IS INCONSISTENT WITH THE INDEPENDENCE, INTEGRITY, OR IMPARTIALITY OF THE JUDICIARY

4.1	Political and Campaign Activities of Judges and Judicial Candidates in General	763

Rule **Page**

4.2 Political and Campaign Activities of Judicial Candidates in Public Elections 766

4.3 Activities of Candidates for Appointive Judicial Office 768

4.4 Campaign Committees 769

4.5 Activities of Judges Who Become Candidates for Nonjudicial Office 770

PREAMBLE

[1]   An independent, fair and impartial judiciary is indispensable to our system of justice. The United States legal system is based upon the principle that an independent, impartial, and competent judiciary, composed of men and women of integrity, will interpret and apply the law that governs our society. Thus, the judiciary plays a central role in preserving the principles of justice and the rule of law. Inherent in all the Rules contained in this Code are the precepts that judges, individually and collectively, must respect and honor the judicial office as a public trust and strive to maintain and enhance confidence in the legal system.

[2]   Judges should maintain the dignity of judicial office at all times, and avoid both impropriety and the appearance of impropriety in their professional and personal lives. They should aspire at all times to conduct that ensures the greatest possible public confidence in their independence, impartiality, integrity, and competence.

[3]   The Model Code of Judicial Conduct establishes standards for the ethical conduct of judges and judicial candidates. It is not intended as an exhaustive guide for the conduct of judges and judicial candidates, who are governed in their judicial and personal conduct by general ethical standards as well as by the Code. The Code is intended, however, to provide guidance and assist judges in maintaining the highest standards of judicial and personal conduct, and to provide a basis for regulating their conduct through disciplinary agencies.

SCOPE

[1]   The Model Code of Judicial Conduct consists of four Canons, numbered Rules under each Canon, and Comments that generally follow and explain each Rule. Scope and Terminology sections provide additional guidance in interpreting and applying the Code. An Application section establishes when the various Rules apply to a judge or judicial candidate.

[2]   The Canons state overarching principles of judicial ethics that all judges must observe. Although a judge may be disciplined only for violating a Rule, the Canons provide important guidance in interpreting the Rules. Where a Rule contains a permissive term, such as "may" or "should," the conduct being addressed is committed to the personal and professional discretion of the judge or candidate in question, and no disciplinary action should be taken for action or inaction within the bounds of such discretion.

[3]   The Comments that accompany the Rules serve two functions. First, they provide guidance regarding the purpose, meaning, and proper application of the Rules. They contain explanatory material and, in some instances, provide examples of permitted or prohibited conduct. Comments neither add to nor subtract from the binding obligations set forth in the Rules. Therefore, when a Comment contains the term "must," it does not mean that the Comment itself is binding or enforceable; it signifies that the Rule in question, properly understood, is obligatory as to the conduct at issue.

[4] Second, the Comments identify aspirational goals for judges. To implement fully the principles of this Code as articulated in the Canons, judges should strive to exceed the standards of conduct established by the Rules, holding themselves to the highest ethical standards and seeking to achieve those aspirational goals, thereby enhancing the dignity of the judicial office.

[5] The Rules of the Model Code of Judicial Conduct are rules of reason that should be applied consistent with constitutional requirements, statutes, other court rules, and decisional law, and with due regard for all relevant circumstances. The Rules should not be interpreted to impinge upon the essential independence of judges in making judicial decisions.

[6] Although the black letter of the Rules is binding and enforceable, it is not contemplated that every transgression will result in the imposition of discipline. Whether discipline should be imposed should be determined through a reasonable and reasoned application of the Rules, and should depend upon factors such as the seriousness of the transgression, the facts and circumstances that existed at the time of the transgression, the extent of any pattern of improper activity, whether there have been previous violations, and the effect of the improper activity upon the judicial system or others.

[7] The Code is not designed or intended as a basis for civil or criminal liability. Neither is it intended to be the basis for litigants to seek collateral remedies against each other or to obtain tactical advantages in proceedings before a court.

TERMINOLOGY

The first time any term listed below is used in a Rule in its defined sense, it is followed by an asterisk (*).

"Aggregate," in relation to contributions for a candidate, means not only contributions in cash or in kind made directly to a candidate's campaign committee, but also all contributions made indirectly with the understanding that they will be used to support the election of a candidate or to oppose the election of the candidate's opponent. See Rules 2.11 and 4.4.

"Appropriate authority" means the authority having responsibility for initiation of disciplinary process in connection with the violation to be reported. See Rules 2.14 and 2.15.

"Contribution" means both financial and in-kind contributions, such as goods, professional or volunteer services, advertising, and other types of assistance, which, if obtained by the recipient otherwise, would require a financial expenditure. See Rules 2.11, 2.13, 3.7, 4.1, and 4.4.

"De minimis," in the context of interests pertaining to disqualification of a judge, means an insignificant interest that could not raise a reasonable question regarding the judge's impartiality. See Rule 2.11.

"Domestic partner" means a person with whom another person maintains a household and an intimate relationship, other than a person to whom he or she is legally married. See Rules 2.11, 2.13, 3.13, and 3.14.

"Economic interest" means ownership of more than a de minimis legal or equitable interest. Except for situations in which the judge participates in the management of such a legal or equitable interest, or the interest could be substantially affected by the outcome of a proceeding before a judge, it does not include:

(1)   an interest in the individual holdings within a mutual or common investment fund;

(2)   an interest in securities held by an educational, religious, charitable, fraternal, or civic organization in which the judge or the judge's spouse, domestic partner, parent, or child serves as a director, an officer, an advisor, or other participant;

(3)   a deposit in a financial institution or deposits or proprietary interests the judge may maintain as a member of a mutual savings association or credit union, or similar proprietary interests; or

(4)   an interest in the issuer of government securities held by the judge.

See Rules 1.3 and 2.11.

"Fiduciary" includes relationships such as executor, administrator, trustee, or guardian. See Rules 2.11, 3.2, and 3.8.

"Impartial," "impartiality," and **"impartially"** mean absence of bias or prejudice in favor of, or against, particular parties or classes of parties, as well as maintenance of an open mind in considering issues that may come before a judge. See Canons 1, 2, and 4, and Rules 1.2, 2.2, 2.10, 2.11, 2.13, 3.1, 3.12, 3.13, 4.1, and 4.2.

"Impending matter" is a matter that is imminent or expected to occur in the near future. See Rules 2.9, 2.10, 3.13, and 4.1.

"Impropriety" includes conduct that violates the law, court rules, or provisions of this Code, and conduct that undermines a judge's independence, integrity, or impartiality. See Canon 1 and Rule 1.2.

"Independence" means a judge's freedom from influence or controls other than those established by law. See Canons 1 and 4, and Rules 1.2, 3.1, 3.12, 3.13, and 4.2.

"Integrity" means probity, fairness, honesty, uprightness, and soundness of character. See Canons 1 and 4, and Rules 1.2, 3.1, 3.12, 3.13, and 4.2.

"Judicial candidate" means any person, including a sitting judge, who is seeking selection for or retention in judicial office by election or appointment. A person becomes a candidate for judicial office as soon as he or she makes a public announcement of candidacy, declares or files as a candidate with the election or appointment authority, authorizes or, where permitted, engages in solicitation or acceptance of contributions or support, or is nominated for election or appointment to office. See Rules 2.11, 4.1, 4.2, and 4.4.

"Knowingly," "knowledge," "known," and **"knows"** mean actual knowledge of the fact in question. A person's knowledge may be inferred from circumstances. See Rules 2.11, 2.13, 2.15, 2.16, 3.6, and 4.1.

"Law" encompasses court rules as well as statutes, constitutional provisions, and decisional law. See Rules 1.1, 2.1, 2.2, 2.6, 2.7, 2.9, 3.1, 3.4, 3.9, 3.12, 3.13, 3.14, 3.15, 4.1, 4.2, 4.4, and 4.5.

"Member of the candidate's family" means a spouse, domestic partner, child, grandchild, parent, grandparent, or other relative or person with whom the candidate maintains a close familial relationship.

"Member of the judge's family" means a spouse, domestic partner, child, grandchild, parent, grandparent, or other relative or person with whom the judge maintains a close familial relationship. See Rules 3.7, 3.8, 3.10, and 3.11.

"Member of a judge's family residing in the judge's household" means any relative of a judge by blood or marriage, or a person treated by a judge as a member of the judge's family, who resides in the judge's household. See Rules 2.11 and 3.13.

"Nonpublic information" means information that is not available to the public. Nonpublic information may include, but is not limited to, information that is sealed by statute or court order or impounded or communicated in camera, and information offered in grand jury proceedings, presentencing reports, dependency cases, or psychiatric reports. See Rule 3.5.

"Pending matter" is a matter that has commenced. A matter continues to be pending through any appellate process until final disposition. See Rules 2.9, 2.10, 3.13, and 4.1.

"Personally solicit" means a direct request made by a judge or a judicial candidate for financial support or in-kind services, whether made by letter, telephone, or any other means of communication. See Rule 4.1.

"Political organization" means a political party or other group sponsored by or affiliated with a political party or candidate, the principal purpose of which is to further the election or appointment of candidates for political office. For purposes of this Code, the term does not include a judicial candidate's campaign committee created as authorized by Rule 4.4. See Rules 4.1 and 4.2.

"Public election" includes primary and general elections, partisan elections, nonpartisan elections, and retention elections. See Rules 4.2 and 4.4.

"Third degree of relationship" includes the following persons: great-grandparent, grandparent, parent, uncle, aunt, brother, sister, child, grandchild, great-grandchild, nephew, and niece. See Rule 2.11.

APPLICATION

The Application section establishes when the various Rules apply to a judge or judicial candidate.

I.   APPLICABILITY OF THIS CODE

(A)   The provisions of the Code apply to all full-time judges. Parts II through V of this section identify provisions that apply to four categories of part-time judges only while they are serving as judges, and provisions that do not apply to part-time judges at any time. All other Rules are therefore applicable to part-time judges at all times. The four categories of judicial service in other than a full-time capacity are necessarily defined in general terms because of the widely varying forms of judicial service. Canon 4 applies to judicial candidates.

(B)   A judge, within the meaning of this Code, is anyone who is authorized to perform judicial functions, including an officer such as a justice of the peace, magistrate, court commissioner, special master, referee, or member of the administrative law judiciary.[1]

Comment

[1]   The Rules in this Code have been formulated to address the ethical obligations of any person who serves a judicial function, and are premised upon the supposition that a uniform system of ethical principles should apply to all those authorized to perform judicial functions.

[2]   The determination of which category and, accordingly, which specific Rules apply to an individual judicial officer, depends upon the facts of the particular judicial service.

[3]   In recent years many jurisdictions have created what are often called "problem solving" courts, in which judges are authorized by court rules to act in nontraditional ways. For example, judges presiding in drug courts and monitoring the progress of participants in those courts' programs may be authorized and even encouraged to communicate directly with social workers, probation officers, and others outside the context of their usual judicial role as independent decision makers on issues of fact and law. When local rules specifically authorize conduct not otherwise permitted under these Rules, they take precedence over the provisions set forth in the Code. Nevertheless, judges serv-

---

[1]   Each jurisdiction should consider the characteristics of particular positions within the administrative law judiciary in adopting, adapting, applying, and enforcing the Code for the administrative law judiciary. *See, e.g.,* Model Code of Judicial Conduct for Federal Administrative Law Judges (1989) and Model Code of Judicial Conduct for State Administrative Law Judges (1995). Both Model Codes are endorsed by the ABA National Conference of Administrative Law Judiciary.

ing on "problem solving" courts shall comply with this Code except to the extent local rules provide and permit otherwise.

II. RETIRED JUDGE SUBJECT TO RECALL

A retired judge subject to recall for service, who by law is not permitted to practice law, is not required to comply:

> **(A)   with Rule 3.9 (Service as Arbitrator or Mediator), except while serving as a judge.**

> **(B)   at any time with Rule 3.8(A) (Appointments to Fiduciary Positions).**

Comment

[1]   For the purposes of this section, as long as a retired judge is subject to being recalled for service, the judge is considered to "perform judicial functions."

III. CONTINUING PART-TIME JUDGE

A judge who serves repeatedly on a part-time basis by election or under a continuing appointment, including a retired judge subject to recall who is permitted to practice law ("continuing part-time judge"),

> **(A)   is not required to comply:**

> > **(1)   with Rule 4.1 (Political and Campaign Activities of Judges and Judicial Candidates in General) (A)(1) through (7), except while serving as a judge; or**

> > **(2)   at any time with Rules 3.4 (Appointments to Governmental Positions), 3.8(A) (Appointments to Fiduciary Positions), 3.9 (Service as Arbitrator or Mediator), 3.10 (Practice of Law), and 3.11(B) (Financial, Business, or Remunerative Activities); and**

> **(B)   shall not practice law in the court on which the judge serves or in any court subject to the appellate jurisdiction of the court on which the judge serves, and shall not act as a lawyer in a proceeding in which the judge has served as a judge or in any other proceeding related thereto.**

Comment

[1]   When a person who has been a continuing part-time judge is no longer a continuing part-time judge, including a retired judge no longer subject to recall, that person may act as a lawyer in a proceeding in which he or she has served as a judge or in any other proceeding related thereto only with the informed consent of all parties, and pursuant to any applicable Model Rules of Professional Conduct. An adopting jurisdiction should substitute a reference to its applicable rule.

IV. PERIODIC PART-TIME JUDGE

A periodic part-time judge who serves or expects to serve repeatedly on a part-time basis, but under a separate appointment for each limited period of service or for each matter,

    (A)   is not required to comply:

        (1)   with Rule 4.1 (Political and Campaign Activities of Judges and Judicial Candidates in General) (A)(1) through (7), except while serving as a judge; or

        (2)   at any time with Rules 3.4 (Appointments to Governmental Positions), 3.8(A) (Appointments to Fiduciary Positions), 3.9 (Service as Arbitrator or Mediator), 3.10 (Practice of Law), and 3.11(B) (Financial, Business, or Remunerative Activities); and

    (B)   shall not practice law in the court on which the judge serves or in any court subject to the appellate jurisdiction of the court on which the judge serves, and shall not act as a lawyer in a proceeding in which the judge has served as a judge or in any other proceeding related thereto.

V. PRO TEMPORE PART-TIME JUDGE

A pro tempore part-time judge who serves or expects to serve once or only sporadically on a part-time basis under a separate appointment for each period of service or for each case heard is not required to comply:

    (A)   except while serving as a judge, with Rules 2.4 (External Influences on Judicial Conduct), 3.2 (Appearances before Governmental Bodies and Consultation with Government Officials), and 4.1 (Political and Campaign Activities of Judges and Judicial Candidates in General) (A)(1) through (7); or

    (B)   at any time with Rules 3.4 (Appointments to Governmental Positions), 3.8(A) (Appointments to Fiduciary Positions), 3.9 (Service as Arbitrator or Mediator), 3.10 (Practice of Law), and 3.11(B) (Financial, Business, or Remunerative Activities).

VI. TIME FOR COMPLIANCE

A person to whom this Code becomes applicable shall comply immediately with its provisions, except that those judges to whom Rules 3.8 (Appointments to Fiduciary Positions) and 3.11 (Financial, Business, or Remunerative Activities) apply shall comply with those Rules as soon as reasonably possible, but in no event later than one year after the Code becomes applicable to the judge.

Comment

[1]   If serving as a fiduciary when selected as judge, a new judge may, notwithstanding the prohibitions in Rule 3.8, continue to serve as fiduciary, but only for that period of time necessary to avoid serious adverse consequences to the beneficiaries of the fiduciary relationship and in no event longer than one year. Similarly, if engaged at the time of judicial selection in a business activity, a new judge may, notwithstanding the prohibitions in Rule 3.11, continue in that activity for a reasonable period but in no event longer than one year.

CANON 1

A JUDGE SHALL UPHOLD AND PROMOTE THE INDEPENDENCE, INTEGRITY, AND IMPARTIALITY OF THE JUDICIARY, AND SHALL AVOID IMPROPRIETY AND THE APPEARANCE OF IMPROPRIETY.

RULE 1.1 COMPLIANCE WITH THE LAW

A judge shall comply with the law,* including the Code of Judicial Conduct.

RULE 1.2 PROMOTING CONFIDENCE IN THE JUDICIARY

A judge shall act at all times in a manner that promotes public confidence in the independence,* integrity,* and impartiality* of the judiciary, and shall avoid impropriety and the appearance of impropriety.

Comment

[1]   Public confidence in the judiciary is eroded by improper conduct and conduct that creates the appearance of impropriety. This principle applies to both the professional and personal conduct of a judge.

[2]   A judge should expect to be the subject of public scrutiny that might be viewed as burdensome if applied to other citizens, and must accept the restrictions imposed by the Code.

[3]   Conduct that compromises or appears to compromise the independence, integrity, and impartiality of a judge undermines public confidence in the judiciary. Because it is not practicable to list all such conduct, the Rule is necessarily cast in general terms.

[4]   Judges should participate in activities that promote ethical conduct among judges and lawyers, support professionalism within the judiciary and the legal profession, and promote access to justice for all.

[5]   Actual improprieties include violations of law, court rules or provisions of this Code. The test for appearance of impropriety is whether the conduct would create in reasonable minds a perception that the judge violated this Code or engaged in other conduct that reflects adversely on the judge's honesty, impartiality, temperament, or fitness to serve as a judge.

[6]   A judge should initiate and participate in community outreach activities for the purpose of promoting public understanding of and confidence in the administration of justice. In conducting such activities, the judge must act in a manner consistent with this Code.

RULE 1.3 AVOIDING ABUSE OF THE PRESTIGE OF JUDICIAL OFFICE

A judge shall not abuse the prestige of judicial office to advance the personal or economic interests* of the judge or others, or allow others to do so.

Comment

[1]   It is improper for a judge to use or attempt to use his or her position to gain personal advantage or deferential treatment of any kind. For example, it would be improper for a judge to allude to his or her judicial status to gain favorable treatment in encounters with traffic officials. Similarly, a judge must not use judicial letterhead to gain an advantage in conducting his or her personal business.

[2]   A judge may provide a reference or recommendation for an individual based upon the judge's personal knowledge. The judge may use official letterhead if the judge indicates that the reference is personal and if there is no likelihood that the use of the letterhead would reasonably be perceived as an attempt to exert pressure by reason of the judicial office.

[3]   Judges may participate in the process of judicial selection by cooperating with appointing authorities and screening committees, and by responding to inquiries from such entities concerning the professional qualifications of a person being considered for judicial office.

[4]   Special considerations arise when judges write or contribute to publications of for- profit entities, whether related or unrelated to the law. A judge should not permit anyone associated with the publication of such materials to exploit the judge's office in a manner that violates this Rule or other applicable law. In contracts for publication of a judge's writing, the judge should retain sufficient control over the advertising to avoid such exploitation.

CANON 2

A JUDGE SHALL PERFORM THE DUTIES OF JUDICIAL OFFICE IMPARTIALLY, COMPETENTLY, AND DILIGENTLY.

RULE 2.1 GIVING PRECEDENCE TO THE DUTIES OF JUDICIAL OFFICE

The duties of judicial office, as prescribed by law,* shall take precedence over all of a judge's personal and extrajudicial activities.

Comment

[1]   To ensure that judges are available to fulfill their judicial duties, judges must conduct their personal and extrajudicial activities to minimize the risk of conflicts that would result in frequent disqualification. See Canon 3.

[2]   Although it is not a duty of judicial office unless prescribed by law, judges are encouraged to participate in activities that promote public understanding of and confidence in the justice system.

RULE 2.2 IMPARTIALITY AND FAIRNESS

A judge shall uphold and apply the law,* and shall perform all duties of judicial office fairly and impartially.*

Comment

[1]   To ensure impartiality and fairness to all parties, a judge must be objective and open-minded.

[2]   Although each judge comes to the bench with a unique background and personal philosophy, a judge must interpret and apply the law without regard to whether the judge approves or disapproves of the law in question.

[3]   When applying and interpreting the law, a judge sometimes may make good-faith errors of fact or law. Errors of this kind do not violate this Rule.

[4]   It is not a violation of this Rule for a judge to make reasonable accommodations to ensure pro se litigants the opportunity to have their matters fairly heard.

RULE 2.3 BIAS, PREJUDICE, AND HARASSMENT

(A)   A judge shall perform the duties of judicial office, including administrative duties, without bias or prejudice.

(B)   A judge shall not, in the performance of judicial duties, by words or conduct manifest bias or prejudice, or engage in harassment, including but not limited to bias, prejudice, or harassment based upon race, sex, gender, religion, national origin, ethnicity, disability, age, sexual orientation, marital status, socioeconomic status, or political affiliation, and shall not permit court staff, court officials, or others subject to the judge's direction and control to do so.

(C)   A judge shall require lawyers in proceedings before the court to refrain from manifesting bias or prejudice, or engaging in harassment, based upon attributes including but not limited to race, sex, gender, religion, national origin, ethnicity, disability, age, sexual orientation, marital status, socioeconomic status, or political affiliation, against parties, witnesses, lawyers, or others.

(D)   The restrictions of paragraphs (B) and (C) do not preclude judges or lawyers from making legitimate reference to the listed factors, or similar factors, when they are relevant to an issue in a proceeding.

Comment

[1]   A judge who manifests bias or prejudice in a proceeding impairs the fairness of the proceeding and brings the judiciary into disrepute.

[2]   Examples of manifestations of bias or prejudice include but are not limited to epithets; slurs; demeaning nicknames; negative stereotyping; attempted humor based upon stereotypes; threatening, intimidating, or hostile acts; suggestions of connections between race, ethnicity, or nationality and crime; and irrelevant references to personal characteristics. Even facial expressions and body language can convey to parties and lawyers in the proceeding, jurors, the media, and others an appearance of bias or prejudice. A judge must avoid conduct that may reasonably be perceived as prejudiced or biased.

[3]   Harassment, as referred to in paragraphs (B) and (C), is verbal or physical conduct that denigrates or shows hostility or aversion toward a person on bases such as race, sex, gender, religion, national origin, ethnicity, disability, age, sexual orientation, marital status, socioeconomic status, or political affiliation.

[4]   Sexual harassment includes but is not limited to sexual advances, requests for sexual favors, and other verbal or physical conduct of a sexual nature that is unwelcome.

RULE 2.4 EXTERNAL INFLUENCES ON JUDICIAL CONDUCT

(A)   A judge shall not be swayed by public clamor or fear of criticism.

(B)   A judge shall not permit family, social, political, financial, or other interests or relationships to influence the judge's judicial conduct or judgment.

(C)   A judge shall not convey or permit others to convey the impression that any person or organization is in a position to influence the judge.

Comment

[1]   An independent judiciary requires that judges decide cases according to the law and facts, without regard to whether particular laws or litigants are popular or unpopular with the public, the media, government officials, or the judge's friends or family. Confidence in the judiciary is eroded if judicial decision making is perceived to be subject to inappropriate outside influences.

RULE 2.5 COMPETENCE, DILIGENCE, AND COOPERATION

(A)   A judge shall perform judicial and administrative duties, competently and diligently.

(B) **A judge shall cooperate with other judges and court officials in the administration of court business.**

Comment

[1]   Competence in the performance of judicial duties requires the legal knowledge, skill, thoroughness, and preparation reasonably necessary to perform a judge's responsibilities of judicial office.

[2]   A judge should seek the necessary docket time, court staff, expertise, and resources to discharge all adjudicative and administrative responsibilities.

[3]   Prompt disposition of the court's business requires a judge to devote adequate time to judicial duties, to be punctual in attending court and expeditious in determining matters under submission, and to take reasonable measures to ensure that court officials, litigants, and their lawyers cooperate with the judge to that end.

[4]   In disposing of matters promptly and efficiently, a judge must demonstrate due regard for the rights of parties to be heard and to have issues resolved without unnecessary cost or delay. A judge should monitor and supervise cases in ways that reduce or eliminate dilatory practices, avoidable delays, and unnecessary costs.

RULE 2.6 ENSURING THE RIGHT TO BE HEARD

(A) **A judge shall accord to every person who has a legal interest in a proceeding, or that person's lawyer, the right to be heard according to law.***

(B) **A judge may encourage parties to a proceeding and their lawyers to settle matters in dispute but shall not act in a manner that coerces any party into settlement.**

Comment

[1]   The right to be heard is an essential component of a fair and impartial system of justice. Substantive rights of litigants can be protected only if procedures protecting the right to be heard are observed.

[2]   The judge plays an important role in overseeing the settlement of disputes, but should be careful that efforts to further settlement do not undermine any party's right to be heard according to law. The judge should keep in mind the effect that the judge's participation in settlement discussions may have, not only on the judge's own views of the case, but also on the perceptions of the lawyers and the parties if the case remains with the judge after settlement efforts are unsuccessful. Among the factors that a judge should consider when deciding upon an appropriate settlement practice for a case are (1) whether the parties have requested or voluntarily consented to a certain level of participation by the judge in settlement discussions, (2) whether the parties and their counsel are relatively sophisticated in legal matters, (3) whether the case will be tried by the judge or a jury, (4) whether the parties participate with

their counsel in settlement discussions, (5) whether any parties are unrepresented by counsel, and (6) whether the matter is civil or criminal.

[3]   Judges must be mindful of the effect settlement discussions can have, not only on their objectivity and impartiality, but also on the appearance of their objectivity and impartiality. Despite a judge's best efforts, there may be instances when information obtained during settlement discussions could influence a judge's decision making during trial, and, in such instances, the judge should consider whether disqualification may be appropriate. See Rule 2.11(A)(1).

RULE 2.7 RESPONSIBILITY TO DECIDE

A judge shall hear and decide matters assigned to the judge, except when disqualification is required by Rule 2.11 or other law.*

Comment

[1]   Judges must be available to decide the matters that come before the court. Although there are times when disqualification is necessary to protect the rights of litigants and preserve public confidence in the independence, integrity, and impartiality of the judiciary, judges must be available to decide matters that come before the courts. Unwarranted disqualification may bring public disfavor to the court and to the judge personally. The dignity of the court, the judge's respect for fulfillment of judicial duties, and a proper concern for the burdens that may be imposed upon the judge's colleagues require that a judge not use disqualification to avoid cases that present difficult, controversial, or unpopular issues.

RULE 2.8 DECORUM, DEMEANOR, AND COMMUNICATION WITH JURORS

(A)   A judge shall require order and decorum in proceedings before the court.

(B)   A judge shall be patient, dignified, and courteous to litigants, jurors, witnesses, lawyers, court staff, court officials, and others with whom the judge deals in an official capacity, and shall require similar conduct of lawyers, court staff, court officials, and others subject to the judge's direction and control.

(C)   A judge shall not commend or criticize jurors for their verdict other than in a court order or opinion in a proceeding.

Comment

[1]   The duty to hear all proceedings with patience and courtesy is not inconsistent with the duty imposed in Rule 2.5 to dispose promptly of the business of the court. Judges can be efficient and businesslike while being patient and deliberate.

[2]   Commending or criticizing jurors for their verdict may imply a judicial expectation in future cases and may impair a juror's ability to be fair and impartial in a subsequent case.

[3]   A judge who is not otherwise prohibited by law from doing so may meet with jurors who choose to remain after trial but should be careful not to discuss the merits of the case.

RULE 2.9 EX PARTE COMMUNICATIONS

(A)   A judge shall not initiate, permit, or consider ex parte communications, or consider other communications made to the judge outside the presence of the parties or their lawyers, concerning a pending* or impending matter,* except as follows:

(1)   When circumstances require it, ex parte communication for scheduling, administrative, or emergency purposes, which does not address substantive matters, is permitted, provided:

(a)   the judge reasonably believes that no party will gain a procedural, substantive, or tactical advantage as a result of the ex parte communication; and

(b)   the judge makes provision promptly to notify all other parties of the substance of the ex parte communication, and gives the parties an opportunity to respond.

(2)   A judge may obtain the written advice of a disinterested expert on the law applicable to a proceeding before the judge, if the judge gives advance notice to the parties of the person to be consulted and the subject matter of the advice to be solicited, and affords the parties a reasonable opportunity to object and respond to the notice and to the advice received.

(3)   A judge may consult with court staff and court officials whose functions are to aid the judge in carrying out the judge's adjudicative responsibilities, or with other judges, provided the judge makes reasonable efforts to avoid receiving factual information that is not part of the record, and does not abrogate the responsibility personally to decide the matter.

(4)   A judge may, with the consent of the parties, confer separately with the parties and their lawyers in an effort to settle matters pending before the judge.

(5)   A judge may initiate, permit, or consider any ex parte communication when expressly authorized by law* to do so.

(B)   If a judge inadvertently receives an unauthorized ex parte communication bearing upon the substance of a matter, the judge shall make provision promptly to notify the parties of the substance of the communication and provide the parties with an opportunity to respond.

(C)   A judge shall not investigate facts in a matter independently, and shall consider only the evidence presented and any facts that may properly be judicially noticed.

(D)   A judge shall make reasonable efforts, including providing appropriate supervision, to ensure that this Rule is not violated by court staff, court officials, and others subject to the judge's direction and control.

Comment

[1]   To the extent reasonably possible, all parties or their lawyers shall be included in communications with a judge.

[2]   Whenever the presence of a party or notice to a party is required by this Rule, it is the party's lawyer, or if the party is unrepresented, the party, who is to be present or to whom notice is to be given.

[3]   The proscription against communications concerning a proceeding includes communications with lawyers, law teachers, and other persons who are not participants in the proceeding, except to the limited extent permitted by this Rule.

[4]   A judge may initiate, permit, or consider ex parte communications expressly authorized by law, such as when serving on therapeutic or problem-solving courts, mental health courts, or drug courts. In this capacity, judges may assume a more interactive role with parties, treatment providers, probation officers, social workers, and others.

[5]   A judge may consult with other judges on pending matters, but must avoid ex parte discussions of a case with judges who have previously been disqualified from hearing the matter, and with judges who have appellate jurisdiction over the matter.

[6]   The prohibition against a judge investigating the facts in a matter extends to information available in all mediums, including electronic.

[7]   A judge may consult ethics advisory committees, outside counsel, or legal experts concerning the judge's compliance with this Code. Such consultations are not subject to the restrictions of paragraph (A)(2).

RULE 2.10 JUDICIAL STATEMENTS ON PENDING AND IMPENDING CASES

(A)   A judge shall not make any public statement that might reasonably be expected to affect the outcome or impair the fairness of a matter pending* or impending* in any court, or make any nonpublic statement that might substantially interfere with a fair trial or hearing.

(B)   A judge shall not, in connection with cases, controversies, or issues that are likely to come before the court, make pledges, promises, or commitments that are inconsistent with the impartial* performance of the adjudicative duties of judicial office.

(C)   A judge shall require court staff, court officials, and others subject to the judge's direction and control to refrain from making statements that the judge would be prohibited from making by paragraphs (A) and (B).

(D)   Notwithstanding the restrictions in paragraph (A), a judge may make public statements in the course of official duties, may explain court procedures, and may comment on any proceeding in which the judge is a litigant in a personal capacity.

(E)   Subject to the requirements of paragraph (A), a judge may respond directly or through a third party to allegations in the media or elsewhere concerning the judge's conduct in a matter.

Comment

[1]   This Rule's restrictions on judicial speech are essential to the maintenance of the independence, integrity, and impartiality of the judiciary.

[2]   This Rule does not prohibit a judge from commenting on proceedings in which the judge is a litigant in a personal capacity, or represents a client as permitted by these Rules. In cases in which the judge is a litigant in an official capacity, such as a writ of mandamus, the judge must not comment publicly.

[3]   Depending upon the circumstances, the judge should consider whether it may be preferable for a third party, rather than the judge, to respond or issue statements in connection with allegations concerning the judge's conduct in a matter.

RULE 2.11 DISQUALIFICATION

(A)   A judge shall disqualify himself or herself in any proceeding in which the judge's impartiality* might reasonably be questioned, including but not limited to the following circumstances:

> **(1)**   The judge has a personal bias or prejudice concerning a party or a party's lawyer, or personal knowledge* of facts that are in dispute in the proceeding.
>
> **(2)**   The judge knows* that the judge, the judge's spouse or domestic partner,* or a person within the third degree of relationship* to either of them, or the spouse or domestic partner of such a person is:
>
>> **(a)**   a party to the proceeding, or an officer, director, general partner, managing member, or trustee of a party;
>>
>> **(b)**   acting as a lawyer in the proceeding;
>>
>> **(c)**   a person who has more than a de minimis* interest that could be substantially affected by the proceeding; or
>>
>> **(d)**   likely to be a material witness in the proceeding.

(3)   The judge knows that he or she, individually or as a fiduciary,* or the judge's spouse, domestic partner, parent, or child, or any other member of the judge's family residing in the judge's household,* has an economic interest* in the subject matter in controversy or is a party to the proceeding.

(4)   The judge knows or learns by means of a timely motion that a party, a party's lawyer, or the law firm of a party's lawyer has within the previous [insert number] year[s] made aggregate* contributions* to the judge's campaign in an amount that [is greater than $[insert amount] for an individual or $[insert amount] for an entity] [is reasonable and appropriate for an individual or an entity].

(5)   The judge, while a judge or a judicial candidate,* has made a public statement, other than in a court proceeding, judicial decision, or opinion, that commits or appears to commit the judge to reach a particular result or rule in a particular way in the proceeding or controversy.

(6)   The judge:

    (a)   served as a lawyer in the matter in controversy, or was associated with a lawyer who participated substantially as a lawyer in the matter during such association;

    (b)   served in governmental employment, and in such capacity participated personally and substantially as a lawyer or public official concerning the proceeding, or has publicly expressed in such capacity an opinion concerning the merits of the particular matter in controversy;

    (c)   was a material witness concerning the matter; or

    (d)   previously presided as a judge over the matter in another court.

(B)   A judge shall keep informed about the judge's personal and fiduciary economic interests, and make a reasonable effort to keep informed about the personal economic interests of the judge's spouse or domestic partner and minor children residing in the judge's household.

(C)   A judge subject to disqualification under this Rule, other than for bias or prejudice under paragraph (A)(1), may disclose on the record the basis of the judge's disqualification and may ask the parties and their lawyers to consider, outside the presence of the judge and court personnel, whether to waive disqualification. If, following the disclosure, the parties and lawyers agree, without participation by the judge or court personnel, that the judge should not be disqualified, the judge may

participate in the proceeding. The agreement shall be incorporated into the record of the proceeding.

Comment

[1]   Under this Rule, a judge is disqualified whenever the judge's impartiality might reasonably be questioned, regardless of whether any of the specific provisions of paragraphs (A)(1) through (6) apply. In many jurisdictions, the term "recusal" is used interchangeably with the term "disqualification."

[2]   A judge's obligation not to hear or decide matters in which disqualification is required applies regardless of whether a motion to disqualify is filed.

[3]   The rule of necessity may override the rule of disqualification. For example, a judge might be required to participate in judicial review of a judicial salary statute, or might be the only judge available in a matter requiring immediate judicial action, such as a hearing on probable cause or a temporary restraining order. In matters that require immediate action, the judge must disclose on the record the basis for possible disqualification and make reasonable efforts to transfer the matter to another judge as soon as practicable.

[4]   The fact that a lawyer in a proceeding is affiliated with a law firm with which a relative of the judge is affiliated does not itself disqualify the judge. If, however, the judge's impartiality might reasonably be questioned under paragraph (A), or the relative is known by the judge to have an interest in the law firm that could be substantially affected by the proceeding under paragraph (A)(2)(c), the judge's disqualification is required.

[5]   A judge should disclose on the record information that the judge believes the parties or their lawyers might reasonably consider relevant to a possible motion for disqualification, even if the judge believes there is no basis for disqualification.

[6]   "Economic interest," as set forth in the Terminology section, means ownership of more than a de minimis legal or equitable interest. Except for situations in which a judge participates in the management of such a legal or equitable interest, or the interest could be substantially affected by the outcome of a proceeding before a judge, it does not include:

> (1)   an interest in the individual holdings within a mutual or common investment fund;
>
> (2)   an interest in securities held by an educational, religious, charitable, fraternal, or civic organization in which the judge or the judge's spouse, domestic partner, parent, or child serves as a director, officer, advisor, or other participant;
>
> (3)   a deposit in a financial institution or deposits or proprietary interests the judge may maintain as a member of a mutual savings association or credit union, or similar proprietary interests; or
>
> (4)   an interest in the issuer of government securities held by the judge.

RULE 2.12 SUPERVISORY DUTIES

(A)   A judge shall require court staff, court officials, and others subject to the judge's direction and control to act in a manner consistent with the judge's obligations under this Code.

(B)   A judge with supervisory authority for the performance of other judges shall take reasonable measures to ensure that those judges properly discharge their judicial responsibilities, including the prompt disposition of matters before them.

Comment

[1]   A judge is responsible for his or her own conduct and for the conduct of others, such as staff, when those persons are acting at the judge's direction or control. A judge may not direct court personnel to engage in conduct on the judge's behalf or as the judge's representative when such conduct would violate the Code if undertaken by the judge.

[2]   Public confidence in the judicial system depends upon timely justice. To promote the efficient administration of justice, a judge with supervisory authority must take the steps needed to ensure that judges under his or her supervision administer their workloads promptly.

RULE 2.13 ADMINISTRATIVE APPOINTMENTS

(A)   In making administrative appointments, a judge:

(1)   shall exercise the power of appointment impartially* and on the basis of merit; and

(2)   shall avoid nepotism, favoritism, and unnecessary appointments.

(B)   A judge shall not appoint a lawyer to a position if the judge either knows* that the lawyer, or the lawyer's spouse or domestic partner,* has contributed more than $[insert amount] within the prior [insert number] year[s] to the judge's election campaign, or learns of such a contribution* by means of a timely motion by a party or other person properly interested in the matter, unless:

(1)   the position is substantially uncompensated;

(2)   the lawyer has been selected in rotation from a list of qualified and available lawyers compiled without regard to their having made political contributions; or

(3)   the judge or another presiding or administrative judge affirmatively finds that no other lawyer is willing, competent, and able to accept the position.

(C)   A judge shall not approve compensation of appointees beyond the fair value of services rendered.

Comment

[1]   Appointees of a judge include assigned counsel, officials such as referees, commissioners, special masters, receivers, and guardians, and personnel such as clerks, secretaries, and bailiffs. Consent by the parties to an appointment or an award of compensation does not relieve the judge of the obligation prescribed by paragraph (A).

[2]   Unless otherwise defined by law, nepotism is the appointment or hiring of any relative within the third degree of relationship of either the judge or the judge's spouse or domestic partner, or the spouse or domestic partner of such relative.

[3]   The rule against making administrative appointments of lawyers who have contributed in excess of a specified dollar amount to a judge's election campaign includes an exception for positions that are substantially uncompensated, such as those for which the lawyer's compensation is limited to reimbursement for out-of-pocket expenses.

RULE 2.14 DISABILITY AND IMPAIRMENT

A judge having a reasonable belief that the performance of a lawyer or another judge is impaired by drugs or alcohol, or by a mental, emotional, or physical condition, shall take appropriate action, which may include a confidential referral to a lawyer or judicial assistance program.

Comment

[1]   "Appropriate action" means action intended and reasonably likely to help the judge or lawyer in question address the problem and prevent harm to the justice system. Depending upon the circumstances, appropriate action may include but is not limited to speaking directly to the impaired person, notifying an individual with supervisory responsibility over the impaired person, or making a referral to an assistance program.

[2]   Taking or initiating corrective action by way of referral to an assistance program may satisfy a judge's responsibility under this Rule. Assistance programs have many approaches for offering help to impaired judges and lawyers, such as intervention, counseling, or referral to appropriate health care professionals. Depending upon the gravity of the conduct that has come to the judge's attention, however, the judge may be required to take other action, such as reporting the impaired judge or lawyer to the appropriate authority, agency, or body. See Rule 2.15.

RULE 2.15 RESPONDING TO JUDICIAL AND LAWYER MISCONDUCT

(A)   A judge having knowledge* that another judge has committed a violation of this Code that raises a substantial question regarding the judge's honesty, trustworthiness, or fitness as a judge in other respects shall inform the appropriate authority.*

(B) A judge having knowledge that a lawyer has committed a violation of the Rules of Professional Conduct that raises a substantial question regarding the lawyer's honesty, trustworthiness, or fitness as a lawyer in other respects shall inform the appropriate authority.

(C) A judge who receives information indicating a substantial likelihood that another judge has committed a violation of this Code shall take appropriate action.

(D) A judge who receives information indicating a substantial likelihood that a lawyer has committed a violation of the Rules of Professional Conduct shall take appropriate action.

Comment

[1] Taking action to address known misconduct is a judge's obligation. Paragraphs (A) and (B) impose an obligation on the judge to report to the appropriate disciplinary authority the known misconduct of another judge or a lawyer that raises a substantial question regarding the honesty, trustworthiness, or fitness of that judge or lawyer. Ignoring or denying known misconduct among one's judicial colleagues or members of the legal profession undermines a judge's responsibility to participate in efforts to ensure public respect for the justice system. This Rule limits the reporting obligation to those offenses that an independent judiciary must vigorously endeavor to prevent.

[2] A judge who does not have actual knowledge that another judge or a lawyer may have committed misconduct, but receives information indicating a substantial likelihood of such misconduct, is required to take appropriate action under paragraphs (C) and (D). Appropriate action may include, but is not limited to, communicating directly with the judge who may have violated this Code, communicating with a supervising judge, or reporting the suspected violation to the appropriate authority or other agency or body. Similarly, actions to be taken in response to information indicating that a lawyer has committed a violation of the Rules of Professional Conduct may include but are not limited to communicating directly with the lawyer who may have committed the violation, or reporting the suspected violation to the appropriate authority or other agency or body.

RULE 2.16 COOPERATION WITH DISCIPLINARY AUTHORITIES

(A) A judge shall cooperate and be candid and honest with judicial and lawyer disciplinary agencies.

(B) A judge shall not retaliate, directly or indirectly, against a person known* or suspected to have assisted or cooperated with an investigation of a judge or a lawyer.

Comment

[1] Cooperation with investigations and proceedings of judicial and lawyer discipline agencies, as required in paragraph (A), instills confidence in judges' commitment to the integrity of the judicial system and the protection of the public.

CANON 3

A JUDGE SHALL CONDUCT THE JUDGE'S PERSONAL AND EXTRAJUDICIAL ACTIVITIES TO MINIMIZE THE RISK OF CONFLICT WITH THE OBLIGATIONS OF JUDICIAL OFFICE.

RULE 3.1 EXTRAJUDICIAL ACTIVITIES IN GENERAL

A judge may engage in extrajudicial activities, except as prohibited by law* or this Code. However, when engaging in extrajudicial activities, a judge shall not:

(A)   participate in activities that will interfere with the proper performance of the judge's judicial duties;

(B)   participate in activities that will lead to frequent disqualification of the judge;

(C)   participate in activities that would appear to a reasonable person to undermine the judge's independence,* integrity,* or impartiality;*

(D)   engage in conduct that would appear to a reasonable person to be coercive; or

(E)   make use of court premises, staff, stationery, equipment, or other resources, except for incidental use for activities that concern the law, the legal system, or the administration of justice, or unless such additional use is permitted by law.

Comment

[1]   To the extent that time permits, and judicial independence and impartiality are not compromised, judges are encouraged to engage in appropriate extrajudicial activities. Judges are uniquely qualified to engage in extrajudicial activities that concern the law, the legal system, and the administration of justice, such as by speaking, writing, teaching, or participating in scholarly research projects. In addition, judges are permitted and encouraged to engage in educational, religious, charitable, fraternal or civic extrajudicial activities not conducted for profit, even when the activities do not involve the law. See Rule 3.7.

[2]   Participation in both law-related and other extrajudicial activities helps integrate judges into their communities, and furthers public understanding of and respect for courts and the judicial system.

[3]   Discriminatory actions and expressions of bias or prejudice by a judge, even outside the judge's official or judicial actions, are likely to appear to a reasonable person to call into question the judge's integrity and impartiality. Examples include jokes or other remarks that demean individuals based upon their race, sex, gender, religion, national origin, ethnicity, disability, age, sexual orientation, or socioeconomic status. For the same reason, a judge's extrajudicial activities must not be conducted in connection or affiliation with an organization that practices invidious discrimination. See Rule 3.6.

[4]   While engaged in permitted extrajudicial activities, judges must not coerce others or take action that would reasonably be perceived as coercive. For example, depending upon the circumstances, a judge's solicitation

of contributions or memberships for an organization, even as permitted by Rule 3.7(A), might create the risk that the person solicited would feel obligated to respond favorably, or would do so to curry favor with the judge.

RULE 3.2 APPEARANCES BEFORE GOVERNMENTAL BODIES AND CONSULTATION WITH GOVERNMENT OFFICIALS

A judge shall not appear voluntarily at a public hearing before, or otherwise consult with, an executive or a legislative body or official, except:

> **(A)**   in connection with matters concerning the law, the legal system, or the administration of justice;

> **(B)**   in connection with matters about which the judge acquired knowledge or expertise in the course of the judge's judicial duties; or

> **(C)**   when the judge is acting pro se in a matter involving the judge's legal or economic interests, or when the judge is acting in a fiduciary* capacity.

Comment

[1]   Judges possess special expertise in matters of law, the legal system, and the administration of justice, and may properly share that expertise with governmental bodies and executive or legislative branch officials.

[2]   In appearing before governmental bodies or consulting with government officials, judges must be mindful that they remain subject to other provisions of this Code, such as Rule 1.3, prohibiting judges from using the prestige of office to advance their own or others' interests, Rule 2.10, governing public comment on pending and impending matters, and Rule 3.1(C), prohibiting judges from engaging in extrajudicial activities that would appear to a reasonable person to undermine the judge's independence, integrity, or impartiality.

[3]   In general, it would be an unnecessary and unfair burden to prohibit judges from appearing before governmental bodies or consulting with government officials on matters that are likely to affect them as private citizens, such as zoning proposals affecting their real property. In engaging in such activities, however, judges must not refer to their judicial positions, and must otherwise exercise caution to avoid using the prestige of judicial office.

RULE 3.3 TESTIFYING AS A CHARACTER WITNESS

A judge shall not testify as a character witness in a judicial, administrative, or other adjudicatory proceeding or otherwise vouch for the character of a person in a legal proceeding, except when duly summoned.

Comment

[1]   A judge who, without being subpoenaed, testifies as a character witness abuses the prestige of judicial office to advance the interests of another. See Rule 1.3. Except in unusual circumstances where the demands

of justice require, a judge should discourage a party from requiring the judge to testify as a character witness.

RULE 3.4 APPOINTMENTS TO GOVERNMENTAL POSITIONS

A judge shall not accept appointment to a governmental committee, board, commission, or other governmental position, unless it is one that concerns the law, the legal system, or the administration of justice.

Comment

[1]   Rule 3.4 implicitly acknowledges the value of judges accepting appointments to entities that concern the law, the legal system, or the administration of justice. Even in such instances, however, a judge should assess the appropriateness of accepting an appointment, paying particular attention to the subject matter of the appointment and the availability and allocation of judicial resources, including the judge's time commitments, and giving due regard to the requirements of the independence and impartiality of the judiciary.

[2]   A judge may represent his or her country, state, or locality on ceremonial occasions or in connection with historical, educational, or cultural activities. Such representation does not constitute acceptance of a government position.

RULE 3.5 USE OF NONPUBLIC INFORMATION

A judge shall not intentionally disclose or use nonpublic information* acquired in a judicial capacity for any purpose unrelated to the judge's judicial duties.

Comment

[1]   In the course of performing judicial duties, a judge may acquire information of commercial or other value that is unavailable to the public. The judge must not reveal or use such information for personal gain or for any purpose unrelated to his or her judicial duties.

[2]   This rule is not intended, however, to affect a judge's ability to act on information as necessary to protect the health or safety of the judge or a member of a judge's family, court personnel, or other judicial officers if consistent with other provisions of this Code.

RULE 3.6 AFFILIATION WITH DISCRIMINATORY ORGANIZATIONS

(A)   A judge shall not hold membership in any organization that practices invidious discrimination on the basis of race, sex, gender, religion, national origin, ethnicity, or sexual orientation.

(B)   A judge shall not use the benefits or facilities of an organization if the judge knows* or should know that the organiza-

tion practices invidious discrimination on one or more of the bases identified in paragraph (A). A judge's attendance at an event in a facility of an organization that the judge is not permitted to join is not a violation of this Rule when the judge's attendance is an isolated event that could not reasonably be perceived as an endorsement of the organization's practices.

Comment

[1]   A judge's public manifestation of approval of invidious discrimination on any basis gives rise to the appearance of impropriety and diminishes public confidence in the integrity and impartiality of the judiciary. A judge's membership in an organization that practices invidious discrimination creates the perception that the judge's impartiality is impaired.

[2]   An organization is generally said to discriminate invidiously if it arbitrarily excludes from membership on the basis of race, sex, gender, religion, national origin, ethnicity, or sexual orientation persons who would otherwise be eligible for admission. Whether an organization practices invidious discrimination is a complex question to which judges should be attentive. The answer cannot be determined from a mere examination of an organization's current membership rolls, but rather, depends upon how the organization selects members, as well as other relevant factors, such as whether the organization is dedicated to the preservation of religious, ethnic, or cultural values of legitimate common interest to its members, or whether it is an intimate, purely private organization whose membership limitations could not constitutionally be prohibited.

[3]   When a judge learns that an organization to which the judge belongs engages in invidious discrimination, the judge must resign immediately from the organization.

[4]   A judge's membership in a religious organization as a lawful exercise of the freedom of religion is not a violation of this Rule.

[5]   This Rule does not apply to national or state military service.

RULE 3.7 PARTICIPATION IN EDUCATIONAL, RELIGIOUS, CHARITABLE, FRATERNAL, OR CIVIC ORGANIZATIONS AND ACTIVITIES

(A)   Subject to the requirements of Rule 3.1, a judge may participate in activities sponsored by organizations or governmental entities concerned with the law, the legal system, or the administration of justice, and those sponsored by or on behalf of educational, religious, charitable, fraternal, or civic organizations not conducted for profit, including but not limited to the following activities:

(1)   assisting such an organization or entity in planning related to fund-raising, and participating in the management and investment of the organization's or entity's funds;

(2)   soliciting* contributions* for such an organization or entity, but only from members of the judge's family,* or from judges over whom the judge does not exercise supervisory or appellate authority; (3) soliciting membership for such an organization or entity, even though the membership dues or fees generated may be used to support the objectives of the organization or entity, but only if the organization or entity is concerned with the law, the legal system, or the administration of justice;

(4)   appearing or speaking at, receiving an award or other recognition at, being featured on the program of, and permitting his or her title to be used in connection with an event of such an organization or entity, but if the event serves a fund-raising purpose, the judge may participate only if the event concerns the law, the legal system, or the administration of justice;

(5)   making recommendations to such a public or private fund- granting organization or entity in connection with its programs and activities, but only if the organization or entity is concerned with the law, the legal system, or the administration of justice; and

(6)   serving as an officer, director, trustee, or nonlegal advisor of such an organization or entity, unless it is likely that the organization or entity:

> (a)   will be engaged in proceedings that would ordinarily come before the judge; or

> (b)   will frequently be engaged in adversary proceedings in the court of which the judge is a member, or in any court subject to the appellate jurisdiction of the court of which the judge is a member.

(B)   A judge may encourage lawyers to provide pro bono publico legal services.

Comment

[1]   The activities permitted by paragraph (A) generally include those sponsored by or undertaken on behalf of public or private not-for-profit educational institutions, and other not-for-profit organizations, including law-related, charitable, and other organizations.

[2]   Even for law-related organizations, a judge should consider whether the membership and purposes of the organization, or the nature of the judge's participation in or association with the organization, would conflict with the judge's obligation to refrain from activities that reflect adversely upon a judge's independence, integrity, and impartiality.

[3]   Mere attendance at an event, whether or not the event serves a fund raising purpose, does not constitute a violation of paragraph 4(A). It is

also generally permissible for a judge to serve as an usher or a food server or preparer, or to perform similar functions, at fund-raising events sponsored by educational, religious, charitable, fraternal, or civic organizations. Such activities are not solicitation and do not present an element of coercion or abuse the prestige of judicial office.

[4]   Identification of a judge's position in educational, religious, charitable, fraternal, or civic organizations on letterhead used for fund-raising or membership solicitation does not violate this Rule. The letterhead may list the judge's title or judicial office if comparable designations are used for other persons.

[5]   In addition to appointing lawyers to serve as counsel for indigent parties in individual cases, a judge may promote broader access to justice by encouraging lawyers to participate in pro bono publico legal services, if in doing so the judge does not employ coercion, or abuse the prestige of judicial office. Such encouragement may take many forms, including providing lists of available programs, training lawyers to do pro bono publico legal work, and participating in events recognizing lawyers who have done pro bono publico work.

RULE 3.8 APPOINTMENTS TO FIDUCIARY POSITIONS

(A)   A judge shall not accept appointment to serve in a fiduciary* position, such as executor, administrator, trustee, guardian, attorney in fact, or other personal representative, except for the estate, trust, or person of a member of the judge's family,* and then only if such service will not interfere with the proper performance of judicial duties.

(B)   A judge shall not serve in a fiduciary position if the judge as fiduciary will likely be engaged in proceedings that would ordinarily come before the judge, or if the estate, trust, or ward becomes involved in adversary proceedings in the court on which the judge serves, or one under its appellate jurisdiction.

(C)   A judge acting in a fiduciary capacity shall be subject to the same restrictions on engaging in financial activities that apply to a judge personally.

(D)   If a person who is serving in a fiduciary position becomes a judge, he or she must comply with this Rule as soon as reasonably practicable, but in no event later than [one year] after becoming a judge.

Comment

[1]   A judge should recognize that other restrictions imposed by this Code may conflict with a judge's obligations as a fiduciary; in such circumstances, a judge should resign as fiduciary. For example, serving as a fiduciary might require frequent disqualification of a judge under Rule 2.11 because a judge is deemed to have an economic interest in shares of stock held by a trust if the amount of stock held is more than de minimis.

RULE 3.9 SERVICE AS ARBITRATOR OR MEDIATOR

A judge shall not act as an arbitrator or a mediator or perform other judicial functions apart from the judge's official duties unless expressly authorized by law.*

Comment

[1]   This Rule does not prohibit a judge from participating in arbitration, mediation, or settlement conferences performed as part of assigned judicial duties. Rendering dispute resolution services apart from those duties, whether or not for economic gain, is prohibited unless it is expressly authorized by law.

RULE 3.10 PRACTICE OF LAW

A judge shall not practice law. A judge may act pro se and may, without compensation, give legal advice to and draft or review documents for a member of the judge's family,* but is prohibited from serving as the family member's lawyer in any forum.

Comment

[1]   A judge may act pro se in all legal matters, including matters involving litigation and matters involving appearances before or other dealings with governmental bodies. A judge must not use the prestige of office to advance the judge's personal or family interests. See Rule 1.3.

RULE 3.11 FINANCIAL, BUSINESS, OR REMUNERATIVE ACTIVITIES

(A)   A judge may hold and manage investments of the judge and members of the judge's family.*

(B)   A judge shall not serve as an officer, director, manager, general partner, advisor, or employee of any business entity except that a judge may manage or participate in:

(1)   a business closely held by the judge or members of the judge's family; or

(2)   a business entity primarily engaged in investment of the financial resources of the judge or members of the judge's family.

(C)   A judge shall not engage in financial activities permitted under paragraphs (A) and (B) if they will:

(1)   interfere with the proper performance of judicial duties;

(2)   lead to frequent disqualification of the judge;

(3)   involve the judge in frequent transactions or continuing business relationships with lawyers or other

persons likely to come before the court on which the judge serves; or

(4)   **result in violation of other provisions of this Code.**

Comment

[1]   Judges are generally permitted to engage in financial activities, including managing real estate and other investments for themselves or for members of their families. Participation in these activities, like participation in other extrajudicial activities, is subject to the requirements of this Code. For example, it would be improper for a judge to spend so much time on business activities that it interferes with the performance of judicial duties. See Rule 2.1. Similarly, it would be improper for a judge to use his or her official title or appear in judicial robes in business advertising, or to conduct his or her business or financial affairs in such a way that disqualification is frequently required. See Rules 1.3 and 2.11.

[2]   As soon as practicable without serious financial detriment, the judge must divest himself or herself of investments and other financial interests that might require frequent disqualification or otherwise violate this Rule.

RULE 3.12 COMPENSATION FOR EXTRAJUDICIAL ACTIVITIES

A judge may accept reasonable compensation for extrajudicial activities permitted by this Code or other law* unless such acceptance would appear to a reasonable person to undermine the judge's independence,* integrity,* or impartiality.*

Comment

[1]   A judge is permitted to accept honoraria, stipends, fees, wages, salaries, royalties, or other compensation for speaking, teaching, writing, and other extrajudicial activities, provided the compensation is reasonable and commensurate with the task performed. The judge should be mindful, however, that judicial duties must take precedence over other activities. See Rule 2.1.

[2]   Compensation derived from extrajudicial activities may be subject to public reporting. See Rule 3.15.

RULE 3.13 ACCEPTANCE AND REPORTING OF GIFTS, LOANS, BEQUESTS, BENEFITS, OR OTHER THINGS OF VALUE

(A)   A judge shall not accept any gifts, loans, bequests, benefits, or other things of value, if acceptance is prohibited by law* or would appear to a reasonable person to undermine the judge's independence,* integrity,* or impartiality.*

(B)   Unless otherwise prohibited by law, or by paragraph (A), a judge may accept the following without publicly reporting such acceptance:

(1)   items with little intrinsic value, such as plaques, certificates, trophies, and greeting cards;

(2)   gifts, loans, bequests, benefits, or other things of value from friends, relatives, or other persons, including lawyers, whose appearance or interest in a proceeding pending* or impending* before the judge would in any event require disqualification of the judge under Rule 2.11;

(3)   ordinary social hospitality;

(4)   commercial or financial opportunities and benefits, including special pricing and discounts, and loans from lending institutions in their regular course of business, if the same opportunities and benefits or loans are made available on the same terms to similarly situated persons who are not judges;

(5)   rewards and prizes given to competitors or participants in random drawings, contests, or other events that are open to persons who are not judges;

(6)   scholarships, fellowships, and similar benefits or awards, if they are available to similarly situated persons who are not judges, based upon the same terms and criteria;

(7)   books, magazines, journals, audiovisual materials, and other resource materials supplied by publishers on a complimentary basis for official use; or

(8)   gifts, awards, or benefits associated with the business, profession, or other separate activity of a spouse, a domestic partner,* or other family member of a judge residing in the judge's household,* but that incidentally benefit the judge.

(C)   Unless otherwise prohibited by law or by paragraph (A), a judge may accept the following items, and must report such acceptance to the extent required by Rule 3.15:

(1)   gifts incident to a public testimonial;

(2)   invitations to the judge and the judge's spouse, domestic partner, or guest to attend without charge:

(a)   an event associated with a bar-related function or other activity relating to the law, the legal system, or the administration of justice; or

(b)   an event associated with any of the judge's educational, religious, charitable, fraternal or civic activities permitted by this Code, if the same invitation is offered to nonjudges who are engaged in similar ways in the activity as is the judge; and

(3)   gifts, loans, bequests, benefits, or other things of value, if the source is a party or other person, including

a lawyer, who has come or is likely to come before the judge, or whose interests have come or are likely to come before the judge.

Comment

[1]   Whenever a judge accepts a gift or other thing of value without paying fair market value, there is a risk that the benefit might be viewed as intended to influence the judge's decision in a case. Rule 3.13 imposes restrictions upon the acceptance of such benefits, according to the magnitude of the risk. Paragraph (B) identifies circumstances in which the risk that the acceptance would appear to undermine the judge's independence, integrity, or impartiality is low, and explicitly provides that such items need not be publicly reported. As the value of the benefit or the likelihood that the source of the benefit will appear before the judge increases, the judge is either prohibited under paragraph (A) from accepting the gift, or required under paragraph (C) to publicly report it.

[2]   Gift-giving between friends and relatives is a common occurrence, and ordinarily does not create an appearance of impropriety or cause reasonable persons to believe that the judge's independence, integrity, or impartiality has been compromised. In addition, when the appearance of friends or relatives in a case would require the judge's disqualification under Rule 2.11, there would be no opportunity for a gift to influence the judge's decision making. Paragraph (B)(2) places no restrictions upon the ability of a judge to accept gifts or other things of value from friends or relatives under these circumstances, and does not require public reporting.

[3]   Businesses and financial institutions frequently make available special pricing, discounts, and other benefits, either in connection with a temporary promotion or for preferred customers, based upon longevity of the relationship, volume of business transacted, and other factors. A judge may freely accept such benefits if they are available to the general public, or if the judge qualifies for the special price or discount according to the same criteria as are applied to persons who are not judges. As an example, loans provided at generally prevailing interest rates are not gifts, but a judge could not accept a loan from a financial institution at below-market interest rates unless the same rate was being made available to the general public for a certain period of time or only to borrowers with specified qualifications that the judge also possesses.

[4]   Rule 3.13 applies only to acceptance of gifts or other things of value by a judge. Nonetheless, if a gift or other benefit is given to the judge's spouse, domestic partner, or member of the judge's family residing in the judge's household, it may be viewed as an attempt to evade Rule 3.13 and influence the judge indirectly. Where the gift or benefit is being made primarily to such other persons, and the judge is merely an incidental beneficiary, this concern is reduced. A judge should, however, remind family and household members of the restrictions imposed upon judges, and urge them to take these restrictions into account when making decisions about accepting such gifts or benefits.

[5]   Rule 3.13 does not apply to contributions to a judge's campaign for judicial office. Such contributions are governed by other Rules of this Code, including Rules 4.3 and 4.4.

RULE 3.14 REIMBURSEMENT OF EXPENSES AND WAIVERS OF FEES OR CHARGES

(A)   Unless otherwise prohibited by Rules 3.1 and 3.13(A) or other law,* a judge may accept reimbursement of necessary and reasonable expenses for travel, food, lodging, or other incidental expenses, or a waiver or partial waiver of fees or charges for registration, tuition, and similar items, from sources other than the judge's employing entity, if the expenses or charges are associated with the judge's participation in extra-judicial activities permitted by this Code.

(B)   Reimbursement of expenses for necessary travel, food, lodging, or other incidental expenses shall be limited to the actual costs reasonably incurred by the judge and, when appropriate to the occasion, by the judge's spouse, domestic partner,* or guest.

(C)   A judge who accepts reimbursement of expenses or waivers or partial waivers of fees or charges on behalf of the judge or the judge's spouse, domestic partner, or guest shall publicly report such acceptance as required by Rule 3.15.

Comment

[1]   Educational, civic, religious, fraternal, and charitable organizations often sponsor meetings, seminars, symposia, dinners, awards ceremonies, and similar events. Judges are encouraged to attend educational programs, as both teachers and participants, in law-related and academic disciplines, in furtherance of their duty to remain competent in the law. Participation in a variety of other extrajudicial activity is also permitted and encouraged by this Code.

[2]   Not infrequently, sponsoring organizations invite certain judges to attend seminars or other events on a fee-waived or partial-fee-waived basis, and sometimes include reimbursement for necessary travel, food, lodging, or other incidental expenses. A judge's decision whether to accept reimbursement of expenses or a waiver or partial waiver of fees or charges in connection with these or other extrajudicial activities must be based upon an assessment of all the circumstances. The judge must undertake a reasonable inquiry to obtain the information necessary to make an informed judgment about whether acceptance would be consistent with the requirements of this Code.

[3]   A judge must assure himself or herself that acceptance of reimbursement or fee waivers would not appear to a reasonable person to undermine the judge's independence, integrity, or impartiality. The factors that a

judge should consider when deciding whether to accept reimbursement or a fee waiver for attendance at a particular activity include:

(a) whether the sponsor is an accredited educational institution or bar association rather than a trade association or a for-profit entity;

(b) whether the funding comes largely from numerous contributors rather than from a single entity and is earmarked for programs with specific content;

(c) whether the content is related or unrelated to the subject matter of litigation pending or impending before the judge, or to matters that are likely to come before the judge;

(d) whether the activity is primarily educational rather than recreational, and whether the costs of the event are reasonable and comparable to those associated with similar events sponsored by the judiciary, bar associations, or similar groups;

(e) whether information concerning the activity and its funding sources is available upon inquiry;

(f) whether the sponsor or source of funding is generally associated with particular parties or interests currently appearing or likely to appear in the judge's court, thus possibly requiring disqualification of the judge under Rule 2.11;

(g) whether differing viewpoints are presented; and

(h) whether a broad range of judicial and nonjudicial participants are invited, whether a large number of participants are invited, and whether the program is designed specifically for judges.

RULE 3.15 REPORTING REQUIREMENTS

(A)   A judge shall publicly report the amount or value of:

(1)   compensation received for extrajudicial activities as permitted by Rule 3.12;

(2)   gifts and other things of value as permitted by Rule 3.13(C), unless the value of such items, alone or in the aggregate with other items received from the same source in the same calendar year, does not exceed $[insert amount]; and

(3)   reimbursement of expenses and waiver of fees or charges permitted by Rule 3.14(A), unless the amount of reimbursement or waiver, alone or in the aggregate with other reimbursements or waivers received from the same source in the same calendar year, does not exceed $[insert amount].

(B)   When public reporting is required by paragraph (A), a judge shall report the date, place, and nature of the activity for which the judge received any compensation; the description of any gift, loan, bequest, benefit, or other thing of value accepted; and the source of reimbursement of expenses or waiver or partial waiver of fees or charges.

(C) The public report required by paragraph (A) shall be made at least annually, except that for reimbursement of expenses and waiver or partial waiver of fees or charges, the report shall be made within thirty days following the conclusion of the event or program.

(D) Reports made in compliance with this Rule shall be filed as public documents in the office of the clerk of the court on which the judge serves or other office designated by law,* and, when technically feasible, posted by the court or office personnel on the court's website.

CANON 4

JUDGE OR CANDIDATE FOR JUDICIAL OFFICE SHALL NOT ENGAGE IN POLITICAL OR CAMPAIGN ACTIVITY THAT IS INCONSISTENT WITH THE INDEPENDENCE, INTEGRITY, OR IMPARTIALITY OF THE JUDICIARY.

RULE 4.1 POLITICAL AND CAMPAIGN ACTIVITIES OF JUDGES AND JUDICIAL CANDIDATES IN GENERAL

(A) Except as permitted by law,* or by Rules 4.2, 4.3, and 4.4, a judge or a judicial candidate* shall not:

(1) act as a leader in, or hold an office in, a political organization;*

(2) make speeches on behalf of a political organization;

(3) publicly endorse or oppose a candidate for any public office;

(4) solicit funds for, pay an assessment to, or make a contribution* to a political organization or a candidate for public office;

(5) attend or purchase tickets for dinners or other events sponsored by a political organization or a candidate for public office;

(6) publicly identify himself or herself as a candidate of a political organization;

(7) seek, accept, or use endorsements from a political organization;

(8) personally solicit* or accept campaign contributions other than through a campaign committee authorized by Rule 4.4;

(9) use or permit the use of campaign contributions for the private benefit of the judge, the candidate, or others;

(10) use court staff, facilities, or other court resources in a campaign for judicial office;

(11) knowingly,* or with reckless disregard for the truth, make any false or misleading statement;

(12) make any statement that would reasonably be expected to affect the outcome or impair the fairness of a matter pending* or impending* in any court; or

(13) in connection with cases, controversies, or issues that are likely to come before the court, make pledges, promises, or commitments that are inconsistent with the impartial* performance of the adjudicative duties of judicial office.

(B) A judge or judicial candidate shall take reasonable measures to ensure that other persons do not undertake, on behalf of the judge or judicial candidate, any activities prohibited under paragraph (A).

Comment

GENERAL CONSIDERATIONS

[1] Even when subject to public election, a judge plays a role different from that of a legislator or executive branch official. Rather than making decisions based upon the expressed views or preferences of the electorate, a judge makes decisions based upon the law and the facts of every case. Therefore, in furtherance of this interest, judges and judicial candidates must, to the greatest extent possible, be free and appear to be free from political influence and political pressure. This Canon imposes narrowly tailored restrictions upon the political and campaign activities of all judges and judicial candidates, taking into account the various methods of selecting judges.

[2] When a person becomes a judicial candidate, this Canon becomes applicable to his or her conduct.

PARTICIPATION IN POLITICAL ACTIVITIES

[3] Public confidence in the independence and impartiality of the judiciary is eroded if judges or judicial candidates are perceived to be subject to political influence. Although judges and judicial candidates may register to vote as members of a political party, they are prohibited by paragraph (A)(1) from assuming leadership roles in political organizations.

[4] Paragraphs (A)(2) and (A)(3) prohibit judges and judicial candidates from making speeches on behalf of political organizations or publicly endorsing or opposing candidates for public office, respectively, to prevent them from abusing the prestige of judicial office to advance the interests of others. See Rule 1.3. These Rules do not prohibit candidates from campaigning on their own behalf, or from endorsing or opposing candidates for the same judicial office for which they are running. See Rules 4.2(B)(2) and 4.2(B)(3).

[5]   Although members of the families of judges and judicial candidates are free to engage in their own political activity, including running for public office, there is no "family exception" to the prohibition in paragraph (A)(3) against a judge or candidate publicly endorsing candidates for public office. A judge or judicial candidate must not become involved in, or publicly associated with, a family member's political activity or campaign for public office. To avoid public misunderstanding, judges and judicial candidates should take, and should urge members of their families to take, reasonable steps to avoid any implication that they endorse any family member's candidacy or other political activity.

[6]   Judges and judicial candidates retain the right to participate in the political process as voters in both primary and general elections. For purposes of this Canon, participation in a caucus-type election procedure does not constitute public support for or endorsement of a political organization or candidate, and is not prohibited by paragraphs (A)(2) or (A)(3).

STATEMENTS AND COMMENTS MADE DURING A CAMPAIGN FOR JUDICIAL OFFICE

[7]   Judicial candidates must be scrupulously fair and accurate in all statements made by them and by their campaign committees. Paragraph (A)(11) obligates candidates and their committees to refrain from making statements that are false or misleading, or that omit facts necessary to make the communication considered as a whole not materially misleading.

[8]   Judicial candidates are sometimes the subject of false, misleading, or unfair allegations made by opposing candidates, third parties, or the media. For example, false or misleading statements might be made regarding the identity, present position, experience, qualifications, or judicial rulings of a candidate. In other situations, false or misleading allegations may be made that bear upon a candidate's integrity or fitness for judicial office. As long as the candidate does not violate paragraphs (A)(11), (A)(12), or (A)(13), the candidate may make a factually accurate public response. In addition, when an independent third party has made unwarranted attacks on a candidate's opponent, the candidate may disavow the attacks, and request the third party to cease and desist.

[9]   Subject to paragraph (A)(12), a judicial candidate is permitted to respond directly to false, misleading, or unfair allegations made against him or her during a campaign, although it is preferable for someone else to respond if the allegations relate to a pending case.

[10]   Paragraph (A)(12) prohibits judicial candidates from making comments that might impair the fairness of pending or impending judicial proceedings. This provision does not restrict arguments or statements to the court or jury by a lawyer who is a judicial candidate, or rulings, statements, or instructions by a judge that may appropriately affect the outcome of a matter.

PLEDGES, PROMISES, OR COMMITMENTS INCONSISTENT WITH IMPARTIAL PERFORMANCE OF THE ADJUDICATIVE DUTIES OF JUDICIAL OFFICE

[11]   The role of a judge is different from that of a legislator or executive branch official, even when the judge is subject to public election. Campaigns for judicial office must be conducted differently from campaigns for

other offices. The narrowly drafted restrictions upon political and campaign activities of judicial candidates provided in Canon 4 allow candidates to conduct campaigns that provide voters with sufficient information to permit them to distinguish between candidates and make informed electoral choices.

[12]   Paragraph (A)(13) makes applicable to both judges and judicial candidates the prohibition that applies to judges in Rule 2.10(B), relating to pledges, promises, or commitments that are inconsistent with the impartial performance of the adjudicative duties of judicial office.

[13]   The making of a pledge, promise, or commitment is not dependent upon, or limited to, the use of any specific words or phrases; instead, the totality of the statement must be examined to determine if a reasonable person would believe that the candidate for judicial office has specifically undertaken to reach a particular result. Pledges, promises, or commitments must be contrasted with statements or announcements of personal views on legal, political, or other issues, which are not prohibited. When making such statements, a judge should acknowledge the overarching judicial obligation to apply and uphold the law, without regard to his or her personal views.

[14]   A judicial candidate may make campaign promises related to judicial organization, administration, and court management, such as a promise to dispose of a backlog of cases, start court sessions on time, or avoid favoritism in appointments and hiring. A candidate may also pledge to take action outside the courtroom, such as working toward an improved jury selection system, or advocating for more funds to improve the physical plant and amenities of the courthouse.

[15]   Judicial candidates may receive questionnaires or requests for interviews from the media and from issue advocacy or other community organizations that seek to learn their views on disputed or controversial legal or political issues. Paragraph (A)(13) does not specifically address judicial responses to such inquiries. Depending upon the wording and format of such questionnaires, candidates' responses might be viewed as pledges, promises, or commitments to perform the adjudicative duties of office other than in an impartial way. To avoid violating paragraph (A)(13), therefore, candidates who respond to media and other inquiries should also give assurances that they will keep an open mind and will carry out their adjudicative duties faithfully and impartially if elected. Candidates who do not respond may state their reasons for not responding, such as the danger that answering might be perceived by a reasonable person as undermining a successful candidate's independence or impartiality, or that it might lead to frequent disqualification. See Rule 2.11.

RULE 4.2 POLITICAL AND CAMPAIGN ACTIVITIES OF JUDICIAL CANDIDATES IN PUBLIC ELECTIONS

(A)   **A judicial candidate* in a partisan, nonpartisan, or retention public election* shall:**

      (1)   act at all times in a manner consistent with the independence,* integrity,* and impartiality* of the judiciary;

(2)   comply with all applicable election, election campaign, and election campaign fund-raising laws and regulations of this jurisdiction;

(3)   review and approve the content of all campaign statements and materials produced by the candidate or his or her campaign committee, as authorized by Rule 4.4, before their dissemination; and

(4)   take reasonable measures to ensure that other persons do not undertake on behalf of the candidate activities, other than those described in Rule 4.4, that the candidate is prohibited from doing by Rule 4.1.

(B)   A candidate for elective judicial office may, unless prohibited by law,* and not earlier than [insert amount of time] before the first applicable primary election, caucus, or general or retention election:

(1)   establish a campaign committee pursuant to the provisions of Rule 4.4;

(2)   speak on behalf of his or her candidacy through any medium, including but not limited to advertisements, websites, or other campaign literature;

(3)   publicly endorse or oppose candidates for the same judicial office for which he or she is running;

(4)   attend or purchase tickets for dinners or other events sponsored by a political organization* or a candidate for public office;

(5)   seek, accept, or use endorsements from any person or organization other than a partisan political organization; and

(6)   contribute to a political organization or candidate for public office, but not more than $[insert amount] to any one organization or candidate.

(C)   A judicial candidate in a partisan public election may, unless prohibited by law, and not earlier than [insert amount of time] before the first applicable primary election, caucus, or general election:

(1)   identify himself or herself as a candidate of a political organization; and

(2)   seek, accept, and use endorsements of a political organization.

Comment

[1]   Paragraphs (B) and (C) permit judicial candidates in public elections to engage in some political and campaign activities otherwise prohibited by Rule 4.1. Candidates may not engage in these activities earlier than

[insert amount of time] before the first applicable electoral event, such as a caucus or a primary election.

[2] Despite paragraphs (B) and (C), judicial candidates for public election remain subject to many of the provisions of Rule 4.1. For example, a candidate continues to be prohibited from soliciting funds for a political organization, knowingly making false or misleading statements during a campaign, or making certain promises, pledges, or commitments related to future adjudicative duties. See Rule 4.1(A), paragraphs (4), (11), and (13).

[3] In partisan public elections for judicial office, a candidate may be nominated by, affiliated with, or otherwise publicly identified or associated with a political organization, including a political party. This relationship may be maintained throughout the period of the public campaign, and may include use of political party or similar designations on campaign literature and on the ballot.

[4] In nonpartisan public elections or retention elections, paragraph (B)(5) prohibits a candidate from seeking, accepting, or using nominations or endorsements from a partisan political organization.

[5] Judicial candidates are permitted to attend or purchase tickets for dinners and other events sponsored by political organizations.

[6] For purposes of paragraph (B)(3), candidates are considered to be running for the same judicial office if they are competing for a single judgeship or if several judgeships on the same court are to be filled as a result of the election. In endorsing or opposing another candidate for a position on the same court, a judicial candidate must abide by the same rules governing campaign conduct and speech as apply to the candidate's own campaign.

[7] Although judicial candidates in nonpartisan public elections are prohibited from running on a ticket or slate associated with a political organization, they may group themselves into slates or other alliances to conduct their campaigns more effectively. Candidates who have grouped themselves together are considered to be running for the same judicial office if they satisfy the conditions described in Comment [6].

RULE 4.3 ACTIVITIES OF CANDIDATES FOR APPOINTIVE JUDICIAL OFFICE

A candidate for appointment to judicial office may:

(A) communicate with the appointing or confirming authority, including any selection, screening, or nominating commission or similar agency; and

(B) seek endorsements for the appointment from any person or organization other than a partisan political organization.

Comment

[1] When seeking support or endorsement, or when communicating directly with an appointing or confirming authority, a candidate for appointive

judicial office must not make any pledges, promises, or commitments that are inconsistent with the impartial performance of the adjudicative duties of the office. See Rule 4.1(A)(13).

RULE 4.4 CAMPAIGN COMMITTEES

(A)   A judicial candidate* subject to public election* may establish a campaign committee to manage and conduct a campaign for the candidate, subject to the provisions of this Code. The candidate is responsible for ensuring that his or her campaign committee complies with applicable provisions of this Code and other applicable law.*

(B)   A judicial candidate subject to public election shall direct his or her campaign committee:

> **(1)   to solicit and accept only such campaign contributions* as are reasonable, in any event not to exceed, in the aggregate,* $[insert amount] from any individual or $[insert amount] from any entity or organization;**

> **(2)   not to solicit or accept contributions for a candidate's current campaign more than [insert amount of time] before the applicable primary election, caucus, or general or retention election, nor more than [insert number] days after the last election in which the candidate participated; and**

> **(3)   to comply with all applicable statutory requirements for disclosure and divestiture of campaign contributions, and to file with [name of appropriate regulatory authority] a report stating the name, address, occupation, and employer of each person who has made campaign contributions to the committee in an aggregate value exceeding $[insert amount]. The report must be filed within [insert number] days following an election, or within such other period as is provided by law.**

Comment

[1]   Judicial candidates are prohibited from personally soliciting campaign contributions or personally accepting campaign contributions. See Rule 4.1(A)(8). This Rule recognizes that in many jurisdictions, judicial candidates must raise campaign funds to support their candidacies, and permits candidates, other than candidates for appointive judicial office, to establish campaign committees to solicit and accept reasonable financial contributions or in-kind contributions.

[2]   Campaign committees may solicit and accept campaign contributions, manage the expenditure of campaign funds, and generally conduct campaigns. Candidates are responsible for compliance with the requirements of election law and other applicable law, and for the activities of their campaign committees.

[3]   At the start of a campaign, the candidate must instruct the campaign committee to solicit or accept only such contributions as are reasonable in amount, appropriate under the circumstances, and in conformity with applicable law. Although lawyers and others who might appear before a successful candidate for judicial office are permitted to make campaign contributions, the candidate should instruct his or her campaign committee to be especially cautious in connection with such contributions, so they do not create grounds for disqualification if the candidate is elected to judicial office. See Rule 2.11.

RULE 4.5 ACTIVITIES OF JUDGES WHO BECOME CANDIDATES FOR NONJUDICIAL OFFICE

(A)   **Upon becoming a candidate for a nonjudicial elective office, a judge shall resign from judicial office, unless permitted by law* to continue to hold judicial office.**

(B)   **Upon becoming a candidate for a nonjudicial appointive office, a judge is not required to resign from judicial office, provided that the judge complies with the other provisions of this Code.**

Comment

[1]   In campaigns for nonjudicial elective public office, candidates may make pledges, promises, or commitments related to positions they would take and ways they would act if elected to office. Although appropriate in nonjudicial campaigns, this manner of campaigning is inconsistent with the role of a judge, who must remain fair and impartial to all who come before him or her. The potential for misuse of the judicial office, and the political promises that the judge would be compelled to make in the course of campaigning for nonjudicial elective office, together dictate that a judge who wishes to run for such an office must resign upon becoming a candidate.

[2]   The "resign to run" rule set forth in paragraph (A) ensures that a judge cannot use the judicial office to promote his or her candidacy, and prevents post-campaign retaliation from the judge in the event the judge is defeated in the election. When a judge is seeking appointive nonjudicial office, however, the dangers are not sufficient to warrant imposing the "resign to run" rule.

CALIFORNIA CODE OF JUDICIAL ETHICS

Amended by the Supreme Court of California effective January 21, 2016; originally adopted effective January 15, 1996; previously amended March 4, 1999, December 13, 2000, December 30, 2002, June 18, 2003, December 22, 2003, January 1, 2005, June 1, 2005, July 1, 2006, January 1, 2007, January 1, 2008, and April 29, 2009, January 1, 2013, and January 21, 2015.

Preface 772

Preamble 772

Terminology 773

Canon 1. A judge shall uphold the integrity and independence
of the judiciary. 776

Canon 2. A judge shall avoid impropriety and the appearance
of impropriety in all of the judge's activities. 777

Canon 3. A judge shall perform the duties of judicial office impartially,
competently, and diligently. 781

Canon 4. A judge shall so conduct the judge's quasi-judicial and
extrajudicial activities as to minimize the risk of conflict
with judicial obligations. 795

Canon 5. A judge or candidate for judicial office shall not engage in political or
campaign activity that is inconsistent with the independence,
integrity, or impartiality of the judiciary. 805

Canon 6. Compliance with the code of judicial ethics. 808

PREFACE

Formal standards of judicial conduct have existed for more than 50 years. The original Canons of Judicial Ethics promulgated by the American Bar Association were modified and adopted in 1949 for application in California by the Conference of California Judges (now the California Judges Association).

In 1969, the American Bar Association determined that current needs and problems warranted revision of the canons. In the revision process, a special American Bar Association committee, headed by former California Chief Justice Roger Traynor, sought and considered the views of the bench and bar and other interested persons. The American Bar Association Code of Judicial Conduct was adopted by the House of Delegates of the American Bar Association August 16, 1972.

Effective January 5, 1975, the California Judges Association adopted a new California Code of Judicial Conduct adapted from the American Bar Association 1972 Model Code. The California code was recast in gender-neutral form in 1986.

In 1990, the American Bar Association Model Code was further revised after a lengthy study. The California Judges Association again reviewed the model code and adopted a revised California Code of Judicial Conduct on October 5, 1992.

Proposition 190 (amending Cal. Const., art. VI, § 18(m), effective March 1, 1995) created a new constitutional provision that states, "The Supreme Court shall make rules for the conduct of judges, both on and off the bench, and for judicial candidates in the conduct of their campaigns. These rules shall be referred to as the Code of Judicial Ethics."

The Supreme Court formally adopted the 1992 Code of Judicial Conduct in March 1995, as a transitional measure pending further review.

The Supreme Court formally adopted the Code of Judicial Ethics effective January 15, 1996.

The Supreme Court has formally adopted amendments to the Code of Judicial Ethics on several occasions. The Advisory Committee Commentary is published by the Supreme Court Advisory Committee on the Code of Judicial Ethics.

PREAMBLE

Our legal system is based on the principle that an independent, fair, and competent judiciary will interpret and apply the laws that govern us. The role of the judiciary is central to American concepts of justice and the rule of law. Intrinsic to this code are the precepts that judges, individually and collectively, must respect and honor the judicial office as a public trust and strive to enhance and maintain confidence in our legal system. The judge is an arbiter of facts and law for the resolution of disputes and a highly visible member of government under the rule of law.

The Code of Judicial Ethics ("code") establishes standards for ethical conduct of judges on and off the bench and for candidates for judicial office.* The code consists of broad declarations called canons, with subparts, and a terminology section. Following each canon is a commentary section prepared by the Supreme Court Advisory Committee on the Code of Judicial Ethics. The commentary, by explanation and example, provides guidance as to the purpose and meaning of the canons. The commentary does not constitute additional rules and should not be so construed. All members of the judiciary must comply with the code. Compliance is required to preserve the integrity* of the bench and to ensure the confidence of the public.

The canons should be read together as a whole, and each provision should be construed in context and consistent with every other provision. They are to be applied in conformance with constitutional requirements, statutes, other court rules, and decisional law. Nothing in the code shall either impair the essential independence* of judges in making judicial decisions or provide a separate basis for civil liability or criminal prosecution.

The code governs the conduct of judges and candidates for judicial office* and is binding upon them. Whether disciplinary action is appropriate, and the degree of discipline to be imposed, requires a reasoned application of the text and consideration of such factors as the seriousness of the transgression, whether there is a pattern of improper activity, and the effect of the improper activity on others or on the judicial system.

TERMINOLOGY

Terms explained below are noted with an asterisk (*) in the canons where they appear. In addition, the canons in which terms appear are cited after the explanation of each term below.

"Candidate for judicial office" is a person seeking election to or retention of judicial office. A person becomes a candidate for judicial office as soon as he or she makes a public announcement of candidacy, declares or files as a candidate with the election authority, or authorizes solicitation or acceptance of contributions or support. See Preamble and Canons 3E(2)(b)(i), 3E(3)(a), 5, 5A, 5A (Commentary), 5B(1), 5B(2), 5B(3), 5B (Commentary), 5C, 5D, and 6E.

"Fiduciary" includes such relationships as executor, administrator, trustee, and guardian. See Canons 3E(5)(d), 4E(1), 4E(2), 4E(3), 4E (Commentary), 6B, and 6F (Commentary).

"Gift" denotes anything of value to the extent that consideration of equal or greater value is not received and includes a rebate or discount in the price of anything of value unless the rebate or discount is made in the regular course of business to members of the public without regard to official status. See Canons 4D(5), 4D(5) (Commentary), 4D(6), 4D(6)(a), 4D(6)(b), 4D(6)(b) (Commentary), 4D(6)(d), 4D(6)(f), 4H (Commentary), 5A (Commentary), 6D(2)(c), and 6D(7).

"Impartial," "impartiality," and **"impartially"** mean absence of bias or prejudice in favor of, or against, particular parties or classes of parties, as well as maintenance of an open mind in considering issues that may come before a judge. See Canons 1, 1 (Commentary), 2A, 2A (Commentary), 2B (Commentary), 2C (Commentary), 3, 3B(9) (Commentary), 3B(10) (Commentary), 3B(12), 3B(12) (Commentary), 3C(1), 3C(5), 3E(4)(b), 3E(4)(c), 4A(1), 4A (Commentary), 4C(3)(b) (Commentary), 4C(3)(c) (Commentary), 4D(1) (Commentary), 4D(6)(a) (Commentary), 4D(6)(b) (Commentary), 4D(6)(g) (Commentary), 4H (Commentary), 5, 5A, 5A (Commentary), 5B (Commentary), 6D(2)(a), and 6D(3)(vii).

"Impending proceeding" is a proceeding or matter that is imminent or expected to occur in the near future. The words "proceeding" and "matter" are used interchangeably, and are intended to have the same meaning. See Canons 3B(7), 3B(7)(a), 3B(9), 3B(9) (Commentary), 4H (Commentary), and 6D(6). "Pending proceeding" is defined below.

"Impropriety" includes conduct that violates the law, court rules, or provisions of this code, and conduct that undermines a judge's independence, integrity, or impartiality. See Canons 2, 2A (Commentary), 2B (Commentary), 2C (Commentary), 3B(9) (Commentary), 4D(1)(b) (Commentary), 4D(6)(g) (Commentary), 4H, 5, and 5A (Commentary).

"Independence" means a judge's freedom from influence or controls other than those established by law. See Preamble, Canons 1, 1 (Commentary), 4C(2) (Commentary), 4D(6)(a) (Commentary), 4D(6)(g) (Commentary), 4H(3) (Commentary), 5, 5A (Commentary), 5B (Commentary), and 6D(1).

"Integrity" means probity, fairness, honesty, uprightness, and soundness of character. See Preamble, Canons 1, 1 (Commentary), 2A, 2A (Commentary), 2B (Commentary), 2C (Commentary), 3B(9) (Commentary), 3C(1), 3C(5), 4D(6)(a) (Commentary), 4D(6)(b) (Commentary), 4D(6)(g) (Commentary), 4H (Commentary), 5, 5A (Commentary), 5B (Commentary), and 6D(1).

"Knowingly," "knowledge," "known," and **"knows"** mean actual knowledge of the fact in question. A person's knowledge may be inferred from circumstances. See Canons 2B(2)(b), 2B(2)(e), 2C (Commentary), 3B(2) (Commentary), 3B(7)(a), 3B(7)(a) (Commentary), 3D(2), 3D(5), 3E(5)(f), 5B(1)(b), 6D(3)(a)(i), 6D(3)(a) (Commentary), 6D(4) (Commentary), and 6D(5)(a).

"Law" denotes court rules as well as statutes, constitutional provisions, and decisional law. See Canons 1 (Commentary), 2A, 2C (Commentary), 3A, 3B(2), 3B(7), 3B(7)(c), 3B(8), 3B(8) (Commentary), 3B(12) (Commentary), 3E(1), 4C(3)(c) (Commentary), 4F, and 4H.

"Law, the legal system, or the administration of justice." When a judge engages in an activity that relates to the law, the legal system, or the administration of justice, the judge should also consider factors such as whether the activity upholds the integrity, impartiality, and independence of the judiciary (Canons 1 and 2A), whether it impairs public confidence in the judiciary (Canon 2), whether the judge is allowing the activity to take precedence over judicial duties (Canon 3A), and whether engaging in the activity would cause the judge to be disqualified (Canon 4A(4)). See Canons 4B (Commentary), 4C(1), 4C(1) (Commentary), 4C(2), 4C(2) (Commentary), 4C(3)(a), 4C(3)(b) (Commentary), 4C(3)(d)(ii), 4C(3)(d) (Commentary), 4D(6)(d), 4D(6)(e), 5A (Commentary), 5D, and 5D (Commentary).

"Member of the judge's family" denotes a spouse, registered domestic partner, child, grandchild, parent, grandparent, or other relative or person with whom the judge maintains a close familial relationship. See Canons 2B(3)(c), 2B (Commentary), 4C(3)(d)(i), 4D(1) (Commentary), 4D(2), 4D(5) (Commentary), 4E(1), and 4G (Commentary).

"Member of the judge's family residing in the judge's household" denotes a spouse or registered domestic partner and those persons who reside in the judge's household and who are relatives of the judge including relatives by marriage, or persons with whom the judge maintains a close familial relationship. See Canons 4D(5), 4D(5) (Commentary), 4D(6), 4D(6)(b) (Commentary), 4D(6)(f) and 6D(2)(c).

"Nonpublic information" denotes information that, by law, is not available to the public. Nonpublic information may include, but is not limited to, information that is sealed by statute or court order, impounded, or communicated in camera, and information offered in grand jury proceedings, presentencing reports, dependency cases, or psychiatric reports. See Canons 3B(11) and 6D(8)(a).

"Pending proceeding" is a proceeding or matter that has commenced. A proceeding continues to be pending through any period during which an appeal may be filed and any appellate process until final disposition. The words "proceeding" and "matter" are used interchangeably, and are intended to have the same meaning. See Canons 2A (Commentary), 2B(3)(a), 3B(7), 3B(9), 3B(9) (Commentary), 3E(5)(a), 4H (Commentary), and 6D(6). "Impending proceeding" is defined above.

"Political organization" denotes a political party, political action committee, or other group, the principal purpose of which is to further the election or appointment of candidates to nonjudicial office. See Canon 5A.

"Registered domestic partner" denotes a person who has registered for domestic partnership pursuant to state law or who is recognized as a domestic partner pursuant to Family Code section 299.2. See Canons 3E(5)(d), 3E(5)(e), 3E(5)(i), 4D(6)(d), 4D(6)(f), 4D(6)(j), 4H(2), 5A (Commentary), 6D(3)(a)(v), and 6D(3)(a)(vi).

"Require." Any canon prescribing that a judge "require" certain conduct of others means that a judge is to exercise reasonable direction and control over the conduct of those persons subject to the judge's direction and control. See Canons 3B(3), 3B(4), 3B(6), 3B(8) (Commentary), 3B(9), 3C(3), 6D(1), 6D(2)(a), and 6D(6).

"Service organization" includes any organization commonly referred to as a "fraternal organization." See Canons 3E(5)(d), 4C(2) (Commentary),

4C(3)(b), 4C(3)(b) (Commentary), 4C(3)(d) (Commentary), 4D(6)(j), and 6D(2)(b). **"Subordinate judicial officer."** A subordinate judicial officer is, for the purposes of this code, a person appointed pursuant to article VI, section 22 of the California Constitution, including, but not limited to, a commissioner, referee, and hearing officer. See Canons 3D(3), 4G (Commentary), and 6A.

"Temporary Judge." A temporary judge is an active or inactive member of the bar who, pursuant to article VI, section 21 of the California Constitution, serves or expects to serve as a judge once, sporadically, or regularly on a part-time basis under a separate court appointment for each period of service or for each case heard. See Canons 3E(5)(h), 4C(3)(d)(i), 4C(3)(d) (Commentary), 6A, and 6D.

"Third degree of relationship" includes the following persons: great-grandparent, grandparent, parent, uncle, aunt, brother, sister, child, grandchild, great- grandchild, nephew, and niece. See Canons 3E(5)(e), 3E(5)(i), and 6D(3)(a)(v).

CANON 1

A JUDGE SHALL UPHOLD THE INTEGRITY* AND INDEPENDENCE* OF THE JUDICIARY

An independent, impartial,* and honorable judiciary is indispensable to justice in our society. A judge should participate in establishing, maintaining, and enforcing high standards of conduct, and shall personally observe those standards so that the integrity* and independence* of the judiciary will be preserved. The provisions of this code are to be construed and applied to further that objective. A judicial decision or administrative act later determined to be incorrect legally is not itself a violation of this code.

ADVISORY COMMITTEE COMMENTARY

Deference to the judgments and rulings of courts depends upon public confidence in the integrity* and independence* of judges. The integrity* and independence* of judges depend in turn upon their acting without fear or favor. Although judges should be independent, they must comply with the law* and the provisions of this code. Public confidence in the impartiality* of the judiciary is maintained by the adherence of each judge to this responsibility. Conversely, violations of this code diminish public confidence in the judiciary and thereby do injury to the system of government under law.

The basic function of an independent, impartial,* and honorable judiciary is to maintain the utmost integrity* in decision making, and this code should be read and interpreted with that function in mind.

CANON 2

A JUDGE SHALL AVOID IMPROPRIETY* AND THE APPEARANCE OF IMPROPRIETY* IN ALL OF THE JUDGE'S ACTIVITIES

A. Promoting Public Confidence

A judge shall respect and comply with the law* and shall act at all times in a manner that promotes public confidence in the integrity* and impartiality* of the judiciary. A judge shall not make statements, whether public or nonpublic, that commit the judge with respect to cases, controversies, or issues that are likely to come before the courts or that are inconsistent with the impartial performance of the adjudicative duties of judicial office.

ADVISORY COMMITTEE COMMENTARY

Public confidence in the judiciary is eroded by irresponsible or improper conduct by judges.

A judge must avoid all impropriety* and appearance of impropriety.* A judge must expect to be the subject of constant public scrutiny. A judge must therefore accept restrictions on the judge's conduct that might be viewed as burdensome by other members of the community and should do so freely and willingly.

The prohibition against behaving with impropriety* or the appearance of impropriety* applies to both the professional and personal conduct of a judge.

The test for the appearance of impropriety* is whether a person aware of the facts might reasonably entertain a doubt that the judge would be able to act with integrity,* impartiality,* and competence.

As to membership in organizations that practice invidious discrimination, see also Commentary under Canon 2C.

As to judges making statements that commit the judge with respect to cases, controversies, or issues that are likely to come before the courts, see also Canon 3B(9) and its commentary concerning comments about pending proceedings,* Canon 3E(3)(a) concerning disqualification of judges who make statements that commit the judge to a particular result, and Canon 5B(1)(a) concerning statements made during an election campaign that commit the candidate to a particular result. In addition, Code of Civil Procedure section 170.2, subdivision (b), provides that, with certain exceptions, a judge is not disqualified on the ground that the judge has, in any capacity, expressed a view on a legal or factual issue presented in the proceeding before the judge.

B. Use of the Prestige of Judicial Office

(1)   A judge shall not allow family, social, political, or other relationships to influence the judge's judicial conduct or judgment, nor shall a judge convey or permit others to convey the impression that any individual is in a special position to influence the judge.

(2)   A judge shall not lend the prestige of judicial office or use the judicial title in any manner, including any oral or written communication, to advance the pecuniary or personal interests of the judge or others. This canon does not prohibit the following:

(a)   A judge may testify as a character witness, provided the judge does so only when subpoenaed.

(b)   A judge may, without a subpoena, provide the Commission on Judicial Performance with a written communication containing (i) factual information regarding a matter pending before the commission, or (ii) information related to the character of a judge who has a matter pending before the commission, provided that any such factual or character information is based on personal knowledge.* In commission proceedings, a judge shall provide information responsive to a subpoena or when officially requested to do so by the commission.

(c)   A judge may provide factual information in State Bar disciplinary proceedings and shall provide information responsive to a subpoena or when officially requested to do so by the State Bar.

(d)   A judge may respond to judicial selection inquiries, provide recommendations (including a general character reference, relating to the evaluation of persons being considered for a judgeship), and otherwise participate in the process of judicial selection.

(e)   A judge may serve as a reference or provide a letter of recommendation only if based on the judge's personal knowledge* of the individual. These written communications may include the judge's title and may be written on stationery that uses the judicial title.

(3)   Except as permitted in subdivision (c) or otherwise authorized by law* or these canons:

(a)   A judge shall not advance the pecuniary or personal interests of the judge or others by initiating communications with a sentencing judge or a representative of a probation department about a proceeding pending* before the sentencing judge, but may provide information in response to an official request. "Sentencing judge" includes a judge who makes a disposition pursuant to Welfare and Institutions Code section 725.

(b)   A judge, other than the judge who presided over the trial of or sentenced the person seeking parole, pardon, or commutation of sentence, shall not initiate communications with the Board of Parole Hearings regarding parole, or the Office of the Governor regarding parole, pardon, or commutation of sentence, but may provide these entities with information for the record in response to an official request.

(c)   A judge may initiate communications concerning a member of the judge's family* with a representative of a probation department regarding sentencing, the Board of Parole Hearings regarding parole, or the Office of the Governor regarding parole, pardon, or commutation of sentence, provided the judge is not identified as a judge in the communication.

ADVISORY COMMITTEE COMMENTARY

A strong judicial branch, based on the prestige that comes from effective and ethical performance, is essential to a system of government in which the judiciary functions independently of the executive and legislative branches. Judges should distinguish between proper and improper use of the prestige of office in all of their activities.

As to those communications that are permitted under this canon, a judge must keep in mind the general obligations to maintain high standards of conduct, as set forth in Canon 1, and to avoid any impropriety* or the appearance of impropriety* as set forth in Canon 2. A judge must also be mindful of Canon 2A, which requires a judge to act at all times in a manner that promotes public confidence in the integrity* and impartiality* of the courts.

A judge must avoid lending the prestige of judicial office for the advancement of the private interests of the judge or others. For example, a judge must not use the judicial position to gain advantage in a civil suit involving a member of the judge's family;* or use his or her position to gain deferential treatment when stopped by a police officer for a traffic offense.

As to the use of a judge's title to identify a judge's role in the presentation and creation of legal education programs and materials, see Commentary to Canon 4B. In contracts for publication of a judge's writings, a judge should retain control over the advertising, to the extent feasible, to avoid exploitation of the judge's office. As to the acceptance of awards, see Canon 4D(6).

This canon does not afford judges a privilege against testifying in response to any official summons.

See also Canons 3D(1) and 3D(2) concerning a judge's obligation to take appropriate corrective action regarding other judges who violate any provision of the Code of Judicial Ethics and attorneys who violate any provision of the Rules of Professional Conduct.

Except as set forth in Canon 2B(3)(a), this canon does not preclude consultations among judges. Additional limitations on such consultations among judges are set forth in Canon 3B(7)(a).

C. Membership in Organizations

A judge shall not hold membership in any organization that practices invidious discrimination on the basis of race, sex, gender, religion, national origin, ethnicity, or sexual orientation.

This canon does not apply to membership in a religious organization.

ADVISORY COMMITTEE COMMENTARY

Membership by a judge in an organization that practices invidious discrimination on the basis of race, sex, gender, religion, national origin, ethnicity, or sexual orientation gives rise to a perception that the judge's impartiality* is impaired. The code prohibits such membership by judges to preserve the fairness, impartiality,* independence,* and honor of the judiciary, to treat all parties equally under the law,* and to avoid impropriety* and the appearance of impropriety.*

Previously, Canon 2C contained exceptions to this prohibition for membership in religious organizations, membership in an official military organization of the United States and, so long as membership did not violate Canon 4A, membership in a nonprofit youth organization. The exceptions for membership in an official military organization of the United States and nonprofit youth organizations have been eliminated as exceptions to the canon. The exception for membership in religious organizations has been preserved.

Canon 2C refers to the current practices of the organization. Whether an organization practices invidious discrimination is often a complex question to which judges should be sensitive. The answer cannot be determined from a mere examination of an organization's current membership rolls but rather depends on how the organization selects members and other relevant factors, such as whether the organization is dedicated to the preservation of religious, ethnic, or cultural values of legitimate common interest to its members, or whether it is in fact and effect an intimate, purely private organization whose membership limitations could not be constitutionally prohibited. Absent such factors, an organization is generally said to discriminate invidiously if it arbitrarily excludes from membership on the basis of race, religion, sex, gender, national origin, ethnicity, or sexual orientation persons who would otherwise be admitted to membership.

Although Canon 2C relates only to membership in organizations that invidiously discriminate on the basis of race, sex, gender, religion, national origin, ethnicity, or sexual orientation, a judge's membership in an organization that engages in any discriminatory membership practices prohibited by law* also violates Canon 2 and Canon 2A and gives the appearance of impropriety.* In addition, it would be a violation of Canon 2 and Canon 2A for a judge to arrange a meeting at a club that the judge knows* practices such invidious *discrimination or for the judge to use such a club regularly. Moreover, public manifestation by a judge of the judge's knowing* approval of invidious discrimination on any basis gives the appearance of impropriety* under Canon 2 and diminishes public confidence in the integrity* and impartiality* of the judiciary in violation of Canon 2A.*

CANON 3

A JUDGE SHALL PERFORM THE DUTIES OF JUDICIAL OFFICE IMPARTIALLY,* COMPETENTLY, AND DILIGENTLY

A. Judicial Duties in General

All of the judicial duties prescribed by law* shall take precedence over all other activities of every judge. In the performance of these duties, the following standards apply.

B. Adjudicative Responsibilities

(1)   A judge shall hear and decide all matters assigned to the judge except those in which he or she is disqualified.

ADVISORY COMMITTEE COMMENTARY

Canon 3B(1) is based upon the affirmative obligation contained in Code of Civil Procedure section 170.

(2)   A judge shall be faithful to the law* regardless of partisan interests, public clamor, or fear of criticism, and shall maintain professional competence in the law.*

ADVISORY COMMITTEE COMMENTARY

Competence in the performance of judicial duties requires the legal knowledge,* skill, thoroughness, and preparation reasonably necessary to perform a judge's responsibilities of judicial office. Canon 1 provides that an incorrect legal ruling is not itself a violation of this code.

(3)   A judge shall require* order and decorum in proceedings before the judge.

(4)   A judge shall be patient, dignified, and courteous to litigants, jurors, witnesses, lawyers, and others with whom the judge deals in an official capacity, and shall require* similar conduct of lawyers and of all staff and court personnel under the judge's direction and control.

(5)   A judge shall perform judicial duties without bias or prejudice. A judge shall not, in the performance of judicial duties, engage in speech, gestures, or other conduct that would reasonably be perceived as (1) bias or prejudice, including but not limited to bias or prejudice based upon race, sex, gender, reli-

gion, national origin, ethnicity, disability, age, sexual orientation, marital status, socioeconomic status, or political affiliation, or (2) sexual harassment.

(6)   A judge shall require* lawyers in proceedings before the judge to refrain from manifesting, by words or conduct, bias or prejudice based upon race, sex, gender, religion, national origin, ethnicity, disability, age, sexual orientation, marital status, socioeconomic status, or political affiliation against parties, witnesses, counsel, or others. This canon does not preclude legitimate advocacy when race, sex, gender, religion, national origin, ethnicity, disability, age, sexual orientation, marital status, socioeconomic status, political affiliation, or other similar factors are issues in the proceeding.

(7)   A judge shall accord to every person who has a legal interest in a proceeding, or that person's lawyer, full right to be heard according to law.* Unless otherwise authorized by law,* a judge shall not independently investigate facts in a proceeding and shall consider only the evidence presented or facts that may be properly judicially noticed. This prohibition extends to information available in all media, including electronic. A judge shall not initiate, permit, or consider ex parte communications, that is, any communications to or from the judge outside the presence of the parties concerning a pending* or impending* proceeding, and shall make reasonable efforts to avoid such communications, except as follows:

> (a)   Except as stated below, a judge may consult with other judges. A judge shall not engage in discussions about a case with a judge who has previously been disqualified from hearing that matter; likewise, a judge who knows* he or she is or would be disqualified from hearing a case shall not discuss that matter with the judge assigned to the case. A judge also shall not engage in discussions with a judge who may participate in appellate review of the matter, nor shall a judge who may participate in appellate review of a matter engage in discussions with the judge presiding over the case.
>
> A judge may consult with court personnel or others authorized by law,* so long as the communication relates to that person's duty to aid the judge in carrying out the judge's adjudicative responsibilities.
>
> In any discussion with judges or court personnel, the judge shall make reasonable efforts to avoid receiving factual information that is not part of the record or an evaluation of that factual information. In such consultations, the judge shall not abrogate the responsibility personally to decide the matter.
>
> For purposes of Canon 3B(7)(a), "court personnel" includes bailiffs, court reporters, court externs, research attorneys, courtroom clerks, and other employees of the court, but does not include the lawyers in a proceeding before a judge, persons who are appointed by the court to serve in some capacity in a proceeding, or employees of other governmental entities, such as lawyers, social workers, or representatives of the probation department.

ADVISORY COMMITTEE COMMENTARY

Regarding communications between a judge presiding over a matter and a judge of a court with appellate jurisdiction over that matter, see also Government Code section 68070.5.

Though a judge may have ex parte discussions with appropriate court personnel, a judge may do so only on matters that are within the proper performance of that person's duties. For example, a bailiff may inform the judge of a threat to the judge or to the safety and security of the courtroom, but may not tell the judge ex parte that a defendant was overheard making an incriminating statement during a court recess. A clerk may point out to the judge a technical defect in a proposed sentence, but may not suggest to the judge that a defendant deserves a certain sentence.

A sentencing judge may not consult ex parte with a representative of the probation department about a matter pending before the sentencing judge.

This canon prohibits a judge from discussing a case with another judge who has already been disqualified. A judge also must be careful not to talk to a judge whom the judge knows* would be disqualified from hearing the matter.

(b)   A judge may initiate, permit, or consider ex parte communications, where circumstances require, for scheduling, administrative purposes, or emergencies that do not deal with substantive matters provided:

   (i)   the judge reasonably believes that no party will gain a procedural or tactical advantage as a result of the ex parte communication, and

   (ii)   the judge makes provision promptly to notify all other parties of the substance of the ex parte communication and allows an opportunity to respond.

(c)   A judge may initiate, permit, or consider any ex parte communication when expressly authorized by law* to do so or when authorized to do so by stipulation of the parties.

(d)   If a judge receives an unauthorized ex parte communication bearing upon the substance of a matter, the judge shall make provision promptly to notify the parties of the substance of the communication and provide the parties with an opportunity to respond.

ADVISORY COMMITTEE COMMENTARY

An exception allowing a judge, under certain circumstances, to obtain the advice of a disinterested expert on the law* has been eliminated from Canon 3B(7) because consulting with legal experts outside the presence of the parties is inconsistent with core tenets of the adversarial system. Therefore, a judge shall not consult with legal experts *outside the presence of the parties. Evidence Code section 730 provides for the appointment of an expert if a judge determines that expert testimony is necessary. A court may also invite the filing of amicus curiae briefs.*

An exception allowing a judge to confer with the parties separately in an effort to settle the matter before the judge has been moved from this canon to Canon 3B(12).

This canon does not prohibit court personnel from communicating scheduling information or carrying out similar administrative functions.

A judge is statutorily authorized to investigate and consult witnesses informally in small claims cases. Code of Civil Procedure section 116.520, subdivision (c).

(8)   A judge shall dispose of all judicial matters fairly, promptly, and efficiently. A judge shall manage the courtroom in a manner that provides all litigants the opportunity to have their matters fairly adjudicated in accordance with the law.*

ADVISORY COMMITTEE COMMENTARY

The obligation of a judge to dispose of matters promptly and efficiently must not take precedence over the judge's obligation to dispose of the matters fairly and with patience. For example, when a litigant is self-represented, a judge has the discretion to take reasonable steps, appropriate under the circumstances and consistent with the law and the canons, to enable the litigant to be heard. A judge should monitor and supervise cases so as to reduce or eliminate dilatory practices, avoidable delays, and unnecessary costs.*

Prompt disposition of the court's business requires a judge to devote adequate time to judicial duties, to be punctual in attending court and expeditious in determining matters under submission, and to require that court officials, litigants, and their lawyers cooperate with the judge to that end.*

(9)   A judge shall not make any public comment about a pending* or impending* proceeding in any court, and shall not make any nonpublic comment that might substantially interfere with a fair trial or hearing. The judge shall require* similar abstention on the part of staff and court personnel subject to the judge's direction and control. This canon does not prohibit judges from making statements in the course of their official duties or from explaining the procedures of the court, and does not apply to proceedings in which the judge is a litigant in a personal capacity. Other than cases in which the judge has personally participated, this canon does not prohibit judges from discussing in legal education programs and materials, cases and issues pending in appellate courts. This educational exemption does not apply to cases over which the judge has presided or to comments or discussions that might interfere with a fair hearing of the case.

ADVISORY COMMITTEE COMMENTARY

The requirement that judges abstain from public comment regarding a pending* or impending* proceeding continues during any appellate process and until final disposition. A judge shall make reasonable efforts to ascertain whether a case is pending* or impending* before commenting on it. This canon does not prohibit a judge from commenting on proceedings in which the judge is a litigant in a personal capacity, but in cases such as a writ of mandamus where the judge is a litigant in an official capacity, the judge must not comment publicly.

"Making statements in the course of their official duties" and "explaining the procedures of the court" include providing an official transcript or partial official transcript of a court proceeding open to the public and explaining the rules of court and procedures related to a decision rendered by a judge.

Although this canon does not prohibit a judge from commenting on cases that are not pending* or impending* in any court, a judge must be cognizant of the general prohibition in Canon 2 against conduct involving impropriety* or the appearance of impropriety.* A judge should also be aware of the mandate in Canon 2A that a judge must act at all times in a manner that promotes public confidence in the integrity* and impartiality* of the judiciary. In addition, when commenting on a case pursuant to this canon, a judge must maintain high standards of conduct, as set forth in Canon 1.

Although a judge is permitted to make nonpublic comments about pending* or impending* cases that will not substantially interfere with a fair trial or hearing, the judge should be cautious when making any such comments. There is always a risk that a comment can be misheard, misinterpreted, or repeated. A judge making such a comment must be mindful of the judge's obligation under Canon 2A to act at all times in a manner that promotes public confidence in the integrity* and impartiality* of the judiciary. When a judge makes a nonpublic comment about a case pending* before that judge, the judge must keep an open mind and not form an opinion prematurely or create the appearance of having formed an opinion prematurely.

(10)   A judge shall not commend or criticize jurors for their verdict other than in a court order or opinion in a proceeding, but may express appreciation to jurors for their service to the judicial system and the community.

ADVISORY COMMITTEE COMMENTARY

Commending or criticizing jurors for their verdict may imply a judicial expectation in future cases and may impair a juror's ability to be fair and impartial* in a subsequent case.

(11)   A judge shall not disclose or use, for any purpose unrelated to judicial duties, nonpublic information* acquired in a judicial capacity.

ADVISORY COMMITTEE COMMENTARY

This canon makes it clear that judges cannot make use of information from affidavits, jury results, or court rulings, before they become public information, in order to gain a personal advantage.

(12)   A judge may participate in settlement conferences or in other efforts to resolve matters in dispute, including matters pending before the judge. A judge may, with the express consent of the parties or their lawyers, confer separately with the parties and/or their lawyers during such resolution efforts. At all times during such resolution efforts, a judge shall remain impartial* and shall not engage in conduct that may reasonably be perceived as coercive.

ADVISORY COMMITTEE COMMENTARY

While the judge plays an important role in overseeing efforts to resolve disputes, including conducting settlement discussions, a judge should be careful that efforts to resolve disputes do not undermine any party's right to be heard according to law.*

The judge should keep in mind the effect that the judge's participation in dispute resolution efforts may have on the judge's impartiality* or the appearance of impartiality* if the case remains with the judge for trial after resolution efforts are unsuccessful. Accordingly, a judge may wish to consider: (1) whether the parties or their counsel have requested or objected to the participation by the trial judge in such discussions; (2) whether the parties and their counsel are relatively sophisticated in legal matters or the particular legal issues involved in the case; (3) whether a party is unrepresented; (4) whether the case will be tried by the judge or a jury; (5) whether the parties will participate with their counsel in settlement discussions and, if so, the effect of personal contact between the judge and parties; and (6) whether it is appropriate during the settlement conference for the judge to express an opinion on the merits or worth of the case or express an opinion on the legal issues that the judge may later have to rule upon.

If a judge assigned to preside over a trial believes participation in resolution efforts could influence the judge's decision making during trial, the judge may decline to engage in such efforts.

Where dispute resolution efforts of any type are unsuccessful, the judge should consider whether, due to events that occurred during the resolution efforts, the judge may be disqualified under the law* from presiding over the trial. See, e.g., Code of Civil Procedure section 170.1, subdivision (a)(6)(A).

C.   Administrative Responsibilities

(1)   A judge shall diligently discharge the judge's administrative responsibilities 7impartially,* on the basis of merit, without bias or prejudice, free of conflict of 8interest, and in a manner that promotes public confidence in the integrity* of the judiciary. A judge shall not, in the performance of administrative duties, engage in speech, gestures, or other conduct that would reasonably be

perceived as (i) bias or prejudice, including but not limited to bias or prejudice based upon race, sex, gender, religion, national origin, ethnicity, disability, age, sexual orientation, marital status, socioeconomic status, or political affiliation, or (ii) sexual harassment.

ADVISORY COMMITTEE COMMENTARY

In considering what constitutes a conflict of interest under this canon, a judge should be informed by Code of Civil Procedure section 170.1, subdivision (a)(6).

(2)   A judge shall maintain professional competence in judicial administration, and shall cooperate with other judges and court officials in the administration of court business.

(3)   A judge shall require* staff and court personnel under the judge's direction and control to observe appropriate standards of conduct and to refrain from manifesting bias or prejudice based upon race, sex, gender, religion, national origin, ethnicity, disability, age, sexual orientation, marital status, socioeconomic status, or political affiliation in the performance of their official duties.

(4)   A judge with supervisory authority for the judicial performance of other judges shall take reasonable measures to ensure the prompt disposition of matters before them and the proper performance of their other judicial responsibilities.

(5)   A judge shall not make unnecessary court appointments. A judge shall exercise the power of appointment impartially,* on the basis of merit, without bias or prejudice, free of conflict of interest, and in a manner that promotes public confidence in the integrity* of the judiciary. A judge shall avoid nepotism and favoritism. A judge shall not approve compensation of appointees above the reasonable value of services rendered.

ADVISORY COMMITTEE COMMENTARY

Appointees of a judge include assigned counsel and officials such as referees, commissioners, special masters, receivers, and guardians. Consent by the parties to an appointment or an award of compensation does not relieve the judge of the obligation prescribed by Canon 3C(5).

D. Disciplinary Responsibilities

(1)   Whenever a judge has reliable information that another judge has violated any provision of the Code of Judicial Ethics, the judge shall take appropriate corrective action, which may include reporting the violation to the appropriate authority. (See Commentary following Canon 3D(2).)

(2)   Whenever a judge has personal knowledge,* or concludes in a judicial decision, that a lawyer has committed misconduct or has violated any provision of the Rules of Professional Conduct, the judge shall take appropriate corrective action, which may include reporting the violation to the appropriate authority.

ADVISORY COMMITTEE COMMENTARY

Appropriate corrective action could include direct communication with the judge or lawyer who has committed the violation, other direct action, such as a confidential referral to a judicial or lawyer assistance program, or a report of the violation to the presiding judge, appropriate authority, or other agency or body. Judges should note that in addition to the action required by Canon 3D(2), California law imposes mandatory additional reporting requirements on judges regarding lawyer misconduct. See Business and Professions Code section 6086.7.

"Appropriate authority" denotes the authority with responsibility for initiation of the disciplinary process with respect to a violation to be reported.

(3)   A judge shall promptly report in writing to the Commission on Judicial Performance when he or she is charged in court by misdemeanor citation, prosecutorial complaint, information, or indictment, with any crime in the United States as specified below. Crimes that must be reported are: (1) all crimes, other than those that would be considered misdemeanors not involving moral turpitude or infractions under California law; and (2) all misdemeanors involving violence (including assaults), the use or possession of controlled substances, the misuse of prescriptions, or the personal use or furnishing of alcohol. A judge also shall promptly report in writing upon conviction of such crimes.

If the judge is a retired judge serving in the Assigned Judges Program, he or she shall promptly report such information in writing to the Chief Justice rather than to the Commission on Judicial Performance. If the judge is a subordinate judicial officer,* he or she shall promptly report such information in writing to both the presiding judge of the court in which the subordinate judicial officer* sits and the Commission on Judicial Performance.

(4)   A judge shall cooperate with judicial and lawyer disciplinary agencies.

ADVISORY COMMITTEE COMMENTARY

See Government Code section 68725, which requires judges to cooperate with and give reasonable assistance and information to the Commission on Judicial Performance, and rule 104 of the Rules of the Commission on Judicial Performance, which requires a respondent judge to cooperate with the commission in all proceedings in accordance with section 68725.

(5)   A judge shall not retaliate, directly or indirectly, against a person known* or suspected to have assisted or cooperated with an investigation of a judge or a lawyer.

E. Disqualification and Disclosure

(1)   A judge shall disqualify himself or herself in any proceeding in which disqualification is required by law.*

(2)   In all trial court proceedings, a judge shall disclose on the record as follows:

(a)   Information relevant to disqualification A judge shall disclose information that is reasonably relevant to the question of disqualification under Code of Civil Procedure section 170.1, even if the judge believes there is no actual basis for disqualification.

(b)   Campaign contributions in trial court elections

(i)   Information required to be disclosed

In any matter before a judge who is or was a candidate for judicial office* in a trial court election, the judge shall disclose any contribution or loan of $100 or more from a party, individual lawyer, or law office or firm in that matter as required by this canon, even if the amount of the contribution or loan would not require disqualification. Such disclosure shall consist of the name of the contributor or lender, the amount of each contribution or loan, the cumulative amount of the contributor's contributions or lender's loans, and the date(s) of each contribution or loan. The judge shall make reasonable efforts to obtain current information regarding contributions or loans received by his or her campaign and shall disclose the required information on the record.

(ii)   Manner of disclosure

The judge shall ensure that the required information is conveyed on the record to the parties and lawyers appearing in the matter before the judge. The judge has discretion to select the manner of disclosure, but the manner used shall avoid the appearance that the judge is soliciting campaign contributions.

(iii)   Timing of disclosure

Disclosure shall be made at the earliest reasonable opportunity after receiving each contribution or loan. The duty commences no later than one week after receipt of the first contribution or loan, and continues for a period of two years after the candidate takes the oath of office, or two years from the date of the contribution or loan, whichever event is later.

ADVISORY COMMITTEE COMMENTARY

Code of Civil Procedure section 170.1(a)(9)(C) requires a judge to "disclose any contribution from a party or lawyer in a matter that is before the court that is required to be reported under subdivision (f) of Section 84211 of the Government Code, even if the amount would not require disqualification under this paragraph." This statute further provides that the "manner of disclosure shall be the same as that provided in Canon 3E of the Code of Judicial Ethics." Canon 3E(2)(b) sets forth the information the judge must disclose, the manner for making such disclosure, and the timing thereof.

"Contribution" includes monetary and in-kind contributions. See Cal. Code Regs., tit. 2, § 18215, subd. (b)(3). See generally Government Code section 84211(f).

Disclosure of campaign contributions is intended to provide parties and lawyers appearing before a judge during and after a judicial campaign with easy access to information about campaign contributions that may not require disqualification but could be relevant to the question of disqualification of the judge. Depending upon the circumstances, the judge may conclude that the most effective and efficient manner of providing disclosure is to state the required information on the record in open court. In the alternative, a judge may determine that it is more appropriate to disclose on the record that parties and lawyers may obtain the required information at an easily accessible location in the courthouse, and provide an opportunity for the parties and lawyers to review the available information.

In addition to the disclosure obligations set forth in Canon 3E(2) (b), a judge must, pursuant to Canon 3E(2)(a), disclose on the record any other information that may be relevant to the question of disqualification. As examples, such an obligation may arise as a result of contributions or loans of which the judge is aware made by a party, lawyer, or law office or firm appearing before the judge to a third party in support of the judge or in opposition to the judge's opponent; a party, lawyer, or law office or firm's relationship to the judge or role in the campaign; or the aggregate contributions or loans from lawyers in one law office or firm.

Canon 3E(2)(b) does not eliminate the obligation of the judge to recuse where the nature of the contribution or loan, the extent of the contributor's or lender's involvement in the judicial campaign, the relationship of the contributor or lender, or other circumstance requires recusal under Code of Civil Procedure section 170.1, and particularly section 170.1, subdivision (a)(6)(A).

(3)   Judges shall disqualify themselves in accordance with the following:

   (a)   Statements that commit the judge to a particular result

         A judge is disqualified if the judge, while a judge or candidate for judicial office,* has made a statement, other than in a court proceeding, judicial decision, or opinion, that a person aware of the facts might reasonably believe commits the judge to reach a particular result or rule in a particular way in a proceeding.

   (b)   Bond ownership

         Ownership of a corporate bond issued by a party to a proceeding and having a fair market value exceeding $1,500 is disqualifying. Ownership of government bonds issued by a party to a proceeding is disqualifying only if the outcome of the proceeding could substantially affect the value of the judge's bond. Ownership in a mutual or common investment fund that holds bonds is not a disqualifying financial interest.

ADVISORY COMMITTEE COMMENTARY

The distinction between corporate and government bonds is consistent with the Political Reform Act (see Gov. Code, § 82034), which requires disclosure of corporate bonds, but not government bonds. Canon 3E(3) is intended to assist judges in complying with Code of Civil Procedure section 170.1, subdivision (a)(3) and Canon 3E(5)(d).

(4)　　　An appellate justice shall disqualify himself or herself in any proceeding if for any reason:

(a)　the justice believes his or her recusal would further the interests of justice; or

(b)　the justice substantially doubts his or her capacity to be impartial;* or

(c)　the circumstances are such that a reasonable person aware of the facts would doubt the justice's ability to be impartial.*

(5)　　　Disqualification of an appellate justice is also required in the following instances:

(a)　The appellate justice has appeared or otherwise served as a lawyer in the pending* proceeding, or has appeared or served as a lawyer in any other proceeding involving any of the same parties if that other proceeding related to the same contested issues of fact and law as the present proceeding, or has given advice to any party in the present proceeding upon any issue involved in the proceeding.

ADVISORY COMMITTEE COMMENTARY

Canon 3E(5)(a) is consistent with Code of Civil Procedure section 170.1, subdivision (a)(2), which addresses disqualification of trial court judges based on prior representation of a party in the proceeding.

(b)　Within the last two years, (i) a party to the proceeding, or an officer, director or trustee thereof, either was a client of the justice when the justice was engaged in the private practice of law or was a client of a lawyer with whom the justice was associated in the private practice of law; or (ii) a lawyer in the proceeding was associated with the justice in the private practice of law.

(c)　The appellate justice represented a public officer or entity and personally advised or in any way represented such officer or entity concerning the factual or legal issues in the present proceeding in which the public officer or entity now appears.

(d)　The appellate justice, or his or her spouse or registered domestic partner,* or a minor child residing in the household, has a financial interest or is a fiduciary* who has a financial interest in the proceeding, or is a director, advisor, or other active participant in the affairs of a party. A financial interest is defined as ownership of more than a 1 percent legal or equitable interest in a party, or a legal or equitable interest in a party of a fair market value exceeding $1,500. Ownership in a mutual or common investment fund that holds securities does not itself constitute a financial interest; holding office in an educational, religious, charitable, service,* or civic organization does not confer a financial interest in the organization's securities; and a proprietary interest of a policyholder in a mutual insurance company or mutual savings association or similar interest is not a financial interest unless the outcome of the proceeding could substantially affect the value of the interest. A justice shall make reasonable efforts to keep informed about his or her personal and fiduciary* interests and those of his or her spouse or registered domestic partner* and of minor children living in the household.

(e)   The justice or his or her spouse or registered domestic partner,* or a person within the third degree of relationship* to either of them, or the spouse or registered domestic partner* thereof, is a party or an officer, director, or trustee of a party to the proceeding, or a lawyer or spouse or registered domestic partner* of a lawyer in the proceeding is the spouse, registered domestic partner,* former spouse, former registered domestic partner,* child, sibling, or parent of the justice or of the justice's spouse or registered domestic partner,* or such a person is associated in the private practice of law with a lawyer in the proceeding.

(f)   The justice (i) served as the judge before whom the proceeding was tried or heard in the lower court, (ii) has personal knowledge* of disputed evidentiary facts concerning the proceeding, or (iii) has a personal bias or prejudice concerning a party or a party's lawyer.

(g)   A temporary or permanent physical impairment renders the justice unable properly to perceive the evidence or conduct the proceedings.

(h)   The justice has a current arrangement concerning prospective employment or other compensated service as a dispute resolution neutral or is participating in, or, within the last two years has participated in, discussions regarding prospective employment or service as a dispute resolution neutral, or has been engaged in such employment or service, and any of the following applies:

     (i)   The arrangement is, or the prior employment or discussion was, with a party to the proceeding;

     (ii)   The matter before the justice includes issues relating to the enforcement of either an agreement to submit a dispute to an alternative dispute resolution process or an award or other final decision by a dispute resolution neutral;

     (iii)   The justice directs the parties to participate in an alternative dispute resolution process in which the dispute resolution neutral will be an individual or entity with whom the justice has the arrangement, has previously been employed or served, or is discussing or has discussed the employment or service; or

(iv)   The justice will select a dispute resolution neutral or entity to conduct an alternative dispute resolution process in the matter before the justice, and among those available for selection is an individual or entity with whom the justice has the arrangement, with whom the justice has previously been employed or served, or with whom the justice is discussing or has discussed the employment or service.

For purposes of Canon 3E(5)(h), "participating in discussions" or "has participated in discussions" means that the justice solicited or otherwise indicated an interest in accepting or negotiating possible employment or service as an alternative dispute resolution neutral or responded to an unsolicited statement regarding, or an offer of, such employment or service by expressing an interest in that employment or service, making any inquiry regarding the employment or service, or encouraging the person making the statement or offer to provide additional information about that possible employment or service. If a justice's response to an unsolicited statement regarding, a question about, or offer of, prospective employment or other compensated service as a dispute resolution neutral is limited to responding negatively, declining the offer, or declining to discuss such employment or service, that response does not constitute participating in discussions.

For purposes of Canon 3E(5)(h), "party" includes the parent, subsidiary, or other legal affiliate of any entity that is a party and is involved in the transaction, contract, or facts that gave rise to the issues subject to the proceeding.

For purposes of Canon 3E(5)(h), "dispute resolution neutral" means an arbitrator, a mediator, a temporary judge* appointed under section 21 of article VI of the California Constitution, a referee appointed under Code of Civil Procedure section 638 or 639, a special master, a neutral evaluator, a settlement officer, or a settlement facilitator.

(i)   The justice's spouse or registered domestic partner *or a person within the third degree of relationship* to the justice or his or her spouse or registered domestic partner,* or the person's spouse or registered domestic partner,* was a witness in the proceeding.

(j)   The justice has received a campaign contribution of $5,000 or more from a party or lawyer in a matter that is before the court, and either of the following applies:

(i)   The contribution was received in support of the justice's last election, if the last election was within the last six years; or

(ii)   The contribution was received in anticipation of an upcoming election.

Notwithstanding Canon 3E(5)(j), a justice shall be disqualified based on a contribution of a lesser amount if required by Canon 3E(4).

The disqualification required under Canon 3E(5)(j) may be waived if all parties that did not make the contribution agree to waive the disqualification.

ADVISORY COMMITTEE COMMENTARY

Canon 3E(1) sets forth the general duty to disqualify applicable to a judge of any court. Sources for determining when recusal or disqualification is appropriate may include the applicable provisions of the Code of Civil Procedure, other provisions of the Code of Judicial Ethics, the Code of Conduct for United States Judges, the American Bar Association's Model Code of Judicial Conduct, and related case law.

The decision whether to disclose information under Canon 3E(2) is a decision based on the facts of the case before the judge. A judge is required to disclose only information that is related to the grounds for disqualification set forth in Code of Civil Procedure section 170.1.

Canon 3E(4) sets forth the general standards for recusal of an appellate justice. The term "appellate justice" includes justices of both the Courts of Appeal and the Supreme Court. Generally, the provisions concerning disqualification of an appellate justice are intended to assist justices in determining whether recusal is appropriate and to inform the public why recusal may occur.

However, the rule of necessity may override the rule of disqualification. For example, a judge might be required to participate in judicial review of a judicial salary statute, or might be the only judge available in a matter requiring judicial action, such as a hearing on probable cause or a temporary restraining order. In the latter case, the judge must promptly disclose on the record the basis for possible disqualification and use reasonable efforts to transfer the matter to another judge as soon as practicable.

In some instances, membership in certain organizations may have the potential to give an appearance of partiality, although membership in the organization generally may not be barred by Canon 2C, Canon 4, or any other specific canon. A judge holding membership in an organization should disqualify himself or herself whenever doing so would be appropriate in accordance with Canon 3E(1), 3E(4), or 3E(5) or statutory requirements. In addition, in some circumstances, the parties or their lawyers may consider a judge's membership in an organization relevant to the question of disqualification, even if the judge believes there is no actual basis for disqualification. In accordance with this canon, a judge should disclose to the parties his or her membership in an organization, in any proceeding in which that information is reasonably relevant to the question of disqualification under Code of Civil Procedure section 170.1, even if the judge concludes there is no actual basis for disqualification.

CANON 4

A JUDGE SHALL SO CONDUCT THE JUDGE'S QUASI-JUDICIAL AND EXTRAJUDICIAL ACTIVITIES AS TO MINIMIZE THE RISK OF CONFLICT WITH JUDICIAL OBLIGATIONS

A. Extrajudicial Activities in General

A judge shall conduct all of the judge's extrajudicial activities so that they do not

(1)   cast reasonable doubt on the judge's capacity to act impartially;*

(2)   demean the judicial office;

(3)   interfere with the proper performance of judicial duties; or

(4)   lead to frequent disqualification of the judge.

ADVISORY COMMITTEE COMMENTARY

Complete separation of a judge from extrajudicial activities is neither possible nor wise; a judge should not become isolated from the community in which he or she lives. Expressions of bias or prejudice by a judge, even outside the judge's judicial activities, may cast reasonable doubt on the judge's capacity to act impartially* as a judge. Expressions that may do so include inappropriate use of humor or the use of demeaning remarks. See Canon 2C and accompanying Commentary.

Because a judge's judicial duties take precedence over all other activities (see Canon 3A), a judge must avoid extrajudicial activities that might reasonably result in the judge being disqualified.

B. Quasi-Judicial and Avocational Activities

A judge may speak, write, lecture, teach, and participate in activities concerning legal and nonlegal subject matters, subject to the requirements of this code.

ADVISORY COMMITTEE COMMENTARY

As a judicial officer and person specially learned in the law,* a judge is in a unique position to contribute to the improvement of the law, the legal system, and the administration of justice,* including revision of substantive and procedural law* and improvement of criminal and juvenile justice. To the extent that time permits, a judge may do so, either independently or through a bar or judicial association or other group dedicated to the improvement of the law.* It may be necessary to promote legal education programs and materials by iden-

tifying authors and speakers by judicial title. This is permissible, provided such use of the judicial title does not contravene Canons 2A and 2B.

Judges are not precluded by their office from engaging in other social, community, and intellectual endeavors so long as they do not interfere with the obligations under Canons 2C and 4A.

C. Governmental, Civic, or Charitable Activities

(1)   A judge shall not appear at a public hearing or officially consult with an executive or legislative body or public official except on matters concerning the law, the legal system, or the administration of justice* or in matters involving the judge's private economic or personal interests.

ADVISORY COMMITTEE COMMENTARY

When deciding whether to appear at a public hearing or whether to consult with an executive or legislative body or public official on matters concerning the law, the legal system, or the administration of justice, a judge should consider whether that conduct would violate any other provisions of this code. For a list of factors to consider, see the explanation of "law, the legal system, or the administration of justice" in the terminology section. See also Canon 2B regarding the obligation to avoid improper influence.*

(2)   A judge shall not accept appointment to a governmental committee or commission or other governmental position that is concerned with issues of fact or policy on matters other than the improvement of the law, the legal system, or the administration of justice.* A judge may, however, serve in the military reserve or represent a national, state, or local government on ceremonial occasions or in connection with historical, educational, or cultural activities.

ADVISORY COMMITTEE COMMENTARY

Canon 4C(2) prohibits a judge from accepting any governmental position except one relating to the law, legal system, or administration of justice as authorized by Canon 4C(3). The appropriateness of accepting extrajudicial assignments must be assessed in light of the demands on judicial resources and the need to protect the courts from involvement in extrajudicial matters that may prove to be controversial. Judges shall not accept governmental appointments that are likely to interfere with the effectiveness and independence* of the judiciary, or that constitute a public office within the meaning of the California Constitution, article VI, section 17.*

Canon 4C(2) does not govern a judge's service in a nongovernmental position. See Canon 4C(3) permitting service by a judge with organizations devoted to the improvement of the law, the legal system, or the administration of justice and with educational, religious, charitable, service,* or civic organizations not conducted for profit. For* *example, service on the board of a public educational institution, other than a law school, would be prohibited under Canon 4C(2), but service on the board of a public law school or any private educational institution would generally be permitted under Canon 4C(3).*

(3)   Subject to the following limitations and the other requirements of this code,

(a)   a judge may serve as an officer, director, trustee, or nonlegal advisor of an organization or governmental agency devoted to the improvement of the law, the legal system, or the administration of justice* provided that such position does not constitute a public office within the meaning of the California Constitution, article VI, section 17;

(b)   a judge may serve as an officer, director, trustee, or nonlegal advisor of an educational, religious, charitable, service,* or civic organization not conducted for profit;

ADVISORY COMMITTEE COMMENTARY

Canon 4C(3) does not apply to a judge's service in a governmental position unconnected with the improvement of the law, the legal system, or the administration of justice.* See Canon 4C(2).

Canon 4C(3) uses the phrase, "Subject to the following limitations and the other requirements of this code." As an example of the meaning of the phrase, a judge permitted by Canon 4C(3) to serve on the board of a service organization* may be prohibited from such service by Canon 2C or 4A if the institution practices invidious discrimination or if service on the board otherwise casts reasonable doubt on the judge's capacity to act impartially* as a judge.

Service by a judge on behalf of a civic or charitable organization may be governed by other provisions of Canon 4 in addition to Canon 4C. For example, a judge is prohibited by Canon 4G from serving as a legal advisor to a civic or charitable organization.

Service on the board of a homeowners' association or a neighborhood protective group is proper if it is related to the protection of the judge's own economic interests. See Canons 4D(2) and 4D(4). See Canon 2B regarding the obligation to avoid improper use of the prestige of a judge's office.

(c)   a judge shall not serve as an officer, director, trustee, or nonlegal advisor if it is likely that the organization

(i)   will be engaged in judicial proceedings that would ordinarily come before the judge, or

(ii)   will be engaged frequently in adversary proceedings in the court of which the judge is a member or in any court subject to the appellate jurisdiction of the court of which the judge is a member.

ADVISORY COMMITTEE COMMENTARY

The changing nature of some organizations and of their relationship to the law* makes it necessary for the judge regularly to reexamine the activities of each organization with which the judge is affiliated to determine if it is proper for the judge to continue the affiliation. Some organizations regularly engage in litigation to achieve their goals or fulfill their purposes. Judges should avoid a leadership role in such organizations as it could compromise the appearance of impartiality.*

(d) a judge as an officer, director, trustee, or nonlegal advisor, or as a member or otherwise

(i) may assist such an organization in planning fundraising and may participate in the management and investment of the organization's funds. However, a judge shall not personally participate in the solicitation of funds or other fundraising activities, except that a judge may privately solicit funds for such an organization from members of the judge's family* or from other judges (excluding court commissioners, referees, retired judges, court-appointed arbitrators, hearing officers, and temporary judges*);

(ii) may make recommendations to public and private fund-granting organizations on projects and programs concerning the law, the legal system, or the administration of justice;*

(iii) shall not personally participate in membership solicitation if the solicitation might reasonably be perceived as coercive or if the membership solicitation is essentially a fundraising mechanism, except as permitted in Canon 4C(3)(d)(i);

(iv) shall not permit the use of the prestige of his or her judicial office for fundraising or membership solicitation but may be a speaker, guest of honor, or recipient of an award for public or charitable service provided the judge does not personally solicit funds and complies with Canons 4A(1), (2), (3), and (4).

ADVISORY COMMITTEE COMMENTARY

A judge may solicit membership or endorse or encourage membership efforts for an organization devoted to the improvement of the law, the legal system, or the administration of justice,* or a nonprofit educational, religious, charitable, service,* or civic organization as long as the solicitation cannot reasonably be perceived as coercive and is not essentially a fundraising mechanism. Solicitation of funds or memberships for an organization similarly involves the danger that the person solicited will feel obligated to respond favorably if the solicitor is in a position of influence or control. A judge must not engage in direct, individual solicitation of funds or memberships in person, in writing, or by telephone except in the following cases: (1) a judge may solicit other judges (excluding court commis-

sioners, referees, retired judges, court-appointed arbitrators, hearing officers, and temporary judges*) for funds or memberships; (2) a judge may solicit other persons for membership in the organizations described above if neither those persons nor persons with whom they are affiliated are likely ever to appear before the court on which the judge serves; and (3) a judge who is an officer of such an organization may send a general membership solicitation mailing over the judge's signature.

When deciding whether to make recommendations to public and private fund-granting organizations on projects and programs concerning the law, the legal system, or the administration of justice,* a judge should consider whether that conduct would violate any other provision of this code. For a list of factors to consider, see the explanation of "law, the legal system, or the administration of justice" in the terminology section.

Use of an organization letterhead for fundraising or membership solicitation does not violate Canon 4C(3)(d), provided the letterhead lists only the judge's name and office or other position in the organization, and designates the judge's judicial title only if other persons whose names appear on the letterhead have comparable designations. In addition, a judge must also make reasonable efforts to ensure that the judge's staff, court officials, and others subject to the judge's direction and control do not solicit funds on the judge's behalf for any purpose, charitable or otherwise.

(e)   A judge may encourage lawyers to provide pro bono publico legal services.

ADVISORY COMMITTEE COMMENTARY

In addition to appointing lawyers to serve as counsel for indigent parties in individual cases, a judge may promote broader access to justice by encouraging lawyers to participate in pro bono publico legal services, as long as the judge does not employ coercion or abuse the prestige of judicial office.

D.   Financial Activities

(1)   A judge shall not engage in financial and business dealings that

(a)   may reasonably be perceived to exploit the judge's judicial position, or

(b)   involve the judge in frequent transactions or continuing business relationships with lawyers or other persons likely to appear before the court on which the judge serves.

ADVISORY COMMITTEE COMMENTARY

The Time for Compliance provision of this code (Canon 6F) postpones the time for compliance with certain provisions of this canon in some cases.

A judge must avoid financial and business dealings that involve the judge in frequent transactions or continuing business relationships with persons likely to appear either before the judge personally or before other judges on the judge's court. A judge shall discourage members of the judge's family* from engaging in dealings that would reasonably appear to exploit the judge's judicial position or that involve family members in frequent transactions or continuing business relationships with persons likely to appear before the judge. This rule is necessary to avoid creating an appearance of exploitation of office or favoritism and to minimize the potential for disqualification.

Participation by a judge in financial and business dealings is subject to the general prohibitions in Canon 4A against activities that tend to reflect adversely on impartiality,* demean the judicial office, or interfere with the proper performance of judicial duties. Such participation is also subject to the general prohibition in Canon 2 against activities involving impropriety* or the appearance of impropriety* and the prohibition in Canon 2B against the misuse of the prestige of judicial office.

In addition, a judge must maintain high standards of conduct in all of the judge's activities, as set forth in Canon 1.

(2)　　A judge may, subject to the requirements of this code, hold and manage investments of the judge and members of the judge's family,* including real estate, and engage in other remunerative activities. A judge shall not participate in, nor permit the judge's name to be used in connection with, any business venture or commercial advertising that indicates the judge's title or affiliation with the judiciary or otherwise lend the power or prestige of his or her office to promote a business or any commercial venture.

(3)　　A judge shall not serve as an officer, director, manager, or employee of a business affected with a public interest, including, without limitation, a financial institution, insurance company, or public utility.

ADVISORY COMMITTEE COMMENTARY

Although participation by a judge in business activities might otherwise be permitted by Canon 4D, a judge may be prohibited from participation by other provisions of this code when, for example, the business entity frequently appears before the judge's court or the participation requires significant time away from judicial duties. Similarly, a judge must avoid participating in any business activity if the judge's participation would involve misuse of the prestige of judicial office. See Canon 2B.

(4)　　A judge shall manage personal investments and financial activities so as to minimize the necessity for disqualification. As soon as reasonably possible, a judge shall divest himself or herself of investments and other financial interests that would require frequent disqualification.

(5)   Under no circumstance shall a judge accept a gift,* bequest, or favor if the donor is a party whose interests have come or are reasonably likely to come before the judge. A judge shall discourage members of the judge's family residing in the judge's household* from accepting similar benefits from parties who have come or are reasonably likely to come before the judge.

ADVISORY COMMITTEE COMMENTARY

In addition to the prohibitions set forth in Canon 4D(5) regarding gifts, other laws* may be applicable to judges, including, for example, Code of Civil Procedure section 170.9 and the Political Reform Act of 1974 (Gov. Code, § 81000 et seq.).*

Canon 4D(5) does not apply to contributions to a judge's campaign for judicial office, a matter governed by Canon 5.

Because a gift, bequest, or favor to a member of the judge's family residing in the judge's household* might be viewed as intended to influence the judge, a judge must inform those family members of the relevant ethical constraints upon the judge in this regard and urge them to take these constraints into account when making decisions about accepting such gifts,* bequests, or favors. A judge cannot, however, reasonably be expected to know or control all of the financial or business activities of all family members residing in the judge's household.**

The application of Canon 4D(5) requires recognition that a judge cannot reasonably be expected to anticipate all persons or interests that may come before the court.

(6)   A judge shall not accept and shall discourage members of the judge's family residing in the judge's household* from accepting a gift,* bequest, favor, or loan from anyone except as hereinafter set forth, provided that acceptance would not reasonably be perceived as intended to influence the judge in the performance of judicial duties:

(a)   a gift,* bequest, favor, or loan from a person whose preexisting relationship with a judge would prevent the judge under Canon 3E from hearing a case involving that person;

ADVISORY COMMITTEE COMMENTARY

Upon appointment or election as a judge or within a reasonable period of time thereafter, a judge may attend an event honoring the judge's appointment or election as a judge provided that (1) the judge would otherwise be disqualified from hearing any matter involving the person or entity holding or funding the event, and (2) a reasonable person would not conclude that attendance at the event undermines the judge's integrity, impartiality,* or independence.**

(b)   a gift* for a special occasion from a relative or friend, if the gift* is fairly commensurate with the occasion and the relationship;

ADVISORY COMMITTEE COMMENTARY

A gift* to a judge, or to a member of the judge's family residing in the judge's household,* that is excessive in value raises questions about the judge's impartiality* and the integrity* of the judicial office and might require disqualification of the judge where disqualification would not otherwise be required. See, however, Canon 4D(6)(a).

(c) commercial or financial opportunities and benefits, including special pricing and discounts, and loans from lending institutions in their regular course of business, if the same opportunities and benefits or loans are made available on the same terms to similarly situated persons who are not judges;

(d) any gift* incidental to a public testimonial, or educational or resource materials supplied by publishers on a complimentary basis for official use, or an invitation to the judge and the judge's spouse or registered domestic partner* or guest to attend a bar-related function or an activity devoted to the improvement of the law, the legal system, or the administration of justice;*

(e) advances or reimbursement for the reasonable cost of travel, transportation, lodging, and subsistence that is directly related to participation in any judicial, educational, civic, or governmental program or bar-related function or activity devoted to the improvement of the law, the legal system, or the administration of justice;*

ADVISORY COMMITTEE COMMENTARY

Acceptance of an invitation to a law-related function is governed by Canon 4D(6)(d); acceptance of an invitation paid for by an individual lawyer or group of lawyers is governed by Canon 4D(6)(g). See also Canon 4H(2) and accompanying Commentary.

(f) a gift,* award, or benefit incident to the business, profession, or other separate activity of a spouse or registered domestic partner* or other member of the judge's family residing in the judge's household,* including gifts,* awards, and benefits for the use of both the spouse or registered domestic partner* or other family member and the judge;

(g) ordinary social hospitality;

ADVISORY COMMITTEE COMMENTARY

Although Canon 4D(6)(g) does not preclude ordinary social hospitality, a judge should carefully weigh acceptance of such hospitality to avoid any appearance of impropriety* or bias or any appearance that the judge is misusing the prestige of judicial office. See Canons 2 and 2B. A judge should also consider whether acceptance would affect the integrity,* impartiality,* or independence* of the judiciary. See Canon 2A.

(h) a scholarship or fellowship awarded on the same terms and based on the same criteria applied to other applicants;

(i)   rewards and prizes given to competitors or participants in random drawings, contests, or other events that are open to persons who are not judges;

(j)   an invitation to the judge and the judge's spouse, registered domestic partner,* or guest to attend an event sponsored by an educational, religious, charitable, service,* or civic organization with which the judge is associated or involved, if the same invitation is offered to persons who are not judges and who are similarly engaged with the organization.

E. Fiduciary* Activities

(1)   A judge shall not serve as executor, administrator, or other personal representative, trustee, guardian, attorney in fact, or other fiduciary,* except for the estate, trust, or person of a member of the judge's family,* and then only if such service will not interfere with the proper performance of judicial duties.

(2)   A judge shall not serve as a fiduciary* if it is likely that the judge as a fiduciary* will be engaged in proceedings that would ordinarily come before the judge, or if the estate, trust, or minor or conservatee becomes engaged in contested proceedings in the court on which the judge serves or one under its appellate jurisdiction.

(3)   The same restrictions on financial activities that apply to a judge personally also apply to the judge while acting in a fiduciary* capacity.

ADVISORY COMMITTEE COMMENTARY

The Time for Compliance provision of this code (Canon 6F) postpones the time for compliance with certain provisions of this canon in some cases. The restrictions imposed by this canon may conflict with the judge's obligation as a fiduciary.* For example, a judge shall resign as trustee if detriment to the trust would result from divestiture of trust holdings the retention of which would place the judge in violation of Canon 4D(4).

F. Service as Arbitrator or Mediator

A judge shall not act as an arbitrator or mediator or otherwise perform judicial functions in a private capacity unless expressly authorized by law.*

ADVISORY COMMITTEE COMMENTARY

Canon 4F does not prohibit a judge from participating in arbitration, mediation, or settlement conferences performed as part of his or her judicial duties.

G. Practice of Law

A judge shall not practice law.

ADVISORY COMMITTEE COMMENTARY

This prohibition refers to the practice of law in a representative capacity and not in a pro se capacity. A judge may act for himself or *herself in all legal matters, including matters involving litigation and matters involving appearances before or other dealings with legislative and other governmental bodies. However, in so doing, a judge must not abuse the prestige of office to advance the interests of the judge or member of the judge's family.* See Canon 2B.*

This prohibition applies to subordinate judicial officers,* magistrates, special masters, and judges of the State Bar Court.

H. Compensation, and Reimbursement, and Honoraria

A judge may receive compensation and reimbursement of expenses as provided by law* for the extrajudicial activities permitted by this code, if the source of such payments does not give the appearance of influencing the judge's performance of judicial duties or otherwise give the appearance of impropriety.*

(1)   Compensation shall not exceed a reasonable amount nor shall it exceed what a person who is not a judge would receive for the same activity.

(2)   Expense reimbursement shall be limited to the actual cost of travel, food, lodging, and other costs reasonably incurred by the judge and, where appropriate to the occasion, by the judge's spouse or registered domestic partner* or guest. Any payment in excess of such an amount is compensation.

(3)   No judge shall accept any honorarium. "Honorarium" means any payment made in consideration for any speech given, article published, or attendance at any public or private conference, convention, meeting, social event, meal, or like gathering. "Honorarium" does not include earned income for personal services that are customarily provided in connection with the practice of a bona fide business, trade, or profession, such as teaching or writing for a publisher, and does not include fees or other things of value received pursuant to Penal Code section 94.5 for performance of a marriage. For purposes of this canon, "teaching" shall include presentations to impart educational information to lawyers in events qualifying for credit under Mandatory Continuing Legal Education, to students in bona fide educational institutions, and to associations or groups of judges.

ADVISORY COMMITTEE COMMENTARY

Judges should not accept compensation or reimbursement of expenses if acceptance would appear to a reasonable person to undermine the judge's integrity,* impartiality,* or independence.*

A judge must assure himself or herself that acceptance of reimbursement or fee waivers would not appear to a reasonable person to undermine the judge's independence,* integrity,* or impartiality.* The factors a judge should consider when deciding whether to accept reimbursement or a fee waiver for attendance at a particular activity include:

(a)   whether the sponsor is an accredited educational institution or bar association rather than a trade association or a for-profit entity;

(b) whether the funding comes largely from numerous contributors rather than from a single entity, and whether the funding is earmarked for programs with specific content;

(c) whether the content is related or unrelated to the subject matter of a pending* or impending* proceeding before the judge, or to matters that are likely to come before the judge;

(d) whether the activity is primarily educational rather than recreational, and whether the costs of the event are reasonable and comparable to those associated with similar events sponsored by the judiciary, bar associations, or similar groups;

(e) whether information concerning the activity and its funding sources is available upon inquiry;

(f) whether the sponsor or source of funding is generally associated with particular parties or interests currently appearing or likely to appear in the judge's court, thus possibly requiring disqualification of the judge;

(g) whether differing viewpoints are presented;

(h) whether a broad range of judicial and nonjudicial participants are invited; and

(i) whether the program is designed specifically for judges.

Judges should be aware of the statutory limitations on accepting gifts.*

CANON 5

A JUDGE OR CANDIDATE FOR JUDICIAL OFFICE* SHALL NOT ENGAGE IN POLITICAL OR CAMPAIGN ACTIVITY THAT IS INCONSISTENT WITH THE INDEPENDENCE*, INTEGRITY*, OR IMPARTIALITY* OF THE JUDICIARY

Judges and candidates for judicial office* are entitled to entertain their personal views on political questions. They are not required to surrender their rights or opinions as citizens. They shall, however, not engage in political activity that may create the appearance of political bias or impropriety.* Judicial independence,* impartiality,* and integrity* shall dictate the conduct of judges and candidates for judicial office.*

Judges and candidates for judicial office* shall comply with all applicable election, election campaign, and election campaign fundraising laws* and regulations.

A. Political Organizations*

Judges and candidates for judicial office* shall not

(1)   act as leaders or hold any office in a political organization;*

(2)   make speeches for a political organization* or candidate for nonjudicial office or publicly endorse or publicly oppose a candidate for nonjudicial office; or

(3)   personally solicit funds for a political organization* or nonjudicial candidate; or make contributions to a political party or political organization* or to a nonjudicial candidate in excess of $500 in any calendar year per political party or political organization* or candidate, or in excess of an aggregate of $1,000 in any calendar year for all political parties or political organizations* or nonjudicial candidates.

ADVISORY COMMITTEE COMMENTARY

The term "political activity" should not be construed so narrowly as to prevent private comment.

This provision does not prohibit a judge or a candidate for judicial office* from signing a petition to qualify a measure for the ballot, provided the judge does not use his or her official title.

In judicial elections, judges are neither required to shield themselves from campaign contributions nor are they prohibited from soliciting contributions from anyone, including attorneys. Nevertheless, there are necessary limits on judges facing election if the appearance of impropriety* is to be avoided. In soliciting campaign contributions or endorsements, a judge shall not use the prestige of judicial office in a manner that would reasonably be perceived as coercive. See Canons 1, 2, 2A, and 2B. Although it is improper for a judge to receive a gift* from an attorney subject to exceptions noted in Canon 4D(6), a judge's campaign may receive attorney contributions.

Although attendance at political gatherings is not prohibited, any such attendance should be restricted so that it would not constitute an express public endorsement of a nonjudicial candidate or a measure not affecting the law, the legal system, or the administration of justice* otherwise prohibited by this canon.

Subject to the monetary limitation herein to political contributions, a judge or a candidate for judicial office* may purchase tickets for political dinners or other similar dinner functions. Any admission price to such a political dinner or function in excess of the actual cost of the meal shall be considered a political contribution. The prohibition in Canon 5A(3) does not preclude judges from contributing to a campaign fund for distribution among judges who are candidates for reelection or retention, nor does it apply to contributions to any judge or candidate for judicial office.*

Under this canon, a judge may publicly endorse a candidate for judicial office.* Such endorsements are permitted because judicial officers have a special obligation to uphold the integrity,* impartiality,* and independence* of the judiciary and are in a unique position to *know the qualifications necessary to serve as a competent judicial officer.*

Although family members of the judge or candidate for judicial office* are not subject to the provisions of this code, a judge or candidate for judicial office* shall not avoid compliance with this code by making contributions through a spouse or registered domestic partner* or other family member.

B. Conduct During Judicial Campaigns and Appointment Process

(1)   A candidate for judicial office* or an applicant seeking appointment to judicial office shall not:

> (a)   make statements to the electorate or the appointing authority that commit the candidate or the applicant with respect to cases, controversies, or issues that are likely to come before the courts, or

> (b)   knowingly,* or with reckless disregard for the truth, misrepresent the identity, qualifications, present position, or any other fact concerning himself or herself or his or her opponent or other applicants.

(2)   A candidate for judicial office* shall review and approve the content of all campaign statements and materials produced by the candidate or his or her campaign committee before their dissemination. A candidate shall take appropriate corrective action if the candidate learns of any misrepresentations made in his or her campaign statements or materials. A candidate shall take reasonable measures to prevent any misrepresentations being made in his or her support by third parties. A candidate shall take reasonable measures to ensure that appropriate corrective action is taken if the candidate learns of any misrepresentations being made in his or her support by third parties.

(3)   Every candidate for judicial office* shall complete a judicial campaign ethics course approved by the Supreme Court no earlier than one year before or no later than 60 days after either the filing of a declaration of intention by the candidate, the formation of a campaign committee, or the receipt of any campaign contribution, whichever is earliest. This requirement does not apply to judges who are unopposed for election and will not appear on the ballot. This requirement also does not apply to appellate justices who have not formed a campaign committee.

ADVISORY COMMITTEE COMMENTARY

The purpose of Canon 5B is to preserve the integrity* of the appointive and elective process for judicial office and to ensure that the public has accurate information about candidates for judicial office.* Compliance with these provisions will enhance the integrity,* impartiality,* and independence* of the judiciary and better inform the public about qualifications of candidates for judicial office.*

This code does not contain the "announce clause" that was the subject of the United States Supreme Court's decision in Republican Party of Minnesota v. White (2002) 536 U.S. 765. That opinion did not address the "commit clause," which is contained in Canon 5B(1)(a). The phrase "appear to commit" has been deleted because, although candidates for judicial office* cannot promise to take a particular position on cases, controversies, or issues prior to taking the bench and presiding over individual cases, the phrase may have been overinclusive.

Canon 5B(1)(b) prohibits making knowing misrepresentations, including false or misleading statements, during an election campaign because doing so would violate Canons 1 and 2A, and may violate other canons.

Candidates for judicial office* must disclose campaign contributions in accordance with Canon 3E(2)(b).

The time limit for completing a judicial campaign ethics course in Canon 5B(3) is triggered by the earliest of either the filing of a declaration of intention, formation of a campaign committee, or receipt of any campaign contribution. A financial contribution by a candidate for judicial office* to his or her own campaign constitutes receipt of a campaign contribution.

C. Speaking at Political Gatherings

Candidates for judicial office* may speak to political gatherings only on their own behalf or on behalf of another candidate for judicial office.*

D. Measures to Improve the Law

A judge or candidate for judicial office* may engage in activity in relation to measures concerning improvement of the law, the legal system, or the administration of justice,* only if the conduct is consistent with this code.

ADVISORY COMMITTEE COMMENTARY

When deciding whether to engage in activity relating to measures concerning the law, the legal system, or the administration of justice,* such as commenting publicly on ballot measures, a judge must consider whether the conduct would violate any other provisions of this code. See explanation of "law, the legal system, or the administration of justice" in the terminology section.

CANON 6

COMPLIANCE WITH THE CODE OF JUDICIAL ETHICS

A. Judges

Anyone who is an officer of the state judicial system and who performs judicial functions, including, but not limited to, a subordinate judicial officer,* magistrate, court-appointed arbitrator, judge of the State Bar Court, temporary judge,* and special master, is a judge within the meaning of this code. All judges shall comply with this code except as provided below.

ADVISORY COMMITTEE COMMENTARY

For the purposes of this canon, if a retired judge is serving in the Assigned Judges Program, the judge is considered to "perform judicial functions." Because retired judges who are privately retained may perform judicial functions, their conduct while performing those functions should be guided by this code.

B. Retired Judge Serving in the Assigned Judges Program

A retired judge who has filed an application to serve on assignment, meets the eligibility requirements set by the Chief Justice for service, and has received an acknowledgment of participation in the Assigned Judges Program shall comply with all provisions of this code, except for the following:

> 4C(2)—Appointment to governmental positions
>
> 4E—Fiduciary* activities

C. Retired Judge as Arbitrator or Mediator

A retired judge serving in the Assigned Judges Program is not required to comply with Canon 4F of this code relating to serving as an arbitrator or mediator, or performing judicial functions in a private capacity, except as otherwise provided in the Standards and Guidelines for Judicial Assignments promulgated by the Chief Justice.

ADVISORY COMMITTEE COMMENTARY

In California, article VI, section 6 of the California Constitution provides that a "retired judge who consents may be assigned to any court" by the Chief Justice. Retired judges who are serving in the Assigned Judges Program pursuant to the above provision are bound by Canon 6B, including the requirement of Canon 4G barring the practice of law. Other provisions of California law,* and standards and guidelines for eligibility and service set by the Chief Justice, further define the limitations on who may serve on assignment.

D. Temporary Judge,* Referee, or Court-Appointed Arbitrator[2]

A temporary judge,* a person serving as a referee pursuant to Code of Civil Procedure section 638 or 639, or a court-appointed arbitrator shall comply only with the following code provisions:

(1)   A temporary judge,* referee, or court-appointed arbitrator shall comply with Canons 1 [integrity* and independence* of the judiciary], 2A [promoting public confidence], 3B(3) [order and decorum], 3B(4) [patient, dignified, and courteous treatment], 3B(6) [require* lawyers to refrain from manifestations of any form of bias or prejudice], 3D(1) [action regarding misconduct by another judge], and 3D(2) [action regarding misconduct by a lawyer], when the temporary judge,* referee, or court-appointed arbitrator is actually presiding

---

[2] Reference should be made to relevant commentary to analogous or individual canons cited or described in this canon and appearing elsewhere in this code.

in a proceeding or communicating with the parties, counsel, or staff or court personnel while serving in the capacity of a temporary judge,* referee, or court-appointed arbitrator in the case.

(2)   A temporary judge,* referee, or court-appointed arbitrator shall, from the time of notice and acceptance of appointment until termination of the appointment:

(a)   Comply with Canons 2B(1) [not allow family or other relationships to influence judicial conduct], 3B(1) [hear and decide all matters unless disqualified], 3B(2) [be faithful to and maintain competence in the law*], 3B(5) [perform judicial duties without bias or prejudice], 3B(7) [accord full right to be heard to those entitled; avoid ex parte communications, except as specified], 3B(8) [dispose of matters fairly and promptly], 3B(12) [remain impartial* and not engage in coercive conduct during efforts to resolve disputes], 3C(1) [discharge administrative responsibilities without bias and with competence and cooperatively], 3C(3) [require* staff and court personnel to observe standards of conduct and refrain from bias and prejudice], and 3C(5) [make only fair, necessary, and appropriate appointments];

(b)   Not personally solicit memberships or donations for religious, service,* educational, civic, or charitable organizations from the parties and lawyers appearing before the temporary judge,* referee, or court-appointed arbitrator;

(c)   Under no circumstance accept a gift,* bequest, or favor if the donor is a party, person, or entity whose interests are reasonably likely to come before the temporary judge,* referee, or court-appointed arbitrator. A temporary judge,* referee, or court-appointed arbitrator shall discourage members of the judge's family residing in the judge's household* from accepting benefits from parties who are reasonably likely to come before the temporary judge,* referee, or court- appointed arbitrator.

(3)   A temporary judge* shall, from the time of notice and acceptance of appointment until termination of the appointment, disqualify himself or herself in any proceeding as follows:

(a)   A temporary judge*—other than a temporary judge solely conducting settlement conferences—is disqualified to serve in a proceeding if any one or more of the following is true:

(i)   the temporary judge* has personal knowledge* (as defined in Code of Civil Procedure section 170.1, subdivision (a)(1)) of disputed evidentiary facts concerning the proceeding;

(ii) the temporary judge* has served as a lawyer (as defined in Code of Civil Procedure section 170.1, subdivision (a)(2)) in the proceeding;

(iii) the temporary judge,* within the past five years, has given legal advice to, or served as a lawyer (as defined in Code of Civil

Procedure section 170.1, subdivision (a)(2), except that this provision requires disqualification if the temporary judge* represented a party in the past five years rather than the two-year period specified in section 170.1, subdivision (a)(2)) for a party in the present proceeding;

(iv) the temporary judge* has a financial interest (as defined in Code of Civil Procedure sections 170.1, subdivision (a)(3) and 170.5) in the subject matter in the proceeding or in a party to the proceeding;

(v) the temporary judge,* or the spouse or registered domestic partner* of the temporary judge,* or a person within the third degree of relationship* to either of them, or the spouse or registered domestic partner* of such a person is a party to the proceeding or is an officer, director, or trustee of a party;

(vi) a lawyer or a spouse or registered domestic partner* of a lawyer in the proceeding is the spouse, former spouse, registered domestic partner,* former registered domestic partner,* child, sibling, or parent of the temporary judge* or the temporary judge's spouse or registered domestic partner,* or if such a person is associated in the private practice of law with a lawyer in the proceeding; or

(vii) for any reason:

(A)   the temporary judge* believes his or her recusal would further the interests of justice;

(B)   the temporary judge* believes there is a substantial doubt as to his or her capacity to be impartial;* or

(C)   a person aware of the facts might reasonably entertain a doubt that the temporary judge* would be able to be impartial.* Bias or prejudice toward an attorney in the proceeding may be grounds for disqualification.

(viii)   the temporary judge* has received a campaign contribution of $1,500 or more from a party or lawyer in a matter that is before the court and the contribution was received in anticipation of an upcoming election.

ADVISORY COMMITTEE COMMENTARY

The application of Canon 6D(3)(a)(iii), providing that a temporary judge is disqualified if he or she has given legal advice or served as a lawyer for a party to the proceeding in the past five years, may depend on the type of assignment and the amount of time available to investigate whether the temporary judge* has previously represented a party. If time permits, the temporary judge* must conduct such an investigation. Thus, if a temporary judge* is privately compensated by the parties or is presiding over a particular matter known* in advance of the hearing, the temporary judge* is presumed to have adequate* *time to investigate. If, however, a temporary judge* is assigned to a high volume calendar, such as traffic or small claims, and has not been provided with the names of the parties prior to the assignment, the temporary judge* may rely on his or her memory to determine whether he or she has previously represented a party.*

(b) A temporary judge* before whom a proceeding was tried or heard is disqualified from participating in any appellate review of that proceeding.

(c) If the temporary judge* has a current arrangement concerning prospective employment or other compensated service as a dispute resolution neutral or is participating in, or, within the last two years has participated in, discussions regarding prospective employment or service as a dispute resolution neutral, or has been engaged in such employment or service, and any of the following applies:

(i) The arrangement or current employment is, or the prior employment or discussion was, with a party to the proceeding.

(ii) The temporary judge* directs the parties to participate in an alternative dispute resolution process in which the dispute resolution neutral will be an individual or entity with whom the temporary judge* has the arrangement, is currently employed or serves, has previously been employed or served, or is discussing or has discussed the employment or service.

(iii) The temporary judge* will select a dispute resolution neutral or entity to conduct an alternative dispute resolution process in the matter before the temporary judge,* and among those available for selection is an individual or entity with whom the temporary judge* has the arrangement, is currently employed or serves, has previously been employed or served, or is discussing or has discussed the employment or service.

For the purposes of canon 6D(3)(c), the definitions of "participating in discussions," "has participated in discussions," "party," and "dispute resolution neutral" are set forth in Code of Civil Procedure section 170.1, subdivision (a)(8), except that the words "temporary judge" shall be substituted for the word "judge" in such definitions.[3]

---

[3] **Editors' Note**: Cal. Civ. Proc. Code § 170.1(a)(8)(B)(i) provides:

"Participating in discussions" or "has participated in discussion" means that the judge solicited or otherwise indicated an interest in accepting or negotiating possible employment or service as an alternative dispute resolution neutral, or responded to an unsolicited statement regarding, or an offer of, that employment or service by expressing an interest in that employment or service, making an inquiry regarding the employment or service, or encouraging the person making the statement or offer to provide additional information about that possible employment or service. If a judge's response to an unsolicited statement regarding,

(d) A lawyer is disqualified from serving as a temporary judge* in a family law or unlawful detainer proceeding if in the same type of proceeding:

(i) the lawyer holds himself or herself out to the public as representing exclusively one side; or

(ii) the lawyer represents one side in 90 percent or more of the cases in which he or she appears.

ADVISORY COMMITTEE COMMENTARY

Under Canon 6D(3)(d), "one side" means a category of persons such as landlords, tenants, or litigants exclusively of one gender.

(4) After a temporary judge* who has determined himself or herself to be disqualified from serving under Canon 6D(3)(a)–(d) has disclosed the basis for his or her disqualification on the record, the parties and their lawyers may agree to waive the disqualification and the temporary judge* may accept the waiver. The temporary judge* shall not seek to induce a waiver and shall avoid any effort to discover which lawyers or parties favored or opposed a waiver.

ADVISORY COMMITTEE COMMENTARY

Provisions addressing waiver of mandatory disqualifications or limitations, late discovery of grounds for disqualification or limitation, notification of the court when a disqualification or limitation applies, and requests for disqualification by the parties are located in rule 2.818 of the California Rules of Court. Rule 2.818 states that the waiver must be in writing, must recite the basis for the disqualification or limitation, and must state that it was knowingly* made. It also states that the waiver is effective only when signed by all parties and their attorneys and filed in the record.

(5) A temporary judge,* referee, or court-appointed arbitrator shall, from the time of notice and acceptance of appointment until termination of the appointment:

(a) In all proceedings, disclose in writing or on the record information as required by law,* or information that is reasonably relevant to the

---

a question about, or offer of, prospective employment or other compensated service as a dispute resolution neutral is limited to responding negatively, declining the offer, or declining to discuss that employment or service, that response does not constitute participating in discussions.

Cal. Civ. Proc. Code § 170.1(a)(8)(B)(iii) provides:

"Dispute resolution neutral" means an arbitrator, mediator, temporary judge appointed under Section 21 of Article VI of the California Constitution, referee appointed under Section 638 or 639, special master, neutral evaluator, settlement officer, or settlement facilitator.

question of disqualification under Canon 6D(3), including personal or professional relationships known* to the temporary judge,* referee, or court-appointed arbitrator, that he or she or his or her law firm has had with a party, lawyer, or law firm in the current proceeding, even though the temporary judge,* referee, or court-appointed arbitrator concludes that there is no actual basis for disqualification; and

(b)   In all proceedings, disclose in writing or on the record membership of the temporary judge,* referee, or court-appointed arbitrator, in any organization that practices invidious discrimination on the basis of race, sex, gender, religion, national origin, ethnicity, or sexual orientation, except for membership in a religious organization.

(6)   A temporary judge,* referee, or court-appointed arbitrator, from the time of notice and acceptance of appointment until the case is no longer pending in any court, shall not make any public comment about a pending* or impending* proceeding in which the temporary judge,* referee, or court-appointed arbitrator has been engaged, and shall not make any nonpublic comment that might substantially interfere with such proceeding. The temporary judge,* referee, or court-appointed arbitrator shall require* similar abstention on the part of staff and court personnel subject to his or her control. This canon does not prohibit the following:

(a)   Statements made in the course of the official duties of the temporary judge,* referee, or court-appointed arbitrator; and

(b)   Explanations about the procedures of the court.

(7)   From the time of appointment and continuing for two years after the case is no longer pending* in any court, a temporary judge,* referee, or court-appointed arbitrator shall under no circumstances accept a gift,* bequest, or favor from a party, person, or entity whose interests have come before the temporary judge,* referee, or court-appointed arbitrator in the matter. The temporary judge,* referee, or court-appointed arbitrator shall discourage family members residing in the household of the temporary judge,* referee, or court-appointed arbitrator from accepting any benefits from such parties, persons or entities during the time period stated in this subdivision. The demand for or receipt by a temporary judge,* referee, or court-appointed arbitrator of a fee for his or her services rendered or to be rendered shall not be a violation of this canon.

(8)   A temporary judge,* referee, or court-appointed arbitrator shall, from time of notice and acceptance of appointment and continuing indefinitely after the termination of the appointment:

(a)   Comply with Canon 3B(11) [no disclosure of nonpublic information* acquired in a judicial capacity] (except as required by law*);

(b)   Not commend or criticize jurors sitting in a proceeding before the temporary judge,* referee, or court-appointed arbitrator for their verdict other than in a court order or opinion in such proceeding, but may express appreciation to jurors for their service to the judicial system and the community; and

(c)   Not lend the prestige of judicial office to advance his, her, or another person's pecuniary or personal interests and not use his or her judicial title in any written communication intended to advance his, her, or another person's pecuniary or personal interests, except to show his, her, or another person's qualifications.

(9)(a)   A temporary judge* appointed under rule 2.810 of the California Rules of Court, from the time of appointment and continuing indefinitely after the termination of the appointment, shall not use his or her title or service as a temporary judge* (1) as a description of the lawyer's current or former principal profession, vocation, or occupation on a ballot designation for judicial or other elected office, (2) in an advertisement about the lawyer's law firm or business, or (3) on a letterhead, business card, or other document that is distributed to the public identifying the lawyer or the lawyer's law firm.

(b)   This canon does not prohibit a temporary judge* appointed under rule 2.810 of the California Rules of Court from using his or her title or service as a temporary judge* on an application to serve as a temporary judge,* including an application in other courts, on an application for employment or for an appointment to a judicial position, on an individual resume or a descriptive statement submitted in connection with an application for employment or for appointment or election to a judicial position, or in response to a request for information about the public service in which the lawyer has engaged.

(10)   A temporary judge,* referee, or court-appointed arbitrator shall comply with Canon 6D(2) until the appointment has been terminated formally or until there is no reasonable probability that the temporary judge,* referee, or court-appointed arbitrator will further participate in the matter. A rebuttable presumption that the appointment has been formally terminated shall arise if, within one year from the appointment or from the date of the last hearing scheduled in the matter, whichever is later, neither the appointing court nor counsel for any party in the matter has informed the temporary judge,* referee, or court-appointed arbitrator that the appointment remains in effect.

(11)   A lawyer who has been a temporary judge,* referee, or court-appointed arbitrator in a matter shall not accept any representation relating to the matter without the informed written consent of all parties.

(12)   When by reason of serving as a temporary judge,* referee, or court-appointed arbitrator in a matter, he or she has received confidential information from a party, the person shall not, without the informed written consent of the party, accept employment in another matter in which the confidential information is material.

ADVISORY COMMITTEE COMMENTARY

Any exceptions to the canons do not excuse a judicial officer's separate statutory duty to disclose information that may result in the judicial officer's recusal or disqualification.

E. Judicial Candidate

A candidate for judicial office* shall comply with the provisions of Canon 5.

F. Time for Compliance

A person to whom this code becomes applicable shall comply immediately with all provisions of this code except Canons 4D(4) and 4E and shall comply with these canons as soon as reasonably possible and shall do so in any event within a period of one year.

ADVISORY COMMITTEE COMMENTARY

If serving as a fiduciary* when selected as a judge, a new judge may, notwithstanding the prohibitions in Canon 4E, continue to serve as fiduciary* but only for that period of time necessary to avoid adverse consequences to the beneficiary of the fiduciary* relationship and in no event longer than one year.

G. (Canon 6G repealed effective June 1, 2005; adopted December 30, 2002.)

H. Judges on Leave Running for Other Public Office

A judge who is on leave while running for other public office pursuant to article VI, section 17 of the California Constitution shall comply with all provisions of this code, except for the following, insofar as the conduct relates to the campaign for public office for which the judge is on leave:

2B(2)—Lending the prestige of judicial office to advance the judge's personal interest

4C(1)—Appearing at public hearings

5—Engaging in political activity (including soliciting and accepting campaign contributions for the other public office).

ADVISORY COMMITTEE COMMENTARY

These exceptions are applicable only during the time the judge is on leave while running for other public office. All of the provisions of this code will become applicable at the time a judge resumes his or her position as a judge. Conduct during elections for judicial office is governed by Canon 5.

PART VI

SEC FINAL STANDARDS OF PROFESSIONAL CONDUCT

SEC Final Rules Issued January 29, 2003 (effective August 5, 2003)

PART 205 - STANDARDS OF PROFESSIONAL CONDUCT FOR ATTORNEYS APPEARING AND PRACTICING BEFORE THE COMMISSION IN THE REPRESENTATION OF AN ISSUER*

Sec.

205.1   Purpose and scope.

205.2   Definitions.

205.3   Issuer as client.

205.4   Responsibilities of supervisory attorneys.

205.5   Responsibilities of a subordinate attorney.

205.6   Sanctions and discipline.

205.7   No private right of action.

Authority: 15 U.S.C. 77s, 78d-3, 78w, 80a-37, 80a-38, 80b-11, 7202, 7245, and 7262.

§205.1   Purpose and scope.

This part sets forth minimum standards of professional conduct for attorneys appearing and practicing before the Commission in the representation of an issuer. These standards supplement applicable standards of any jurisdiction where an attorney is admitted or practices and are not intended to limit the

---

* Rules authorized by 15 USC 7245 (section 307 of the Sarbanes-Oxley Act), which states:

Not later than 180 days after the date of enactment of this Act, the Commission shall issue rules, in the public interest and for the protection of investors, setting forth minimum standards of professional conduct for attorneys appearing and practicing before the Commission in any way in the representation of issuers, including a rule —

(1)   requiring an attorney to report evidence of a material violation of securities law or breach of fiduciary duty or similar violation by the company or any agent thereof, to the chief legal counsel or the chief executive officer of the company (or the equivalent thereof); and

(2)   if the counsel or officer does not appropriately respond to the evidence (adopting, as necessary, appropriate remedial measures or sanctions with the respect to the violation), requiring the attorney to report the evidence to the audit committee of the board of directors of the issuer or to another committee of the board of directors comprised solely of directors not employed directly or indirectly by the issuer, or to the board of directors.

ability of any jurisdiction to impose additional obligations on an attorney not inconsistent with the application of this part. Where the standards of a state or other United States jurisdiction where an attorney is admitted or practices conflict with this part, this part shall govern.

§205.2   Definitions.

For purposes of this part, the following definitions apply:

(a) Appearing and practicing before the Commission:

(1) Means:

(i) Transacting any business with the Commission, including communications in any form;

(ii) Representing an issuer in a Commission administrative proceeding or in connection with any Commission investigation, inquiry, information request, or subpoena;

(iii)Providing advice in respect of the United States securities laws or the Commission's rules or regulations thereunder regarding any document that the attorney has notice will be filed with or submitted to, or incorporated into any document that will be filed with or submitted to, the Commission, including the provision of such advice in the context of preparing, or participating in the preparation of, any such document; or

(iv) Advising an issuer as to whether information or a statement, opinion, or other writing is required under the United States securities laws or the Commission's rules or regulations thereunder to be filed with or submitted to, or incorporated into any document that will be filed with or submitted to, the Commission; but

(2) Does not include an attorney who:

(i) Conducts the activities in paragraphs (a)(1)(i) through (a)(1)(iv) of this section other than in the context of providing legal services to an issuer with whom the attorney has an attorney-client relationship; or

(ii) Is a non-appearing foreign attorney.

(b) Appropriate response means a response to an attorney regarding reported evidence of a material violation as a result of which the attorney reasonably believes:

(1) That no material violation, as defined in paragraph (i) of this section, has occurred, is ongoing, or is about to occur;

(2) That the issuer has, as necessary, adopted appropriate remedial measures, including appropriate steps or sanctions to stop any material violations that are ongoing, to prevent any material violation that has yet to occur, and to remedy or otherwise appropriately address any material violation that has already occurred and to minimize the likelihood of its recurrence; or

(3) That the issuer, with the consent of the issuer's board of directors, a committee thereof to whom a report could be made pursuant to §205.3(b)(3), or

a qualified legal compliance committee, has retained or directed an attorney to review the reported evidence of a material violation and either:

(i) Has substantially implemented any remedial recommendations made by such attorney after a reasonable investigation and evaluation of the reported evidence; or

(ii) Has been advised that such attorney may, consistent with his or her professional obligations, assert a colorable defense on behalf of the issuer (or the issuer's officer, director, employee, or agent, as the case may be) in any investigation or judicial or administrative proceeding relating to the reported evidence of a material violation.

(c) Attorney means any person who is admitted, licensed, or otherwise qualified to practice law in any jurisdiction, domestic or foreign, or who holds himself or herself out as admitted, licensed, or otherwise qualified to practice law.

(d) Breach of fiduciary duty refers to any breach of fiduciary or similar duty to the issuer recognized under an applicable federal or state statute or at common law, including but not limited to misfeasance, nonfeasance, abdication of duty, abuse of trust, and approval of unlawful transactions.

(e) Evidence of a material violation means credible evidence, based upon which it would be unreasonable, under the circumstances, for a prudent and competent attorney not to conclude that it is reasonably likely that a material violation has occurred, is ongoing, or is about to occur.

(f) Foreign government issuer means a foreign issuer as defined in 17 CFR 230.405 eligible to register securities on Schedule B of the Securities Act of 1933 (15 U.S.C. 77a et seq., Schedule B).

(g) In the representation of an issuer means providing legal services as an attorney for an issuer, regardless of whether the attorney is employed or retained by the issuer.

(h) Issuer means an issuer (as defined in section 3 of the Securities Exchange Act of 1934 (15 U.S.C. 78c)), the securities of which are registered under section 12 of that Act (15 U.S.C. 78l), or that is required to file reports under section 15(d) of that Act (15 U.S.C. 78o(d)), or that files or has filed a registration statement that has not yet become effective under the Securities Act of 1933 (15 U.S.C. 77a et seq.), and that it has not withdrawn, but does not include a foreign government issuer. For purposes of paragraphs (a) and (g) of this section, the term "issuer" includes any person controlled by an issuer, where an attorney provides legal services to such person on behalf of, or at the behest, or for the benefit of the issuer, regardless of whether the attorney is employed or retained by the issuer.

(i) Material violation means a material violation of an applicable United States federal or state securities law, a material breach of fiduciary duty arising under United States federal or state law, or a similar material violation of any United States federal or state law.

(j) Non-appearing foreign attorney means an attorney:

(1) Who is admitted to practice law in a jurisdiction outside the United States;

(2) Who does not hold himself or herself out as practicing, and does not give legal advice regarding, United States federal or state securities or other laws (except as provided in paragraph (j)(3)(ii) of this section); and

(3) Who:

(i) Conducts activities that would constitute appearing and practicing before the Commission only incidentally to, and in the ordinary course of, the practice of law in a jurisdiction outside the United States; or

(ii) Is appearing and practicing before the Commission only in consultation with counsel, other than a non-appearing foreign attorney, admitted or licensed to practice in a state or other United States jurisdiction.

(k) Qualified legal compliance committee means a committee of an issuer (which also may be an audit or other committee of the issuer) that:

(1) Consists of at least one member of the issuer's audit committee (or, if the issuer has no audit committee, one member from an equivalent committee of independent directors) and two or more members of the issuer's board of directors who are not employed, directly or indirectly, by the issuer and who are not, in the case of a registered investment company, "interested persons" as defined in section 2(a)(19) of the Investment Company Act of 1940 (15 U.S.C. 80a-2(a)(19));

(2) Has adopted written procedures for the confidential receipt, retention, and consideration of any report of evidence of a material violation under §205.3;

(3) Has been duly established by the issuer's board of directors, with the authority and responsibility:

(i) To inform the issuer's chief legal officer and chief executive officer (or the equivalents thereof) of any report of evidence of a material violation (except in the circumstances described in §205.3(b)(4));

(ii) To determine whether an investigation is necessary regarding any report of evidence of a material violation by the issuer, its officers, directors, employees or agents and, if it determines an investigation is necessary or appropriate, to:

(A) Notify the audit committee or the full board of directors;

(B) Initiate an investigation, which may be conducted either by the chief legal officer (or the equivalent thereof) or by outside attorneys; and

(C) Retain such additional expert personnel as the committee deems necessary; and

(iii)At the conclusion of any such investigation, to:

(A) Recommend, by majority vote, that the issuer implement an appropriate response to evidence of a material violation; and

(B) Inform the chief legal officer and the chief executive officer (or the equivalents thereof) and the board of directors of the results of any such investigation under this section and the appropriate remedial measures to be adopted; and

(4) Has the authority and responsibility, acting by majority vote, to take all other appropriate action, including the authority to notify the Commission in the event that the issuer fails in any material respect to implement an appropriate response that the qualified legal compliance committee has recommended the issuer to take.

(l) Reasonable or reasonably denotes, with respect to the actions of an attorney, conduct that would not be unreasonable for a prudent and competent attorney.

(m) Reasonably believes means that an attorney believes the matter in question and that the circumstances are such that the belief is not unreasonable.

(n) Report means to make known to directly, either in person, by telephone, by e-mail, electronically, or in writing.

§205.3   Issuer as client.

(a) <u>Representing an issuer</u>. An attorney appearing and practicing before the Commission in the representation of an issuer owes his or her professional and ethical duties to the issuer as an organization. That the attorney may work with and advise the issuer's officers, directors, or employees in the course of representing the issuer does not make such individuals the attorney's clients.

(b) <u>Duty to report evidence of a material violation</u>. (1) If an attorney, appearing and practicing before the Commission in the representation of an issuer, becomes aware of evidence of a material violation by the issuer or by any officer, director, employee, or agent of the issuer, the attorney shall report such evidence to the issuer's chief legal officer (or the equivalent thereof) or to both the issuer's chief legal officer and its chief executive officer (or the equivalents thereof) forthwith. By communicating such information to the issuer's officers or directors, an attorney does not reveal client confidences or secrets or privileged or otherwise protected information related to the attorney's representation of an issuer.

(2) The chief legal officer (or the equivalent thereof) shall cause such inquiry into the evidence of a material violation as he or she reasonably believes is appropriate to determine whether the material violation described in the report has occurred, is ongoing, or is about to occur. If the chief legal officer (or the equivalent thereof) determines no material violation has occurred, is ongoing, or is about to occur, he or she shall notify the reporting attorney and advise the reporting attorney of the basis for such determination. Unless the chief legal officer (or the equivalent thereof) reasonably believes that no material violation has occurred, is ongoing, or is about to occur, he or she shall take all reasonable steps to cause the issuer to adopt an appropriate response, and shall advise the reporting attorney thereof. In lieu of causing an inquiry under this paragraph (b), a chief legal officer (or the equivalent thereof) may refer a report of evidence of a material violation to a qualified legal compliance committee under paragraph (c)(2) of this section if the issuer has duly

established a qualified legal compliance committee prior to the report of evidence of a material violation.

(3) Unless an attorney who has made a report under paragraph (b)(1) of this section reasonably believes that the chief legal officer or the chief executive officer of the issuer (or the equivalent thereof) has provided an appropriate response within a reasonable time, the attorney shall report the evidence of a material violation to:

(i) The audit committee of the issuer's board of directors;

(ii) Another committee of the issuer's board of directors consisting solely of directors who are not employed, directly or indirectly, by the issuer and are not, in the case of a registered investment company, "interested persons" as defined in section 2(a)(19) of the Investment Company Act of 1940 (15 U.S.C. 80a-2(a) (19)) (if the issuer's board of directors has no audit committee); or

(iii) The issuer's board of directors (if the issuer's board of directors has no committee consisting solely of directors who are not employed, directly or indirectly, by the issuer and are not, in the case of a registered investment company, "interested persons" as defined in section 2(a)(19) of the Investment Company Act of 1940 (15 U.S.C. 80a-2(a)(19))).

(4) If an attorney reasonably believes that it would be futile to report evidence of a material violation to the issuer's chief legal officer and chief executive officer (or the equivalents thereof) under paragraph (b)(1) of this section, the attorney may report such evidence as provided under paragraph (b)(3) of this section.

(5) An attorney retained or directed by an issuer to investigate evidence of a material violation reported under paragraph (b)(1), (b)(3), or (b)(4) of this section shall be deemed to be appearing and practicing before the Commission. Directing or retaining an attorney to investigate reported evidence of a material violation does not relieve an officer or director of the issuer to whom such evidence has been reported under paragraph (b)(1), (b)(3), or (b)(4) of this section from a duty to respond to the reporting attorney.

(6) An attorney shall not have any obligation to report evidence of a material violation under this paragraph (b) if:

(i) The attorney was retained or directed by the issuer's chief legal officer (or the equivalent thereof) to investigate such evidence of a material violation and:

(A) The attorney reports the results of such investigation to the chief legal officer (or the equivalent thereof); and

(B) Except where the attorney and the chief legal officer (or the equivalent thereof) each reasonably believes that no material violation has occurred, is ongoing, or is about to occur, the chief legal officer (or the equivalent thereof) reports the results of the investigation to the issuer's board of directors, a committee thereof to whom a report could be made pursuant to paragraph (b) (3) of this section, or a qualified legal compliance committee; or

(ii) The attorney was retained or directed by the chief legal officer (or the equivalent thereof) to assert, consistent with his or her professional obligations, a colorable defense on behalf of the issuer (or the issuer's officer, director, employee, or agent, as the case may be) in any investigation or judicial or administrative proceeding relating to such evidence of a material violation, and the chief legal officer (or the equivalent thereof) provides reasonable and timely reports on the progress and outcome of such proceeding to the issuer's board of directors, a committee thereof to whom a report could be made pursuant to paragraph (b)(3) of this section, or a qualified legal compliance committee.

(7) An attorney shall not have any obligation to report evidence of a material violation under this paragraph (b) if such attorney was retained or directed by a qualified legal compliance committee:

(i) To investigate such evidence of a material violation; or

(ii) To assert, consistent with his or her professional obligations, a colorable defense on behalf of the issuer (or the issuer's officer, director, employee, or agent, as the case may be) in any investigation or judicial or administrative proceeding relating to such evidence of a material violation.

(8) An attorney who receives what he or she reasonably believes is an appropriate and timely response to a report he or she has made pursuant to paragraph (b)(1), (b)(3), or (b)(4) of this section need do nothing more under this section with respect to his or her report.

(9) An attorney who does not reasonably believe that the issuer has made an appropriate response within a reasonable time to the report or reports made pursuant to paragraph (b)(1), (b)(3), or (b)(4) of this section shall explain his or her reasons therefor to the chief legal officer (or the equivalent thereof), the chief executive officer (or the equivalent thereof), and directors to whom the attorney reported the evidence of a material violation pursuant to paragraph (b)(1), (b)(3), or (b)(4) of this section.

(10) An attorney formerly employed or retained by an issuer who has reported evidence of a material violation under this part and reasonably believes that he or she has been discharged for so doing may notify the issuer's board of directors or any committee thereof that he or she believes that he or she has been discharged for reporting evidence of a material violation under this section.

(c) Alternative reporting procedures for attorneys retained or employed by an issuer that has established a qualified legal compliance committee. (1) If an attorney, appearing and practicing before the Commission in the representation of an issuer, becomes aware of evidence of a material violation by the issuer or by any officer, director, employee, or agent of the issuer, the attorney may, as an alternative to the reporting requirements of paragraph (b) of this section, report such evidence to a qualified legal compliance committee, if the issuer has previously formed such a committee. An attorney who reports evidence of a material violation to such a qualified legal compliance committee has satisfied his or her obligation to report such evidence and is not required to assess the issuer's response to the reported evidence of a material violation.

(2) A chief legal officer (or the equivalent thereof) may refer a report of evidence of a material violation to a previously established qualifi ed legal compliance committee in lieu of causing an inquiry to be conducted under paragraph (b)(2) of this section. The chief legal officer (or the equivalent thereof) shall inform the reporting attorney that the report has been referred to a qualified legal compliance committee. Thereafter, pursuant to the requirements under §205.2(k), the qualified legal compliance committee shall be responsible for responding to the evidence of a material violation reported to it under this paragraph (c).

(d) <u>Issuer confidences</u>. (1) Any report under this section (or the contemporaneous record thereof) or any response thereto (or the contemporaneous record thereof) may be used by an attorney in connection with any investigation, proceeding, or litigation in which the attorney's compliance with this part is in issue.

(2) An attorney appearing and practicing before the Commission in the representation of an issuer may reveal to the Commission, without the issuer's consent, confidential information related to the representation to the extent the attorney reasonably believes necessary:

(i) To prevent the issuer from committing a material violation that is likely to cause substantial injury to the financial interest or property of the issuer or investors;

(ii) To prevent the issuer, in a Commission investigation or administrative proceeding from committing perjury, proscribed in 18 U.S.C. 1621; suborning perjury, proscribed in 18 U.S.C. 1622; or committing any act proscribed in 18 U.S.C. 1001 that is likely to perpetrate a fraud upon the Commission; or

(iii) To rectify the consequences of a material violation by the issuer that caused, or may cause, substantial injury to the financial interest or property of the issuer or investors in the furtherance of which the attorney's services were used.

§205.4   Responsibilities of supervisory attorneys.

(a) An attorney supervising or directing another attorney who is appearing and practicing before the Commission in the representation of an issuer is a supervisory attorney. An issuer's chief legal officer (or the equivalent thereof) is a supervisory attorney under this section.

(b) A supervisory attorney shall make reasonable efforts to ensure that a subordinate attorney, as defined in §205.5(a), that he or she supervises or directs conforms to this part. To the extent a subordinate attorney appears and practices before the Commission in the representation of an issuer, that subordinate attorney's supervisory attorneys also appear and practice before the Commission.

(c) A supervisory attorney is responsible for complying with the reporting requirements in §205.3 when a subordinate attorney has reported to the supervisory attorney evidence of a material violation.

(d) A supervisory attorney who has received a report of evidence of a material violation from a subordinate attorney under §205.3 may report such evidence to the issuer's qualified legal compliance committee if the issuer has duly formed such a committee.

§205.5   Responsibilities of a subordinate attorney.

(a) An attorney who appears and practices before the Commission in the representation of an issuer on a matter under the supervision or direction of another attorney (other than under the direct supervision or direction of the issuer's chief legal officer (or the equivalent thereof)) is a subordinate attorney.

(b) A subordinate attorney shall comply with this part notwithstanding that the subordinate attorney acted at the direction of or under the supervision of another person.

(c) A subordinate attorney complies with §205.3 if the subordinate attorney reports to his or her supervising attorney under §205.3(b) evidence of a material violation of which the subordinate attorney has become aware in appearing and practicing before the Commission.

(d) A subordinate attorney may take the steps permitted or required by §205.3(b) or (c) if the subordinate attorney reasonably believes that a supervisory attorney to whom he or she has reported evidence of a material violation under §205.3(b) has failed to comply with §205.3.

§205.6   Sanctions and discipline.

(a) A violation of this part by any attorney appearing and practicing before the Commission in the representation of an issuer shall subject such attorney to the civil penalties and remedies for a violation of the federal securities laws available to the Commission in an action brought by the Commission thereunder.

(b) An attorney appearing and practicing before the Commission who violates any provision of this part is subject to the disciplinary authority of the Commission, regardless of whether the attorney may also be subject to discipline for the same conduct in a jurisdiction where the attorney is admitted or practices. An administrative disciplinary proceeding initiated by the Commission for violation of this part may result in an attorney being censured, or being temporarily or permanently denied the privilege of appearing or practicing before the Commission.

(c) An attorney who complies in good faith with the provisions of this part shall not be subject to discipline or otherwise liable under inconsistent standards imposed by any state or other United States jurisdiction where the attorney is admitted or practices.

(d) An attorney practicing outside the United States shall not be required to comply with the requirements of this part to the extent that such compliance is prohibited by applicable foreign law.

§205.7   No private right of action.

(a)   Nothing in this part is intended to, or does, create a private right of action against any attorney, law firm, or issuer based upon compliance or non-compliance with its provisions.

(b)   Authority to enforce compliance with this part is vested exclusively in the Commission.